THE BANTAM GREAT OUTDOORS
VACATION & LODGING GUIDE

Eastern United States • Western United States and Alaska • Canada

The Bantam Great Outdoors Guide, the first book of this trail-blazing series, was hailed from coast-to-coast as the most comprehensive, authoritative travel encyclopedia and wilderness guide ever published to the U.S. and Canada. A beautifully illustrated wilderness library in one fact-packed volume, it was selected by the Literary Guild Book Club, L.L. Bean and Montgomery Ward catalogs, Reader's Digest Books, and designated one of the "Outstanding Reference Books of the Year" by the American Library Association.

The new three-volume *Bantam Great Outdoors Vacation & Lodging Guide* was created for the family on the go as well as the lone nature lover. Its revolutionary format will provide you with the most useful and complete all-year-round vacation and lodging information ever published to the Eastern United States, Western United States and Alaska, and Canada.

No other guide offers the breadth and depth of coverage you'll get in *The Bantam Great Outdoors Vacation & Lodging Guide.* Here, finally, is all the hard-to-find information you'll ever need to make planning your next vacation or weekend trip easier than ever before. Organized in an easy-to-use A-Z format, it provides the indispensable details on all major vacation and outdoor recreation areas; gateways, cities and towns; information sources, maps and access; accommodations, lodges and resorts; transportation and outfitting services.

The perfect gift for you and everyone who loves the great outdoors!

Book-of-the-Month Club Selection
Quality Paperback Book Club Selection

Bantam Books by Val Landi
Ask your bookseller for the books you have missed

THE BANTAM GREAT OUTDOORS GUIDE
THE BANTAM GREAT OUTDOORS VACATION AND LODGING
   GUIDE: Canada
THE BANTAM GREAT OUTDOORS VACATION AND LODGING
   GUIDE: Eastern U.S.
THE BANTAM GREAT OUTDOORS VACATION AND LODGING
   GUIDE: Western U.S. and Alaska

THE BANTAM
GREAT OUTDOORS
VACATION &
LODGING GUIDE

Eastern United States

BY VAL LANDI

Illustrated by Gordon Allen

PHOTO CREDITS

We are grateful to the following United States Government agencies, firms, lodge and resort operators for granting us permission to reproduce their photos in the Bantam *Great Outdoors Vacation Travel & Lodging Guide to the Eastern United States:* U.S. Dept. of Interior—National Park Service, U.S. Fish & Wildlife Service, U.S. Forest Service, U.S. Geological Survey, Fontana Village, Grand Hotel—Mackinac Island, Snowshoe Resort, Trees For Tomorrow Environmental Center, Snowy Owl Inn, Green Trails Inn by the Floating Bridge, Northpoint Outfitters, The Inn at Long Trail, Gunflint Lodge, Dana Place Inn, Nicatous Lodge & Camps, Sapphire Valley Resort, Michael Hannau Enterprises, Trapp Family Lodge, Frank Stern, Killington Vermont Resort, The Birches on Moosehead & North Country Outfitters, Country Hills Farm, Woodstock Inn, Indian Cave Lodge, The Darby Field Inn, Olson's Resort, Wildcat Lodge, Canaan Realty—Mirror Lake Resort, Cobb's Bosebuck Mountain Camps, Overland Rolls, The Beresford Farms, Bryce Resort, Mountain Meadows Lodge.

THE BANTAM GREAT OUTDOORS VACATION AND LODGING GUIDE:
EASTERN U.S.
A Bantam Book / April 1980

Cover photos courtesy Cobb's Bosebuk Mountain Camps, U.S. Dept. of Interior—Natl. Park Service, Trapp Family Lodge, Green Trails Inn by the Floating Bridge, and the Blue Ridge Natl. Park Service (Woodbridge Williams).

ISBN 0-553-01231-2

Published simultaneously in the United States and Canada

Bantam Books are published by Bantam Books, Inc. Its trademark, consisting of the words "Bantam Books" and the portrayal of a bantam, is Registered in U.S. Patent and Trademark Office and in other countries. Marca Registrada. Bantam Books, Inc., 666 Fifth Avenue, New York, New York 10019.

PRINTED IN THE UNITED STATES OF AMERICA

0 9 8 7 6 5 4 3 2 1

ACKNOWLEDGMENTS

I am deeply grateful to the hundreds of United States government travel, forestry, fish and wildlife, park, and conservation authorities and their agencies (listed throughout the book) and to the lodge, resort, inn, hotel, and motel operators and local chambers of commerce and state travel officials who contributed their time and expertise, and provided much of the source material that made the compilation of the Bantam *Great Outdoors Vacation/Lodging Guide to the Eastern United States* possible. I also wish to acknowledge the kind assistance given by the members of the American Hotel & Motel Assn. and the useful *AHMA Redbook*.

Special thanks go to the members of the Great Outdoors Vacation/Lodging Guide Series editorial research and field staff—especially A. Donald Grosset, Jr., Jason Mackenzie, Marilyn Young, Anne Ashely, and Judy May—for their valuable contributions. For much of the fascinating local historical information found throughout the guide, we are indebted to the useful Federal Writers' Project guides to Maine, New Hampshire, Vermont, Rhode Island, Massachusetts, Connecticut, New York, New Jersey, Pennsylvania, Delaware, Maryland, Ohio, Kentucky, North Carolina, South Carolina, Virginia, West Virginia, Alabama, Florida, Mississippi, Indiana, Michigan, Wisconsin, Minnesota, and Illinois.

My thanks go also to Beverly Susswein and Ken Leish of Bantam Books; and to Gordon Allen, for his superb and powerful drawings of the great outdoors.

CONTENTS

Lodging Symbols & Rates

The Eastern United States lodges, resorts, inns, ski centers, motels, and hotels described in the pages that follow have been listed, after rigorous evaluation, as a service for vacation travelers. Be sure to contact lodgings of interest directly for possible changes in conditions or rates, due to the constant cost increases caused by the rate of inflation. In most instances, we have provided summer and/or ski season rates.

Please note that rates have been included only as a guide to help you plan a trip to fit your budget. It's advisable to check references provided by the vacation lodges and resorts, and make your reservations at the earliest possible dates. Most of the outstanding lodges, resorts, and ski centers are booked up months in advance. In almost all cases, a deposit is required to hold your reservation.

The following rating symbols are used throughout the book:

★★★★—Outstanding
★★★—Excellent
★★—Very Good
★—Good

In rating lodges, resorts, country inns, and ski centers, we have given considerable weight to location and the quality of the outdoor recreation opportunities of the surrounding area, in addition to the quality of facilities and services.

Eastern United States Youth Hostels

American Youth Hostels, a non-profit youth service organization, sponsors a nationwide system of inexpensive overnight accommodations, many of which are located in major outdoor recreation areas, with responsible adult supervision, owned or chartered by one of the 50 national hosteling associations affiliated with the International Youth Hostel Federation. These inexpensive lodgings—in such outdoor meccas as New Hampshire's White Mountains, the Maine Coast, and Minnesota's Boundary Waters Canoe Country—are ideally suited for young people on the go—backpacking, canoeing, skiing, sailing, bicycling, or bird watching.

A 192–page *American Youth Hostels Guide* ($1.75, plus 50¢ postage and handling) and information may be obtained from: American Youth Hostels, Inc., National Headquarters, Delaplane, VA 22025 (703–592–3271).

Maps & Trip Planning Information

The fabled outdoor recreation areas of the Eastern United States are shown on the full-color U.S. Geological Survey topographic maps, which may be ordered using the *Topographic Map Indexes*, available free for each state upon request from the Distribution Office at the following address: U.S. Geological Survey, 1200 South Eads St., Arlington, VA 22202. These eminently useful maps show man-made and natural features, including contours, forests, lakes and streams, mountain ranges, roads, villages, trails, bogs, portages, rapids and falls, wilderness cabins, and much more.

If you're planning an extended backcountry vacation, it pays to get in top physical condition before you depart. Watch out for bad sunburns from the bright reflecting surfaces of lakes and rivers. To avoid exposure, wear a wide-brimmed hat and a pair of quality sunglasses, along with an effective sunscreen such as Almay Deep Tanning Oil, Sun Block Gel, Pabanol, Pre-Sun, and Bain de Soleil Suntan Foam—all of which contain a concentration of 5 percent para-aminobenzoic acid in 50–70 percent ethanol. A supply of salt tablets will help restore sodium lost through perspiration. Be sure to pack a good supply of bug dope and a head net and cotton gloves for travel during the black fly and mosquito season. Recommended insect repellents include Muskol, Mosquitone, Off!, and Cutters, all of which contain a 50 percent plus concentration of DEET—the most effective known repellent against insect pests.

For detailed travel information on the area you plan to visit contact the addresses and/or phone numbers listed under the "Information Sources, Maps & Access" sections found throughout the *Great Outdoors Vacation/Lodging Guide*. Listings and descriptions of all national forest and wilderness area maps, national park maps, state highway and road maps, and regional guidebooks are listed throughout the book. Perhaps the best source of information about the area you plan to visit are the local lodges and resorts, as well as outfitters.

Traveler's Field Guides to Wildlife and Flora

In addition to the proper maps, equipment, and accessories, no outdoor traveler is complete without a good set of field

guides to the wildlife and flora of the major life zones he is likely to travel through. Among the classic, time-tested field guides are *Roger Tory Peterson's Field Guide Series*—to the Birds, Mammals, Rocks & Minerals, Animal Tracks, Ferns, Trees and Shrubs, Reptiles and Amphibians—all published by Houghton Mifflin Co. The *Golden Field Guide to the Birds of North America* is thought by many to be the best bird guide ever published—its color paintings are without parallel for identification of field markings. The *Golden Field Guide Series* includes useful, full-color guides to Trees of North America, Rocks and Minerals, and Seashells.

The new all-photographic, full-color *Audubon Society Field Guides* to North American Birds—Eastern Region, North American Wildflowers—Eastern Region, and Rocks and Minerals, have set a new standard for field guides, with exclusive use of full-color photographs, new visual identification systems, fullness of textual data, and a handy, waterproof, pocket-sized format. Each guide has 864 pages, with between 650 and 700 color photographs which show the individual species as you would see them with the naked eye or through a pair of binoculars. Radically new identification keys make it possible to identify birds, wildflowers, or rock specimens quickly and accurately without special knowledge or training. The breadth of coverage is far greater than in competing guides, and the text provides scientific facts and background notes on habitat and environment, use, folklore, and more. The texts are supplemented with dozens of black and white drawings.

ALABAMA

Introduction

Alabama's Gulf of Mexico coastal waters, inland lakes, reservoirs, scenic rivers, and national forest and state wildlife-management-area game lands offer some outstanding fishing, hiking, canoeing, and hunting opportunities.

Accommodations & Travel Information

For information on Alabama's vacation lodges and resorts, motels, and hotels, write the Alabama Travel Department, State Capitol, Montgomery 36104 (call toll free (800)633–5761). Additional information may be obtained by writing to the local Chamber of Commerce of the area you plan to visit.

Alabama's state-park recreation areas provide a complete range of camping facilities, from primitive backcountry campsites to modern family campgrounds with complete connections for large motor homes or trailers. A comprehensive listing of state-park and Corps of Engineers campgrounds, including descriptions of facilities and recreation activities, is contained in the 58–page *Alabama Travel Guide*, available free upon request from the Alabama Travel Department, State Capitol, Montgomery 36104. Alabama's state parks range from De Soto State Park on Lookout Mountain in the foothills of the Smokies, surrounded by pine forests, with fishing and canoeing in Little River Canyon, to Gulf State Park, overlooking the Gulf of Mexico. A free guide, *Alabama State Parks*, may be obtained by writing: Division of State Parks, 64 North Union St., Montgomery 36104.

Highways & Maps

A free *Alabama State Highway Map* is available from the Alabama Travel Dept., State Capitol, Montgomery 36104. It shows all major and minor routes, mileage between major points, points of interest, state parks, airports, rest areas, and national and state forests. It includes a state-park index and many color pictures of the state's attractions. A free travel guide to vacation highlights off the Interstate highway system, *Interstate Interludes*, may be obtained by writing the Alabama Travel Dept. (address above).

**VACATION/
LODGING GUIDE**

Alabama Lakes, Forests & Coastal Recreation Areas

The Cotton State's sprawling reservoirs, ranging in size from 560 acres to 67,086 acres, dot the Mountain Lake Country of the northern region and the Black Belt Country of the central region, and provide good seasonal angling for a wide variety of fish, including chain pickerel, largemouth, smallmouth, and spotted bass, crappie, walleye, bluegill, white bass, warmouth, and a few stocked striped bass up to trophy weights. The major impoundments in central Alabama include 9,200–acre Bankhead Lake on the Black Warrior River, with a sinuous shoreline of over 400 miles; Warrior Lock and Dam Lake on the Black Warrior River, which covers 7,800 acres with a 300–mile shoreline; 5,850–acre Lake Tuscaloosa on the North River, with a 177–mile shoreline; 10,000–acre Demopolis Reservoir on the Tombigbee River; deep, rocky 6,800–acre Lake Jordan, which offers striped-bass fishing below Mitchell Dam; 22,000–acre Miller's Ferry Reservoir on the Alabama River, which provides good spring fishing for chain pickerel, channel catfish and a few striped bass; and sprawling Lake Eufaula, once considered by many to be one of the nation's top trophy largemouth-bass lakes, which covers 45,000 acres on the Chattahoochee River. Other productive central Alabama lakes include Holt, Oliver Pool, Claiborne, Big Creek, Shelby, Jones Bluff, Yates, Thurlow, Bartlett's Ferry, Goat Rock, Oliver, Columbia, and Gantt.

The great reservoirs of northern Alabama, surrounded by the rolling foothills of the ancient Appalachian Mountains, offer some of the nation's top-ranked trophy largemouth and smallmouth bass fishing. Pickwick Lake, which straddles the Alabama-Tennessee border on the Tennessee River, is one of the nation's top smallmouth-bass lakes, as is Wilson Lake, the oldest of the four TVA reservoirs in Alabama. Impounded in 1924, Wilson has yielded smallmouths that grow to trophy weights of 10½ pounds, feeding on the large schools of gizzard shad found in all the TVA impoundments. Wheeler Lake, a 67,100–acre TVA impoundment, is noted for its crappie, bass, bream, and striped-bass fishing. Huge 69,100–acre Guntersville Lake, the largest lake in the state, provides often spectacular fishing for crappie and bream during the June willow-fly hatchings, and trophy largemouth bass during the spring and early summer. The hundreds of acres of flooded woodlands in 12,000–acre Lay Lake yield huge stringers of big largemouth and spotted bass and crappies. Other major lakes of the northern mountain country include Smith, Weiss, Neely, Henry, Logan Martin, Mitchell, and Martin lakes and the beautiful unspoiled Inland Lake, which provides good fishing for rainbow trout. The beautiful, wild West Fork of the Sipsey River, a feeder stream of the Lewis-Smith Reservoir, rises in the rugged backcountry of northwest Alabama and flows through the Bee Branch Scenic Area and a wilderness of narrow ridges, canyons, deep valleys, waterfalls, sheer rock bluffs, and lush vegetation in the Bankhead National Forest to its mouth on the reservoir. This beautiful stream offers unspoiled float fishing for spotted bass, white bass, and fat bluegills. May, June, September, and October are the most productive months to float the Sipsey. The beautiful Cahaba River rises in Lake-of-the-Woods in the Central Region and flows for 162 miles past scenic woodlands—with thick undergrowths of colorful dogwood, wild azalea, and mountain laurel—and sheer rock bluffs to its mouth on the Alabama River at Old Cahaba. The Cahaba provides good float fishing along its entire length for walleye and river redhorse and for bream and spotted bass in the upper stretches, and largemouth bass, crappie, and bluegill along the lower coastal-plain stretches. Numerous sand and gravel bars provide natural campsites. The sunken logs and weed beds of the Tallapoosa River, upstream from Lake Martin, provide excellent fishing for scrappy spotted bass and largemouths. The scenic, wild, boulder-strewn waters of the upper river provide superb float-fishing opportunities. Other top-ranked float-fishing streams that offer long stretches of wild country include the upper Black Warrior River, Coosa River, and Little River.

Alabama offers an interesting variety of saltwater fishing in its bays, tidal streams, and offshore waters. The rivers and bayous of the great 40–mile long Mobile Delta—including the bays of the lower delta, Tensaw River, Johns Bend, and the bayous and lakes of the middle and upper delta—provide fishing for crappie, yellow bass, white bass, striped bass, catfish, huge alligator gars often in excess of 100 pounds, as well as for speckled trout (weakfish) and white trout, redfish, croaker, and flounder in the bays and tidal streams. Charter boats and skiffs provide seasonal offshore fishing for tarpon—the state fish—and for king mackerel, kingfish, bluefish, barracuda, blackfin tuna, dolphin, snapper, cobia, ladyfish, pompano, big sharks, amberjack, channel bass, sea trout, and sailfish.

Information Sources, Maps & Access

For detailed hunting and fishing information, regulations, and free *Wildlife Management Area Maps*, write: Department of Conservation & Natural Resources, Montgomery 36130. A full-color map, *Alabama National Forests*, showing major roads, trails, trail shelters, boat ramps, forest-service recreation sites, lookout stations, and hunting camps, may be obtained for 50¢ from the Forest Supervisor, P.O. Box 40, Montgomery 36101. This useful map shows the fishing, hunting, and camping areas of the 360,000–acre Talladega National Forest in the northeast corner of the state at the southernmost thrust of the Appalachian Mountains, including the South Sandy Wildlife Management Area, 2,407–foot Mount Cheaha (the highest point in the state), Lake Chinnabee, Choccolocco Wildlife Management Area and Sweetwater Lake, Hollins Wildlife Management Area, and the scenic Skyway Motorway and Talladega Scenic Drive; the 181,000–acre Bankhead National Forest, in the northwest region of the state, which includes the bass waters of sprawling Lake Lewis Smith with its sheer rock-wall-lined shoreline, the famed Black Warrior Wildlife Management Area, Bee Branch Scenic Area, and the deep canyons of the wild Sipsey River; the 85,000–acre Conecuh National Forest; and the 11,000–acre Tuskegee National Forest. *Recreation on TVA Lakes*, available free from the TVA Map Sales Office, Union Bldg., Knoxville, TN 37902, describes the entire region, provides information on public access, public parks, boat docks and resorts, fishing, boating, camping, water safety, and the Land Between the Lakes Recreational Area. The map shows lakes, rivers, forests, state parks, and roads and includes a close-up of the Land Between the Lakes. Complete listings are given for boat docks, resorts, state parks, U.S. Forest Service camp areas, and county and municipal parks with docks or camping areas.

Recreation Maps of Pickwick Lake, Guntersville Lake, and *Wheeler Reservoir* are available free from TVA Map Sales (address above). They show public-use areas, public lands, commercial recreation areas, commercial boat docks, public parks, wildlife-management areas, boat-launching sites, and private lands. They also show roads, lakes, rivers, and parks. A free *Index to Navigation Charts & Maps of TVA Reservoirs* may be obtained upon request from the TVA Map Sales Office.

Lodges & Resorts

★★★*Cheaha State Park Resort in Talladega National Forest* commands spectacular views from 2,500 feet on Cheaha Mountain, the highest point in Alabama. Hiking and biking trails wind throughout the dense woods, mountain streams and lakes of the 2,700–acre state park. There is a 73–site campground, fishing in Cheaha lake, a large swimming pool, a putt-putt golf course, and new tennis courts will soon be completed. The restaurant is open year-round, and provides stunning views of the surrounding countryside. Cheaha Resort Hotel has 30 spacious, air-conditioned rooms, with color TV, wall-to-wall carpeting, private bath and phone. Single rates are $21; double rates, $25. Winter rates are $18, single; $21 double occupancy. In addition there are modern A-frame chalets and stone cabins, each with a fireplace and fully equipped modern kitchens. Cabins accommodate eight persons; chalets six. Rates are $22 for two persons; $32–36 for four. The Bald Rock Lodge can accommodate up to 50 persons, and is completely furnished with a large kitchen and dining area. This facility is popular for retreats, and rents overnight for $185. For more information write: Cheaha State Park Resort, PO Box 546, Lineville, AL 36266 (205)488–5115.

★★★*De Soto State Park Resort—Grand Canyon of the South* is located on the Little River, the only river in America that flows its entire length on top of a mountain. Little River forms in Northwest Georgia and Northeast Alabama and flows down the middle of Lookout Mountain, leaving the mountain at Little River Canyon Mouth Park and flowing into Weiss Lake. This beautiful river is classified as an Alabama Wild and Scenic River. The Little River Canyon area of De Soto State Park is located 10 miles south of the Information Center. The Little River flows in the bottom of this canyon, which is the deepest canyon east of the Rocky Mountains. Little River Canyon is approximately 16 miles long and has an average depth of 400 feet, being 600 feet at its deepest point. It is approximately three-fourths of a mile wide at its widest point. Little River Canyon Rim Parkway, a 22 mile scenic drive, follows the west rim of the canyon, with picnic tables available at the scenic overlooks. The De Soto Falls Area of De Soto State Park is located seven miles north of the Information Center on De Soto Parkway. In this

area, in addition to a beautiful 100–foot waterfall, is a historic dam creating a beautiful mountain lake which provides swimming, fishing, and boating. In this spectacular setting, the rustic lodge features a skyview lobby, craft and gift shop, dining rooms and 25 modern guest rooms with color television. The main dining room, with its giant fireplace, has a seating capacity of 90. Adjoining the main dining room, there are two private dining rooms, seating up to 40 persons. Closeby are the cabins—22 in all. Twelve are modern chalet-type cabins, each offering air-conditioning and electric heating, fireplace, kitchenette, two downstairs rooms, and sleeping loft. The park's outdoor facilities include a swimming pool, playground, ball-field, picnic area, country store, and 60–site campground. Rhodo-dendron trails are located along the west bank of Little River and east of the picnic and cottage area. Along these trails will be found many of the park's 15 waterfalls. Catawba rhododendron and moun-tain laurel blooms turn this area into a riot of color in May and June. There are approximately 20 miles of hiking trails within the park area. Rustic foot bridges span many of the rushing mountain streams. Unusual rock formations and many rare and endangered forms of plant life will be found along these trails. The Park resort is located 80 miles northeast of Birmingham and 50 miles southwest of Chattanooga, Tennessee. For information, rates, and reservations, contact: De Soto State Park, Rt. 1, Box 210, Fort Payne, AL 35967 (205)845–0051.

★★★*The Grand Hotel-Gulf Coast Resort* is on a peninsula on Mobile Bay in the Gulf of Mexico. This Gulf Coast resort has been on the site since 1847, and retains the charm and ambience of the old days. It is a peaceful resort with moss-covered oaks and white sandy beaches. The Grand Hotel is especially famous for its Lakewood Golf Club which has 27 championship holes, including nine dozen well-raked traps. The course has a view of the bayous with wooden bridges over lazy creeks, and even an alligator in a lagoon on the Dogwood nine. Green fees are $11 per day and $6 for 9 holes. There are golf packages which include unlimited greens fees. The Club also has a pro shop, a clubhouse bar, locker service, a sauna, and golf lessons. There are bicycles for rent, as well as tandem bikes and tricycles. Bicycle trails start at the Lakewood Club. Sailors can rent "Rhodes 19" class sailboats by the hour. There is also water skiing, with or without instruction; a 53–foot Hatteras rigged for game fishing, and other charter boats. Guests can enjoy skeet and trap shooting from 9–5 or evenings by appointment. The Hotel has its own fishing pier, with fishing poles, crab nets, and bait available free. On the pier are lounges for sunning. Free facilities include shuffleboard courts, lawn bowling, croquet, ping-pong, swimming in the hotel pool or on the sandy beach, use of the putting greens, and the children's playground. During the summer months, there is a program of supervised activities for five to nine year olds and 10 to 16 year olds. The hotel has ten Rubico tennis courts, a tennis pro shop, racquets for rent and instruction. Tennis shoes and attire are required and there is a court fee. Dress is casual during the day, but at night, guests dress up with ladies in long skirts and gentlemen in coats and ties. The Hotel Dining Room serves elegant meals. In the Bird Cage cocktail lounge complimentary hors d'oeuvres are served during cocktail hour, and after dinner there is music and danc-ing. Box lunches are available; there is lunch at the Golf Club and sandwiches are served in season at the pool. Rates are quoted on the American Plan (modified) with breakfast and dinner. Per person, double occupancy rooms in the Main Building are $39.50 to $51 depending on the season and the location of the room. The Bay House is $48.75 to $53.50 per person per day double occupancy. Bay House rooms have sitting rooms and terraces or balconies. There are also cottages for two to eight people, rates for children and

for extra persons in a room. For more information contact: The Grand Hotel, Point Clear, AL 36564 (305)928–9201.

★★★*Gulf State Park Resort* is located on the beach in a beautiful setting east of Gulf Shores on Alabama Highway 182. Area attractions include superb surf and off-shore fishing, tennis, golf, and historic sites. The resort offers attractively designed motel units facing the Gulf of Mexico, swimming pool, surf beach, and complete dining facilities. All rooms have two double beds, bath, color TV, telephone, and a private balcony overlooking the Gulf. Seasonal rates range from $37 to $74 daily, based on double occupancy. For additional information, contact: Gulf State Park Resort, P.O. Box 437, Gulf Shores, AL 36542 (205)968–7531.

★★★*Lake Guntersville State Park Lodge* is situated on a 500 foot bluff overlooking the spectacular Guntersville Reservoir, and 5,550 acres of dense forests, open meadows, and high mountain ridges of Lake Guntersville State Park. Built of natural stone, the center has eight meeting rooms, accommodating groups up to 450, and a gourmet restaurant, a gift shop, game room, swimming pool, and lounge areas. There is a wide sandy beach and modern bath house on the lake front below, and a complete fishing center and marina with boat rentals. In addition, there is an 18–hole golf course with pro shop and cart rental, tennis courts, hiking trails and picnic areas. The Resort Inn has 100 wood panelled rooms, with individual patios and balconies overlooking Guntersville Reservoir, and the deep woods and valleys of the park. Lodge rooms are $24–27 for one or two persons in season (March 15–Nov. 30) and $22–25 winter rate. Suites, with bedroom, living room with bar, refrigerator and sink are $45 for one to two persons winter and summer. Chalets, dotting the high ridge overlooking the lake, have two bedrooms, a living room with fireplace, private bath, dressing rooms and fully equipped kitch-ens. Rates are $55 all year round. Lakeshore cottages have two bedrooms, a living room, two baths, and fully equipped modern kitchens, and can accommodate one-four persons. Rates are $42.50. Along the lakefront there is a 300 site camping ground, with tables, grills, bath houses, hot showers, a camp store, and children's playground. For more information write: Lake Guntersville State Park Lodge, Star Route 52, Guntersville, AL 35976 (205)582–2061.

CONNECTICUT

Introduction

Connecticut is very industrialized, urbanized, and heavily populated, containing more than 3 million people. However, there are numerous state forests and parks, the scenic Appalachian Trail, winding along the Housatonic River in the northwest section, and some exquisitely beautiful countryside. Parts of northwestern Connecticut look as though a giant hand had carved a slice out of Vermont and placed it there; and portions of the central, northern, and eastern regions are composed of rolling hills, forests, streams and lakes of comparable quality. The southern margin of Connecticut rests on Long Island Sound, and the coastline area is famous for its beautiful sandy beaches, productive, rock-ribbed shoreline and points, tidal marshes, offshore islands, and the fish-filled sweep of the sound. There is much more to Connecticut than suburbia, factory whistles, and superhighways; yet many local sportsmen, unaware of the excellent opportunities right at their doorstep, pack up the station wagon and head for the Adirondacks, Maine, Canada, or other points.

Accommodations & Travel Information

Connecticut has few full-service resorts and lodges. For information on accommodations and travel in the state, contact: Travel Information, Dept. of Commerce, 210 Washington St., Hartford, CT 06106 (203)566-3977. Campers have their choice of more than 1,500 campsites in 18 recreation sites located in the state park and forest reserve system. Campsite reservations are available for most campgrounds. For information and applications contact: Parks & Recreation Unit, Dept. of Environmental Protection, State Office Bldg., Hartford 06115. The state also has commercial campsites of all types, and a comprehensive listing of these areas can be found in an informative brochure, *Connecticut Campgrounds*. You can obtain a free copy by writing: Secretary, Connecticut Campground Owners' Assn., Woodstock 06281. The publication contains a listing and brief description of each camping area, and each area is location-keyed to the map provided on the reverse side of the brochure. The map will also show you how to get to the campsites, with major highways indicated. There is a chart showing the services provided at each campsite, along with information on rates.

Highways & Maps

Connecticut's beautiful countryside—deep, wooded hills, stunning river valleys, charming old villages and towns, not far from modern cities—offers many scenic routes that are resplendent with beauty throughout the year. The Dept. of Commerce, 210 Washington St., Hartford 06106, will send you a free information booklet, *Connecticut Scenic Tours*. Different types of tours are described. There is a 4–day scenic tour, a 2–day historical tour, a 3–day family trip, and a 2–day maritime tour. Explicit directions are provided for automobile travel, and there are small maps to aid the motorist. Distances between destinations are noted, and the booklet is attractively illustrated with photographs. The department will also send, at no charge, the official *Highway Map of Connecticut*, which shows all roads and highways; recreation features, such as state parks and forests, fishing areas, and ski areas; and miscellaneous features, such as airports, heliports, and fish hatcheries. There is a chart listing state parks and forests, location-keyed to the road map, showing what services are available at each area. Capsule information on fishing and hunting, and state parks and forests, is also shown. A list of public boat-launching sites, also location-keyed, is provided. For additional information on scenic routes and highways in Connecticut, write to: Dept. of Commerce (address above) for the following publications: *Connecticut, So Much So Near; Points of Interest; Connecticut in Fall;* and *Connecticut in Winter.*

VACATION/ LODGING GUIDE

Connecticut Forests, Lakes & Coastal Recreation Areas

The Nutmeg State's scenic forestlands, rolling hills, trails, lakes, ponds and streams, and beautiful Atlantic coastline offer excellent opportunities for hiking, fishing, canoeing, and cross-country skiing. For the angler and hunter, Connecticut is a state of many surprises— 10–pound sea trout, 60–pound striped bass, 22–pound northern pike, 16–pound brown trout, 9–pound shad, rafts of scaup, black ducks, Canada geese, ruffed grouse, woodcock, 355–pound bucks, and rabbits. While no one would attempt to equate the Nutmeg State's outdoor potential with Maine, Michigan, Wyoming, Washington, or Quebec, a progressive, hardworking Department of Environmental Protection has done a creative job of protecting and maintaining the fishing and hunting opportunities, as well as introducing new, compatible species. Trout are found in every section of the state in streams, lakes, and ponds, and trophy fish are taken every season. Connecticut stocks more than 250 streams with trout, but because of watershed limitations and hot summer temperatures, a large percentage of the streams are "put and take," being reduced to trickles during July, August, and September. There are a number of all-season rivers, and these can provide some surprising sport throughout the state's long open fishing period. The Housatonic River, source of the state record 4–pound 6–ounce brook trout, dominates the western side of the state, winding its way from the Berkshire foothills of the northwest corner south to Long Island Sound. This verdant country furnishes some of Connecticut's finest trout fishing in the deep pools, swift runs, and riffles of the "Hous." The best water consists of the 20 or so miles between Kent and Lime Rock; the stream runs beside U.S. 7. Brown trout, rainbows, and brookies are stocked, and there are holdover browns to 7 or 8 pounds. The 2½ miles in the Housatonic Meadows State Park are for fly fishing only, and the energetic Housatonic Fly Fishermen's Association does an enormous amount of work, including stocking, to maintain the quality of the fishing. Some of the Housatonic's tributaries produce good fishing, including the attractive Blackberry, Shepaug (a lot of private land is a problem on this one) flowing through Aspeterck, the excellent Pomperaug—an all-season producer—and the Pequonnock. These streams all yield some big holdover browns each season, in addition to the "stockers." Lake Lillinonah, an impoundment near Brookfield Center on Route 133, is a long sinuous section of the Housatonic which produces first-rate fishing for largemouth and smallmouth bass, pickerel, and panfish. Lake Zoar, another dammed-up stretch of the river a few miles upstream from Derby, is also a consistent producer of these species.

The great Connecticut River splits the state as it flows south to the sound at the picturesque towns of Old Saybrook and Old Lyme. The Connecticut is not a trout producer, but some of its tributaries are noted streams. The Scantic, above Hartford, yields good fishing throughout the season, and big browns are taken in the fall in the stretch near its confluence with the Connecticut. The Salmon River, which springs from feeder streams in the Salmon River State Forest, and its tributaries, such as Jeremy's River, Blackledge River, Fawn Brook, and Dickinson Creek, offer good spring fishing, and the main Salmon produces throughout the season.

Much of the best all-season trout fishing can be found in the state's many lakes and ponds. Good trout ponds and lakes are found in every part of the state, including a group of reclaimed and heavily stocked "put and take" waters. There are a number of bodies of water which contain large holdover fish, and a significant proportion of these have been stocked with landlocked alewives and/or smelt to

feed the big trout. East Twin Lake, in northwestern Connecticut near Salisbury, has some of the finest kokanee fishing in the East, with many fish near 2 pounds in weight, and offers excellent angling for brown and rainbow trout, bass, and panfish. Wononscopomuc, to the south at Lakeville, is another great producer in this beautiful section of New England villages and forested ridges. This lake holds the 29–pound 13–ounce record for lake trout, but lakers are now only an incidental catch. However, the excellent kokanee, brown, and rainbow populations make up for the laker's decline, and this body of water yields lunker trout, as well as largemouth and smallmouth bass, pickerel, and panfish. The Colebrook River-Hogsback reservoirs, a double impoundment, in the Algonquin-Tunxis State Forest area near Colebrook, is a scenic piece of water bordered by Route 8. Rainbow trout create most of the excitement, but there are some big browns cruising the depths of this impoundment. Highland Lake, near Winsted, holds some lunker browns, and has fine angling for kokanee salmon, rainbow trout, both kinds of bass, pickerel, and panfish. West Hill Pond, a few miles southeast of Winsted, is considered by many knowledgeable Connecticut anglers to be the best trout lake in the state. Browns to 8 pounds are taken fairly regularly and there are some real busters in the cold depths, as well as some good-sized rainbows, kokanee, bass, pickerel, and panfish.

Connecticut offers some of the best warmwater fishing in New England. There are hundreds of public and private lakes and ponds that produce largemouth bass to 9 or 10 pounds, and any fisherman can find a good, nearby bass lake where he is allowed to fish, or where permission can be secured. An exciting sport in which the state stands at the top of the list is fishing for swift, rugged shad, the "poor man's salmon." Shad are taken in a few rivers such as the Thames at Greenville Dam in Norwich, the Salmon and the Eight Mile rivers, both Connecticut River tributaries, but the best location in the state and probably in the United States is the Connecticut River above Hartford, including the mouth of the Farmington River, the Bissell Bridge area, the mouth of the Scantic River, the Windsor Locks area, and the finest shad stretch of all, Enfield Dam.

The Connecticut provides good fishing for other species too. White perch and whitefish are found all along the river; striped bass are caught as far upstream as Enfield Dam. Largemouth bass, pickerel, and northern pike are caught at various points along the river. Pike are savage opponents in the Connecticut's currents and hit plugs, spoons, bucktail baits, minnows, and big spinners. Atlantic salmon restoration efforts are beginning to show some small victories, and it is hoped that the great expenditure of time, money, effort, and devotion of federal, state, and private groups will bear fruit.

Another great warmwater fishing area, also noted for northern pike, is Bantam Lake in northwest Connecticut, south of Litchfield. Pike were stocked in Bantam to thin out an overly abundant white perch population and the management step has worked out to the benefit of both species. A new state record 22–pound 4–ounce pike was taken in 1976, and other large specimens are taken throughout the season. Both kinds of bass, and pickerel and panfish, are abundant. Lake Wangumbaug at Coventry is considered to be one of the best, possibly the best smallmouth bass lake in the state, with little competition from other game fish. Other fine bass producers include Lake of Isles at North Stonington, which holds quantities of pickerel, perch, and crappies; Pachaug Pond on the edge of Pachaug State Forest, and Moodus Reservoir and Bashan Lake in East Haddam.

Other exceptional warmwater fishing places are described in the descriptions of trout fishing above, being "two-story" lakes managed for both types of fish.

Connecticut has exceptional, unpublicized saltwater fishing, and fishermen passing through the state on their way to Cape Cod, Montauk Point, and other popular areas are overlooking some of the finest saltwater angling on the East Coast. Bluefish to 20 pounds and striped bass to 60 pounds are taken from the productive shores of Greenwich on the New York border at the west to the Pawcatuck River on the Rhode Island line to the east. The state's rocky shores, marshy coves, and rocky ledges provide optimum bass water, and the sound with its 250 miles of shoreline produces steady fishing during a long season. Bluefish appear in July and are present until fall storms drive them south; they are often caught along with stripers.

Weakfish (squeteague), mackerel, sea bass, porgies (scup), blackfish (tautog), fluke and winter flounders, cod, pollack, tomcods, and hordes of snappers (small bluefish) are other popular fish. The troutlike, iridescent weakfish has made a dramatic comeback after a long absence. These trim, orange-finned game fish weigh from about 2 to 12 pounds and prefer spoons, spinners, jigs, shrimptail lures, small bucktails, spinner and worm rigs, sea worms, squid, killies, spearing, and shrimp. Mackerel and snappers hit small chrome jigs, spoons, spinners, flies, bucktails, and minnows. The bottom fish take the baits described above, plus clams and small crabs—fiddlers and green crabs for blackfish. Cod and pollack hit jigs or other lures and can be taken on bait.

Connecticut's state forest reserves and wildlife management areas (WMAs) encompass a varied topography of mixed hardwoods and evergreens with laurel thickets, beaver flowage, meadows, wetlands, lakes, ponds, and streams, and offer excellent opportunities for backcountry hiking, camping, fishing, canoeing, cross-country skiing, and hunting in season for ruffed grouse, woodcock, gray squirrel, cottontails, raccoon, deer, pheasant, and ducks and geese. The Connecticut segment of the Appalachian Trail enters the state at the Massachusetts border and winds for 55 miles through the Housatonic and Mohawk state forests, and parallels the Housatonic River for much of its length before it ascends to the New York border at the Schagticoke Mountain Indian Reservation.

Connecticut offers some surprising scenic canoe routes and trout streams surrounded by beautiful upland forests of mixed hardwoods and conifers, meadows, rolling hills, beaver flows, and marshlands. It has over 500 lakes and ponds, and roughly 250 miles of coastline on Fishers Island and Long Island sounds. The state's major canoe routes are the Housatonic (the Indian name for "river beyond the mountains"), Connecticut, and Thames rivers, and the scenic 80-mile-long Farmington River, which provides excellent whitewater runs. Although the state is heavily populated, there are many areas where the canoeist can enjoy smooth canoeing with scenic panoramas, or whitewater canoeing during the spring runoff.

Information Sources, Maps & Access

Several publications of interest to the Connecticut fisherman and hunter are available free on request (single copies only) from: Dept. of Environmental Protection, State Office Bldg., Hartford 06115 (203)566–5599: *Public Access to Connecticut Fishing Waters, Connecticut Shad Fisher, Connecticut Trout Stocking Report, Hunting-Trapping & Sportfishing Regulations, Deer Season Field Guide, A Hunting Guide to Game Management Areas,* and *Waterfowl Hunting & Duck Identification Guide.* A useful large-format 202-page guide, *Trout and Salmon Fishing in New England Lakes and Ponds* ($8 postpaid), contains detailed descriptions and lake survey maps of

East Twin, Wononscopomuc, Mashapaug, and Crystal lakes and West Hill Pond. It may be ordered from: Partridge Press, Box 422, Campton, NH 03223. The free 54-page *Hunting Guide to Wildlife Management Areas* may be obtained by writing: Wildlife Unit, Dept. of Environmental Protection, State Office Bldg., Hartford 06115. For information and hiking and wild country camping in the state forest reserves, write: Connecticut Forest and Parks Assn., 1010 Main St., East Hartford 06108. Depth contour maps for several of Connecticut's major lakes are available free (single copies only) from: Information Office, Dept. of Environmental Protection, State Office Bldg., Hartford 06115. These useful maps show depth contour intervals, which will allow the angler to determine his drifting and trolling patterns based on the lake's thermal stratification, and boat landings. Each map contains a detailed description of the lake's physical characteristics, fish species present, and fishing history and potential. Contour maps are available for the following lakes: *Wononscopomuc* (kokanee and trophy browns from 2 to 12 pounds), *West Hill Pond* (the former state record 31-inch, 13-pound brown trout was caught here in 1964), *Black Pond* (Meriden and Middlefield), *Quonnipaug* (largemouth bass and brown trout), *Mashapaug* (producer of state record fish), *Amos, Ball, Highland* (kokanee), *Silver, Cedar* (browns up to 7 pounds), *Dooley Pond, East Twin Lake* (considered the most productive kokanee lake east of the Rockies), *Pataganset* (trophy black crappie), *Bantam* (northern pike, trophy smallmouth and largemouth bass), *Beach, Billings, Black Pond, Crystal* (large holdover browns), *Gardner, Green Falls Reservoir, Halls Pond, Lantern Hill Pond, Long Pond* (New London County, trophy bass and browns up to 7 pounds), *Mohawk Pond, North Farms Reservoir, Pickerel Lake, Quaddick Reservoir, Rogers Lake* (large holdover browns up to 5 pounds), *Candlewood Lake*. The invaluable *EMS Ski Touring Guide to New England* ($5.95) contains detailed descriptions, topo maps, and mileage charts of the state's major abandoned railroad beds and ski touring trails, including Tunxis State Forest, State Bridle Trail, McLean Game Refuge, and the Copper Hill area. It may be obtained by writing: Eastern Mountain Sports, 1047 Commonwealth Ave., Boston, MA 02215. Hikers planning to travel the Connecticut segment of this trail should be sure to purchase the *Guide to the Appalachian Trail in Massachusetts and Connecticut.* Order your copy ($5.85) from: Appalachian Trail Conference, Box 236, Harpers Ferry, WV 25425. Though the state is heavily populated, there are many areas where the canoeist can enjoy smooth canoeing with scenic panoramas, or whitewater canoeing during the spring runoff. Anybody planning a canoe trip in Connecticut should send for the excellent *Connecticut Canoeing Guide,* available free from: Public Information & Education, Dept. of Environmental Protection, State Office Bldg., Hartford 06115. Consult the *AMC River Guide Volume II: Central & Southern New England,* before setting out, which contains detailed descriptions of Connecticut rivers. It costs $6.00, and can be obtained from: Appalachian Mountain Club, 5 Joy St., Boston, MA 02108. The *Connecticut River Guide* ($4.50), Connecticut River Watershed Council, 125 Combs Rd., Easthampton, MA 01027, contains much information for the canoeist as well as three detailed maps of the Connecticut River.

Lodges & Resorts

★★★★*Woodbury Ski & Racquet* is a small club tucked away in Woodbury, Connecticut, only 1½ hours from New York or Boston. A full selection of skiing and racquet facilities are available. Woodbury's alpine trails offer the most challenging skiing in Connecticut, as well as excellent beginner and intermediate trails. Rod Taylor, former member of the U.S. Olympic Ski Team and National Downhill Champion in 1970, operates the ski school, with instructions on all

levels. Bilingual instruction is available from international instructors, including former Olympic skiers. The Alpine Racing Program includes Slalom course training, video tape replays and recreational races every Sunday afternoon. There is a complete Ski Pro Shop, open daily with rentals and mounting and repair service available. Cross-country skiing on miles of groomed touring trails at nearby Woodbury and Steep Rock Park is available with touring instructors, complete cross-country equipment and rentals. Woodbury offers four Har-tu tennis courts for outdoor playing from April 1 to November 15. Indoor tennis is provided year round with two heated Bubble courts. A Paddle Tennis court, lighted for night use, is another Woodbury feature. Single, family and junior tennis lessons are available. Ski rates: $8.50 weekends full day/$6 weekdays full day. Night skiing $5.50 with a $3.50 Monday night special. Family, unlimited day and night rates and group rates are available. Woodbury holds ski camps Christmas and Washington's Birthday weeks for all levels. Package includes four days of intensive skiing, ten hours total, including lifts, lunch and lessons $50, or $70 with rentals. Full season outdoor tennis membership including all court time, special lesson rate, Round Robins, guest privileges, is $100/single $160/family. Private lessons for members $12, non-members $15. For full information, write: Woodbury Ski & Racquet, Route 47, Woodbury, CT 06798 (203)263–2203.

Travel Services

Great World Wilderness Outfitters & Ski Touring Center rent and sell equipment for most summer and winter outdoor, active participant sports and activities. They also offer instruction, repair of equipment and guided wilderness trips. Their facility is located in West Simsbury, approximately 12 miles from Hartford. Canoes with paddles and a life jacket rent for $13 per day, kayaks with helmet, paddle and spray skirt are $15 per day and the daily rates decrease with each additional day. They rent car racks, tents from light backpacking tents to the six person Space–10, packs, sleeping bags, pads, reflector ovens, cooking gear, grills, etc. In winter they operate the Great World Ski Touring Center. With agreements from local landowners, the Ethel Walker School, the State of Connecticut, and the Simsbury Cultural & Recreational Dept., the center has inter-

connected a widespread system of trails in West Simsbury Valley, to produce 20 miles of marked and groomed ski trails through woods, meadows and foothills. The rental package for adults for a full day including skis, boots and poles is $7.50 weekends and $6 weekdays. There are rates for half days and juniors. The Great World Cross-Country Ski School has only EPSTI-certified instructors teaching group and private lessons. NASTAR races are run on Sundays and several family and citizen races are planned. There is no trail fee, but a 50¢ fee for the trail map. The Ski Touring Center is open from 8:30 AM to 5:00 PM. For more information contact: Great World Wilderness Outfitters, 250 Farms Village Rd., W. Simsbury, CT 06092 (203)658–4461.

River Running Expeditions Ltd are canoe and kayak outfitting specialists in the summer and run a cross-country ski touring center in the winter. From RRE Ltd's base in downtown Falls Village, ski tourers can ski Battle Hill, the River Trail, Sugar Hill or the Appalachian Trail. The Ski shop has equipment and accessories for sale and a complete rental package for an adult for a full day is $5 weekdays and $8 weekends. Children can rent cross-country ski equipment for $4 per day weekdays and $7 per day weekends. The trail fee is $2 for adults and $1 for children. Group and private lessons are available and RRE Ltd runs moonlight tours. The Ski Center is open six days a week, closed Tuesdays. Weekend reservations are a must. In the summer, RRE Ltd has a complete rental program of river running equipment. Canoes and kayaks rent for $13 per day on weekdays and $15 per day weekends and holidays. Paddles, vests and helmets are $1.50 per day weekdays and $2 per day weekends. Wet suits are $6 weekdays and $8 weekends. There is a complete retail sales showroom and service department. A weekend whitewater school with 10 students in five canoes for two days with all equipment included is $65 per person. The kayak course is $115. Guided weekend trips on the Housatonic River leave RRE Ltd on Friday evening and return Sunday afternoon: $69 per person includes all equipment, food for two dinners, two lunches and two breakfasts, guides and shuttle service. For reservations or more information write: River Running Expeditions, Main Street, Falls Village, CT 06031 (203)824–5579.

DELAWARE

Introduction

Delaware is known primarily for its superb coastal recreation areas and saltwater fishing, off the surf and in the Baltimore Canyon, Indian River Inlet, and Dewey Beach offshore areas.

Accommodations & Travel Information

Delaware has a variety of accommodations available to the traveler. For the free 16–page *Delaware Hotel Guide* and information on where to stay, write to: Visitors Service, Division of Economic Development, 45 The Green, Dover 19901 (302)678–4254. You may also contact local chambers of commerce. State campgrounds are maintained at Lum's Pond State Park in the Chesapeake & Delaware Canal Wildlife Area, in northern Delaware, and at Trap Pond State Park, in southern Delaware. Trap Pond is surrounded by picturesque pine and hardwood forests, and contains the northernmost natural stands of cypress trees in the United States. Primitive camping and backpacking opportunities are available in several of the state forest and wildlife area game lands. For information on camping regulations, seasons, and reservations, write: Division of Parks, Recreation, & Forestry, Dept. of Natural Resources, William Penn St., Dover 19901.

Highways & Maps

The motorist will need the essential *Delaware Highways Map*, which shows principal highways and other roads, route markers, access points, airports, fish hatcheries, charter boat fishing, state park or recreation areas, state police offices, campsites, lighthouses, and other features. Populations of cities and towns are also indicated. There are insets showing Dover, Wilmington, northern New Castle County, and the Atlantic Ocean area. There is an index of cities and towns whose locations are shown on the map.

The reverse side contains an *Outdoor Recreation Guide to Delaware*. Some scenic and historic routes are described, and outlined on an illustrative map. There is a chart of state parks and state forests showing the facilities available at each area. A chart of areas managed by the Division of Fish & Wildlife is also shown. Each area is location-keyed to the road map, and the chart shows which activities are available to sportsmen and vacationers (hunting, fishing, boat launching, etc.) at each area. There are capsule descriptions of state parks and state forests. The map is attractively illustrated with photos of Delaware attractions. To get your free map, write to: Visitors Service, 45 The Green, Dover 19901 (302)678–4254.

Delaware Woodlands, Streams & Coastal Recreation Areas

Tiny Delaware, the nation's second-smallest state, offers some surprisingly good freshwater and saltwater fishing and hunting. Its 2,057–square-mile area, which is divided into two natural regions—the Piedmont Plateau in the extreme north and the lowlying Coastal Plain—is drained by the Delaware River, and the Murderkill, Mispillion, Indian, and Nanticoke rivers. During the spring, summer, and fall, its 50 ponds and streams yield largemouth and smallmouth bass, chain pickerel, black crappie, bluegills, trout, and white and yellow perch, shad, and striped bass in the tidewater areas. The Diamond State, which is in the eastern part of the Delaware Peninsula, formed by Chesapeake Bay and the estuary of the Delaware River, has long been known for the quality of its coastal waterfowl shooting and surf and offshore saltwater fishing in the Bower Beach, Slaughter Beach, Mispillion Light, Breakwater Harbor, Lewes Beach, and Indian River areas.

Warmwater species are found in all Delaware's heavily fished ponds and larger streams, including Trap Pond in Trap Pond State Forest, Killen Pond in Killen Pond State Park, and Tub Mill, Coursey, Ingrams, Blair's, Griffith, McGinnis, Garrison's, Becks, and Lum's ponds, as well as the state record-producing waters listed above. Rainbow, brook, and brown trout are stocked seasonally in White Clay Creek, Brandywine Creek, Christina Creek, Beaver Run, Red Clay Creek, and Wilsons Run. Red Clay Creek from the Pennsylvania line to Yorklyn is restricted to fly fishing only. Fishing and hunting regulations may be obtained by writing: Division of Fish & Wildlife (address below).

Delaware's coastal wetland areas and central farmlands provide some of the East's finest shooting for Canada geese and ducks. The scenic interior woodlands and swamp areas provide good hunting in season for whitetail deer, rabbit and squirrel, bobwhite quail, mourning doves, woodcock, red fox, raccoon, and woodchuck. Canoeing in Delaware is limited by the terrain. Most of the state is situated in the Atlantic Coastal Plain. The relatively flat courses of the rivers and creeks do not lend themselves to extensive canoeing.

The northern portion of the state is in the hilly Piedmont Plateau. The chief waterway in this area is historic Brandywine Creek. This is a lovely 1–day trip by canoe. The creek flows through a very picturesque area. Symmetrical slopes, rising 200 feet above the water, line the shores of the upper course. Although the upper river is aesthetically more pleasing, the white-water enthusiast will enjoy views of the terracing slopes of the Brandywine battlefield above the northeastern shore. In the lower reaches of the Brandywine much of the industrial history of the United States and Delaware was written. Gristmills, textile mills, and other water-powered factories once stood on these shores. Most impressive are the mills of the Hagley Yards where the Du Pont company was founded in 1802 and where black powder was manufactured until the mid-1920's. It is now an industrial museum.

The Brandywine course begins at Lenape (PA), State Route 52, and ends directly above the Market Street Bridge in Wilmington at the tidewater mark. For further information, write: Division of Economic Development, 45 The Green, Dover 19901.

Information Sources, Maps & Access

Detailed fishing and hunting information and free *Wildlife Area Maps* may be obtained by writing: Division of Fish & Wildlife, D St., Dover, DE 19901. A daily *Fishing Forecast for Delaware Tidal Waters* may be obtained by dialing (1–800)282-8511. The

VACATION/ LODGING GUIDE

climate is generally humid and mild, with cool winds warmed by the ocean currents. A healthy supply of insect repellent is advised during the mosquito-plagued summer months.

Lodges & Resorts

Delaware has a very limited number of full-service vacation lodges and resorts. For detailed information, see "Accommodations & Travel Information" above.

Introduction

Florida is nationally famous for its scenic inland and coastal recreation areas. This 447–mile-long peninsula is divided into four geographic regions: the eastern Atlantic coastal strip, bordering the Atlantic to Key West; the rolling central lake district; the western coastal region; and the western panhandle, which includes the hill country along the north shore of the Gulf of Mexico. The Everglades, until 1842 a mysterious, unexplored region known only to the Seminole Indians, form one of the nation's largest wilderness areas. The famous snook and tarpon waters of the Ten Thousand Islands, fringing the lower gulf and the Whitewater Bay and Florida Bay, are a labyrinth of mangrove-tangled islets broken by swift-running tide channels. An estimated 30,000 lakes dot the low-lying terrain of the Sunshine State, ranging in depth from 2 to 27 feet and in size from small ponds to giant Lake Okeechobee, which has a surface area of 717 square miles.

FLORIDA

Accommodations & Travel Information

Descriptions of outstanding Florida resorts are contained in the "Vacation/Lodging Guide" which follows. Travelers in Florida should consult the *Florida Hotel & Motel Guide* for information on where to stay. This free publication is available from the Florida Hotel & Motel Association, Inc., P.O. Box 8788, Jacksonville 32211. The booklet contains information about rates and facilities of all Florida Hotel & Motel Association members at the time of compilation of the publication. The accommodations are listed alphabetically by town, and there is a handy form included so that you can make reservations by mail if you wish. Several toll-free reservations numbers (for phoning in Florida only) are provided, should you wish to reserve or obtain additional information.

For further information on any of the Dept. of Natural Resources vacation facilities, write to the Department, Bureau of Education and Information, Room 321, Crown Building, Tallahassee 32304; phone (904)488–7326. The Dept. of Natural Resources will send you a free *Vacation Cottages and Group Camping* describing the cabins and camping areas and providing information on current rates and reservation policies of each park. Another helpful agency is the Dept. of Commerce, Tallahassee 32304. They will be glad to provide you with information on accommodations and vacation resorts in Florida.

Florida offers unlimited opportunities for pleasure cruising, exploration, and fishing along its 8,426 miles of coastal shoreline and hundreds of navigable lakes and scenic rivers. The Sunshine State's major waterways, including the Hawk Channel from Miami to Key West, West Coast Intercoastal waterway, Okeechobee Waterway, St. Johns River, Oklawaha River, Kissimmee Waterway, Apalachicola River, and Suwannee River, are described in the free 100-page booklet *Florida Boating Safety*, available from the Division of Marine Resources, Crown Bldg., Tallahassee 32304.

This excellent booklet is chock-full of information on all aspects of boating—including tips on selecting and using a trailer to transport your boat, safety equipment (both that required by law and equipment not required but good to have on board), facts about fueling, boarding a boat, launching, "rules of the road," and a comprehensive directory of marine facilities in Florida listed by county. The booklet also has information on navigation, buoys, and weather, and includes a number of small maps. There are also brief sections on skin diving, sailing, and canoeing. Emergency measures and a glossary of nautical terms are also provided. This is a publication that every boater, from novice to expert, should have before setting out on a Florida boat trip.

Another useful publication is *Facts for Florida Boat Owners*, available free from the Dept. of Natural Resources, Crown Bldg., Tallahassee 32304. This brochure contains helpful facts on registration, fees, classification, and other rules and regulations regarding boat ownership and operation in Florida. For additional information, contact the Division of Marine Resources (at address above).

Florida is a year-round camping paradise, and the Sunshine State offers extensive public and privately owned facilities, ranging from fully developed parks to remote, primitive retreats. There are a number of booklets and brochures that provide listings and descriptions of Florida's many camping areas, so that you can select one that fits your desires and requirements.

The Florida Dept. of Commerce, Crown Bldg., Tallahassee 32304, has prepared an extensive, informative, free booklet, *Florida Camping*, which lists, by region, camping areas in chart form, indicating available facilities in each area. A map inside the back cover will show you the location of each region. The ownership or administration of each area is also given (private, state park, national forest, etc.). It is wise to contact the campsite you are considering for current information on fees and availability of space (most private and public campgrounds accept reservations by phone only). If you write to the Florida Campground Assn., Inc., P.O. Box 10084, Tallahassee 32302, they will send you their free brochure *Private Campgrounds in Florida*, which contains a listing and brief description of Florida's private campgrounds. Their locations are shown on a road map, and the campgrounds are also listed in chart form, showing facilities available and proximity of facilities if they are not on the campground itself.

Two comprehensive guides to state parks and camping facilities— *Florida Camping & State Parks Guide* and *Camping in Florida's State Parks*—may be obtained from the Dept. of Commerce, Tallahassee 32304.

The Florida Dept. of Natural Resources has established the Canoe Trail System, currently composed of sixteen wild and scenic rivers and creeks, including the Suwannee Wild and Scenic River, and the Kissimmee, St. Johns, Loxahatchee, Manatee, Escambia, Oklawaha, Withlacoochee, Peace, Chipola, Wacissa, Econfina, and Yellow rivers. These waters include renowned bass meccas that produce fish in the 10–pound class up to weights of 20 pounds. If you are planning a canoe trip in Florida, send for the free *Florida Canoe Trail Guide*. This useful, interesting 40–page booklet describes all the Florida canoe trails, and has illustrative maps showing the exact courses the trails take. The maps also show campsites, boat ramps, and wayside parks. You can get your copy by writing to the Dept. of Natural Resources, Division of Recreation and Parks, Larson Bldg., Tallahassee 32301.

Highways & Maps

If you are driving in Florida, you should obtain a copy of the *Florida Official Road Map*. This excellent road map shows all roads and highways, including Florida toll roads (which are conveniently broken down in a separate legend, state parks and recreation areas with and without campsites), airports, welcome stations, rest areas, and points of interest. There is a list of the Florida Trail sites (see section on this trail), with each point location keyed on a small map. A chart of public recreation areas (state parks and historic memorials), U.S. Park and Forest Service, and Division of Forestry (state forest) areas is provided, showing the facilities available in each area. There is a handy mileage index, showing distances in miles between major points on the map. The map is attractively illustrated with color photographs. For your copy, or further information, write to: Florida Dept. of Commerce, Collings Bldg., Tallahassee 32304.

Florida Lakes & Coastal Recreation Areas

Florida's east and west coasts and the Florida Keys have long been famous for the quality of their saltwater fishing. The cooler waters of the eastern Atlantic coast provide seasonal fishing for bluefish, Spanish mackerel, giant spotted sea trout up to 13 pounds, red and black drum, sheepshead, whiting, crevalle, ladyfish, snook, and tarpon, and Gulf Stream gamefish including sailfish, blue marlin, blackfin tuna, dolphin, kingfish, yellowtail, amberjack, and wahoo. Popular east-coast fishing areas include the inshore tidal waters and offshore waters in the St. Augustine, Daytona, Jacksonville, New Smyrna, Halifax, and Tomoka rivers, Indian River, Banana River, Mosquito Lagoon, Cocoa Beach, St. Lucie River, Stuart, Palm Beach, Boynton, and the tidal canals and offshore waters of the Miami area. Excellent seasonal fishing is found in Biscayne Bay (Miami) for bonefish along the grassy flats, mackerel, bluefish, ladyfish, big schools of marauding jack crevalle, barracuda, snook, tarpon, and permit along the edges of the deep flats.

The western coast, along the Gulf of Mexico, offers nationally famous spin and fly fishing for giant tarpon to well over 100 pounds, and snook along the beautiful mangrove-tangled Ten Thousand Islands and the Shark River wilderness in Everglades National Park; Boca Grande, at the mouth of the Myakka and Peace rivers; and at nearly every point along the coast north to Pensacola for most marine gamefish, including red drum, mangrove snappers, spotted sea trout, grouper, bluefish, sheepshead, red snapper, and king and Spanish mackerel. Along the northwest coastal areas, sailfish move in close to the shoreline and remain until the cold water forces them to follow the "Loop" current south. A dramatic run of cobia, or "ling," occurs off northwest Florida's "Miracle Strip" on the Gulf Coast beaches after the first of April.

Hundreds of party boats, locally called "head boats," for drifting and bottom fishing, and charter boats for deep-water trolling and drifting the reefs for sailfish, marlin, dolphin, bonito, kingfish, mackerel, and an occasional tuna, are anchored at the major fishing centers up and down both coasts and provide convenient access to the offshore hot spots. "Tarpon boats," used for shoalwater fishing, are common in the Keys and along the lower west coast. Skiffs and other small craft (available at hundreds of fishing camps that dot the Florida coastal areas) are used along the Inland Waterway, Key Flats, and the thousands of bays, passes, and tidal rivers.

Mangrove snappers, channel bass, snook, and jack crevalle are easily reached by inshore small-craft boaters. Tarpon, which are caught on trolled spoons, plugs, and flies with feathers, are present during the spring and year-round in the Keys and on the southern coast. Trophy snook are taken along the east-coast Inland Waterway in the Lake Worth vicinity during the summer on plugs and live mullet. Big snook, which reach record weights of up to 50 1/2 pounds, are best caught during the ebb tide, when the receding waters pull schools of baitfish out of the mangrove mazes into the open holes.

The beautiful Florida Keys, curving into the Gulf of Mexico from Florida's southern tip for over 100 miles from Key Largo to Key West, are world-famous for their year-round fishing for bonefish, permit, tarpon, barracuda, snook, jacks, ladyfish, blackfin tuna, sharks, kingfish, mackerel, and redfish. The elusive, spooky bonefish, commonly known as the "gray ghost," are caught on weighted jigs, shrimp, and flies along the shallow, sun-drenched flats of the Keys. Stalking this aristocratic powerhouse—infamous for its searing, tackle-busting runs—is as much a matter of trophy hunting as it is

VACATION/ LODGING GUIDE

fishing. Fly fishing along the grassy flats for "tailing" bonefish ranks among the world's most challenging (and often frustrating) sports. The inexperienced angler is strongly advised to hire the services of a knowledgeable local guide, with a skiff and pole. The major fishing areas include the Islamorada Area, Marathon Area, and Smith Shoals, Demolition Key, Fleming Key, Northwest Channel, Boca Grande Key, Snipe and Barracuda keys, and Calda Banks in the Key West area. The chain of islands is connected by the Florida Overseas Highway.

The famous Everglades National Park takes in the largest subtropical forest in the United States. The reserve covers a vast wildland of beautiful, mangrove-bordered waterways along the famous trophy tarpon- and snook-fishing areas of the Ten Thousand Islands, inland to limestone flats, cypress swamps, sloughs, hammocks, dense tropical hardwood forests, and open woods of slash pine and saw palmetto inhabited by bald eagles, man-o'-war birds, wood ibis, rare manatees, alligators, flocks of white ibis, deer, and bear. The thousands of miles of interconnecting waterways and lakes, including vast Lake Okeechobee and the Loxahatchee Slough, offer some of the finest fishing in the country for tarpon, snook, and largemouth bass up to 18 pounds. Other features of the region include Okaloochee Swamp, Corkscrew Swamp, Big Cypress Indian Reserve, and Tamiami Canal. Some of the biggest tarpon caught in the state are found along the passes, creek mouths, and outside channels of the Ten Thousand Islands.

Florida's shallow, weedy, stump-filled lakes and meandering cypress-lined rivers are inhabited by a subspecies of the northern bass known as the Florida largemouth—a strain that grows to trophy weights of more than 20 pounds and provides the legendary fishing that gave birth to the state's nickname as "The Bass Capital of the World". Other freshwater species caught in Florida's lakes and streams include chain pickerel, several sunfishes, catfishes, crappie, and gar.

Each year, hundreds of trophy bass in the 10- to 14-pound class are caught in the lakes and streams throughout the state. The trophy waters of the western panhandle region include the Chipola River and Dead Lake—tributaries of the Apalachicola River, sprawling Lake Seminole, which straddles the Florida-Georgia border; Lake Talquin, on the Ochlockonee River, which flows through the Apalachicola National Forest, and Lake Iamonia and Lake Jackson. The moody Ochlockonee River flows through banks of high, pine-clad bluffs and dense cypress and hardwood forests. It can be treacherous during the flood season. Dead Lake, named for the countless dead cypress, oak, and pine trees submerged in the overflow from the Chipola River, offers some excellent fly fishing for big bass in the shallow, stump-filled areas and along the maze of forest-covered islands. Lodging and fishing guide service in the Apalachicola Swamp and Dead Lakes area is provided by *Breakaway Lodge*, Box 606, and *Bay City Lodge*, Box 172, both Apalachicola 32320.

The trophy bass waters in the famous northeast region of the Sunshine State include the Suwannee River, St. Johns River, Lake George, Lake Crescent, Oklawaha Lake and River, Waccasassa Bay, and Lochloosa, Orange, Newmans, and Magnolia lakes. The St. Johns River, whose nationally famous bass waters are suffering from the environment effects of an increasing population, still provides stretches of pastoral beauty along its shores, and excellent fishing in the cathedral-like cypress backwaters and sloughs. The St. Johns—the only major river in the United States that does not freeze over—rises in the flat, marshy treeless plains near Lake Helen Blazes and meanders north through a famed chain of bass lakes that include Sawgrass, Winder, Washington, Poinsett, Puzzle, Harney, Monroe, Mullet, Jessup, Beresford, Woodruff, Dexter, and Spring Garden, and huge Lake George. The central section of the St. Johns provides excellent fishing during the winter for American shad. Salt Cove, on the northwest side of Lake George, and the eastern shore of the lake yield good-size bass. The mouth of the Oklawaha River is a popular area, as are the waters around Turkey Island and Seven Sisters Islands. The prime fishing months are December through April for bass and January through April for crappie. The *Bass Capital Sportsman's Assn.* will provide free maps and information on big-bass spots and resorts in the St. Johns area; write: Box 550 C, Palatka 32077.

The fabled central lake region of Florida contains the largest number of trophy largemouth bass waters, including the cypress-lined shores of the wild Withlacoochee River, Rainbow and Hillsborough rivers, and Apopka, Tsala, Rousseau, Hamilton, Larkin, Louisa, Hart, Tohopekaliga, Myrtle, Preston, Cypress, Hatchineha, Kissimmee, Weohyakapka, Caloosa, Tiger, Marion, Pierce, June in Winter, and Istokpoga lakes. These scenic lakes and rivers, fringed with hammock growth of oak, hickory, cypress, and magnolia, provide fishing for pickerel, perch, bream, and catfish, in addition to lunker bass in the tangled, shallow, weedy, and dead-timber areas. Write to the *Hunting and Fishing Association*, Dunnellon 32630, for free information on fishing, guides, and lodges in the Withlacoochee and Rainbow river areas. Free recreation map/guides to the *Kissimmee Waterway* may be obtained by writing: Central and Southern Florida Flood Control District, P.O. Box V, West Palm Beach 33402.

The 475-mile Florida Trail, which will eventually stretch for 1,300 miles as a national scenic hiking trail, begins in the Big Cypress Swamp just north of the Everglades National Park and ends in the Blackwater River State Forest near Pensacola. The trail passes through some of the wildest and most scenic portions of Florida's interior, and provides access to many seldom-explored bass lakes and wilderness

camping areas. The best time to hike the trail is winter, when temperatures are moderate and insects less troublesome than during the spring and summer.

The scenic Ocala National Forest takes in 336,000 acres of vast sand-pine forests, meandering crystal-clear streams, huge bubbling springs, and hundreds of natural lakes between the Oklawaha and St. Johns rivers in central Florida. The major features of the region include Junipers and Alexander Creek canoe trails, Ocala Trail, Buckskin Prairie, and the renowned largemouth-bass waters of Lake George and of Dorr, Ker, Bryant, Dexter, and Halfmoon lakes, and the Lake Woodruff National Wildlife Refuge. The forest also includes the whitetail-deer, black-bear, and wild-turkey hunting areas of the F. McCoy and Lochloosa wildlife-management areas.

The Ocala Trail, a 64–mile portion of the Florida Trail, which eventually will run the 700–mile length of Florida in much the same way as the Appalachian Trail crosses the eastern mountains, passes about 60 natural ponds and plunges through cypress and gum swamps on winding boardwalks. The trail also traverses the rolling, open, longleaf-pine forests and scattered clumps of dwarf live oaks. The rolling sand dunes of the ancient Florida coastline are now covered with sand pine. This unusual tree, with its dense scrub understory, is the only major species of tree capable of growing on these very dry dunes.

The 556,480–acre Apalachicola National Forest, from the Indian word meaning "people on the other side," lies in the eastern portion of the Florida panhandle and includes the renowned bass waters of the Ochlockonee River (Indian for "red oak") canoe trail, Lake Talquin, and the New, Sopchoppy, and Apalachicola rivers. Wildlife includes whitetail deer, black bear, the beautiful wood duck, southern bald eagle, sandhill crane, alligator, and panther. Campgrounds are located at Wright, Silver, Lost, and Moore lakes and at Trout Pond. The entire forest is a designated wildlife-management area, with hunting by special permit only.

Information Sources, Maps & Access

For detailed fishing and hunting information, regulations, and the following free publications, write to the Information Office, Dept. of Natural Resources, Crown Bldg., 302 Blount St., Tallahassee 32304 (904)488–1234: *Florida's Fish Management Areas; Florida Sport Fishing Guide*, which includes full-color illustrations of freshwater and saltwater game fish, fishing tips, laws, first aid, fishing rigs and natural baits, and a chart for regional fishing areas and species present; *Facts for Florida Fishermen; Archery and Special Managed Hunt Information, Migratory Game Bird Regulations; State Forest Maps*; and *Hunting & Freshwater Fishing Regulations*.

Southern Guide Fishing Maps showing all man-made and natural features including camps, boat-ramps, roads, water depths, stump and lily pad areas, and trophy bass spots are available for Juniper, Dead, Talquin, Jackson-Orange-Lochloosa, Rodman, George, Tohopekaliga, Kissimmee, and Okeechobee lakes. Each map sells for $1.90 (postpaid) and may be ordered from: Southern Guide Fishing Maps, 1325 E. Tennessee St., P.O. Box 1106, Tallahassee 32302.

For a free *Everglades National Park Map/Brochure* and information about Everglades National Park guided park tours, hikes, and canoe adventures, write: Superintendent, Everglades National Park, Box 279, Homestead 33030 (305)247–6211. For free maps that show the canal system of Florida from Orlando to the Everglades National Park, detailing locks, spillways, pump stations, and major roads, as well as a booklet, *Recreation in the Everglades*, containing maps

described above and also launching ramps, write to: Central and Southern Florida Flood Control District, P.O. Box V. West Palm Beach 33402. The park is reached via the Tamiami Trail, U.S. Route 41, and Florida 27 from Miami. Lodging, meals, marina services, charter fishing boats, and sightseeing boat trips are provided by *Everglades Park Catering Inc.*, 301 Miamarina Parkway Dr., Miami 33132; phone (305)358–5480.

For information, a free *Florida Trail* pamphlet, and a *Florida Trail Map Kit* ($2.50, postpaid), write: Florida Trail Assn., Office, P.O. Box 13708, Gainesville 32604.

A descriptive folder on the *Ocala National Forest* is available free from the Forest Service, P.O. Box 1050, Tallahassee 32302 (904)878–1131. This attractive full-color brochure provides the forest visitor with a map showing all primary and secondary recreation areas and roads. A brief description of the extent of the forest's variety and beauty is also included. For further information on the forest, you may contact: Lake George Ranger District, Ocala 32670, phone (904)622–6577; Seminole Ranger District, Eustis 32726, phone (904)357–3721; or Forest Supervisor, P.O. Box 1050, Tallahassee 32302. The Forest Service will also provide a free folder on the *Ocala National Trail*. It contains a map of the trail, showing campgrounds, water sources, lookout towers, roads, and other useful points of interest to the hiker. Mileage between points on the trail is also provided, and different vegetation areas are also delineated. This brochure is useful not only to the beginner, but to anyone who is planning to hike this most interesting trail for the first time.

Professional guide service for the trophy bass waters of the Ocala National Forest and Central Florida is provided by Bass Champions, Route 2, Box 2047, Ft. McCoy 32637. Bass Champions also arranges guided bass fishing trips throughout the Southern United States, plug big-game saltwater fishing trips.

All visitors to the Ocala National Forest should obtain a copy of the *Ocala National Forest Map*, available for 50¢ from the Forest Supervisor (address above). This excellent map shows all boundaries, roads, canoe runs, developed and primitive recreation sites, boat ramps, swamps and marshes, lakes and ponds, wayside areas, and other points of interest. A legend of federal recreation symbols is also provided to aid motorists. The map includes a chart showing principal, secondary, and primitive recreation areas, their locations on the map, and the facilities available at each individual area. Free maps/guides to the *Alexander Springs Recreation Area* and *Juniper Creek Canoe Run* may be obtained by writing to the Forest Supervisor's Office.

Visitors to the Apalachicola National Forest will want to send for the *Apalachicola National Forest Map*. A copy can be obtained for 50¢ from the Forest Supervisor, P.O. Box 1050, Tallahassee 32302 (904)878–1131. This map shows roads and highways, wildlife-management areas, recreation areas, undeveloped sites, ranger headquarters, and work centers. The Forest Service also has available a free pamphlet describing the *Silver Lake Recreation Area*, noting the facilities available in the area, along with a map. For further information on Silver Lake, contact the District Ranger, P.O. Box 68, Crawfordville 32327. The forest is reached by U.S. highways 98 and 319 and Florida 20, 65, and 369. Accommodations, supplies, and equipment rentals are available at Apalachicola, Blountstown, Bristol, and Tallahassee.

Lodges & Coastal Resorts

★★★★*Amelia Island Plantation*, located on the southernmost sea island in the "Golden Isles" chain of barrier islands, is an outstanding 850–acre resort community located 32 miles northeast of Jacksonville, with superb surf and offshore charter-boat fishing, a 27–hole golf course, 19 tennis courts, beach club, inn, nature and bicycle paths, playgrounds, and nature preserves. The Plantation is located at the southern end of Amelia Island between the Atlantic Ocean and the Intracoastal Waterway, only 30 minutes by car from Jacksonville International Airport. There are 27 holes of golf masterfully designed by noted golf course architect Pete Dye, who is also golf course consultant to the Plantation. Dye has described the Amelia Links as "The only true links on the East Coast". The three "nines" offer a host of challenges to amateur and professional alike: Oakmarsh and Oysterbay nines are 6,372 yards of winding fairways, with marsh edges and undulating greens. Oceanside, the third nine, includes

three holes nestled between sand dunes, paralleling the sea. There is a pro shop with snack-beverage bar, sportswear shop, plus a golf-cart barn to accommodate 100 carts. There is also a driving range and putting green, and individual lessons are available from a staff of teaching professionals. The Plantation's Racquet Park has 19 composition tennis courts, one a stadium court for tournaments. Tennis camps featuring four- and seven-day options are conducted by All-American Sports, September through May. Private and group lessons are available, using video teaching equipment and ball machines. Racquet Park also includes a restaurant, specializing in local seafood, banquet room, veranda bar, tennis pro shop, and complete health club with sauna, whirlpool, steam and exercise room. There are over 200 kinds of birds on the Plantation, in addition to raccoons, opossum, squirrels, and an occasional armadillo or alligator. All of the lagoon systems hold a wide variety of fish indigenous to Florida. Four environment "awareness walks" with interpretive signs explaining the ecology, have been developed for the enjoyment of nature lovers. *The Sunken Forest:* An 850–foot cypress boardwalk winds through a rare sunken forest between dune lines and then climbs to an observation deck on top of a 50–foot dune overlooking the ocean. The forest is a dense canopy of trees which offers protection to birds, reptiles, and small mammals from the salt spray and ocean winds. Approximately two acres in size, the Sunken Forest area has been designated a perpetual forest. *Willow Pond Conservancy:* The low wetland and thick woods are a haven for the Plantation's marsh wildlife. Bordering the conservancy on the east is the Landmark Oak, a tree of monumental size. Paths wind near this and other ancient oaks, palms, and willows in the area. *Drummond Point Park:* Almost seven acres of tidal marsh, mixed broadleaf forest and a transitional area mixing the two offer a quiet walk on coquina paths and 800 feet of cypress boardwalks along the edge of the marsh. Picnic tables and benches are provided so that guests can relax and enjoy the sight of waterbirds feeding in the marshlands. *Walker's Landing:* This marsh-side area centers around an Indian burial mound dating from 800–1200 A.D. Here the Plantation has built a camp for cookouts, picnics and oyster roasts. Fishing and crabbing are popular along the creek banks. Many of the Plantation's informal social events are held here on weekends and holidays. A network of about five miles of bicycle trails connects all parts of the Plantation. These trails lead through some of the most scenic parts of the Plantation and avoid the main road systems. Bicycles can be rented at the Village Store. Fishing is excellent, both within the Plantation and on Amelia Island itself. Freshwater lagoons on the Plantation are stocked with bream and largemouth bass, and landlocked tarpon and snook are often found here. Crabbing is popular at Walker's Landing. Offshore catches on the island include king mackerel, cobia, crevalle, dolphin, sailfish, amberjack, bonita, barracuda, blue marlin, red snapper and grouper. Giant tarpon can be found at the mouth of St. Marys River from April through late October. Inshore fishing offers record black drum, tarpon, channel bass, striped bass, spotted sea trout, bluefish, flounder and sheepshead. The fishing is especially good between Cumberland Inlet and Amelia Island (at the northern end of the Island). Surf fishing is excellent near the Plantation on the south end of the Island. Charter boats can be rented through Amelia Angler Shop. The Amelia Angler, Terry Lacoss, arranges fishing expeditions both on and off the Plantation. He can also supply equipment, bait and advice. The Beach Clubhouse contains an 85–seat restaurant, disco and cocktail lounge, an Olympic-sized pool, a baby pool, and children's playground. The Clubhouse is headquarters for the Plantation's summer youth program, directed by Tom Purvis. There are also dressing rooms, and a beach rental shop with chaise lounges, sailboats, rafts, and beach umbrellas available. A lifeguard is on duty during the spring, summer and

early fall. The Plantation has over two miles of beach with a strand over 300 feet wide at low tide. The hardpacked, white sandy stretch is beautiful and uncluttered. Sand dunes of up to 50 feet rise behind the beach, and boardwalks lead from the beach club and all oceanfront villas to the beach. The Plantation's fishing guide, the Amelia Angler, is also headquartered at the Beach Club. The Sea Horse Stables are located about two miles from the Plantation on the southern end of the Island. Saddle horses can be rented here for individual and group rides through trails and along the beach. Riding lessons are also available. The Shopping Village at the Plantation includes two gift boutiques, a ladies shop, beauty parlor, a delicatessen and sandwich shop, an ice cream parlor, bicycle rental shop and a village store, a general and package store. The Paddle Loft Lounge, a local pub, is located above the Village Store. The Amelia Island Inn, with its 125–seat oceanview restaurant and cocktail lounge, is the social center of the Plantation. The Inn contains 24 spacious guest suites, each with private balcony or terrace offering views of the Atlantic Ocean and the Amelia Links. Many of the privately-owned villas on the Plantation are available for vacation rental by the day, week or month. These villas offer complete accommodations and are available in a variety of architectural styles, floor plans and locations, which range from ocean-front to fairway and marsh. All are within walking distance or a bicycle ride of the Inn, beach, tennis center, pools, golf course and shopping village. Villas have from one to four bedrooms. All have central air and heat and are equipped with complete kitchens, linens and towels. Inn and villa rates range from $51 to $156 per person per day depending on season and location and include daily maid service. Amelia Island Plantation shares the Island with the charming and picturesque seaport community of Fernandina Beach, once a favorite winter resort for turn-of-the-century "snowbirds" and the birthplace of the offshore shrimping industry. The little Victorian town, which is the first stop in Florida on the Intracoastal Waterway, has been named an Historic District in the National Register of Historic Places since its recent 30–block restoration. Fernandina's walking or driving tour for visitors begins with a look at the shrimp fleet, docked next to the old brick railroad station, now the Chamber of Commerce Building. The tour goes down Centre Street, past the famous old Palace Saloon, the oldest bar in Florida, and winds through side streets past old Steamboat Gothic and Queen Anne houses dating as far back as 1857. The restored 1878 Steak House is noted today for its steaks, shrimp and oysters. The tour takes you to Fort Clinch, on the northern end of the Island looking out to Cumberland Island, now a National Park. Begun prior to Civil War but never finished, Fort Clinch illustrates a European-style brick masonry, unique in this country. The Fort's museum includes a summary of Amelia Island history. For additional information and reservations, contact: Amelia Island Plantation, Amelia Island, FL 32034 (800)874–6878. In Florida, call (904)261–6161.

★★★★*Cheeca Lodge on Islamorada in the Florida Keys* has the most complete year-round sports facilities in the area. For the golfer, there is an executive golf course designed by the people who build all Jack Nicklaus' championship courses. Fishermen will enjoy the 525–foot lighted fishing pier. Or they can join Islamorada's captains and guides for off-shore fishing for bonefish, permit and tarpon. Tennis players will enjoy the four all-weather lighted courts and the well-stocked pro shop, and they may learn some new techniques from the teaching pro on staff. For water sports there are two pools, diving and snorkeling on the nearby coral reefs, or wading in the ocean along the 1,100–foot white sandy beach. One of the longest stretches of private beach in the Keys, it is also perfect for strolling at sunset or jogging at dawn. For dining pleasure there is the oceanfront restaurant in the lodge, a snack bar, or dining outdoors at umbrellaed tables. There are drinks and evening entertainment in the Light Tackle Lounge. And, while the atmosphere is luxurious, it is also informal. Accommodations are luxurious. There are villas, lodge rooms and cottage bedrooms. Rates are quoted on the European Plan. From May 2 through December 14, lodge rooms rent for $45 to $50, a villa bedroom with screened porch is $55 to $60, a studio kitchenette with Bahamas beds is $60 to $65 and a cottage bedroom is $40. Winter rates from December 15 through May 1, start at $65 for a cottage bedroom and go up to $100 for a studio/kitchenette. Greens fees are $5 per person per day including unlimited play. Tennis is free in the summer season and $5 per day from December 15 to May 1. For information write: Cheeca Lodge, P.O. Box 527, Islamorada, FL 33036 (305)664–4651 or call toll free outside Florida (800)327–2888.

★★★*Flamingo Inn at Everglades National Park* is located on the edge of Florida Bay providing a full range of activities for the novice or experienced angler. From the Bay, or the Everglades Backcountry, fishermen can catch tarpon, snook, redfish, snapper and sea trout. Chartered boats and skiffs are available. The marina at Flamingo has 100 rental slips, and a full range of fishing paraphernalia. There are boat rentals, including canoes, skiffs, and outboard. Cruising houseboats are outfitted for an excursion of several days. Backcountry cruises travel into Coot Bay, with wildlife spotted along Buttonwood Canal, and stops at Cape Sable, the southernmost point in the continental United States. Vessels departing the marina from Flamingo each day offer spectators a fine view of the famous Everglades sunsets and colorful flights of birds. A wilderness tram

travels into the underbrush through mangrove forests, with views of wildlife along the Snake Bight Trail. The National Park Service and Flamingo Inn offer a variety of guided trips—or explore on your own. The Visitor Center and Museum offering area displays is staffed by Park Service naturalists. Accommodations at Flamingo Inn include guest rooms in the motel, with maid service, two double beds, bath, pool privileges and TV. There are also housekeeping cottages, with kitchens, separate bedrooms, living rooms, dishes, flatware, maid service, air-conditioning, and pool privileges. Rates do not include meals, which are available at the Inn's restaurant overlooking Florida Bay. Rates: guest rooms, winter $35, summer $26 double occupancy. Housekeeping cottages, winter $38, summer $29. For further information contact: Flamingo Inn, Flamingo, FL 33030 (813)695-3101, or (305)253-2241.

★★★★*Grenelefe Golf & Racquet Club* offers tennis and 36 holes of golf right at your doorstep. Only minutes away are Florida's most popular attractions: Sea World, Cypress Gardens, Disney World, Stars Hall of Fame, Bok Singing Tower and Mountain Lake Sanctuary, and Circus World, the home of the Ringling Bros. and Barnum & Bailey Circus. Grenelefe's Tennis Village features a large tennis clubhouse and pro shop with an observation tower overlooking the 12 Har-tru courts below. Four courts are lit for night play, Grenelefe's staff of professionals are on hand to offer the finest instruction. Tennis tournaments, and court side barbeques, and a variety of tennis vacation packages make Grenelefe one of the nation's top tennis resorts. Two lush, undulating golf courses provide 36 challenging holes of golf, relaxed and uncrowded, with plenty of well-designed sand traps and sparkling lagoons to challenge every golfer. Grenelefe has a golf pro shop, a professional teaching staff, and a variety of golf vacation packages to insure a delightful golfing vacation, in any season. Fisherman will appreciate nearby Lake Marion, which holds big bass, perch and bluegill. There are also two pools, intimate lounges, and two fine restaurants offering a variety of cuisine and nightly entertainment. All Grenelefe's deluxe hotel rooms are handsomely furnished and overlook the fairways. Rates are $26-32 daily, depending on the season. Grenelefe also offers plush, one, two and three bedroom suites, beautifully furnished with living room, private balconies, and complete kitchens. Rates are $46-76 from June 1 to September 30, and $52-104 in season. For more information write: Grenelefe Resort, P.O. Box 143, Cypress Gardens, FL 33880 toll free, (800)228-9822.

★★★*Indies Inn on Duck Key*, one of the remote Florida Keys, is about 90 minutes south of Miami via the Overseas Highway. Boat owners can arrive by boat from the Intracoastal Waterway; the channel is 85 feet wide and a minimum depth of 10 feet at low tide. Marina facilities include 110 and 220 voltage, fresh water, fuel, dry storage, a laundromat and "botels." The Indies Inn is luxurious but casual and has an "out islands" feeling to it. Guests can enjoy skin diving on the continent's only living coral reef. There is swimming in a freshwater pool, a saltwater pool and the ocean. The hotel has a 9–hole, par–3 course and the Sombrero Country Club nearby has a challenging 18–hole course. Several all-weather tennis courts, located just steps from their rooms, will please tennis buffs. Anglers can charter fishing boats at the Marina, and there are also sailing and outboard rentals. The Inn also has bicycling, shuffleboard, volleyball, ladies programs and activities for the children. The Island Dining Room serves lobster, snapper, pompano, shrimp and grouper as well as meat dishes, or for dining, dancing and entertainment, guests can choose the Ship's In Supper Club. For a relaxing drink there is the Bamboo Lounge. Rooms are large with patio balconies and two double beds in each. There are also suites, two-bedroom "botels" and apartments and one-bedroom Marina Apartments with

kitchens. For more information write: Indies Inn, Duck Key, FL 33050 (305)289-1000.

★★★★*Innisbrook Resort at Tarpon Springs* is nestled on 1000 acres of spacious grounds and blue lakes near the Gulf of Mexico beaches in Tarpon Springs. Three undulating championship golf courses, banked by lakes and tree-lined fairways, provide 63 holes of superlative golf. Golf director Mike Souchak, world record holder for the lowest 72–hole total ever recorded in a PGA tournament, heads the professional staff that makes golfing at Innisbrook unique. Tennis buffs will enjoy Innisbrook's superior courts, 17 in all, many lit for a brisk evening set. Round robins and guest tournaments offer singles and doubles play, and Innisbrook offers expert daily instruction featuring the finest electronic equipment to analyse form and strengthen every level of ability. Fishermen will enjoy the variety of lakes and ponds that lace the quiet woods and open lawns. Children will find special activities including tennis, swimming, fishing, volleyball, basketball and trips to the nearby gulf beaches, led by a trained, enthusiastic staff of counselors. Other amenities include 5 swimming pools, a sauna, professional massage, bike rentals, daily shuttles to the Gulf beaches, 3 restaurants serving a variety of fine cuisine, lounges, discos and live entertainment nightly. All deluxe hotel rooms are luxuriously furnished and have private balconies and patios. Plush suites have wall-to-wall carpeting, modern fully equipped kitchens and sumptuous decor. Innisbrook offers a variety of honeymoon packages, golf and tennis specials. Innisbrook also has twin conference centers with 30 individual modern seminar rooms for groups from 10–2000. For details, write: Innisbrook Resort, P.O. Drawer 1088, Tarpon Springs, FL 33589 (800)237-0157.

★★★★*Rainbow Bend Fishing Club on Grassy Key* combines the friendly atmosphere of the old Florida Keys fishing clubs with modern facilities. It is family owned and operated, just 92 miles south of Miami via the Overseas Highway. Room rates include use of one of their 15–foot Boston Whalers with 25–hp motors. They also have sailboats for the use of guests and expert instruction for the beginner. Captain Kris Karelius runs daily fishing or diving trips from the dock. Their specialty is saltwater fly fishing and there are tarpon, bonefish, grouper, mackerel, kingfish, dolphin and others to be caught. There is a fresh water swimming pool as well as a hot therapy pool. For salt water swimming, guests can swim near the dock at high tide, or walk out through shallow water to a deep "swimming hole." Or guests can motor south about a mile to the sandbars which can be seen from the dock. For those who like to get underwater, there is snorkeling in clear water at Coffin's Patch, a shallow coral area. Rarely visited deep diving spots are farther out. The resort supplies masks and snorkels, and scuba gear and air are available in Marathon Shores, three miles south. Guests can relax on the sandy beach or in the enclosed sub-tropical gardens. The Rainbow Bend Restaurant serves local specialties such as conch chowder, Florida lobster and key lime pie, as well as specialties of the house including lasagna and Argentine mixed grill. For refreshments, the Rainbow Room has wines and beer on draft and overlooks the dock, beach and ocean. Accommodations are in large rooms, efficiencies and cottages with two bedrooms, bath, living room and kitchen. The off season rate from May through December is $50 for a room, $52 for a small efficiency, $56 for one or two bedrooms with kitchen, and $65 for oceanfront cottages with kitchens. All units are air conditioned and heated. A full American breakfast is included and rates are based on single or double occupancy. There is no charge for children under 7 and rates are slightly higher in season. For reservations, write or phone: Kris and Virginia Karelius, P.O. Box 2447, Marathon Shores, FL 33052 (305)289-1505.

★★★★*South Seas Plantation* is secluded on the north shore of lush tropical Captiva Island. Legend has it that Pirate Jose Gasper, who plundered the west coast of Florida, hid beautiful captive women on this island, believing they would bring a finer ransom if protected from his own men. Now Captiva Island harbors one of the nation's finest resorts, South Seas Plantation, offering luxurious accommodations, a rolling golf course bordered by the azure Gulf waters, 17 championship tennis courts, three restaurants, 13 fresh water pools, miles of white sandy beaches strewn with rare shells, and a deep marina harboring yachts to 100 feet. Gulf and backbay waters yield trout, grouper, Spanish mackerel, snook, jack crevalle, redfish, pompano, and other species, depending on the season. The Plantation charters 22-foot open boats for fishing parties up to four persons, and will arrange wildlife tours and rare-shell hunts to the remote Gulf islands. Sunfish, paddleboats, and Hobie Cat sailboats are available at the marina, which also has a well-stocked Ships Store, complete with all necessary charts and supplies. Tennis clinics led by professionals, tournaments, and day and nightly challenge on South Seas 17 championship courts offer unique opportunities for players on all levels. Bicycles, tandems, and three-wheel bicycles are available to explore the back beaches and bayous of Captiva Island. Three exciting restaurants provide a variety of atmosphere and cuisine; the Kings Crown offers continental dining in the gracious atmosphere of the old south; native specialties and sumptuous seafood buffets are served in the Chadwicks; and Captain Als' Pub is a popular spot for an informal meal overlooking the marina. All deluxe hotel rooms are beautifully furnished and carpeted, with color TV and private balconies. Rates are $37 daily, double occupancy. There are also plush villas, with one or two bedrooms, living room, kitchen, and private porches. All are fully equipped with modern conveniences, and luxurious decor. Rates are $50–$70 daily. Tennis fees, golf fees, bike rentals and fishing charters are additional. South Seas Plantation has three modern, tastefully appointed conference centers for groups to 300. For details, write: South Seas

Plantation, P.O. Box 194, Captiva Island, FL 33924 (within Florida, (800)282–3402; out of state (800)237–3102).

★★★★*Sugar Loaf Lodge in the Florida Keys* is an out-island resort and is as beautiful as any to be found anywhere in the Caribbean. It is situated on 120 acres, secluded, peaceful and relaxing, yet brimming with activity—a complete resort community. Enjoy the fresh water pool or swim in the clear waters of the Gulf, play tennis, miniature golf, shuffleboard, go sailing, water skiing, skin diving or canoeing, roam the shoreline, take a nature tour or go shelling or bicycling. Fish the ocean side aboard a charter boat, fish the Gulf side with a guide, or go it alone. The waters abound with sail, dolphin, tarpon and king, bonefish, permit, snapper, and grouper—it's truly a fisherman's paradise. You can also arrange for an exciting flight ($45) to Fort Jefferson, the most inaccessible National Monument in America, on Dry Tortugas. There you can fish, snorkel, lunch or just walk around the beach and historic fort. Rooms at the lodge are European plan and have patios overlooking the crystal waters of Sugar Loaf Sound and the Gulf of Mexico; some are poolside. Rates range from $30–45 depending on season. Some efficiencies are also available. Contact Sugar Loaf Lodge, Box 148, Sugar Loaf Key, FL 33044 (305)745–3211.

Travel Services

Worldwide Sportsman, Inc.—Safaris and Outfitters, of Islamorada, offers complete travel-planning and trip-outfitting services (including air transportation, lodging, and guides) for vacations at several world-renowned trophy fishing meccas, including the tarpon and bonefish waters of the Florida Keys, Mexico's Pez Maya on the Yucatan Peninsula; Casa Mar Camp on the northeast Caribbean coast of Costa Rica for giant snook and tarpon; and the famed bonefish flats of the Turneffe Islands in Central America. For free literature, rates, and information, write Worldwide Sportsman, Inc., P.O. Drawer 787, Islamorada, FL 33036; or call, toll free, (800)327–2880.

GEORGIA

Introduction

The State of Georgia contains several renowned outdoor recreation areas within its 58,876 square miles: the southernmost segment of the Appalachian Trail, winding along the scenic crest of the 4,000–foot Blue Ridge Mountains; the famed Blue Ridge fish and game country of the Chattahoochee National Forest; the Chattooga National Wild River; the waters of Lake Burton, Chestatee River, Lake Sidney Lanier, and Lake Seminole; the legendary Okefenokee National Wildlife Refuge and the headwaters of the historic Suwannee National Scenic River; and the beautiful Atlantic barrier islands and fishing areas of the famous "Golden Isles."

Accommodations & Travel Information

For information on hotel and motel accommodations in Georgia write: Georgia Hotel and Motel Assn., 1410 Rhodes Haverty Bldg., Atlanta 30303. Specific details on state parks and historical points of interest can be obtained from: Public Relations and Information Section, Dept. of Natural Resources, 270 Washington St., SW, Atlanta 30334. The Bureau of Industry and Trade, Tourist Division, P.O. Box 38097, Atlanta 30334, will be glad to provide information and suggestions on vacation and travel within the state.

Georgia Days, a handsome, illustrated 47–page booklet, available free from the Bureau of Industry and Trade at the above address, contains a wealth of interesting information on the state's many outdoor attractions. Divided into three major sections on the mountains, piedmont, and coastal plain, the guide offers town-by-town listings of camps and camping areas, historical sites, lakes, hunting areas, state parks and cabins, fishing, and annual events. Charts for the various state parks indicate number and kinds of facilities available: picnic areas, campsites, hiking trails, boat rentals, etc. Detailed and comprehensive road maps for each region are also included. For more specific information on any area, activity, or attraction, the authors of *Georgia Days* advise writing the Chamber of Commerce of the community listed.

Campgrounds in the Blue Ridge include the Lake Blue Ridge Camping Area, off U.S. 76 near the town of Blue Ridge. Open between May 1 and October 31, the area is operated by the U.S. Forest Service and offers tent and trailer camping, water skiing, swimming, nature trails, fishing, and a boat ramp, all on 15 forested acres adjoining the lake. Slightly northwest of the Lake Blue Ridge Camping Area, Morgantown Point, also off U.S. 76, offers similar opportunities for outdoor recreation on 12 acres of national forest land. The privately owned Skeenah Creek Campgrounds, 16 miles east of Blue Ridge via State Highway 60, is open year round for trailer and primitive camping, hiking and bicycle trails, and trout fishing. Also privately owned, Whispering Pines Camping Area, 8 miles east of Blue Ridge, features year-round tent and trailer camping, nature trails, fishing, a swimming pool, and a campground. A third Forest Service campground 18 miles east of Blue Ridge via State Highway 60, Deep Hole Recreation Area, offers camping, hiking, and fishing between May 1 and October 31. Many other campsites are scattered throughout the state, providing facilities and activities for every taste and budget. Consult the *Georgia Days* booklet or write to: Georgia Campground Owners Assn., P.O. Box 5487, Columbus 31902. Supervisors of the state parks and national forest will also be glad to supply details on camping areas within their jurisdiction.

Georgia Forests, Lakes & the "Golden Isles"

Georgia, the largest state east of the Mississippi, is famous for its beautiful chain of barrier islands—known as the "Golden Isles"—and superb saltwater fishing as well as some of the finest freshwater fishing in the eastern U.S. for bass and chain pickerel up to world's record size, brown trout up to 8 pounds, rainbows to 12 pounds, walleye to 11 pounds, acrobatic bronzebacks up to 7 pounds, giant stripers up to 60 pounds, and schools of perch, crappie, and bluegills in its 17 major reservoirs, 3,500 miles of warmwater streams, 40,000 small lakes and ponds, and some 700 miles of scenic mountain trout streams in the northern Blue Ridge wildlands in the vast Chattahoochee National Forest (q.v.). The state is divided into five major physiographic provinces: the Appalachian plateau, the valley and ridge region, the Blue Ridge country, the Piedmont plateau, and the coastal plain.

The extreme northwestern corner of the state, separated by mountain ridges from the rest of Georgia, ranges in altitude from 800 to 2,000 feet. Most of north Georgia is covered by ranges of the southern Appalachians, the Blue Ridge mountains on the east and the Cohuttas—a continuation of the Smoky Mountains—on the west. Numerous cross ranges are separated by valleys such as the Hiawassee and Nottely river valleys. The ridge separating these two valleys features Georgia's highest peak, Brasstown Bald or Mount Etowah, 4,784 feet in altitude. Many of the state's major rivers—the Savannah, Toccoa, Chattahoochee, and Tennessee—have their sources in the Blue Ridge, where the clear, swift-flowing headwaters descend in many waterfalls.

Almost a third of Georgia's territory and most of its major cities fall within the rolling uplands of the middle or Piedmont region. The landscape here is broken occasionally by deep rivers and a few bold

VACATION/ LODGING GUIDE

ridges and hills rising as high as 1,000 feet above the surrounding terrain. Formed of a highly resistant rock, the most conspicuous of these hills are Kennesaw Mountain near Marietta and Stone Mountain outside Atlanta. The red or reddish-yellow waters of the Savannah, Ocmulgee, Oconee, and Chattahoochee rivers drain the Piedmont. Below the fall line, which extends from Augusta to Columbus, the southern half of Georgia is part of the coastal plain. Rivers descend in many small rapids from hills along the highlands, some of which exceed elevations of 600 feet. Five coastal "terraces" cover the southeastern corner of the plain; the best known of these, the Okefenokee Terrace, ranges in elevation from 100 to 160 feet and contains the magnificent Okefenokee Swamp, second-largest freshwater swamp in the country. Often submerged at flood tide, the shorelands of the coastal plain are cut by tidal rivers and studded with grassy marshes. The beautiful "Golden Isles"—including St. Catherines, St. Simon, Jekyll, Cumberland, and Sapelo—fringe the Georgia coastline.

The Chattahoochee National Forest, a renowned hunting, fishing, hiking, and canoe-camping area, once the hunting grounds of the Cherokee Indian Nation, covers 700,000 acres of Blue Ridge wilderness country in northern Georgia. The forest is joined on the north by the Cherokee and Nantahala national forests of Tennessee and North Carolina. Two of the Chattahoochee's major features are the Appalachian Trail and a 50–mile stretch of the Chattooga National Wild River, rated by experts as one of the most perilous whitewater canoe runs in the United States. The wild Chattooga roars through a deep gorge with sheer walls up to 400 feet high.

The forest offers excellent hunting for whitetail deer, ruffed grouse, and wild turkey in the interior wildlands of the Warwoman, Russell Lake, Swallow Creek, Lake Burton, Chattahoochee, Chestatee, Cooper's Creek, Blue Ridge, Rich Mountain, Cohutta, and Johns Mountain wildlife management areas. There is good fishing for brook, brown, and rainbow trout in the highland streams and fine canoe camping along the Toccoa, Nottely, Hiawassee, Jacks, Conasauga, and Tallulah rivers.

Primitive hiking trails and old abandoned logging roads provide access to the distant pools and riffles of the forest's premier fly fishing waters, where rainbow, brook, and brown trout grow to record weights. These picturesque streams, which are managed for artificial lures and flies only, are located in scenic mountain valleys surrounded by mixed hardwoods and dense thickets of laurel and rhododendron. The major streams include the Chattahoochee River, Coleman River, Jones and Noontootla creeks on the Blue Ridge WMA (Wildlife Management Area), Moccasin Creek on the Lake Burton WMA, Mountaintown Creek on the Cohutta WMA, Stanley Creek on the Rich Mountain WMA, Tate Branch on the Coleman River WMA, scenic Tuckaluge Creek, and Walnut Fork and Hood creeks on the Warwoman WMA. Water Creek on the Chestatee WMA produced the state record 5–pound 5–ounce brook trout, is managed as a "trophy" stream for barbless hooks only, and annually yields rainbows up to 10 pounds and brown trout to 8 pounds. Rock Creek on the Blue Ridge WMA produced the state record 18–pound 3–ounce brown trout, and consistently yields trophy browns up to weights of 8 pounds.

In the northwestern portion of the forest is the Cohutta Wilderness, 61,500 acres of primitive mountains and forest, the largest protected Forest Service Wilderness in the East. The land here is steep and deeply scored by the Conasauga and Jacks rivers and their many tributary streams. The rough topography, rocky bluffs, and absence of major roads make the area almost completely inaccessible except to hikers and backpackers, who will find innumerable deep, quiet pools interrupting the boulder-strewn stretches of river. The Jacks River flows through a wild gorge, dropping over 400 feet in 2 miles, and is additionally enhanced by a spectacular waterfall, Ball-Peen Falls. The waters of the two adjacent watersheds of the Conasauga and Jacks rivers harbor naturally reproducing stocks of trout, testimony to the quality and purity of these streams as they flow through virtually undisturbed areas. In the southern reaches of the wilderness, tall stands of virgin hemlock and oak blanket the slopes of Cohutta Mountain. Camping facilities are available on Conasauga Lake at the foot of the mountain. Huge island-dotted Lake Lanier, located south of the Chattahoochee National Forest, where it is fed by the clear, frigid waters of the Chestatee and Chattahoochee rivers, provides some of the state's best fishing for trophy largemouth bass and brown trout. The clear, 30–mile long tailrace waters below Lake Lanier provide some of the best float fishing in the South for large rainbows and buckskin-flanked browns up to 9 pounds. Lake Allatoona to the west on the Etowah River holds some lunker bass, and Lakes Rabun, Seed, Tugaloo, and Hartwell on the Tallulah River to the east hold large bass and a few trophy-sized rainbows and browns. The lakes of northern Georgia are generally clear year round with excellent launching and rental facilities scattered along the access area.

The huge Clark Hill Reservoir, Lake Blackshear, Walter F. George Reservoir, and Lake Seminole—often referred to as the bass capital of the world—with their sprawling, stump-filled irregularly shaped shorelines in central and southern Georgia, offer some of the South's finest fishing for trophy largemouth bass. The meandering, deep, dark waters of the scenic Flint, Chattahoochee, Ocmulgee, Oconee, Ogeechee, Ohoopee, Altamaha, Savannah, and Satilla rivers, which flow through the central plateau and coastal lowlands surrounded by moss-draped cypress trees, thick green floodplain forests, and swamplands, provide excellent canoe camping and float fishing for big largemouth bass, bluegills, redear sunfish, and voracious chain pickerel as long as your arm. Fishing camps and float fishing outfitters are located along most of the rivers. The lower reaches and tidewater areas of the coastal streams provide good seasonal fishing for migrating shad and striped bass up to 50 pounds. The limpid green headwaters of the beautiful Suwannee River in the vast primitive wildlands of Okefenokee National Wildlife Refuge hold some monster largemouth bass and lean green chain pickerel.

A few miles south of Waycross, the Okefenokee Swamp spreads across the southeastern corner of the state to an indefinite termination south of the Florida line. Covering an area of close to half a million acres, the Okefenokee is some 40 miles long and up to 25 miles wide. Geologists believe the swamp was once a shallow ocean sound, cut off by a 100–mile-long sandbar now called the Trail Ridge. Sometime during the Pleistocene era, a half million to a million years ago, the large body of water was trapped and its salt content gradually flushed away by heavy rains. Sandbars scattered beyond the Trail Ridge became islands. Aquatic plants first found a favorable environment in the tepid shallows, then decayed and formed layers of peat, rich deposits capable of supporting other forms of plant life. Eventually a forest took root throughout the swamp. Fires leveled the forest growth, resulting in the swamp prairies of today.

In this vast swamp, sizable bodies of water stretch through dense mazes of moss-covered cypress trees. Against the prevailing silvery-green of cypress and tupelos, white and golden water lilies along with other flowering plants add bright splashes of color. Lakes, islands, and prairies interrupt the moist expanse. "Houses," clumps of bushes and trees underlain by smaller plants, are formed when gases produced by decaying vegetable matter force masses of plant growth from the bottom of the water. The surface of this mucky stuff rises several inches above the surrounding water and becomes covered in time by bushes, water weeds, and grass. This living island floats until it becomes entangled in a thicket of trees, gathering seeds from cypress and other trees until it forms a "house." Many houses never stabilize but sway and tremble under the slightest disturbance, hence the origin of the area's name. Okefenokee is derived from a Choctaw Indian term meaning "quivering earth." Some nine-tenths of the area has been designated a wildlife refuge. Ring-necked, pintailed, and black ducks make their winter home here, sharing the terrain with robins, cardinals, buzzards, red-winged blackbirds, owls, catbirds, osprey, and many other species. Except during the stillness of mid-day, the squealing cries of wood ducks and the discordant squawks of herons and egrets are heard repeatedly. Add to this the constant plops and splashes of over twenty species of frogs, the hammering of woodpeckers, and the occasional deep-throated bellowing of alligators in the canals, lakes, and deeper pools, and you have a veritable symphony of the swamp. In the tangled forests of cypress, bay, and gum adorned with streamers of Spanish moss are raccoons, bobcats, opossums, and otter.

Canoe trails allow you to explore the boundaries of Billy's Island (named for the Seminole chief Billy Bowlegs), for many years the home of Daniel Less and his family, the only white people living in the swamp's interior. When timber crews first arrived in the late 19th century, the Less evacuated the island but were so homesick they returned a few months later. A lumber camp, stores, a school, and a movie house thrived on the island for a short time but have long been abandoned. Floyd's Island, a favorite overnight stop for canoers, features bogs of muck and moss so dense it is impossible to walk on them. Hundreds of spotted pitcher plants, able to ensnare flies in their tubelike leaves, are found here growing to the unusual height of 3 feet. Canoers will have to use their paddle every inch of the way, as there is no fast-moving water within the swamp. Because there is little dry land and much shallow water, you may have to get out of your craft and push across peat blowups and low-water pools. Reservations for canoe trips are advisable but not necessary. Permits are required. For both reservations and permits, write: Refuge Manager (address below).

Three public entrances provide access to the Okefenokee Wildlife Refuge: the west entrance at Stephen C. Foster State Park near Fargo, the Suwannee Canal Recreation Area near Folkston on the east, and the northern entrance in Okefenokee Swamp Park. At each entry point guided tours, walking trails, swamp exhibits, and picnic facilities are available. Typical activities include guided boat tours leaving several times daily for trips over watery swamp trails into the heart of the refuge, a mile-long boardwalk trek over the wetlands to an observation tower; and self-guiding canoe and motorboat rentals over marked water trails. Camping is not permitted in the swamp itself, but camping facilities, hotels, motels, and restaurants are available at Folkston.

Georgia's warm Gulf Stream waters and irregularly shaped coastline, with the Inland Waterway, bays, and scenic islands, provide good surf (particularly on the beautiful unspoiled Golden Isles) and off-shore fishing in season for tarpon up to 100 pounds, red drum, sailfish, barracuda, the "mad chopper" (bluefish), weakfish (called summer trout locally), albacore, cobia, kingfish, striped bass, and during the winter months for spotted sea trout and American shad.

Information Sources, Maps & Access

A free *Guide to Georgia Freshwater Sportfishing Regulations* and a free 30–page *Georgia Hunting Regulations and Game Management Area Guide* may be obtained from: Information Office, DNR, 270 Washington St., SW, Atlanta 30334 (404)656–3530. The management area guide contains detailed descriptions of Georgia's game management areas and a map of Georgia's Hunting Areas.

An overview of northern Georgia's trout streams and rugged wildlife management is provided by a full-color *Chattahoochee National Forest Recreation Map* (50¢), available from: Forest Supervisor, Chattahoochee National Forest, U.S. Forest Service, P.O. Box 1437, Gainesville 30501 (404)536–0541. A set of full-color U.S. Geological Survey large-scale topo maps will prove an invaluable aid to the wilderness fly fisherman. Nonrelief *Wildlife Management Area Maps* are available free from: Information Section, DNR, 270 Washington St., SW, Atlanta 30334, phone (404)656–3530. Nonrelief *County Maps* showing roads, many smaller trout streams, and boundaries of wildlife management areas may be obtained for 25¢ each from: Department of Transportation, Rm. 354, 2 Capitol Sq., Atlanta 30334. The *Guide to Georgia Trout Regulations* contains a detailed map of the Chattahoochee River from Buford Dam to Morgan Falls Dam, a map of Georgia's streams, rivers, and reservoirs, a map of trout streams of Georgia, and regulations of managed stream directions and fishing schedule. An *Oconee National Forest Map* (50¢) showing all fish and game lands, campgrounds, trails and forest roads may be obtained from the Supervisor, Oconee National Forest, Monticello 31064.

Forest maps and the free *Canoeing Routes Guide, Trail Guide*, and *Guide to Outdoor Recreation on the Cohutta District* are available from: Forest Supervisor, Chattahoochee National Forest, U.S. Forest Service (address above). Another useful guide to the wilderness, *Wildlife on the Chattahoochee National Forest*, describes and illustrates the black bear, deer, bobcat, raccoon, and other animals found in the forest. The booklet contains much useful information concerning animal habits and habitats, tracks, breeding patterns, and the like and is available free from the Forest Supervisor at the above address.

The Chattahoochee National Forest is easily reached via State Highway 11 north of Gainesville. Other nearby towns include Toccoa, Clarkesville, and Chatsworth. For an *Okefenokee National Wildlife Map-Guide* and other free information, call or write: Okefenokee Swamp Park, Waycross 31501 (912)283–0583.

A map and folder on *Wilderness Canoeing in Okefenokee*, describing trips over Floyd's Island, through Minnie's and Big Water lakes, and across Chase and Mizell prairies, is available free from: Refuge Manager, Okefenokee Wildlife Refuge, P.O. Box 117, Waycross 31501.

Lodges & Coastal Resorts

★★★★*The Cloister at Sea Island* is a year round resort, situated between the Black River and bordered by five miles of open beach. The Cloister has complete facilities for inshore fishing, and deep sea ventures. Transportation is provided to and from the Sea Island Golf Courses, riding stables, and gun club featuring skeet and trap shooting. There are biking and hiking trails which wind over the lush grounds and Marshes of Glynn bordering the resort, and shuffleboard and croquet are played on the open lawns. The Cloister Racquet Club features 18 courts, a pro shop, and a teaching staff headed by experienced pros. The oceanside dining room has full-course menus, and offers plantation suppers under sprawling oaks, and dinner dances throughout the week. An orchestra plays nightly, and there are a variety of cocktail lounges in the hotel, and beach and golf clubs. The Cloister's main hotel building sits back several yards from the beach. The mediterranean terraces of the River House overlook the Black River and the marshes. The beach houses hug the shore, each room with an open view. The guest houses adjacent to the beach houses and the beach club, have rooms that will connect, providing a suite with living rooms, with complete bars and TV. Rates vary according to the season, the size of the room and the number of people in each party. Generally, Spring rates are $46–82 double occupancy, and $66–138 single occupancy. Summer rates are $41–78 double occupancy, and $56–130 single occupancy. Winter rates, $54–94 single occupancy, $41–78 double occupancy. For more information write: Cloister Hotel, Sea Island, GA 31561 (912)638–3611; out of state call toll free: (800)841–3223.

★★★★*Pineisle* is nestled on pine-studded Lake Lanier Island overlooking the crystal clear waters of Lake Lanier, with its 550 miles of shoreline. Pineisle, amidst 1200 wooded acres, offers a unique blend of beach and forest. This lavish 256-room hotel features luxurious penthouse suites with fireplaces, wet bars, and sun decks for your vacation or convention stay. Meeting and banquet facilities are complete and up-to-date; ballrooms can accommodate groups of 10 or 500. Leisure activities include golf—on an 18–hole professional course designed by Ron Kirby and Gary Player; tennis—on four outdoor or three indoor courts (lighted for nighttime play); swimming—in an indoor/outdoor heated pool or therapeutic pool; there is also a sauna, game room, and shuffleboard at the hotel. The Islands provide horseback riding, sailing charters, fishing for trout or bass; houseboat and pontoon boat rentals, miniature golf, water skiing. There are also a wide variety of tours available—shopping, historic, craft shows and fashion shows and activities for children can be arranged as well. Dress at the hotel is casual; after 6:00 p.m. jackets are preferred. The cuisine is continental and excellent, entertainment is provided nightly. There is a charge for most of the activities and rates at the hotel range from $35–53 (singles); $42–63 (doubles) and $112–225 (suites). For further information or reservations call toll free (800)323–4455 or write the Management, Pineisle, P.O. Drawer 545, Buford, GA 30518 (404)945–8921.

Travel Services

Wilderness Southeast is a non-profit organization made up of naturalists and environmental educators who organize wilderness camping, backpacking, canoeing and snorkeling trips to explore the coast, rivers and mountains of Georgia, Florida, North Carolina and other locations. On each expedition, they provide leaders who know the natural history of the area. Teaching is done, not with lectures, but with questions and answers, discussion and discoveries on the trip. All trips bring participants back to nature with minimal impact camping. Individuals, couples, families and groups can participate. They don't have to be expert or even experienced campers, since leaders will teach all skills needed. But, more than camping skills, Wilderness Southeast teaches about the plants, animals and environment of the area visited. Groups are small (16 or less) and include people of all ages and both sexes. Wilderness Southeast provides leaders; trip information; tent space; canoes as needed; backpacks for hiking expeditions; mask, fins, and snorkel for snorkeling trips; all meals; commissary gear; transportation within the trip; reference library; first aid equipment; field study equipment and all permits. The director is Dick Murlless, a noted naturalist and graduate in zoology from Duke University. Trips are sponsored by Savannah Science Museum, The Georgia Conservancy, Jacksonville Museum of Arts & Sciences and Macon Museum of Arts and Sciences. They offer

two basic types of programs: the scheduled, open to the public expedition listed in the brochures and scheduled year around; and contractual, custom-designed for groups. A sampling of some of the planned trips are:

Sea Islands Photographic Workshop is a weeklong program in photographing wildlife conducted by Bill Weems, a freelance photographer whose work appears in National Geographic. Participants set up a base camp on a private, wild island off the Georgia coast. They will visit other islands, including Wassaw, the National Wildlife Refuge. This trip is $260.

Dry Tortugas Snorkeling is a trip to study the underwater life of the coral reef in the most remote corner of the Florida Keys. Participants will camp at seaside campgrounds and spend considerable time aboard a boat. Everyone must know how to swim, but snorkeling skills can be learned on the trip. Cost $305; minimum age is 10.

The Okefenokee Swamp trips start at Stephen Foster State Park where participants launch canoes into the swamp. The trip includes canoeing down the Suwannee River, camping in the swamps and looking for alligators, egrets, carnivorous plants and other unique natural sights in the Swamp. A three-day trip is $75; one-week trip, $175.

Other trips include tagging Loggerhead Sea Turtles on the remote beaches of Georgia; discovering Mayan ruins, lush jungles and native markets in Guatemala; exploring Cataloochee cove in the Great Smokies with Frank Garrett, well known mushroom collector extraordinaire; learning how to catch shellfish and seafood in Coastal Georgia, paddling down the crystal clear Florida springs and drifting on the Santa Fe and Suwannee Rivers, hiking in the Great Smoky Mountains, sailing and snorkling the lower Keys, and visiting the Everglades, land of the Seminole Indians. For information on these and other trips write to Wilderness Southeast, Route 3, Box 619, Savannah, GA 31406 (912)355-8008.

Wolfcreek Wilderness is a non-profit educational organization that runs outdoor programs to help participants develop basic outdoor skills, as well as to explore themselves, others and their environment. It is under the directorship of Keith W. Evans. College credit is available for some courses, and Wolfcreek Wilderness also designs and implements programs for business, educational and service groups. The most comprehensive course is their wilderness experience for youngsters 14 to 22 which lasts 21 days. Participants experience the mountains, the rivers and underground. The entire time is spent outdoors in a group of 8 or 10 individuals and two instructors. The group backpacks through the woods, makes camps, learns outdoor cooking, braves deep water crossing and cuts through unmarked territory. Then they move on to rock climbing, blending technique, skill and concentration. Participants then learn canoe camping and paddling techniques on lazy Georgia rivers and on rushing white water. Then a cave is explored, to the extent of eating and sleeping in it. The program ends with a three-day solo, completely alone. Fees for all programs include all food, accommodations, equipment and transportation during the course. Participants must provide clothing, sturdy footwear and rain gear, as well as medical and accident insurance. The 21–day course described above is $545. Other courses offered by Wolfcreek Wilderness are a 10–day adult wilderness experience which includes backpacking, outdoor living, rock climbing and whitewater canoeing. The cost is $295. There is an 8–day course for "women in the wilderness" for $240 and a 2–day wilderness emergency medical aid seminar for $65. A five-day winter program teaches emergency techniques in cold and winter environmental adaptions. For information on all programs, contact Wolfcreek Wilderness, P.O. Box 596, Blairsville, GA 30512 (404)745–6460.

ILLINOIS

Introduction

The heavily populated Inland Empire, as the state is popularly known, offers some surprisingly good, if limited, fishing, canoeing, hiking, and hunting opportunities. This river-slashed, intensely farmed and settled plains state contains 56,400 square miles bordered on the north and northeast by the glacial uplands of Wisconsin and Lake Michigan; on the east and southeast by Indiana and the Wabash and Ohio rivers; on the west by Iowa, Missouri, and the Mississippi River; and on the south by Kentucky and the Ohio River. The great Mississippi Flyway has long made the state famous for its Canada goose and duck hunting. Inland some excellent goose and duck shooting is found on crop fields, marshes, lakes, and river bottomlands. The scenic Shawnee National Forest and state forests and wildlife areas offer good, but crowded, hunting in season for whitetail deer and upland game birds, as well as cottontails, squirrels, crows, red and gray fox, raccoon, and woodchuck.

Accommodations & Travel Information

For information about Illinois's wide variety of motels and hotels, write: Division of Tourism, 222 S. College St., Springfield 62704. For information and reservations for state park cabins and lodges, write: *Giant City State Park*, Makanda 62958, phone (618)457–4921; *Illinois Beach State Park*, Zion 60099, phone (312)244–2400; *Pere Marquette State Park*, Box 325, Grafton 62037, phone (618)786–3351; *Starved Rock State Park*, Box 116, Utica 61373, phone (815)667–4211; and *White Pines Forest State Park*, RR1, Mount Morris 61054, phone (815)946–3817. Illinois provides many opportunities for campers to enjoy the beauties of the state's natural areas. Campers should obtain the free booklet *Illinois Camping Guide*, available from: Division of Tourism, 222 S. College St., Springfield 62704. This publication lists and describes Illinois's major camping areas, organizing them by region. The camping areas are presented in chart form, noting the season open, number of campsites, facilities, and other information available for each area.

A useful free brochure, *Illinois Department of Conservation Recreation Areas*, provides a handy chart listing state parks, historical memorials, conservation areas, and state forests, and the facilities available at each area. Each area is location-keyed to a map. Camping permits must be obtained upon arrival at each campsite from the manager or nightwatchperson. Camping is limited to 14 nights. Boat rentals in some areas are in operation only during the summer or on weekends, and in some areas, such as refuge areas, motors are not allowed at certain times of the year. It is advisable to check with the management of the area you're planning to visit in advance. For additional information on state recreation areas and campgrounds, write to: Information/Education Section, Dept. of Conservation, 605 State Office Bldg., Springfield 62706.

Highways & Maps

Anyone planning on driving in Illinois should have a copy of the free *Illinois Highway Map*. It can be obtained by writing: Division of Tourism, 222 S. College St., Springfield 62704. It indicates all roads and highways, route markers, access points, and junctions. Also shown on the map are the Great River Road, Lincoln Heritage Trail, state parks or conservation areas, rest areas, airports, and other points of interest. A location index of cities and villages and points of interest is provided, as well as a chart of recreation areas showing facilities available in each, and its location on the map. A mileage distance chart showing distances between principal towns and cities is also included.

**VACATION/
LODGING GUIDE**

Illinois Forests, Lakes & Recreation Areas

The state's premier trophy fishery is Lake Michigan—the sixth largest lake in the world, 22,400 square miles in surface area. The Illinois portion of the lake takes in 7% of its total surface area and offers top-ranked fishing for brown trout up to 28 pounds, brook trout up to 4 pounds, rainbow trout in the 20–pound-plus class, tiger trout and rod-busting coho and Chinook salmon, as well as lake trout and yellow perch. Lake Michigan has a relatively smooth, gently sloping bottom in its southern region and an irregular bottom, with numerous scenic islands in the northern regions. Salmon were first introduced, unsuccessfully, into the lake between 1873 and 1880. The recent, spectacularly successful introduction into Lake Michigan began when the Michigan Department of Natural Resources obtained 1 million coho salmon eggs from Oregon in 1964. The fish were hatched and reared in a Michigan hatchery for 18 months until they reached smolt size and were released into the Big Huron River in the Upper Peninsula, and the Platte River and Bear Creek in the Lower Peninsula. In the fall of 1966 several thousand coho jacks ranging from 2 to 7 pounds returned to their parent streams. The following fall, 35% of the original stock returned to spawn and complete their life cycle. The results of this first spawning run have become a modern legend, with coho and Chinook salmon growing to record weights on the enormous alewife population found throughout the lake and its tributaries. Illinois's Lake Michigan hot spots include the Great Lakes Naval Station, Belmont, Waukegan, Diversey Harbor, Jackson Harbor, Winnetka, Chicago, Illinois Beach, Poevell Park, Kellog Ditch, Roosevelt Park, Burnham Harbor, and Highland Park areas.

While not as dramatic as the spectacular Great Lakes trophy salmon and trout fishery, the lakes and streams of the Inland Empire provide often excellent fishing for largemouth and smallmouth bass, walleye, northern pike, crappie, sunfish, and a few trout. The glacially formed waters of Fox Chain O'Lakes in the northeast region of the state—comprised of Fox, Long, Nippersink, Pistakee, Grass, Petite, Bluff, Marie, Katherine, and Channel lakes—hold walleye, channel catfish, panfish, bass, and northern pike. Marie Lake produced the state record 22–pound 12–ounce northern pike. Beautiful Grass Lake, with its large beds of snow-white lotus lilies, is one of the chain's best producers of largemouth bass. Several northern Illinois rivers—among them the Rock, Kishwaukee, Sugar, Coon, Du Page, Fox, Kankakee, Iroquois, and Vermilion rivers and Big Indian Creek—provide fishing for smallmouth bass, walleye, yellow perch, and channel and flathead catfish. Cliff-lined Apple River in the rugged uplands of northwest Illinois is one of the state's top rainbow and brown trout streams. The major fishing waters in central Illinois include the primitive Spoon River—immortalized in Edgar Lee Masters's *Spoon River Anthology*—the club-owned Strip Mines lakes, Sangamon River, La Moine Creek, Kickapoo River, Salt Creek, Middle Fork of the Vermilion River, and the wild and scenic Mackinaw River. The fishing is primarily for smallmouth bass, walleye, and catfish. The Little Vermilion River, a fine limestone smallmouth bass stream, flows past numerous cliffs and Troy Grove—the birthplace of Wild Bill Hickok. The rugged backcountry lakes and streams of southern Illinois, known as "Little Egypt," provide the state's top trophy largemouth bass fishing. Little Grassy, Devil's Kitchen, and Crab Orchard lakes in the Crab Orchard National Wildlife Refuge, situated in the heart of the Shawnee National Forest region, provide consistently good fishing for largemouth bass up to 6, 7, and 8 pounds in the numerous shallow submerged timber areas. Other productive lakes in the Shawnee Hills region

include Kincaid, Horseshoe, Dutchman, Lake of Egypt, Glendale, and Glen O. Jones Lake in the Wildcat Hills country. The rugged Cache and Big Muddy (Aux Vases) rivers are the region's top streams. The giant navigation pools, sloughs, backwater lakes, and weed-filled bays of the island-dotted, meandering Mississippi River provide often excellent fishing for lunker bass, crappie, walleye to 10 pounds, and giant catfish.

The historic Fox Valley Canoe Trail between Yorkville and Wedron in northeast Illinois is the state's most popular canoe route, flowing past caves, springs, numerous islands, exotic plants, and a relic glacial forest. The major features along this scenic wild river include Old Mill, Glass House, the Slooper Settlement of Norway, Dells of the Fox, Sank Ford where Lincoln is believed to have camped, and the Indian Creek Massacre site. The Kankakee River, traveled by La Salle into the Illinois country in 1683, is one of the state's top-ranked fishing streams and canoe routes. The Kankakee flows over a limestone bed past bayous, islands, canyons, caves, rapids, and large beds of mallow and lotus. The "Big" Vermilion River, famous for its spring run of striped bass, is one of the best whitewater streams in the state. The beautiful, unspoiled Mackinaw River flows past high bluffs and the Bloomington Moraine—a remnant of the Wisconsin Ice Age. The scenic, gravel-bottomed Kishwaukee River flows through wooded hills and meadows with good fishing for walleye, smallmouth bass, and northern pike. The Sangamon—the first Illinois stream to be dedicated as a canoe trail—is a beautiful, winding woodland stream that flows through the heart of Lincolnland. The 70–mile stretch known as the "Lincoln Heritage Canoe Trail" flows past the sternwheeler Talisman—a replica of the one young Lincoln once piloted down the river. The majestic Rock River—known as the "Hudson of the West"—flows for 150 miles through Black Hawk country past many islands, rolling hills, and pine-clad bluffs. The Cache River, named by the French-Canadian voyageurs, flows through towering forests past numerous islands, ancient Indian campsites, beaver dams, cypress swamps, cliff and fossil beds. Overnight campers on the Illinois canoe trails should be alert for rattlesnakes, copperheads, and cottonmouths.

The 240,000–acre Shawnee National Forest is made up of rolling hills, lakes, and towering limestone bluffs, stretching across southern Illinois from the Mississippi River to the Ohio. The major features include the La Rue-Pine Hills Ecological Area, Oakwood Bottoms, Greentree Reservoir, Garden of the Gods, Rimrock Forest Trail, Bell Smith Springs, Lusk Creek Wild Area, Lake of Egypt, Crab Orchard National Wildlife Refuge, Kincaid, Devil's Kitchen, and Little Grassy lakes, and prehistoric stone forts and Indian burial mounds. The forest is an outstanding fishing, hunting, and camping area. Game animals include whitetail deer, drumming grouse, red fox, and raccoon.

The La Rue-Pine Hills Wilderness is one of the outstanding hiking and natural areas in the Midwest, embracing 19,000 acres of deep, forested ravines, hill prairie, wet pine-oak flatlands, spring-field swamps, and sheer limestone river bluffs in the northwestern section of the Shawnee National Forest. Wildlife includes whitetail deer, bobcat, red fox, raccoon, and beaver. The 15,000–acre Lusk Creek Wild Area is located in the Greater Shawnee Hills in the eastern section of the Shawnee National Forest, embracing the spectacular Indian Kitchen of Lusk Creek Canyon. The area, renowned for its natural beauty, is an outstanding hiking and hunting region.

Information Sources, Maps & Access

Single copies of the following booklets may be obtained free upon request from the Dept. of Conservation, Division of Fisheries, 605 State Office Bldg., Springfield 62706: *Carlyle Lake Fishing Guide, Lake Shelbyville Fishing Guide, Rend Lake Fishing Guide, Fishing the Mississippi, Fishing the Rock, Pond Fish & Fishing, Fishing the Kankakee, Fishing the Big Muddy.* The following brochures may be obtained free from the Southern Illinois Tourism Council, 2209 W. Main, Marion 62959: *Southern Illinois Lake Guide* and *Recreation Map of Southern Illinois.*

An *Illinois Fishing Information* brochure (which contains regulations, seasons, and a listing of state-managed public fishing areas and facilities) and *Illinois Hunting Information* brochure (with regulations, seasons, and public hunting areas) may be obtained free from: Dept. of Conservation, 605 State Office Bldg., Springfield 62706 (217)782–2964. For info on daily condition and salmon fishing on Lake Michigan, call the *Salmon Unlimited Hotline* (312)282–7100. A useful 47–page guide, *Illinois Fishery of Lake Michigan*, shows boat and bank fishing areas, rigs, launch sites, and contains charter boat information. It may be obtained free upon request from: Dept. of Conservation, Division of Fisheries, 605 State Office Bldg., Springfield 62706. For info on Lake Michigan trout and salmon charters, write or call: *Chicago Sportfishing Assn.*, 25 E. Washington, Suite 823, Chicago 60602 (312)922–1100 or *Waukegan Charter Assn.*, 207 Water St., Waukegan 60085 (312)244–3474.

Illinois's major canoeable waterways, several of which were originally traveled by the French-Canadian voyageurs, are described in the 64–page *Illinois Canoeing Guide* available free from the Dept. of Conservation, 605 State Office Bldg., Springfield 62706. The major routes—including the Cache, Des Plaines, Embarras, Fox, Illinois, Kankakee, Iroquois, Mackinaw, Pecatonica, Rock, Sangamon, Vermilion, and Spoon rivers—are presented in detail, with maps accompanying each route, indicating access, bridges, dams, campsite locations, points of interest, and locations of state parks. There is also a useful equipment checklist.

The Chicagoland Canoe Base, 4017 N. Narragansett Ave., Chicago 60634, phone (312)777–1489, offers complete canoe rental and trip outfitting services. It also offers free *Chicagoland Canoe Trails* and *Historic Fox Valley Canoe Trail* guides, a *Des Plaines River Mara-*

thon Canoe Map (50¢), *Midwest Canoe Livery Guide* ($1.50), *Illinois Country Canoe Trails, Vol. I*: Fox, Mazon, Vermilion, and Little Vermilion ($1.25), and *Illinois Country Canoe Trails, Vol. II*: Du Page, Kankakee, Des Plaines, and Au Sable ($1.25). Add 25¢ per copy to cover postage and handling.

Visitors to the Shawnee National Forest should obtain a copy of the *Shawnee National Forest Map*, available for 50¢ from: Supervisor's Office, Shawnee National Forest, Harrisburg 62946 (618)253–7114. This excellent map of the entire Shawnee area shows all roads and highways, boundaries, trails, mines, recreation sites with and without camping facilities, horse trails, boat-launching sites, ranger stations, and other points of interest. A chart of the various recreation areas and facilities provided in each is also included. The map is attractively illustrated with full-color photographs and some information on the various recreational opportunities offered in the forest. The forest is reached via U.S. Highways 45 and 51 and Illinois routes 1, 3, 34, 127, 144, 145, 146, and 151. Overnight accommodations, supplies, and equipment rentals are available at Anna, Cairo, Carbondale, Harrisburg, Metropolis, and Murphysboro; also, Paducah, Kentucky, and St. Louis, Missouri.

Lodges & Resorts

For details, see "Accommodations & Travel Information" above.

Travel Services

PanAngling Travel Service, one of the nation's finest outdoor recreation travel firms, matches the fisherman with the type of fishing he desires. The firm arranges all air travel, lodging and guide service, and provides its clients with recommended lists of clothing, tackle, and detailed information about the specific area he plans to visit. PanAngling Travel Service offers a wide spectrum of different fishing trips available throughout the world. While the firm is heavily involved with Canada and Central America, its scope is almost world-wide. To give you an idea of their range here are some species and fishing trips available through the services of PanAngling: *Black Marlin*: Cairns, Australia, Club Pacifico of Panama, and Tropic Star (also Panama); *Striped Marlin*: Salinas, Ecuador, Mazatlan, Mexico, Baja California; *Pacific Sailfish*: Club Pacifico of Panama, Tropic Star, and Costa Rica's Bahia Pez Vila; *Atlantic Sailfish*: Cozumel, Mexico; *Pacific Blue Marlin*: Kona, Hawaii; *Wahoo*: Club Pacifico of Panama, Bahia Pez Vela; *Tarpon & Snook*: several camps on East Coast of Costa Rica; *Bonefish*: Boca Paila, Mexico, Turnefee Islands in Belize, Deep Water Cay Club in Bahamas, Mexico; *Trophy Rainbow Trout*: Alaskan camps, North Island of New Zealand, Argentian; *Brown Trout*: South Island of New Zealand and Argentina; *Trophy Brook Trout*: Minipi Waters of Labrador, several Quebec Rivers, and Argentian; *Arctic Char*: Umiakovik Camp in Labrador, Tree River and Victoria Island in Canada's Northwest Territories, and Ilkalu Lodge in northern Quebec; *Northern Pike*: throughout Canada, but Brabant Lodge in N.W.T. among the best; *Arctic Grayling*: numerous Canadian waters, particularly Kasba Lake Lodge in N.W.T.; *Lake Trout* throughout northern Canada, particularly Great Bear Lake in N.W.T.; *Atlantic Salmon*: Alta River in Norway, Laxa i Kjos in Iceland, and the Restigouche in Quebec; *Smallmouth Bass*: Rainy Lake (with Fontana's Houseboats) and other lakes in Ontario. PanAngling caters to fishermen who are interested in fly fishing for relatively small species, such as trout or grayling, and to those anglers who like to tussle with big marlin for several hours. Some clients like to fish for exotic species in remote areas regardless of whether sport is good or not, while others are interested in a great deal of action. For detailed trip brochures, rates, and travel planning information, write: PanAngling Travel Service, 180 N. Michigan Ave., Chicago 60601 (312)263–0328.

INDIANA

Introduction

From the scenic woodlands of the northern lake country through the central agricultural plain to the rugged hills, shard ridges, rounded knolls, and waterfalls of the southern lowlands, the Hoosier State offers some surprisingly varied fishing, camping, hiking, and hunting opportunities. The state-managed forests and fish and game areas, and the Hoosier National Forest lands provide hunting in season for bobwhite quail, pheasant, ruffed grouse, whitetail deer, cottontails, fox and gray squirrels, red fox, raccoons, and fair hunting in wetland areas for a few Canada geese and ducks. The major public hunting areas include the Pigeon River, Jasper-Pulaski, Kingsbury, Winamac, Atterbury, Patoka, Monroe, Hovey Lake, Springs Valley, Brush Creek, Willow Slough, Kankakee, and La Salle state fish and game areas and the Yellowwood, Salamonie River, Clark, Pike, Harrison-Crawford, Ferdinand, Jackson-Washington, Frances Slocum, Martin, Monroe-Morgan, Owen-Putnam, and Greene-Sullivan state forest reserves.

Accommodations & Travel Information

For complete information on where to stay in Indiana, send for the free 124–page booklet *Indiana Camping & Outdoor Recreation Guide*. This publication lists and describes camping areas and resorts, giving locations, facilities available, length of the season, rates, and of course, addresses and phone numbers. Each area is location-keyed to a map on the inside front cover of the book. The booklet and additional information may be obtained from: Dept. of Commerce, Rm. 336, State House, Indianapolis 46204.

Indiana's national and state forests, parks, and wildlife management areas provide excellent scenic and primitive camping, hiking, and backpacking areas. Several of the major state-managed areas include the Pike State Forest, Patoka Fish and Wildlife Area, Green-Sullivan State Forest, Starve Hollow State Forest, Pigeon River Fish and Wildlife Area, and Salamonie River and Yellowwood state forests. Other scenic camping and backpacking areas include the large tracts of virgin forest and deep, rock-walled canyons and gorges of the Turkey Run area; the dense stands of pines, juniper, blueberry thickets, shifting dunes of the famous Indiana Dunes on Lake Michigan; the Chain O'Lakes area with its nine natural connecting lakes; the ravines, sinkholes, abandoned quarries, and deep stone gullies of the McCormick's Creek area; and scenic woodlands, lakes, streams, and rolling hills of the Brown County backcountry. Free maps of Indiana state forest reserves and wildlife management areas may be obtained from: Dept. of Natural Resources, Indianapolis 46204.

Highways & Maps

A free *Official Indiana Highway Map* showing all interstate, U.S., and state routes, points of interest, airports, recreation sites, fish hatcheries, national and state forests, cities, and towns, is available upon request from: Dept. of Commerce, Rm. 336, State House, Indianapolis 46204.

Indiana Sceni-Circle Drives is an excellent, informative 126–page booklet designed to get the traveler off the speedy interstate road system and onto leisurely secondary roads where a wealth of scenic wonders and points of interest await discovery. Visitors may trace Abraham Lincoln's footsteps along the Lincoln Heritage Trail, or recapture the life-style of simpler days in Amishville, near Berne. This free booklet describes 13 scenic drives ranging from 82 to 268 miles. It is attractively illustrated with line drawings. You can obtain a copy free of charge by writing to: Dept. of Commerce (address above).

VACATION/ LODGING GUIDE

Indiana Forests, Lakes & Recreation Areas

The 117,906–acre Hoosier National Forest is located in the Crawford and Norman uplands in southern Indiana. It is a scenic area of rolling hills, sharp ridges, numerous lakes and streams, and colorful stands of hardwoods and evergreens with an understory of dogwood and redbud; it embraces the old buffalo migration trail between the western plains and French Lick. The major features of this outstanding hiking, camping, fishing, and hunting region include German Ridge, French Lick, and Monroe reservoirs; the Patoka, White, Salt, Lost, Little Blue, and Anderson rivers, the Yellowwood, Washington, Wyandotte Caves, and Harrison-Crawford state forests; Brown County State Park; and lakes Celina, Indian, Tipsaw, Saddle, and Starve Hollow. Wildlife includes deer, red fox, raccoon, upland game birds, and wild turkey.

The proposed Hoosier Wilderness takes in 80 square miles of rolling hills, marshlands, and woodlands in the northern division of the Hoosier National Forest, Brown County State Park, and Yellowwood State Forest. This is the largest roadless wild area in the state and is an outstanding hiking and hunting zone. The major features in the area include Lemon, Yellowwood, Ogte, and Strahl lakes, Hardin Ridge Recreation Area, and the North, Middle, and South Forks of the Salt River.

The vast, wave-capped waters of Lake Michigan in the extreme western corner of the northern lake region are the state's premier trophy fishery. More than 50,000 coho and Chinook salmon, steelhead trout, brown trout, and lake trout are caught along Indiana's Lake Michigan shoreline each year. Brown trout and lake trout are stocked directly in the lake, while coho and Chinook salmon and steelhead trout from the Mixawbah State Hatchery are introduced into Trail Creek and the east branch of the Little Calumet River. The giant, state record 18–pound 13–ounce brown trout was caught in Trail Creek in 1975. Fishing for coho from 4 to 10 pounds and Chinook from 12 to 30 pounds and over is excellent in the tributary streams during the fall spawning run. Most of the steelhead are in the streams by October, where they remain until February or March of the following year. Although fewer fish are caught during the fall than in the spring, their average size is much larger.

The state's premier lake and stream fishing for holdover rainbow and brown trout, northern pike, walleye, largemouth bass, crappie, and huge catfish is found in the northern lake country with its hundreds of small lakes, ponds, and streams surrounded by low rolling hills left by retreating glaciers. The swift flowing waters of the historic Tippecanoe River, once considered one of the top smallmouth bass streams in the nation, yields smallmouth bass, northern pike, rock and white bass, and channel and flathead catfish up to trophy weights. In the scenic lake-dotted northeast region are several of the state's top trout and bass streams and lakes, including famous Gage Lake, Lake James, Oliver Lake, Pigeon River, Lake Hamilton, and Fawn, Emma, Little Elkhart, Elkhart, and St. Joseph rivers. Deep, clear Lake Gage yielded the state record 13–pound 5–ounce rainbow and 3–pound 15–ounce brook trout. Other premier lakes and streams in the northern lake country include the Indian Lakes, Pine Creek, and Hudson, Koontz, Freeman, Wolf, Flint, Pine, Stone, Clear, Ball, Snow, Troxall, Fox, Fish, Story, Flatbelly, Waldron, Chain O'Lakes, Wawasee, Syracuse, Bixler, and Tippecanoe lakes. The Kankakee River yields northern pike and walleye up to record weights.

The major streams in the central region of Indiana—a great level till plain of deep glacial deposits of soil and gravel—and the east-to-west

succession of lowlands and uplands in the southern region are the White River and its tributaries: the Wabash, Eel, West Fork White River, East Fork White River, Blue River, Patoka River, and Muscatatuck River tributaries. The fishing is primarily for largemouth bass, white crappie, rock bass, yellow perch, channel and flathead catfish, a few walleye and smallmouth bass, as well as for freshwater drum, buffalo, and the primitive paddlefish (also known as the spoonbill). A few small muskellunge up to 12 pounds are taken from the Blue River and its tributaries. The major lakes in the central and southern region include Hominy Ridge, Prairie Creek, Mississinewa, Loon, Salamonie, Palestine, Mansfield Reservoir, Rockville, Brookville Reservoir, Waveland, Whitewater, Manlove, Monroe, Dogwood, West Boggs Creek Reservoir, Wampler Pit, West Twin Pit, Island Pit, Indian, Celina, Ferdinand, Tipsaw, Saddle, Versailles, Cypress, Grouse Ridge, Greensburg Reservoir, Hardy, Crosley Fish & Wildlife Area, Clark State Forest, and Starve Hollow. Yellowwood Lake in the scenic Yellowwood State Forest east of Bloomington in Brown County and the Willow Slough State Fish & Wildlife Area north of Morocco in Newton County are two of the state's top lunker largemouth areas.

Several of the Hoosier State's streams and rivers—including the historic Tippecanoe, Iroquois, Kankakee, Fawn, St. Joseph, Elkhart, Salamonie, Wild Cat, Deer, Wabash, Eel, and White rivers—provide excellent scenic canoeing and float fishing opportunities. Many of the waterways are rich in historic Indian and exploration lore. The Eel River, near the town of Hoosier Highlands, served as a common hunting ground for the Indian tribes in the area. Old legends have it that they panned gold here from the highland streams. The river was called *Shakamak* by the Delaware Indians and *Kena Pocomoco* by the Miami—both meaning "eel" or "snakefish." The Kankakee, used by the French explorer La Salle and the voyageurs as a connecting waterway between the Mississippi and Great Lakes, is derived from the Indian word A-ki-ki, meaning "wolf." Near Argos, on the south bank of the famed Tippecanoe, is the site of the Chippewanuing Indian village, one of the last of the Potawatomi Indian villages.

Information Sources, Maps & Access

A comprehensive listing and description of the state's fish and wildlife areas, state forests, hunting preserves, state recreation areas, and state park and forest resorts is contained in the 61–page booklet *Indiana Hunting, Fishing, Boating*, available free upon request from: Dept. of Commerce, Rm. 336, State House, Indianapolis 46204. The following publications may be obtained free upon request from the Dept. of Natural Resources, Division of Fish & Wildlife, Indianapolis 46204: *Where to Fish in Indiana, Indiana Fishing Regulations, Indiana Hunting & Trapping Regulations, Deer Distribution Map, Pheasant & Quail Distribution Map*, and *DNR Property Guide*, as well as free maps of Indiana state forests and fish and wildlife areas. The DNR also publishes a 53–page *Guide to Indiana Lakes* (52¢). *Lake Survey Reports*, free from the Division of Fish & Wildlife; are available for about 100 lakes. Be sure to specify both lake name and the county it's in when ordering. For additional information, write for the free publication *Fishing Indiana's Lake Michigan Shoreline*, available from: Dept. of Natural Resources, Indianapolis 46204. A wealth of useful information is contained in the 128–page *The Compleat Guide to Fishing the Great Lakes*, available for $5.95 (include 50¢ postage and handling) from: Great Lakes Living Press, 3634 W. 216th St., Matteson, IL 60443.

Fishermen and boaters will be interested in the lake maps available from: Dept. of Natural Resources, Map Sales, Rm. 604, State Office Bldg., Indianapolis 46204. Maps of Indiana's major lakes; *Reservoir Depth Maps* (Morse, Geist, Hardy, Cataract); *Reservoir Area Maps* (Monroe, Mansfield, Salamonie, Mississinewa, Huntington, Eagle Creek), size 22 × 28 inches, are available at 60¢ each. The following state maps are also available: *Streams and Lakes of Indiana*, scale 1: 250,000, size 47 × 72 inches, $2; and *Streams and Lakes of Indiana*, scale 1:500,000, size 24 × 36 inches, 50¢. A 10% postage and handling charge must be enclosed with all mail orders. Prepayment must accompany the orders (no stamps). Make your check or money order payable to Dept. of Natural Resources. The lake and reservoir maps show fishing ponds, stumps, brush piles, standing timber, picnic areas, boat ramps, and areas where shoreline fishing is permitted. Mooring areas, camping sites, and other important features are also shown.

If you are planning to visit the Hoosier National Forest, write to: U.S. Forest Service, Bedford 47421, for the useful full-color *Hoosier National Forest Map* (50¢), which shows all roads and highways, state parks, state forest lands, state fish and game areas, forest service and other recreation sites with or without camping facilities, and boat-launching sites, district ranger stations, and other points. There is also an index of recreation sites showing their locations on the map and facilities available in each area. Rules, regulations, and addresses of forest rangers are provided on the reverse side. The map is attractively illustrated with color photographs. The Forest Service also has available a free map of the *Hardin Ridge Recreation Area*. This map shows the location of the various areas and on the reverse side provides a chart showing three locations on the map and what facilities are available in the different areas. It would also be wise to read the Forest Service's pamphlet *Regulations Governing the Occupancy and Use of National Forest Recreation Sites and Areas*. A helpful booklet entitled *Outdoor Safety Tips* is also available free from the Forest Service. It has a number of useful tips, and would be a good item to carry with you not only on your trip to the Hoosier National Forest, but anywhere you camp, hunt, fish, or go boating. The Hoosier National Forest is reached via U.S. Highways 50 and 150 and Indiana routes 37, 46, 62 and 64. Overnight accommodations, supplies, and equipment rentals are available at Bedford, Evansville, Jasper, Paoli, Tell City, and Bloomington. Paddlers with an interest in Indian history and lore should send for the 24 × 36–inch *Historic Indian Map* (Publication 122), available for 50¢ from: Dept. of Natural Resources, Map Sales, Rm. 604, State Office Bldg., Indianapolis 46204. If you are interested in renting canoes and related equipment, contact *Whitewater Valley Canoe Rental*, P.O. Box 2, Brookville, 47012, or RR1, Metamora 47030, 24–hour telephone (317)647–5434, which runs many canoe trips of varying lengths through the Whitewater River and historic Whitewater Canal. The firm also rents and sells equipment, and arranges field trips and outdoor recreation programs.

Lodges & Resorts

Indiana has a limited number of full-service lodges and resorts. For details, see "Accommodations & Travel Information" above.

KENTUCKY

Introduction

The Bluegrass State's great reservoirs, streams, thousands of productive farm ponds, national and state forest lands, and wildlife management areas offer superb outdoor recreation opportunities. Kentucky's topography consists of a scenic blend of mountains and gently rolling uplands. The eastern mountain region contains the state's highest elevations, slashed by hundreds of rushing creeks and streams. Moving westward from the Daniel Boone National Forest, the mountains gradually give way to an irregular plain known as the Knobs and the famous bluegrass country; at the southern end of the central plain are broad valleys, gently rolling farmlands, and rocky forested hillsides. The terrain gradually levels off into plains and the swampy bottomlands along the Mississippi and Ohio rivers which form the state's western boundary.

Accommodations & Travel Information

For detailed information on all aspects of vacation travel in Kentucky, contact: Div. of Travel & Promotion, Dept. of Public Information, Frankfort, KY 40601 (502)564–4930. The Division of Travel & Promotion will also provide free booklets on *Kentucky Lake Vacationland* and *Kentucky's Lake Cumberland-Dale Hollow* and *Green River Lake.* Kentucky Lake is extremely popular all year round for fishing and water sports. The booklet provides information on the different kinds of fish in the lake, seasonal weather and recreation, annual events in the area, and complete listings of motels, resorts, campgrounds, houseboats, attractions, restaurants, realtors and subdivisions, grocery supplies, and other general services. A pullout map of the whole area is included.

The 46–page *Kentucky Campgrounds Guide* contains a comprehensive listing of all public and commercial campgrounds with descriptions of facilities and recreation activities available. The guide covers all state park, forest, wildlife management and recreation areas, including the Turkey Foot, Hurricane Creek, Grand Rivers, Rockcastle, Mammoth Cave, Rodburn Hollow, and Windy Hollow lakes. The campgrounds guide may be obtained free upon request from: Division of Travel & Promotion, Dept. of Public Information (address above).

Highways & Maps

The Dept. of Public Information, Frankfort 40601, will provide a free *Kentucky Official Highway & Parkway Map.* It shows all cities and towns, roads and highways, airports, forests and parks, lakes and rivers, plus populations and mileage markers. Close-up maps of Ashland, Owensboro, Lexington, Louisville, and Covington-Newport are provided, as well as detail maps of major parkways and highways. These include Pennyrile Parkway, Cumberland Parkway, Audubon Parkway, Daniel Boone Parkway, Mountain Parkway, Blue Grass Parkway, Purchase Parkway, Western Kentucky Parkway, Green River Parkway, and Interstates 64, 71, 65, and 75. Toll charts are included, plus an index of state park facilities. A mileage chart showing distances between major points is featured.

Kentucky Forests, Lakes & Recreation Areas

Several of the nation's top-ranked bass and walleye lakes are found in Kentucky. The famous Dale Hollow Lake, covering 4,300 acres, straddles the central Kentucky-Tennessee border. The world's record 11–pound 15–ounce smallmouth bass was taken from the deep, clear waters along the Kentucky side of the lake in 1955. In addition to trophy bronzebacks, Dale Hollow yields hordes of white bass and crappie, as well as large rainbow trout and an occasional muskie. The gently rolling creek bottoms and steep ridges of the 3,000–acre Dale Hollow Wildlife Management Area wind along the shoreline of the lake. Just north of Dale Hollow are the sprawling waters of huge 50,250–acre Lake Cumberland—one of the most scenic and productive fishing areas in the state for trophy largemouth, small-mouth, and Kentucky bass, white bass, crappie, big rainbow trout, walleye, and landlocked striped bass. Cumberland yielded the state record 21–pound 8–ounce walleye. The big frigid tailrace waters below the Wolf Creek Dam hold trophy metallic-flanked rainbow trout up to 14 pounds. During the hot summer months night is the most productive time to fish for the big Lake Cumberland rainbows. The gently sloping creek bottoms, ridges, hardwood forests, old farmlands, and wildlife food plots of the 23,000–acre Lake Cumberland Wildlife Management Area border portions of the lake's irregularly shaped shoreline. Beautiful 6,000–acre Laurel River Lake lies due east of Lake Cumberland, surrounded by the forested hills and rocky bluffs of the Daniel Boone National Forest. This incredibly scenic lake yields smallmouth bass, panfish, and rainbows.

VACATION/ LODGING GUIDE

The rugged uplands of eastern Kentucky shelter several outstanding lakes and streams. Buckhorn Lake has 1,250 acres surrounded by mountains and yields good strings of largemouth bass around submerged brush areas as well as white bass, crappie, and bluegill. Rainbows are caught beneath the dam from spring through fall. Portions of the shoreline are hemmed by the primitive gamelands of the 2,580–acre Buckhorn Lake Wildlife Management Area. Scenic Fishtrap Lake, the easternmost of Kentucky's major lakes, covers 1,130 acres in Pike County with fishing for bluegill, channel catfish, smallmouth, and white bass. The dense hardwood forests and steep mountainous terrain of the 10,000–acre Fishtrap Lake Wildlife Management Area border portions of the lake's shoreline. Cave Run Lake on the Licking River covers 8,300 acres in the northern part of the Daniel Boone National Forest and yields smallmouth bass, crappie, bluegill, and a large population of elusive muskellunge. The deep-flowing pools of the Licking River and its tributaries provide some of the state's best smallmouth bass and muskie float fishing. Other top-ranked eastern Kentucky fisheries include Kinniconick Creek for muskie, bass, and trout; Tygart Creek, a renowned muskie stream; Grayson and Greenbo lakes on the Little Sandy River for trophy bass, crappie, bluegill, and trout; Red River for smallmouth bass and muskie; and the scenic South Fork of the Cumberland and Dewey Lake on Levisa Fork.

Several major lakes and float streams are located in the beautiful, gently rolling central bluegrass country. Herrington Lake stretches for 35 miles and has a huge spring spawning run of white bass up the Dix River. Herrington's 1,860 acres also produce good catches of largemouth bass, crappie, and bluegill. Green River Lake in south central Kentucky yields trophy largemouth bass, crappie, and bluegill. The wooded hills of the 14,625–acre Green River Wildlife Management Area border portions of the lake's shoreline. The North, South, and Middle forks of the Kentucky River provide excellent float fishing for muskellunge and smallmouth bass. The Little Kentucky River is an excellent early season smallmouth bass stream. The scenic and wild, gravel-bottomed Elkhorn Creek is considered

one of the nation's top smallmouth bass streams. Other productive central Kentucky game-fish streams include the Rolling Fork and its Beech Fork, Chaplin River, and Little Beech Fork tributaries; Salt River and Floyd's Fork; Guist Creek Lake; and Eagle Creek, a good panfish stream.

Information Sources, Maps & Access

Several useful free fishing and hunting guides, maps, and booklets may be obtained by writing to: Division of Public Relations, Dept. of Fish & Wildlife Resources, Capitol Plaza Tower, Frankfort 40601. The 29–page guide *Fishing in Kentucky* contains descriptions of all major lakes and streams, as well as a "Kentucky Fishing Map," regulations, and a handy fishing resort and marina guide. The 29–page guide *Hunting in Kentucky* contains regulations and license information, seasons and limits, and descriptions of game species. Additional free Fish & Wildlife Resources publications include a *Kentucky Trout Waters Map*, *Guide to 28 Public Fishing Lakes*, *Kentucky Lake Fish & Fishing*, *Hunting Digest*, *Deer Hunting Guide*, *Waterfowl Hunting Guide*, *Waterfowl Identification*, and *Places to Hunt—a Guide to 45 Public Hunting Areas in Kentucky*, which describes all state forest reserves and fish and wildlife management areas. Boating information and regulations may be obtained from: Division of Boating, Dept. of Transportation, State Office Bldg., Frankfort 40601.

The *Daniel Boone National Forest Map* shows recreation sites and facilities, boundaries, highways and roads, trails, railroads, lookout stations, boat launches, natural arches, points of interest, historical points, and lakes and streams. Information is also given on hunting and fishing, camping, wildlife, climate, and boating. The map is available for 50¢ as well as information from: Forest Supervisor, Winchester 40391. Free map-brochures are available from the same address for the *Pioneer Weapons Hunting Area*, *Red River Gorge*, *Natural Bridge*, and *Yahoo Falls Scenic Area*. The primitive weapons area map shows gravel roads, trails, primitive camping areas, water holes, bottomlands, and wildlife openings.

The forest is reached via U.S. Highways 25, 27, 60, 421, and 460. Motels and cottages are available at the boat docks on Lake Cumberland at the confluence of the Laurel and Rockcastle rivers. Accommodations, supplies, and equipment rentals are available at Boonesboro, Corbin, and Lexington. For backpacking and camping info in the Cumberland Gap backcountry, write: Superintendent, Cumberland Gap National Historic Park, Box 340, Middlesboro 40965 (606)248–2817. Contact the Superintendent's Office, Land Between the Lakes, Golden Pond, KY 42231 (502)924–5602 for information and the following free publications: *Land Between the Lakes Map & Guide*, TVA's *Land Between the Lakes Guide*, *Long Creek Trail*, *Field Guide to Mammals*, *Field Guide to Wading & Upland Game Birds*, *Bald Eagles*, *Hiking & Riding Trails*, and *Woodland Walk*. The major auto access routes serving Kentucky include Interstate Highways 75, 65, 64, and 24.

Recreation Areas

Cumberland Gap National Historic Park

The Cumberland Gap Roadless Area embraces 20,169 acres of mixed hardwood forests, knifelike ridges, valleys, streams, caves, and limestone sinks along the Allegheny Plateau in the Cumberland Gap National Historic Park. A backpacking trail winds across the length of the park, passing through scenic forests of pine, oak, and hickory, with a lush understory of rhododendron, mountain laurel, dogwood, and redbud inhabited by deer, ruffed grouse, raccoon, and red fox.

The historic Boone Trace, and its successor, the Wilderness Road,

one of the most famous trails in American history, originated at Cumberland Gap and crossed the Cumberland River where it followed the ancient Warriors Path—known to the Indians as Athiamionee, meaning "path of the armed one"—across the state to the Daniel Boone National Forest and beyond through the Great Valley to Pennsylvania. The legendary Boone Trace, originally a game trail followed by the buffalo and Indians, and later by the French fur trappers, was blazed by Daniel Boone and 30 companions. From about 50 miles north of Cumberland Gap, Boone followed the Warriors Path. The Boone Trace later became the Wilderness Road, followed by intrepid pioneers heading west. The old route of the Boone Trace and Wilderness Road will be followed by the proposed Daniel Boone National Scenic Trail, which will extend from North Carolina to Fort Boonesborough State Park, Kentucky.

Daniel Boone National Forest

This forest reserve takes in 460,000 acres of towering sandstone bluffs, woodlands, waterfalls, natural arches, and rolling hills on the western rim of the Cumberland Plateau between the mountains of eastern Kentucky and the bluegrass country. The major features of this hunting, camping, and canoeing region include the 7,000–acre Pioneer Weapons Hunting Area—set up for the use of only old-time weapons including flintlock and percussion cap rifles, muzzle-loading shotguns, longbows, and crossbows—the Red River Gorge Scenic Area, Licking River, Beaver Creek Wilderness, Rockcastle River, and Lake Cumberland. The Big South Fork of the Cumberland, a proposed national wild and scenic river, is one of the most spectacular rivers in the eastern U.S.; it flows through the forest surrounded by a wild country of giant sandstone bluffs, scenic waterfalls, and deep woodland valleys. There is good hunting in season for gray squirrel, ruffed grouse, whitetail deer, and wild turkey. Cave Run, Wood Creek, Buckhorn, and Laurel River lakes provide good fishing for trophy bass and pan fish. Lake Cumberland, created by Wolf Creek

Dam, provides 250 miles of national forest shoreline and provides top-ranked fishing for trophy walleye, largemouth bass, white bass, and crappie. The scenic Red River yields muskellunge up to 20 pounds. Fly fishermen will find large holdover rainbow trout along the remote backcountry streams. A segment of the Boone Trace or Wilderness Road has been marked at several places in the forest, including the site of Wood's Block House at "Hazelpatch," which furnished the only refuge from the Indians to pioneers on their way to Boonesborough.

Land Between the Lakes

Land Between the Lakes is a 170,000 acre peninsula located between Kentucky Lake and Lake Barkley in western Kentucky and Tennessee. The area is being developed by the Tennessee Valley Authority (TVA) as a national demonstration in multiple-use land for outdoor recreation, environmental, educational and resource management. Oak-hickory type hardwood forests comprise about 145,000 acres of the land and meadows, open areas and reverting fields occupy about 25,000 acres, primarily concentrated in long narrow valleys. There are more than 300 miles of shoreline on Kentucky Lake and Lake Barkley, which almost completely surrounds the Land Between the Lakes. These two giant lakes are joined by a canal and combined with Land Between the Lake's shores and the other lands touched by the lakes, a body of water with about 3,500 miles of shoreline. Within the land area of the peninsula there are about 1,000 surface acres of water, with three subimpoundments of Lake Barkley, a small interior lake and over 300 ponds and wildlife waterholes.

Lake Kentucky and Lake Barkley are two of the top bass and crappie fishing lakes in the United States. Fishermen can pass through the free flowing canal between these two lakes in less than five minutes. The slight, but constant water flow caused by changes in the water

levels of the two lakes makes an ideal fishing environment. During a plentiful year over two million crappie, some reaching record weights, are taken from these lakes. Black bass is also one of the twin lakes' premier fishing attractions. Both species are best during the spring and fall, and excellent mid-summer catches are reported from the old creek and river beds. The current world record for blue catfish was caught in 1971 in the Tennessee portion of Kentucky Lake. The fish, which weighed in at 115 pounds was estimated to have weighed 125 pounds when taken in four days earlier. Anglers also cast for bluegills, whitebass, and delicious saugers. Fall and winter are prime times for hunting at Land Between the Lakes. The area game includes wild turkey (a population of about 800 birds), deer, squirrel, quail, rabbit, dove, snipe, woodcock, raccoon, opossum, woodchuck and gray fox. Waterfowl enthusiasts will find that Kentucky and Barkley Lakes are wintering habitat for up to 5,000 geese and 5,500 ducks.

Nature buffs will marvel at Land Between the Lake's offerings. During the winter months bald and golden eagles can be seen soaring above the deep, quiet coves of the lakes or perched high above the lakeshore. Mourning doves, green and blue herons, egrets and bobwhite quail inhabit the area's shores and wooded areas. Beavers, bobcats, gray and red foxes, deer, mink, raccoon, squirrels, and other small mammals comprise Land Between the Lake's wildlife. An added feature of the Land Between the Lake region is the herd of buffalo that roam a 200 acre pasture. Buffalo were once native to the Tennessee and Cumberland River area and the small herd that has been brought to the area is symbolic of the TVA's conservation efforts. There are over 400 backwood trails winding throughout

Land Between the Lakes, including specialty trails and trails for wheelchairs. Hikers can follow the historical, 26–mile Ft. Henry trail of which a portion traces General Grant's troops' movements. There is a 60–mile North-South trail with a wide variety of hiking experiences for both novices and experts. The self-explaining Blue-Gray Trail, the Songbird Trail and a Resource Motor Trail help round out the offerings.

The pleasures of Land Between the Lakes continue beyond the recreational. A well developed environmental education program with a variety of presentations may be found here as well. Many demonstrations are held at the Environmental Educational Center, a 5,000 acre wooded area near Lake Barkley's shoreline. The Center has an interpretive facility where displays and slide presentations can be viewed; Silo Overlook, a platform atop a silo which overlooks Lake Barkley; the two internal lakes of Hematite and Honker; and Empire Farm, where children can see farm animals and learn about life on the farm. Farming methods and household patterns of the mid–1800's can be seen in The Homeplace—a two generation farm typical of the Land Between the Lakes area in 1850. The planners of Land Between the Lakes area deliberately restricted commercial enterprises from the area. Camping facilities are in the area, but visitors wishing to stay in hotels or motels must use privately owned resorts and motels which are within close driving range. Food stands, gas stations, grocery stores and restaurants are conveniently located along the opposite shores of Kentucky Lake and Lake Barkley.

Lodges & Resorts

★★★★*Apple Valley Resort at Lake Cumberland* is a condominium development situated within Lake Cumberland State Resort Park in south central Kentucky. Guests enjoy the privacy of the 100 townhouses and exclusive recreation facilities, as well as the public recreation provided by the State Park. Apple Valley is on 12 acres of a wooded peninsula jutting out into Lake Cumberland. Facilities include a heated swimming pool, saunas, four tennis courts, horse-shoe pits, a volleyball court, and a clubhouse with kitchen, fireplace, bar, card tables and ping-pong. On the 3,000 acres of the State Park, visitors will find boat launching and docking facilities, a 9–hole golf course, horseback riding, playgrounds, hiking trails, and indoor and outdoor programs and group activities. Lake Cumberland has excellent fishing for bass and holds the national record for brown trout. The lake is so clear that skin and scuba diving is enjoyed there. Overlooking the water is the newly-expanded Lure Lodge, offering fine dining with a panoramic view. The townhouses are all air-conditioned and have two levels with aproximately 980 square feet including upper and lower balconies. There is an entry foyer with doors separating the upper and lower levels for privacy when renting only one floor. Each floor has a full bath and closet space. From May 15 through September 15 the daily rate is $45 for up to four persons and $10 each additional person (over 15 years of age). The weekly rate is seven days for the price of six. Kitchens are fully equipped with utensils and dinnerware. To rent one level, rates are $26 a day for the bedroom level and $28 a day for the efficiency level (with kitchen). For reservations and information contact: Apple Valley Resort, Townhouse Association Inc., RR 2, Jamestown, KY 42629 (502)343–3121.

★★*Barkley Inn* offers deluxe accommodations and private suites overlooking Lake Barkley, just across from the Land Between the Lakes region. All deluxe rooms are beautifully furnished, with plush wall-to-wall carpeting, TV and fully equipped modern kitchens, which are optional. Private three- and four-bedroom chalets are also available. The Barkley Inn has a large swimming pool, private boat docking facilities, and a variety of fishing boats and ski boats to enjoy

on the lake. Rates are $12.50–20 for a single room depending on the season, $19–28 for a double room, and $27–43 for a suite with kitchen. Cottages accommodating six persons are $55. For more information write: Barkley Inn, Route 2, Box 129, Cadiz, KY 42211 (502)924–5659.

★★★*Barren River Lake State Resort Park* is located in the gently rolling country of southcentral Kentucky. Lake Barren's 10,000 acres and the park's 1,799 acres provide a full range of recreational opportunities. Guests can enjoy fishing in the lake for white, largemouth and smallmouth bass, channel catfish, bluegill, walleye, and muskie. There is a sand beach and bathhouse for swimming and a year-round marina with 100 open slips, 40 covered slips, a launching ramp and fishing boats, pontoon boats, and ski boat rentals. The resort also offers: camping on 101 suites with electric and water hookups; horseback riding trails around the lake; a 9–hole golf course with instruction available; a pool; handball on a lighted court; two lighted tennis courts; two lighted paddle tennis courts with lessons; picnicking facilities; shuffleboard; bicycle rentals; lighted basketball courts and a recreation room. The resort's gift shop has the largest selection of Kentucky cookbooks in the parks system. Children can enjoy the two playgrounds plus planned activities. During the summer months singing groups perform, and year-round entertainment is arranged by the recreation director. Accommodations at the resort include lodge rooms and two-bedroom executive cottages. Five rooms in the lodge have special facilities for the handicapped. Meals, not included in the rates, are available in the lodge's dining room or snack bar. Rates: lodge rooms $19.25–28 double occupancy depending on season. For further information contact: Barren River Lake State Resort Park, Lucas KY 42156 (502)646–2151 or toll-free in Kentucky (800)372–2961.

★★★*Big Bear Resort at Kentucky Lake* offers air-conditioned deluxe motel rooms, private housekeeping cottages, and open and shady campsites in a secluded cove. Big Bear Resort rents fishing boats, sailboats, and pontoon boats from a private marina, and also provides covered boat slips for private boats on a daily, weekly, or monthly basis. The lake holds bass, crappie, perch, channel catfish, walleye, and bluegill. There is no closed season on game fish. The resort has a complete bait and tackle store at the Marina, a sandy beach for swimming with a diving float, and waterski rentals. Nearby horseback riding stables, golf courses, antique shops, and 170,000 acres of backwoods in the Land Between the Lakes region offer a variety of family entertainment. Private motel rooms are $12 daily and $72 weekly. Rooms with efficiency kitchens are also available for $20 daily and $120 weekly. All private cottages have air-conditioning, TV's, full kitchens and plush wall-to-wall carpeting. Rates are $30 daily, and $180 weekly for a one-bedroom, and $33 daily, $198 weekly for a two-bedroom. Cottages must be reserved for a minimum of three days, and on a weekly basis only throughout the summer months. Special rates are available in spring and fall. Big Bear Resort also offers a rustic log cabin with a completely modernized, deluxe interior for 12–14 guests. All three bedrooms are air-conditioned; there is a full kitchen and a glassed-in porch overlooking Kentucky Lake. Rates are $50 daily, $300 weekly. For more information write: Big Bear Resort, Box 156, Route 4, Benton, KY 42025 (502)354–6414.

★★★*Buckhorn Lake State Resort Park* is tucked away amid the eastern mountains on 1,200 acre Lake Buckhorn on the edge of beautiful Daniel Boone National Forest. Vacationers will find relaxing, peaceful scenery and tranquil settings. There is hiking on Leatherwood Trail and Moonshiner Hollow, an interpretive trail with nature stations identifying various plants and trees. Marina services are available and there are 60 open slips, two launching ramps, rental pontoon boats, fishing boats, and towboats. Fishing catches include largemouth and smallmouth bass, crappies, bluegill, and channel fish. The lake has a sand beach with a bathhouse complex. The lodge also has a pool for guests. There are 72 camping sites with electrical hook-ups. Tennis courts, bicycle rentals, miniature golf and picnicking facilities are available. A playground and planned recreational activities are provided for children. During the summer season performances by singing groups, square dances, special events and social activities are arranged by the recreation director. Accommodations at the resort consist of lodge rooms open May 1–October 31. Each room has two double beds, bath, maid service, phone, air-conditioning and private patio or balcony with lake view. Meals, not included in rates, are available three times a day in the dining room. Rates: $23.75–28 double occupancy depending on season. For further information contact: Buckhorn Lake State Park, Buckhorn KY 41721 (606)398–7510 or toll-free (800)372–2961 in Kentucky.

★★★*Carter Caves State Resort Park* is located on 1,239 acres of ruggedly beautiful terrain. Guided tours through three eerie, awe-inspiring caves on the park's grounds provide guests with a fascinating underworld nature study. Both lighted and unlighted tours are available. Interpretive exhibits on the area's geology, wildflowers, wildlife and cave diorama can be enjoyed in the Nature Center. Organized canoeing trips on Tygart Creek are very popular at the resort. Catfish, muskie, bass, bream, and crappie can be caught in local streams. There is hiking over miles of trails. The park's major facilities are connected by the trails leading over the natural bridges and to the caves. Horseback riding, a 9–hole golf course, picnicking and tennis facilities are available for guests. Swimming is provided in the lodge's pool and a community pool free to camping guests. There are camping facilities on 86 recreational and tent sites. Children's playgrounds are provided, as well as planned recreation. During the summer musical entertainment is offered and movies and nature films are shown in the amphitheater. A park naturalist arranges nature programs, special events and other social activities year round. Accommodations include modern lodge rooms and housekeeping cottage units. The 28 lodge rooms all have baths, two double beds, TV, wall-to-wall carpeting and individually controlled heating and air-conditioning. Cottages include efficiencies, one bedroom and two bedroom units. All have phones, TV, air-conditioning and heat. Tableware, cooking utensils and linens are furnished. Meals, not included in rates, are available in the main dining room three times a day, or in the snack bar, which operates on a seasonal basis. Rates: Lodge rooms $19.25–28 double occupancy, depending on season. Cottages: $25.75–40.25 per night depending on accommodation. For further information contact: Carter Caves State Resort Park, Olive Hill, KY 41164 (606)286–4411, or toll-free reservation (1–800)372–2911 from any point in Kentucky.

★★★*Cumberland Falls State Resort Park in Daniel Boone National Forest* is located on Lake Cumberland in the Cumberland Plateau area of eastern Kentucky. The 1,794-acre state park is surrounded by the Daniel Boone National Forest. Cumberland Falls, nicknamed "The Niagara of the South," is the only falls in the Western World to reflect a moonbow when the moon is full. Eleven miles of backpacking trails connect with Moonbow Trail through Daniel Boone National Forest, with two shelters. Hiking can be enjoyed on 15 miles of trails, ranging from ¼ mile to seven miles in length. There are two camping areas, with a total of 73 sites for tents or recreational vehicles. Horseback riding trails run through scenic wooded trails around the lodge. Bass, catfish, panfish and rough fish can all be caught in the Cumberland River. Tennis facilities, an Olympic-size pool, horseshoe and picnic areas are available to guests. Children's

activities are planned and playgrounds are provided. Adult entertainment includes an 80–person amphitheater hosting movies, nature films, and sing-alongs; performances by singing groups, and square dancing. Additional planned activities and special events are arranged by recreational directors including sports, games, dances, drama and nature crafts. The resort has a lodge, woodland suites, and housekeeping cottage accommodations. The lodge maintains the rustic feeling of the area, with 60 rooms all including air-conditioning, TV, phone and wall-to-wall carpeting. Woodland suites are two-bedroom units located in wooded areas near the lodge. Each has three double beds, TV, air-conditioning and maid service. Housekeeping cottages include one- and two-bedroom units. All have air-conditioning, TV and phone. Tableware, cooking utensils and linens are furnished. Meals, not included, are available three times a day in the main dining room or in the coffee shop which operates on· a seasonal basis. Rates: Lodge rooms and Woodland suite rooms: $19.25–28 depending on season, double occupancy. Cottages: $30.75–40.25 per night. For further information contact: Cumberland Falls State Resort Park, Corbin, KY 40701 (606)528–4121 or toll-free reservations (800)372–2911 in Kentucky.

★★★*General Butler State Resort Park*, located in north central Kentucky is a beautiful, totally modern resort in an area of outstanding natural beauty. The furnished and restored mansion of General Butler is on the park grounds, and open for viewing. Three miles of hiking trails lead from the lodge to the Ohio River to overlook the mansion. The park's lake provides opportunities for row boating, pedal boats and a sand beach. Fish include bass, crappie, and catfish. Bicycle rentals, tennis, a miniature golf course, 9–hole golf course, recreation room, horseback riding, picnicking areas and shuffleboard are all offered at the resort. There are 135 camping sites with electrical and water hookups. Children can enjoy three playgrounds, with one featuring rides on the Kentucky Flyer, a miniature train. During summer months the resort hosts singing groups and square dances. Year round daily activities and special events are planned by the recreation director for both children and adults. Accommodations include lodge rooms, efficiency cottages, one-bedroom cottages and three-bedroom cottages. Lodge rooms have maid service, two double beds, individual climate control, baths, TV, phone and private balcony or patio. All cottages have TV's, phones, and air-conditioning, with tableware, cooking utensils and linens provided. Meals, not included in rates, are available in the dining room. Meeting rooms are available. Rates: Lodge rooms $19.25–28 double occupancy depending on season. Efficiency cottages $25.75; one-bedroom $30.75; three-bedroom cottage for six $54.50 per person. For further information contact: General Butler State Resort Park, Carrollton, KY 41008 (502)732–4384 or toll-free (1–800)372–2961.

★★★*Greenbo Lake State Resort Park* is located on the shore of Greenbo Lake on 3,330 wooded acres of park land. Every article in the lodge—from the draperies down to the faucets—was made in Kentucky. The resort's lodge also boasts a massive fireplace with a copper hood reflecting the tiniest spark. Marina facilities are nearby with 105 open slips, a launching ramp and rowboats, motorboats, pedal boats, and pontoon boats for rent. The lake holds big black bass, bluegill, and channel catfish. The lake also provides swimming off its sand beach. There are several hiking trails in the park, some linking with other state park trails. Camping facilities for 63 recreational vehicles with electrical hookups are available. Horseback riding, picnicking, pool swimming, shuffleboard, and a recreation room can all be enjoyed from the resort. Playgrounds are provided for children, plus additional planned activities. During summer months singing groups perform and dance. Special events and other activi-

ties are planned by the recreational director year round. Accommodations at the resort consist of lodge rooms, with two double beds, TV, phone, bath, and private balcony or patio overlooking the lake. Maid service is provided daily. The first floor of the resort is equipped to handle wheelchairs. Rates: Lodge rooms $19.25–28 double occupancy, depending on season. For further information contact: Greenbo Lake State Resort Park, Greenup, KY 41144 (606)473–7324 or toll-free (1–800)372–2911.

★★★*Hendricks Creek Resort on Dale Hollow Lake* offers superb fishing for smallmouth bass, scrappy bluegills, big walleye, striped bass, largemouth bass and rainbow trout. The resort holds the state's record for the largest muskie catch. Dale Hollow Lake has an annual $5,000 Fall Fishing Rodeo, and the resort offers special rates for early reservations. The resort will gladly arrange a group fishing trip and provide food, houseboats, and/or cottages, fishing boats and motors. The resort has lakeside cottages for two-six persons. All are completely furnished and have cooking utensils, pillows, and blankets. Linens are not provided. The specialty of the resort is its houseboats—available in six sizes. Choose from a number of plans differing in space and facilities. For example, Plan 10 offers a 38–foot Captain Craft with accommodations for two-four adults or a family of six with small children. There's a 7 × 11 covered deck area, 45 hp outboard motor, and bunk beds. Plan 60 features a 55–foot President's Cruiser for up to ten adults. There are five double beds, a large galley, a stereo tape deck, a 12 × 13 front deck for fishing and sightseeing, a comfortable dining area and all the equipment needed for cruising. Various additional plans are

available to suit needs. Guests can take "Maxi Cruises" which last seven days, or a "Mini Cruise" for three days. Boats come with a full tank of fuel, and a charge is made only for fuel used. The resort has a fully-stocked country store. Rates: Cottage: daily, two persons, $20 daily, $116 weekly. Houseboat rates: Mini Cruises in-season, $190–360; Maxi Cruises in-season, $335–695. For further information contact: Hendricks Creek Resort, P.O Box 2107, 8215 Arlington Ave., N.W., North Canton, OH 44720 (216)854–4151 or (502)433–7172.

★★★*Indian Creek Lodge at Lake Cumberland* is nestled on the wide shores of the 100–square-mile lake, a fisherman's paradise. Grider Hill dock rents fishing boats with or without motors, and water ski boats, and will also provide overnight dockage for guests' boats. Fishermen can troll the clear lake for bass, perch, crappie, blue gill, and rainbow trout. Nearby the spectacular 76 Falls spill over a high ledge from Indian Creek. Golfers are welcome guests at the nearby 76 Fall Country Club, which sports a rugged, championship course. The main lodge has a pleasant dining room with a breathtaking lake view, and a lounge for relaxing after hours. The lodge offers spacious rooms with a view over Lake Cumberland, private cottages along the lakeshore, and family houseboats, fully equipped to accommodate up to eight persons. Rates are $14 single and $18 for a lodge room, and $84–108 weekly. Private cottages with kitchenettes are $20 daily, $132 weekly. Cottages with full kitchens, living room/dining areas, and private bath accommodate up to six and are $34–40 daily, $204–240 weekly. Luxurious houseboats, from 34–46 feet, accommodate four to ten, and are $55–90 daily. For more information write: Indian Creek Lodge & Grider Hill Dock, Albany, KY 42602 (606)387–5501.

★★★*Jamestown Dock Village at Lake Cumberland* hugs the shores of this spectacular 100–square-mile lake. Green hills surround the lake providing shelter from high winds along the 1,255-mile wooded shoreline. Expert fishing guides will show anglers the best spots for largemouth bass, walleye, and rainbow trout. Fishermen are welcome to cast from shore, or take advantage of Jamestown Dock's complete marina of round- or flat-bottom fishing boats, outboard motors, and pontoon boats. The modern dock is completely equipped with private moorings, tackle, bait ice, individual lockers, and cleaning and storage space for the day's catch. Deluxe houseboats and private two-, three-, and four-bedroom cottages with fully equipped modern kitchens, air-conditioning and screened-in porches offering a lake view are available. Other amenities include a large outdoor swimming pool, a children's playground, and a pleasant dining room serving three hearty country-style meals daily. For details write: Jamestown Dock Village, Rt. 2, Jamestown, KY 42629 (502)343–3535.

★★★*Jenny Wiley State Resort Park* is located on 1,700 acres of highlands near a 1,150-acre lake. There is boating from two docks with 199 open slips, 40 covered slips, and a launching ramp. Guests can rent pontoon boats, fishing boats and pedal boats. Fishing in the area includes largemouth, smallmouth, and white bass, rock bass, crappie, catfish and bluegill. The resort is popular for its skylift, which carries riders to and from a point about two miles north of the lodge to the top of Sugar Camp Mountain for a scenic view of the surrounding mountains, lakes, and valleys. Miles of picturesque hiking trails lead through the mountains around the lodge. Seasonal horseback riding, a 9–hole golf course, an 18–hole miniature golf course, waterskiing on a four mile strip, shuffleboard, picnicking and a recreation room are available to guests. Camping facilities include 128 sites with electrical hookups. Children's playgrounds are provided, as well as planned recreation. A trained recreation director plans daily activities, special events and social activities. There is a summer music

theatre in a 900–capacity amphitheater. Accommodations at the resort include lodge rooms, duplex cottages for two, and two-bedroom cottages. The lodge rooms each have maid service, two double beds, bath, TV, phone and air-conditioning. Cottages have TV, phone, air-conditioning and electric heat. Tableware, cooking utensils and linens are furnished. Meals, not included in rates, are provided three times a day in the lodge's dining room. A snack shop operates on a seasonal basis. Rates: Lodge is $19.25–28 double occupancy depending on season. Duplex cottages are $25.75 per night, double occupancy. Two bedroom cottage is $40.25 per night per person for four people. For further information contact: Jenny Wiley State Resort Park, Prestonsbury, KY 41653 (606)886–2711 or toll-free in Kentucky (1–800)372–2961.

★★★*Kenlake State Resort Park* is a year-round resort located about midway down the western side of Kentucky Lake, is compact in comparison to other Kentucky State resorts although the park area totals 1,800 acres. Its position in the Western Kentucky Waterland makes boating both accessible and popular. Marina facilities operate year-round, with 75 open slips, 140 covered slips, rental boats, and full service facilities for anglers. The lake is one of the state's finest sailboating areas and home of the annual Watkins Cup and Governor's Cup sailboat regattas. The lake is noted for its fine catches of largemouth, smallmouth, white and Kentucky bass; channel blue catfish, bluegill, rockfish, and crappies. Summer months offer lake swimming with a sand beach and bathhouse. The lodge also has a pool. Horseback riding, picnicking, a 9–hole golf course, shuffleboard, a recreation room, and six tennis courts, with a lighted multi-purpose court are provided for guests. Camping sites for both tents and recreational vehicles are available, with water and electrical hookups. The lodge is equipped to accommodate the handicapped. Daily activities and special events are planned by a recreation director for both children and adults. Four playgrounds are provided throughout the park for children. Accommodations at the resort include lodge rooms, efficiency cottages and one-, two-, and three-bedroom cottages. The lodge rooms all have maid service, bath, view of the lake or park, TV, phone, wall-to-wall carpeting and air-conditioning. Cottages have phones, TV, air-conditioning and linen service. Meals, which are not included in the rates, are available three times a day at the lodge. Rates: Lodge rooms $19.25–28 double occupancy depending on season. Cottages: efficiency $25.75 double occupancy per night; one-bedroom cottage $30.75 double occupancy per night; two-bedroom cottage $40.25 per night, four people; three bedroom cottage for six people $47.75 per night. For further information contact: Kenlake State Resort Park, Hardin, KY 42048 (502)474–2211 or toll free in Kentucky (1–800)372–2961.

★★★*Kentucky Dam Village State Resort Park*, located in western Kentucky on 160,300–acre Kentucky Lake, is one of the largest and most popular vacation resorts in Kentucky. There are 225 camping sites with water hookups, electricity and grills. A miniature golf course is located in the camping area, and the 18–hole Village Green Course is within walking distance from the lodge. Nature enthusiasts can enjoy the scenery and wildlife on the resort's several hiking, bicycling, and horseback riding trails. Kentucky Dam Village has the largest docking facilities in the state's park system. Fishing boats, houseboats, rowboats, pontoon and pedal boats can all be rented. The lake also provides fine bass fishing and a sand beach for swimmers. Additional recreational activities include swimming in the lodge's pool; two tennis courts; picnicking facilities and a recreation room. Children can enjoy playgrounds located throughout the park and planned activities. Accommodations at the resort are in lodge rooms; one- and two- bedroom cottages; two-bedroom deluxe cottages with living room, 1½ baths, dining area and garages; three-bed-

room cottages; three-bedroom deluxe cottages with living rooms, 1½ baths; dining areas and garage; three-bedroom executive cottages with living room, dining area, custom kitchen, two baths and maid service. Meals, not included in rates, are available at the lodge's dining room. A coffee shop and snack bar also operate on the park's premises. Conference and meeting rooms are available. Rates: Lodge rooms are $19.25–28 double occupancy depending on season; one-bedroom cottages are $30.75 double occupancy. For further information contact: Kentucky Dam Village State Resort Park, Gilbertsville, KY 42044 (502)362–4271 or toll-free in Kentucky (1–800)372–2961.

★★★*Lake Barkley State Resort Park* is located in Kentucky's Western Waterland area on the scenic Little River embayment of Lake Barkley. Lake Barkley's area totals 57,920 acres with 42,020 in Kentucky. Just about every sort of water sport can be enjoyed here. There is a year round marina with 118 covered slips, 46 open slips, and a launching ramp. Fishing and waterskiing boats can be rented. Organized canoe trips are arranged by the resort. Fishing is superb for Kentucky, white, largemouth and smallmouth bass. Nature enthusiasts will enjoy the huge outdoor conservation area at the Land Between the Lakes. There are backpacking hikes through the park with skill and techniques of backpacking demonstrated, hiking on three trails with brochures available to point out unusual trees and plants, and bird feeders to attract rare and lovely birds. Lake Barkley Resort has a trapshooting range, which is unique to the state's park system. Equipment and instruction are available. Horseback riding, picnicking, a recreation room, shuffleboard, four tennis courts with free instruction (and two lighted courts), 80 camping sites; swimming off a sand beach or in the lodge's pool and an 18–hole golf course with instruction can all be found at the resort. There are playgrounds and planned activities for children. During the summer months singing groups perform and there is year round entertainment provided under the guidance of the recreation director. Accommodations at the resort include lodge rooms, lodge suites and two-bedroom executive cottages. Lodge rooms have two double beds, radio, TV, split-area dressing room and bath and private balconies. Lodge suites each have two bedrooms, a kitchenette and the same facilities as lodge rooms. Executive cottages are two-bedroom units with custom kitchens, bath, phone, and TV. Tableware, cooking utensils and linens are furnished. Four rooms in the lodge have facilities for the handicapped. Meals, not included in the rates, are provided three times a day in the dining room. A coffee shop operates on a seasonal basis. Meeting rooms are available. Rates: Lodge rooms: $19.25–30.25 per person double occupancy, depending on season. Lodge suites for six people are $64.50 per night; executive cottages for six people $54.50 per night. For further information contact: Lake Barkley State Resort Park, P.O. Box 790, Cadiz, KY 42211, (502)924–1171 or toll free (1–800)372–2961 in Kentucky.

★★★*Lake Cumberland State Resort Park* is located on the shore of 100–square-mile Lake Cumberland in the wooded forests of south-central Kentucky. The area offers a wide assortment of wildlife and plants, many of which can be seen in the resort's Nature Center. Displays on local history, as well as wildlife of the region are on view. From the Nature Center, two trails lead to the lodge. A 3½-mile self-guided trail has interpretive signs along the way. Horseback riding on trails overlooking the lake and bicycle trails provides nature enthusiasts additional opportunities to enjoy the scenery. Water sports include fine fishing, swimming in the lodge's pool, and boating with houseboats, skiboats, fishing and pontoon boats. There are 150 camping sites with electrical and water hookups available; two tennis courts; a multipurpose court; picnicking facilities; a 9–hole golf course; a miniature golf course; shuffleboard and a recreation room. Children can take advantage of two playgrounds as well as

planned activities. The Activities' Center hosts singers June through Labor Day. Dances, special events and entertainment are arranged year-round by the recreation director. Accommodations at the resort are in lodge rooms, one- and two-bedroom cottages and two-bedroom wildwood cottages with living/dining rooms, kitchen, bath, fireplace and porch deck. Maid service is provided in lodge rooms, and fresh linens are available daily to cottage guests. Four rooms in the Lodge have facilities for the handicapped. Meeting and conference rooms are available. Rates: Lodge rooms are $19.25–28 double occupancy depending on season; one bedroom cottages for two are $30.75 per night; two bedroom cottages for four are $30.75 per night; two bedroom wildwood cottages for four are $40.25. For further information contact: Lake Cumberland State Resort Park, Jamestown, KY 42629 (502)343–3111 or toll-free in Kentucky (1–800)372–2961.

★★★*Lake Malone Inn* is nestled on the wooded shores of a private lake, bordered by Lake Malone State Park in the rolling hills of western Kentucky. Fisherman can cast in the quiet waters of the small lake stocked with catfish, or troll fish the deep clear waters of the 900–acre Lake Malone for big bass and crappie and gamefish year-round. Lake Malone Inn has private tennis courts, secluded sandy beaches, shuffleboard courts, badminton and volleyball nets, and a golf driving range. All deluxe rooms are air-conditioned, with plush wall-to-wall carpeting, AM-FM radio, and sumptuous decor. Many have private balconies overlooking the lake, and wood-burning fireplaces. Generous country-style meals are enjoyed in the candlelit dining room, and there is a spacious lounge warmed by a rustic stone hearth and many cozy parlors to relax in after hours. Two private meeting rooms are available for conference groups as large as 130. Private catering services are available. Rates are $26 daily single occupancy, and $32 double occupancy. For more information write: Lake Malone Inn, P.O. Box 56, Dunmor, KY 42339 (502)657–2121.

Mammoth Cave National Park is built around the spectacular Mammoth Cave with tours to the world's longest network of cavern corridors, and beautiful stalactite and stalagmite formations. The park also has campfire programs, guided and self-guided nature trails, naturalist walks, scenic boat trips on the Green River and tennis and shuffleboard courts. There has been hotel service at Mammoth Cave since 1814. Today there is the hotel, a lodge and cottages.

★★★*Mammoth Cave Hotel* is a large, new brick motor-hotel near the historic entrance to the cave. It is completely air-conditioned, carpeted and equipped with tiled baths in all rooms. There are private patios and balconies, a spacious lounge, and a gift shop featuring local crafts. The daily rate for one person is $18.50 and for two persons $23. The hotel is open all year and off-season rates are $13.50 and $17.

★★★*Sunset Point Motor Lodge* is on the edge of the forest, overlooking Sunset Point Bluffs. The large modern rooms have two double beds, TV, air-conditioning, electric heat, and carpeting. Three persons to a room are $25 and four are $28. There is a special family rate for two parents and children under twelve with two double beds for $22 and off season rates are also available.

★★★*Hotel Cottages* are furnished in early American, have air-conditioning, heat, carpeting and a shower bath. A cottage is $17.50 for one person and $22 for two.

★★★*Woodland Cottages* are secluded in the forest and provide privacy for quiet enjoyment of the national park. There are single, two-, three- and four-bedroom units. Rates range from $13 to $27.

Reservations can be made for all types of accommodations by writing

to National Park Concessions, Mammoth Cave Hotel, Mammoth Cave, Kentucky 42259 (502)758–2225. There are no accommodations available with cooking facilities. There is a 145-site campground with a fee.

★★★*The Moors on Kentucky Lake* is a modern resort with a marina, housekeeping cottages, and a waterfront campground. The resort is located on Kentucky Lake at the mouth of Big Bear Creek, 10 miles above the Kentucky Dam, situated in a cove protected by breakwater seawalls. Besides offering protected dockage, the marina also has covered boat slips; accommodations for large cruisers; a boat and motor repair service; rentals of 16–foot fishing boats, 24– and 28–foot pontoon boats, and six and nine horsepower motors; guides; bait; fishing licenses; fuel and boating accessories. The Moors also has a restaurant and a store selling groceries. Daily rates for cottages start at $25 for two in a one-bedroom duplex. Two-bedroom units rent for $30 to $42.50, three-bedroom cottages are $45 to $52.50, four-bedrooms are $55 to $65 and the six-bedroom lodge for large groups is $100 a day. The weekly rate is six times the daily rate and there are lower rates in fall and spring. Each lake-front cottage is air-conditioned, has a TV and a kitchenette and is fully equipped with linens and cooking utensils. Many are wood paneled and all are in rustic settings. For information and reservations write: Moors Resort, Inc., Route 2, Gilbertsville, KY 42044 (502)362–4356.

★★★*Natural Bridge State Resort Park in the Daniel Boone National Forest* is noted for a great natural sandstone bridge that sets the tone of scenic beauty throughout the park. A skylift takes passengers to the National Bridge for viewing. There are hiking trails centering around Natural Bridge as well as park areas with legendary names like Lovers Leap, Devil's Gutch and Lookout Point. The resort has a pool for swimming and a lake for additional water activities, including fishing for rainbow trout, bream, crappie and largemouth and smallmouth bass and boating. Camping is available in the park's 95 sites with electric and water hookups. The resort also features a Nature Center and a recreation room. Children can enjoy the two playgrounds as well as additional planned activities. Year round recreation and activities are planned for adults plus seasonal activities such as tours through Red River Gorge and summer performances by singers. The park's lodge rests on a ledge overlooking a deep valley and is encircled by hemlock which provides shade and a tranquil environment. Housekeeping cottages are also available and have been paneled in pine in keeping with the natural motif. Meals, which are not included in the rates, are available at the lodge's dining room. Meeting rooms are available. Rates: Lodge rooms are $19.25–28, double occupancy. Cottages: Efficiency, $25.75 double occupancy. One-bedroom cottages, $30.75 double occupancy. For further information contact: Natural Bridge State Resort Park, Slade, KY 40376 (606)663–2214 or toll-free in Kentucky (1–800)372–2961.

★★★*Paradise Resort on Kentucky Lake* is a quiet vacation retreat, offering housekeeping cottages and recreational facilities reserved for the exclusive use of guests. Along the shoreline, there is a play-area for children, and a gradually tapering sandy beach for swimming. The resort will teach any swimming guest how to ride an aquaplane one afternoon per week at no charge during June, July, and August. There is a private dock with launching ramp and dockage for guests who bring their own boats; and rental boats and motors for other guests. The resort also has bait, licenses and free freezer service. Other recreational facilities include badminton, shuffleboard, horseshoes and basketball. The cottages along the shoreline are all air-conditioned and range in size from small units sleeping four to larger ones accommodating up to ten. The resort is

open from April 1st to November 1st and there is a minimum rental of three days. All cottages are equipped for housekeeping with range, refrigerator, hot and cold water, utensils, dishes and cutlery. There is a private bath in each and bed linens are furnished. Cottages are 80 to 150 feet from the water. They range from $17 per day to $102 per week for two people in a one-bedroom cottage with kitchen; $31 per day or $186 per week for four people in a two-bedroom unit with living room, dining room, and kitchen. For reservations or additional information write: Carol and Bill Loyd, Kentucky Lake's Paradise Resort, Route 6, Box 239, Murray, KY 42071 (502)436-5414.

★★★*Pennyrile Forest State Resort Park* is located in a scenic woodland area of Western Kentucky on 435 acres with a 55–acre lake. The 15,000–acre Pennyrile State Forest surrounds the resort, with numerous hiking and horseback riding trails. Lake Beshear, four miles from the lodge, holds largemouth bass, crappie, bluegill and channel catfish. Rowboats and pedal boats are available for rental. A 9–hole golf course, miniature golf, picnicking, shuffleboard, two tennis courts, swimming lakeside or in the lodge's pool and 68 camping sites are available at the resort. Children can enjoy the two playgrounds plus additional planned activities. Accommodations include lodge rooms, efficiency cottages, one-bedroom and two-bedroom cottages. Rooms have two double beds, maid service, phone, TV, bath and private balcony or patio. All cottages have TV's, phones, air-conditioning and electric heat. Tableware, cooking utensils and linens are furnished. Meals, not included in rates, are available in the lodge's dining room. Rates: Lodge rooms are $23.75–28 double occupancy depending on season. Cottages are $25.75 to $40.75 depending on accommodations. For further information contact: Pennyrile Forest State Resort Park, Dawson Springs, KY 42408 (502)797-3421 or toll free (1–800)372-2961 in Kentucky.

★★★*Pine Mountain State Resort Park* stands on a pinnacle of one of the steep mountains of the Kentucky Ridge Forest. The resort has a nature center within walking distance of the lodge where interpretive displays on nature, area history, native plants and rare orchids can be viewed. Activities include seven hiking trails from the lodge; horseback riding; picnicking; shuffleboard; fishing for bass, crappie, and catfish; a 9–hole golf course; miniature golf; swimming pool and a recreation room. There are 36 camping sites with electricity and water hookups. Three playgrounds and planned activities are provided for children. During July and August the 3,000 capacity Laurel Cove Amphitheater presents the "Book of Job". Singing groups, dances and other social activities are also planned. Accommodations at the resort include lodge rooms, rustic log cottages and one-bedroom and two-bedroom cottages. Maid service, TV, and private balconies are included with lodge rooms. Cottages have phones, TV, air-conditioning and heat. Tableware, linens and cooking utensils are furnished. Meals, not included in the rates, are available in the lodge's dining room. Meeting rooms are available. Rates: $19.25–28 for lodge rooms, double occupancy depending on season; rustic efficiency cottages for two, $18.75 nightly; rustic one-bedroom cottages, $23.75 nightly; two-bedroom cottages for four people, $35.75– 40.25 nightly. For further information contact: Pine Mountain State Resort Park, Pineville, KY 40977 (606)337-3066 or toll free (1–800)372-2961 in Kentucky.

★★★*Rough River Dam State Resort Park* is located in western Kentucky on the 4,860–acre Rough River Lake, which holds big largemouth and smallmouth bass, crappie, bluegill, channel catfish, and walleye. The "Lady of the Lake" cruise boat makes daily excursions on the lake, and fishing boats, rowboats, pedal boats and pontoon boats can be rented. The resort has a launching ramp, 38 open slips, and 18 covered slips. There is a sand beach with bath-

house for swimming in the lake, plus a lodge pool. Archery, a 9–hole golf course, hiking trails, picnicking, shuffleboard, three tennis courts, and a recreation room are available at the resort. Camping facilities include 50 paved sites with electric and water hookups. There are three playgrounds for children, plus planned recreational activities. Accommodations at this resort consist of lodge rooms and two-bedroom cottages. Meals, which are not included in the rates, are available in the dining room or in the coffee shop. Meeting rooms are available. Rates: Lodge rooms are $19.25–28 double occupancy, depending on season. Two-bedroom cottages for four people are $40.25 nightly. For further information contact: Rough River Resort Falls, of Rough, KY 40119 (502)257-2311 or toll free (1–800)372-2961 in Kentucky.

★★★*Shawnee Bay Resort on Kentucky Lake* is situated on 15 wooded acres surrounded by water on three sides. The lake is considered one of the nation's finest year-round fishing spots for crappie, pike, sauger, striped bass, catfish, bluegill, and rockfish. The resort has a full-service private marina, complete with covered and open slips, skis, bait and sailboat rentals. Skiing instruction is provided free of charge. The lake also has a large, private sandy beach with excellent swimming and is especially safe for children. An adjacent playground, complete with tame ducks and rabbits, is also provided for children. There is hiking on rustic trails which wind throughout the peninsula and golf courses are nearby. The resort has facilities for horseshoes, badminton, volleyball, and basketball. Accommodations at the resort are completely furnished one-, two-, and three-bedroom cottages with screen porches overlooking the lake. Rates: Spring, for two $28 daily, $157 weekly. Summer rates, $218–265 weekly. Fall rates, $28 daily, $157 weekly. During the fall a 14–foot deluxe aluminum fishing boat is included with cottage rental. For further information contact: Shawnee Bay Resort, Route 4, Box 253–B, Benton, KY 42025 (502)354–8360.

★★★*Wisdom Fishing Camp on Dale Hollow Lake* offers superlative fishing and services. The world's record smallmouth bass, 11 lbs. 15 oz., was caught here. Anglers can fish from the luxury of their own private houseboat, complete with deck chairs, barbeque grills, and picnic tables, kitchen, bar, living room/dining area, private bedrooms accommodating six-ten persons, dressing rooms, showers, and sundecks. Wisdom Fishing Camp also has a variety of camping sites and private cabins with complete kitchens along the wooded shoreline. A complete camp store offers groceries, film, charcoal, bait and tackle; everything to make a fishing vacation complete. Houseboats are available on a weekly basis only through the summer season, from Memorial Day through Labor Day. In the spring and fall they may be rented on a three-day weekend basis, or on a daily basis mid-week. Weekly rates are $420–595 depending on the size of the houseboat, and weekend rates, $85–125 daily. Mid-week daily rates are $75–115. Cabin rates are available on request. For more information write: Wisdom Fishing Camp, Albany, KY 42602 (606)387–5011.

★★★*Wolf River Resort and Marina on Dale Hollow Lake*, in the foothills of the Cumberland mountains, offers superb fishing for big walleye and bass. The resort has a full-service marina, providing instant access to the lake's fishing and varied water sports. Covered slips and mooring for most sizes of boats can be found at the marina, along with fishing, skiing, pontoon boats and motors, and houseboat rentals. The resort has facilities for camping on the shores of Dale Hollow Lake at Wolf River. Campsites with hookups for water, electricity and sewer are available, as well as sites without hookups, for rustic camping. The resort has a grocery store and restaurant on the premises. Accommodations include motel units, cabins and

mobile homes. Motel units have beds, bath with linens, and a view of the marina. Cabins have two, three, or four bedrooms and overlook the lake. They are available with or without light house-keeping facilities and have bed linens, cooking utensils, silverware and dishes. Mobile home accommodations have one-two bedrooms, housekeeping facilities, bath and TV. There is a mobile home park providing spacious, well-shaded rental sites. Rates: Motel double $16 nightly, $90 weekly. Cabins small $14–22 per night, $100–130 weekly. Large cabins, $28–42 nightly, $165–250 weekly. Mobile homes, $18–24 nightly, $105–140 weekly. For further information contact: Wolf River Resort and Marina, Route 2, State Route 738, Albany, KY 42602 (606)387–5841.

Travel Services

Green River Canoe Livery runs day, overnight, and four-day trips down the beautiful Green River. The river cuts through lush woods and rolling pastureland, changing from deep pools to light rapids. Overnight canoeists find camping accommodations provided for them at the popular Legion Park. Green River Canoe Livery offers the finest aluminum canoes, all transportation, and complete safety equipment. Rates range from $2.50 per person for a brief two-mile canoe trip to $12.50 per person for an overnight trip. For more information write: Green River Canoe Livery, P.O. Box 156, Greensburg, KY 42743 (502)932–5683.

MAINE

Introduction

The Pine Tree State contains some of the wildest and most beautiful country east of the Rocky Mountains: sprawling glacial lakes dotting the lowlands as well as the high; mountains reaching above 5,000 feet, some still pathless; thousands of miles of wild and scenic rivers, strewn with giant boulders, rapids, chutes, and silent, deep-flowing pools; a rugged, wave-pounded coastline with many bays, islets, islands, and sand dunes broken by rocky headlands; and wide expanses of unbroken forests of northern hardwoods and conifers with colorful undergrowths which include hobblebush, holly, meadow sweet, alder, mountain ash, blueberry, starflower, heath shrubs, swamp candles, Indian cucumber root, painted trillium, skunk currant, shadbush, dogberry, and honeysuckle. The Northern Appalachians are an ancient range, bearing the marks of aeons of erosion. The famed Appalachian Trail and thousands of miles of spur trails and old logging roads climb along the summits and through the forests and valleys of the ancient chain, providing access to seldom explored fishing, hunting, and wilderness camping areas.

The legendary Maine Woods conjure images of big orange-bellied native brook trout; spring-powered, deep-shouldered landlocked salmon; massive, baleful bull moose; trophy whitetail bucks; vast green seas of spruce, fir, and pine; lean, rugged woodsmen, skilled with deer rifle, fishing rod, canoe paddle, and ax; icy, deep, boulder-girded lakes carving a jagged blue path into the forest; and pure white-water rivers, grinding tortured streambeds through the thick layers of glacial rock. These are some of the facets of the Maine outdoor experience that have attracted sportsmen for generations. Some of the finest fishing and hunting on the North American continent may be enjoyed in this beautiful state, which has almost 18 million acres of forestland. Maine is 90% wooded, harboring the largest expanses of wilderness in the East, and contains over 2,500 lakes and ponds, as well as more than 5,000 streams. The state occupies 33,215 square miles, almost exactly the same as the rest of New England combined. Much of the northern half of Maine, which protrudes into Canada, and Washington County, is a wilderness of vast forests of spruce, fir, white pine, larch or tamarack, cedar, birch, beech, and maple, hundreds of lakes, ponds, and streams, few roads, and a sparse population. Paper companies and private landowners hold much of this territory, and individually, or through the North Maine Woods Association, maintain road networks—

some of which may be driven by the public at no charge, while others require a modest fee.

Maine features a long rocky coastline, vast expanses of northern forests, wild rivers, sprawling glacial lakes, and wave upon wave of ancient rounded summits, culminating at 5,268–foot Mount Katahdin, the state's highest peak. The Pine Tree State contains several of North America's most legendary fishing, hunting, and wilderness camping and canoeing areas set amid its vast reaches of north country forests and mountains; the Chiputneticook Lakes, Fish River Chain of Lakes, Grand Lake Chain, North Maine Woods Tract, Allagash Wilderness Waterway, Mahoosuc Range, Machias River, Moosehead Lake, Mount Desert Island, Rangeley Lakes, St. John River, West Branch of the Penobscot River, Baxter State Park, Sebago Lake, Belgrade Lakes, Piscataquis Mountains, Kennebec River, Magalloway River, and the Red River, Musquacook, and Munsungan lakes country. Some 1,200 incredibly scenic conifer-clad islands, some little more than giant rocks, form an intricate maze of green off the rocky headlands of the Maine coast.

Accommodations & Travel Information

Maine's major vacation lodges, resorts, inns and famous north country sporting camps are described in detail in the "Vacation/Lodging Guide" which follows. For additional travel information, you may wish to contact any of the following agencies: Publicity Bureau, 1 Gateway Circle, Portland 04102 (207)289–2423. Maine Vacation Center, 1268 Ave. of the Americas, New York, NY 10020 (212) 757–4455. Information Center, Mount Royal Hotel, 1455 Peel St., Montreal, Quebec H3A 1T5; Maine Campsites-Forest Service, State Office Bldg., Augusta 04333.

Information & Services

Official Lake Survey Maps, published by the Department of Inland Fisheries & Wildlife, are available for more than 1,000 Maine lakes and ponds, including Sabattus, Moosehead, Deboullie, East Grand, West Grand, Spednic, Fish River, Musquacook, Presque Isle, Chain of Ponds, Cupsuptic, Kennebago, Rangeley, Sysladobsis, China, B Pond, Azisconos, Green, Parmachenee, Katahdin, Umbagog, Pemadumcook Chain of Lakes, Allagash, Caucomgomoc, Chamberlain, Telos, Chemquasabamticook, Chesuncook, Big, Eagle, Horserace Ponds, Millinocket, Nahmakanta, Penobscot, Munsungan, Machias, Meddybemps, Great East, Sebago, and other trophy land-

locked salmon, lake trout, squaretail, and smallmouth bass waters. These useful maps show lake depth and major features and contain detailed descriptions of each lake along with lake bottom composition and fish species present. The maps cost 15¢ each and may be ordered from the *Maine Lakes Index*, available free from the Department of Inland Fisheries & Wildlife, 284 State St., Augusta 04333.

The Maine Forest Service maintains hundreds of forest campsites scattered throughout the state, from the wave-pounded, rockbound coast, with its breathtaking scenic views, offshore islands, and jagged peninsulas, to the remote wild rivers, glistening mountain ponds, and sprawling, island-dotted glacial lakes of the North Maine Woods wilderness. A trip spent along one of the forest campsites will provide lasting memories of wind-swept blue lakes surrounded by the ancient rolling hills of the evergreen-carpeted Appalachians, wild deep-flowing streams and turbulent rivers, soaring gulls and hawks, and the fragrant smells of pine and wood smoke. An excellent, informative free brochure entitled *Forest Campsites* can be obtained by writing: Forest Service, Dept. of Conservation, State Office Bldg., Augusta 04333. This brochure contains a map of Maine showing public and private roads, tollgates, North Woods, Forest Service campsites (free and those which charge), private campgrounds, Forest Service ranger stations, and other points of interest to campers. The reverse side contains a chart showing the Forest Service campsites broken down by district showing township, description, access routes, and available recreational facilities, and whether or not a fee is charged. The brochure also provides helpful information on fees, access, fire permits, forest and fire laws, equipment and services. The Forest Service welcomes requests for additional information.

A free 56–page booklet, *Camping in Maine*, can be obtained from: Publicity Bureau, 1 Gateway Circle, Portland 04102. This booklet contains brief descriptions of camping and tenting areas in Maine, organized by region. Each camping area's location is shown on a map, which also shows U.S. routes and turnpikes. Campers should write or phone individual camping areas that interest them to obtain information on rates, reservations, etc. The mist-shrouded, boulder-studded pools, roaring rapids, rips, falls, eddies, and flat-water drifts of Maine's wild rivers and the windswept, island-dotted waters of the great North Maine Woods lakes provide some of the finest wilderness canoeing-camping opportunities in the nation. The old tramways, beaver dams, osprey, moose, logjams, bogs, legendary brook trout and togue, landlocked salmon, and fragrant evergreen forests found along the legendary canoe routes and Indian trails of the Allagash, St. John, West and East branches of the Penobscot, Fish River Chain of Lakes, Dead River, Aroostook River, Grand Lakes Chain, and the wild Machias River, which flows through a vast plateau of "blueberry barrens," combine to provide a wilderness canoeing paradise matched in the United States only by Minnesota's Boundary Waters Canoe Area. The North Maine Woods canoe country is also home to hordes of blackflies, mosquitos, and cute little fellows known as "no-see-ums." If you forget to bring a good supply of insect dope you're sure to have a trip you'll long remember. If you are planing a canoe fishing trip, you will vastly improve your enjoyment, success, and knowledge of the Maine Woods by hiring the services of a registered guide. A listing of *Canoeing Guides* may be obtained by writing to: Dept. of Inland Fisheries & Game, State House, Augusta 04333. The *AMC River Guide* vol. 1, *Northeastern New England* ($6), Appalachian Mountain Club, 5 Joy St., Boston, MA 02108, contains descriptions of the wild and scenic rivers in the Androscoggin, Kennebec, and Penobscot watersheds, the Allagash Wilderness Waterway, and the St. John, Mid-Coastal, and Eastern Coastal watersheds. Each stream is concisely described, indicating

class, location, length of trip, surrounding wilderness, history, topographic maps. The book describes virtually every important Maine river in a clear, easy-to-read format. Maps show the locations. The helpful introduction contains notes on the format, explanation of terms, scenery descriptions, and river classifications, water levels, etc., that will aid you in getting the most out of this guide.

For detailed fishing and hunting information, laws, regulations and the following useful, free booklets, write to the Maine Dept. of Inland Fisheries & Wildlife, 284 State St., Augusta, ME 04333 (207)289–2871: *Fishing & Hunting in Maine, Maine Open Water Fishing Laws, Ice Fishing Regulations, Hunting Regulations Summary, Bear Hunting in Maine, Discover Maine's Wilderness Trout Ponds* (B–308, 25¢). Write: Dept. of Inland Fisheries & Wildlife (address above) for their free *Publications Catalog.* Select subjects tailored to your particular needs and you will gain a great deal of helpful knowledge, including a wealth of where-to-go and technique information, because almost all of the articles are written by the department's in-the-field professionals. A subscription to the quarterly *Maine Fish and Wildlife* costs $2.50 for 1 year, $4.00 for 2 years, $5.50 for 3 years, and is an excellent way to keep current about the

status of fishing and hunting, as well as projects affecting the future. An eminently useful 225–page guide, *Trout and Salmon Fishing in New England Lakes and Ponds*, by Dick Devlin, may be obtained for $8 (postpaid) from Partridge Press, Box 422, Campton, NH 03223. It includes all you need to know about the trophy lakes, fishing techniques, bait fishing lures, fly patterns and colors for all six New England states, from the Maine North Woods to Connecticut and contains 35 detailed lake fishing maps showing boat launching sites and actual trolling routes in each for landlocks and trout.

Anyone wishing to hike the Appalachian Trail in Maine can obtain information from excellent publication by the Appalachian Mountain Club and the Appalachian Trail Conference, two organizations involved in the support and maintenance of the trail. Suggestions for *Appalachian Trail Users* (ATC Publication No. 15) is available from: Appalachian Trail Conference, Box 236, Harpers Ferry, WV 25425, for 50¢. This 35–page booklet contains information for those contemplating trips over the Appalachian Trail. Subjects covered include the nature of the trail; the Appalachian Trail Conference, use of the trail; horse, bicycle, and motor vehicle guide; planning trips; maps; guidebooks, etc.; lean-to use; food and equipment; trail marking and maintenance; etc. *Guide to the Appalachian Trail in Maine* (Maine Appalachian Trail Club) is published in two volumes that can be purchased separately. *The Appalachian Trail in Maine* (356 pp., 9 maps) contains information for planning trips in Maine, generalized description of the trail route, approaches to the trail, detailed trail data (24 sections) for the Appalachian Trail in Maine reading in both directions, and a chapter on side trails. This volume is indexed, is issued in a loose-leaf format, and costs $7.25. The second volume, *Katahdin Section* (202 pp., 2 maps) is a complete guide to the Katahdin region, containing a description of the area, the approaches, trails, and accommodations, with chapters on the Katahdinauguoh and Deadwater mountains. This volume is also loose-leaf; it costs $2.50. *The Map: The Katahdin Region* (MATC No. 3), 35¢, covers terrain between the East and West branches of the Penobscot River, it contains a sketch map of Katahdin trails.

The *AMC Maine Mountain Guide* contains summary trail mileages and mountain elevations in English and metric equivalents; durable, plastic pouch to carry books and maps, and other small hiking paraphernalia; and it has a soft, flexible, water-resistant binding. This volume contains about 290 pages and five maps, and costs $6.50. The *AMC Maine Mountain Guide* covers all trails in the Katahdin area, Aroostook, Mount Desert Island, East Branch of the Penobscot, Camden Hills, southwestern Maine, Oxford Hills, Grafton Notch area, Wild Region, Rangeley and Stratton area, Upper Kennebec and Piscataquis mountains. It is available from: Appalachian Mountain Club, 5 Joy St., Boston, MA 02108. Also available from the AMC are the following latex maps, at $1 each: *Carter-Mahoosuc*; *Baxter Park-Katahdin*; and *Mount Desert Island*. The following paper maps are available at 50¢ each: *Carter-Mahoosuc/Monadnock/Cardigan*; *Carter-Mahoosuc/Rangeley-Stratton*; and *Mount Desert Island/Weld*.

Maine, with its mountainous forest terrain, is a veritable paradise for the winter sports enthusiast. The state's major ski touring areas—including the abandoned railroad beds of the "Old Eastern" and Greenville-Derby branch of the Bangor & Aroostock railroads and the Pleasant Mountain, Sunday River, Mount Blue-State Park, Saddleback Mountain, Pineland Ski Club, Sugarloaf Mountain,

Narrow Gauge Trail, University Forest, Bald Mountain, Acadia National Park, Appalachian Trail, Wolfe Neck Woods, Holbrook Hills, and Camden Hills State Park areas—are described in the *EMS Ski Touring Guide to New England*, along with regional maps, driving directions, ski trail mileages, and available facilities. This 228–page bible may be obtained for $5.95 (plus 50¢ postage) from: Eastern Mountain Sports, 1047 Commonwealth Ave., Boston, MA 02215.

Highways & Maps

To get to your destination without getting lost, the *Official Maine Transportation Map* is indispensable. It shows the entire state, featuring all roads and highways (scenic highways are noted), route markers and access points, mileage between designated points, and approximate populations of cities and towns. Also shown are state boat-launching sites, seacoast ferry routes, highway rest areas and other lunch grounds, campsites, forest ranger headquarters, forest lookout stations, lighthouses, airports, state police stations, toll ferries and bridges, ports of entry, major ski areas, fish hatcheries, railroads, and state parks (indicating those places where camping is and is not permitted). This informative map may be obtained free from: Publicity Bureau, 1 Gateway Circle, Portland 04102.

The state's Publicity Bureau also has available the free 100–page booklet *Motoring Through Maine*, a directory which contains a description of principal highway routes, along with an alphabetical gazetteer of towns and place names in Maine, including notes of interest on each, location on the *Official Maine Transportation Map*, and suggested places to shop and eat. A classified index of advertisers is also included. The booklet also provides handy lists of state and national parks. This is a fine companion publication that should be used with the road map to make getting around in Maine easy and enjoyable.

The most comprehensive road maps to Maine are in the excellent *Maine Road Atlas*. This large-format (18x25 inch) spiral-bound atlas is available for $6 from: Dept. of Transportation, Augusta 04333. General highway maps are provided for each county, as well as details of urban or congested areas. In addition to showing all roads and highways, airports, water features, boundaries, bridges, and city and village areas, the map also shows natural features, as well as scenic sites, campsites, tourist accommodations, camps or lodges, small state or municipal parks, roadside rest areas, ski areas, forest ranger stations, forest service towers, fish hatcheries, bird sanctuaries, game farms and preserves, and extensive recreational areas. The maps are printed in black and white and are clear and easy to read.

Prentiss & Carlisle Co., 107 Court Street, Bangor 04401, publishes excellent State of Maine County Maps, indispensable to campers, guides, tourists, fishermen, and hunters. These maps have a scale of 1 inch to 3 miles and are detailed and accurate. They show features such as roads and highways (including private roads), trails, railroads, town lines, state lookout stations, and bodies of water. The maps are priced from $1.25 to $1.75 depending on which county map you order. A complete set, flat for mounting, costs $12.50. Prices are subject to 5% sales tax for Maine residents, plus handling charge of 35¢ per order, prepaid. A current price list of the maps can be obtained from Prentiss & Carlisle.

A beautiful, full-color *Illustrated Map of the Maine Coast* from Kittery to Bar Harbor, 6' x 2', with 22 blow-ups of coastal towns showing street names, special historical and natural points of interest, and 13 watercolor reproductions of coastal scenes, is available for $2 post-paid (folded) from: DeLorme Publishing, P.O. Box 81, Yarmouth, ME 04096.

**VACATION/
LODGING GUIDE**

Eastern Maine Lakes Region
& Acadia National Park

Washington County, on Maine's and the nation's easternmost border, has been blessed with an abundance of natural riches and is an outdoors enthusiast's paradise. The 5,000–square–mile region is bordered on the south by the jagged, spruce-clad, rocky Atlantic coastline, on the north by the pastoral potato lands of Aroostook County, on the west by the Penobscot River, and on the east by the Maine-New Brunswick border. Within this area lies the greatest variety of fish and game species and terrain in the state. Graceful, aristocratic Atlantic salmon, acrobatic landlocked salmon, pugnacious smallmouth bass, native brook trout, lunker togue (lake trout), voracious pickerel, and white and yellow perch await the fisherman, and you can fish for more species of game fish in a single day than in any other place in Maine. The smallmouth bass fishing is so good that landing 50 fish a day weighing over 1 1/2 pounds each is possible in many of the better waters. There are also a few bronzebacks here exceeding five pounds in weight.

The topography is richly varied and includes the beautiful fjord-like and island-studded coast, the cool, deep spruce and fir forests, thousands of acres of fish-laden lakes and ponds, many miles of productive streams and canoe trails, the fragrant blueberry barrens, granite mountains, and glacial bogs. The growing moose herd finds the swamps particularly to its liking, and some of the finest deer and black bear hunting in the East is found here. Ruffed grouse, woodcock, pheasant, wildfowl, and small game abound, and the observant outdoorsman may see beaver, otter, mink, bobcat, marten, fisher, ospreys, and eagles. Nestled on the Maine-New Brunswick border in the northeast corner of the region are the irregular-shaped shorelines of the Chiputneticook Lakes, East Grand and Spednic, which are also the headwaters of the St. Croix River. Sprawling, rocky East Grand is one of the blue-ribbon landlocked salmon and togue lakes in Maine and one of the least known, considering the quality fishing it offers. Salmon and togue run big, with some salmon topping five pounds and togue exceeding ten pounds. The outlet spills through a dam and runs into Spednic, and offers the chance to hook one of these big, silvery acrobats in fast water. Jagged Spednic has a well deserved reputation for big bass and lots of them, and offers some excellent salmon fishing as well.

The St. Croix River, a famous canoeing and fishing stream, spills through a dam on the end of Spednic at Vanceboro and flows southeast for about 100 miles to the sea, forming the border between Maine and New Brunswick. Fishing is good for landlocks and bass, and the many miles of white water will test the wilderness paddler's skills. Among the popular stretches are Elbow, Mile, Joe George's, and Hall's rips and the dangerous class IV rapids at Little Falls. The Grand Lake Chain, which is the inundated West Branch of the St. Croix, merges with the main river at Grand Falls Flowage. Names that are dear to the hearts of smallmouth bass fans include Sysladobsis, Junior, Scraggly, Big, Long, Lewey, Pocumus, Pocomoonshine, Clifford, and Wabassus lakes. When conditions are right you can hook bass until your arms won't take any more, and there are a number of fish weighing more than three pounds. Paddling along the dri-ki-strewn shore of these waters, your solitude will be broken only by the cry of a loon, the malevolent gaze of a feeding moose, or the electrifying strike of a lunker smallmouth. Some of the heftiest pickerel to be found in the United States add variety to the day's fishing. West Grand Lake, one of the original homes of the landlocked salmon, provides excellent fishing for this species, as well as for togue. Its outlet, Grand Lake Stream, which runs into Big Lake, offers superb fly fishing for landlocks, if you are there at the right time. The Musquash Lakes are also good salmon waters, as are Sysladobsis, Scraggly, and Junior lakes, where bass and salmon seem to tolerate each other. Tomah Stream is famous for brook trout and gave its name to the beautiful Tomah Jo fly. Adjacent waters which are famous for fishing include Nicatous and Gassabias lakes and the Pistol group, all of which are part of the Passadumkeag River headwaters, and Crawford and Meddybemps lakes to the south of Grand Falls Flowage.

Maine is the only state where the spectacular Atlantic salmon can still be caught in its original habitat. The Dennys, Machias, Pleasant, and Narraguagus, four Washington County rivers, are managed for salmon, and a great deal of effort and expense has been employed by the state and federal governments and concerned sportsmen. The runs seem to be on the increase, and the commitment has been worthwhile. The Dennys River drains Meddybemps Lake and joins the sea near Dennysville. Fly fishermen try their luck in the beautiful rocky pools of this exquisite little river, especially during June and July. Canoeists will enjoy the exciting trip of about 20 miles and will encounter some rugged white-water stretches, most notably the formidable Little Falls. The rapid-strewn Machias River, a few miles to the west of the Dennys on U.S. 1, is another popular salmon and canoeing stream. An awesome natural ravine, the Machias Gorge at the tideline in the town of Machias, hinders the upstream migration of salmon, except during periods of low stream flow. The hordes of fish at the foot of the ravine were easy pickings for the nets of Indians and colonists 200 years ago. Those who know the river take salmon on local fly patterns year after year, and there is some fine trout fishing, particularly around the mouths of feeder brooks. Fifth Machias Lake in the headwaters produces good squaretail fishing. Fourth, Third, Second, and First Machias Lakes offer warmwater species. Mopang Lake at the head of Mopang Stream, a feeder, has

a sizable population of scrappy landlocks. Canoeists will find the Machias a worthwhile challenge, particularly in the early season. The long Wigwams Rapids and Carrot and Boot rips will test your mettle. Upper Holmes Falls, a 30-foot drop through a canyon, and Little Falls must be portaged or lined. The Machias is a river for experienced canoeists, and the trip is well worth the effort, because you will pass through some wild, lonely country in which surprising

a moose or black bear are distinct possibilities. Between the blueberry barrens at Cherryfield on the western edge of Washington County and the Penobscot River lies fine fishing for landlocks and togue. Beautiful Tunk Lake is rumored to have produced a 20-pound landlocked salmon during the 1920's. It is the deepest lake in eastern Maine, with a maximum depth of 222 feet. With its boulder-strewn shoreline set in an area of forested hills and mountains, Beech Hill Pond, near Ellsworth, produced the state-record togue in 1958, which is remarkable when one thinks of all of the famous remote togue waters in Maine. Green and Branch lakes are neighboring waters which produce good catches of salmon and togue. Floods Pond has the only population in Maine of the rare Sunapee trout, a relative of the arctic char. Sprawling Graham Lake has superb fishing for bass, pickerel, and perch, as do many other lakes and ponds in Hancock County. Brown trout have been selectively stocked in places like the Union River, and some browns find their way to the ocean to return later as sea trout.

Information Sources, Maps & Access

Three free paper company maps show area campsites, public and private roads, fire towers, land holdings, and much other useful information. *Eastern Maine Timberlands Sportsman's Map* is produced by the Dead River Company and Eastern Woodlands Division of Standard Packaging Corporation. This excellent map covers most of Hancock and Washington countries and the lower part of Aroostook County and is packed with a great deal of valuable material. The publication describes the area, facilities, fishing, hunting, and camping details, and can be obtained from: Dead River Co., 55 Broadway, Bangor 04401, or Standard Packaging Corp., Brewer 04412. Write to: Penobscot Development Co., Great Works 04468, for the *Sportsman's Map, Penobscot Tree Farm*, which covers 20 townships in the Nicatous Lake-Penobscot River area and includes an interesting history of the company. Woodland Division, Georgia Pacific Corp., Mill St., Woodland 04694, produces the free, colorful, informative *Sportsmen's Map of Washington County and Western New Brunswick*. Three beautiful large-size maps of the Eastern Maine Region, *Phillips' Map of Washington County, Phillips' Map of Hancock County,* and *Phillips' East of Katadhin Map* ($1.50 each, plus 40¢ postage) show all man-made and natural features, including trails, portages, gravel roads and highways, Forest Service and paper company campsites, fly-in services, fish hatcheries, and boat-launching sites. They may be ordered from Augustus D. Phillips & Son, Northeast Harbor 04662. For detailed information on Acadia National Park and a free *Acadia National Park Map/Brochure, Acadia National Park Hiking Map, Camping & Campsites* and *Wintertime Activities* leaflets, contact: Superintendent's Office, Acadia National Park, RFD 1, Box 1, Bar Harbor, ME 04609 (207)288-3338. For more detailed information about the park, write to the park for the free *Eastern Park and Monument Association Publication List*. There are books and articles on every subject from blueberries to seals. A handy *AMC Trail Guide to Mount Desert Island and Acadia National Park* may be obtained by sending a check or money order for $2 to: Appalachian Mountain Club Books, 5 Joy St., Boston, MA 02108. A useful *AMC Latex Map of Mt. Desert Island* ($1.95) may be obtained from the same address. A beautiful full-color *Acadia National Park Topographic Map* (23 × 27 inches) may be ordered for $2 from: Distribution Branch, U.S. Geological Survey, 1200 S. Eads St., Arlington, VA 22202. For detailed refuge information and a free *Moosehorn National Wildlife Refuge* brochure, contact: Manager, Moosehorn National Wildlife Refuge, Calais, ME 04619. The eastern Maine region is reached by U.S. 95 or U.S. 1 and is crossed by Maine 9, called the Airline, and by Maine 6. Lodging, supplies, guides, and outfitters are available at the towns of Calais, Bar

Harbor, Eastport, Lubec, Machias, Dennysville, Whiting, Northfield, Wesley, Cooper, Grove, Meddybemps, Baring, Woodland, Princeton, Waite, Topsfield, Brookton, Forest City, Danforth, Forest Station, Cherryfield, Debois, Great Pond, Franklin, Eastbrook, Waltham, Green Lake, Ellsworth, Bucksport, and Dedham.

Recreation Areas

Acadia National Park & Mount Desert Island

Acadia National Park (33,000 acres) is a magnificent expanse of rugged, glacial seacoast indented by fjords, fir-clad mountains, sparkling lakes and ponds, rushing streams, and forested valleys; it is crisscrossed by an excellent network of trails. The major section of the park is located on Mount Desert Island, which is dominated by Cadillac Mountain (1,580 feet), the highest point on the New England coast. The fjord of Somes Sound divides the park into eastern and western sections. The island was named by the great French explorer Samuel de Champlain in 1604, who incorrectly thought the land was inhabited. The famous summer resort town of Bar Harbor is found on the eastern side of the island in the shadow of Cadillac Mountain. Two additional segments, Schoodic Point on the mainland and Isle au Haut to the southwest, complete the park. Major features include Long Pond, Eagle Lake, Big Heath, the Black Woods, Penobscot Mountain, Jordan Pond, and the Bubbles. Summer resort activities are blended with outstanding hiking and naturalist pursuits, and bird-watchers, botanists, and geologists find plenty to keep them occupied. There is some trout, salmon, bass and pickerel fishing available, and the quality is fairly good, considering the numbers of people.

Moosehorn National Wildlife Refuge

Moosehorn National Wildlife Refuge, in the southeast corner of Washington County, consists of the Baring Unit (16,065 acres) near Calais, and the Edmunds Unit (6,600 acres) on Cobscook Bay near Dennysville. The topography bears witness to the awesome force of the glaciers during the Ice Age. The effects of thousands of years of massive weight and grinding can be seen in the rocky outcroppings, hills, boreal forests, lakes, streams, bogs, and marshes of the refuge. The tidal bores exceed 20 feet and are the greatest to be found in the United States, with the exception of Alaska's Cook Inlet. Moosehorn is primarily managed for migratory birds such as woodcock, ducks, and geese, and there is an abundance of small-game animals and birds, such as snowshoe hares and ruffed grouse. For a change of pace the nature lover will find some good fishing for brook trout, smallmouth bass, and pickerel.

Gateways & Accommodations

Bangor—Gateway to the Eastern Maine Lakes & Woods

(Pop. 40,000; zip code 04401; area code 207) on the great Penobscot River, was once the rugged lumber town and capital of Maine. Bangor was the terminus of log drives of massive white pines down the Penobscot that began far to the north in the Allagash Country. More than fifty sawmills once lined the banks of the river extending north from Bangor to Old Town. The city today is surrounded by gently rolling farmlands dotted by quaint villages with white churches and country stores. Bangor is a popular stopover for fishermen, hunters, and family vacationers heading east to the St. Croix Watershed and New Brunswick, Canada. The once great runs of Atlantic salmon up the Penobscot have been revived somewhat and salmon are regularly taken on the fly from the famous Bangor Salmon Pool. The famous Old Town Canoe Factory is located in Old Town northeast of Bangor on U.S. 2. Old Town is also the site

of the Penobscot Indian Reservation. Accommodations: *Holiday Inn Downtown* (rates: $40–44 double), with 128 excellent rooms, restaurant, cocktail lounge, at 500 Main St. (947–8651); *Holiday Inn-West* (rates: $40–44 double), with 140 excellent rooms, restaurant, cocktail lounge, heated pool, at the junction of U.S. 2 and I–95 Hermon exit (947–0101); *Howard Johnson's Motor Lodge* (rates: $33.60–39.90 double), with 58 good rooms, restaurant, cocktail lounge off U.S. 2 at I–95 Hermon exit (942–5251); *Ramada Inn* (rates: $44–48 double), with 116 excellent rooms, restaurant, cocktail lounge, indoor heated pool and sauna, off U.S. 2 at I–95 Hermon exit at 357 Odlin Rd. (947–6961).

Bar Harbor—Gateway to Acadia National Park

(Pop. 3,000; zip code 04609; area code 207) is a nationally famous summer vacation center overlooking Frenchman Bay on the rocky, lake-dotted mountainous expanse of beautiful Mount Desert Island, first discovered by Samuel de Champlain in 1604. The town serves as the major gateway to Acadia National Park and the wave-pounded Cranberry Isles and the quaint Mount Desert coastal villages of the lobster pot and dory country to the south—Southwest Harbor, Seal Cove, Tremont, Seal Harbor, and Northeast Harbor. Area attractions include the Acadia National Park Visitor's Center at Hulls Cove, Islesford Historical Museum on Little Cranberry Island, scenic park interior and coastal drives, Abbe Museum of Archeology near Bar Harbor, and the M/V *Bluenose Ferry Service* to Yarmouth, New Brunswick (288–3395 or toll-free (800)341–7981 outside of Maine). Accommodations: *Atlantic Oakes By the Sea* (rates: $44 double), with 66 excellent rooms and family units in former estate mansion, breakfast service, heated pool, poolside bar, tennis courts, boats and sailing, dock, next to ferry terminal, 1¾ miles north of town on Ellen St. or Maine Highway 3 (288–5218); *Bar Harbor Motor Inn & Dining Room* (rates: $48–75 double), with 74 superb rooms in beautiful location overlooking Frenchman Bay, excellent dining, heated

pool, in town at pier on Newport Dr. (288–5169); *Golden Anchor Inn & Lobster Pound Restaurant* (rates: $50 double), with 75 excellent rooms overlooking the harbor with swimming pool, dock, and sailboat sightseeing trips, cocktail lounge at Granite Point off West Street in town (288–5033); *Kimball Terrace Inn at Northeast Harbor* (rates: $41–46 double), with 50 excellent guest rooms, the Mast & Rudder Restaurant, heated pool overlooking the Municipal

Pier on Huntington Rd. (276–3383); *Moorings Motor Sail Inn at Southwest Harbor* (rates: $20–40 double), with excellent guest rooms and cottage facilities overlooking harbor with good maritime restaurant, cocktail lounge, boats and sailboats available (244–5523); *Park Entrance Motel at Bar Harbor* (rates: $35.70–39.90 double), with 53 excellent rooms and family units, in beautiful location overlooking Frenchman Bay, with heated pool, fishing and boat mooring facilities on Hamor Ave., 2½ miles north of town on Maine Highway 3 (288–3306).

Calais—Gateway to Moosehorn National Wildlife Refuge

(Pop. 4,000; zip code 04619; area code 207) is located on the bank of the historic St. Croix River across from New Brunswick, Canada. Area attractions include the famous landlocked salmon and small-mouth bass waters of Meddybemps and Pocomoonshine lakes, Moosehorn National Wildlife Refuge (four miles to the north on U.S. Highway 1), and the St. Croix Island National Monument (eight miles south of town on U.S. 1). Accommodations: *Heslin's Motel & Dining Room* (rates: $24–31 double), with 26 good guest rooms and family units in a nice location overlooking the St. Croix River, cocktail lounge, heated pool, 5½ miles south of town on U.S. 1 (454–3762).

Ellsworth—Gateway to Mt. Desert Island & the East Maine Coast

(Pop. 4,600; zip code 04605; area code 207) is the commercial center of Hancock County and a popular stopover for vacationers heading south to Acadia National Park and the rugged eastern Maine coast. The surrounding forestlands and lakes offer excellent hunting and fishing opportunities—particularly the Union River for Atlantic salmon, and beautiful Green Lake, Beech Hill Pond, and Graham Lake for trout and landlocked salmon. Beech Hill Pond produced the state record 31 lb. 8 oz. lake trout. Other area attractions include the John Black House on West Main St., built in 1802, and the Stanwood Museum, and Birdsacre Sanctuary, of unusual interest to bird watchers two miles south of town off Maine Highway 3 on Bar Harbor Rd. Accommodations: *Holiday Inn* (rates: $54 double), with 101 excellent rooms and family units, restaurant, cocktail lounge, heated indoor pool, and tennis court (667–9341).

Rockland—Gateway to the Eastern Maine Coast & Islands

(Pop. 9,000; zip code 04841; area code 207) is the commercial center of the Penobscot Bay Region and a favorite stopover for vacationers heading east on U.S. Highway 1 to Acadia National Park and eastern Maine. Ferry service to several of the coastal islands is provided by the *Maine State Ferry Service* at 517 Main St. (594–5543). Accommodations: *Trade Winds Motor Inn* (rates: $40 double), with 71 excellent rooms, restaurant, cocktail lounge, heated pool and sauna overlooking the harbor at 303 Main St. (596–6661).

Lodges & Sporting Camps

Appalachian Mountain Club North Woods & Coastal Camps (see "Southern Maine Vacationlands" lodges, inns & sporting camps).

★★★*Goose Cove Lodge at Deer Isle* is secluded on 70 wooded acres by a sandy beach on Deer Island, surrounded by the blue waters of Penobscot Bay. Small sailboats and rowboats are available to explore the rocky coves and craggy inlets. Clearly marked hiking trails meander through the pine forests with sudden views of the bay waters. The offshore fishing and deep-sea fishing are excellent. Fresh Maine lobster picnics are held each week on the beach, a favorite sunbathing spot. Island-hopping boat trips leave the dock

each day. The main dining room, overlooking the bay, features fresh seafood. There are seven private cabins nestled on the shoreline, secluded by pines. Each has a private bath, a living room with a fireplace, and an individual sundeck, with sea view. Rates are daily, per person $35 double occupancy; $33 per person daily triple occupancy; and $31 per person daily for four persons. Weekly rates are $245 each for two persons, $231 for three, and $217 weekly for four persons. All rates include three meals daily. Spacious motel rooms are available, with fireplace or old fashioned wood-burning stoves for cool nights. Rates are daily $40–44 single occupancy; $26–32 per person double occupancy; $26–30 per person triple occupancy, and $25–28 per person daily for four persons. Duplex cottages, with two bedrooms, private bath, open fireplace and bay view are $33–29 daily for each of two-four persons, and $231–203 weekly. For more information write: Goose Cove Lodge, Sunset, ME 04683 (207)348–2508.

★★*Grand Lake Lodge* is located on the southeastern shore of beautiful West Grand Lake, about two blocks from quaint Grand Lake Stream Village, the dam, and the fabled Grand Lake Stream—a noted landlocked salmon, brown and brook trout fishery. The lodge offers fishing in West Grand Lake from "ice-out" in mid-May till fall for landlocked salmon and lake trout, and easy access to the famed smallmouth bass waters at nearby Big, Pocumus, Wabassus, and Sysladobsis lakes. The rustic lodge and guest cabins overlook the lake and offer spacious, comfortable accommodations. The log-panelled housekeeping cabins offer complete baths with showers, hardwood-burning stoves, and large furnished porches which are completely screened. The lodge rooms are big, airy and nicely appointed, each with a view of the lake. Boats and motor rentals are available for guests. Cabin rates for two guests are $120 per week and $210 per week for a party of six. Special family rates are available for July and August. Modified American Plan lodge rates are $35 per person per day. Grand Lake Lodge is reached via a private road from the village. For additional information, contact: Al and Peggy Smith, Grand Lake Lodge, Grand Lake Stream, ME 04637 (207)796–5584.

★★★*Hiram Blake Camp*, with 12 secluded cottages and a spacious coastal lodge, hugs the eastern shores of Cape Rosier in Penobscot Bay. The surrounding 100 wooded acres provide many quiet trails for hiking, with observation points overlooking the windy bay. The camp rents rowboats to explore the craggy inlets, tidal pools, and seal ledges of the nearby islands. The camp passenger boat, the "Hazel R", often used on TV, makes weekly trips to the outer islands, carrying guests to remote picturesque spots for lobster cook-outs. Golf courses are within a 20-minute drive at Castine, Bluehill, and Deer Isle. Hiram Blake Camp has a recreation room with ping pong tables, and card tables. Every Sunday night sea-chanteys are sung, and tales spun. There is a quiet chapel in the pines overlooking the sea, and simple services are held here Sunday mornings. Nearby Blueberry Hill is covered with wild blueberries which find their way into fresh pancakes, and home-baked blueberry pies all summer. Hot, homemade donuts are served every morning, a camp specialty. Dinners offer a variety of seafood specialties such as fresh scallops, clam chowders, lobster newburg, and St. John salmon. Oven-baked meat dishes, down-east baked beans, and fresh raspberries and watermelon are some other favorites at the camp. Rooms in the Oak Lodge, which has seven bedrooms, three baths, a large living room and a screened-in porch with a bay view, are on the American Plan. Weekly rates only. Rates for a single room are $137.50. A double room in Oaks Lodge is $231 weekly. Cottages have two-five rooms, with fully equipped kitchens, private bath, screened-in porches with bay view, and wood heat. Cottage guests may choose to cook for themselves, or reserve with rates including breakfast and dinner. Rates are from $200–355 per week per cabin without meals, and start at $356 per couple per week, with breakfast and dinner. For more information write: Manager, Hiram Blake Camp, Harborside, P.O. Cape Rosier, ME 04642 (207)356–4951.

★★★★*Leen's Lodge* is one of the nation's finest wilderness family retreats. This beautiful, rustic resort is located in the heart of eastern Maine's great salmon, trout, and canoe country. Leen's is located at the mouth of Grand Lake Stream on sprawling, island-dotted West Grand Lake and offers outstanding fishing for landlocked salmon, smallmouth bass, lake trout, and brook trout. For guests who like to get off the beaten path, a number of unspoiled wilderness lakes may be reached by the lodge's four-wheel drive station wagon. Lodge accommodations are in private, secluded log cabins with full modern luxury surrounded by forest pines and spruce. The guest cabins have a living room, picture window, refrigerator, automatic gas heat, and Franklin stoves. Artesian well water is piped to each camp. The finest meals—lobster, steak, buffets, homemade breads and pastries—are served in a relaxing and pleasant North Country style

linens provided. One-bedroom cabins are weekly, $145. Two bedroom housekeeping cabins are $155, weekly. Shelter cabins, on the forest edge, sleep four persons in double bunk accommodations, with kitchens, outdoor fireplace and private picnic tables. They are $160 weekly. Tent cabins, secluded in the pine woods have wooden floors, bunk beds and individual picnic tables and outdoor fireplaces. Tent cabins sleep four and are $70 weekly. Centrally located bathrooms with hot and cold running water, and hot showers serve the shelter cabins and the tent cabins. Wilderness tent sites are also available for $5 a night, or $30 weekly. Outboard motor boats and sailboats can be rented to skim the sparkling lake waters, which are also ideal for swimming. Nearby clear running streams provide excellent fishing. Canoes are rented for $10 a day, and complete outfits, including canoe, pack, tent, food and cooking equipment are available for $17 daily. The Canoe Basin staff offers training and practice in portaging, paddling strokes, navigation and map reading, swimming safety skills, setting up a proper camp, and campfire cooking. The staff will help you design a wilderness adventure to suit your abilities from overnights to month-long adventures along the Grand Lake Chain, just ¼ mile portage from Pleasant Lake offer-

lodge. The rustic Tannery Room features individually stocked liquor cabinets, color TV, plus game and card tables. Both the Tannery Room and dining area face west, overlooking the lake. The Lodge has a fleet of aluminum fishing boats, motors, and Grand Lake Canoes, and will arrange for guide service if desired. A full-service float-plane dock is located off the Guides' Headquarters. Daily Modified American Plan rates (includes breakfast and dinner, with cook-out and picnic lunches optional) are $33 per person for a one-bedroom cabin; $38 per person for a two-bedroom cabin; $38 per person for a three-bedroom cabin; $31 per person for four or more in a cabin. The lodge is reached by auto off Route 1 via Woodland and Princeton. For additional information, contact: (summer) Leen's Lodge, Grand Lake Stream, ME 04637 (207)796–5575; (Oct.-May) Box 100, Brewer, ME 04412 (207)989–7363.

★★★★*Maine Wilderness Canoe Basin & Deer Isle Sailing Center* is secluded on the wilderness shores of the four-mile-long Pleasant Lake, the headwaters of the Grand Lake Chain. Private housekeeping cabins, commanding a southwest view of Pleasant Lake, accommodate five-seven persons with private bath, complete kitchens, and

ing white waters, placid streams, wilderness islands to explore, a glimpse of moose or bear in the dense pine forests, and excellent fishing for landlocked salmon, trout and bass. Transportation for groups or individuals, their gear and canoes is available from the Canoe Basin to any location in Maine, for 40¢ a mile. Wilderness Canoe Basin also opens a two-week base-camp program for ages 10–18 in the summer, including fishing, backpacking, swimming, overnight wilderness canoe trips in the back country. Also there are special white-water kayaking programs, backpacking trips, cycling in Nova Scotia, and salt water sailing at the Deer Isle Outpost. Deer Isle is a large wooded, rocky island off the Maine coast in the Penobscot Bay. Here, and on the jewellike Isle au Haut (Island of Heights) directly across from Deer Isle in the bay, is the Deer Isle Sailing Center. The surrounding waters offer access to hundreds of tiny wilderness islands, deserted beaches, picturesque harbors, unparalleled open seas for sailing, and unlimited camping on the rocky coast. 12–20-foot boats equip the camp and are also available for charter. Navigation, seamanship, and swimming skills are emphasized the first few days of the program, and then the boats are taken on extended trips to explore the tiny islands and the rugged

coastline. Oceanside camping cabins, accommodating four-five persons are available at the Deer Isle Sailing Center for $10 a night. From August 14–24 Deer Isle Sailing Center hosts family camps, where everyone can enjoy hearty evening meals and breakfasts in the spacious dining room, take overnight cruises, hike the wooded paths, play golf at the nearby country club or tennis at Deer Isle courts, or fish the clear-running island streams. Campfire stories, sing-a-longs, and squaredances highlight the summer evenings. The cost of a family camp outing is $25 per person. For more information write: summer address—Maine Wilderness Canoe Basin and Deer Isle Sailing Center, Springfield, Maine 04487 (207)989–3636 ext. 631. Winter address—Capt. Carl Selin, 223 Neptune Drive, Groton, CT. 06340 (203)536–7980.

★★★*Nicatous Lodge & Camps* is located in the heart of thousands of acres of evergreen forests on the shore of beautiful, 12–mile long Nicatous Lake, noted for its picturesque uninhabited islands and jagged shoreline. Hiking, cross-country skiing and snowmobile trails are beautiful and virtually limitless. Lake and brook fishing are excellent for brook trout, landlocked salmon, smallmouth bass, pickerel, and perch. Deer, bear, fox and upland game abound for the hunter. Wildlife in the camp area includes moose, bobcat, hawk, otter, beaver, raccoon. The surrounding territory is literally dotted with lakes, ponds and streams. One of the most popular with guests is West Lake, only a twenty-minute walk from the Lodge over a well-marked trail. There are also many uninhabited islands on the lake, and beaches for camping and cookouts. The rustic, fully-equipped log camps are on the lake on either side of the lake outlet where salmon can be seen in fall returning to the lake after spawning downstream. All camps are on the lakeshore, have stone fireplaces, screened porches, complete kitchen and bathroom facilities. The meals served in the rustic main lodge are homecooked, family style featuring Downeast specialties, homemade breads, etc. No one leaves the table hungry. Picnic lunches are prepared and packed on request. After the meal, you can relax in front of the main lounge fireplace or on the screened porch overlooking the lake, or take a walk over the old woods trails handy to camp. A fully stocked store, hunting, fishing licenses, boat and motor rentals are available. American Plan rates are $24 per person per day (children under 10, half price) and include lodge or cabin accommodations, three meals in lodge dining room, and daily maid service. Modified American Plan rates are $20 per person per day (children under 10,

half price) and include cabin accommodations, main evening meal in lodge dining room, daily maid service. Housekeeping plan daily rates are $12 per person; weekly rates (up to four persons) are $135 (each additional person $10 per week). Boat and motor per day, plus gas is $10.00. Boat only per day $4.00. The lodge and camps are located 65 miles northeast of Bangor, six miles in on a good woods road at the northern end of Nicatous Lake. For additional information and reservations, contact: Barry and Joan Tyne, Nicatous Lodge & Camps, Burlington, ME 04417.

★★*Pocomoonshine Lake Lodges* is nestled on the unspoiled lake shore, surrounded by rolling hills and deep forests. Four pound bass are not an uncommon catch in Pocomoonshine Lake, and perch and pickerel are also abundant. The surrounding streams, remote lakes, and free running rivers provide excellent fishing for brook trout, landlocked salmon, and, in tidewater, sea-run stripers. Pocomoonshine Lake Lodges operates a 12-mile trip into the remote, backcountry fishing waters. Only an hour's drive from the wild rocky northern Atlantic coast, fishermen can charter deep-sea boats and fish for flounder, cod, and haddock. In the autumn, when the lake mirrors the crimson hills, Pocomoonshine offers some of the finest bird hunting in Maine. For more information write: Gene & Estelle Moriarty, Pocomoonshine Lake Lodges, Alexander, ME 04610 (207)454–2310.

★★★*Rideout's Lodge & Cottages* is located on the water's edge overlooking East Grand Lake in Danforth. The view from the recreation and dining rooms extends from Rideout's cove to the Canadian shore of New Brunswick, four miles away. Deep in the North Woods, Rideout's offers access to thousands of acres of woodland offering excellent hunting for small game, bear and deer. East Grand Lake, over twenty-two miles in length has salmon, lake trout, smallmouth bass and perch, and it's great for boating and water skiing as well as fishing. Baxter State Park is only two hours away with its many miles of well-marked trails and the mile-high Mt. Katahdin. Accommodations include American Plan cottages with double beds, showers and daily maid service and housekeeping cottages, equipped with electric stove and refrigerator, dishes and bed linen for six people. Each group of cottages has its own boat dock for convenience. The lodge has a recreation room, extending over the lake with ping-pong tables, a lounge with TV, a small store with fishing tackle and drugstore items, and a dining room with the best of Down East cooking. Meals are served family style and the menu features steaks, roasts, "Down East home-baked beans" and a Sunday turkey dinner. American Plan private cottages cost $29 per day per person including three meals. Housekeeping cabins range from $140 to $225 per week for up to six people. There is an additional charge of $20 per person per week over six people. For reservations and information contact George and Jean Graham, Rideout's Lodge and Cottages, East Grand Lake, Danforth, ME 04424 (207)448–2440 from April 1 until December 1. From December 1 until April 1, the address is Iron Ore Hill Road, Bridgewater, CT 06752 (203)354–6302.

★★★*Tripps' Lodge & Cabins* is located in the fabled St. Croix River Region. Washington County has long been Maine's outstanding deer country. Its vast forests offer hunters freedom away from other hunters and a chance at independently stalking the largest bucks on the American Continent (many over 300 pounds). Bear and partridge hunting are also excellent. As for fishing, the St. Croix River and Big Lake Country has some of the greatest smallmouth bass waters in the nation. Mingling with the waters of the Big Lake are those of Western Grand Lake and West Musquash Lake, two of Maine's top salmon and togue lakes. Bass season runs from June 1– Oct. 30, and salmon and togue season is from ice-out (early May) to

Sept. 30. This country offers fishing that can't be beat and the lodge will provide you with a guide and boats and motors if you wish. The cabins are situated on Lake Lewy, which is the outlet to Big Lake and the beginning of the St. Croix River. There is an airport about a mile from the cabins and if you fly in by private plane, the camp car will meet you. The cabins themselves are new and modern in every respect—hot and cold running water, shower, flush toilet, electric refrigerator, gas cooking—and fully equipped for housekeeping. If you prefer, you can stay at the lodge—the rooms are large and comfortable. The lodge serves homecooked meals—Maine family style. There is a swimming area for children and two excellent golf courses a short drive away. There are both fishing and hunting non-resident licenses available at the lodge. Rates, per day, per person, for a lodge room are $20 (with meals). A cabin, per day, runs $18 (one bedroom) up to $28 (two bedrooms). There are also family rates available. Your hosts are Walter and Lois Tripp. You can reach them at (207)796–2324 or by writing Tripps' Lodge and Cabins, Princeton, ME 04668.

★★*Wantalfego Lodge & Cabins* is located in the scenic Penobscot Acadia region within an hour of Maine's coast and Acadia National Park. Roosevelt's summer estate on Campobello is two hours' drive along Maine's rugged coastline. The lodge and cabins are located in a secluded grove on the shore of Webb Pond, with good bass, pickerel and perch fishing. Sightseeing, hiking, antiquing, bird watching and just relaxing are good ways to pass the time. The lodge will provide you with boats and canoes; motors can be rented by the day or week. Indoors, there is a well stocked library, piano and game

room. There is good home cooking, with breakfast and dinner served family style. The lodge has a short season—June 16–Sept. 30. Hunting parties in season by arrangement. Cabins are rented on a weekly basis, from Sat.-Sat. and are $140 for double occupancy. Daily rates are on a space available basis only, and are slightly higher. All cabins have heat, flush toilet and shower. For further information contact Dot and Bob Dunton, Wantalfego Lodge, R.F.D. #1, Franklin, ME 04634 (207)565–3530. Winter address is 2343 Croydon Rd., Sebring, FL 33870.

★★★★*Weatherby's—The Fisherman's Resort* is one of Maine's grand old sporting camps and vacation retreats, situated on picturesque Grand Lake Stream at Grand Lake in the heart of the legendary Eastern Maine fish and game country. The camp offers fishing from ice-out in May through September for landlocked salmon and lake trout in Grand and Big Lakes and for smallmouth bass up to trophy weights in Grand, Big, Wabassus, Pug, Junior, and Scraggly. Grand Lake Stream is restricted to fly-fishing only for landlocked salmon and smallmouth bass. There are 15 rustic cottages, most of which have living rooms with fireplace or open Franklin stove fireplace and from one to two double bedrooms. All cottages have full bath with tub and shower, electric heaters, long beds and screened porches. The cottages are widely spaced on a tree-shaded knoll facing the stream and assuring privacy. Electric blankets are provided if desired. There is daily maid service and a cabin boy who supplies ice and fills your wood box. The large and early American decorated dining room is in the lodge. The food, graciously served, is varied and of the best quality, including Government-inspected meats,

native turkeys, chicken, and Maine lobster with fresh vegetables and berries from the garden. Cooks artfully prepare and cook rolls, bread, pies, cookies and other fancy pastries as well as popular Down-East fish chowder and lobster stew. At noon, guests are provided with either picnic box lunches or hot cook-out basket lunches that your guide cooks on the lakeshore. July and August are the months for family fishing fun. Swimming in the clear, pure water of Grand Lake is delightful. There are many interesting smaller lakes for boating, discovering Indian relics, dri-ki gathering or admiring the pond lilies and wildlife in their natural habitat. There are trails for hiking, leading to a "look-out tower", a study of wild flowers or bird watching by the stream or in the woods. There are over 100 species of birds in the area. Outdoor games, badminton, horseshoes and basketball can be enjoyed on the spacious grounds. Modified American Plan rates (breakfast and dinner) are $26 per person daily based on double occupancy. Family rates available on request. For additional information, contact: Weatherby's, Grand Lake Stream, ME 04637 (207)796–5558.

Travel Services

Island/Wilderness Expeditions, Ltd. offers four one-week expeditions for photography buffs with some experience in camping and wilderness living. The destination of each expedition is a single, (in most cases) uninhabited island. These small islands, generally less than 10 acres in size, are located in Penobscot Bay on the edge of the Atlantic Ocean. They offer a variety of topography and vegetation, plus clam and mussel beds, a beach near which the cook site is established, and provide a microcosm of unique wilderness. Each island destination calls for an all-day sail (or row) from Rockport. The expedition's sole link with civilization is two 22–foot wooden Cape Ann dories. Built expressly for I/WE in Bath, Maine, by the Apprenticeshop (a school for traditional boat building), these stout boats are extremely seaworthy and able sailors. Their stability and shallow draft allow them to navigate comfortably among the islands and inlets of the Maine coast. Their design was taken from plans of the traditional Cape Ann dories used off Gloucester, Massachusetts, over 100 years ago. With no engines, their only means of propulsion is sail and oars. I/WE provides all specialized equipment: cooking equipment, cook tent, boats, safety equipment, etc. Participants are required to bring their own sleeping bag, rain gear, and camera equipment. A small two- or three-man tent is also required. A complete list of required and recommended equipment will be sent each applicant. The food on each expedition is simple, hardy, and ample. There are no frills, except those invented and added by the party members themselves. There is a basic menu from which the expedition can work, leaving enough room for inventiveness and ingenuity. Enough food is provided for all but one of the days on the islands, forcing the participants to forage for wild native food: fish, clams, mussels, berries, wild greens, beach peas, rose hips, sea urchin roe, etc. Wine for dinner is provided, but no beer. Alcoholic beverages are allowed, but if you bring them expect to share. Fees are $195, and include all meals, Monday lunch through Friday lunch—but not parking and ferry fees, and accommodations on these nights spent on the mainland. For additional information, contact: Mr. Bill Cole, Island/Wilderness Expeditions, Ltd., Rockport, ME 04856 (207)236–8581.

Victory Chimes Windjammer offers a delightful week of sailing along the Maine Coast. Leaving Rockland, Maine, each Monday morning and returning each Saturday night, from early June through September, the *Victory Chimes* visits many of Maine's fascinating outer islands. The cruising area offers a great variety of interesting sails and ports of calls. Each day's run is determined by winds, tides and weather. The sail may be a brisk 60 mile run at sea with a slashing fair wind or a leisurely sail among the islands in a gentle southerly breeze. Each night, weather permitting, the *Victory Chimes* anchors in a different harbor and passengers may go ashore to explore places such as Monhegan Island, Isle au Haut, Swan's Island and Mount Desert. The *Victory Chimes* is the largest passenger sailing vessel under the American flag. Built in 1900 for the cargo trade, the *Victory Chimes* operates today with the very best equipment and under regulations and a certificate of inspection issued by the U.S. Coast Guard. Staterooms are well equipped with hot and cold running water. There are six modern flush toilets. The large main saloon accommodates all passengers at meal time and is a comfortable gathering place for social activities. The meals are generously served to satisfy sea-going appetites. The Captain's dinner is a highlight of the cruise and includes fresh lobsters right out of the water. Homemade breads, popover, pies, and cakes are also featured. Meals start with breakfast Monday morning and continue through Saturday lunch. The cruise fare is $325 per person per week. For reservations and more information, contact Schr. *Victory*

Chimes, Windjammer Wharf, Rockland, ME 04841 (207)596–6060 summer; (207)326–8856 winter.

Moosehead Lake Region & Mt. Katahdin

This vast northern lakes and forests region encompasses huge Piscataquis, the "county of lakes," and the northern parts of Somerset and Penobscot counties. The Moosehead Lake country, one of the great, historic fishing, canoeing, camping, and hiking areas in the Northeast, is dominated by Maine's largest lake, Moosehead, 40 miles long and 20 miles wide, the Kennebec and Penobscot watersheds, and Baxter State Park. This territory is bordered to the north by the North Maine Woods tract, to the south by a line drawn between Stratton and Millinocket, to the west by the Maine-Quebec border, and to the east by Baxter State Park and the East Branch of the Penobscot. Within this region lie over 5,000 square miles of cold, deep, rockbound lakes, gouged out by the great glacial ice cap, wilderness trout ponds, hundreds of miles of classic canoeing water, thick evergreen forests, and scores of mountains dominated by majestic Mt. Katahdin. The lakes and river waters hold brook trout and landlocked salmon of better than seven pounds and togue well in excess of 15 pounds. Some of the famous names are Spencer, Brassua, Chesuncook, Lobster, Penobscot, Schoodic, Canada Falls, and Sebec Lakes. Schoodic is one of the original homes of the landlocked salmon, and Schoodic fish have been stocked all over the state. Pierce Pond is the home of Maine's record brook trout, taken in 1958. The state record blueback was taken at nearby Basin Pond in 1973. The fragrant balsam and spruce mantle is the habitat of bear, moose, deer, ruffed grouse, marten, wildcat, lynx, fisher, beaver, mink, otter, loon, osprey, and eagle. Miles of hiking trails, such as the famed Appalachian, afford a good opportunity to view some of these natives. Other, less friendly, natives were the Abenaki Indians, who made their home in the Moosehead-Kennebec area. Their raids on coastal settlements made much of Maine uninhabitable for more than 100 years. This area is also one of the earliest centers of Maine's immense timber industry. In season, pulpwood drives still fill some of the rivers bank to bank with seething masses of 4–foot-long "sticks."

Moosehead Lake has attracted sportsmen since the early 19th century. This greatest of all New England lakes cuts through the north Maine wilderness for a stretch of about 35 miles, hemmed by rugged mountains and flanked by dense forests. Mt. Kineo thrusts itself above the waters and far-flung forests of the lake's eastern shores. The mountain is composed of flint. Many of the New England Indian tribes came here for flint and it is believed that this mountain was also the source of iron pyrites used by the ancient Red Paint People for firestones. When Henry David Thoreau made a trip into the Moosehead-Katahdin region in 1846, his party remarked on the size, abundance, and voracity of the trout. The philosopher's comrades did not observe the niceties of angling, however, and harvested their squaretails with salt pork and stout lines. The lake holds sizable populations of trout, togue, and salmon. You can enjoy the recreational activities of one of Moosehead's many luxury resorts one minute, and in half an hour be fly casting on a remote trout pond. The Kennebec River discharges from the East and West Outlets of Moosehead, which drain into a dammed lake, Indian Pond. The East Outlet offers 3½ miles of heavy rapids before it flows into Indian Pond. The river holds some good trout and salmon all the way to Wyman Lake at Bingham. One of its tributaries, the Dead River, was the scene of Benedict Arnold's ill-fated march to Quebec in 1775. Fans of novelist Kenneth Roberts will recall his account of the epic.

Information Sources, Maps & Access

For detailed information on the Moosehead Lake Region and Forest Service Campsite Permits, contact: Maine Forest Service, Greenville, ME 04441 (207)695–3721. Scott Paper Company produces an excellent free map and brochure titled *Maine USA and Scott Paper Company Timberlands*. This colorful publication includes a map of the area around Moosehead Lake and west to Coburn Gore and contains a wealth of detail about the private road network, campsites, boat-launching sites, ski areas, gasoline locations (in remote areas), landing strips, fish species in principal waters, and much other valuable data. To obtain this worthwhile brochure, write to: Paper Industry Information Office, 133 State St., Augusta 04330. The Great Northern Paper Co., Millinocket 04462, produces a free pamphlet, *Your Road Guide to the West Branch Region*, which traces the GNP road system around Moosehead, Lobster, Seboomook, Caucomgomoc, Chesuncook, and Telos lakes and the western approaches to Baxter State Park. Rules of the road, safety regulations, registration, and forestry management are discussed too.

For detailed information on Baxter State Park and the free *Baxter State Park Map/Brochure* and *Baxter State Park Rules & Regulations Bulletin* contact: Reservations Clerk, Baxter State Park, Millinocket, ME 04462 (207)723–5140. A useful *AMC Latex Map of Baxter State Park* ($1.95) may be ordered from: Appalachian Mountain Club, 5 Joy St., Boston, MA 02108. You can telephone ahead for up-to-the-minute park conditions. The leaflet contains a schematic map which shows the park features, road, and trail network, campground locations, access, park history, it lists all of the trails and their lengths. The bulletin gives the rules and essential information, such as fees, registration, length-of-stay regulations, reservations, and other details of park use. You are advised to place reservations months in advance of your trip.

Two beautiful, useful maps, *Phillips' Map of Northern Maine's Moosehead-Allagash Region: Headwaters of the Kennebec, St. John & Penobscot* and *Phillips' Map of Baxter Park* ($1.50 each, plus 40¢ postage) may be ordered from Augustus D. Phillips & Son, Northeast Harbor 04662. Both maps show all man-made and natural

features, including trails, portages, logging roads, fly-in services, and Forest Service and paper company campsites. A free map of the *Moosehead & Upper Kennebec Waterways* may be obtained from: Scott Paper Co., Northwest Div., Winslow, ME 04901.

The Moosehead Lake and Katahdin region is reached via U.S. Highway 201, Interstate 95 and Maine Highways 6–15, 11, and the Baxter State Park Road. Lodging, guides, supplies, and outfitters are available at Jackman—the "Switzerland of Maine"—Medway, Millinocket, Moosehead, Tarratine, Greenville, Rockwood, Kokadjo, and Grindstone. Remote interior areas are reached via charter float plane service from Greenville and Millinocket.

Recreational Areas

Baxter State Park & Mt. Katahdin

Baxter State Park, a magnificent tract of more than 200,000 acres, is the gift of former Governor Percival P. Baxter. The park is a magnificent expanse of evergreen-clad mountains, cold glacial lakes, remote ponds, and streams famous for trout, togue, and salmon fishing, dense forests, and rugged alpine bogs. The park is crowned by Maine's highest mountain, Katahdin (5,268 feet), known to the Abenaki Indians as Ktaadn, the "Greatest Mountain." Mt. Katahdin (shown in three dimensions on a beautiful full-color, shaded relief U.S. Geological Survey Map of Katahdin) is a perfect example of a monadnock, a single remnant of a former highland which rises as an isolated rock mass above a plain, and is said to be the first point on which the morning sun shines in the continental United States. The mountain is one of the highest points east of the Rockies and dominates a vast expanse of territory whose lakes and streams are famous among fishermen and whose forest depths outside the park are among the best deer, black bear, and upland game bird hunting grounds in the state. Katahdin, the eastern terminus of the Appala-

chian Trail, was climbed in 1804 by Charles Potter, a Boston surveyor, who so far as is known was the first white man to stand on its summit. Forty-two years later, Thoreau wrote of the view from the summit that "the surrounding world looked as if a huge mirror had been shattered, and glittering bits thrown on the grass." There are 46 peaks in Baxter which exceed 3,000 feet. Major features surrounding Mt. Katahdin include Grand Lake Matagamon, Nesowadnehunk (Sourdnahunk) Lake and Stream, the Wassataquoik watershed (the lake contains some bluebacks), Kidney Pond, Upper Togue, Daicey, and Chimney ponds, the Klondike, the Cross Range, and Traveler Mountain. The rare Sunapee golden trout, a relative of the arctic char, was stocked in the South Branch Ponds in 1971. Woodland caribou, long absent from Maine, were reintroduced (unsuccessfully) into the park in 1973. One hundred and forty miles of trails, including the old Hunt and Abol Trails, spread through Baxter, ranging in length from ½ to 22 miles; they afford every degree of hiking difficulty. You can take a short Sunday stroll to a quiet pond, or tackle imposing Mt. Katahdin. Campgrounds are conveniently located, except for two sites, which require a hike.

West Branch of the Penobscot & Chesuncook Lake

To the north, northeast, and east of Moosehead lie the wilderness waterways of the West and East Branches of the Penobscot, which include Baxter State Park. The West Branch, one of America's famed canoe trails, has two major segments. The top portion from Seboomook Lake to Chesuncook is mostly easy going. It passes close to Lobster Lake, a beautiful salmon and togue spot, picking up its outlet, receives the two Ragmuff streams, and merges with Chesuncook for the final paddle to Ripogenus Dam, 92 feet high at the head of West Branch Gorge. The swift Penobscot currents at the foot of the dam hold some salmon of better than 10 pounds and some eyepopping trout. The fisherman may find himself with the trophy of a lifetime or some smashed tackle, depending on his brand of luck.

The upper stretch of the West Branch (from Seboomook Lake Dam downstream past the North East Carry to Chesuncook Lake) and huge Chesuncook Lake offer some of Maine's finest trophy fishing for landlocked salmon up to nine pounds. The major fishing pools along the upper West Branch, bordered by a dense northern forest of spruce, pine, poplar, and tamarack, include the Big Island area, the legendary Fox Hole with its sheer granite cliffs, and the boulder-studded Rocky Rips area near the mouth of Pine Stream (an excellent early season stream which yields big squaretails from its meandering, tea-colored waters). The top fishing areas in Chesuncook Lake include the rock ledges along beautiful Gero Island, mouth of Red Brook, Togue Point, and the Caribou Lake area. The nearby lakes and streams of Chesuncook Country—which is dominated on the east by Majestic Mount Katahdin, and is believed to be the Algonquin word for "land of many waters"—provide some excellent early and late season fishing for salmon and squaretails up to trophy weights. The most productive waters (particularly during the early season smelt run for 10 days after ice out for salmon, during the May spawning run of suckers for squaretails, and during the upstream spawning migration of landlocked salmon from late August to October 1st) which feed into Chesuncook Lake are Duck Pond—a perennial hotspot for squaretails up to four-six pounds, Cuxabexis Stream and Lake, Umbazooksus Stream, beautiful Caucomgomoc Lake and Stream, and remote Loon Lake—one of the state's least explored trophy salmon waters.

The wilderness traveler in Chesuncook Country—one of the state's most productive trapping, logging, and big game and upland game bird hunting areas—will often see osprey, the phantom-like goshawk, red-tailed and sharp-shinned hawks, pine marten, loons, grebes, mergansers, teal, ruffed grouse, woodcock, river otter, beaver, red fox, goldeneye, moose, whitetail deer, and the sign of black bear, lynx, and the large eastern coyote, known locally as "brush wolves," which are descended from the Ontario timberwolf and reach weights up to 120 pounds.

The lower West Branch from Chesuncook to Ambajejus Lake, an arm of sprawling Pemadumcook, is quite different from the upper portion. This is a trip for experts. Here the West Branch is full of boiling rapids, falls, chutes, and everything an experienced canoeist could desire. The tongue-twisting names are indicative of the brawling nature of the water: Ambejackmockamus, Nesowadnehunk, and Pickwockamus Falls, as well as Horserace Rapids.

The formidable East Branch spills from Grand Lake Matagamon at the northeast corner of Baxter State Park. It is considered more fearsome, if less well known, than the West Branch. The name of some of the stretches tell the story; Grand Pitch, the Hulling Machine, Spencer Rips, and Grindstone Falls. These are not names to inspire confidence in the inexperienced or timid. Rampaging white water, seething currents, falls, and jagged rocks await the expert. This river segment is considered by many knowledgeable enthusiasts to be the finest canoe run in the eastern United States.

Gateways & Accommodations

Dover-Foxcroft—Gateway to the Moosehead Lake Country

(Pop. 4,200; zip code 04426; area code 207) is located on the Piscataquis River just south of Sebec Lake (noted for its lake trout and landlocked salmon fishing), the site of Peaks-Kenny State Park. A fascinating Blacksmith Shop Museum on Chandler Road is open to visitors daily. Accommodations: *Blethen House Motel & Dining Room* (rates: $18–23 double), with 30 guest rooms at 37 East Main Street (564-2481).

Greenville—Gateway to Moosehead Lake & the North Maine Woods

(Pop. 2,000; zip code 04441; area code 207) has been famous since the late 19th century as the major gateway for sportsmen heading for Moosehead Lake and the headwaters of the St. John, West Branch of the Penobscot, and Allagash rivers. This colorful vacation center,

with its red, brown, and green wood-front stores, cigar store Indian and general store, jumbled along the island-dotted south antler of sprawling Moosehead Lake, is the base of several Northern Maine charter float-plane and sight-seeing flight and guide services. Area attractions include Mt. Kineo—made of solid flint and site of arrowheads made by the ancient "Red Paint" people, Squaw Mountain Ski Area, and Lily Bay State Park eight miles north of town on the lake. Accommodations: *Indian Hill Motel* (rates: $21 double), with 12 good guest rooms on Maine Highway 15, ½ mile south of town (695-2623).

Jackman—Gateway to the Moose River Country

(Pop. 800; zip code 04945; area code 207.) This northwoods village on U.S. 201 has long been a popular jumping-off place for fishermen, hunters, and canoeists heading into the Moose River headwaters, and Wood River country. Several registered Maine guides and sporting camps are based here. Accommodations: *Hillcrest Motel* (rates: $20.50–$21.50 double), with 14 good rooms and restaurant, 2½ miles north of town on U.S. 201 (688-2721); *Sky Lodge* (rates: $23–30 double), in Moose River Village with 25 good rooms and family units in log cabin lodge with dining room and cocktail lounge, two miles north of Jackman on U.S. 201 (688-2171).

Millinocket—Gateway to Baxter State Park & Mt. Katahdin

(Pop. 9,000; zip code 04462; area code 207) is a historic forest products town on the West Branch of the Penobscot River, due south of Mt. Katahdin and the Baxter State Park Wilderness. The town is a popular jumping-off point to the legendary fishing, hunting, and canoeing areas of the North Maine Woods. North of Millinocket is the fascinating Lumberman's Museum on Maine 159 in Patten which houses an exact replica of a 19th–century Maine Woods

lumber camp, a blacksmith's shop, a steam log hauler and assorted collections of lumberjack tools and old photographs. Accommodations: *Heritage Motor Inn* (rates: $22–24 double), with 42 excellent rooms and dining room east of town on Maine Highways 11 and 157 (723–9777).

Rockwood—Gateway to Moosehead Lake & the "West Branch"

(Pop. 300; zip code 04478; area code 207) is a beautiful North Country vacation center on the northern antler of Moosehead Lake at the mouth of the Moose River and head of the famous Kennebec. Registered Maine fishing and hunting guides and charter float-plane service are available. Several old-style country stores overlook beautiful Moosehead, surrounded by evergreen forests and rolling hills. The town is located northwest of Greenville on Maine 6/15 across from Mt. Kineo. Area attractions include auto tours of the Scott Paper Co. forestlands and logging service on the Kennebec and Pittston Farm at Seboomook Lake on the West Branch and the North East carry—both historic logging settlements developed at the turn of the century by the Great Northern Paper Company. Accommodations: *Moosehead Motel* (rates: $24–32 double), with 28 excellent guest rooms and family units at Moosehead Lake, view of Mt. Kineo, dining room, cocktail lounge, heated pool, boats, motors, canoes, guide service and boat tours of the lake, one mile north of town on Maine 6/15 (534–7787).

Lodges & Sporting Camps

★★★*Attean Lake Resort* is an island vacation resort in an unspoiled mountain lake area of the Moose River Country. North of Waterville and near the Canadian border, it is the only resort on Attean Lake. The atmosphere of the area is beautiful and serene, and the resort itself rustic and comfortable. There is a private beach, fishing, swimming, water skiing, boating, hiking and climbing. Spring brings the season for landlocked salmon and brook trout and in summer, the lake is good for trolling. Fishing tackle is sold at the camp and licenses are available in Jackman—10 minutes away. The highlight of your stay might be a 42-mile canoe trip along Moose River. There are also 17 other lakes and streams in the immediate area and canoes are available for exploring them. The resort is convenient to major routes, and in addition, offers its own seaplane service. The resort has 21 private log cabins—accommodating from two-six persons, containing bath, fireplace and porch, overlooking the lake and mountains. Spring drinking water and pitchers of ice are supplied as well as wood for the fireplace, and there is daily maid service. Rates, on the American Plan (three meals a day) are $40 per person daily, $215 weekly. Further information is available from the Attean Lake Resort, the Langdon Holdens, Jackman, ME 04945 (207)668–3792 summer; or (207)668–3321 winter.

★★★*The Birches at Moosehead* consist of 17 log cabins built of native timber, secluded in hardwood groves on the edge of sprawling Moosehead Lake. Sailfish, outboards, and canoes are available at the lake dock, and the 42-mile shoreline, with its rugged evergreen coves and secluded beaches, provides superlative fishing for trout, landlocked salmon, and togue. The Birches has a private marina to moor guests' boats, a swimming area, and water skiing instruction. Fresh vegetables from the garden, hot fresh baked rolls, and homemade pies and cakes are a part of each evening's meal. The log cabins accommodate two-eight persons, and are open all year round. Each has a private bath, and a fireplace, or an old-fashioned Franklin stove to take the edge off cool nights. The open porches overlook the lake to the surrounding mountains. Brilliant autumn days and windy nights bring hunters to the birches in pursuit of small game. In the winter, cross-country skiers and snowshoers explore the quiet

forests and the frozen lake edge. For details, write: North Country Outfitters, P.O. Box 81, Rockwood, ME 04478 (207)534–7305.

★★★*Buckhorn Camps* are located on Middle Jo-Mary Lake of the famous Jo-Mary Lakes Chain of the wild West Branch of the Penobscot River, near beautiful Mt. Katahdin and Baxter State Park. The Jo-Mary Lakes and surrounding lakes and ponds hold landlocked salmon, lake trout, and brook trout up to trophy weights. Buckhorn will fly you to outpost camps on remote wilderness ponds for big brook trout. During the brilliant fall months, Buckhorn offers top-ranked hunting for whitetail and partridge. Buckhorn Camps began in 1889 as a private hunting lodge. Many sturdy log cabins were built of which several remain, including the Guides' Camp. Accommodations are in rustic log cabins with modern comforts, private baths and showers, and wood-burning stoves. Delicious home-cooked meals are served family-style in the camp dining room. American Plan rates are $34 per person per day; housekeeping rates are $150 per person per week and $25 per person for each guest over two per cabin. Children under 16 are free. Boats, canoes, and motors are available for rental. Charter float-plane flying service is available for sightseeing flights, trips to outlying camps and ponds, and service from Delta Airlines at Bangor, direct to camp. For additional information, contact: Buckhorn Camps, Millinocket, ME 04462 (207)723–5658.

★★★*Camp Phoenix* is located northwest of Mt. Katahdin on the west-central boundary of Baxter State Park along the shore of beautiful Nesowadnehunk Lake. The surrounding ponds, wild rivers, and north country wilderness offers superb trout and landlocked salmon fishing, hiking, bird watching, canoeing, and wildlife photography. Nesowadnehunk Lake is undoubtedly one of the best fly fishing lakes for trout in the east. Nesowadnehunk Stream and other streams and brooks are very productive to the patient stream fisherman. Little Nesowadnehunk Lake is reached over a pleasant trail from the main lake. This jewel of a big-trout lake will often produce two- and three-pound scrapping wild brookies to the careful fly fisherman. One may fish for hours without seeing a rise or hearing a splash but suddenly the entire surface of the lake can become alive with monstrous rising trout, creating action that will make the heart of the most hardy fly fisherman race with excitement. This lake is a trophy lake and has a one fish daily bag limit, fly casting only. Thissell Pond is accessible by road and is another good trout pond open to general law fishing (excluding live fish as bait). At Telos and Chamberlain Lakes, a few miles northerly from Thissell, canoeists start the famous Allagash River trip. These two lakes have good trolling for big trout and

togue (lake trout). Ripogenus Dam and Chesuncook Lake are south-westerly from camp and offer good salmon and trout fishing. Its outlet, the West Branch of the Penobscot River, is famous for its landlocked salmon fishing. The Katahdin Range of mountains run from northeast to southeast of camp. The camp offers both a housekeeping plan and American Plan with comfortable, fully-equipped modern cabins with lake views, breakfast and dinner in the main dining room, and a lunch to take out at noon. Boats and canoes are furnished at no additional charge. All meals served in the informal main dining room are the best home-cooked foods. Boat rentals and guide service are available for camp guests. The camp is reached via Baxter State Park Road. It's advisable to bring rain gear and warm clothing as well as light boots or rubbers for hiking to outlying ponds and streams. A camera and binoculars will be handy for observing and photographing the abundant wild-life. For additional information and rates, contact: Camp Phoenix, Box 210, Millinocket, ME 04462 (207)695–2821; (winter) Box 771, Attleboro, MA 02703.

★★Chalet Moosehead is situated on the shore of Moosehead Lake, one of the largest fresh-water lakes within the boundaries of one state. The deep clear water is the natural home for the salmon, trout and togue. The lake opens for fishing immediately after ice-out (early May). Some of the best salmon and togue fishing in Maine is found here. Brook trout are in nearby lakes and ponds. The Inn is located at the foot of Little Squaw Mountain and just ten minutes from the ski trails of Squaw Mt. For snowmobilers there are 40 miles of lake travel and numerous trails in the area. In the summer months, Squaw Mountain offers chair-lift rides to the top of the mountain for horseback riding, golf, a pool and sauna, excellent cuisine and a cocktail lounge. Of course, there's mountain climbing and hiking, swimming and water skiing. There are docks for your own boat, or rentals are available. The Inn is just an hour's drive to the best theatres, horse racing, and summer fairs. The Inn offers flying service to your favorite hunting, fishing or camping areas each day. The lake also has cruises available. Accommodations consist of a motel with eight units or a private chalet cottage—equipped for six—with its own sunporch. The rooms provide a living room-kitchen combination (equipped for light cooking), bedroom, bath, electric heat, wall-to-wall carpeting, and a large picture window overlooking the lake. Cots will be provided if needed. Pets are not allowed. Summer rates, double occupancy, are $28 per day, $180 per week. Winter rates are lower and package plans are available for skiers. Meals are not available although there are many restaurants nearby. Contact Ken and Mary Hughes, Chalet Moosehead, P.O. Box 315, Greenville Junction, ME 04442 (207)695–2950.

★★★Chesuncook Lake House, a national historic landmark visited by Henry David Thoreau on his historic canoe trip through the Maine Woods, is a delightful, unpretentious wilderness lodge located at the top of huge Chesuncook Lake across from Mt. Katahdin near the mouth of the upper West Branch of the Penobscot River, accessible only by float-plane or boat. Owned and operated by Burt McBurnie and his wife Maggie, the lodge offers warm hospitality, North Country charm, great meals with homebaked breads and desserts and fresh, garden-grown vegetables, and superb fishing and wilderness canoeing in the surrounding waterways. Chesuncook Lake, Cau-comgomoc stream, and the West Branch of the Penobscot (particu-larly in the legendary "Fox Hole" and "Rocky Rips" areas) offer often outstanding fly fishing during the spring and fall for landlocked salmon up to six pounds. The seldom-explored waters of meandering Pine Stream and Umbazoskais Stream hold squaretails up to weights usually found only in the Canadian wilds. Beautiful Duck Pond, reached by a 100 yard portage, also holds some eye-popping wild

brookies. The canoeist or fisherman is likely to sight moose, beaver, goshawks, osprey, Cooper's hawks, woodcock, pine marten, goldeneye, mergansers, teal, and an occasional bald eagle. During the fall, the lodge offers guided hunting for whitetail deer and bear in the surrounding big woods country. During the summer, the lodge is a perfect stopover for canoeists heading into the Allagash Country. The lodge offers pick-up service by boat for guests at the South Arm of Chesuncook Lake. Lodge rooms will accommo-date up to ten guests. Housekeeping cabins are clean and simple with everything furnished except your food and bedding. Boats, motors, and canoes are available for rental. American Plan rates are $30 per day per person; housekeeping cabins are $7.50 per day per person or $100 per week for two guests. For additional info, con-tact: Chesuncook Lake House, Chesuncook Village, Greenville, ME 04441 or phone Folsom's Air Service at Greenville (207)695–2821.

★Folsom's Wilderness Fly-In Camps, operated by Folsom's Air Service, are located fifteen miles east of Greenville. There are two camps, one on the east end of the pond and one on the west side of the pond. The pond is slightly less than one mile long and about ½ mile wide. The large camp sleeps eight in four double bunks and the small camp sleeps five in two double bunks and a roll-away bed. Cots can be used in either camp to accommodate larger parties. Three boats go with the large camp and two with the smaller one. Horseshoe Pond is fly-fishing only for wild brook trout with an eight fish limit. Pearl Pond is general law, with an eight fish limit. Fish will run from 6″ to 12″ with an occasional larger one. It is usually easy to meet your limit each day. The camps are completely equipped with cooking utensils and blankets. All the party has to bring is food, fishing equipment, linen and towels. There are gas stoves, gas lights, and gas refrigerators in each camp. The remote Russell Pond camps are 48 miles north of Greenville. There are two camps, each will accommodate a party of four. One other camp can be used for larger parties. There are two boats and three canoes at the camps. This pond is fly fishing only, with an eight fish limit. These fish will run to two pounds. The fishing is usually good, although not as fast as Horseshoe, the brook trout will average larger. Everything is furnished except food and fishing gear. There are gas stoves, gas lights, and gas refrigerators. For additional information and seasonal rates, contact: Folsom's Air Service, Moosehead Lake, Greenville, ME 04441 (207)695–2821.

★★★Frost Pond Camps & Allagash Wilderness Outfitters are in the heart of Maine's North Woods. Nearly forty miles from any town, Frost Pond is surrounded by a forest of hardwood and evergreen.

Frost Pond itself is a brook trout haven, and landlocked salmon are in nearby Chesuncook Lake and the famous West Branch of the Penobscot River. Harrington Lake, a fifteen-minute drive away, provides good fishing for lake trout. Boats, canoes and outboard motors are available for rent and parties can be outfitted for canoe trips over a wide wilderness area, including the Allagash River. Besides fishing, boating, swimming, and canoeing, Frost Pond offers a variety of wildlife from moose to snowshoe hare. The 200,000–acre Baxter State Park, with its trails for hiking and mountain climbing, is only fifteen miles away. In late October and November, there is hunting for deer and an occasional bear and in the winter, there is excellent ice fishing. Snowmobiles are welcome and the numerous logging roads and open hardwood areas are great for ski touring and snowshoeing. The eight rustic housekeeping cabins are all equipped with gas stoves, refrigerators, lights and wood heaters. Seven have no electricity or running water with the water being obtained from the well. One cabin is equipped with "all the luxuries," running hot and cold water, shower and indoor toilet. All cabins contain blankets, bed linens, bath towels, hot pads, dish linens, and all cooking and eating utensils. There are also ten well wooded campsites directly on the pond shores. Rates for cabins without plumbing run from $8.50 per person for one day, $7.00 per person for two or more days and $6.50 per person for five or more days. The cabin with plumbing, with room for at least four to six people, runs $145 a week. Campsites are $3.50 per day, $21 per week. For further information about Forest Pond Camps and canoe trips on the Allagash River, contact Rick and Judy Givens at Frost Pond, Star Route 76, Greenville, ME 04441, radio contact (207)695–2821 from May 1 to November 30. From December 1 to April 30 contact Rick and Judy Givens at 36 Minuteman Drive, Millinocket, ME 04462 (207)723–6622.

★★★*Little Lyford Pond Fly-In Camps* offers some of the best wild trout fly fishing and cross-country skiing in Maine. Fishing at Little Lyford has been consistently excellent for over 50 years because access to the surrounding ponds and streams is limited to those who stay at the camps. Located in Northern Maine near the Moosehead Lake region, this area offers a great variety of fishing opportunities. Each day you can explore a new spot, First and Second Ponds, the Pleasant River, Mountain Brook Pond, the hidden Beaver Bog, Lloyd Pond, Horseshoe Pond, and many others. The camps are beautifully situated next to Little Lyford Pond with an outstanding view of Baker Mountain. They offer simple comfortable accommodations with unusually good food in an atmosphere of relaxation and

pleasure. There are seven attractive log cabins with comfortable beds, a wood stove, gas lamps, running water and a cheerful outhouse. A rustic main lodge provides dining facilities and a small, interesting library. Enjoy the delightful cedar sauna and shower at the end of the day. Other facilities include an overnight cabin on Mountain Brook Pond for guests of Little Lyford. You'll also find boats for your use on four of the ponds. Daily rates are $38.50 per person and include 3 meals a day, accommodations, and full use of facilities. You may also take advantage of the special Little Lyford Pond/Chairback Mountain Camps fishing trip. You'll begin your week with a short float-plane ride over Elephant Mountain for your stay at Little Lyford Pond Camps. You'll stay for three days of fishing for native brook trout at any of the secluded "fly-fishing only" ponds within a short walk of your cabin, or the beautiful West Branch of the Pleasant River. On Wednesday, you'll take a short ride to Chairback Mountain Camps located on the Appalachian Trail, at the edge of Long Pond, just eight miles from Little Lyford. The waters surrounding Chairback Mountain Camps offer you the chance to catch trophy-sized native brook trout and Maine land-locked salmon. Cast your line in the active waters of Long Pond or take a short hike to the outlying waters such as East and West Chairback Ponds, Henderson Brook, Trout Pond, Indian Pond and Gulf Hagas. Most of the fishing spots have boats for your use. You'll stay in one of seven log cabins with gas lights, woodstoves and outhouses. Other facilities include an Octagon library and sandy swimming beach. Breakfast in the main lodge brings hot muffins straight from the oven, doughnuts, bacon and eggs, homefries, pancakes and of course, your fresh cooked trout and salmon. Hearty lunches are packed for your day of fishing. Dinnertime salads and vegetables from camp gardens complement steak and beans, shrimp, roasts and other fine meals. This is a unique fishing trip with a history of over 150 years of experience between the two camps. For additional information and rates, contact: F.H.T. Tours, 52 Beacon St., Boston, MA 02108 (617)742–6076.

★★★★*Penobscot Lake Lodge* is a wilderness fly-in sporting camp at the remote headwaters of the West Branch of the Penobscot River in the North Maine Woods, sheltered in the cathedral-like spruce and fir forest along the shore of beautiful Penobscot Lake. Accessible by private plane, the lodge offers the quiet elegance of the fashionable hunting lodges of an earlier day, with all of the modern amenities that make mid-twentieth century life enjoyable. Running water and electricity help to make your stay carefree and easy. The only camp on the lake, the lodge offers fly and bait fishing for big brook trout

and rare blueback trout. Boats and canoes are available for fishing and exploring. Each cabin accommodates two adults and features comfortable beds, hot and cold running water, plus the warmth of a wood stove for occasional cool summer evenings. There are accommodations for no more than eighteen adults, making your visit relaxing and quiet in an uncrowded atmosphere. Meals at Penobscot combine fine food and Down East cooking carefully prepared by your host and hostess. American Plan rates are $60 per person per day and include meals, cabin, cocktail snacks, boats, motors, fuel, raingear, and fishing tackle if a guest does not have his own. Penobscot Lake Lodge is 50 miles northwest of Greenville, Maine; one and a half miles from the Maine-Canada border. Connections to the lodge can be made via charter airline or rental car from Maine's major airports to Greenville. The 30–minute flight from Greenville to Penobscot is by charter float-plane service. For additional information, contact: P.O. Box 45, Greenville, ME 04441 or call Folsom's Air Service (207)695–2821.

★★★★*Squaw Mountain at Moosehead Lake*, a superb four-season resort, offers excellent alpine and cross-country skiing and a summer northwoods adventure program that includes your choice of canoeing, fishing, hiking, sailing, golf, tennis, scenic boat rides, whitewater rafting, seaplane flying instruction, and expertly guided wilderness canoeing, fishing, and backpacking trips on remote stretches of the Appalachian Trail. Squaw Mountain also offers complete canoe outfitting services. Summer events include the Salty Dog Bluegrass Festival, Logdriver Days, Fly-Fishing Workshop, Nature Photography Workshop, Lumberjack Jamboree, and the International Seaplane Fly-In. Summer rates based on double occupancy range from $16–34 per person. Special rates for children. The lodge offers nursery and playground facilities, special events, and entertainment for children. On a clear day skiers can see 100 miles from the summit of 3,200–foot Squaw Mountain. Fourteen miles of skiing terrain over a 1,750–foot vertical drop offer wide, gentle novice slopes and challenging mogul runs to skiers of every ability. The Squaw Mountain Ski Shop has full equipment sales and rentals. The Squaw Mountain professional ski school offers instruction from beginning to freestyle, and special programs for children. Group lessons are $7 for 1½ hours of instruction, and private lessons are $14 an hour. The Squaw Mountain Ski Touring Center operates 25 miles of wilderness trails throughout the Moosehead Lake area. Cross-country ski rentals and professional ski touring lessons are available. Squaw Lodge, with 55 deluxe units, family rooms and suites, is located on the mountain, with the chairlift right at the door. Other amenities include a heated indoor pool, a sauna, a poolside cocktail lounge, nursery, a cafeteria, game room, TV room, fine dining in the Masquaso Dining Room, and dancing in the Red Eagle Lounge after dinner. Standard rooms at Squaw Mountain are $19; family rooms are $19 per person; suites, which are large, multilevel units with a spacious living room and two full baths, are $19 per person and accommodate a minimum of six persons. In addition, Squaw Mountain offers a variety of ski vacation plans, ski lesson plans, and two, four, and five day ski weeks. For more information write: Squaw Mountain, P.O. Box D, Greenville, ME. 04441 (207)695–2272.

Travel Services

Folsom's North Maine Woods Air Service, located on Moosehead Lake at Greenville, is Maine's largest floatplane operator, founded in 1946 by Dick Folsom. Folsom's offers charter air service to the wilderness sporting camps, lakes, ponds and streams throughout the North Maine Woods for fishing, hunting, and canoeing parties. Folsom's will also outfit you for your wilderness adventure with

boats, canoes, tents, and gear. On St. John and Allagash canoe trips, Folsom's will pick you up at St. Francis due to the better water conditions there during summer. There are several other points along both rivers, however, that they can fly out of. With the exception of the Beaver, Folsom's planes are usually new, current year models. Their standard rates (1979) are as follows.

Destination	Per Person	Destination	Per Person
Augusta	48.00	Mountain Pond	14.00
Baker Lake	32.00	Munsungan Lake	39.00
Bangor	34.00	Nahmakanta Lake	20.00
Buttermilk Pond	18.00	N.E. Carry	21.00
Caucomgomac	32.00	Onawa	16.00
Chamberlain Lake	35.00	Penobscot Lake	28.00
Chesuncook Lake	27.00	Pierce Pond	20.00
Churchill Lake	44.00	Rainbow Lake	22.00
Deer or Sugar Island	12.00	Rockwood	14.00
Eagle Lake	39.00	Ross Lake	44.00
Enchanted Pond	20.00	Round Pond, on	
5th St. John	30.00	Allagash	53.00
Forest Park	12.00	Rum Pond	10.00
Horseshoe Pond	14.00	Russell Pond	28.00
Jackman	22.00	St. Francis	74.00
Johnson Pond	36.00	Sebec Lake	18.00
Kokadjo–1st Roach Pond	16.00	Seboomook	21.00
Little Lyford	15.00	Spencer Lake	
Lobster Lake	21.00	Hardscrabble Lodge	22.00
Long Pond (Chairback)	21.00	Umsaskis Lake	48.00
Millinocket Lake	39.00	Yoke Pond	18.00

Rates are based on two passengers minimum. One passenger rate is 150% of single fare. If canoe is hauled, subtract 150 lb. from allowed weight. If baggage is too bulky, extra plane may be required. Extra charge for canoe hauls depending on distance flown, $5 to $25.

Five models of Cessna Aircraft are usually available. Cessna 172, two passengers, 450 lb. total weight; Cessna 180, three passengers, 700 lb. total weight; Cessna 206, five passengers, 1100 lb. total weight; Cessna 185, four passengers, 900 lb. total weight; DeHavilland Beaver, six passengers, 1300 lb. total weight. 50 lb. weight of baggage allowed per person. Extra charge if larger plane required due to overweight baggage.

For additional information, contact: Folsom's Air Service, Greenville, ME 04441 (207)695–2821.

Maine Whitewater, Inc. runs one-day whitewater trips on the West Branch of the Penobscot and Kennebec River. The operation is headed by Jim Ernst, a master whitewater guide on the Colorado River in the Grand Canyon for nine years, before he returned to his native Maine. He provides rafters with the best equipment, including Professional Type I life preservers. Maine Whitewater runs two kinds of trips: paddle-powered and oar-powered. Paddle-power trips are for people who really want to get involved with the river, but they must be in top physical shape and have experience in rafting, canoeing or kayaking. On the oar-powered trips the guides do most of the work and rafters can sit back and enjoy the scenery. Oar-powered trips are suitable for young and old alike. Besides individual and family reservations, Maine Whitewater will arrange trips for groups of photographers, naturalists, youth organizations or professionals. Reservations are necessary for both individuals and groups. The Kennebec River trip is run on weekdays only over a 12½–mile stretch of rough to moderate rapids, between Harris Station and West Forks. This area of the river was once used for driving logs south to the pulp mills. Rafters gather at West Forks at 9:00 a.m. and are taken to the starting point of the river trip. They return in late afternoon to West Forks. A picnic lunch on shore breaks the day and gives rafters a breather to enjoy the scenery. When the weather is good, hikes into Moxie Falls and Dead Creek may be taken. On weekends, trips are planned to the West Branch of the Penobscot River, running along the southern border of Baxter State Park deep in timberland. This trip starts in Millinocket at 9:00 a.m. and ends there in late afternoon. Noontime is spent having lunch on shore in the shadow of Mt. Katahdin. A highlight of this area of the river is the wildlife. Rafters often see deer, moose and bear. For more information or reservations, write: James A. Ernst, Maine Whitewater, Inc., Suite 454, Bingham, Maine 04920. From May through September call (207)672–4814 and in winter call (207)622–2260.

Millinocket Lake Flying Service has been offering float plane service to remote sporting camps and wilderness areas of the North Maine Woods and Allagash Country—including the headwaters of the Allagash and St. John rivers—for over 30 years. They have 20 canoes and boats cached on several remote ponds for fly-in fishing, camping, and hunting trips, and offer outfitting and canoe rental services. Millinocket Lake Flying Service will help you plan a vacation in some of the most beautiful wilderness left in the United States. Their seaplane base is located between Ambajejus and Millinocket Lakes on the road to Baxter State Park is only minutes by air from Mt. Katahdin, the Appalachian Trail, and the Allagash Wilderness Waterway. For rates and info, contact: Box 171, Millinocket, ME 04462 (207)723–8378 or 9215.

The Moosehead Flying Service is owned and operated by Ramona Morrell, Maine's only lady bush pilot. Ramona offers much more than just flying services, however. She runs air tours for two or three persons; operates an approved floatplane flight school; flies people and equipment to Maine's lakes, ponds and rivers for fishing, camping and outdoor adventures; and puts together fully planned and equipped fly-in canoe and camping trips. Seven different air tours are offered for people who want to see the beautiful, rugged backcountry the easy way. The *Allagash Wilderness* Air Tour is a 2½ hour flight, starting at the southern tip of Moosehead Lake, continuing to Kineo Mountain and on to the West Branch River and Chesuncook, Chamberlain and Allagash Falls and the Canadian border, ending with a view of Mount Katahdin and Ripogenus Dam. Cost is $140 for two or three persons. The *Mount Katahdin* tour lasts an hour, flying over Maine's highest mountain, over waterfalls up to 600 feet in height and past the Ripogenus Dam. It is $55 for two or three

persons. *Northeast Carry* tour flies over 40 miles of unpolluted fresh water to the head of Moosehead Lake, past Spencer Mountain and Kineo Mountain for $38 for two or three. *Kineo Mountain* tour flies over the mountain, rising 700 feet above the clear lake waters. The mountain is the largest mass of hornblende in the world, and Indian implements and weapons made from its flint have been found as far west as the Mississippi. This trip is especially enjoyed by photographers and is $30 for two or three. The *Squaw Mountain* tour flies over miles of mountain trails, the ski lodge and the first fire tower built in the U.S., and over the Kennebec whitewater and Boarstone Mountain. The fly-in trips for those with their own camping, backpacking, fishing, hunting or canoeing equipment go to remote lakes, trout streams, roaring rivers and wilderness areas. The plane can take three passengers with light gear for a total of 650 pounds—subtracting 150 pounds from the total weight for a canoe. She can set a group down in one area and arrange to pick them up elsewhere, after they have canoed down river or backpacked through the wilderness. Vacationers can be picked up in Bangor from commercial airlines or flown to wilderness locations from Moosehead Flying Services' base in Greenville Junction in the northcentral part of the state. All rates quoted for these trips are the one-way cost per plane load. A trip to Chamberlain Lake, the largest lake in the Allagash Region offering trout and togue to the fisherman and challenges and scenery for hunters and vacationers, is $66. Experienced canoeists can be flown to the St. John for approximately $65 and travel down 122 miles of this wild and remote river. A $38 flight takes visitors to Pierce Pond, and a $56 flight to Penobscot can yield brook trout, blueback trout and good hunting. Prices are available for all Maine lakes, ponds and rivers. Guides can be hired at $50.00 per day. Moosehead also does all the planning and equipping for fly-in canoe and backpacking package trips. They plan trips to fit the level of experience of beginners and experts, doing all planning and provisioning, including information on water and trail conditions, location of camping areas and campsites, securing fire permits, providing maps and complete outfitting. Vacationers are flown to the starting point to save all their vacation time for wilderness adventure. The package trip prices quoted below include round trip air transportation to the wilderness area. Outfitting adds $24 per day per person ($20 for children under 12) and includes canoes and camping equipment. For just a canoe, paddles and life jackets for two persons, add $12 per day. Typical trips include the Dead River trip with a flight to Spencer Lake and a two-day ride on the rapids in a canoe along 15 miles of exciting waters, dropping at the rate of 30 feet to the mile. This package is only $58 per person. A trip to Nahmakanta for four to six days is $55. The lake is accessible only by seaplane and nestles in the hills south of Katahdin Mountain. Backpackers can take the trail to the summit of Katahdin. Twelve packages to various areas with optional side trips are offered by Moosehead. There are also deluxe lakeside accommodations available at the Moosehead base in Greenville Junction. They can arrange for any wilderness services, licenses, equipment, guides and air transportation for most any trip. For more information on the air tours, trips and packages, and many more wilderness adventures, write: Ramona Morrell, Moosehead Flying Service, Inc., Moosehead Lake, Greenville Junction, ME. 04442 (207)695–2674.

North Country Outfitters on Moosehead Lake offers complete outfitting services and guided canoe trips for the Allagash Wilderness Waterway, St. John River, West Branch of the Penobscot, and Moose River. North Country Outfitters operate from "The Birches," a set of rustic log cabins on the western shore of Moosehead overlooking Mt. Kineo, where Thoreau camped on his famous north woods canoe trip into the headwaters of the Allagash region a century ago.

For those who wish to plan an independent trip, they offer a complete outfitting service including canoes, tents, camping gear, and food. Their canoes, which are designed for long trips as well as whitewater use, are made from A.B.S. materials, which have been proven tougher than both fiberglass and aluminum. North Country takes pride in offering only the finest quality equipment. They will arrange everything in advance so that all you need bring is a few personal items. For those who already own some equipment they can supply partial outfits. They also have high quality kayaks for the serious whitewater paddler. North Country's organized trips use only Registered Maine Guides. For those who wish to go it alone, a guide, although not essential, can add much to your trip as they know the best fishing spots and campsites. Registered guides are available on request. All of North Country Outfitters' trips begin and end at the Birches. For outfitted parties, ground transportation to and from starting and ending points may be arranged. Ferrying cars around to pick-up points may also be arranged. They have access to a local flying service which is equipped to fly canoes, equipment, and parties into and out of many remote areas. Rates and reservations are available on request. A boat shuttle service is available on Moosehead Lake to North East Carry for those who are limited for time but have a desire to see the north bay. Transportation from Bangor and Greenville to Rockwood can also be arranged. For rates and additional information, contact: North Country Outfitters, P.O. Box 81, Rockwood, ME 04478 (207)534–7305.

Northern Whitewater Expeditions is the oldest rafting company in the Northeast and the first company to take people down the Kennebec, Penobscot and Hudson Rivers, where they still run day trips. They use three sizes of rafts, depending on the water flow, with the largest for big rapids and smaller boats for calmer water to get the most out of any trip. Participants need no whitewater experience. A short instruction and practice session before each trip gives the basics in paddling and river running. Trips are designed for people 15 years of age or older, in reasonably good health and with an adventurous spirit. Special trips for children under 15 and elderly people can be arranged. Guides, life preservers, rafts and hot lunch cooked over an open fire all are provided by Northern Whitewater Expeditions. Rafters must wear tennis shoes and bring a dry change of clothes. Wet suits can be rented for cool weather rafting. The season runs from April through September with April the best month for high water on the Hudson, May the highest water on the Penobscot and June the most reliable month for both weather and water on the Penobscot and Kennebec Rivers. July and August are warm and comfortable and usually have sufficient water for exciting trips. In September, the rivers are deserted and the shoreline colorful. Reservations should be made well in advance. The *Kennebec*

expeditions begin at Harris Dam and run for 12 miles through Kennebec gorge, a total wilderness area. The river winds through a deep rock-walled canyon on one of the longest, steepest drops of any river in the country. Since the river is dam-controlled, there is usually good water from June through September. The trip starts and ends at Northern Whitewater's base in West Forks, with transportation provided to and from the river. Lunch is cooked on shore, where rafters can enjoy a short walk to Moxie Falls, the highest in New England, before returning to the river. The *Penobscot* expeditions go down the West Branch of the Penobscot River, beginning below Ripogenus Dam in high mountain country. The river falls rapidly as it passes Mt. Katahdin and alternates steep drops with calm stretches of water. Rafts are beached at lunchtime while the guides put on a shore cook-out. This trip starts and finishes at Millinocket. *Dead River* trips are special expeditions planned for July 3rd, 4th and Labor Day. This is a 15-mile trip and small four-man rafts are used. For information and reservations from June 2 through the season write Northern Whitewater Expeditions, P.O. Box 100, West Forks, ME 04985 (207)663–2271. From October through June 1st, write Northern Whitewater Expeditions, P.O. Box 57, Rockwood, ME 04478 (207)534–7355.

Scotty's Flying Service is a commercial seaplane operation that provides fly-in service to isolated lakes, ponds, streams, and sporting camps in the North Maine Woods. They have canoe, boat and motor rentals and several rustic housekeeping cabins on unspoiled lakes and ponds for fishing and hunting. These fly-in cabins are $10 per night per person and include gas lights, gas and wood stoves, bunks, cooking utensils, and use of canoes or boats. Special family rates are available. Registered Maine guides are available for fishing, canoeing or hunting trips. Scotty's Flying Service is located at beautiful Shin Pond, just 19 miles from I–95 on Maine 159, due east of Baxter State Park. For detailed information and rates, contact: Scott & Louise Skinner, Scotty's Flying Service, Box 278, Patten, ME 04765 (207)528–2626.

Webb's Wilderness Outfitters offers professionally guided canoeing and fishing trips in the northern Maine Wilderness as well as complete outfitting services from their north woods country store in West Forks. Fish for salmon, trout, togue at a variety of wilderness "hotspots"—miles away from the crowds. They have special "pack-in" type trips and four-wheel-drive power wagons to get you into the backcountry. A choice of trips to fit your budget and schedule start at $35.00 per person. This country offers the best beaver bog fishing you may find anywhere. Their canoe route takes you to several beaver bogs that are full of pan-size trout. Canoe the Moose, Penobscot—Allagash and several other great Wilderness Rivers of the Northeast for only a few dollars per person per day. Webb's will outfit, transport, and pick you up at your destination. Their canoe route also takes you over a deep cold lake that holds lake trout up to 20 pounds and also big salmon and brook trout. Professional Guide Service available by the day or for longer periods if desired. Prices start at $40.00 per day and include four-wheel-drive power wagon and canoe and guide. Webb's is equipped to outfit you or your group and provide transportation to and from your wilderness campsite at a very modest cost. Webb's has several scenic wilderness campsites available for your use. A special three day wilderness canoe and fishing trip with a Maine guide (restricted to a maximum of three per trip plus guide) includes three full days of fishing for salmon, trout and togue plus an overnight stay in a trapper's cabin. All-inclusive trip including food, shelter, and fishing license for $150 per person. For additional information, contact: Webb's Wilderness Outfitters, West Forks, ME 04985 (207)663–2214.

North Maine Woods & The Allagash

The legendary North Maine Woods tract occupies 2.5 million acres of evergreen forest in the northernmost portion of the state and is cut by two great wild rivers, the Allagash and the St. John. The Fish River Lake Chain, renowned for trophy landlocked salmon, has its headwaters in the tract. For centuries the NMW area was the prized fishing and hunting ground of the Abenaki Indians, who harvested the abundant fish and game, especially moose, bear, and woodland caribou. The region is bordered to the south by Baxter State Park and the Moosehead country, to the west by the Quebec border, to the east by Maine Route 11, which is Aroostook County's Potatoland Highway, and to the north by Maine's northernmost point, the Quebec border at Estcourt, Quebec. Hundreds of miles of maintained roads, jeep trails, and rugged logging roads provide access to the remote fishing, hunting, and canoeing areas. The lakes and ponds are justly famous for superb fishing for trout, togue, and whitefish. The streams offer some of the greatest brook trout fishing in the United States. Chamberlain, Churchill, Eagle, Spider, Munsungan, Haymock, Umsaskis, Ross, Chase, Priestly, and Telos are well known. The Musquacook Lakes hold brook trout in excess of six pounds and are considered by many fishermen to be the best trout waters in the state. Big Reed Pond, south of Munsungan, holds a sizable population of blueback trout. Wildlife of the North Maine Woods includes moose, bear, deer, marten, fisher, mink, otter, lynx, bobcat, ruffed grouse, loon, eagle, and osprey.

Information Sources, Maps & Access

For detailed information on travel in the North Maine Woods tract and the free *North Maine Woods Map/Regulations & Information Folder* and the free *St. John River Map/Brochure*, contact: North Maine Woods Association, P.O. Box 552, Presque Isle, ME 04769 (207)764–0016. For detailed information on the Allagash Wilderness Waterway and the free *Allagash Wilderness Waterway Map/Brochure* and *Allagash Wilderness Waterway Laws, Rules & Regulations*, contact: Maine Bureau of Parks & Recreation, Augusta, ME 04330 (207)289–2057. For detailed local information on Allagash and St. John water conditions and travel info, contact: Maine Forest Service Ranger Office, Allagash Village, ME 04774 (207)398–3196. Three extremely useful large-size maps, *Phillips' Map of the St. John-Allagash Wilderness*, *Phillips' East of the Allagash Map* and *Phillips' Map of Northern Maine's Moosehead-Allagash Region* ($1.50 each, plus 40¢ postage) may be ordered from Augustus D. Phillips & Son, Northeast Harbor 04662. These beautiful maps show all man-made and natural features, including trails, portages, fly-in services, Forest Service and paper company campsites, and logging roads. A free *Sportsman's Map of the Allagash, Chesuncook & Chamberlain Canoe Country* may be obtained from: Great Northern Paper Co., 6 State St., Bangor, ME 04401. The North Maine Woods tract and the Allagash Country are reached via State Forest Service Roads off Maine Highways 6/15 and 11. Maine Highway 11 provides direct access to the Fish River Chain and Allagash Village. Primary access to the interior lakes and headwaters areas of the North Maine Woods tract is by charter float plane service from Greenville and Millinocket. Official Lake Survey maps of North Maine Woods lakes and ponds may be ordered from the *Maine Lakes Index*, available free from the Dept. of Inland Fisheries & Wildlife, 284 State St., Augusta, ME 04333.

Recreation Areas

Allagash Wilderness Waterway

The Allagash Wilderness Waterway was established in 1966 by an act of the legislature, thus protecting forever this historic river. The wilderness contains about 200,000 acres, of which roughly 30,000 acres are water. One section of the law establishes a zone along the water where no cutting or building may be done. The Allagash region has been a major source of timber for over 100 years. Great virgin white pines, which once grew to heights in excess of 150 feet with girths of 20 feet, were logged out by the fabled Allagash rivermen, "Moosetowners" as they were called, for the coastal shipbuilders. The "Telos War" in 1846 was a dispute over the use of waterways for the transport of logs to the market. The remains of a 6,000–foot-long tramway on the piece of land separating Chamberlain and Eagle lakes can still be seen. The abandoned Eagle Lake and Umbazookus Railroad, with its two enormous locomotive hulks, is a popular sight. The NMW has attracted sportsmen for many years. Henry David Thoreau visited the Allagash headwaters in 1857; he was the first of many naturalists to recognize the great beauty and value of the Allagash country.

The Allagash, the Abenaki Indian word for "bark cabin," flows north for about 100 miles to its confluence with the St. John River. The trip can start at Telos Lake or at more northerly access points, and will take you through some magnificent country: granite-hemmed blue lakes, a deep green forest, and white-water river segments. The river flows through Telos, Chamberlain, Eagle, and Churchill lakes, through the exciting Chase's Rapids—nine miles of fast water—Umsaskis and Long lakes, Round Pond, past Musquacook Stream, and on to the impassable 40–foot-high Allagash Falls. The Allagash meets the St. John 14 miles downstream from the falls at Allagash Village. The river is not particularly difficult. It is a blend of fast water, dead water, lakes, and ponds. There are few dangerous places. During the brief period between ice-out and the end of June, the Allagash waterways offer often spectacular fishing for coasting lake trout and voracious squaretails up to five pounds. The most

productive "big-river" fishing on the Allagash is found along the pools and eddies of Chase's Rapids, in the 14–mile stretch below Allagash Falls, in the deep holes around the abandoned Long Lake logging dam, and at the mouths of feeder streams, using streamers, nymphs, or worms. There are few portages along the Allagash. Park rangers operate a portaging service at the five-mile Chase's Carry below Churchill Dam. Other portages include a 100–yard trail around Lock Dam at the head of Chamberlain Lake and at Allagash Falls, near journey's end. Maine Forest Service Rangers are stationed at Telos, Churchill and Umsaskis lakes, Long Lake Thoroughfare, and Michaud Farm.

Fish River Chain of Lakes

The Fish River Chain of Lakes lies partly in the NMW tract and offers some of the finest landlocked salmon fishing in the state, as well as good trout fishing. These lakes have yielded salmon of better than 20 pounds. There are eight major lakes in the chain: Fish River, the farthest upstream, followed by Portage, St. Froid, Eagle, Square, Cross, Mud, and Long lakes. Most of the big fish come from the downstream lakes. The Fish River and the thoroughfares between Eagle, Square, Cross, Mud, and Long lakes offer good fishing in the spring during the smelt run and in the fall during the spawning season. Several landlocked salmon weighing 18 pounds each were taken out of these waters in the fall of 1936. Seventeen small ponds on the headwaters of the Red River provide unsurpassed fishing for lunker squaretails. Canoeists will enjoy the Fish River in early season, but the level drops quickly and the river soon becomes impassable. The area is well known for its fall deer and bear hunting. On fishing and hunting trips in this region, guides will frequently call attention to beaver dams and houses, which are particularly numerous in the vicinity of Portage Lake, 60 miles from St. Agatha, a terminus of the Fish River Chain of Lakes canoe trip. The blueback trout is found in Gardner, Deboullie, Pushineer, and Big Black lakes in the Red River area.

St. John River Canoe Country

The St. John Wilderness Canoe Trail offers over 100 miles of prime canoeing and trout fishing water. In the early season fishermen have a good chance of hooking squaretails of better than four pounds. The river flows in a northeasterly direction through remote forest areas, where you are more likely to see a moose than another human, from its headwaters in the St. John Ponds to its meeting with the Allagash, where the upper portion ends. There is a good deal of heavy water in the early season, but the river drops quickly as summer starts and can become a real hull scraper. Highlights of the journey include Poplar, Priestly Brook, Big Black, Long, School House, Fox Brook, Poplar, and Big Rapids. Other points of interest are Depot Lake, Burntland Pond, Clayton Lake, Big Black River, Little East Lake, and Musquacook Mountain.

Gateways & Accommodations

Fort Kent—Gateway to the St. John & Allagash Wilderness Waterway

(Pop. 5,000; zip code 04743; area code 207) is a historic lumbering, fishing and hunting center across from New Brunswick, Canada on U.S. Highway 1 and the St. John River. The town is the terminus of canoe trips down the wild and scenic Allagash and St. John rivers. It's also, of course, the headquarters of numerous registered Maine guides who operate fishing and hunting trips in the vast North Maine Woods tract to the south. A popular area attraction is the restored Fort Kent Block House constructed in 1839 during the "Aroostook War" with Great Britain over the disputed Maine-New Brunswick boundary. Accommodations: *Rock's Motel* (rates: $24 double), with 26 good guest rooms on Main St. (834–3133).

Presque Isle—Gateway to the Fish River Lakes

(Pop. 13,000; zip code 04769; area code 207) is the commercial center of the Aroostook potato country and a popular jumping-off point for fly-in fishing, hunting, and canoeing trips in the Munsungan, Musquacook, and Fish River lakes and Machias River headwaters areas of the North Maine Woods tract. Aroostook State Park is located southwest of town off U.S. 1. Accommodations: *Keddy's Motor Inn* (rates: $36 double), with 82 excellent rooms, dining room, cocktail lounge, heated pool and sauna on U.S. 1, one mile south of town (764–3321).

Lodges & Sporting Camps

★★★★*The Bradford Camps* is a fly-in wilderness fishing and hunting retreat nestled on beautiful Munsungan Lake in the heart of the North Maine Woods. Munsungan Lake and the surrounding lakes, pools, and streams offer some of the finest wilderness fishing, canoeing, and hunting left in the Eastern U.S. The fishing here is for landlocked salmon, brook trout, rare blueback trout, and big lake trout. Fall hunting on the surrounding hardwood ridges is excellent for big whitetails, often in the 200 lb. class, as well as bear and partridge. Mile upon mile of canoe and hiking trails offer the wildlife enthusiast and photographer unlimited opportunities to sight moose, beaver, pine marten, hawks, waterfowl, herons, and bald eagle. Outpost camps are located on several trout ponds for guests who wish to plan overnight stays and who employ a guide. Canoes are available on many unspoiled virgin lakes and ponds that can be reached by air or trail. Camp accommodations consist of rustic guest cabins with panoramic views of Munsungan Lake, built of hand-hewn logs, equipped with modern baths, showers, hot running water, wood burning stoves and gas lights. Home-cooked meals are served at your private dining table in the main lodge dining room, with fresh vegetables and home-baked breads and pastries. American Plan rates are $36 per person per day with special discounts for children. Float-plane pickup service will be arranged for arriving guests. For additional info, contact: (summer) Bradford Camps, Patten, ME 04765; (winter) RFD #1, Turner, ME 04282 (207)225–3057.

★★*Chamberlain Lake—Allagash Headwaters Camps*, pioneered by Al

and Patty Nugent, are true north country sporting camps for the wilderness fisherman and hunter located on the shores of sprawling Chamberlain Lake at the headwaters of the Allagash Wilderness Waterway. Chamberlain Lake and surrounding ponds and streams offer superb early and late season fishing for lake trout and squaretails. During the fall the camps provide access to "big buck" country and superb partridge shooting. Camp accommodations are in hand-hewn log housekeeping cabins available for two or six guests. There are two camps that sleep ten and over. Wood, dishes, gas refrigerator, stove and lights are included. Boats, motors, gas, and guide service are available. Housekeeping cabins are $10 plus tax per person per day. Ideal for those who like to "rough it" in one of the nation's great north woods wilderness areas. The camps are reached by seaplane from Moosehead Lake or by auto along the beautiful scenic route to Chamberlain Bridge. There you will be met by boat and taken on an enchanting four mile trip into the camps. For additional info and reservations, contact: Nugent's Chamberlain Lake Camps, East Millinocket, ME 04430.

★★★*Fish Lake Camps* are located on an island in beautiful Fish Lake—a renowned lake trout, brook trout, and landlocked salmon fishery at the head of the Fish River Chain of Lakes. The original camps, established in 1895 as a sporting camp, have been improved over the years to make this a superb vacation retreat for fishermen and their families. Guest accommodations are in eight genuine, comfortable, picturesque, hand-hewn log cabins with views of the lake. The cabins have modern bathroom facilities and hot showers. Three home-style meals are served daily in the main lodge, noted for its massive twin fireplaces and rustic north country lounge, and library. Noted for their warm hospitality and informality, the camps feature professionally guided backcountry trips to remote wilderness ponds and streams. Boats, canoes, and motors are available for guest rental. Rates are $25 per day per guest and include a private cabin and all meals. The camps are open from ice-out in mid-May to Sept. 30th and are reached via charter float plane from Portage or via the Great Northern Paper Co. Private Road. For additional information and reservations, contact: Rod & Marie James, Fish Lake Camps, P.O. Box 104, Portage, ME 04768.

★★*Jalbert's Allagash Camps* are located in the Allagash Wilderness Waterway of Northwestern Maine, with excellent guides and comfortable cabins, and offer plenty of tasty food. The Allagash Camps specialize in trout fishing and canoeing. Trips can run from five days to two weeks. You have your choice of canoeing the length of the Allagash or using the base camp at Round Pond for side trips to the upriver lakes and downriver to the Allagash Falls. From base camp Jalbert's can also provide you with canoeing on the St. John River. The camps are accessible only by canoe which insures a genuine deep-woods type of vacation. All equipment provided. For information write to: Jalbert's Allagash Camps, P.O. Box 126, Fort Kent, Maine 04743 (207)834-5015.

★★★*Libby's Sporting Camps* are north of majestic Mount Katahdin on beautiful Millinocket Lake at the headwaters of the Aroostook River in the heart of the Maine Woods. This north country fly-in lodge offers superb fishing from the time ice goes out on Millinocket Lake for trout and landlocked salmon. Libby's also maintains completely equipped, remote fly-in outpost camps—Chaniller Camps, Big Caribou Camp, and the River Camp—for wilderness fishing, canoeing, hunting, or hiking. Libby's Home Camp cabins, constructed of peeled spruce logs, stand along the shore of Millinocket Lake. There are cabins to accommodate one to six persons and all are comfortably furnished. A roaring fire in the wood stove in each cabin throws out comforting warmth in the cool of the evening.

Delicious home-cooked meals are served daily. Libby's is reached by a 40 minute float-plane flight from Shin Pond on Maine 159. The camps open at ice-out in May and close at the end of deer season in November. It is recommended that reservations be made as early as possible. Guide service is available. American Plan rates are $28 per person per day—guides, boats and motors are extra. Outpost housekeeping cabin rates are $10 per person per day, plus air fare. Seaplane flights from Shin Pond to Millinocket Lake are $25 per person round trip. For additional information, contact: Libby's Sporting Camps, Ashland, ME 04732 (207)435-4202.

★★★*Moose Point Camps* is a traditional Maine fishing and sporting camp located on the east shore of Fish Lake, the first major body of water that comprises the famous Fish River Chain of Lakes. The lake is five miles in length with an average width of one mile. The surrounding shoreline, unspoiled by civilization, is covered with lush growths of pine, spruce, fir, and cedar blending into stands of hardwood on the hillsides of beech, maple and birch. This area is bounded on the north by the Canadian border, on the west by the Allagash waterway, on the south by the Machias River, and on the east by Route 11 and the town of Portage. Fish Lake and nearby ponds and streams hold landlocked salmon, brook and lake trout. Several virgin wilderness squaretail ponds are accessible by a short hike. Moose Point has an outpost camp on Carr Pond, which contains big lake trout up to 20 lbs. and over. The surrounding forests, ridges, and old logging roads provide good fall hunting for whitetail, bear, and small game. The Carr Pond Camp is equipped for housekeeping rentals during the summer months. The Moose Point Camps consist of separate cabins of hewn log construction located within fifty feet of the shoreline. Each cabin is comfortably furnished and complete with full bath. All meals are served family-style in the main lodge dining room with a commanding view of beautiful Fish Lake. Summer activities include fishing, canoeing, cookouts, hiking, bird watching, and wildlife photography. American Plan rates are $25 per person per day, with special rates for children. For additional information, contact: Moose Point Camps, Portage, ME 04768 (207)435-4091.

★★★★*Red River Camps* is a superb wilderness fishing and hunting retreat situated in the heart of the fabled Red River Lakes Country. This rolling big forest and lake country—noted for its old burns, swamps, beaver ponds, old trails and abandoned logging roads—

offers some of the finest wild brook trout fishing and hunting in Maine for deer, black bear, ruffed grouse, snowshoe rabbit, and bobcat. This area's spring-fed, unspoiled lakes and ponds hold wild brook trout, landlocked salmon, and lake trout, and feed into the famous Fish, Red, and Allagash River watersheds. This is one of the few remaining wilderness sporting camps in the East. The Camp offers superb fishing, hunting, hiking, canoeing, wildlife photography, wildflower study and bird watching, cookouts, and painting. Camp life is informal, with no planned schedules and your privacy is respected. The camps consist of 17 buildings, many constructed at the turn of the century, on the north shore of beautiful Island Pond. The rustic guest camps are constructed of hand-hewn logs and contain complete baths with hot water, gas lights, porch, wood supply and lawn furniture. Cabin girls provide daily cleaning and bedmaking service. A cabin boy tends to the wood supply. Red River Camps has a large library and North Country lounge in the main lodge, where delicious home-cooked meals are served family style.

Homemade bread and pastries are prepared daily. Shore dinners and packed lunches are available. A scenic, remote Island Camp built in 1901 with three bedrooms, a large living room, and stone fireplace is also available for guests. This camp, built of hand-hewn logs, is set high on a knoll on a small island with a beautiful view of the North Maine woods, lakes, and mountains. Canoes for guest use are kept on eight fly-fishing ponds, with boats as well on the larger lakes. Registered Maine guide service is available for fishermen and hunters as is 4-wheel drive rental. American Plan rates are $185 per week per person. Housekeeping rates are $10 per person per day. Special discounts for children. Delta Airlines serves the Presque Isle Airport, about 30 miles away. For additional information, contact: Red River Camps, Portage, ME 04768 (207)435-6000; (winter) 12 Cedar St., Presque Isle, ME 04769 (207)764-1256.

Travel Services

North Maine Woods Float Plane & Outfitting Services. For additional listings of float-plane services and outfitters serving the vast North Maine Woods tract, see "Moosehead Lake Region & Mount Katahdin" section.

Rangeley Lakes Region & The Sugarloaf Ski Area

The beautiful Rangeley Lakes region occupies the western corner of Maine where its border joins with those of New Hampshire and Quebec. Known as the "Switzerland of Maine," this scenic area is dominated by the spruce and fir-clad peaks of the Mahoosuc Mountain Range to the southwest, the Blue Mountain Range to the east, the

Kennebago Mountains to the north, and the cold deep waters, rich in trout and landlocked salmon, of the Rangeley Lakes. This 2,500-square-mile area is covered by a thick northern forest of spruce, fir, pine, birch, and maple, and contains hundreds of miles of fast-flowing streams, and many shimmering blue lakes and wilderness trout ponds. In the fall the crimson of the maples and the bright yellow of the birches are framed in brilliant contrast against the rich green background of balsam, spruce, tamarack, and pine, making a breathtaking sight on a clear blue day. Bear, moose, and deer find the dense forest to their liking, and you may see bobcat, lynx, marten, fisher, mink, otter, grouse, eagles, and ospreys in your travels on forest paths or along a rapid-filled stream. Hunters come back every year to try for deer and bear, and wing shots pursue the abundant partridge and woodcock.

The Rangeley Chain of Lakes descend like a series of steps from Kennebago Lake on the north to Rangeley, Mooselookmeguntic, the largest of the chain, and its arm, Cupsuptic, and Upper and Lower Richardson lakes. Rapid River, which spills through Middle Dam, the outlet of Lower Richardson, is four miles of wild pitches, chutes, ledges, and rips, interrupted by Pond-in-the-River, a 1½ mile pond in the upper third of the river. Rapid River drops 300 feet in elevation between Middle Dam and its foam-flecked merger with Umbagog Lake, the source of the Androscoggin River. Standing on the rock-ribbed bank you can look upstream and see the sharp pitch of the riverbed. This river is reputed to be the fastest piece of white water, for its length, in the East. The final two miles are not for the canoeist, and have only been run once in high water, by two professionals standing up in a freight canoe. Kayakers find the river a great challenge, and enjoy facing rugged stretches such as Hedgehog Pool and the boulder-studded Devil's Hopyard. The 14 deep, magnificent pools scattered the length of Rapid River have drawn fly fishermen for over 100 years to try for trout and landlocked salmon. If you hook a big fish in this heavy water, be prepared to do some fancy acrobatic footwork. The famous Maine author Louise Dickinson Rich and her family lived for many years at Forest Lodge, an old fishing camp on the river below the dam at Pond-in-the-River and wrote of her adventures in the moving 1943 best-seller *We Took to the Woods.*

Squire Rangeley, for whom the region is named, built and operated sawmills in the area in 1825. The great pine, spruce, and balsam forests lured woodsmen to the region throughout the early 19th century, and dams were built at Rangeley, Mooselookmeguntic, Lower Richardson, Pond-in-the-River, and Umbagog Lake to sluice the logs down through the chain to the Androscoggin River and the many lumber and paper mills along its banks. Logs were "boomed" or rafted in vast floating seas of wood and hauled down each lake by picturesque steamboats with raffish names such as the "Alligator." The booms were sluiced through each dam down into the next lake to their ultimate destinations on the Androscoggin. The log drive era, which continued into the 1930's, attracted some hard-bitten lumberjacks of various nationalities, and when these rivermen hit towns such as Berlin, New Hampshire, or Rumford after weeks on the lakes, the townspeople groaned, shuttered their houses, and stayed at home, while their respective communities reverted to the Old West for a few days, and the loggers "let 'er rip."

The Rangeleys are famed as the home of a giant strain of brook trout which grew to weights of 12 pounds. Fed by the hordes of their smaller cousin, the blueback trout, the size and numbers of these great fish were unequaled in the United States, and 19th-century experts argued over whether these outsized trout were indeed squaretails. R.C. Allerton, in *Brook Trout Fishing* (1869), tells about

a week's catch by his party of eight in June of that year. The 30 largest fish weighed from four to nine pounds and averaged 6¼ pounds. By the 1850's word started to spread about the incredible sport to be had in the lakes, particularly at Upper Dam Pool, between Mooselookmeguntic and Upper Richardson, a short piece of fast water at the foot of the dam. The wealthy and famous soon followed, and private railroad cars became a common sight at sidings in Bemis and Rangeley. Some of the well-appointed fishing lodges which sprang up to take care of the creature comforts of the gentleman sportsmen survive to this day. Third- and fourth-generation descendants still return to favored sporting lodges or family camps such as Lakewood Camps at Middle Dam. By the 1870's, fishing for the pressure-vulnerable squaretails had started a long, slow decline, although remarkable catches continued into the 1940's. Not content with the trout bonanza, the Oquossoc Angling Association stocked landlocked salmon in 1875. The more active, aggressive salmon preyed on the bluebacks to such an extent that by 1905 these fish, once so plentiful that farmers loaded wagons with them for use as fertilizer, were extinct in the chain. The bluebacks outlasted, by 50 years, the Abenaki Indians, who used the small char as a food staple. Smelts were introduced in the late 19th century to replace the fading blueback population, and still fuel the trout and salmon in the lakes. Although the fishing is not what it once was, good catches continue to be made, and every once in a while a fisherman will have his sturdy leader shattered by the incredibly powerful strike of one of the remnants of the native strain of giant squaretails.

Brook trout have contributed to the fame of several adjacent lakes and streams. Parmachenee Lake to the northwest of the Rangeleys was an exclusive club for many years and produced some superior fishing. The famed Parmachenee Belle fly was named in the lake's honor. Nearby Aziscohos Lake and its outlet, the Big Magalloway River, have drawn anglers for over 100 years, including President Eisenhower, to try for trout and landlocks. Kennebago Lake and River to the north of Mooselookmeguntic produce great trout and salmon fishing in the spring and fall. The beautiful lake is set in a bowl in the mountains surrounded by peaks, such as East Kennebago (3,791 feet), which exceed 3,000 feet. The scenic Kennebago River rises in the Island Ponds to the north of Kennebago Lake and flows south through a ruggedly mountainous forest area, passing through Little Kennebago Lake, picking up Kennebago's outlet, and flowing through two dams to its mouth at Mooselookmeguntic. In early season canoeists like to run the river and enjoy the exquisite scenery and abundant wildlife. Some vicious, boiling rapids, particularly those below Kennebago Lake, require portaging, but the trip is well worth the effort. The Sandy River rises in the Sandy River Ponds just to the south of Rangeley Lake and flows southeast through Phillips and Farmington to the Kennebec River below the town of Anson. This stream is noted for excellent brown trout fishing and is a popular canoe trip. The Mahoosuc Mountain Range, dominated by Old Speck Mountain (4,180 feet), and the Blue Mountain Range, crowned by Saddleback (4,116 feet) are crisscrossed by trails, including the famed Appalachian, and give the hiker the chance to travel through some exceptionally beautiful scenery and challenge some difficult mountain trails, which ascend most of the peaks. Stunning, panoramic views of the wild mountainous terrain will reward your efforts. In the winter, the mountains and surrounding areas, such as the Sugarloaf complex near Kingfield, offer excellent alpine and cross-country skiing.

The Sugarloaf Ski Area at Carrabassett Valley offers 150 days of superlative skiing on 36 miles of trails, with an average yearly snowfall of 15 feet. A 9,000 ft. four passenger gondola, five double chairlifts, and five T-Bars service this eastern giant, which sports a 2,600–foot vertical drop. The 36 miles of trails include 14 wide novice slopes, 16 panoramic, winding intermediate runs and 14 expert runs, with deep powder moguls and steep terrain to challenge any skier. In the spring, the above timberline snowfields open for spring skiing, to delight late season skiers. The Sugarloaf Ski School offers a variety of ski programs from learn-to-ski weeks and basic lesson plans to concentrated programs designed to make intermediate experts, and experts surpass themselves. The "Intensive Program for Strong Skiers" features introductory racing, on the spot video review, and 3½ hours a day of hard, fast skiing. The "Outer Limits" program uses mind games, muscular control techniques, and film analysis to enable each skier to reach the "outer limits" of his skiing ability. The Little Club School, in association with the Sugarloaf nursery, gets little tots on skis for 1½ hours daily. Sugarloaf also offers a "kids only" ski school program for ages 7–12, where first rate ski instruction is offered by ski instructors who specialize in working with kids. Competitive and freestyle events are well mixed with

Sugarloaf slapstick in the winter calendar of events. The Rossignol program competition commences the zany White, White World Week Winter Carnival, which includes body sliding championships, barrel stave races, torch light parades, fireworks, and nightly costume parties on fifties themes, western, and Italian mafiosi garb. In the spring Peugeot hosts a Grand Prix Pro Classic Giant Slalom, and there is Sugarloaf's world heavy weight skiers race, racers must be a minimum of 225 pounds to qualify. A sunrise service on top of Sugarloaf Mountain begins the Easter festivities, which include a boisterous costume parade on skis. Sugarloaf's most unique feature is the mountain village snuggled at the base of the slopes which includes a health club and sauna, a grocery store, bank, real estate offices, laundromat, six unique specialty shops, and seven delightful restaurants, with food ranging from deli fare to Italian cuisine and hearty steak and prime rib. Night spots offer a variety of entertainment, from single guitarists to folk groups, dance bands and jazz combos. For more information write: Sugarloaf Area Association, Kingfield, Maine 04947 (207)237–2861.

Information Sources, Maps & Access

For detailed information on the Rangeley Lakes Region and a free *Map of the Canoe Routes in the Rangeley Lakes-Aziscohos Area* and *Rangeley Lakes Region Trail Map*, contact: Rangeley Lakes Region Chamber of Commerce, Rangeley, ME 04970 (207)864–5571. For fishing information on lakes and streams in the Rangeley Region and guide service info, write or call: *Rangeley Region Sports Shop*, Box 850, Rangeley 04970, (207)864–3309. The beautiful, large-size *Phillips' Map of the Rangeley Lakes Region* shows all man-made and natural features, including logging roads, portages, fly-in services, fish hatcheries, Forest Service and paper company campsites, boat-launching ramps, and the Appalachian Trail. It may be ordered for $1.50 (plus 40¢ postage) from Augustus D. Phillips & Son, Northeast Harbor 04662. The strikingly beautiful *Phillips' Map of the Arnold Trail* shows the entire route of Benedict Arnold's historic trail from Madison to Eustis as well as the Appalachian Trail. This map shows all natural features, as well as gravel and logging roads, Forest Service and paper company campsites, public boat-launching ramps, and fish hatcheries. It may be ordered by mail for $1.50 (plus 40¢ postage) from Augustus D. Phillips & Son (address above). In the Rangeley Lakes Region, charter fly-in fishing and hunting trips and scenic flights are provided by *Steve's Air Service* (207)864-3347, Rangeley 04970. The Rangeley Lakes region is reached from the south by Maine Highway 4 or Maine Highway 26 and local roads, from east and the west by U.S. Highway 2 and local roads, and from the north by Maine Highway 16. Lodging, supplies, canoes, boats, and guides for fishing and big-game hunting are available at the towns of Oquossoc, Rangeley, Kennebago Lake, Stratton, Andover, Byron, Upton, Wilsons Mills, and Pleasant Island.

Gateways & Accommodations

Farmington—Gateway to Sugarloaf & the Sandy River

(Pop. 6,000; zip code 04938; area code 207) is located on the Sandy River in the beautiful Oxford Hills region. The town is a popular gateway to Mt. Blue State Park, Sugarloaf and Saddleback Mountain Ski Areas, and the Rangeley Lakes. The Sandy River has a well-earned reputation as one of the state's premier brown trout streams. Area attractions include the birthplace of opera singer Lillian Nordica and the Little Red Schoolhouse Museum, two miles west of town on

U.S. 2. Accommodations: *Farmington Motel* (rates: $26–30 double), with 39 excellent rooms, Pioneer House Restaurant, in nice location two miles east of town on U.S. 2 (778–4680).

Rangeley—Gateway to the Rangeley Lakes

(Pop. 950; zip code 04970; area code 207) has been a rustic, historic vacation center and gateway since the turn of the century for the famous Rangeley Lakes Chain, Upper and Middle Dam, Rapid River, Kennebago Lake and River, Parmachenee Lake and the Magalloway River, Saddleback Mountain Ski Area, the Appalachian Trail, and the ancient peaks and forests of the beautiful Mahoosuc Range. Rangeley Lake State Park is situated on Rangeley Lake. Air charter service, guides and outfitters are available in town. Accommodations: *Rangeley Inn & Motor Lodge* (rates: $18–25 double), located in the Rangeley Lakes region, and directly on Haley Pond. The town of Rangeley is a mountain village at 1600' elevation, and in the center of many year-round recreational activities. The Inn offers swimming, boating, hunting, skiing, snowmobiling, tennis, sailing, horseshoes, badminton, and hiking. There is good food—home baked goods, smorgasbords and lobster bakes. The rooms at the inn are spotless, comfortable and have full baths. The cabins, all situated near the shore, are fully equipped for housekeeping and house from two-four people. High season is June 15–October, winter rates slightly lower. Contact the Rangeley Inn and Motor Lodge, Rangeley, ME 04970 (864–3341).

Rumford—Gateway to the Rangeley Lakes

(Pop. 10,000; zip code 04276; area code 207) is a popular gateway for family vacationers, fishermen, cross-country and alpine skiers, and backpackers heading north to the Rangeley Lakes region,

Appalachian Trail, Saddleback Mountain and Sugarloaf Ski Areas, and Mount Blue State Park on Lake Webb. A popular area attraction is guided tours of the Andover Telestar Satellite Earth Station, located in the town of Andover on Maine Highway 120. Accommodations: *Madison Motor Inn* (rates: $30–35 double), with 64 excellent rooms, restaurant, heated pool, on U.S. 2, four miles west of town (364–7973).

Skowhegan—Gateway to the Carrabassett Valley & Moosehead Lake

(Pop. 7,000; zip code 04976; area code 207) is an old shoe and forest products manufacturing town on the Kennebec River and a popular stopover for vacationers heading north to the Moosehead Lake Region. Accommodations: *Lakewood Motor Lodge* (rates: $25–40 double), with 34 rustic guest rooms and family cottages with living rooms and fireplaces, restaurant, cocktail lounge, fishing, tennis, on lake, site of the Lakewood Summer Stock Theatre located five miles north of town on U.S. 201 (474–8513); *Somerset Motor Lodge* (rates: $18–20 double), with 30 good rooms and family guest cottages in nice location with private fishing pond, boat rentals, tennis, one mile north of town on U.S. 201 (474–2227).

Lodges, Inns & Sporting Camps

★★*Arnold Trail Inn* is an old loggers' inn built on Benedict Arnold's route to Quebec. The inn is open year-round with skiing on two of Maine's highest mountains—Sugarloaf and Saddleback—and over 100 miles of cross-country ski trails at the doorstep. The inn offers quick access to great spring and summer fly fishing for landlocked salmon and brook trout. Sprawling Flagstaff Lake is at the inn's back door. Other summer activities include mountain climbing and hiking the Appalachian Trail. Bird, bear, and deer hunting are popular in the rolling woodlands during the fall. There are comfortable guest rooms, two dining rooms featuring home-made soups and pastries, a cozy bar, and a large game room with fireplace. Rates range from $8–24 per person per day, based on a choice of American, Modified American, or European Plans. For additional information, contact: Dick & Elaine Andrews, Arnold Trail Inn, P.O. Box 16, Stratton, ME 04982 (207)246–2000.

★★*Bald Mountain Camps* are located in the famous Rangeley Lakes Region on Mooselookmeguntic Lake near Oquossoc, Maine, in the southwest part of the state. Situated 1,500 feet above sea level, Bald Mountain is truly a family resort with cottages on the lake front. There is excellent salmon and trout fishing in Mooselookmeguntic as well as in surrounding lakes, ponds and streams. There is also a clay tennis court, shuffle board, horseshoes, games and playground equipment for children. Water activities, including sailing, motor boat and canoe trips and water skiing down beautiful mountain streams, are all featured at Bald Mountain Camps. There are golf courses, riding clubs, antique shops and a fish hatchery nearby. All the cottages are on the lake front, with its beautiful white sandy beach. Each cottage offers modern conveniences with one or two private baths and from two to four bedrooms, along with an attractive living room and a wood-burning fireplace. New England-style cooking, with the best in seafood from the Maine Coast, highlights the three meals served daily. Famous Maine Guide cookouts and picnics are a regular feature. Rates for May and June are $33 per day per adult. For July, August and September, $36 per day per adult. Children under 12 are at a lower rate. The rates include three meals a day and lodging. For reservations and information contact Ronald and Aurore Turmenne, Bald Mountain Camps, P.O. Oquossoc Maine 04964 (207)864–7397 or (207)864–3671.

★★★*The Bethel Inn & Club* overlooks the picturesque village common

and the Longfellow Mountains to the west. The six handsome traditional buildings of the Bethel Inn compose a small village. There is a ski touring center, where skis can be rented, lessons arranged and ski trails begin. Toboggan hills surround the inn, and the nearby Sango Pond is popular for fishing and ice skating. T. Abrams downhill ski area, and Sunday River Skiway are skiing an easy distance away. The Bethel Inn has a sauna to relax in after an invigorating day outdoors, and a congenial cocktail lounge. A roaring fireplace in the living room is a favorite gathering place, and the cozy library with its own fireplace and private music room with a Steinway piano, are charming retreats. The dining room serves three meals daily, which feature fresh fish, fresh vegetables and meat dishes. In the summer, the Bethel Inn opens a beach lodge at nearby Sango Pond, popular for boating and fishing. There is a golf pro-shop and adjoining private golf course, tennis courts, and a heated pool. In the evening there is dancing to live music on the terrace. Winter rates at the Bethel Inn are $28–35 daily, single occupancy including breakfast and dinner, and $23–28 per person double occupancy. Ski week plans beginning with Sunday dinner and ending after breakfast Friday morning are $125–140 single occupancy, and $105–115 double occupancy. Summer rates range between $32–42 on the European plan. For more information write: The Bethel Inn and Club, Bethel, Maine 04217 (207)824–2175.

★★*Blue Ox Lodge at Sugarloaf* is a four-season apartment motel on the mountain in the Carrabassett Valley at Kingfield. Sugarloaf is world-famous for its skiing, and at Blue Ox the Birches chair lift is less than a five minute walk away. For Nordic skiers, the network of trails throughout the Carrabassett Valley begins at Blue Ox's front door. Terrain ranges from pure novice to expert with spectacular views of unspoiled mountains. Cozy, well furnished apartments offer ideal vacation homes with a grocery store, health spa and sauna, a laundromat, gas station, and a wide variety of interesting shops, restaurants and lounges nearby. Each vacation apartment is completely furnished with an electric stove with oven and broiler, large refrigerator, dining area with table and chairs, full bath and a convertible double couch, two daybeds, closet and chest of drawers. There are also freshly laundered sheets, towels and blankets. A ski locker room is provided for guests with an individual locker keyed to the room key and a waxing bench. One-, two- and three-room apartments, both with and without balconies, are available. Daily rates during the high season, December 22 through January 1 and February 16 through March 30, for apartments range from $37 for a studio without a balcony sleeping two people to $96 for a three-room apartment with a balcony sleeping seven or eight people. Summer

rates run $28 for a two-bed studio with an extra person at $7. For more information and reservations, contact Albert F. Webber, Blue Ox Lodge, On the Mountain, Sugarloaf, Kingfield, ME 04947 (207)237–2200.

★★*Capricorn Lodge at Sugarloaf*, is near all the essential skiing services and more—lodging, restaurants, shops, banks. A touring center is nearby and day nurseries are also available. The area is also noted for special events which last well into the spring with canoe races and whitewater river races. The Capricorn Lodge is nestled in the pines on the slopes of Sugarloaf Mountain and is a full-service lodge with old world charm and new world comfort. You can enjoy food, beverages by the fire, listening and dancing to the best in entertainment, a comfortable TV room or varied recreational facilities in the game room. Rooms are luxurious and spacious with private dressing rooms and bath—the outstanding feature is the "Thermasol" whirlpool bathtub and steam bath. Rates in the dorm start at $10 per person per day, and lodge rates start at $25 per person per day. European Plan and Modified American Plan are available. For reservations and further information call or write: Capricorn Lodge, P.O. Kingfield, ME 04947 toll free (1–800)631–1601 or (207)237–2801.

★★★*Carrabassett Valley Ski Lodges*, operated by the Sullivan Agency, offer a variety of rental accommodations for skiers at Sugarloaf.

Hotel Carrabassett, built during the winter of 1978, has fourteen oversized rooms with two double beds each, color television, plush carpeting and modern baths. Designed with luxury and comfort, Hotel Carrabassett fills the increasing need in the Sugarloaf area for first class accommodations. On the premises is Tufulio's Restaurant offering casual dining and a lively bar featuring nightly entertainment. A continental breakfast and dinner at Tufulio's can be arranged for hotel guests. There is also a gift shop, clothing store, real estate agency and a full service laundry. Shuttle service to the mountain is available and access to Sugarloaf's many miles of cross-country touring trails is at the doorstep. Rates range from $48 a night for one or two people to $65 a night for four people during the holiday season (Dec. 22 to Jan. 3 and Feb. 16 to Feb. 26) and from $39 a night for one or two people to $51 a night for four people during the regular season (Nov. 18 to Dec. 21, Jan. 4 to Feb. 15 and Feb. 27 to April 15.)

The Left Bank Condominiums are in the heart of the Carrabassett Valley's dining and entertainment center. Studio, one-bedroom and two-bedroom units accommodate from two to eight people at economical family rates. During the regular season, rates for a studio are from $34 for one night to $195 to seven days, and

rates for a two bedroom are from $60 for one night to $375 for seven days. Holiday season rates for a studio for one night are $42.50 and for seven days $243.75. For a two bedroom, $75 for one night, $468.75 for seven days.

Mountain Colony is a comfortable ski apartment complex just three miles from the Sugarloaf access road offering reasonably priced accommodations for families and couples. Mountain Colony offers studio, one-bedroom and two-bedroom apartments with kitchenettes and full baths. Rates range from $40 to 54 for two nights for a motel unit to $104 to 128 for two nights for a two bedroom unit during the regular season, from $50 to 70 for two nights in a motel unit and from $120 to 148 in a two-bedroom unit during the holiday season.

The Sullivan Agency also has ski home rentals at a cost which is generally far lower than hotel accommodations. Located within five miles of Sugarloaf, the rental homes are carefully inspected. Each home, typically, is fully carpeted, attractively furnished and features a Franklin stove or fireplace. Depending on size of home, rates range from $300 to 650 a week during the regular season, $350 to 800 a week during the holiday season. There are also weekend rates. For further information on ski home rentals, Mountain Colony apartments, Left Bank Condominiums and the Hotel Carrabassett, contact: Sullivan Agency, Valley Crossing, Carrabassett Valley, Maine 04947 (207)235–2300.

★★★*Center Lovell Inn*, a delightful country inn overlooking the White Mountains and Lake Kezar, was built in 1805. The inn is located near the Evergreen Valley, Pleasant Mountain, Sunday River, and Mt. Cranmore alpine and cross-country ski areas. Cross-country skiing is available from the inn's back door with miles of quiet, unbroken forest and meadows to explore. The surrounding Western Maine backcountry offers excellent fishing, canoeing, and bird-watching. The inn's dining room features Northern Italian cuisine and a superb wine cellar. The inn is located a half-hour from North Conway and two and a half hours from Boston. Rates are $20 per day double. Contact: Center Lovell Inn, Rt. 5, Center Lovell, ME 04016 (207)925–1575.

★★★★*Cobb's Bosebuck Mountain Camps*, a superb North Country sporting camp which has been in continuous operation for over 60 years, is situated in the heart of a 200,000–acre wilderness at the northern end of 15–mile-long Aziscohos Lake at the junction of the Big and Little Magalloway rivers—noted for their wild brook trout and landlocked salmon. Boats and motors are maintained at famous Parmachenee Lake and Lincoln Pond. Both are accessible by a 30–minute hike. During the fall, the camp is popular with hunters for deer, grouse and woodcock. Guest cabins at the camp, which is located 15 miles from the nearest public road, accommodate two-six people and are equipped with woodburning stoves, electric power and lights, hot and cold running water, showers, and bathrooms. Three delicious homecooked meals, with fresh baked breads and pastries, are served daily, family-style in the rustic lodge dining room. Picnic lunches are packed for those who wish to stay out all day. The main lounge has a panoramic lake view and Franklin fireplace. Boats, motors, or canoes are available for rent. Access to Bosebuck Camp is from Wilsons Mills, where a gate to the area is maintained. A gatekeeper is on duty from 7:00 a.m.–7:00 p.m. American Plan rates are $29–32 per person per day. Contact: Cobb's Bosebuck Mountain Camps, Wilsons Mills, ME 04293 (207)243–2945; (winter) Kingfield, ME 04947 (207)265–5411.

★★★*Country Cupboard Guesthouse at Sugarloaf* is a delightful 100–year-old farmhouse noted for its New England charm and hominess. Country Cupboard, which has recently been renovated,

offers rustic, peaceful year-round accommodations in newly carpeted and redecorated rooms and a new bunkroom with shared bath for skiers, summer hikers, backpackers, and vacationers. All rooms are spotlessly clean. The dining room is open to the public, serving all homemade and homecooked foods, breads, muffins, pies, and soups daily. "The best breakfast in town" is served from 5:30 to 10:30 weekdays and 7:00 to 10:30 on weekends. Call anytime for evening dinner hours and reservations. European Plan daily rates are $8.50–10.50 per person; Modified American Plan rates are $16–23.50 per person. Country Cupboard is located on Route 27 in Kingfield near the Sugarloaf Ski Area. For additional information, contact: Sharon & Bud Jordan, Country Cupboard Guesthouse, Kingfield, ME 04947 (207)265–2193.

★★★★*Deer Farm Camps & Ski Touring Center*, located off a quiet country road that used to be the main road to Canada, is surrounded by 60 acres of wilderness. The 200-year-old farmhouse now serves hearty country breakfasts, with homemade muffins, homefries, ham pancakes, and coffee, and hearty dinners with nourishing soups and hot fresh-baked bread. Skiers are lodged in cozy, rustic cabins which have one to four rooms, private showers, and are heated and carpeted, rates are $21.50 per person daily including breakfast and dinner, and $102.50 on a five day basis, and $143.50 weekly. Twenty six miles of groomed and marked ski trails surround the camps, encircling three frozen ponds, nearing the spectacular 60–foot Reed Brook Falls, and offering spectacular views of Sugarloaf from high ridges. Skis, boots, and poles can be rented from the touring center for $7. Traditional sleigh rides and moonlight ski tours greet winter in the Yankee tradition. Deer Farms is also open in the summer, with swimming, boating, fishing and canoeing on the ponds, tennis nearby, and weekly steak bar-b-que parties, and picnic hikes to Reed Brook Falls. For more information write: Deer Farm Camps, Kingfield, ME 04947 (207)265–2241.

★★★★*Grant's Kennebago Camps* on beautiful Kennebago Lake is one of Maine's great old time fishing camps noted for often superb wild brook trout and landlocked salmon fishing. This rustic lakeshore camp provides easy access to the renowned trout and salmon waters of Little Kennebago Lake and Stream, Seven Pond, Johns Pond, and the historic fly-fishing pools of the Kennebago River—the Pine Stump, Island, Canoe, Drinkwaters Bath, Cedar, Old Canoe, and

Johns Pond pools. Squaretails up to four pounds are taken from these waters each season. Kennebago Lake covers about five miles of good fishing. They have 16–ft. Rangeley boats to take you about the lake; these are equipped with 6½ hp motors, or you can row as you please. These boats are steady enough for two fisherman to stand and fly cast. The stream, with 20 good fishing pools and lots of white water, is approximately nine miles long. In the stream, as in the lake, there are landlocked salmon and wild trout. For the nature lovers, the many birds who live here and migrate through give added pleasure, as does the sighting of moose, deer, bear and many other animals. During the period from July 15th through August 30th, Grant's has fishing, sailboating, fly casting lessons from the docks, swimming, cookouts on the river, and canoeing. At this time a family rate is offered. For those who like to hike and bird watch, there are many trails. West Kennebago Mountain, with its Fire Warden Tower, elevation 370 ft., is a trip to plan for the day. Grant's rustic individual cabins are clean, comfortable and well screened. Cabins have modern facilities, and electric blankets on all beds. In the central dining room, with its "Old Fashioned Home Cooking," three big meals are served daily plus a box lunch when you leave camp for the day. American plan rates are $36 per person per day, with special children and off-season rates. The camps are located on the lake, nine miles into the woods off Maine Highway 16, three miles from the junction of routes 4 and 16 near the town of Oquossoc. For additional information, contact: Walter C. Davenport, Grant's Kennebago Camps, Inc., Oquossoc, ME 04964 (summer (207)864–3608; winter (207)864–3754).

★★★*The Lumberjack at Sugarloaf* is situated at the base of Sugarloaf Mountain and is the closest lodge to the new Carrabassett Valley Touring Center—which is within skiing distance. Although primarily a ski resort, there are activities offered during other seasons as well. In the spring, the area is a fisherman's dream. The lakes and streams abound in trout, salmon, and togue. The summer brings Maine's famous wild blueberry and raspberry season and there is hiking along the Appalachian Trail. The lodge is near fine golfing and swimming areas. Fall is the hunting season and the Sugarloaf region with its variety of terrain has an abundance of game. There are rocky crags for bear and bobcat, fields for partridge, woodcock and quail, heavily wooded lands for deer and moose, with marsh and swamp for duck. The inn itself has two beautiful clay courts for tennis—available spring through fall. The lodge offers 10 "chalet-type efficiency units" under one roof. Plank and beam construction create a warm rustic atmosphere. Each unit is complete with tile bath, wall-to-wall carpeting, kitchenette and dining area, large living room, bedroom and balcony and individual heat controls. Ideal for family groups or couples, the units will accommodate up to eight people. There is also a large central game room with TV, and ski and boot storage is provided. Rates, based on double occupancy, are $32—and are slightly lower from May to November. There are also ski packages available. There is no dining at the lodge, but many elegant restaurants nearby. Your hosts, Dick & Mary Fountain, request no pets, please. For further information contact them at The Lumberjack, Kingfield, ME 04947 (207)237–2141.

★★★★*Mountainside Condominiums at Carrabassett Valley* are clustered along the Buckboard Trail at Sugarloaf, and nestled at the mountain's base, among the shops, restaurants, and lively nightclubs. The plush, spacious apartments range in size from studios to five bedroom townhouses, accommodating two-twelve skiers. All units have spacious living rooms to relax in, many with fireplaces. Linens and firewood are provided. There are modern, fully equipped kitchens with dishwashers, and at least one private bath. Rates generally range from $70 for two in a studio for two nights, $140 for a two

night stay in a one bedroom, $162 for a two night stay in a two bedroom unit, $183 for a two night stay in a condominium with a capacity for six-eight skiers, $304 for a two night stay in a unit accommodating eight-twelve skiers, and $325 for a two night stay in a unit with a capacity for ten-fourteen skiers. Mountainside units are also rented on a five night, and seven night basis. For more information write: Mountainside Rentals, Carrabassett Valley, Maine 04947 (207)237–2000.

★★★*Pleasant Island Lodge & Cottages* is located on a peninsula jutting into an 18–mile lake in the heart of Maine's fishing and hunting country. The area is the center of the scenic Rangeley Lakes region and convenient to and from many other destination points. There are skiffs, and outboards and canoes for hire and many beautiful spots along the lakes or river to reach with them. Water skiing and riding the aqua plane are available—with instruction. Swimming is excellent from any of the docks; there are diving boards from two of them, and two sandy beaches for lounging. Fishing is a paradise in the streams and lakes. Some of Rangeley's finest trout and salmon can be found at the island. June and September are best for fly-fishing for trout, although as the waters warm, trolling for fish is quite successful. The island also provides an anchorage for seaplanes. There are two interesting trails on the island for hiking or drift-wood hunting or watching wildlife. Nearby is Saddleback Mountain for climbing or, if you wish, you can take the chairlift to the top for

the view. Many of the other surrounding mountains have excellent trails as well. The area also offers horseback riding, tennis (on clay), and golf—there are two fine nine-hole courses on the shores of Rangeley Lake. The lodge has basketball and horseshoes and a recreation room with ping-pong and a piano. There is a well stocked library and one television in the main building. Occasionally there are song fests or community games and a weekly lobster cookout. The facilities are rustic and informal and family oriented. There is a dining room serving full meals—but no bar—you must bring your own. Grouped along the lake shore are 13 log cottages—each rustically furnished with an open fireplace, living room, bedroom and bath. Each is separate and private and has a spectacular view. Daily maid service is provided. Some cottages will accommodate up to eight people. Rates, based on double occupancy, and full American Plan (all meals) are $60 daily or $400 weekly. There are reduced rates for children under 10, and no charge for infants. Cribs, etc. are provided. The season is late May to early Sept. For brochure of the Island and map of the area, contact Don and Pamela Young, Pleasant Island Lodge and Cottages, P.O. Address, Oquossoc, Maine 04964 (207)864–3722.

★★★★*Quimby Pond Camps* is a superb, rustic vacation sporting camp secluded in stands of spruce, fir and white birch on the shore of beautiful Quimby Pond, noted for its excellent brook trout fishing. Charming two- and three-bedroom log housekeeping cottages, with automatic heat and Franklin fireplaces, provide the comforts of home in this wilderness paradise. Quimby Pond and the surrounding hidden ponds and rolling woodlands offer trout fishing and hunting in the fall for deer, bear, partridge and woodcock. Quimby Pond is reserved for fly-fishing only and no motors are allowed. Boat and canoes are available at the camp. Fishing and hunting guide service may be arranged. More than 60 miles of hiking, bird watching, and hunting trails provide access to the interior areas. For those who select the American or Modified American Plans, delicious home-cooked meals are served in the main dining area. For the winter enthusiast, the camp offers cross-country and alpine skiing on Saddleback Mountain and guided snowmobile safaris with cookouts and overnights by registered guides along groomed trails. Daily rates are: American Plan, $33 per person; Modified American Plan, $30 per person; housekeeping cottages, two-bedroom camp for four persons, $25 per day or $168 per week. Quimby Pond is off Route 4, five miles from the village of Rangeley. For additional information, contact; Quimby Pond Camps, Rangeley, ME 04970 (207)864–3675.

★★★*Saddleback Lake Lodge* is a large roomy mountain lodge on beautiful Saddleback Lake with cozy pubs and fine country dining, surrounded by rustic cottages and restored log cabins overlooking the crystal waters of Saddleback Lake. Rushing mountain streams hold landlocked salmon, and trout, and the nearby Sandy River—a famous brown trout stream—is still panned for gold. Hikers and backpackers leave from here to hike the northernmost reaches of the Appalachian Trail. The cool lake waters are ideal for swimming, and canoes and rowboats are available to explore the far reaches of the lake. There are two new hard surface tennis courts on the open lawns, and a practice putting green to warm up on before tackling the challenging 18–hole championship golf course nearby. The mountain lodge houses a country dining room with huge picture windows capturing the lake reflection of Saddleback Mountain. Hot, fresh-baked breads, hearty entrees and homemade pastries make up each evening meal. The Milk Pail Pub is a favorite gathering spot when the sun goes down, and the rustic living room is lined with bookshelves full of unusual books, and has a roaring fire to take the edge off cool nights. Each of the rustic cabins has its own fireplace or woodburning stove, and a pine-panelled living room with hand hooked rugs and

old fashioned lamps. One-, two-, and three-bedroom cabins are available. Each has its own screened in porch with a view of the lake and surrounding mountains. The lodge opens in mid-June, when the streams are still swollen with the spring run-off, and closes in mid-October, when the mountains blaze with autumn color, and fires warm starlit nights. Cabin rates vary according to the size of the cabin and the number of people sharing it. Generally, cabin rates range between $31 and $36, including meals. Family rates are available. For more information write: Saddleback Lake Lodge, P.O. Box 620, Rangeley, Maine 04970 (207)864–5501.

★★★★*The Sugarloaf Inn* has a lift at its door, so guests can ski home after an exhilarating day on the slopes. Afternoon tea is served fireside, and cocktails are available in the elegant Victorian Lounge. Sixty ski-touring trails surround the inn, and skis can be rented from the nearby Carrabassett Valley Touring Center. There is a new indoor game room, a library, and ski movies. Hot home-baked breads and pastries, and nourishing home-made soups accompany the evening meals, which feature char-broiled steaks, fresh Maine lobster, and sumptuous buffets. On weekends, there is after-dinner dancing to live music. The 48 cozy rooms of the Inn have recently been renovated, and have soft carpeting, hanging plants, and panoramic views of Sugarloaf Mountain. Rates include both breakfast and dinner, and vary according to what part of the Sugarloaf season guests reserve. Single rooms are not available at the height of the ski season. Sugarloaf Inn offers a five-day ski plan, including lodging, meals and lifts. Plans including lessons and equipment are also available. Ground floor rooms are $35–38 single occupancy, and not available in the high season; $26–31 per person double occupancy throughout the season. Five-day ski week plans are $180–205. Superior rooms, on the second and third floors are $47–50 single occupancy, and $34–36 per person double occupancy, and $220–245 on the five-day ski plan. Deluxe rooms, on the third floor, offering two level suites with sleeping lofts, are $37–40 per person double occupancy, $33–38 per person triple occupancy, and $30–35 per person for four persons. The new Birchwood Condominiums, plush modern wood and glass apartments, are adjacent to Sugarloaf Inn, on the mountainside. The one-, two-, and three-bedroom spacious apartments offer ski-to-your-door convenience, and all the freedom and privacy of your own home in the midst of Sugarloaf skiing excitement, fine dining, and apres-ski entertainment at the Village. Each condominium has a spacious living room to relax in after the day's skiing, and fully equipped kitchens, and at least one full private bath. Guests are welcome to take full advantage of the facilities of the adjacent Sugarloaf Inn. Rates vary according to what part of the season condominiums are rented. Generally they range from $30–50 daily for a one-bedroom with private bath, $40–80 for a one bedroom with kitchen/living room area, and $60–105 for a two bedroom, plus sleeping loft, living room with fireplace, and kitchen, $80–125 for a three bedroom with sleeping loft, living room with fireplace, kitchen dining room area, and two baths. For more information write: Peter Webber's Sugarloaf Inn, Carrabassett, Maine, 04947 (207)237–2701.

★★★*Sunday River Inn & Ski Touring Center* is just a mile down the road from Sunday River Ski Area and minutes away from the Mt. Abram ski slopes. The aroma of fresh-baked breads greets skiers returning home from a day on Sunday River's 25 miles of marked ski trails that meander through the surrounding woods and fields. Sunday River ski rental shop offers a complete line of ski-touring equipment, clothing and supplies, a waxing and warming room. Skis, boots, and poles are available for $6 daily. The living room fireplace blazes continuously with warm fires all winter, and guests are welcome to bring your own and relax before dinner, or after the old-

fashioned, night-ski by kerosene lamplight. Home cooked meals, with hot bread just out of the oven, and homemade desserts close an exuberant winter's day. Cozy inn rooms are $25 daily single occupancy, and $21 per person for a double room. Dormitory space is also available, $15 daily, bring your own bag. All rates include two delicious meals daily. For more information write: Steve and Peggy Wight, Innkeepers, Sunday River Inn, RFD 2 Bethel, ME 04217 (207)824–2410.

★★★*Westways-at-Kezar*, built half a century ago as a getaway for Diamond Match Company executives, combines backwoods charm with up-to-date comforts in the midst of 130 densely forested acres. The lodge itself overlooks lovely Kezar Lake and is accessible from Boston, Hartford, and New York via interstate highways. Accommodations center around the main lodge with its big fieldstone fireplace and rooms for 14 guests. Private guest houses with 2–7 bedrooms are also available on a weekly basis. In winter, the lodge hosts ski touring buffs who come for the miles of trails in White Mountain National Forest—and for the private game rooms, handball courts, ice-fishing, and fine Yankee cooking. Summer activities run the gamut from horseback riding and tennis to hiking, fishing, sailing, canoeing and swimming. Local antique shops and country fairs offer lazy browsing on summer afternoons. Rates: $24–40 daily; $10 for children under 13. Contact: Westways-at-Kezar, Center Lovell, ME 04016 (207)928–2663.

★★*Wildwind Lodge & Camps* is sheltered in tall pine woods at the base of Bald Mountain on Mooselookmeguntic Lake, the largest of the Rangeley Lakes. Private lodge rooms, some with fireplace, are available in the rustic mountain lodge, whose unique root door handles, bark panelling, and bear-skin rugs show evidence of Indian craftsmanship. The old-fashioned wood-burning stove in the large living room warms many a windy night, and families gather around the piano after dinner. Wildwind's lakefront restaurant serves a variety of Swiss and American food. Fishing season begins with ice-out in April, and ends in September, when the lake reflects the brilliant autumn foilage. Troll Mooselookmeguntic Lake for landlocked salmon or brook trout, or fly fish the rushing mountain streams close by. Boats and motors can be rented at Wildwind for $7 daily. Canoes are available for $5. There is a wide sandy beach for swimming, and a log sauna house on the lake shore. Lodge rooms are $9–12 daily for a single room, and $16–20 for a double room. Private cabins have a living-room-kitchen area, complete with refrigerator, gas range, dishes and cookware, private bath, one and two bedrooms, fireplaces or a woodburning stove, and screened-in porches. They can comfortably accommodate two-six persons and

rates range between $110 and $155 weekly. American Plans, including your choice of room or cabin, maid service, and three meals daily are available for $30 per person per day, and economy plans, featuring your choice of lodge room or cabin and three meals daily without maid service, for $20 per person daily. For more information write: The Von Tobel Family, Wildwind Lodge and Camps, Bald Mountain Road, Oquossoc, ME 04964 (winter (207)597–2010; summer (207)864–3845).

★★★★*Winters Inn at Sugarloaf*, a stately turn-of-the-century inn, built on a hill overlooking the picturesque village of Kingfield and across from Sugarloaf Mountain, offers elegance and informal charm near the finest skiing in Maine. The Georgian Inn, with its grand hall, formal staircase, music room with Chickering piano, and 50–seat, candlelit French restaurant overlooking the mountains, is on the national register of historic places. Fifteen bedrooms range from bunkrooms to spacious two-bedroom suites. Winters Inn operates a free ski shuttle daily to Sugarloaf Mountain. Saddleback Mountain, the Bigelow Range, and Mt. Abrams are close by. A variety of weekend plans and winter week specials including apres ski parties, fine dining, lodging and evening entertainment are offered by Winters Inn, ranging from $52–72 for a weekend stay, to $162–222 for a long winter week. The new Balthazar's Pub offers respite by a roaring fire after an exuberant day outdoors. In the summer, the large pool and tennis courts open, with a backdrop of spectacular mountain scenery. The inn is surrounded by cool pine forests to hike in, and there are many country roads, book barns, and auctions to explore. For more information write: The Winters Inn, Box 44, Kingfield, Maine 04947 (207)265–5421.

Travel Services

The Andover Touring Center, operated by Akers Ski Shop, maintains several miles of gentle touring trails which meander through thick pine forests and ascend to 300 feet above the valley. Open forest clearings allow unlimited views of the valley, the picturesque town of Andover, the Telstar earth satellite station, and the surrounding mountains. Andover Touring Center rents waxless skis for $6 including boots and poles. Trail use fee is $1. A series of cross-country racing trails are also maintained by the center. The Akers Ski Shop specializes in Nordic ski clothing and equipment, and maintains a rapidly growing mail order business. Complete "starter sets" including waxable Akers Bear or Bobcat skies, poles, boots and bindings are $90. Non-wax Bear or Bobcat skis are $95–97, including boots, bindings, and poles. Akers also offers a variety of fiberglass skis, and Norwegian light touring skis, and a variety of touring boots, bindings, waxes, and accessories. The full line of racing and ski-jumping competitive

equipment is detailed in "Akers Competition Catalog." For a catalog, or more information about ski touring in Andover write: Akers Ski, Andover, Maine 04216 (207)392–4582.

The Carrabassett Valley Ski Touring & Mountain Recreation Center has 60 miles of ski touring trails over wide logging roads and across bright open fields under the bold face of Sugarloaf and the Bigelow Mountains. A full service log cabin overlooking beautiful Caribou Pond provides accommodations for up to 40 skiers. The new recreation center, recently built by the town of Carrabassett Valley on public reserve land, is a spacious pine and glass building which is solar heated and serves as a winter touring center, and hiking lodge and canoe outfitter in the summer. The center, which may be rented by private parties and recreational groups, has a unique two way fireplace, a ski shop, warming room with wood-burning stove, and a spacious sundeck with outdoor bar-b-ques. The Ski Rack Shop has complete ski touring outfits for sale, featuring high quality skis, and rents Rossignol wax and waxless skis. Complete rental packages, including skis, boots and poles are $7. Group lessons with professional ski touring instructors are offered for $3.50 an hour, and private lessons are $10. The recreation center charges a $2 fee for use of its 60 miles of groomed and wilderness trails. For more information write: Jack Lufkin, Carrabassett Valley, Maine 04947 (207)237–2205.

Pleasant Mountain, the second largest ski resort in Maine, is a 20 minute drive from the New Hampshire border. Three chairlifts, and three T-Bars service 20 miles of trails for every level of ability, from wide gentle novice slopes to challenging expert runs, all for a price a little less dear than is found at most Alpine resorts: lift tickets are $5 weekdays, and $10 weekends and holidays. At the base there are two lodges with cafeterias, a ski shop, rental shop, nursery, night club and lounge. At the top, there is a summit warming hut, offering panoramic views of the White Mountains and the Longfellow Range. Pleasant Mountain Ski School features the American Teaching Method for beginners, and promises to make good skiers better in their "from bumps to boogie" class. Group 1½ hour lessons are $6, private one hour lessons are $12. Good skiers class, $20. In addition, Pleasant Mt. Ski School offers lessons for three-six year olds, known as "mogul mice," for $5. "Mini-Masters", five-ten year olds, are taught different aspects of skiing, such as racing and freestyle, for 1½ hours on Saturday and Sunday, $50. Training for racing and freestyle competition is also offered by the ski school. For more information write: Pleasant Mt. Ski Area, Bridgton, Maine 04009 (207)647–2022.

Southern Maine Vacationlands & The Coastal Islands

The southern Maine vacationland offers traditional summertime vacation activities in populated areas, and at the same time some surprisingly good fishing and hunting, canoeing, camping, and cross-country skiing and hiking in the famous Sebago Lake area, Belgrade Lakes, Oxford Hills, and the Androscoggin River and the lower sections of the Kennebec and Penobscot rivers—the three largest rivers in Maine, which drain the area. The region contains sizable forest areas, hundreds of lakes, ponds, and streams, and rolling green hills and mountains.

The crystal-clear waters of Sebago, the second-largest lake in Maine at 14 miles long and 11 miles wide, reach a depth of 400 feet and are the native habitat of acrobatic landlocked salmon, brook trout, and black bass. On the shore of Sebago in North Windham, where one of the largest Indian burial grounds in the United States was discovered and thousands of Indian relics have been collected, the storied Songo River connects Sebago Lake to the north with Long

Lake. Scores of other lakes and ponds, such as Little Sebago, Panther Pond, Crescent Lake, Thomas and Moose ponds, and Pleasant, Highland, and Woods lakes, dot this area. Sebago Lake is one of the original homes of the landlocked salmon and has been honored by the fish's Latin name, *Salmo salar sebago*. The state record landlock was taken in Sebago Lake in 1907. A giant 36–pound landlock was netted by Fish & Game officials during the previous year. Sebago holds more state records than any other body of water in Maine: landlocked salmon, brown trout, chain pickerel, and whitefish. Moose Pond, a close neighbor, yielded the record largemouth bass. Easterners look forward to the news each spring that the ice has gone out on Sebago, and another Maine fishing season has begun. The Sebago fishery region occupies all of southern Maine to Brunswick and north to Rumford in the Oxford Hills. Major lakes, streams and canoe trails include Long Lake, Little Sebago, the Songo and Saco rivers, and Lake Pennesseewassee. Lovewell Pond is named for a Captain Lovewell who was killed by Indians, after a savage battle in 1725, the so-called Lovewell's War. A more fortunate colonist was a fellow named Frye who, when chased by Indians, scaled down a steep cliff on Sebago's Frye Island, dropped to the beach, and escaped from the amazed war party. The Indians made pictographs on the cliff's face to commemorate the event. The scenic Belgrade Lakes region is located just north of Augusta and near the lower Kennebec River. The Belgrade area has been a popular fishing, canoeing, and vacationing spot for many years. Great, North, East, Ellis, Long, and McGrath ponds and Messalonskee Lake make up the scenic chain. Messalonskee holds the state record for white perch, a hefty four pounds ten ounces.

Warmwater species such as bass, pickerel, and perch predominate, and they run to large size. Some big landlocks and trout are taken from a few of the waters, particularly Messalonskee.

The Oxford Hills region occupies the western border of Maine between the Androscoggin River to the north and Sebago Lake to the south. This mountainous area is dotted with lakes, ponds, streams, and bogs. Major features of the Oxford Hills include the Evans Notch segment of the White Mountain National Forest on the New Hampshire border: Mounts Abram, Black, Caribou, Tir'em, Speckled, Royce, Ames, and Zircon, Lake Kezar, Little Concord Pond, the Bryant Ponds, and the Androscoggin River. The *AMC Maine Mountain Guide* will tell you what you need to know about the extensive trail system in this famous hiking country. Hunting is good in season for deer, ruffed grouse, snowshoe rabbits, and woodcock. Bass, pickerel, and perch are found in most lakes and ponds. Kezar Lake has a good population of salmon and brown trout, as well as warmwater species. Worthley Pond, near Rumford, produces some hefty brown trout exceeding six pounds, but they are extremely wary. Lake surveys are available for most of the lakes and ponds.

To the south, Maine's jagged 2,300–mile coastline angles northeast to southwest in a seemingly endless series of rocky islets and bays bordered by ancient spruce-clad mountains and valleys. More than 1,200 incredibly scenic islands, some little more than giant rocks, jut up from the waters off the wave-pounded, often fog-shrouded coastline. This labyrinth of isles such as famous Mount Desert, Isle au Haut, Cranberry, Duck, and Monhegan, lures thousands of

family vacationers, backpackers, canoeists, and sailors each summer. The islands are inhabited by seals and a great variety of birds, including seagulls, terns, herons, great cormorants, Canadian geese, and ducks. Deer can often be seen feeding along the shore edges of the island forests. Red squirrel, fox, northern cottontail, woodchuck, otter, snowshoe hare, and many species of whale can be seen, as well as seals in the secluded rocks and ledges. Several down east sailing firms operate summer schooner trips along the scenic Maine coast. These magnificent 19th–century sailing ships have been converted to the windjammer trade by the addition of staterooms, fully equipped galleys, and modern safety equipment.

Information Sources, Maps & Access

The following publications may be obtained from the Maine Dept. of Inland Fisheries & Wildlife, State House, Augusta, ME 04333: *Maine's Fishery Regions:* Sebago (B–288, 45¢) and *Maine's Rivers: The Saco* (B–165, 35¢). The southern Maine vacationland is reached via Interstate 95 and U.S Highways 2, 202, and 302. Lodging, supplies, guides, canoes and boats, and gear are available at the hundreds of towns and villages scattered throughout the Sebago-Long Lake region, Belgrade Lakes region, and Oxford Hills.

Gateways & Accommodations

Auburn

(Pop. 23,000; zip code 04210; area code 207) is a major southern Maine gateway to the Androscoggin River Country, Lake Auburn, and Sabattus Pond, situated on Maine Highway 4. The Lost Valley Ski Area is located five miles to the northwest off Maine Highway 11. Accommodations: *Holiday Inn* (rates: $29–37 double), with 120 excellent rooms, restaurant, cocktail lounge, swimming pool and kennel, four miles south of town on U.S. 202 at Maine Turnpike Exit 12 (783–1454).

Augusta

(Pop. 22,000; zip code 04330; area code 207), the capital of the Pine Tree State since 1832, is located off Interstate 95 on the Kennebec River. This one time fur trading center includes Capt. Myles Standish among its original settlers. Area attractions include the state capitol; Maine State Museum with fish and wildlife displays in the State Cultural Building; and the restored Fort Western Museum at Bowman and Cony Streets, originally constructed on the Kennebec River in 1754. Accommodations: *Howard Johnson's Motor Lodge* (rates: $38.50 double), with 103 excellent rooms, restaurant, cocktail lounge, swimming pool off Interstate 95 Augusta-Belgrade Exit on Maine 8 (622–4751).

Boothbay Harbor—Gateway to the Coastal Islands

(Pop. 2,200; zip code 04538; area code 207) with its quaint village streets and old wharfs is a famous coastal vacation spot and center of the picturesque fishing villages of the Boothbay Harbor region, including the towns of Bath, site of the Bath Iron Works shipbuilding center and the Davenport Museum with its paintings of old ships and original half-models; Wiscasset, with its stately old houses, believed to be the setting for Eugene O'Neill's "Mourning Becomes Electra"; North Edgecomb on the Sheepscot River, site of the old block house now at Fort Edgecomb and the Marie Antoinette House; East Boothbay on the western shore of Linnekin Bay, with its old shipyards and the century-old Hodgdon Tide Mill; Damariscotta with its Indian middens built of oyster and clam shells; the gray wharfs, lobster pots, fishing nets, and dories of New Harbor on the Pemaquid Peninsula; Pemaquid Beach, an old fishing and vacation center and the site of a replica of the Tower of Fort William Henry, built in 1692; and Waldboro, a popular summer vacation center and

fishing village. Boothbay Harbor, situated on the peninsula between the Sheepscot and Damariscotta rivers, is a popular jumping-off point to the incredibly scenic coastal islands, such as Monhegan, Squirrel, Mouse, and Damariscove. Area attractions include scenic coastal cruises and fishing trips departing from Fisherman's Wharf, Boothbay Playhouse, Grand Banks Schooner Museum at 100 Commercial St., McKown's Point Marine Aquarium (two miles southeast of town), and the Boothbay Railway Museum, located 3½ miles north of town on Maine Highway 27. Accommodations: *Brown Bros. Wharf & Restaurant* (rates: $47 double), with 46 excellent rooms and family units overlooking the harbor, dining room, cocktail lounge, fishing trips and marina at Atlantic Ave. (633–5440); *Fisherman's Wharf Inn & Motel* (rates $40 double), with 54 superb rooms and family units, dining room, cocktail lounge, overlooking the harbor on Fisherman's Wharf at 42 Commercial St. (633–5090); *Ocean Gate Motor Inn & Restaurant* (rates: $34–44 double), with 60 superb guest rooms and cottages, dining room, cocktail lounge, dock, fishing, boat rentals, tennis in beautiful ocean setting on Maine Highway 27, 2½ miles south of Boothbay Harbor (633–3321); *Rocktide Motor Inn & Restaurant* (rates: $36–52 double), with 52 excellent guest rooms, balconies overlooking the harbor in charming maritime architectural design, and superb dining, cocktail lounge, at 45 Atlantic Ave. (633–4455).

Brunswick—Gateway to the Maine Coast & Islands

(Pop. 17,000; zip code 04011; area code 207), the home of Bowdoin College, is noted for its attractive tree-lined streets and stately mansions. The town is a popular stopover for vacationers heading east to the Maine Coast. Of interest to travelers are the Peary-Mac-Millan Arctic Museum and Art Museum at Bowdoin College and the Penobscot Historical Society Museum at 11 Lincoln St. with displays of early Americana and Civil War exhibits. Accommodations: *Holiday Inn* (rates: $44.75 double), with 110 excellent rooms, restaurant, cocktail lounge, heated pool, on Maine Highway 24 (729–3317); *Stowe House Motor Inn* (rates: $38.50 double), with 54 excellent rooms, dining room, cocktail lounge, at 63 Federal St. (725–5543).

L.L.Bean®
Spring 1979

Freeport—Home of L.L. Bean, Outdoor Sporting Specialists

(Pop. 5,000; zip code 04032; area code 207) is world famous as the headquarters of L.L. Bean Retail Store and the *L.L. Bean Catalog*. Leon Leonwood Bean, known to outdoorsmen nationwide as L.L., launched his famous North Maine Woods empire in 1913 with a borrowed $400 and a parctical, homely creation: the now legendary

Maine hunting shoe. L.L. was tired of trekking home with wet and sore feet from wearing the heavy woodsman boots then in use. Rubber boots were too clammy and clumsy for all-day use. His new boot combined light-weight leather tops with all-rubber bottoms, incorporating the best features of both boots in use, and doing away with the disadvantages. Bean's business grew rapidly as fishermen and hunters discovered the comfort and warmth provided by this curious boot. For bare-ground walking it was light in weight, with a snug fit, cushioned innersole, and a chain tread outersole for traction. The waterproof bottoms proved ideal for hunting in wetlands and on snow. The revolutionary split backstay eliminated chafing. Today the Maine hunting shoe is the most widely used sporting boot in the world. Its success launched the worldwide North Maine Woods mail-order business contained in the pages of the famous *L.L. Bean Catalog*, which is mailed four times a year to a million outdoor enthusiasts in 50 states and 70 foreign countries. Bean's merchandise-packed, 10,000–square-foot retail salesroom is housed in a rambling wooden building in Freeport, accessible by two flights of stairs. The salesroom, visited annually by thousands of North Maine Woods-bound sportsmen and browsers, is open 24 hours a day, 365 days a year. During the peak summer months it's wall to wall with customers until 3:00 or 4:00 a.m. L.L. started keeping the store open all night in 1954 when he tired of being awakened at all hours of the night and early morning to serve newly arrived outdoorsmen and vacationers, who often traveled hundreds and even thousands of miles to visit this north country landmark. A free copy of the *L.L. Bean Catalog* may be obtained by writing L.L. Bean, Freeport 04032. Accommodations: *Casco Bay Motel* (rates: $28 double), with 16 good rooms, two miles south of town on I–95 (865–4925).

Kennebunkport

(Pop. 3,000; zip code 04046; area code 207) is the center of a century-old shipbuilding, fishing, and vacation resort area at the mouth of the Kennebec River. Scenic attractions include the rocky, wave-pounded shores along Cape Arundel, Cape Porpoise, Walker's Point, and Goose Rocks Beach. Of interest is the Seashore Trolley Museum, northeast of town off U.S. 1 on Log Cabin Road. There are two summer theatres in the area—the Kennebunkport Playhouse and the Ogunquit Playhouse. Accommodations: *The Colony* (rates: $88–102 double), with 140 excellent guest rooms, dining room, cocktail lounge, heated pool, deep-sea fishing, sailing, in beautiful location overlooking the ocean at King's Rd. and Ocean Dr. (967–3331); *Old Fort Club* (rates: $40–50 double), with superb units in restored rustic, carriage house with heated pool and tennis court on Old Fort Ave. (967–2709).

Ogunquit

(Pop. 1,000; zip code 03907; area code 207) is a picturesque summer resort and art colony noted for its three-mile-long sand beach and beautiful Perkins Cove, connected to the village by a one-mile-long trail that winds along the rocky shore and cliffs. Each summer, art exhibits are displayed at the Barn Gallery, Ogunquit Museum of Art and the Art Center. Excellent seafood dining is available at the Whistling Oyster and Ogunquit Lobster Pound. Outstanding summer theatre is available at the famous Ogunquit Playhouse. Accommodations: *Cliff House* (rates: $54–60 double), with 73 excellent guest rooms, dining room, cocktail lounge, swimming pool, tennis court at Bald Head Cliff (646–5124); *The Dunes* (rates: $25–42), with 36 excellent rooms and guest cottages with fireplaces, beach, boat rentals in beautiful ocean front location, just north of the village on U.S. 1 (646–2612); *Ogunquit Motel* (rates: $35–39 double), with 47 good rooms, restaurant, heated pool, 1¼ miles north of the village on U.S. 1 (646–2471).

Portland—Gateway to Sebago Lake & the Maine Coast

(Pop. 60,000; zip codes, see below; area code 207) is the Pine Tree State's largest city and commercial center, located off Interstate 95 at the head of beautiful Casco Bay—famous for its picturesque Calendar Islands. Cruises to the Calendar Islands, which number 365, are provided by Casco Bay Lines at the Custom House Wharf (774–7871) and Buccaneer Line at the central wharf off Commercial St. (799–8188), with cruises to House Island. Other area attractions include the Wadsworth-Longfellow House at 487 Congress St., Portland Observatory built in 1807 at 138 Congress St., and the historic Portland Headlight, one of the nation's oldest lighthouses, built in 1791. Accommodations: *Holiday Inn West* (rates: $46 double), with 206 excellent rooms and family units, restaurant, cocktail lounge, heated pool off I–95 exit 8 at 81 Riverside St., Portland 04103 (774–5601); *Howard Johnson's Motor Lodge* (rates: $44–48 double), with 120 excellent rooms, restaurant, heated pool and sauna, cocktail lounge off I–95 exit 8 at 155 Riverside St., Portland 04103 (774–5861).

Portsmouth, New Hampshire— Gateway to the Maine Woods & Coast

(Pop. 30,000; zip code 03801; area code 603) on the Maine-New Hampshire border, once the booming center of the West India Yankee Clipper trade, today is the site of the famous Portsmouth Navy Yard. Portsmouth is a popular stop for vacationers heading east to the Maine Woods and coastal resort areas. A *State of Maine Information Center* is located across the Piscataqua River Bridge just north of the junction of U.S. 1 and Interstate 95 in Kittery. This renowned shipbuilding center at the mouth of the Piscataqua River is noted for its charming Georgian houses and narrow, crooked streets around Puddle Dock, which follow the paths traveled by the early sea captains. The historic 18th–century mansions of Portsmouth include the Moffat-Ladd House on Market St., built in 1763; John Paul Jones House at the corner of Middle and State Sts., built in 1758, and the Warner House, built in 1718. Other beautiful mansions are the Pierce Mansion on Haymarket Square and the Governor John Langdon House. The Portsmouth Navy Yard, situated on an island at the river's mouth, is reached by U.S. 1 across the Piscataqua in Kittery, Maine. Accommodations: *Howard Johnson's Motor Lodge at the Interstate Traffic Circle* (rates: $39.90 double), off I–95 Exit 5 with 54 excellent rooms, restaurant, heated pool (436–7600).

Waterville—Gateway to the Belgrade Lakes

(Pop. 16,000; zip code 04901; area code 207) is a famous manufacturing town on the banks of the Kennebec River. The town is a popular stopover for vacationers on their way to the northern Maine lakes and woods and the nearby Belgrade Lakes—Long, Great, and East ponds. Area attractions include Old Fort Halifax, built in 1754, located one mile east of town on U.S. 201 in Winslow; Redington Museum at 64 Silver St. with displays from 19th–century Waterville; and the Colby College Museum of Art, with collections of famous European and American artists such as Winslow Homer. Accommodations: *Holiday Inn* (rates: $40 double), with 92 excellent rooms, restaurant, coffeeshop, heated pool on Maine Highway 104 off Main St. exit I–95 (873–0111); *Howard Johnson's Motor Lodge* (rates: $34.50 double), with 86 excellent rooms, restaurant, coffeeshop, cocktail lounge, heated pool on Maine Highway 104 off Main St. exit I–95 (873–3335).

Lodges, Inns & Sporting Camps

★★★*Alden Camps* is nestled on the wooded shores of the clear, spring-fed East Lake, the first of the Belgrade chain of Lakes. Spacious cabins, with rustic wood-panelled living room-sleeping

room combinations, and two- and three-bedroom cottages dot the lake shore, shaded in birch and maple groves. Each cabin is brightly carpeted, furnished with handsome beds and old fashioned rocking chairs, and has a screened-in porch, and wood-burning stoves for cool nights. Motor boats are available on a daily and weekly basis to fishermen eager to troll the lake, famous for excellent smallmouth bass fishing. Swimmers can plunge into the cool, clear waters off the dock; sun-bathers enjoy the sandy beach. Afternoon softball games on the open playing fields, and shuffleboard tournaments in the recreation barn are part of the informal recreation program at Alden Camps. Breakfasts, packed picnic lunches, and generous buffet style dinners are all included in cabin rates. Full steak dinners with all the trimmings, and fresh Maine lobster clambakes highlight each week's menu. Tennis courts are open daily, and there is an 18–hole championship golf course at the nearby Waterville Country Club, where Alden guests have privileges. There are a variety of book barns, antique shops, and country fairs in the area to enjoy. Cottage rates, including meals are $26–35 daily in combined living-sleeping rooms accommodating one-three people. Rates vary according to the number of people. Weekly rates are $154–210. Cottages with living rooms and two bedrooms accommodating two-four people range from $26–35 depending on the number of people, and $154–196 weekly. Three bedroom cottages, with living rooms accommodate three-six people. Rates vary from $26–35 daily and $154–182 weekly. Alden Camps also offers fishing vacations and get-away specials for three days at $75. Weekend specials are $52 per person. For more information write: Alden Camps, East Lake, ME 04963 (207)465–7703.

★★*Appalachian Mountain Club North Woods & Coastal Camps* are group summer recreation camping sites for members and nonmembers (at slightly higher rates) that serve as convenient resting areas and base camps for the family camper, backpacker, naturalist, or wilderness paddler. Most of the camps are in scenic north woods backcountry and coastal areas. The *Swan's Falls Campground*, on the banks of the Saco River in Fryeburg, is a family campground in the White Mountains, with many remote, spacious campsites for families, individuals, and organized groups. The camp is open from June 19 through Labor Day and on weekends during the spring and fall. *Walker's Falls*, the most remote of the AMC Saco River campgrounds, is 14 miles downstream from Swan's Falls and is designed to serve as an overnight stop for canoeists, although many campers extend their visit to enjoy its idyllic wilderness setting. The camp is open June 15 through Labor Day. The *Beal Island Camp*, at Georgetown, accessible by canoe or boat from Bath, is 64 acres of

scenic coastal woodlands surrounded by the tidal waters of the Sasanoa River. The island is a scenic wilderness retreat for canoeists of all levels of experience and ability. The primitive *Knubble Bay Camp*, on Georgetown Island, is used by hikers, canoeists, and family vacationers. The idyllic *Fort Island Camp* on the Damariscotta River is open year round and provides the tidewater canoeist with a base camp from which he can explore the Maine coast from Pemaquid Point to Beal Island, 13 miles to the west. The *Swans Island Camp*, once the home of the Abenaki Indians and presently a wildlife refuge, is an ideal year round family campground operated by the Island Fisheries & Game Commission on the Kennebec River. Canoeists can travel upriver with the tidal flow to the old Colburn House—a jumping-off point for Benedict Arnold's 1775 winter expedition to capture Quebec—or canoe downriver with the ebb tide to Merrymeeting Bay, Bath, and Beal Island. This scenic island camp has ten Adirondack shelters around a green meadow. A ferry will provide transportation to the island from the Steve Powell Game Management Area dock in Richmond. The *Echo Lake Camp*, Mount Desert 04660, (207)244–3747, is in the beautiful coastal highlands of Acadia National Park near the south end of Echo Lake just off the road to Southwest Harbor. This is a scenic tent camp with excursions to outer islands and overnight trips to Mount Katahdin and Baxter State Park. For complete information on these and other AMC camps (and for membership info and application forms), write: Appalachian Mountain Club, 5 Joy St., Boston MA 02108 (617) 523–0636.

★★★*The Chute Homestead* is nestled at the edge of Long Lake, a 12–mile-long lake, 30 miles from the seacoast city of Portland, in the foothills of the White Mountains. Long Lake crowns the Sebago chain, a series of lakes and connecting streams forming a 40–mile waterway to fish, canoe, and explore on foot. Every week, the Chute Homestead offers a canoe trip down the unspoiled Crooked River. Near the wide sandy beach is a snack bar, open for breakfast and a light lunch. Waterskiing instruction is sold at the dock. Sailfish, canoes, and rowboats are available to explore the 12–mile reach of Long Lake, or to visit the quaint village of Naples, which can be reached by waterway. Chartered seaplanes take off from Naples every day for more remote waters. The lighted tennis courts can be enjoyed night and day, and there is a new jogging track. Each cottage is nestled in its own private setting, in the pine woods, or on the lake front, with a private dock. Each has its own bar-b-que pit, and the lucky fisherman can grill the day's catch. All cottages have spectacular sunset views of the mountains to the west. Many have their own fireplaces, and fresh logs are delivered daily. Eleven of the cottages are complete housekeeping units, with full kitchens, daily maid service, and linens provided. There are also large chalet guest rooms, with full views of the lake. There is a softball field, a horseshoe pit, and a sauna for leisure, a pitch and putt course for golf. Tuesdays and Fridays highlight the week, with fresh Maine lobster and clam bakes in the outdoor picnic grove. The renovated barn swings weekly with traditional square dances. Rates in the larger cottages are on a weekly basis only, and range from $336–413 depending on the size of the cabin, and the number of people sharing it. Shorter stays are possible in the smaller cabins, for two-three people. Weekly rates range from $196–322, and daily rates range from $32–48. For more information write: Phil Chute and John Mitchell, Chute Homestead Cottages, P.O. Box 127, Naples, ME 04055 (207)693–6425.

★★★*The Craignair Inn at Clark Island* is a superb old-time inn situated on 4 acres of shorefront surrounded by the rocky islands and headlands of the Maine Coast. Built in 1930 to house workers from the granite quarry in the village of Clark Island, the inn's location

and rustic coastal atmosphere make it an ideal vacation retreat. Some guests only wish to sit in the gardens to relax and watch the activities of shorebirds, clammers and lobstermen. Others prefer exploring the coast, along the many miles of paths adjacent to the property, to find the spruce forests, clam flats, offshore islands, tidal pools, and meadows; all abundant with wildflowers, birds, and seals. Also, nearby towns offer such diversions as antiques, art galleries, museums, shops, concerts, golf, tennis, riding, cycling, sailing, and festivals paying homage to seafood, blueberries, chicken, and sailboats, as well as numerous country fairs. During the colder months, one may hike, snowshoe, cross-country ski, or ice skate in the immediate area; or downhill ski at the Camden Snow Bowl, just a short drive away. When the fog rolls in, the comfortable sitting room with its large library and crackling fire, provides a pleasant refuge. Craignair can accommodate twenty-seven guests in fifteen bedrooms overlooking the Atlantic Ocean and Long Cove. Bike tours are available through Overland Rolls Maine Bicycle Touring. Further details below. Daily rates range from $14–24 double. Contact: The Craignair Inn, Clark Island, ME 04859 (207)594–7644.

★★★★*Linekin Bay Resort at Boothbay Harbor*, with five spacious lodges and thirty private cabins, hugs the rugged shores of the sparkling Linekin Bay. Linekin offers complete sailing instruction and unlimited use of the resort's 28 Lightnings and O'Day Rhodes. Sail the protected bay waters, or explore the rocky, wooded coasts of the outer islands. Regattas highlight each week, and sailors of all classes are encouraged to compete. Everyone is offered the chance to handle the lines and take the helm of the 43' Alden Schooner, the "Sea Waif". The picturesque town of Boothbay Harbor, with a 9-hole golf course, lies across the bay, reached by a scenic ride on the Linekin Ferry. Waterskiing instruction is available, and canoeing is possible in the sheltered bay waters. Bay fishing is excellent, and deep-sea ventures can be chartered at the dock. There are shuffleboard courts, several clay courts for tennis, and a large heated salt-water pool, where fresh Maine lobster-clam bakes are held each week. The dining room overlooking the bay specializes in seafood, and is famous for Sunday night smorgasbords, which highlight each week. Lodge rooms are spacious and overlook the water. Many have fireplaces. Lodge room rates range between $22 and 28 daily per person, and $135–168 weekly. Private cabins, accommodating two-four persons range between $21 and $28 per person daily, and $140 and $198 weekly. All rates include complete sailing instruction, unlimited use of all recreational facilities, and three meals daily. For more information write: Robert and Ida Branch, Linekin Bay Resort, Boothbay Harbor, ME 04538 (207)663–2494.

★★*Long Lake Cottages* are located in the Belgrade region deep in the secluded Maine woods yet within driving distance of many towns, golf courses, coastal areas and the famous Lakewood Summer Theatre. The cottages are situated on the east shore of Long Lake, shaded by tall majestic pines, white birches, maples and oaks. The region offers fishing for smallmouth bass, brook trout and landlocked salmon. Spacious grounds and sheltered sandy beaches with a sundeck are featured here. Some of the popular activities are swimming, hiking and boating. Boats and motors are available for rental at reasonable rates. The cedar log housekeeping cottages are well spaced for privacy. They accommodate up to six persons and are well equipped with utensils, blankets, linens and towels and are comfortably furnished. They have electric kitchens with snack bars, baths with showers, electric water heaters and an outdoor porch. Weekly rates from June 18 through Labor Day based on double occupancy begin at $175. Off season rates begin at $147. Pets are not permitted. For more information write to Jim and Doris Williams, Belgrade Lakes, ME 04918 (207)495–2262).

★★★★*Migis Lodge on Lake Sebago* is less than an hour from Maine's seacoast and the White Mountains of New Hampshire. Portland, the nearest city, is 24 miles away. The lodge is situated on 100 acres, 90 of which provide well-marked woodland trails for observing wildlife and flowers. There are 1,400 feet of shorefront on the lake's crystal-clear water. The white sand beach and sunny terraces with lounge chairs are perfect for complete relaxation. There is great swimming, free sailing, water skiing and excellent fishing. Sebago Lake is the original home of the landlocked salmon. July and August are the months for bass, and the lake is heavily stocked with trout. The lodge will provide boats, or you may bring your own and dock it in the yacht basin. On the premises are three well kept tennis courts, two shuffleboard courts, badminton, croquet, volleyball and horseshoes. Golf courses and riding stables are available in the area, as well as boat and canoe trips on nearby rivers. There is a summer theatre 1½ miles from the lodge. For indoor sports, there is a recreation hall with bingo, movies, talent shows, magic shows, an official size pool table, ping-pong, bumper pool, skittles and indoor soccer, a well-stocked library and game closet. Accommodations include a few rooms in the main lodge or private cottages for two-six people. The cottages—all along the shore—are well spaced for privacy, with a good view of the lake. They have twin beds, tile baths with tub and shower, living rooms with TV, porches, and fireplaces. Maid service is provided but there are no housekeeping facilities. Meals are served in the dining room; there are weekly buffets and cookouts, and late breakfasts available if you choose to sleep in. Dinner comes with flowers and soft music—and there is a complimentary cocktail party. Jackets are required at dinner. The

lodge is open June 15 to Sept. 8. Rates, in the main lodge, for two people, start at $62. Cottages, based on double occupancy, start at $74. The lodge provides a full American Plan—and picnics are available, if you choose to be out for lunch. No pets allowed—but there are kennels nearby. For further information contact Migis Lodge, South Casco, ME 04077 (207)655–4524.

★★★★*Quisisana*, is located on the shores of Lake Kezar near Mt. Sabattus on the western edge of Maine, about five miles from the New Hampshire border and within view of the impressive Presidential Range. The lake, of course, is beautiful and refreshing with mountain clear water. All water activities are available including water skiing, swimming, sailing, hiking, canoeing and fishing for bass or salmon. There are clay tennis courts, shuffleboard, badminton, ping pong, a card room, TV lounge and a 9-hole golf course just 3½ minutes away. Its most intriguing highlight is its performing artist staff—a musical tradition started in 1946 and carried on till this day. The camp recruits young artists from Juilliard, the New England Conservatory and other music schools, to do chores by day and perform by night. Consequently, there are many musical evenings of concerts, Broadway musical excerpts, opera, dancing and folk singing—

making the stay at this camp not only relaxing but memorable. Cottages on the lake shore are attractively furnished, with screened-in porches, private baths, from one-three bedrooms and heat. Some have living rooms and fireplaces. The resort is seasonal—open mid-June till after Labor Day—and offers American Plan with continental dining and Sunday night smorgasbords. If you do not want a cottage, you may stay in the lodge. Rooms—double occupancy—are $32–38. Cottages range from $38–48. Your hosts are Leonard Haskell and Elliott Hyman and you can reach them at Quisisana (after May 10), Center Lovell, Maine 04016 (207)925–3500. During the winter months write: P.O. Box 25068, Ft. Lauderdale, FL. 33320 or call: (305)731–7397 or 739–3317.

***Stage Neck Inn** is located on a peninsula, near rustic York Harbor, off the Maine coastline and ¾ miles from Portland. It is a complete resort with activities for every taste. In the summer there is swimming in the ocean or a heated salt-water pool, tennis, fishing and boating of all kinds, plus a scenic 18-hole golf course. There are fishing docks and a breathtaking cliff walk. Nearby is the famous summer theatre—the Ogunquit Playhouse. The spring is the best time for fishing and wildflowers, and the fall, of course, for the magnificent foliage and country fair excursions. Year-round there are historic sites, art galleries and antique shops galore. The inn is elegantly furnished, yet homey and comfortable. Every bedroom has two good twin beds or one king-sized. Each has a private sun porch, luxury

bath, color TV and phone. Suites, with adjoining living room, are also available. Meals are not included in the rates, but are offered separately three times a day. The dining room is especially handsome and offers a European and American menu, and excellent seafood. There is a well-stocked wine cellar and entertainment—a piano bar and weekend dancing; jackets are required at dinner. Rates for the summer season—June 29 thru Sept. 3—range from $58–75 for double occupancy. Off season—May 11–June 28, Sept. 4–Oct. 27—rates range from $45–60 for double occupancy. There are beach, river or ocean-front rooms available. For reservations and information contact the Stage Neck Inn, Off Rt. 1A, York Harbor, ME 03911 (1–207)363–3850.

Whisperwood Lodge & Cottages are located on the shores of Salmon Lake, in the famous Belgrade Lake country. The main attraction, aside from being near many of the children's summer camps, is fishing for brown trout and big bass. Non-resident fishing licenses, and guides are available. The fish you catch can be fixed the way you like it for your evening meal. If you're not a fisherman you can enjoy the bountiful, expertly prepared Maine-style meals available, along with home-cooked pastries and desserts. Other recreation at the lodge includes swimming in crystal-clear Salmon Lake, water skiing, shuffleboard, croquet, ping pong, horseshoes, billiards, TV, and other indoor games. Children will enjoy free pony rides. The cottages face the lake and have completely screened-in porches. They can accommodate one-three people and have separate living rooms, bathrooms, showers, automatic heat and wood-burning stoves. Daily maid service is provided. Rates based on the American Plan start at $18 per day per person and range to $24. For further information contact: Mr. & Mrs. Edgar H. Douglas, Whisperwood Lodge and Cottages, North Belgrade, ME 04959 (207)465–2497.

★★★★*Whitehall Inn* is a country inn in a seacoast village. Located in Camden, Maine, where the mountains meet the sea, Whitehall carries on a tradition begun over 75 years ago when a seacaptain's widow first took in guests. Windjammers under full sail leave Camden every Monday morning throughout the summer season. The fog lifting at daybreak and the sun setting over the mountains are all part of a vacation here. Camden has lots of arts and crafts studios and antique shops for browsing or shopping. Day trips to Bar Harbor, Boothbay Harbor and Islesboro are easily arranged. There are both fresh- and salt-water fishing and swimming and two golf courses are located nearby. Activities at the inn include entertainment nights with old movies, bingo, informal concerts and luncheon cruises to Little Green Island, a nature preserve with eighteen varieties of wild flowers. There's an all-weather tennis court, shuffleboard, a 16–foot Bettle-Cat available for day-sailing and bicycles for scenic tours of the miles of country roads along the shore, back in the farmland, or out to the lakes. The inn itself is furnished with antiques from various periods. There aren't any TV sets but there are hundreds of books to read, jig-saw puzzles to be completed and wicker furniture to sit in while enjoying the fresh sea breeze. Each room is individually decorated and the dining room offers the best of Down-East cooking. Maine blueberries, home-made chowders and fresh seafood are all served. Formal traditions from the past are retained, such as fingerbowls and fine linens. Jackets for men at dinner are requested. Rates for the summer season from June 29 through Labor Day range from $28–36 per person, with breakfast and dinner. From Labor Day through October 15, rates go from $25 to $33 per person, with breakfast and dinner; and from May 25 through June 29, rates go from $18 to $32 including breakfast. For full details and more information, contact Jean and Ed Dewing, Whitehall Inn, Camden, ME 04843 (207)236–3391.

Travel Services

Maine Windjammer Cruises are the first and best known of all sailing vacations, having been in continuous operation since 1935. The schooners are among the last of the American merchant sailing vessels, and offer you a chance to live the adventure of the old days of sail. You can spend a week or longer cruising along the coast of Maine viewing the magnificent islands and rugged coastline. There is no set itinerary followed—only the tides and winds are used, making the cruise more interesting. The area cruised, Penobscot Bay and adjacent waters, is well protected. The sail is not on the high seas, but the variety and scope is plenty—even for the most sophisticated sailor. However, you need no previous sailing experience to enjoy the cruises. You may work the ship as much, or little, as you like. There is a different port of anchor each night with enough time to swim, fish, or go ashore to explore the villages and towns. Maine offers the finest sailing, and an unforgettable experience is guaranteed for those who wish the simple pleasures, with no responsibility and a complete change of scene. Casual clothing, foul weather gear, warm jacket and sweater, rubber-soled shoes are a must. If you wish, you may also bring a sleeping bag, flashlight, camera and binoculars, and scuba gear if you dive. Meals are served New England family style and include roasts, fish and chowders cooked on a wood burning stove. Hearty breakfasts are a special delight, and the lobster bake is the highlight of the cruise. Accommodations are clean, comfortable and plain. There are cabins for two, three or four, each with nearby toilet facilities. Beds are first rate, with foam rubber mattresses and clean fresh linens and blankets. Nobody is cramped or crowded. There are three vessels from which to choose—the *Mattie*, a veteran of the West Indies fruit trade, is 81 feet long and accommodates 29; the *Mercantile*, last of the famous Deer Isle coasters is 78 feet long and takes 26. These ships are unusually roomy, with broad decks and full headroom below. They are operated by a captain and four crew members. The third vessel, the *Mistress*, is a new 40–foot topsail schooner. She accommodates six guests only, with three private double cabins, each complete with toilet, lavatory and companionway. You will have the opportunity to learn to sail and navigate, help the crew or just completely relax. Meals are similar to the other two vessels. The crew consists of captain and mate-cook. Rates for the *Mattie* and *Mercantile*—per week, per person—are $265 (for June and Sept.) and $285 (for July and August). The *Mistress'* rate is $295. Minimum age 16; 13–15 if accompanied by parents. Sails start each Monday from mid-June thru mid-Sept. For reservations and further details, contact Les and Ann Bex, Maine Windjammer Cruises, Inc., P.O. Box 617, Camden ME 04843 (207)236–2938.

Northern Maine Flying Service is located on Pleasant Lake in Island Falls, Maine, just 10 minutes off Route 95. It has two planes—a Cessna 180 and a P.A. 11. Norm Bradley is the pilot, with 35 years of flying experience, and he is also a Registered Maine Guide. He flies groups and individuals to all the Northern Maine lakes and ponds for fishing, canoeing and camping, including the Allagash area. They run sight-seeing trips, flying over the local area and around Mount Katahdin. This family-owned operation accepts only small parties that they can serve efficiently and safely. Their float plane is based at the Birch Point Campground and Recreation Area on Pleasant Lake. There, campsites and cabins are available, as well as recreational facilities including boating and swimming. Families of anglers planning to go on fly-in fishing or hunting trips can stay at the Birch Point facility. The season for the flying service is from ice-out around May 10th until November. Early reservations are recommended. From May through November contact: Norm and Rita Bradley, Island Falls, ME 04747 (207)463–2260 or 2181. From

November to May, contact the Bradleys at RD 1, Norridgewock, ME 04957.

Overland Rolls runs weekend and week-long bicycle tours to some of the finest and prettiest country inns along Maine's spectacular seacoast as well as at the foot of the White Mountains. You'll "roll" through historic villages and settlements, some dating back to the seventeenth century, with time out for lunch, shopping and sightseeing. Follow

your guide or break away on your own—Overland Rolls gives you detailed maps indicating local attractions and outstanding scenery. At night, enjoy New England hospitality, dinner with the group, and snug inn accommodations. Rates: $90–$100 for weekend tours, $225 for 5 days, including meals, double-occupancy lodgings, guide and gratuities. There's also a "Sail 'n Roll" adventure for those who want to alternate days on board a classic sloop with days spent cycling the Maine islands and coastal regions ($550 for 7 days). Rent a bike from Overland Rolls or bring your own. For details contact: Overland Rolls, P.O. Box 4134, Station A, Portland, ME 04101 (207)775–1418.

White Mountain National Forest

For complete details on Maine's portion of the White Mountain National Forest and the Caribou-Speckled Mountain Wilderness and Wild River Wilderness areas, see the "New Hampshire" chapter.

MARYLAND

Introduction

Maryland, the Old Line State, stretches from the Atlantic Ocean to the Allegheny Mountains and takes in the nationally famous striped bass waters and duck and goose hunting grounds of Chesapeake Bay. Inland are the trophy smallmouth bass waters of the North Branch of the Potomac and the backpacking and camping areas of the state forest reserves and game lands, which offer good hunting in season for whitetail deer, wild turkey, upland game birds, and waterfowl. Delaware, to the east, is known primarily for its superb waterfowl hunting and saltwater fishing.

Accommodations & Travel Information

Maryland has accommodations to suite the needs of every vacationer, including hotels, motels, fishing and hunting lodges, resorts, and campsites. For information on where to stay, write to: Division of Tourist Development, Dept. of Economics & Community Development, 1748 Forest Dr., Annapolis 21401 (301)267–5517. A detailed traveler's guide to the state is contained in the *Maryland Guidebook*, available free upon request from the same address. With 9 state forests, 33 state parks, and dozens of private campgrounds, Maryland provides the camper with a variety of choices in every region ranging from full-service family campgrounds to remote primitive sites and Adirondack shelters. The 25–page *Directory of Maryland Campgrounds* lists and describes all privately operated campsites and trailer parks, state forest and park campsites, and national and regional campsites. Most campsites are available on a first-come first-served basis. At Assateague, Deep Creek Lake, and Shad Landing state parks, campsites have been set aside as reserved areas for family groups and may be reserved in advance for 1–week periods. For campsite permit regulations, and reservation information, write: Park Service, Dept. of Natural Resources, State Office Bldg., Annapolis 21401. For 24–hour recorded, up-to-date state park camping information, call (301)768–0895. Detailed *State Park Map-Brochures* are available free upon request for all state park recreation areas from: Park Service (address above). For information on state forest campsites write to: Maryland Forest Service (same address). A free guide, *Maryland—the Mountains, the Bay, the Ocean, Recreation in Maryland's Parks & Forests*, may be obtained from: Park Service (same address).

Highways & Maps

For anyone planning a trip through the state, the *Maryland Highway & Natural Resources Map* is essential. It shows all highways and other roads, route markers, population size of towns and cities, and special features such as forests and parks, information centers, picnic areas, airports, state and federal wildlife areas, camping areas, and rest areas. There is a mileage diagram showing distances between points. A chart of forests and parks is provided, showing facilities available in each. A list of lakes and ponds open to public fishing is provided, and the coordinates for location on the map are shown, as well as winter warmwater fishing areas, fish hatcheries and rearing stations, trout streams, wildlife management areas and sanctuaries, public hunting grounds, and public boat-launching ramps (listed by county). For a free copy, write to: Division of Tourist Development, Dept. of Economics & Community Development, 1748 Forest Dr., Annapolis 21401.

Maryland Forests, Lakes & Coastal Recreation Areas

Although Maryland is small, encompassing only 10,577 square miles, its varied topography provides some of the finest fishing and waterfowl hunting opportunities in the eastern United States, ranging from the flat lowlands of tidewaters of the Coastal Plain, through the low-lying Eastern Shore and the higher Western Shore of the 20,000–square-mile inland area of Chesapeake Bay, and the rolling, orchard-studded hillsides of the Piedmont Plateau region, to the rugged beauty and scenic mountain streams, valleys, and mixed hardwood and conifer forests of the Appalachian Mountains in the western counties—which reach their greatest height at the peak of Backbone Mountain (3,360 feet) in Garrett County. The state's 9 forests and 33 parks and wildlife management areas cover 170,000 acres in the mountains and on the ocean, bays, and rivers. There are 35 public hunting grounds covering 70,788 acres. Seventy-two ponds, lakes, and reservoirs make up the state's freshwater fishing area, along with the historic waters of the Susquehanna River in the northeast corner, the winding riverbanks of the Patapsco, and the famed smallmouth bass waters of the North Branch of the Potomac. The major lakes include scenic Deep Creek Lake, Youghiogheny Lake, and Savage River Reservoir in the western highlands, and

**VACATION/
LODGING GUIDE**

Liberty, Prettyboy, and Loch Raven reservoirs in the north central region. The state's generally moderate climate varies from mild to hot in summer and mild to moderate in winter in the east and south to bitter cold in the winter in the western mountains. The major fishing waters in the Appalachian Highlands and forests of northwest Maryland include Deep Creek Lake, the state's largest body of fresh water, and the brook, rainbow, and brown trout waters of the beautiful Savage River, which flows through Savage River State Forest, torrential Youghiogheny River, Bear Creek, Salt Block Run, Mill Run, Muddy Creek, and Buffalo, Puzzley, and Glade runs in Garrett County and Evitts Creek, Flintstone Creek, and Laurel Run in Allegany County. Scenic Youghiogheny Reservoir, which sprawls across the Maryland-Pennsylvania boundary surrounded by dense conifer forests and highlands, holds muskellunge, northern pike, rainbow and brown trout, walleye, and smallmouth bass up to trophy weights. The waters of the renowned North Branch of the Potomac, with its deep pools and rocky ledges forming the southern boundary of the northwest region at the West Virginia line, are a fly fisherman's paradise for explosive smallmouth bass up to 4 and 5 pounds.

Maryland is famous for its saltwater fishing potential in the Ocean City area—long known as the White Marlin Capital of the World—and the Atlantic shore and ocean and its renowned bays, including the Isle of Wight, Sinepuxent, Assawaman, Assateague, and Chincoteague, some 80 miles from the great inland sea of Chesapeake Bay. Chesapeake Bay, which covers 3,237 square miles, is one of the nation's great fishing, boating, and waterfowl hunting regions. This vast semi-enclosed body of water, a mixture of sea and river some 185 miles long, varies from 3 to 22 miles wide, with an average depth of 21 feet. The deepest area, off Bloody Point at the southern tip of Kent Island, reaches down 174 feet. The food-rich waters of this great bay are fed by 46 rivers and streams, including the "fathers of rivers"—the Susquehanna—and the Northeast, Bohemia, Elk, Bush, Sassafras, Gunpowder, Patapsco, Choptank, Potomac, Pocomoke, and Patuxent rivers. Its 4,100 miles of tidal shoreline in Maryland provide the finest Canada goose shooting on the Atlantic seaboard. More than 430,000 geese and 402,000 ducks winter in the tidewater region during a typical season, along with innumerable quail, dove, rails, woodcock and jacksnipe. The tidal flats and marshlands are also inhabited by whitetail deer and annually produce the nation's second-largest number of muskrat pelts.

The bay is the nation's prime producer of striped bass (known south of the Mason-Dixon line as "rockfish"). The best striper fishing is from mid-June to mid-September when the schools begin the annual fall migration toward their winter homes in the Potomac and Susquehanna rivers. The most popular fishing methods include bait fishing with peeler crabs, drifting soft-shell crabs and live eels, and casting with surface plugs, bucktails, spoons, and surgical hose eels. The bay provides often spectacular fishing for black drum around the marshy islands of Tangier Sound, cobia around wrecks in the lower Chesapeake, and spotted sea trout, bluefish, big largemouth and smallmouth bass, northern pike, chain pickerel, and crappie in the tidewater areas, such as the Susquehanna, Northeast, and Pocomoke rivers, and elsewhere. Fly fishing with streamers, poppers, and shad flies is becoming increasingly popular in the bay region.

The 38-mile Maryland section of the Appalachian Trail parallels the ancient route of the Great Indian Warpath (a system of old Indian trails) along the northernmost Blue Ridge Mountains through Civil War battlefields to the Virginia line at Weaverton. The 35-mile stretch from Pen Mar to Weaverton passes along a narrow ridge crest through a scenic forest area and an area of historic interest. From Weaverton the trail follows the abandoned Chesapeake & Ohio Canal towpath west and crosses the Potomac River via the bridge at Sandy Hook, Virginia.

Information Sources, Maps & Access

A detailed guide to Chesapeake Bay is contained in the 32-page *Tidewater Fishing Guide*, available free from: Dept. of Natural Resources, Tawes State Office Bldg., Annapolis 21401. The guide also contains a synopsis of laws, seasons, dividing lines, public launching ramps, state fishing reefs, full-color hydrographic sectional charts, a Maryland fish table, and a fish identification chart. Chesapeake Bay is shown on *National Ocean Survey Nautical Charts* 12260 and 12220, available for $3.25 each from: Distribution Division (C44), National Ocean Survey, Riverdale 20840.

For complete descriptions of the freshwater, Chesapeake Bay, and Atlantic coast divisions, write for the free *Maryland Sportfishing Tournament* brochure to: Dept. of Natural Resources, Tawes State Office Bldg., Annapolis 21401. The DNR also publishes the following free fishing and hunting guides: *Maryland Sportfishing Guide*, which contains detailed information about licenses, season and special

fishing areas, regulations, trout streams, lakes and ponds open to the public, a fish identification chart, all-purpose fisherman's knots, and live baits; a 32-page detailed *Tidewater Sportfishing Guide*; a 36-page *Maryland Hunting Guide*; a *Marylander's Guide to Venomous Snakes & Snakebite Treatment* (rattlesnakes and copperheads); and *Fish & Wildlife News*, a bimonthly publication available free on request. The DNR also publishes the following free contour maps: *Fisherman's Map of Deep Creek Lake, Fisherman's Map of Triadelphia Lake, Fisherman's Map of Liberty Reservoir, Fisherman's Map of Prettyboy Reservoir,* and *Fisherman's Map of Loch Raven Reservoir.* If you are planning to hike the Appalachian Trail in Maryland, you will want to consult *The Appalachian Trail* (publication #17, 25¢), Appalachian Trail Conference, P.O. Box 236, Harpers Ferry, WV 25425, a

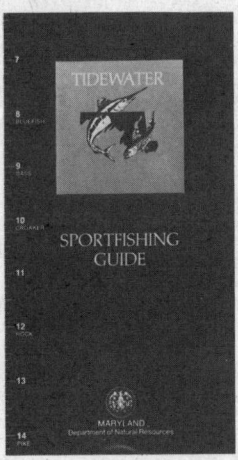

booklet which contains a brief history of the trail and a description of the route, including maps and a complete list of publications sold by the conference. You should also look into *Suggestions for Appalachian Trail Users* (70¢), same publisher, which includes information on trip planning, accommodations, safety precautions, maps, equipment, and other important aspects of using the trail. This publication is essential for all trail users. The *ATC Guidebook—Susquehanna River to Shenandoah National Park* ($4.75) describes the Maryland segment of the Appalachian Trail in detail.

Lodges & Resorts

Maryland has a limited number of full-service vacation resorts. For information, see "Accommodations & Travel Information" above.

MASSACHUSETTS

Introduction

Although heavily populated and industralized, Massachusetts offers some excellent camping, fishing, hunting, backpacking, and cross-country skiing opportunities in extensive state forest reserves and wildlife management areas, as well as some of the nation's finest saltwater fishing along the rocky, deeply indented Atlantic coast and freshwater fishing in the hundreds of lakes, ponds, and swift-flowing freestone streams. Massachusetts' sprawling, island-dotted Quabbin Reservoir, surrounded by beautiful hardwood and evergreen forests, is one of the East's hot spots for trophy-sized landlocked salmon, brown trout, lake trout, northern pike, and walleye.

Accommodations & Travel Information

Description of major Bay State lodges, motels, inns, and resorts are found in the "Vacation/Lodging Guide" which follows. For detailed travel information contact: Vacation Travel Bureau, 100 Cambridge St., Boston, MA 02202 (617)727–3201.

Highways & Maps

The Bay State is filled with many beautiful scenic routes that will delight vacationers. For a guide to these, consult the *Official Massachusetts Transportation Maps*, prepared by the Department of Public Works. You can get one free by writing: Massachusetts, Box 1775, Boston 02105. It is an excellent map of the state showing all highways and other roads. There is a chart showing recreational facilities (state forests, state parks, reservations, and beaches); the location of each area is shown. The chart indicates what facilities are available at each site. More information on scenic areas may be found in the free brochure *Vacationing in the Beautiful State of Massachusetts*. This attractive publication has beautifully illustrated descriptions of suggested scenic trips in different areas of the state. It can be obtained by writing to the address above.

Cape Cod & The Coastal Islands

Cape Cod is the playground of New England. Jutting out like a giant arm, bent at the elbow, the Cape is surrounded by water—Cape Cod Bay, the open Atlantic Ocean, Nantucket Sound and Buzzards Bay. When the Cape Cod Canal was constructed, it cut off the Cape from the mainland, making it an island. From the bridge at the Canal to the tip of the Cape it is about 150 miles. Driving on Route 6, visitors pass quaint old towns, early historical sites, sand dunes, beaches, harbors, reminders of the whaling days and of the Pilgrims, artist's colonies and high-class resorts. The 28,000 acres of the northeastern part of the Cape has been designated the Cape Cod National Seashore. It is open all year. The two visitors' centers with exhibits and information at Salt Pond (Eastham) and Province Lands (near Provincetown) are open from May through November. In the National Seashore there are paved bicycle trails, guided walks and nature trails, four picnic areas, beaches where picnicking is allowed and lifeguards are on duty in the summer, campfire programs, saltwater and freshwater fishing, lighthouses, and historic sites. Scenery in the seashore area includes wind-swept sand dunes, forests, high cliffs and cedar swamps. There is no camping allowed and pets must be on leashes. The rest of Cape Cod is made up of small towns, most of which were once fishing villages or whaling harbors. Most have changed very little over the years and 17th, 18th, and 19th century buildings are still standing, old gristmills still grind grain, the pool where the pilgrims drew their first water is still clear, and relics of the "old days" can be seen in the many Cape Cod museums. Most of the visitors come for the water sports. The Cape has 300 miles of shoreline with protected beaches on the Bay sides and wild, breaking waters on the ocean and sound. Most of the beaches are open and free, but beaches have parking fees which are strictly enforced. Fishermen enjoy the surf casting, deep-sea fishing from private or charter boats and some superb freshwater fishing in the ponds. Much of the offshore fishing is based on Cape Cod, which enables skippers to fish the Nantucket Sound-Block Island waters for the heavyweights, or on Cape Cod Bay and points north. Beautiful Ipswich Bay, on the north coast above Gloucester, is a renowned giant tuna ground, and charter boats are available in the area.

Cape Cod with the southeast shore of the state ranks as one of the best, if not *the* best, striped bass territories on either coast for fish up to 80 pounds. The Elizabeth Islands—including Naushon, Pasque, Nashawena, and fabled Cuttyhunk—with their reefs, boulder-girded shores, holes, and tidal rips are considered by many experts to be the finest stretch of bass water in existence. These superb striper islands are located off Cape Cod at Woods Hole. It was in Vineyard Sound, separating the Elizabeths from Martha's Vineyard, that the long-standing 73–pound world's record fish was taken in 1913 by trolling an eel. Martha's Vineyard and Nantucket Island also offer extraordinary striper fishing. Martha's Vineyard and Cuttyhunk have tradition-laden striper clubs; the preferred bait 70 years ago was lobster tail, with the rest of the animal used as chum—by the bushel! Evidently this practice is no longer followed, and stripers are now caught on plugs, surgical tube lures, bucktails, spoons, other artificials, and all sorts of live bait, including eels, squid, seaworms, live menhaden, herring, mackerel, other small bait fish, and clams. Martha's Vineyard is blessed with miles of beaches, including the excellent stretch under the multihued cliffs of Gay Head, whose minerals reflect blue, green, red, copper, and other colors in the sun. The numerous bays, salt ponds with inlets, rocky shoals, and reefs make this ideal bass country. Light-tackle fans, including fly rodders, enjoy some memorable hours at the mouths of salt ponds, taking fish on light

VACATION/ LODGING GUIDE

popping plugs and swimmers, lures, streamers, and popping bugs. Nantucket offers similar delights, and its beaches are famous throughout the East. Cape Cod itself takes a back seat to no area, and the Cape Cod Canal, the entire south shore including Monomoy Island, Chatham, the Cape Cod National Seashore, which takes up most of the northward "hook," and Race Point, Wellfleet, and Barnstable harbors, and much of the Cape Cod Bay shore produce fine striper fishing. The canal, separating the Cape from mainland Plymouth County, receives enormous runs of bass, but the banks are lined with fishermen and this is not fishing for the dainty or timid. Buzzards Bay (the bay, not the town), between the Elizabeth Islands and New Bedford, offers great bass fishing along its beaches, points, reefs, bays, and in rivers such as the Acushnet, Westport, Taunton, and Weweantic. Bluefish up to 20 pounds are found with stripers in all these coastal areas, and often herd up vast shoals of frantic bait fish such as mackerel, menhaden, and herring, turning the water blood-red as they attack the "balled-up" prey and reduce the fish to table scraps. When the unpredictable stripers turn sullen and refuse to hit, the voracious bluefish often save the day, whether the fisherman is on the beach or in a boat on Cape Cod, the islands, or the mainland coast. The northern weakfish or squeteague has made a comeback and these gleaming, iridescent fish are taken on the beaches and in the bays. Troutlike in appearance, weaks run up to about 12 pounds and prefer natural baits, spoons, small bucktails, rubber or plastic-tailed jigs, and spinners.

Mackerel are taken from late spring until coldwater conditions in the fall and provide sport all along the Massachusetts shores. Bottom fish of one sort of another are taken throughout the year and include scup (porgies), tautog (blackfish), summer and winter flounders, tomcods, smelt, and lesser varieties, plus the offshore species halibut—which reach several hundred pounds—cod, haddock, pollack, hake, and ling. Accommodations on Cape Cod range from small cottages, to rooms in old hotels, to large resorts, to modern motels. There are also campgrounds and housekeeping cottages. Evening entertainment at the Cape includes well-established and well-known summer theatre companies, a Symphony Orchestra, night clubs and lounges with entertainment. A part of the Cape Cod "scene" is the two coastal islands of Martha's Vineyard and Nantucket. The islands that lie in Nantucket Sound are reached by boat from Cape Cod and the mainland. Martha's Vineyard is seven miles from Woods Hole and can be reached via the car ferry from Nantucket or

Woods Hole and by a passenger boat from Falmouth, Hyannis and New Bedford. The triangular-shaped island is less than 20 miles across the base and 10 miles from north to south. Its oldest town is Edgartown, an old whaling center; Edgartown and other villages still have the grand old houses of that era. The State Lobster Hatchery is in Oak Bluffs and open to the public. Power yachts and sailboats can anchor in three protected harbors. There are beaches, golf courses, sailboats and bicycles for rent, tennis courts, and the fishing for bluefish and striped bass is outstanding. Museums include the Dukes County Historical Society Museum of ship models, colonial architecture, and furniture; Thomas Cooke House of whaling and early American memorabilia; and the Indian Memorial to Rev. Thomas Mayhew. At the southwestern tip of the island is Gay Head which has been reserved for the descendants of Indians since 1711. Using the colored clay of the area, they craft bowls and jars for sale to tourists. Accommodations on Martha's Vineyard are designed to please summer vacationers and range from small housekeeping cottages for rent, to huge mansions maintained as summer homes. Nantucket Island is smaller than Martha's Vineyard (less than 50 square miles) and farther from the mainland (30 miles). Visitors can reach the island by car and passenger ferries from Hyannis and Martha's Vineyard in the summer and Woods Hole all year round. Nantucket Island was first settled by Thomas Macy in 1659. It became a fishing port and, in the late 17th century, was the greatest whaling port in the world. Today its main business is tourism, with beaches, golf courses, tennis, boating, fishing and bicycling. In summer there are plays, concerts, sailboat races and art shows. But the island still retains its old-fashioned charm, particularly in Nantucket Town and Siasconset, the two main towns. There are many museums to visit. The Nantucket Historical Society (617)228–1894 has set up a complex of thirteen museums including restored houses, a windmill, a whaling museum, an old lightship, a pre-1930s jail, and firefighting equipment. There are sightseeing tours of the island by boat and by bus. Paved roads connect the main towns to the summer resorts scattered about the island. Accommodations range from single rooms to summer homes, and many tourists come for day trips when staying on Cape Cod.

Information Sources, Maps & Access

For detailed information and a map of the *Cape Cod National Seashore,* contact: Superintendent, Cape Cod National Seashore, South Wellfleet, MA 02663 (617)349–3785. For information on travel attractions and services, contact: Cape Cod Chamber of Commerce, Hyannis, MA 02601 (617)362–3225. For info on charter fishing boats, contact: Cape Cod Charter Assn., P.O. Box 668, West Yarmouth, MA 02673. Cape Cod is reached via U.S. Highway 6.

Gateways & Accommodations

Barnstable

(Pop. 20,000; zip code 02630; area code 617) is the gateway to water sports in Barnstable Harbor, including swimming at Sandy Neck Beach, fishing, and boating. It is the county seat governing all of Cape Cod and has some interesting historic sites and pre-Revolutionary architecture. The buildings include the Sturgis Library (1645), the oldest library building in the country; the Old Customs House (1856) which houses the Donald G. Trayser Museum of nautical paintings, marine equipment, ship models and scrimshaw; and the West Parish Meetinghouse (1717), the oldest Congregational church in the U.S. in which an active congregation still worships.

Bourne

(Pop. 13,000; zip code 02532; area code 617) is a resort town on the south bank of the Cape Cod Canal. Its most interesting attraction is

the reconstruction of a 1627 Dutch trading post. The Aptuxet Trading Post was set up for trade with fur trappers, and is thought to be the oldest North American commercial site. On exhibit are Pilgrim and Indian objects, as well as a rune stone, inscribed with the ancient language, futhark, and believed to have been left by Phoenicians who visited the area over 1,500 years ago. Nearby is the railroad station constructed for summer visits of President Cleveland and an old Dutch windmill. There is picnicking, bicyling, camping and swimming at Bourne Scenic Park and 18 holes to play at Pocasset Golf Club.

Brewster

(Pop. 2,000; zip code 02631; area code 617) is on Cape Cod Bay on the way to the Roland C. Nickerson State Park and camping area. The town has romantic seafarers' homes including Captain Kendrick's house and Crosby Cottage-Mansion. Other historic attractions are the New England Fire and History Museum, displaying firefighting equipment from three centuries; one of the oldest (and still operating) gristmills in the U.S.; and the Drummer Boy Museum with life-size Revolutionary War paintings. Local plant, animal and marine life can be seen live and in exhibits at the Cape Cod Museum of Natural History and Sealand with its dolphin show, aquarium, seals and penguins. Accommodations: *Skyline Motel* (rates: $20–22 double), with 11 good rooms in a nice location, located three miles west of town on Massachusetts Highway 6A (385–3707).

Buzzards Bay

(Pop. 2,500; zip code 02532; area code 617) is on the west side of the Cape Cod Canal and an ideal jumping off point for boating or water sports in both Cape Cod Bay and Buzzards Bay. It is also a gateway to the Shawme Crowell State Forest where there is camping. Accommodations: *Buzzards Bay Motor Lodge* (rates: $26 double), with 31 good rooms and family units, swimming beach and boat dock, just west of town on U.S. 6 and Mass. 28 (759–3466); *Redwood Motel* (rates: $26–28 double), with 20 good rooms and swimming pool, next to restaurant, one mile east of town at the junction of U.S. 6 and Mass. 28 (759–3892).

Chatham

(Pop. 5,000; zip code 02633); area code 617) located at the "elbow" of Cape Cod, is in an excellent position to act as gateway to the Nantucket Sound, the open Atlantic Ocean and the national wildlife refuge on Monomoy Island. Monomoy Island, reached by boat from Chatham harbor, is a wild, sandy isle that is a rookery for sea gulls. From the pier at Chatham, fishermen leave to catch bass, bluefish, and other deep-sea fish. Attractions in the area are the Chatham Railroad Museum and an operating gristmill built in 1797. At the Congregational Church are the famous Wight Murals, depicting Christ as a rugged fisherman and the disciples as contemporary townspeople. There is also a 9–hole golf course at Chatham Bars Inn. Accommodations: *Chatham Bars Inn* (rates: $100–130 American Plan, double), with 68 superb rooms and family guest cottages on spacious ocean grounds with dining room, cocktail lounge, beach house, swimming beach, boats, golf course, on Shore Road (945–0096); *Pleasant Bay Village* (rates: $36–50 double), with 58 excellent rooms and family cottages, breakfast and luncheon room, heated pool in beautiful location three miles north of town on Mass. 28 (945–1133).

Dennis

(Pop. 6,500; zip code 02638; area code 617) is the gateway to the expansive sandy beaches of Cape Cod Bay for swimming, fishing, skin diving, and shelling. Historic attractions in the area are the renovated house of Josiah Dennis Manse for whom the town was named; a barn museum at the Jerico Historical Center and an old schoolhouse on Nobscusset Rd. For a panoramic view, there is the Stone Tower on Scarbo Hill. One of the best known and oldest summer theatres in the country is the Cape Cod Playhouse, located in Dennis. There are famous murals by Rockwell Kent painted on the walls of the Cape Cinema. Accommodations: *Colonial Village Motel* (rates: $32 double), with 59 excellent rooms and guest cottages, heated pool, in nice location on Lower County Road (398–2071); *Edgewater Motor Lodge* (rates: $52–58 double), with 66 excellent rooms and family units, swimming beach, across from restaurant on Chase Ave. (398–6922); *Spouter Whale Motor Inn* (rates: $40–57 double), with 39 excellent rooms and swimming beach on Old Wharf Rd. (398–8010).

Eastham

(Pop. 2,100; zip code 02642; area code 617) is a gateway to the Cape Cod National Seashore. Located at Eastham is the Salt Pond Visitors Center, with an auditorium orientation program, exhibits and evening programs. The oldest windmill on the Cape is here, built in 1793 and restored in 1936. It is known as Seth Knowle's Old Windmill. Other attractions are the Nauset Light and the schoolhouse museum of the Eastham Historical Society featuring Indian, agricultural and nautical exhibits in a building built in 1869. Accommodations: *Salt Pond Motel* (rates: $34–36 double), with 22 good rooms, boats, overlooking inlet near the Cape Cod National Park Visitor Center on U.S. 6 (255–2100); *Sheraton Ocean Park Inn* (rates: $46–58 double), with 100 excellent rooms and suites, restaurant, cocktail lounge, indoor/outdoor heated pool, 1½ miles north of town on U.S. 6 (255–5000).

Falmouth

(Pop. 18,000; zip codes, see below; area code 617) is a gateway town for history buffs. Settled around 1660, Falmouth was the site of naval battles in the Revolutionary War and the War of 1812. It then became a whaling port. Attractions to see are the Saconesset Homestead, including the restored 1678 house, original furniture, tools, wagons and farm equipment, plus live farm animals; the Julia Wood House, built in 1790 and now housing a whaling exhibit, art and artifacts; the bell cast by Paul Revere and hanging in the 1756 Congregational Church; and the Ashumet Holly Reservation, a wildlife sanctuary operated by the Audubon Society and featuring nature trails and a unique collection of holly. Accommodations: *Cape Codder Hotel* (rates: $80–100 Modified American Plan in season), with 132 good rooms with ocean view, restaurant, cocktail lounge, swimming pool and beach on Cape Codder Road, Falmouth 02540 (540–1900); *The Capewind* (rates: $32 double), with 31 excellent rooms, heated pool, dock and boat rentals in beautiful location on the bay at 34 Maravista Extension, Falmouth 02540 (548–3400); *Coonamessett Inn* (rates: $40 double), with 22 excellent inn rooms and Cape Cod cottage units, restaurant, cocktail lounge on lake in superb location at Jones Road and Gifford St., Falmouth 02540 (548–2300); *Sheraton Inn* (rates: $50 double), with 96 good rooms, restaurant, cocktail lounge, heated pool and sauna at 291 Jones Road, Falmouth 02540 (540–2000).

Harwich

(Pop. 7,000; zip code 02645; area code 617) is, for the most part, a summer resort. Located on the south shore of Cape Cod, it offers excellent swimming from a beach on Nantucket Sound. Also at Harwich is the Brooks Library displaying a collection of figurines by John Rogers. Accommodations: *Harwich Port Motor Lodge* (rates: $34 double), with 41 good rooms and heated pool next to good restaurant at 558 Main (432–2424).

Hyannis

(Pop. 8,000; zip code 02601; area code 617) is the gateway to the islands of Nantucket and Martha's Vineyard. There are boats leaving from Pier #1 at the Ocean Street Docks from May to November for day trips (775–7185 for Hyannis schedules) and auto ferry Steamship Authority service to Nantucket (540–2022). Hyannis is also the commercial center of Cape Cod, with the best shopping. Attractions include Aqua Circus with high diving and dolphin shows, exhibits and a zoo; a memorial to President Kennedy on Ocean Street; Melody Tent, a summer theatre-in-the-round featuring musicals. There are also several fine beaches with bathhouse and picnicking facilities, and the harbor can accommodate ocean-going yachts. Accommodations: *Capt. Gosnold Village* (rates: $32 double), with 54 excellent rooms and cottage units, swimming pool at Gosnold St. (775–9111); *Dunfey Hyannis Resort* (rates: $72 double), with 232 superb rooms and suites, dining room, cocktail lounge, indoor/outdoor pool, tennis courts, golf at Main and 137 Saudde Ave. (775–7775); *Green Harbor on the Ocean* (rates: $245 weekly double), with 51 excellent rooms and guest cottages in beautiful location overlooking Nantucket Sound, with heated pool, swimming beach, dock and boat rentals at 182 Baxter Avenue (771–1126); *Holiday Inn*, (rates: $60.25 double) with 120 good rooms, restaurant, cocktail lounge, indoor pool, tennis, on Mass. 132 (775–6600); *Hyannis Harborview Motel* (rates: $41 double), with 67 excellent rooms, restaurant, cocktail lounge, indoor/outdoor pool, sauna at 213 Ocean St. overlooking the harbor (775–4420).

Martha's Vineyard

(Pop. 7,300; zip codes, see below; area code 617)—for description see above. For ferry info, contact: Woods Hole, Martha's Vineyard and Nantucket Steamship Authority, Box 284, Woods Hole, MA 02543 (540–2022). For all the details on accommodations, services, and reservations and a *Martha's Vineyard Vacation Kit* ($1), including maps and a pictorial guide, contact: Martha's Vineyard Information, Vineyard Haven 105, MA 02568 (693–0085). Accommodations: *Daggett House Inn* (rates: $35–55 double), with 26 excellent rooms and traditional Cape Cod cottages in superb setting with swimming beach, gardens, boat dock at North Water St. in Edgartown 02539 (627–4600); *Edgartown Inn* (rates: $24–40 double), with 23 early American rooms, breakfast service, on North Water St. in Edgartown 02539 (627–4794), *Harbor View Hotel* (rates: $60–85 double), with 120 excellent rooms and suites, restaurant, heated pool and swimming beach, boat dock on Water Street in Edgartown 02539 with ocean views (627–4333).

Nantucket Island

(Pop. 2,500; zip code of Nantucket is 02554; area code 617)—for description see above. For ferry information, contact: Woods Hole, Martha's Vineyard & Nantucket Steamship Authority, Box 284, Woods Hole, MA 02543 (540–2022). Accommodations: *Harbor House* (rates: $45–75 double), with 115 excellent rooms, restaurant, cocktail lounge on Beach St. (228–1500); *Jared Coffin House* (rates: $40–55 double), with 40 superb rooms, restaurant, in charming New England mansion at 29 Broad St. (228–2400); *The White Elephant Inn* (rates: $80 double), with 108 excellent rooms and spacious guest cottages overlooking Nantucket Harbor, restaurant, cocktail lounge, swimming beach, heated pool, boat dock on Easton St. (228–2500).

Orleans

(Pop. 1,000; zip code 02653; area code 617) is a gateway to watersports and the shopping area for the many resort towns around it. Swimmers and beachcombers enjoy Nauset Beach, a beautiful Atlantic coast beach within the Cape Cod National Seashore. The beach even has surfing. The prime area for sport fishing charter boats is Rock Harbor, on the Cape Cod Bay side. Other attractions are the cable station which linked Orleans and Brest, France during the years 1897 to 1950 and summer theatre at the Academy Playhouse in the Old Town Hall. Accommodations: *Cove Motel* (rates: $26–29 double), with 46 excellent rooms, coffeeshop, heated pool on town cove on Mass. 28 (255–1203); *Olde Tavern Motel* (rates: $34 double), with 24 excellent rooms, restored early American tavern, near restaurant, west of town on Mass. 6A (255–1565); *Skaket Beach Motel* (rates: $30–39 double), with 37 excellent rooms, heated pool in nice location one mile west of town on Mass. 6A (255–1020).

Provincetown

(Pop. 4,000; zip code 02657; area code 617) is the town with the most history on the Cape. The Pilgrim Memorial Monument, a 252–foot granite tower, commemorates the landing of the Pilgrims and displays a diorama of the Mayflower's arrival. Up Commercial Street is a tablet marking the spot of the first landing. Located on the tip of Cape Cod, Provincetown offers access to both the Atlantic and Cape Cod Bay, as well as to the Cape Cod National Seashore. A visitor's center for the Seashore is located at Province Lands, a wild area of sand dunes and beach grass. Provincetown was a whaling port, and today accommodates commercial fishermen, artists, and tourists. Attractions include Seth Nickerson's House, built in 1746 by a ship's carpenter who used the wood from shipwrecks to build his house; the Provincetown Museum of Art; and the site of Eugene O'Neill's house. In summer, there are plays at the Provincetown Playhouse (487–0955) and concerts by the Symphony Orchestra. A protected swimming beach with bathhouse facilities is found at Provincetown Beach; at the wilder Race Point there is surf fishing. Accommodations: *Best Western Chateau Motor Inn* (rates: $43–48 double), with 60 superb rooms in beautiful setting, heated pool on Bradford St. West (487–1286); *Bradford Gardens Inn* (rates: $47–90 double), with 18 rooms in early American inn, some with fireplaces, guest cottages, free breakfast at 178 Bradford St. (487–1616); *Crows Nest Motel* (rates: $39 double) with 32 excellent rooms and ocean beach located 3½ miles east of town on Mass. 6A (487–9031); *Governor Prence Motor Lodge* (rates: $42–46 double) with 70 excellent rooms in nice bay location, restaurant, cocktail lounge, swimming pool and tennis courts on U.S. 6, 4½ miles southeast of town (487–0629); *The Masthead* (rates: $50 double) with 20 ex-

cellent rooms and spacious cottages in attractive ocean location at 31 Commercial St. (487–0523); *Tides Motor Inn* (rates: $40–46 double) with 64 excellent rooms and family units, coffeeshop, heated pool and swimming beach on Beach Point Rd. (487–1045).

Sandwich
(Pop. 6,000; zip code 02563; area code 617) is best known for its production of the famous pressed glass called Sandwich Glass. The Sandwich Glass Museum (888–0251) in Town Hall Square has thousands of pieces on display dating from 1825 to 1888. Not to be missed is the Heritage Plantation (888–3300) which covers over 70 acres and includes many old buildings and exhibits. In a round stone barn are automobiles from 1899 to the 1930's, a Barney Oldfield race and a film on antique autos. There are exhibits of early American hand crafts; a military museum of firearms and miniature soldiers; an 1800 mill still grinding grain daily; jitney tours of the manicured grounds; a 1912 carousel and nature trails. Sandwich is also the gateway to Scusset Beach State Park and Shawme Crowell State Forest, with camping in both areas. Accommodations: *Daniel Webster Inn* (rates: $44–52 double) with 26 superb rooms, restaurant, cocktail lounge, at 149 Main St. (888–3622); *Sandy's Motor Lodge* (rates: $26–30 double), with 23 excellent rooms, swimming pool, west of town on Mass. 6A (888–2275); *Shady Nook Motel* (rates: $28–32 double), with 24 excellent rooms and family units, heated pool in nice location one mile west of town on Mass. 6A (888–0409).

Truro
(Pop. 1,000; zip code 02666; area code 617) is a gateway town to the Cape Cod National Seashore, a historic area and the region with the most open land on the Cape. Truro is near the Pilgrim Heights area of the Seashore where there are exhibits, swimming, and nature trails. Approaching Truro, you see the Hill of Churches with the spires of early 19th–century houses of worship. At North Truro is Highland Light, a 66–foot lighthouse built in 1795. Nearby is a tablet commemorating the spot where Captain Miles Standish and his scouting party spent their first night on American soil; and Pilgrim Spring, where they found their first fresh water. There is surf fishing on the Atlantic side, swimming at several area beaches and guided tours through the dunes.

Wellfleet
(Pop. 2,000; zip code 02667; area code 617) is a summer resort and a fishing town, once a whaling center and head of the oyster industry. It offers numerous water sports; swimming in the Atlantic or the Bay, or in the tree-lined freshwater ponds; sailing, in rental boats from Wellfleet Marina; boating, using the Marina's launching and docking facilities; fishing in the Atlantic surf or from charter boats available at the Marina; or beachbuggy tours to Nauset Beach. Attractions include the Wellfleet Historical Museum, exhibiting scrimshaw, nautical items, and Marconi artifacts; the Wellfleet Bay Wildlife Sanctuary, which has a day camp for youngsters; and the clock in the Congregational Church which strikes ship's time. Accommodations: *Southfleet Motor Inn* (rates: $33–38 double), with 30 excellent rooms, restaurant, cocktail lounge, outdoor/indoor pool, sauna, located three miles southeast of South Wellfleet on U.S. 6 (349–3580); *Wellfleet Motel* (rates: $38–40 double), with 25 excellent rooms, cocktail lounge, heated pool, four miles south of South Wellfleet on U.S. 6 (349–3535).

Woods Hole
(Pop. 950; zip code 02543; area code 617) is the major gateway to the coastal islands of Nantucket and Martha's Vineyard on the southwestern point of the Cape. For ferry information, contact: Woods Hole, Martha's Vineyard and Nantucket Steamship Authority, Box 284, Woods Hole (540–2022). One of the village's major attractions is the marine aquarium of the National Marine Fisheries on Albatross St., which is open daily, free, during the summer season. Accommodations: *Sands of Time Motor Inn* (rates: $38–42 double), with 27 excellent rooms next to restaurant overlooking the Woods Hole harbor at 549 Woods Hole Rd. (548–6300).

Yarmouth
(Pop. 12,000; zip codes, see below; area code 617) has the best and the most numerous examples of 19th–century architecture. Along Main Street are the "Skippers' Homes," well-preserved and restored homes of seafarers. There is the house of Col. John Thacher which is dated 1680 on its huge chimney; the Winslow Crocker House, furnished with antiques and built in 1780; and the Captain Bangs Hallet House, with furniture from Europe and paraphernalia of the sea. Nearby is swimming in Nantucket Sound and the Cranberry Village. Accommodations: *Blue Rock Motor Inn* (rates: $44–50 double), with 40 excellent rooms, coffeeshop, cocktail lounge, heated pool, golf and tennis off High Bank Rd. in South Yarmouth 02664 (398–6962); *Jolly Captain Motor Lodge* (rates: $33–34 double), with 32 excellent rooms, coffeeshop, heated pool, dock on Bass River with great view on Mass. 28 in South Yarmouth 02664 (398–2253); *Riverview Motor Lodge* (rates: $37 double), with 110 excellent rooms, indoor heated pool, restaurant, free breakfast, overlooking river at 37 Neptune Lane in South Yarmouth 02664 (394–9801).

Massachusetts Lakes, Forests & Trails

Massachusetts, the most populous New England state, with over 5 million residents, provides some surprisingly good backpacking, cross-country skiing, hunting, and fishing in its varied topography, of which almost 70% is forest. Land types include the seacoast with its miles of scrub oak, pine, bayberry, sand plains, bays and surf-pounded beaches; the rolling hills, river valleys, and farmlands of the central interior; and the Berkshire Highlands of the west, crowned by Mount Greylock at 3,491 feet and covered with a green forest mantle of pine, hemlock, white and yellow birch, beech, and maple. Bay State outdoorsmen have over 4,200 miles of streams and rivers, 1,100 lakes and ponds, wildlife management areas, state forests and parks, fish and wildlife private land-owned cooperative tracts, and 2,000 miles of coastline and the island and reef-studded

expanse of the Atlantic Ocean in which to pursue their favorite sports.

Massachusetts furnishes some excellent trout fishing, particularly in the many impoundments, lakes, and ponds. The outstanding body of water in the state is sprawling Quabbin Reservoir, in central Massachusetts, near Belchertown. The deep blue waters of this island-studded lake, the largest expanse of fresh water in the state, cover about 25,000 acres indented with long arms, bogs, and coves, which provide an ideal environment for a long list of game fish. This is the only lake in Massachusetts providing fishing for landlocked salmon (state record, 9 pounds 11 ounces) and lake trout (state record, 17 pounds 13 ounces), which grow to heavy weights in the cold, deep waters. Brown trout to 20 pounds and thick-bodied rainbows are favorite quarry for many of the anglers who fish the big Swift River impoundment each season. Quabbin is one of the quality waters of New England, producing large gray lakers and trophy browns each season, as well as impressive salmon and rainbows. Superb large- and smallmouth bass, pickerel, walleye (state record, 11 pounds), and panfish angling round out the opportunities of this lake. An added dividend is the fact that Quabbin is surrounded by a large, beautiful forest tract which provides top-ranked whitetail deer and wild turkey hunting in season. The Swift River continues out of Quabbin at Windsor Dam, and the 4-mile stretch downstream to Bondsville, including a short piece of "fly fishing only water" from the dam to Route 9, offers some of the state's best trout fishing. The three branches of the Swift that flow into the top of Quabbin have good trout populations and also offer a chance at stream fishing for some of the enormous hook-jawed browns and rainbows which move in and out of the lower portions of these streams to feed on smelts and fly hatches. The spring spawning run of smelts and rainbows makes these feeders particularly attractive.

To the west of Springfield lie the productive waters of Otis Reservoir. Otis yields brook, brown, and rainbow trout, shelters some trophy fish in its deep blue waters, and produced the state record 6-pound 4-ounce squaretail. Smallmouth and largemouth bass and panfish are also present in large numbers and add variety to the angling in this prolific lake. Otis is a tributary lake of the West Branch of the Farmington River, and the stream provides good trout fishing from the town of Otis to the top of Hogsback Reservoir on the Connecticut border. Onota Lake, a couple of miles northwest of Pittsfield near the middle of the border with New York, ranks close to Quabbin in the excellence and variety of its fishing; trophy browns and rainbows are taken every season. It provides the only fishing in the state for the landlocked, red kokanee salmon, and offers fine angling for bass, big northern pike (state record), pickerel, and panfish. Wachusett Reservoir (home of the state record brown trout), northeast of Worcester, holds big rainbows, smallmouths, and lots of browns in the 4–5–pound-and-over class.

Some of the best trout fishing in New England is found on Cape Cod. Because it is situated in the middle of a hotbed of saltwater angling, the Cape does not receive the pressure its quality would ordinarily attract. There are more than 50 "kettle" ponds, a heritage of the Ice Age, which provide exceptional angling in their cool, spring-fed depths. Among the best of these are the set of ponds at Nickerson State Park, near Orleans, composed of Cliff (brown and rainbow), Little Cliff (brook), Higgins (brook), and Flax (brook and rainbow). A brown trout tipping the scales at almost 20 pounds was found dead of old age on the shores of Cliff Pond! Mashpee Pond and its connected sister, Wakeby, are noted producers of brook and brown trout as well as smallmouth bass, perch, and

pickerel. These two bodies of water are near Otis Air Force Base on Route 130 at the town of Mashpee. The Mashpee River, draining south to Popponesset Bay, is an excellent sea-run brook and brown trout stream producing those big silver-bodied fish to weights of better than 2 pounds and occasional fish to 6 pounds. Other famous Cape Cod trout ponds include Gull Pond, Crystal Lake, Sheep, Shubael, Scargo, and Hamblin. Rivers containing stream and sea-run trout include the Pamet, Marston Mills, Quashnet, and Santuit rivers, and Scorton Creek, which flows north to Cape Cod Bay at Scorton Harbor. The sea trout are very wary and difficult to raise to a lure, fly, or bait. Flies and lures which imitate spearing, shrimp, killies, and other natural baits, as well as the naturals themselves, are preferred tackle. Other popular trout lakes include Richmond Pond, a few miles southwest of Pittsfield, which contains large brown trout, both kinds of bass, pickerel, and panfish; Laurel Lake in the central Berkshires, which holds lunker browns, bass, pickerel, and panfish; the Congamond Lakes, on the Connecticut border below Southwick, which produce big browns and rainbows in the northern pond, and excellent smallmouths and largemouths, pickerel and panfish in the other two sections; Asnacomet Pond, in central Worcester County, which has a reputation for good, steady brown and rainbow trout angling, and shelters bass, pickerel, and panfish to add variety; Quacumquosit Pond, southwest of Worcester, which produces browns and rainbows, its sister, Quaboag Pond, yeilding bass and pickerel; the Quaboag River; the Chicopee River; and Lake Quinsigamond, east of Worcester, which is heavily stocked with brook, brown, and rainbow trout, and provides good warmwater fishing too.

In addition to these streams, Massachusetts has some scenic, productive rivers scattered about the state. The most famous trout river is the beautiful Deerfield, which rises in Vermont and meanders southeast through a heavily forested valley of mixed evergreens and hardwoods to the Connecticut at Greenfield. The lower part contains some trout, including an occasional trophy brown or brook trout, but the best fishing is from Shelburne Falls to the Vermont border at Sherman Reservoir. Power dams make the flow *highly* changeable, and you will have to watch the flow carefully or you may end up stranded on a midstream boulder for several hours, unless you are willing and able to swim for shore. The Deerfield is a beautiful piece of water to fish. Many of the Deerfield's tributaries, such as the east and west branches of the North River, yield good trout fishing; many of the little feeder brooks, rising high in the heavily wooded ridges, produce native trout for anyone willing to leg it up the steep, heavily forested slopes. The Green River rises in Vermont to the east of the Deerfield headwaters and flows south to meet the latter in Greenfield. Its limestone bed gives the Green a soft, emerald tint and the stream produces some enjoyable angling for all three stream trout. The many stretches of riffles found along the tight, hemlock-shaded river valley hold good-sized rainbows.

Two other Connecticut tributaries are popular with Bay State trout fishermen. The Westfield River drainage, that is, the Little River (west, east, and middle branches), is productive from Huntington north and yields some fine creels of brook, brown, and rainbow trout. The Millers River, flowing west to the Connecticut at Millers Falls, provides good trout fishing from its headwaters to the Otter River State Forest in northern Worcester County. The Squannacook, which flows east from the central New Hampshire border near Ashby to the Nashua near West Groton, holds trout; some big browns are taken in the deep holes above the Nashua. The Ware River drainage parallels the east side of Quabbin Reservoir and consists of east and west branches. A glance at a map will show you

how parts of the branches flow away from roads, and these sections have the best trout fishing. The Nisitissit, near the New Hampshire border in Middlesex County, and the suburban Ipswich, flowing through Middlesex and Essex counties, also receive a good deal of attention from trout fishermen. Massachusetts offers excellent warmwater fishing opportunities throughout the state, including both species of black bass, northern pike, walleyes, pickerel, shad, white and yellow perch, crappies, bluegills, bullheads, and other panfish. Largemouth and smallmouth bass are present everywhere, from the ponds and brackish tidal basins of Martha's Vineyard and Nantucket Island to the forested upland waters of the Berkshires at the western border with New York. The Cranberry Bay area of southeastern Massachusetts in Plymouth County continues to produce outsized largemouths. The state record largemouth came from Sampson's Pond near South Carver, and in 1976 a 13–pounder was taken from Muddy Pond, a few miles north, which has a reputation for lunkers, even though it only covers 90 acres.

Many of the premier bass, pike, walleye, and pickerel waters were covered in the discussion of trout fishing above, but there are a number of productive spots that merit special mention. The Assawompset-Great Quitticas-Long Pond System, at Lakeville, furnishes fine angling for both species of bass, trophy walleyes and pickerel, and panfish. To the northwest of Taunton lies Norton Reservoir, which consistently yields lunker smallmouth and largemouth bass—the latter to 10 pounds, pickerel, and panfish, big white and yellow perch, crappies, and bluegills. Lake Savvatia, on the northern outskirts of Taunton, is considered another bass hot spot, and also holds pickerel and perch. Chauncy Lake at Westboro in eastern Worcester County provides some of the best smallmouth bass fishing in the state and has a healthy population of walleyes, in addition to largemouths and panfish. Singletary Pond, a few miles south of Auburn, is another exceptional bronzeback-largemouth producer and contains trout, pickerel, and panfish, with good fishing for all species.

On the Connecticut border near the town of Webster is Lake Chargoggagoggmanchaugagoggchaubunagungamaug (also known as Lake Webster, this is the famous "joke lake" which translates from the Indian dialect as "You fish on your side of the lake, I'll fish on mine, and nobody fishes in the middle"), which furnishes superb bass fishing for both species—some trout, pickerel, and panfish. The lake is somewhat off the beaten path and well worth the effort. East Brimfield Reservoir, an impoundment of the Quinebaug River at Sturbridge, produces bass, trout, pickerel, and panfish and also contains a few northern pike. At the northern tip of Worcester County, northwest of Fitchburg, are upper and lower Naukeag and Winnekeag lakes, which combine some fine scenery with bass, pickerel, and panfishing of top-notch quality. In western Massachusetts, the Connecticut River produces shad to 10 pounds in the

waters at the foot of the Holyoke Dam, in the Chicopee River at Chicopee, and in the Springfield area. Shad are also found in a few coastal rivers such as the South (state record) at Marshfield and the North at Scituate, both south of Boston. The best fishing in the Connecticut is from the Vermont border to Millers Falls where the Millers River enters. In this stretch of water paralleling I–91, smallmouths, largemouths, walleyes, northern pike, and assorted panfish are taken. Massachusetts is involved in the Atlantic salmon restoration program, and it is hoped that in the future silvery legions will again ascend the Connecticut. Other top-ranked Massachusetts lakes include Walden Pond near Concord, once Thoreau's base camp for his philosophical musings, which holds brown, rainbows, and smallmouths; Lake Mattawa in Franklin County, which holds rainbows and some giant browns; and Wallum Lake in the Douglas State Forest at the Rhode Island border, which holds some whopper brown trout.

Massachusetts, with its wide range of terrain, offers hunting for deer, pheasants, ruffed grouse, quail, woodcock, waterfowl, rabbits, and gray squirrels, and has a severely restricted black bear season by limited permits. A few moose are known to exist in isolated parts of the northwest corner of the state, and wild turkeys have been reintroduced into appropriate areas, particularly the Quabbin forestlands and the Berkshires along the Appalachian Trail area northwest of Great Barrington, but there is currently no season for either species. Deer are hunted in December during a very short 1–week season in which shotguns only are permitted. Bow hunters and muzzle-loaders are granted special seasons at other times. Whitetails are found all over the state, the best areas being the Berkshires, the northern portion of Worcester County, Franklin County, and Cape Cod.

The great mountain footpath known as the Appalachian Trail winds through the backcountry of Massachusetts from the Vermont boundary over Mount Greylock south to Cheshire and along woodland roads to Dalton, Warner Hill, and Washington Town Hall before entering the scenic highlands of the October Mountain State Forest, beyond which it winds past Goose Pond and across Tyringham Valley, through the Beartown-East Mountain State Forest in the Berkshires to the Housatonic Valley and the Connecticut line.

Information Sources, Maps & Access

For detailed Bay State fishing and hunting information and regulations, and the following free publications, contact the Division of Fisheries & Wildlife, Leverett Saltonstall Bldg., 100 Cambridge St., Boston, MA 02202 (617)727–3151: *Massachusetts Fish and Game Laws Folder, Migratory Birds Regulations, Public Access to Waters of Massachusetts,* and *Stocked Trout Waters of Massachusetts.* The Information & Education Section, Division of Fisheries & Wildlife, Westboro 01581, will send a free list of *Wildlife Management Area Maps* available, which include a majority of the tracts. Single copies of each map, not more than five areas per person, will be mailed free if the request for maps is accompanied by a stamped, self-addressed envelope. An eminently useful large-format 202–page guide, *Trout and Salmon Fishing in New England Lakes and Ponds* ($8 postpaid), contains detailed descriptions and lake survey maps of Quabbin Reservoir and Cape Cod Ponds. It may be ordered from: Partridge Press, Box 422, Campton, NH 03223. *Great Pond Maps* of the top-ranked fishing lakes, showing depth contours, boat-launching areas, locations of key structures, and areas where shore fishing is permitted, are available free (single copies) from: Information & Education Section, Division of Fisheries & Wildlife, Westboro 01581. Due to limited quantity, only single copies of up to five

different maps will be furnished to each angler who sends a stamped, self-addressed, legal-sized envelope. Be sure to indicate the lake or ponds that you desire. Great Pond Maps are available for such renowned trout, salmon and bass waters as Land Pond, Lake Quacumquosit, Lake Nippennicket, Onota Lake, Otis Reservoir, Quabbin Reservoir, Mashpee-Wakeby Pond, Metacomet Lakes, Nissitissit River, Pontoosuc Lake, Lake Beul, Lake Garfield, Lake Mattawa, Spy Pond, Lake Quannapowitt, Walden Pond—memorialized by Henry David Thoreau—Watuppa Pond, Quaboag Pond, Furnace Pond, Manchaug Pond, and Assawompset, Packsha, and Great Quitticas Ponds. A free *Listing of Great Pond Maps* may be obtained from the Division of Fisheries & Wildlife (address above). For a handy overview of Cape Cod fresh and saltwater fishing, write to: Cape Cod Chamber of Commerce, Hyannis 02601, for *Sportsman's Guide to Cape Cod*, a free folder which lists all of the trout, bass, pickerel, and perch ponds and streams by town, and lists the species present in each, the availability of boat-launching sites, and whether or not the pond is reclaimed. Detailed descriptions of the state's major cross-country skiing areas, including abandoned railroad beds, state forests and reserves, are contained in the *EMS Ski Touring Guide to New England* ($5.95), available from: Eastern Mountain Sports, 1047 Commonwealth Ave., Boston 02215.

There are many areas in Massachusetts where one can find good canoe trails and trout water. The canoeist would do well to consult the authoritative *AMC River Guide: Volume II Central & Southern New England* ($6.00), published by: Appalachian Mountain Club, 5 Joy St., Boston 02108. It lists rivers arranged by watershed, except for coastal rivers which are arranged by areas. Rivers are described from source to mouth, since downstream travel is most common; but upstream travel has been indicated where it is necessary to make connections with other rivers. Lakes are described as parts of the watershed or stream in which they are located. There are maps included which will show the exact location of the river, and also describe the type of canoeing to be found. You will find detailed descriptions of the Housatonic ("river beyond the mountains") and Merrimack rivers, and the Rhode Island–Massachusetts coast. Detailed mile-by-mile descriptions of the Massachusetts segment of the trail are contained in the *ATC Guide to the Appalachian Trail in Massachusetts & Connecticut* ($5.85), available from: Appalachian Trail Conference, Box 236, Harpers Ferry, WV 25425; and in the *AMC Massachusetts–Rhode Island Trail Guide* ($6.75), available from: AMC Books, 5 Joy St., Boston, 02108. The *Guide to the Metacomet-Monadnock Trail in Massachusetts and New Hampshire* ($1), which describes the scenic route of this trail from Hanging Hills, Connecticut to the summit of Grand Monadnock in New Hampshire, may be ordered from: AMC, 5 Joy St., Boston 02108. For information on camping and backpacking in the state forests and parks, and for free *State Forest Maps*, write: Division of Forests & Parks, 100 Cambridge St., Boston 02202. Massachusetts' scenic state forest lands and reservations provide numerous camping and backcountry hiking opportunities. An excellent brochure to consult is *Camping in Massachusetts*, available free from: Dept. of Commerce & Tourism, Box 1775, Boston 02105. It constains a listing and descriptions, regulations, and fee schedules for private campsites, state campgrounds, city and town campsites, and state day-use areas, whose locations are shown on easy-to-read maps. The major Interstate Highway routes serving Massachusetts are 90, 91, 86, and 290.

Lodges & Cross-Country Ski Centers

★★★★*Cummington Farm* is a small rustic ski lodge located on a 700–acre farm in the northern Berkshire Mountains. This location, plus its base elevation of 1250 feet, has helped the farm to receive and hold snow longer than other nearby areas. The lodge has a 45 kilometer trail system, which is well marked and groomed daily, as the base for cross-country facilities. A night track of 2½ kilometers is lighted five nights a week. A fully stocked, newly renovated shop holds everything one needs for outfitting. Eastern professional ski touring instructors are on hand. Easy trails for beginners to more challenging advanced trails are provided to accommodate all levels of skiers. Trails take skiers over the rolling Berkshire hills and through woods of beautiful, still fir and maple. A full-moon night tour takes skiers through moonlit fields and woodlands and returns them to the farm lodge, where cheese, homemade breads and hot mulled wine are served around an open fireplace. The old Cummington Farm Sugar House has been renovated for 30 guests. Modestly decorated in New England style, the house is heated by two wood stoves. Rustic cabins with wood stoves are available for stays. Guests bring sleeping bags and ski out to the cabins. The Cummington Farm Restaurant prepares hearty meals for skier appetites. Rates (based on four-person occupancy): winter lodging, $19.90 adults per night. A mid-week package from Tuesday-Thursday is $42.36 for adults. These rates include dinner and entertainment at the Farm Restaurant the evening of arrival, breakfast the morning after and trail pass. Instruction is $6 group, $12 private. Rentals are $8 day, $4 night. Trail fee $3. Children's rates, special group rates and other special packages are available on request. For further information contact: Cummington Farm Ski Touring Center, South Road, Cummington, MA 01026 (413)634–2111.

★★★*Jug End*, tucked away on 1,200 acres in the scenic Berkshires, is a fine area for just about any recreational activity. Jug End is a rustic, year-round resort hotel featuring everything from skiing to swimming. On the grounds two slopes are available for downhill skiing, with lessons and rentals. Many of the resort's guests visit Catamont, a favorite Berkshire ski spot three miles away. Special discount tickets are available for Jug End's guests. Cross-country skiing trails running through the Berkshire's scenic hills are part of the resort's on-premise offerings. An 18–hole (72 par) golf course awaits golfers. There are indoor and outdoor swimming pools, indoor and outdoor tennis courts, plus horseback riding and lessons. The area offers beautiful hiking in all seasons. Other resort activities include music, dancing and entertainment. The resort is laid out with motel units and the main lodge spread apart to maintain a spacious feeling. Most accommodations are deluxe, with some offering patios. The atmosphere is sophisticated but informal. Meals are served country-style and the mountain air is as relaxing as it is invigorating. Modified American Plan or European Plans are available. Swimming and outdoor tennis are included in rates. Rates: Peak season, $44–52 per person, double occupancy with MAP, European Plan $29–37. Off season, $35–42 per person double occupancy with MAP, European $20–27. Rates include taxes and gratuities. Children's rates available. For further information contact: Jug End in the Berkshires, So. Egremont, MA 01258 (413)528–0434.

MICHIGAN

Introduction

Michigan's 58,216 square miles border on four of the five Great Lakes, divided into an Upper and Lower Peninsula by the picturesque Straits of Mackinac, which links Lake Michigan with Lake Huron. The two peninsulas are connected by the Mackinac Bridge, with its 3,800–foot suspension span—the third longest in the U.S. The Wolverine State is one of North America's most popular fishing, hunting, camping, canoeing, and family-vacation areas. The awesomely productive trophy fishing waters of lakes Michigan, Huron, and Superior, managed by Michigan's progressive Department of Natural Resources, hold, without a doubt, yet-to-be-caught world-record muskellunge, brown trout, northern pike, rainbow trout, walleye, and coho salmon. The mitt-shaped Lower Peninsula, a low-lying region of rolling hills and mixed hardwood and coniferous forests, contains several nationally famous recreation areas, including the historic trout waters of the Au Sable and Pere Marquette rivers, the famed ruffed-grouse lands of the Pigeon River State Forest, and the nationally renowned salmon and steelhead waters of the wild Big Manistee, Boardman, Platte, Au Gres, and St. Joseph rivers.

The remote wildlands of the beautiful Upper Peninsula, with its ancient mountains, sandy plains, rocky ridges, vast swamplands, and boreal forests, boasts the renowned trout waters of the scenic Big Two Hearted and Tahquamenon rivers and the rugged, picturesque South Shore of Lake Superior, Lake Huron's beautiful Les Chenaux Islands, the Porcupine Mountains Wilderness, the famed fishing and game lands of the Ottawa and Hiawatha national forests, and the remote Isle Royale of Lake Superior. The sandy plains areas, in part burned over by the Indians, are covered with jack pine, scrub oak, aspen, and huckleberry bushes. The tea-colored cedar swamps of the Upper Peninsula, with their numerous beaver flows, offer one of the nation's last remaining wild brook trout frontiers. Michigan, the ancient home and hunting grounds of the Chippewa, Ottawa, and Huron Indians, was an important center of the fur-trade era, with a major fort at Michilimackinac (Mackinac Island), and later became a part of the United States' old North-West Territory.

Accommodations & Travel Information

Michigan's major vacation lodges, sporting camps, inns, ski resorts, and cross-country ski centers are described in detail in the "Vacation/ Lodging Guide" which follows. Information on all aspects of travel in the state may be obtained from the Michigan Travel Bureau, P.O. Box 30226, Law Bldg., Lansing, MI 48909 (toll free (1–800)248–5700) and the Upper Peninsula Travel & Recreation Assn., P.O. Box 400, Iron Mountain, MI 49801 (906)774–5480. Visitors to the Upper Peninsula can obtain a number of free publications especially written to increase enjoyment of this wilderness playground. The *Upper Peninsula Campground Directory* lists almost all camping areas in the region, both public and private, with sections on sites with state parks, state forests, and national forests. Location, activities available, special regulations, and number of acres are all included. *Finest Attractions in Michigan's Upper Peninsula*, a glove-compartment-size brochure, describes various highlights, including the Pictured Rocks boat cruises, Copper Peak, Mackinac Island boat cruises, the Soo Locks tour train, and other activities. Over 150 waterfalls are found along the Upper Peninsula's swift, roaring streams, many of which can be easily reached by car. Grand Sable Falls at Grand Marais, Presque Isle River Falls north of Wakefield, and the famous Tahquamenon Falls between Newberry and Paradise are included in the *Upper Peninsula Waterfalls Guide*, a brochure listing 117 superb cascades with a keyed map and brief

directions for finding the falls. For those interested in touring the peninsula by car, the folder entitled *Fall Color Tours* describes eight trips, from 70 to 223 miles in length, that thoroughly explore some of the region's most spectacular natural attractions. Included are tours through the remote Keweenaw Peninsula, along the shores of lakes Superior and Michigan, beside sand dunes and tumbling rivers, and through several ghost towns, abandoned since nineteenth-century mining days. Explicit directions and maps are provided. Fine introductory descriptions of attractions in the region are offered on the reverse of the *Map and Guide to Travel and Recreation in Michigan's Upper Peninsula*, a special edition of the Michigan State Highway Map. Historic forts, Mackinac Island, shoreline drives, mountains, fishing, hunting, boating and water sports, winter activities, and many other features are described, while the detailed road and highway map will help you find your way. All of the above publications are available free from the Upper Peninsula Travel & Recreation Assn., P.O. Box 400, Iron Mountain 49801.

For winter-sports enthusiasts, the Travel & Recreation Association also publishes a free *Winter Activities and Recreation Guide* listing ski areas and snowmobile trails. Slopes, lifts, trails, rentals, accommodations, and other facilities are all indicated for such prominent skiing attractions as Porcupine Mountain, Big Powderhorn, Pine and Brule Mountains, Ottawa National Forest, and other areas. The *Calendar of Winter Events* lists special races and winter festivals. Write to the Michigan Dept. of Natural Resources (DNR), 905-A Southland Dr., Lansing 48926, for the free *Michigan Fishing Guide* booklet, which defines the seasons, bag limits, and approved fishing methods for the various game fish, and lists the general laws, waters with special rules, and the location and telephone number of DNR field offices. For detailed, statewide fishing information, call the *Michigan Fishing Hotline*, operated by the DNR, (517)373–0908. Other free publications published by the DNR of interest to the fisherman and hunter are: *Michigan's Fishing Waters, Fishing in Michigan, Michigan Boat Launching Directory, Michigan Hunting, Michigan Big Game/Small Game Hunting Guide, Waterfowl Hunting Guide, Catching Great Lakes Salmon & Trout, Know Your Great Lakes Salmon & Trout, Michigan Harbors Guide*, and *Coho, Chinook & Steelhead in Michigan*. Fishermen planning to charter a boat and guide to pursue salmon, lakers, and steelhead should write to the Michigan Travel Commission, Lansing 48913, for the free booklet *Michigan Charter Boat Directory by Port*, which lists boats and captains by lake and alphabetically within each lake region by port. Boat lengths, rates, and address and telephone numbers of the skippers are provided in each listing.

Catching Great Lakes Salmon & Trout

Michigan Department of Natural Resources

The standard reference book for non-resident and resident anglers alike, *Trout Streams of Michigan*, published by the Michigan United Conservation Clubs, contains detailed descriptions and maps of more than 300 trout streams, including such nationally renowned north country trout, steelhead, and salmon streams as the Escanaba, Fox, Ontonagon, Paint, Whitefish, Blind Sucker, and Big Two Hearted rivers in the Upper Peninsula and the Jordan, Pere Marquette, Rifle, and Little Manistee rivers in the Lower Peninsula. Individual stream descriptions cover species present, habitat, insect life, access, stream bottom composition, tributaries, holding pools, historical info, and topography. This eminently useful large-format book is edited by Thomas E. Huggler and contains an introduction by Robert Traver. It may be ordered for $2.95 (plus 50¢ postage) from: MUCC, Box 30235, Lansing 48909.

Contour lake maps are available for all major Michigan lakes, including Cisco, Lac Vieux Desert, Indian, Michigamme, Caribou, and Gogebic, for 75¢ each (plus 40¢ postage and handling) from the Michigan United Conservation Clubs, P.O. Box 30235, Lansing 48909. A handy catalog, *Michigan Mapped Lakes and Campgrounds*, offers both a county-by-county index of contour maps and a useful explanation of how such maps allow you to determine the best fishing spots. The catalog also contains a guide to forest and private campgrounds throughout the state, with charts indicating location and recreational opportunities, including fish species available in nearby lakes. At the end of the catalog is a "Michigan Guide to Easy Canoeing" describing rivers in the state that can be navigated by canoe easily, leisurely, and with a minimum of danger. The *Michigan Mapped Lakes and Campgrounds* guide is available for $1.00 from the Michigan United Conservation Clubs at the above address.

A paperbound volume, *25 Upper Peninsula Hydrographic Lake Maps*, offers 12–by–16–inch contour maps for 25 lakes, including Thousand Island, Brevoort, Gogebic, Manistique, Au Train, Caribou, Deer, Lac Vieux Desert, Michigamme, and other favorite fishing lakes in the Upper Peninsula. Similar volumes of *24 Southern Michigan Hydrographic Lake Maps* and *25 Central Michigan Hydrographic Lake Maps* are available at a price of $2.00 each from the Clarkson Map Co., Kaukauna, WI 54130. Clarkson will also mail you a complete list of approximately 2,200 hydrographic maps available from the Michigan Conservation Department if you send a stamped, self-addressed envelope to the above address.

Canoeists planning to ply the waters of the Wolverine State will find that an astounding repertory of trips is possible. With its 34 major river systems, the state offers streams differing markedly in character and difficulty, from the gentle, pastoral rivers of the Lower Peninsula to the brawling and wild waters of the Upper Peninsula.

The names of Michigan's rivers testify to the prominent role they have played in the history of the state, beginning with the days when Indians paddled the waterways in search of game, through the times of early settlement. Names like Au Sable, Pere Marquette, and Brule are reminders of the loosely-knit empire of the fur trade in the seventeenth and eighteenth centuries, when rugged French voyageurs, 10 hardy men to a 36–foot canoe, paddled the thousand-mile journey from Michigan posts to the great Northwest, then returned over the same route in a single summer.

Many rivers in the Lower Peninsula such as the Au Sable, Muskegon and Pigeon, offer fine opportunities for canoeing, with numerous possibilities for extended trips along adjoining streams. The Little Manistee's fast waters pass an old ghost town by the same name; the historic Pere Marquette features many quick turns, and crosses several tricky rapids; the scenic Ocqueoc, for experts only, flows north

through several small lakes, swamps, forests, and plains; and the placid waters of the Clinton offer easygoing waters with minimum portaging. The above rivers, as well as the St. Joseph, Black, Thornapple, Paw Paw, Flat, Red Cedar, Rifle, Chippewa, and many others are described in *Canoeing in Michigan*, a booklet available free from the Michigan Dept. of Natural Resources, 905–A Southland Dr., Lansing 48901. Directions, put-in and takeout points, length, points of interest, location of campsites, and the possibilities for extended trips are all described. Maps and details on Upper Peninsula rivers such as the Carp, Sturgeon, Escanaba, Brule, Menominee and others are included as well. Sections on "paddling pointers" and "reading white water," with several illustrations, are also provided, and the short introduction will help you decide which streams are best suited to your interests and abilities. The Department of Natural Resources also publishes a free pamphlet, *Michigan's Natural Rivers Program*, that describes the state's proposed wild and scenic rivers. For those who are not familiar with Michigan's camping facilities, the Department of Natural Resources publishes a free map/guide, *Michigan State Parks*, including a checklist of campgrounds with addresses, number of sites, general camping information (toilets, showers, fees, boat-launching sites, etc.), day-use facilities, activities, and special features.

Michigan State Forests Campground Directory lists camping facilities in all 33 state forests and correlates individual campgrounds with highway maps of the Upper and Lower peninsulas. Various charts for each forest give all information relevant to campers: number of sites, special attractions, addresses, phone numbers, and opportunities for boating, canoeing, fishing, and hiking. Write to the Dept. of Natural Resources, Forestry Division, Lansing 48926, for a free copy of the brochure and further information on campgrounds in the state forests. For detailed, state-wide camping information (after Memorial Day), call the *Michigan Camping Hotline*, operated by the DNR, (517)373–1279.

Michigan's Shore-to-Shore Riding-Hiking Trail is a fine way to see the state on horseback or on foot. The trail stretches from the Lake Michigan shore on the west to the shores of Lake Huron on the east, crossing scenic countryside, beautiful rivers, and dense hardwood and pine forests. Public trail camps along the route, as well as private facilities and services, are available for trail users. Two brochures offer information on the trail—*Michigan's Shore-to-Shore Riding-Hiking Trail* and *Michigan Riding & Hiking Trails*—and include a map of the route, approximate distances between major points, and general information on trail camps. Both brochures are available free from the Michigan Dept. of Natural Resources, Lansing 48926.

Highways & Maps

Visitors to Michigan's numerous lakes and wilderness areas will find the *Michigan Official Transportation Map* an invaluable guide to routes within the Upper and Lower peninsulas. All interstate U.S. and state routes are indicated, as well as country roads, state parks, rest areas, roadside parks, airports, seaports, county lines, ferries and boatlines, cities, towns, villages, and many other features. The map is available free from the Michigan Dept. of State Highways and Transportation, Lansing 48904. The same office also offers free maps to individual counties, showing roads and recreation facilities (total map limit: 1).

A useful *Map Guide to Michigan* is a large bound book that contains individual color maps for each of Michigan's 83 counties, packed with info about hunting, state forests, public access sites, game and fish reports, and campgrounds. It may be ordered for $5.80 from Michigan United Conservation Clubs, P.O. Box 30235, Lansing 48909. A fascinating Map of *Ghost Towns, Old Mining and Logging Towns of Northern Wisconsin and Michigan* may be obtained for $3 from Wisconsin Sportsman Inc., P.O. Box 1307, Oshkosh, WI 54901. It contains historical descriptions of all ghost towns shown on the maps.

**VACATION/
LODGING GUIDE**

Hiawatha National Forest
& Les Cheneaux Islands

This famous 860,000–acre forest embraces a wild, lake-dotted country of dense evergreens and mixed hardwoods, wetlands, and scattered rolling hills interlaced by hundreds of miles of rushing, free-stone streams and wild rivers. The forest takes its name from Henry Wadsworth Longfellow's famous *Song of Hiawatha*, the epic poem celebrating the deeds of an extraordinary Indian brave. Stretched across the eastern segment of Michigan's Upper Peninsula, the two units of the Hiawatha National Forest open onto the wave-pounded shorelines of Lakes Huron, Michigan, and Superior, the last of which was described by Longfellow as the "Shining Big-Sea Waters." Here are ancient Indian cliff paintings and the famed smallmouth bass, steelhead, brown trout, and northern pike waters of Big and Little Bay de Noc of Lake Huron, and the beautiful Laughing Whitefish Falls. Remote trails and old logging and Forest Service roads provide access to the brook-trout and steelhead waters of the Indian, Manistique, Au Train, Rapid, and Tahquamenon rivers and to the wild, scenic Rock River Canyon, Betchler Lake Wilderness, and to the swamps, glacial moraines, and giant buck trees of the Big Island Lake Wilderness. The proposed 23,000–acre Betchler Lake Wilderness contains the Laurentian Divide and the headwaters of streams that flow into both Lake Superior and Lake Michigan, surrounded by swamps, eskers, and chaotic glacial moraines. The wild fish and game lands of the Munuscong, Mackinac, Manistique, Lake Superior, Escanaba River, and Grand Sable state forests lie adjacent to the national forest boundaries. To the north are the Grand Sable Sand Dunes and ancient Indian burial grounds at Grand Island and Lake Superior.

The forest's domain includes Round and Government islands surrounded by the clear waters of Lake Huron off the southern shores of the eastern unit. Government Island is the only one of the beautiful Les Cheneaux Islands in public ownership. Like the other 34 members of this archipelago located just south of Cedarville and Hessel, the island is heavily wooded and offers superb fishing offshore for northern pike, yellow perch, and smallmouth bass, as well as hunting in season for deer and small game. Government Island was a popular stopover for explorers and voyageurs en route from Montreal and Mackinac, and from 1874 to 1939 it served as a U.S. Coast Guard station. On the northwest end of this uninhabited island are the remains of a dock and manmade clearings. Water channels leading to Government Island are popular for small boating and fishing, and small craft can be beached at two widely separated primitive picnic sites on the sheltered side of the island. The name "Les Cheneaux" derives from the French word for "the channels." Known locally as "The Snows," the islands vary in size from Marquette Island, over six miles long, to Dollar Island, barely large enough to accommodate a single summer cottage. Les Cheneaux have been popular with summer vacationers since the turn of the century. All the islands are heavily wooded, with numerous trails leading through forests of cedar, pine, and balsam. From a distance, the group gives the appearance of floating rafts of greenery, while tall conifers lend an illusion of great height.

Sandwiched between Mackinac and Bois Blanc islands, Round Island has changed very little since the Indians called it *Minnisais* ("little island"). An old lighthouse on the northwest end of the island, built in 1873 and abandoned in 1935, is the only permanent testimony to the white man's presence here. Round Island can be reached by boat in summer or over ice in wintertime. Both Government and Round islands have been classified as scenic areas and

are carefully managed to preserve the natural wilderness conditions favorable to forest plant and animal life. A varied and fascinating community of plant life flourishes on the islands throughout the spring and summer. Bunchberry and bearberry carpet wide areas; twin flowers, trillium, ground hemlock, and pyrola thrive deep in the woods; and rare and delicate orchids are found growing wild and undisturbed. Present everywhere is a variety of trees, shrubs, ferns, lichens, and mosses. Wildlife of the mainland, varying in size from the deer mouse to the whitetail deer, can cross the water to visit or live on the islands. Bird life of the area includes ducks, woodpeckers, sparrows, warblers, sandpipers, hawks, and owls. No campgrounds have been developed on either Round or Government Island, but picnic sites and primitive trails make both areas ideal for day trips.

Other attractions of the Hiawatha National Forest's eastern unit include the Point Iroquois Lighthouse, a picturesque abandoned structure at the mouth of the St. Marys River affording splendid views of Canada, Lake Superior, and of oceangoing freighters, or "salties," plying the river and lake. The Big Sea Water Area offers miles of sandy Lake Superior shoreline with handsome scenery and panoramic overlooks. The Bay View and Monocle Lake campgrounds near Lake Superior offer 24 and 59 campsites respectively and opportunities for fishing and boating. Other campgrounds in the eastern unit are located on the shores of Brevoort Lake, along Carp River, at Soldier Lake, and near Foley Creek. Just outside the forest's southern boundary is St. Ignace, second oldest settlement in Michigan, officially founded by Father Jacques Marquette and visited during its early history by such notables as Jean Nicolet and the Sieur de La Salle.

In the western part of the forest is the famous Grand Island-Bay de Noc Trail, following an old Indian route along the Whitefish River bluff. Au Train, just north of the lake of the same name, was a favorite camping ground for Chippewa Indians and an important stop for voyageurs on their trips along the south shore of Lake Superior. A modern campground with opportunities for fishing and boating is nestled among Norway pines on the south shore of Au Train Lake. Many other campgrounds in the western unit are situated near lakes, including Camp, Little Bass, Petes, Pole Creek, and Corner. Canoeing is popular on the Whitefish, Sturgeon, and Au Train rivers. Innumerable species of wildlife contribute to the beauty and fascination of the national forest. Whitetail deer and black bear are among the largest species, but there are also snowshoe hare, beaver, squirrel, porcupine, coyote, weasel, red fox, and raccoon. In addition, the rare pine marten, previously extinct in this part of

the country because of trapping and changes in habitat, has been reintroduced. Although the chances of sighting them are extremely remote, there have been reports of both timber wolves and moose in the Hiawatha. In addition to the wide variety of mammals, game birds—including ruffed and sharp-tailed grouse, woodcock, and a diversity of waterfowl—provide top hunting opportunities. In the waters of the Hiawatha, Thunder, Hulbert, Pendrills, Manistique, and Brevoort lakes, and the forest's many rivers hold trophy-sized trout, bass, perch, walleye, northerns, coho salmon, smelt, and steelhead.

Information Sources, Maps & Access

For detailed vacation travel and recreation information, a full-color *Hiawatha National Forest Map* (50¢) and a free map/brochure of *The Islands*, contact: Supervisor, Hiawatha National Forest, Escanaba, MI 49829 (906)786-4062. For information and a free *Seney Wildlife Refuge & Wilderness Tract Map*, contact: Manager, Seney National Wildlife Refuge, Seney, MI 49883. The Hiawatha Forest is reached from Sault Ste. Marie: take U.S. 75 south, then State Highway 28 west. U.S. 75 also leads north from Mackinaw City and St. Ignace. From Escanaba and Gladstone, take U.S. 41 north. The Upper Peninsula is connected to the Lower Peninsula by the Mackinac Bridge, which spans the awesomely beautiful Straits of Mackinac between lakes Huron and Michigan—dominated on the east by the historic wilderness fur trade capital of Mackinac Island.

A free map/brochure, *Pictured Rocks National Lakeshore*, showing major park features, roads, lakes, and other points of interest, is available from the Superintendent, Pictured Rocks National Lakeshore, Munising 49862 (906)387-2607. The Park Service also publishes free fliers on hiking, skiing, snowshoeing, boating, fishing, hunting, and camping. Guided cruises of the area are provided by *Pictured Rocks Cruises, Inc.*, Box 355, Munising 49862 (906)387-2379.

Recreation Areas

Drummond Island—"Gem of Lake Huron"

This "Gem of Lake Huron" is located just off the eastern shoreline of the Upper Peninsula and is reached by ferry from the village of De Tour. Outlined by high, rocky shores facing numerous irregular coves and bays, Drummond Island features 136 square miles of forested wilderness interrupted by more than 40 inland lakes. The many bays, protected by small, rocky islands, afford excellent anchorage for boats and provide superb fishing for lake trout and salmon year round. Potagannissing Bay offers some of the finest duck hunting in the north while inland wooded areas contain deer, bear, and an occasional moose. Hiking trails, a yacht club, campgrounds, and three stocked trout streams are additional attractions.

The island is named after the British commander of the lake district, Sir Gordon Drummond. After losing Mackinac Island to the Americans following the War of 1812, the British constructed a fort here in 1815. When title to the island was settled in favor of the United States in 1822, the British abandoned their fort, leaving behind extensive fortifications including some 14 buildings. The remains of Fort Drummond—faint traces of foundation walls, a cemetery, chimneys, and huge fireplaces—are still visible on the southwestern promontory of the island, two miles from the channel landing.

Lake Superior State Forest

Stretched across Luce and Chippewa counties in the unsettled wilderness of the Upper Peninsula, this 175,749–acre area offers unparalleled canoeing, hunting, and fishing just north of the Hiawatha National Forest. The forest encompasses both the rugged Lake

Superior shoreline and several major inland bodies of water, including Muskellonge, Betsy, Little Two Hearted, Bear and Sheephead lakes, which hold wild brook trout, bass northern pike, and walleye. Two historic north country gems, the Tahquamenon and Big Two Hearted rivers, are top-rank canoe routes and fishing streams for wild red-bellied brook trout and rainbows, surrounded by scenic conifers and mixed hardwoods, beaver meadows, tag alder, cedar and spruce swamps. The Tahquamenon, sometimes called the "dark" or "golden" river, flows through marshy lowlands, past densely wooded ridges, and between towering rock cliffs as it makes its way through the forest and neighboring Mackinac State Forest to the waters of Whitefish Bay. The river figures prominently in Longfellow's epic poem *Hiawatha*, where it makes the watery grave of Kwasind, the friend of Hiawatha who is killed in a mighty battle with the scheming otters. Between the town of Newberry and Paradise are the legendary Tahquamenon Falls, known as the "Little Niagara," tumbling down the face of a 40–foot cliff. Six miles downstream from the Big Falls are the Cataracts, or Lower Falls, from which point the river broadens

over wide ledges, then swirls through impressive stretches of thundering rapids until it finally comes to rest in Lake Superior. The Tahquamenon offers good canoeing between McMillan and Whitefish Bay during all months except June and July, when black flies make the trip unbearable. Canoeists should plan on paddling 15 miles the first day, since campsites are not available in the extensive willow marshes that line this first stretch of the route. The upper and lower falls must be portaged. A 25–mile trip for experts is also possible on the Two Hearted River between the High Bridge on County Road 407 and the stream's mouth at Lake Superior. Fast water, occasional portages, and wild and rolling country are the characteristics of this particular run. About seven miles downstream is the Two Hearted River Canoe Campground, and another state campground is five miles farther, at Reed and Green Bridge, a good spot for pickup or overnight camping. Beyond the Two Hearted River Forest Campground, another state facility at the river's mouth, the land adjoining the river is suitable for camping almost anywhere.

Besides canoeing and trout fishing, the interior wildlands of this old logging country provide top-ranked hunting for whitetail deer, black bear, and ruffed grouse. Nearby attractions and major features of the forest include the Tahquamenon Falls State Park, Grand Sable Sand Dunes, Seney National Wildlife Refuge, and the Hiawatha National Forest. Campgrounds are located on Pratt, Holland, Perch, Culhane, and Bodi lakes, and at the High and the Reed and Green bridges.

Mackinac Island & the Straits of Mackinac

Rising from the Straits of Mackinac between Lakes Huron and Michigan, Mackinac Island has been called a modern summer resort in a nineteenth century setting. No automobiles are permitted on the island, which is reached by ferry from St. Ignace, and visitors must tour the area via horseback, bicycle, or horse-drawn carriage. Graced by large summer houses, rolling green slopes, and lush gardens, Mackinac offers a taste of bygone elegance on a solid-rock island free from swamps, mosquitoes, or polluted waters. The island's first inhabitants were nomadic Indians who gathered here to trade or to take refuge from the fierce Iroquois tribes. Natives called the island *Michilimackinac*, or "the great turtle," because they believed it rose from the straits like a giant reptile coming up for air. The more prosaic geologic evidence indicates that the island was once covered by an inland sea which gradually receded. As the waters lowered, the limestone pinnacle gradually emerged, terrace by terrace, until the Great Lakes settled to their present levels. Water erosion carved Mackinac's many natural wonders—the Devil's Kitchen, Arch Rock, Scott's Cave and other rock formations and wore down the huge limestone cliffs which at one time overshadowed the eastern and southern shores of the island. With neither rich soil nor ready sources of irrigation, the island was never a great attraction for settlers. Visitors today, however, find that the absence of lakes or streams on Mackinac Island is offset by the many natural springs and the surrounding sparkling waters of Lake Huron. Jean Nicolet was the first white man to venture near the island when he canoed through the straits on his futile voyage toward the Orient. For almost fifty years thereafter traders, missionaries and voyageurs passed the island's rocky cliffs on their way to and from the great Northwest. Father Marquette visited the island after founding his mission at St. Ignace in 1671, and the Sieur de la Salle passed Mackinac in 1679 in the *Griffon*, the first commercial sailing vessel to explore the Great Lakes. French traders dominated the entire area surrounding the island until the end of the French and Indian War when the victorious British moved the regional headquarters from the old French post near Mackinaw City on the Lower Peninsula to the more strategic setting of Mackinac Island in 1781.

Sharply aware of the island's many assets, John Jacob Astor in 1817 centered the activities of his American Fur Company on Mackinac. Astor's endeavors peaked around the middle of the 1820's, when the company annually employed as many as 2,000 voyageurs and 400 clerks and traded pelts valued at three million dollars. Until the decline of the fur empire toward 1830, the Mackinac post was a hub of furious activity inhabited by a cross-section of humanity never rivalled since: French voyageurs and coureurs de bois, American soldiers and businessmen, and hundreds of Indians who sometimes camped along the beach in tents two and three rows deep. The island developed a civilization unto itself where the irregular life led by most of its occupants was punctuated by impromptu celebrations, drunken brawling, and an occasional fracas ending in the murder of some unfortunate trader.

After fur traders abandoned the island, Mackinac began to be promoted as a resort center. Several wealthy Southern planters built summer homes there, but the Civil War put an end to Dixie prosperity and the colony disappeared. The resort movement revived after the war when the island began to attract vacationers from Chicago. Ferry service was started in 1881, by 1887 the huge Grand Hotel was constructed to cater to prosperous visitors, and in 1895 the island was declared a State Park. Fort Mackinac has been restored in its original location on a high, steep bluff overlooking the harbor, and today dominates the island much as it did in 1781. Carriage and

walking tours are available of the Avenue of Flags, blockhouse and officers' quarters. The Mackinac Tea Room offers refreshments in reconstructed period building overlooking the entire impressive straits area. Write to the Mackinac Island State Park Commission for a free brochure describing the fort and for information on nearby Fort Michilimackinac on the mainland in Mackinaw City. For detailed Mackinac Island information, contact the Chamber of Commerce at (906)847–3783.

Everywhere on the island are natural rock formations sculpted by wind and water over long periods of time. Arch Rock, located 149 feet above Lake Huron on the eastern shoreline, has a span of 50 feet and appears from certain angles to be suspended in air. Indians believed the bridge was fashioned by spirits as a gateway to the island. Not far from Arch Rock is Skull Cave, a narrow opening in the solid limestone which widens to a cave large enough to accommodate a man sitting upright. Friendly natives hid the fur trader Alexander Henry here after a massacre known as Pontiac's Conspiracy at Fort Michilimackinac in 1763. When Henry awakened the following morning, he discovered that he had spent the night on a pile of human skulls and bones, the remains of Indian prisoners who had been sacrificed or perhaps eaten at war feasts. Sugar Loaf Rock, a towering limestone pinnacle on the eastern side of Mackinac, offers sweeping views of the island and surrounding waters from its lofty summit. According to Indian legend, the great spirit Menabozho, who recreated the world after the deluge, lived inside the rock tower. A few miles beyond Sugar Loaf Rock is the Devil's Kitchen, a smoke-darkened opening in the rock once used for cooking by picnickers.

Other attractions on the island include the many historic buildings such as St. Anne's Church built in 1874 with a parish record reaching back to the seventeenth century. Built in 1829–30, the Old Mission Church offers a square tower and clapboard exterior reminiscent of New England architecture. There is also the long, white-washed Astor House, headquarters of the American Fur Company, originally constructed of hand-hewn timbers and fused glass.

Pictured Rocks National Lakeshore

Along a 15–mile stretch of the Lake Superior shoreline are the multicolored sandstone cliffs of the Pictured Rocks escarpment, rising abruptly to heights of 200 feet and overshadowing the coastal waters northeast of Munising. Wind, driving rain, and the erosive action of ice during glacial periods have carved many weird and beautiful formations: columns, arches, towers, domes, promontories, and thunder caves. Over the years, soluble oxide deposits have stained the intricate patterns incised by nature on the exposed sandstone, creating tableaux colorful enough to rival any artist's canvas.

The Pictured Rocks National Lakeshore offers outstanding opportunities for wilderness camping, backpacking, and encompasses the scenic trophy trout and steelhead waters of the Miners, Mosquito, and Hurricane rivers, surrounded by tag alder, wooded dunes, conifer and mixed hardwood forests. These wild north country streams are noted for their deep pools, log jams, falls, and overhanging brush. In the eastern section of the national lakeshore are the spectacular Grand Sable Banks and Dunes. Extending for five miles along the Lake Superior shorelines and rising to a height of 275 feet above the lake level, the Grand Sable Banks are the remnant of a vast glacial deposit left by melting sheets of ice thousands of years ago. Perched on top of the banks are the Grand Sable Dunes, rising an additional 85 feet and covering an area of five square miles. The sand was blown into great dunes at the edge of the ancient lake that

preceded Superior. Wind off the lake is slowly blowing the dunes island, where they are partially stabilized by plant growth. Much of the inland portion of the national lakeshore is thickly wooded with northern hardwoods, pine, spruce, hemlock, and fir. Spring flowers and autumn foliage make the area particularly spectacular in season. In some burned-over areas, there are large, almost pure stands of lovely white birches. Arborvitae and tamarack, along with leatherleaf and other northern bog plants, are common in marshy areas and around ponds and lakes. At Hurricane River, Little Beaver Lake, and Twelve-Mile Beach there are primitive camping areas accessible by car. Backcountry camping is permitted in many remote areas of the park, but a special camping permit, available from park headquarters or any park ranger, should be obtained first. Winter activities in the national lakeshore include snowmobiling, cross-country skiing, and snowshoeing. Pictured Rocks National Lakeshore is accessible via County road H58 from Grand Marais to the northeast of the park and via State Highway 28 from Munising and Marquette. From Manistique, take State Highway 94 north. Other nearby outfitting centers include Wetmore, Shingleton, and Meistrand.

Gateways & Accommodations

Cheboygan—Gateway to Les Cheneaux & Bois Blanc Islands

(Pop. 5,500; zip code 49721; area code 616). Gateway to St. Ignace, Mackinac Island and Les Cheneaux Islands, Cheboygan is named after an Indian word for "place of entrance" or "harbor"—an allusion, no doubt, to the Cheboygan River, which is an outlet for numerous streams and lakes, including Mullett and Bird lakes, both famous for bass and muskie fishing. The town and its environs have long been noted for a healthful climate, especially for hayfever sufferers. Accommodations: *Continental Motor Court* (rates: $26–31 double), 40 excellent rooms and suites, color TV, free airport bus, nearby restaurant, at 613 N. Main St., one block north of town on U.S. Hwy. 23 (627–7164); *River Terrace Motel* (rates: $30–36 double), 26 excellent rooms, five with kitchens, on nicely landscaped grounds along the Cheboygan River, color TV, sundeck, restaurant adjacent, at 847 S. Main St., one mile south on Michigan State Hwy. 27 (627–5688).

Escanaba

(Pop. 15,000; zip code 49829; area code 906). The only iron ore shipping port on Lake Michigan, Escanaba boasts a long and varied history as a lumbering center, commercial fishing port, and vacation gateway to unspoiled streams and primitive wilderness areas. The

town is headquarters for the Hiawatha National Forest with its rugged shoreline on three of the Great Lakes. Other area attractions include the trout waters of the Escanaba River and state forest; Ludington Park, off Michigan State Hwy. 35, overlooking Little Bay de Noc; and the Delta County Historical Museum within the park featuring displays of local historical artifacts. Accommodations: *Best Western Pioneer Motor Inn* (rates: $31–34 double), 50 attractive rooms, color TV, heated indoor pool, dining room and cocktail lounge, at 2635 Ludington St. (786–0602); *Hiawatha Motel* (rates: $24–26 double), 21 comfortable rooms, one two-bedroom housekeeping cottage, free continental breakfast, nearby restaurant opposite, 4½ miles north of town via U.S. Hwy. 2 (786–1341); *Terrace Motor Inn* (rates: $36–40 double), 71 excellent rooms overlooking Little Bay de Noc, color TV, heated pool, sauna, some private patios and balconies, locally popular restaurant and cocktail lounge, 4½ miles north of town via U.S. Hwy. 2 (786–7554).

Grand Marais—Gateway to Pictured Rocks & Lake Superior State Forest

(Pop. 400; zip code 49839; area code 906). The only harbor on the Lake Superior coast between Munising and Sault Ste. Marie, Grand Marais is the gateway to an area of exceptional natural beauty:

crystal-clear lakes, secluded trout streams, and unspoiled beaches. At the edge of town are the Pictured Rocks National Lakeshore (see above) and several renowned steelhead fishing streams. Also within easy driving distance are Grand Sable Falls, where the Grand Sable River tumbles down rocky shelves on its way to Lake Superior, and the Grand Sable Dunes, a series of ever-changing, wind-whipped dunes that stretch for seven miles between Lake Superior and Grand Sable Lake. Accommodations: *Alverson's Motel* (rates: $18–20 double), 15 attractive rooms, color TV, overlooking Lake Superior, restaurant opposite, ½ block east of Michigan State Hwy. 77 (494–2681); *Welker's Lodge* (rates: $17–21 double), 20 motel rooms, eight housekeeping cottages, TV, boats and motors for rent, playground, grocery, restaurant, on Canal St., one mile east of Michigan State Hwy. 77 (494–2361).

Mackinaw City—Gateway to Mackinac Island & the Upper Peninsula

(Pop. 900; zip code 49701; area code 616) situated at the northernmost tip of the Lower Peninsula on Interstate 75 at the beautiful Straits of Mackinac joining Lake Huron and Lake Michigan, is the major gateway and stopover for fishermen, canoeists, and vacation travelers heading north across the Mackinac Bridge into the famous Upper Peninsula region. The town is the site of old Fort Michilimackinac in Michilimackinac State Park (436–5563) at the rear of the South end of Mackinac Bridge. This legendary fort—framed in the epic novel *Northwest Pasage* (based on the Kenneth Roberts novel)—was a major stopover and jumping-off point for voyageurs on their trips between Lake Huron and Lake Michigan. Several transportation companies (see below) provide ferry service from the town to adjacent Mackinac Island. Other area attractions include beautiful Wilderness State Park (436–5381) on Lake Michigan at the straits, eight miles west off I-75; Lake Paradise; the Mackinac Maritime Museum at the Old Mackinac Point Lighthouse, built in 1872; and Teysen's Talking Bear Museum, across from the ferry docks at 416 S. Huron Avenue Accommodations: *Colonial Inn* (rates: $38 double), with 23 excellent rooms and heated pool at 517 N. Huron. (436–5543); *International Inn* (rates: $38–44 double), with 77 excellent rooms and heated pool, ½ mile south of town on U.S. 31 (436–5332); *Ramada Inn* (rates: $44–48 double), with 114 excellent rooms, restaurant, cocktail lounge, heated pool, tennis, sauna, off I-75 exit 338, ½ mile south of Mackinac Bridge (436–5535); *Travelodge* (rates: $38–44 double), with 60 excellent rooms, coffeeshop, heated pool, one mile south of town on U.S. 31 (436–5544).

Manistique

(Pop. 4,300; zip code 49854; area code 906.) Surrounded by over 300 lakes and streams and located at the mouth of the Manistique River, this town is a popular jumping-off point for fishermen, canoeists, and visitors to the Hiawatha National Forest. Nearby Palms Brook State Park, 12 miles northwest on Michigan State Hwy. 149, encompasses the state's largest spring, called Kitch-iti-kippi, 200 feet wide and 40 feet deep. Accommodations: *Beachcomber Motel* (rates: $24–26 double), 20 rooms overlooking Lake Michigan, color TV, restaurant adjacent, one mile east of town via U.S. Hwy. 2 (341–2567); *Best Western Breakers Motel* (rates: $24–26 double), 20 rooms overlooking Lake Michigan, color TV, heated pool, playground, attractive restaurant adjacent, 3½ miles east of town via U.S. Hwy. 2 (341–2410); *Maple Leaf Motel* (rates: $20–22 double), 13 rooms, opposite Lake Michigan, color TV, 1½ miles east of town on U.S. Hwy. 2 (341–6014); *Ramada Inn* (rates: $38.50 double), 40 excellent rooms overlooking Lake Michigan, color TV, indoor pool, sauna, playground, restaurant and cocktail lounge, two miles east of town via U.S. Hwy. 2 (341–6911).

Marquette

(Pop. 23,300; zip code 49855; area code 906). Named for the missionary-explorer Father Jacques Marquette, the city occupies a series of rocky headlands on the south shore of Lake Superior. Marquette is one of the main shipping points of the Upper Peninsula and a vacation gateway for visitors to the Hiawatha National Forest and Pictured Rocks National Lakeshore. East of town is a sweeping shoreline with crescent-shaped beaches; to the west and south are forests and granite-bearing mountains. Area attractions include Presque Isle Park, a beautiful wooded peninsula with a small zoo and fine beaches, just north of the city; Northern Michigan University campus; the Marquette and Huron Railroad, 4½ miles north of town on Presque Isle and Lake Shore Blvds., where visitors embark on a scenic 1½ hour ride aboard a refurbished steam train built in 1910 (phone 228–8785 for schedule); the Marquette County Historical Society Museum, at 213 N. Front St., housing exhibits of local historical interest (open Mon.-Fri., 9 am–4:30 pm); and Sugar Loaf Mountain, north of the city, the summit of which is reached by rail and offers a superb view of Lake Superior, Accommodations: *Bavarian Inn* (rates: $32 double), 26 good to excellent rooms, color TV, restaurant and cocktail lounge, three miles west of town via U.S. 41 and Michigan State Hwy. 28 (226–2314); *Holiday Inn* (rates: $42.50 double), 206 rooms, color TV, heated indoor pool, saunas, airport bus, restaurant and cocktail lounge, on Washington St., one mile west of town via U.S. Hwy. 41 bypass (225–1351); *Imperial Motel* (rates: $22–26 double), 28 excellent rooms, color TV, nearby restaurant, two miles west of town via U.S. Hwy. 41 and Michigan State Hwy. 28 (228–7430); *Queen City Motel* (rates: $22–26 double), 31 attractive rooms, two efficiency units with two bedrooms each, color TV, airport bus, nearby restaurant, 2½ miles west of town via U.S. Hwy. 41 and Michigan State Hwy. 28 (225–1336); *Tiroler Hof Motel* (rates: $34 double), 44 excellent rooms and suites on beautiful, wooded grounds overlooking Lake Superior, private balconies and patios, stocked trout pond, fishing, sauna, lighted skiing, restaurant and cocktail lounge, at 150 Carp River Hills, 1¾ miles southeast of town via U.S. Hwy. 41 and Michigan State Hwy. 28 (226–7516).

Munising—Gateway to Pictured Rocks

(Pop. 3,700; zip code 49862; area code 906). Ringed on three sides by sharply rising hills, Munising is a gateway to both the Hiawatha National Forest and Pictured Rocks National Lakeshore. For centuries, the area was the camping place of Ojibway Indians, who called Grand Island across the harbor "Gitchi Menesing" (place of the big island). The latter half of this name, slightly altered, was eventually adopted by white settlers for their community on the mainland. Boat cruises to the National Lakeshore leave the City Pier on Elm Avenue, June 15–mid-October, at scheduled intervals. The 2½-to-3-hour tours explore the colored rock formations which rise along Lake Superior to heights of 200 feet (call 387–2379 for information). Accommodations: *Alger Falls Motel* (rates: $18–20 double), 16 rooms and one cottage in wooded area, TV, snowmobile trails, playground, two miles east of town via Michigan State Hwys. 28 and 94 (387–3536); *Terrace Motel* (rates: $16–20 double), 18 rooms, four 2–room units, TV, snowmobile guide service in winter, at 420 Prospect, ½ mile east of town via Michigan State Hwy. 28 (387–2735); *Vacationer Motel* (rates: $22–28 double), 20 rooms, TV, restaurant opposite, five blocks southeast of town via Michigan State Hwy. 28 (387–3400).

Newberry—Gateway to Tahquamenon Falls & Lake Superior State Forest

(Pop. 2,400; zip code 49868; area code 906) is the gateway to Lake Superior State Forest and beautiful Tahquamenon Falls State Park

(492–3415), 30 miles northeast of town via Michigan State Hwy. 123, a 20,000–acre preserve encompassing the upper and lower falls of the Tahquamenon River. The falls are accessible by regularly scheduled boat service from Hulbert and Soo Junction. Tom Sawyer Riverboat Cruise, a 4½–hour tour down the Tahquamenon River through virgin hardwood forests to Upper Tahquamenon Falls, leaves Slater's Landing, 10 miles north of Hulbert via Michigan State Hwy. 28, twice daily, June 15–Labor Day (phone 876–2331 for information). Accommodations: *Green Acres Motel* (rates: $26–30 double), 11 attractive rooms and six two-room units, color TV, playground, restaurant opposite, four miles southeast of town on Michigan State Hwy. 28 (293–5932); *Park-a-Way Motel* (rates: $22–26 double), 24 rooms, six with kitchens, color TV, heated indoor pool, restaurant opposite, ¾ mile south of town via Michigan State Hwy. 123 (293–5771).

St. Ignace—Gateway to the Upper Peninsula & Hiawatha National Forest

(Pop. 2,900; zip code 49781; area code 906). Second oldest city in Michigan, St. Ignace is on the Straits of Mackinac and connected by bridge with Mackinaw City. Points of interest include the five-mile long Mackinac Straits Bridge, one of the longest suspension bridges in the world; Castle Rock, four miles north of town, an ancient outlook of the Algonquin Indians with impressive views; and Marquette Park, at State and Marquette Sts., encompassing a French and Indian Museum and the grave of Pere Marquette. West of the city, U.S. Hwy. 2 offers a scenic drive along the lakeshore then up through rolling, wooded hills. Accommodations: *Belle Isle Motel* (rates: $28–37 double), 47 attractive rooms on five acres of landscaped grounds overlooking Lake Huron, color TV, sun deck and patio, heated pool, putting green, restaurant adjacent, 2½ miles north of Bridge via Interstate 75 business rt., 1030 N. State St. (643–8060); *Best Western Georgian House* (rates: $38 double), 46 fine rooms overlooking the straits, color TV, heated indoor pool, sundeck, dining room and cocktail lounge, on Interstate 75 business loop, three miles north of bridge (643–8411); *Chalet North Motel* (rates: $26–32 double), 70 attractive rooms overlooking Lake Huron, TV, heated pool, beach, playground, restaurant nearby, at 1140 North State St., three miles north of bridge via Interstate 75 business rt. (643–9141); *Dettman's Motel* (rates: $34 double), 77 rooms, four two-bedroom units, TV, landscaped grounds overlooking the straits, heated pool, nice views of island, nearby restaurant, at 797 N. State St., two miles north of bridge via Interstate 75 business rt. (643–9882); *Thunderbird Motor Inn* (rates: $29–34 double), 34 rooms, color TV, nearby restaurant, opposite Mackinac Island Ferry, at 10 S. State St. (643–8900); *Tradewinds Motel* (rates: $27–30 double), 25 rooms, pleasant grounds opposite Lake Huron, color TV, heated pool, playground, next to restaurant, at 1190 N. State St., three miles north of bridge via Interstate 75 business rt. (643–9388).

Sault Ste. Marie

(Pop. 17,000; zip code 49783; area code 906). The city known as "Sweet Soo" stands at the northeastern tip of the Upper Peninsula, on the south shore of the St. Marys River just across from its Canadian twin, Sault Ste. Marie, Ontario. The famous series of locks along the St. Marys are in operation all year round, raising and lowering lake- and sea-going vessels 21 feet between Lake Superior and Lake Huron in approximately five to fifteen minutes. Boat tours of the locks leave the city docks at 500 and 1155 East Portage Avenue daily, Memorial Day to October. Once described by Henry Clay as "the remotest settlement in the United States, if not on the moon," Sault Ste. Marie was the first permanent settlement in Michigan. When Father Jacques Marquette built a church here in

1669, the site became the center of missionary activities for the region. The town takes its name from the falls of the St. Marys River ("sault" means cascades or leap in French), which necessitated the building of the "Soo" Locks during the 1870's and 1880's. Sault Ste. Marie, the only entrance into Canada for almost 300 miles, boasts a beautiful setting against high hills that afford spectacular views of the river and its islands. Visitors can also enjoy panoramic views of the locks from the 21–story Tower of History, at 326 East Portage Ave.; the building houses artifacts from Sault Ste. Marie's early days and a slide show depicting the history of the city and the Great Lakes. Accommodations: *Best Western Colonial Inn* (rates: $32–36 double), 32 attractive rooms, color TV, airport bus, just south of town via Interstate 75 business route (632–2170); *La France Terrace Motel* (rates: $22–36 double), 30 rooms, including two-room family units, TV, heated pool, playground, nearby restaurant, at 1608 Ashmun St., ¾ mile south of town via Interstate 75 business route (632–7823); *Mid-City Motel* (rates: $20–25 double), 20 attractive rooms, color TV, in town adjacent to Tower of History, 304 E. Portage Ave. (632–6832); *Skyline Motel* (rates: $30–32 double), 24 rooms, some with oversize beds, color TV, restaurant adjacent, 1¾ miles south of town via Interstate 75 Business route, at 2601 Business Spur I-75 (632–3393).

Lodges & Mackinac Island Resort Hotels

★★★*Bark's Resort on Au Train Lake* is located in the heart of the Hiawatha National Forest. It is 12 miles west and three miles south of Munising in the Upper Peninsula and is open from May 1 through October 15th. Au Train lake has great fishing for walleyes, northern pike, bass and panfish. Trips can be arranged to troll Lake Superior or fish the trout streams. In season, there is hunting for snowshoe rabbit, partridge, ducks and deer. Bark's has a playground and a sandy, safe beach. There is a fish house, and each cottage comes with a free boat. In the area, there is hiking, bird and animal watching, sighting natural wonders on walks, auto tours and boat trips. Cabins have two and three bedrooms, automatic heat and are fully equipped for housekeeping. They have rustic northwoods furniture and many have fireplaces. From June 16 through Sept. 1, cabins are rented by the week only and are $130 to $140 for two persons, $140 to $150 for three or four, and $160 for five or six. A three-bedroom cabin on the Lake will accommodate six or eight people with a rollaway and rents for $175 per week. For more information, write to Cyril & Virginia Bark, Bark's Resort, Au Train, MI 49806 (906)892–8300.

★★★★*The Grand Hotel at Mackinac Island* is the landmark of the island, and epitomizes the 300–year-old history and charm of this island where no automobiles are allowed and the busy world stops. The Grand is a huge, white elegant old hotel with the longest porch in the world, manicured lawns, outstanding recreational facilities and impeccable service. The hotel has a large heated pool, surrounded by a patio and lush gardens. It has its own adjoining golf course, with a putting green for warming up, a fully-equipped pro shop and clubs for sale or rent. Lunch can be enjoyed beneath the umbrellaed tables of the Snack Bar. There are four all-weather tennis courts, with lessons and equipment available; a baseball diamond, complete with bats and balls; shuffleboard courts and indoor games in the Game Room. Guests can explore the island on foot, in a surrey, on the 18½ miles of bicycle trails or on the 40 miles of bridle paths. Bicycles can be rented at the Grand and horses hired nearby. The Grand is operated on the American Plan, including all three meals. Morning brings a country breakfast, there is a sumptuous luncheon buffet, complimentary tea in the afternoon with freshly baked cakes and cookies, followed by the incomparable dinner. Dinner in the Main Dining Room is formal with men in jackets and

ties. Coffee can be enjoyed in the main lobby during the after-dinner concert hour. There is a piano bar for a night cap, the Terrace Room for dancing and entertainment with never a cover or minimum, and the Grand Stand for late night entertainment. Visitors will also enjoy shopping in the village and waterfront area of Mackinac Island; seeing the 1789 Fort Mackinac, preserved exactly as it was; touring Astor Fur Post, headquarters of the original American Fur Co. founded by John Jacob Astor; visiting an Indian Dormitory built in 1838 and seeing many other Revolutionary-era sights and landmarks. Rooms at the Grand match the elegance of the rest of the hotel with high ceilings, modern furniture and beautiful views. The Grand is open from May through October. Daily room rates including all meals are $47.50 to $75.00 per person (double occupancy). There are rates for children, and suites are also available. A 15% gratuity charge is added to the bill, but there is absolutely no tipping permitted at the Grand Hotel, including all waiters, bellmen, doormen, porters, chambermaids, etc. For reservations and information write: The Grand Hotel, Mackinac Island, MI 49757 (906)847–3331. Winter offices are at 222 W. 1st St., Lake Forest, Ill. 60045 (312)234–6540.

★★★*Hotel Iroquois on the Beach* is on the southern tip of Mackinac Island overlooking the Straits. It is a traditional hotel in keeping with the historic and charming flavor of the island. Mackinac Island does not allow automobiles, so visitors must leave their cars in the ample parking facilities at Mackinaw City or St. Ignace and take the ferry across the Straits. There is also a private airstrip on the island for small planes. The hotel offers charming rooms in the Inn, and each room has a water view. There is dining in the Carriage House with an informal style. Guests can relax in the sun on the large sun-deck, enjoy the white sandy beach or sip cocktails outside under umbrellas. The Hotel Iroquois also has a Cycle Shop with bicycles to rent. Visitors can then tour Old Fort Mackinac, Beaumont Memorial and Skull Cave or visit natural scenic spots such as Arch Rock and Sugar Loaf. Nearby are golf courses, horseback riding, horse-drawn carriages and shopping in the busy downtown area. Room rates are based on double occupancy, European Plan and vary by size of the room, its view of the water and location in the hotel. They are $52 to $94 per day in full season and $38 to $60 for off season dates. For more information write: Hotel Iroquois on the Beach, Mackinac Island, MI 49757 (906)847–3321 or 847–3322.

★★★★*Lakeview Resort on Drummond Island* overlooks beautiful Potagannissing Bay in the northern Great Lakes area. Essentially an outdoor activity resort, it boasts hunting and an especially wide range of fishing. There are over 40 islands in the Potagannissing Bay area from which to fish. The resort makes available a 16–foot Lone Star boat; 6 and 10 mph Mercury motors; an enclosed fish cleaning house with running water; your own launching ramp for your use. Bait, gas and oil are also always available. Fishing enthusiasts can fish for perch, smelt, walleye, northern pike, and bass. Four months of the year provide excellent hunting. September through November there's grouse; October through November hunt for duck, geese and woodcock. Deer and bear hunting with bow and arrow is September through November, and the month of December. The rifle season for deer and bear runs November 15–31. A variety of wildlife can be seen while canoeing up the unspoiled Potagannissing Bay. Birdwatchers will have a chance to catch sight of some of the 207 species of birds on Drummond Island. There are miles of backwood trails for both hikers and trail bikers, tennis courts and a nine-hole golf course. Children can participate in the resort's Youth Center every Tuesday and Friday night of the summer season. There are seven furnished cottages snuggled between pines and white birch. Each has complete kitchen facilities and all linen is included. Supplies can be picked up at any of the four grocery stores, the liquor store, hardware store and clothing store. Restaurants and taverns are nearby. Presbyterian and Catholic worship services are held on Sundays. Rates: daily $18–23; weekly $120–130 depending on number of people. There are regularly scheduled ferries between the mainland and Drummond Island. For further information contact: Lakeview Resort, Steve and Karen Kemppainen, Drummond Island, MI 49726 (906)493–5241.

★★*The Murray & the Chateau Beaumont at Mackinac Island* have been greeting visitors to the Island since 1882. Despite modernization of the facilities, the quaint, old-fashioned atmosphere is preserved as a tradition on Main Street. While enjoying the home-style cooking, diners in the Lamplighter room can look out onto the charming harbor. As a tribute to its popularity, the Murray has an annex, the equally comfortable and charming Chateau Beaumont. Rates per person: The Murray $30 to $40 in season, $20 to $30 off season; Chateau Beaumont $28–32 in season, $18 to $22 off-season. Contact: The Murray and Chateau Beaumont, Mackinac Island, MI 49757 (906)847–3361; October-April, (313)769–4222.

★★*The Pines Hotel at Bois Blanc Island* offers 22,000 acres of prime wilderness hunting area, and approximately 60% of it is owned and open to hunting. Some of the best deer hunting in Michigan is here, not to mention exceptional partridge and woodcock hunting. For the waterfowl hunter, there are great flights of mallards, bluebills, teal, and Canadian geese; blinds and boats are available. Whether you aim with gun, bow or camera, the true sportsman will appreciate the thousands of acres of virgin forest, sparkling lakes, and lush meadows. Bois Blanc Island is serviced by two ferries each having spring, summer, and fall schedules. Guests must call or write ferry companies for reservations. Facilities include a fine hotel, restaurant, a sport shop, boat rentals, taxi service from airport or ferry, island tours, fishing, hunting, and non-denominational church services during the summer months. Lodging is of two types: rustic hotel rooms at $18 per day and modern motel rooms at $22 per day and $2.50 for each additional person. The hotel offers 11 rooms that share three baths; the motel rooms will sleep up to four and have private baths. Special discounts are available for family groups and extended stays. A special deer hunting package includes three meals and one night's lodging at $25 per day, per person, based on double occupancy. The special vacation package for two, including two nights lodging, all meals, taxi service from ferry or airport, is available at $76.92. For information, ferry schedules, and special rates, contact: The Pines Hotel, Pte. Aux Pins, P.O. Box 941, Bois Blanc Isle, MI 49775 (616)634–5381.

★★★*Rustic Resort on Lake Huron* is sheltered by 36 Les Cheneaux Islands of Lake Huron. This beautiful area of wooded islands and crystal-clear channels is approximately 15 miles east of Interstate 75 near the towns of Hessel and Cedarville. The resort is open year around, has everything for a family vacation and is specially equipped to please the fisherman and the hunter. The resort has 14 housekeeping cottages; space for trailers, campers or motor homes with hookups; a grocery store; a bait and tackle shop with bait available all year; a dock with launching ramp, gas, oil and water; and recreational facilities for all ages. In the winter, there is ice fishing, and the resort rents ice-fishing shanties and runs an ice fishing taxi service. There are hundreds of miles of trails for snowmobiling and cross-country skiing. Fall and winter seasons offer partridge, bear, duck, snowshoe rabbit and deer hunting. In the summer, guests can rent 14–foot aluminum or wooden boats with or without motors; 18– and 23–foot inboard launches or aqua cycles to enjoy the waters or explore Les Cheneaux Islands. Fishing tackle is available for rent and the rustic resort broadcasts the daily fishing report over local radio stations. There is a fish cleaning house and fish freezing service, plus freezers to keep fish and small game. The sandy beach has a swimming area with a giant water slide and a raft. There is a playground for children, an adult gymnastic set, tether ball, volley ball and basketball. Hiking and backpacking trails lead through evergreens, where wildflowers, mushrooms and a wide variety of birds may be seen. Cottages range from one-bedroom units to four-bedroom units which sleep 10 or 11 persons. Weekly

rates range from $65 to $195, and there are daily rates available for some seasons. For more information and reservations contact: Lew & Patricia Johns, Rustic Resort, RR 1, Box 33, Cedarville, MI 49719 (906)484–2558.

★★★★*Stonecliffe at Mackinac Island* is a magnificent edifice built on 160 rolling acres of cliffs on the island's west shore. Built in 1904, the mansion stands as one of the most luxurious homes in Michigan. Guests may stay in rooms tastefully appointed with the finest in furnishings from an era long since past. Facilities include tennis, horseback riding, swimming and bicycling. Room rates from $30 per person. For further information, write: Stonecliffe, P.O. Box 338, Mackinac Island, Mich. 49757 (906)847–3882.

Travel Services

Mackinac Charter on Mackinac Island provides five-hour fishing trips on the "Vera Mae", a 28–foot, fully-equipped Chris Craft. In addition to complete safety and fishing equipment, "Vera Mae" has a recording fish finder to ensure a successful trip. All the guests' fish will be cleaned and bagged in ice by the crew. Rates are $90 to $160 for two to six people; inquire also about day and night tours of the area. Contact: Capt. Jim Francis, P.O. Box 293, Mackinac Island, MI 49757 (906)847–3749.

Northland Wilderness Canoeing Outfitters offers complete outfitting services for canoe-camping trips and fishing in the Hiawatha National Forest wilderness, Manistique River, Fox River, and Manistique Lake. Northland Outfitters is located on the border of the Seney National Wildlife Refuge. The Manistique River flows through both the refuge and the Manistique State Forest, offering a true wilderness experience. Both wildlife areas offer an opportunity to see birds and animals in their natural habitat. Established campsites are located at several locations to allow moderate one-day paddling to each. With the cooperation of the Michigan Forestry Service NWCO is able to offer several wilderness camping areas in the Manistique River State

Forest. Their trips take you through nearly all State and Federal lands, offering miles of wooded scenery. Both hardwoods and pines dominate the area. The 96,000 acres of the Seney Wildlife Refuge contain over 200 species of birds and many varieties of animals. An intensive forest management program is conducted throughout the area to improve wildlife habitat. For detailed rates, information, and reservations, contact: Northland Outfitters, P.O. Box 65, Germfask, MI 49836 (906)586–9801.

Shepler's Mackinac Island Ferry safely speeds between Mackinaw City and the island in just 18 minutes. "The Welcome", "Felicity", and "The Hope" are fully-equipped, hydrofoil-type boats with completely padded seats for comfort. Dockside parking is provided with optional valet service. The crew is friendly and handles you and your luggage with care. One-way fares are $2.75 adults, $2.00 children; round trip, $3.75 and $2.50. A bicycle can travel too for $1.50. Group and charter rates are available as are bridge and other cruises. Contact: Shepler's Inc., P.O. Box 261, Mackinaw City, MI 49701 (616)436–9891.

Huron National Forest & The Au Sable Country

Stretching west from the shores of Lake Huron, this renowned forest covers some 415,000 acres in east-central Michigan. The Au Sable River, lifeline of the Huron National Forest, is the largest of over 650 miles of streams that crisscross the wooded landscape and form a network of prime canoeing and fishing waters. During the days of Michigan's lumber boom, the Au Sable was one of the principal channels down which logs were floated to Lake Huron. Today the fertile, insect-rich alkaline waters of the Au Sable are renowned for excellent brown-trout fishing and challenging canoe trips, especially below Mio, where the waters are faster and dams must be portaged. Grayling, a sizable town along the Au Sable a few miles west of the forest is named for the now-extinct game fish that once flourished in these waters. Grayling were caught by the thousands until the early 1880's, when the species began to dwindle, then virtually disappeared because of extensive logging activities. Brook trout, introduced in 1884, and subsequent stockings of brown trout, and the famous June mayfly hatch have earned the Au Sable the reputation of one of the finest trout streams in the nation.

The Au Sable, named the Riviére aux Sables—the "River of Sands"—by the French voyageurs, was traveled for centuries by the Chippewa and Ottawa Indians, trappers, and explorers and provided a valuable waterway between 1870 and 1890 for logs destined for the sawmills of East Tawas, Tawas City, and Oscoda. This classic limestone trout stream, noted for its mazes of deadfalls, log jams, and sweepers, rises in the marl swamps of Otsego County and flows southeast for 200 miles through sandy country of jack-pine forests, bogs, cedar swamps and limestone outcroppings to its mouth on Lake Huron at Oscoda. Its famous tributaries—including the tea-colored Middle Branch; the East Branch, which rises in the marl bogs and spring-fed Loon Lake above Grayling; the legendary North Branch, which rises in the frigid springheads above Lovells; and the famed fly-fishing waters of the South Branch's Mason Tract—offer another 300 miles of highly alkaline, insect-rich trout water. The once awesome runs of big Lake Huron steelhead up the Au Sable were brought to an abrupt end with the construction of six dams along the lower river. Today, fishing for the big lake-run rainbows up to 20 pounds is confined to a stretch of river below Foote Dam. This great historic river, which has contributed immeasurably to American angling lore, has been floated by fishermen since the turn of the

century in the fabled flat-bottomed Au Sable longboats. The forest itself includes other fine fishing streams and lakes, such as the East and Middle branches of Big Creek, the North Branch of the Au Sable, Little Shupac, and Lost and Big Blue lakes. Many of the lakes are also stocked with rainbow trout. Foremost among these are Log, Bear, Starvation, Big Blue, Twin, Big Guernsey, Oxbow, and Selkirk.

Other attractions of the Huron National Forest include the winter-sports areas at Mio, Oxbow, and Pioneer Hills, the last of which is just outside the forest's southwest corner. Twelve campgrounds are scattered throughout the area, many offering opportunities for fishing, swimming, and boating. In addition to the Au Sable River, there are numerous fine fishing streams and lakes, including Horseshoe, Island, Jewell, Kneff, Round, Loon, and Mack lakes. The Huron is also one of the best hunting areas in the state for black bear, deer, and upland game birds.

Information Sources, Maps & Access

For detailed information and a full-color *Huron National Forest Map* (50¢), contact: Supervisor, Huron National Forest, Cadillac, MI 49601 (616)775–2421. Trout and salmon stream maps ($2 each) showing fishing, wading, boating conditions, width and depths of channel, trout population, public access areas, and campgrounds are available for the *Sturgeon, Pigeon, Black, Au Sable,* and *Rifle* rivers. They may be ordered by mail from Hendrickson's, P.O. Box 207, New Glarus, WI 53574. For additional info on vacation lodging and services, write: East Michigan Tourist Association, 1 Wenonah Park, Bay City 48706 (517)895–8823. The Huron National Forest is accessible via Highway 55 from Tawas City and East Tawas. From West Branch, take State Highway 55 east, then 33 north. From Alpena, take U.S. 23 south. Lodging, guides, supplies, and canoe rentals are available at numerous towns within the forest, including East Tawas, Glennie, Mio, South Branch, Luzerne, Eldorado, and Grayling.

Gateways & Accommodations

Alpena

(Pop. 14,000; zip code 49707; area code 517). Area attractions of this gateway town on beautiful Thunder Bay include the Dinosaur Gardens Prehistorical Zoo, 10 miles south via U.S. Hwy. 23 near Ossineke, with its life-sized reproductions of prehistoric animals in a 40–acre forest (open daily, May 1– Oct. 31); the Jesse Besser Museum, at 491 S. Johnson St., a collection of restored 19th-century buildings and historical exhibits (open daily, July–Aug., Sunday-Monday, rest of the year); and the Old Lighthouse on Presque Isle Harbor, 23 miles north of town via U.S. Hwy. 53, a restored lighthouse and keeper's home (open daily, 8am–8pm, May 30–Oct. 31). Accommodations: *Best Western of Alpena* (rates: $24–28 double), 36 excellent rooms, color TV, heated indoor pool, free continental breakfast, at 1286 Hwy. 32, 1½ miles west of town (356–9087); *Fletcher's Motel* (rates: $30 double), 92 attractive rooms, color TV, heated indoor pool, sauna, tennis, beach opposite, restaurant and cocktail lounge, one mile north of town via U.S. Hwy. 23 (354–4191); *Kentucky Motor Lodge* (rates: $18–20 double), 44 rooms and suites, restaurant and bar, at 234 W. Chisholm St. (356–2271); *Parker House Motel* (rates: $18 double), 11 rooms and four cottages with kitchens on lovely shaded grounds along Long Lake, beach, swimming, rental boats, 12 miles north of town via U.S. Hwy. 23 (595–6484).

Gaylord

(Pop. 3,000; zip code 49735; area code 517.) Area attractions of this blustling town, the seat of Otsego County, include the Call of the

Wild Museum (732–4336), at 850 South Wisconsin Ave., with its scenic displays of 150 North American mammals and game birds (open daily, May 1–Sept. 5, 8am–9pm; 8:30am–6pm, rest of the year); Otsego Lake State Park (732–5485), seven miles south of town off Interstate 75, a 62–acre preserve with facilities for swimming, boating, camping, fishing, and waterskiing; and the Sylvan Knob Ski Area, five miles east of town via Michigan State Hwys. 32 and 44. Accommodations: *Best Western Chalet Motor Lodge* (rates: $31.20–39.52 double), 117 excellent rooms and suites, 20 with kitchens, color TV, two heated pools, sauna, tennis courts, putting green, airport bus, restaurant and cocktail lounge, at 1042 W. Main St., on Michigan State Hwy. 32 at junction with Interstate 75 (732–5193); *Golfview Motel* (rates: $19–24 double), 16 attractive rooms on quiet, shady grounds, color TV, one mile south of town via Old U.S. Hwy. 27 (732–5138); *Holiday Inn* (rates: $34 double), 140 excellent rooms and suites, heated pool, wading pool, airport bus, kennel, restaurant and cocktail lounge, at 833 W. Main St., ¼ mile west of town via Michigan State Hwy. 32 near junction with Interstate 75 (732–2431); *Timberley Motel* (rates: $24.96 double), 30 rooms and suites, color TV, ski trails, recreation room, restaurant opposite, at 881 South Otsego Ave., ¾ mile south of town via Old U.S. Hwy. 27 (732–5166).

Grayling—Gateway to the Middle Branch Au Sable River

(Pop. 2,200; zip code 49738; area code 517). Gateway to the Huron National Forest, the town is located on the Middle Branch of the Au Sable River, one of Michigan's finest trout streams. Grayling is named for the species of game fish that once inhabited the upper Au Sable; the fish is now extinct in Michigan waters because of logging pressure at the turn of the century. Area attractions include the Hartwick Pines State Park (348–7068), seven miles northeast of town via Michigan State Hwy. 93, a 9,200–acre preserve containing impressive stands of virgin pine and hemlock; and the Fred Bear Museum (348–9822), two miles west of town on Michigan State Hwy. 93, an extensive collection of trophy game animals, primitive weapons, and artwork (open daily, 10am–6pm except holidays). Grayling is a popular outfitting center for canoe trips on the area's numerous waterways. Accommodations: *Best Western Aquarama Motor Lodge* (rates: $28 double), 31 excellent rooms, color TV, restaurant adjacent, ½ mile south of town on Interstate 75 business route (348–3141); *Holiday Inn* (rates: $36–40 double), 102 attractive rooms, color TV, heated pool, wading pool, steam baths, restaurant and cocktail lounge, ¾ mile south of town on Interstate 75 business loop (348–7611); *Marshall Hospitality House* (rates: $27–30 double), 31 rooms and suites, color TV, playground, putting green, ski trails, indoor pool, free airport bus, at 405 McClellan Ave., ¼ mile north of town on Interstate 75 Business Rt. (348–3861).

Houghton Lake

(Pop. 800; zip code 48629; area code 517). The town is perched on the shores of Houghton Lake, the largest inland lake in Michigan and the source of the Muskegon River. Two other nearby lakes, St. Helen and Higgins, boast beautiful sandy beaches, and pine-fringed shorelines. Accommodations: *Bill Oliver's Lakefront Motor Lodge* (rates: $21–22.50 double), 34 attractive lodge rooms and nine cottages with kitchens and fireplaces, shady lakeside grounds, private beach, dock, pool privileges, nice dining room and cocktail lounge, in Prudenville 48651, five miles east of town on Michigan State Hwy. 55 (366–5910); *Val Halla Motel* (rates: $23–26 double), 12 excellent rooms, two with kitchens, color TV, heated pool, wading pool, at 9869 Old Hwy. 27, ¾ mile north of Michigan State Hwy. 55 (422–5137).

Oscoda

(Pop. 2,200; zip code 48750; area code 517). The town is a key gateway to the Huron National Forest and marks the spot where the famous Au Sable River empties into Lake Huron. Paddlewheel boat cruises are available along the Au Sable to Cooke Dam and back, a total of 19 miles, with narratives on historic and scenic points of interest. The *River Queen I* (728–9891) departs from Five Channels Dam, 19 miles west of town at the junction of Michigan State Hwy. 65 and W. River Road, twice daily, Memorial Day to Labor Day. The *River Queen II* (739–7351) features a cocktail bar and glass-enclosed decks and leaves Foote Dam, six miles west of town on W. River Rd., twice daily, Memorial Day to Labor Day; twilight cruises also available. Accommodations: *Aurora Resort Motel* (rates: $23.50 double), 18 units, 10 with kitchens, on Lake Huron, TV, beach, playground, restaurant opposite, two miles south of town via U.S. Hwy. 23 (739–9801); *Crescent Motel* (rates: $19–21 double), 12 rooms on attractive grounds, two efficiency units, heated pool, coffeeshop, six miles south of town on U.S. Hwy. 23 (362–3354); *Lake Trail Motel* (rates: $24.96 double), 19 excellent rooms overlooking Lake Huron, beach, lighted tennis courts, one mile north of town on U.S. Hwy. 23 (739–2096); *Redwood Motor Lodge* (rates: $23–28 double), 17 excellent rooms and five housekeeping cottages with two-three bedrooms, TV, heated pool, playground, private beach on Lake Huron opposite, 2½ miles south of town via U.S. Hwy. 23 (739–2021).

Lodges & Resorts

★★★★*Hinchman Acres Resort on the Au Sable River* in the Huron National Forest is a year round facility with housekeeping cottages, excellent recreational facilities, organized canoe trips in warm weather and cross-country skiing in the snow months. The resort spreads out over wooded land on the banks of the river. In summer there is trout fishing for rainbow, brown, and brook trout, sun bathing on the private sand beach, or swimming in the spring-fed lake. Children 12 and under fish free and can catch up to two fish per day from the resort's own trout pond. There is a playground, badminton, basketball, shuffleboard, horseshoes, ping pong and miniature golf. Serious golfers will find two 19–hole courses just minutes away. A horse ranch, with guided rides through the Huron National Forest is also nearby. The resort also operates Hinchman Acres Canoe Service, with canoes and equipment for rent, pick up service and overnight trips planned for the Au Sable River from Grayling to Oscoda—a 240–mile run. They have 15–foot, 17–foot and 18–foot aluminum canoes, life jackets for adults and children, cushions and paddles. The Au Sable is a gentle river with average depths from 1½ to 3 feet and no "white water." Cost of rentals depends on the length of the trip and the number of canoes rented. For one canoe, a 2½ hour (10 mile) trip from the resort to Comins Flats is $10 and the 40–mile nine-hour trip to the Alcona Dam is $17. Overnight trips add $8.00 for each additional day. A four-day 160–mile trip in one canoe, for example, would cost $56. The Canoe Service also specializes in organized groups. They have 200 canoes and school buses for land transportation, and can easily handle large clubs or organizations. The Canoe Service is available separately from the resort facilities and reservations for canoes can be made by calling (517)826–3991. In the winter Hinchman Acres becomes a cross-country skiing resort. They have complete rental equipment for the whole family. New skiers can take the free instruction—a ten-minute basic course on fundamentals of ski touring given on a special practice trail on the resort grounds. Then it's off to the measured, marked and well-groomed trails. There are six loops of 1.5 to 16.0 kilometers (1–10 miles) which start and loop back to the resort. Trails wind

through the wooded Huron National Forest and along the Au Sable River. There are easy trails for beginners, rolling and hilly trails for intermediates and steep hills for expert skiers. Plus, beyond the resort trails, there are miles of remote wooded trails in the National Forest and on the river banks. A free trail map is given to each group and use of the resort trails is free to guests at the cottages. Others pay a $1 parking fee which includes a map and use of the warming hut, game room, fireplace, restrooms and snack counter. Other winter sports at the resort are sledding on two hills safe for children, down hill skiing at Mio Mountain, five minutes away, ice skating on the pond lighted for night skating, and ice fishing. The cottages and the two new chalets are scattered throughout the resort property for privacy and are fully equipped with kitchens, bed linens, towels, TV, grill, gas heat, private bath and a living room. There are one-, two- and three-bedroom cottages sleeping two to ten people. Reservations from mid-June through Labor Day are for one week minimums from Saturday to Saturday. Other seasons, reservations are accepted by the day or week, with a two day minimum. Cottages range from $20–24 per day or $100–120 per week for a one-bedroom unit for two people. A two-bedroom for four people is $28–32 per day and $145–165 per week. A three-bedroom cottage for two families or eight to ten people is $250 a week. There are special off-season midweek rates. For reservations, or information about the resort, the canoe service or the cross-country skiing contact: Sam and Natalie Giardina, Box 146, Mio, MI 48647 (517)826–3991.

★★★★*Northwood Resort* is situated on the west shore of beautiful Otsego Lake in the north country of Michigan. Its eight well-spaced, lakefront cottages are situated on 700 feet of lake frontage. Winter months provide fine skiing and wonderful snowmobile trails. Hunting in Otsego County is excellent. Partridge, rabbit and deer are among the available game. Fishing for bass, northern pike and panfish can be done right from your door step. There is a safe, sandy beach for swimming with a large shallow area roped off for small children and a diving raft in the deeper water. Waterskiing is ideal on Otsego Lake. A golf course and horseback riding facilities are nearby. Spring is mushroom hunting season at the resort and there are "color tours" of the fall foliage the last week of September and the beginning of October. Additional activities include, shuffleboard, ping-pong, basketball, volleyball, badminton, horseshoes, tetherball and a playground. All of the cottages have fireplaces and automatic heat and are set up for housekeeping. Linens are provided free during the hunting and skiing seasons, and at a slight charge during the summer season. Rates: three-bedroom cottages, weekly for six persons $225, overnight for six persons $38. Two bedroom cottages, weekly for four persons $195, overnight for four persons $30. For further information contact: Northwood Resort, Route No. 2, Box 600, Gaylord, MI 49735 (517)732–5094.

★*Penrod's Au Sable River Resort*, on the banks of the Au Sable River, offers a series of rustic cabins and cottages convenient for canoe-trippers, hikers and hunters. Aluminum canoes are provided with each cabin and the resort also arranges for day and over-night canoe trips for its guests, returning them by car from their downriver excursions. Though not offered directly on the premises, scenic lumber trails, fishing, lake swimming, deer and bird hunting, saddle horses, skeet shooting and shopping facilities are all within a few minutes' drive. There are seven housekeeping cottages, and four cabins with breakfast units only. All have private showers, heat and TV. Linens, blankets, dishes and kitchen equipment furnished. Rates—one bedroom with kitchen: $22 per day, $130 per week. One bedroom without kitchen: $18 per day, $100 per week. Housekeeping cottages can be rented for full weeks only, from mid-June through July and August. Space is also available for trailers, campers, and

group outings such as scouts and clubs. For more information, contact: Penrod's Au Sable River Resort, 100 Maple Street, P.O. Box 432, Grayling, Mich. 49738 (517)348–3711. In winter, (313) 626–1356.

Travel Services

Carlisle Canoe Rentals on the Au Sable River rents canoes and camping gear, plans trips on the Au Sable River, as well as the Manistee River, and gives instructions to beginners on canoe handling. Carlisle offers trips ranging from two hours to seven days on quiet waters, and will provide pickup service at the end of the trip, so that all canoeing can be downstream. The Au Sable is a peaceful river, bordered by stately pines and green meadows. The current is gentle and the river is wadeable in most areas from Grayling to McMaster Bridge, so it is an excellent location for learning to canoe and for bringing the whole family. On day trips, canoeists can stop at picnic sites complete with drinking water and picnic tables; or they can choose a remote backcountry area for lunch. At Carlisle, there are many canoes from which to choose and all are aluminum and equipped with paddles and cushions. Rental for day trips depends on the number of canoes rented, the day of the week and the length on the river run. All canoe rentals include pickup at a pre-arranged spot on the river, where a driver will pick up the canoe and drive canoeists back to their car. Camping trips on the Au Sable River include pickup charges in the rate, as well. Rates vary by the number of canoes, the number of days and the length of the run. For example, for one canoe, a two day trip to McMaster Bridge, a 40–mile, 8½–hour run, is $26. A five-day trip to Lake Huron including 240 miles or 40 hours of canoeing is $82.00. There are special rates for more canoes, also, with four paid days, the fifth is free; and with five paid days, the sixth and seventh are free. For all rates, maps of the Au Sable and further information write: Carlisle Canoe Rentals, 110 State Street, P.O. Box 150, Grayling, MI 49738 (517)348–2301.

Isle Royale National Park of Lake Superior

The largest of Michigan's islands, Isle Royale forms a majestic forested wilderness camping, backpacking, and fishing paradise 15 miles from the mainland shores of the Keweenaw Peninsula in the extreme northern part of the Upper Peninsula. Isle Royale is renowned for the scenic beauty of its wild, log-strewn beaches, dense forests, 1,000–foot-high hills, fjordlike natural harbors, deep blue lakes, and fast-flowing streams. The island is approximately 45 miles long and three to nine miles wide, with a rugged, irregular coastline notched with excellent harbors, including Rock Harbor in the northeast, considered by many to be the finest port of anchorage in the Great Lakes. The surrounding waters of Lake Superior are studded with more than 200 small (often fog-shrouded) islands and atoll-like reefs, visited regularly by excursion and fishing boats. The interior of Isle Royale offers a truly unspoiled landscape, free from roads or towns. Spruce and balsam forest alternate with fine stands of white and black birch; pure hardwoods grace the upland regions; and the cool, moist shores and lake borders support mixed evergreens. A few crystal-clear streams and emerald-blue lakes, such as Lake Desor, Siskiwit Lake, Sargent Lake, the Little and Big Siskiwit rivers, and Tobin Creek, dot the rugged forest mantle.

Isle Royale's history began millions of years ago with the glaciers that covered the island time and again. Massive sheets of ice ground smooth the surfaces of its rocks, gouged out basins that are now lakes, and exposed layers of sandstone, subsequently eroded by water into valleys extending the length of the island. Between the valleys are rock beds of hard basalt forming long ridges, including the massive Greenstone Ridge, Isle Royale's bulky and impressive spine. At frequent intervals, the linear ridges are broken by cross-cutting ravines or depressions, much to the dismay of the less hardy hiker, who finds himself going endlessly up and down on the more than 160 miles of foot trails. Unusual geological features include Monument Rock, one of the numerous "sea stacks" lining the coast, and the huge wave-cut arches on Amygdaloid Island to the northwest of Isle Royale.

Long after the retreat of the glaciers, prehistoric races settled here and mined the extensive copper deposits, using alternate applications of hot and cold water to cause the rock to crack, then pounding out the small particles of copper with stone hammers. Archaeologists have excavated their primitive shallow mining pits and the remains of crude tools, some of which date as far back as 4,500 years. Theories concerning the identity of these tribes range from Phoenicians from the Near East to Norsemen to early American Indians. When the French took possession of the island in 1671, they found Indians living here who could not remember the copper miners of old.

The first white man known to have visited Isle Royale was Etienne Anton Brule, followed by Jean Nicolet in 1643. Nicolet's report on the island, stating that "gold, rubies, and precious stones are found in abundance," caused considerable excitement in Paris and Montreal and probably did a great deal to incite further exploration in the New World. French traders, lured to the island in pursuit of fur-bearing animals, gave the area its name. Isle Royale passed into American hands in 1783, largely through the insistence of Ben Franklin, who had heard tales of the rich copper deposits and was determined to obtain the island in the terms of the Treaty of Paris.

One of the island's most valuable and fascinating natural resources is its varied wildlife. The only animals that live here today are those that could fly, swim, drift across the water barrier, or cross the ice that occasionally forms a bridge to Canada. Of the many common mammals that make their home here—including beaver, red fox, coyote, muskrat, and weasel—undoubtedly the most spectacular is the moose. Standing almost seven feet high and weighing as much as 1,000 pounds, these impressive beasts have been on Isle Royale since 1912, when a few of them straggled fifteen miles over ice from Canada and became stranded during the spring thaw. Although they are most often seen wading in the shallow inland lakes, moose are common throughout the park and form one of the largest herds in the United States. Wolves, rarely seen by visitors, prey upon the moose population, culling the herds and keeping the numbers down to levels the island can support. Bird life on the island is largely dominated by waterfowl, including the wild ducks and geese that

feed on the lakes throughout the warm weather. By day, the raucous cries of gulls fill the air, while summer nights are often interrupted by the shrill laugh of native loons. Eagles, red-shouldered hawks, and great horned owls prey on the island's smaller birds and rodents. Other species common to the area are robins, warblers, wrens, and redheaded and downy woodpeckers.

Hunting is not allowed on the island, but Isle Royale has long been a favorite rendezvous for fishermen eager to try their luck on the more than 70 inland lakes and connecting streams, and in the frigid waters of Lake Superior. Brook, brown, rainbow, and lake trout, steelhead, northern pike, and muskellunge up to 25 pounds are the most common species taken. A few fortunate anglers have landed lake trout weighing over 30 pounds. Michigan fishing regulations apply on Isle Royale, and a state license is required in all Lake Superior waters, but no license is necessary for the island's inland lakes or streams. Both the store at Rock Harbor and the Windigo Inn offer complete outfitting.

Despite a relatively short summer growing season, the island offers several hundred species of wildflowers, which greatly enhance the pleasure of hiking trips and form a delicate counterpoint to the lofty green of Isle Royale's forests. Early spring brings bluebells and common violets, while white daisies, over 30 varieties of wild orchids, and jack-in-the-pulpits appear in full force during the summer months. In addition to fishing, camping and hiking are perhaps the most popular activities on the island. Because motor vehicles are prohibited in the park, travel must be accomplished solely by boat or on foot, with the latter form of transport fast becoming the most enjoyable way to explore the rocky, wooded wilderness. An extensive trail system offers hikes to suit just about every taste—long, short, easy, or rugged, each revealing a different corner of the island's unspoiled beauty. One of the longer routes in the park, the Rock Harbor Trail, follows the rocky shore of the harbor to its head some 10½ miles away, passing an inland sea arch and the Daisy Farm Lakeside Camp, one of the largest campgrounds in the park. The 2.2–mile Mount Franklin Trail leads from Rock Harbor to Mount Franklin and continuously alternates between ridge and valley until it reaches the summit with its spectacular view of the north side of the island. By far the longest and most rugged path in the park is the wild and primitive Greenstone Ridge Trail, recommended for the seasoned hiker only. Winding across the forested interior of the island atop the Greenstone Ridge some 40 miles between Rock Harbor Lodge and Windigo Inn, the footpath passes through diverse scenery within easy reach of three lakeside campgrounds.

The island offers 24 lakeside and trailside campsites with a maximum of 23 tent spaces. All camping parties, including those traveling in their own boats, are required to obtain a camping permit and/or boat registration upon arrival. No fee is charged for admission to the park or for camping. Campsites cannot be reserved and are operated on a first-come basis. Basic food staples, specialized camping foods, and white gasoline may be purchased at the Rock Harbor store or at Windigo. Disposable items such as bottles, cans, and other nonburnables are prohibited in Isle Royale's backcountry.

Information Sources, Maps & Access

For detailed information and the free *Isle Royale Map/Brochure* and *Camping & Hiking in Isle Royale National Park* booklet, contact: Superintendent, Isle Royale National Park, 87 N. Ripley St., Houghton, MI 49931 (906)482–3310. A beautiful 39" x 54" *U.S. Geological Survey Isle Royale National Park Shaded-Relief Map* ($2, also available in a full-color topographic edition) showing man-made and natural features may be ordered from: Distribution Branch,

U.S. Geological Survey, 1200 S. Eads St., Arlington, VA 22202. The following publications may be ordered direct (request current prices) from Isle Royale Natural History Assn., P.O. Box 27, Houghton, MI 49931; *The Wolves of Isle Royale* ($1.75, 200 pp.), *Birds of Isle Royale National Park* (60¢), *Fishes & Sport Fishing in Isle Royale National Park* (60¢), *Wildflowers of Isle Royale National Park* ($1.00), *Wilderness Trails—A Guide to the Trails in Isle Royale National Park* (75¢), *Forests & Trees of Isle Royale* (60¢).

Isle Royale National Park is open to visitors from about May 15 to October 20. Transportation from the mainland to the island is by boat or floatplane only. For schedules, rates, and reservations on the National Park Service boat *Ranger III* from Houghton to Rock Harbor (May to October), write or call the Superintendent, Isle Royale National Park (address above). The *Isle Royale Queen II* (Copper Harbor 49918) runs between Copper Harbor and Rock Harbor between late June and Labor Day and also offers pre- and post-season charter trips. For information on boat service between Grand Portage and Windigo (late June to Labor Day) and between Grand Portage and Rock Harbor via Windigo, write to *Sivertson Brothers*, 366 Lake Ave. S., Duluth, MN 55802. One boat circumnavigates Isle Royale and will discharge and pick up passengers at various points. The *Isle Royale Seaplane Service* (Box 371, Houghton 49931) offers flights between Houghton and Windigo via Rock Harbor from late June to Labor Day. Because the waters of Lake Superior are often rough, it is not safe to use boats of 20 feet or less to go to the island. However, such boats can be transported to Isle Royale on the *Ranger III*. The private boat operators mentioned above will transport small runabouts and canoes. Gasoline for your boat cannot be carried on commercial boats or planes, but may be purchased at Rock Harbor and Windigo.

FORESTS AND TREES

OF ISLE ROYALE NATIONAL PARK

Gateways & Accommodations

Duluth, Minn.

(See "Superior National Forest" in Minnesota chapter.)

Houghton

(Pop. 6,300; zip code 49931; area code 906.) Mainland headquarters for Isle Royale National Park, Houghton lies on the shores of narrow Portage Lake, facing its twin city of Hancock (which see). The area was the scene of the first important mineral strike in the Western

Hemisphere. Between 1855 and 1870, more than 200 locations were prospected south of Portage Lake, many of which yielded rich bonanzas in copper. The great mining rush attracted hundreds of European settlers, including the Cornish master miners and Finnish immigrants who have given the town its unusual ethnic stamp. Accommodations: *Best Western King's Inn* (rates: $24–27 double), 50 rooms, color TV, nearby restaurant, in town at 215 Sheldon Ave. (482–5000); *College Motel* (rates: $25–27 double), 24 rooms, color TV, restaurant adjacent, ½ miles east of town on U.S. 41, 1308 College Ave. (482–2202); *Vacationland Motel* (rates: $24–30 double), 25 rooms, TV, swimming pool, beach opposite, 3½ miles southeast of town on U.S. Hwy. 41 (482–5351).

Lodges

★★★*Isle Royale Rock Harbor Lodge* offers excellent accommodations at the northern end of Isle Royale. The lodge, which is located along the shore of picturesque Rock Harbor, includes lodge and housekeeping rooms with private bath. Other facilities and services include dining room, store, snack bar, gift shop, marina, motorboats, guided fishing and sightseeing tours. Rock Harbor Lodge is famous for hospitality, excellent food and service. Sixty motel-type rooms are included in the lodge units located along Rock Harbor. Each room has private bath and steam heat, and is attractively decorated and furnished for your comfort and enjoyment. Picture windows provide colorful vistas of the harbor and islands. The superlative food served at the lodge will add to the enjoyment of your Isle Royale vacation. All American Plan guests at Rock Harbor Lodge take meals in the Lodge Dining Room. Table d'hote meals are available to housekeeping guests and other park visitors. Twenty Housekeeping Rooms are located convenient to the central lodge area and store. Each room is furnished with electric stove, refrigerator, utensils, and china; private bath with dressing room; one double bed and two bunk beds with linen and blankets; studio-type living area; no maid service. A wide selection of groceries are available at the Marina Store. Groceries including canned goods, assorted frozen and canned meats, eggs, milk, vegetables, freeze dry foods and other staple foods are sold in the Marina Store. Fishing tackle, camping and hiking assessories, Coleman fuel, photographic supplies, post cards, boating accessories, sundries are also offered. Laundry and showers are available for your convenience. American Plan rates for lodge rooms are $62.50 per day for two persons to a room. Daily housekeeping rates are $32 for one or two persons to a room. Early reservations are recommended. The beautiful Windigo area is situated on the shore of Washington Harbor, at the southwestern end of Isle Royale, and is only 22 miles from the Minnesota shore. It is easily accessible by daily boat service from Grand Portage. You can enjoy camping, hiking and stalking moose with your camera. Secluded Washington Harbor invites boating and trout fishing while nearby Grace and Washington Creeks will please the most ardent brook trout angler. You will be delighted with the colorful vistas on the south end of Isle Royale. No overnight lodging facilities available at Windigo area. The grocery store offers cold sandwiches, freeze dry foods, canned goods, soft drinks, candy and other sundry items. Fishing tackle, license, gifts and photographic supplies can be purchased at the store. 14 ft. boats, outboard motor rentals and gasoline are available. Charter fishing trips for lake trout, boat and motor rentals, water taxi service to area attractions and islands, and sightseeing cruises—to Daisy Farm, Lookout Louise, Rock Harbor lighthouse, Mott Island and Raspberry Island—are available at Rock Harbor Lodge. For additional information, contact (summer) Rock Harbor Lodge, Isle Royale National Park, P.O. Box 405, Houghton, MI 49931 (906)482–2890; (winter) National Park Concessions, Inc., Mammoth Cave, KY 42259 (502)758–2217.

Travel Services

Isle Royale Seaplane Service offers regularly scheduled charter seaplane service to beautiful Isle Royale National Park. "Sky Ranger" flight service to the island is available daily for individuals and groups. Scheduled service from Houghton to Rock Harbor or Windigo and back is $20.00 or 25.00 per person. Charter service is available to the island from Copper Harbor, Grand Portage, MN, Houghton, and Thunder Bay, Ont. Rates for five persons vary from $125–150; and from $150–210 for six. For details, write: Isle Royale Seaplane Service, P.O. Box 371, Houghton MI 49931 (906)482–8850.

Manistee National Forest & The Lake Michigan Coast

This 500,000–acre mixed hardwood and conifer forest is located in the northwestern part of the Lower Peninsula east of Lake Michigan and is renowned for its salmon, trout, and steelhead streams and canoe-camping routes. The major features include the historic Pere Marquette and wild Big Manistee rivers—both are truly great fishing streams for large, hook-jawed brown trout to eight pounds, steelhead to 20 pounds, and coho and Chinook salmon up to 36 pounds. Manistee Lake, bordering the Manistee River State Game Area, is well-stocked with largemouth bass, perch, and pike and offers excellent duck hunting as well. Flowing out of the lake, the Big Manistee River twists through cedar swamps and forests with campgrounds situated all along the route north of the lake as far as Crawford County. The legendary Little Manistee, located between the Big Manistee and Pere Marquette rivers, is one of the Wolverine State's finest trophy fishing streams for giant metallic-flanked steelheads and brown trout. This wild, turbulent river, noted for its deep pools and log jams and scenic red and white pine borders, was once the scene of numerous logging drives. Its famous Indian Club, Old Grade, Bear Track, and Sawdust Pile pools have been immortalized in angling history. Named for the seventeenth-century Jesuit missionary who founded St. Ignace, the Pere Marquette River flows through lake-studded regions of the forest on its swift course, marked by numerous tricky rapids, deep pools, overhangs, log jams, and eddies. The legendary Pere Marquette (once renowned for its grayling fishing) and its historic trout pools—the Birch Hole, Whirlpool, Claybanks, Grayling Hole, and First Rollway—offers some of the nation's finest fishing for trophy brown and lake-run rainbows. The main Pere Marquette and its tributaries provide 138 miles of trout water noted for its deep pools and log jams, surrounded by scenic forests, jack pine plains, and marshes. Its backwaters hold big northern pike. A good put-in site for canoeists is the public access site south of Baldwin. Numerous campgrounds line the river's course with canoes and supplies available at Baldwin, Branch, Custer, and Scottville. The seven-mile stretch of the river from M–37 down to Gleason's Landing is fly fishing only, year-round.

Hunting is also excellent in the Manistee National Forest. Deer are found throughout Manistee County, but the best hunting is on the public lands near swamps, river bottoms, and in jack-pine and oak forests. Grouse and snowshoe hare inhabit the swamp edges, some pine plantations, and brushy areas adjacent to swamps. Rivers, lakes, and Lake Michigan shoreline provide hunting for dabbling ducks, divers, and geese. Wild turkey are found in some parts of the forest, but special regulations govern hunting.

Nearby attractions in the vicinity of the forest include the Mena Creek Waterfowl Area; the White, Muskegon, and Little Manistee river canoe routes; Pentwater River State Game Area; Lake Michigan Recreation Area; Big Star, Tippy Dam, Hamlin, and Mitchell

lakes; and the adjacent Fife Lake and Pere Marquette state forests. Campgrounds are located beside Lake Mitchell, near the Hodenpyle Dam, at the Peterson Bridge, on Dorner Lake, and near the Deer Lake Bayou. Grand Traverse Bay, Little Traverse Bay, Leelanau, and Charlevoix lakes in the north offer excellent angling for big sleek rainbow, brown, and lake trout. Charlevoix contains some Atlantic salmon, and the two Traverse bays are renowned for superb coho and Chinook fishing. Several of the state's outstanding vacation areas are located to the north of the Manistee National Forest.

Information Sources, Maps & Access

For detailed information and a full-color *Manistee National Forest Map* (50¢), contact: Supervisor, Manistee National Forest, 421 S. Mitchell St., Cadillac, MI 49601 (616)775–2421. For information on steelhead and salmon fishing, stream and lake conditions, equipment, canoe rentals, and guide service, contact: *Trout & Salmon Pro Shop*, Bear Lake, MI 49614 (616)864–3000. *Trout and Salmon Stream Maps* ($2 each) showing fishing, wading, boating, conditions, width and depth of channel, trout population, public access areas, and campgrounds are available for the Pere Marquette, Manistee, Boardman, Pigeon, and Black rivers. They may be ordered by mail from Hendrickson's, P.O. Box 207, New Glarus, WI 53574.

For more information on the Sleeping Bear Dunes National Lakeshore, write to the Superintendent, 400½ Main Street, Frankfort 49635 (616)352–9611. A free *Sleeping Bear Dunes Map/Brochure* describing the area, as well as a flyer on South Manitou Island, is available. For information on accommodations and services in the area, write to the Sleeping Bear Dunes Area Chamber of Commerce, P.O. Box 505, Beulah 49617. Ferry service to the Manitou Islands is provided by *Manitou Islands Boat Cruise*, Fishtown Harbor, Leland 49654 (616)256–9061. Manistee National Forest is accessible via State Highway 55 from the town of Manistee. From Cadillac, take the Cadillac Highway (M115) northwest. State 42, leading west from Manton, also offers access to forestlands. Lodging, supplies, guides, canoe rentals, and outfitters are available at numerous towns within and surrounding the forest, including Muskegon, Leland, Big Rapids, Ludington, Pentwater, Scottville, Walhalla, Manistee, Little Manistee, and Boon.

Recreation Areas

Beaver Island

Known as "America's Emerald Isle", Beaver Island lies in upper Lake Michigan, 32 miles west of the harbor of Charlevoix. The island is 14 miles long and up to six miles wide, the largest of a group of thirteen that includes Hog, Gull, Squaw, Trout, Garden and Whiskey Islands. To the southwest of Beaver Island are the Fox Islands and the Manitou, two small groups which complete the archipelago. Archaeological evidence indicates that the first people to inhabit the island were mound builders, primitive tribes whose mounds for burial and for worship mark the terrain in many places. In the seventeenth century, Chippewa and Ottawa Indians owned the archipelago and became notorious for their canoe-raiding par-

ties. When a passing vessel was sighted, groups of Indians would swiftly paddle out in their birchbark craft, board the ship, torture the crew, and make off with all valuables. The first white men in the area were French *coureurs de bois*, itinerant adventurers who roamed the woods and trespassed on Indian hunting grounds for possibly a century before permanent settlements were made in Michigan. Calling Beaver Island *Ile du Castor*, they set up headquarters and makeshift farms near St. James as early as 1603. After the disappearance of the French, no attempt was made to settle the islands until the territory came into American possession, even though the archipelago remained a popular stop-over for missionaries and voyageurs on their way west and north.

In 1847, a scouting party for the eastern branch of the Mormons led by James Jesse Strang found Beaver Island admirably suited for a religious colony where members could live and worship undisturbed by outsiders. By 1850 Strang had laid out the town of St. James, built a tabernacle and persuaded most of the Mormons from the inland settlement of Voree, Wisconsin to join him on Beaver Island. Two years earlier the public lands of the archipelago had been opened to general homesteading. Violent clashes between the religious sect and "outsiders" became common, but the Mormons remained in control and soon outnumbered non-members. Once Strang and his followers were firmly entrenched on Beaver Island, the islands were incorporated into a Mormon kingdom and Strang was crowned king with much pomp and ceremony. Strang's rule was supreme and absolute; harsh and repressive measures were taken against those who questioned his authority, and the island was ruled like a tiny dictatorship. When rumors of corruption and abuse reached the Federal Government, Strang and many of his followers were investigated and arrested on charges that included tampering with the mails, counterfeiting, and stealing public timbers. King Strang's eloquent and persuasive address to a Detroit jury turned the tide of public opinion in favor of the tiny colony, and he and 12 other defendants were acquitted. A born politician with a readymade constituency, Strang next got himself elected to the Michigan House of Representatives, largely through the efforts of loyal Mormon disciples. Political success abroad led to ever more tyrannical measures at home, including an edict that all women must wear bloomers or knee-length skirts. Husbands of women who defied the decree were sent to the whipping post or stripped of any and all political rights. Strang was eventually shot by rebellious followers during the summer of 1856. With Strang out of the way, non-Mormons seized the island and forced the inhabitants from the archipelago. No official count was made at the time, but it is estimated that some 2600 colonists were ordered to vacate the island and take nothing with them.

Today only a few buildings in the town of St. James bear witness to this short and fascinating chapter in Beaver Island's history. The tension and conflict of an earlier era have vanished, and the island is now one of the world's most unique vacation retreats. Seven inland lakes, including Lake Geneserath and Fox, Greens, and Font lakes, offer fine fishing for pike, bass, and panfish. The run of perch in St. James Bay each spring and fall is rated among the finest in the Great Lakes. The island also has improved dock and marina facilities in a fine natural harbor. Charter boats are available to Garden Island, renowned for smallmouth bass and pike fishing, and the site of numerous burial mounds, some of them thousands of years old. The island's 54 square miles are covered with dense forest growth, providing cover and fall hunting for grouse, deer, geese, ducks, squirrels and rabbits.

Fife Lake State Forest

This lake-dotted 103,000 acre reserve stretches north from Manistee National Forest to the wild shores of Lake Michigan and Grand Traverse Bay in the northwestern section of the Lower Peninsula. The major features shown include the renowned canoe routes and salmon and steelhead waters of the Boardman, Platte, and Betsie rivers, and Long, Glen, Green, Duck, Arbutus, Elk and Woodcock lakes. Lake Leelanau, a long, slender body of water in the Chippewa "Land of Delight", is especially famous for its lunker brown trout, with catches up to 15 pounds. Just outside a southeastern segment of the forest, Fife Lake itself with its two small islands is well-stocked with fish, while the jack pine stands north of the nearby village offer fine hunting for deer, birds, and rabbit.

Within easy reach of the forest are Crystal and Glen lakes, the Sleeping Bear Dunes, South Manitou Island, and the Betsie River State Game area. Deer are plentiful throughout the region but most numerous in the brushy, forested lands. Cut-over timber lands are favorite feeding places, especially when adjacent to heavy pine, cedar or balsam swamp cover. Grouse and woodcock are plentiful in brushy stream and swamp edges. Three campgrounds are situated in the Arbutus Lake area with additional sites located on Lake Ann, near the Grass Lake Flooding, at Brown's Dam and on the Boardman River. The lengthy Shore-to-Shore Trail also crosses sections of the Forest.

Hardwood State Forest

This scenic northcountry reserve takes in 188,000 acres of coniferous and mixed hardwood forests, rolling hills, swamps, large blue lakes, and wild streams, south from the majestic Straits of Mackinac in the northernmost part of the Lower Peninsula. Stretched across Emmet and Cheboygan counties, the forest begins west of Lake Michigan and extends northeast to Lake Huron. Hardwood State Forest includes a southern arm of Mullett Lake, second largest of Michigan's inland waters, offering excellent beaches, boating, and good fishing near the northern and eastern shores. Fishermen will also find excellent sport in the renowned trout and smallmouth bass waters of the Pigeon, Sturgeon, Carp, Bear, and Black rivers, and the walleye, northern pike, muskellunge and lake trout waters of Burt and Douglas Lakes. Little Traverse Bay in Emmet County is famous as one of Michigan's salmon and lake trout fishing "hot spots."

Other popular activities in the forest include canoeing on the nearby Cheboygan, Black, and Indian rivers, and hunting in the remote wilderness areas for deer, black bear, grouse and wild turkey. Campgrounds are located at Pine Grove on the Pigeon River and at Tin Bridge near Cornwall Creek. Complete outfitting services are available in Cheboygan, Indian River, and Petoskey.

Pigeon River State Forest

This majestic 90,000-acre northcountry reserve includes the wildlands surrounding the Pigeon River watershed in the northern Lower Peninsula and the scenic wilderness and trout fishing waters of Beaver Island west of the Straits of Mackinac in Lake Michigan. A top-ranked trout fishing and hunting region for deer, black bear and wild turkey, the Pigeon River State Forest also offers the finest grouse cover in the state. Geese flights are common with flocks frequently landing to feed on large green grass and corn fields in the vicinity of Torch Lake during their fall migrations. A sizeable herd of wild elk, at one time native to northern Michigan, was imported about 40 years ago, and today the forest supports a modest number of these shy and relatively rare animals.

Because the forest falls within rolling hardwood hill country, the landscape is especially spectacular during the first half of October when the trees burst into full color. Scenic drives surrounding Torch Lake and from the District Headquarters at Gaylord to the Otsego-Crawford County line are popular at this time of year. Just outside the forest is Torch Lake in Antrim County, so-called because Indian natives speared fish there at night, using torches as a source of light. The lake's white sand beaches and dark green trees form a striking setting for clear, spring-fed waters which range in color from palest blue near the shoreline to a deep cobalt, almost purple, at the center of the lake. Fishing is good at the north and south ends of Torch Lake as well as in Otsego, Opal, Big Bass, Big, Bradford, and Emerald lakes. Rivers popular with fishermen include the Jordan, Big Manistee, Sturgeon, Black, and Pigeon. Campgrounds in the Pigeon River State Forest are situated on Lake Marjory, at the Pigeon Bridge, near Round Lake, and just north of Hardwood Lake Road.

Sleeping Bear Dunes National Lakeshore & the Manitou Islands

An old Chippewa Indian legend tells of a mother bear who once attempted to swim across Lake Michigan with her two cubs. As the trio approached the shoreline, the exhausted cubs began to lag behind. On reaching dry land, the mother bear climbed to the top of a high bluff to watch and wait for her offspring, but they never

rejoined their anxious parent, who can still be seen today as the "Sleeping Bear," a solitary dune covered with dark trees and shrubs in the wilderness of northwestern Michigan. Her unfortunate cubs, now the Manitou Islands, lie a few miles offshore.

The Sleeping Bear Sand Dunes, today part of a varied and fascinating national lakeshore, rise as much as 460 feet above Lake Michigan. These and other dunes along the shoreline are in a state of constant flux; wind continually blows sand off the beaches and up the side of the dunes. A living essay in the geologic history of the area, the national lakeshore's sinuous outline, consisting of rounded headlands and sweeping embankments, traces the rough outline of the last great glacier as it paused in its retreat northward. As the ice disappeared during the great thaw, a tremendous quantity of rock, sand, and silt was deposited by the glacier or sluiced by its meltwater to create the ridges, hills, lowlands, and lakes of the present park landscape. Today this variety of landforms supports a rich diversity of plant and animal life. Sanddune deserts form a striking contrast with hardwood forests that explode in a glow of color during the fall season. Beech, basswood, maple, and oak alternate with dense stands of green and aromatic pines, cedar swamps, chalk-white birches, and an occasional unsteady bog of sphagnum moss. Where there are trees, there are also porcupines, sometimes seen gnawing on the green inner bark of a young tree. Deer hide in the aspen thickets; and in winter, bobcat tracks can be sighted in the fresh snow.

Seven miles by water from Glen Haven, South Manitou Island also forms part of the Sleeping Bear Dunes National Lakeshore. The island's 12 miles of shoreline, deep natural harbor, and thick virgin forests attracted European settlers as early as 1830. Since that time South Manitou's natural resources have been used by various interests—lumbermen, farmers, the coast guard, and more recently vacationers and fishermen. The Valley of the Giants in the southwestern part of the island offers a remnant of the magnificent forest that once covered the whole region: tall white cedars, some more than 500 years old, common and redberry elder, white ash, basswood, mountain and sugar maple. The native understory of shrubs and flowers makes hiking in the region a particularly inviting adventure. Gull Point, the island's northwestern "hook," is a major nesting area for herring and ringbilled gulls. Although the point is closed to visitors, a trail around the colony permits observation of these noisy but graceful winged residents. Perched more than 350 feet above Lake Michigan, the high dunes on the west side of the island rest on bluffs of glacial moraine and are intersected by marked paths leading to spectacular views of the lake. Three camping areas with primitive facilities are located on the east side of the island. On the mainland, the Platte River and D.H. Day campgrounds, operated by the National Park Service, are also available to visitors. Camping is limited to 14 days, and campgrounds are usually filled to capacity during the summer.

The park's numerous lakes, including Platte, Crystal, Loon, Glen, and giant Lake Michigan, offer trophy fishing for salmon, walleye, trout, northern pike, and bass. During the autumn season, when coho salmon run, fishing fervor reaches its greatest peak. Canoeists will enjoy the quiet waters of the Platte River, running through some of the loveliest scenery in northern Michigan.

Gateways & Accommodations

Boyne Falls

(Pop. 400; zip code 49713; area code 616.) Straddling the Boyne River near its source, Boyne Falls is the gateway to two popular ski areas, Thunder Mountain, five miles east of town on Thumb Lake

Rd. (two chairlifts, rentals, school, patrol, cafeteria, phone 549–2941) and Boyne Mountain, ½ mile southwest of town, off U.S. Hwy. 131 (eight chairlifts, rentals, school, patrol, restaurant, bar, nursery, phone 549–2441). In warm weather, the Boyne River offers good trout fishing. Accommodations: *Cliff Dweller Lodge* (rates: $30 per person, double occupancy, American plan), 50 rooms, pool, sauna, meeting and recreation rooms, one block south of town on U.S. Hwy. 131 (549–2466).

Cadillac

(Pop. 12,500; zip code 49601; area code 616.) The town was named for Antoine de la Mothe Cadillac, founder of Detroit, and was once a lumber boomtown, thanks to its central location and the presence of two railroads. Today Cadillac supports diversified industries, ranging from automobile tires to snowmaking equipment. Located on the shores of lakes Cadillac and Mitchell, it is also headquarters for the Manistee and Huron National Forests. District Ranger's offices for both forests are located in town. Accommodations: *Cadillac Sands Motor Inn* (rates: $32.50–40.50 double), 55 excellent rooms and suites, attractive grounds on Lake Cadillac, some patios and balconies, private beach, heated indoor pool, golf course, restaurant and cocktail lounge, four miles west of town via Michigan State Hwy. 55 (775–2407); *McGuire's Motor Lodge* (rates: $27–41 double), 91 rooms and suites, eight condominiums, resort-type complex on spacious, beautifully landscaped grounds, heated indoor pool, sauna, ski trails, sundeck, tennis, golf course, dining room and cocktail lounge, two miles south of town via the Mackinaw Trail, at 7880 Mackinaw Trail (775–9947); *South Shore Motel* (rates: $24–26 double), 15 attractive units, five with kitchens, on Lake Cadillac, private beach, fishing, rental boats, nearby restaurant, at 1246 Sunnyside Drive (775–7641); *Sun n' Snow Lodge* (rates: $22–30 double), 32 rooms and suites, private beach on Lake Mitchell, swimming, dock, fishing, restaurant adjacent, 4½ miles west of town via Michigan State Hwy. 115, at 301 S. Lake Mitchell (775–9961).

Charlevoix—Gateway to Beaver Island

(Pop. 3,500; zip code 49720; area code 616.) The town was named for the French explorer Pierre François Xavier de Charlevoix, and owes its popularity as a resort to the three lakes on which it fronts: lakes Michigan, Round, and Charlevoix. This is a favorite outfitting center for canoeists bound for the many connecting waterways within easy reach of Charlevoix. *The Beaver Island Boat Dock.*, at 103 Bridge St. by the city dock, offers 2½–hour trips to Beaver Island, mid-April to December (call 547–2311 for information). Fall color cruises also leave the boat dock for leisurely autumn sightseeing trips along the shoreline of Lake Charlevoix (phone 547–2101 for information). Accommodations: *The Lodge at Charlevoix* (rates: $34–36 double), 40 excellent rooms and suites, some with balconies, heated indoor pool, charter fishing boats, putting green, overlooks harbor, on U.S. Hwy. 31 at Harbor Bridge (547–6565); *Weathervane Terrace* (rates: $38–48 double), 37 excellent rooms, four with kitchens, color TV, pool, sundecks overlooking lake and river, fine restaurant opposite, at 111 Pine River Lane off U.S. Hwy. 31 (547–9955).

Harbor Springs

(Pop. 2,000; zip code 49740; area code 616.) Located on Little Traverse Bay, the town was once the permanent home of a large tribe of Ottawa Indians. Today Harbor Springs and nearby Harbor Point (where transportation is by horse-and-carriage only) are the site of numerous resorts and impressive summer houses. The Lake Shore Scenic Drive, along Michigan State Hwy. 131, runs from Harbor Springs to Cross Village for 19 miles, following a high bluff

with splendid views of Lake Michigan. Other points of interest include the Chief Andrew J. Blackbird Museum, in town on Michigan State Hwy. 131, housing displays of Indian relics and artifacts (daily, 10am–noon and 1–5pm, July 1–Labor Day); and the excellent downhill and cross-country ski facilities at Nub's Nob, six miles northeast of town on Pleasantview Rd. (phone 526–2131) and Boyne Highlands, 4½ miles northeast of town off Michigan State Hwy. 131 (phone 526–2171). Accommodations: *Berchwood Inn* (rates: $36–40 double), 43 attractive rooms, two units with kitchens, TV, recreation room, playground, country club privileges, also vacation cottages with two-four bedrooms ($450–500 weekly), 3½ miles west of town on Michigan State Hwy. 131 (526–2151).

Indian River

(Pop. 300; zip code 49749; area code 616). Located on the Indian and Sturgeon rivers, the town is a gateway to the Lower Peninsula's northern lake country. Just south of Indian River via Interstate 75 is Burt Lake State Park, which offers excellent fishing, boating, swimming and waterskiing. Game Haven, 12 miles south of town on old U.S. Hwy. 27, is an unusual wildlife ranch where live buffalo, deer, elk and other animals may be seen in natural habitats. Accommodations: *Coach House Motel* (rates: $22 double), 11 rooms and six mobile homes, TV, playground, trout pond, fireplace in motel rooms, at 6100 Hwy. 68 (238–9370); *Nor Gate Motel* (rates: $20–24 double), 12 rooms and family suites, TV, playground, at 4846 S. Straits Hwy., 1½ miles south of Interstate 75 via old U.S. Hwy. 27 (238–7788).

Ludington—Gateway to the Pere Marquette River

(Pop. 10,000; zip code 49431; area code 616.) Vacationers are drawn to Ludington for its long stretch of beach on Lake Michigan and the many lakes and rivers surrounding the town, including the Pere Marquette River and Hamlin Lake. Just east of town is the Manistee National Forest. Other area attractions include Pioneer Village (843–4808), five miles south of town on S. Lakeshore Drive, encompassing many buildings restored to 1880's period style (open Memorial Day-Labor Day); Ludington State Park (843–8671), 8½ miles north of town on Michigan State Hwy. 116, with beaches on lakes Michigan and Hamlin and the Big Sable River; and the Marquette Memorial Cross, overlooking the harbor and Lake Michigan. Accommodations: *Four Seasons Motel* (rates: $35–42 double), 30 attractive rooms, color TV, at 717 E. Ludington Ave. (843–3448); *Holiday Inn* (rates: $38 double), 116 excellent rooms, color TV, heated indoor pool, saunas, putting green, restaurant and cocktail lounge, two miles east of town via U.S. Hwy. 10 (845–7311); *Miller's Lakeside Motel* (rates: $26–27 double), 52 rooms, four two-room units, color TV, heated pool, public beach opposite, at 808 W. Ludington Ave. (843–2177); *Viking Arms Motel* (rates: $29–39 double), 21 rooms, color TV, free airport bus, at 930 E. Ludington Ave. (843–3441).

Manistee

(Pop. 8,000; zip code 49660; area code 616.) The town was once the permanent camp of 1,000 Chippewa Indians, who gave the site its name, Manistee, or "spirit of the woods." In later years, Manistee was developed by Swedish and Norwegian settlers into a vacation center and one of the nation's leading producers of salt. Framed by Lake Michigan on the west and Manistee Lake on the east, the town is the major gateway to the Manistee National Forest. A District Ranger's office is located in town. Accommodations: *Bella Vista Motor Lodge* (rates: $29 double), 20 attractive rooms in Early American decor, swimming pool, color TV, tennis, restaurant adjacent, 16 miles north of town via U.S. 31 (864–3000); *Best Western*

Carriage Inn Motel (rates: $28–38 double), 63 excellent rooms and suites, color TV, heated indoor pool, sauna, tennis, dining room and cocktail lounge, ¾ mile north of town via U.S. 31, at 200 Arthur St. (723–9949).

Muskegon

(Pop. 45,000; zip codes, see below; area code 616.) The largest city on the east bank of Lake Michigan, Muskegon is a bustling industrial center, manufacturing hub, and jumping-off point for fishermen and canoeists. The former "Lumber Queen of the World," so-called because it supported 47 sawmills during the logging heyday, is surrounded by excellent lakes and streams which are restocked with fish annually. During the perch run each year, scores of fishermen line the channel and breakwater walls on Lake Michigan. Points of interest include the Hackley Art Museum at 296 W. Webster Ave.; the Muskegon County Museum, at 30 W. Muskegon Ave., housing displays of the area's history (both museums are zip code 49440); and Deer Park, eight miles north of town on old U.S. Hwy. 31, an amusement park and deer preserve. Accommodations: *Holiday Inn* (rates: $29–30 double), 199 excellent rooms and suites, color TV, heated pool, restaurant and cocktail lounge, 4½ miles south of town on Interstate 96 business route, at 3450 Hoyt St., 49444 (733–2601); *Ramada Inn of Muskegon* (rates: $28–30 double), 112 excellent rooms and suites, heated indoor pool, sauna, color TV, restaurant and cocktail lounge, at 2967 Henry St., 49441, three miles south of town via U.S. Hwy. 31 business rt. (733–2651).

Saugatuck

(Pop. 1,000; zip code 49453; area code 616.) A small, picturesque resort town in the Lake Michigan dune country, Saugatuck has long been one of the major summer art colonies of the Middle West. Landscape painters come here for the spectacular views of the lake, dunes, and surrounding countryside. Archaeological excavations at the north end of town have uncovered an ancient Potawatomi Indian burial ground. Accommodations: *Shangri-La Motel* (rates: $22–28 double), 20 rooms on attractively landscaped grounds, TV, heated pool, playground, free airport bus, on Blue Star Hwy. ½ mile northeast off Interstate 196, exit 41 (857–2040); *Timberline Motel* (rates: $24–36 double), 17 rooms on quiet landscaped grounds, TV, heated pool, playground, free airport bus, on Blue Star Hwy., one mile north of Saugatuck, Douglas Bridge (857–2070).

Traverse City—Gateway to the Sleeping Bear Dunes

(Pop. 18,000; zip code 49684; area code 616.) The heart of Michigan's fruit-growing district, Traverse City is a gateway to the Lower Peninsula's northwestern lake country and to the Sleeping Bear Sand Dunes National Lakeshore. Area attractions include the Interlochen State Park and Arts Center (276–9511), 15 miles southwest via Michigan State Hwy. 137; Hickory Hills Ski Area, two miles west of town on Randolph Rd. (phone 947-8566 for information); and Sugar Loaf Village ski area, 18 miles northeast of Traverse City in Cedar via U.S. Hwy. 31 (phone 228–5461, see below for details). Of the area's many scenic drives, perhaps the most spectacular is that along Michigan State Hwy. 37, especially during the May cherry blossom season. The drive extends the length of the Old Mission Peninsula, the tip of which stands midway between the North Pole and the Equator and is marked by the Old Mission Lighthouse. Accommodations: *Best Western Pinestead Reef* (rates: $45 double), 88 excellent rooms and two-bedroom kitchen units, many with balconies overlooking East Bay, heated indoor pool, sauna, sundeck, private beach, charter fishing boats, restaurant and cocktail lounge, 3½ miles northeast of town via U.S. Hwy. 31, at 1265 Shore Dr. (947–4010); *Colonial Inn* (rates: $38 double), 27 excellent rooms,

color TV, heated pool, sauna, restaurant adjacent, 2½ miles northeast of town via U.S. Hwy. 31 and Michigan State Hwy. 72, at 460 Munson Ave. (947–5436); *Days Inn Motel* (rates: $25.88 double), 114 rooms, color TV, heated pool, playground, restaurant adjacent, two blocks from Grand Traverse Bay at 420 Munson Avenue (941–0208); *Holiday Inn* (rates: $44–46 double), 180 excellent rooms overlooking private beach on Lake Michigan, color TV, two heated pools, dock, sauna, rental boats and canoes, dining room and cocktail lounge, at 615 E. Front St., ½ mile east of town via U.S. Hwy. 31 (947–3700); *Park Place Motor Inn* (rates: $41–55 double), 146 attractive rooms, balconies, color TV, large heated indoor pool, sauna, health club, three dining rooms, ski and hunting package plans available, free airport bus, adjacent to summer theater, in town at 300 East State St. (946–5410).

Lodges & Resorts

★★★*American Resort on Little Platte Lake*, near Honor, the "Coho Capital of the World," is run as a family resort by Buss & Charlene Maddock and Tom & Lois Mullins. They have 15 modern cottages and a small campground, and are open year-around. In winter, there is snowmobiling and cross-country skiing on hundreds of miles of marked trails. Crystal Mountain Ski Lodge is only 12 miles away. And every winter, they hunt snowshoe rabbits in the pines. Spring brings rainbow and brown trout to the Platte River and morel mushrooms to the forests. There is fishing for perch, bass, and northern pike in Little Platte Lake, coho, chinook and steelhead swim up the Platte to spawn in October and there is good salmon and steelhead fishing in the Betsie River. They offer free guide service for spring steelhead fishing, fall salmon fishing; and deer hunting. There is freezer service for all guests. Visitors can also canoe the Platte River all the way to Lake Michigan, or ice fish in a shanty on Crystal Lake or Platte Lake. A 14–foot aluminum boat is free with each cottage and motors are available for rent. The resort provides life jackets, cushions, and grills free to guests. Cabins have two bedrooms and housekeeping facilities. They rent from $75 a week to $105 a week with linens extra. Cabin price is based on two people or one family with children under 17. There is an extra charge for extra persons over 17. American Resort also operates some campsites with hookups for electricity at $4.00 per day. For reservations and information: The American Resort, Rt. #1, Box 64, Honor, MI 49640 (616)325–2981.

★★★★*Barothy Lodge at the Pere Marquette* provides luxury condominium-style living units within a rustic, Michigan northcountry setting. The lodge, situated on a scenic hillside overlooking the Pere Marquette River, offers year-round activities for the nature lover within its 200 acres of recreation area. These activities include trout and salmon fishing in the river or in their private trout ponds, swimming in their heated pool, use of twin tennis courts and nearby canoeing, hiking, snowmobiling and skiing facilities. There are several private lodge-units within the resort complex, each a total apartment in its own right. Each unit is tastefully furnished, fully carpeted, has bath and shower, bedrooms, living rooms with fireplace, and complete, modern kitchens. These units can be rented on a daily, weekly or monthly basis. Daily rates, approximately $22 per person, double occupancy; weekly rates, $17 per person per day, double occupancy. There are also monthly rentals at reduced rates. Children 12 and under, ½ price. Rates do not include linen cleaning service (available upon request). Complete catering service is also available. For more information, contact: Barothy Lodge, P.O. Box 165, Walhalla, MI 49458 (616)898–2340.

★★★★*The Bartley House* is located on the grounds of the Boyne Highlands ski resort. The hotel is at the foot of the Boyne Highlands

chairlift and has been designed specifically for skiing families and groups. There is also an outdoor heated swimming pool and saunas open daily all winter-long. During the summer, there is a par-three golf course located directly in front of the lodge. Guests also get golfing privileges at two nearby 18–hole championship courses, tennis courts, both grass and hard surface, are just a short walk from the door, and the heated pool remains an ideal spot for sunning and swimming. Other recreation in the area includes fishing, boating, riding, hiking, sightseeing and shopping in famous resort shops. The Bartley House has 70 spacious guest rooms. Summer rates run from $35–55 per day, double occupancy. Winter rates run from about $37–40 per person, per day, double occupancy, but this includes lodging, breakfast, lift ticket and use of all lodge facilities. Ski, golf, and weekend packages also available. For more information contact: The Bartley House, Harbor Springs, MI 49740 (616)526–2183.

★★★*The Birchwood Inn at Harbor Springs*, three miles west of Harbor Springs on scenic Little Traverse Bay, is surrounded by hills and forests. The inn has its own pool, four newly surfaced tennis courts, and a modern conference center, with fieldstone fireplace. Closeby are the scenic Boyne Highlands, and Nubs Nob. Sailing, fishing, golf, hunting and horseback riding, and alpine skiing can all be enjoyed in the area. The large firelit lounge with exposed beam ceilings, comfortable sofas and cardtables looks out to the surrounding hills and deep blue waters of the bay. The cozy rooms are elegantly furnished with early American touches, soft carpeting, color TV and private phones. Rates are $26–44 for bed and breakfast in the summer season, and $20–32 in the winter. Rooms with kitchenettes are $48 in the summer, and $36, ski season. For more information write: The Birchwood Inn, Shore Drive, Harbor Springs, MI 49740 (616)526–2151.

★★★★*Boyne Country Ski Areas & Lodges* is a superb resort complex on the northern Michigan peninsula. *Boyne Highlands*, the northernmost of the two, features 17 slopes, six chairlifts, and a complete winter sports and recreation program which includes heated outdoor swimming pools, saunas, ice skating, and apres ski activities. Because it is designed with families in mind, the resort even offers special children's programs and a nursery for preskiing tots. Accommodations and meals are available at the new Boyne Highlands Inn, which has 170 rooms, each with private bath, TV & phone. Rates start at $295 per person, double occupancy, for a five-day ski week. This includes lodging, breakfast, lunch and dinner daily, heated pool, unlimited use of lifts, daily ski instruction, and planned evening recreation. Ski weekends and special discount periods are also available. For details, contact: Boyne Highlands, Harbor Springs, MI 49740 (616)526–2171. *Boyne Mountain*, owned and operated by the same company, is just a few miles to the south and offers one of the largest and best-equipped facilities in the country. Crowds are kept to a minimum on these magnificently-groomed slopes, though, with plenty of chairlifts and tows to handle thousands of skiers per hour. And after skiing, there's ice skating, heated outdoor pools, and a wide variety of apres-ski activities to choose from. Here, too, there are nursery and babysitting services for the very young. Boyne Mountain has its own lodging facilities—Boyne Mountain Lodge, with 350 luxury rooms, each with private bath, TV and phone. Rates here are $250 per person, double occupancy for a five day ski week (same extras as at the Highlands). For more info contact: Boyne Mountain, Boyne Falls, MI 49713 (616)549–2441 or (1–800)632–7174.

★★★*The Colonial Inn at Harbor Springs*, surrounded by shady landscaped grounds, and bright flower gardens, faithfully captures early American charm and revives it on the shores of Little Traverse Bay.

The inn has a private dock and sandy beach on the water, and a heated pool as well, where sumptuous buffets are served daily in the adjacent pavillion. Intimate dinners are served in a quiet, crystal and candlelight tradition. Breakfast will be served in bed, or in the early American dining room. Light from the crystal chandelier glimmers on the inlaid tile floor, and the chimes of the grandfather clock echo throughout the lobby, furnished with authentic period furniture, reminiscent of 18th century elegance. The inn has a modern air-conditioned convention room with a seating capacity of 200. It is open year round, and in winter is near the fine ski slopes of northern Michigan. Rooms in the "Olde Inn" accommodate two-four persons, and are $32 for a twin bedded room, and $23 per room for connecting room with shared bath. Garden apartments, complete with living room, bedroom, bath and kitchen are $49 daily. Rooms in the Colony Plaza are $60 daily for a studio room, $65 with fireplace, and $70 with fireplace and kitchenette. Private cottages have two-five bedrooms and two-three baths, living rooms with fireplaces, and fully equipped kitchens. Rates vary and are $60–100 daily. Monthly rates are also available. For more information write: The Colonial Inn, Harbor Springs, MI 49740 (616)526–2111.

★★★★*Hilton Shanty Creek & Nordic Ski Center* is a four-season recreational resort, commanding a hill top view of the surrounding hills, Lake Bellaire, Torch Lake, and Grand Traverse Bay. Shanty Creek has its own alpine ski area, with 14 runs ranging from novice to expert, professional ski instruction, night skiing, and complete equipment rentals. The nordic ski center grooms and maintains 28 km. of trails over the rolling golf course terrain, and throughout the surrounding woods. Touring skis are available at the center. Afterwards, enjoy the heated indoor pool, and the wide variety of apres ski activities offered by Shanty Creek including wine, cheese and fondue parties, gourmet dining, ice skating, ski movies, game rooms, and after dinner dancing. In the spring the moist shady woods offer hours of hiking and morel mushroom hunting, for which northern Michigan is famous. There are a myriad of bridle trails, and two fine riding stables nearby. Hilton Shanty Creek has 350 feet of sandy beach to enjoy on Lake Bellaire, and sailboats, paddleboats, canoes, rowboats, and outboard motors are available. March 1 to May 31 the silver smelt are running, and catches number in the hundreds. The season for coho, bass, Kokanee, salmon, rainbow, brown and lake trout extends from late April until early October. Shanty Creek has a rolling 18-hole golf course, with manicured greens and watered fairways and several competition tennis courts. In addition there is fall hunting, bowling, bicycling, snowmobiling, Hilton Shanty Creek Festivals and a wide variety of live entertainment throughout the year. For more information write: Hilton Shanty Creek, P.O. Box 355, Bellaire, MI 49615 (616)533–8621.

★★★★*Honeysuckle Creek Ranch—A Wildlife & Forest Preserve*, located in the Manistee National Forest, is a rustic deluxe lodge set on a 160–acre forest preserve of outstanding scenic beauty. The ranch is organized and equipped for small groups (up to 10) or families. The historic Pere Marquette River—which offers 138 miles of some of the finest trout fishing and canoeing water in the nation—is less than a 10 minute drive away. Also minutes away are the scenic trout and canoe waters of the Little Manistee and Pine rivers. The Honeysuckle Creek Ranch forest preserve offers a wide variety of wildlife and nature trails on 160 acres of rolling, wooded deer country. Spring-fed Honeysuckle Creek is noted for its watercress beds and trout fishing. The fall colors here are spectacular. Deer, wild turkey, and partridge are abundant. The plush ranch lodge offers three pine-panelled bedrooms. The modern ranch kitchen is fully-equipped for your use. Cooking and/or maid service can be arranged. Lodge rental rates from two to four guests are $100–150

per night; weekly rates, two to four guests, are $250. For additional information, contact: Mr. Harold Curtice, Sr., Honeysuckle Creek Ranch, RR 2, Box 66, Bitely, MI 49309 (616)745–3960 or 1605A Woodcutter Lane, Wheaton, IL 60187.

★★★*Long Lake Resort* is located 17 miles east of Ludington on Long Lake, and is a family vacation spot. It is open year around, welcoming anglers and vacationers in the summer, skiers and snowmobilers in the winter, mushroom pickers and hunters in the fall, hikers and canoeists in the spring and people who want to get away from it all throughout the year. Accommodations are in six modern knotty pine housekeeping cottages and one housekeeping apartment for two people. With each cottage, guests get the use of a boat, and motors, gasoline and safety cushions are available. There are also water bikes, paddle boards, a raft and a diving board for water fun. Other outdoor facilities are swings and playground equipment for the youngsters, picnic tables, barbecue grills, and games including badminton, horseshoes, croquet, volleyball, and basketball. The surrounding national forest, Pere Marquette River and the many lakes offer outstanding fishing, canoeing, and hiking. In nearby Ludington on Lake Michigan, ferry boat trips cross the lake to Milwaukee. The cottages at Long Lake Resort have two or three bedrooms, hot and cold water, modern bathrooms and gas heat. They are equipped for cooking with kitchenettes featuring a gas range, electric refrigerator and all utensils. The porches of all cottages face the lake and the large cottage sleeping ten has its own pier. The housekeeping apartment adjoins the home of Gordon and Gertrude Lied, the owners, and has its own entrance, seven windows facing the lake, and all knotty pine interior. The two-bedroom cottage for four people is $25 daily and $140 weekly. A three-bedroom for six is $35 daily and $155 weekly. The large cottage for ten people is $50 daily and $180 weekly. The apartment for two is $18 daily and $105 weekly. For information and reservations: Long Lake Resort, Box 161, Walhalla, MI 49458 (616) 757-2142.

★★★*North Arm Resort at Walloon Lake* is a four-season facility in the heart of the Boyne Mountain ski country. The accommodations are outstanding. The chalets are wood panelled, carpeted, fully equipped for housekeeping and accommodate up to seven persons. Each chalet has instant hot water, refrigeration and thermostatically

controlled heat. The chalets look out on a sandy beach, safe for swimming and equipped with lounge chairs for relaxing in the sun. Wolloon Lake has 54 miles of shoreline and is known for its clean, clear waters. The lodge furnishes indoor fun for guests with a large stone fireplace set up as a focal point for congregating, pool tables, pinball machines, bowling and music. Outdoors, there is fishing, boating, softball, waterskiing and a playground for the children. Mushrooming and game hunting are popular in season. In the winter, there are the snow sports—cross-country skiing, snowshoeing and snowmobiling start right outside the front door of each chalet. And Boyne County ski areas, including Thunder Mountain, Walloon Hills, Boyne Highlands, Nub's Nob and Boyne Mountain, are minutes away. Other nearby attractions are Mackinaw Island and Fort Mackinac, Cross Village Indian Settlement and Museum, Indian River Catholic Shrine and Beaver Island. For further information contact the hosts, Bob and Patti Brown at: North Arm Resort, Route 3, Petoskey, MI 49770 (616)347–8432.

★★*Portage Point Inn* is tucked away on a peninsula with one side facing Lake Michigan and the other Portage Lake. The peninsula is a lovely pine-scented haven with beautiful shores. The inn is a simple, relaxed family place with a full-range of water activities. Swimming, boating, sailing, water-skiing, and fishing can be enjoyed. The inn also has a heated pool. Golf is available at either Manistee Country Club or the Crystal Downs Course, both providing 18–hole courses. Fine 9–hole courses can be found at Frankfort and Bear Lake. There is also a driving range adjacent to the inn for practicing. Tennis courts and archery ranges are popular at the inn, as is croquet, volley ball, soft ball and badminton. Bikes are provided by the inn free of charge for scenic rides. Children four to ten can participate in supervised classes every morning with a graduation ceremony at the end of the week. There is evening entertainment at the casino, with impromptu dancing. The inn includes three meals a day in the rates, with snacks and refreshment available. The dining room has a beautiful view of Portage Lake and boasts excellent cuisine. Men are requested to wear coats and ties to dinner. Accommodations available at the inn range from a private room with bath to a deluxe Terrace Town House with two bedrooms, living room, bath and TV. All facilities are included in rates. Rates: Private room with bath $222, double occupancy per person, Saturday to Saturday booking. A "Doll House", an individual unit $227 double occupancy, per person. Hotel suites with bedroom, bath, studio living room $257 per person, double occupancy. Terrace Town House, as described above $242, per person, double occupancy. There are children's rates, special weekend and holiday specials and group packages also available. For further information contact: The Portage Point Inn, Onekama, MI 49675 (616)889–4222.

★★★★*Ranch Rudolf Lodge & Cross-country Ski Center* is an outstanding family vacation, cross-country skiing, canoeing, and fishing center in the evergreen forests and woods of the beautiful Boardman River Valley. The Boardman is one of the Wolverine State's top-ranked steelhead and salmon fishing streams. The ranch, surrounded by 100,000 acres of the Fife Lake State Forest, offers cross-country skiing on the Muncie Lakes Trail and marked and groomed ranch trails, with rest stops and shelters. The ranch offers rustic accommodations for up to 78 guests in 16 lodge suites and rooms. Skiers and fishermen will enjoy the rustic Homestead Bunkhouse which can accommodate groups of up to 12 people. For backcountry explorers the ranch offers wilderness campsites. Hearty meals and drinks are available at the main lodge. The ranch operated Boardman Valley Outfitting Company offers cross-country instruction and complete outfitting for nordic skiing, snowshoeing, canoeing, backpacking,

skijouring (cross-country skiing behind Siberian Huskies), and dog-sled excursions. Ranch Rudolf daily rates range from $35 per person to $45 per person. Homestead rates are $10 per person. For additional information, contact: Ranch Rudolf, P.O. Box 587, Traverse City, MI 49684 (616)947–9529 or call free in Michigan (1–800)632–1702.

★★★*Rustic Resort at Big Platte Lake* is situated at the entrance to the Sleeping Bear Dunes, and the National Lakeshore. At spring thaw, steelhead trout, rainbows and brook trout offer superb fishing in the Platte River. A 14-foot fiberglass boat, private dock, and swim raft are included in the cabin rates. Nearby are the Sleeping Bear Dunes, the worlds largest shifting sand dunes, to hike in or drive through. Concerts and plays are given throughout the summer at Interlochen Music Camp, a nationally famous training program for young American artists. Fall fishing, amidst the brilliant fall foliage yields Chinook salmon in the Platte River and Platte Bay. In winter, the frozen lake is a favorite spot for ice fishing and ice skating. The hushed woods offer hundreds of scenic trails for ski touring and snowshoeing. The rustic cabins are lake front on Big Platte Lake, accommodate two-eight persons, have wall-to-wall carpeting, private bath, and complete kitchens. Each has its own outdoor fireplace and picnic tables on the lake. Daily rates range between $17.50 and $24 and weekly rates range between $120 and $227 depending on the size of the cabin and the number of people in the party. Cabins are rented by the week only throughout July and August. For more information write: Rustic Resort, 8867 Deadstream Road, Honor, MI 49640 (616)325–6992.

★★★★*Schuss Mountain Village & Ski Area* is a four-season resort village with old-world Bavarian architecture, located in Northern Michigan's Grand Traverse region. In the winter, Schuss Mountain is one of the finest ski resorts in the midwest. For the downhill skier, there are 13 slopes, three double and triple chairlifts, a T-bar, plenty of snow and snowmaking equipment for times when Mother Nature doesn't do her job. The resort has also expanded its facilities for cross-country skiing. There are 15 miles of new trails, groomed, patrolled and marked according to difficulty. All trails have reverse mile and metric signs. There are NASTAR races on the weekends, a full service ski shop for sales and rental of equipment, ski movies in the evening and a Ski School operated under the direction of Dave Hofacker and Dave Peterson. Winter guests also enjoy the heated outdoor

swimming pool, the ice skating rink, sleigh rides and snowshoeing in the Enchanted Forest. There are many different ski plans and packages which include lessons, lodging, meals, etc. Children under 12 ski and sleep free when staying in the same room with two adults. Parents will especially like the Royal Elf Club ski program. For children ages five to nine, this program gives them supervised skiing all day, plus planned activities after skiing so that parents are free to enjoy their own activities. In the evening, guests enjoy the Ivanhof Restaurant, the Royal Pub or the Camelot Lounge or plan a cheese fondue party, hot wine party or just relaxation. In the summer, Schuss Mountain specializes in tennis, golf and other warm weather activities. There are six hard-surfaced tennis courts. Professional instruction, use of a ball machine and practise walls are all available. Five-day tennis packages are offered from May 29 through September 1, Sunday through Friday. Golfers come to the resort for the unique Schuss Royal Golf Course, set in natural terrain, with no fairways side by side. Three day golf packages include unlimited golf, two nights lodging and use of a pull cart. In summer, there are two heated swimming pools. There is trout stream fishing, shuffleboard, croquet, badminton and facilities for cook-outs. Hiking trails are marked, there are rides on the royal trolley and on the sky tramway and an indoor game room designed for teens. The Royal Elf Club operates in the summer, as well as winter. Children four to twelve are taken on nature hikes and royal trolley tours, supervised in arts and crafts and outdoor games, and introduced to other children their own age. Three meals a day are served in the Ivanhof Restaurant and the Sunday Brunch there with over 40 items is famous. There is professional entertainment six nights a week from June 16 through Sept. 2 in Ivan's Attic. Accommodations, summer and winter, offer something for every taste and every size group. Village rooms are deluxe accommodations in the Village Square with private bath, air-conditioning, color TV, phone, dressing vanity and carpeting in each room. Suites can accommodate up to four people and have cooking facilities and a private sundeck. The Sudendorf Condominiums are a half-mile from the Village Square with their own community house and private pool. These units have kitchens, electric heat, private baths, phones and most have sundecks, fireplaces and air-conditioning. They can sleep up to 12 people with a variety of interior arrangements including sleeping lofts and convertible couches. The Chalets are deluxe accommodations and are scattered throughout the Enchanted Forest. They have two to four bedrooms and are equipped for cooking.

Minimum occupancy is for two nights, and the children's "sleep-free" program is not applicable in Chalets. Rates vary substantially by the number of persons in the unit, the season and the sports package chosen. Village rooms start at $30 a night in the off season and a Chalet for twelve is $140–160 a day. There are rates for children, for six-day stays, golf, tennis, downhill ski, and cross-country touring packages; and special holiday rates. For all the rate information, reservations or literature on Schuss Mountain, contact: The Kingdom of Schuss, Mancelona, MI 49659 (616)587–9162 or in Michigan toll-free (800)632–7170.

★★★★*Sugar Loaf Village & Ski Center* is a luxury mountain resort with outstanding year-round recreation facilities. It is located just 20 miles northwest of Traverse City, surrounded by lakes, rivers, and hills, on 2,000 acres overlooking Lake Michigan. Golf is played on the resort's championship 7,000 yard 18-hole course. There is instruction for adults and children, rental equipment and a new 2,800 square foot Pro Shop. Tennis buffs can enjoy the four Sportsface carpeted indoor tennis courts in the "Sugar Barn" all year long. There are also five outdoor courts and a practice wall for warm weather use. There is a tennis shop, locker rooms, a spectators' deck and professional instruction. Guests can swim in two outdoor pools, one of which is heated for year-round use. The resort has its own airport with a 4,300–foot lighted year-round landing strip only 100 yards from the main lodge. Their sky sailing instructors teach hang-gliding. Eight to twelve hours of instruction can introduce a guest to the thrills of soaring free. Indoors there is a sauna, the Four Seasons dining room, the Top of the Leaf evening entertainment center and two cocktail lounges with live entertainment. But, it is the snow sports that have really given Sugar Loaf its name. These are Lower Michigan's highest slopes. Twenty runs are reached by five double chair lifts and one J-bar. Eighty per cent of the runs are for beginners and intermediate skiers. But there is a 600–foot vertical drop, a nationally known Ski School and excellent equipment available for rent. For guests who prefer cross-country skiing, there are over 13 miles of marked wooded trails. Guides, instructors and rental equipment are available. Accommodations include lodge rooms and two- and four-bedroom townhouses. They are newly built, air-conditioned, beautifully furnished and have outstanding views. Rates vary with the sports package and the season. A mid-week winter American Plan, for example, would include room, dinner, breakfast, lift ticket, a group lesson and one hour of tennis for a daily rate of $48.50 per person (double occupancy). A two-bedroom townhouse with no meals included, sleeping up to eight people is $110 a day and $450 for five days. A four-bedroom townhouse sleeping up to 12 is $150 for one day and $600 for five days. For reservations and more information contact: Sugar Loaf Village, Route One, Cedar, MI 49621 (616)228–5461.

★★*Village Resort at Walloon Lake*, nestled on the eastern edge of Walloon Lake's 54 mile shore line, offers deluxe apartments, two and three bedroom brick cottages with fireplaces, and luxurious two bedroom houses, available by the week or the month. Dotted with white sails in the summer, the blue waters of Walloon Lake offer fishing, swimming off the sandy beach, boating and water skiing. Fishing licences are available at the Village Resort Store, which also rents fishing boats, sells live bait, tackle, and carry-out beer and wine. The surrounding hills, brilliant with autumn foliage provide excellent hunting, and ice fishing and skating are popular in the winter months. All of the Village Resort cottages are winterized and may be rented for the entire ski season, ideally located in the center of Michigan's "Big Six" ski facilities. For more information write: Kay and Howard Bills, The Village Resort, P.O. Box 220, Walloon Lake, MI 49796 (616)535–2296.

Ottawa National Forest & The Keweenaw Peninsula

The famous fishing, hunting, and canoe-camping areas of the 910,000–acre Ottawa National Forest embrace wild, second-growth hardwoods and conifers, rolling hills, remote blue lakes, and fast deep-flowing streams, located in the western section of the Upper Peninsula, south of Lake Superior and the Keweenaw Peninsula. The forest terrain varies from the level, sandy plains covered with second-growth pine to the rugged hills of the Gogebic Range. Black River Harbor, in the westernmost sections of the forest, has been called the most picturesque harbor in Michigan and offers charter boats for salmon, steelhead, and lake trout in Lake Superior. The wild and scenic Black River is one of the north country's most picturesque streams, with 11 scenic cascades and rapids. The Black is also renowned for its superb trout fishing and canoe-camping. The Ottawa Country contains several of the Wolverine State's outstanding trophy fisheries for northern pike, walleye, smallmouth bass, and muskellunge, including Lake Gogebic, Lac Vieux Desert on the Wisconsin boundary, Thousand Island Lake, Cisco Chain of Lakes, Presque Isle Flowage, Chaney and Langford Lakes, and the adjacent rainbow, salmon, and brook trout waters of the Montreal and Brule rivers. The Ontonagon River system, including its nationally renowned Middle Branch and its famous Agate Falls pool, provides fishing for brook and brown trout up to trophy weights, and Lake Superior steelhead. The Middle Branch from Bond Falls to Agate Falls— surrounded by an evergreen wilderness—is considered the top brook and brown trout water in the Upper Peninsula. Other attractions of the forest include the series of waterfalls south of Black River Harbor, including Rainbow, Standstone, Potawatomi, Great Conglomerate, and Algonquin Falls. Southwest of Paynesville, the Agate Falls, reached by a 200–yard footpath along the riverbank, drop over an 80–foot ledge that crosses the Ontonagon River. The four branches of the Ontonagon offer some very good canoe stretches, including the main stream from Military Bridge on U.S. 45 to Lake Superior, a pleasant 30–mile paddle with a few rapids that are easily portaged. The scenery along the river is wild and rugged, with little or no development near the shoreline. Nestled in a deep valley with steep clay bluffs to either side, the Ontonagon is particularly lovely in late spring, when banks of delicate lady's slippers bloom near the shoreline.

The Paint River and its North and South branches also offer excellent canoeing in the southwestern reaches of the forest.

Once the hunting and trapping grounds of the Ottawa Indians, the forest still provides excellent hunting for whitetail deer, black bear, and upland game birds. The forest is a top-ranked fishing area for large steelhead and brown trout from Lake Superior found in the many miles of deep-flowing streams, including the Ontonagon, Deer Creek, Presque Isle River, and Cherry and Warbler creeks. In fall, these two species, plus salmon, enter forest streams on their annual spawning runs. Walleye and northern pike, brook, rainbow, and brown trout; splake; muskies; and small and largemouth bass are other game fish found in the 700–odd lakes and 2,000 miles of streams.

In wintertime, downhill skiers can enjoy the major ski hills near Ironwood, Iron River, and in the Porcupine Mountains just north of the forest. In the western part of the Ottawa is the Copper Peak Ski Flying Hill, the largest ski jump in the Western Hemisphere, offering breathtaking views of Lake Superior from its lofty summit. Many trails wind through all sections of the wilderness, exploring remote woodlands, clear blue lakes, and cascading streams. The Beaver Lodge Trail, beginning at the Bob Lake Campground, passes an active beaver colony near Leveque Creek. Strategically located in the most rugged country of Michigan's Upper Peninsula, the Ottawa National Forest forms a jump-off point for extended wilderness travel. To the north are the Porcupine Mountains, the Copper Range State Forest, and the wild Keweenaw Peninsula. The Baraga and Iron Range state forests lie just west of the Ottawa, and to the south is the renowned Nicolet National Forest of Wisconsin. The possibilities for canoeing, camping, hunting, and fishing trips, and adventurous backpacking are virtually unlimited.

Information Sources, Maps & Access

Detailed information and a full-color *Ottawa National Forest Map* (50¢) may be obtained from: Supervisor, Ottawa National Forest, Ironwood, MI 49938 (906)932–1330. The map shows forest roads, recreation areas, ski areas, hiking trails, lakes, streams, rivers, boat-access sites, and other attractions of the Ottawa, including nearby towns, the Porcupine Mountains State Park, and adjoining lands of the Nicolet National Forest, Copper Range State Forest, and Baraga

State Forest. A *Sylvania Recreation Area Map-Brochure* showing hiking trails, canoe routes, campsites, boat-launching sites, lakes, forest roads, picnic grounds, and other features of the region is available free from the Forest Supervisor. A free *Porcupine Mountains Wilderness Map/Brochure* may be obtained free from: Porcupine Mountains State Park, Star Route, Ontonagon, MI 49953 (906)885–5798. The map/brochure also contains information on modern and rustic campgrounds and trailside cabins. The cabins are available for rent between April 1 and November 30, and reservations should be made in advance with the Park Supervisor. Adirondack shelters have also been developed for trail hikers and are available on a first-come basis. Backpackers must register at the park office before entering the wilderness. Ottawa National Forest is easily reached on State Highway 2 from Ironwood, Bessemer, and Ramsay. From Ontonagon, take State Highway 45 south. State Highway 2 also leads to the forest on the east from Iron River, Stambaugh, and Caspian.

Recreation Areas

Keweenaw Peninsula

Michigan's most northerly arm, the Keweenaw Peninsula, forms a giant hook reaching into the waters of Lake Superior above the Northern Peninsula. Sometimes called the "Treasure Chest of Michigan" or "Copper Country," the peninsula has produced billions of pounds of copper and has been extensively mined since prehistoric days. It is believed that primitive races using crude fire-and-water or stone-hammer methods extracted deposits of pure copper and silver from the mines and fashioned them into weapons and ornaments. Who these people were and where they came from remains an open question. Some say the work was done by American Indians who fashioned metal implements for trading purposes, others believe that Vikings in the tenth and eleventh centuries made expeditions to the Great Lakes for copper cargos. Still other anthropologists maintain that Aztecs from Mexico sent mining expeditions up the Mississippi to procure the valuable metal or that Phoenicians, famous for their skilled bronzework, worked the mines centuries before the Christian era.

The first white men to systematically explore the region and its riches were English and French, but full-scale exploitation of the area did not begin until the survey made by Dr. Douglass Houghton, the state's first geologist, in 1840–43. After that date, nearly a thousand claims were filed in the Lake Superior district. While some mines proved worthless, others produced fortunes in copper. The copper boom peaked shortly before World War I and has declined since then, although some mines continue to be profitable. Today this remote, lake-studded region offers fine opportunities for outdoor activities. Fort Wilkins, an historic army post established in 1844 on Lake Fanny Hooe, has now been converted into a State Park with campgrounds and excellent lake fishing. Michigan's northernmost town, Copper Harbor, is a summer resort of great beauty offering passenger service to Isle Royale. Stretching between Copper Harbor and Eagle Harbor is the Brockway Mountain Drive, perhaps the most scenic route in the state. The road passes precipitous cliffs and offers access to Brockway's Knoll, a high peak overlooking the entire breadth of the peninsula. Views from the drive of rolling, tree-covered hills are particularly outstanding in the fall when bright leaves add to the overall beauty. Other attractions of the area include the numerous units of the Baraga State Forest and the Devil's Washtub, a cool, dark inlet near the water's edge where swirling and pounding waves rush in during periods of high water. The peninsula offers both first rate hunting for deer, black bear, and ruffed grouse, and fishing in the many crystal-clear lakes, including Lac la Belle, Gratiot and Deer Lakes, and Lake Medora.

Porcupine Mountains Wilderness

One of the wildest areas left in the Midwest, the Porcupine Mountains Wilderness State Park covers 58,000 acres along the shores of Lake Superior about 17 miles west of Ontonagon in Michigan's Upper Peninsula. Towering stands of virgin pine and hemlock, four secluded lakes, and miles of wild rivers and streams combine to make this one of the most beautiful and challenging areas in the state for backpacking, fishing, and camping. The "Porkies," densely wooded mountains reaching heights of 1,900 feet, were named by Chippewa Indians who thought their rolling, forested outlines resembled crouching porcupines. The only road in this primitive wilderness skirts the south and east borders of the park and leads motorists to within a quarter-mile of spectacular views of the Lake of the Clouds.

The Department of Natural Resources maintains over 80 miles of foot trails and rustic trailside cabins for use by the public. Strategically designed to reward hikers with breathtaking views of tree–rimmed lakes and forested ridges, the trails are rugged with steep grades and many stream crossings. The 16–mile Lake Superior Trail, longest in the park, follows the rugged lake shoreline and offers both outstanding views and excellent fishing for lake trout, rainbows, and salmon at the mouths of the many streams that empty into Lake Superior. Two short trails, the East and West River trails, follow the Presque Isle River, largest and most beautiful of the streams in the Porcupines. Before it reaches the waters of Lake Superior, the Presque Isle rushes from the tableland through narrow, precipitous gorges over a series of spectacular waterfalls and rapids. The Big Carp River Trail, nine miles in length, offers perhaps the widest variety of wilderness scenery in the park. For the first two miles the trail parallels the escarpment; then it descends into the valley of the Big Carp River, where excellent brook trout fishing and turbulent rapids are found all the way to the river's mouth. Shining Cloud Falls, the second longest in the park, are located approximately one mile upstream from the mouth. The four-mile Escarpment Trail begins where the Carp River route leaves off and leads over Cloud and Coyahoga peaks, then down to the north end of the Government Peak Trail. Striking rock formations and panoramic views of Lake of the Clouds are the major attractions of this footpath. Hunting for deer in season and cross-country skiing are other favorite activities in the Porcupine Mountains. Write to the Park Supervisor at the above address for ski and snowshoe trail maps and information on hunting. For canoeists there is the Carp River canoe trail, with its many beautiful cascades, including the Explorers. Trappers, Trader, Greenstone, and Shining Cloud falls. Complete outfitting and resort-type accommodations are available in nearby Ontonagon.

Sylvania Recreation Area

Perhaps the most spectacular region on the Ottawa is the Sylvania Recreation Area, encompassing Whitefish, Clark, Loon, Deer Island, Devils Head, and Duck lakes in the southern reaches of the forest. Spread out over 21,000 acres, the old-growth forests of birch, maple, hemlock, pine, spruce, and fir are still largely virgin timber, huge trees that burst into full color during the fall season. The water quality of the lakes here is as high as or higher than most other inland lakes in the United States, with a transparency seldom exceeded in lakes of other regions. Because these lakes were at one time inaccessible to fishermen, a virgin-type fish population developed. Most fish, though relatively large, are quite old, making the fish population similar to what might have been found by the first white men to visit the Upper Peninsula. The lakes contain bass, lake trout, walleye, northern pike, perch, and sunfish. Mammals of the Sylvania area include whitetail deer, black bear, skunk, otter, raccoon, beaver, muskrat, coyote, mink, and fox. A variety of water and forest

birds, including the loon and bald eagle, may be seen in their natural habitats. Hunting and fishing are permitted in season with a valid state license. Numerous campsites, many of them situated on lakeshores, are scattered throughout the area and are available on a first-come basis. Fine hiking trails wind around the southern shores of Clark Lake, around Deer Island Lake, and through dense, unspoiled forests. Lake canoeing is also popular, with the major lakes linked by established portage routes.

Gateways & Accommodations

Calumet

(Pop. 1,000; zip code 49913; area code 906.) Named after an Indian word for peace pipe, Calumet owes its growth to copper mines in the area. The town is also a gateway to the rugged northwestern tip of the Upper Peninsula and to the Ottawa National Forest. Accommodations: *Elms Motel* (rates: $20–23 double), 15 rooms, color TV, nearby restaurant, at 6th and Elm Sts., ¼ mile west of U.S. Hwy. 41 (337–2620); *Northgate Motel* (rates: $26 double), 29 rooms, color TV, playground, one mile north of town via U.S. Hwy. 41 (337–1000).

Copper Harbor

(Pop. 25; zip code 49918; area code 906.) Northernmost village in the state, Copper Harbor is named for the lumps of pure copper that were once found along the lakeshore here and attracted the first explorers to the area. When copper deposits petered out in the late 19th century, the town prospered for a time as a lumbering center. Today Copper Harbor is a remote and beautiful resort town, a gateway to Isle Royale National Park and the wild Keweenaw Peninsula. Fort Wilkins State Park (289–4215), one mile east of town on U.S. 41, contains a restored army outpost, officers' quarters, a museum, and 190 acres of parkland. In town is the Astor House Museum (see below) with a large collection of antique dolls and toys, Indian relics, and exhibits of local historical interest. Accommodations: *Bella Vista Motel* (rates: $22–26 double), 20 attractive rooms, eight cottages with kitchens, overlooking Lake Superior, one block north of town, just off the junction of U.S. Hwy. 41 and Michigan State Hwy. 26 (289–4213); *Minnetonka Resort & Astor House Motel* (rates: $20–22 double), 13 motel rooms and 17 cottages, 10 with kitchens, TV, saunas, bicycles, attractive rustic decor, Astor House Museum on premises, at junction of U.S. Hwy. 41 and Michigan State Hwy. 26 (289–4449).

Hancock

(Pop. 4,700; zip code 49930; area code 906.) Named for the patriot John Hancock, the town is located on Portage Lake at its narrowest point, just across the water from its sister city, Houghton. Area attractions include the Arcadian Copper Mine, one mile east of town on Michigan State Hwy. 26, where visitors can view the mine in operation (open daily June-Oct. 15); and the Quincy Mine Steam Hoist, one mile north of town on U.S. 41, the 790-ton hoist used at the Quincy Mine during the 1920's. Accommodations: *Best Western Copper Crown Motel* (rates: $24.96 double), 40 attractive rooms, color TV, indoor pool, saunas, restaurant adjacent, at 235 Hancock Ave. (482–6111); *Whispering Pines* (rates: $18–22 double), 16 rooms, TV, free airport bus, pleasant pine-shaded grounds, on Rte. 1 in Calumet (zip 49913), six miles north of Hancock via U.S. Hwy. 41 (482–5887).

Iron Mountain

(Pop. 9,000; zip code 49801; area code 906.) The city takes its name from a nearby bluff heavily stratified with iron ore. From 1879 well into the 1930's, mines in the area were in continuous production, yielding the richest deposits of Menominee hematite in the district. Abandoned mine pits, cave-ins, and the huge Chapin Mine Pump are reminders of Iron Mountain's boom days. Tours of the underground drifts and tunnels of the Iron Mountain Iron Mine (eight miles east of town via U.S. Hwy. 2) are offered daily, 9am–6pm, May 15–Oct. 15. Other area attractions include the House of Yesteryear Museum, three miles southeast of town via U.S. Hwy. 2 (open May 15–Oct. 15) and the Pine Mt. Lodge ski area (which see). Accommodations: *Dickinson Inn* (rates: $17.50 double), 54 fine rooms, colonial decor, TV, excellent steak house, bar and grill on the premises, at 101 W. B St., one block west of U.S. Hwy. 2 (774–5000); *Holiday Motel* (rates: $23–25 double), 68 attractive rooms, color TV, heated pool, restaurant adjacent, at 1609 Stephenson Ave. (774–6220).

Ironwood

(Pop. 8,500; zip code 49938; area code 906.) Gateway to the Ottawa National Forest, Ironwood was the first town established in the rich mining country of the Gogebic Range. Today Ironwood is the jumping-off point for the vast recreation lands of the western Upper Peninsula, including several noteworthy ski areas: Mt. Zion, ¾ miles north of town via U.S. 2, one of the highest points in the Gogebic Range, with spectacular views of the surrounding countryside (phone 932–9879 for information) and Big Powderhorn Mt., four miles northeast of town off U.S. Hwy. 2 on Powderhorn Rd. (phone 932–3100 for information). Black River Drive on County Road 513 follows the twisting course of the Black River to Lake Superior. The 17–mile scenic drive passes eight beautiful waterfalls, all of which are accessible on foot. Other points of interest are the Ironwood Historical Museum, at 226 E. McLeod Ave., housing exhibits of the city's past, and Copper Peak Ski Flying Hill, 12 miles north of town on County Road 513, where a chairlift and elevator take visitors to the top of Copper Peak, a spectacular vantage point with views of Lake Superior and surrounding forests (open May–Oct., phone 932–3500 for hours). Accommodations: *Best Western Cloverland Motel* (rates: $22–24 double), 30 attractive rooms and suites, color TV, queen-size beds, playground, nearby restaurant, at 477 W. Cloverland Dr., ¾ mile northwest of town via U.S. Hwy. 2 (932–1260); *Sandpiper Motel* (rates $16–20 double), 29 attractive rooms, color TV, saunas, restaurant opposite, at 1200 Cloverland Drive, one mile east of town via U.S. Hwy. 2 (932–2000).

Ontonagon—Gateway to Porcupine Mountains Wilderness

(Pop. 2,400; zip code 49953; area code 906.) Once the site of a Chippewa village, Ontonagan takes its name from an Indian word meaning "place of the bowl." The town is a gateway to both the Ottawa National Forest and Porcupine Mountains Wilderness State Park (which see), a rugged, semi-primitive wilderness area encompassing 58,000 acres, numerous lakes and streams, hiking trails, and an excellent ski area. Other area attractions include the renowned trout and steelhead waters of the Ontonagon River system. Accommodations: *Hokans Chalet Cottages* (rates: $18–22 double) two motel rooms and seven cottages with one-two bedrooms and kitchens, pleasant wooded area along Lake Superior, private beach, rental boats, playground, groceries, cross-country ski trails, 1½ miles west of town via Michigan State Hwy. 64 (884–4230); *Silver Sands Motor Lodge* (rates: $23 double), 20 rooms overlooking Lake Superior, beach opposite, swimming, fishing, in Porcupine Mountains State Park, 16 miles west of town via Michigan State Hwy. 107, two miles west of Silver City (885–5643).

Lodges & Resorts

Arrow Lodge at Thousand Island Lake, in the Ottawa National Forest, is situated on a beautiful bay, just 1½ miles from Sylvania, the national wilderness of 18,000 acres of virgin forest and 36 unspoiled lakes. The largest of the 15 lakes in the Cisco Chain, Thousand Island Lake offers numerous islands and bays with superb fishing for walleyes, muskie, pike, huge perch, small- and largemouth bass, and trophy-size trout. Boating and hiking are other popular summer activities. In the winter, Arrow Lodge is a jumping-off point for cross-country skiing, ice-fishing, and hunting. Modern, comfortable housekeeping cottages begin at $125 per week for four persons. Boat and motor rentals are additional. The lodge restaurant offers home-style cooking, and there is also a general store. For information, write: Arrow Lodge, Thousand Island Lake Road, Watersmeet, MI 49969 (906)358–4390.

Bailey's Rustic Resort at Lake Gogebic is noted for excellent walleye and perch fishing, as well as deer and bear hunting. The resort has housekeeping cabins, boats and motors for rent to guests and offers good fishing and hunting. The two-bedroom cabins have double beds, plus sofa beds in the living rooms. There is a complete bath and fully equipped kitchen in each cabin. Blankets, bed linen and towels are provided. Rates are $100 per week for two persons and $10 per week for each additional person. Boats are $15 a week and motors, with gas and oil included, are $30 to $40. The resort is open all year, and special deer season and skiing rates are available on request. For more information, contact: Bailey's Rustic Resort, Star Route, Box 207, Marenisco, MI 49947 (906)842–3336.

Indianhead Ski Resort has been said to have some of the best skiing, combined with the most beautiful views, in the Mid-West. Overlooking the Black River Valley and Lake Superior, Indianhead gets an average of 200 inches of snow each ski season. Add to that their snowmaking capabilities and you get a ski season that lasts from early fall into late spring. There are 12 slopes, seven lifts, a ski school, ski shop, equipment rentals and special holiday "happenings" including costumed carnivals, bikini races, sundeck barbeques and trailside parties. There is also a disco, bar, and three fine dining rooms. For extended stays, even in the summertime, there is a mountain-top Lodge offering sauna, heated outdoor pool, game room, babysitting service, tennis courts and golf course. Mid-week rates are $35–39 per person per night, double occupancy. This includes lodging, breakfast, dinner and lift. There are also the Indian Hills Chalets, perfect for families or large groups, which offer the privacy of a total apartment, within walking distance of the lifts. Rental of a chalet, about $70 per day. Ski week special: Sun.-Fri., including five nights' lodging, lift tickets, dinners and ski lessons costs about $171 per person at the Lodge, $187 per person in a chalet (double occupancy). Weekend packages and holiday rates also available. For details, contact: Indianhead Mountain, Wakefield, MI 49968 (in Wisconsin, Ill., Minn., & Northern Indiana (800)338–1243; elsewhere (906)229–5181.

Keweenaw Mountain Lodge is located at Copper Harbor, the gateway town to Isle Royale National Park. Jutting out into Lake Superior, this finger of land is reached from the south via Wisconsin or from the east by the Straits of Mackinac. Daily round trip boat transportation to Isle Royale is available at Copper Harbor. Guests at Keweenaw Mountain Lodge can find much to do on the mainland as well as the island. The resort has free tennis and shuffleboard. Greens fees for golf are only $4.95 per day—and $3.00 for guests in cottages. The main lodge has two big fireplaces, an elegant dining room and a lounge with exotic drinks. Nearby, there are old ghost towns and the famed copper mines of this area. Guests can drive along the 9½

mile Brockway Mountain Drive with its vistas of Lake Superior, collect rock throughout Keweenaw County or launch their own boats for canoeing or boating. The lodge is open from June 10 through October 15. Accommodations are in one- and two-bedroom cottages each with a fireplace, and two beds in every bedroom. Rates for a one-bedroom duplex cottage for one or two persons is $24.75 and for a two-bedroom cottage for one to four guests is $41.80 per night. For further information or reservations write Keweenaw Mountain Lodge, Copper Harbor, MI 49918 (906)289–4403.

Lac La Belle Resort on Thousand Island Lake, the largest lake in the Cisco Chain of Lakes, is 11 miles from Watermeet, Michigan and 16 miles from Land O'Lakes, Wisconsin. The resort is designed for families, with six cottages facing the lake and a large lawn with a playground for children. The safe swimming beach is within easy sight and distance of all cottages. A 14–foot aluminum boat is provided free with each cottage, and guests can explore 271 miles of wooded shoreline in the Chain of Lakes; fish for walleye, muskie, lake trout, bass, northern pike and panfish; or, in season, hunt for deer, bear, duck and partridge. There is a launching ramp for those with their own boat, a screened fish-cleaning house and freezer facilities. Motors, extra boats, gas, bait and canoes are available. Sylvania Recreation Area is only 1½ miles away and has hiking trails, canoeing, swimming, picnicking, hunting, fishing and boating. The cottages accommodate two to six people and have fully equipped kitchens, automatic heat, running water and showers. Three of the six cottages are available for rental year around. Lac La Belle also has a trailer park with complete hook-ups for travel trailers and pickup campers. The area is secluded and scenic, and can be reserved by the day, week or month. For information and reservations: Don and Iolah Vernier, Lac La Belle Resort, Thousand Island Lake, Watersmeet, MI 49969 (906)368–4396.

North Shore Resort on Cisco Lake has housekeeping cottages, rooms in the lodge, boats and motors for rent, as well as tackle, bait, fishing and hunting licenses and groceries for sale. It is minutes from the Sylvania Wilderness in the National Forest, and is open from May 15th through late fall. Meals are served in the dining room at the resort only from May 15th to June 15th and Sept. 15th to closing. During the summer season, guests cook in the fully-equipped cottages or visit nearby restaurants. A boat is provided with each cottage and boaters can reach 14 of the 16 lakes in the Cisco Chain for hours of fishing and scenic boating. The lakes offer superb

fishing and walleye fishing is especially good in spring and fall. The resort has a dock and guests can enjoy swimming and waterskiing in the lake. Cottages have gas stoves and electric refrigerators, all cooking utensils, linens and blankets. Groceries are available at the resort store. A one-bedroom housekeeping cottage sleeping four rents for $135 a week, and a two-bedroom cottage for up to six is $160 per week. Lodge rooms are $14 single and $18 double per day. For information and reservations write Don and Shirley Murphy, North Shore Resort, Watersmeet, MI 49969 (906)358–4309.

★★★★*Pine Mountain Lodge* serves both as a winter ski resort and a summer country club. The Swiss-style Alpine Lodge rests at the foot of a majestic skier's mountain, boasting about a dozen slopes of varying degrees of difficulty, six lifts, an Olympic ski jump and all the necessary ski facilities including school, shop and rentals. The lodge itself has an indoor heated pool, a chalet cafeteria, an elegant dining room, cocktail lounge, fireplace lounge, and a separate "Pine Cone" eatery atop the slopes. During the summer there is 18–hole golf at the Pine Grove Country Club, a tennis court, lake fishing only five minutes away at Lake Antoine, and river and backwater fishing at the headwaters of the Menominee River. Tours of the iron mines and spectacular water shows at nearby Iron Mountain recreational center are also a plus. Rates in peak season: $170 per person (double occupancy) for a five-day stay. Prices include room, breakfast, dinner, lift, ski lessons and use of the pool. Complete facilities for conventions also available. Write: Pine Mountain Lodge, Pine Mountain Road, Star Route 2, Iron Mountain, MI 49801 (906)774–2747.

Travel Services

Sylvania Outfitters equips and guides vacationers for canoe trips, camping, and cross-country ski touring. Owner/operator Bob Zelinski is a native of the Sylvania Recreation Area and his advice is invaluable when planning trips. Sylvania is 21,000 acres of virgin northwoods. There are 36 lakes and 19 ponds, most of which are connected by short portages. This seemingly endless chain of lakes can be traversed by canoe. In 1966 the area was purchased by the Federal Government and is now part of Ottawa National Forest. Sylvania is located one mile west of Watersmeet on U.S. Rte. 2. They have lightweight Grumman canoes, life jackets, tents, sleeping bags, freeze-dried food and everything else needed for an outing. Canoes rent for $7 a day or $42 a week including paddles, flotation cushions or life vests, carrying yoke and cartop carrier. Complete outfitting (based on two persons per canoe) is $15 and includes all canoeing and camping equipment. Sylvania Outfitters also arranges trips on the wild and scenic Ontonagon and Paint Rivers. The heavier river canoes rent for $10 a day. For lake sailing in Ottawa National Forest they can provide canoes with sail rigging. In the winter, the center turns to ski touring. The outfitting post becomes a skier's lounge and the camp store a ski shop. They rent and sell skis and equipment, help plan cross-country ski routes over the marked week-end and novice routes. They offer skiing instruction for the beginner and for the hearty expert, there is winter camping on skiis. Rental equipment for all seasons should be reserved in advance if possible. For rentals and more information contact: Sylvania Outfitters, West U.S. 2, Watersmeet, MI 49969 (906)358–4766.

MINNESOTA

Introduction

Minnesota, known as the "Land of 10,000 Lakes," the westernmost of the Great Lakes States, bounded on the east by Lake Superior and Wisconsin, contains the headwaters of the mighty Mississippi—which begin its long, meandering 3,710–mile journey south into the Gulf of Mexico from its source in beautiful Lake Itasca in the north-central part of the state—and several of the nation's outstanding fishing, canoeing, and wild and scenic northwoods vacation areas, including the famous trophy muskellunge of lakes Leech, Cass, and Winnibigoshish in the Mississippi headwaters country of the Chippewa National Forest; the Red Lake canoe country; the great glacially gouged Boundary Lakes, such as Rainy, Namakan, Lac La Croix, Basswood, Gunflint, Saganaga, Kabetogama, and Mountain—which stretch like a ragged necklace of blue jewels along the Minnesota-Ontario border; the wild rivers and remote blue lakes of the Boundary Waters Canoe Area in the Superior National Forest; the historic Grand Portage Trail and brawling, deep-flowing trophy steelhead streams along Lake Superior's rugged North Shore.

The "North Star State," located in the geographic center of North America, contains several distinct outdoor recreation regions within its 84,068 square miles: the "Arrowhead" region in the northeast—a southern extension of the great Canadian Shield, with rocky highlands, swampy marshes, and ancient volcanic rock, and both the highest and lowest elevations in the state (and 660 feet at Lake Superior); the central hill and lake country, with its mixed hardwood and coniferous forests and wetlands; the ancient bed of glacial Lake Agassiz in the northwest—which at one time covered an area 700 miles long and 200 miles wide, leaving traces of its lowering beach lines in the many sandy ridges still visible here—dominated by the southern reaches of beautiful island-dotted Lake of the Woods (1,485 square miles), Rainy Lake (345 square miles) and Red Lake, the state's largest body of water, covering an area of 494 square miles, all draining northward into Canada's Hudson Bay. The virgin forests and waterways of Minnesota, the original home and hunting grounds of the Chippewa and Sioux Indians, were first explored by the hardy fur traders and voyageurs of the old Northwest Company, followed by Lieutenant Zebulon Pike, who took possession of the region for the United States under President Thomas Jefferson.

Accommodations & Travel Information

The North Star State's famous north country vacation lodges and resorts are listed and described in the "Vacation/Lodging Guide" which follows.

The following guides to Minnesota's outdoor vacation regions may be obtained free upon request: *Arrowhead Country*, a guide to the state's scenic and wild northeastern corner, may be obtained from the Minnesota Arrowhead Association, Hotel Duluth, Duluth 55802 (218)722–0874; *Tip o'the Arrow* is a 23–page booklet on rugged Cook County—the easternmost point of Arrowhead country between Saganaga Lake, Jacoinette Harbor, and Grand Portage—available from the Tip of the Arrowhead Association, Grand Marais 55604; *Heartland*, a 55–page guide to north-central Minnesota, known as the "Muskie Capital of the World," is available from Heartland Inc., P.O. Box 443, 411 Laurel St., Brainerd 56401 (218)829–1615; *Viking Land U.S.A.*, a 23–page booklet about the northwest region, believed to have been visited by the Norsemen in 1362, may be obtained from Viking-Land U.S.A., Box 545, Battle Lake 56515; *Hiawathaland*, a 55–page guide to the southeastern region, is available from Hiawathaland, 212 1st Ave., SW, Rochester 55901; *Pioneerland*, a guide to the state's southeastern corner, is available

from Pioneerland Inc., Chamber of Commerce Bldg., Box 999, Mankato 56001.

Further information on resorts throughout the state can be obtained from the Minnesota Resort Association, 2001 University Ave., St. Paul 55104. The Minnesota Hotel and Motor Hotel Association, at the same address, will also be glad to provide details on statewide accommodations. Information on motels alone is also available from the Minnesota Motel Association, 2901 Pleasant Avenue, Minneapolis, MN 55408.

A toll–free phone number is also available to Minnesota's visitors for information on Minnesota vacations. Dial (1–800)652–9008 for information on resorts, hotels, motels, attractions, calendar events, camping, and driving tours of the state. Twin Cities residents should use the regular tourist center number, (612)296–5029. Residents of Illinois, Iowa, Kansas, Michigan, Missouri, Nebraska, North and South Dakota, and Wisconsin should call toll–free (1–800)382–9161 for Minnesota vacation information.

Information & Services

The North Star State's huge expanses of scenic northern hardwood and evergreen forests, wetlands, and 4,900 square miles of water (excluding the state's portion of Lake Superior), including more than 10,000 "sky-blue" lakes and wild, twisting rivers, provide unrivaled fishing and hunting opportunities.

Fishing and hunting regulations, seasons, permits, and specific area information are available from the Division of Fish & Wildlife, Dept. of Natural Resources, 390 Centennial Bldg., St. Paul 55155. For waterfowl hunters, the Division of Fish & Wildlife publishes a useful, free *Minnesota Wildlife Lands Map*, showing the locations of 848 wildlife-management-area wetlands. Department of Natural resources Five Plan Maps are available to sportsmen who hunt in Minnesota. Each map covers 36 square miles (except in border areas). The scale is two inches to one mile, and details shown include rivers, lakes, railroad tracks, fire towers, and the logging roads. The maps are reproduced on plastic-coated paper and sell for 75¢. A free *Index to Fire Plan Maps*, giving range, township, and ordering instructions, may be obtained by writing: Documents Section, Room 140 Centennial Bldg., 658 Cedar St., St. Paul 55155. Several useful field guides are available from the Documents Section of the Division of Fish & Wildlife (address above): *Beaver in Minnesota* (9–14, $1.50, 87 pp.) describes the history of the beaver and contains a guide to beaver trapping and grading; *Big Game in Minnesota* (9–15, $2.50) provides a useful, fascinating guide to the state's big-game past and present, including whitetail deer, bear, moose,

elk, and caribou; *Steelhead of the Minnesota North Shore* (9–8, $1.00) provides a technical study of the steelhead trout of the Great Lakes; *Timber Wolf in Minnesota* (9–18, $1.15) is a field study of the timber wolf on the Superior National Forest. *Make checks or money orders payable to:* State of Minnesota, Documents Section.

Two publications, *The Story of the Walleye* and *The Story of Minnesota's Pike*, available free from the Dept. of Natural Resources, Information & Education, 350 Centennial Office Bldg., St. Paul 55155, include a wealth of facts about walleye, northern pike, and muskie fishing in Minnesota, including spawning and growing patterns and fishing methods. Minnesota's innumerable lakes, rugged wilderness areas, and scenic mixed hardwood and evergreen forests offer excellent opportunities for camping. The *Minnesota Camping Guide*, a 57–page sourcebook for campers, lists almost all campgrounds and recreation areas in the state. The booklet is divided into sections on state, national forest, and private camping sites and Mississippi River recreation areas. Listings are alphabetical by townsite and include location, rates, telephone numbers, activities and facilities, fireplaces, picnic tables, swimming beaches, fishing outfitters, and the like. The *Minnesota Camping Guide* is available free from the Publicity and Promotion Division, Dept. of Economic Development, 480 Cedar St., St. Paul 55101.

Another *Minnesota Camping Guide*, prepared by the Minnesota Association of Campground Operators, lists state-licensed association members throughout the state. Again, listings are alphabetical by town and indicate addresses, number of sites, facilities, telephone numbers, and directions to the campsite from many of the major cities. A road map showing the various campgrounds and major highways is included. The 23–page booklet is available free from the Minnesota Assn. of Campground Operators, P.O. Box 3440, Elk River 55330. MACO recommends making all reservations for campsites in advance, and will be happy to answer any questions you have about camping in Minnesota.

Minnesota, "the Land of Sky-blue Waters," offers a canoeist's jackpot in swift-flowing rivers and intricate networks of waterways. Inland waters alone cover an area equal in size to that of the combined areas of Rhode Island and Connecticut. Together with the hundreds of tributary systems, the Mississippi, Minnesota, St. Croix, Red, and St. Louis rivers make up more than 25,000 miles of flowing water. But of all the state's renowned canoe routes, perhaps those of the far north and northwestern regions, including the unparalleled complex of the Boundary Waters Canoe Area, offer the finest opportunities for challenging white-water runs and extended trips through vast labyrinths of inter-connected rivers and lakes. Here rock-bottomed, swift streams with many waterfalls flow along the forested North Shore, while others find their origin in the "Big Bog" of northwestern Minnesota, a muskeg wilderness of tamarack, low shrubs, black spruce, and spongy sphagnum moss lying in the ancient basin of glacial Lake Agassiz. Streams originating in this swampy wilderness feed the Red River, eventually reaching the waters of Hudson Bay.

Many different publications offer excellent guides to these waters; some are pocket-sized, providing only maps and basic route information, and others are more extensive, covering many runs and offering explicit and detailed information on technique, equipment, and even the history of the area traversed. Of the latter category, *Whitewater, Quietwater—The Wild Rivers of Wisconsin, Upper Michigan, & NE Minnesota*, by Bob and Jody Palzer, is a 157–page guide to canoe streams and rivers personally traveled and recorded by the authors. *Whitewater, Quietwater* is concerned with those waters that are still mainly for canoes; hence, wide rivers, lakes, and flowages are not described. Over 80 trips are mapped and detailed; in addition, fifteen

trips are outlined without maps. Each river run is a one-day trip between landings accessible by car. Length of the run, time required, gradient, hazard rating, and water conditions are described for each route. Also included are comments on the scenery, geology, fishing, campgrounds, and local history. The 32–page introductory section describes equipment, including the various types of canoes—open, decked, and kayaks—paddles, protective aids, rafts, and other important gear. Descriptions of canoeing techniques, paddling methods, portaging, and tips on maneuvering in rapids and water safety are also offered. Profusely illustrated, this section contains detailed but highly readable explanations of all data relevant to the canoeist. A substantial bibliography is also provided. Appendixes at the end of the guide offer additional river information, an explanation of the International Scale of River Difficulty, plus lists of periodicals, clubs, maps, technique manuals, and equipment sources. Priced at $7.95, *Whitewater, Quietwater* is available from Evergreen Paddleways, 1416 21st St., Two Rivers, WI 54241.

Another comprehensive guide to canoe runs along the state's waterways, *Minnesota Voyageur Trails*, outlines many routes originally traveled by French fur traders and early explorers. Seventeen routes on such rivers as the Big Fork, Kettle, Des Moines, Mississippi, Snake, and Rum are described in abundant detail. Additional facts on the history of the region are woven into the text. Also provided is a mile-by-mile guide to the terrain and local points of interest, along with names and addresses of contacts who will be glad to supply additional information. *Minnesota Voyageur Trails* is available for $2.00, tax included, from the Minnesota Dept. of Natural Resources, Division of Parks and Recreation, 320 Centennial Bldg., St. Paul 55155.

Also available from the department are six pocket-size, spiral-bound boating guides providing aerial photographic descriptions of canoe routes along Minnesota's rivers. Written descriptions of the trips are brief, detailing mileage, scenic areas, locations of rapids, bridges, etc., but the numerous maps following, showing each stretch of the route, contain abundant directions superimposed in code. Small (about 4 to 6 inches), lightweight, and easily portable, the guides are available for each of the following runs: *Crow River*, from Forest City to Albright Mills County Park (9–46; $1.49); *Kettle River*, between Willow Road and the confluence with the St. Croix River through Hell's Gate Rapids, white water navigable only by seasoned experts (9–41; $1.20); *Rum River*, from Princeton to the Mississippi River in Anoka (9–42; $1.49); *St. Croix River, Book I*, from Danbury to Taylors Falls (9–43; $1.49); *St. Croix River, Book II*, from Taylors Falls to the Mississippi River (9–44; $1.20); and the *Snake River* from McGrath to Gaston (9–45; $1.20). Booklets may be ordered by the code numbers and at the prices cited above, tax included, from the Minnesota Dept. of Natural Resources, 140 Centennial Bldg., St. Paul 55155.

A second series of free, compact, brochure-type guides describes 10 different canoe trips in Minnesota. A detailed map for each run, indicating campsites, rest areas, rapids, portages, and mileage is accompanied by a mile-by-mile route description, general trip information, tips on packing and safety, and, in some guides, a checklist of equipment. In addition, the surrounding terrain is briefly described—the landscape, wildlife, and possibilities for fishing. The following routes are each described in individual brochures: *Pine River*, from Cross Lake Dam through Pine Lake to the Mississippi River; *Mississippi River*, from Lake Winnibigoshish through Schoolcraft State Park and Grand Rapids to Jackson, the *Mississippi Headwaters*, from Lake Itasca past Rice and Boat lakes and through Lake Irving to Lake Bemidji; *Vermilion River*, from Vermilion Lake past

Shively and Liftover falls, across De Caigny Rapids to Crane Lake; *St. Louis River*, from the access point near U.S. 53 across the White Face River through Boulderfield Rapids to Spafford Park at Cloquet; *Kettle River*, from the access point near Kennedy bridge through heavily forested Banning State Park and Hell's Gate Rapids to State Highway 27; *Rum River*, from Lake Koronis Dam through Forest City and the Crow Hassan Park Reserve to the Mississippi; and *Root River*, from Houston over a lengthy stretch of white water between Rushford and Chatfield. The canoe routes are free from the Minnesota Department of Natural Resources at the above address.

The Grand Marais Municipal Airport at Devils Track Lake offers facilities for both land-based aircraft and seaplanes. Customs officers are on duty here for flights returning from Canada. *Wilderness Wings Airways*, Box 188, Ely 55731, phone (218)365–4449, offers fly-in service, hunting trips, seaplane training, and tours in the heart of the Superior National Forest and surrounding Arrowhead terrain. *Lac La Croix Quetico Air Service*, Crane Lake 55725, phone (218)993–2361, provides charter fly-in and pickup service throughout the famed Quetico-Superior canoeing and fishing country.

Based at Duluth International Airport (Duluth, 55811), *Halvair Airways* features a charter service, scenic rides, and air-taxi facilities. *Mesabi Airlines* in Grand Rapids, 55744 phone (218)326–6657, has scheduled daily flights from Minneapolis, St. Paul and will provide charter flights anywhere. Rentals, Cessna sales and service, and float certification are also provided.

Highways & Maps

The first roads in what is now Minnesota were trails of the American Indians, followed by wilderness routes forged by the voyageurs and fur traders—down from Hudson Bay and Fort Garry in the Red River Valley, from Pembina as far as Red Lake and Lake Traverse. Grand Portage, the most notable of these trails, still exists and retains the primitive and rough character of 200 years ago.

Today, the state boasts a vast network of roads and highways, including some spectacular scenic drives such as the North Shore Drive along the craggy cliffs bordering Lake Superior and the wilderness Gunflint and Arrowhead trails, paved roads open to automobiles leading through the rugged terrain of northeast Minnesota. These and other roads and highways are shown on the *Minnesota State Highway Map*, available free from the Minnesota Highway Dept., Administrative Services Section, State Highway Bldg., St. Paul 55165. The map shows all varieties of goods, including interstate highways, divided and undivided highways, gravel-surfaced roads, railroads, airports, towns and cities, parks, forests, rest areas, and historical sites.

Minnetours, an attractive booklet with many handsome photographs, describes 11 tours by automobile through every part of Minnesota, including the "voyageurs' empire," the Lake Superior region, and the heartlands of the old Sioux Indian nation. Explicit directions and alternate routes are provided for each trip, along with information on accommodations, campgrounds, rest areas, picnic sites, restaurants, and other facilities along the route. Points of historical and natural interest are also described, with directions for finding the best "lookouts" and panoramic views. The booklet is available free from the State of Minnesota, Dept. of Economic Development, 480 Cedar St., St. Paul 55101.

VACATION/ LODGING GUIDE

Chippewa National Forest & The Mississippi Headwaters

Located in north-central Wisconsin, the Chippewa National Forest covers 640,000 acres of mixed hardwood and conifer forests, swamps, sparkling lakes, and meandering wilderness streams. The Mississippi River, the "father of waters," little more than a country stream at its Lake Itasca headwaters, enters the forest on the western boundary at Andrusia Lake. It sweeps past the end of Star Island in Cass Lake, through Knulson Dam, where seasonal boat passage is provided, winds into Lake Winnibigoshish—the fifth-largest body of water in Minnesota—then travels southeast across the forest on its long journey to the Gulf of Mexico. The river's waters are swollen by Leech Lake River and by major rivers in the watershed: Steamboat, Turtle, Pigeon, Boy, Bear, Shingobee, and others.

The many tongue-twisting and exotic names given to the major forest landmarks—Winnibigoshish (locally shortened to "Winnie"), Inguadona, Shingobee, Ah-gwah-ching, Wabana—are reminders of this area's early inhabitants, the Chippewa Indians, properly called the Ojibway. The tribe was named for its moccasins, since Ojibway literally means "gathering" and describes the leather footgear gathered over toe and instep worn by these people. One of the largest Algonquian tribes north of Mexico, the Chippewa lived in loosely federated villages across the north-central Midwest. They lived off the land, harvesting planted crops, hunting, gathering wild rice, and intermittently making war on their neighbors, the Sioux and Fox Indians. From the outset, they depended on the intricate travel routes provided by inland waterways, and they learned to navigate the huge network of lakes and rivers—eventually guiding the trappers and explorers who first discovered the area's rich beaver lands and mighty forests in the mid-seventeenth century. The introduction of firearms a short time later gave the Chippewa temporary sway over rival tribes, but by 1832 the discovery of the Mississippi's source attracted increasing numbers of white men. The influx of fur traders, trappers, lumbermen, and settlers brought many changes to the wilderness, most of them detrimental to the forest's primeval glory. The loggers who came to Minnesota, romanticized in the folklore of Paul Bunyan, came from the East, where a growing nation's demand for timber had all but exhausted the land. Pressure from conserva-

tionists gradually persuaded a sympathetic government of the need for protection of forest lands, and in 1908 President Theodore Roosevelt proclaimed this area the Minnesota National Forest. Lands were purchased from the Chippewa Indians; the region's name was changed in 1928 to honor the original rulers of the forest.

Today many areas of the forest offer a wilderness experience as rugged and unspoiled as that encountered by the Indians and first white men. Canoe tours explore the same waters braved by trappers in search of a fortune in furs. While the Mississippi remains a favorite route for canoeists, other rivers with rich historical pasts are becoming equally popular. The Turtle River, for instance, was first navigated by followers of La Salle in vain pursuit of the elusive Northwest Passage.

The Turtle River Canoe Route flows from Lake Julia through Turtle and Three Island lakes into Turtle River Lake, where it enters Chippewa National Forest and finally Cass Lake. Sights along the way include blue herons, wild-rice beds, remains of an old splash dam and sawmill, and the site of an American Fur Company post operative around 1820. The Rice River canoe route flows from Clubhouse Lake in the forest's northeastern corner through East, Slauson, and Cameron lakes to the terminus at Big Fork, a total length of 18 miles. The tour covers clear, usually tranquil waters as they wind through the forest and past the remains of old logging camps, the homestead of an early settler and a farm reputedly taken over by a small population of skunks.

The Inguadona canoe route flows from Lower Trelipe Lake southeast of Leech Lake through Inguadona Lake along the Boy River to a terminus some 20 miles north. A generally easy route, with one stretch of fast-moving water, the tour explores an early "highway" of the fur trade called "Equademog," meaning edge of a slope, by the Chippewa who paddled these waters in canoes laden with pelts. The name eventually metamorphosed into Inguadona, perhaps because it was found more manageable by French and English tongues. Points of interest along the way include the site of an early Chippewa village, nests of native bald eagles, and the extensive beds of wild rice in the area.

In addition to the innumerable streams and rivers in Chippewa National Forest, there are 499 major lakes, of which the most popular, at least with fishermen, are probably Winnie, Leech, and Cass. The two latter have gained national reputations as muskie lakes and offer excellent northern pike and walleye fishing as well. Most of the lakes in the forest are ideal for boating and are generally fine for canoeing, although squalls can develop quickly on the large lakes, and it is always best to skirt the shoreline. The remote unspoiled wilderness areas of Upper and Lower Red Lake—the state's largest body of water—located to the north in the Red Lake Indian Reservation, and the meandering Red Lake River, provide outstanding canoeing and fishing opportunities.

Many species of wildlife inhabit the forest, including the rare and majestic bald eagle. Of the estimated 600 breeding pairs in the United States today, Chippewa National Forest supports about one-sixth of the population of our endangered national emblem. Most readily sighted between March 15 and November 30, the bald eagle is distinguished from vultures and osprey of the area by its magnificent flat wings spreading over seven feet. Huge nest structures, sometimes measuring ten feet in diameter, are easily spotted in tall pine trees along the lakeshores.

Other winged residents of the forest include the Canada goose, mallard, loon, goldeneye, teal, and many other waterfowl and songbirds. Whitetailed deer, bear, moose, gophers, otter, mink, and bobcats roam the open lands, swamps and forests of birch and pine. While the most common species of trees include Norway and jack pines, aspen, and spruce, the various swamplands offer certain seldom-seen varieties: black spruce, northern white cedar, and tamarack. The Avenue of Pines, a scenic drive along State Highway 46, offers a fine introduction to the different pine trees of the forest, including 100-year-old red pines.

Itasca State Park, north of Park Rapids, encompasses more than 32,000 acres of dense, virgin forests and 157 lakes, the largest of which, Lake Itasca, marks the source of the mighty Mississippi River. Two explanations have been offered for the origin of the lake's name. One claims it derives from a contraction of the Latin term *veritas caput*, meaning "true head". The second, more romantic, explanation traces the name to the legendary daughter of the Chippewa hero Hiawatha, Iteska, who was abducted by the god of the underworld. Tears shed by the Indian maiden on leaving her homeland formed the headwaters of the Mississippi. Within the park are picnic grounds, hiking trails, cabins, campsites, and facilities for swimming, boating, snowmobiling, and daily launch excursions. Aiten Heights, a lookout station in the southeastern section, provides panoramic views of the park. Indian mounds scattered throughout the preserve are reminders of the area's Chippewa history. In the summer, the University of Minnesota School of Forestry offers naturalist programs, plant and animal exhibits, evening movies, and guided hikes.

Information Sources, Maps & Access

Detailed information on the Chippewa National Forest and the following publications may be obtained from: Supervisor's Office, Chippewa National Forest, Cass Lake, MN 56633 (218)335–2226. The *Chippewa National Forest Map* (50¢) lists and locates these facilities and shows lakes, rivers, highways, trails, roads, canoe routes, and boat-launching sites as well. Also included are descriptions of the forest's history and many points of interest. The *Bald Eagle in the Chippewa National Forest*, a six-page brochure summarizing the life patterns and habits of this regal bird, is available free from the Forest Supervisor. The Forest Supervisor's Office also offers free map/brochures of the *Turtle River Canoe Tour*, *Rice River Canoe Tour*, and *Inguadona Canoe Tour*. Enlarged hydrographic maps are also available for *Leech Lake* (E–18, 22½ by 29¼ inches, scale 1-1/6 inches to one mile, waterproof) and for *Lake Winnibigoshish* (E–21, 22½ by 35 inches, scale 1¼ inches to one mile, waterproof) showing contour intervals at five feet, reefs, buoys, and shallows. Each hydrographic map is priced at $1.00 each and may be ordered direct (add 50¢ for postage) from: W.A. Fisher Co., Box 1107, Virginia, MN 55792. Chippewa National Forest is easily reached via State Highway 46 from Deer River and Grand Rapids east of the forest. Cass Lake, another major outfitting and supply center, provides access to the forest at its western boundary. Other towns within and near the area include Walker, Blackduck, Bigfork, and Northome.

*The
Inguadona
Canoe Tour*
CHIPPEWA NATIONAL
FOREST

Gateways & Accommodations

Bemidji

(Pop. 12,700; zip code 56601; area code 218.) The city takes its name from a Chippewa Indian chief whose band of about 50 made their home on the present site at the foot of Lake Bemidji. A lumber boomtown at the turn of the century, Bemidji today is surrounded by second growth forests, scenic rivers, and prime year-round recreation areas. The Bunyan House Information Center, on 3rd St. and Bemidji Ave. at the lakefront, contains displays of outsized Paul Bunyan tools with amusing descriptions. Statues of the legendary lumberjack and his blue ox stand near the lakefront. Adjacent to the Information Center is the Historical and Wildlife Museum, housing

exhibits of regional wildlife, Indian artifacts, and antiques. Accommodations: *Bel-Air Motel* (rates: $25–32 double), 22 air-conditioned rooms, eight two-room units, color TV, playground, restaurant nearby, free airport bus, open all year, two miles west of town on U.S. Hwy. 2, just west of junction with U.S. 71 (751-3222). *Edgewater Motel* (rates: $24–30 double), 74 comfortable rooms and seven with kitchens, attractive setting on Lake Bemidji, sand beach, swimming, boats, canoes, dock, restaurant opposite, open all year, at 1015 Midway Dr., ¾ mile southeast of town on U.S. 2(751-3600); *Holiday Inn* (rates: $38 double), 120 excellent rooms, color TV, indoor pool, sauna, whirlpool, snowmobile trails, dining room, coffeeshop, cocktail lounge, three miles west of town on U.S. 2 (751-9500).

Brainerd

(Pop. 13,000; zip code 56401; area code 218.) Located on the Mississippi River at the geographical center of the state, the city is an important gateway to a vast outdoor playground which includes some 460 evergreen-fringed lakes within a 25–mile radius. Brainerd has been a lumber center since the 1870's when the Northern Pacific Railroad first arrived and the then unpaved streets were lined with shacks, tents, and 36 busy saloons. Known as "the hometown of Paul Bunyan," the city's attractions include the Paul Bunyan Center, west of town at the junction of Minnesota State Hwys. 371 and 210, an amusement park with animated figures, trained animals, rides, and picnic grounds; and Lumbertown, U.S.A., four miles north on U.S. 371 and eight miles west on county road 77, a replica of a 19th–century logging town, including a general store, schoolhouse, saloon, pioneer home, and other buildings. A replica of the first Northern Pacific train and an old-time riverboat operate daily at 40 minute intervals (open mid-June–Labor Day, 10a.m.–6p.m. daily, after Labor Day to mid-Sept., 10a.m.–4:30p.m.; closed rest of the year). Accommodations: *Holiday Inn* (rates: $44 double), 150 excellent rooms, color TV, heated indoor pool, saunas, therapy pool, free airport transportation, recreation room, dining room and cocktail lounge, one mile south of town via Minnesota State Hwy. 371 (829–1441); *Paul Bunyan Motel* (rates: $18–33 double), 36 fine air-conditioned rooms, color TV, heated indoor pool, sauna, whirlpool, 24-hr. restaurant adjacent, next to Paul Bunyan Center, two miles west of Brainerd at junction of Hwys. 210 and 371 (829–3571).

Deer River

(Pop. 800; zip code 56636; area code 218.) The town is a key gateway to the Chippewa National Forest and numerous north-central Minnesota lakes, including Leech and Winnibigoshish. Northwest of town via Minnesota State Hwy. 46 is Cut Foot Sioux Lake. Along the lake's shoreline is a 30–foot long mound in the shape of a turtle surrounded by a snake of proportionate size. The Turtle and Snake Indian Mound was supposedly built by jubilant Sioux Indians to commemorate a victory over Chippewa warriors. The turtle's head points north, signifying the enemy's retreat in that direction. Accommodations: *Bahr's Motel* (rates: $20–29 double), 22 fine air-conditioned rooms, five with kitchens, two two-room units, color TV, playground, cross country ski trails, fish freezer, fishing guide available, at junction of U.S. Hwy. 2 and Minnesota State Hwy. 6 (246–8271).

Detroit Lakes

(Pop. 6,500; zip code 56501; area code 218.) Within a 25–mile radius of this town are some 412 lakes in five separate chains. A French missionary first called the site *détroit*, or narrows, over 200 years ago, and the name was used thereafter by voyageurs and

fur-traders to describe the immediate vicinity. Area attractions include the city park at the foot of Washington Ave., with its playgrounds, boat rentals, and mile-long public beach; Fort Detroit, 3½ miles west of town via U.S. 10, a replica of a frontier stockade; and the Tamarac National Wildlife Refuge, eight miles east on Minnesota State Hwy. 34, then 10 miles north on County Rd. 29, a 43,000–acre preserve encompassing 18 lakes, wild rice beds, and a flyway sanctuary for waterfowl. Accommodations: *Best Western Holland Motel* (rates: $25–28 double), 38 excellent rooms and suites, color TV, heated indoor pool, saunas, putting green, restaurant adjacent, one mile east of town via U.S. 10 (847–4483); *Holiday Haven Motel* (rates: $25 double), ten attractive rooms, nine with kitchens, opposite Lake Detroit, color TV, beach and marina, at 220 W. Lake Dr. (847–5605); *Holiday Inn* (rates: $36–40 double), 103 excellent rooms and suites, some with balconies, color TV, heated indoor pool, saunas, whirlpool, on lake with private beach and dockage, dining room and cocktail lounge, 1½ miles southeast on U.S. 10 (847–2121).

Grand Rapids

(Pop. 7,300; zip code 55744; area code 218.) Gateway to the Chippewa National Forest, Grand Rapids lies at the head of navigation on the Mississippi River and encompasses four beautiful lakes within its city limits. The surrounding forests and hundreds of lakes offer a wealth of recreational opportunities: canoeing on the Mississippi to nearby bodies of water—or as far south as the Gulf of Mexico, hiking the national forest, swimming off local beaches, and fishing remote lakes. Sugar Hills (which see), 14 miles southwest of town via U.S. 169, is a year-round, 1,000–acre complex with a ski area, golf course, private airport, marina, lakes, and forests. Skiers will also find downhill and cross-country trails at the Quadna Mountain Ski Area, 20 miles south of Grand Rapids on U.S. 169 (see below). For more information on area attractions, visit the Chamber of Commerce Welcome House (326–6619) at the junction of U.S. Hwys. 2 and 69. Accommodations: *Holiday Inn* (rates: $32.50–33.50 double), 125 attractive rooms and suites, color TV, heated indoor pool, sauna, putting green, recreation room, restaurant and cocktail lounge, at 2301 Pokegama Ave. S., two miles of town via U.S. 69 (326–8501); *Holiday Village* (rates: $20–26 double), 34 rooms, color TV, swimming pool, restaurant adjacent, six blocks east of town at junction of U.S. Hwys. 2 and 169 (326–3457).

Hackensack

(Pop. 200; zip code 56452; area code 218.) Gateway to Minnesota's north-central lake country and the Chippewa National Forest, Hackensack was named for the city in New Jersey by its first postmaster. A popular local restaurant, *Bromley's Ten Mile Inn*, serves excellent steaks and prime ribs in a pleasant dining room overlooking Ten Mile Lake; three miles north of town on Minnesota State Hwy. 371 (675–6576).

Park Rapids—Gateway to Itasca State Park

(Pop. 2,800; zip code 56470; area code 218.) The town is surrounded by excellent fishing lakes, unspoiled forests, and numerous fine resorts. Itasca State Park (which see), 28 miles north of town via U.S. 71, embraces virgin forests and the headwaters of the Mississippi. Other area attractions include Deer Town, one mile north on U.S. 71, an old frontier town and wildlife refuge, and Aqua Park Aquarium and Deer Farm, at 1008 E. First St. off Minnesota State Hwy. 34. Accommodations: *Riverside Resort Motel* (rates: $16–24 double), nine efficiency and housekeeping cottages on attractive grounds beside the Fish Hook River, color TV, beach, dock, fishing, boat and canoe rentals, weekly rates available, at 700 N. Park Ave., ½ mile north of town via U.S. 71 (732–9711).

Pipestone

(Pop. 5,300; zip code 56164; area code 507.) Many of the city's buildings are constructed of the beautiful red granite from quarries in the Pipestone National Monument, a 283–acre tract at the north edge of town. The pipestone deposits, which were highly prized by the Indians for use in ceremonial pipes, are known as catlinite in honor of George Catlin, the American painter who first described the stone. Tribes from the Great Plains states once gathered here because the grounds were considered sacred by Indians of differing loyalties and outlook. The national monument was established in 1937 to protect the remaining stone and preserve it for use by all Indian tribes. A self-guided circle trail leads visitors to the quarries, Winnewissa Falls, and unusual rock formations such as the group of glacial boulders known as the Three Maidens. Also within the monument is the Nicollet Marker, a boulder bearing an inscription made by the famous explorer in 1838. The Upper Midwest Indian Cultural Center features exhibits of Indian artifacts, including the famous ceremonial pipes. (Open Memorial Day-Labor Day, 8a.m.–9p.m.; rest of the year, 8a.m.–5p.m.; admission free). Accommodations: *Arrow Motel* (rates: $16–18 double), 17 air-conditioned rooms on attractive shaded grounds, color TV, playground, restaurant opposite, at 600 8th Ave., N.E., ½ mile north of town on U.S. 75 (825–3331).

Thief River Falls

(Pop. 9,000; zip code 56701; area code 218.) The area surrounding Thief River Falls was once the favorite hunting grounds of Dakota Indians, who built embankments of dirt and twigs around their lodges to conceal them from their warring Chippewa neighbors. Because of these embankments, the Chippewa named the stream that flows through town Secret Earth River. Through some error in translation, fur-traders called the stream Stealing Earth River, which eventually metamorphosed into Thief River. The town is a popular gateway for fishermen and canoeists headed for the lakes and rivers of northwestern Minnesota. Accommodations: *Best Western of Thief River Falls* (rates: $27 double), 81 excellent rooms, color TV, heated indoor pool, saunas, free airport bus, dining room and cocktail lounge, one mile southwest of town on Minnesota State Hwy. 32 (681–7555); *Country Inn* (rates: $18–21 double), 47 comfortable rooms, oversize beds, color TV, restaurant adjacent, two miles southeast of town on U.S. 59 (681–6205).

Walker

(Pop. 1,300; zip code 56484; area code 218.) Perched on the southwest shore of Leech Lake, Walker is a jumping-off point for the Chippewa National Forest and Minnesota's north-central lake country. A District Ranger's Office of the national forest is located here. On the east edge of town off U.S. 371 is the Museum of Natural History and Indian Arts and Crafts, housing exhibits of area wildlife and Indian crafts (open daily 9a.m.–5p.m., June 1–Labor Day). Accommodations: *Chase on the Lake* (rates: $20–27 double), 65 rooms in hotel and air-conditioned motel, TV, restaurant and bar, sand beach, boat launching, free airport transportation, off Minnesota State Hwy. 200 near junction with State Hwy. 371 (547–1531); *Peterson's Northwood Beach Motel* (rates: $25 double), seven apartments with kitchens, one or two bedrooms, TV, sand beach, rooms overlook Leech Lake, pleasant grounds, boats and motors available, free airport bus, restaurant adjacent, nearby grocery, off Minnesota State Hwy. 200 (547–1702).

Lodges & Resorts

★★*Bay Lake Lodge* is a year round resort located on Bay Lake, outside of Deerwood. Nearby is Mille Lacs National Wildlife Refuge

and Mille Lacs Lake, the largest lake in central Minnesota. Outdoor activities available to guests include tennis, golf, horseback riding (with guides), fishing, sailing, water skiing, and swimming. Both an indoor and an outdoor pool, a sauna, and a whirlpool are maintained. There is a supervised playground for children. Local points of interest include Ak-Sar-Ben (flower gardens and tame animals), the Paul Bunyan Amusement Center, and an Indian museum (near Garrison). In the winter guests can use the snowmobiling trails and skating rink, or go cross-country skiing. The outdoor pool is also available. Cabins are completely winterized, and some have fireplaces. American plan accommodations include two home-cooked meals a day, featuring home-made breads and pastries. Rates vary depending upon the size of the accommodation and the number of people in the party. Cabins average $235 per week, $35 per day. There are a variety of special plans and packages: Memorial and Labor Day weekends are $99 per person, complete; weekday specials (available in May, June, September, and October) are $96 per person for four days/three nights; $157 per person for six days/five nights. Winter rates are somewhat less. Rooms in the lodge are $27.50 per person (for two persons); January weekends are $55 per person, complete. For additional information, contact Jack Ruttger, Bay Lake Lodge, Deerwood, MN 56444 (218)678–2885.

★★*Big Rock Resort* is centrally located on Leech Lake, famous for muskie, walleye, and great northern pike. A variety of outdoor activities may be enjoyed by guests of the resort, including fishing, swimming, water skiing, tennis, boating, and canoeing. A golf course and horseback riding stable are located nearby. In addition there is a recreation room in the main lodge. Also in the lodge are a small store—selling groceries, beverages, tackle, bait and fishing licenses—and a lounge where snacks and beverages are available. Additional services include fish cleaning and freezer storage. A special feature of the resort is its heated swimming pool. There are twenty housekeeping cabins and a small campground. Cabin rentals include the use of an 18–foot boat. Pets are permitted, but must be leashed. All cabins are carpeted, heated, panelled, and equipped for light housekeeping. Cabins range from $150 per week, $28 per day (for two persons) to $260 per week, $52 per day (for six persons). Additional guests in cabins are $20 per week, $4 per day. Campsites rent for $6 per day, $35 per week; trailer sites (with complete hookups) are $8 per day, $50 per week. Campers are entitled to use of all resort facilities. For additional information, contact: Ed Kotula, Big Rock Resort, Walker, MN 56484 (218)547–1066.

★★*Bord du Lac Lodge in Paul Bunyan State Forest* is located on Benedict Lake, thirty miles northeast of Park Rapids. The lodge is set amidst 100 acres of pine, spruce, balsam, and white birch. The lake is spring-fed, cool and deep, with a gradually sloping, sandy beach. Benedict Lake flows by a channel into famous Leech Lake, one of Minnesota's largest lakes. Hiking, fishing, swimming, boating and canoeing are among the activities offered in the summer. Hunting—for grouse, deer, and duck—is available in the fall; winter activities include skiing and snowmobiling. Walleye, northern pike, black bass, panfish, and muskie are all fished locally. Among the services offered at Bord du Lac are: fish cleaning house, use of deep freeze, boat dock, a launch (for guided fishing trips), and a game room. A golf course is located nearby. There is a snack bar, and a small store sells bait, tackle, and beverages. Pets are allowed but must be leashed. There are twelve winterized cabins, completely equipped for light housekeeping, all of which face the lake. Use of a boat is included with each weekly rental. Cabins rent for $140 per week, $28 per day (for two persons); $165 per week (for four persons), $33 per day; additional persons are $15 per week, $5 per day. Launch service, to Leech Lake, is $20 per day (per person). For

additional information, contact: E.K. (Bud) Crowell, Bord du Lac Lodge, P.O. Benedict, MN 56436 (218)224–2384.

★★★*Bowstring Northwoods Resort* is located on the shore of Bowstring Lake, just northwest of Grand Rapids, in the Chippewa National Forest. Recreational opportunities are numerous: fishing for walleye and northern pike, swimming in the lake and heated pool, boating, golf, hiking, and volleyball. In the winter snowmobiling, ice fishing, and cross-country skiing are featured. Supervised children's programs are offered regularly. Additional services include boat and motor rentals and guide service. A game room, cocktail lounge, and dining room are located in the main lodge. Nearby points of interest include the Mississippi headwaters and the Mesabi iron mines. A variety of accommodations is available—there are rooms in the lodge and fully furnished cabins. American plan (including lodging and all meals), modified American plan (including lodging and breakfast and dinner) and light housekeeping plan (lodging only) are all offered. American plan is $15 per day per person. Housekeeping plan runs from $245 per week for four persons to $280 per week for six. Rooms in the lodge are $30 per day (for two persons). For additional information contact: Fred and Carol Branham, Bowstring Northwoods Resort, 101 Inger Rt., Deer River, MN 56636 (218)556–4321.

★★*Cragun's on Pine Beach* is located on the south end of Gull Lake near Brainerd. Among the many outdoor activities enjoyed by guests are swimming, fishing, sailing, canoeing, golf (at the adjacent 45–hole Pine Beach Golf Course), tennis, and volleyball. Nearby Pillsbury State Forest offers opportunities for hiking, bicycling, and birdwatching. Supervised activities are planned daily for children (swimming, pony rides, and games). A new swimming pool, whirlpool spa, and sauna are open to guests. Two basic types of accommodations are offered: modified American plan (including breakfast and dinner) and European plan (which does not include meals, golf, tennis, or supervised recreation). Each cottage and room has a view of the lake, heating and air-conditioning, carpeting, and a telephone. Some cottages have kitchenettes and fireplaces. Weekly rates are $234 per person, daily rates are $35 per person (less for children). Pets, which must be leashed, are charged $4.50/day. There is a $45 minimum per unit per day. European plan is less expensive. For additional information, contact Merrill and Irma Cragun, Cragun's on Pine Beach, Route 6, Box 484, Brainerd, MN 56401 (218)829–3591.

★★★★*Douglas Lodge at Itasca State Park* is a historic log hotel built in 1905, just 14 years after the park was established to protect the headwaters of the mighty Mississippi River and this beautiful timberland. Guests at the lodge can enjoy all of the facilities and natural sites of Itasca State Park. The park lies within the Pine Moraine Region, a belt of steep hills deposited by the glaciers during the Ice Age, and encompasses the glacier lake, Lake Itasca. Woodland life includes over 60 types of animals and more than 100 species of birds, the second largest living Norway pine on record, beaver lodges, bald eagles, great blue herons and whitetailed deer. The park has a variety of planned programs, including forestry and biological courses for students, self-guided and naturalist-led hikes and tours, children's activities and evening programs. The Forest Inn, a massive log and stone structure, has a snack bar and souvenir shop, and is a popular warmup spot for cross-country skiers in the winter. Brower Inn and Natural History Museum has craft demonstrations and sales of local handicrafts. There is an Interpretive Center at the Mississippi headwaters, 1475 feet above sea level. The Observation Tower and Peace Pipe Vista offer wide angle views of Lake Itasca. Boats are available for rent at Squaw Lake, Elk Lake and Mary Lake, and there are many historic and natural landmarks to explore. The

park has an extensive system of marked trails for hiking, bicycling, snowmobiling and cross-country skiing. Detailed maps of all trails are available free. Douglas Lodge is open from Memorial Day-September, and there are cabins as well as rooms in the lodge. Most accommodations have a private bath and some have fireplaces, screened-in porches, and dressing rooms. One to three bedroom cabins rent from $28 for two to $46 for four. Rooms in the two-story motel unit, Nicollet Court, range from $24 to $26 double occupancy and plain sleeping rooms are $16 double occupancy. Additional adults are $4 per day and there are children's rates. Club House rates range from $16 to $24 double occupancy. All rates are for lodging only. Six log cabins are located in the campground area and are equipped for housekeeping. These rent for $24 a night for two with special rates for extra adults and children. For visitors who want to get closer to nature there are 237 family campsites at Bear Paw Campground on the lake and at Pine Ridge Campground just east of Park Headquarters. Campgrounds have showers and flush toilets. Primitive group camp sites are available at Squaw Lake and Elk Lake by reservation only. Backpacking and camping are permitted along the trails but a permit must be applied for. For information on Douglas Lodge or other facilities within the park write to Itasca State Park, Lake Itasca, MN 56460 (218)266–3656.

★★*Evergreen Lodge* is situated in a grove of pinetrees on the shores of Big Sand Lake, just outside of Park Rapids. The 1,660–acre lake is well known for walleye, northern pike, muskie, and largemouth bass. In addition to fishing, guests of the lodge enjoy tennis, volleyball, shuffleboard, swimming, water skiing, hiking, canoeing and boating (pontoons and sailboats are available for guests' use). A golf course is located nearby. Evergreen features a 1000–foot sandy beach. There are 17 lakefront wood-panelled cabins, all fully furnished, heated, and equipped for light housekeeping. Two additional units, comparable to the lakefront cabins, are located near the tennis court. All rentals include the use of a boat. A two-bedroom cabin ranges from $130 per week to $220 per week (for up to four persons), depending upon the time of year (July and August are the more expensive months). For additional information contact: Karl and Kay Dyer, Evergreen Lodge, Park Rapids MN 56470 (218)732–4766.

★★★*Finn 'n Feather Resort Inn* is located on Lake Andrusia, in the Chippewa National Forest. Lake Andrusia, one of the Mississippi chain of lakes, produces walleye, northern pike, bass, and muskie. Five connecting lakes are easily reached by boat. The resort comprises 45 acres of forest and lawns and 1,200 feet of shoreline. Outdoor activities, in addition to fishing, include swimming (either at the beach or in a heated pool), volleyball, and other sports. Supervised recreational programs for children are offered. Finn 'n Feather is open all year with hiking, fishing and skiing available in season. In the main lodge are a game room, reading area, dining room, and small store. Bait and licenses are available on the premises. Included in each weekly rental is use of one boat; extra boats and/or motors may be rented. A variety of accommodations is possible: American plan (includes all meals), continental plan (includes dinner only), and light housekeeping plan. Most cabins are located on the lakefront. American plan rates for one person are $42 per day, $241 per week; for two persons the rate is $30 per day (each), $168 per week. Children are charged at a lower rate. Housekeeping rates range from $20 per day, $135 per week (for two persons) to $41 per day, $239 per week (for six persons). Rates depend upon the number of persons in the party, the type of accommodation chosen, and the time of the year. Winter rates range from $31 to $37 per day. Meals are by arrangement during the winter. For additional information contact: Finn 'n Feather Resort, Route #4, Box 208, Bemidji, MN 56601 (218)335–6598.

★★★*Grand View Lodge,* situated amid Norway pines and white birch on the north shore of Gull Lake, features excellent facilities for golf and tennis buffs. The golf-tennis building has rental clubs, pull and electric carts, and a sportswear shop. Golf lessons, given by a pro, are available to guests. Other outdoor activities include fishing, sailing, boating, canoeing, water skiing, and swimming. There is a semi-enclosed heated pool. Within the vicinity of the lodge are many places of interest, including animal parks, iron mines, the Lindbergh Museum, the Paul Bunyan Center, and the Indian Museum (at Mille Lacs). A special program for children is offered, and there is also an adult social program of golf and tennis tournaments, and local sight-seeing. The management prefers no pets, however if you must bring yours, please consult with them when you make your reservation. The lodge is open from early May to early October. American and modified American plans are available; a

housekeeping plan is offered only during early and late season. A wide choice of meals is provided, including a smorgasbord on Sundays. Over fifty completely furnished cottages are nestled among the pines, all with views of the lake. Some units have kitchenettes, air-conditioning, fireplaces, and decks. There are also seventeen rooms in the lodge, designed for one or two persons. Daily maid service is provided with each room and/or cottage. Rates vary depending upon the type of accommodation chosen and the number of people in your party. Deposits are required. For additional information, contact: Grand View Lodge, Route 6, Box 22, Brainerd, MN 56401 (218)963–2234. In winter, the office is at: Curtis Hotel, Minneapolis, MN 55404 (612)332–1667.

**Lost Lake Lodge*, located at the north end of Gull Lake outside of Brainerd, caters to a limited clientele—only thirty-five guests at a time—and is situated on ninety beautifully wooded acres. There is a fine, sandy beach ideal for swimming. Other outdoor activities include canoeing, boating, fishing, badminton, and volleyball. Nearby are tennis courts, golf courses, and horseback riding stables. Evening entertainment, including movies, picnics, and barbeques, is also offered. In addition there are many opportunities for hiking, birdwatching, and photography. The dining room at Lost Lake features home-made breads made from stone-ground flour from the lodge's own grist mill. Log cabins with rustic interiors are completely furnished and heated. Accommodations are American plan and include three meals a day, lodging, and use of a boat. Cabins range from $58 per day (for two persons) to $116 per day (for four). Weekly rates are $378 per two persons. Children (under 10) are charged a lower rate. Special rates are available for conventions, fishing parties, and private groups of 20 or more. For additional information, contact: Bill and Ethelmae Carter, Lost Lake Lodge, Route 6, Box 115, Brainerd, MN 56401 (218)963–2681 or (612)922–6064.

★★★★*Madden Resorts*, a recreational complex on the shore of Gull Lake, encompasses four fine resort hotels offering a total of 274 air-conditioned rooms, three dining rooms, 23 meeting rooms, 45 holes of golf, six tennis courts, six indoor and outdoor pools, three saunas, three whirlpools, three sand beaches and marinas, plus unlimited fishing, canoeing, sailing, shuffleboard, indoor game rooms, paddle tennis, and anything else you could ask for in summer-time sports. The Madden Inn and Golf Course is a golfer's paradise with three golf courses, a sandy beach, spa, comfortable cabins and rooms, and a clubhouse. Cabins vary in size from a single bedroom to the lakehouse with its eight bedrooms and large lakeview living room. Rates for two, European Plan, run about $24–37 per night, with a minimum stay of three nights. The Madden Voyageur is planned for those who want to live in luxury. It has 41 units, of which 24 are efficiency apartments. Kitchens in the efficiencies have apartment-size gas stoves, full-size refrigerators, dishes and silverware, and porcelain cabinet sinks. Each efficiency and bedroom has a

private porch-patio facing the lake. Rates for two about $37 per night in an efficiency, $36 per night in a bedroom. The Madden Lodge has eleven suites in the main lodge, all carpeted and colorfully furnished. There are also nearly 40 cottages ranging in size from one bedroom to four bedrooms, all with a view of the lake. The Lodge prides itself on the fine home cooking served in its dining area. There is entertainment for old and young, including a special children's program. Rates on the Modified American Plan run from about $30–38 per person, per day, double occupancy. Pine Portage, the fourth of the Madden resorts, is a rustic northwoods lodge operated as a convention and group meeting facility. There are 32 air-conditioned cottages each with fireplace and four lodge bedrooms. The main lodge has a lakeview dining room. Group rates are available. For information on all four resorts, contact: Madden Resorts, Box 387, Brainerd, MN 56401 (218)829–6936 from May 1–Sept. 30 and (218)829–8100 from Oct. 1–April 3.

★★★*McArdle's* is a modern resort located on sprawling Lake Winnibigoshish in the Chippewa National Forest, north of Bena. The lake is one of the headwaters of the Mississippi River and is best known for its walleye and northern pike fishing. The lodge offers swimming (including a heated pool) and fishing. At the main lodge there is a store that sells fishing tackle, licenses, and groceries. A fish filleting service is available to guests as is use of a deep freeze. McArdle's has complete facilities; bait and fuel are always on hand. Use of one boat is included with each weekly rental. All cabins are fully equipped and heated. Cabins range in price from $20 to $45 per day, depending upon the size of the cabin. Weekly rate is 10% less. American plan (including all meals) is also available. The dining room is open every day for breakfast, lunch, and dinner. In addition, extra boats and motors may be rented. Fishing trips— launch service with an experienced guide—are $18 per day per person ($11 for a half-day trip); charter service is more expensive. These trips include bait. For additional information, contact: McArdle's, Star Route, Bena MN 56626 (218)665–2212.

★★★*Quadna Mountain Lodge* is a year-round resort located on the shore of Hill Lake, between Bemidji and Duluth. Among the many activities offered in the summer are golf, tennis, swimming (pool or lake) boating, fishing, bicycling, and hiking. Boats and motors are available for rental. An indoor pool and sauna are in the lodge. Winter sports include skiing, swimming, indoor tennis, and snowmobiling. Ski equipment (for both cross-country and downhill) may be rented. A fee is charged for some activities. Quadna is a complete resort offering a wide variety of accommodations: lodge, motel, townhouses, and campsites. The lodge is rustic and comfortable. Rooms overlook the water, and a bar and gameroom are housed there as well. The dining room is open everyday. A general store sells sundries; and there are laundry facilities at the campground. Lodge rooms are $25 per day (for one person); $33 per day (for two); $175 per week. Winter weekends and holiday periods, including lift tickets, are $34 per day (for one); $51 per day (for two); $78 per day (for four). Larger rooms are available at a higher cost. Motel rooms are $24 per night (for two persons); $140 per week. Townhouses are completely furnished. They range in price from $35 per day (for two persons) to $60 per day (for six); additional persons are charged $6 per day. A general store is open in season. For additional information, contact: Quadna Mountain Lodge, Hill City MN 55748; (218)697–2324; collect calls are accepted; in Minnesota, call toll-free: (800)662–5796.

★★★★*Sugar Hills Resort* is a total recreational village, combining every sort of outdoor activity imaginable within a series of lodges,

inns and sports areas built around Sugar Lake in Minnesota's northwoods. Sugar Hills boasts one of the midwest's major ski areas, with 23 slopes, nine lifts and tows, a ski school and rental facilities, 20 miles of cross-country ski trails, a skating rink on Sugar Lake, Belgian-horse sleigh rides, children's sliding area, nine-hole golf course, tennis, fishing, water skiing, sailing, canoeing, pontoon boat, crafts program, lawn games, saddle horses, heated pools and saunas. Among the special activities offered are a sailing school with a three-day "Learn to Sail Program", a summer-time native crafts demonstration run by skilled craftsmen from all over the northern states and Canada, and various planned group activities and lessons. Lodging facilities include: The Sugar Hills Inn, at the base of the ski slopes, with 22 compact units, each with one double bed and two twin-sized bunk beds. These small rooms are equipped with private or connecting baths and are attractive to those who desire active surroundings right at the ski area. The inn has an indoor swimming pool, sauna, dining room and bar. There are also bunk rooms (accommodating six-ten people each) which share baths. Rates for bedrooms, double occupancy, about $32 per night. The Sugar Lake Lodge, about three miles from the ski area, has 17 rooms, two family suites and nine cabins, with complete resort facilities. Rates for one bedroom cabins, about $30 per night, double occupancy; rates for lodge rooms available upon request. There are now also the recently built Sugar Wood Townhouses situated in a wooded area convenient to golf courses and the main lodge. Rates for one, two and three bedroom townhouses are also available upon request. For more information about any of these, contact: Sugar Hills, Box 369, Grand Rapids, Minn. 55744 (218)326–3473.

★★*Timberland Lodge* is a year-round resort on Long Lake, just outside of Park Rapids. The lodge is situated amidst 150 acres of pine, spruce, oak, maple, and birch, with ½ mile of lake frontage. Long Lake is ten miles long and is well-known for bass fishing. Other activities offered at the lodge include swimming (either at the beach or in a heated pool), water skiing, and tennis. There is a special program for children. In the winter, guests enjoy skiing, skating, ice fishing, and swimming in the indoor pool. Horseback riding and golf are available nearby. Summer rates are as follows. American plan cabins average $140 per week per person. Housekeeping rates range from $135 per week (for two persons) to $285 per week (for six). Children are charged a lower rate, based on their age. Additional guests are charged $5 per day each. Housekeeping guests may take meals at the main lodge. Cabins are fully equipped. Pets are not welcome. For additional information, contact: Al and Crystal Gustafson, Timberland Lodge, PO Box A168, Park Rapids MN 56470 (218)732–4364.

★*White Forest Resort* is located on Long Lake in George Washington State Forest, adjacent to the Chippewa National Forest, north of Grand Rapids, with good fishing for bass, walleye, northern pike, and panfish. The irregular shoreline and occasional islands offer an interesting challenge to anglers. Swimming, hiking, berry picking (in season), and birdwatching can be enjoyed by guests. There is a playground for children. White Forest is open from mid-May to the end of September. Use of a boat is included with each weekly rental. All cabins are equipped for housekeeping and all have a view of the lake. Available on the premises are fuel, bait and tackle, beverages and sandwiches, and free freezer space. Pets are welcome but dogs must be leashed. Cabins range from $90 per week (for two persons) to $120 per week (for six). Daily rates average $20 per cabin. For additional information, contact: Dave and Dianne Giessinger, White Forest Resort, RR 2, Bigfork MN 56628 (218)245–2218. Winter address is: 113–22 St., NW, Minot ND 58701 (701)838–3112.

★★*Wolfview Resort* is situated on Wolf Lake, near the Chippewa National Forest, one of a chain of nine lakes connected by the Mississippi River. At Wolfview, water skiing, swimming, and fishing are offered. The resort also features a heated pool. Wolf Lake is known for fine fishing for bass walleye, northern pike, and muskie. Many other lakes are easily accessible without portaging. The main lodge has a game room, lounge, and snack bar. Fishing licenses, tackle, fuel, and bait are available. A boat is included with each weekly rental, and extra boats and motors may be rented. All cabins are fully equipped for light housekeeping. Cabins are heated and carpeted and have modern kitchens and bathrooms. Weeks run from Saturday to Saturday. Cabins range from $150 per week (for two persons) to $260 per week (for six persons; additional guests are charged $25 per week). The daily rate (three-day minimum) is $30 per day (for two persons), $52 per day (for six). For additional information, contact: Carl and Nancy Henninger, Wolfview Resort, Box 505, Cass Lake, MN 56633 (218)335–2352.

Travel Services

Huntersville Outfitters are located on the Crow Wing River in central Minnesota. The Crow Wing River offers many miles of canoeing and the Crow Wing Wilderness Trail, which parallels the river, offers hiking and horseback riding opportunities. There are 13 public campsites located along the river, and there are no dams, rapids, or portages. While on the river, supplies may be purchased at Huntersville, Nimrod, Oylen, and Wahoo Valley. Huntersville Outfitters supply complete or partial outfits for a canoeing or a horseback riding trip. An experienced wrangler guides all trail rides. For canoe trips, Huntersville Outfitters will arrange to meet you at the end of your trip. They also offer a shuttle service for those who have their own equipment. A five-day horseback riding and camping trip, including horse, tack, guide, all camping and cooking gear, and food is $100 per person, based on a party of four to ten persons. A complete canoe outfit (does not include food) is $6 per day per person. Partial outfits are also available. For additional information, contact Dorothy Kennelly, Huntersville Outfitters, Route 4, Menahga MN 56464 (218)564–4279.

Irv Funk Canoe Outfitters is located along the Crow Wing River just 1½ miles north of Nimrod. Running through central Minnesota, the Crow Wing River runs parallel to the 90–mile Crow Wing Wilderness Trail. Irv Funk and his family will help you to plan your trip through this scenic area. They have ample parking and will also help you by moving your car or by picking you up at the end of your trip. The 75–mile Crow Wing Trail is ideal for beginners as there are no portages or dangerous rapids. Several campgrounds have sandy beaches; and most campgrounds also have road access and telephones. You may start and end your trip where you choose. Any type of outfit and/or trip is available, from an afternoon out on the river to a week-long canoe trip. Guide services are available, although not necessary. A complete outfit (does not include food) is $6 per day per person. For additional information, contact Irv Funk Canoe Outfitters, Route 2, Box 51, Sebeka MN 56477 (218)472–3272.

Papoose Bay Resort & Outfitters is located on Potato Lake, near Park Rapids, in the Mississippi headwaters region. Potato Lake is a good producer of walleye, crappie, bass, bluegill, and northern pike. In addition to fishing, guests may enjoy swimming, hiking, volleyball, and archery at the resort. Services on the premises include a fenced-in fishing dock, boat dock, fish cleaning house, and a small store. There are six cabins, all fronting on the lake. Each cabin is heated and furnished. Use of a 14–foot boat is included with each weekly rental. Cabins are equipped with cooking utensils and dishes. Two of the cabins are winterized. During the winter, guests may ski, ice skate, and ice fish. Cabin rentals (in the summer) range from $95 per week (for two persons) to $163 per week (for eight persons). A sauna, laundry, and recreation room have been recently added to the resort. Pets are not permitted. Papoose Bay is also a complete outfitter—both for canoeing and backpacking trips. Canoe trips are available on the following rivers: Mississippi, Schoolcraft, Necktie, Fish Hook, and Crow Wing, and also along the Mantrap Lake Chain. A wide variety of wildlife may be seen along the rivers, including deer, beaver, otter, black bear, fisher, and marten. Partial and/or complete outfits can be supplied. For additional information, contact: Papoose Bay Resort and Outfitters, Niawa Star Route, Park Rapids MN 56470 (218)732–3065.

Lake of the Woods

With a lakeshore shared by both Canada and Minnesota, Lake of the Woods, in the remote northern wilderness, covers more than 200 square miles of surface and offers some of the finest fishing in the nation for smallmouth bass, northern pike, walleye, muskellunge, perch, and whitefish. Warroad, the only American port on Lake of the Woods, is the starting point for vacationers and anglers bound for this famous body of water studded with 14,000 islands and offering more miles of shoreline than any other lake on the North American continent.

When the treaty that gave the United States her independence was signed in Paris in 1783, the Mississippi River was commonly believed to be west of Lake of the Woods. This geographical mistake gave the United States not only the southern shore of the lake, but also many islands and the Northwest Angle, the most northerly point of the forty-eight contiguous states. Entirely isolated from the mainland, the Angle offers true wilderness country with few roads and magnificent forests of spruce and pine. The area is rich in the history of explorers and fur traders. The famous French explorer and first man from the east to see the Rocky Mountains and the Sioux, La Vérendrye, founded Fort St. Charles on the Angle in 1732. Four years later, 21 Frenchmen—including La Vérendrye's son—perished in a surprise attack of Sioux Indians on what today is known as Massacre Island. Their bodies were brought back to the fort and buried under the chapel. A reconstruction of Fort St. Charles can be visited today by air charter.

All of the U.S. islands in the lake are magnificently forested with spruce and pine, in spite of their predominantly rocky composition. Cracked and broken rock surfaces here alternate with ankle-deep carpet moss and scrubby underbrush. Intricate designs are traced on craggy outcroppings by a gray-green lichen indigenous to the area; and rare flowering plants, saxifrage and fleabane, grow on rough ledges.

Seventeen miles southeast of Lake of the Woods is Baudette, billed as the "walleye capital of the world" and situated on the cold, deep waters of the Rainy River. Boats by the hundreds use the Rainy River as a highway to such famous fishing areas as Morris Point, Four Mile Bay, Light House Gap, Wheeler Point, and Pine, Sable, and Curry islands. Almost 3,000 acres of wild land just west of Baudette on the south shore of Lake of the Woods are now being developed as Nipped Bay State Park, with primitive campsites now available. A 50-mile wilderness trail just south of Baudette offers visitors a chance to see deer, bear, grouse, moose, and other wildlife. Write the Chamber of Commerce in Baudette or Warroad for more information on accommodations and outfitters. While in the Lake of the Woods area, be prepared for lengthy bouts of daylight. Baudette boasts the longest vacation day in the U.S., with as many as 18 hours from sunrise to sundown.

Information Sources, Maps & Access

The following Lake of the Woods charts showing navigation routes, portage trails, and topography of the surrounding North Country wilderness are available from the Distribution Division (C44), National Ocean Survey, Riverdale, MD 20840. The following chart sells for $1.25 each (be sure to order by chart number and make checks payable to NOS-Dept. of Commerce) 14999 *Lake of the Woods* (1:120,000).

Accessible only by air or water, a number of resorts are located on the Angle and on nearby Flag, Oak, and Penasse islands. The Chamber of Commerce, Box 34, Warroad 56763, will supply information on vacation, fishing, and moose and waterfowl hunting accommodations and outfitters in these and other Lake of the Woods areas. The Baudette International Airport is an international (U.S.-Canada) point of entry with both land and seaplane facilities. An airport at Warroad offers three charter, seaplane, and fly-in services: *Carlson Flying Service, Hartson's,* and *Warroad,* write c/o Warroad Airport, Warroad 56763 (218)386–1691, for details. Lake of the Woods is accessible via State Highway 11 from Roseau, Roosevelt, and Williams; and via Minnesota 172 from Baudette. Lake of the Woods is shown on U.S. Geological Survey 1:250,000–scale map: Kenora available for $2 from: Distribution Branch, U.S. Geological Survey, 1200 S. Eads St., Arlington, VA 22202.

Gateways

Baudette—Gateway to Lake of the Woods

(Pop. 1,600; zip code 56623; area code 218.) Gateway to the sprawling, island-dotted Lake of the Woods area, Baudette is located on the Rainy River, just across from Ontario, and is an official Port of Entry connected by bridge to Canada. West of town on Minnesota State Hwy. 11 is Beltrami Island State Forest and the Red Lake Management Area, a 415,000–acre habitat for moose, elk, bear, lynx, and other native wildlife (seasonal hunting permitted in public grounds surrounding refuge).

Lodges

★★*Sportsman's Lodge* is located at the mouth of the Rainy River on sprawling, island dotted Lake of the Woods, the northernmost lake in Minnesota. At the lodge, guests may participate in a variety of activities including swimming (either in the lake or in the indoor heated pool), boating, water skiing, and fishing for muskellunge, walleye, northern pike, and smallmouth bass up to trophy weights. A golf course is located nearby. Entertainment is provided every night in the cocktail lounge, and there is a game room in the lodge. A year-round resort, one can go hunting in the fall; and ice fishing, skiing, or snowmobiling in the winter. Special fly-in ice fishing trips are offered. The cost—including flight, house (on the ice), bait, and tackle—is $65 per person for a two-day (one-night) trip. The dining room is open daily, and the chef will prepare your day's catch. Additional services offered to guests include: fish cleaning services and freezers, launches and guides, and boat and motor rentals. There are rooms in the lodge and housekeeping cabins. Rooms are $31 per day (for two persons); suites are $40 per day (for two). Housekeeping cabins are fully equipped. Cabin rentals range from $21 per day (for one bedroom) to $54 per day (for three bedrooms). For additional information, contact: Mr. Beckel, Sportsman's Lodge, Inc., Baudette, MN 56623 (218)634–1342.

Superior National Forest & Boundary Waters Canoe Area

Encompassing the famous Boundary Waters Canoe Area and most of Minnesota's Arrowhead Country, the three-million acre Superior National Forest contains 2,000 portage-linked lakes and streams, dense evergreen forests, muskeg, islands, stark outcroppings of weathered granite, and the ancient Mesabi and Vermilion mountain ranges. The forest straddles the southern extension of the vast Canadian Shield, a 2½–billion-year-old granite intrusion that covers a total area in excess of two million square miles. Great glaciers stretched across the area three times during the Ice Age, carving countless valleys and ridges, and leaving over 5,000 lakes, ranging in size from a few acres to 70 square miles, in their wake. For hundreds of years Indians paddled the quiet waters and braved the treacherous

river rapids between the shores of Lake Superior and the international boundary. Later, Jesuit fathers, traders, and voyageurs became the first white men to explore this wilderness. While the white traders of the rival Hudson's Bay and North West companies fought for supremacy of the fur empire, Chippewa and Sioux tribes fought vicious battles over the land itself. Eventually, both the Chippewa and Hudson's Bay were victorious, each according to its own methods.

The forest, of course, remained neutral to human differences, and today offers little testimony to its rich history, beyond the portages blazed by voyageurs or wild-rice beds harvested by Indians. Even the effects of the logging industry have been largely effaced. From a nucleus of 36,000 acres established in 1909, the forest has grown to its present mammoth size, blanketed by healthy stands of balsam, spruce, tamarack, aspen, and paper birch. The forest cover is complemented by lichen-quilted rock outcroppings and numerous plants and flowers, among them the delicate pink lady slipper, Minnesota's state flower. Other varieties of flowers include wild iris, marsh, marigold, wild rose, daisies, and dogwood. Mushrooms and several kinds of berries—raspberry, strawberry, chokeberry, and juneberry—are also abundant throughout the forest.

The forest is a top-ranked hunting area for whitetail deer and upland game birds. Moose, protected in Minnesota since 1922, range across the forest's 185–mile long northern tip. Woodland caribou, once common to the region, were last seen in the Red Lake area more than 30 years ago, and are presumed to be extinct. Other common game species include black bear, red and gray fox, raccoon, upland game birds, and waterfowl. Diligent wildlife watchers may be lucky enough to sight the tracks of the elusive eastern timber wolf. Classified as an endangered species, the timber-wolf today is limited largely to Minnesota and Superior National Forest, the latter offering refuge to about half the nation's wolf population.

At least thirty different species of fish are found in the lakes and streams of the Superior National Forest and its famous Boundary Waters Canoe Area. Among others, these include muskellunge, northern pike, lake trout, walleye, and large and smallmouth bass up to record weights in such famed Boundary Waters lakes as huge

Saganaga—considered one of the nation's top trophy walleye lakes—Gunflint, Vermilion, Sea Gull, Namakan, Basswood, and sprawling, island-dotted Lac La Croix. Lac La Croix and the Bottle River and the hidden bays and coves of Iron, Crooked, and Knife lakes along the boundary waters chain provide some of the premier smallmouth bass fishing in North America. Inland, the forest's deep, cold-water lakes offer almost every kind of fishing challenge, from deep-water trolling for lake trout and splake to fly fishing for lake-run steelhead, browns, and trophy brook trout in the deep pools of the turbulent North Shore streams.

In the north, abutting the Quetico Provincial Park in Ontario, is the largest water-based wild region in the country, the Boundary Waters Canoe Area. Set aside in 1926 as a roadless area to preserve its primitive character, the BWCA consists of more than one million acres of land and water covering the northern third of the forest. Stretching approximately 200 miles along the Canadian boundary, the BWCA offers more than 1,200 miles of canoe routes. Portages here, worn deep from use over several centuries, were used by such notables as Jacques de Noyons, believed to be the first white man to travel the border waters; Sieur de La Vérendrye, who left a record of his travels through the area; and Alexander Mackenzie, a traveler along this route on his epic journey to the Pacific. The real fame of the area came in 1731 with the arrival of Vérendrye and the opening of the fur trade. In the spring of 1732, the Vérendrye party and others paddled their narrow birchbark canoes over what are now the waters of the BWCA, establishing posts on the border lakes. Later, settlers, loggers, missionaries, miners, and farmers plied these waters on their way across Minnesota to the north and inland. A number of outfitters headquartered at Ely and Grand Marais supply everything needed except personal articles at very reasonable rates, which include food, canoe, tent, ax, cook kits, and detailed items such as insect repellent. They will also rent any item of equipment needed.

The most popular entry routes into the Boundary Waters Canoe Area include the Ely area entry points at Moose Lake, Fall Lake, and Lake One; at Saganaga, Seagull, and Sawbill lakes on the east; and the more remote wilderness entry points such as those at Crab Lake, Fourtown Lake, and Horse Lake (20 miles to the northwest of Ely), at Moose River (at the Echo Trail crossing, 40 miles northwest of Ely), at Little Indian Sioux River (50 miles northwest of Ely on the Echo Trail), and at Magnetic and Round Lakes (45 miles from Grand Marais on the Gunflint Trail). Be sure to check with the Forest Supervisor's Office for the "BWCA User Distribution Program" regulations. Entry points into Canada's Quetico Wilderness from the BWCA are located at Basswood Lake, the Cache Bay Ranger Station, and Saganaga Lake Customs.

The Superior Forest-Boundary Waters Canoe Area contains literally hundreds of renowned historic canoe-camping and wilderness fishing lakes and streams, including the famous tributaries of Minnesota's North Shore region of Lake Superior. Many plants not found elsewhere in Minnesota grow along the North Shore and in the surrounding forests: stands of leatherleaf cover; acres of muskeg; abundant Labrador tea; billberry, which grows only in this upper tip of the state. Swamp laurel, bog and autumn willow, and black currant are plants characteristic of the region. Trailing arbutus is found in the sandy forests, and aromatic wintergreen covers the forest bed in much of the drier area. The major features of the North Shore region include the Grand Portage Trail (this nine-mile portage was used by voyageurs and fur traders to avoid falls and rapids in the Pigeon River) and the famous black-water trout and steelhead waters of the Reservation River, Arrowhead and Cascade rivers, and the Temperance, Knife, Poplar, Devil Track, Manitou, and Brule

rivers—the last named after Etienne Brule, who explored the foot of Lake Superior in 1622—which rise out of tamarack and alder swamps along the southern slope of the Laurentian Divide and flow along wild boulder-studded courses into frigid Lake Superior. Crane Lake, to the northwest, is renowned for its walleye and northern pike fishing and serves as a gateway to the chain of wilderness boundary lakes.

From Crane Lake are accessible some of the greatest inland canoeing-fishing waters on the continent, and the scenic wilderness camping areas of Voyageurs National Park. The great chain of border lakes—including Rainy, Namakan, Lac La Croix, Iron, Crooked, Basswood, Knife, Saganaga, Gunflint, Mountain, and South Fowl—now so sparsely settled, was once the scene of great historic conflicts. It was on these lakes that the Sioux fought losing battles in their retreat before the ruthless, savage Chippewa, who had determined to secure for themselves the rewards of the fur trade. The region's remote lakeshores and rivers contain numerous Indian petroglyphs and ancient dams constructed of huge rounded boulders, often several tons in weight, and situated where such boulders are naturally scarce. To the south and east of Crane Lake lies beautiful Vermilion Lake, known to the Chippewa as the "Lake of the Sunset Glow," and the famous Boundary Waters outfitting center of Ely. The region was developed through the Vermilion Iron Range mining industry. Campgrounds and excellent smallmouth bass, walleye, and northern pike fishing in the Ely area are found at the South Kawishiwi River, Birch Lake, Burntside Lake, Moose River, South Hegman, Fenske, Big, and Second lakes, and along the Moose, Sioux, and Hunting Shack rivers.

Information Sources, Maps & Access

For detailed information, a full-color *Superior National Forest Map* (50¢) and a free *Boundary Waters Canoe Area Map/Brochure*, contact: Supervisor, Superior National Forest, Duluth, MN 55801 (218)727–6692 or 727–4945 or the District Ranger's Office at Ely, MN 55731 (218)365–6185 or at Grand Marais, MN 55604 (218) 387–1750. *Grand Portage*, a brochure available free from the Grand Portage National Monument, Grand Portage 55605 (218)387–2788, describes the various buildings and local trails and offers a concise but fascinating history of the fur trade. Daily boat service from Grand Portage to Isle Royale National Park (see "Michigan") is provided by *Grand Portage-Isle Royale Transportation Lines, Inc.*, 363–6 Lake Ave., South, Duluth 55802 (218)722–2609.

Maps compiled, lithographed, and published by the W.A. Fisher Company are designed as aids for those who travel the waters in northern Minnesota and southern Ontario. All maps of the border waters show shorelines, lakes, streams, rivers, BWCA motor and snowmobile routes, roads, highways, and other features, and may be ordered at the prices quoted below from the W.A. Fisher Co., Box 1107, Virginia 55792 (218)741–9544. Be sure to indicate code numbers and titles when ordering, and request a free chart index.

The basic Superior-Quetico map series (size 17 by 22 inches, scale ⅝ inch to one mile, waterproof) includes fifteen maps, numbered 101 to 115. The Minnesota-Canadian border country between Grand Portage on Lake Superior and International Falls on Rainy Lake is mapped in detail. All of the Canadian Quetico Park, Boundary Waters Canoe Area, and most of Minnesota's Superior National

Forest are covered. Campsites and portages are updated annually. These maps are specifically designed for the fisherman and canoeist. An index chart illustrating the 15 maps and the area they cover is available on request. Maps are priced at 50¢ each.

All 15 maps in the Superior-Quetico series have been combined in book form (17 by 22 inches, printed on regular paper). Also included is a historical map of the entire area. The *Superior-Quetico Map Book* costs $4.00 plus postage.

Enlarged Superior-Quetico maps (22 by 34 inches, scale 1¼ inches to one mile, waterproof), which are similar in nature to the regular maps, place greater emphasis on detail, such as incorporation of some reef markers, water levels, campsites, BWCA boundaries, motor routes, etc. The following maps are available in these editions: E–1 *Crane, Sandpoint, Namakan*; E–2 *Lac La Croix*; E–3 *Crooked, Basswood, Agnes*; E–4 *Saganaga, Saganagons, Seagull*; E–5 *Brule, Alice, Sawbill*; E–19 *Winchell, Arrow, Fowl lakes* (slightly smaller scale); E–20 *Namakan*. The above maps are priced at $1 each.

Enlarged maps of both *Saganaga Lake* (E–6) and *Northern Lights Lake* (E–7) are 17 by 22 inches, at a scale of 1½ inches to one mile, and show most of the islands and landmarks. They are waterproof and cost 50¢ each. The *Seagull Lake Hydrographic Map* (E–8, 17 by 22 inches, scale 3½ inches to one mile, waterproof) is similarly enlarged and designed for maximum detail, showing the lake-bottom contour at depth intervals of 10 feet. Price is also 50¢. Enlarged maps are also available for *Kabetogama Lake* (E–9) and *Namakan Lake* (E–10), 17 by 22 inches, at a scale of one inch to one mile, priced at 50¢ each.

The *Rainy Lake Boaters Map* (E–11, 22½ by 35 inches, scale ⅝ inch to one mile, waterproof) is priced at $1.00 and shows all of the lake, with special attention to accuracy of shoreline detail. The *Pelican Lake Hydrographic Map* (E–12, 17 by 22 inches, scale 2½ inches to one mile, waterproof) shows bottom contours, landmarks, islands, and reefs, and is priced at 50¢. Divided into its east and west sections, the *Lake Vermilion Hydrographic Map* (East E–13, West E–14, 22 by 33⅝ inches, scale 2⅛ inches to one mile, waterproof) shows the lake bottom contour, reefs and buoy information. The two maps overlap and cost $1.00 each.

A comprehensive map of the area within, and of the surrounding Boundary Waters Canoe Area, the *Minnesota-Canadian Wilderness Area Map* (E–15, 22 by 34 inches, scale one inch to three miles, waterproof) shows the region from Crane Lake on the west to Gunflint Lake on the east. Also designated are the Superior National Forest, Quetico Provincial Park, BWCA, and international boundaries. Outboard-motor and snowmobile routes within the BWCA are also shown. Maps cost $1.00 each.

The *Trout Lake Hydrographic Map* (E–16, 17 by 22 inches, scale 2⅛ inches to one mile, waterproof) is priced at 50¢ and shows Trout and surrounding lakes. Lake-bottom contours are shown at depth intervals of 20 feet. The adjacent portion of Lake Vermilion and connecting motorized portage are also indicated. *Kabetogama Lake Hydrographic Maps* (E–17, 22 by 34 inches, scale 2⅛ inches to one mile, waterproof) shows coast-guard buoys, reefs, shallows, and lake-bottom contours at intervals of 10 feet. Maps cost $1.00 each.

The Fisher map of *Southwestern Ontario* (R–2, 22 by 27¼ inches, scale ¼ inch to one mile, waterproof) also costs $1.00 and shows Rainy Lake, the western portion of Lake of the Woods, and the area east of Lake of the Woods, spanning a distance of about 125 miles.

The map is of interest primarily to those traveling north and east of International Falls, Minnesota, and south and east of Kenora, Ontario, Canada.

A small map is also available of the *Orr Region* (R–3, 11 by 17 inches, scale ⅜ inch to one mile, waterproof), including Pelican Lake and the area to the immediate north and west, at a price of 35¢. The *Ely Area Map* (R–4, 17 by 22 inches, scale ¼ inch to one mile, regular paper) shows lakes in the Superior-Quetico region from Atikokan on the north to Babbitt on the south and is also priced at 35¢. A similar edition of the *Gunflint Trail Area* (R–5) at the same scale, size, and price shows lakes in the Superior-Quetico region from Basswood Lake on the west to Whitefish Lake on the east. Maps are also available for the *Western Entry to the Canoe Country* (R–6, 17 by 22 inches, scale one inch to three miles, regular paper) at a price of $.50 each, indicating the Minnesota Canadian border lakes accessible from Crane Lake, including Lac La Croix, Beaverhouse, Basswood, and Crooked lakes.

W.A. Fisher also publishes a special map of the *Old Voyageurs Highway* (C–1, 19 by 24 inches, embossed-finish paper), colorfully decorated with sketches and historical information, showing the country from Grand Portage on Lake Superior to Rainy Lake, 50¢.

Beginning at Grand Marais on Lake Superior, the Gunflint Trail winds inland for 58 miles through the heavily forested terrain of the huge Superior National Forest. Originally used by Chippewa Indians as a winter trail, the route later became the main transportation link for travel into the vast forest and lakes area by explorers and trappers. Today, most of the road is well-paved and open to automobiles.

The trail passes through the magnificent stands of pine, spruce, balsam, birch, and aspen that cover the ancient Laurentian Highlands, the geologic reminder of the prehistoric chain of hills that once covered a large area of Minnesota. Along much of the route, the famous chain of glacial lakes bordering the Boundary Waters Canoe Area offers excellent opportunities for camping, canoeing, and fishing for lake trout, brookies, walleyes, northerns, and bass. Near Poplar Lake, the trail crosses the Laurentian Divide, where the watershed divides, with water falling on the south side flowing into Lake Superior, and water falling on the north side traveling toward Hudson Bay. The route ends near the cold, clear waters of Saganaga Lake, named for a Chippewa term meaning "lake with many islands."

East of the Gunflint Trail, the 18–mile-long Arrowhead Trail pursues a parallel route through the wilderness of Grand Portage State Forest. Beginning at Hovland on Highway 61, the trail winds through dense spruce, balsam, birch, and pines and terminates at McFarland Lake, a short distance south of the Canadian border. Like the Gunflint trail, this paved road offers an introduction to the remote wilderness of Minnesota's Arrowhead Country: pine forests as far as the eye can see, and clear lakes and swift-flowing streams that hold smallmouth bass, walleye, steelhead, and salmon.

Two other scenic trails explore the wilds of Arrowhead country and lead to the famous Boundary Waters Canoe Area. The region's first major entrance to the BWCA, the 24–mile Sawbill Trail, begins near Tofte and runs paralled with the Temperance River for several miles. The route then crosses Parent Lake Road and ends at Sawbill Lake, a long L-shaped body of water studded with numerous small islands. Caribou Trail, beginning just north of Lutsen, winds its way into the interior of the Arrowhead region along many smaller lakes and rivers, ending at Brule Lake, the second major boundary lake for the BWCA.

The Lake Superior North Shore Scenic Drive passes through Grand Marais as it makes its way between Duluth and Thunder Bay in

THE
GREAT OUTDOORS
ROAD ATLAS
EASTERN
UNITED STATES

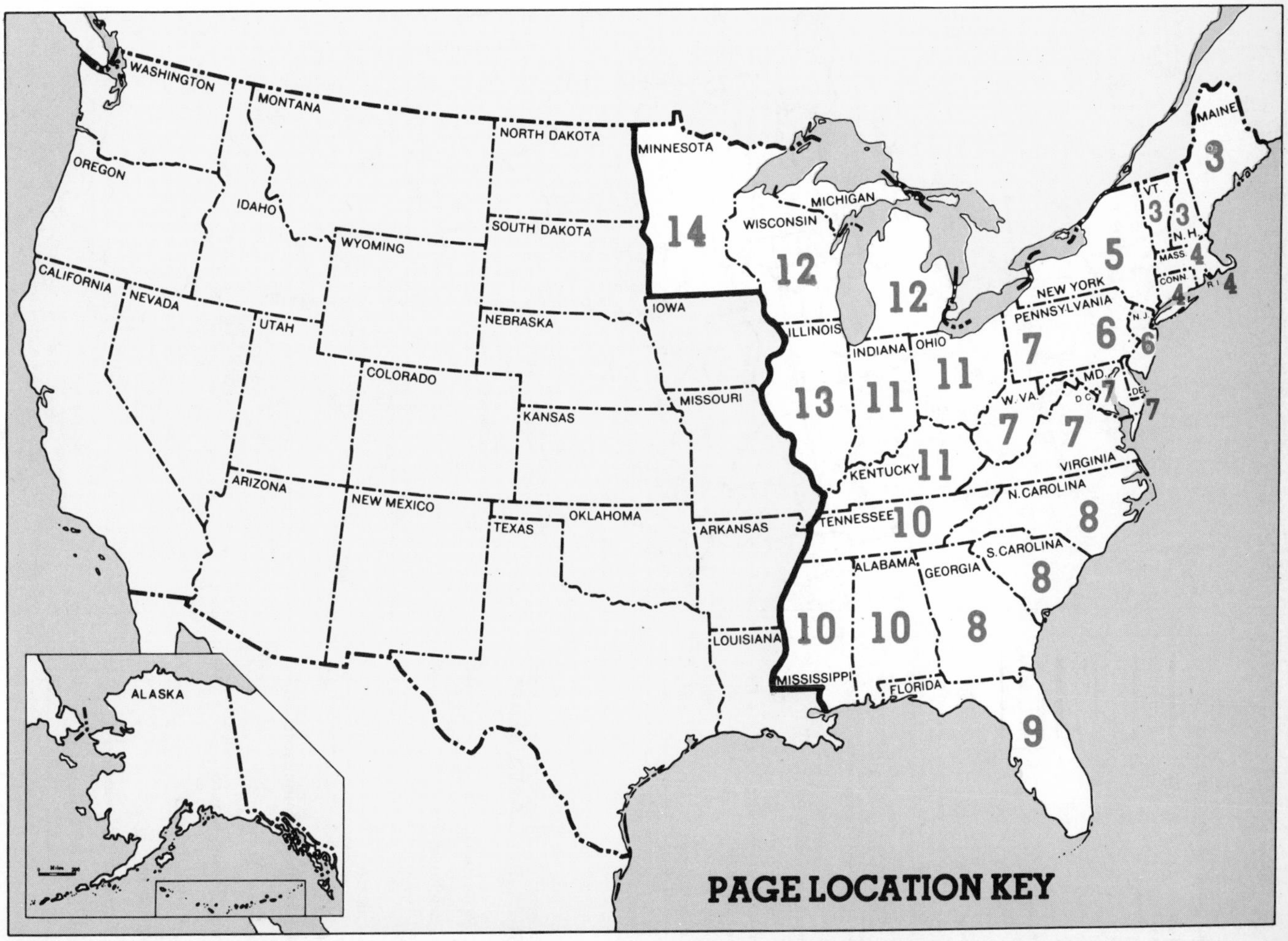

PAGE LOCATION KEY

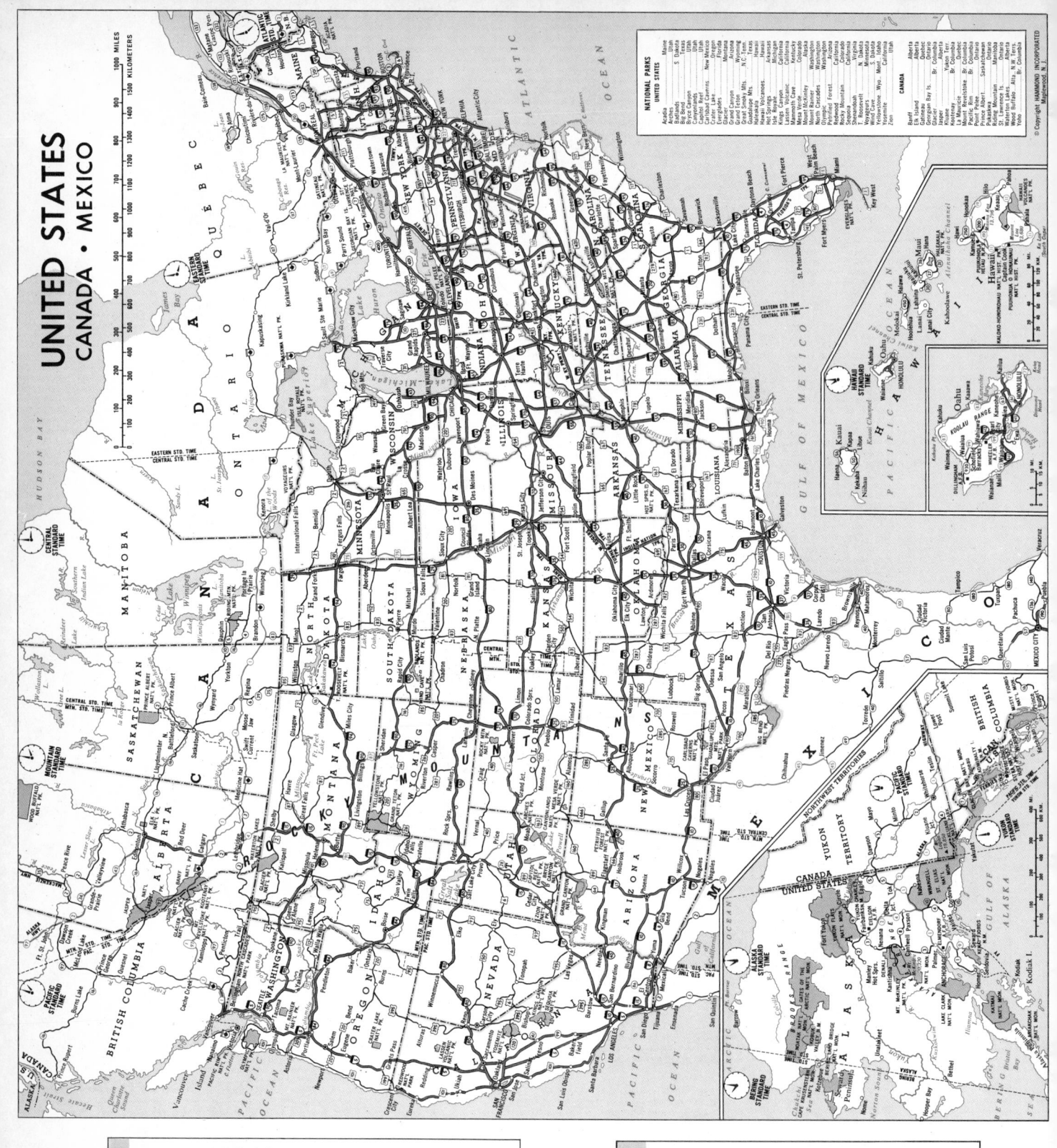

SYMBOLS USED IN THIS ATLAS

- Limited Access Highways
- National Parkways
- Toll Roads and Interchanges
- Major Highways
- Other Important Roads
- Mileage Between Dots
- Selected Scenic Routes
- Ferries
- U.S. Interstate Route Numbers

Routes with odd numbers run north and south, the even-numbered routes east and west. Numbers progress lowest to highest from west to east and from south to north. Major routes have one- or two-digit numbers and the long, evenly spaced routes have numbers ending in 0 or 5. Connecting full or partial circumferential routes around or in urban areas carry a three-digit number, using the main route number with an even number prefix. Radial and spur routes are also three-digit, using the main route number with an odd number prefix. For example: an auxiliary route to I-80 might be classified as I-180 or I-280.

- Federal Route Numbers
- State and Other Route Numbers
- Trans-Canada Highway
- Points of Interest, Recreation Areas
- Major Commercial Airports
- National Capitals
- State and Provincial Capitals

METROPOLITAN AREA MAPS

POINTS OF INTEREST

VERMONT

Barre (A4)—Granite quarries, tours, Maple Sugar Museum; nearby: ski areas.
Bennington (A5)—Revolutionary War Battle Monument, Historical Museum & Art Gallery, Old First Church; nearby: scenic Green Mountain National Forest.
Brattleboro (A5)—Winter resort, national ski jumping matches; nearby: Santa's Land, miniature railroad.
Manchester Center (A5)—Resort town; nearby: fine ski areas, Southern Vermont Art Center, scenic road on Mt. Equinox.

NEW HAMPSHIRE

Concord (B5)—State capital, State House, Historical Museum, Arts & Crafts Shop, Franklin Pierce House; nearby: Shaker Village, Daniel Webster Birthplace.
Laconia (B5)—Popular vacation town in lake region; nearby: Lake Winnipesaukee recreation area, Auto Museum.
Manchester (B5)—Institute of Arts & Sciences, Art Gallery, Historical Museum, General Stark's Home; nearby: Wild Animal Farm, Natural History Museum.
North Conway (B4)—Ski center, Skimobile Tramway; nearby: White Mountain National Forest, Mt. Washington cog railway.
North Woodstock (A4)—Scenic town, many nearby attractions: Franconia Notch, Old Man of the Mountains, Indian Head, Nature-land, Lost River, ski areas.
Portsmouth (B5)—Historic seaport, John Paul Jones House, Pitt Tavern, Jackson House, Warner House, Governor Langdon Mansion; nearby: Governor Wentworth's Mansion, excellent beaches, historic town of Exeter.

MAINE

Acadia National Park (C4)—Rocky seashore area, Mt. Cadillac scenic drive; nearby: Bar Harbor resort, archaeological museum, Fort Western, Blaine House.
Augusta (C4)—State capital, State House & museum, restored Fort Western, Blaine House.
Bath (C5)—Historic shipbuilding town, Historical Museum, Old Jail, historic Fort Edgecomb; nearby: Art gallery at Wiscasset, aquarium in Boothbay Harbor, Old Fort Popham, reconstructed Fort William Henry.
Baxter State Park (C3)—Large wilderness area, terminus of Appalachian Trail, mountain climbing, hiking, water sports; nearby: Allagash Wilderness Waterway.
Eastport (D4)—Easternmost town in United States, spectacular tides; nearby: Franklin D. Roosevelt's home on Campobello Island, museum, scenic Quoddy Head State Park.
Kennebunk (B5)—Historic town; nearby: Old Gaol Museum, Brick Store Museum, Trolley Museum; nearby: Old Gaol Museum, seashore resorts of Kennebunkport & Old Orchard Beach.
Portland (B5)—Victoria Mansion, Wadsworth-Longfellow House, Victoria Mansion, scenic Promenades, boat cruises; nearby: old lighthouse, Sebago Lake, water sports.
Rockland (C4)—Lobster fishing center, art museum; nearby: Owl's Head Light, General Knox Mansion, picturesque coastal fishing villages.
Searsport (C4)—Marine Museum; nearby: Fort Knox State Park, Fort George.

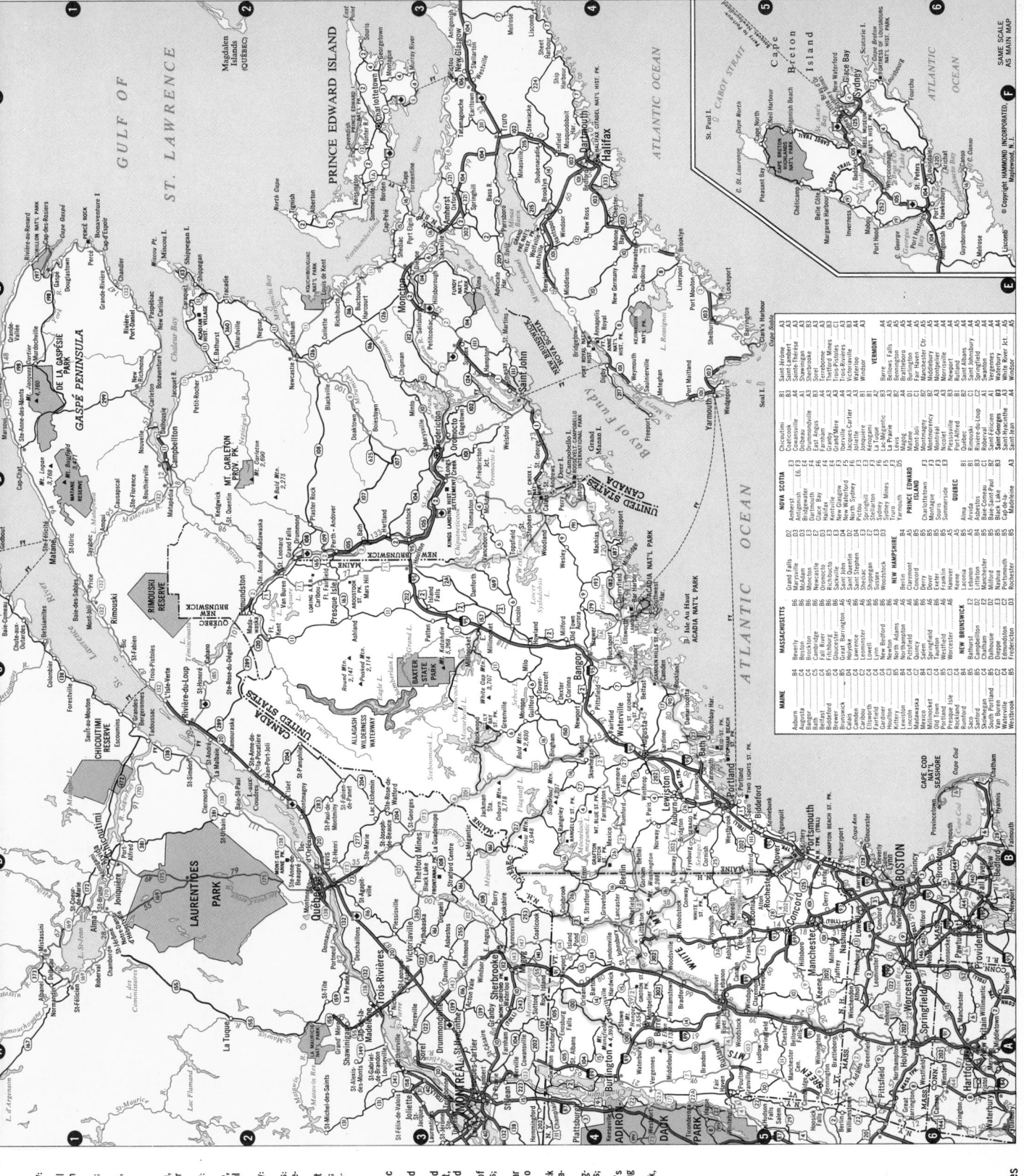

Map scale: 1 inch=68 miles

A3

A 4

POINTS OF INTEREST

SOUTHERN VERMONT

Bennington (B2)—Revolutionary War Battle Monument, Historical Museum & Art Gallery, Old First Church; nearby: scenic Green Mountain National Forest.

Brattleboro (C2)—Winter resort, national ski jumping matches; nearby: Santa's Land, miniature railroad.

Manchester Center (B1)—Resort town; nearby: fine ski areas, Southern Vermont Art Center, scenic road on Mt. Equinox.

SOUTHERN NEW HAMPSHIRE

Concord (D1)—State capital, State House, Historical Museum, Arts & Crafts Shop, Franklin Pierce House; nearby: Shaker Village, Daniel Webster Birthplace.

Laconia (D1)—Popular vacation town in lake region; nearby: Lake Winnipesaukee recreation area, Auto Museum.

Manchester (D2)—Institute of Arts & Sciences, Art Gallery, Historical Museum, General Stark's Home; nearby: Wild Animal Farm, Natural History Museum.

Portsmouth (E1)—Historic seaport, John Paul Jones House, Pitt Tavern, Jackson House, Warner House, Governor Langdon Mansion; nearby: Governor Wentworth's Mansion, excellent beaches, historic town of Exeter.

MASSACHUSETTS

Boston (E3, F6)—Freedom Trail Walking Tour (including State House, King's Chapel, Old State House & Massacre site, Faneuil Hall, Paul Revere House, Old North Church), The Common, Athenaeum, Old South Meeting House, Historical Museum, Fine Arts Museum, Symphony Hall, Children's Museum, Gardner Museum, Science Museum, Planetarium; nearby: Bunker Hill Monument, USS Constitution at Charlestown, Art Museum, University Museum (Peabody & Botanical Museums), Longfellow House in Cambridge, Concord Battlefield Site, Walden Pond at Concord, Minute Man National Historical Park, Hancock-Clarke House at Lexington, Adams National Historic Site, John & John Quincy Adams Houses in Quincy.

Cape Cod (F4)—Summer resort area, National Seashore, unspoiled beaches & sand dunes, historic towns, old windmill, Kennedy Home, Pilgrim Memorial Monument, Historical & Art Museum, Pilgrim Spring, Oceanographic Institution, U.S. Marine Biological Laboratory.

Deerfield (C2)—Scenic historic village, Memorial Hall, Indian House, Hall Tavern.

Gloucester (E2)—Fishing port & art colony, Beauport Mansion, Art Museum.

Martha's Vineyard (E5)—Unspoiled vacation area, excellent beaches, colored cliffs.

Nantucket (F5)—Old famous whaling port, Whaling Museum, historic homes.

Pittsfield (B3)—Berkshire Museum; nearby: Tanglewood music festivals, historic homes and Indian burial ground.

Plymouth (F4)—Plymouth Rock, reconstructed Plimoth Plantation, Mayflower II berth, Pilgrim Hall, National Monument to the Forefathers, Harlow House; nearby: Pilgrim Village.

Salem (E2)—Site of old witchcraft trials, Essex Institute, Pioneers' Village, Salem Maritime National Historic Site, Maritime Museum, House of Seven Gables, Witch House & Gallows Hill; nearby: yachting center at Marblehead.

RHODE ISLAND

Block Island (D5)—Summer seashore resort, deep-sea fishing, high clay cliffs.

Newport (E4)—Touro Synagogue National Historic Site, old summer homes (The Breakers, The Elms, Belcourt Castle), scenic Ocean Drive, Cliff Walk, Tennis Hall of Fame, Naval Base.

Providence (D4)—State House, Historical Museum, Art Museum, Planetarium, Natural History Museum, Roger Williams National Memorial, John Brown House, Art Museum, Stephen Hopkins House.

CONNECTICUT

Bridgeport (B5)—Barnum Museum, Tom Thumb statue; nearby: summer Shakespearean Festivals in Stratford.

Greenwich (B5)—Yachting center, Putnam Cottage, Bruce Museum; nearby: Audubon Nature Center, museum & nature trails.

Hartford (C4)—State Capitol, Colt gun collection in State Library, Old State House, Historical Museum, Art Museum, Mark Twain House; nearby: Clock Museum in Bristol.

New Haven (B5)—University Art Gallery, Sterling Library, Natural History Museum, Gun Museum, Bowditch House; nearby: Sleeping Giant State Park, Trolley Museum.

New London (C5)—Former whaling port, modern submarine base, nearby: Shaw Mansion, Old Town Mill, Court House, Hempstead House, Art Museum; nearby: Battle Monument, Submarine Library, Mystic Seaport & Marine Museum, Gillette Castle State Park.

POINTS OF INTEREST

NEW YORK

Albany (E5)—State Capitol, State Museum & Library, Institute of History & Art, Schuyler Mansion, Ten Broeck Mansion; nearby: Fort Crailo, Shaker Museum, Fire Fighting Museum.

Buffalo (B4)—Major Great Lakes port, Museum of Science, T. Roosevelt Inaugural National Historic Site, art gallery, historical museum.

Cooperstown (E4)—Baseball Hall of Fame Museum, Farmers Museum, James Fenimore Cooper Home; nearby: Howe Caverns.

Corning (C5)—Famous Glass Center, displays, plant tours; nearby: scenic Finger Lakes region, gorge & waterfalls at Watkins Glen.

Kingston (E5)—Restored State Senate House, Historical Museum; nearby: Huguenot stone houses, Franklin D. Roosevelt Home & Vanderbilt Mansion National Historic Sites.

Lake George (E4)—Center of popular resort area, restored Fort William Henry, ruins of Fort George and battlefield site, Gaslight Village, Automobile Museum; nearby: National Museum of Racing, Saratoga National Historical Park, Schuyler House, Petrified Gardens, mineral-water baths at Saratoga Springs.

Lake Placid (E3)—Adirondack resort surrounded by outdoor recreation facilities; nearby: Robert L. Stevenson's former home at Saranac Lake, Olympic Ice Arena & Bobsled Run, Santa's Workshop, Adirondack Center Museum.

New York City (E6, see also page 15)—Statue of Liberty National Monument, Empire State Building, Broadway & Times Square, Rockefeller Center, United Nations Buildings, Wall Street, Stock Exchange, Lincoln Center for the Performing Arts, Metropolitan Art Museum, Modern Art Gallery, Museum of Natural History, Planetarium, Chinatown, Greenwich Village, exclusive Fifth Avenue shops, Museum, City Hall, General Grant National Memorial, The Cloisters, Bronx Zoo, Botanical Gardens, Coney Island, Verrazano-Narrows Bridge, Washington Irving home & Philipse Manor, Old Dutch Church, Van Cortlandt Manor. Metropolitan Area map on page 48.

Newburgh (E6)—Hasbrouck House & other historic buildings; nearby: General Knox's Headquarters House, Incline Railway at Beacon, U.S. Military Academy at West Point, Bear Mountain State Park, Palisades Interstate Park.

Niagara Falls (B4)—Spectacular waterfalls, boat trips, Cave of the Winds, Seagram Observation Tower, Queen Victoria Park, Table Rock House, Wax Museum; nearby: Old Fort Niagara.

Oyster Bay (E6-near Mineola)—Theodore Roosevelt's former home, Sagamore Hill; nearby: Vanderbilt Mansion, Marine Museum.

Rochester (C4)—Eastman Kodak plant tours, Museum of Photography, Museum of Arts & Sciences.

Southampton (F6)—Seashore resort & artist colony, Art Museum, Automotive Museum, historic homes.

Syracuse (D4)—French Fort, Salt Museum, Art & Historical Museums.

Thousand Islands (D3)—Vacation area, boat cruises, Boldt Castle, island parks; nearby: Seaway Locks.

Ticonderoga (E3)—Restored American Revolution fort, museum; nearby: Lake Champlain recreation areas.

Map scale: 1 inch=58 miles

A 5

POINTS OF INTEREST

EASTERN PENNSYLVANIA

Bethlehem (C2)—Former Moravian settlement, Gemein Haus, Old Chapel, Brethren's House, museum; nearby: Lost River Caverns.
Chester (C4)—Old Courthouse, shipyard tours; nearby: Caleb Pusey House, Morton Homestead, Longwood Gardens, Brandywine Battlefield State Park.
Gettysburg (A4)—National Military Park, Battlefield Tower, Visitor Center, Eternal Light Peace Monument, General Meade's Headquarters museum; nearby: National Museum, electric battle map, Civil War Wax Museum.
Harrisburg (A3)—State Capitol, Museum, William Penn Memorial Museum & Archives Building; nearby: Fort Hunter Museum, Old Barracks, Historical Museum at Carlisle, chocolate plant tours, Hersheypark, Rose Gardens at Hershey, Indian Echo Caverns.
Lancaster (B4)—Old state capital, Amish Farmers' Markets, nearby: James Buchanan Home, Farm Museum, Amish Farm & House, Amish Homestead, farm tours, steam railroad tours at Strasburg, Mercer Museum at Doylestown.
New Hope (D3)—Scenic Delaware Canal, barge trips; nearby: Washington Crossing State Park, historic buildings.
Philadelphia (D4, A1)—Independence National Historical Park (Independence Hall, Congress Hall, Carpenters' Hall, Supreme Court Building, other historical buildings and landmarks), Betsy Ross House, Elfreth's Alley, Old Swedes' Church, Civic Center, Franklin Institute & Fels Planetarium, City Hall, Museum of Art, Academies of Natural Sciences, Music and Fine Arts, zoo, University Museum, Rodin Museum, aquarium, Admiral Dewey Flagship, U.S. Mint, Fairmount Park mansions; nearby: Valley Forge National Historical Park, Fort Washington State Park.
Reading (C3)—Public Museum & Art Gallery, Pagoda Observation Tower; nearby: Hopewell Village National Historic Site, old iron-making settlement, American Wonderland, Boone Homestead, historic buildings.
Scranton (C1)—Natural History, Science & Art Museum, zoo; nearby: Historical Museum, coal mine tours.
Stroudsburg (D2)—Gateway to Pocono Mountains resort area, outdoor sports; nearby: scenic waterfalls, Pocono Wild Animal Farm.
York (A4)—Temporary Revolutionary War state capital, Plough Tavern, Friends Meeting House, Gates House, Historical Museum.

NEW JERSEY

Asbury Park (E3)—Shore resort, deep-sea fishing; nearby: Gateway National Recreation Area at Sandy Hook, Monmouth Battlefield Site, abandoned village in Allaire State Park.
Atlantic City (E5)—Seashore resort, famous boardwalk, amusement piers, excellent beaches; nearby: restored 19th century town of Batsto, Somers Mansion.
Camden (D4, B2)—Walt Whitman House, County Historical Museum; nearby: historic Indian King Tavern.
High Point State Park (D1)—Scenic area, observation tower; nearby: Old Dutch Parsonage, Duke Gardens at Somerville.
Morristown National Historical Park (E2)—George Washington's Headquarters (Ford Mansion), museum, Fort Nonsense earthworks, historic Jockey Hollow, reconstructed huts.
Newark (E2)—City Museum, Historical Museum, brewery tours; nearby: Edison National Historic Site, Grover Cleveland Birthplace, Meadowlands Sports Complex.
New Brunswick (E3)—Boy Scout Museum; nearby: Wallace House, Old Dutch Parsonage, Duke Gardens at Somerville.
Trenton (D3)—State Capitol, Revolutionary War Battle Monument, Old Barracks, historic homes, State Museum; nearby: historic Crosswicks town, Princeton Battlefield National Historic Site, Great Adventure near Jackson.

BALTIMORE and WASHINGTON

Baltimore (A5, F5)—National Anthem City, Fort McHenry National Monument, famous U.S.S. Constellation, Washington Monument, Flag House, Art Museums, Railroad Museum; nearby: Ordnance Museum at Aberdeen, Ellicott City's B & O R.R. sta. Museum.
Washington (A6, F6)—Capitol Building, White House, Jefferson Memorial, Lincoln Memorial, Washington Monument, Smithsonian Institution, FBI Headquarters, Supreme Court Building, Constitution Hall, historical museum, Library of Congress, Bureau of Engraving & Printing, Blair House, Shakespeare Library, Freer Art Gallery, Islamic Center, Pan American Union, Potomac Park's scenic cherry trees, zoo, historic Georgetown area; nearby: Arlington National Cemetery, Tomb of the Unknowns, Kennedy Grave, Marine Corps Memorial, The Pentagon.

POINTS OF INTEREST

WEST VIRGINIA

Beckley (B5)—Exhibit Coal Mine; nearby: Coal Town Museum.

Charleston (B4)—State Capitol, State Museum, Art Gallery, Planetarium. Children's Museum.

Harpers Ferry National Historical Park (D3)—John Brown's Monument, Civil War sites.

Wheeling (C3)—Fort Henry site, historic Mansion House, industrial tours; nearby: Oglebay Park, nature center, museum, Indian Burial Mound at Moundsville.

White Sulphur Springs (C5)—Health resort, President's Cottage; nearby: fish hatchery.

PENNSYLVANIA

Erie (C1)—Restored Perry's flagship, Planetarium, General Wayne's Blockhouse; nearby: Land Lighthouse, Perry Victory Monument.

Fort Necessity National Battlefield Site (C3)—Restored fort, museum, Old Mt. Washington Tavern.

Grand Canyon of Pennsylvania (E1–near Wellsboro)—Outstanding scenery, deep gorge; nearby: scenic state parks and recreation areas.

Philadelphia & Eastern Pennsylvania—See page 6.

Pittsburgh (A2, C2)—Major world iron and steel center, "Golden Triangle" business district and park area, Fort Pitt Blockhouse, Carnegie Institute Museums, Phipps Conservatory, Zoo, Civic Arena, Planetarium & Institute of Modern Science; nearby: restored Harmony Society Village at Ambridge.

DELAWARE

Dover (F3)—State Capitol, Old Statehouse, State Museum, historic churches; nearby: restored John Dickinson Mansion.

Rehoboth Beach (F4)—Seashore resort; nearby: Zwaanendael Museum at Lewes, Delaware Dunes, African Wild Animal Park at Milford.

Wilmington (F3)—Fort Christina, Old Swedes Church, Old Town Hall, Historical Museum; nearby: Winterthur Museum, Industrial Arts Museum, first DuPont powder mill.

MARYLAND

Annapolis (E4)—Picturesque State Capitol, U.S. Naval Academy, museum, Old Treasury Building; nearby: Chesapeake Bay Maritime Museum near Easton.

Baltimore—See page 6.

Frederick (E3)—Barbara Fritchie Museum; nearby: Antietam National Battlefield Site, Chesapeake & Ohio Canal National Monument.

Ocean City (F4)—Seashore resort, boardwalk; nearby: Assateague Island National Seashore.

VIRGINIA

Alexandria (E4)—Historic Christ Church, Gadsby's Tavern, Carlyle House & other historic buildings; nearby: Custis-Lee Mansion, Manassas National Battlefield Park, George Washington's plantation, Mount Vernon.

Appomattox Courthouse National Historical Park (D5)—Civil War Surrender Site, McLean House & other restored buildings; nearby: Red Hill Shrine (Patrick Henry's former home).

Charlottesville (D4)—Town designed by Thomas Jefferson (Monticello, Ash Lawn, Serpentine Walls), historic Michie Tavern; nearby: Stratford Hall-George Washington Birthplace National Monument.

Cumberland Gap National Historical Park (A5)—Famous transmountain pass used by early explorers and pioneers; Allegheny mountain pass (see page 6).

Fredericksburg (E4)—James Monroe Law Office & Library, Kenmore Mansion, Hugh Mercer Apothecary, John Paul Jones House, historic Masonic Lodge, Rising Sun Tavern; nearby: George Washington's Boyhood Home, National Military Park (several battle sites), electric map, Stratford Hall-George Washington Birthplace National Monument.

Lexington (C5)—Homes of Robert E. Lee & "Stonewall" Jackson; nearby: Natural Bridge.

Norfolk, Newport News-Hampton (E5)—Largest U.S. Naval Base, tours, Naval Shipyard Museum, Mariners Museum, old Fort Monroe (Casemate Museum), General MacArthur Memorial, Arts & Sciences Museum, many historic buildings; nearby: restored Jamestown & Williamsburg, Folk Art Collection, craft shops, Yorktown Battlefield, museum, old mansions, Virginia Beach resort area, Fort Story.

Richmond (E5)—State Capitol, Confederate Museum, Battle Abbey, Art Museum, Edgar Allan Poe Shrine, National Battlefield Park; nearby: Petersburg National Military Park.

Shenandoah National Park (D4)—Scenic Skyline Drive, overlooks, outdoor recreation facilities, famous caverns.

WASHINGTON, D.C. (See page 6)

Map scale: 1 inch=58 miles

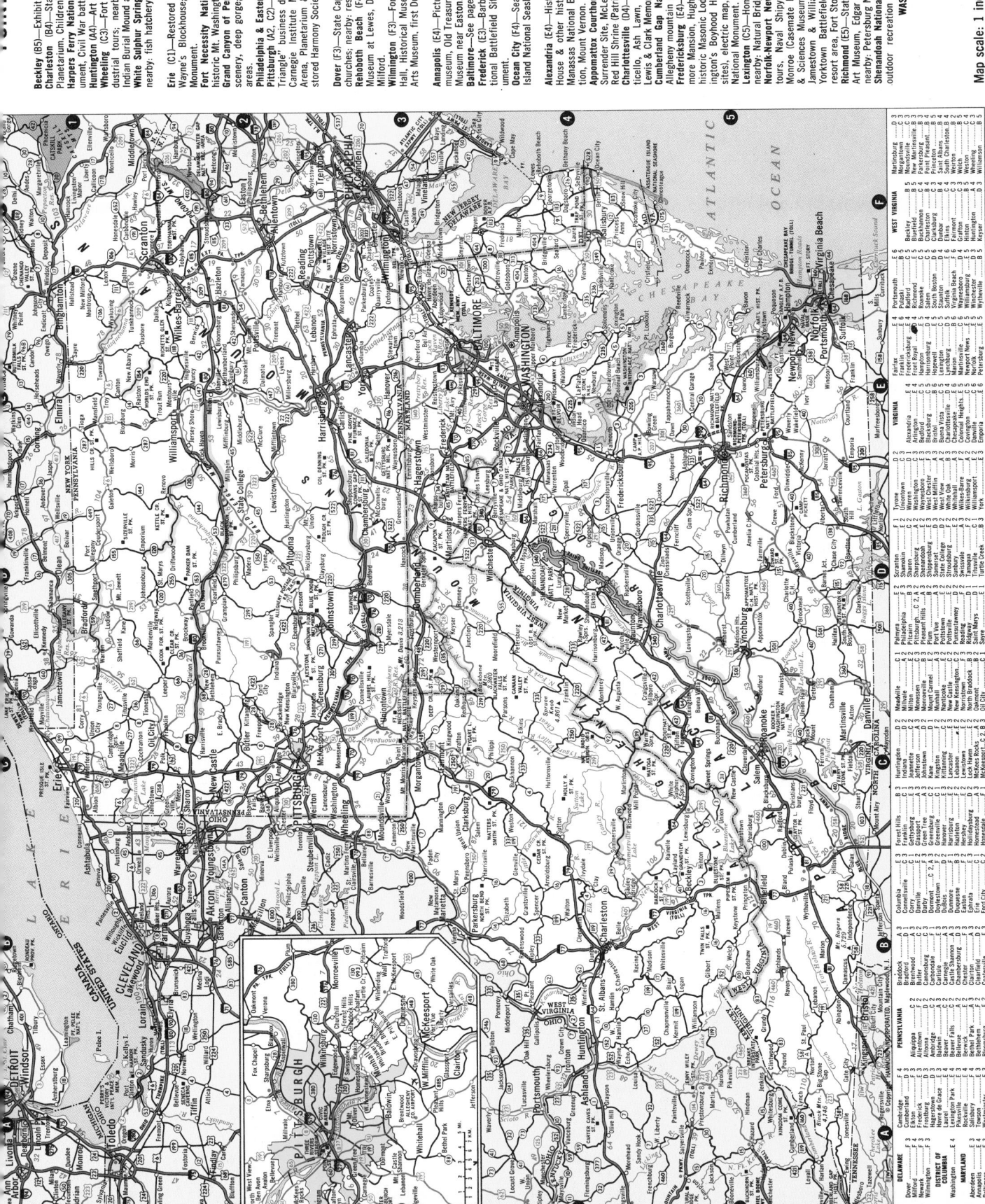

A7

POINTS OF INTEREST

GEORGIA

Atlanta (A3)—Gold-gilded State Capitol, Battle of Atlanta Cyclorama, Science & Industry Museum, Art Museum, Thornton House, Wren's Nest, Joel C. Harris House, Piedmont Park, Six Flags over Georgia (theme park), zoo, steel mill tours; nearby: Stone Mountain Memorial Park, Kennesaw Mountain National Battlefield Park.
Augusta (C4)—Art Institute, National Golf Club, historic houses.
Brunswick (C5)—Shrimp fleet, seafood processing plants, tours; nearby: Jekyll Island, St. Simons Island & Sea Island resorts, Fort Frederica National Monument, scenic Cumberland Island National Seashore.
Chickamauga & Chattanooga National Military Park (A2)—Nation's oldest military park, museum, Point Lookout & Missionary Ridge.
Columbus (A4)—Confederate Naval Museum, textile plant tours, historic home tours.
Macon (B4)—Greek-Revival architecture; nearby: Ocmulgee National Monument, Indian village excavations.
Milledgeville (B4)—Old State Capitol, Historical Museum; nearby: Lake Sinclair, water sports.
Okefenokee Swamp (B5)—Swamp wilderness area, abundant wildlife, nature trails, fishing.
Savannah (C5)—Picturesque riverfront, Pirates' House, Owens-Thomas House, Art Museum, Girl Scout Museum; nearby: Fort Pulaski National Monument, Fort Screven, lighthouse.
Warm Springs (A4)—Health resort, F. D. Roosevelt Home, park, museum.

SOUTH CAROLINA

Beaufort (C4)—Antebellum homes, Old Arsenal, Fort Walker; nearby: Parris Island Marine Base, historic Port Royal, Hilton Head resort, Sheldon Church ruins.
Charleston (D4)—Historic homes & churches, Old Slave Exchange, Battery Park, Dock Street Theatre, Old Powder Magazine, Art Gallery, Museum; nearby: Fort Sumter National Monument, Fort Moultrie, Cypress Gardens, Middleton Gardens, Magnolia Gardens.
Columbia (C3)—State House, Confederate Museum, Art Museum, planetarium, Woodrow Wilson's Boyhood Home, historic churches; nearby: Lake Murray, water sports, Congaree Swamp National Monument.
Georgetown (D4)—Historic homes; nearby: Belle Isle Gardens, Civil War fort, Brookgreen Gardens, Hampton Plantation, Myrtle Beach resort area.
Greenville (B3)—Sacred Art Museum, Bible collection, Arboretum, historic homes; nearby: Caesar's Head resort area.
Greenwood (C3)—Carillon foundry; nearby: Lake Greenwood.
Kings Mountain National Military Park (C2)—Museum; nearby: Cowpens National Battlefield.
Orangeburg (C4)—Edisto Memorial Gardens, American Rose Society garden.
Rock Hill (C2)—Glencairn Gardens, Nature Museum; nearby: Jackson's Birthplace.
Summerville (D4)—Historic Fort Dorchester, Pine Hurst Gardens; nearby: Lake Moultrie, water sports.
Sumter (D3)—Swan Lake Iris Gardens; nearby: Dunndell Gardens, Lake Marion recreation area.

NORTH CAROLINA

Asheville (B2)—Biltmore Estate, Thomas Wolfe Memorial; nearby: Craggy Gardens, Chimney Rock Park.
Cape Hatteras National Seashore (F2)—Unspoiled island chain, lighthouse, museum, beaches, bird refuges; nearby: Wright Brothers National Memorial, Fort Raleigh National Historic Site.
Charlotte (C2)—Art Museum, textile plant tours; nearby: Lake Norman, water sports.
Durham (D2)—Cigarette factory tours, tobacco auctions, Sarah Duke Gardens, Planetarium.
Great Smoky Mountains National Park (B2)—Picturesque mountain area, Cherokee Indian Village, museum, outdoor theater; nearby: Maggie Valley Railroad, Fontana Dam.
Morehead City (F3)—Deep-sea fishing center, fine beaches; nearby: Fort Macon State Park, fortifications, Cape Lookout National Seashore.
New Bern (E2)—First State Capitol, Tryon Palace, Firemen's Museum, historic churches.
Raleigh (E2)—State Capitol, State Museum, Historical Museum, Art Museum, Nuclear Reactor Building.
Wilmington (E3)—Resort city, Greenfield Gardens, Art Gallery; nearby: Orton Plantation, Airlie Gardens, historic Fort Fisher, Fort Caswell, Moores Creek National Military Park.
Winston-Salem (D2)—Cigarette factory tours, Old Salem (restored Moravian buildings), Reynolda Gardens; nearby: Guilford Courthouse National Military Park.

ALABAMA
- Dothan ... A 5
- Eufaula ... A 5
- Fort Payne ... A 3
- Opelika ... A 4
- Phenix City ... A 4

FLORIDA
- Chattahoochee ... A 6
- Fernandina Beach C 6
- Gainesville ... B 6
- Jacksonville ... C 6
- Jacksonville Beach ... C 6
- Lake City ... B 6
- Live Oak ... B 6
- Marianna ... A 6
- Palatka ... C 6
- Perry ... B 6
- Quincy ... A 6
- Saint Augustine ... C 6
- Tallahassee ... A 6

GEORGIA
- Adel ... B 5
- Albany ... A 5
- Alma ... B 5
- Americus ... A 5
- Arco ... C 5
- Athens ... B 3
- Atlanta ... A 3
- Augusta ... C 4
- Bainbridge ... A 5
- Barnesville ... A 4
- Baxley ... B 5
- Blakely ... A 5
- Brunswick ... C 5
- Buford ... B 3
- Cairo ... A 6
- Calhoun ... A 3
- Camilla ... A 5
- Carrollton ... A 3
- Cartersville ... A 3
- Cedartown ... A 3
- Cochran ... B 4
- College Park ... A 3
- Columbus ... A 4
- Commerce ... B 3
- Cordele ... B 5
- Covington ... B 3
- Cuthbert ... A 5
- Dalton ... A 3
- Dawson ... A 5
- Decatur ... A 3
- Douglas ... B 5
- Douglasville ... A 3
- Dublin ... B 4
- East Point ... A 3
- Eastman ... B 5
- Elberton ... B 3
- Fitzgerald ... B 5
- Forest Park ... A 3
- Forsyth ... B 4
- Fort Valley ... B 4
- Gainesville ... B 3
- Garden City ... C 5
- Griffin ... A 4
- Hartwell ... B 3
- Hawkinsville ... B 4
- Hazlehurst ... B 5
- Hogansville ... A 4
- Jesup ... C 5
- LaFayette ... A 3
- LaGrange ... A 4
- Lawrenceville ... B 3
- Macon ... B 4
- Manchester ... A 4
- Marietta ... A 3
- Milledgeville ... B 4
- Monroe ... B 3
- Montezuma ... A 4
- Moultrie ... B 5
- Nashville ... B 5
- Newnan ... A 4
- North Atlanta ... A 3
- Pelham ... A 5
- Perry ... B 4
- Quitman ... B 6
- Rockmart ... A 3
- Rome ... A 3
- Rossville ... A 2
- Savannah ... C 5
- Smyrna ... A 3
- Statesboro ... C 4
- Summerville ... A 3
- Swainsboro ... B 4
- Sylvania ... C 4
- Sylvester ... B 5
- Thomaston ... A 4
- Thomasville ... A 6
- Thomson ... B 4
- Tifton ... B 5
- Toccoa ... B 3
- Valdosta ... B 6
- Vidalia ... B 5
- Warner Robins ... B 4
- Washington ... B 3
- Waycross ... B 5
- Waynesboro ... C 4
- West Point ... A 4
- Winder ... B 3

KENTUCKY
- Campbellsville ... A 1
- Corbin ... A 1
- Hazard ... B 1
- Middlesboro ... B 1

NORTH CAROLINA
- Ahoskie ... F 1
- Albemarle ... D 2
- Asheboro ... D 2
- Asheville ... B 2
- Boone ... C 1
- Brevard ... B 2
- Burlington ... D 2
- Canton ... B 2
- Cary ... E 2
- Chapel Hill ... D 2
- Charlotte ... C 2
- Cherryville ... C 2
- Clinton ... E 2
- Concord ... D 2
- Dunn ... E 2
- Durham ... D 2
- Eden ... D 1
- Edenton ... F 2
- Elizabeth City ... F 1
- Farmville ... E 2
- Fayetteville ... D 2
- Forest City ... C 2
- Gastonia ... C 2
- Goldsboro ... E 2
- Graham ... D 2
- Greensboro ... D 2
- Greenville ... E 2
- Hamlet ... D 3
- Henderson ... E 1
- Hendersonville ... B 2
- Hickory ... C 2
- High Point ... D 2
- Jacksonville ... E 3
- Kannapolis ... C 2
- Kings Mountain ... C 2
- Kinston ... E 2
- Laurinburg ... D 3
- Lenoir ... C 2
- Lexington ... D 2
- Lincolnton ... C 2
- Lumberton ... D 3
- Midway Park ... E 3
- Monroe ... D 2
- Mooresville ... C 2
- Morehead City ... F 3
- Morganton ... C 2
- Mount Airy ... C 1
- Mount Olive ... E 2
- New Bern ... E 2
- Newton ... C 2
- North Wilkesboro ... C 2
- Oxford ... E 1
- Plymouth ... F 2
- Raleigh ... E 2
- Reidsville ... D 1
- Roanoke Rapids ... E 1
- Rocky Mount ... E 2
- Roxboro ... D 1
- Salisbury ... D 2
- Sanford ... D 2
- Shelby ... C 2
- Siler City ... D 2
- Smithfield ... E 2
- Southern Pines ... D 2
- Spindale ... C 2
- Spring Lake ... D 2
- Statesville ... C 2
- Tarboro ... E 2
- Thomasville ... D 2
- Wadesboro ... D 2
- Washington ... F 2
- Waynesville ... B 2
- Whiteville ... E 3
- Williamston ... F 2
- Wilmington ... E 3
- Wilson ... E 2
- Winston-Salem ... D 2

SOUTH CAROLINA
- Abbeville ... B 3
- Aiken ... C 4
- Allendale ... C 4
- Anderson ... B 3
- Barnwell ... C 4
- Batesburg ... C 3
- Beaufort ... C 4
- Bennettsville ... D 3
- Bishopville ... D 3
- Camden ... C 3
- Cayce ... C 3
- Charleston ... D 4
- Cheraw ... D 3
- Chester ... C 3
- Clinton ... C 3
- Clover ... C 2
- Columbia ... C 3
- Conway ... D 3
- Darlington ... D 3
- Denmark ... C 4
- Dillon ... D 3
- Easley ... B 3
- Florence ... D 3
- Gaffney ... C 2
- Georgetown ... D 4
- Great Falls ... C 3
- Greenville ... B 3
- Greenwood ... C 3
- Greer ... B 2
- Hartsville ... D 3
- Kingstree ... D 3
- Lake City ... D 3
- Lancaster ... C 3
- Laurens ... C 3
- Manning ... D 3
- Mount Pleasant ... D 4
- Mullins ... D 3
- Myrtle Beach ... E 3
- Newberry ... C 3
- Orangeburg ... C 4
- Rock Hill ... C 2
- Seneca ... B 3
- Spartanburg ... C 2
- Sumter ... D 3
- Union ... C 3
- Walterboro ... C 4
- Winnsboro ... C 3
- Woodruff ... C 3
- York ... C 2

TENNESSEE
- Athens ... A 2
- Bristol ... C 1
- Chattanooga ... A 2
- Cleveland ... A 2
- Cookeville ... A 1
- Elizabethton ... C 1
- Greeneville ... B 2
- Harriman ... A 2
- Johnson City ... B 1
- Kingsport ... B 1
- Knoxville ... B 2
- LaFollette ... A 1
- Maryville ... B 2
- McMinnville ... A 2
- Morristown ... B 1
- Newport ... B 2
- Oak Ridge ... A 2

VIRGINIA
- Bedford ... D 1
- Blacksburg ... D 1
- Bristol ... C 1
- Chesapeake ... F 1
- Colonial Heights ... E 1
- Danville ... D 1
- Emporia ... E 1
- Hampton ... F 1
- Hopewell ... E 1
- Lynchburg ... D 1
- Marion ... C 1
- Martinsville ... D 1
- Newport News ... F 1
- Norfolk ... F 1
- Norton ... B 1
- Petersburg ... E 1
- Portsmouth ... F 1
- Radford ... D 1
- Roanoke ... D 1
- Salem ... D 1
- South Boston ... D 1
- Suffolk ... F 1
- Virginia Beach ... F 1

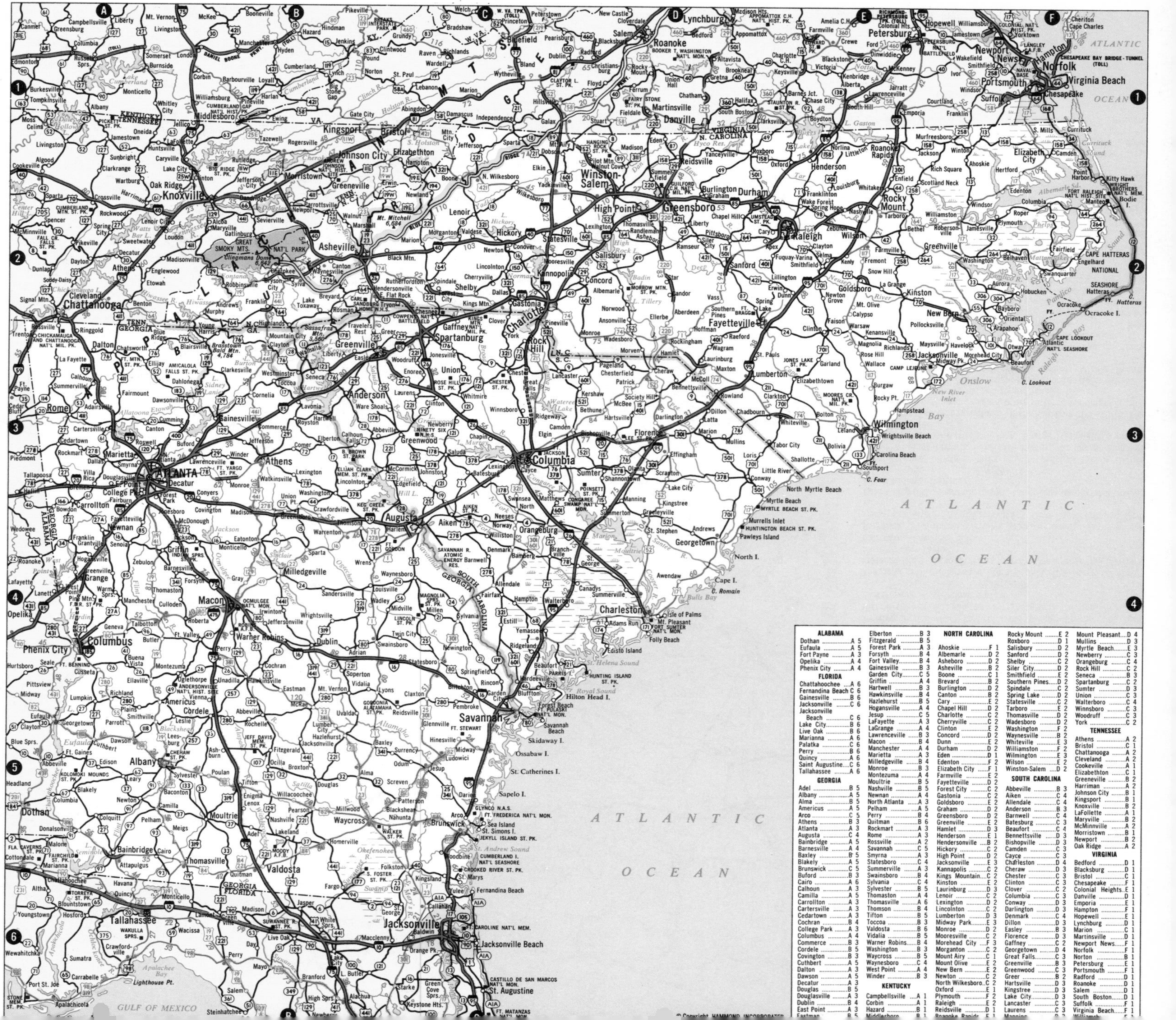

FLORIDA

Cape Canaveral (F3)—John F. Kennedy Space Center, drive-through tours only, Space Museum; nearby: Patrick Air Force Base, missile exhibit; Real Eight Treasure Gallery.

Daytona Beach (E2)—Leading seashore vacation area, International Speedway, greyhound racing; nearby: scenic Tomoka State Park.

Everglades National Park (F6)—Subtropical Wilderness area, mangrove swamps, rare birds, fish & plants, Seminole Indian Village, Wilderness Tram Train, nature trails, museum, boat rides; nearby: Orchid Jungle, Coral Castle.

Florida Caverns State Park (B1)—Underground tours.

Fort Lauderdale (F5, A4)—Vacation center, fine beaches, cruises from Port Everglades, scenic Hugh Taylor Birch State Park, Bahia Mar Marina, deep-sea fishing; nearby: Seminole Indian Village, greyhound racing, jai-alai fronton.

Fort Myers (E5)—Former winter home of Edison, house & laboratory tour, Marine Museum, shell factory; nearby: shell collecting on Captiva & Sanibel Islands, Cape Coral Gardens, Koreshan State Park, former religious settlement, museum.

Fort Pierce (F4)—Sport-fishing center, citrus packing & canning plants, tours; nearby: McKee Jungle Garden.

Gainesville (D2)—State Museum, antebellum mansions.

Jacksonville (E1)—Oriental Gardens, Art Museum, Harriet B. Stowe Home, Gator Bowl, zoo; nearby: Fort Caroline National Memorial, Fort Clinch & Fort George.

Key Largo (F6)—Off-shore exploration of living coral reef at John Pennekamp Coral Reef State Park, glass-bottom boats nearby: Sunken Treasure Fortress, Theater-of-the-Sea.

Key West (E6)—Hemingway House, Audubon House, Aquarium; nearby: Fort Jefferson National Monument, reached by boat.

Lake Wales (E3)—Mountain lake, Sanctuary, Singing Bok Tower, carillon recitals, Passion Play; nearby: mosaic replica of da Vinci's masterpiece "The Last Supper."

Miami (F5, A6)—Luxurious resort city, Seaquarium, Vizcaya (County Museum), Spanish monastery, Historical Museum, International Design Centre, Wax Museum, zoo, greyhound racing, jai-alai fronton; nearby: Serpentarium, Parrot Jungle, Monkey Jungle, living coral reef at Biscayne National Monument.

Miami Beach (F5)—Famous "Hotel Row," recreation pier, Museum of Art.

Ocala (E2)—Horse-breeding center; nearby: Silver Springs, glass-bottom boats, Early American Museum, Reptile Institute, Rainbow Springs.

Orlando (E3)—Exposition Park, Observatory; nearby: Mead Botanical Gardens, Citrus Tower.

Panama City (B1)—Sport-fishing center, fine beaches; nearby: scenic St. Andrews State Park.

Pensacola (A1)—Naval Aviation Museum, Fort San Carlos, Fort Barrancas, historic Fort Pickens State Park, fine beaches.

St. Augustine (E2)—Nation's oldest city, Castillo de San Marcos National Monument, Oldest House, Oldest Wooden Schoolhouse, Mission, Fountain of Youth, Indian Burial Mound, Wax Museum, alligator farms, Museum of Hobbies, Outdoor Amphitheater; nearby: Marineland, Fort Matanzas National Monument.

St. Petersburg (D4, B3)—Popular retirement city, Sunken Gardens, Art Museum, greyhound racing; nearby: Fort De Soto Park, Aquatarium, Wax Museum.

Sarasota (D4)—Ringling Museum of Art, Ringling residence, Museum of American Circus, Circus Hall of Fame, Cars of Yesterday Exhibit, Jungle Gardens; nearby: De Soto National Monument, Floridaland, Gamble Mansion.

Stephen Foster Memorial (D1-near White Springs)—Museum, boat rides on Suwannee River, carillon recitals.

Tallahassee (C1)—State Capitol, tours, antebellum homes; nearby: Maclay Gardens State Park, Wakulla Springs, boat cruises.

Tampa (D3, B2)—Busch Gardens, brewery tours, cigar factory tours, Latin Quarter, Lowry Park Fairyland, jai-alai fronton; nearby: Weeki Wachee Springs.

Walt Disney World (E3)—Family amusement center.

Weeki Wachee Springs (D3)—Underwater ballet, glass-bottom boats, river cruises.

West Palm Beach (F4)—Art Galleries, Flagler Mansion, museum, greyhound racing, sightseeing boats; nearby: Jonathan Dickinson State Park, excellent beaches.

Winter Haven (E3)—Citrus Museum; nearby: Cypress Gardens, water-skiing shows, cruises.

Map scale: 1 inch=58 miles

A9

POINTS OF INTEREST

TENNESSEE

Chattanooga (E2)—Rock City Gardens, Confederama, Incline Railroad; nearby: National Military Park, Ruby Falls, Chickamauga Dam.
Fort Donelson National Military Park (D1–near Dover)—Civil War battlefield, earthworks; nearby: Land Between The Lakes National Recreation Area.
Great Smoky Mountains National Park (F2)—Scenic mountainous area, hiking & nature trails, camping, waterfalls, Cherokee Indian Village, museum, outdoor theater.
Greeneville (F1)—Andrew Johnson National Historic Site, homestead, shop, burial site.
Knoxville (E2)—Confederate Memorial Hall, Blount House; nearby: Museum of Atomic Energy at Oak Ridge, Norris Lake, water sports, Confederate Park; nearby: restored Chucalissa Indian Village.
Memphis (C2)—Cotton Exchange, City Museum, Art Gallery, Confederate Park; nearby: restored Chucalissa Indian Village.
Murfreesboro (D2)—Former state capital; nearby: Stones River National Military Park.
Nashville (D2)—State Capitol, The Parthenon (art museum), Fort Nashborough replica, State Museum & Planetarium, Children's Museum; nearby: Andrew Jackson's Hermitage.
Shiloh National Military Park (C2)—Famous Peach Orchard, Hornet's Nest, relic museum.

MISSISSIPPI

Biloxi (C5)—Oldest Mississippi settlement, Old Lighthouse, Beauvoir (Jefferson Davis home), All Southern Museum, shrimp boat fleet; nearby: Old Spanish Fort.
Gulf Islands National Seashore (C5)—Beautiful beaches, abundant waterfowl.
Gulfport (C5)—Beach resort; nearby: Dixie White House at Pass Christian, colorful gardens.
Jackson (C4)—State Capitol, Historical Museum, model of Mississippi River Basin, Mynelle Gardens.
Natchez (B4)—Historic mansions (Dunleith, Stanton Hall, Longwood, Auburn, Holly Hedges, The Elms), Connelly's Tavern; nearby: scenic Natchez Trace Parkway.
Tupelo (C3)—National Battlefield Site, federal fish hatchery; nearby: Brices Cross Roads National Battlefield Site.
Vicksburg (B4)—Historic river port, National Military Park, fortifications & trenches, museum, Old Court House Museum, sternwheel river boats, U.S. Army Engineer Waterways Experiment Station.

ALABAMA

Birmingham (D3)—Vulcan Statue, Arlington Confederate Shrine, Art Museum; nearby: Vestavia, Greek temple replica.
Gadsden (E3)—Scenic Noccalula Falls; nearby: Little River Canyon.
De Soto Falls.
Gulf State Park (D5)—Beach resorts, water sports; nearby: historic Fort Morgan.
Huntsville (D2)—Space Orientation Center, exhibits; nearby: Cathedral Caverns.
Mobile (D5)—Scenic Azalea Trail, Clarke, Oakleigh & Long Gardens, USS Alabama memorial; nearby: Bellingrath Gardens, Fort Gaines.
Montgomery (D4)—State Capitol, Confederate Monument, Jefferson Davis Home, White House of the Confederacy.
Russell Cave National Monument (E2)—Important archaeological site, Visitor Center.

Map Scale: 1 inch=25 miles

A10

POINTS OF INTEREST

INDIANA

Corydon (C4)—Old State Capitol; nearby: National Steamboat Museum, Wyandotte and Marengo Caves.

Fort Wayne (C2)—Lincoln Museum, Cathedral of the Immaculate Conception.

Indianapolis (C3)—Copper-domed State Capitol, State Library & Historical Building, War Memorial Plaza, Soldiers' & Sailors' Monument, Children's Museum, Observatory & Planetarium, Auto Speedway & Museum.

Lafayette (B3)—Tippecanoe Historical Museum; nearby: Tippecanoe Battleground, restored Fort Ouiatenon.

Lincoln Boyhood National Memorial (B5-near Lincoln State Park)—Site of Family Homestead and grave of Lincoln's mother; nearby: Lincoln Pioneer Village.

Michigan City (B1)—International Friendship Gardens, European Antiques Museum; nearby: scenic Indiana Dunes National Lakeshore.

Mounds State Park (C3)—Well-preserved earthworks of ancient Indian Mound Builders.

New Harmony (B5)—Site of two 19th century social experiments in communal living, Old Rappite Fort, Rapp-Maclure-Owen Roofless Church, Workingmen's Institute.

South Bend (C1)—Council Oak Tree, Pierre Navarre Cabin, Courthouse Museum, University Art Gallery.

Vincennes (B4)—Oldest state city, first Territorial Capitol, George Rogers Clark Memorial, William Henry Harrison House, Old Cathedral of St. Xavier.

OHIO

Akron (F2)—Rubber center, plant tours; Goodyear Air Dock, John Brown Home, 65-room Stan Hywet Hall, Children's Zoo, annual Soap Box Derby.

Bellefontaine (D3)—Center of scenic and historic region; nearby: Indian Lake State Park recreation areas, Ohio and Zane Caverns.

Canton (F2)—McKinley Monument, Art Institute, Pro Football Hall of Fame.

Chillicothe (E3)—Greek-revival mansions, Adena Mansion; nearby: Mound City Group National Monument.

Cincinnati (D4)—Taft Museum, Museum of Natural History, Art Museum, conservatory, zoo, Stowe House, Union Terminal; nearby: Grant Birthplace, McGuffey Museum.

Cleveland (F1)—Terminal Tower, Museum of Art, Museum of Natural History, Health Museum, Auto & Aviation Museum, Dunham Tavern, Lighting Institute, aquarium, planetarium.

Columbus (E3)—State Capitol, Historical Society Museum, Fine Arts Gallery, Leveque-Lincoln Tower, Park of Roses, zoo; nearby: Perkins Observatory, Olentangy Caverns.

Dayton (D3)—Art Institute, Dunbar House, Newcom Tavern, Deeds Carillon; nearby: Wright Brothers Memorial, Air Force Museum.

Marietta (F3)—Oldest state settlement, Campus Martius Historical Museum, Snyder Sternwheeler, Mound Cemetery.

New Philadelphia (F2)—Warther Museum (wood carvings); nearby: Schoenbrunn and Zoar Village State Memorials.

Sandusky (E2)—Tourist center, island cruises; nearby: Perry's Victory and International Peace Memorial, Kelleys Island (glacial grooves, pictographs), Blue Hole spring and grotto, Edison Birthplace, Marine Museum.

Toledo (D1)—Museum of Art, Museum of Science & Natural History, Zoo, aquarium.

Youngstown (F2)—Institute of American Art, Mill Creek Park (Natural History Museum, Pioneer Pavilion, Old Mill Museum).

KENTUCKY

Bardstown (C5)—"My Old Kentucky Home" shrine, St. Joseph's Cathedral; nearby: Abraham Lincoln Birthplace National Historic Site.

Cumberland Gap National Historic Park (D6)—Famous transallegheny mountain pass used by early explorers and pioneers.

Frankfort (D4)—State Capitol, Old State House Museum, Daniel Boone Monument.

Harrodsburg (D5)—Pioneer Memorial State Park with reconstructed frontier settlement.

Henderson (B5)—Audubon Park bird sanctuary and memorial to the famous naturalist.

Lexington (D5)—Center of Bluegrass Region, horse farms, Henry Clay Home.

Louisville (C4)—Annual Kentucky Derby, Derby Museum, Railway Museum, Art Museum, Farmington Home; nearby: Fort Knox Gold Depository, Patton Military Museum.

Mammoth Cave National Park (C5)—150 miles of explored underground passages.

Map scale: 1 inch=58 miles

INDEX

ILLINOIS

Benton	A5
Cairo	A6
Carbondale	A6
Carmi	A5
Chicago Heights	B2
Cicero	B2
Du Quoin	A5
Eldorado	A5
Harrisburg	A5
Highland Park	B1
Joliet	B2
Kankakee	B3
Lake Forest	B1
Marion	A5
Metropolis	A6
Mound City	A6
Murphysboro	A5
Normal	A4
North Chicago	B1
Paris	B4
Robinson	B4
Shawnee	A5
Waukegan	B1
Zion	B1

KENTUCKY

Ashland	E4
Bardstown	C5
Campbellsville	C5
Corbin	D6
Danville	D5
Elizabethtown	C5
Georgetown	D4
Glasgow	C5
Hopkinsville	B5
Lexington	D5
Louisville	C4
Madisonville	B5
Mayfield	A6
Maysville	E4
Middlesboro	E6
Murray	A6
Owensboro	B5
Paducah	A5
Paris	D4
Pikeville	F5
Richmond	D5
Winchester	D5

MICHIGAN

Adrian	D1
Albion	C1
Battle Creek	C1
Benton Harbor	B1
Coldwater	C1
Dearborn	D1
Detroit	D1
Jackson	C1
Kalamazoo	B1
Lansing	C1
Lincoln Park	D1
Livonia	D1
Monroe	D1
Niles	B1
Pontiac	D1
Royal Oak	D1
Saint Clair Shores	D1
Saint Joseph	B1
Sturgis	C1
Warren	D1

INDIANA

Anderson	C3
Auburn	C2
Bedford	C4
Bloomington	C4
Brazil	B4
Columbus	C4
Connersville	C4
Crawfordsville	B3
Decatur	C3
Elkhart	C1
Elwood	C3
Evansville	B5
Fort Wayne	C2
Frankfort	B3
Franklin	C4
Gary	B1
Goshen	C1
Greencastle	B4
Greenfield	C3
Hammond	B1
Hobart	B1
Huntington	C2
Indianapolis	C3
Jasper	B5
Jeffersonville	C5
Kokomo	C3
LaPorte	B1
Lafayette	B3
Lebanon	B3
Linton	B4
Logansport	B3
Madison	C5
Marion	C3
Michigan City	B1
Mishawaka	C1
Muncie	C3
New Albany	C5
New Castle	C3
Peru	C3
Plainfield	B4
Princeton	B5
Richmond	C3
Rochester	C2
Seymour	C4
Shelbyville	C4
South Bend	C1
Terre Haute	B4
Tipton	C3
Valparaiso	B1
Vincennes	B4
Wabash	C3
Warsaw	C2
Washington	B4
Winchester	C3
West Lafayette	B3

OHIO

Akron	E1
Alliance	F2
Ashland	E2
Ashtabula	F1
Athens	E3
Barberton	E2
Bellaire	F2
Bellefontaine	D3
Bowling Green	D1
Brunswick	E1
Bucyrus	E2
Cambridge	F2
Canton	F2
Celina	C3
Chillicothe	E3
Cincinnati	D4
Circleville	E3
Cleveland	E1
Columbus	E3
Conneaut	F1
Coshocton	E2
Dayton	D3
Defiance	C2
Delaware	E3
Delphos	D2
East Liverpool	F2
Elyria	E1
Findlay	D2
Fostoria	D2
Franklin	D3
Fremont	D1
Gallipolis	E4
Greenville	C3
Hamilton	D3
Huntington	E2

POINTS OF INTEREST

WISCONSIN

Apostle Islands National Lakeshore (B2)—Wilderness area, explorer trails.

Appleton (C4)—Paper Chemistry Museum.

Baraboo (B5)—Circus World Museum, County Historical Museum; nearby: quartzite cliffs of Devils Lake State Park.

Fond du Lac (C5)—Galloway House, St. Paul's Cathedral.

Green Bay (C4)—Oldest Wisconsin settlement; Roi-Porlier-Tank Cottage, Fort Howard Hospital Museum, National Railroad Museum.

Interstate State Park (A3)—Scenic gorge, "Old Man of the Dalles" rock formation.

La Crosse (A5)—Grandad Bluff Overlook, scenic drive.

Lake Winnebago (C5)—Popular year-round vacation area.

Madison (B5)—State Capitol, U.S. Forest Products Laboratory, Historical Society Museum, Observatory & Planetarium, University Arboretum; nearby: Swiss Village and Chalet of the Golden Fleece, Little Norway.

Milwaukee (C5)—Civic Center, Art Center, Public Museum (science and history), Washington Park and County Zoos, Brewery Tours.

Mineral Point (B5)—Restored homes of Cornish lead miners.

Oshkosh (C4)—Art Center & Arboretum.

Portage (B5)—Old Fort Winnebago Surgeon's Quarters, Indian Agency House.

Prairie du Chien (A5)—Villa Louis historic mansion, Museum of Medical Progress, Michel Brisbois House.

Racine (C5)—Johnson Wax Research Center, Art Center.

Rhinelander (B3)—Vacation area, Logging Museum.

Ripon (C5)—Little White Schoolhouse (birthplace of Republican Party), Long House historic community center.

Spooner (A3)—Woodcarving Museum; nearby: "Historyland" Indian village and logging camp.

Sturgeon Bay (C4)—Center of the peninsular vacation area.

Superior (A2)—World's tallest grain elevator and largest iron ore docks, Historical Museum.

Watertown (C5)—57-room Octagon House and nearby restored "first kindergarten" in the United States.

Wisconsin Dells (B5)—Picturesque intricate rock shapes formed by erosion of sandstone.

MICHIGAN

Battle Creek (D6)—"Cereal capital of the world," factory tours, Leila Arboretum.

Benton Harbor (D6)—World's largest wholesale noncitrus fruit and vegetable market, House of David religious colony.

Detroit (F6, F1)—Automotive center of the world, plant tours; Civic Center, Institute of Arts, Historical Museum, International Institute, Children's Museum, Belle Isle Park (Conservatory, Children's Zoo, Aquarium, Great Lakes Museum), Fort Wayne Military Museum, Zoo; nearby: Greenfield Village and Ford Museum in Dearborn, Cranbrook Art Galleries.

Flint (E5)—Automobile center, plant tours, Cultural Center.

Grand Rapids (D5)—Furniture Museum, Public Museum, Art Gallery, Zoo.

Holland (D5)—Dutch heritage community, annual Tulip Time Festival, Netherlands Museum, Little Netherlands, Windmill Island, Wooden Shoe Factory, Furniture Museum.

Houghton-Hancock (C2)—Center of copper region, mine tours, Mineralogical Museum.

Iron Mountain (C3)—Winter sports center, tours of underground Iron Mountain Iron Mine.

Ishpeming (C3)—National Ski Hall of Fame & Ski Museum, large Mather Iron Mine.

Isle Royale National Park (C2)—Scenic wilderness and wildlife sanctuary including moose, wolves and numerous species of birds.

Lansing (E5)—State Capitol & War Relic Museum, Historical Museum, auto plant tours.

Mackinac Island (D4)—Famous resort center, restored Old Fort Mackinac, John Jacob Astor House; nearby: five-mile long Mackinac Bridge, reconstructed Fort Michilimackinac.

Manistee (D4)—Historic Ramsdell Opera House, Historical Museum, salt plant tours.

Munising (D3)—Cruises to Pictured Rocks immortalized in Longfellow's "Hiawatha."

Sault Ste. Marie (E3)—Locks of St. Mary's River (Soo Locks), boat cruises through locks.

Sleeping Bear Dunes National Lakeshore (D4-6 mi. north of Empire)—High sand dunes, glacial deposits.

Tahquamenon Falls State Park (D3-8 mi. southwest of Paradise)—Picturesque 40-foot falls.

A12

ILLINOIS

Cahokia (F6)—Oldest town in Illinois, Log Cabin Courthouse, Old Church of the Holy Family.

Cairo (E6)—Levee protected at confluence of Ohio and Mississippi Rivers, Magnolia Manor.

Champaign-Urbana (E3)—University of Illinois' Natural History Building, Classical and European Culture Museum and Art Museum.

Chicago (E2)—The Loop, Merchandise Mart, Mercantile Exchange, Board of Trade Building, Midwest Stock Exchange, Grant Park (Art Institute, Natural History Museum, Aquarium, Planetarium & Astronomical Museum), Lincoln Park (Zoo, Conservatory, Academy of Science, Historical Society, Museum of Science & Industry, Oriental Institute, Soldier Field, Marina City; nearby: Chicago Zoological Park, Baha'i Temple, Hinsdale Health Museum, Great Lakes Naval Training Station, Great America (theme park).

Dickson Mounds State Memorial (D3-near Lewistown)—Remains of more than 200 Indian mounds, artifacts.

Elgin (E2)—Academy of Fine Arts, Audubon Museum.

Galena (D1)—Ulysses S. Grant Home, restored Market House, Historical Society Museum.

Nauvoo (C3)—Former Mormon settlement, Joseph Smith Home & Mansion House, old Carthage Jail.

New Salem State Park (D3)—Authentically restored village where Lincoln lived, museum.

Rockford (D2)—Tinker Swiss Cottage.

Springfield (D4)—State Capitol, restored Lincoln Home National Historic Site, Lincoln Tomb, Old State Capitol, State Museum (history and science).

Map scale: 1 inch=68 miles

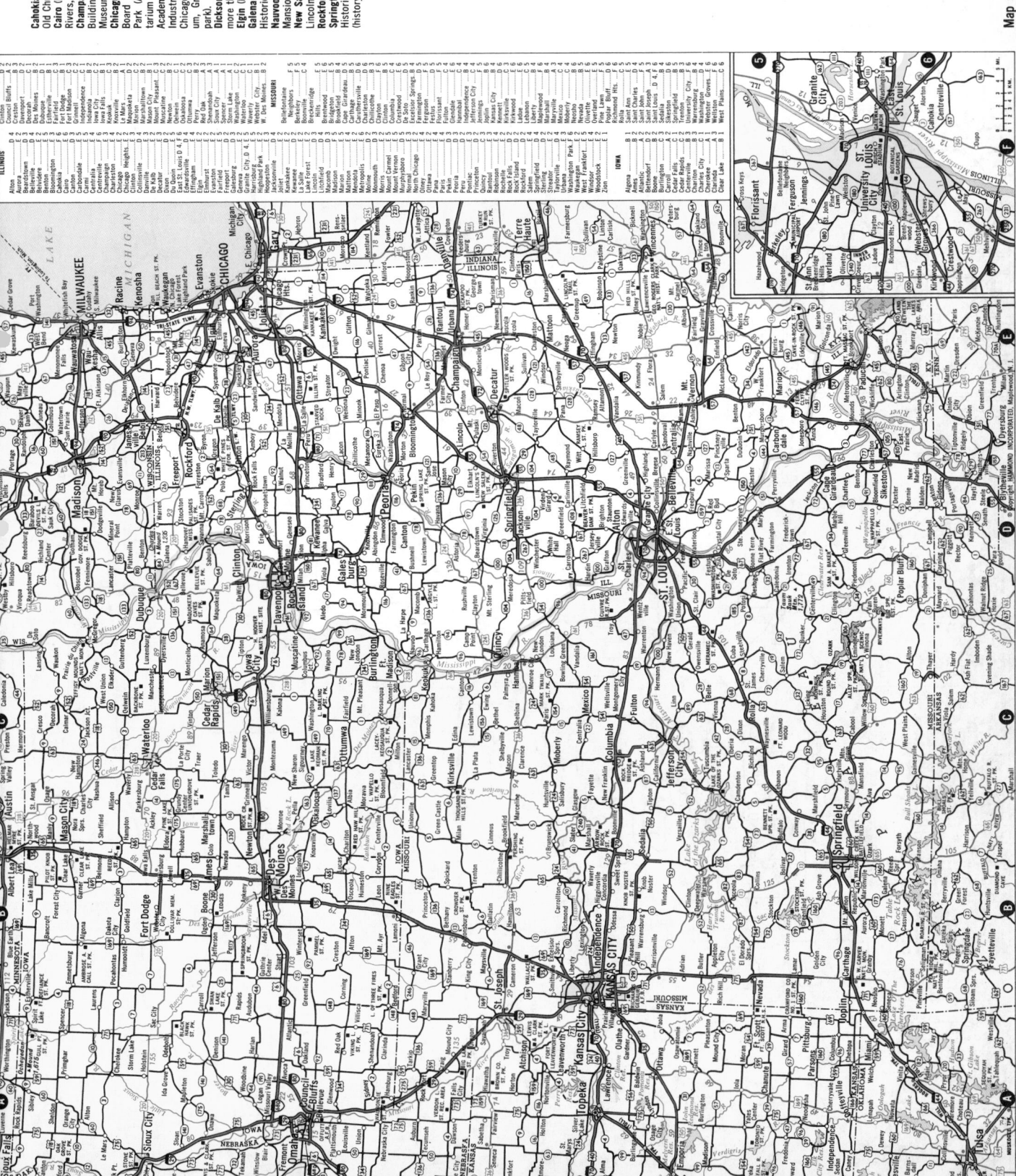

POINTS OF INTEREST

MINNESOTA

Bemidji (D3)—Giant statues of Paul Bunyan and his Blue Ox, wildlife museum, aquarium.

Brainerd (E4)—Paul Bunyan Center; nearby: Lumbertown, U.S.A. (replica of 1870 town).

Duluth (F4)—Aerial Lift Bridge, Skyline Parkway, Bible House, Leif Erikson boat replica.

Ely (F3)—Gateway to Superior National Forest recreation areas, wilderness tours, hunting.

Grand Portage National Monument (F3)—Nine-mile land trail, route of explorers; reconstructed North West Company settlement.

Hibbing (E3)—Center of vast iron ore region, world's largest open pit mine, other large mines; nearby: Museum of Mining at Chisholm.

Itasca State Park (D4)—Forested vacation area, source of Mississippi River.

Minneapolis (E5, E1)—Grain Exchange, Minnehaha Park (Falls, Hiawatha & Minnehaha Statues), St. Anthony Falls, Foshay Tower, Guthrie Theater, Art Center, American Swedish Museum, Art Institute, Natural History Museum.

Pipestone National Monument (D5)—Red-stone quarries from which Indians obtained materials for making ceremonial peace pipes.

Rochester (E5)—World-renowned Mayo Clinic.

Saint Paul (E5, F1)—State Capitol, Sibley House Museum, Historical Society Museum, Science Museum, Zoo, Indian Mounds Park.

Voyageurs National Park (E3)—Scenic lake and forest area, historic canoe routes.

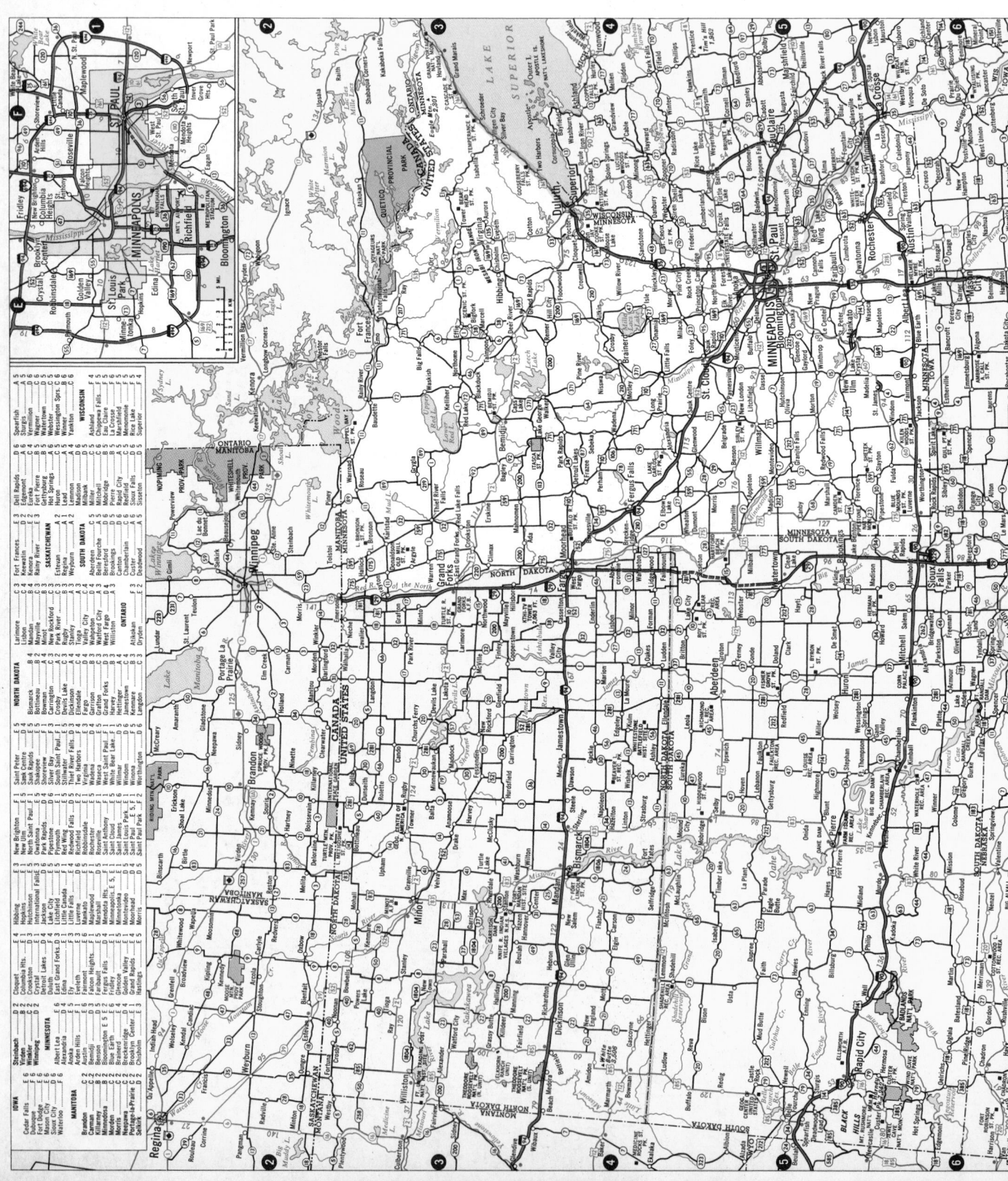

NEW YORK METROPOLITAN AREA

CHICAGO METROPOLITAN AREA

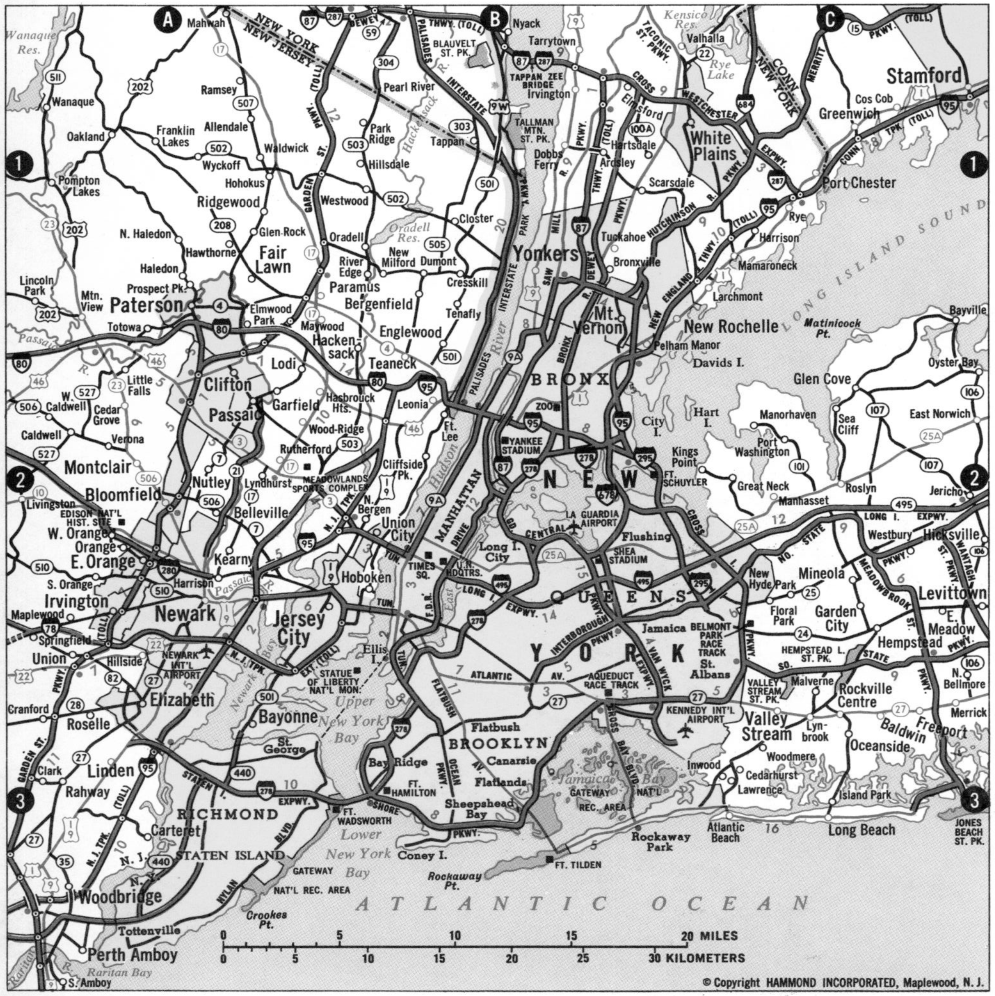

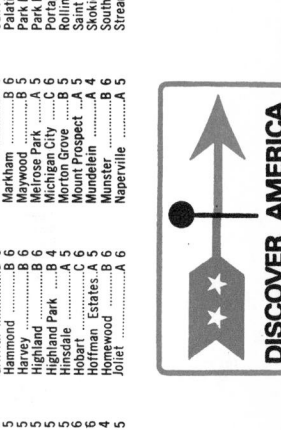

DISCOVER AMERICA

© Copyright HAMMOND INCORPORATED, Maplewood, N.J.

New York Metropolitan Area Index

City	Ref	City	Ref
Baldwin	C 3	Maplewood	A 2
Bayonne	A 3	Maywood	A 2
Belleville	A 2	Merrick	C 3
Bergenfield	B 1	Mineola	C 2
Bloomfield	A 2	Montclair	A 2
Caldwell	A 2	Mount Vernon	B 1
Carteret	A 3	New Hyde Park	C 2
Cedar Grove	A 2	New Milford	B 1
Clark	A 3	New Rochelle	B 2
Cliffside Park	B 2	New York	B 2
Clifton	A 2	Newark	A 2
Cranford	A 3	North Bellmore	C 3
Dumont	B 1	North Bergen	B 2
Dobbs Ferry	B 1	Nutley	A 2
East Meadow	C 2	Nyack	B 1
East Orange	A 2	Oakland	A 1
East Paterson	A 1	Oceanside	C 3
Elizabeth	A 3	Orange	A 2
Elmsford	B 1	Paramus	A 1
Englewood	B 2	Passaic	A 2
Fair Lawn	A 1	Paterson	A 1
Floral Park	C 2	Perth Amboy	A 3
Fort Lee	B 2	Pompton Lakes	A 1
Freeport	C 3	Port Chester	C 1
Garden City	C 2	Port Washington	C 2
Garfield	A 1	Rahway	A 3
Glen Cove	C 1	Ramsey	A 1
Glen Rock	A 1	Ridgewood	A 1
Great Neck	C 2	River Edge	B 1
Greenwich	C 1	Rockville Centre	C 3
Hackensack	B 2	Roselle	A 3
Harrison, N.J.	A 2	Rutherford	A 2
Harrison, N.Y.	C 1	Rye	C 1
Hawthorne	A 1	Scarsdale	B 1
Hempstead	C 2	South Orange	A 2
Hicksville	C 2	Springfield	A 2
Hillsdale	B 1	Stamford	C 1
Hillside	A 3	Tarrytown	B 1
Hoboken	B 2	Teaneck	B 2
Irvington	A 2	Tenafly	B 1
Jericho	C 2	Totowa	A 1
Jersey City	B 2	Union	A 2
Kearny	A 2	Union City	B 2
Kings Point	C 2	Valley Stream	C 3
Larchmont	C 1	Verona	A 2
Levittown	C 2	Waldwick	A 1
Linden	A 3	West Caldwell	A 2
Little Falls	A 2	West Orange	A 2
Livingston	A 2	Westbury	C 2
Lodi	A 1	Westwood	B 1
Long Beach	C 3	White Plains	B 1
Lyndhurst	A 2	Woodbridge	A 3
Malverne	C 2	Woodmere	C 3
Mamaroneck	C 1	Wyckoff	A 1
		Yonkers	B 1

© Copyright HAMMOND INCORPORATED, Maplewood, N.J.

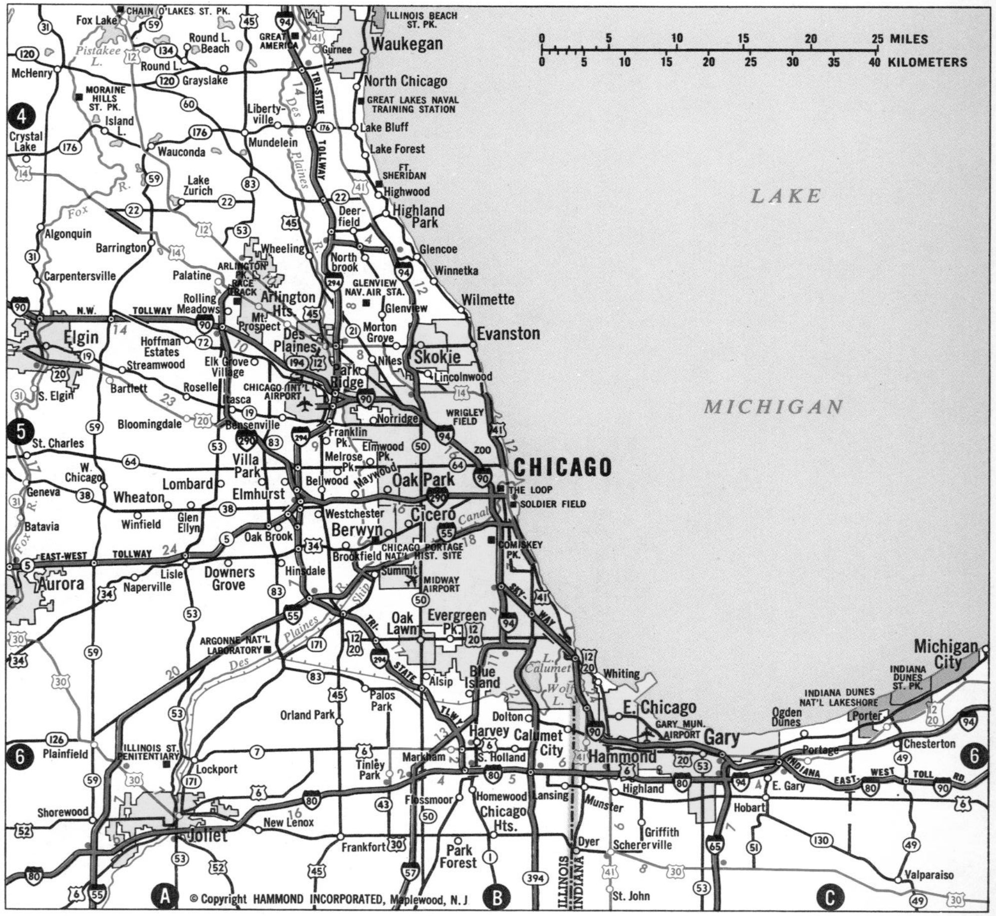

Chicago Metropolitan Area Index

City	Ref	City	Ref
Arlington Heights	A 5	Lake Forest	B 4
Aurora	A 5	Lansing	B 6
Barrington	A 4	Libertyville	B 4
Batavia	A 5	Lincolnwood	B 5
Bellwood	B 5	Lockport	A 6
Bensenville	B 5	Lombard	B 5
Berwyn	B 5	Markham	B 6
Blue Island	B 6	Maywood	B 5
Brookfield	B 5	Melrose Park	B 5
Calumet City	B 6	Michigan City	C 6
Carpentersville	A 4	Morton Grove	B 4
Chicago	B 5	Mount Prospect	A 5
Chicago Heights	B 6	Mundelein	B 4
Cicero	B 5	Munster	B 6
Crystal Lake	A 4	Naperville	A 5
Deerfield	B 4	Niles	B 5
Des Plaines	A 5	Norridge	B 5
Dolton	B 6	North Chicago	B 4
Downers Grove	A 5	Northbrook	B 5
East Chicago	C 6	Oak Lawn	B 6
East Gary	C 6	Oak Park	B 5
Elgin	A 4	Palatine	A 5
Elk Grove Village	A 5	Park Forest	B 6
Elmhurst	B 5	Park Ridge	B 5
Elmwood Park	B 5	Portage	C 6
Evanston	B 5	Rolling Meadows	A 5
Evergreen Park	B 6	Saint Charles	A 5
Flossmoor	B 6	Skokie	B 5
Fox Lake	A 4	South Holland	B 6
Franklin Park	A 5	Streamwood	A 5
Gary	C 6	Summit	B 5
Geneva	A 5	Tinley Park	B 6
Glen Ellyn	B 5	Valparaiso	C 6
Glencoe	B 4	Villa Park	B 5
Glenview	B 5	Waukegan	B 4
Griffith	C 6	West Chicago	A 5
Hammond	B 6	Westchester	B 5
Harvey	B 6	Wheaton	A 5
Highland	C 6	Wheeling	A 4
Highland Park	B 4	Whiting	B 6
Hinsdale	A 5	Wilmette	B 5
Hobart	C 6	Winnetka	B 5
Hoffman Estates	A 5		
Homewood	B 6		
Joliet	A 5		

A15

Ontario. The drive follows a hard-paved road near the edge of Lake Superior and passes through almost all towns along the lakeshore: Two Harbors, Castle Danger, Beaver Bay, Little Marais, Grand Marais, Hovland, and Grand Portage. Sprawling vistas of the lake are available from craggy cliffs all along the drive. North of Two Harbors, picnic and camping sites offer fine views of the cascading waters of Gooseberry Falls.

Gateways & Accommodations

Cloquet

(Pop. 8,700; zip code 55720; area code 218.) Located just west of Duluth, the city is a gateway to the state's northeastern lake country. The nearby Fond Du Lac Indian Reservation covers 25,000 acres and supports a small population of Chippewa Indians. Accommodations: *Golden Gate Motel* (rates: $20–25 double), 25 air-conditioned rooms, color TV, restaurant adjacent, two miles southeast of town via Hwy. 61 (879–6752).

Cook

(Pop. 700; zip code 55723; area code 218.) Western gateway to the Superior National Forest, Cook is also an outfitting center for the excellent fishing waters of nearby Vermilion and Pelican lakes. A District Ranger's office of the national forest is located here. Just outside of town is one of the two known deposits of rare green granite; the other is in Germany.

Duluth

(Pop. 101,000; zip codes, see below; area code 218.) A major inland port on the westerly tip of Lake Superior, Duluth boasts one of the finest harbors in the country, protected by high bluffs that rise from the lakeshore. The city's 49 miles of docks are lined with grain elevators, ore docks, and ships of many different countries. Because of its excellent harbor and commanding views of the lake and St. Louis River, Duluth has a long history as a trading center, beginning in 1660 when the first sizeable shipment of furs—60 canoes' worth—left the twin ports of Duluth and Superior. The city takes its name from the French explorer Daniel Greysolon, Sieur du Luth, who landed here in 1679. Just beyond the city limits begin the great Minnesota north woods and recreation areas. The Lake Shore Drive (U.S. Hwy. 61) runs for 150 miles along Lake Superior from Duluth northeast to the Grand Portage National Monument and Canada. The city is headquarters for the Superior National Forest. Area attractions: Aerial Lift Bridge, at the foot of Lake Ave., spans the canal entrance to Duluth Harbor (136 feet), lifting 138 feet in less than a minute to let ships through; Canal Park Marine Museum, next to the Aerial Lift Bridge on First Ave., E., houses exhibits illustrating the history of Lake Superior shipping and the Duluth harbor (open daily, except Sundays and holidays; admission free); Duluth-Superior sightseeing excursions aboard the *S.S. Vista Queen* and *S.S. Vista King* leave from the Arena-Auditorium Door at the foot of 5th Ave., W. (daily; call 722–6218 for hours and information); Fairmont Park Zoo, at 72nd Ave., W. and Grand Ave., encompasses a zoo with animals from all over the world, a wildlife museum, and picnic grounds (open daily till 8p.m. summers, till 4p.m. rest of year); The University of Minnesota campus at Oakland Ave. and College St. includes the Tweed Museum of Art (18th and 19th century paintings, contemporary art, and traveling exhibits) and the Marshall W. Alworth Planetarium; St. Louis County Heritage and Arts Center (727–8025), at 506 W. Michigan St., is a complex of museums and exhibits illustrating the area's natural, social, and cultural history, including one of the most powerful steam locomotives ever built (open Mon-Sat., 10a.m.–5p.m.; Sun., noon–5p.m.); Skyline Parkway Drive is a scenic boulevard along the city bluffs

overlooking the harbor, lake, and docks; the Spirit Mountain Recreation Area (628–2891), ten miles south of town via Interstate 35, encompasses lakes, riding stables, picnic and campgrounds, hiking trails, and a ski area with five chairlifts and cross-country trails (open year round). Recommended restaurants in the Duluth area include the *Chinese Lantern*, at 403 W. Superior St., a popular spot for first-rate Oriental cuisine (722–7481); the *Highland Supper Club*, at 1301 Miller Trunk Hwy. two miles north of town via U.S. 53, an elegant dining room specializing in prime ribs and seafood (722–7713); and the *Top of the Harbor* (see Radisson-Duluth Hotel below), a 16th–floor revolving restaurant with superb views of the city (727–8981). Accommodations: *Best Western Edgewater East Motel* (rates: $30.75–37.75 double), 80 excellent rooms, overlooking Lake Superior, color TV, heated indoor pool, saunas, tennis court, restaurant adjacent, at 2330 London Rd. (zip 55812), two miles northeast of town via U.S. 61 (728–3601); *Best Western Edgewater West Motel* (rates: $37.75 double), 60 excellent rooms and suites, adjacent to Edgewater East Motel above, same facilities plus beauty shop, game room, at 2211 London Rd. (zip 55812), two miles northeast of town on U.S. 61 (728–5141); *Lake-Aire Motel* (rates: $25.50–27.50 double), 51 rooms and suites, overlooking Lake Superior, color TV, tennis courts, sauna, queen-size beds, at 2416 London Rd. (zip 55812), 2¼ miles northeast of town via U.S. 61 (724–8513); *Normandy Inn-Best Western* (rates: $38.50–41.50 double), 242 excellent rooms and suites, color TV, heated indoor pool, saunas, dining room and cocktail lounge, at 209 W. Superior (zip 55802) (722–1202); *Radisson-Duluth Hotel* (rates: $39.50 double), 268 excellent rooms, overlooking harbor and Lake Superior, heated indoor pool, saunas, rooftop revolving dining room, coffeeshop, cocktail lounge, at 505 E. Superior St. (zip 55802), downtown via U.S. 61 (727–8981).

Ely—Gateway to the Boundary Waters Canoe Area

(Pop. 5,000; zip code 55731; area code 218.) Gateway to the country's most extensive canoeing waters, Ely is located on the shores of Lake Shagawa in the heart of the Superior National Forest. The town has long been famous with canoeists, fishermen, and outdoor travelers as an outfitting center and jumping-off point to Minnesota's lake country, Ontario's Quetico Provincial Park, and the Boundary Waters Canoe Area. Area attractions include the Voyageur Visitor Center (365–6162), ¼ mile east of town on Minnesota State Hwy. 169, containing extensive exhibits of the area's history and geology; the Hidden Valley Winter Sports Area (365–3097), one mile east

REFLECTIONS FROM THE
NORTH COUNTRY
Sigurd F. Olson

on Minnesota State Hwy. 169, encompassing ski slopes, lifts, toboggan runs and a skating rink; and the 2–billion year old greenstone outcropping at 13th Ave. E. and Main St., the only surface ellipsoidal greenstone in the country. For detailed area information, contact the Ely Chamber of Commerce at 365–6123. Ely is the home of Sigurd Olson, considered by many to be the country's most famous living woodsman and author. This modern-day voyageur, who over the years has explored the ancient Indian water trails and canoe routes throughout the Superior-Quetico Wilderness and the remote, seldom-explored hinterlands of Canada's Great North Woods, has described his adventures in the vast grandeur of the north country and the lonely lands of the Canadian Northwest in a series of classic books that are required reading for the wilderness paddler. The following books (hardbound) by Sigurd Olson may be obtained from Alfred A. Knopf Inc., Mail Order Dept., 400 Hahn Rd., Westminster, MD 21157: *The Lonely Land, Reflections from the North Country, Runes of the North, Listening Point, The Singing Wilderness, The Wilderness Days.* A District Ranger's Office of the Superior National Forest is located in town. Accommodations: *Motel Ely* (rates: $24–31 double), 15 airconditioned rooms, color TV, restaurant nearby, at 1047 E. Sheridan St., six blocks east on Minnesota State Hwy. 1 (365–3237); *Kasir's Motel* (rates: $23–25 double), 15 airconditioned rooms, three 2–room cottages, color TV, fish freezer, restaurant opposite, at 1314 E. Sheridan St., 10 blocks east on Minnesota State Hwy. 1 (365–3392).

Eveleth

(Pop. 5,000; zip code 55734; area code 218.) "The Hill Top City" is the capital of extensive iron ore mining operations that supply a large part of the nation's iron requirements. Points of interest include the U.S. Hockey Hall of Fame, on Hat Trick Ave. via U.S. 53, and the attractive Veterans' Park, two miles south of town on County Rd. 132. Just north of Eveleth is the Superior National Forest. Accommodations: *Holiday Inn* (rates: $31–37 double), 146 excellent rooms, color TV, heated indoor pool, saunas, recreation room, putting green, dining room and cocktail lounge, two miles east of town via U.S. 53, on Hat Trick Ave. (749–2703).

Grand Marais—Gateway to the Gunflint Trail

(Pop. 1,400; zip code 55604; area code 218.) Situated on the rocky north shore of Lake Superior, this north country village is the starting point for the scenic Gunflint Trail, which winds northwest through the Superior National Forest to Saganaga Lake at the Canadian border. Another memorable route, the North Shore Drive on U.S. 61, follows the Lake Superior Shoreline from Duluth to Pigeon River and is considered one of the most beautiful lakeside

thoroughfares in the U.S. Grand Marais (French for "great marsh") is a popular outfitting center for canoeists, fishermen, and other visitors to Minnesota's famed Boundary Waters and Arrowhead Country. Accommodations: *Best Western Superior Inn* (rates $28 double), 20 comfortable rooms, color TV, restaurant adjacent, on 1st Ave. E., just off U.S. 61 (387–2240); *Gladmanor Motel* (rates: $20 double), 14 rooms, TV, nearby restaurant, three blocks northeast of town on U.S. 61 (387–2727); *Shoreline Motor Lodge* (rates: $25–29 double), 28 comfortable rooms on Lake Superior shore, color TV, private beach, open year round, two blocks south of U.S. 61 (387–2633); *Wedgewood Motel* (rates: $20–22), 10 rooms, opposite Lake Superior, TV, nature trails, 2½ miles northeast of town via U.S. 61 (387–2944).

Grand Portage

(Pop. 150; zip code 55605; area code 218.) Located at the tip of Minnesota's Arrowhead Country, Grand Portage was once a flourishing depot for fur traders of the North West Company. The Grand Portage National Monument is a recreation of this busy settlement, which is said to have included a police force, numerous buildings, even shops for French fashions—all before the signing of the Declaration of Independence 1,000 miles away. Among the carefully researched reconstructions on the excavated site of the original village are a stockade and gate house, the Great Hall where officers lived and dined, a canoe warehouse, and storage buildings. The Grand Portage hiking trail, retracing the route of the voyageurs, begins at the stockade and runs 8½ miles northwest from Lake Superior to the Pigeon River. Passenger ferry service is available from Grand Portage to Isle Royale National Park in Michigan state waters, 20 miles away (daily, mid-June to Labor Day). For further information, write: Superintendent, Grand Portage National Monument, Box 666, Grand Marais, MN 55604. Accommodations: (see "Radisson Inn—Grand Portage" below).

Hibbing

(Pop. 17,000; zip code 55746; area code 218.) The largest town on the Mesabi Iron Range, Hibbing is often called the "Iron Ore Capital of the World" because of its prodigious output of taconite, an ore-bearing rock which yields a rich iron concentrate. At the Hull-Rust Mahoning Mine, northwest of town, visitors can tour a 4–mile long mining area from which more than a billion tons of material have been removed. At its deepest, the mine dips 535 feet into the earth. Hibbing is also a gateway to the Superior National Forest. Accommodations: *Best Western Kahler's Motel* (rates: $31.20–32.20 double), 126 excellent rooms and suites, most with oversize beds, color TV, heated indoor pool, sauna, dining room, coffee-shop, cocktail lounge, at 1402 E. Howard St., ½ mile east of town via U.S. 169 (262–3481); *Iron Man Motel* (rates: $18.72–20.80 double), 44 air-conditioned rooms, color TV, restaurant adjacent, ½ mile southwest via U.S. 169 (254–3393).

Lutsen

(Pop. 100; zip code 55612; area code 218.) On the shores of Lake Superior southwest of Grand Marais, Lutsen is a gateway to the Superior National Forest and northern Minnesota lake country. The Lutsen Ski Area (see below) off U.S. 61, has downhill and cross-country trails, a lodge, and complete ski facilities. A scenic chairlift ride and alpine slide are in operation from mid-May to mid-October. Accommodations: (see "Lutsen Resort" below).

Tower

(Pop. 700; zip code 55790; area code 218.) Located on the shores of Lake Vermilion, Tower is the oldest mining town in northern

Minnesota and a gateway to the Superior National Forest. Points of interest include a museum of pioneer and Indian history housed in an old steam locomotive and coach (at the west end of Main St.) and Tower Soudan State Park, two miles east of town via Minnesota State Hwy. 169, site of the state's first underground iron mine; 1–hour guided tours, including a train ride, are available June-Sept., 9a.m.–4p.m. Accommodations: *Bay View Lodge* (rates: $42–59 double, American Plan), on Lake Vermilion with 16 1–3 bedroom cottages, housekeeping units, motel rooms, beach, water sports, dock, boat rentals, sundeck, recreation room, dining room and cocktail lounge, two-day minimum stay, five miles west of Tower via Minnesota State Hwy. 1, then 4½ miles north on County Road 77 (753–4825).

Virginia

(Pop. 12,000; zip code 55792; area code 218.) Second largest city on the Mesabi iron range, Virginia is surrounded by cavernous open mine pits and green countryside. Just north of town is the Superior National Forest; a District Ranger's office is located here. Area attractions include the Rochleau Mine, on the southern edge of town, an operating open pit mine with a visitor observation tower and Olcott Park, at N. 9th St. and 9th Ave., comprising a multicolored lighted fountain, a greenhouse with unusual floral displays, and a free 18–hole golf course. Accommodations: *Best Western Ski-View Motel* (rates: $20.80–22.88 double), 59 comfortable rooms and suites, color TV, saunas, restaurant opposite, 15 miles from Giant's Ridge Ski Area, at 903 N. 17th St., 1½ miles north of town on U.S. 53 business rt. (741–8918); *Rico's Voyageur Motor Lodge* (rates: $25.22 double), 18 attractive, spacious rooms, color TV, near shopping mall, family restaurants, and cocktail lounge, one mile southwest of town via U.S. 53, at junction with 13th St. S. (741–9235).

Lodges & Sporting Camps

★★*Aspenwood Resort-Motel on Lake Superior* is located on the scenic North Shore Drive. Grand Portage National Monument is nearby as are Isle Royale National Park and the Boundary Waters Canoe Area. Guests can enjoy fishing, hiking, canoeing, or swimming in the summer. In the winter there is skiing (both cross-country and downhill), snowshoeing, and snowmobiling at Lutsen Resort or in Superior National Forest. All of these activities are easily accessible from Aspenwood. Aspenwood has its own private beach, with coffee shop, game room, and sauna located in the main building. The resort has a motel on the lakeshore and cabins on a cliff overlooking the lake. The motel has some housekeeping units. These and the cabins are completely furnished, heated, and fully equipped for light housekeeping. Motel rooms range from $22 per day (for one person) to $31 per day (for four). Housekeeping units are $32 per day (for two persons). Weekly rates for cabins are $160 (for two persons). Extra persons are charged $5 per day; children are charged a lower rate. For additional information contact: Aspenwood Resort-Motel, Tofte MN 55615 (218)663–7978.

★★★*Beaver Lodge on the Echo Trail* is on the east side of Burntside Lake, just north of Ely, one of the largest and most beautiful lakes in the area—crystal clear and dotted with many islands, holding big walleye, lake trout, northern pike, and bass. Beaver Lodge offers superb fishing, swimming (there is a sandy beach) and canoeing. A golf course is available in nearby Ely. Baby-sitting services are available to guests. The lodge has a lounge, grocery store, and snack bar, fishing licenses, tackle, gas, and live bait. In addition guests have use of dock service, the fish house and freezer. Guide services are offered; and fly-in trips to more remote areas can be arranged. A 14–foot boat is included with each weekly rental. Modern, com-

pletely furnished two-bedroom cabins are situated along the lake. Beaver Lodge offers ice fishing, hunting, and skiing in the winter. Championship dog sled races are held in January. Housekeeping cabins are $100 per week for two persons, $20 per each additional person; children (under six) are $10 per week. Larger housekeeping units (accommodating up to eight people) are $120 per week for two persons, $20 each additional person, with a minimum charge of $140 per week (for four persons). For additional information, contact: Basil and Alberta Georgeff, Beaver Lodge, S.R. 2, Box 8295, Ely MN 55731 (218)365–5286.

★★★★*Bill Zup's Lac La Croix Fishing Camp & Outfitters* will put you on to some of the nation's most spectacular canoeing and northern-pike and smallmouth-bass fishing country. Their float-plane base is on Crane Lake, off the scenic Echo Trail; the main fishing camp and cabins are on huge, island-dotted Lac La Croix, on the Boundary Waters Lakes chain. To the north in Ontario's Quetico Provincial Park, are over a thousand remote lakes. Canoe trips of every description are available. And there are no roads, nothing to spoil the vast wilderness. The main lodge has a dining room, lounge, and small trading post. Homemade bread is baked daily, and guests on special diets can be accommodated. Big breakfasts and shore lunches are also served. Guide services are available, as are Indian packers and paddlers. They know the waters and the area and are experienced boat handlers. Your fish are cleaned and packed and there is a smoke house, too. Cabins are located near the lodge, Some have kitchen facilities. There is a sauna in the main lodge. Rates vary with the type of accommodation desired. A five-day

trip to Pine Island for private camping—including tent cabin with cots, stove, canoe or boat, and fifteen meals—is $125 per person (minimum of two persons). A Quetico canoe trip is $16 per day per person. At the main camp, housekeeping cabins are $12 per day; European plan cabins are $30 per day per person (including dinner). American plan is $35–40 per day per person (double occupancy) and includes all meals. Other types of trips and accommodations are available; rates on request. The camp is open from May to October. For additional information, contact: Bill Zup, 611 E. Harvey St., Ely MN 55731 (218)365–4018; in the summer: Box ZUP, Crane Lake MN 55725 (218)993–2273.

★★★*Burntside Lodge*, a resort since 1913, is on the shores of Burntside Lake, near Ely, in Superior National Forest. Towering cliffs form much of the shoreline of this beautiful 7000–acre lake, a well known for smallmouth bass, northern pike and lake trout fishing. Guided canoe-fishing trips to Basswood Lake via portage can be arranged as can fly-in trips to other wilderness areas. Other outdoor recreational opportunities and facilities include swimming and water skiing, a playground for children, a game room, tennis courts, and a sauna. There are twenty-five modern cabins, all located on or near the lakeshore. Most have housekeeping facilities, and there is a variety of sizes—up to three bedrooms. The lodge has a large, beamed dining room that is open daily to guests and to the public. There is a salad bar and fresh fish are always on the menu. Bait, motors, boats, fuel, and tackle are available. Pets are permitted but not encouraged; there is a $1 per day charge for dogs. Dogs must be kept leashed and may not be left alone in the cabins. Guests also have use of the fish cleaning house and there is freezer space available for your catch. A variety of vacation plans are available: modified American plan (which includes breakfast and dinner, a boat or canoe, and daily maid service) is $31 per day per person; $195 per week per person. (Children are charged a lower rate.) European plan (which includes a cabin and maid service—no meals, no cooking facilities) ranges from $32 per person to $55 per person, depending on the type of accommodation. The housekeeping plan (for a cabin with cooking facilities, bed linens, dishes, boat) ranges from $169 per week to $311 per week, depending upon the size of accommodation. Extra persons are $5 per day with rollaway. For additional information, contact: Mr. Ray LaMontagne, Burntside Lodge, SR 2, Box 4215, Ely MN 55731 (218)365–3894.

★★*Canadian Border Lodge* is situated on Moose Lake, in Superior National Forest, just 30 minutes from the Canadian border. The Moose Lake chain includes Newfound, Sucker, and Birch Lakes. Access to nearby Basswood Lake is from Prairie Portage, operated under the supervision of the U.S. Forest Service. Fishing, swimming, hiking, berry picking (in season), and boating are all enjoyed by guests at Canadian Border Lodge. The lodge offers complete dock services: fuel, live bait, ice, a fish-filleting service, and use of the freezer. For those guests wishing to bring their own boats, a launching ramp is available. In addition, groceries, fishing licenses and tackle may be purchased. All cabins are heated and fully equipped and feature either log or knotty pine interiors. A 14–foot boat is included with each weekly rental. In addition to the resort accommodations, there is a small campground with 20 campsites and a trailer park with six sites. Full hookups are available at the trailer park. Cabins are $125 per week for two persons (one-bedroom cabin), larger cabins are more expensive. Additional guests are charged $30 per week, children are $20 per week. Daily rates are $10 per person. Boats are extra on the daily rate. Weeks run from Saturday to Saturday. Reservations should be made in advance. For additional information, contact: Ron and Kim Stockdill, P.O. Box 58, Ely MN 55731 (218)365–5486.

★★★*Cascade Lodge on Lake Superior* offers the warmth and friendliness of a family lodge nestled in a virgin forest of evergreens and birch on Lake Superior. During the summer, you can hike any of five wilderness trails which start right outside the lodge, where the scenery is breathtaking and the birds, deer, and other wildlife are plentiful. Take a guided trip to Hidden Falls, or join in group activities such as handicraft classes, and evening fireside forums. There is also camping, canoeing, fishing, golf, and horseback riding just a few miles down the road. In the winter, cross-country ski touring, snowshoeing, and alpine skiing are available at the Lutsen Ski Area. Cascade offers rooms in the main lodge, as well as cabins—some with housekeeping facilities. There is also a restaurant and gift shop on the premises. Rates for two are about $20–25 per day. There are also mini-vacation plans on the modified American plan. For details, contact: Cascade Lodge, P.O. Grand Marais, MN 55604 (218)387–9980.

★★*Chik-Wauk Lodge on Saganaga Lake*, a sprawling, island-dotted lake, near Grand Marais in Superior National Forest, is famed for its fishing for walleye, northern pike, lake trout, and smallmouth bass up to record weights. Other recreational opportunities at the lodge include swimming, hiking, and canoeing. There is a playground for children, a putting green, and a sauna. In addition, visitors have use of freezer service; and fuel, tackle, and bait are available. The trading post sells fishing licenses, and beverages, and there is also a small grocery store. Boundary Waters Canoe Area permits are available. Pets, too, are welcome. Should a visitor wish to "rough it," Chik-Wauk also has a complete outfitting service. They maintain outpost cabins on beautiful Northern Lights Lake (in Canada) 25 miles from the lodge by water (with only a short mechanical railroad portage). Fly-in trips can also be arranged—a visitor may either camp out or be based at an established tent camp on remote wilderness lakes. A variety of wilderness trips and accommodations are available. Rustic housekeeping cabins of log construction, comfortably furnished, fully screened, and well equipped are available at the lodge. A 16–foot boat or canoe is included with each weekly rental. For two persons, rates are $130 per week, $30 per day (minimum stay of three days). For three or four persons, a cabin is $145 per week, $40 per day; for six or more persons, the rate is $175 per week, $50 per day. Children are charged at a lower rate. Additional persons are charged $15 per week, $4 per day. Extra boats and motors can also be rented. A complete outfitting, per person, is $12.50 per day (without food the charge is $7). Partial outfitting is also available. For additional information, contact Ralph and Bea Griffis, Grand Marais MN 55604 (218)388–2281. In winter, contact them at: 1609 North Parkwood Drive, Harlingen, TX 78550 (512)423–1504.

★★★★*Gunflint Northwoods Lodge & Outfitters* is located at beautiful Gunflint Lake on the Canadian border in wilderness canoe country. Gunflint Northwoods Outfitters will route each canoe trip to individual specifications, what kind of country you want to see, and what kind of fish you want to catch. There are over 50 routes to choose from, with clear waters, open skies, and dense timber country, home of beavers, moose, and bear. The Boundary Waters Canoe Area surrounds Gunflint Northwoods Outfitters on three sides, and the Canadian wilderness is across the lake to the north. Park service maintains a forest quota entry system which ensures the area remains just as it was 100 years ago, when Indians and trappers carried furs and trade goods down river. Gunflint will outfit you with an Old Town Chipewyan canoe, or Alumnacraft and Gruman. Complete outfitting includes canoe, Stearns Gatsby vests, sleeping bags, foam pads, cookkits, lightweight "A" tents, which are erected without poles, a soft pack that fits well in canoes, lightweight tarps, camp axe, and personal pack with everything from face soap to matches. Every canoeist has a choice of lightweight foods from Gunflint's long and varied selection of Richmoor, Drilite, and Seidel foods, along with little extras, like home-baked bread from the lodge kitchen. Old Town Chipewyan canoes are $9 daily and $60 weekly. Alumnacraft and Gruman canoes are $8 daily and $50 weekly. complete outfitting with Old Town canoes $20.50 per person daily for three-five day trips, $18.50 for six-seven day trips, and $17.50 per person for each day of an extended trip of eight days or more. Gruman and Alumnacraft outfits are $1 less on each rate. Children are $12 for three-five day trips, $11 each day for six-seven day trips and $10 a day for trips lasting eight days or more. Gunflint Northwoods Outfitters also offer spring packages from May 1–15, for early fishing when the woods are a new green, kids and parents packages, and Indian summer packages, when the woods are changing colors, and northern light displays are most frequent. At Gunflint Lodge, life is casual in the northwoods. Most people come up to fish, and the biggest strings are heavy with walleye, lake trout, northern pike, and smallmouth bass. Deep 16–foot aluminum boats are available with good cushions and a choice of live bait for $8 daily, $19 with late-model Mercury motors. Gunflint Lodge has a new 20–foot pontoon boat for group outings and picnics; $30 daily with gas. It

warms up enough to swim in the lake in July, and water skiing and sailing, and use of the lakeside sauna are free to guests. There are many breathtaking bridle paths throughout the surrounding hills, that begin at Gunflint stables. Shuffleboard, badminton, archery, horseshoes, and a children's playground surround the lodge. The lodge has big picture windows looking out across the lake to Canada. There is a big fire blazing in the open hearth, comfortable redwood furniture, Indian rugs, and a good library. The dining room serves fresh squeezed orange juice with your choice of breakfast which may include blueberry wheat cakes, bacon and strong coffee. Hot, home-baked bread is placed on every dinner table, and the entrees are varied; fried shrimp, fresh pork, baked chicken. All the desserts are home made, from baked Alaska to frozen peppermint pie. Sunday smorgasbords highlight the week, and there are afternoon barbeques with everything from spareribs to mooseburgers. Cabins are modern, have electric heat, electric blankets, and fireplaces for chill north country nights. Open deck porches overlook the forest and the lake. A-frame chalets have complete kitchens, and several other cottages have kitchenettes. Rates including three meals daily, barbeques, and smorgasbord are $35–39 per adult daily, and $225–250 weekly, double occupancy. Children ages 3–14 are $12 daily and $65 weekly. For more information write: Bruce and Sue

Kerfoot, Gunflint Lodge and Outfitters Inc., Grand Marais, MN 55604 (218)388–2294 or 2296.

★★★*Jackpine Lodge* is located on beautiful, island-dotted Snowbank Lake in Superior National Forest, at the border of Boundary Waters Canoe Area. Snowbank Lake is famous for its walleyed pike, lake trout, largemouth bass, and smallmouth bass. For guests' convenience there is a fish cleaning house and deep freeze. Other activities include swimming, boating, water skiing, hiking, and photography. In season, berry-picking parties can be organized. Housekeeping cabins, all of which are located on the lakeshore, are completely equipped—including all cooking and eating utensils and bed linens—and the use of one boat is included with each weekly rental. Services include fuel, bait, refreshments, licenses, daily grocery and mail pickup, as well as guides and baby sitters. In addition there is a main lodge which offers guest rooms and where meals are served daily. The dining room is open to the public and features a weekly smorgasbord. American plan (rooms in the main lodge and complete meals) is $160 per week per person; $135 per week (each) for two or more persons. The daily rate is $29 per person; $24 per person (for two or more persons). Children under 10 are charged half price. Cabin accommodations range from $150 to $185 per week; $28 to $38 per day per person. Housekeeping cabins (no meals provided) are $140 per week (for two) and up. For additional information, contact: The Stocks, Jackpine Lodge, Box 570, Ely MN 55731 (218)365–5700.

★★*Jasper Lake Resort* is the only resort on scenic Jasper Lake in Superior National Forest, located 16 miles northeast of Ely on the Fernberg Road, immediately adjacent to the Boundary Waters Canoe Area. Jasper is a small, quiet fishing resort in a wilderness setting. Wildlife—including deer, bear, moose, and occasional wolf tracks—can be sighted along trails in the area. There is also an abundance of birdlife. Look for loons, scaup, and mallard among other species. Fishing tackle, bait, ice, and groceries are available at resort's store as are locally handcrafted gifts. There is also freezer service for fish storage. Accommodations at Jasper Lake Resort include completely equipped housekeeping cabins. Each rental includes a 14–foot boat. There are seven cabins ranging from $80 per week to $95 per week for two persons; each additional person is charged $15 per week. For additional information, contact: Joe Baltich, Jasper Lake Resort, 239 W. Harvey Street, Ely MN 55731 (218)365–3957 or 5489.

★★★*Jocko's Clearwater Lodge* is a small, family-owned and operated resort on the evergreen-fringed shores of Clearwater Lake, a long, narrow lake with high palisades forming part of its shoreline within the Boundary Waters Canoe Area. The water is clear, the air pine-scented. Fishing, canoeing, hiking, swimming (either in the lake or a heated pool) are all enjoyed by visitors. Jocko's also maintains a complete outfitting service. They will help guests to plan their wilderness canoe trips and provide instruction in canoeing, portaging, packing of gear, and camping. Guide services, while not necessary, are available. Partial outfits can also be supplied. At the main lodge meals are served daily. There is also a small store where beverages, licenses, tackle, and souvenirs may be purchased. The log cabins are completely equipped for housekeeping and will accommodate from two to eight persons. In addition there are two suites with housekeeping facilities located upstairs in the main lodge. Cabins rent from $95–230 per week depending upon the size of the cabin and the number of people in the party. For American plan, add $27 per day per person; continental plan is an additional $35 per week per person. Children are charged at a lower rate. A boat is included in each weekly cabin rental. A complete outfit—minimum outfitting is for two persons for three days—is $16 per day per person for a four-six day trip; longer trips are less expensive per day as are parties of more than two. Children are charged at a lower rate, and there are special group rates. For additional information, contact Jocko and Lee Nelson, Jocko's Clearwater Lodge, Gunflint Trail Box 31, Grand Marais MN 55604 (218)388–2254; in winter, contact the Nelsons at: 8624 Kell Avenue South, Bloomington MN 55437 (612)831–0755.

★★★*Loon Lake Lodge* is a superb family vacation resort located on scenic Loon Lake, off the famous Gunflint Trail, in the Superior National Forest. Fishing, swimming, hiking, and berry picking (in season) can all be enjoyed by guests of the lodge. Loon Lake is located near the Boundary Waters Canoe Area and guests can portage to fish a number of lakes in the area. Loon Lake is best known for its lake trout fishing, but there are also walleyes, northerns, and smallmouth bass. Guide service is available and fly-in trips to remote wilderness areas can be arranged. The lodge is in a beautiful setting; the hills surrounding the lake are covered with birch, aspen, and pine. The lodge is open in the fall for deer, bear, and grouse hunting. Meals feature delicious home-made breads and pastries. All cabins are constructed of peeled logs and have private bathrooms (with shower), heat, kitchens, and linens. Maid service is also offered. American plan cabins are $149–161 per week per person, $22–24 per day per person; children (under 10) are charged half price. For additional information, contact: Willard and Kermit Johnson, Loon Lake Lodge, Gunflint Trail, Grand Marais MN 55604 (218)388–2232.

★★★★*Lutsen Resort & Ski Center on Lake Superior*, just south of historic Grand Marais, offers a variety of accommodations ranging from the rustic, economy-styled Cliff House to luxurious Sea Villas, with facilities for cooking and entertaining. Lodge activities include tennis, swimming, horseback riding in the mountainous backcountry, backpacking, hiking, and nine holes of golf. Fishermen can charter Lake Superior deep-sea boats or try their luck in the many smaller lakes nearby. Northerns and walleyes are abundant, and the nearby Poplar River is privately stocked with rainbow trout. The rugged, hilly Lake Superior terrain is excellent for winter skiing, with its 630 feet of vertical slope and 1½ to three-mile runs, Lutsen is one of the largest ski areas in the Midwest. Both downhill and cross-country skiing are offered, and there is swimming in the heated pool. Ski rentals and instruction are available. A wide variety of accommodations and packages is offered. Summer rates in the main lodge

(including breakfast and dinner) average $34 per day, $225 per week for each of two persons. Rooms in the Cliff House are less expensive. In addition, apartments and Sea Villas are available. These are fully equipped and furnished. A three-day sports package is $101 per person (in the lodge). And lodging only (in the lodge) for three days, averages $51 per person (based on double occupancy). Winter rates range from $26 per day per person in the Cliff House to $38 per day, per person, in the main lodge. Apartments range from $38 (for two) to $62 (for four). Lift fees are $11 per day on weekends, less during the week. Weekend skiing packages are as little as $28 per day (per person). These include lodging, breakfast, and lift fees. The ski season at Lutsen is from the end of November to the middle of April. For additional information, contact: Lutsen Resort, Lutsen MN 55612 (218)663–7212; in Minnesota, call toll-free: (800)232–0071.

★★★*Moose Lake Lodges* owns and operates Moose Lake Lodge and North Country Lodge, both on Moose Lake; the former is accessible by boat only, the latter is on the mainland. Moose Lake is 20 miles north of Ely in Superior National Forest, on the border of the Boundary Waters Canoe Area, and only six miles by water from the Canadian border with easy access to Basswood Lake and to many other Minnesota and Canadian wilderness lakes inhabited by walleye, lake trout, large and smallmouth bass, and northern pike. Moose Lake lodge is a brand new resort, with completely equipped A-frame cabins, and modern kitchens and baths. There is a main lodge with a dining room, lounge (complete with fireplace), tackle shop, grocery store, and snack bar. There is a network of scenic hiking trails; and guided canoe trips into the wilderness canoe country may be arranged. Fish packing and freezer services are also available at the lodge. The North Country Lodge, a rustic fishing camp, features completely furnished cabins. A boat is included with each weekly rental. Motors can be rented; and fuel, bait, and fishing licenses can be purchased at the lodge. Guests also have the use of the deep freeze for their fish. Swimming, water skiing, fishing, hiking, and photography are among the activities enjoyed by guests here. Rates depend upon which type of accommodation is chosen: Cabins at Moose Lake Lodge are $176 per week for two persons; $45 per week for each additional person; children (under 12) are $20 per week. Cabins are also rented on a daily basis at $30 per day. Moose Lake Lodge is open from 1 May to 1 October. Cabins at North Country Lodge are from $125 per week to $160 per week year-round depending upon size of the cabin and number of persons. For additional information, contact Don Beland, Moose Lake Lodges, Box 808, Ely MN 55731 (218)365–6256 or 5811.

★★★*National Forest Lodge* is located in Superior National Forest on 143 acres on the south shore of Lake Gegoka, just south of the Boundary Waters Canoe Area. In the summer, canoeing and fishing are featured; in the winter guests enjoy ice fishing, skiing, snowshoeing, and tobogganing. Housekeeping cabins, available in the summer only, are fully furnished and completely equipped. Rooms are available in the lodge as well. Meals are served family-style in the spacious dining room. Rates vary widely depending upon the type of accommodation, number of persons, length of stay, and time of year. In the winter a weekend package costs $54 per person. This includes lodging, all meals, and use of all lodge facilities. Extra days are $27 per person. Children (under 12) are charged half the adult rate. Ski equipment and snowshoes may be rented at a nominal charge. For additional information, contact: Bob Hunger, National Forest Lodge, Isabella MN 55607 (218)323–441,1.

★★*Northernair Lodge*, on beautiful Mitchell Lake, is located 3½ miles south of Ely. Walleye and northern pike are plentiful at Mitchell Lake, while largemouth bass and northern pike are found at Twin Lakes, a nearby wilderness spot. The lodge can arrange float-plane trips for those visitors wishing to fish the remote Canadian border lakes. For those who wish to take extended canoe-fishing trips, arrangements can be made with a local outfitter. The comfortable log cabins have fireplaces and are fully equipped. A fishing boat is included with each cabin rental. Groceries, fishing licenses, bait, motors, and gasoline are all available. Arrangements to meet buses and private planes in Ely can be made. Rates range from $100 per week for a one-bedroom cabin for two persons to $150 per week for a two-bedroom cabin for four persons. For additional information, contact Jean and Jon Barkdoll, Northernair Lodge, Star Route 1, Box 1212, Ely MN 55731 (218)365–4882.

★★★★*Nor'Wester Lodge* is a family-owned, year-round lodge located on the famous Gunflint Trail on the evergreen shores of Poplar Lake in Superior National Forest, only 30 miles north of Grand Marais. Year-round activities include fishing—for walleye, bass, northern pike, lake trout, brook trout, and rainbow trout—canoeing, swimming, waterskiing, boating, hiking, and snowshoeing. Barbecues and picnics are popular, and there is a putting green at the lodge. In the main lodge—a sturdy building of log construction—there is a small gift shop, laundromat, and trading post. At the post, beverages, licenses, tackle, maps, and groceries are available. Nor'Wester Lodge features home-cooked meals and special diets can be accommodated as well. If a canoe trip is desired, Nor'Wester operates a complete outfitting service. A variety of accommodations is available: American plan (including all meals); continental plan (includes dinner only); and housekeeping plan. All cabins are equipped for light housekeeping complete with linens, towels, and bedding. They range in size from two to five rooms. Maid service can be arranged. There are also wilderness lake villas, completely winterized for year round occupancy with knotty pine interiors. Each unit will sleep up to twelve persons, and all are completely equipped for housekeeping. All cabins have a private dock on the lake. Rates vary depending upon the type of plan chosen. Rustic pine cabins, for two persons, are $180 per week, $30 per week for each additional person, $20 per week for children. Nor'Wester cabins are $125–155 per week for two persons. Wilderness lake villas are $155 per week for two persons. American plan is an additional $80 per week, $15 per day; continental plan is $45 per week, $7 per day. Children are charged a lower rate. In addition, there are discounts in May, June, and September as well as discounts for persons over 65 in June, September, and October. Extended vacations (longer than one week) are also discounted—up to 20%. Boats and canoes rent from $30–50 per week, $6–10 per day. Guide services are available at $45 per day. For additional information, contact: Carl and Luana Brandt, Nor'Wester Lodge, Gunflint Trail, Grand Marais, MN 55604 (218)388-2252.

★★★★*Olsen's Borderland Lodge & Outfitters* is located on beautiful Crane Lake, in the Superior National Forest, bordering on Voyageurs National Park. From here one can take off on a real wilderness canoe trip: over 60 miles of wilderness lakes, 1000 miles of canoe routes and some of the nation's finest smallmouth bass fishing lie before you. Borderland Lodge offers a complete (or partial) outfitting service; guests who choose to remain at the lodge may enjoy swimming, fishing, canoeing, and hiking. A small store is located at the lodge where tackle, sporting goods, groceries are available. Bait and fuel are also for sale, and guests have use of a deep freeze as well. Picturesque pine forests and sky-blue lakes make this area a photographer's paradise. American plan accommodations may be had in the lodge or in the cabins with maid service furnished. All cabins are heated and have modern kitchens and bathrooms, with knotty pine interiors. The cabins are completely furnished and

are equipped with dishes, cooking utensils, and bedding. Cabins rent for $85 per week (for two persons); $110 per week (for four persons). Larger cabins are more expensive. Lodge rooms (American plan) are $25 per day per person; children (under 10) are $20 per day. Boats are $30 to $40 per week with a cabin rental. Olsen's Borderland Outfitters will completely outfit canoe parties for wilderness travel in the Boundary Waters with modern equipment, including canoes, tents, sleeping bags, and packs. Experienced guides are available. The store carries a complete line of groceries suitable for a canoe trip, and there is also a large assortment of fishing tackle in stock. Experienced people will help you to plan your trip and will give instruction in paddling, portaging, and setting up camp. A complete outfit (*not* including food) is $8 per day per person. Food averages $7 per day per person. Partial outfits are also available. For additional information, contact: Olsen's Borderland Lodge and Outfitters, Crane Lake, MN 55725 (218)993–2233.

***Radisson Inn—Grand Portage* is located in historic Grand Portage, the oldest white settlement in Minnesota. The Grand Portage band of the Chippewa Indians created this unique inn and join with Radisson Hotels in offering it for your enjoyment. Nestled between towering spruce and birch, overlooking Lake Superior, Radisson Inn is a prime place for bird watchers, photographers and nature lovers. Deer, moose and small game are readily seen; canoeing and fishing are excellent, and there are miles of hiking trails for both the novice and serious backpacker. There are a swimming pool and tennis courts on the premises, plus snowmobiling and a 50–mile network of cross-country ski trails for winter enjoyment. Guide service and ski rentals are available. There is also a daily liner service to Isle Royale National Park, a beautiful island nature preserve and camping area. Radisson—Inn has 100 luxurious guest rooms, each with color TV and a view of either the lake or forests. There are also dining facilities. Rates, for two, $26–28 per night for regular room, $51 for lakeside suites (including parlor). For more information, contact: Radisson Inn—Grand Portage, Grand Portage, MN 55605 (218)475–2401.

****Rockwood Lodge on the Gunflint Trail* in the Superior National Forest is located on 70 acres on the cool north shore of Poplar Lake, a sparkling north country lake just four miles from the Canadian border. Poplar Lake has a wooded, irregular shoreline and is dotted with nearly 30 pine-studded islands. Outdoor activities available at Rockwood include fishing, canoeing, hiking, and birdwatching. Guide service is available, and an outfitting service is provided for those guests who want to take a canoe and camping trip into the Boundary Waters Canoe Area. Everything, including planning,

equipment, food, maps, and supplies, is provided. The entire country surrounding Rockwood Lodge is a photographer's and nature lover's delight. Among the many species of birds and animals to be seen in the area are: loon, mallard, merganser, ruffed grouse, hermit thrush, deer, bear, moose, beaver, otter, fox, and snowshoe rabbits. Nearby points of interest include historic Grand Portage Fort and Stockade, Isle Royale National Park, and the Rose Lake waterfall. In the main lodge, there is a lounge with fireplace, game room, trading post, bar, and dining room. The dining room, furnished with many antiques, is open daily. All cabins, equipped for light housekeeping, are well spaced along the lakeshore and range in size from one to five rooms, with modern kitchens and bathrooms. A sauna is located near the main lodge. Rates vary depending upon the type of plan desired and upon the number of people in the party. American plan, for two persons, is $130 per week; $47 per day. Modified plan, for two persons, is $220 per week; $34 per day. The housekeeping plan, for two persons, is $135 per week; $22 per day; for four persons, it is $150 per week; $27 per day. Children are charged at a lower rate. Boats rent for $5 per day, $35 per week. For additional information, contact: Rick Whitney and Don Lobdell, Rockwood Lodge, Gunflint Trail, Grand Marais MN 55604 (218)388–2242.

**Sawbill Lodge & Canoe Outfitters* on Sawbill Lake in the Superior National Forest is surrounded by gently rolling, wooded terrain in spectacular wilderness lake country. Nearby streams flowing into Lake Superior offer fine fishing for brook trout; the waters of Sawbill Lake itself and connecting chains hold big walleye, smallmouth bass, and northern pike. Deer are abundant, and moose and bear are often sighted along the scenic hiking trails. Log cabins, a rustic log lodge, and an excellent marina are available. There are also hotel-type sleeping accommodations for groups, adventure education seminars, conference accommodations, and cross-country skiing, as well as a nearby national forest campground and wilderness canoe outfitters. For detailed information and rates, contact: Sawbill Lodge, Box 2128, Tofte, MN 55615 (218)387–1360.

***Sea Gull Resort & Arrow Tip Canoe Outfitters* is located on beautiful Sea Gull Lake, in Superior National Forest, just off the Gunflint Trail. Sea Gull Lake, seven miles long and dotted with over 125 picturesque islands, and the surrounding evergreen forests offer fishing, boating, canoeing, and hiking. Boats, canoes, motors, fuel, bait and tackle are all available. A small grocery store stocks plenty of fresh items (milk, bread, vegetables), frozen foods, and staples. Affiliated with the resort is Arrow Tip Canoe Outfitters. Complete outfits run from $17.50 per day per person to $19.50 per day per person, depending upon the length of the trip. Children are charged at a lower rate. The fully modern, heated cabins face the lake and each has large windows to enjoy the view, with knotty pine panelling. All linens, bedding, cooking utensils, and dishes are furnished. The dining room features char-broiled steaks, fish, and home-made soups. Cabins range from $135 per week (for two persons) to $285 per week (for ten persons). Daily rates range from $27 to $57. There are also a few motel units available; these range from $20 to $32 per day. For the American plan, add $13.50 per day; $92 per week per person. For the continental plan, add $7.50 per day; $52 per week per person. Children are charged at a lower rate. Boats and canoes rent from $6.50 to $7 per day. Motors may also be rented. For additional information, contact: Al and Lois Danielson, Sea Gull Resort, Gunflint Trail, Grand Marais, MN 55604 (218)388–2251.

**Shig-Wak Resort on the Echo Trail* is located six miles north of Ely on Little Long Lake, in the Superior National Forest. Modern family housekeeping cabins are well spaced along the shores of the

lake, known for its excellent fishing for northern pike, walleye, and large- and smallmouth bass. A wide variety of recreational activities is offered, including swimming (there is a sandy beach), canoeing, and water skiing. In winter, ice fishing and cross country skiing are among the activities offered. Shig-Wak Resort also has supervised pet care and baby sitting services. There is a trading post that sells refreshments and supplies. The main lodge has a convivial atmosphere where evenings may be spent around the fireplace reading or talking. Visitors may also participate in various evening activities which include amateur night, movies, and so forth. Weekly rates are as follows: one-bedroom cabins are $130 per week for two persons, $150 per week for three or four persons; two-bedroom cabins are $180 per week; and three-bedroom cabins are $210 per week for up to six persons; $20 per each additional person. A 14–foot fishing boat is included with each rental as are use of the fish-cleaning house, dock service, and freezer service. For additional information contact: Shig-Wak Resort, P.O. Box 388, Ely MN 55731 (218)365–5285.

★★*Snowbank Beach Resort* is located at the southern end of beautiful 5–mile long Snowbank Lake in the Superior National Forest, on the border of Boundary Waters Canoe Area. Outdoor activities include fishing, camping, canoeing, hiking over old logging roads, berry picking (in season), photography, birdwatching. Nearby are golf courses and tennis courts. Snowbank Lake is best known for its walleye, lake trout, and large- and smallmouth bass fishing. The lodge is also open for fall hunting. Canoe trips (with or without guides) are featured. Services include licenses, tackle, groceries, freezing and fish cleaning, and ice. In addition, car-top carriers are available should a guest wish to fish any of the many nearby lakes. Baby sitting services can be provided, there are also a playground and recreation room. A limited number of guest rooms are located in the main lodge. Meals are available on request in the area. There is also a sauna that is open to all guests. Each cabin comes furnished with one boat, and dock space is available for those who wish to bring their own boats. Extra boats and canoes can also be rented. Pets are welcome but must be leashed. All cabins are fully furnished and heated, with modern baths and showers. Rates for housekeeping cabins are $140 per week for two persons, $30 per week for each additional person, $20 per week for children. The daily rate is $12 per person. For additional information, contact: Bob and Margaret Ellis, Box 357, Ely MN 55731 (218)365–4313.

★★★*Snowbank Lodge* is situated on a 52–acre peninsula in Snowbank Lake, a spring-fed, crystal-clear lake located in Superior National Forest, on the edge of the Boundary Waters Canoe Area. Fishing is the primary outdoor activity here, and Snowbank is well known for its smallmouth bass, walleye, lake trout, and northern pike. In addition, there is a 23–mile trail around the lake which offers a chance to sight moose, deer, bear, hawks and other wildlife, including bald eagles. Other recreational activities include swimming, water skiing, camping, and boating. Canoe guide service is available for overnight trips. Other services include a complete tackle shop, fish cleaning and freezing, grocery and mail service. Both motel accommodations (with complete meals) and housekeeping cabins are offered. Box lunches are available for those who wish to spend the entire day on the lake. The cabins are fully equipped, modern, and comfortable. The main lodge is a massive log structure with two fireplaces, a game room, lounge, bar, and dining room. The lodge itself is actually the famous Basswood Lodge (originally on the shores of Basswood Lake) rebuilt. A variety of accommodations is available and rates vary depending on which type is chosen. Rooms in the lodge (American plan, including all meals) are $20 per day, $100 per week per person. American plan cabins (including all meals) are $40 per day per person, $230 per week; $335 per week for two persons.

Housekeeping cabins are $27 per day, $135 per week for one person; $30 per day, $155 per week for two persons. Boats and motors are available at a nominal charge. For additional information, contact Snowbank Lodge, Box 128, Ely, MN 55731 (218)365–5800; from October to April, call 365–5801 or 5802.

★★★*Squaw Bay Resort* is located at Fall Lake on 60 acres, just outside of Ely, in Superior National Forest. Hiking along old logging trails provide the visitor with a close look at the beauty of nature in this area. Guided one-day fishing trips to Basswood Lake in Boundary Waters Canoe Area are offered. There is also a heated swimming pool, sauna, and a sand beach. Tennis courts are on the premises; a golf course is only three miles away in Ely. In Ely, the U.S. Forest Service maintains a Voyageur Visitors' Center with a variety of interpretive programs and exhibits. Nearby, in Tower, tours of an underground iron mine are offered. Squaw Bay offers 21 cabins, a motel unit, and a main lodge. All units are on the lakeshore, and come complete with light housekeeping facilities. In the main lodge is the dining room where home-cooked meals are served daily featuring fresh-baked breads, pies, and cakes. American plan starts at $30 per day per person; $205 per week (includes three meals a day, cabin, maid service, and a boat). The combination plan starts at $20 per day per person; $135 per week (includes two meals a day, cabin). The housekeeping plan ranges from $120 per week to $230 per week depending on number of persons, size of cabin, and time of year. Children are charged at a lower rate. Guests can make arrangements to be picked up in Ely. For additional information, contact Joseph and Carol Skala, Star Route 1, Box 3425, Ely MN 55731 (218)365–4197.

★★★*Tanglewood Trail Resort* is located on beautiful Moose Lake, near Ely, in Superior National Forest. Moose Lake is one of a chain of four lakes offering excellent fishing for walleye (in mid-May) and bass (in June and July), and northern pike in the fall. Canoe trips into Boundary Waters Canoe Area can be arranged. Camping and hiking are also available in the surrounding forestlands. Tanglewood offers fish cleaning and freezing services, and there are also docking and launching facilities for those who wish to bring their own boat. The main lodge has a game room, library, fireplace, and rustic dining room that serves home-cooked, family-style meals daily. All housekeeping cabins are well spaced along the lakeshore for privacy. Log cabins are cozy and rustic, yet fully furnished with cooking utensils, dishes, and linens. Other services available include boat rentals, guide services, gas, bait and tackle, ice and beverages, BWCA permits, licenses, and portage service to Basswood Lake. Pets are permitted but must be leashed. Several types of accommodations are offered—full American plan (rates on request); wilderness plan,

which includes a cabin, boat, and dinner at the lodge ($240 per week for two persons; $80 per week each additional person); and the housekeeping plan, which includes a cabin and a boat ($150 per week for two persons; $35 per week each additional person). Tanglewood is open from May to September. Arrangements to be met in Ely can be made. For additional information, contact: Ted Cleys, Tanglewood Trail Resort, Box 209, Ely MN 55731 (218)365–4977.

★★*Timber Trail Resort* is right on the edge of the Boundary Waters Canoe Area, only 7½ miles east of Ely. Hiking, boating, canoeing, fishing, birdwatching, and berry picking (in season) are among the activities available to guests. From the resort you can travel to Farm, South Farm, White Iron and Garden Lakes with no portages, where you can fish for walleye, northern pike, crappie, and bass, hike along the beautiful Kawishiwi Trail, or explore abandoned logging camps. Guide services are available and fly-in wilderness trips can be arranged. Timber Trail features fully equipped modern cabins. A boat is included with each weekly cabin rental and motors can be rented. Cabins with private bathrooms are $110 per week for two persons, $20 per week for each additional person. Cabins with central showers and restrooms are $90 per week for two persons, $15 per week for each additional person. (The above rates are for two-bedroom cabins.) Additional boats may be rented $8 per day or $50 per week. For additional information, contact: Bob and Shirley Kalesqs, Star Route 1, Box 3111, Ely MN 55731 (218)365–4879.

★★★*Tuscarora Lodge & Outfitters on the Gunflint Trail*, not far from Grand Marais, is in Superior National Forest on Round Lake, at the border of the Boundary Waters Canoe Area, with easy access to Quetico Provincial Park. Tow service across Saganaga Lake is available if a visitor prefers not to paddle to the park entrance. There are fully modern cabins as well as a bunkhouse, and meals are served in the main lodge. Guests who prefer not to take wilderness trips may stay at the lodge and enjoy fishing, swimming, and boating on Round Lake. Each wilderness trip is individually planned, and trips can be started at a variety of points along the Gunflint Trail. Tuscarora Outfitters will plan your route, and point out campsites, points of interest, and fishing spots. Instructions on canoe handling and portaging, packing of gear, and tent pitching will be given if needed. A complete outfit for a three-day trip for two persons is $18 per day (minimum outfitting is for two persons for three days). A four-six day trip for two persons is $16.50 per day per person; for four persons it is $15.50 per day per person. Longer trips are less expensive; children are charged a lower rate. Partial outfitting is also available. Cabin rentals are $19 per day for two persons, $20.50 per day for three persons, and $22 per day for four persons. For additional information, contact Kerry Leeds, Tuscarora Lodge and Outfitters, Gunflint Trail, Grand Marais MN 55604 (218)388–2221.

★★*Whispering Pines Lodge on the Echo Trail* is 20 miles north of Ely in the Superior National Forest, set among tall pines on the shore of Big Lake. Fishing, hunting, and hiking are among the

recreational opportunities available. Services include fishing tackle, fish cleaning, packing, and freezing; boat and canoe rentals; licenses, maps, bait, and groceries. The guest cabins are all fully equipped and heated. There is also a sauna, a library, and boat launching service. Pets are allowed, but must be kept leashed. There are 11 cabins which vary in size—"Cedar" has two bedrooms, "Red Pine" has three—which range, for two persons, from $135 per week to $170 per week; additional persons are $10 per week. A boat is included with each weekly rental. Rates are reduced in September and October. For additional information, contact: G. S. Sjobeck, Whispering Pines Lodge, Box 326, Ely MN 55731. Radio Phone: ZB8–7422. For making reservations, collect calls are accepted.

Travel Services

Bear Track Outfitting Co. operates out of Grand Marais year 'round. Winter trips include guided cross-country ski touring and winter camping. These planned expeditions are from three to five days and are spent in Superior National Forest. All camping equipment and food is provided, and tents are heated. An experienced musher will transport all gear by dog sled to the base camp. Campers must provide their own skis. In the summer, canoe trips are outfitted as are backpacking trips. Canoeists may depart into the Superior-Quetico area from many points. Backpackers may wish to take the ferry (from Grand Portage) to Isle Royale National Park or travel the many hiking trails found in the Arrowhead Region. Among the trails are the rugged 38–mile Kekekabic Trail, the Border Trail, and many shorter trails along Lake Superior or in Superior National Forest. Isle Royale National Park, open from 15 May to 1 October, is an extremely rugged island and is only open to foot travel. Permits to visit Isle Royale are required by the park service. Bear Track Outfitting Co. also offers a traveling camp for children. Planned expeditions in canoeing and backpacking offer an outdoor educational program. Age limits for these trips are 11–17. Transportation to and from Duluth and all equipment (except for sleeping bags) are included. Guided trips for adults, too, can be arranged. A complete outfit with canoe is $16.25 per day per person (one-three days); $15.50 per day per person (four-six days); $14.75 per day per person (seven or more days). Children are charged at a lower rate. A complete backpacking outfit is $14 per day per person (one-three days), $13.25 per day per person (four-six days), and $12.50 per day per person (seven or more days). Partial outfits are also available. For additional information, contact: David and Cathi Williams, Bear Track Outfitting Co., Box 51, Grand Marais MN 55604 (218)387–1162; winter address is: Box 505, Mazomanie, WI 53560 (608)795–4745.

Bill Rom's Canoe Country Outfitters is an experienced outfitter located in Ely. Their routing service plans individual trips for each guest or party. A modern motel in Ely is maintained for those who wish to spend the night(s) before and/or after their trips. Guide service, while not necessary, is available. The guides are all experienced and will lead you to remote, unspoiled fishing areas, set up camp, and so forth. There is a livery service to all trip starting points, and there are also motorboat tows available. Complete outfits include a canoe and accessories, tents, packsacks, axe, sleeping bags and foam pads, cook kit and eating utensils, and all food. Optional additional gear is available, as are partial outfits. Fly-in canoe trips are also available to wilderness lakeshore cabins in Ontario. These rent for $279 per person per week and are fully equipped including boats, canoes, food, and flying in and out. Deluxe outfitting for a seven-day canoe trip is $133 per person; children (under 16) are charged $105 per week. Daily outfitting is $20 per person; children $16. However, a wide range of trips and outfits is available. For additional information,

contact: Bob Olsen, 629 East Sheridan Street, Box 30, Ely MN 55731 (218)365–4046 or 6416.

Canadian Border Outfitters maintain a base on Moose Lake, in Superior National Forest, just north of Ely. This is a family-run outfitter and has been in business for over 20 years. At their Moose Lake base are a motel, bunkhouse, shower and sauna, coffee shop, parking lot (attended), tackle shop, boat launching ramp, and float-plane service. They also maintain fly-in wilderness outpost camps in Ontario, which are fully equipped with sleeping bags, gas cooking, eating utensils, lanterns, and a 14–foot boat with a motor. Fresh linens are flown up with each party. The food box includes fresh meat, eggs, fruits and vegetables, and staples (such as coffee, tea, sugar, soap, and so forth). Canadian Border Outfitters will gladly help you plan your trip. They will also handle all paperwork involved with forest service permits. Guide service is available at $40 per day plus the cost of outfitting for the guide; packers are available for $25 per day plus outfitting. By prearrangement, guests arriving at Ely can be met. Rates vary depending upon the kind of trip one wishes to take. A five-day fly-in trip to one of the camps in Ontario (discussed above) is $325 per person. Complete outfitting (lightweight) is $20 per person per day for trips up to five days; six- or seven-day trips are $19 per person per day; and trips of eight days or more are $18 per person per day. Children (under 15) are charged $5 less per day. Rooms in the lakeside motel are $17 per night for two persons. Bunks in the bunkhouses (with use of sleeping bags and central showers) are $13 per night per person. A lightweight outfit includes: canoe, portage yoke, paddles, life jackets, tent and poles, mattress, sleeping bag, saw, axe, shovel, cook kit, eating utensils, rope, rain gear, packsacks and waterproof liners, reflector oven, and food. For additional information, contact: Tom Harristhal, Canadian Border Outfitters, Box 117, Ely, MN 55731 (218)365–5847.

Canadian Waters, Inc. is a long-established outfitter located in Ely. Each party's trip is individually planned and routed on large-scale waterproof maps; and such details as suggested campsites, productive fishing areas, historical sites, Indian rock paintings, rapids, and waterfalls are all carefully marked. Trip plans are filed in the main office so that parties can be reached in the event of an emergency. Although guide service is not required for a successful trip, professional guides are available at a charge of $40 per day plus outfitting charges. For those customers taking the complete outfitting service, free transportation is provided to and from Fall Lake, Lake One, Moose Lake, Snowbank Lake, South Kawishiwi River, and the Echo Trail. Fly-in service to remote wilderness lakes is also offered. It is also possible to fly-in and paddle back. A wide variety of trips

and plans are offered, and rates depend upon which type of trip is chosen. A complete lightweight outfitting trip is $133 per week per person; a complete deluxe ultra-lightweight outfitting trip is $175 per week per person; and a complete deluxe boat-fishing trip is $185 per person for a five-day package. Children are charged at a lower rate, and there are daily rates for all trips. Partial outfitting is also available. Additional services include flight pickups and motel accommodations (in Ely). For additional information, contact Jon Waters, Canadian Waters, Inc., 111 East Sheridan Street, Ely MN 55731 (218)365–3202.

Carlson's Quetico-Superior Outfitters is a family-owned outfitter on Moose Lake, just 20 miles northeast of Ely. Carlson's has been outfitting canoe parties for 30 years. Each trip is individually planned and routed; and by beginning trips at their Moose Lake dock, one can save a day's paddle over starting points in Ely or Winton. Travel permits are required for the Boundary Waters Canoe Area and Quetico Provincial Park. Carlson's will secure these permits for their guests, but need to know the trip's starting date and entry point. Parties who plan ahead and who are somewhat flexible should have little trouble canoeing the area. Since weekends are usually the busiest, it is advisable to begin one's trip during the week. Overnight cabins are available for rental for those who wish accommodations at the base camp. Guests who wish to start from points other than Moose Lake will be transported, free of charge, to other points including Lake One and Snowbank Lake. Minimum outfitting is for two persons for three days. Minnesota fishing licenses are available at Carlson's, as are canoe motors, fuel, fishing tackle, and refreshments. A complete outfit is $18 per day per person; $14 per day for children (under 16). A cabin for two persons is $15 per night, $18 per night for three, $22 per night for four. Eating arrangements (at a nearby lodge) can be made for guests. For additional information, contact: Bernie Carlson, Carlson's Quetico-Superior Outfitters, P.O. Box 89, Ely MN 55731 (218)365–5480.

Duane's Outfitters is a complete outfitting service located near Ely in the Superior National Forest. Motel accommodations are available and a lowcost bunkhouse at the base serves people arriving late in the day. They will transport canoes and all equipment to various put-in places—usually Fall Lake, Moose Lake, or Lake One. You may embark from one point and return to another. All trips are individually planned; and Duane's will provide assistance in basic canoeing methods, portaging, packing of gear, and setting up camp. Duane's issues BWCA permits and sells fishing licenses. Their food packs conform to the U.S. Forest Service regulations and do not contain either cans or bottles. Fly-in trips can be arranged. Partial outfits are available; canoes are $7 per day; other equipment may be rented separately. Complete outfits are $49 per person (for three days); $62 per person (for four days); $99 per person (for seven days). Children (under 16) are charged a lower rate. For additional information, contact: Duane and Elsie Arvola, Highway 21, Babbitt MN 55706 (218)827–2710.

Graystone Outfitters have their headquarters outside of Ely. Two short portages from their Fall Lake base is famous Basswood Lake—a beautiful island-dotted fishing mecca in the heart of the Boundary Waters Canoe Area. Graystone is a complete wilderness canoe outfitting service and can accommodate individuals, families, or groups. Their expert staff will help you to choose a route and plan the details of your trip. Graystone also maintains a campground located near Lake One, Moose Lake, and Snowbank Lake. It is suitable for the nights before and after a canoe trip. Guests may also base themselves there and take day trips in the area—by canoe, boat, or hike the famous Kekekabic Trail. Graystone can arrange fly-in trips (to Canada) as well. They also maintain a tent camp on Basswood Lake. Canoeing, camping, fishing, hunting—Graystone is fully equipped to outfit any trip. Rates vary with the outfit chosen: a complete outfit (including canoe, yoke, paddles, tent, tarp, cooking and eating utensils, food, and so on) is $16 per day per

person for a trip from one to three days; $13 per person for a trip from four to seven days; and $12 per person for a trip of eight days or more. Groups of more than three persons are charged somewhat less per person. Children are $9 per day when accompanied by at least one adult. Parties being outfitted must supply their own clothing, compass, first-aid kit, and fishing equipment. For additional information, contact Arlan Ladwig, Graystone Outfitters, 1829 East Sheridan Street, Ely MN 55731 (218)365–3251.

Lynx Track Winter Travel, a nonprofit educational organization, offers seminars in all forms of winter travel in the northern forest wilderness—including dog-sledding, cross-country skiing, snowshoeing, winter camping, maps and compass use, igloo buildings, ice safety, first aid, fire, survival techniques, stargazing, and winter nature lore. The seminars include all meals and sleeping-bag accommodations at their base camp north of Ely near the Boundary Waters Canoe Area in heated arctic tents and Indian tepees. Advanced courses include a nine-day crossing of the Boundary Waters Canoe Area via cross-country skills, snowshoes, and dog sled, and a ski-touring expedition in Wyoming's Cloud Peak Wilderness in the Bighorn Mountains. For rates and free literature, write: 5375 Eureka Rd., Excelsior 55331 (612)474–5190.

Northpoint Canoe Outfitters, one of the nation's first north country canoe services, has its base on sprawling Saganaga Lake off the Gunflint Trail, at the edge of the Boundary Waters Canoe Area in the Superior National Forest. Northpoint will help you to custom plan your wilderness canoe trip; it will be tailored to your interests: scenery, fishing, wildlife photography, whatever you prefer. Their planning kit includes detailed maps showing campsites, portages, and points of interest. At their base on Saganaga Lake, there are private cabins where you can spend either the night before or the night after your canoe trip. The cabins are nestled among jack pine and birch trees along the Seagull River. You can start out at a variety of points along the Gunflint Trail; Northpoint will transport you free of charge. Head start (motor) service is also available; the charge ranges from $12 to $40 depending on where you want to be towed to (or from). Guide service, while not necessary, is available; and fly-in service to the Quetico Wilderness is also offered. A minimum complete outfit is for two persons for three days. A four-six day trip is $18 per day per person; children are charged at a lower rate. There are also group rates. Partial outfits are also available. Canoe rentals are $7–$9 per day; outfitting, food is $7.50 per day per person. For additional information, contact: Fred Zopff, Northpoint Canoe Outfitters, Gunflint Trail 152, Grand Marais MN 55604 (218)388–2283; winter (314)843–7199.

Pipestone Canoe Outfitting Company is located on Fall Lake in the Superior National Forest only two miles from the Boundary Waters Canoe Area. This is wilderness country, where one can canoe, camp, and fish virtually undisturbed. At Fall Lake there are log cabins with complete light housekeeping facilities. Linens are supplied and the cabins are heated. A 14-foot boat is included with each cabin. Pets are not allowed. Pipestone Outfitting Company will provide complete or partial outfitting service: canoe, all camping equipment, and food supplies. All food packs meet the regulations of the U.S. Forest Service for carrying into Boundary Waters Canoe Area. For those entering BWCA, Pipestone is authorized to issue travel permits. In addition, motors, motorboats, and fishing tackle may be rented. Experienced guides are also available. Pipestone is well equipped to help canoeists who may be making their first trip. Since they are located right on the lake, it is easy for them to give instruction in paddling, loading, and portaging. Good maps are available and instruction is yours for the asking. For those who wish to start their trip elsewhere, fly-in service and motorboat tows are available. There is a nominal charge for transportation for canoeists who want to put in at Moose Lake or at other locations along the Echo Trail (or elsewhere). Free cartop carriers (for canoes) are available for visitors who want to drive themselves to put-in points. The Forest Service maintains free parking facilities at nearly all frequently used canoe put-in points. Pipestone is easy to reach from Ely—just take Route 169 north to Winton and continue to the sign that indicates the Fall Lake turn-off. Rates for a cabin (for two people), including one boat, are $95 per week; each additional person: $10 per week. A complete, ultra-lightweight outfit is $16.50 per person, per day for two persons (for a trip of five days or less).

There are special rates for longer trips and/or for larger parties. For additional information, contact: Toni and Jack Dulinsky (owners), Pipestone Canoe Outfitting Company, P.O. Box 780, Ely MN 55731 (218)365–3788.

Portage Outfitters have their headquarters off the scenic Gunflint Trail on Seagull Lake. Seagull is one of the thousands of lakes in Superior National Forest adjacent to Quetico Provincial Park offering immediate access to Boundary Waters Canoe Area. Numerous canoe trips are possible and the fishing is excellent here for walleye, northern pike, bass, and lake trout. Portage sells fishing licenses and issues permits for BWCA. Rustic sleeping facilities are available at headquarters for either the night before or the night after your canoe trip. In Grand Marais a variety of accommodations is available. Both complete and partial outfitting are offered. Minimum complete outfitting is for two persons for three days. A three-day trip for two persons is $17 per day per person; for four persons it is $16.75 per day per person. A four-six day trip is $16.50 per day per person (for two persons), $16.25 per day per person (for four persons). Children are charged at a lower rate. A student discount is also available. For additional information, contact: Portage Canoe Outfitters, Gunflint Trail, Grand Marais MN 55604 (218)388–2216.

Saganaga Outfitters are located on the Gunflint Trail in Grand Marais, at the eastern entry to the Boundary Waters Canoe Area. Canoeists beginning their trip at the landing on Saganaga Lake have direct access—without rapids or portage—to the wilderness lakes in the BWCA and Quetico Park. Saganaga Outfitters will instruct the novice in canoeing, portaging, packing gear, cooking, map reading, and general camping. They will mark on large-scale maps the better campsites, points of interest, fishing areas, and portages. For those wishing accommodation at the base camp for the night(s) before and/or after a trip, Adirondack cabins and bunkhouse are available. Saganaga Outfitters will also start or meet parties at a variety of locations without extra charge. Partial outfitting is also available. Rates vary depending upon the length of the trip and the number of people involved. Minimum outfitting is for two persons for three days. Examples of costs are: a three- or four-day trip for two persons is $18 per day per person; five- or six-day trip for four persons is $15.50 per day per person; trips seven days or longer are $15.25 per day per person (for two persons). Children are charged a lower rate. Base camp charges for completely outfitted persons are free for one night, $1.50 per person for each additional night. Sauna, shower, and parking are all available. For additional information, contact: Don and Carole Germain, Saganaga Outfitters, Gunflint Trail, Grand Marais MN 55604 (218)388–2217.

Superior Forest Outfitters are located on Farm Lake, east of Ely, in Superior National Forest, near the border of the Boundary Waters Canoe Area. A campground and lodge are also located here. Directly across Farm Lake is the Kawishiwi River which is an entry point to BWCA. Permits to enter BWCA must be obtained in advance, and Superior Outfitters will reserve permits for you. All food packs conform to U.S. Forest Service regulations. Each trip is individually planned and Superior Outfitters will give instruction in canoe paddling and portaging and camping tips. Guides are available, but are not necessary. Complete outfitting includes bunk-house accommodations for the first and last night, sauna, breakfast on the first day, canoe, tent, pack, cooking utensils, life jacket, saw, axe, and food. A complete outfit is $14.50 per day per person. A seven-day package if $87 per person. Children (under 12) are charged a lower rate. There are special rates for organized groups of eight or more. Partial outfits are also available. For additional information, contact: Gene and Carol Johnson, Star Route 1, Box 3199, Ely MN 55731 (218)365–4870.

Tip of the Trail Canoe Outfitters are experienced outfitters located off the Gunflint Trail, outside of Grand Marais, with their base on Saganaga Lake, a jumping-off point to the Boundary Waters Canoe Area and the Quetico Wilderness. The Douglases—owners and operators of Tip of the Trail—will personally supervise the preparations of your wilderness canoe trip. They will help you plan your trip, outline your route, indicate the exact location of campsites, prime fishing spots, scenic areas, and dangerous rapids. Before you leave their base, they will offer camping tips and instruction in paddling, portaging, and water safety. At the base one may purchase maps, gloves and hats, gas, fishing licenses and tackle, and beverages. Permits for entering BWCA will be reserved for you and will be issued upon your arrival. Guides, while not necessary, are available upon request. The fee for a guide is $40 per day plus outfit. Equipment included in outfits is lightweight and sturdy and all provisions have been trail-tested by the Douglases. Overnight accommodations, showers, and a sauna are available at their base. There is also a campground. Campsites are $4 per day (tent); $7 per day (RV). Services available include boat docking, showers, sauna, dumping station, boat and canoe rental, and provisions. Boat-fishing trips are also offered. A five-day package (per person) is $150; $175

for seven days. Children are charged a lower rate. Packages include food, boat, motor, and all necessary camping gear. A complete outfit for a four-six day canoe trip is $18.50 per day per person. A three-day trip is $19.50 per day per person; longer trips are less expensive per day. There is a discount for students, and children (under 16) are charged a lower rate. Partial outfitting is also available. For additional information, contact: Bill and Sue Douglas, Tip of the Trail Canoe Outfitters, Box 147, Gunflint Trail, Grand Marais MN 55604 (218)388–2225.

Wilderness Outfitters, Inc. maintain a variety of camps: fly-in outpost cabins in Canada located on Baril Bay of Mille Lacs Lake and deluxe tent cabins on famous Basswood Lake, located in the Boundary Waters Canoe Area. In addition, there is a base camp at Moose Lake, a convenient starting point for wilderness canoe trips. The trading post has a restaurant, and there are tent cabins for those who wish to spend the night before starting off. Advance reservations for these cabins are required. Private landings for the guests of Wilderness Outfitters are maintained at Fall Lake and at Moose Lake where there are lighted parking areas and where canoes are available. In addition, launch service to all points on Basswood Lake is maintained as is launch service to various other portages (Ensign, Prairie, and Carp Lake). Wilderness Outfitters' post is located in Ely, on Camp Street. Guide service is also available, but is not necessary for a successful trip. Fishing licenses are available at the outfitting post. Wilderness Outfitters can supply a complete or partial outfit. There is a wide range of rates, depending upon which type of outfit and/or trip is chosen. A complete outfit (including canoe, camping equipment, and food) is $20 per person per day for trips up to seven days, each day after the seventh is $15 per person. Children (under 16) are charged $16 per day. Tent cabins on Basswood Lake for five days are $205 per person; $30 per person for each additional day; canoes are $8 per day. Wilderness Outfitters' season runs from 20 May to 20 September. Since such a variety of trips is possible, it would be wise to write for their brochure. For additional information, contact Jim Pascoe and Bob LaTourell (owners and operators), 1 East Camp Street, Ely MN 55731 (218)365–3211 or 4785.

Voyageurs National Park

This 219,400–acre wilderness encompasses the picturesque Kabetogama Peninsula, a heavily forested region of fir, spruce, pine, aspen, and birch, broken by bogs, ancient rock outcroppings, sandy beaches, and towering cliffs. Bounded in part by three major glacial lakes—Rainy, Kabetogama, and Namakan—Voyageurs National Park offers top-ranked trophy fishing, canoeing, and wilderness lakeshore camping. The main body of land, the 75,000–acre Kabetogama Peninsula, is accessible principally by water, and its interior holds a number of lakes that can be reached only on foot. The north shore of the peninsula features a sharply broken front with many small bays and hidden coves. Off the south shore lie innumerable tiny islands, smooth, glaciated rocks along both shores offer ideal sites for camping.

The earliest chapters in the human history of the North American continent opened in the forested lake country of Minnesota's northern border when descendants of the Asiatic people wandered south thousands of years ago and settled along the shoreline. These people are known to have been in Minnesota as early as 11,000 years ago, the first known existence of man in America. The remains of one of their descendants, "Minnesota Man," was found in 1931 near Pelican Rapids. "Minnesota Man" was actually a teenage girl who drowned in glacial Lake Pelican, part of the vast waters of ancient Lake Agassiz. From these early people the Sioux Indians evolved into the first tribal inhabitants of the area. Thanks to the rich sources of

game—deer, moose, and woodland caribou—and the abundant fish in the lakes and streams, the Sioux developed a highly prosperous hunting and gathering society which thrived until 300 years ago, when Algonquian Indians, also known as Ojibways, and their relatives the Ottawas moved westward from the Ohio and Michigan area. The Ojibways, commonly called Chippewas, intruded upon the highly desirable lands of the Sioux. After many battles lasting several generations, the Sioux were forced from northern Minnesota by Chippewa tribes, who then held sway over the lakes and forests until the coming of the white man.

Beginning in the mid-seventeenth century and for a century and a half thereafter, French Canadian voyageurs, led or assisted by Indians, plied this maze of lakes and streams in slender canoes, transporting huge quantities of furs and goods between Montreal and the far Northwest. Thus opened one of the most colorful and adventurous eras in the history of the great Northwest, names like Sieur de La Vérendrye, Pierre Esprit Radisson, and Sieur des Broseillers still evoke an aura of romance and daring, of incredible prosperity coupled with hard work, tremendous hardship, danger, and sheer cunning. The portage paths blazed by the Indians and French Canadian explorers were traveled during the nineteenth century by the fur traders of the American Fur Company, who established trading posts in the North Country at Fond-du-Lac, Grand Portage, Grand Marais, Vermilion Lake, Moose Lake, Basswood Lake, Rainy River, Rainy Lake, Rosseau Lake and Lake of the Woods. The latter part of the nineteenth and early twentieth centuries saw the influx of loggers and gold prospectors, who followed the old Indian trail from Duluth to beautiful Lake Vermilion, called *Sak-Ga-Ee-Gum-Wah-Ma-Mah-Nec*, or "Lake of the Sunset Glow," by the Chippewa.

Though the hardy voyageur—with his lusty songs, colorful sash, red stocking cap, pipe, and vermilion-tipped paddle—is gone, the land is not. From the water this stretch of lake country looks today much as it did during the heyday of trapping and trading. It has all the wildness and immense scale associated with the northern lakes region—a land surface shaped by glaciers into an endless and intricate system of waterways complemented by the vast green mantle of lush forests.

Water sports have naturally become the major attraction of the area. Game-fish populations, especially walleyes, provide excellent fishing opportunities in Kabetogama, Namakan, and Rainy lakes. Northern pike, lake trout, and smallmouth bass are other frequently caught species. Boating is also popular on the many lakes. Boaters not familiar with the waters are advised to obtain the services of a guide or detailed charts, which are available locally. The large lakes can

quickly become very rough, and it is imperative to keep an eye on weather conditions at all times. Users of small boats and canoes should be particularly cautious and prepared to wait out rough water. The park's wildlife is also a source of continuing fascination and delight. Black bear and deer are common sights, as are ruffed grouse and snowshoe hare. Shorebirds are fairly scarce, although the solitary sandpiper sometimes nests in the area. Northern owls, the great gray, boreal, and hawk owls can often be seen silhouetted against the winter sky, along with merlins and ravens. The principal species sought by the voyageur—beaver, otter, mink, Canada lynx, muskrat, and fox—are still found in good numbers throughout the park, with over 200 beaver colonies scattered along inland streams.

Information Sources, Maps & Access

For detailed park information and the free *Voyageurs National Park Map/Brochure*, *Voyageurs National Park Backcountry Travel*, and *Fish & Wildlife of Voyageurs National Park*, contact: Superintendent's Office, Voyageurs National Park, 405 2nd St., International Falls, MN 56649 (218)283–9821. Voyageurs National Park is easily approached by surfaced roads from four points along U.S. 53 traveling from Duluth. County Route 23 from Orr leads to Crane Lake at the eastern end of the planned park; County Route 122, just south of International Falls, provides access to the south shore of Lake Kabetogama; Minnesota 11 from International Falls approaches the park area at Black Bay and Neil Point; County Route 765, or Ash River Trail, provides access to Namakan Lake. There are no roads into the interior, so access is primarily by boat. Major outfitting centers are Crane Lake and International Falls (which see).

Gateways & Accommodations

International Falls—Gateway to Voyageurs National Park

(Pop. 7,000; zip code 56649; area code 218). Named for a 35–foot drop of the Rainy River, International Falls is a port of entry to Canada and the gateway to a vast wilderness of lakes, rivers, and forests. Points of interest include the Koochiching County Historical Museum, in Municipal Park, containing displays of local historical interest, and Voyageurs National Park, just east of town via Minnesota State Hwy. 11. Accommodations: *Best Western Rambler* (rates: $19–22 double), 22 rooms, color TV, free airport bus, restaurant nearby, 1½ mile south of town on U.S. 53 (283–8454); *Holiday Inn* (rates: $34.50 double), 125 excellent rooms and suites, color TV, heated indoor pool, sauna, putting green, free airport bus, restaurant and cocktail lounge, on Sherwood Drive, two miles west of town via U.S. 71 (283–4451). *International Motor Lodge* (rates: $20–24 double), 32 rooms, color TV, restaurant nearby, on Riverview Blvd., one mile west of town on U.S. 71 (283–2577); *Tee Pee Motel* (rates: $20–22 double), 42 rooms, color TV, restaurant nearby, ½ mile south of town via U.S. 53 (283–8494).

Lodges & Resorts

***Currie's Ash-Ka-Nam Resort*, at the entrance to the Voyageurs National Park, has full resort facilities for vacationers and caters to fishermen. It is located on the Ash River above the junction of Kabetogama and Namakan Lakes. Fishermen and boaters starting out at the resort's dock have quick access to either lake. There is an ice cream parlor for guests, a fireside lounge with a bar, and a dock with gas, bait, and boat rentals. Accommodations are in modern cabins overlooking the water. Rates are $155 per week for two people and $10 per week for each extra person or $30 per day for two people plus $2.50 per day for each extra person. A new deluxe cabin can accommodate up to 12 people at a rate of $330

per week for four people plus $15 per week for each additional person. A 16–foot boat is included with each cabin that is rented by the week. Canoes, 16–foot boats, 25–hp motors and an 18–foot guide boat with a 50–hp motor are all available for rent. For further information contact: Currie's Ash-Ka-Nam Resort, Ash River Trail, Orr, MN 55771 (218) 374–3181.

★*Minnesota Voyageur Houseboats'* base is located on the scenic Ash River Trail in Superior National Forest, on the border of Voyageurs National Park. This spectacular wilderness park was created for the canoer who must camp to appreciate its unspoiled beauty. The Ebels help each party plan their trip. At the main lodge, provisions, beverages, tackle, ice, licenses, and bait may be purchased. Complete navigation charts are provided, at no extra charge. Walleye, smallmouth bass, crappie, and muskie can all be caught here. A 14–foot boat is included with each rental. Motors are not included but may be rented. An ice cooler is also included, in addition to the refrigerator. However, it is a good idea to bring your own live bait container. All houseboats are equipped with life jackets and Coast Guard approved life-saving devices. Guide service is available, at prevailing rates. The cost of all outboard motor gas is additional; the average amount used is 45 gallons. The rental season is from the beginning of May to the beginning of October. Week-long rentals *only* are accepted from mid-June to the end of August; at other times a three-day rental is the minimum. Included in each rental are: gas heater, refrigerator, cooking facilities, hot and cold running water, bedding and linens, all dishes and cooking utensils, an anchor with steel cable and winch, and deck chairs. Rates vary depending on the size of the boat. A 42–foot boat that sleeps up to nine persons is $675 per week. A 48–foot boat (also sleeps nine) is $745 per week. The deluxe, 50–foot boat (sleeps 10) is $840 per week. For additional information, contact: Gordy Ebel, Minnesota Voyageur Houseboats, Ash River Trail, Orr MN 55771 (218)374–3571.

★★*Burchell's Moosehorn Resort* is located on the evergreen shores of beautiful Kabetogama Lake, north of Ray, bordered by dense pine forests. Kabetogama Lake, one of the four entry points to Voyageurs National Park, is 22 miles long and six miles wide, dotted with numerous evergreen islands and its shoreline embraces many inlets and bays, making it possible to fish in all kinds of weather. Walleye, muskellunge, northern pike, and jumbo perch are found here. One may travel a distance of 65 miles without portaging. Guide services, while not necessary, can easily be arranged. Other services include fish filleting and use of the fish cleaning house and freezer. Bait, tackle, motors, and fuel are available. Housekeeping cabins are fully

furnished and have modern bathrooms and kitchens, with picture windows facing the lake. Use of a 16–foot boat is included with each weekly rental. Pets are not permitted. Rates for cabins range from $120 per week to $180 per week depending upon the number of persons in the party and the size of the cabin. Additional persons are charged $20 per week. A nightly rate (minimum of three nights) is available at one-fifth the weekly rate. Additional boats and motors may be rented. For additional information, contact: Burchell's Moosehorn Resort, Ray MN 56669 (218)875–3491.

★*Northernaire Floating Lodges* is a houseboat rental concern. Their base camp is located seven miles east of International Falls on North Jackfish Bay of huge Rainy Lake, which borders on Voyageurs National Park and holds big walleye, smallmouth bass, crappie, muskie, and northern pike. Guide service is recommended. Northernaire's guides are fully experienced and are available either full- or part-time. If this is your first houseboating venture, a guide is required for at least part of the first day. Complete navigation charts are provided and each trip is individually planned. Outboard motor gas is not included. Small boats may also be rented, with or without motors. All houseboats have gas heaters, screened windows, an anchor with winch, and Coast Guard approved life-saving devices. Included with each rental are: all cooking and eating utensils, cleaning equipment, blankets and bedding, towels, gas for heating and cooking, and ice for coolers. Food may be purchased at the base. As the refrigeration compartment on the boats is not large, it is suggested that guests bring their own coolers as a supplement. Food can be supplied at a cost of $15 per day, $75 per week per person. Rates for guides are $35 minimum. Houseboat rentals vary depending upon the type of boat and the length of the rental. Rates range from a 36–foot boat at $495 per week, $100 per day to a 50–foot boat at $935 per week, $200 per day. The former will accommodate up to four persons, the latter up to ten. For additional information, contact: Charles and Jane Levene, Box 510, Island View Route, International Falls MN 56649 (218)286–5221 or 5222.

★★*Rocky Point Resort* is located on sprawling, island-dotted Kabetogama Lake outside of Ray, near Voyageurs National Park. There is excellent fishing in Kabetogama for northern pike, walleye, smallmouth bass, and perch. Cabins are nestled among tall pines in a wilderness setting. Each housekeeping cabin has a knotty pine interior, is carpeted and heated, and is completely furnished with modern kitchens and bathrooms. Cabin rentals range from $130 per week to $150 per week for two persons; each additional guest is charged $20 per week. During the summer, children (under 12) are not charged. A 16–foot boat is included with each rental (or dock space for your own boat). Extra boats and motors can also be rented. There is a small store that sells gas, tackle, beverages, and groceries. Fish filleting and freezing services are also available. Boat tours and guide services can be arranged. For additional information, contact: Gene and Jean Juelich, Rocky Point Resort, Ray MN 56669 (218)875–2411.

★★*Thunderbird Lodge* is a year-round resort located east of International Falls on Rainy Lake, near Voyageurs National Park. Fishing for big walleye, smallmouth bass and northern pike is the most popular activity at the lodge. In summer guests may also enjoy hiking, berry picking, swimming, and boating and canoeing. Fall is the hunting season; and in winter one can ski, go snowmobiling, or go ice fishing. There are tennis courts and a heated swimming pool at the lodge. Fly-in fishing trips can be arranged and expert guide service is available. Cabins are heated and completely furnished and have efficiency cooking units. The base rate for American plan (including lodging and all meals) is $32 per day per person. Actual rate may be slightly higher or lower depending upon accommodations and length of stay. Modified American plan (including lodging, breakfast, and dinner) is $28.50 per day per person. Rooms at the lodge range from $22 to $32 per day per person; additional persons are charged $5 per day; children (under 12) are not charged. The European plan (no meals) is offered at the cabins. These range from $175 per week (for one or two persons) to $260 per week (for four persons); and $300 per week (for six). Canoes, boats and motors may also be rented. For additional information, contact: Thunderbird Lodge, Box 407, Island View Route, International Falls MN 56649 (218)286–3151.

★★★*Voyageurs Park Lodge* occupies a high 20–acre peninsula jutting 1,500 feet into Lake Kabetogama in Voyageurs National Park, which together with Rainy, Namakan, Sandpoint, and Crane Lake, forms a spectacular scenic chain of wilderness lakes stretching for 100 miles along the Minnesota-Ontario border. Lake Kabetogama offers some of the best walleye, northern pike, and smallmouth bass fishing in the state. The scenic 75,000–acre Kabetogama peninsula is just a few minutes away by boat. Wilderness hiking trails penetrate its interior leading to seldom fished lake trout and muskie lakes. The rustic Voyageurs Park Lodge is one of the largest log structures in the area. The lodge dining room and lounge are open to all guests. The guest cabins sleep from two to eight people and are well spaced for privacy. The cottages are scattered on the peninsula with a picturesque trail leading to each cabin for convenient parking. On each end of the peninsula there is a sandy beach for swimming. Virgin timber, blueberries, and many kinds of wildlife are found among the huge lakeshore rocks, enhancing the wilderness setting. Each cottage is spacious and heated for chilly nights. All are carpeted, warm natural wood interior, and have a completely modern kitchen and bathroom. Weekly cabin rates are $150 for two people, one-bedroom; $225 for four people, two-bedroom; $300 for six people, three-bedroom; $375 for eight people, four-bedroom. The lodge offers excellent services as well as canoe rentals, boats and motors, and excursion trips by boat in Voyageurs National Park. The lodge is reached by Minnesota Highway 122 from U.S. 53. For additional information, write or call: Voyageurs Park Lodge, Ray, MN 56669 (218)875–2131.

MISSISSIPPI

Introduction

Mississippi's scenic pine and hardwood forests, rolling fields, coastal waters, lakes, streams, reservoirs, cypress-shaded bayous, and marshlands provide excellent fishing and hunting opportunities. The state's major freshwater fish species include largemouth, spotted, striped, and white bass; blue and channel catfish; and hordes of white perch, bream, and crappie. The state's 19 upland wildlife areas, national-forest game lands, 9 waterfowl areas, and 2 national wildlife refuges provide outstanding hunting in season for whitetail deer, gray (or cat) fox and squirrel, rabbits, wild turkey, and rafts of dove, quail, mallards, black ducks, and pheasant. In addition to the public game lands, the state licenses 75 shooting preserves, where hunting is permitted on payment of a fee.

Accommodations & Travel Information

For detailed information on fishing and hunting lodges, vacation resorts, motels, and hotels throughout the state, write to the Travel/Tourism Department, Mississippi Agricultural & Industrial Board, P.O. Box 849, Jackson 39205, or to the local Chamber of Commerce of the area you plan to visit. A complete listing of state-park lodges and cabin facilities is contained in the 95–page *Mississippi Travel Guide*, available free upon request from the Travel/Tourism Department (address above).

Comprehensive listings and descriptions of all commercial, state-park, and national-forest campgrounds are contained in the free 95–page *Mississippi Travel Guide*. This indispensable guide also contains a listing of all Mississippi lake and reservoir campgrounds, and descriptions of types of facilities available, including trailer camping, tent camping, group camping, and primitive camping as well as boat-launching sites, trailer-hook-up sites, tent showers, and recreation attractions.

Highways & Maps

Detailed highway maps of the state, including the Lakes and Hills, the Delta, the Plains, the Old and New South, and the Gulf Coast vacation regions, are contained in the 95–page *Mississippi Travel Guide*, available free upon request from the Travel/Tourism Department, address above. This eminently useful travel guide is packed full with information about Mississippi's weather and climate, little-known facts, natural resources, national forests, geography, hunting and fishing, pilgrimages, and region-by region/county-by-county descriptions of historic sites and buildings, county fairs and festivals, scenic attractions and museums, recreational activities, reservoirs, campgrounds, rock- and fossil-collecting areas, and shooting preserves.

The "travel guide" also contains a detailed *Natchez Trace Parkway Map* as well as descriptions of all major recreation and historic attractions along this famed scenic route, which winds from Natchez,

Mississippi, to Nashville, Tennessee. This national parkway, maintained and administered by the National Park Service, crosses the state from its northeast corner to its southwest boundary, passing through beautiful forests of majestic pines and moss-hung oaks, along the ancient Natchez Trace Indian Trail and pioneer route. The major features shown along the trace include Emerald Mound— a temple mound built by an unknown tribe of Indians—Owl Creek Indian Mounds, Pigeon Roost, Bynum Mounds, the legendary Witch Dance, De Soto's Crossing, and old Chickasaw Village. This ancient wilderness route once connected the Natchez, Choctaw, and Chickasaw Indian villages. For detailed recreation travel information along the route, write: Natchez Trace Parkway, P.O. Box 948, Tupelo 38801. An excellent guide, *Fossil & Mineral Collecting Localities in Mississippi*, available for $1.50 from the Geological Economic & Topographical Survey, 2525 Northwest St., P.O. Box 4915, Jackson 39216, gives explicit directions and maps to collections throughout the state.

**VACATION/
LODGING GUIDE**

Mississippi Lakes, Forests & Coastal Recreation Areas

The northern Lakes and Hills Region of the Magnolia State contains the foothills of the Great Smokies and the "great lakes"—huge reservoirs that have hundreds of miles of shoreline, marvelous fishing for trophy bass and bream, and some of the nation's top duck-hunting lands. Pickwick Lake, on Tennessee's TVA Pickwick Dam on the Tennessee River in the northeast corner of the state, offers fishing for largemouth bass, striped or white bass, walleye, crappie, and bream. Pickwick is Mississippi's largest body of freshwater. Other major bass lakes and streams include Arkabutla Reservoir, which covers 52 square miles, surrounded by 28,200 acres of public hunting lands; Y-shaped Grenada Reservoir, with 75,000 acres of public game lands; and Log Loader Lake, Sunflower River, Black Bayou, Six-Mile Lake, and Horn, Beaver, Lamar Bruce, Lee, and Dumas lakes and the Sardis River, which extends up the Little Tallahatchie River for 30 miles. The prime public game lands in the northern lake and hill country include Holly Springs National Forest and the reservoir waterfowl areas, and Malmaison and John Bell Williams wildlife-management areas, and Yellow Creek Waterfowl Area on Pickwick Reservoir.

The fertile Mississippi Delta Region, which stretches along the western boundary of the state, has good fishing for bass, crappie, bream, and catfish in the innumerable lakes formed by the ever-changing Mississippi, Sunflower, and Yazoo rivers. The major lakes of the region include Beulah, Bolivar, Old River, De Soto, Horseshoe, Tchula, Little Eagle, Chotard, Yazoo, McIntyre Scatters, Lower Ossy, Mink, Buzzard Bayou, and 17–mile-long Tunica cut-off lake (an old bed of the Mississippi), Moon Lake (a cut-off bend in the "Ole Miss"), and Ferguson, Washington, and Deer lakes. The 30,000–acre Ross Barnett Reservoir, in the southwest quadrant of the state, is the site of the annual National Bass Anglers Sportsman Society Tournament (BASS). The lake's 150 miles of shoreline, with its numerous bays and dead timber areas, provide top-ranked fishing for trophy black bass, sea-run striped bass, crappie, bluegill, and catfish. The acorn-bearing hardwood forests, marshlands, and beautiful moss-hung, cypress-studded bayous provide good hunting for deer, dove, duck, quail, rabbit, squirrel, and turkey. The major public hunting areas include the Assaquena and Sunflower wildlife-management areas, Delta and Homochitto national forests, and the Indian Bayou Waterfowl Area, and Pearl River Waterfowl and Upland Birch Area.

The lakes, streams, gently rolling hills, extensive cornfields, and woodland borders on the Plains Region, in the east-central part of the state, the legendary hunting grounds of the Choctaw Indians, provide numerous hunting and fishing opportunities. Within the region is Nanih Waiya, an Indian mound considered to be the fabled birthplace of the Choctaw nation. The Chickasawhay River, which flows for 96 miles through the plains past high bluffs and limestone banks lined with southern pines and cypress, provides good float fishing for bass and bream. The major lakes include Long Creek Reservoir, American Legion Lake, Bluff and Loakfona lakes in the Noxubee National Wildlife Refuge, Lake Tiak-O'Khata, and the Big Noxubee River and Lobutchia, Noxapater, and Tallalaga creeks. The Plains Region provides good hunting in season for deer, wild turkey, mallard and black duck, and pheasant on its numerous private shooting preserves and on the Tombigbee and Bienville National Forest game lands, and the Tallalaga Creek Wildlife Management Area and Noxubee National Wildlife Refuge.

The southern Gulf Coast Region, with its hundreds of fishing

camps, provides excellent bass, crappie, and bream fishing in the scenic Black and Beaver Dam creeks, Lake Bogue Homa, and countless remote lakes, ponds, and bayous. Hunting in season is for deer, turkey, rabbit, quail, and waterfowl on the De Soto National Forest game lands and on the Red Creek, Chickasawhay, Hugh L. White, Wolf River, Leaf River, and Little Biloxi state wildlife-management areas, as well as on several licensed shooting preserves. The tidal waters of the Gulf Coast and Mississippi Sound are havens for big redfish, speckled trout, white trout, flounders, bluefish, croaker, sheepshead, and tripletail. Famous Chandeleur Island and the isles of the Gulf Islands National Seashore—Ship, Horn, and Petit Bois—provide scenic unspoiled surf fishing. This beautiful string of islands protects the sound from the offshore winds. Charter boats from Biloxi and Gulfport provide offshore fishing for saltwater big-game fish, including tarpon.

Mississippi's 1.5 million acres of national forestlands range from flat, black marshlands and spectacular bluffs to cypress-shaded bayous and dense cathedral-like pine and hardwood forests. The 177,000–acre *Bienville National Forest*, located in central Mississippi, includes Coastal Plain second-growth pine and hardwood forests and the 189–acre virgin loblolly pine forest surrounding the Bienville Ranger Station. The 23–mile Shockaloe Riding Trail provides access to the scenic interior areas. The forest game lands provide hunting in season for quail, deer, and wild turkey. The forest is reached via U.S. 80 and State Highway 85. The 59,000–acre *Delta National Forest* in the west-central part of the state contains the Greentree Reservoir waterfowl-hunting area and the Red Gum Natural Area, a natural bottomland hardwood stand. The forest is reached along U.S. 61 and state routes 16, 14, and 3. The 500,000–acre *De Soto National Forest*, situated in the southeast corner of the state, is the site of the South Mississippi Gun and Dog Club field trails and includes the Tuxachanie Trail, which winds through pine forests and scenic bottomland hardwoods, and two of the nation's most scenic float-fishing streams, Black Creek and Beaver Dam Creek. The forest's acorn-bearing hardwoods make the area a hunter's mecca for deer, wild turkey, and waterfowl. Other features in the forest include Airey Lake, Big Biloxi River, and Thompson Creek. The forest is reached via U.S. 11, 49, and 90 and State Highway 26. *Holly Springs National Forest*, which encompasses 145,000 acres in northern Mississippi is the site of annual bird-dog field trails at Holly Springs, and the Chewalla Lake and Pusksu Lake fish and game areas. The forest provides top-ranked hunting in season for whitetailed deer, quail, squirrel, and wild turkey. The forest is reached via U.S. 72 and 78 and Mississippi 7 and 15. The 192,000–acre *Homochitto National Forest* in southwest Mississippi offers fishing, hiking, and primitive camping opportunities in the Clear Lake, Woodman Springs, and Pie's Lake areas, and top hunting in the Amite and Franklin wildlife-management areas for deer, wild turkey, and squirrel. The forest is reached via U.S. highways 61 and 84 and State Route 33. *Tombigbee National Forest*, encompassing 65,000 acres in the northern portion of the state, contains Upper Coastal Plain pine and hardwood forests, ancient Indian mounds, Davis and Choctaw lakes recreation areas, and a portion of the Natchez Trace Parkway. Beautiful 200–acre Davis Lake, near the Owl Creek Indian Mounds, is close to the site of explorer Hernando de Soto's winter camp. The forest provides good hunting in season for deer and quail. Access is via U.S. 82, the Natchez Trace Parkway, and Mississippi routes 8 and 15.

Information Sources, Maps & Access

For additional Magnolia State fishing and hunting regulations and information, write to the Game & Fish Commission, Box 451, Jackson 39205. The commission has available upon request the free publications *Hunt in Mississippi*, *Mississippi Commission Lakes*, and wildlife-management-area regulations sheets. The bimonthly magazine *Mississippi Game & Fish* is available free upon request to residents of the state from the commission (address above). A complete listing and description of state wildlife-management and waterfowl areas, lakes, reservoirs, streams, and fishing camps and licensed shooting preserves is contained in the 95–page full-color *Mississippi Travel Guide*, available free from the Travel/Tourism Department, P.O. Box 849, Jackson 39205. Specific fishing, hunting, camping, hiking, and canoeing information may be obtained from the Forest Supervisor, National Forests in Mississippi, Box 1291, Jackson 39205. A full-color *De Soto National Forest Recreation Map* (50¢) may be obtained from the Supervisor's office, along with the following free publications: *Outdoors in Your Southern National Forests*, *National Forests in Mississippi*, *Black Creek Float Trip* (De Soto National Forest), *Tuxachanie Trail* (De Soto National Forest), *Chewalla Recreation Area* (Holly Springs National Forest), *Clear Springs Recreation Area* (Homochitto National Forest), *Big Foot Horse Trails* (De Soto National Forest), and *Shockaloe Trail* (Bienville National Forest).

Lodges & Resorts

See "Accommodations & Travel Information" above for details.

NEW HAMPSHIRE

Introduction

New Hampshire's cloud-wreathed, glaciated mountain ranges, remote wilderness ponds, boulder-fringed lakes, swift, rocky streams, and fragrant northern forest tracts provide some of New England's outstanding fishing, hunting, backpacking, alpine and cross-country skiing at Waterville Valley, Loon Mountain, Bretton Woods and Franconia in one of New England's spectacularly beautiful regions. The state contains four major divisions: the industrial valleys, foothills, and brief seacoast of the south; the lake-dotted landscape of the midsection uplands; the rugged summits of the White Mountains, interspersed by steep river valleys, culminating in the windswept crowns of the magnificent Presidential Range, and the vast, largely roadless evergreen expanse of New Hampshire's North Country, occupied by trophy deer, bear, beaver, native trout, and salmon. The traveler will find picturesque New England villages with treelined streets and neat colonial houses, high country peaks with tundra meadows containing alpine plants, and the brooding silences of the north woods, a land of impenetrable forest, spruce swamps, and pure watersheds stretching to the wild borders of Maine, Vermont, and Quebec.

New Hampshire encompasses the beautiful White Mountain National Forest, dominated by the spectacular Presidential Range, with its towering peaks reaching up 6,000 feet, and arctic-like tundra above timberline. Old logging roads, abandoned railroad beds, and hundreds of miles of hiking trails provide access to the remote lakes, ponds, streams, and mountain bogs of the Pemigewasset Wilderness, Wild River area, Sandwich Range, Great Gulf Wilderness, Carter-Moriah Range, Franconia Notch, Carr Mountain Wilderness, and the Pilot and Pliny ranges in the Kilkenny Wilderness area. South of the White Mountains lies the famous Lakes Region, dominated by a cluster of the state's finest landlocked salmon, trout, and smallmouth bass lakes: Winnipesaukee, Squam, Ossipee, and Winnisquam. The remote, lightly traveled North Country Region of the Granite State is a vast wilderness of great evergreen and northern hardwood forests and rolling hills, broken by turbulent rivers and the sprawling blue headwater lakes of the Connecticut River.

Accommodations & Travel Information

The Granite State's major vacation lodges, sporting camps, ski resorts, and charming country inns are described in detail in the "Vacation/ Lodging Guide" which follows. For additional travel info, contact: *New Hampshire Vacation Center*, 1268 Ave. of the Americas, New York, NY 10020 (212)757-4455. For more detailed information on a specific region, write to one of the following addresses: *Dartmouth-Lake Sunapee Region*, Box 246, Lebanon 03766; *Lakes Region Assn.*, Box 300, Wolfeboro 03894; *Merrimack Valley Region Assn.*, Box 634, Manchester 03105; *Monadnock Region Assn.*, Box 269, Peterborough 03458; *New Hampshire Seacoast Regional Development Assn.*, Box 476, Exeter 03833. The *White Mountains Attraction Assn.* (Box 176, North Woodstock 03262) publishes a free guide to the White Mountains area along with a brochure on the Lakes Region, and free publications on Lost River, Loon Mountain, and Franconia Notch State Park, and a highway map of the state.

Information & Services

New Hampshire's majestic winter wilderness, with its whitened forests, fields, and slopes laced by hundreds of miles of trails, old logging roads, abandoned railroad beds, old carriage paths, and frozen lakes and streams, offers some of the nation's top cross-country skiing. The Granite State's major ski touring areas are described in the 288-page *EMS New England Ski Touring Guide*— including the abandoned railroad beds of the old Suncook Valley

Railroad and Claremont and Concord Railroad. The EMS guide, which also contains regional maps, driving directions, ski trail mileages, and facilities, may be obtained for $5.95 (plus 50¢ postage) from: Eastern Mountain Sports, 1047 Commonwealth Ave., Boston, MA 02215.

The *New Hampshire Four-Seasons State Camping Guide* lists privately and publicly operated campgrounds in each of the state's six regions, including location, facilities and services, recreational opportunities, and season rates. The guide is available free from: Lee Bosworth, New Hampshire Campground Owners Assn., Harbor Hill CA, Rte. 25, Meredith 03253. *The Clean Getaway* describes the state's 32 state parks and their camping facilities, recreational opportunities, and outstanding features. Order the guide from: Division of Parks, Dept. of Natural Resources, P.O. Box 856, State House Annex, Concord 03301. For information on camping in the White Mountain National Forest, write to: Supervisor, White Mountain National Forest, Laconia 03246.

The state's major rivers are described in detail in *Summer Canoeing and Kayaking in the White Mountains of New Hampshire*, a free booklet available from: White Mountains Region Assn., Lancaster 03584. The booklet describes the major rapids in the main canoe and kayak streams, and lists larger lakes and ponds in the region which have public boat accesses.

The *AMC River Guide: Volume 1 Northeastern New England* ($6) is available from: Appalachian Mountain Club, 5 Joy St., Boston, MA 02108, and gives comprehensive descriptions of most of the canoeable waters in New England, including difficulty ratings, historical notes, and descriptions of features along the way. It includes a "Canoeist's Map of Vermont and New Hampshire," which shows ratings of rapids and the scenery of the areas surrounding the streams. The map also shows divides, communities, and major topographical features.

An official angling rules and regulations booklet, *New Hampshire Freshwater and Saltwater Fishing Guide*, may be obtained free from: Fish & Game Dept. 34 Bridge St., Concord, NH 03301 (603)271–3421, it provides the usual ordinances, a list of trout lakes and ponds, which are marked by an asterisk if reclaimed, a list of togue lakes, and special laws by county or border water. The department also publishes the free *New Hampshire Fishing & Hunting* booklet which describes the fishing and hunting opportunities in the state, license details, seasons, and boat and snowmobile regulations and the free *Wildlife Management Area Guide* and *New Hampshire Game & Furbearers: A History*. A useful, large-format, 202–page guide, *Trout and Salmon Fishing in New England Lakes and Ponds* ($8 postpaid), contains detailed descriptions and lake survey maps of Silver, Winnipesaukee, Sunapee, Squam, Newfound, Ossipee, First Connecticut, and Winnisquam lakes. It may be ordered from: Partridge Press, Box 422, Campton 03223.

Highways & Maps

The *New Hampshire Official Highway Map* is distributed free by: Division of Economic Development, Concord 03301. This full-color map keys the locations of highways (express or interstate, U.S., primary state, secondary state), town or local roads, foot trails, historical markers, points of interest, cities and towns, public recreation areas, picnic areas, roadside rest areas, mountain passes or notches, airports, fire lookout stations, fish hatcheries, covered bridges, ski areas, high mountain peaks, and water features. A chart of public recreation areas given the map locations, nearest towns, and types of available recreation for state parks, White Mountain National Forest, and other areas.

The Kancamagus Highway winds through the White Mountain National Forest for 34½ miles between Lincoln and Conway, offering marvelous views of towering mountain peaks, plunging mountain streams, and vistas of unspoiled wilderness. The Forest Service maintains recreation facilities, picnic sites, developed campgrounds, and scenic areas of outstanding natural beauty along the highway. Trails head along the highway for hikes ranging from an hour's to several days' duration. A free brochure on the *Kancamagus Highway* is available from: Forest Supervisor, White Mountain National Forest, Laconia 03246. The brochure describes the facilities and scenic areas along the highway, and includes a map of the highway showing the locations of national forest boundaries, campgrounds, picnic sites, scenic areas, overlooks, and water features.

Eight tours in the White Mountains are listed and mapped in a free brochure, *Shunpike Fall Foliage in New Hampshire's White Mountain Region*. The brochure is free from: White Mountain Region Assn., Lancaster 03584.

VACATION/ LODGING GUIDE

The Lakes Region

South of the White Mountains is a group of famous landlocked salmon and lake trout waters, forming the largest and most beautiful of the state's 1,300 lakes, dominated by the jagged shoreline and blue island-dotted waters of Lake Winnipesaukee (the Indian name meaning "The Smile of the Great Spirit"), the second largest lake in New England. Algonquin Indians once fished these abundant lakes and hunted in the surrounding Squam, Ossipee, and Belknap mountains. The scenic mountain forests of this region harbor a variety of game, and provide good hunting for deer, woodcock, pheasants, and ducks. Smaller numbers of black bear and bobcat also roam the conifer and mixed hardwood forests surrounding the lakes.

The Indians who once inhabited these lands were of two confederacies: the Abenakis, "those living at the sunrise," and the Penacooks, "living at the bottom of the hill." Among the most powerful tribes of these confederacies were Winnipesaukees (Penacooks), and the Abenaki Ossipees. Winnipesaukees inhabited the fishing village of Aquadochtan at the weirs on the lake that bears their name; it lay on the north side of a stony stream that led to huge W-shaped fish traps made of stone and woven-together saplings. Here at the source of the Winnipesaukee River the Indians made great catches of shad, which were dried and stored for winter use.

New Hampshire's largest body of water, Lake Winnipesaukee, is 22 miles long and from one to ten miles wide, with depths ranging to 300 feet, has a 240-mile shoreline and more than 250 scenic islands. Spring is naturally the best season for the coldwater salmon and trout. Winter fishing is also popular here; during the cold, snowy months hundreds of small ice-fishing huts dot the lake's frozen surface. Winnisquam Lake, covering 4,264 acres with a maximum depth of 154 feet, provides excellent fishing for lake trout and landlocked salmon, as well as for smallmouth and largemouth bass, and pickerel. Nearby Squam and Little Squam lakes, connected by a short, navigable neck of water, are known primarily for lake trout and landlocked salmon fishing.

The Ossipees fished beautiful Ossipee Lake and River, and the Pine and Bearcamp rivers. The remains of what was thought to be their burial place were found near the lake in the 1870s. Arrowheads, stone knives, and other artifacts lie along trails and in open fields throughout the area. Ossipee is a small lake, about 3.5 by 2 miles, with a pine-fringed shoreline. There are some summer homes around its shore. The lake holds large black bass, landlocked salmon, brook trout, and pickerel.

Mount Chocorua and its neighboring peaks tower above the forested shores of Big Squam Lake, one of the state's top-ranked salmon lakes, annually yielding landlocks up to 12 pounds. Both Big Squam and Little Squam dominate a scenic area known to the Indians as Wonnasquamsaukee—"the beautiful place surrounded by water." Other features of the region include the famous lake trout and landlocked salmon waters of Newfound Lake (known to the Indians as Pasquaney—"the place where birch bark is found"), with its sheer 800-foot-high rock ledges and the Bearcamp River, Pine River, Pemigewasset River, Merrymeeting Lake, Hemmenway and Belknap state reservations, and Sky Pond and Green Mountain state forests. White Lake State Park, near Tamworth, offers trout fishing and camping. Other state parks in the region are Ellacoya, on the southwest shore of Lake Winnipesaukee, and Wentworth, on the shore of the lake of that name. Most of the state reserves have camping facilities. White Lake State Park, the largest camping area, limits stays to two weeks in the period July 1 to August 15. Reservations

for White Lake camping should be made in person at the park office.

Hundreds of miles of scenic trails lace through the backcountry of the Squam, Ossipee, and Belknap mountains, good for hiking or ski touring. In addition, many towns and alpine ski areas have miles of marked cross-country trails.

Information Sources, Maps & Access

For detailed vacation travel and recreation information, contact: Lakes Region Assn., Wolfeboro, NH 03894 (603)569–1117. Special lake contour sounding maps of the region's major lakes are available for 50¢ each, or $2.00 for a package set of the larger lakes, from: Fish & Game Department, 34 Bridge St., Concord 03301. These useful maps provide the angler with information about the composition of the lake bottom and show depths and contours, islands, feeder streams, and boat-launching sites. Individual maps are available for *Winnipesaukee*, *Winnisquam*, *Newfound*, *Ossipee*, *Dan Hole*, *Merrymeeting*, *Pleasant*, *Silver*, *Waukewan*, and *Nubanusit* lakes. The package set includes Winnipesaukee, Winnisquam, Newfound, Ossipee, Dan Hole, and First and Second Connecticut Lakes. Gilford, Laconia, Center Harbor, and Melvin Village on Lake Winnipesaukee, Holderness on Squam Lake, and West and Center Ossipee on Ossipee Lake are among the many outfitting and supply centers in the Lakes Region that offer boat and canoe rentals, fishing gear, and family vacation lodging. The area may be reached by driving north on State Routes 106 or 28, or U.S. 202/4. U.S. 3/Interstate 93 is the main artery entering the Lakes Region from the White Mountains National Forest to the north.

Gateways & Accommodations

Holderness

(Pop. 250; zip code 03245; area code 603) is the major gateway for tourists, hikers, backpackers, hunters, canoeists and fisherman on Squam Lake, the second largest lake in New Hampshire. Early colonists who settled the region in 1751 hoped it would become a major city to rival Boston. Now it is the major gateway south of the White Mountains to recreation areas in this densely wooded, mountainous lake region. Area attractions include the Squam Lakes Science Center featuring nature trails, exhibits of New England wildlife, a blacksmith shop, and an operating steam-powered saw mill, and craft demonstrations at Sandwich Home Industries. Accommodations: *Olde Colonial Eagle on Squam Lake* (rates: $25.50 double), with 16 good rooms, swimming beach, outdoor recreation activities and rentals, on U.S. 3 and New Hampshire 25 (968–3233); *Squam Lake Resort* (rates: $36 double), with 13 guest rooms and cottages, dining room, outdoor recreation activities, on U.S. 3 (968–3348).

Laconia

(Pop. 14,500; zip code 03246; area code 603) is the western gateway for summer and winter recreation in the Lakes Region of New Hampshire. Bordered by three lakes, the Winnisquam, Opechee, and Paugus, and neighboring Lake Winnipesaukee, this bustling industrial center is surrounded by the Belknap Mountains and the Sanbornton Hills. The headquarters of the White Mountain National Forest is situated here. Area attractions include the Alpine Ski Area, Gunstock Recreation Area with downhill skiing all winter and summer rides in the chairlift, lake cruises on the *Mt. Washington*, summer regattas, and the annual winter highlight, the World Championship Dog Sled Races, a Laconian tradition. Accommodations: *Belknap Point Motel* (rates: $40 double), with 18 superb rooms and family units on Lake Winnipesaukee with swimming beach and

dock located four miles east of town on New Hampshire Highway 11 (293–4454); *Lord Hampshire Motel & Cottages* (rates: $31–33 double), with 20 excellent rooms and family units, housekeeping cottages, swimming beach, and outdoor recreation facilities and rentals on Lake Winnipesaukee on U.S. Highway 3, four miles south of town, (524–4331); another popular attraction is the *Hickory Stick Farm Dining Room* in a refurbished country farm house barn (524–3333).

Wolfeboro

(Pop. 1,500; zip code 03894; area code 603) on Lake Winnipesaukee is the eastern gateway to the spectacular New Hampshire Lakes region. The largest town on the 22–mile lake, Wolfeboro is an important port, and a quaint summer resort, the oldest in the United States. Cross-country skiing has become increasingly popular in winter. Area attractions include two-hour scenic rides through the Lakes district on the old fashioned Wolfeboro Railroad, boat cruises on the lake steamer *The Mt. Washington*, Wentworth state park, and the historical Libby Museum and Clark House. Accommodations: *The Lake Motel* (rates: $28–34 double), with 35 excellent guest rooms and family units, restaurant, on Crescent Lake with four-season outdoor recreation activities and rentals, on New Hampshire 28 southeast of town (569–1100); *Lakeview Inn & Motor Lodge* (rates: $31.50–33.50 double), with 14 good rooms and family units, dining room, cocktail lounge, on Lake Winnipesaukee at 120 N. Main St. (569–1335).

Lodges & Resorts

★★*Christmas Island Resort*, on the shores of the Lake Winnipesaukee, offers private sand beaches for swimming and sunbathing, rowboats to explore the lake's quiet coves and private dock and marina for guests' boats. In the winter, cross-country ski trails surround the lake,

and Mt. Gunstock downhill ski area is close by. Ice fishing and skating are popular on the lake. Christmas Island's indoor heated pool, saunas, and whirlpool bath are popular year round. The Steak House will prepare hearty steaks and prime ribs to your liking over an open pit. The Drummer Boy Lounge features dancing to live music nightly. Modern motel rooms are available for $24–30 off season, and $32–40 at the height of summer season. Two bedroom family suites are $200 a week from January 1–June 24, and $250 for four persons, $300 per week for two and $350 a week for four from June 24 through September 2. Private cottages, which accommodate from two-six persons and have living rooms with fireplaces, range between $220 and $325 per week depending on the size of the cottage and the number of people reserving it. For more information write: Christmas Island Resort, Weirs Boulevard, Route 3, Laconia, NH 03246 (603)366–4378.

★★★★*Pasquaney Inn on Newfound Lake* is nestled in a valley at the edge of the White Mountain region, on Newfound Lake, one of the clearest lakes in the world. The inn dates back to 1840 and the innkeepers offer 150 years of family tradition to welcome you and provide you with a pleasant stay. The inn has its own sand beach on the lake and skiffs for rowing around the cove. Sailboats are also available from nearby marinas. The grounds contain courts for shuffle board, croquet, badminton, lawn-bowling, and horseshoes. There is a recreation barn with basketball, ping-pong and square dancing in the evenings. Golf and tennis are available within a short drive, as well as country stores, auctions and antique shops. In the winter, some good ski areas are within minutes or a short drive away, offering both down-hill and cross-country terrain. In the fall, fishing—for landlocked salmon or trout—is the primary pastime and is excellent in this area. The location is beautiful, any time of year, for just strolling along the back woods or hiking on the mountain trails—Bridgewater Mountain is right behind the inn.

Dining is relaxed and informal. All meals are New England country style, with a slight French accent. Vegetables, always fresh, come from the inn's garden or local markets. Special desserts are prepared in the pastry kitchen. The guest rooms are bright, airy and attractive. They offer a magnificent view of Newfound Lake and the surrounding mountains. There are both private and shared baths. Rates start at $20 for double occupancy, depending on plan or season. European and Modified American plans are available. Your innkeepers are Mary Jo and Jim Shipe. Contact them for additional information at Pasquaney Inn, Bridgewater, NH 03222 (603)744–2712.

★★★*Pick Point Lodge* is located in a pine forest directly on Lake Winnipesaukee. There are 75 acres of a wildlife sanctuary with deer, duck, birds and other wildlife, including approximately three miles of trails through dense forest with a wide variety of trees, shrubs, ferns and especially peace and quiet. The lodge is situated on a point of land with ½ mile shore frontage—cottages are well spaced for greater privacy. The main lodge stands 150 feet from the water's edge, has an indoor and outdoor cocktail lounge, buffet breakfasts, four large fireplaces, game room, TV writing room, dining room and library. Daily maid service for cottages and motel rooms with a no tipping policy. There is a sandy swimming area with a gentle slope and a 200' sundeck jutting into the lake. All types of boats are available—and a professional-size clay tennis court as well as pool table, ping pong, shuffleboard, lawn games, horseshoes, putting, and an 18–hole golf course nearby, as well as horsebackriding. There is a weekly get together and cook out. Cottages are near the lake and under the pines—and have furnished kitchens, porches, and picture windows. Removable phones are in all cottages. Motel rooms from late June-Labor Day are $24.50 per day per person or $294 a week for two. Cottages range from $195–750 per week. For further information Dick Newcomb, Pick Point Enterprises, Inc., P.O. Mirror Lake, NH 03853 (603)569–1338.

★*Piping Rock Cottages and Motel*, nestled amongst the foothills of the White Mountains, is located on the shore of island-studded Lake Winnipesaukee. Piping Rock welcomes vacationers year round on its nine acres and 400 feet of shore frontage. It's a natural playground with badminton, volley ball, horsehoes, waterskiing, boating, sailing, swimming, fishing. Theatre, horseback riding, shops, churches, and many other facilities are only moments away. The new and modern cottages provide a fireplace, picture window, a fully equipped kitchen, thermostatic heat, comfortable furnishings and a choice of one-four bedrooms, all with linens supplied. The motel rooms, each with a terrace or balcony, offer a superb view of the lake. The rooms also include twin double beds, full carpeting, TV, bath-shower combinations, electric heat, through ventilation and maid service. Motel rates, based on double occupancy, range from $30–43 per day. Cottage rentals range from $32–50 daily, two-eight persons. Off season rates are lower. No pets allowed. For further information contact Bill and Marjorie Long, Piping Rock Cottages and Motel, North Main St., Wolfeboro, NH 03894 (603)569–1915.

★★*Sandy Point Beach Resort* is the largest family resort on Lake Winnipesaukee with 2,000 feet of beach front property on its own peninsula. There is free docking available for your own boat or you can take advantage of a boat tour around the lake. The resort has a game room and shuffleboard and there is tennis, golf, horseback riding, hiking, mountain climbing and airplane rides nearby, as well as day trips to Mt. Washington, Old Man of the Mountains, Kancamagus Highway, Polar Caves, the Flume and Aerial Highway. Sandy Point is a seasonal resort open from May thru October. Early spring is the best time to enjoy salmon fishing when the fish are on the surface. The fall, of course, provides the splendor of the New

Hampshire foliage. The resort's restaurant, with cocktail lounge, is famous for fine food and courteous service and specializes in lobster at the lowest prices around. There are 77 units from motel rooms to individual cottages. If you choose a cottage, you must bring your own supplies, although linen may be rented at a nominal charge. Cottages are rented on a weekly basis and range from $160–250 per week, accommodating two-six people. Motel rooms can be rented daily from $23–35, double occupancy. There are also three-day specials available. Off season rates are slightly lower. Contact your hosts, the Quellette family, at (603)875–6000 or write Sandy Point Beach Resort, Route 11, Alton Bay, N.H. 03810.

★★★★*Village at Winnipesaukee* is a group of superb condominiums in the heart of the Lake Region, situated on a gentle rise overlooking beautiful Lake Winnipesaukee. Each season brings a new outdoor treat to the area. During the winters guests can ski from their door to adjacent Brickyard Mountain. Gunstock, Waterville Valley, Loon, Rowe and Tenny Mountain are nearby offering fine skiing. Groomed trails and unbroken fields are available for cross-country enthusiasts and sites for ski jumping, tobogganing or sledding are all nearby. There is snowmobiling on Lake Winnipesaukee, plus ice skating and ice fishing. Spring and summer activities run the full range from swimming, fishing, cruising, to sailing and waterskiing. The Village has both outdoor and indoor tennis courts and an outdoor swimming pool. Instruction is available for both. An 18–hole golf course is nearby, along with a driving range, and miniature golf. You can go horseback riding through the woods or bicycle on the scenic roads. The condominiums are completely furnished in comfortable, attractive, contemporary style. Each has two or three bedrooms, two baths and enough space to sleep six to eight. All units are air-conditioned, carpeted, furnished with linen and essential kitchen utensils and cable TV. Sliding glass doors lead to private balconies. There is a babysitting service and laundry room on the Village's premises. Rates per day: weekends, $40, mid-week, $35; per week $200. Monthly rates start at $325 depending on month. Units with fireplaces are slightly more. For further information contact: The Village at Winnipesaukee, P.O. Box 284, Weirs Beach, NH 03246 (603)366–2272.

★★★*Wolfeboro Inn.* Sprawling oaks shade this handsome colonial inn, built in 1812 and overlooking Lake Winnipesaukee. The inn has been carefully restored to blend modern convenience with charm of the past. The spacious dining room with brick fireplace, high beamed ceiling, and large picture windows overlooking the lake, serves fresh fish, fruits and vegetables along with hearty meat entrees. Old fashioned saloon type doors open onto the large panelled bar, with red leather barrel backed seats. The village of Wolfeboro is within walking distance, with quaint antique shops, and the busy dock, where an impressive ship, the *Mt. Washington*, picks up her passengers. The beautiful lake is the center of one of New England's oldest summer resorts, where you can swim, sail, canoe or fish. Rates in the Wolfeboro Inn are $24 for a double room, and $16 for a single. For information write: The Wolfeboro Inn, 44 Main Street, Wolfeboro, NH 03894 (603)569–3016.

Travel Services

The Nordic Skier, in Wolfeboro, is the headquarters for ski touring in the Lakes region. The colonial town on the shores of Lake Winnipesaukee is known as one of New England's oldest summer resorts, and is now becoming popular in winter, as cross-country skiers discover the enjoyment of lake touring. There are 20 miles of groomed and mapped trails, which are free, offered with the permission of private land owners, and maintained by volunteers. The Nordic skier specializes in cross country ski sales and rentals, tours, sportswear,

and accessories. Lessons are offered on Saturday and Sunday mornings at 10:30, and Tuesday afternoons at 1:00. Private lessons can be arranged at the center by appointment. Wax workshops are held on Fridays. Stop in the Nordic Ski Center for information about the many motels and unusual restaurants in the area. If possible, try to plan your trip around a full moon. The Nordic skier offers moonlight tours every month, and moon-light touring in the Lakes region is something not to be missed. For more information write: The Nordic Skier, 10 N. Main Street, Wolfeboro, NH (603)569–3151.

North Country & The Connecticut Lakes

This magnificent evergreen forest and wilderness lake country includes the entire northern section of New Hampshire from the Upper Ammonoosuc River on the south to the Maine-New Hampshire border on the east, and the headwater lakes of the Connecticut River area along the Vermont and Quebec borders to the east and north. The vast North Country interior is among the northeast's last vestiges of wilderness. Few foot trails lead through the forests and rolling hills, but logging operations have created an intricate network of gravel roads that provide the fisherman, hunter, and camper with access to remote pockets of the hinterlands.

The Connecticut River finds its source near the Canadian boundary and flows southwest forming a series of beautiful blue lakes as it flows south. The First Connecticut Lake, the largest of the lakes (5½ miles long), mirrors the unbroken fir and spruce forests of its northern and eastern shores, brilliant with red, yellow, and orange colors in the fall. Mountains rise up beyond the shores, among them the forested slopes of Magalloway Mountain (3,360 feet). Trails to Magalloway Mountain head on the eastern side of the lake, but directions from local inhabitants are necessary, and a guide would be helpful. The lake holds trophy landlocked salmon, and lake, rainbow, and brook trout. This majestic glacial lake is one of New England's premier landlocked salmon meccas. Back in the 1930's it was known for its population of chinook salmon, which reached weights of up to 12 pounds. Camping is available nearby. Several sporting lodges (which see) are located on the lake's western shore.

The Second Connecticut Lake lies among forested hills, eight miles from the wide swells of Bosebuck (3,149 feet) and Rump (3,647 feet) mountains. Second Lake is framed on the west by the scenic conifers and hardwoods of the Connecticut Lakes State Forest. Third Lake, also known as Lake St. Sophia, surrounded by hills, embodies the

primeval beauty of the northlands. Guides and trail information are available at nearby Pittsburg, the Glen or Camp Idlewild. The headwaters of the Connecticut River, where it flows from the Connecticut Lakes, downstream to North Stratford holds some lunker wild brook, brown, and rainbow trout.

The United States and Canada both claimed the Connecticut Lakes Region in the early years of its settlement. Finally the settlers formed their own government, and by 1829 the area was known as the Indian Stream Territory, named for the river which rises at the northern tip of the state and flows through this region. In 1832 settlers formed the Republic of Indian Stream, with its own courts, constitution, council, and assembly. The republic died in 1836 when the New Hampshire militia occupied the region after a dispute with the Canadian authorities.

U.S. 3, one of three main highways in the whole of the North Country, provides access or near access to all the lakes but the Fourth. For the most part, even secondary roads are few and short in the North Country, and few of the mountains have trails. Inexperienced hikers should not attempt this sparsely settled, undeveloped region. For current trail information contact the state district chief conservation officer or the state district fire chiefs.

Some of the best areas for backcountry trekking and wilderness fly fishing in the Connecticut Lakes Region are old logging roads running from First Lake to Hell Gate on the Dead Diamond River, through the heart of the North Country woods; the Grouse Survey line from the Balsams hotel in Dixville Notch to the dam at the lower end of Second Lake; Rump Mountain; and Deer Mountain Trail from Moose Campground north of Second Lake to the mountain summit. Both the Swift Diamond and Dead Diamond rivers hold large, wild brook trout. The Swift Diamond is fed by Big Diamond Pond in Coleman State Park and offers several miles of wild, deep-flowing water accessible by trail along its bank.

The brawling Androscoggin River watershed tops the eastern section of the North County and provides some of its wildest country and best fishing. At the top of the drainage are the Dead Diamond and Swift Diamond rivers, which form a Y and flow southeast and east respectively to meet and spill into the famed Magalloway River. Located in the swampy and mountainous academic grant country along the Maine border, this area is penetrated by a few dirt logging roads and provides some of New England's prime native trout fishing. Most of the feeders, flowing through tight valleys between domes up to 3,000 feet high, also hold wild brookies. Big and Little Diamond ponds at the head of the Swift Diamond, above Kidderville on Route 26, have fishing for rainbow trout; Big Diamond holds togue, while Little Diamond contains squaretails.

The Magalloway flows for a short, meandering distance along the New Hampshire-Maine border before spilling into Umbagog Lake. There are some lunker squaretails and landlocks in this stretch of the Magalloway, although this lowermost portion is full of warmwater fish, particularly yellow perch. Umbagog is rated by the state as a warmwater lake, but knowledgeable anglers take some big salmon in the spring, as well as an occasional togue, and a few landlocks run up the Magalloway in the fall to spawn.

The Androscoggin flows out of Umbagog through a dam at Errol and runs south for about 25 miles along Route 16 to Berlin. This piece of water is one of the great rainbow streams in the East, and holds a few brook trout and landlocks.

Information Sources, Maps & Access

New Hampshire's North Country is shown on U.S. Geological Survey 1:250,000–scale (four miles to 1″) maps Lewiston and Sherbrooke. They may be ordered for $2 each from: Distribution Branch, U.S. Geological Survey, 1200 S. Eads St., Arlington, VA 22202. *Official Lake Survey Maps of First and Second Connecticut Lakes* may be obtained for 50¢ each from: Fish & Game Dept., 34 Bridge St., Concord, NH 03301. U.S. Highway 3 parallels the Connecticut River from West Stewartstown northeast along the western shorelines of Lake Francis and Second Connecticut Lake where it merges into State Route 3 and enters the Connecticut Lakes State Forest, passing Second and Third Connecticut lakes to the Quebec border. Lodging, boat and canoe rentals, gear, supplies, and guides are available at Pittsburg, West Stewartstown and the Glen. State Highway 26 passes through the heart of the North Country and provides access to Umbagog Lake, Dixville Wilderness Ski Area, Mohawk River, and Coleman State Park. The region is reached along the west via U.S. 3 and on the east via State Route 16 which parallels the Androscoggin River. The North Country's southern boundary is traversed by State Route 110.

Gateways & Accommodations

Colebrook

(Pop. 1,100; zip code 03576; area code 603.) Historic Colebrook, nestled below Vermont's Mt. Manadnock on the junction of the Mohawk and the Connecticut Rivers, is the gateway to hunting, fishing, canoeing and backpacking in New Hampshire's northern mountains, and the lovely Connecticut Lakes area. Many of the buildings date back to the 1700's when the town was first incorporated. Area attractions include the State Fish Hatchery, Beaver Brook Falls, Coleman State Park, and the historic Columbia Covered Bridge. Accommodations: *Country Club Motel* (rates: $26–28 double) with 18 excellent guest rooms, restaurant, cocktail lounge, heated pool just east of town on New Hampshire Highway 26 (237–5566).

Dixville Notch

(Pop. 10; zip code 03576; area code 603), the most northern and rugged gap in the White Mountains, is a spectacular gateway for hunters, hikers, skiers and fishermen heading into the northeastern mountains of New Hampshire and the Rangeley Lakes region in Maine. Dixville Notch is the most jagged, wild mountain pass in New Hampshire. Area features include the nearby Wilderness Ski Area, Table Rock offering spectacular views of the northern White Mountains, Quebec, and Maine, and beautiful Lake Gloriette, nestled in the open valley at the end of the notch. Accommodations: (see "The Balsams" below).

Lodges, Resorts & Sporting Camps

★★★*The Balsams at Dixville Notch* is a spectacular 15,000-acre resort high in the White Mountains of New Hampshire. Known as the "Switzerland of America," the Balsams offers both summer and winter activities. There's an 18–hole, par–72 championship golf course and a 9–hole par–32 executive course, plus six tennis courts, three red-clay and three all-weather, plus tennis instruction. There's an olympic-sized heated outdoor swimming pool and trout fishing in a private lake. There's boating and canoeing, and two trap shooting fields. The wide lawns of the Balsams sweep down to the outdoor pool and terrace on the edge of Lake Gloriette, and 1,000 feet above the lake towers Table Rock, one of the mountain walls of Dixville Notch. There are scenic roads for bicycling and walking, crystal clear streams, cascades and waterfalls. For winter pleasures, there's the Dixville Wilderness, a major New England ski area, on the property with convenient shuttle service to the slopes, and a dozen trails up to two miles long with terrain for experts, intermediates and

beginners. Cross-country skiing is popular on miles of marked trails which explore the thousands of acres of Balsams wilderness and professional instruction and a modern ski shop with equipment sales and rentals is available. The Balsams has room for 425 guests with all of the services of a complete village. There are six different lounges offering a variety of settings, a game room, a coffee shop as well as a dining room, a library and a number of shops. Activities include lectures, craft demonstrations, sport clinics, hay rides, torchlight parades, maple sugar and snow parties as well as both indoor and outdoor games. There's a children's game room and a complete supervised play program for children between the ages of four and twelve. For more information and rates, contact The Balsams, Dixville Notch, NH 03576 (603)255–3400; Boston (617) 227–8288, N.Y. (212)563–4383.

★★★*The Glenn*, situated high in the north country, on the shores of First Connecticut Lake near the Quebec border, offers spacious rooms, generous family-style meals, and private wooded or lake front cabins to hunters, fishermen, and wilderness lovers. Landlocked salmon, lake trout, rainbows, browns, and squaretails are abundant in the deep blue lake, and in the pools of the clear rushing mountain streams. Boats are available on a dozen different fishing waters suitable for fly, spin, or bait fishing, for $6 a day. Trips into the remoter fishing waters of New Hampshire and Maine can be arranged. Sightseeing trips by float plane are available, and there are innumerable trails to satisfy any hiker with a yen to wander. Swimming is possible, off the modern dock, on a hot summer's day. In the early morning hours, and the cool of the evening, many varieties of birds may be seen and heard. This area is known to attract the greatest variety of birds in New Hampshire. Salmon and lake trout season runs from "ice out" to October 1. Rainbow, brook, and brown trout season runs from May 1 to October 15. September brings the first tinge of frost to this country, and the surrounding mountains explode with color. Hunting for small game begins October 1. Rates for a spacious, twin bedded room in the lodge are, per person and including meals, $21 daily and $140 weekly. Cabins which comfortably accommodate two-eight persons run from $24 daily per person including meals, and $160 weekly, for a wooded cabin. Lake front cabins are $27 daily, and $180 on a weekly basis. Special rates for children are ½ off for children two-five years and ⅓ off for children

six-twelve. For more information, contact Betty Falton & Family, The Glenn, First Connecticut Lake, Pittsburg, NH 03592 (603)538–6500.

★*Harmony Lodge* is located on the north shore of beautiful First Connecticut Lake, 14 miles from the Canadian border, surrounded by miles of unbroken evergreen forest, inhabited by deer, bear, snow shoe rabbits, woodcock, partridge, and other small game. The five large lakes of the area—the First, Second and Third Connecticuts, Lake Francis and Back Lake—offer excellent salmon, lake trout, rainbow, and pickerel fishing. The region also has some of the finest waters in New England for brook trout in the many beaver ponds, bogs, and streams. Accommodations include three cabins located on the lakeshore, widely spaced for a maximum of privacy. The cabins, with modern furnishings, have hot and cold water and are completely equipped for light housekeeping. There are gas stoves for cooking, electric refrigerators, and gas heat. Meals are served in the many dining rooms in the area—one within walking distance. Rates are $10 per person per night and $110 per couple per week. For further information contact Fred and Kathleen Taeger, Harmony Lodge, Box 61, RFD #1, Pittsburg, NH 03592 (603)538–6541.

★★*Partridge Lodge & Cabins*, located on First Connecticut Lake, provides four seasons of enjoyment for the vacationer. Landlocked salmon, rainbows and lake trout, well stocked in the lake, and the Connecticut River, excellent for brookies and rainbows make the area a paradise for fishermen. The hunter will enjoy the vast forests, hardwood ridges and flowage land surrounding the lodge, inhabited by deer, bear, grouse, rabbit, partridge and duck. For the hunter and fisherman, the lodge will provide motors, tackle, bait, boats, maps, guides and licenses. If you are a snowmobiling fan, you will enjoy the many miles of logging roads, ice covered lakes, and groomed trails. The unspoiled beauty of this northern woodland region is magnificent and there are miles of wilderness trails for hiking. There is also a well protected cove for swimming or sun bathing in the summer months. For sightseers there is the famous Franconia Notch, Indian Head, the Flume, Profile Lake, The Old Man, Echo Lake and The Aerial Tramway. This area also has the added attraction of being free from causes of hay fever. The lodge's restaurant is noted for its excellent and hearty home-cooked meals. Accommodations include seven rustic housekeeping log-cabins, situated among pines on the shore of the First Connecticut Lake. The cabins are winterized with gas heaters, and each cabin has a private bath and can comfortably house four to eight people. For rates and further information contact Gerald Boutin or Ed and Lise Bunnens at Partridge Lodge and Cabins, Pittsburg, NH 03592, (603)538–6380 or 6522.

★★★*Tall Timber Lodge* is surrounded by evergreens on remote Back Lake in the north country. The lake offers excellent brook and rainbow trout fishing. The lodge has a fleet of wooden and aluminum motor boats on the lake for guests. Lake trout and salmon can be found in nearby lakes, streams and ponds, where boats are also docked. Guides can be arranged for, and bait, tackle and a large selection of flies are sold at the main lodge. Licenses are also sold at the lodge and your catch will be frozen for your trip home. The lake also provides swimming in clean, clear water. The area is popular for birdwatching (there is a great variety of species) as well as camera buffs and hikers. Both large and small game can be hunted in fall including deer, bear, grouse, woodcock, rabbit, and fox for either firearm or bow hunters. Wintertime sports include snowmobiling in the back country. There are many trails, plus miles of logging roads. Accommodations are available in the main lodge or separate cabins. The main lodge includes the dining room, serving home

cooked meals, and the front room for gathering and relaxing. The log cabins are located on the lakeshore with cooking and refrigeration, controlled heating and plumbing. Both the cabins and lodge rooms are finished in knotty pine. The lodge also offers a large private cabin on the shore of First Connecticut Lake, on Dry-Ki Cove. The lodge operates on the American plan, and maid service is included. Rates: cabins, $22 per guest per day; rooms, $20 per day per guest. Housekeeping cabins available during the first two weeks in June and the month of October and all winter, $10 per day per guest. Boats and motor including fuel and accessories, $10 per day. For further information contact: Harold & Barbara Webster, Back Lake Road, Pittsburg, NH 03592 (603)538–6651.

★★*Timberland Camps*, on the First Connecticut Lake, offers superb fishing and hunting and quick access to old logging roads, remote ponds and wilderness trails. Highlights of the area include Indian Head, the Flume, Profile Lake, The Old Man, Echo Lake and The Aerial Tramway. The experienced snowmobiler will find Magalloway

Mountain an exciting challenge and Timberland provides access to the Quebec groomed-trail system. There are guides for cross-country travel and detailed trail maps are available. First Connecticut Lake provides good fishing for landlocked salmon and lake trout. The main Connecticut River, just below the lake, and the streams surrounding Timberland, hold speckled and rainbow trout. Guides, licenses and maps are all available for the hunter and motors, boats, licenses, tackles and bait for the fisherman. Timberland has seven housekeeping log cabins, each completely winterized with gas heaters or wood stoves, a private bath with hot and cold running water, electricity and kitchen facilities. Meals are available by reservation in the Timberland dining room. The cabins sleep three to eight people and rates are $8 per night per person with weekly family rates available during July and August. For further information regarding rates and reservations, contact Bill and Elaina Johnson, Timberland Camps, Pittsburg, NH 03592 (603)538–6613.

White Mountain National Forest & The Presidential Range

The White Mountain National Forest encompasses New England's largest and most majestic fishing, backpacking, alpine and nordic skiing, hunting, and wilderness camping area, covering 727,000 acres crowned by the towering peaks of the Presidential Range. The White Mountains, once the home and hunting grounds of the Algonquin Indians and known to them as *Waumbeck Methna* ("white rock"), sweep across more than 1,200 square miles in the northern

half of the state into Maine, covered by forests of fir, hemlock, spruce, and lovely stands of mature white birch. The only higher mountains east of the Rockies are in North Carolina and Tennessee. Eight of the White Mountains are more than a mile high, culminating at Mt. Washington (6,288 ft.), 22 are 4,000 to 5,000 feet; and 26, 3,000 to 4,000 feet high. Many of these mountains rise higher from the surrounding country than do the Rockies. The headwaters of four great rivers rise on the slopes and notches of the mountains. Hundreds of miles of forest roads and trails, including the Appalachian Trail, from Kinsman Notch at the north base of Mount Moosilauke to the summit of Old Speck Mountain in Maine, wind through the renowned high country fishing, hunting, and camping areas. Numerous spur trails, including the Tuckerman Ravine, Lion Head, Boot Spur, Alpine Garden, and Lake-of-the-Cloud, provide access to the high peaks and surrounding valleys.

Great ridges stretch through the surrounding arcs of the White Mountains, bearing huge cirques, among them the outstandingly scenic King Ravine, the Great Gulf, Huntington, and Tuckerman, flanked by Lion's Head and Boot Spur to the east and Oakes to the south. The Montalban (white mountain), a 10–mile ridge, rises from the south. The most famous of the mountains in this ridge are the terraced Stairs (3,425 feet). The Rocky Branch parallels the Montalban to the east. The proposed Presidential Range Wilderness embraces some 26,000 acres of some of the most scenic geological relief in the northeast, with more than eight miles of ridge above timberline. The wilderness is bordered on the north by the lower slopes of the northern peaks, on the west by Jefferson Notch and Mount Clinton roads, on the south by the Appalachian, Camel, and Boot Spur trails, and on the east by the Great Gulf.

The higher, wind-swept slopes of the Presidential Range, noted for weather conditions approaching arctic severity, have a number of alpine flora above the timberline, including ancient, gnomelike spruces, scrub birch, and mountain alder. Labrador tea is found frequently mingled with extensive patches of bilberry below the timberline along with large mats of colorful Greenland sandwort, beds of three-toothed cinquefoil, bearberry, moss campion, and alpine azalea. High up on the summits of the Presidential Range are found arctic rushes, sedges, colorful lichens, and infrequently, Lapland rosebay, an alpine relative of the great laurel. Lichens are so extensive on some of the high peaks that the color of the summit will occasionally change after a heavy rain, when lichens alter from brownish gray to green.

The proposed Pemigewasset Wilderness stretches through the mountain country, bisected by Kancamagus Highway. This renowned back-packing, fishing, and hunting area is the largest roadless area on the national forests of the Appalachian Mountain Chain, embracing 100,000 acres surrounding the East Branch of Pemigewasset River— noted for its wild, orange-bellied brook trout. Several scenic trails wind through the backcountry and provide access to Black Pond, Franconia Brook, Cedar Brook, Thoreau Falls, Signal Ridge, Shoal Pond, Carrigan Notch, Sawyer River, Hancock Notch, Nancy Pond, Arethusa-Ripley Falls, and Lincoln Brook. The East Branch of the Pemigewasset is not recommended for canoeing because of its severe rapids.

The proposed Sandwich Range Wilderness area lies southeast of these highlands. This famous range rises abruptly from the surrounding lake country to towering 4,000–foot peaks, and extends for about 30 miles from Conway or the Saco River westward to Campton on the Pemigewasset. The wilderness area encompasses 60,000 acres of steep ridges, wooded valleys, glacial basins, passes, and remote uplands. Many trails wind to the summit of prominent Mount

Chocorua (3,475 feet), the most accessible of which is the Piper Trail. More than 25 other trails ascend its surrounding peaks, including Scarred Whiteface (3,985 feet), Paugus (3,200 feet), and Sandwich Dome (3,993 feet).

The 5,552-acre Great Gulf Wilderness Area lies between Mount Washington and the northern peaks of the Presidential Range, embracing a huge valley 1,100 to 1,600 feet deep, formed by glacial action and drained by the West Branch of the Peabody River. A fairly accessible trail system leads through the rugged cirque. Waterfalls plunge down the steep walls of the gulf, and Spaulding and Star lakes sparkle in the uppermost reaches of the wilderness. Elevations range from 1,700 feet in the east to 5,800 feet near Mount Washington's summit. Spruce, fir, and northern hardwoods grow on the lower slopes. Violent winds often lash the barren high country.

Whitetail deer range the country to 3,500 feet, and snowshoe rabbit flourish here. Lynx, bobcat, mink, marten, fisher cat, ruffed grouse, and spruce partridge also inhabit the gulf. Hunting is difficult, however, because of the area's inaccessibility. The lower mile of Peabody River holds brook trout. Two backcountry shelters in the gulf are available on a first-come, first-served basis. The 29,000 roadless acres of the proposed Dry River-Rocky Branch Wilderness embrace the southern Presidential Range, large portions of the Dry River and Rocky Branch valleys, the above-mentioned Montalban Ridge, and some of the most spectacular "big mountain" terrain in the White Mountain National Forest. Dense hardwood forests cloak the river valleys and provide cover for good deer and black bear populations. Numerous trails wind through the rough landscape of the valleys, and five Appalachian Mountain Club shelters are located in the area. One of the most scenic of these footpaths is the Dry River Trail, which follows the river through a steep-walled chasm and winds over the headwall of Oakes Cirque to the Crawford path of Mount Washington. The AMC Mizpah Springs Hut and Lake of the Clouds Hut are located just outside the northern boundary of the wilderness.

The gorge of the Devil's Hopyard cuts through the dense forests of the proposed 24,000-acre Killkenny Wilderness Area, which embraces the Pilot and Pliny ranges in the northernmost part of the White Mountain Forest. This remote upland region contains the headwaters of the Upper Ammonoosuc River and a portion of the Israel River. Panoramic views of the surrounding White Mountain highlands can be had from the summits of Mount Cabot (4,180 feet) and Mount Waumbek (4,020 feet). Large herds of whitetails use the conifer stands throughout the area as winter yarding sites. The Killkenny Wildlife Management Area lies in the southeastern portion of the wilderness and has a large number of eastern coyote. The northern half of the area has seven small high country trout ponds, the largest being Unknown Pond in the shadow of the Horn, and a sizable beaver and moose population. Numerous hiking trails wind through the wilds to such scenic spots as Mount Crescent, Mount Forist and the frozen caves of Ice Gulch.

Hugging the New Hampshire-Maine border of the forest is a remote, roadless hiking, fishing, and hunting area embraced by the proposed 20,000-acre Wild River Wilderness, surrounding the beautiful Wild River. The Carter Range forms the western border and the mountains from North Baldface to West Royce form the eastern border. Many mountain streams flow out of these two ranges and converge at No-Ketchum Pond in the broad, gentle valley floor to form the Wild River. The marshy grasslands attract moose and beaver and provide fine open vistas of the surrounding mountains. Following the Wild River northward, the land changes from marsh to a dark climax forest of birch, balsam, and spruce. Except for a stand of virgin forest along the Black Angel Trail, most of the wilderness was either burned by the fire of 1903 or has been cut in logging operations. There are four shelters and 40 miles of primitive trails, including the Appalachian Trail, which follows the western boundary. Brook trout fishing is good along the broad, flat Wild River Trail. Wildlife includes deer, black bear, bobcat, fox, coyote, and fisher.

The proposed 10,000-acre Carr Mountain Wilderness Area includes Mount Carr and Mount Kineo, and the lowlands between the two mountains in the southwestern section of the White Mountain National Forest. To the west are many mountain brooks which drain into the Baker River. To the east, the brooks from Mounts Carr and Kineo empty into the marshy basin and form Three Ponds—tarns left by receding glaciers—and numerous beaver ponds. The Brown Brook marshes are considered the best waterfowl habitat in the Pemigewasset ranger district. The brook trout fishing is at times excellent. There is a shelter at Three Ponds and an old logging road converted into a trail for access.

In the Maine portion of the forest lies the proposed Caribou-Speckled Mountain Wilderness in the scenic Oxford Hills region, some 12 miles southwest of Bethel. This mountainous 12,000-acre area of heaths, stunted conifers and pine and spruce forests is a popular backpacking and hunting area, inhabited by whitetail deer, black bear, moose, upland game birds, and eastern coyote, or "brush wolves" as they are called locally.

Much of the White Mountain area is accessible by car, but vast expanses of undeveloped wilderness preserve the rugged beauty and the challenge of the mountains. Deer range the mountains below 3,000 feet; bear, partridge, ruffed grouse, and rabbits are other game animals of the forest. Among the better known hunting areas of the forest are the Killkenny, Wild River, Swift River, Zealand River, Sawyer River, Chatham, Jackson, and Waterville areas.

Many of the forest's rivers carve their paths through the remote backcountry areas; a canoe or kayak trip is one of the most pleasant ways to travel the undisturbed wildlands. The Magalloway, Androscoggin, Connecticut, Saco, Pemigewasset, and Ammonoosuc offer some of the best canoe water in the state.

Information Sources, Maps & Access

For detailed outdoor recreation information contact the Supervisor's Office, White Mountain National Forest, Laconia, NH 03246 (603)524-6450. The forest includes more than 30 developed recreation sites, many of which include camping areas. Huts and trail shelters dot the mountain paths, and the backcountry areas have a wide

variety of sites for primitive camping. The *White Mountain National Forest Map* (50¢) includes a directory of these recreation sites. Locations of the sites are shown on the full-color topographic map, as are wilderness areas, state forest areas, highways and roads (good, poor), trails (including the Appalachian trail), railroads, landing fields, ranger stations, campsites, recreation sites, winter sports areas, points of interest, and trail huts, cabins, and shelters.

The forest requires wilderness permits for travel in the Great Gulf and Presidential Range areas. Applications for wilderness permits are available by mail from: White Mountain National Forest, Laconia 03246. Included with the application form is information on where within the forest you may obtain permits, rules and regulations for wilderness use, and a map showing entry points for the wilderness areas. A map and text on *Off-Road Vehicle Conditions of Use* is available from the Forest Supervisor, White Mountain National Forest, which gives regulations for the use of such vehicles, and shows use areas.

Write to: Forest Supervisor, P.O. Box 638, Laconia 03246, for additional trail, camping, wilderness use, and other recreational information. In addition, information on backcountry and wilderness use regulations, weather, and snow conditions may be obtained daily between 8:00 am and 10:00 pm at the main desk in the trading post at the AMC Pinkham Notch Camp, Gorham 03581 (603)466–3994.

Perhaps the most important resource book for visitors to this region is the *AMC White Mountain Guide*. This 550–page guide describes the entire White Mountain region in detail, noting the topography and natural features, wildlife, and plant life, and trails and crosscountry routes to take through each area. The guide also describes skiing and rock-climbing areas, gives distances and times between points, and includes other information of interest to hikers, canoers, ski tourers, and campers. The guide includes contour maps of Mount Monadnock, Mount Cardigan, Chocorua-Waterville, Franconia, Mount Washington Range, Carter-Mahoosuc, and the Pilot Range. These show the locations of surfaced, unsurfaced, and abandoned roads, paths and trails, railroads, summits, camps, trail huts, shelters, abandoned buildings, abandoned trails, water features, and the Appalachian Trail. This compact, hardbound guide costs $8.00 and may be ordered from: AMC Books, 5 Joy St. Boston, MA 02108. Individual AMC maps of *Mount Chocorua, Mount Monadnock, Mount Cardigan, Waterville,* and the *Pilot Range* are available

from the same source for 25¢ each; maps of *Mount Washington, The Franconia Area,* and the *Carter-Mahoosuc Region* cost 50¢; and *Plastic-Coated Maps of the Franconia and Mount Washington Areas* cost $1.00 each.

The club also publishes the *AMC Guide to Mount Washington and the Presidential Range* ($3.95). This eminently useful guide describes the mountain environment, weather, man's impact, management policies, accident reporting, camping facilities, and other wilderness information. The 160–page paperback book includes a map and is packaged in a waterproof bag.

Peter Randall's *Mount Washington,* $3.95 from: University Press of New England, Hanover 03755, offers a history of the mountain and its legends, and a guide to its rugged slopes. Diane M. Kostecke edited the *Franconia Notch* guide, which includes helpful facts for visitors, human history, natural history, major attractions in the area, rock climbing, fishing, winter activities, and hikes and trails. The 100–page guide ($2.95) is published by: Society for the Protection of New Hampshire Forests, 5 S. State St., Concord 03301. If you plan to hike the upper reaches of the mountains, L.C. Bliss's *Alpine Zone of the Presidential Range* ($1.50) will provide a helpful guide to the geology, climate, and flora and fauna of this area. This book and the others listed in this paragraph may be ordered by mail from: AMC Books (address above).

For local fishing and stream conditions, information, and equipment and accessories, contact: *Dick Surette Fly Fishing Shop,* North Conway, NH 03860 (603)356–5091. The forest is reached by way of U.S. Highway 302 and State Route 10 from the west, Interstate 93 from the south, and State Route 16/25 from the southeast. Outfitting and supply centers for the region include Berlin and Gorham to the north, Conway near the southeast boundary. Plymouth to the south on U.S. 3, and Littleton to the northwest on Interstate 93. Lodging, supplies, canoe rentals, and outfitters within the forest are available at Warren, Rumney, Benton, Woodstock, Waterville Valley, Bretton Woods, Jackson, Glen, Bartlett Willey House, Intervale, Chatham, Shelburne, Gileas, and Stowe.

Gateways & Accommodations

Berlin

(Pop. 15,300; zip code 03570; area code 603) is a northern gateway for skiers, backpackers, hikers, fisherman, and hunters situated halfway between the northernmost section of the White Mountain National Forest and the Appalachian Trail as it passes from New Hampshire into Maine. The mighty Androscoggin River spills through this historic logging town, home of the Nansen Ski Club, the first ski club in the United States. Area attractions include the Nansen Ski Jump (182 ft.), Jasper Cave, Milan Hill State Park, and Moose Brook State Park. Accommodations: *Traveler Motel* (rates: $20–24 double), with 28 good rooms in town at 25 Pleasant St. (752–2500).

Crawford Notch

(Area code 603) is the major gateway for tourists, hunters, skiers, snowshoers, hikers and fisherman heading into the spectacular high country of the central White Mountains. A natural mountain pass cut by the Saco river through a wooded valley hemmed in by high mountains, Crawford Notch was discovered in 1771 by two hunters, and opened up a route into the north country in the revolutionary days. Today the Appalachian Trail crosses here, heading into the Presidential Range. Area attractions include Arethusa Falls, the highest in the state; Silver Cascade (1,000 ft.), on Mt. Webster; and Crawford Notch State Park, the site of the Wiley Family tragedy in 1826, when the family fled their home and perished in an

avalanche, which changed its course and left their home intact. Accommodations: (see below under "Lodges, Resorts & Inns").

Franconia Notch & Village

(Pop. 500; zip code 03580; area code 603), dividing the impressive Franconia and Kinsman Ranges, is the most popular of the White Mountain passes, and a major gateway for tourists, skiers, backpackers, and hikers who seek the rugged beauty of its unique geological features, clear lakes, rocky gorges, and surrounding untracked wilderness. Special features include the following. The Old Man of the Mountains: 48 feet high and composed of three granite ledges, a gigantic profile on Cannon Mountain and the best loved geological feature of the White Mountains; The Flume: public walks and bridges follow Flume Brook as it tumbles wildly through the spectacular Flume Gorge, with sheer rock walls 70' high in places; The Basin: a clear alpine tarn, in a smooth granite bowl near the highway; Echo Lake: a clear lake below the jagged walls of Eagle Cliff, hemmed in by Artists Bluff, Bald Mountain and Cannon Mountain; Cannon Mountain Aerial Tramway: ascends 2,200 feet from May 27–Oct. 15 to Summit observation platform; Cannon Mt. Ski Area and Mitterhill Ski Area. The Appalachian Trail crosses Franconia Notch and ascends Mt. Lafayette (5,249 ft.) offering spectacular views of Mt. Washington and the Presidential Range, and the mountains of Vermont to the west. Accommodations: *Notchway Motel* (rates: $24–34 double), with 25 excellent rooms and family units, dining room, coffeeshop, swimming pool at Franconia Notch entrance on U.S. Highway 3 (823–5525); *Raynor's Motor Lodge* (rates: $24–30 double), with 31 excellent rooms and family units, heated pool ¾ miles south of village at junction of New Hampshire 18 and 142 (823–5651).

Gorham

(Pop. 2,000; zip code 03581; area code 603), situated north of Pinkham Notch where the Peabody River tumbles into the Androscoggin, is the northern gateway to the Presidential Range. Only a path led south from Gorham to the Connecticut River Valley when it was first settled in 1805. In 1852 the Atlantic and St. Lawrence Railroad in 1852 made Gorham a bustling tourist center, the nearest approach to the White Mountain by railroad. Today, surrounded by the high peaks of the northern Presidentials, Gorham is a gateway for hikers, backpackers, skiers and fisherman heading into the spectacular high country of the White Mountain National Forest. There is a district ranger office here. Area attractions include the Moose Brook State Park; the Libby Memorial Pool and Recreation area, with a natural pool; and the Dolly Copp Campground, named for a pipe smoking pioneer woman who, with her husband, lived alone in the wilds for 19 years before any one else came to settle, and by crafting such beautiful hand-sewn linens and woolens gained quite a reputation when guests came to stay in the first Glen House in 1852. Accommodations: *Mount Madison Motel* (rates: $25 double), with 37 good guest rooms and family units, heated pool at 365 Main St. (466–3622); *Northern Peaks Motel* (rates: $22–28 double), with 27 good guest rooms and heated pool at 289 Main St. (466–3374); *Town & Country Motor Inn* (rates: $26–36 double), with 74 excellent rooms and family units, and superb dining room just east of town on U.S. Highway 2 (466–3315).

Jackson

(Pop. 300; zip code 03846; area code 603.) South of Pinkham and Crawford Notches, Jackson is a major gateway to the White Mountain National Forest and skiing in New Hampshire. The Wildcat River spills through this colonial town, dominated by a high church spire. Area attractions include the Jackson Ski Touring Foundation which maintains a large network of ski trails over public and private property, Tyrol Mountain Ski Area, and Black Mountain Ski Area. Heritage New Hampshire in nearby Glen recreates 30 historical events by animation. Accommodations: *Covered Bridge Motel* (rates: $22–30 double), with 25 excellent guest rooms, and family units, heated pool, tennis, golf, and skiing ½ mile south of town on New Hampshire Highway 16 (383–6630).

Jefferson

(Pop. 100; zip code 03583; area code 603.) High on the slopes of Mt. Starr King, Jefferson is the gateway to the northern reaches of the White Mountain National Forest. Known locally as Jefferson Hill, the town offers some of the finest views of the White Mountains. The Israel River flows through its center. One of the first prominent settlers of Jefferson, a Colonel Whipple, brought with him a girl named Nancy to work as a domestic servant. Nancy is said to have been the first woman to pass through Crawford Notch, when, in 1778, she set out in pursuit of her lover and died in a howling snow storm. Mt. Nancy is said to have been named for her. Area attractions include the Annual White Mountains Festival of the Arts in July and August, Weeks State Park, Santa's Village and Gingerbread Forest with tame deer, tropical birds, and a variety of rides. Accommodations: *Evergreen Motel* (rates: $22–24 double), with 18 excellent guest rooms one mile west of town on U.S. Highway 2 (586–4449).

Littleton

(Pop. 4,200; zip code 03561; area code 603), on the Vermont border north of Franconia Notch, is the northwest gateway to the White Mountain National Forest. The Ammonoosuc River spills through the town, descending 235 feet, providing the power for the early industry which spurred the town's growth. Today Littleton is a commercial center and a scenic gateway to the western edge of the White Mountains. Area attractions include Mt. Eustis with a ski tow in Littleton, Forest Lake State Park, Mettersill Ski Area, and picnicking and recreation at Moose Reservoir. The Samuel C. Moore Station, the largest hydroelectric plant in New England, on Moose Reservoir, has a visitor center open to the public in the summer months. Accommodations: *Beal House Inn* (rates: $17–18 double), with 13 charming Old New England guest rooms with old style country breakfast at 247 W. Main St. (444–2661); *Littleton Motel* (rates: $24 double), with 19 excellent rooms, heated pool, at 187 Main St. (444–5780).

North Conway

(Pop. 1,700; zip code 03860; area code 603), centered in the Mt. Washington Valley, is a gateway for tourists, skiers, hikers, snowshoers, hunters and fishermen heading into the spectacular high country of the White Mountains. Situated on the Saco River, North Conway provides one of the most breathtaking scenic approaches to the Presidential Range. Area highlights include Echo Lake State Park, Cathedral Ledge and White Cliffs, Conway Scenic Railroad, Attitash and Mt. Cranmore ski areas, and scenic mountain flights by biplane from the White Mountain Airport. Accommodations: *Junges Motel* (rates: $30–32 double) with 25 excellent guest rooms and family units, heated pool, in scenic location 1¾ miles south of town on U.S. 302 (356–2886); *Old Field House Motor Lodge in Intervale* (rates: $28–36 double), with 13 excellent guest rooms and services, 3½ miles north of town on New Hampshire Highway 16A (356–5478); *Red Jacket Mountain View Inn* (rates: $44–56 double), with 159 excellent alpine guest rooms and housekeeping apartments in spectacular setting with dining room, indoor and outdoor heated pools, sauna, tennis courts, Birchmont Tavern Lounge, 1 mile

south of town on U.S. 302 and New Hampshire 16 (356–5411); *Swiss Chalets Motel in Intervale* (rates: $34 double), with 24 excellent guest rooms and family units, swimming pool, four miles north of town on New Hampshire 16A (356–2232).

North Woodstock

(Pop. 650; zip code 03262; area code 603) is the junction for tourists, backpackers, skiers, hikers, and fishermen heading north to Franconia Notch, or west to Kinsman Notch. The Moosilauke River flows west of the town, which offers superb views of Franconia Notch to the north. Area attractions include Loon Mountain Ski Area, Joseph Story Fay Wayside Picnic Area, Elbow Pond, and the Lost River Reservation, with a nature garden featuring rare wildflowers, large caves, trout ponds, and Paradise Falls. Accommodations: *Jack O' Lantern Resort* (rates: $60 double), with 65 superb guest rooms and family cottages and chalets on pine-shaded grounds in the beautiful Pemi Valley with restaurant, cocktail lounge, heated pool, tennis court, and trout fishing, 5½ miles south of town on U.S. 3, off I-93 Exit 30 (745–8121); *Woodward's Motor Inn & Open Hearth Steak House* (rates: $36 double), with 42 excellent rooms, heated pool, tennis court 3½ miles north of town on U.S. 3 (745–8141).

Pinkham Notch—Gateway to Mount Washington

Pinkham Notch, the easternmost gap in the White Mountains, is the major gateway for tourists, backpackers, hikers, skiers and fisherman to Mt. Washington and the magnificent Presidential Range. Here the Appalachian Mountain Club has its headquarters and maintains a series of eight huts within a day's hike of one another amid the rocky clefts, alpine lakes, and lofty peaks of the Presidential Range. Wildcat Mountain Ski Area, and the dramatic Tuckerman Ravine, make Pinkham Notch one of the leading ski areas of the east. Special area features include the Glen Ellis Falls, the Crystal Cascade, and the Wildcat Gondola Tramway, which ascends to the summit of Wildcat Mt. from May-Oct. offering spectacular views of Mt. Washington and the Presidential Range. Other area attractions include the spectacular Mount Washington Auto Road and the scenic Mount Washington Cog Railway, built in 1869. Eight steam locomotives operate from base station six miles off U.S. 302 from Fabyans-Bretton Woods daily from 8–5 on the hour June 24 to Labor Day, (603)846–5404. Please note that the Mount Washington Auto Road should be attempted only by experienced high country drivers. Chauffeured station wagon service is available in Pinkham Notch for those not wishing to drive. Accommodations: (see below, "AMC Mountain Hut System").

Plymouth

(Pop. 3,100; zip code 03264; area code 603.) South of Franconia Notch, and north of the spectacular New Hampshire Lakes region, Plymouth is a crossroads for tourists, hikers, skiers, hunters, fishermen and sailors. Industry has played an important part in the development of this colonial town above the Pemigewasset River. Area attractions include Tenny Mountain Ski area, the Polar Caves, Squam Lake, Mad River Run Ski Area, and spectacular Waterville Valley. Accommodations: *Holiday Inn* (rates: $38.50 double), with 103 excellent guest rooms, restaurant, cocktail lounge, indoor heated pool and sauna four miles north of town off Interstate 93 Exit 27 (536–3520).

Twin Mountain—Gateway to Mount Washington

(Pop. 300; zip code 03595; area code 603.) North of the White Mountain National Forest between Crawford Notch and Franconia Notch, Twin Mountain is a gateway for skiers, hikers, backpackers, and hunters to the Franconia and Presidential Ranges. Lying in the beautiful Ammonoosuc Valley, Twin Mountain is surrounded by the towering peaks of North Twin Mountain, Mt. Lafayette, Mt. Garfield, and in the distance, Mt. Washington. Area features include the Bretton Woods Ski Area, downhill and cross-country skiing in a spectacular setting, and the Mt. Washington Cog Railway. This hardy little train climbs one foot for every four traveled, until it reaches the very summit of Mt. Washington. Views from here extend over 100 miles, including parts of Maine, Quebec, Vermont, New York, and the Atlantic Ocean. Accommodations: *Charlmont Motor Inn* (rates: $20–25 double), with 38 excellent guest rooms and family units, dining room, cocktail lounge, tennis courts, just south of town on U.S. 3 at junction of U.S. 302 (846–5549); *Seven Dwarfs Motel* (rates: $20–25 double), with 14 excellent rooms and family units, some with fireplaces, in scenic location with trout fishing south of town off U.S. 3 (846–5535).

Waterville Valley Village & Ski Touring Center

(Pop. 100; zip code 03223; area code 603.) Waterville Valley is a major gateway to skiing, hiking, canoeing, backpacking and fishing in the White Mountain National Forest. Nathaniel Greeley built the first house here in 1833 and took in boarders. Waterville Valley has been welcoming guests ever since, and is now one of New Hampshire's largest and best loved four-season resorts. Special area attractions are the Waterville Valley Tennis Center and Tennis Programs, Golf Club and Golf Programs, Jamboree Recreational Program, Wings Day Camp and Nursery, Waterville Valley Ski Area, and the Waterville Valley Ski Touring Center. Mt. Tecumseh, an official site for the U.S. Alpine Ski Team, is the ideal place to learn how to ski. Classes are small and geared to individual abilities. With the GLM method, you parallel from the beginning, and enjoy yourself. Instructors are enthusiastic, equipped with great patience and a sense of humor. The five-day ski program is crowned with a race at the end (on an intermediate slope) and an optional awards banquet, where skiers and their families are seated with their instructor at one of the nine high quality restaurants in the valley. All eight lifts to Mt. Tecumseh begin at a central point, so it is easy to meet with group members who may be skiing any of the mountain's 32 runs. Two expert runs, True Grit and Bobby's Run, were the site of the first National Professional Freestyle Championships. Skiers with wanderlust can take advantage of the five-day ski pass called "Ski the White Mountains" that offers skiing in Waterville Valley, Loon, Mt. Cannon, Bretton Woods, Mt. Cranmore, Wildcat,

and Attitash. Snow's Mountain, opposite Mt. Tecumseh in Waterville Valley, offers excellent intermediate skiing, and features a lighted skating rink. Centered between these two mountains, on the valley floor, is the Waterville Valley Ski Touring Center, offering cross country skiing on 30 miles of groomed and patrolled ski trails. The warming hut offers wax, advice, hot chocolate and coffee. Rentals are available at the ski center, and it is a starting point for lessons, guided tours, citizen races, and other events. All trails form a loop, so you need never retrace your steps, and all can meet at the adjacent Finish Line Restaurant for a hearty lunch. The national forest surrounding Waterville Valley, has many wilderness trails for adventurous cross-country skiers. Nearby or right in Waterville Valley there are 23 country inns, two bunkhouses, and 300 luxurious condominiums with fully equipped kitchens and fireplaces. All tastefully blend with the environment, so the beauty of the National Forest is not lost. Winter campgrounds are open for those who have warm sleeping bags and lots of nerve. Saunas, whirlpool baths, indoor pools, a skating rink, heated and lighted platform tennis courts, and game rooms are located throughout the valley. There are many fine restaurants, featuring hearty steaks and prime ribs, Italian dishes, and fresh seafood. Free shuttle bus service runs between all accommodations, restaurants, and skiing in the valley. For more information write: The Waterville Valley Co., Waterville Valley. Accommodations: *Silver Squirrel Inn* (rates: $34–42 double), with 30 excellent guest rooms off New Hampshire 49 on Snow's Brook Rd. (236–8366).

Lodges, Resorts & Inns

****Appalachian Mountain Club Hut System*. The Appalachian Mountain Club is the oldest mountaineering and conservation club in the United States. In New Hampshire, they have established the AMC Hut system, a four-season network of eight cabins spaced a day's hike apart in the White Mountain National Forest, one of the few, large, backcountry areas in the northeast. Within its boundaries are most of New England's highest peaks.

Pinkham Notch Camp, in Gorham, serves as a base camp for all the other cabins, and is only ½ mile from the Wildcat Ski area. Located right off Route 16, and a stop on the Continental Trailways Bus system, Pinkham Notch is the largest facility, accommodating 100 guests in rooms with two, three, and four bunks. There is a library, living room, dining room and snack bar serving hot drinks and snacks for the trail. Lodging with breakfast is $11 per person, with dinner, $12.75; lodging, meals, and downhill skiing rates are $98 midweek and $209.50 full week; lessons as well as lodging, meals, lifts and rentals, $164 midweek and $254.50 full week. Cross-country ski rentals, with meals and lodging run $77.50 midweek and $125 on a full-week basis. Reservations are necessary. There is a 60 seat lodge conference room which may be reserved by any group or organization. In addition, there is a pack-up room where all skiers, snowshoers, and hikers are welcome to relax, shower, repack their gear, and pick up trail maps and AMC guidebooks. Two of the AMC Huts, the Zealand Hut and the Carter Notch Hut, are open to skiers and snowshoers in the winter on a caretaker basis. Bring your own sleeping bag and food. A caretaker will let you in, and you are welcome to use the stove and utensils for cooking. Reservations for the huts may be made at the Pinkham Notch Camp.

Zealand Falls Hut is accessible to skiers, backpackers, and snowshoers by the Zealand Falls trail, which starts at the end of Zealand Road, an old logging road that forks off to the left of 302. Since the Zealand Road is still used for logging operations in the winter, and is popular with snowmobilers, skiers may wish to take a ski trail, which veers off the road 50 yards after the first bridge. This trail parallels Zealand Road, and meets up with it again at the trailhead of the Zealand Trail. From there it is 2.7 miles of easy skiing, until it gets steep right before the hut, along the snow bound fall. Altogether it is six miles from where Zealand Road cuts off of 302 to the hut, and AMC cautions skiers and snowshoers not to leave any later than 1:00 pm.

Carter Notch Hut, an old stone hut tucked deep in the cleft between Carter Dome and Wildcat Mountain, is accessible by a four mile section of the 19 mile Brook Trail, which begins off Route 16. Since the Carter Notch Hut is built in one of the most rugged mountain notches, only expert cross country skiers will take on the challenge of skiing there. Most people prefer to snowshoe in. The hut has a capacity for 40 people, and features two bunkhouses, separate from the main hut, which are divided into four and six bunks. AMC cautions adventurers to leave for the hut by 12 p.m. The view from the Carter Notch Hut is one of the most spectacular views of the mountains in New England.

The other six huts along the Appalachian Trail, are open from June through September. *Lonesome Lake Hut*, nestled by the lake under the jagged face of Cannon Mountain, has a sleeping capacity of 44. *Greenleaf Hut*, near Eagle Lake with a spectacular view of Franconia Notch is sometimes called the sunset hut, known for the

beauty and fire of sunsets that linger in memory. Capacity is 36. The *Galehead Hut* is the most remote, surrounded by 4,000 ft. mountains on three sides, and overlooking the Pemigewasset Wilderness, with a capacity of 38. The *Lake of the Clouds Hut*, 1.4 miles from the summit of Mt. Washington, is the largest of the high huts, with a capacity of 90. On a rare, cloud-free day you can see the mountains of Vermont and Canada, and the distant lights of Montreal twinkling, 140 miles away. *Mitzah Spring* is the newest hut in the system, with a capacity for 60 people. Tucked away at 3,800 feet on the eastern flank of Mt. Clinton, in the southern Presidentials, Mitzah Spring offers beautiful view of the Dry River wilderness and the Chocorua region. *Madison Spring Hut*, above tree line of the Madison-Adams col has a capacity to serve 50 people.

Reservations along the hut system, including Pinkham Notch Camp are required, and can be made by writing: Reservations Secretary, Pinkham Notch Camp, Gorham, NH 03581 or calling (603)466–2727.

***Baker Brook Resort*, situated on its own private lake, is centrally located in the White Mountain National Forest region, with hiking trails and 130 acres of pine forest. The north hiking trail leads to a secluded trout pond with a sandy beach. The south trail winds

through a pine forest alongside the lake to a large trout stream with several pools. The 15–acre private lake is stocked with bass and pickerel. The lakes, pools and streams are all license-free to Baker Brook guests. The grounds surrounding the resort are woodsy and spacious. The resort offers two heated swimming pools, shuffleboard courts, pedal boating on the lake, a children's playground and outdoor barbecue fireplaces. Mountain attractions are available in the area and side trips can be taken to Mt. Washington Cog Railway and Auto Road, Cannon Mt. Aerial Tramway, Franconia Notch State Park or Crawford Notch State Park. Two 18–hole golf courses and tennis courts are also nearby. The lodgings are in harmony with the natural beauty of the area. Knotty pine walls and beamed ceilings add to the relaxed informality. Each lodge has a kitchen unit and private bath and is fully equipped with all utensils and supplies. Daily maid service is provided, as well as free cribs, cots and TV. Some of the lodges are located directly on the lake and some have fireplaces, with fire logs provided free of charge. There are also three separate motel units on the property—all rooms have private baths, TV and air-conditioning, central heating and individual thermostats. The resort's restaurant and cocktail lounge overlooks the lake and offers delicious food and beverages at affordable prices. Baker Brook is open all year. Motel rates range from $24–30 for double occupancy, daily. Lodge rates, for two-four people, range from $32–47 daily, or $189–322 weekly. Off season rates are slightly lower. For further information call or write Baker Brook Resort, Route 302, Littleton, NH 03561 (603)444–2147.

★★★★*Bretton Woods Ski Resort & Touring Center*. At the base of Mt. Washington and the Presidential Mountain Range, offers a downhill ski area, lodge, motel, and cross-country ski-touring center surrounded by breathtaking alpine scenery. Two double chairlifts and one T-Bar service the seven miles of downhill runs. The sports lodge at the mountain base houses alpine ski rentals, a nursery, a spacious lounge and fireplace, game rooms and live entertainment in the restaurant, which serves hot and cold sandwiches, soups and brew. The professional ski school offers group lessons for $7, and private lessons for $14 to skiers of every ability. In addition, there are

daily recreational races and freestyle events. Ski rentals are $10 daily, for a complete package. A variety of mid-week specials, ski lesson and lift packages and reduced rental rates for three days or more are available. The 84 kilometers of trails at the Bretton Woods Ski Touring Center forms one of the largest ski trail networks in the east. Trail systems follow both forks of the wide, snow-laden Ammonoosuc River and reach the sparkling upper falls, cross tiny springs, encircle beaver ponds and penetrate the Pemigewasset Wilderness Area. Sudden clearings on mountain ridges afford spectacular views of Mt. Washington and the Presidential Range. Professional instruction on all levels of ski touring is available. Lessons are $7, skis, boots, and poles can be rented in the center for $7. Photography tours, moonlight tours, and overnight wilderness expeditions are all available, and there are regularly scheduled races. The ski center has a roaring fire to return to, and serves hot drinks and refreshments. All trails converge at the Bretton Woods Sports Lodge. The Bretton Woods Motor Inn offers deluxe rooms, fully carpeted with color TV, private bath, and spectacular view. Darbys Tavern, located in the inn, offers hearty food and drink with live entertainment, overlooking the Presidential Range. Rooms in the Motor Inn are $14 weekdays for a single, and $25 weekends. Double occupancy, per person $10 weekdays, $16 weekends. Triple occupancy, per person $8 weekdays, $11 weekends and quads are $7 weekdays, $9 weekends, per person. Slightly more economical is the Silver Fox Inn, offering rooms with two double beds and TV for $12 weekdays and $23 weekends, single occupancy; $8 weekdays and $14 weekends per person double occupancy; $6 weekdays, $9 weekends per person triple occupancy and $5 weekdays, $7 weekends per person quad. Fabyan's Station, a restored railway depot on the Cog Railway Road offers weekend entertainment, sandwiches, burgers, seafood and steaks. For more information call toll free outside NH (800)258–0330 and within NH (603)278–1000 or write: Bretton Woods Ski Resort, Bretton Woods, NH 03575.

★★★*Cannon Mountain House & Cottage*, located within a short distance of the White Mountain National Forest and its thousand acres of woodlands, mountains, streams and well-marked trails, is situated on its own 200 acres. A trout brook runs through the property and fishing, deer hunting, hiking and exploring are excellent. For skiers, the base of the Tucker Brook Ski Trail is in the "front yard" and Coppermine, Bridal Veil Falls and Mt. Kinsman Trails of the Appalachian Mountain Club network are all within a short distance. Golf, tennis, skating and horseback riding can also be found within the immediate area. Franconia Village, with its superb stores and restaurants, is only 2½ miles away. The famed Franconia Notch with the Great Stone Face, the Flume, Aerial Tramway, ski schools and ski lifts are only four miles away. The inn, which dates back to colonial times, provides an informal and congenial atmosphere where one can relax on the huge porch and enjoy the unsurpassed view of the surrounding mountain range. Activities on the premises include shuffleboard, croquet, badminton, horseshoes, dancing, music, singing and TV. Day tours are offered to the area sights. The rooms in the main house are pleasant and comfortable, and the full-course meals provided include vegetables grown right on the property. There is also a duplex cottage available, with its own wide porch. Each unit has a bed-living-room, bath and shower, and kitchen equipped for light housekeeping. It's fully insulated and has controlled heat and hot water. The units can accommodate from two to six people and are perfect for privacy. Your host of the past 43 years, Jerry Kosch, looks forward to helping make your stay a pleasant one. Rates, for double occupancy on the Modified American plan, start at $16 daily. (European plan is also available starting at $8 daily.) Contact him at (603)823–9574 or write Cannon Mt. House and Cottage, Franconia, NH 03580.

★★Cranmore Inn. Just off the main street in North Conway a hand painted, white colonial sign indicates the Cranmore Inn, one of the inviting, traditional inns that makes New England so unique. Close to all five ski areas of the Mt. Washington Valley, and surrounded by cross country ski trails, Cranmore offers package ski plans with interchangable lift tickets to all guests. Special group and family rates are available. The town of North Conway has many quaint shops, a movie theater, bowling alleys, and a skating rink. The inn has a comfortable living room with a fireplace, a television room and a game room. The dining room serves excellent home-cooked food, with fresh baked bread, and a variety of homemade desserts. The 25 guest rooms offer a variety of accommodations ranging from $15–24, depending on the type of accommodations, and the number of people. In the summer, huge oak trees shade the porch. The atmosphere is quiet, and unrushed. There is a pool to sun by, and endless trails in the mountains to hike. For more information write: Cranmore Inn, North Conway, NH 03860 (603)356–5502.

★★★Cranmore Mountain Lodge at Mt. Washington Valley, a year-round retreat within minutes of five major ski areas; Cranmore, Mt. Attitash, Wildcat, Tyrol and Black Mt., surrounded by hundreds of miles of cross-country ski paths, and offers hospitality of a traditional New England country inn. There is a pond on the grounds for ice skating, a toboggan hill, and an alpine ski rental center. The attractive inn has 11 spacious bedrooms, a sitting room with a roaring fire, and a dining room which serves hearty country breakfasts daily, and home-cooked dinners on weekends only. An adjoining barn has been renovated into a large, carpeted dormitory to house groups in bunk style rooms. The basement is a recreation room with a crackling fire. Pizza parties and weekend snowmobile rides highlight each week, and the Volvo World Pro Ski races on Cranmore Mt..highlight the season. In the summer, the surrounding forest offers trails for hiking, and the Cranmore's own trout pond is stocked for fly fishing. There is a new, all-weather tennis court, a 40 ft. swimming pool, and a jacuzzi to relax in. Outdoor bar-b-ques highlight the summer evenings. The Mt. Washington Valley offers indoor and outdoor tennis, golf, horseback riding, kayaking, canoeing, and summer theater shows. Rates are $10 daily per person double occupancy, $12 with breakfast, and on weekends when dinner is served, $16 daily with two meals. Rooms sleeping three people are $8.50 per person daily, $10.50 with breakfast, and $14.50 on weekends with breakfast and dinner. Four-six in a room are $7.50 without meals, $9.50 with breakfast, and $13.50 per person on weekends with two meals. Dorm rates are $7 per person without meals, $9 per person with breakfast, and $13 per person on weekends with both breakfast and dinner. Special group rates are available on request, and mid-week ski specials, offering five night stays for the price of four nights, and a 20% discount on ski rentals, are also offered. For more information write: Cranmore Mountain Lodge, Box 1194, North Conway, NH 03860 or call (603)356–2044.

★★★★Dana Place Inn at Mount Washington Valley is located at the foot of Mt. Washington and is surrounded by 600,000 acres of unspoiled national forest. The inn offers 300 acres of lawns, gardens, streams, meadows and woodland trails. There is mountain climbing and hiking, with Mt. Washington and the Presidential Range offering the most challenging variety of trails in the Appalachian Range. Scenic points of interest within a short drive are the Wildcat Mountain Gondolas, Mt. Washington Auto Road, Glen Ellis Falls (one of the highest in New Hampshire) and the Jackson covered bridge. You can quietly explore the Ellis River, which cascades for more than a mile through the inn's meadows and woodlands, or swim in a crystal-clear natural river pool, or in their pool located in the apple orchard. There are two all-weather tennis courts, trout fishing and four golf courses only

minutes away. In the winter this is the central location for the best ski trails around—Wildcat, Black Mountain, Tyrol, Attatish, and Cranmore. It is also the center of the most popular cross-country trails—over 80 miles of the well marked network of the Jackson Ski Touring Foundation—and right next to the beautiful Ellis River Trail. For further skiing convenience, a courtesy car is provided for transportation, there is a heated waxing room for your skis, and the inn keeps in constant touch with trail conditions. Afterwards, there is a comfortable reading lounge and television room. The inn offers country gourmet dining and the meals are outstanding, with a good wine list and excellent service. The Pub, for informal relaxing at the end of the day, provides intimate piano music. Accommodations are available either at the inn, (the rooms are charming and tastefully restored) or in one of the more luxurious condominiums. These feature outside decks, floor to ceiling picture windows, spiral staircases and cathedral ceilings. They are located in a wooded area close to the tennis courts, have spectacular views, and are fully equipped units. The rooms, based on double occupancy, range from $28–44, bath either shared or private, breakfast included. Condominium rates per unit, weekly, range from $180–495, daily from $28–75. Rates slightly higher in winter months. For further information contact Betty and Mal Jennings, Dana Place Inn, Box F, Jackson, NH 03846 (603)383–6822.

★★★*Darby Field Inn at Mt. Washington Valley* is an enchanting four-season country inn set high atop Bald Hill in the White Mountains. Located one thousand feet above the surrounding Mt. Washington Valley and only 1½ miles from Conway, the Darby Field commands a magnificent panorama of alpine scenery. The Mt. Washington valley has activities for everyone. In the summer there is hiking and a swimming pool at the inn, and golf, fishing, theater, shopping and a variety of attractions nearby. Winter brings down-hill skiing at five mountains, and cross-country skiing and snowshoeing right from the inn's door. The accommodations at the inn, named after the first white man to climb Mt. Washington in 1642, are superb. Each bedroom has a charm of its own—some are decorated with gingham checks and calicos, others more formally. Each room has its own bath and most have a view of the valley. Downstairs is a huge stone fireplace, old fashioned pub, and a dining room where dinners are elegantly served by candlelight. Daily Modified American Plan rates for room with private bath (double occupancy) are $28–30. For additional information contact

Marc & Marilyn Donaldson, Darby Field Inn, Bald Hill, Conway, NH 03818 (603) 447–2181.

★★★*Eagle Mountain House at Mount Washington Valley* is in the very heart of ski country in Jackson. The magnificent 125–kilometer Jackson Ski Touring Trail system starts at the front door. Within minutes are five Mt. Washington downhill-ski areas. Along with skiing, winter sports include skating, snowshoeing and toboganing. Coffee, tea, hot chocolate and cookies greet guests as they return from the slopes each afternoon. Other wintertime activities include ping-pong, pool and other games in the well-equipped recreation room, entertainment in the Highlander Pub, and relaxation in front of one of the fireplaces. The Mountain House has its own 9–hole golf course plus tennis, swimming, badminton, shuffleboard and miles of hiking trails. A trout stream flows through the property to the famous Jackson Falls. A variety of accommodations is available, including connecting rooms, ideal for families. Most rooms have a beautiful mountain view. A Saturday night buffet dinner dance is a regular feature and early risers' coffee is served in the lobby every morning at 6:30 a.m. The dining room offers delicious breakfasts and dinners. Home-baked breads and pastries are featured. Lunch is also available. Modified American Plan rates per person range from $25–35 per night for doubles with bath, $15–20 for doubles with private baths and $20–30 for two or three room suites. Weekend specials and ski week plans are available. For further information or reservations, contact Eagle Mountain House, Mount Washington Valley, Route 16B, Jackson, NH 03846 (603)383–4264.

★★★*Eastern Mountain Sports Lodge.* Just a short distance from its touring center in Jackson, EMS operates a large swiss-style chalet in North Conway. Twenty six spacious, modern rooms with private bath are available. A 50% discount is available to guests on cross-country and alpine ski rentals. Cross-country touring begins at the back door of the lodge, and there are miles of scenic trails along the banks of the Saco River. The Great Eastern Restaurant features delicious chef specialties, fresh seafood, a salad bar, prime ribs and steak. On Sundays there is a special brunch. The EMS shop adjacent to the lodge sells the fine high-quality outdoor clothing and cross-country and downhill ski equipment they are famous for. In the summer, enjoy hiking the White Mountains, swim in the large outdoor pool after a set of tennis or, if you are someone who enjoys the adrenaline laced precision of rock climbing, the EMS Climbing School offers expert instruction. Rates: $20 single and $24 double room. For more information write: Manager, Eastern Mountain Sports Lodge, Main Street, North Conway, NH 03860(603)356–3686.

★★★*The Franconia Inn & Ski Touring Center* is nestled in the broad Easton Valley, with breath-taking views of Mt. Lafayette, Franconia Notch, and the Franconia and Kinsman Ranges of the White Mountains, and offers 60 miles of ski trails, 40 of them carefully groomed, traversing sunny meadows and winding through deep woods and over mountain ridges. If downhill skiing is your sport, Cannon Mountain and Mettersill are just minutes away. The old barn, next to the inn, houses the cross-country ski center. Skis, boots, poles, and the wax of the day are offered for $6 daily and $20 weekly. One-hour group lessons are available for $5, private lessons are $10. Guided tours are available for $5. In addition, the ski touring center organizes weekly events such as soccer on skis—sounds impossible? Nights of the full moon are no time to stay inside, with guided tours through the moon shadows highlighted by wine and cheese parties beside a warm fire. There are a variety of special events such as the black coffee ski tour on New Year's Day, which promises to get you going again, and the Bushwater Obstacle Ski Race. With a tradition of hospitality since the post-Civil War days, the Franconia Inn offers

comfortable lodging in pleasant, spacious rooms, many pine pan-elled. The large sunlit dining room, embellished with hanging plants and polished wooden floor, promises hearty country breakfasts and superb dinners. Rates are daily, including breakfast and dinner $40–50 single; $34–40 per person double occupancy. Children (14 and under) $17–20. Three day ski vacation plans are $114–141 single and $96–114 double occupancy. Five day winter vacation rates $180–225 single; $153–180 double occupancy. Special five day savings vacations, offered during lulls in the season, $160–200 single occupancy and $144–160 double occupancy. Contact: Franconia Inn, Franconia, NH 03580 (603)823–5542.

**The Jackson Lodge* is situated on a quiet knoll overlooking the village of Jackson, nestled in the White Mountain National Forest. It is just minutes away from five major mountain ski areas—Tyrol, Black, Cranmore, Attitash and Wildcat. The Jackson Ski Touring Foundation is at the doorstep. It is the focal point of 125km of well maintained cross-country trails. The area also provides three golf courses, swimming, hiking, tennis, and cycling. The lodge and pub have great food, comfortable rooms, a tranquil atmosphere, spectacular mountain views and a fine porch and patio (for dining). Rates, based on double occupancy, including a hearty breakfast, range from approximately $20–30, depending on whether you choose a dorm room or bedroom with private bath. There are numerous ski packages and family rates available. For information, contact The Jackson Lodge, Jackson, NH 03846 (603)383–4226.

Lime Kiln Camps is located in the White Mountain National Forest region, and situated so that you can take advantage of all the forest and mountain activities. Black Mountain and Sugar Loaf nearby (2800 ft. high) are for climbing, with mountain streams and trails to stroll along, mushrooms to pick, flowers and birds to photograph or just watch, and trout fishing. The camp itself offers ping-pong, badminton, volleyball, croquet, baseball and swimming and horseback riding, either English or Western. It is within a short driving distance of golf, tennis and hang gliding, as well as the local auctions, antique dealers and country stores. There are 14 campsites and 12 rustic housekeeping units, and a six bedroom lodge house. The campsites, with table, fireplace, flush toilets and hot showers are $3.50 per night for two (50¢ each additional person). The housekeeping units with bedrooms, living rooms, kitchen and bath are $79 for four people per week. Contact the O'Shaughnessys, at The Lime Kilns, North Haverhill, NH 03774, (1–603)989–5656. Their winter address is: Loomis Street, Southwick, MA 01077 (1–413)569–6015.

**Lovett's Inn by Lafayette Brook* is a traditional New England inn located in Franconia, surrounded by brooks, ponds, pine woods and the White Mountains. There's winter and spring skiing and Lovett's is a 15–minute drive to three major ski areas. Cross-country ski touring facilities in the area are excellent and ice skating and snowshoeing are available. There are antique, flower, and horse shows, plus country fairs and summer stock theater. Half a dozen golf courses are in the immediate vicinity and tennis, horseback riding and bicycling are readily available. There are a couple of trout streams on the premises and a mountain pond for hardy swimmers as well as a splendid, new heated pool. The inn itself is a rambling connection of comfortable rooms, some small, some quite large. There are also self-contained cottages with studio/bedroom, bath and a protected terrace. Some have fireplaces and all have views of the Franconia Range. An extra nice touch is the tea served in the winter. Lovett's own herb garden adds spice to the meals. A com-fortable bar, a sun-porch game room, and a sitting room are all part of the Lovett's scene. Rates range from $20 to $34 per person,

double occupancy, with complete dinner and full breakfast. Winter package plans are available. For information and reservations, con-tact Lovett's Inn by Lafayette Brook, Franconia, NH 03580 (603)823–7761.

**Moose Mountain Lodge*. Nestled high on the western slope of Moose Mountain, this rustic lodge, built of hand-hewn logs and stone, offers a cozy armchair before a crackling fire to those who have spent the day wandering amid the blazing crimson slopes of the surrounding mountains in the fall. In winter, when snow covers the fields and forests, cross-country ski trails begin at the front door. Rental skis are available for $6 a day and $10 a weekend. Snowshoes are also available. Ideal for skiers of all abilities, trails wander over bright meadows and along meandering brooks. High ridge trails offer spectacular views of the White and Green mountains. Many connect with the Dartmouth Outing Club trails and the Appalachian Trail for extended touring. A nearby beaver pond provides ice skating in the winter. The proprietors, Peter and Kay Shumway, serve three meals daily; home baked breads and nourishing soups are a specialty. Rates are $26 per person for a double room with meals included, and $23 for a dormitory room, also with meals. Children ten and under are given special rates. Package rates are available for a minimum of four nights. For more information, contact: Peter and Kay Shumway, Moose Mountain Lodge, Etna, NH 03750 (603)643–3529.

★★★★*Mountain View House* is a 350–acre estate situated in the center of the White Mountains, with the picturesque beauty of the highest peaks, and the relaxing atmosphere of the clean, healthful mountain air all around you. The forest areas offer a natural setting for watching wildlife, and the hotel's spacious grounds offer a myriad of recreational activities. There is an excellent golf course, four tennis courts (two all-weather), an Olympic-size heated swimming pool, a putting green, shuffleboard, a children's playground. The Sports House offers a well stocked pro shop, locker rooms, a refreshment lounge, a poolside buffet and an upper deck for viewing the activities. You can take a hike along the mountain trails, or the hotel's beautiful garden, or try fishing in the nearby streams. In the evening, the hotel offers shows and dancing to an orchestra. The cuisine is superb. Fresh breads, desserts and pastries are baked daily and there is an excellent wine cellar. The rooms have walk-in closets, spacious chests and bureaus, a chaise longue, arm chairs, wall-to-wall carpeting—each a bit different in decor—to provide a home away from home. The hotel is open seasonally—from May to October. Rates, based on double occupancy, and full American Plan (all meals) range from $80–100 per day. There are family plans and packages also available. For further information contact: Stuart W. Hamilton, Jr., Mountain View House, Whitefield, NH 03598 (603)837–2511.

★★★*The Robbins Nest*, snuggled in a grove of hemlock and birch, on the banks of the Pemigewasset River in the heart of the White Mountains, offers cozy rooms, each with a view of the river or its tributary Burleigh Brook, at reasonable prices ($15–22 daily for a double room, or $18 per person on the American plan). But most people know of it because of its unique restaurant. Live trees grow up through the roof, and some of the finest home cooking in the northeast is served on the table. Hot baked breads and nourishing soups are served along with salads and hearty entrees. Homemade cakes and pies promise to tempt even the most prudent. Prices for complete dinners range from $5–8. New Hampshires major ski areas, Waterville Valley, Loon Mountain, Mitterhill, and Cannon Mountain are all within easy reach. The area around the lodge is perfect for cross-country skiing. In the summer, fish the river, or hike the cool mountains. The fishing in this area is very good. In autumn, perhaps the most beautiful season in the northeast, hunting is excellent. For more information contact: Alan and Bev Murray, RFD 1, Campton, NH 03223 (603)726–3341.

★★★*Snowvillage Lodge* is a European style country inn, located 1,100 feet up in the White Mountains. Many major ski areas provide slopes of all descriptions within a short drive and cross-country trails of incredible beauty and tranquility wind through fields and woods and along the rivers. The lodge's trails border Foss Mountain's miles of unplowed road and the Foss Mountain Ski Touring School. The Mt. Washington Valley offers scenic beauty throughout the year. A good clay tennis court and fragrant woods all around beckon guests to the outdoors. Each room is large, sunny and elegantly furnished with a beautiful view of the White Mountains. The double rooms have either twin beds or double beds. Snowvillage Lodge offers the hospitality and warmth of yesterday with the convenience and comfort of today. The dining room specializes in memorable continental cuisine plus the best home made breads and soups. The bar/lounge is open before and after dinner. Rates including a four course dinner and full breakfast range from $28–37 per person for double occupancy. Weekly rates range from $168 to $180 per person for double occupancy and $210–222 per person for single occupancy. There are special midweek, Sunday through Thursday, rates. For reservations and information contact Pat and Ginger Blymyer, Snowvillage Lodge, Snowville, NH 03849 (603)447–2818.

★★★★*Snowy Owl Inn*, one of the nation's most beautiful four-season family mountain resorts, is located in the center of Waterville Valley bordered by scenic woodlands and Snow's Brook in the heart of the White Mountain National Forest. Blending natural wood and native stone, the rooms are functional, comfortable and attractive. Inside and out, its lines reflect the warmth and hospitality you expect in a fine New England inn. In the main living room, a massive fieldstone fireplace rises three stories to the rooftop. Handsome furnishings, antique accessories and a profusion of plants and flowers give the Inn an air of casual elegance. Other facilities include an apres ski lounge and recreation room, heated outdoor pool, 18 championship clay tennis courts and expert instruction, and a challenging 9–hole golf course with PGA pro. Summer activities include hiking, bicycling, climbing, fishing, bird watching, and the Waterville Valley Jamboree—a daily recreation program for adults and children. For cross-country and alpine ski buffs there are 30 miles of groomed trails and Tecumseh and Snow's Mountain with 32 slopes. For children under 10, the Wings Day Camp and Nursery offers supervised sports, games, arts and crafts. The rustic accommodations include soundproofed rooms with two double beds; a family room with bunk-bed sleeping loft for children; or a dormer-windowed room with double bed and sitting area. All rooms have individual temperature control, telephone and private bath. Lodge rates range from $30–42 per day double occupancy. For additional information, contact: Tish and Roger Hamblin, Snowy Owl Inn, Waterville Valley, NH 03223 (603)236–8383.

★★*Stonybrook Motor Lodge* provides year-round recreation facilities in a quiet, friendly atmosphere. It is located within minutes of some of the best White Mountain sports areas and scenic wonders. The Cannon Mountain Aerial Tramway, Alpine Slide, Mt. Washington Cog Railway, the Flume, Appalachian Trail and Old Man of the Mountains at Franconia Notch are in the area surrounding Stonybrook. White Mountain winter sports available close by include Cannon Mountain and Mettersill for 3.9 miles of downhill skiing. There is a cross-country ski trail hookup on the lodge's premises as well as ice skating and snowmobiling. In other seasons, you can try trout fishing—in the pond or river—hunting, hiking, tennis, golf or swimming—in the pool or Echo Lake. The lodge, situated on quiet, landscaped grounds with beautiful mountain views, provides modern, clean and comfortable accommodations. The rooms are spacious, each with private bath, color TV, and individual heat controls. The family style restaurant, with huge fireplace and lounge, offers a relaxing and peaceful evening after any activity. Rates, subject to change for seasons, are $20–28 for double occupancy. Your hosts, the Sandy family, look forward to meeting you. Contact them at Stonybrook Motor Lodge, Route 18, Franconia, NH 03580 (603)823–8192 or 8196.

★★★★*Sunset Hill House*, a fine old north country inn, welcomes guests with warmth and hospitality unique to people who love the mountains. Inside, the rooms are decorated with quiet elegance, reminiscent of colonial days. A traditional Thanksgiving is celebrated every year when the surrounding mountains of the Presidential and Franconia Ranges are brilliant with color and the air is crisp and clear. If you come along Thanksgiving weekend, the Sunset House will put you to work, offering reduced lodging to those who will help make Christmas decorations, set up the ski shop, or bring in wood for the fireplaces for three hours in the morning. All those who participate in this "work-a-bee" weekend will be served large family style Thanksgiving dinners, in the New England tradition. In the winter, when the White Mountains are truly white, the Sunset Hill Ski Shop opens. Special five-day lift and lodging packages are available for downhill skiing on nearby Cannon Mountain. Cross-country ski rentals and instruction are offered through the ski shop. The Sunset Hill House is a part of a 75–mile touring network connecting inns throughout Sugar Hill and Franconia. Moonlight tours, followed by wine and cheese parties, highlight the season. In the summer, play the 9–hole golf course high on the mountain ridge. A teaching professional, caddies and lockers are always available. The Sunset House has just added a brand new pool, with a unique whirlpool spa. Rates, including breakfast and dinner are $54–58 double occupancy, and $30–35 single occupancy. Special five day ski package rates are cross-country $150 per person double occupancy, and $175 single occupancy for lodging, meals, lessons and ski rentals. The five day downhill ski package offers lodging, meals and a five day lift ticket on Cannon mountain for $150 per person. The downhill package with ski rentals and lessons added runs $185 per person. For more information write: Sunset Hill House, Sugar Hill, 03585 (603)823–5522.

★★★★*Thorn Hill Lodge.* Three of the Jackson Ski Touring trails begin right at the door of the Thorn Hill Lodge, an old fashioned country inn with twelve charming bedrooms and a large living room, with a fireplace and windows looking out across fields to Mt. Washington beyond. Rooms in the main inn run, per person, $29 for a large room with full bath, and $22 and $24 for rooms with a sink and shared bath. In addition there are four private mountain chalets with one-seven bedrooms, all sumptuously decorated, and each with private bath. Thorn Mountain Chalet, the grandaddy of them all, has seven bedrooms, a large living room with a stone fireplace, piano, color TV, and windows looking out at Thorn Mountain. Rates for the chalets range from $26–30 per person. The restaurant at the Thorn Hill Lodge is a favorite in Jackson. Fresh baked breads and pastries are a part of each evening meal. Specialties

such as traditional New England turkey dinner and Yankee pot roast are offered every day along with the regular selections, such as homemade Thorn Hill chicken pie and pan-fried stuffed trout. Winter packages, Wildcat Mountain packages, special cross-country packages and four Mt. Washington Valley interchangeable lift ticket packages are available. For details write: The Thorn Hill Lodge, Jackson, NH 03846 (603)383–4242.

★★★*The Valley Inn at Waterville Valley* offers superb vacations year-round. The Valley is known as one of the top ski resorts—even to the point of guaranteeing snow by Thanksgiving. There's a good ski school for children and the ski touring center offers tours, instruction, and complete rental service. In summer they offer a 9–hole golf course, a swimming pool that's heated year-round, and fine clay tennis courts. Resident golf and tennis pros are available for instruction. The surrounding countryside offers fishing, hiking, and bicycling at the front door. A fully-equipped exercise room, complete with massage and sauna is located on the premises. All rooms in the inn have either a private balcony or a private patio-terrace. Each room has two double beds, TV, phone, and private bath. Special Loft rooms are available for families who need extra sleeping room for children. Rates vary from a low of $22 per night to $60 for the special loft rooms. All rates given are for during the season. Deduct 15% for dates prior to December 15 and after March 24. No pets are allowed. Modified American Plan meal packages are available at the new Valley Tavern restaurant. For further information contact Jack and Andrea Carnevale, Innkeepers, The Valley Inn, Waterville Valley, NH 03223 (603)236–8336.

★★★★*The Waterville Valley Bunkhouse & Touring Center* is in the center of the White Mountain National Forest, near excellent skiing areas as well as summer recreation areas. The bunkhouse offers inexpensive lodging, meals, and entertainment in a new lodge that is impressive both architecturally and in its relationship with the environment. Winter guests can enjoy over 35 miles of cross-country skiing trails that start right at the door of the bunkhouse. The U.S. Cross-Country Team trained on these trails. Across the road at the ski touring center, guests can sign on for ski tours or environmental lectures. The bunkhouse offers free shuttle service to Mt. Tecumseh, where 32 slopes and miles of trails offering skiing opportunities for all abilities. Or, skiers can walk from the bunkhouse to Snow's Mountain ski lift and skating rink for day and night sport. When the snow is gone, visitors enjoy hiking the mountain trails, swimming, fishing, canoeing and exploring. Nearby, there is a 9–hole golf course and 19 championship clay tennis courts. After a long day of summer or winter fun, guests can enjoy a hearty meal served family style in the beautiful dining room. Huge stone fireplaces are a focal point for the living and game rooms which have Fuss-Ball, TV games and even a special ski preparation room. Sleeping accommodations are in colorful rooms with six bunks in each room. Reservations can be made for groups or individuals. The group rate applies to twenty or more persons and includes all meals. One free package is included with each twenty one people in a group. Two-day weekends range from $23.25 to $31.25 depending on the season. Two days midweek range from $18.25 to $31.25 and five days midweek are $50 to $80. Individual rates are $5 to $12 midweek and $8 to $11 weekends without meals. Individual dinners are $3.75 and breakfasts are $2.00. For information and reservations, write: The Waterville Valley Bunkhouse, Waterville Valley, NH 03223 (603)236–8326.

★★★*Whitney's Inn at Mt. Washington Valley*, at the base of Black Mountain, is a charming, cheerful, comfortable inn. Nestled at the edge of the White Mountain National Forest, it provides year-

round outdoor activities in the majestic Presidential Range. On the premises, you can take advantage of shuffleboard, badminton, horseshoes, ping pong, croquet or a 9–hole putting green. Their pond allows you a refreshing dip in the summer or ice skating in the winter and their trails and brooks provide hours of enjoyment for hiking and trout fishing. The famous ski terrain of Black Mountain is right at your doorstep. Other activities nearby include horseback riding, golf, tennis, bowling, bicycling, canoeing, summer theatre and movies, antiquing and scenic flying. The inn itself has a large library of books. Sunday evenings bring their famous smorgasbord suppers and in the summer there are weekly cookouts. The altitude assures comfortable nights for sleeping in any of the diverse accommodations from individual rooms to cottages to chalet suites, all with private baths. Rates, based on Modified American plan double occupancy, range from $22–28 daily. (European plan is also available.) Don and Kathy Murray, your hosts, will be happy to send you their detailed rate card and further information on package plans and weekly rates. Contact them by phone (603)383–4291 or by writing Whitneys', Jackson, NH 03846.

Travel Services

Eastern Mountain Sports Nordic Ski Touring Center, located near North Conway, has well-qualified instructors, maintained trails and facilities for nordic skiers. Bob Wilcox and other ski enthusiasts developed the natural cross-country trails. They connected over 30 miles of well marked trails which all lead back to the ski center. The degree of difficulty of each trail is marked yellow for easy, green for intermediate and blue for most difficult. All trails are safe with steep sections marked and bridges built over all major water crossings. Everyone is invited to use the trails free of charge. The Ski School has certified nordic instructors who offer private and group lessons. Every Tuesday afternoon, there are races from five to seven kilometers in length for all classes and abilities. The Center Ski Shop has a complete inventory of skis and accessories; and in the rental department there are 200 pairs of skis, boots and poles of all sizes. For the tired and hungry skier, there is a snack bar. The trails and facilities are open seven days a week, nine to five, from December 1st to April 15th. For information write Eastern Mountain Sports Nordic Ski Center, Intervale, NH 03845 or phone the snow-condition number (603) 356–5606.

Jackson Ski Touring Foundation. Surrounded by the impressive Presidential Range in the lovely Mt. Washington Valley, the village of Jackson, still retains an extraordinary colonial charm. White clapboard buildings with shingled roofs line the streets, and the Wildcat River spills through the center of town. Two-thirds of Jackson is in the White Mountain National Forest. The Jackson Ski Touring Foundation is a non-profit organization that originated in the early 70's to create and maintain 125 km of trails offering some of the finest cross-country trails in the country. The trail network extends over privately owned property, and through the national forest, connecting inns, ponds, rivers and mountain trails in its unique system. A donation of $3 a day is asked of adults for trail maintenance, and $1 for children under 12. Special two day ($5), three day ($7), and five day ($12) donations are suggested. The foundation hosts cross-country tours, clinics, races, and citizen events. For more information write: The Jackson Ski Foundation, Box 90B, Jackson, NH 03846 (603)383–9355.

Killington Adventure, see "Vermont" chapter for details.

Saco Bound/Northern Waters specializes in canoeing and kayaking. Its programs include full outfitting, rentals, guided trips, white-water school, raft trips, and its shops are well stocked with canoes, kayaks, accessories, and related camping gear. The Saco River rises in Crawford Notch in the New Hampshire White Mountains and flows 115 miles to the Atlantic. Over its length, the river offers a wide variety of navigable waters; during the spring the upper Saco offers a challenging white-water run. During the summer months the river is very gentle, offering little hazard to even novice canoeists. The Northern Waters Whitewater School offers instruction in canoeing and kayaking for groups from beginners to experts. These classes are five day programs with instruction and practise supervised by the expert staff. Raft trips are available on five to ten person rafts on different parts of the rivers at different times of the season. The shops offer absolutely everything one might need for outdoor fun in this vacation area. For further information, write P.O. Box 113, Center Conway, NH 03813 (603)447–2177.

Other Granite State Gateways and Accommodations

Hanover

(Pop. 6,200; zip code 03755; area code 603.) Dartmouth College

and the colonial town of Hanover have grown together ever since 1769 when Dartmouth was founded by Rev. Eleazar Wheelock "for the instruction of the youth of Indian tribes . . . and others." Since then Dartmouth has grown to be one of America's most distinguished colleges and Hanover has changed from a tiny farming settlement on a broad plateau above the Connecticut River to a cultural and recreational center of western New Hampshire and eastern Vermont. The campus, radiating from the college green, is a combination of modern and colonial buildings; the oldest of these, along Old Dartmouth Row, date from as early as 1784. The Baker Memorial Library contains over a million volumes, including medieval manuscripts illuminated by hand. The Orozco Frescoes, painted in 1934 by the Mexican artist Jose Orozco, portray the development of civilization on the American Continent in brilliant colors over 3,000 square feet of space. Hopkins Center for the Arts hosts concerts, plays and a variety of art exhibits throughout the year. Daniel Webster, who fought in the Supreme Court for Dartmouth's survival as a private institution, is remembered in the Webster House. The Dartmouth Ski Bowl, Whaleback Mountain Ski Area, and 120 miles of hiking and ski-touring trails organized by the Dartmouth Outing Club have made Hanover a center for skiers, hikers, backpackers, and fishermen. Seven shelters maintained by the Outing Club dot the mountain paths. The Dartmouth Outing Club House is a popular meeting place for skiers and snowshoers in the winter, and opens a restaurant in the summer. There is a sauna open to the public on the Dartmouth campus. Accommodations: *Hanover Inn* (rates: $50–53 double), with 102 superb rooms and suites, dining room, coffeeshop, cocktail lounge in the center of town off Dartmouth College lawns (643–4300).

Portsmouth—Gateway to the Maine Woods & Coast
See "Maine" Chapter for details.

Sunapee—Gateway to Mt. Sunapee
(Pop. 700; zip code 03782; area code 603) on the western shores of the beautiful lake of the same name, is a gateway for tourists, skiers, hikers, hunters, fishermen and canoeists heading into the mountainous lake region from the west. Surrounded by lakes, ponds, rolling hills and mountains, Sunapee is a popular year-round resort. Special area attractions include: Mt. Sunapee State Park, an alpine ski area, which offers scenic rides to the summit in its four passenger gondola in summer, Kings Ridge Ski Area, lake cruises in Sunapee Harbor, and the annual crafts fair in Sunapee State Park during August. Sunapee Lake was once the home of the rare Sunapee trout, a remnant species of the arctic char, which survived the last Ice Age in a handful of New England lakes and ponds. The beautiful, mysterious Sunapee—with its steel-green back, cream sides, and brilliant gold and ruby colored spots, and dazzling orange belly—was first discovered in the deep cold waters of Sunapee Lake in 1888. Toward the close of the 19th century, anglers reported catching a large number of big, deep-feeding Sunapee reaching weights of up to 12 pounds, with odd tales of this golden char reaching 15 to 20 pounds. As word of this rare and beautiful fish spread, fishermen came to the scenic, mountain-rimmed, blue waters of Sunapee, sporting camps and lodges sprang up, and the fishing for this fragile char rapidly declined with the increased pressure and interbreeding problems with lake trout. Accommodations: *Mt. Sunapee Motel* (rates: $24–28 double), with 22 good rooms and family units, swimming pool, just east of Mt. Sunapee State Park entrance on New Hampshire (103)763–5592.

Other Lodges & Resorts

★★★*Dexter's inn & Tennis Club*, close to both Mt. Sunapee and Kings Ridge downhill ski areas, at 1,400 ft. elevation, has its own Nordic Ski Center. Dexter's Inn owns 200 acres of rolling wood lands, bird sanctuary, and open meadows, or the adjacent village-owned trails totalling 400 acres. The lakes and ponds in this region offer opportunity for fishing, ice boating, and skating. Built in 1801, this handsome colonial inn is decorated with antiques and hand hooked rugs. A warm fire crackles in the wood panelled living room, and a library of 500 books is at the guests' disposal. The Nordic Ski Center is housed in the barn located on the property, and stocked with rental skis and waxing gear. Group lessons are held every day and are $5. Rental skis, boots and poles run $6. In the summer, the restored gardens bloom by the fullsize swimming pool. Three plexicushion tennis courts are in constant use, and a resident tennis pro is on hand. The Nordic Ski Center becomes a game center, featuring ping pong and bumper pool. Sailboats skim across Lake Sunapee, and there is a fine summer theater program in nearby Dartmouth. The restaurant in Dexter's Inn is well known for its excellent food. The 25 rooms of the inn are all individually decorated. In addition Dexter's Inn offers "A place at the inn," apartments, suites and a special Sugar House, all located ¼ mile from the main inn in the quiet of the woods. The Sugar House is a log cabin nestled back in a grove of maple and birch. All these accommodations have fully equipped kitchens, complete with china. Rates for a double room in the main inn vary, depending on size and location, from $27–33 per person including meals. Single rooms range from $36–43 per person. "A place at the inn" rates range from $50–90 a night, depending on the number of people. These accommodations must be reserved for a minimum of two nights, and the rates do not include meals in the main inn. For more information write: Dexter's Inn and Tennis Club, Stagecoach Road, Sunapee, NH 03782 (603)763–5571.

★★*Gray Ledges* is at the hub of the Dartmouth-Lake Sunapee region located on a 1,400 ft. mountain top. The lodge is a 200–year-old estate with spacious grounds and a panoramic view in all directions. Wintertime activities include cross-country skiing right from the lodge's doors with miles of marked, scenic trails. Downhill skiing can be selected from one of the five nearby slopes, including Whaleback, Mt. Sunapee, Dartmouth Skiway, Ragged Mountain and King Ridge. These slopes include skiing for beginners, intermediates and experts. During spring and summer the lodge has facilities for swimming, croquet, horseshoes, badminton, volleyball, archery and skeet. Golf, horseback riding, tennis, boating and fishing are minutes away. This is a lovely area in all seasons for scenic hiking. The lodge maintains a Chapel on the grounds for Christian-oriented groups, and accommodations for 100 or more guests. Accommodations range from bunk houses with 40 beds to motel units for two. The bunk and family rooms are frequently used by bicycle, hiking, cross-country ski groups. The lodge provides cots, blankets and pillows. Guests should bring their own sleeping bags. The motels are simple country units with pine paneling and private baths. The lodge has a restaurant for family style and a la carte meals. Rates: motel, double occupancy $19. Bunkhouses $4.50–$6 per person, per night. Family rooms have accommodations for three to ten beds ranging from $19–50 per night. Special arrangements for groups over 50. Daily and weekly rates with meals available. For further information contact: Grey Ledges, Grantham, NH 03753 (603)863–1002.

★★★★*Indian Cave Lodge at Lake Sunapee* is a large family guest lodge nestled below Mt. Sunapee. Nearby trails lead to the large Indian cave, or to the summit of Mt. Sunapee and Mt. Kearsage for breath taking views. Once a week there are breakfast hikes on Mt. Sunapee; guests enjoy fresh pancakes with mountain blueberries and hot coffee while the sun burns the mist off the mountains. There

are lakeside barbeques, with hot roasted corn and hearty steaks, disco nights, square dancing and talent show. The stately "Sunapee Belle," a replica of a Mississippi river boat cruises the lake waters, offering luncheons and dinners. Sailboats, paddleboats and canoes are available at the lake front, where Indian Cave Lodge also hosts canoe races, shuffleboard and bocci tournaments. There is also a large outdoor pool, water-skiing instruction, badminton and volley ball nets, a playbarn, children's playground, staff/guest softball games, bicycles, Wednesday night outdoor band concerts on the town green, and summer theater productions. Airy spacious rooms are available in the main lodge, and there are also private cottages secluded on the lakeshore. Breakfast and dinner are served in the main dining room, where sumptuous buffets are prepared every Sunday. The lodge cook grills hot dogs and hamburgers by the pool every day at noon. Rates include breakfast and dinner daily and are $36 per person daily for a lodge room, $47 for singles, and $31 per person for a cottage and $42 per person single occupancy for a cottage. There are no housekeeping facilities. Special rates are available in May, June, September and October. For more information write: Jim and Nancy Becker, Indian Cave Lodge, Sunapee, New Hampshire 03782 (603) 763–2762.

★★★★*The John Hancock Inn* is the oldest operating inn in New Hampshire and offers "food for the hungry, drink for the thirsty, and lodging for the weary." Built in 1789, the inn is located right in the center of the picturesque village of Hancock. The area has hardly changed in the last hundred years and offers swimming in Norway Pond, skiing within a 15–minute drive, mountain climbing, bird-watching, snow-shoeing, and horseback riding. Hancock can be reached easily by car, or the inn will arrange to pick up guests arriving by bus at Peterborough or by plane at Keene or Manchester. Hearty New England food is served at the inn and the portions are generous. A large garden is maintained on the premises and guests are often served home-grown vegetables. Drinks are served in the Carriage Room, a quaint room once used as a movie set. Tables are made from the bellows of an old blacksmith shop, seats are from old carriages and the room has a working fireplace. Guests sleeping at the inn really step back in history. Furnishing are early American with braided rugs and authentic antiques. And the board floors, beams and fireplaces are the ones that have been in the building since 1789. Rates are $29.00 per day double occupancy and $25.00 single occupancy, European Plan. Innkeepers Glynn & Pat Wells welcome all to sample New Hampshire past. For reservations write them at: The John Hancock Inn, Hancock, NH 03449 (603)525–3318.

★★★*Loch Lyme Lodge*, a year-round lodge, a renovated farmhouse built in 1784, nestled on the shores of Post Pond, offers three twin bedrooms, and one double room to cross-country skiers, who take off over the silent lake into the surrounding snow-covered hills, or ice fisherman, who cut through the ice, drop a line, and wait under the clear winter sky. Downhill skiers enjoy the nearby Dartmouth Skiway, with two chairlifts and one T-bar servicing two mountain slopes. Informal cross-country ski lessons are available, and with advanced notice, ski rentals can be arranged. The roaring fireplace is a favorite gathering spot, and the dining room serves hearty homecooked meals. In the summer, when the mountains turn a lush green, 25 guest cottages open, accommodating two-six people. Fishing, boating and canoeing are popular in the clear lake, and there is a modern dock and floats for swimming. The surrounding 100–acre forest provides many cool, shady trails for hiking, and trout streams for fishing. There are two high-quality tennis courts, and croquet and badminton on the lawn. The dining room serves fresh vegetables from the garden, and Sunday night lakeside buffets highlight each week. There is a summer theater to enjoy in nearby Dartmouth, craft fairs and auctions, and band concerts on the green. All cottages have living rooms with fireplaces, and private porches. Eleven are housekeeping cabins, with linen provided, and modern, fully equipped kitchens. Winter rates in the lodge are $14, for bed and breakfast. Summer rates may be arranged with or without meals included. Cabin rates with meals are $28 daily, per person, and $165 weekly. Without meals, cottage rates are daily, per person, $14.50, and weekly, $100. Summer rates in the lodge rooms including meals are $21 daily, per person, and $147 weekly. Without meals, lodge rates are $7 daily and $49 weekly, per person. Housekeeping cottages range from $130–225 weekly, depending on the size of the cabin. For more information write: Loch Lyme Lodge, Lyme, New Hampshire, 03768 (603)795–2141.

★★★★*Lyme Inn* is a charming country inn located in the historic town of Lyme. Situated on the Connecticut River, Lyme dates back to 1761. Although skiing is the sport usually attributed to New England, the Lyme area offers recreation facilities during all four seasons. In addition to viewing the sports at Dartmouth College— such as basketball, hockey, track and gymnastics—the public can participate in bowling, squash, tennis and handball. There is a local golf course and canoeing on the Connecticut River. Cultural activities are also available with concerts, plays, film festivals and art exhibits offered throughout the year. Of course the local auctions, fairs, flea markets, country stores and antique dealers will keep you pretty busy as well. The Appalachian Trail, which passes through Lyme, the foot path to the summit of Smart's Mountain, and the many back roads offer a variety of hiking opportunities. Many wildlife sanctuaries are located in the area—two in Lyme itself, and secluded ponds, hidden in the hills away from roads, are accessible to the fisherman and local streams are annually stocked with trout. Winter activities include ice skating on a night-lighted pond, alpine skating at the Dartmouth Skiway, and five other ski areas within an hour's drive from Lyme. There is also cross-country skiing and snowshoeing throughout the area. The location is a one-three hour drive from other regional points of interest in Maine, Canada, and Vermont. The inn itself dates back to 1809 and offers quiet, comfortable rooms furnished in antiques—with poster beds, hooked rugs, hand stitched quilts, wide pine floorboards—each room with a unique character of its own. Dining, in an informal country setting, offers home cooked meals with a continually changing menu of recipes from many countries, as well as traditional New England fare—with fresh seafood a specialty. There is also an antique tavern beside the dining room. The inn offers only one TV—in the sitting room, but has quite an extensive library of books from which to choose. Stenciled wallpaper, wingback chairs, wicker furniture on the huge screened porch, Currier & Ives samplers, and ten fireplaces add to the charm of the inn. Rates, based on double occupancy, range from $22–32 nightly, on the European Plan (no meals). No children under eight years of age, and no pets. For further information, contact the inn's owners, Fred and Judy Siemons, Lyme Inn, Lyme, NH 03768 (603)795–2222.

★★★★*The Wentworth-by-the-Sea* offers true elegance in a New England setting with scenic beauty, historical landmarks, and a location at Portsmouth, New Hampshire, on the Atlantic Ocean. Facilities abound; they include absolutely deluxe accommodations at the gracious 105–year-old hotel. Seven charming New England cottages with panoramic ocean views and deluxe facilities are also available, as are charter accommodations aboard the yacht "Dandideb." Wentworth's magnificent sports facilities include a private oceanside golf course with specially designed water holes, four professional top-maintained clay tennis courts, three all-weather tennis courts, an Olympic-size heated pool, and boating, either aboard yacht, sailboat, or sloop. Horseback riding, supervised sports for youngsters (July-August) and a special Dolphin pool will keep children busy and happy. The surrounding area is unique for its historical importance; Fort Constitution, where the American Revolution began, is one mile away. For the gourmet diner, there are sumptuous buffets, seaside clam-lobster bakes on the private beach, and a wide variety of lunchtime menus are available whether it be poolside at the Ocean Terrace Room, mid-game at the Fairways, at the Yacht Club, or for snacks at the Round Robin. Evenings are busy; the Wentworth has a complete schedule of nighttime entertainment including dancing, floor shows, movies, lectures, bingo, cards, fashion shows, and comfortable cocktail lounges. The Wentworth operates on full American Plan in May, June, after Labor Day, and in October. The Modified Plan with breakfast and dinner is in effect during the guest season from July 1–Labor Day. Rates during this season range from holiday budget to intermediate to deluxe at costs from $35–46 per day, twin. Lanai suites for two persons are available at $46–58 per day. Special children's rates apply up to age 13. Special tennis and golf packages for those enthusiasts are at a per person rate ranging from $105 for three days, and two nights to $295 per person for eight days, seven nights. For further information regarding charters, reservations, special group rates, and facilities, contact the Wentworth-by-the-Sea, Portsmouth, NH 03801 (603)436–3100.

★★*Woodbound Inn* is located in the Monadnock region of Southern New Hampshire, in Rindge, a beautiful unspoiled New England town with attractive homes and farms. With its own nine-hole golf course and sandy beach on the Contoocook Lake, Woodbound offers guests a charming vacation environment. There's swimming, canoeing, rowing, water skiing and kayaking on Contoocook Lake which is over two miles long. And there's fishing in both the lake and in a half-acre trout pond which has been developed in the woods on the inn property. In the Play Barn, there are square dance parties, ping-pong, pool and shuffleboard and the inn has its own tennis court. Within the immediate vicinity, their four golf courses and a fine stable of saddle horses. Families are especially welcome and programs and activities for children are arranged and supervised. The inn is open from late May to the end of October and in the winter from December 26 until mid-March. Winter sports include down-hill and cross-country skiing, skating, tobogganing and sleigh rides. There are 18 miles of easy cross-country trails starting right at the inn and beginner and intermediate down-hill runs on the property. Major ski areas are within a half hour drive with slopes for beginners as well as experts. Furnished in the colonial New England tradition, Woodbound has both rooms and cottages. All rooms, except four, have private baths and there are several large rooms and suites with connecting baths available. The cottages are pine-panelled and vary in size, accommodating two to eight people. Three meals a day are provided with all cooking supervised by real New England cooks. Special diets are followed and cook-outs take place weekly. Weekly double rates for the summer season run from $163 to $219 including three meals per person a day. Children's rates are lower. Daily rates, double occupancy, with three meals, for winter run from $28 to $36. For further information, contact Woodbound Inn, P.O. Jaffrey, NH 03452 (603)532–8341.

Other Travel Services

King Ridge Ski Area, in New London is a family ski resort, with reserved skiing on weekends. Seven lifts serve 17 novice and intermediate runs, with fanciful names from the Alice in Wonderland books. The longest, Brillig Run, is 5,000 ft. A new modern lodge at the bottom serves 460 in its restaurant, and has a capacity for 200 picnickers. Children four months-six years are cared for in the nursery. One of the things that makes King Ridge unique is the staff who return year after year, and soon get to know you and your family. Another special feature of King Ridge is the lift ticket system, which offers lift ticket rates at hourly intervals as well as ½ day $18 and full day $10. This allows you to ski for just a few hours without losing money. Specials include weekday reduced lift tickets $5.95, and Tuesday, Wednesday and Thursday package specials including lifts, lessons and lunch for $9.50. For more information about King Ridge write: King Ridge, RFD 2, New London, NH 03257.

Mt. Sunapee Ski Area, surrounded by state park woods, and overlooking Lake Sunapee, is the largest downhill ski area in southern New Hampshire. Five double chairlifts, a T-bar, J-bar and rope tow all provide access to Mt. Sunapee's 20 runs, providing a variety of novice and intermediate skiing. There is a park headquarters and rental shop at the bottom, and a summit lodge on the very top offering panoramic views of southern New Hampshire, and Massachusetts, from a 2,743 ft. elevation. Group lessons are kept limited to a maximum of six people, to assure individualized instruction. One hour group lessons run $7 adults, $4 children. There is a separate novice area with its own lifts. Intermediate slopes are wide and high, with exhilarating views. Ski rentals run $8.50 for a complete package. Adult lift tickets are $7 midweek, and $10 weekends. Children, $5 and $7. For more information write: The Sunapee Region Ski Association, Box 377, Sunapee, New Hampshire 03782 (603)763–2301.

Summers Ski & Mountain Touring Center. If you are planning to cross-country ski in the southern New Hampshire this winter, Summers Ski & Mountain Touring Center, located ½ mile west of the intersection of routes 137 and 101 in Dublin will provide expert advice on lodging, ski touring, and snow shoe trips in the Mt. Monadock region. The center, open seven days a week has 20 miles of groomed and maintained trails of its own, ranging from novice loop trails and practice fields to intermediate and advanced trails

with excellent views of Mt. Monadock. Ski across a scenic wooden bridge, along meandering brooks, back into the silent, deep woods. Guided tours can be arranged at $5, advanced reservations required. Skis can be rented in the shop for $5 a day if used on the ski center trails and $6 a day, plus a $30 deposit if taken elsewhere. Special beginner lessons are offered for $5.50 per person including equipment, and more advanced lessons begin at $2.50 per person for a group lesson of six or more, to $10 for an individual, advanced lesson. Free instruction is offered on Wednesday nights, be sure to call for a reservation. Coffee, tea, and hot chocolate are served in the warming hut on weekends. Nearby lodging ranges from $12.50–26.50. Winter camping permits can be secured at the center. For more information contact: Jack Summers, The Summers Ski & Mountain Ski Touring Center, Route 101, Dublin, NH 03444 (603)563–8556.

Temple Mountain Ski Area, owned by the Beebe family since 1937, is a small family ski resort, the perfect place to take the kids and learn how to ski. Two T-Bars and three rope tows service thirteen slopes, half of which are beginner, so you can explore the whole mountain, and test out every run, as you become a better and better skier. Short lift lines, a maximum 10 minutes on weekends, are guaranteed by the Beebes' limited ticket sales policy, so you are assured plenty of skiing every day. After a good snowfaull, it is wise to call ahead and reserve lift tickets. Thirty instructors, under the direction of Mike Beebe, teach skiing by the GLM method. Group lessons are $7 and private lessons $12. A special "first timers" package, including lifts, lessons and ski rentals is offered for $17. On Sunday mornings, the "little tots" ski program is offered for ages three-five. The ski school also offers an eight week tow and lesson program for older kids. The Beebe family also operates a complete ski touring center located on the 23 mile Wapack trail, adjacent to the Temple Mountain Ski area. Eight miles of groomed trails traverse rolling hills, pine woods, and high mountain ridges with views for 75 miles. Free monthly ski touring clinics are held the first Saturday of each month from October to April. All the basics are covered, and they are open to everyone. Group instruction is offered by the five professional skiing instructors, group lessons, $7 and private, $12. Skis can be rented at $8 for a complete package. A "first-timers" special package including lessons, rentals and trail fee, for $14 is offered to those who've never experienced, but would like to try "skinny skis". Moonlight tours and annual group tours of six and fifteen miles are offered by the Temple Mountain Ski Touring Center. Temple Mountain Ski area lifts $9. Ski Touring Center trail fee: $2.75. For more information contact: Mike and Sandy Beebe, Temple Mt. Ski Area, Route 101, Peterborough, NH 03458 (603)924–6949.

Windblown is a small, rustic cross-country ski lodge, off the beaten track in the wooded Monadnock region of New Hampshire near the Massachusetts border. Eighteen miles of well maintained trails meander through pine woods, and past brooks black against the snow. All meet up at the warming hut, which serves lunch and offers basic sleeping accommodations for $3.50 a night (bring your own bag and food). The ski shop, warm with the heat of a woodburning stove, rents ski touring equipment $6.50 per day for adults. Skis for children are free. Snowshoes are available for rent at $4.50 a day. Lessons are $4 an hour. There is a $2.50 trail use fee for those who bring their own equipment. The Windblown also offers reasonable prices on new skis. The Windblown season starts in mid-December, and usually continues into April. In February host Al Jenks invites you to join the "Robins Run", a ski tour from the Windblown to Temple Mountain along the Wapack Trail. For information write Al Jenks, Windblown, New Ipswich, NH 03071 (603)878–2869.

Introduction

New Jersey, known as the Garden State, embraces beautiful Atlantic Coast recreation areas and state forests; one of the nation's largest wild areas, the haunting Pine Barrens, with its primeval swamps, bogs, cranberry glades, and tea-colored "cedar" rivers, which hold voracious, arm-length chain pickerel; the renowned trout waters of Big Flat Brook; the beautiful island-dotted waters of Lake Hopatcong, one of the East's top-ranked lakes for tackle-busting brown trout and largemouth bass; the trophy rainbow and brown trout waters of Spruce Run and Round Valley reservoirs; and the long famous saltwater fishing meccas of the Jersey coast.

Accommodations & Travel Information

For information on where to stay in New Jersey, whether it's a hotel, motel, resort, campsite, guesthouse, or anything in between, write to the local chambers of commerce of the areas you plan to visit or to: Chamber of Commerce, 54 Park Place, Newark 07102. Hikers in the state forest areas of New Jersey will want to explore the Batona Trail, which traverses the Pine Barrens in the Wharton and Lebanon state forests. The 30–mile trail, chartered and built in 1961 by the Batona Hiking Club in Philadelphia, passes through a vast wilderness area rich in historic lore as well as interesting flora, bird, and animal life, including white-tailed deer. This trail has no hardships and can be easily walked. Since the trail intersects many roads, it can be reached by car from many points and a variety of hikes can be planned. *Maps of the Batona Trail* and all the other New Jersey state forests can be obtained at no charge from: Bureau of Parks, P.O. Box 1420, Trenton 08625. The maps show roads, footpaths, bodies of water, camping areas, recreation areas, etc. Some state forests that have particularly good hiking opportunities (Bass River, Jenny Jump, and Stokes) supply free trail guides for hikers, which outline and describe suggested hikes, pointing out features of special interest, such as flora and fauna or outstanding scenic views. Also available from the Bureau of Parks is the free booklet *Guide to New Jersey State Forests, Parks, Recreation Areas, Natural Areas, Historic Sites*. It contains capsule descriptions of these areas, with maps to illustrate their locations. The *New Jersey Official Highway Map and Travel Guide* (see below), shows state park and forest areas and includes a facilities chart for all state forest and parks. A helpful map to consult is the free Map of Open Spaces and Recreation Areas.

Highways & Maps

Anyone planning on driving in New Jersey should obtain the free *New Jersey Official Highway Map and Travel Guide* from: Dept. of Transportation, 1035 Parkway Ave., Trenton 08618. The map shows all roads and highways, parks and forests, and recreation areas with and without campsites, winter sport areas, airports, railroads, state agencies, and other places of interest. The map provides a location index of towns and cities, a facility chart of state park, forest, and recreation areas, and a facility chart for fish and wildlife management areas. There is a list of New Jersey ski areas, also location-keyed, as well as brief descriptions of places of interest (monuments, museums, etc.).

NEW JERSEY

VACATION/ LODGING GUIDE

New Jersey Forests, Lakes & Coastal Recreation Areas

Although it is a small state, with only 7,836 square miles, and one of the nation's most populous, New Jersey is long famous for the quality of its hiking trails in scenic State Forests and Parks, hunting, and for its often amazing saltwater and freshwater fishing. The scenic highlands of the Appalachian Mountains cross the northwest corner of the state and include the Kittatinny Mountain and Valley. Crossing the Delaware River at the Delaware Water Gap and continuing in a southwest direction into Pennsylvania to the east are the famous lakes, streams, and hills of northern New Jersey, which include the renowned fishing waters of Lake Hopatcong and Wawayanda, Musconetcong River, and the Spruce Run and Round Valley reservoirs. To the south are the Watchungs and central New Jersey, the great game lands and fishing waters of the Pine Barrens, and the nationally renowned saltwater fishing meccas of the Jersey shore.

The remote wild country waters of the Pine Barrens, the famous big-lake waters of Hopatcong, Spruce Run, Round Valley, Greenwood, Wawayanda and Wanaque, and the hundreds of small back-country and farm ponds and classic freestone streams offer often excellent fishing for pickerel, perch, largemouth bass, and trout—both stocked and a few holdovers. In 1912 New Jersey pioneered one of the first state hatcheries in the country, the Hackettstown Fish Hatchery, which expanded into one of the world's largest and implemented one of the first full-time trout float stocking programs. Sprawling, irregular-shaped Lake Hopatcong, with its numerous bays, coves, islands, and deep river channels, is the focal point of northern New Jersey's lake country. This 2,685–acre lake, with its meandering shoreline and thick underwater vegetation, provides the state's premier fishing year in and year out for trophy-sized brook, brown, rainbow, golden and tiger trout (a cross between a female brown trout and a male brook trout), and for big largemouth bass, walleye, and pickerel. The quality of the trout fishing in Hopatcong has been greatly improved over the years by the stocking efforts of the Knee-Deep Club. The best trophy fishing in the lake is for tackle-busting brown trout in the 8–to–12 pound class (particularly in the Nolan's Point area). Fly fishing from boats is productive along the shoreline during the early season. The most productive way to fish the lake is by drift fishing or slow trolling with a herring rig. Boat rentals, marinas, docking facilities, and launch sites are available at many locations along the shoreline.

The northern lakes country to the west of Lake Hopatcong offers good fishing for bass and pickerel: Swartswood, Owassa, Culvers, Kemak, Mohawk, Budd, Cranberry, Lackawanna, and Ginmill lakes and New Wawayanda Lake—home of the state record landlocked salmon. Brown and rainbow trout are found in Budd and Cranberry lakes and in Lake Ocquittunk in Stokes State Forest. The major bass and pickerel waters to the east of Lake Hopatcong include Morris, Beaver, Canister, Highland, Denmark, Splitrock, Echo, Clinton, Upper Greenwood, Shepherds, Wawayanda, and Greenwood lakes and Green Pond—the home of a longtime former world's record (8-pound) pickerel. The Wanaque Reservoir (fishing by permit only), surrounded by beautiful uplands and mixed hardwood and evergreen forests, holds some monster largemouth bass, pickerel, and rainbow and brown trout—which congregate at the Wanaque River during their fall migrations. Greenwood Lake, to the north of Wanaque, is famed for its trophy brown trout up to state record weight, as well as rainbow trout, largemouth bass, pickerel, and channel catfish to 20 pounds and over. Lake Wawayanda, surrounded by a wild backcountry

of hardwood and spruce forests, holds lunker bass, pickerel, rainbow and brown trout, and northern pike to 20 pounds and over.

The deep waters of Round Valley Reservoir in Hunterdon County, to the south of Lake Hopatcong, surrounded by scenic woodlands and rolling hills, hold large schools of landlocked alewifes (herring), which in turn produce fat trophy rainbows and hook-jawed browns in the 4-to-9-pound class. Round Valley is considered the state's top-ranked rainbow trout water. The deep, clear waters of this lake average 75 feet in depth with a maximum depth of 160 feet, and cover 2,350 acres. The reservoir also holds the state's largest lake population of acrobatic bronzeback smallmouth bass. Spruce Run Reservoir, almost due west of Round Valley, surrounded by scenic woodlands and the Clinton Fish and Wildlife Management Area, is renowed statewide for its superb fishing for trophy rainbow and brown trout to 8 and 10 pounds, and for its large population of big northern pike. Fly fishing for giant buckskin-flanked brown trout is often excellent during the fall spawning run up the lake's Mulhockaway and Spruce Run creeks and tributaries. Mulhockaway Creek is a state-designated natural trout fishing area, limited to dry flies, wet flies, bucktails, nymphs, and streamers. Spruce Run and Round Valley reservoirs are best fished by boat, either drifting or trolling along the drop-offs or old stream channel beds. For detailed info, regulations, and a free *Round Valley Reservoir* and *Spruce Run Reservoir Lake Contour Map*, write: Round Valley-Spruce Run Recreation Areas, Van Syckels Rd., Clinton 08809.

The majestic upper Delaware River, which forms the western boundary of the state, flows south from the New York line through the scenic upper Delaware Valley, rich in Indian lore, paralleled on the east by the historic Old Mine Road, forests, and beautiful thickets of mountain laurel, rhododendron, and dogwood, and the Appalachian Highlands. The upper Delaware is the state's premier big-fish water above the Delaware Water Gap for trophy walleye up to 12 pounds, smallmouth bass up to 6 pounds, pickerel, and a few lunker rainbow and brown trout up to 4 pounds in the deep, swift-flowing pools and riffles. The Delaware produced the state record muskellunge. Dunnfield Creek, a clear, rock-strewn tributary of the Delaware in Worthington State Forest, is one of the state's few streams supporting a population of wild brook trout. An abandoned road, departing from the Appalachian Trail, follows the creek for two-thirds of its length, then climbs a ravine to join the Appalachian Trail.

Big Flatbrook, a tributary of the Delaware in Sussex County and New Jersey's top-ranked trout stream, flows southwest for 20 miles from its headwaters at High Point in the Kittatinny Mountains through the scenic high country woodlands and evergreen forests of Stokes State Forest and the Flatbrook Fish and Wildlife Management Area, through the fly fishing-only stretch in the famous Blewett Tract, to the beautiful historic Junction Pool at the confluence of Little Flatbrook and Big Flatbrook. Downstream from Junction Pool, Big Flatbrook enters its famed deepwater trophy trout area and flows through the lovely "Rhododendron Stretch" on past Flatbrookville to its marriage with the Delaware. The deep pools and riffles of Big Flatbrook hold large, extremely selective brown and rainbow trout up to trophy weights. Another famous tributary of the Delaware, the Musconetcong River, known locally as the "Musky," has a large holdover population of rainbow and brown trout. It flows from its headwaters near Lake Hopatcong southwest for 30 miles past the Hackettstown Fish Hatchery, over numerous small dams and Saxton Falls to its confluence with the Delaware at Riegelsville, Pennsylvania.

In the southern region of populous New Jersey, less than 100 miles south of New York, is one of the nation's most unusual wilderness areas. With its nearly 650,000 acres it is comparable in size to Yosemite and Grand Canyon national parks. This great wild country, known as the Pine Barrens, gives rise to the unspoiled tea-colored "cedar waters" of the Wading and Oswego, Batsto and Mullica rivers, which take twisting, tortuous, deep-flowing courses—similar to the rivers of Canada's Great North Woods canoe country— through dark canopies of white pine surrounded by quaking bogs, cranberry bogs, white cedar swamps of mosses and hummocks and fallen rotting logs, vast plains of stunted dwarf forests of scrub oak and pitch pine, and brush and thickets of foxtail mosses, giant fern, cat briar, blueberry, sphagnum moss, huckleberry, crowberry, greenbriers, bearberry, shadbush, poison sumac, orchids, and sweet pepperbush, once inhabited by panther, timber wolf, black bear, and bobcat. Today this paradise provides excellent hunting in season for whitetail deer, gray fox, and raccoon. The Mullica and Wading rivers and their innumerable sloughs, tributaries, and backwaters offer top-ranked fishing for largemouth bass and giant chain pickerel that grow to arm length in the seldom fished interior reaches.

More than 84 species of birds nest in the Pine Barrens, including Cooper's hawks, green herons, great horned owls, black ducks, whippoorwills, nighthawks, and bald eagles. In the deep swamps and ponds monster snapping turtles up to 50 pounds feed on ducks. Mink, otter, and muskrats inhabit the Barrens along with beaver, whose dams and ponds are often seen by the wilderness paddler. There are timber rattlers in the pines, along with puff adders and red-bodied corn snakes up to 5 feet long.

The Barrens encompass the Wharton, Penn, Bass River, and Lebanon state forests, and most of Atlantic, Ocean, and Burlington counties. Old sand roads and trails wind through the interior areas of the Barrens past several ghost towns to such interesting places as the Hog Wallow (bulls and hogs once ran wild here), the site of the old Lebanon Glass Works, and the Bear Swamp Observation Tower in the Penn State Forest—which provides an unbroken panorama of forest wilderness, broken by an occasional ribbon of flowing water and a few wildly scattered ponds, and of the eerie "dwarf" forests of the plains to the north. Several campsites are located along the trails. The longest pathway is the Batona Trail, which winds for 30 miles through the heart of the Pines, in the Batsto and Lebanon state forests, running parallel for most of its length to the twisting course of the Batsto River.

The state's famed, year-round saltwater fishing and tidewater areas stretch from the renowned bluefish, weakfish, and striped bass waters of Sandy Hook Bay, south along the Atlantic Coast past the surf-casting beaches, inlets, bays, jetties, and marina centers at Sea Bright, Long Branch, Deal, Asbury Park, Manasquan, Point Pleasant Beach, Mantoloking, Lavallette, Seaside Park, and the scenic bluefish and striped bass surf-casting areas of Island Beach State Park, Barnegat Inlet, and Long Beach Island, to Atlantic City and Cape May. For

detailed surf-fishing information and season permit, and four-wheel dune buggy use regulations on Island Beach State Park, write: Superintendent, Island Beach State Park, Seaside Park 08752.

Information Sources, Maps & Access

State forests, park, and recreation areas, which provide scenic eastern woodland hiking, fishing, and camping areas are described in the *Guide to State Forests, Parks, Recreation Areas, Natural Areas, & Historic Sites*, available free, along with detailed camping and hiking information from: Bureau of Parks, P.O. Box 1420, Trenton 08625. The free 40–page booklet *Campsites of New Jersey* contains listings and descriptions of all state-managed campgrounds. For info on privately owned campgrounds, write: New Jersey Private Campgrounds Assn., RD 1, Box 14–H, Tuckerton 08087, (609)296–8789. The camper and backpacker should send for the useful *Map of Open Spaces & Recreation Areas*, available free from: Bureau of Parks (address above). It shows major federal recreation areas, fish and wildlife lands, the Delaware Water Gap National Recreation Areas, Palisades Interstate Park, state parks and forests, and major county and public and private watershed areas, all color-keyed on the map for easy use.

A complete set of 10 *Outdoor Recreation Maps of the Delaware River* describe in detail the characteristics of the river along its entire nontidal main stem—a distance of 200 miles from Hancock, New York, in the western Catskill Mountains to Trenton, on the upstream edge of the tidal estuary that runs to the sea. Elevation of the river over this 200–mile reach drops from about 900 feet to zero. Shown are parks, forests, game lands, river launching locations and recreation areas; rapids, riffles, and pools; channel and water depths, and stream-flow characteristics. The maps point out the hazardous reaches of the river, including the rough waters below Lambertville and New Hope, Pennsylvania. You can obtain copies of these maps by sending $1 to: Delaware River Basin Commission, P.O. Box 360, Trenton 08603.

Anyone planning to hike the Appalachian Trail in New Jersey should obtain the comprehensive *Guide to the Appalachian Trail in New York and New Jersey* (including maps; $6.70), compiled by the New York-New Jersey Trail Conference. To obtain a copy, write to: Appalachian Trail Conference, P.O. Box 236, Harpers Ferry, WV 25425. Locations of lean-tos and other accommodations available to hikers are noted. The descriptions contain very detailed trail data and summaries of distances. In addition, there are sections on the development of the trail; facts you should be aware of before setting out, such as trail maintenance, trail registers, trail markers, trail precautions, and New Jersey forest fires and conservation laws. A

free *Map of Appalachian Trail Campsites* may be obtained along with free maps of the Worthington, Jenny Jump, and Stokes state forests and High Point State Park, from: Bureau of Parks, P.O. Box 1420, Trenton 08625, phone (609)292–2797.

Detailed fishing and hunting regulations, and information about access, boating, seasons, and special permits may be obtained from; Division of Fish, Game, & Shellfisheries, P.O. Box 1809, Trenton 08625. The division publishes the following free publications: *Compendium of Game Laws, Compendium of Fish Laws, List of Stocked Trout Waters, Places to Fish in New Jersey*, and the *New Jersey Deer Season Map-Guide*—including deer management zone locations and permit quotas. For comprehensive information on the state's wildlife management areas, send for the useful 112–page *Guide to Wildlife Management Areas* ($3) published by the Division.

Lodges & Resorts

New Jersey has a very limited number of full-service vacation resorts. For information, see "Accommodations & Travel Information" in the previous section.

Travel Services

Odyssey, the mountain travel agency of the eastern United States, offers guided trips with top-notch professionals throughout North America and the world. During the spring, summer, and fall it has a mountaineering school which runs wet-bend guiding and instruction in the Shawangunks and conducts 2–week summer climbing camps in the Bugaboos in British Columbia. From December through March it runs weekend cross-country ski trips (with certified instructors in Nordic skiing) to Lake Placid, New York, Vermont's Long Trail, and the White Mountains of New Hampshire, plus week-long ski touring trips to Aspen, Yellowstone, and the Canadian Rockies. The Canadian Rockies form the basis for the Odyssey summer program, which includes four backpacks, two mountaineering camps, and two 4–week Youthpack Wilderness Adventures. This renowned firm also offers the following guided trips: trekking in Nepal to the base of Mount Everest with Sherpa porters; cross-country skiing in the Canadian Laurentians; canoing on the Shenandoah in Virginia's magnificent Blue Ridge Mountains; Grand Canyon combination backpack and raft trip; Mexican volcano climbing; mountaineering in the Bugaboos of British Columbia; and weekend canoeing trips and instruction on the Delaware from Bushkill down through the Water Gap, with camping on Tocks Island and hikes through historic Jockey Hollow—studded with Revolutionary War lore. For detailed information, rates, and literature, write: Art Fitch or Denise Van Lear, Odyssey, 26 Hilltop Ave., Berkeley Heights 07922, (201)322–8414.

South Branch Canoe Cruises offers day, weekend, or five day river trips through spectacular scenery on the finest white-water rivers in the east, the Delaware, the Shenandoah, the Lehigh, and the New River. Day trips average six hours, and include an hour picnic lunch and swim. South Branch provides expert instruction on all levels from beginner to expert, guides, equipment, car shuttle and an optional, all-you-can-eat lunch. Day trips are $21 per person, or $19 per person in groups of twenty or more. Weekend trips run the Delaware through the breath taking Delaware Water Gap, the Lehigh River, as it winds through the Appalachian Mountains, or the mysterious red rivers in the dense pine barrens of New Jersey. Instruction, guides, equipment, camping gear, and food are all provided for $82.50 per person on a two day weekend, and $115 for three days. In early May and late September South Branch offers five day canoe trips on the Shenandoah, through rolling Virginia

pastureland and deep woods, lush in spring and brilliant in autumn. The price is $165 per person. The New River trip in August is only for intermediate and advanced canoeists, who can handle fast rapids of this ancient river as it cuts through a spectacular mountain gorge in the Alleghenies; $195 per person, $175 per person in groups of six or more. Five day trips on the Delaware run all season, take on the challenging foul rift rapids, and camp on islands; $115 per person. South Branch Canoe Cruises also offers three day beginner courses, or will arrange special group trips throughout the season. For more information write: South Branch Canoe Cruises, P.O. Box 173, Lebanon, NJ 08833 (201)782–9700.

Vernon Valley—Great Gorge offers year-round facilities for outdoor recreation and alpine and cross-country skiing in winter. The area is accessible from all major highways. Ski facilities are available daily, contingent on weather conditions, from 9 a.m. until 10:45 p.m.

weekdays and from 8:30 a.m. until 10:45 p.m. on weekends. Slopes are designed for the novice to expert skier. Rentals are inexpensive; a ski school and cross-country skiing facilities are also offered. Nursery supervision for children three to nine is available from 9 a.m. until noon and again from 1 p.m. until 4 p.m. at a nominal charge. Ski packages for lift tickets and lessons are also offered. Food facilities for visitors include a cafeteria, dining rooms overlooking the slopes, and cocktail lounges. Vernon Valley Action Park is a multi-recreational facility for summer fun that's open from May until November, offering various amusements including the Alpine Slide, Skateboard Park, Dune Buggies, Water Slide, Rapids Ride, Bumper Boats, Go-Karts, and Lola Formula Race Cars. Other facilities include a swimming pool, tennis courts, Arcades, a disco, and gift shops. They offer a special Night Package price for all rides from 6 p.m. to closing. Overnight accommodations are available at nearby locations in hotels, motels and campsites. For information on ski facilities call (201)827–2000.

Introduction

The vast reaches of New York State, with its coastal saltwater fishing areas, historic trout streams, extensive game lands, and sprawling island-dotted north country lakes, wild rivers, and high peaks, form one of the nation's most popular outdoor recreation areas. The Empire State's major attractions include the world-famous striped bass runs off Montauk Point; the nationally renowned brown-trout fly-fishing streams of the Catskill Forest Preserve; the trophy lake and rainbow trout, walleye, and northern pike waters of the Finger Lakes region; the beautiful northwoods canoe routes, fishing, hunting, cross-country skiing, and wilderness camping areas of the vast Adirondack State Park and Forest Preserve; and the muskellunge, walleye, smallmouth bass, and northern pike waters surrounding the beautiful Thousand Islands of the St. Lawrence River.

Accommodations & Travel Information

For information on all aspects of vacation travel in New York State, contact: New York State Vacation Information, 99 Washington Ave., Albany 12210, phone toll free (800)342–3810. For daily ski conditions call (212)755–8100 or (518)474–5677. The state's major vacation lodges, north country sporting camps, inns, ski resorts and cross-country skiing centers are described in detail in the "Vaction/Lodging Guide" which follows.

Information & Services

For detailed ourdoor recreation information and the following free publications, contact the Information Office, Dept. of Environmental Conservation, 50 Wolf Rd., Albany N.Y. 12333 (518)474–2121: *Sportfishing Guide, Freshwater Fishing in New York, Big-Game Hunting Guide, Small-Game Hunting Guide, County Maps (50¢ each), Outdoor Recreation Guide, Boat-Launching Sites, Camping in New York State, Hiking Areas of New York State, Access Point Maps for the Catskill Forest Preserve, Great Lakes Salmon Sport Fishery, Leaping Rainbows of the Finger Lakes, Panfishes of New York, Red Salmon, Salmon in New York, Smelt, Trout Fishing in the Catskills, Marine Game Fish of New York, Sport Fishing for Cod, Catskill Forest Preserve, Wild Rivers, Surf-fishing,* and *Trout Fishing in the Catskills.* If you plan to walk the Appalachian Trail through New York, obtain the *Guide to the Appalachian Trail in*

NEW YORK

Protecting Our Natural Rivers

New York & New Jersey ($6), available from: Appalachian Trail Conference, P.O. Box 236, Harpers Ferry, WV 25425. The book describes the trail in depth throughout New York and New Jersey, noting topography, ground cover, distances between points, trail markings, special features nearby, and other information of interest to the hiker. The 247–page compact book includes an introduction to traveling the trail, noting rules and regulations in effect throughout the section, a short history of the trail, and 4 maps. A free *Canoe Trips* brochure, available from the DEC, Publications Distribution Unit, 50 Wolf Rd., Albany 12233, describes many of the state's wild and scenic canoe routes, including Black Creek, Cayuta Lake, Upper Mohawk River, West Canada Creek, the Kunjamuk, Fall Stream to Piseco and Vly Lakes, Unadilla River, Upper Delaware River, Ramapo River, the Susquehanna, Chenango River, Upper Hudson River, Champlain Canal-Lake George, Allegheny River, West Branch of the Sacandaga River—a beautiful Adirondack meadowland stream—Oswegatchie River Primitive Area, Indian River, and Long Island's Nissequogue River. Canoe trips are keyed on a state map showing counties throughout the state. Outstanding features and fishing are noted.

Highways & Maps

New York's four-lane expressways include the Governor Thomas E. Dewey Thruway (Interstate 87 and 90), Adirondack Northway (Interstate 87), North-South Expressway (Interstate 81), Long Island Expressway (Interstate 495), and the partly completed Route 17–Southern Tier Expressway. The New York Thruway runs from the state's western border 559 miles to New York City, inscribing an arc across the state and connecting with the Pennsylvania, Massachusetts, and Connecticut turnpikes, the Garden State Parkway, and other major highways. The thruway is a toll way. No accommodations are available on the highway, but there are accommodations just off most of the Thruway's 103 interchanges. For road condition information, call (914)631–6100. Interstate 495 runs from New York

City's Queens Midtown Tunnel to eastern Long Island. Route 17–Southern Tier Expressway runs from Harriman to Allegany. The Taconic State Parkway runs up the east side of the Hudson to connect with the Berkshire Spur of the thruway. The Palisades Interstate Parkway runs from the George Washington Bridge at New York City to Bear Mountain State Park. Other parkways include the Bronx River, Hutchinson, Sprain Brook, and Saw Mill River parkways in Westchester County, Robert Moses Parkway near Niagara Falls, and the Lake Ontario Parkway. The Adirondack Trail (Route 30), which crosses the Adirondack Mountains between the Canadian border and the thruway at Amsterdam and Fultonville, is among the state's most scenic highways. For more information on it, write to: Hamilton Co. Publicity Bureau, Long Lake 12847. Among the scenic highways through the Catskills are the Shawangunk Trail (Route 52 from Newburgh), Minnewaska Trail (Routes 44 and 55 from Poughkeepsie), Onteora Trail (Route 28 from Kingston), Rip Van Winkle Trail (Route 23A from Catskill), and Mohican Trail (Route 23 from Catskill). The Hawk's Nest Drive, a portion of Route 97 between Port Jervis and Hancock, offers spectacular views of the Delaware River Gorge. The Seneca Trail follows an old Indian trail from the Pennsylvania border through Limestone, Salamanca, Little Valley, Cattaraugus, and Gowanda to Hamburg. The St. Lawrence Scenic Highway (Route 12) runs along the river between Alexandria Bay and Morristown. Route 30 in Schoharie County is known as the Timothy Murphy Trail. All New York highways, with the exception of a few parkways, permit trailers. Trailers more than 8 feet wide or 13½ feet high require special hauling permits. For more information about travel trailers, write: Director of Operations, Thruway Authority, Box 189, Albany 12201, or: Highway Permit Agent, Dept. of Transportation, 1220 Washington Ave., Albany 12232. For a free full-color *Official New York State Road Map*, which shows all outdoor recreation areas, state parks and forests, and provides a wealth of useful information, write or call New York State Vacation Information, 99 Washington Ave., Albany 12210 (800)342–3810.

VACATION/ LODGING GUIDE

Adirondack Park & Forest Preserve

The vast Adirondack Park and Forest Preserve embraces some 8,000 square miles of sprawling north country lakes, streams, ponds, wild brawling rivers, and high country trails, surrounded by extensive tracts of evergreen forests, bogs, rolling hills, and high peaks in northern New York State; it contains several nationally renowned fishing, hunting, backpacking, and wilderness canoe-camping areas. Indians once knew these coveted hunting grounds as "the Dark and Bloody Ground." They were the scene of repeated wars between the Iroquois and the Algonquin tribes of the north. Among the Algonquin tribes were the Montaignais Indians, who traveled a great distance to this land from the lower St. Lawrence. As the journey used up their supplies of fish and venison, they were forced to subsist on the buds of moosebushes and the bark of trees. The Mohawks scornfully labeled these unwelcome tribes the bark eaters; in Iroquois, that name was Ad-i-ron-daks. The forest preserve lies, for the most part, within the boundaries of Adirondack Park, established in 1892 based on the explorations and surveys of Verplank Colvin. The park's 5,693,000 acres, or 8,895 square miles, make it larger than any other national or state park in the United States—larger in fact than Massachusetts. This magnificent north country paradise, first penetrated by the great French explorer Samuel de Champlain, and followed over the years by fur trappers, pioneers, lumbermen, miners, woodsmen, hordes of sportsmen, and such celebrated personalities as James Fenimore Cooper, Frederic Remington, Mark Twain, Nessmuk, and the members of the Philosophers' Camp—Louis Agassiz, James Russell Lowell, and Ralph Waldo Emerson—is protected for all time by New York State's "forever wild" statute of 1895. The Adirondack Mountains form the southern tip of the ancient rock-bound plateau known as the Laurentian Upland or Canadian Shield. In the southeast lie the low hills and lakes of the Lake George resort country, the most highly developed region of the Adirondacks. The northeast contains the majestic High Peaks and the headwaters of the Hudson, the earliest settled villages, and the busy centers of Lake Placid and Saranac Lake. Low rolling hills, hundreds of ponds, beaver flows, meandering rivers, and beautiful lakes such as Cranberry Lake lie in the least traveled northwestern quarter. The network of lakes and waterways stretches deep into the southwestern portion of the region; here and there, low hills push up from the boggy land. The riches of this country lie within easy reach of the densely populated Northeast. The land would doubtless lie bereft of all natural beauty if not for the state-owned forest preserve encompassing half its 5 million acres. More than a score of rivers lace the Adirondack country, among them the Hudson, Oswegatchie, Raquette, Grass, Black, and Saranac. The Hudson rises in the heights of Mount Marcy, in Lake Tear-of-the-Clouds. It begins as a small, clear-flowing stream before it opens into the course southward, a course that once bore the prize of the north country—its lumber. The Raquette River meanders along its course from Blue Mountain Lake through Long Lake and 170–odd miles to the St. Lawrence, though a straight line from its source to its junction with the St. Lawrence is only half this distance. The Moose River flows south from the Fulton Chain, connecting more than a hundred lakes and ponds. The Schroon, St. Regis, and the Oswegatchie attract trout fisherman in the spring. The smaller rivers of the region, among them the Cold, Chazy, Bog, Opalescent, Jordan, Cedar, and Chub, are the size of small mountain brooks over most of their lengths. Since the first large-scale lumbering of the region these rivers have shrunk in their water volume. Several of them supported log runs and boat travel during the 19th century, but most are virtually impassable by boat today. The evergreen and mixed hardwood forests of the Adirondacks—once inhabited by

herds of majestic elk, moose, timber wolves, fisher, marten, and the Indian "devil of the north," the wolverine—crown her mountain heights and border the shores of her rivers and lakes. The woods go on and on, surprisingly undaunted by the highways that have opened the area and the millions of visitors they have brought. The woods have changed since the first white explorers saw them. The once dominant great white pines and spruces have given way to hardwoods in many areas. Cherry, poplar, birch, and beech have reforested extensive stands decimated by lumbering or fire, and large areas are covered by scrub. Elsewhere maple and spruce have reseeded themselves. Ground pine, partridge and other berries, ferns and mosses form a luxuriant undergrowth, brightened by trilliums, lady's slippers, and other wildflowers in the spring.

Information Sources, Maps & Access

For detailed information, contact the Adirondack Park Agency, Adirondack, NY 12808 (518)494–2515. For information on Adirondack wild and scenic rivers, contact the Adirondack Park Agency or the Natural Rivers Program, DEC, 50 Wolf Rd., Albany, NY 12233. Wilderness fishing, hunting, canoeing fly-in service and sightseeing tours are provided by *Bird's Seaplane Service*, 6th Lake, Inlet 13360 (315)357–3631 and *Helms Aero Service*, Long Lake 12847 (518)624–3931. For additional fishing and hunting information, stream and lake conditions, hatches, and where-to-go advice, write or call the *Adirondack Sport Shop*, Wilmington 12997 (518)946–2605. Several eminently useful map-guides of the Adirondack backpacking and canoeing areas are available free upon request from: Publications Distribution Unit, Dept. of Environmental Conservation, 50 Wolf Rd., Albany 12233. *Adirondack Canoe Routes* describes the famous 125–mile canoe route originally traveled by the Indians and trappers through the Fulton Chain, Raquette Lake, Long Lake, Tupper Lake, Saranac Lake, and Paul Smiths country; *Hiking Lesser-Known Adirondack Wilds* describes trails in the remote Pepperbox Wilderness, Tongue Mountain, Shaker Mountain Tract, and Soda Range areas; *Moose River Recreation Area* shows roads, trails, lean-tos, fire towers, and camping areas; *Trails in the Schroon Lake Region* shows and describes several primitive trails, including the Long Swing, Peaked Hill, Pharaoh Mountain Fire Tower, Berrymill Pond, and Pharaoh Lake trails; *Trails in the Lake George Region* shows and describes the Prospect Mountain, Tongue Mountain Range, and Black Mountain Fire Tower trails; *Trails in the Blue Mountain Lake Region* describes the Northville-Placid, Cascade Lake, Sargent Ponds, and Tirrell Pond trails; *Trails in the Cranberry Lake Region* describes the Loop, Plains, Five Ponds-Wolf Pond-Sand Lake, Big Deer Pond, Buck

Pond, and Cat Mountain trails; *Trails in the Old Forge-Big Moose Region* describes the Big Otter Lake, Moose River Mountain, Scenic Mountain, Cascade Lake-Queer Lake, and Windfall Lake trails as well as trails in the Beaver River flow region; *Trails to Marcy* describes the trails in the High Peaks country—including the northern approaches via the Van Hoevenberg, Avalanche Lake and Lake Golden, and Indian Pass trails, the trail to Scott and Wallface Ponds, the eastern approaches from Keene Valley via the John Brook, Hopkins, and Range trails, the southern approaches from Tahawus and Elk Lake, and western approaches from Tupper Lake. A detailed foldout *Map of the Mount Marcy Region* shows foot trails, roads, and lean-tos. A free *Indian River Canoe Route Map* is available from: Indian River Lakes Chamber of Commerce, Theresa 13691. The map is on a scale of 1 inch to 1 mile, and shows put-in points, historic sites, towns, and riverside recreation areas.

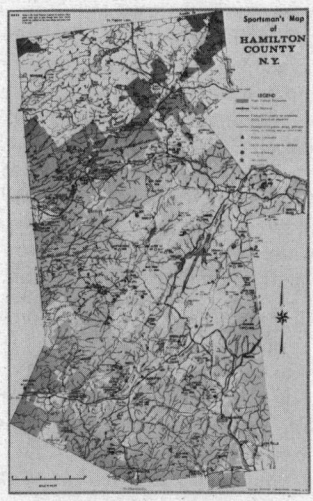

The Adirondack Mountain Club publishes two useful canoeing guides to the Adirondacks. *Adirondack Canoe Waters—North Flow* (299 pp.), by Paul F. Jamieson, outlines canoe travel on the waterways of the Adirondack wilderness, describing excursions down the West, Middle, and East branches of the Oswegatchie River, Little River, Middle, North, and South branches of the Grass River, the Raquette River, Cold River, Bog River, Jordan River, West, Middle, and East branches of the St. Regis River, Osgood River, Deer River, Salmon River, and the Chateaugay River in the northwest watershed of the Adirondack area, and the Great Chazy, Saranac (North Branch). West, East, and Main Branches of the Au Sable River, the Bouquet River, and Lakes Champlain and George. The book relates the courses of each of these streams, describing rapids, falls, dams, obstructions, natural features, and flora and fauna of the rivers and their lands. The book is embellished with historical notes on the people who have inhabited the river country. It includes a chapter on canoe camping by Robert Bliss. The book costs $5.50 (when ordering by mail, be sure to include 50¢ per book for postage and handling). It is available from: Adirondack Mountain Club, 172 Ridge St., Glens Falls 12801. The canoe waters of the south central Adirondacks are described in Barbara McMartin Patterson's 171–page *Walks and Waterways* ($4.75 plus 50¢ for postage and handling, same source). The portion of the Adirondack region covered by this book is the least known; it includes some of the wildest country in the state. Canoe routes described include trips on the Big Bay, Piseco, Clockmill Pond, Fall Stream, Good Luck Lake, Kunjamuk Stream, North Flow of the East Canada, Piseco Outlet, Stewart's

Landing, the West Branch of the Sacandaga (East), and the West Branch of the Sacandaga (North). Nearly 100 canoe routes, walks, and bushwhacks in the East Canada Creek and West Branch of the Sacandaga River regions are described; their natural features, wildlife, and plant life are noted. The book includes 5 simple maps, and should be used in conjunction with U.S. Geological Survey Topographical Maps. The most important single source of information on trails of the High Peaks region is probably the *Guide to Adirondack Trails*, published by: Adirondack Mountain Club (address above, $6). It covers trails in the Keene Valley, St. Huberts, Upper Au Sable Lake, Elk Lake, Sanford Lake, Heart Lake, Cascade-Keene-Hurricane, Bouquet Valley, Lake Placid, and Saranac Lake regions, the outlying mountains of the High Peaks, and the trailless peaks. The book gives distances between points on the trails and identifies natural features, shelters, and camping areas along the way. Its introductory section describes the region, and includes information on preparation and essential camping skills. A topographical map shows trails of the High Peaks region on a scale of about 1 inch to the mile. The map shows water features, roads (heavy duty, medium duty, unimproved dirt, light duty), highways, horse trails, AMC lodges (which see), other lodges, ranger stations, and public lean-tos. The book also covers the Northville-Placid Trail which leads north from the Adirondack foothills and the High Peaks through the heart of the Adirondack wilderness lowlands. It passes through about 133 miles of forest, shot through with myriad lakes and ponds and laced by streams which offer excellent trout fishing in the spring, and bass, pickerel, and pike fishing in the summer and fall.

The Dept. of Environmental Conservation (address above) publishes a free leaflet on The *Northville-Placid Trail*. It describes the six major sections of the trails, features along these routes, and mileage between points. For a complete listing of Adirondack fishing and hunting guides write for the *Register of Guides*, available free from: Bureau of Forest Recreation, DEC, 50 Wolf Rd., Albany 12233. A free pamphlet describing and mapping *Adirondak Loj Ski Touring Trails* is available from: AMC, P.O. Box 867, Lake Placid, NY 12946. *Guide to Trout Waters in the Adirondack Mountains* ($1.50), by N. B. Cole: Outdoor Publications, Box 355, Ithaca 14850, describes the area contained in the park along with its history, sketches important facts about the principal trout species, provides

helpful information about finding good public fishing areas in the park, and includes a review of the principal trout lakes, ponds, and streams. Of particular interest is a list of lakes and ponds which have been reclaimed and stocked with trout. Outdoor Publications has also issued the useful *Sportsman's Map of the Adirondack Mountains* ($2.50, 42 × 50 inches) and *Sportsman's Map of Hamilton Country* (the central Adirondacks, 16 × 24 inches, $1), which show fishing access areas, public campsites, lean-to shelters, hiking and access trails, lookout towers, trout streams, lakes and ponds, roadways, and other features. The maps are printed in color. A useful *Adirondack Area Fishing Waters* guide may be obtained free upon request from the Adirondack Park Agency, Adirondack 12808. *Official lake contour maps of the Adirondack Lakes* are available free from: Publications Distribution Unit, DEC, 50 Wolf Rd., Albany, NY 12233. Charts for *Chautauqua* ($3.50), *Cranberry* ($3), *George* ($4.50), *Great Sacandaga* ($4.50), *Long* ($3), *Owasco* ($3.50), *Placid* ($2), *Raquette* ($2.50), *Saranac Chain* ($2), *Schroon* ($2), *Tupper* ($3), and *Upper Saranac* ($2.50) lakes are available from: Bureau of Marine & Recreational Vehicles, Parks & Recreation Dept. Albany 12238. Special full-color U.S. Geological Survey Topographic maps at a scale of 1:25,000 are available for $2 each for the following Adirondack recreation areas: *Lake Placid Area*, *Saranac Lake Area*, and the *Keene Valley Area*. The maps may be ordered from U.S. Geological Survey, Distribution Branch, 1200 S. Eads St., Arlington, VA 22202. The Adirondack Park and Forest Preserve is reached via the scenic Adirondack Northway (Interstate 87), Interstate 90 and 81, and connecting New York 30, 10, 8, 28, 12, 3, 56, 73, and 86. Overnight accommodations, guides, supplies, and equipment rentals are available at almost all Adirondack villages, such as Lake George, Lake Luzerne, Indian Lake, North River, Warrensburg (known as the "queen village of the Adirondacks"), Schroon Lake, Lake Placid, Saranac Lake, Tupper Lake, Cranberry Lake, Raquette Lake, Piseco, Blue Mountain Lake, Old Forge, Big Moose, and Nehasane.

Recreation Areas

Headwaters of the Hudson

The Adirondack Forest Preserve section of the Hudson River drainage system includes some of the state's premier fishing and canoe-camping waters. The mighty Hudson stems from tiny rivulets in the secluded slopes and glens of the High Peaks. One feeder rises near the summit of soaring Mount Marcy at the outlet of Lake Tear-of-the-Clouds, the most alpine source of the great river. Another origin is the series of spring brooks feeding Lake Henderson, dominated by the imposing masses of Mount McIntyre, and the rugged Santanoni Range. The upper section of the Hudson provides wilderness brook trout fishing in both the Lake Henderson spur and the Opalescent River, which flows into it at Sanford Lake. The Opalescent receives Lake Tear-of-the-Cloud's outlet and begins a wild ride to the valley through a precipitous flume. This river derives its name from mineral-bearing rocks that catch the sun's rays and reflect brilliant bursts of color through the stream's clear waters. The Upper Hudson flows southeast from the High Peaks through the remote and spectacular "Little Grand Canyons" of the Hudson Gorge Primitive Area (lunker brown trout are occasionally caught along this stretch) to its confluence with the Boreas River, continuing south past Loon and Friends lakes, along the placid stretches to Corinth.

High Peaks Wilderness

The majestic 219,570–acre High Peaks Wilderness ranges from small areas of low-lying swamplands along the Raquette and Saranac rivers to the highest point in New York, the summit of Mount Marcy (5,344 feet), which was once known as Tahawus ("cloud

splitter") to the Indians. Mount Marcy is surrounded by the other high peaks of the MacIntyre Range, which extends through the west central portion of Essex County. The Hudson-St. Lawrence River Divide passes over its summit. Lake Tear-of-the-Clouds lies at the base of Mount Marcy and is the highest lake source of the Hudson River. The Range Trail, which traverses a series of mountain summits above timberline from Mount Marcy and Mount Algonquin to the Keene Valley, has long been considered the most rugged and scenic trail in the state. More than 174 miles of trails, including a segment of the Northville-Placid Trail, provide access to the waterfalls and deep trout pools of the Opalescent River, Johns Brook Primitive Area, Flowed Lands, Cold Brook, Moose Creek, Hurricane Mountain Primitive Area, Dix Mountain Wilderness, Klondike Brook, Duck Hole, Cold River Wilderness Canoe Trail, Ampersand Primitive Area, and Sanford Lake. The trails to Mount Marcy from Adirondak Loj via Indian Falls or Lake Colden are perhaps the most heavily used trails in the Adirondacks. The wilderness contains 49 lean-tos. The region is a top-ranking deer and bear hunting area.

Lake Placid Area

Beautiful Lake Placid, with its two major islands—Buck and Moose—and numerous coves, is one of the state's better producers of large lakers and rainbows. Like many of the Adirondack lakes, Lake Placid is island dotted, the islands stretch down the middle of the 5-mile-long lake (it is about 2 miles wide at its broadest point). Hills and mountains surround this lake, shielding it from the high winds and severe storms that whip over less protected areas. Many camps and resort hotels have sprung up along its irregular shores. This lake was once a major camping base for the Algonquins, who journeyed down from the lower St. Lawrence to hunt the Adirondacks. Later the Mohawks built stockaded bark houses near what are now Keene and Elizabethtown, and conquered their enemies from the north. About a thousand Mohawks live on the St. Regis Reservation, just north of the lake, today.

Moose River Country

The wild and scenic Moose River joins the Black at Lyons Falls and its drainage provides some of the best stream and wilderness pond fishing for brook trout in the Adirondacks, as well as lake fishing for bass, salmon, and splake. The South Branch begins in the shadows of steep Little Moose Mountain and flows through the heart of the wild Moose River Recreation Area. Wilderness brook trout fishing is available in the river and its numerous tributary streams and remote ponds. The Middle Branch drains the famous Fulton Chain before joining the South Branch above McKeever. This group of eight lakes, just north of the resort town of Old Forge on Route 28, all contain smallmouths; Second Fulton is the only one that does not hold trout. Rainbows are found in the other lakes, lakers in Third, Fourth, Seventh, and Eighth Fulton, and landlocked salmon and splake in Seventh. The North Branch flows out of Big Moose Lake, which holds lake trout and some brookies, and flows to the Middle Branch at Old Forge. This northerly fork contains excellent headwater squaretail fishing in magnificent surroundings. The 50,000-acre Moose River Plains Area is made up of the plains of the Moose and Red rivers, in Hamilton and Herkimer counties between Route 28, and the West Canada Lakes Wilderness. These flat zones of herb and grass vegetation contrast vividly with the adjacent dense green forests. A maze of abandoned logging roads of the old Gould Paper Company wind through the region. Major features of this top whitetail deer and brook trout area include the Cedar River Flow, Moose River Cliffs, Mitchell Ponds, Lost Ponds, Icehouse and Helldiver ponds, Cedar Lakes, Brook Trout Lake, Indian River Canoe Trail, Beaver, Limekiln, Indian, Sly, and Wolf lakes, and the length of the

South Branch of the Moose River. Nearly 30 miles of access trails lead to the interior fishing and wilderness camping areas; these are open to foot travel only. The area is closed to snowmobile traffic until the close of the big-game hunting season, unless snow makes access roads impassable to other vehicles.

Northville–Placid Trail to the High Peaks

The famous Northville–Placid Trail, blazed by the Adirondack Mountain Club in 1922-23, passes through the heart of the Adirondack Forest Preserve wilderness along a northerly 133–mile-long course connecting the scenic lake-dotted southern Adirondack foothills with the majestic 219,750–acre High Peaks Wilderness to the north— dominated by Mount Marcy and the surrounding peaks of the Mac-Intyre Range and the Hudson-St. Lawrence Divide. The trail passes through several of the East's premier wilderness fishing, hunting, camping, and canoeing areas, including the 106,650–acre Silver Lake Wilderness—a wild country of low rolling hills, dense conifer forests, cedar swamps, and beaver flows dominated by the famed brook trout waters of the wild West Branch of the Sacandaga River; the 160,320–acre West Canada Lakes Wilderness, famous for its wild brook trout waters, spruce and balsam swamp flats, beaver meadows, and rolling hills, including the Moose River Plains, Piseco Lake, Cedar Lakes, Jessup River Wild Forest, Spruce Lake, Cedar River Flow, and Indian River, and Blue Mountain Lake country and beyond, hugging the eastern shore of Long Lake through the heart of the Adirondacks along old logging roads to Lake Placid and the High Peaks. Old tote roads and spur trails provide access to seldom explored game lands and remote high country lakes, many of which hold wild brook trout up to 5 pounds, northern pike, and smallmouth bass. There are several tent sites and Adirondack shelters along the trail.

Old Adirondack Canoe Trail & the Fulton Chain

The lakes, streams, swamps, beaver flows, and wild forests of the Moose River country surround the famous Fulton Chain canoe route, often referred to as the western gateway to the Adirondacks. The old Adirondack Canoe Trail starts at Old Forge, extends through the Fulton Chain and numerous lakes and interconnecting streams, and goes for nearly 100 miles to the northeast. The North Branch of the Moose River and its tributaries provide the greatest drainage of the region. The Independence River and Otter Creek flow into the Black River Valley, surrounded by the beaver meadows and low rolling hills of the 26,600–acre Ha-De-Ron-Dah Wilderness. The Pigeon Lake Wilderness embraces 50,800 acres of brook trout ponds and vast expanses of swamplands adjacent to the Stillwater Reservoir. The famous John Brown Tract lies just southeast of the wilderness. The wetland of alder swamp, marsh, and beaver flows of the 14,600–acre Pepperbox Wilderness has for its southern boundary the Stillwater Reservoir and for its northern boundary the John Brown Tract.

Wild & Scenic Fishing Waters

The boulder-filled runs and deep pools of the East and West branches of the Au Sable, which rise in the majestic High Peaks, hold trophy-sized brown and rainbow trout. The fabled West Branch flows for 7½ miles to Lake Placid and North Elba. The smaller East Branch has excellent fishing for all three species of trout from its headwaters in Upper Au Sable Lake, flowing northeast for 25 miles through beautiful Keene Valley to its confluence with the West Branch at Au Sable Forks. The lower main Au Sable flows through the Ausable Chasm to its mouth on Lake Champlain. Lake Placid, with its two large islands, Buck and Moose, lies in the shadow of Mount Whiteface and holds big lake trout, rainbow and brook trout,

whitefish, smallmouth bass, and northern pike. The wild, boulder-filled runs and beautiful evergreen, fringed pools of the legendary West Branch of the Au Sable provide shelter for some of the largest rainbow and brown trout in the Northeast. A topographic map will show you where the more inaccessible areas are, and it is in these rugged, sometimes precipitous stretches that superlative fishing can be found. Natural baits and deeply fished lures take a lot of trout, but the fly fisherman comes into his own on these magnificent sections of the stream. The trout follow the hatch cycle in the spring, and the fortunate angler who is present during a major emergence of March browns or gray foxes will experience unforgettable fishing. This fork of the river produces well all summer, and during the fall the cooling waters encourage another feeding splurge. Fishing this great stream when crisp weather has turned the maples and birches into torches of crimson and yellow is a feast of the senses. Remember to include some large flies in your kit, such as the Muddler Minnow, Gray Ghost, Black Ghost, and assorted maribou patterns for those trophy trout, particularly the fall-spawning browns. Stonefly and Caddis imitations are particularly effective on this river, and big Stonefly nymphs account for numbers of lunker trout. Other renowned Adirondack wild and scenic trout streams include the Bouquet River, rising in the lofty domes to the west of Keene Valley and boasting quite a reputation for trophy brown, rainbow, and brook trout; the beautiful and wild Boreas River, noted for its numerous white-water stretches interspersed with quiet deep pools and quality brook, brown, and rainbow trout, the brook, brown, and rainbow trout waters of the complex Black River system, surrounded by the interconnecting streams, lakes, ponds, wild tangled swamps, and beaver ponds of the Black River Wild Forest; the rainbow, brown, and brook trout waters of the Little Salmon and Great Chazy rivers, and the famed Saranac River and its North Branch; the rainbow and wild brown trout pools of the Chateaugay River and its Upper and Lower lakes, which hold smallmouth bass and lake, rainbow, brook, and brown trout; the brook and brown trout waters of the Trout River and its eastern branch, the Little Trout, which rise in the deep evergreen forests of the Owls Head Range; the famous brown trout waters of the Big Salmon River; the wild trout waters of the sprawling St. Regis River watershed, which drains a vast wilderness of evergreen forests and clear spring-fed ponds in the northern tip of the Adirondacks, and includes the East, West, and Middle branches of the St. Regis, the Deer River, and Big Fish, St. Regis, and Long ponds; the broad Raquette River system, which starts at Little Tupper Lake and flows north through the smallmouth bass, walleye, and northern pike waters of Round Lake, Big Tupper, Raquette Pond, and Carry Falls Reservoir into the St. Lawrence River; the wild, aptly named Cold River, which holds large brook trout in the rushing feeders which cascade down the steep, forested flanks of its wilderness headwaters; the famous wilderness brook waters of the Moose River and its Middle, North, and South branches; the renowned trout waters of the wild and scenic Independence, Upper Hudson, Red, Opalescent, Indian, Jessup, Rock, Cedar, Boreas, Marion, Schroon, South Branch Grasse, and West Branch Sacandaga rivers; and the famed squaretail waters of West Canada Creek and the Silver Lake Wilderness.

The Adirondack lakes, with their many coves, bays, island-and evergreen-fringed, jagged shorelines offer some of the nation's top fishing for smallmouth bass, lake trout, rainbow trout, northern pike, landlocked salmon, and yellow perch. The major Adirondack lakes include the smallmouth bass haunts of island-dotted Cranberry Lake, bordered by the wild brook trout waters and beaver flows of the vast Five Ponds Wilderness and the Oswegatchie Primitive Area; Upper, Middle, and Lower Saranac lakes, which yield trophy smallmouth bass, northern pike, landlocked salmon (Upper Lake), and lake trout and are bordered by a vast network of remote streams, lakes, and ponds in the Saranac Wild Forest; Schroon Lake, famous for its landlocked salmon and lake and rainbow trout, bordered by the fragrant pine and spruce forests, bogs, and crystal-clear ponds of the Pharaoh Lake Wilderness; the sprawling Fulton Chain Lakes, which hold smallmouth, bass, splake, landlocked salmon, and lake and rainbow trout; beautiful arrowhead-shaped Indian Lake and its smaller sister, Lewey Lake, which hold big smallmouth bass and northern pike to 20 pounds and over; narrow Long Lake, which stretches for 14 miles and holds smallmouth and largemouth bass, and some giant northern pike; jagged Piseco Lake, which produces lake trout, rainbows, whitefish, and smallmouth bass, bordered by the spruce and balsam swamp flats, beaver ponds, lakes, and rolling hills of the West Canada Lakes Wilderness; beautiful, island-dotted Lake George, whose deep, cold waters yield giant landlocked salmon up to 16 pounds, rainbows, lake trout, great northern pike, and smallmouth bass; and Great Sacandaga Reservoir, which produces giant northern pike—the water wolf of the north—as well as largemouth and smallmouth bass and hordes of panfish along the shallow weedy bays and coves of its lengthy arms. Other productive lakes nestled among the scenic rolling hills and conifer forests of the Adirondacks include the Cedar River flow, Beaver River Flow (Stillwater Reservoir) and Lila, Forked, Blue Mountain, Round, Catlin, Newcomb, Sanford, Meacham, Fern, Ampersand, Follensby Pond, Elk, Canachagala, Honnedaga, Pleasant, Big Moose, Wolf, Paradox, Eatong, Loon, Osgood, Canada, and Piercefield Flow. Due west of the forest preserve boundaries are the famous black bass waters of Butterfield, Bonaparte, and Black Lakes. Bonaparte Lake was named for Napoleon's older brother Joseph, who purchased more than 160,000 acres of Adirondack land, hoping to establish a New France for his exiled brother.

Gateways & Accommodations

Blue Mountain Lake

(Pop. 250; zip code 12812; area code 518), a small resort town on the lake's edge, is a cross roads for skiers, hikers, fishermen, tourists, backpackers and hunters centered in the Adirondacks. Area attractions include Blue Mountain Observation Tower, which overlooks the sweeping panorama of rivers, lakes, forests, ravines and high ridges of Adirondack Park from the summit of Blue Mountain, the famous Adirondack Museum, and the Adirondack Lakes Center for the Arts. Accommodations: See listings below under "Lodges & Resorts."

Bolton Landing

(Pop. 1,500; zip code 12814; area code 518), once an exclusive resort for millionaires and still dominated by large estates and manor resorts, is a popular gateway to the spectacular Lake George region. Area attractions include excursion boats, and swimming, fishing and picnic sites in Veterans and Rogers Memorial Park. Area accommodations: *Bonnie View Resort & Motel* (rates: $24–39 double), with 48 excellent rooms and guest cottages on Lake George with heated pool, swimming beach, dock, boats and motors on New York 9N (644–5591); *Melody Manor Resort Motel* (rates: $42–51 double), with 29 superb rooms in a beautiful lakefront location with heated pool, swimming beach and dock on New York 9N (644–9750); *Victorian Village Lodge* (rates: $29–37 double), with 32 excellent rooms and guest cottages, swimming beach, dock, boat rentals on Lake George, south of town on New York 9N (644–9401).

Inlet Village & Ski Touring Center

(Pop. 200; zip code 13360; area code 315) is a major gateway for canoeists, Nordic skiers, hunters, tourists and fishermen heading into

the spectacular lake region of the Central Adirondacks. Nestled on the shore of Fourth Lake, the largest of the Fulton Lake Chain, Inlet also borders the Fifth and Sixth of this lovely strand of lakes. The Inlet Ski Touring Center offers 50 miles of scenic backcountry trails, connecting with Old Forge via the state trail system. The center offers area trail maps and equipment rentals. For information, contact: Inlet Ski Touring Center, South Shore Road (357–3453). Accommodations: see listings below under "Lodges & Resorts."

Jay—Gateway to the High Peaks

(Pop. 2,100; zip code 12941; area code 518). Surrounded by the towering peaks of the northern Adirondacks, is a major gateway for tourists, hikers, backpackers, and skiers heading to Whiteface Mt., Mt. Marcy, Wilmington Mountain and Lake Placid region. Area attractions include the Land of Make Believe, a story book village with steam trains, stagecoaches, and a small zoo, Whiteface Mountain ski area, High Falls Gorge, and Wilmington Notch. Accommodations: *Ark Lodge* (rates: $22 double), with 14 good rooms in nice location on the Au Sable River in Upper Jay, restaurant, coffeeshop, trout fishing, on New York 9N (946–2276); *Swissaire Motelodge* (rates: $26 double), with 27 good rooms, swimming pool next to restaurant, located 4 miles south of the village on New York 9N 12987 (946–2229); *Tirolerland Motel* (rates: $26 double), with 27 good alpine style rooms, restaurant, cocktail lounge, in nice location, just north of town on New York 9N (946–2690).

Lake George

(Pop. 1,000; zip code 12845; area code 518), hugging the southern shore of Lake George in the foothills of the Adirondacks, is a major gateway for tourists, fisherman, boaters, swimmers and hikers approaching the breathtaking Lake George Region. Situated on a valuable portage route between the Hudson River and Lake George, the village was defended throughout the French and Indian Wars by Fort Williams until it was destroyed by the French in 1757 after an Indian massacre. Guided tours of the ruins of Fort Williams are led daily from May-October. Picnic spots and camping sites dot the grassy ruins of Lake George Battlefield State Park. Other attractions include scenic lake cruises and moonlight dance cruises on Lake George operated by the *Lake George Steamboat Company* at Steel Pier, on Beach Road (668–5777), and swimming, boating, and fishing at Lake George Beach State Park. Gore Mountain ski area is within a ten minute drive. Accommodations: *Alpine Village* (rates:

$37 double), with 37 rustic lodge rooms and log cabins in nice setting on Lake George with swimming beach, dock, boat rentals, tennis, 1¼ miles north of the village on New York 9N (668–2193); *Fort William Henry Motel* (rates: $60–65 double), with 64 excellent rooms, restaurant, cocktail lounge, heated pool overlooking the lake on Canada St. (668–3081); *The Georgian* (rates: $63 double), with 100 excellent rooms and family units, dining rooms, cocktail lounge, swimming beach, heated pool, dock, on the lake at 384 Canada St. (668–5401); *Holiday Inn of Lake George* (rates: $65–80 double), with 106 excellent rooms and family units, restaurant, coffeeshop, cocktail lounge, indoor-outdoor heated pools, sauna, ¾ mile south of the village on US Highway 9 and New York 9N (668–5781); *Lake Crest Motel* (rates: $48 double), with 25 excellent rooms and family guest cottages, coffeeshop, heated pool, swimming beach, dock on Lake George at 366 Canada St. (668–3374); *Mohawk Motel & Cottages* (rates: $38–46 double), with 29 excellent rooms and cottages with wood-burning fireplaces, heated pool in central location next to restaurant at 477 Canada St. (668–2143).

Lake Placid

(Pop. 2,700; zip code 12946; area code 518), U.S. headquarters for the 1980 Olympics, is the most popular resort in New York State for skiing, skating, mountain climbing, hiking, swimming, boating, hunting and fishing. Surrounded by the towering peaks of the Northern Adirondacks, including Mt. Marcy, New York State's highest peak, Lake Placid Village borders two lakes, Mirror Lake and Lake Placid. Area attractions include John Brown Farm, home of the famed abolitionist, Mt. Marcy Cross-Country Ski Trails, The Lake Placid Olympic Arena and Convention Hall, Olympic Ski Jump, Whiteface Mountain Alpine Ski Area, Mt. Hoevenberg Olympic Cross-Country Ski area and adjacent Olympic Bobsled and Luge Runs, and scenic lake cruises operated by Holiday Harbor. Accommodations: *Art Devlin's Olympic Motor Inn* (rates: $46 double), with 45 excellent rooms and family units, coffeeshop, heated pool in beautiful location with views of the high peaks at 350 Main St. (523–3700); *Best Western Golden Arrow Motor Inn* (rates: $40–56 double), with 56 excellent rooms in lakeshore setting with restaurant, cocktail lounge, indoor heated pool and sauna, dock and boat rentals at 150 Main St. (523–3353); *Holiday Inn* (rates: $54–65 double), with 131 superb rooms with private balconies in nice location with restaurant, cocktail lounge, indoor/outdoor heated pools and sauna, indoor tennis at 1 Olympic Dr. (523–2556); *Howard Johnson's Motor Lodge* (rates: $38–55 double), with 76 excellent rooms and family units in nice location with restaurant, cocktail lounge, indoor/outdoor heated pools, dock and boat rentals, cross-country ski trails on Saranac Ave. (523–9555); *Lake Placid Hilton* (rates: $58–70 double), with 73 superb rooms in beautiful lakeshore setting with coffeeshop, cocktail lounge, indoor/outdoor heated pools, boat rentals at 1 Mirror Lake Dr. (523–4411); *Town House Motel* (rates: $30–36 double), with 25 excellent rooms and family units in lovely location with heated pool, dock and boat rentals at 40–44 Saranac Ave. (523–2532).

Long Lake

(Pop. 500; zip code 12847; area code 518), nestled on the southern shore of this long narrow lake, welcomes hunters, fishermen, hikers, canoeists and backpackers into the wilderness of the central Adirondacks, surrounded by tiny ponds, clear lakes, rocky islands, and freestone trout streams. Accommodations: *Long Lake Motel* (rates: $20–28 double), with 16 good rooms and family cottages overlooking the lake with dock and fishing on Public Boat Landing Rd. (624–2613); *Long View Lodge* (rates: $23.50–28 double with three meals), situated on beautiful Long Lake with good country

inn rooms and cottages, dining room, sand beach, boats and motors on New York 30/28N (624–2862).

Old Forge Village & Ski Touring Center

(Pop. 950; zip code 13420; area code 315) is the major gateway for hunters, canoeists, fishermen, backpackers, and cross-country skiers approaching the Fulton and Raquette Lake regions. Lake cruises begin here for the Fulton Lake chain, and canoe trips, day, overnight and weekly, extend as far as 125 miles to the town of Paul Smiths, north of Saranac Lakes. Old Forge Ski area operates from December through March as an alpine ski area with skating rink, and carries sightseers to the summit for unparalleled views of this mountainous lake region in the summer. The Old Forge area offers 12 miles of marked and maintained ski-touring trails. For information, contact: Central Adirondacks Assn. at Old Forge (369–6983). Other area attractions include public beaches for swimming, and the annual State Fiddlers Contest in June, held in Enchanted Forest Park, an amusement park based on fairytale themes. Accommodations: *Blue Spruce Motel* (rates: $24–26 double), with 12 good rooms and heated pool next to restaurant on Main St. and New York 28 (369–3817); *The Forge Motel* (rates: $29 double), with 61 excellent rooms in nice lakefront location next to restaurant with heated pool on New York 28, 2¼ miles southwest of town (369–3313).

Plattsburgh—Gateway to Lake Champlain

(Pop. 23,000; zip code 12901; area code 518), dominating the shore of Lake Champlain at the mouth of the Saranac River, is a major gateway for tourists, boaters, hikers, hunters, and fishermen approaching the spectacular Lake Champlain region. Rich in history, Plattsburgh played a key role in land and naval battles between the Americans and the British in the Revolutionary War and the War of 1812. The Macdonough Memorial and the Kent-Delord House Museum commemorate these events. The Alice T. Miner Colonial Collection of antiques and authentic household items of the Colonial period is housed in a restored homestead in Plattsburgh, dating from 1824. Other area attractions include cruises on Lake Champlain; boating, fishing, and camping on Lake Champlain is available at Ausable Beach. Accommodations: *Holiday Inn* (rates: $42 double), with 102 excellent rooms, restaurant, cocktail lounge, heated pool located one mile west of town on New York 3 at junction of Northway exit 37 (561–5000); *Howard Johnson's Motor Lodge* (rates: $40 double), with 96 excellent rooms, restaurant, coffeeshop, cocktail lounge, indoor heated pool and sauna, located one mile west of town on New York 3 at junction of Northway exit 37 (561–7750).

Saranac Lake

(Pop. 6,000; zip code 12983; area code 518). The ideal climate and the clear air of Saranac Lake once made it a world famous restorative health resort. Today it is a major gateway into the breathtaking Adirondack region and its largest resort community. Area attractions include the Mt. Pisgah Ski Center, beach swimming on Lake Colby, and the Robert Louis Stevenson Memorial Cottage. The annual winter carnival is in February. Accommodations (see "Wawbeek Inn" below): *Burke's Lake Flower Motel* (rates $34 double), with 14 excellent rooms, heated pool, boat rentals at 143 Lake Flower Ave. (891–2310).

Schroon Lake

(Pop. 3,000; zip code 12870; area code 518), a small resort town hugging the shores of the lovely Schroon Lake, is a major gateway for canoeists, fishermen, hikers, backpackers and hunters with 70 lakes within its five-mile radius. Area attractions include daily lake cruises, beach swimming, and scenic Eagle Point. Accommodations: *Frontier Town Motel* (rates: $28–34 double), with 28 good rooms, restaurant, swimming area, at Frontier Town—an early pioneer outpost and fort with replicas of an old iron mine, stagecoach museum, etc.—located 8 miles north of town on Interstate 87 at exit 29 (532–7660); *Woods Lodge* (rates: $35 double), with 26 good rooms and family cottages on lake with sand swimming beach, boat rentals, tennis on East St. (532–7529).

Ticonderoga

(Pop. 3,300; zip code 12883; area code 518), a resort town whose Indian name means "where the waters meet," dominates a narrow strip of land between Lake George and Lake Champlain. With a long history of battle between the Indians, French, Canadians, British and American colonists, Ticonderoga now commands a peaceful view of the spectacular mountains and dense forests of the Lake region, and has become a major gateway for tourists, hikers, hunters, backpackers and fishermen. Area attractions include Fort Ticonderoga with a historical museum (585–2821), guided tours and daily exhibitions of cannon shooting, fife-playing, and drum rolling, and a ferry, which operates daily across Lake Champlain to Shoreham, Vermont. Campsites are available at Putnam Pond Campsite in Adirondack Park. Accommodations: *Burgoyne Motel* (rates: $26 double), with 36 good rooms and family units, swimming pool located one mile north of town on New York 74/22 (585–7353).

Tupper Lake

(Pop. 4,850; zip code 12986; area code 518) is the gateway for fishermen, hunters, canoeists, hikers, and skiers, heading into the densely wooded lake region of the northern Adirondacks. Area attractions include the Big Tupper Ski area, a sightseeing lift in the summer months, and Lake Tupper Country Club, with an 18–hole golf course. Little Wolf beach area is open for swimming, and the Fish Creek Pond Campsite in Adirondack Park provides camping, boating, picnicking, and swimming areas. Accommodations: *Shaheen's Motel* (rates: $26–28 double), with 35 excellent rooms, heated pool, next to restaurant at 310 Park St. on New York 3/30 (359–3384); *Tupper Lake Motel* (rates: $24–28 double), with 18 good rooms, heated pool, at 259 Park St. on New York 3/30 (359–3381).

Wilmington—Gateway to the Au Sable & High Peaks

(Pop. 500; zip code 12997; area code 518), a small resort town nestled below the towering face of Whiteface Mountain, is a major gateway for alpine and cross-country skiers, hikers, backpackers, and fishermen heading into the Whiteface Mountain Recreation area. Here the Whiteface Memorial Highway climbs near the summit, providing unparalleled views of northern New York State. Area attractions include the Whiteface Mountain Alpine Ski Area (946–2223), open from December through March, and the breath-taking High Falls Gorge. Accommodations: *High Valley Motel* (rates: $24–26 double), with 20 excellent guest rooms, heated pool, dock, and boat rentals in scenic location one mile southwest of town on New York 86 (946–2355); *Holiday Lodge at North Pole* (rates: $25–38 double), with 29 attractive rooms with private balconies overlooking Whiteface Mountain and restaurant, cocktail lounge, heated pool in center of town at the junction of New York 86 and 431 (946–2251); *Hungry Trout Motel* (rates: $33–42 double), on Au Sable River with 20 excellent rooms and family units with scenic mountain views, restaurant, trout fishing, swimming pool, located two miles southwest of town on New York 86 (946–2217); *Landmark Motor Lodge* (rates: $34–38 double), with 24 excellent rooms, restaurant, coffeeshop, fishing information, special weekly Au Sable fishing and ski plans, just west of town at the junction of New York 86 and 431 (946–2247); *Ledge Rock Motel* (rates: $36–40 double), with 18 excellent rooms in beautiful alpine location, heated pool, trout fishing, ski season packages, across from restaurant, located opposite the Whiteface Mountain Ski Center, on Placid Rd. and N.Y. 86 (946–2302).

Lodges & Resorts

★★★★*Adirondack Mountain Club Lodges in the High Peaks* are connected by the scenic Klondike trail which requires a one-way trek of approximately four hours. The club is a membership organization for conservation, recreation and education, but non-members are welcome to stay at the lodge and use the facilities.

The Adirondak Loj is located eight miles south of Lake Placid at an elevation of 2,178 feet, situated at the point where the trails begin to the Adirondack High Peaks wilderness area, and is on the historic site of the Henry Van Hoevenberg original log hotel. The Loj has four rooms with twin beds, four larger bunk rooms for families or groups of women and a large bunkroom for men. In the Loj is the dining room where Chef Brad serves family-style meals with homemade bread, soups and desserts. After dinner, guests can enjoy the lounge with a fireplace and a small library. There is also a campground with 40 campsites and a dozen lean-tos open year 'round. Sites for trailers and campers are usually inaccessible in the snow, but the lean-tos and campsites are open for winter camping. For day-hikers and campers just passing through, the Campers and Hikers Building has a large public room, hot showers and laundry facilities. A trading post in the building carries camping and skiing supplies, snacks and publications and dispenses hot stews and soups. Parking for persons entering the mountains is available for $1 a day per car or $5 per week. Parking for guests at the Loj or Campgrounds is free. For guests at the Adirondak Loj not planning to take the Klondike Trail, there are many other activities and facilities. Cross-country ski trails and snowshoe trails of various lengths and degrees of difficulty wind through the Loj property and onto the adjoining state land. There are no fees for using these ADK trails and complimentary ski trail maps are available. There are also free mid-week ski lessons and guided gourmet ski tours into the High Peaks for Loj guests. And the Whiteface Mountain downhill ski area, one of the East's greatest vertical drops, is just a short drive away. Many of the 46 major peaks with elevations of 4000 feet or over are within easy reach of both the AMC lodges. Rates at the Adirondak Loj for a bunk with three meals is $21 and a double room with meals is $25. A bunk without meals is $7.75. There are also special meal rates, mid-week packages and member rates. At the campgrounds, lean-tos are $3.25 per person with a minimum charge of $5 a day and a maximum of $14 a day. Campsites per day are $3 for one person, $4 for two and 50¢ for each additional person up to six. For reservations, contact John Stacey or Brad Streeter at: Adirondak Loj, Box 867, Lake Placid NY 12946 (518)523–3441.

Johns Brook Lodge is 3½ miles up the Klondike Trail at an elevation of 2,315 feet. It is accessible only on foot via a network of hiking, snowshoeing and cross-country skiing trails. The Main Lodge is open only during July and August. Camps and lean-tos are used in the winter months. Winter Camp has two rooms with six bunks and a wood stove in one room; and six bunks, a heating stove, dining table, gas stove-top burners and cooking equipment in the main room. Grace Camp has one room, equipped like the Winter Camp main room. Campers must supply their own winter-weight sleeping bags and all food and supplies, since there are none at the Johns Brook Lodge. Crandall, Goodwin and Myers lean-tos sleep six adults each. No camping other than in the lean-tos is permitted on the property, and outdoor fires can be made only in lean-to fireplaces. Winter Camp daily rates are $2.50 for non-club-members and $2.00 for members with a minimum of $10 per day. Grace Camp rates are the same with a $7.50 minimum. The lean-tos are $1 for non-members and 75¢ for members with a minimum of 4 a day. Rooms in the main lodge in the summer are $12 and $13 per day. For reservations write: Johns Brook Lodge, R.F.D., Keene Valley, NY 12943 or call Mrs. Ronald Dubay at (518)576–9833 between 6:30–7:30 a.m. or 6:00–9:00 p.m.

Information on membership, all lodge facilities, and the Adirondack High Peaks area can be obtained from the Adirondack Mountain Club, 172 Ridge St., Glens Falls, NY 12801 (518)793–7737.

★★★*Bark Eater Lodge & Cross-Country Ski Center* is secluded on a small farm in the heart of the Adirondack Mountains. Skis are available for rent at the Ski Center, and lessons, guided picnic tours, and moonlight tours can be arranged. Trails surround the center, and the more adventurous can take off and explore the miles of untracked wilderness surrounding the Bark Eater. Mt. Van Hoevenberg Olympic Cross-Country Ski Area is only minutes away, and offers adjacent bobsled and luge runs. Within a 20 minute drive is the Whiteface Mt. Alpine Ski Area, Mt. Marcy Cross-Country Trails, and Lake Placid, headquarters of the 1980 Winter Olympics. From the Coronation of the King and Queen of Winter in December until the Indoor Speed Skating Championships in late March, Lake

Placid offers a complete ongoing schedule of championship events, ski races, world-cup giant slalom races, bobsled races, cross-country ski races, and international hockey tournaments. All of this can be enjoyed along with quiet country living, home-cooked meals, and a roaring fire at the Bark Eater. Rates are $32 for a double room including abundant country-style breakfasts, and $12 per child under 12. The Bark Eater Lodge also offers a special five-day rate including lodging and meals from Saturday evening till lunch on Friday for $160 a couple. For more information call (518)576–2221), or write, The Bark Eater, Alstead Mill Road, Keene, NY 12942.

★★★*Beckers Resort on the Fulton Chain of Lakes* is a family-owned resort, hugging the shores of the beautiful Fourth Lake. Open year-round, Beckers offers boating, fishing, swimming, shuffleboard, tennis, volleyball, and complete seaplane service in the summer. Daily nature hikes, trips to the Adirondack Museum, and mountain

climbs are part of the family atmosphere of Beckers Resort. The resort is open in the fall when the brilliant colors are reflected in the lake and hunting season begins, and throughout the winter, when cross-country skiers seek the serenity of the fields and woods. Beckers has 21 cottages, with 1–6 bedrooms, accommodating 4–11 persons. All have completely equipped modern kitchens, and there are many cottages with fireplaces. Rates range between $35–70 daily, depending on the size of the cottage and the number of people reserving it, and $210–385 weekly. There are modern motel units, with electric heat and private baths available for $35 daily single occupancy, to $50 daily for four. The hotel has 15 rooms which are available for $25–40 daily with private bath, and $20–40 daily with running water and shared bath. After Labor Day a new hotel with 100 luxurious rooms, an indoor swimming pool, jacuzzi, saunas, steam rooms, a massage room and an exercise gym will replace the hotel. The new hotel will have banquet rooms to seat 400, a large restaurant and cocktail lounge, gift shops, sports shops, and game rooms. Many of the deluxe rooms will have fireplaces, and there will be plush condominiums available on the top floor. The new hotel is scheduled to open July 1, 1980. For more information write: Beckers Resort, Fourth Lake, Old Forge, New York 13420 (315)357–4251).

★★★*Canoe Island Lodge on Lake George* in the Adirondack Mountains has an added plus of Canoe Island, just ¾ mile off the Main Lodge's shore. You can paddle a canoe or go via the lodge's Chris Craft. A five-acre, woodsy haven, Canoe Island has a sand beach and swimming, sailing and boating. Weekly Bar-B-Ques and twilight songfests have become popular activities at the island. There is mainland swimming from sand beaches and sheltered coves. The lodge has three sailboats for guest use, plus powerboats, rowboats, canoes and water-skiing in the morning and afternoon. There are two outdoor tennis courts surrounded by pines and oaks and one all weather court. Activities, including dances and movies, are planned Monday through Saturday. The resort's alpine architecture blends into the beautiful mountain setting of Lake George and maintains a relaxed outdoor-activity atmosphere. Cottages, cabins and suites in the Main Lodge all feature a rustic charm, while providing modern conveniences. Dining is in a cozy dining room, complete with fireplace and rich wood paneling. The resort operates on the modified American plan, and rates include all lodge activities. Rates: daily $30–46 per person, double occupancy. Weekly $189–285 per person double occupancy. Before June 30 and after Sept. 5 weekday rates are 10% less for all rooms. Children's rates are available. For further information contact: Canoe Island Lodge, P.O. Diamond Point, N.Y. 12824 (518)668–5592.

★★★*Covewood Lodge on Big Moose Lake* is a rustic, hand-built inn made of native wood and stone collected from the surrounding forests and fields. The lodge accommodates 100 guests in hotel rooms and apartments, some with glassed-in porches overlooking the lake, and the surrounding 1,300 acre wildlife sanctuary. Deluxe cottages face the lake, and have large living rooms, fireplaces, 1–4 bedrooms, and furnace heat. Smaller cottages accommodate one to three persons. Many new cottages have been built on Buzz Point, and guests cross the Moose River by footbridge to reach the lodge. In the summer, the clear waters of Big Moose Lake are ideal for fishing, swimming and waterskiing. Rowboats and sailboats are available at the dock. There are tennis courts, badminton nets, shuffleboard courts, and horseshoe pits on the open lawns. A jogging trail leads away from the cottages into the woods. Two experienced counselors supervise the children's program, planning games, trips, crafts, and picnics for different age groups. There is a sandy children's beach, a large playroom, and a supervised children's dining room. Handsome fireplaces built by hand dominate the rustic wood paneled living

room and dining room in the main inn, and panoramic windows overlook the lake. The inn also has a library, and a TV room. Because of the spectacular fall foliage, and the popularity of cross-country skiing, Covewood has winterized eleven of its cottages. The dining room is not open in these seasons, but there are many fine restaurants nearby. The spectacular beauty of the crimson hills reflected in the still lake waters and the hushed woods in winter make these seasons at Covewood unforgettable. For details, write: Covewood Lodge, Big Moose, NY 13331 (315)357–9744.

★★★*Geandreau's at Indian Lake* is located on the east edge of the village, adjacent to Lake Adirondack and nestled within the main ridges which form the Adirondack Mountains. The elevation is nearly 1,800 feet above sea level. The bodies of water in the area are numerous—six rivers, nine lakes, 65 ponds, and over 150 streams. Brown, brook, rainbow and lake trout, northern pike, bass, whitefish are found in these waters. Four of the highest mountains are south of Mt. Marcy. White-tailed deer, black bear, raccoon, fox, fisher, beaver, coyotes, rabbits, grouse and partridge inhabit the evergreen and hardwood forests. There are public swimming beaches, tennis courts and hiking trails. Ski centers are within a 20–minute drive, as well as an ice-skating rink, snowmobile trails, and cross-country ski trails in the immediate area. Two golf courses are within five minutes, the famous Adirondack Museum is 11 miles away and the Enchanted Forest, Storytown, and Frontier Town are nearby. Accommodations are in fully-carpeted, one-and-two bedroom house-keeping cabins open year round. They have hot water, electric or gas ranges, refrigerators, screened porches and private bathrooms. All linens, towels, blankets, dishes, cooking utensils, etc. are provided. Rowboats, canoes and cross-country ski equipment and instructions and a New York State licensed guide are available. The camp has playgrounds, picnic areas, safe forest trails—and indoors a lounge with TV and cardtables. Well behaved pets are welcome. Cabins range from $16–20 per person per night or $150–170 per week. Contact Dot & Bob Geandreau, (516)648–550 or write to them c/o Geandreau's, Box 408, Rt 28 East, Indian Lake, NY 12842.

★★★★*The Hedges on Blue Mountain Lake* in the Adirondack Mountains is a tranquil setting for outdoor relaxation and recreation. A 60–foot sand beach with boat dock and sun chairs provides safe, shallow swimming for children and deep water swimming off the dock for adults. The beauty of the lake can be further appreciated with a canoe, provided by the Hedges. Sailboats and powerboats are available at the town livery. The lake offers excellent fishing for lake trout, smallmouth bass, and rainbow trout. On shore, there's hiking and cross-country skiing along the scenic marked trails in Adirondack Park. A clay tennis court and volleyball and badminton facilities are on the Hedges grounds. Two 9–hole golf courses, a riding stable, plus a new bicycle path along the winding mountain roads are nearby features. Breakfast and dinner are served family-style daily at the Hedges, and each meal is simple and solid. Log cabins with all the modern comforts or lodging in one of the three lodges is available. The cottages and lodges are furnished with simple antiques in keeping with the unpretentious, relaxed family-oriented atmosphere of the resort. The resort operates on the modified American plan with its summer season from May 25 to Oct. 8. Rates: daily, $24–33 per person double occupancy. Weekly, $155–222 per person double occupancy. For off-season rates deduct 10%. Children's rates available. For further information contact: The Hedges, Blue Mountain Lake, NY 12812 (518)352–7325.

★★★*Hemlock Hall on Blue Mountain Lake*, surrounded by a mountain wilderness, opens for spring fishing in May, and stays open through the long days of summer until the brilliant days and cool nights in October. There are over 60 miles of hiking trails throughout the adjacent forest preserve lands. Rushing streams and remote lakes afford excellent fishing, and Hemlock Hall has many sailboats, canoes and rowboats for guest use at no extra charge. There is a diving float and sandy beach for swimmers and sunbathers. In addition, there is a recreation room offering ping-pong, and badminton on the lawns. The walls of the living room are lined with books for guest use. In addition to the lodge, there are heated one-and-two-room cottages, nestled on the wooded slope overlooking the lake. Rooms in the lodge include large country breakfasts, and family-style dinners, and are $50 per couple in a twin-bedded room, and $48 per couple in a room with a double bed. Rates for double rooms with running water and shared bath are $44 per couple with twin beds, and $42 per couple for a room with a double bed. The lodge also has special two-room suites, with private porch, for $54 per couple. Cottage rates are $54. Each additional person in any accommodation is $16. For more information write: Mr. and Mrs. L.R. Webb, Blue Mountain Lake, NY 12812 (518)352–7706.

★★*Hidden Valley* is located in the rolling Adirondack Mountains on Lake Vanare, between Lake George and Lake Luzerne. The resort has an Old West flavor maintained in the log cabin buildings and the wrangler guides who will take you along trails for gentle horse-back riding. Riding instruction is available and there is winter riding on specially shod horses. Warm weather activities include pool or lake swimming, relaxing on the sand beach, boating and canoeing. Fishing is good at Lake Vanare, and many guests head for Lake George's waters. Warm weather also brings picnics in the spring and autumn, golf at nearby courses, three tennis courts, badminton, archery, shuffleboard, billiards, bicycling, surrey rides and specially planned activities. In the winter Hidden Valley offers on-premises skiing, with a double chair lift. The ski school at the resort provides instruction for beginners. Nearby Gore Mountain and West Mountain have facilities for advanced skiers. There is also a lighted skating rink, 100 miles of snowmobile trails and old-fashioned sleigh rides. Meals served in Hidden Valley Frontier Room reflect the western ambience. Specialties include western-grilled steaks, fresh fish, and roast duckling. The '49er cocktail lounge serves drinks and features live entertainment. The resort has 250 guest rooms in its modern log cabin-style lodge. Rates: European plan, daily $38–62. Special ski and escape package available. For further information contact: Hidden Valley Ranch Resort, Lake Luzerne, N.Y. 12846 (518)696–2431.

★★★★*Holl's Inn on the Fulton Chain*, a spacious lakeside resort, dominates 2,000 feet of private lakeshore on the clear Fourth Lake. The inn offers spacious hotel rooms with lake views on the upper two floors of the main inn, and ground floor rooms in the annex, which is connected to the inn by a covered walkway. You can swim on the sandy beach right outside your room, and sailing, waterskiing, and seaplane rides are available at the dock. Tennis courts, badminton and volleyball nets, and shuffleboard courts dot the sprawling lawns of the 150–acre estate. A nine-hole golf course is only a mile away, and two 18–hole championship golf courses are within easy distance. Forty-six of the nearby mountain peaks are over 4,000 feet high, and offer panoramic views of the surrounding countryside. The spacious lobby of the inn, with its exposed beam ceilings and open hearth, is a quiet place to relax. The glassed-in porch looks over the sparkling lake to the surrounding mountains. Outdoor bar-b-ques are popular on sunny afternoons, and the spacious, glassed-in dining room overlooking the lake offers excellent meals in a spectacular setting. The mini-cinema provides nightly entertainment, with feature length pictures. The Holl's Inn season is only during July and August. Rooms in the main lodge offer one to four beds, with picture windows and private bath. Rates range between $23–48

daily, depending on the size of the room and the number of people sharing it. Weekly rates are between $155–305. Annex rooms range between $29–46 daily and $166–331 weekly. All rates include meals; picnic lunches are packed for daily outings. Mid-week and weekend specials are available. For more information write: Holl's Inn, Inlet, NY 13360 (call pre-season, before July and August (315)733–2748; in season: (315)257–2941).

**★★*Knowlhurst Lodge* is a family operated inn in the Adirondack State Park in New York near Stony Creek. Eight hundred acres of private forest and open land have been set aside for hiking, fishing, hunting, and cross-country ski touring. Trails start at the door and provide direct access to state lands. The mixture of forest and open land, creeks, lakes and ponds results in excellent deer, bird and waterfowl hunting and trout fishing. There's swimming in forest lakes and ponds. There is also a skating rink and a library. This rustic inn has three bedrooms with two single or one double bed each and one bedroom with three double beds. Weekends begin on Friday with dinner being served. A full-course dinner is served on Saturday night plus breakfast and box lunches on both Saturday and Sunday. Rates including meals are $20 to $22 per day per adults, $10 to $12 per day for children under 12 in rooms with parents. Weekly and holiday arrangements for groups are available. Contact Henry Maag, P.O. Box 95, Castleton on Hudson, New York 12033. Monday through Friday (518)732–7994; weekends (518)696–3335.

**★★★★*Lake Placid Club Resort* is located in the shadow of the majestic Whiteface Mountain on the east shore of Mirror Lake across from the village of Lake Placid. Founded by Melvil Dewey, who invented the Dewey Decimal System, Lake Placid Resort Hotel has been a favorite vacation site since 1895. The largest complex in the Adirondacks, the hotel incorporates many modern facilities while retaining its luxury-in-the-wilderness heritage. At Lake Placid, there are the world renowned Olympic bobsled run and the Olympic Arena for skating and hockey. The hotel has its own mountain, Mt. Whitney, with day/night skiing. There are two high speed T-Bars and six well-groomed slopes from beginner to expert. A ski lodge with a fireside lounge features food and bar service and a sun-deck facing the slopes. Mt. Marcy, with its own seven miles of cross-county ski trails and the touring system at Adirondak Loj are not far away. There are thirty miles of patrolled trails and frozen lakes surrounding the hotel for snowmobiling, and the Toboggan Chute provides a high speed slide down and then out across frozen Mirror Lake. There's a large outdoor skating rink adjacent to the main hotel building and the nearby Olympic Arena where private lessons can be taken. The hotel has two regulation platform paddle tennis courts and two indoor squash courts. Summer facilities include two 18–hole championship golf courses, a 9–hole course for the beginner, putting greens and a practice range. There are 14 tennis courts including eight clay courts. For horseback riders, there are 40 miles of scenic trails. The hotel's Intervales Gun Club has five skeet and four trap fields for shooters. Mirror Lake offers fine swimming and sailing, and Lake Placid offers power boating, water skiing and scenic cruises. Both lakes are well-stocked for fishing; the famous Au Sable River is only a short trip from the hotel. There are also many small ponds and streams nearby. The hotel has its own outdoor heated swimming pool, and the 1,000 richly wooded acres provide excellent opportunities for hikers, bird-watchers and photographers. The hotel operates a Summer Day Camp for children in grades one through six and babysitting services are available. The hotel offers a varied program of social activities for the different seasons. There are costume parties, feature motion pictures, dancing and dance exhibitions, poolside luncheons, bridge parties and the Forest Library of some 12,000 volumes. There are a variety of outstanding shops on the premises and a wide range of accommodations—suites, single and double rooms—within the central clubhouse and in a variety of adjacent cottages. The spacious dining rooms permit uncrowded, informal table arrangements. There are several lounges and public rooms. For rates and more information, contact Lake Placid Club Resort, Lake Placid, NY 12946 toll free in NY (800)342–9501; other areas (518)523–3361.

**★★★*Mirror Lake Inn* is situated on scenic Mirror Lake, only minutes away from Whiteface Mountain and Lake Placid. A year-round resort, Mirror Lake offers swimming, boating, tennis, indoor ice skating and an indoor health spa with sauna, hydrotherapy whirlpool and exercise room, on seven acres of grounds. In the winter, there's a downhill skiing on Whiteface Mountain and cross-country skiing on the Mt. Van Hoevenberg Olympic Cross-Country trails. Tobogganing, bobsledding, dogsled rides, figure skating and snow-mobiling are all available at Lake Placid, only minutes away. There are packages for both downhill and cross-country skiing, including lessons, lift tickets, films and technical clinics, wine and cheese parties and food and lodging. A gourmet menu has over 23 entrees to choose from and there is a special children's menu. Rooms range from cozy bedrooms to lakeview terrace rooms with breathtaking views of the Adirondack high peaks. All rooms have television and fireplaces. Rates range from $50 to $76 per day for two people, including breakfast and dinner daily through the summer, Christmas and New Year's and February. From November 1 through December 15 and from March 19 through June 1, rates range from $46 to $58 per person, double occupancy, Modified American Plan. During the rest of the year, rates go from $48 to $66 per person, double occupancy, Modified American Plan. Special packages are available. For more information and reservations, contact Mirror Lake Inn, Lake Placid, NY 12946 (518)523–2544.

**★★★*The Mohawk Inn on the Fulton Chain of Lakes* was built on the shores of the spectacular Fourth Lake in the Adirondacks in 1896. This picturesque inn offers spacious lodge rooms and rustic guest cottages, swimming, fishing and water sports on the lake, and delicious home cooking with warm hospitality. In the winter, a crackling fire awaits cross-country skiers and ice skaters, and downhill skiers returning from nearby McCauley Mountain Ski Center. Private boat docking facilities are available for guests, and Mohawk Inn also has 1,400 feet of sand beach for swimming, an 18–hole putting green and all-weather courts for the tennis buff. Shuffleboard courts, volleyball and badminton nets dot the open lawns and there is also a game room featuring pool tables, ping-pong, and electronic games. Movies and dancing are enjoyed by all in the evenings. Children will find a full schedule of activities awaiting them in the summer months, including arts and crafts, hikes, waterfront events, indoor and outdoor games, and visits to nearby attractions. Each Sunday there is a sumptuous buffet with free champagne served in the pleasant dining room. Single inn rooms with shared bath are $14 daily and $91 weekly; with private bath, single room rates are $20 daily and $130 weekly. Double room rates are $31 daily and $201 weekly. One-bedroom cottages with private bath are $33 daily and $214 weekly. With kitchens, fireplaces and living room; rates vary, depending on the size of the cottage and the number of people sharing it, from $53–66 daily and $334–429 weekly. Two-bedroom cottages with private bath, living room/dining area with fireplace are $54–77 daily, and $301–500 weekly. Three-bedroom cottages with living/room dining area, fireplace, and private bath are $77–83 daily and $500–539 weekly. Many three-bedroom cottages are two story. For details write: The Mohawk Inn, Fourth Lake, Old Forge, NY 13420 (315)357–2401, or 2491.

★★★*Paleface Lodge & Ski Center*, located in the Whitehorn Mountains, is only 15 miles from Lake Placid, site of the 1980 Winter Olympics. Lots of snow and varied terrain on Paleface and nearby slopes make this a fine skiing area. Paleface has 16 slopes for beginners to experts. Numerous wide trails, a 730–foot vertical drop, top elevation of 1,750 feet and a chair lift 200 feet from the door are some of the resort's downhill ski features. The resort has 15 miles of evergreen forest cross-country skiing trails, starting right across from the lodge. Snowmobiling also starts at the lodge's door. Rentals and lessons are available. The lodge is five miles from Whiteface Mountain and 17 miles from Mt. Van Hoevenberg, the only bobsled run in North America. Guests can take advantage of the lodge's indoor heated swimming pool, sundeck, game room and fireplace lounge facilities. Movies, dance bands and other live entertainment are also provided free of charge. The lodge operates on the European plan, but provides breakfast, lunch and dinner in the dining room. All of the 16 overnight rooms are in the A-frame style main lodge, along with a courteous staff and relaxed, family-oriented atmosphere. Rates: weekends and holidays, $28 per couple; weekdays $24 per couple. Ski rates, adults $5–8. Season passes range from $120–180. Group lessons $5, one-hour private lesson $12. Junior and special group rates available. For further information contact: Paleface Lodge and Ski Center, Route 86, Jay, NY 12941 (518)946–2272.

★★★*Placid Manor at Lake Placid* was chosen by ABC Sports as the headquarters for the 1980 Olympics. It offers continental charm that's not to be found elsewhere in this area. Its lakefront location overlooks Whiteface Mountain and the 16 miles of lakefront property offer access to the lake, with a private beach, sundecks, a large swimming area, waterskiing, tennis on the four courts, free canoeing, fishing boats, paddle floats, and water bicycles; motor boats are available at low rates. An 18–hole golf course with clubhouse and snack bar has modest rates. The main house offers a cocktail lounge, music, cards, TV, and a lakefront coffeeshop serves up delicious breakfasts. Rooms are offered in the main house and cottages, many with terraces, balconies, and porches. Rates are from $28 to $56 per person for two persons, European plan in July and August. Before July and after Labor Day, rates are $24 to $36. Contact: Ted or Mae Frankel, Lake Placid, NY 12946 (518)523–2573. The winter address is 2774 South Ocean Blvd., Palm Beach, FL 33480.

★★★★*The Potter Camp at Blue Mountain Lake* is a cozy summer resort situated in the Adirondack Mountains. Blue Mountain Lake is on a plateau 1,800 feet above sea level, completely encircled by mountains. Blue Mountain towers 3,800 above sea level, dominating the scene. A trail leads up for three miles to the summit of the mountain for a view of this beautiful area. Miles and miles of lakes and mountain trails extend in all directions. Bathing in the area is considered especially safe. Boats and canoes are available. There is lake trout, brook trout and smallmouth bass fishing in the lake and streams. Potter has a new tennis court and is near several golf links. The cabins are situated on the resort's grounds to provide ample space for privacy, with several located on the beach and others scattered among trees on a hill for an excellent view of the lake. Cabins range from a one-bedroom with bath and shower, for two, to a three bedroom cabin with a large living room and fireplace, 1½ baths with shower and a kitchenette, for eight. Meals, all of which are supervised by a dietitian, are served in the main lodge, a Swiss chalet type of building. Cabins may be rented overnight, weekly, monthly or for a season. American or European plans and housekeeping cottages are available. Rates: Lakeshore cottages for two, double occupancy: $240 weekly, $40 daily. Lakeview units for two, double occupancy: $150–156 weekly, $25–26 daily. Housekeeping cottages with accommodations for three to eight range from $175–365 weekly. Meals are not included in housekeeping cottage rates. For further information contact: The Potter Camp, Inc., Blue Mountain Lake, N.Y. 12812 (518)352–7331.

★★★★*Roaring Brook Ranch & Tennis Resort*, located two miles away from Lake George, is a modern resort-ranch surrounded by trees and the Adirondacks. Horses and wranglers are transported annually from Montana to assure the best available facilities. Rides are given in groups, according to experience, with the accompaniment of a Montana wrangler. Riding instructions are free, and beginners are welcome. Bridle trails cover wide, cool, scenic woodlands of the Adirondacks. There are five all-weather double tennis courts on the resort's grounds with a resident tennis pro on hand. The area offers some of the best skiing in New York at nearby Gore Mountain Ski Center and West Mountain, plus miles of beautiful snowmobile trails. Three swimming pools, outdoor and indoors are on the resort's grounds plus two Finnish saunas. Children are given special attention from trained counselors in a regularly conducted program at the ranch. Nightly entertainment, dancing and a poolside bar cater to the adults. Accommodations are comfortable and pleasant motel-type units with about ten rooms per unit. They have been recently renovated and are spacious and nicely furnished with private baths and wall to wall carpeting. Rooms are available in three types, with all heated and types two and three with air-conditioning. The resort operates on the modified American plan, including breakfast and dinner in the room rate. There is a dining room and coffee shop with moderately priced lunches. Rates: Type 1 rooms: $25–39 per person nightly. Type 2: $27–41 per person nightly. Type 3: $13–45. Weekly discounts and special children rates are available. For further information contact: Roaring Brook Ranch and Tennis Resort, Lake George, NY 12845 (518)668–5767.

★*Roberts' Four Season Cottages & Lodge* is right on the shore of Fourth Lake in the beautiful Old Forge area of the Adirondack Mountains. In the winter, it is the number one snowmobile area of the northeast, with well-maintained trails surrounding the camp. The location is near the Moose River Recreation Area, and of course, snowmobiling on the lake itself, which is seven miles long, provides plenty of space for racing in safety. You can also try ski-joring—skiing behind a snowmobile. In the summer, there is swimming, fishing, hiking and boating (dock available for your own

boat). There is a golf course nearby, and Bald Mountain or McCauley Mountain to climb, as well as the Enchanted Forest and the Blue Mountain Museum to visit. Summer season is June-September. There are six housekeeping cottages available—sleeping 4–10 people—and ranging from $140–330 per week (blankets are furnished, but no linen). Rooms at the lodge, double occupancy, range from $16–20 per day (linens, towels and coffee provided). Winter season December-April—there are four cottages available, sleeping from 6–12 persons and ranging from $7–12 per person per night. Rooms at the lodge range from $7–11 per person per night. Rates are reduced for spring and fall. Group rates on request. Contact Roberts' Four Season Cottages and Lodge, Fourth Lake, Old Forge, NY 13420 (315)369–6779 or 337–1314.

★★★*Rocky Point Inn on the Fulton Chain* is in the central Adirondack region located deep in the heart of mountain wilderness. To the north and south of the inn are miles of virtually untouched forest land. This family vacation resort offers deluxe lakeside cottages and spacious rooms at the main inn, all with lovely views of water and surrounding mountain ranges. There is swimming and sunbathing on 300 yards of natural sand beach and almost a mile of boardwalk for long leisurely strolls. Other outdoor activities include fishing, mountain climbing, hikes, and horseback riding. There are five all weather tennis courts and two nearby golf courses. The kids can be dropped off with the children's hostesses who supervise and entertain them on the beach, on hikes and with games, cookouts and picnics. This service is free of charge, and after dinner there's story hour or a movie. Indoor recreation can be enjoyed in the gymnasium, on the volleyball courts or at the ping-pong tables. Late breakfast and the two other daily meals are served in the dining room which overlooks the lake through sliding glass window-walls. A separate dining room is available for children. The inn is open all year round. Winter activities include skiing, snowmobiles, and skating. Rooms at the inn based on daily rates per room start at $30 for double occupancy. Rates for the lakeside cottages start at $39, also based on double occupancy. Special midweek and group rates are available. The dress is casual except for dinner when gentlemen are required to wear a jacket or cardigan sweater. Reservations and further information can be obtained by writing Rocky Point Inn, P.O. 447, Inlet, NY 13360 (315)357–3751.

★★★★*Timberlock on Indian Lake* is a superb Adirondack forest resort. Its position on Indian Lake offers a magnificent lake and mountain setting. Rustic cabins are scattered along a half mile of the lake's front, which stretches in its entirety 15 miles and has 88 miles of shoreline. The 5–million acre area of the Adirondack Forest Preserve surrounds the resort, providing a spectacular combination of wilderness mountains, lakes and rivers. Indian Lake, which is ringed with mountains, and the resort's 1,700 foot altitude make it a perfect get-away for family vacationers. The resort has no preplanned programs, other than meal hours, and guests are free to take advantage of the activities or just relax in the tranquil, beautiful setting. There are three well-maintained red-clay tennis courts and an 18–hole golf course; two nine-hole courses are nearby. Guided horseback rides on woodland trails are conducted several times a day. Less experienced riders can receive instruction at the resort and more experienced riders can take a picnic lunch ride up Pinnacle Mountain. A full range of canoeing is available and the resort will happily provide instruction. Trips for one or two nights with guides are offered, covering beautiful lake chains connected by streams and portages. Delightful moonlight paddles to distant islands are also popular. Guests can sail with Sunfish or more advanced Hobie Cats, with instruction available. Waterskiing is on a request basis and the resort provides everything, including the instruction. Swimming in

Indian Lake is excellent, clean and clear. The resort has a sand beach or guests can swim in the privacy of their cabin front and there are many island beaches to visit. Fishing for all levels can be found at the resort. Children can catch bass and perch right from the resort's dock. Indian Lake is famed for its smallmouth bass and northern pike up to trophy weights. Feeder streams and Indian River provide exciting trout fishing for early morning fishermen, and the resort will gladly cook the catch up for breakfast. Backpacking into the remote West Canadian Lakes Wilderness provides the fisherman with superb trout fishing only accessible by foot. The area provides the nature enthusiast with a variety of fascinating sights. Nature walks will unfold wildlife, varied plant life and quiet wooded settings. Birding is excellent with a huge resident colony of barn and tree swallows, and old apple trees attracting a variety of species. Over 56 species were identified in one week by an Audubon member. The resort furnishes bird and wildflower lists and has keyed nature trails. Guided overnight trips include picnic hikes; canoe and boat picnics; rugged climbing up 4,000–foot Snowy Mountain; easy walking up Pinnacle Mountain and Chimney Mountain with its ice caves. Car tours around the area can also be arranged, with trips to Lake Placid and Lake George available. The resort belongs to the Sierra Club and is recommended by the American Forestry Association. Backpacking in the area is also splendid. The resort will set you up with everything you need, except a sleeping bag, and you can take off from any trail leading out from the resort. Short guided trips and a full range of backpacking technique instruction are available. The atmosphere at the resort is easy-going, warm and friendly. The management and staff are deliberately low-key, with the environment providing the real pleasures. The resort has no electricity; lighting is provided with gas lamps, water is supplied by gravity from mountain springs, and refrigeration gas-driven power. Accommodations have wood stoves for warmth and converters are provided so electric shavers can be used from car cigarette lighters. There is a main lodge with a great stone fireplace. Meals are served on a covered porch with sides open for sun, mountain breezes, and lake views. The food is hearty and simple, with weekly bar-b-ques and Thanksgiving-style turkey dinners served every Sunday. Accommodations include sturdy tents at the water's edge; one-room cabins with or without bath and a lakeview; and cottages with two to four rooms with baths. All units are simple, utilitarian and comfortable. All accommodations have hotel-style beds for adults, blankets and linen. Rates include three meals a day, picnic lunches, hot coffee or tea anytime, ice, all bedding, towels, kerosene lamps, fuel, stove wood, cribs, sailboats and instruction, Big-Chief launch trips, guided day picnic trips, tennis, water skiing on Sunday afternoons, boat cushions, life preservers and all facilities except horseback riding, boats and canoes, and tennis lessons. Tipping is not permitted 10% service charge is added to the bill. Rates: Tent on platform, daily $29 per person, weekly $175 per person. Cabin with trail bath, daily $31 per person, weekly $196 per person. Cabin with bath $36 daily, $210 weekly. Cottage, with accommodations for up to eight, some offering sitting rooms, second floor bunkrooms and attractive A-frame styling, $36 daily per person, weekly $210 per person. Some deluxe cottages have minimum rates from $525–630. Children's rates and special off season rates are available. For further information contact: Timberlock Resort, Indian Lake, Sabael, NY 12864 (518)648–5494 summers; (802)457–1621 winters.

★★★*Trout House Village on Lake George* is surrounded by towering ancient, evergreens and rolling mountains. It is a four-season family resort providing activities for each season. There is year-round fishing to be enjoyed from Lake George for perch, rainbow trout, salmon, and bass as well as hunting in the fall for deer and fowl. Just about every type of winter sport is available at the resort or nearby. Fine downhill skiing is at the slopes of Gore Mountain and other nearby spots. The resort has ice skating on the lake and miles and miles of snowmobiling trails extending to Lake George Village. Cross-country skiing covers equally extensive trails. Warm weather offers an opportunity to play golf at nearby Ticonderoga Country Club, as well as tennis at nearby courts. The resort has 300 feet of sandy beach by the lake with a 75-foot dock for swimming, sunbathing and boat docking. Canoes, row boats, kayaks and bikes are provided to guests free of charge. A variety of games including croquet, badminton, volleyball and ping-pong are available. In the fall, the foliage is breathtaking and it's the prime fishing season. Historic sites, including Fort Ticonderoga and Penfield Heritage Museum, are easily accessible. Accommodations at the resort include log-cabin chalets, cottages, lodge and motel units. Housekeeping facilities are available. Meals are served only on weekends as part of a package. There are many restaurants in the village for all meals. Rates: Summer season, motel units $21–25, lodge $17–25, housekeeping cabins, $32–56 daily. Winter season, motel units $17–19, lodge $15–19, housekeeping cabins $29–42. A weekend package including meals from Friday night dinner to Sunday brunch, $43 per person. Children's rates and weekly rates are available. For further information contact: The Patchetts, Trout House Village Resort, Hague, NY 12836 (518)543–6088.

★★★*Twin Bay Village on Lake George* is located directly on the lakeshore among 35 acres of pine woodland. The lovely waterfront property provides free docking for guests who bring their own boats. The private lakefront beach is ideal for children, and the two pools make swimming a popular sport. Other activities include water skiing, row boating, canoeing, speed boat rides, fishing, badminton, shuffleboard, barbecuing, and picnics. Accommodations include non-housekeeping units, all with lakefront views, priced between $30 and $35 daily and $195–230 weekly. Housekeeping units including cooking facilities, dishes, utensils, linens, and blankets are at $40 per person daily and $260 weekly. The efficiency motel units complete with kitchens, modern baths, air-conditioning, TV, and living rooms are offered at between $42 and $50 daily, and at $275–325 weekly. Trained pets are welcome. Children's rates are low when sharing rooms with adults. For further information, contact Twin Bay Village Inc., Bolton Landing, NY 12814 (518)644–9777.

★★*The Wawbeek on Upper Saranac Lake*, located in the center of the Adirondack Range, is a unique resort offering all the comforts and conveniences of a hotel, combined with the old-fashioned warmth and congeniality found in an early American inn. There are two private beaches shallow enough for children. You can also enjoy water skiing, boating, canoeing, sailing, hiking, tennis, fishing, and golf. There is a playground for children. One-day sightseeing trips can be arranged to Santa's Workshop, Whiteface Mountain, Lake Placid, Land of Make Believe, Ausable Chasm, and Adirondack Museum. The exhilarating mountain air and breathtaking scenery will provide you with a satisfying, relaxing and pleasurable holiday. The cuisine is excellent, and the modern hotel rooms and spacious housekeeping units with efficiency kitchens will make your stay comfortable. All linens, blankets and utensils are supplied. The units have wall-to-wall carpeting, private bathrooms and controlled heating. The cabins range from $32–62 per day and rooms at the Inn (on European Plan) range from $18–28 per day per person. For further information write The Wawbeek Inn, P.O. Tupper Lake, NY 12986 (518)359–3800 or 3280; winter phone (315)386–8522.

★★★★*Whiteface Chalet in the High Peaks* is a rustic four-season lodge overlooking Whiteface Mountain, the headquarters of the

Winter Olympics in 1980. Spacious wood-paneled rooms comfortably accommodate a family of six. A complete schedule of championship events, ski races, bobsled races, World Cup Giant Slalom, cross-country ski races, indoor speed skating championships, 90 meter ski jump training, and figure skating competitions continues throughout the season from December 'till April. The Whiteface Chalet offers a "learn to ski" week at Whiteface Mountain Alpine Ski Area, including lodging, meals, daily lessons, and unlimited skiing for $139–149. The cozy wood-paneled lounge with flagstone floor, piano, billiard table and crackling fire, is a favorite place to unwind, after a full day's skiing. The large picture windows capture the bold face of Whiteface Mountain and complement the excellent dinners served in the dining room. For the summer, when the snow melts and leaves the mountains a lush green, Whiteface Chalet has a private tennis court, a large heated pool, and badminton and

shuffleboard on the 10 acres of private lawns which surround the chalet, nestled in the heart of spectacular, mountainous country. There is a special playground for children, complete with swings and a large sandbox. Minutes away are championship golf courses, boating, Au Sable River trout fishing, and spectacular waterfalls. Rooms in the lodge are $22 per person in bunk accommodations, including meals; $22 per person in rooms with twin beds or a double bed; $30 per person in a room with twin double beds and a studio couch. All rates include breakfast and dinner. Rates without meals can be arranged. For more information write: The Whiteface Chalet, Wilmington, New York 12997 (518)946–2207.

★★★★*The Willis Lodges on the Fulton Chain of Lakes* are located on 12 acres in the heart of the Adirondacks, 1,900 feet above sea level on the shores of Seventh Lake. The Central Adirondack area has one of the heaviest annual snowfalls in the northeast. The snow season lasts from mid-December to mid-April, and the lodge has miles of snowmobile trails, logging roads, and snow covered side roads for snow sports. A well-marked network of over 300 miles of groomed cross-country ski trails are part of the lodges' offerings. Willis Lodges are in the center of the trail system, connecting with the whole Central Adirondack area. There is fine downhill skiing at

McCauley Mountain Ski Area 12 miles away, and a town skating rink. Seventh Lake holds trout and bass, and bordering Bottle Brook is an excellent trout stream. In the winter guests can enjoy ice fishing. During warm weather the wooded Seventh Lake area provides a wealth of mountain beauty. Guests can use the lodges' aluminum boats, rent canoes, water ski, and enjoy a pontoon-boat available from a nearby livery. Seaplanes call at the lodges' dock for those wishing rides. Swimming is very safe in the lake. Additional activities include tetherball, badminton court, basketball nets, horse shoes, shuffle board and croquet. A lakeside fireplace is the site of get-togethers and cookouts. The Adirondack Museum and the Enchanted Forest are a half-hour away. The Lodges are recently built with new furnishings, situated to provide a lake view and to avoid crowding. They are set up for housekeeping, each with two bedrooms, a sofa sleeper, bath with shower and a sundeck porch. Nearby Inlet and Eagle Bay provide groceries, churches, gift-shops, well-equipped garages, ski shops and restaurants. Rates: Weekly $200 for up to four in a lodge, $25 weekly for each additional person. Limit six per lodge. Daily $30 for three or less, $10 for each additional person. For further information contact: The Willis Lodges on Seventh Lake, Route 28, Inlet, NY 13360 (315)357–3904.

Travel Services

Big Tupper Ski Area is only 45 minutes from Lake Placid, the 1980 Winter Olympic site. The area offers some of the finest New York skiing facilities. Wide, well-groomed trails are accessible from the 2,800–foot and 3,050–foot chairlifts and the 2,800–foot T-bar. There is also a 600–foot beginners' lift. Trails vary in difficulty from novice to expert. There is skiing under lights on the T-bar area Wednesday and Friday. The sheltered location, combined with the northeast exposure and base elevation of 2,000 feet, affords some of the best snow conditions in the area. An additional chairlift has been recently added at nearby Mt. Morris. The new lift is 2,200 ft. in length and can transport 800 people to the summit per hour. The completion of this new lift has given Big Tupper a vertical drop of 1,152 feet—the third largest in northeastern New York State. A total of six new trails will be out off this new lift, giving the area some of the best skiing in the northeast with a north exposure. The new chair at Mt. Morris is accessible from three previous lifts. Big Tupper provides lessons, and rentals for alpine and cross-country. There is a cafeteria and cocktail lounge on Big Tupper's premises. Parking facilities have recently been expanded. Rates: three-day package deals from Friday-Sunday or Saturday-Monday: with lessons, rentals and skiing $41; without rentals $26 for adults. A five-day deal from Monday-Friday (excluding holiday weeks and weekends) with lessons and skiing and rentals $60, without rentals $35. Big Tupper holds special days with ski school for senior citizens, ladies and men, giving a one hour lesson for $7. Private lessons are $15, group $6.50; lift tickets for all day $8–10. Half-day $7–8. Season tickets, special night skiing rates, college student, and junior rates are available. For lodging information contact Chamber of Commerce, Tupper Lake, NY 12986 (518) 359–3328. For further information about Big Tupper contact: Big Tupper Ski Area, P.O. Box 820, Tupper Lake, NY 12986 (518) 359–3651.

Killington Adventure, see listing under "Green Mountain National Forest & The Long Trail" in the Vermont chapter.

Catskill Park & Forest Preserve

The Indians knew the beautiful rolling hills, swift flowing streams, and forests of the Catskills as *Onteora* ("land in the sky," the dwelling place of the Great Spirit). They held Onteora sacred, and left its wilderness virtually untouched. By the 17th century Dutch settlers inhabited the eastern foothills. Eventually lumber companies entered the forest and blazed trails through its interior. The great hemlock stands of the forest had vanished by 1870 to supply the tanbark industry, but the dense mixed hardwoods remain today, painting the mountains and countryside brilliant red, orange, and crimson in the fall. A network of trails leads to most of the region's major peaks; highways serve the forest area, providing easy access. Today the heart of the region is encompassed within the boundaries of the famous 250,000–acre Catskill Forest Preserve, which itself lies within the 650,000–acre Catskill State Park and contains several of the finest fishing, hunting, camping, and backpacking areas in the eastern United States. Its scenic mixed hardwood and conifer forests and thick undergrowths of huckleberry, alder, rhododendrons, mountain laurel, and wintergreen provide cover for whitetail deer, black bear, ruffed grouse, a few wild turkey, and red fox. The ancient, glacially scoured mountains and forests are slashed by several of the nation's most historic trout streams which gave birth to American fly fishing: the famous Beaverkill, Neversink, Esopus, Willowemoc, and Schoharie, rising from springs in the hinterlands of the Catskill high country. By the 1880's extensive lumbering and farm clearance had changed the watersheds, causing a substantial rise in median temperature. Coupled with better transportation and increased fishing pressure, warmer water spelled the end of the Catskills as prime brook trout waters. Toward the end of the decade brown trout were introduced from Europe to replace the diminishing population of native squaretails. Not only were the immigrants hardier, but they were far more wary than the naive brookies, and fishermen soon learned that the newcomers would not take such standard flies as the gaudy Parmachene Belles, Silver Doctors, and Scarlet Ibises which were so attractive to the natives. Encouraged by the British masters of the art, pioneer fly fishermen such as Theodore Gordon, Edward R. Hewitt, and George M. L. LaBranche developed techniques and patterns, including the then revolutionary dry fly, which were better suited to the selective, hatch-feeding habits of the brown trout. Bait fishermen, too, learned the delicate methods of presenting a wide range of naturals in a realistic manner. Generations of dedicated anglers have come to know and appreciate the deep, hemlock-shaded pools of these great trout streams, which at times will humble the most experienced fisherman, or conversely, amaze him with a sudden frenzy of feeding activity. The Beaverkill River and Willowemoc Creek join at the town of Roscoe. A legendary two-headed brown trout of immense proportions, the "Beamoc," is said to inhabit the Junction Pool, one head pointing up the waters of the Beaverkill, the other into the flow of the Willowemoc, destined by indecision to remain forever rooted in its hold.

The Big Beaverkill flows west from Roscoe through a series of beautiful pools (Ferdons, Horse Run, Wagon Wheel, Mountain, and Painter Bend, to name a few) to its confluence with the East Branch of the Delaware. The lower river holds some lunker browns, as well as rainbows and a few brookies. The bottom pools also yield some smallmouths. The East Branch of the Delaware was one of the great trout streams of the East before the water demands of New York City raised havoc with the flow of cold water issuing from Pepacton Reservoir, impounding the waters of the East Branch at Downsville. At times the flow is reduced to a trickle, and the pools below the dam don't produce the great numbers of hefty browns which were once the trademark of this section of river. Above Pepacton, through the picturesque village of Margaretville, there is some quality trout water, and natives are found in the feeder brooks of the upper reaches. Pepacton Reservoir contains some of the most spectacular brown trout fishing in the East. Thick, deep-bodied lunkers roam the depths of the impoundment, and fish in excess of 15 pounds are not rare. Trolling, still fishing, and drifting with live bait produce a lot of big trout, 3 to 6 pounds in weight. Smallmouth bass, pickerel, and panfish contribute a lot of action too.

Other top-ranked Catskill trout waters include the upper West Branch of the Delaware; the upper Neversink, home river of the legendary Theodore Gordon, creator of the deadly Quill Gordon fly; Esopus Creek, which provides exciting fishing during the spring for big rainbos migrating up from Ashokan Reservoir; Schoharie Creek and its West Kill, Batavia Kill, and East Kill tributaries, which hold some good-sized browns; and Rondout and Kaaterskill creeks and the remote Catskill headwaters for fat, orange-bellied native brookies.

The Upper Delaware River at the western boundary of the Catskills forms the state's western border with Pennsylvania and New Jersey and offers top-ranked canoe camping and fishing for trout, smallmouth, bass, walleye, pickerel, shad, and panfish along the numerous riffles, pools, and eddies. Some of the best rainbow trout fishing in the East is found in this lengthy segment of river by those who know where and when to fish. The prime trout stretches produce rainbows,

which average 15 inches, and fish to 24 inches are taken regularly. Fishing hot spots along the Upper Delaware are located at the Maples, Frisbie Island, Equimunk Eddy, Lordville Rift, Lacey's Bend Eddy, Baskett Riffle, Killams Bridge, Whitehouse Curve, and Plum Island areas. A small silver-bodied Adams is an effective dry fly, and when conditions are right the action is fast and furious. Shad are found in the main river and both branches and attract a great many fishermen in May, who take the big, silvery scrappers on beaded shad flies, shad darts, spinners, and small wobblers. The average fish weighs about 4 pounds, but many fish reach 7 pounds. Walleye and bass occupy most stretches of the Delaware and furnish exciting angling. Live bait, such as small lampreys, spinner and worm combinations, hellgrammites, and live minnows are effective on both species, as well as standard spoons, jigs, and

plugs. Fly fishermen score well with streamers, the deadly Muddler Minnow, and bass bugs, in quieter stretches.

Some of the finest fishing and camping opportunities in the forest preserve are found off the major trails by traveling cross-country with topo map and compass to the remote high country lakes, ponds, and streams in the central Catskill Mountains. Among the more challenging trails through the forest is the Devil's Path (Indian Head-Hunter Mountain Range Trail), which traverses the Catskill highlands from Platte Cove on the east over Indian Head, Twin, Sugarloaf, Plateau, and Hunter mountains to Spruceton Valley on the west. Other trails through the Catskills (more than 200 miles of them) include the Wittenberg-Cornell-Slide Trail, John Burroughs's inspiration place; the Phoenicia-East Branch Trail; the Pine Hill-Eagle Mountain-West Branch Trail, with its many mountain byways; Seager-Big Indian Mountain Trail; the Delaware Trails, a network of trails through forest preserve lands south of the Pepacton Reservoir in Delaware County; the Mink Hollow Trail from Lake Hill north to the Platte Cove Highway; the Diamond Notch Trail from Lanesville to Spruceton; and the Escarpment Trail from Kaaterskill Creek north to East Windham.

Information Sources, Maps & Access

For information and a free *Catskill Trails Map/Brochure* and a free *Catskill Forest Preserve Brochure*, contact: Information Office, DEC, 50 Wolf Rd., Albany, NY 12233 (516)474–2121. Several useful full-color maps of the Catskill country are published by: Outdoor Publications, Box 355, Ithaca 14850 (add 50¢ on all orders less than $6). *Sportsman's Map of the Catskill Mountains*) $1.50, 23 × 35 inches) locates some 250,000 acres of public land in Delaware, Sullivan, Ulster, and Greene counties and shows more than 300 miles of hiking, cross-country skiing, and access trails, campsites, lean-to shelters, ski centers, lookout towers, and 800 miles of trout streams, with stretches open to public fishing and state-stocked areas; *Sportsman's Map of Ulster County* ($1.50, 27 × 30 inches) shows all man-made and natural features in this heart of the Catskills; *Sportsman's Map of Delaware County* ($1.50, 27 × 27 inches) shows all major features, as do the *Sportsman's Map of Sullivan County* ($1, 28 × 30 inches), *Sportsman's Map of Greene County* ($1, 18 ×

27 inches), and *Sportsman's Map of the Central Catskill Mountains* ($1, 18 × 30 inches). Outdoor Publications, publishes two booklets which are invaluable aids for anyone planning to fish in the Catskills. *Guide to Trout Streams in the Catskill Mountains* ($1.50), by Crane Hanover, describes the general area of the Catskills, the park, forest preserve, and principal watersheds, major roadways through the region, public fishing stretches, and access. The book includes tips on securing permission to fish private lands, campsite information, and a thorough description of each major trout stream. A general schematic watershed map showing the internal road system is provided. For anyone planning to try the beautiful Catskill waters, this book will save hours of wasted time, and furnish a useful basic knowledge of the region and what is offered. A companion book is *New York City Reservoirs in the Catskill Mountains* ($1.50), by C. Austin Glenn, which provides information about six major New York City reservoirs in the Catskills: Pepacton, Cannonsville, Neversink, Rondout, Ashokan, and Schoharie. Outdoor Publications also publishes a valuable *Fishing Map of the Catskill Mountains* ($1.50, 22 × 37 inches), which shows more than 1,000 miles of mountain streams, lakes, ponds, and reservoirs, describes fishing

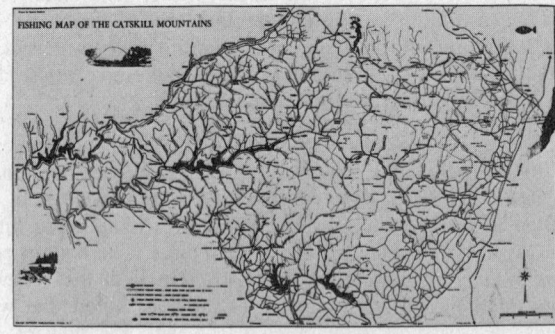

rights areas and reservoirs open by permit, and pinpoints some 30 fishing hot spots; *Sportsman's Map of Pepacton Reservoir*, which shows water depths at 10– to 20–foot intervals, roadways, hollows, coves, and little-known fishing spots and feeder streams; *Sportsman's Map of the Central Catskill Mountains* ($2, 22 × 25 inches), showing all natural and man-made features, with contour lines; and a *Sportsman's Map of the Ashokan Reservoir* ($1, 18 × 30 inches), showing depth contours, roads, coves, and points favored by local guides and fishermen. For info on Catskill lake and trout stream conditions and where-to-go advice, write or call: Beaverkill Sportsman, Roscoe 12776 (607)498–4677. The following maps and guides of the Upper Delaware are available from: Upper Delaware Publications, Rte. 97, Barryville 12719 (all prices post-paid). The *Upper Delaware River Recreation Map Set* ($2.60) is published in two sections; both show fishing access, boat rentals, boat-launching sites, fishing hot spots, springs, rapids, and weirs, rock shelters, eddies, rifts, and streamflow characteristics. Section One ($1.50, 13 x 31 inches) shows the remote, wild section of the river from Hancock to Cochecton; Section Two ($1.50, 12 x 37 inches), the famous white-water and fishing areas of the river from Cochecton to Port Jervis. *Whitewater Boating on the Upper Delaware River* ($1.75) is the standard guide to canoeing, camping, and kayaking on the river (order from address above). The Catskill Park and Forest Preserve are reached via New York 44, 209, 28, and 23 off the New York State Thruway (Interstate 87) and spur roads off New York 17. The Catskill region contains literally hundreds of towns and rural hamlets which offer overnight accommodations, supplies, and equipment rentals.

Gateways & Accommodations

Catskill

(Pop. 5,300; zip code 12414; area code 518) is the eastern gateway to the high peaks and narrow valleys of the Catskills, where Rip van Winkle is said to have slept for twenty years. Catskill Creek cascades through this resort town, which is situated in a narrow valley and surrounded by hills. Nearby Beaverkill Creek, Neversink and Willowemoc Creeks place Catskill near some of the finest fishing in New York State. Area attractions include the Catskill Game Farm and the 260,000–acre Catskill Forest Preserve. Accommodations: *Carl's Rip van Winkle Motor Lodge* (rates: $18–28 double), with 37 excellent rooms and rustic cabin units, next to restaurant, swimming pool on Old New York Route 23 west of Interstate 87 exit 21, (943-3303); *Catskill Motor Lodge* (rates: $21–29 double), with 73 excellent rooms and family units, restaurant, cocktail lounge, swimming pool on New York Highway 23B at Interstate 87 exit 21, (943–5800).

Fishkill

(Pop. 913; zip code 12524; area code 914). Situated on the Hudson River, is the major gateway for skiers, snowshoers, hikers, hunters, backpackers and fishermen heading into the rolling hills, open farmland, and dense forests of Dutchess County. The Fahnstock Ski Area is located here. Accommodations: *Holiday Inn* (rates: $33–37 double), with 100 excellent rooms, restaurant, cocktail lounge, swimming pool on U.S. Highway 9 at the junction of Interstate 84 exit 13 (896–6281).

Livingston Manor

(Pop. 1,500; zip code 12758; area code 914). On the banks of the Beaverkill and Willowemoc Rivers, is the major gateway for hunters, hikers and fishermen heading into the Catskill Forest Preserve in search of some of the finest fishing and hunting in the region. Accommodations: *Willowemoc Motel* (rates: $18–24 double), with 24 good rooms off New York Highway 17 exit 96 (439-4220).

Roscoe

(Pop. 300; zip code 12776; area code 607), in the foothills of the Catskill Mountains, welcomes tourists, hunters, hikers, backpackers, skiers, and fishermen into Catskill Mountain Park. Roscoe is a major jumping-off point for fly fishing on the Beaverkill and is the home of several of the nation's famed fly tiers. Accommodations: *Roscoe Motel* (rates: $21–23 double), on the Beaverkill with 15 good rooms and swimming pool just northwest of town on old New York 17 (498–5220).

Lodges & Resorts

★★★*Bonnie View on the Beaverkill* is a famous sportsman's guest house featuring fine food, clean rooms, fresh air, personal attention, the otherwise unobtainable trout fishing on their section of the world-famous Beaverkill as well as 60 acres of fields and woods in a prime deer and upland game bird hunting area. Bonnie View is located just slightly over a two hour drive from the metropolitan area and 9 miles from the new express Route 17. Bonnie View caters to the sportsman and sportsmen's families, nature lovers, and bird watchers. It is easily accessible but off the main highways with its own private driveway, and is kept secluded by the spacious lawn around the property and the nearby fields and woods. The waters immediately above and below the property are privately owned. There are a succession of wealthy clubs who control most of the area and they do extensive stocking of the stream. There are brown, rainbow and brook trout . . . most of them "eating" size but there are numerous fish over

a foot long and enough lunkers to keep you trying. It is beautiful fly fishing water and an average fly fisherman can often catch and release several fish a day. An exceptional 8–year old brown, 26" long and weighing 6 pounds was caught in July, 1972, on a home-tied wet fly in the Bonnie View waters. For those who may not wish to wade the stream and for younger children and guests who might be learning to fish, a trout pool in the backyard is kept well stocked for easy catching. Almost every weekend there are experienced fly fishermen at Bonnie View. These experts are most willing to act as voluntary instructors and help you improve your fly fishing techniques or teach you to become a fly fisherman, if you are not presently one. Daily American Plan rates (double occupancy) per person are $26.50. Fishing by the day rates are $12.50 with one meal. Deer season rates are available on request. For additional information, write or call: Bonnie View on the Beaverkill, Lewbeach, NY 12753 (914)439–4844.

★★★*The Campbell Inn in the Catskills* is a perfect base for fishing, hunting, and backpacking trips in the surrounding forest lands. The inn, one half mile from the village of Roscoe, is a fine old Catskill resort hotel directly overlooking the famous Junction Pool of the Beaverkill and Willowemoc Rivers. These classic eastern trout waters include three "no-kill" stretches—over 6 miles of water open year round. The inn is situated on 200 acres with a scenic forest-fringed lake, beautiful landscaped grounds with open meadows, rolling hills and mountains. The inn offers comfortable rooms with nice views, dining room, and pool. Daily summer rates (double occupancy) are $21–29. Guest cottages facing the lake are $26–35 daily. Weekly and pre-season rates available. For additional information, contact: The Campbell Inn, Roscoe, NY 12776 (607)498–4111.

★★★*Eldred Preserve in the Catskills*, located in a natural woodland setting, is a renowned vacation retreat noted for its unusual trout preserve. The preserve has harnessed a Catskill trout stream, forming a series of broad, deep-flowing pools stocked with browns, rainbows, and tiger trout up to 26 inches. The trout preserve is open to fishing for guests free of charge. Other features of the preserve include expert fly-casting instruction, fish cleaning service, tennis, golf, swimming pool, and access to 600 acres of hiking and cross-country ski trails. Rustic accommodations in this mountain estate setting include modern, attractively furnished units in a quiet, secluded setting. A gourmet dining room serves delicious meals and offers views of the surrounding countryside. The preserve is located on New York 55 between Barryville and White Lake. Daily rates are $35 double occupancy in season. For reservations and information, contact: Eldred Preserve, Eldred, NY 12732 (914) 557–8316.

★★★★*Lake Minnewaska Resort & Ski Touring Center* is a 1,300–acre, privately owned resort, surrounded by an additional 1,379 acres of state park. Set in the Shawangunk Mountains (the Indian word for white rock) on Lake Minnewaska, it is bordered on three sides by grey cliffs that rise 150 feet into the air. The lake is crystal clear and on a bright day one can easily see 20 or 30 feet below the surface. The area and resort offer a plethora of sports and activities. Hiking is one of the most popular, and the resort considers its walking trails its most precious asset. There are miles of scenic hiking trails and paths, clearly marked, with little gazebos strategically placed along the way for rests. The resort gives suggested hiking trails, maps and estimated walking mileage. The resort is well equipped for dozens of other activities. Select from six clay tennis courts with instruction available; a dozen horses for riding through private bridle paths English or Western style; a nine-hole golf course; a putting green; swimming in the lake; paddle boats, sail boats, and canoes. The resort also has rustic campsites and recreational vehicle spaces. And if you can't find what you want, see the sports director,

who provides games and sport equipment not at hand. In the winter Lake Minnewaska is one of the finest ski-touring areas in the eastern U.S. Over 150 miles of trails wind throughout the mountain's crest, and its elevation of 1,800 feet helps hold the snow. Downhill skiing is also part of the resort's offerings, with a complete range of facilities. Tobogganing, ice-skating, snowmobiling and horse-drawn sleigh rides are also part of the winter's activities. The atmosphere at Minnewaska is quiet, easy-going and full of yesteryear charm. The Wildmere House, a 225–room Victorian Chateau overlooking the lake, was first opened in 1887. Wildmere is filled with Victorian and French provincial furniture, and has 138 wood-burning fireplaces. There are two very large Victorian sitting rooms, and numerous more intimate sitting rooms, each with a charm of its own. The Wine Cellar, with rough hewn beams, granite walls and a cozy fireplace located in Wildmere's basement, is an intriguing resort feature, with dancing at night. The resort also has musical recitals and other quiet entertainment in the evenings. The resort operates on the modified American plan with buffets and a snack bar located on the resort's premises. Rates: Double occupancy, room with running water $27–28.50; room with running water and toilet $29–31.50; room with private bath $30–36. Children's rates are available, as well as ski touring rates and packages. For further information contact: Lake Minnewaska Resort, Lake Minnewaska, NY 12561 (914)255–6000.

★★★★*Mohonk Mountain House & Ski Touring Center* is a beautiful castle-like resort, tucked away in the Shawangunk Mountain range, on Mohonk Mountain. The house's grounds are part of the mountainside, with picture-book scenery, a deep, blue-green glacial lake, clean air and quiet. The house with 305 rooms, 258 balconies overlooking the Catskill mountains and 151 fireplaces, was established in 1869 by Albert Smiley. Its unique character of graciousness and hospitality have been maintained by the Smiley family for over 100 years. The house and area offer just about every kind of activity. Guests can go swimming in the lake and sun on one of the dramatic rock formations. There's fine trout fishing in the stocked lake, golf, tennis, horseback riding on mountain trails (with instruction during season), shuffleboard, lawn bowling, putting, softball and soccer games. Enjoy a caving expedition or explore the quiet of a cloistered natural niche or one of the many arbor seats or thatched summerhouses on the property. There are dozens of trails for hiking, plus nature walks and garden tours conducted by experts. Warm weather activities also include carriage and hay rides, breakfast cook-outs, barbeques and clambakes. Popular winter sports include ice-skating on the lake, sledding and horse drawn sleigh rides. Mohonk Ski Touring Center provides guests with 19 miles of marked maintained cross-country trails, plus unmarked trails and paths. Private and group lessons, guided ski tours, and complete equipment rentals are available. Downhill skiing for beginners and intermediates is also

offered with instruction and rentals. During any season Mohonk is an excellent place to visit if you want to enjoy scenery. The striking stone Sky Top Tower, perched high atop Mohonk Mountain, offers a spectacular view. You can hike up Sky Top Road, enjoying the view all the way. In addition to all this Mohonk offers classes in yoga, art and craftwork projects, concerts, lectures, slide shows and dances. A recent series of programs included "Pioneer Sugaring"; "Earth Watch"; "Tune into Life"; "Runner's Rally"; "October Fest of Chamber Music". Guests can stay in the main house, a charming Victorian style castle-like building with accommodations for 500 guests. It's filled with cozy sitting rooms, parlors, and turn-of-the-century furniture. For a real treat, stay in a unique, spacious tower room. Housekeeping cottages with fireplaces are available early May to late October. The house operates on the full American Plan. There is no bar or cocktail lounge at Mohonk, but guests may order alcoholic beverages at dinner and purchase bottled liquor at the Guest Service Desk. Rates: Towers $55 daily, double occupancy. Rooms with private bath $45 ($10 extra for fireplace). Two rooms with connected bath $39–50. Weekly rates for Tower, per night $43. Rooms with bath $35; two rooms with connecting bath $33–40. There are special packages for several-night stays and ski packages. Children's rates are available. For further information contact: Mohonk Mountain House, Mohonk Lake, New Paltz, NY 12561 (914) 255–1000; NY direct dialing (212)233–2244.

Travel Services

The Wulff's Fly Fishing School is located on Lewbeach on the fabled Beaverkill River in New York's Catskill Mountains—the birthplace of dry-fly fishing in America. Joan and Lee Wulff, the owners and teachers at the school, have impressive backgrounds. Joan has been a national and international casting champion for the past 16 years and is the only woman ever to have won a national distance casting event against all-male competition. Lee Wulff has designed the original fly fisherman's vest and the Wulff series of flies which first brought high-floating animal hair to trout flies. He has written many books and articles and has been a pioneer in light-tackle fishing and conservation. Together Joan and Lee have worked out the "Constant Pressure" system of fly casting which simplifies the learning process and develops maximum capability in the shortest time. A variety of courses offered includes the weekend basic fly-fishing school for beginners and intermediates, the weekend Atlantic salmon fishing school, the weekend fly-casting school and the extended (four day) basic fly-fishing school for beginners and intermediates. Classes teach students to understand the fish, their food and habits, types of flies and effective presentation casting and playing fish. Lee Wulff presents fishing films for added illustration, and video tape recording is used to improve casting techniques. There are three ponds for casting and pond fishing. A stretch of the Beaverkill River is used to teach students how to present wet flies, dry flies and nymphs to the right spots while they practice wading techniques. Students with additional time are encouraged to fish some of the famous streams in the area such as the Esopus, the Delaware and the "No-Kill" stretches of the Beaverkill and Willowemoc. Bonnie View, a half-mile from the school, one of the Catskill's oldest and best-known fishing hotels, accommodates guests of the school. Use of the private three-quarter-mile stream on the hotel's property is free to guests. Rates for weekend schools: Basic fishing, Atlantic salmon, fly casting Friday-Sunday with five meals and two nights lodging, $235 double occupancy. Extended (four day) basic fishing school, Sunday-Thursday, eleven meals, four nights lodging, $360 double occupancy. For further information contact: Joan and Lee Wulff Fishing Schools, Beaverkill Road, Lewbeach, NY 12753 (914)439–4060.

Finger Lakes Region

The Finger Lakes occupy a long arc of land in west-central New York, stretching for about 100 miles east to west, and are nationally famous for their spectacular trout fishing, resorts, and wine vineyards. The lakes are deep glacial gouges set in the rolling Lake Ontario plain, and look as if a giant, multiclawed bear had raked the earth's surface from south to north. This scenic lakeland was once the home and hunting grounds of the Seneca Indians—among them were the great Seneca statesman Red Jacket, and Hiawatha, the Onondaga chieftain who inspired Longfellow's immortal poem—who believed that they lived atop the back of a giant turtle, with pools between the ridges of the turtle's back forming the great finger-shaped lakes. A group of the larger lakes (ranging from 11 to 40 miles long)—Canandaigua, Keuka, Seneca, Cayuga, Owasco, and Skaneateles—and the smaller ones, Conesus, Hemlock, Canadice, Honeoye, and Otisco, drain north to Lake Ontario, primarily through the Seneca and Genesee River networks. These nationally renowned lakes and their feeder streams offer often spectacular fishing for big, metallic-flanked rainbows and lake trout which grow to the 10- to-20-pound class on the abundant schools of smelt and sawbellies, as well as trophy brown trout, landlocked salmon, walleye, smallmouth bass, muskellunge, and northern pike. Seneca Lake, stretching north from the auto racing town of Watkins Glen for almost 40 miles, is one of the deepest bodies of water in the eastern United States, with depths exceeding 600 feet. Most anglers consider this the best member of the chain, and quantities of big lake trout, rainbows, smallmouth bass, and pike are taken from the clear waters. An incredible scene, reminiscent of a bargain basement sale, takes place on April 1 each year when the opening of the fishing season and the fabulous Catherine Creek rainbow run coincide. The creek, which runs through Watkins Glen, is not large to begin with and hordes of hopeful anglers assault the banks, jockey for the best spots, and bombard the stream with fish-roe imitations (spawn is prohibited) such as dyed vaseline balls and gumdrops, spinners, and night crawlers, in the hopes of hooking one of the enormous rainbows that reach weights to 20 pounds. Many trout of 5 pounds or better are caught during this period, and the great enthusiasm is understandable.

Information Sources, Maps & Access

A useful *Finger Lakes Regional Travel Guide* (75¢), available from: Finger Lakes Assn., 309 Lake St., Rte. 54, Penn Yan 14527 (315)536–6621 or 536–4232 describes the fishing, boating, and hunting opportunities available, as well as fishing and hunting vacation resorts, camping facilities, and tourist services. The highway access routes to the Finger Lakes Region are Interstate 90, 81, and 390.

Gateways & Accommodations

Auburn

(Pop. 32,000; zip code 13021; area code 315), a large manufacturing city on the north shore of Owasco Lake, is a major gateway for tourists, hikers, canoeists and fishermen approaching the spectacular Finger Lakes Region. Once the refuge of Harriet Tubman who dedicated herself to freeing slaves by the underground railroad, Auburn is now the resort headquarters for the region. Accommodations: *Auburn Travelodge* (rates: $27–30 double), with 50 good rooms at 37 William Street off New York Route 34 (252–7567); *Sleepy Hollow Motel* (rates: $22–28 double), with 15 excellent rooms and heated pool two miles east of town on U.S. Highway 20 (253–3281).

Canandaigua

(Pop. 13,000; zip code 14424; area code 716) on the northern shores of the first finger lake is the western gateway for fishermen, hunters,

canoeists and hikers heading into the spectacular Finger Lakes region. Here Susan B. Anthony and the suffragettes were tried in 1873, after they had the audacity to vote in a national election. Area attractions include stunning Sonneberg Gardens, Granger Homestead and Carriage Museum, Roseland Park, a large amusement park open June-Labor Day, and the annual 56–mile Canandaigua Lake Cup Bicycle Race. Accommodations: *Sheraton Motor Inn* (rates: $39–46 double), with 115 excellent rooms, restaurant, cocktail lounge, heated pool and sauna, next to Marina at 770 South Main (394–7800).

Skaneateles

(Pop. 3,000; zip code 13152; area code 315) is a small resort town nestled on the northern shore of the easternmost finger lake. Once an important stop on the underground railroad, Skaneateles now welcomes hikers, canoeists, backpackers, hunters, and fishermen into the Finger Lakes region. Area attractions include lake cruises and sandy beaches. Accommodations: *Birds Nest Motel* (rates: $24–29 double), with 19 good rooms and family units, swimming pool 1¾ miles east of town on US 20 (685–5641); *Colonial Motel* (rates: $26–28 double), with 19 good rooms and heated pool, 1½ miles west of town on US 20 (685–5751).

Watkins Glen—Gateway to Seneca Lake

(Pop. 2,700; zip code 14891; area code 607) at the head of the 36–mile Seneca Lake is a major gateway for the Finger Lakes region. Surrounded by rolling hills dotted with orchards, vineyards, and lake shore, Watkins Glen is built on a wild, picturesque gorge. Area attractions include world famous racing events at the Watkins Glen Grand Prix Circuit, site of the United States Grand Prix in October, and the Glen Tripleheader weekend in July. Watkins Glen State Park stairs and bridges explore the rocky gorge, and picnic sites, swimming and camping in Clute Memorial Park. Accommodations: *Chiefton Motel* (rates: $17–19 double), with 14 good rooms and family units on New York 14 at junction of 14A, three miles north of town (535–4759); *Glen Motor Inn* (rates: $35 double), with 40 good rooms, restaurant, cocktail lounge, swimming pool, dock, boat rentals, on Seneca Lake one mile north of town on New York 14 (535–2706); *Rainbow Cove Motel* (rates: $23–28 double), with 24 good colonial style rooms, dining room, landscaped gardens, swimming beach, dock, boat rentals, on Seneca Lake in Himrod off New York 14, 14 miles north of Watkins Glen (243–7535).

Other New York State Gateways & Accommodations

Alexandria Bay—Gateway to the 1,000 Islands

(Pop. 1,440; zip code 13607; area code 315) is the northern gateway to the spectacular Thousand Islands of the St. Lawrence. Cruise boats leave the bay shore through the myriad islands, numbering over 1,700. Many stop at Boldt's Castle, a fairytale structure built for his wife by George Boldt, who worked his way up from a dishwasher to the president of the company owning New York's Waldorf Astoria. The United States entrance to the Thousand Islands International Bridge is located here, spanning the St. Lawrence River from island to island. For area information, call the Chamber of Commerce at 482–9531. On the Ontario side there is a Thousand Island Skydeck with observation tower. Accommodations: *Capt. Thomson's Motor Lodge* (rates: $33–45 double), with 67 excellent guest rooms, heated pool, dock on the St. Lawrence in town on James St. (482–9961); *Edgewood Resort Hotel & Motel* (rates: $36–56 double), with 135 excellent rooms, restaurant, cocktail lounge, heated pool and swimming beach, dock on the St. Lawrence one mile south of town

off New York 26 and 12 (482–9922); *Pine Tree Point* (rates: $30–48 double), with 50 excellent rooms and family units, restaurant, cocktail lounge, heated pool and sauna, dock, on the St. Lawrence located one mile northeast of town off New York 12 (482–9911).

Clayton—Gateway to the Thousand Islands

(Pop. 2,000; zip code 13624; area code 315) is a popular resort town at the head of a peninsula in the midst of the Thousand Islands. Clayton, the home of the Thousand Islands Shipyard Museum (686–4104), provides a snug harbor for pleasure boats, yachts, fishing yawls and sightseeing boats that crowd the Thousand Islands region. For information, call Chamber of Commerce at 686–3771. Scenic areas for picnicking, boating, fishing, camping and swimming are provided by three local state parks, on Cedar Point, Grass Point, and Burnham Point. Accommodations: *Fairwind Lodge Motel* (rates: $24–25 double), with 18 rooms and family cottages on the St. Lawrence with breakfast, boats, and fishing, located three miles southwest of town on New York Highway 12E (686–5251).

Montauk

(Pop. 1,300; zip code 11954; area code 516), a windy old New England-style fishing village on Long Island's eastern tip of the South Fork, is a mecca for fishermen, beachcombers, sailors, swimmers, and waterskiers, ideally situated between Long Island Sound and the pounding Atlantic surf. The easternmost village in New York State, Montauk is actually closer to Block Island, Rhode Island, than to New York City. Area attractions include deep-sea fishing ventures, Montauk State Park and Lighthouse, Gorman's Dock and Restaurant, Montauk Downs State Park, and Hither Hills State Park. For detailed information on fishing charters for bluefish, striped bass, shark, tuna, marlin and so forth call Tuma's Dock & Fishing Center at 668–2707. Accommodations: *Driftwood Motel* (rates: $46–55 in season), with 50 superb rooms and guest cottages, heated pool, tennis courts, at the ocean, five miles west of town on New York 27 (668–5744); *Gurney's Inn* (rates: $98–126 double in season), a famous summer retreat on the Old Montauk Highway, with 125 excellent rooms and guest cottages, restaurant, cocktail lounge, three miles west of town (668–2345); *Montauk Yacht Club & Inn* (rates: $150 Modified American Plan double in season) and 84 superb rooms and balconies, restaurant, coffeeshop, cocktail lounge, indoor/outdoor heated pools, swimming beach, marina and fishing charters, on Lake Montauk on Star Island Rd. (668–3100).

Shelter Island

(Pop. 1,000; zip code 11964; area code 516). Nestled in the jaws of Long Island's eastern tip, Shelter Island is warmed by Gulf Stream currents and is known to grow the only wild bamboo plants found north of the Carolinas. This summer resort, serviced by ferries from North Haven and Greenport, offers superb surf-fishing for striped bass and bluefish. Accommodations: *Dering Harbor Resort Motel* (rates: $69–114 double in summer), with 29 excellent rooms, restaurant, cocktail lounge, boat dock overlooking the harbor on Winthrop Rd. (749–0900).

Other New York State Lodges & Travel Services

Belleayre-Gore-Whiteface Mountains are known as "the big 3" and offer superb skiing in New York State. Specifically, Belleayre has the highest base elevation in the Northeast, seven lifts including chair and T-bar (and J-bar), 25 trails and slopes, a ski school, three lodges, a ski shop and a nursery. In addition to its excellent annual snowfall, it has one of the most sophisticated snowmaking systems in the U.S. Over 100 days of skiing per season is the average December through spring. The Catskill Forest Preserve surrounding Belleayre offers year-round recreation—fishing, canoeing, deer hunting, scenic mountains for hiking, golf, tennis, riding, cycling and picnicking as well as antiquing and strolling through quaint villages add to your fun and relaxation. There are many good hotels, motels and restaurants available. Gore Mountain in the Lake George region is noted for the only gondola lift in NY State. It also has eight lifts, chair and T-bar (and J-bar), 25 trails and slopes, skating rink, two lodges, ski touring and snowshoe trails, ski school, nursery, toboggan and sled slopes. It also provides lessons for the handicapped and offers outriggers and specially modified equipment. Whiteface, in the spectacular High Peaks region of the Adirondacks, has been chosen as the site of the 1980 Olympics and has the greatest vertical drop in the East. It also offers seven lifts—chair, T-bar, J-bar, 28 trails and slopes, two lodges, ski school, ski shop and snowmaking. The mountain has the most varied terrain for the beginner, intermediate and advanced skier. All three offer expert ski instruction and specialized children's classes. Gore and Belleayre offer a choice of the American Teaching Method or the Graduated Length Method—each will meet your specific skill development and needs. Education and skill development is a never-ending process and these schools offer teaching professionals to help you with your style and techniques. There are several packages available. For further information call: Belleayre (914) 254–5601; Gore (518)251–2411, Whiteface (518)946–2223. For accommodations: Belleayre, Central Catskill Association, Fleischmanns, NY; Gore-Warren County Publicity, Lake George, NY, or North Creek Chamber of Commerce (518)251–2612; Whiteface, Chamber of Commerce, Wilmington, NY or Lake Placid, NY.

Beresford Farms Ski Touring Center is located in the rolling hills of upstate New York. There are over 13 miles of groomed trails on 800 acres, with an elevation range from 950 feet to 1200 feet. Trails are mostly wooded and take the cross-country skier through a variety of terrain with ponds and streams along the way. Well marked trails are for beginners to advanced skiers. Night-skiing is conducted on two miles of lighted trails. Ski instruction is offered daily by qualified instructors in group lessons. Guests bringing their own equipment can ice skate at no charge. The lodge also hosts the Northeastern Alaskan Malamute Association Dog Sled Races. Beresford Farms has a ski lodge called the Horse Barn, built over 130 years ago. It still retains the original construction, including hand-hewn beams. Skiers can enjoy the huge fieldstone fireplace along with homemade soup and hot food from the charcoal grill. The rustic ski shop, originally a corn crib, carries a wide range of cross-country equipment and clothing. A complete line of ski accessories, including waxes, wax kits, ski books, back packs, gaiters, etc., is also available. Over 175 sets of cross-country skis are available for rent, including skis for children of all ages. Hotel accommodations are available in nearby Duanesburg. Rates: Trail use $2. Rentals (including tax & trail use), days $8, nights $6.50. Groups, weekdays $6, nights $5. Instruction $6, instruction with rental $12 days, $10.50 nights. Season trail passes, single $15, couple $25, family $30. For further information contact: Beresford Farms, Ski Touring Center, Delanson NY 12053 (518)895–2345.

Country Hills Farms & Ski Touring Center is located on 400 acres in the rolling hills of central New York. Once a dairy farm, it now offers a full four seasons' worth of activities. From mid-March to mid-April guests can take part in maple syrup gathering; gather sap, take a self-guided tour into the woods and ride a horse-drawn sleigh. The "Woodshed" dining room provides maple treats from the kitchen. A weekend summer program at Country Hills offers a farm-fresh variety of foods from the full-course buffet. Tranquil walks in the woods, hay rides and outdoor children's education programs are part of the summer's activities. Fall foliage along the nature trails can be spectacular. In winter take advantage of 18 miles of marked and graded trails including extensive trails for night skiing. A portion of the trail network is left untracked, while an equal amount is mechanically groomed and tracked. Guests can select terrain and trails to suit their abilities. Lessons for beginners to advanced skiers are available from E.P.S.T.I. certified professional instructors. There is a ski shop with complete cross-country equipment and clothing for adults and children. Night skiing is available six

nights a week, and the kitchen stays open for late appetites. Accommodations at Country Hills include suites and private rooms with baths available for individuals, families or groups. The lodge operates on the Modified American Plan with wholesome breakfasts and dinners served in the dining room. Lunch is available cafeteria-style. Rates: Private room $29 per person. Rentals: Skis or snowshoes, $7 day, $5 for ½ day and evening. Mid-week daily rental is $5. Guest rate for a day and evening is $6.50. All rentals include trail fee and sales tax. Trail rates $2 per person. Season rates available. Country Hills Farms also provides information about any cross-country ski matters. For further information contact: Country Hills Farms, Tully, NY 13159 (315)696–8774.

NORTH CAROLINA

Introduction

North Carolina, known variously as the Tar Heel or Old North State, rises from the low coastal plain, dominated by the fabled saltwater fishing grounds of Cape Hatteras and the Outer Banks, to the central Piedmont plateau, and in the west, to the scenic highlands of the Nantahala, Blue Ridge, and Great Smoky mountains, culminating at 6,684–foot Mount Mitchell—the highest point in the East. Within the state's 52,586 square miles are 300 miles of the Appalachian Trail, the famed wildlands and backpacking trails of Great Smoky Mountains National Park; the Pisgah National Forest and the Linville Gorge and Shining Rock Wilderness Areas; the Nantahala National Forest; the Snowbird Creek Wilderness and wilderness camping areas of the Joyce Kilmer Forest and Standing Indian Country; and the nationally renowned fishing waters of beautiful Fontana Lake, Big Pigeon River, Nantahala Lake and River, Hiwassee River and Lake, New River, and Lakes Santeetlah and Chatuge.

Accommodations & Travel Information

Descriptions of North Carolina's major lodges, resorts, and vacation motels, hotels, and inns are found in the "Vacation/Lodging Guide" which follows. For detailed information on all aspects of vacation travel, contact: Travel and Tourism Section, Dept. of Natural & Economic Resources, Raleigh, N.C. 27611 (919)733–4171. North Carolina's scenic high country wilderness areas provide excellent opportunities for camping and hiking. *Camping in North Carolina*, a 28–page guide available free from: Travel Development Section, Dept. of Natural & Economic Resources, Raleigh 27611, lists public and private campgrounds within the state. Number and kinds of campsites, location, seasons, nearby attractions and activities available at each campground in the major forests and parks are described. In addition to the 60 public campgrounds, there are over 300 private camping facilities in North Carolina, many of which are listed. The directory also includes a short description of parks and forests giving the location of ranger headquarters and nearby towns. At the back is a handy equipment checklist for the camper.

Another valuable guide for campers and hikers is *North Carolina Outdoors*, available free from the same address. The booklet is basically an expanded version of *Camping in North Carolina* with the listings of outdoor recreation areas keyed to coordinates of the official North Carolina Highway Map. In addition to the detailed descriptions of camping facilities, both public and private, the brochure includes brief paragraphs on fishing and hiking opportunities, wildlife, and scenic attractions in the various parks and forests. Concise directions to the different campsites and a list of campgrounds near the Blue Ridge Parkway are also included.

North Carolina offers hundreds of miles of hiking trails winding through nearly impenetrable forests, over lofty summits in the western part of the state and through lowlands, pocosins, and along fine sandy beaches in the east. *Trails and Streams of North Carolina*, a 20–page booklet free from the Travel Development Section (same address), offers a brief guide to the 200 miles of Appalachian Trail and its system of trail blazes and to other mountain trails within the state: Clingmans Dome, Cheoah Bald, Black Mountain, Mount Mitchell, Table Rock, and many others. Trail data is concise, giving mileage, access and exit points, difficulty, and sights to watch out for along the way. Trails within the state parks, such as Mount Jefferson, Morrow Mountain, and William B. Umstead, are also briefly outlined. Canoers and rock climbers will appreciate the brochure's list of favorite river runs and rugged rock faces within the state. The Travel Development Section also publishes the free booklet *The Mountains of North Carolina*. This attractive guide provides interesting infor-

mation about the state's high country and contains beautiful full-color photographs.

The 18–page *Directory of National Forest Recreation Areas* in North Carolina is a must for the camper, fisherman, canoeist, hunter, or wilderness traveler planning a visit to the Croatan, Pisgah, or Nantahala national forests. This free booklet will help you locate both developed and primitive recreation areas and campsites in the national forests, and provides information on the facilities you will find at each site and tells you how to get there. Primitive camping is allowed anywhere in the national forests unless posted otherwise. Permits are not needed for primitive camping. However, permits are required for entrance to Linville Gorge and Shining Rock Wilderness; they can be obtained at the district ranger stations that administer these areas. Canoeing is a favorite activity in all parts of North Carolina. The western region of the state, with its many hairraising white-water runs along the French Broad, Nantahala, South Fork New, Little Tennessee, and Oconaluftee rivers, offers maximum excitement and the greatest challenge to experienced canoers. Although streams and rivers in eastern North Carolina are not as rapid as those in the highlands, some of the coastal streams offer many rich and rewarding experiences to the canoer in search of uncommon species of wildlife such as the osprey, alligator, and bald eagle. Amateurs and experts will enjoy runs along the fast-moving swamp water of the Lumber River, through the cypress forests lining Merchants Millpond, and down the fine fishing waters of the Black River. Another favorite coastal run follows the White Oak River through Croatan National Forest, where alligators, unusual vegetation, and rare bird species are commonly sighted. The 27–mile wilderness stretch of the South Fork of the New National Wild and Scenic River offers some of the finest white-water canoeing in the state. For detailed information, write: Stone Mountain State Park, Star Route 1, Box 17, Roaring Gap 28668.

The U.S. Forest Service publishes maps of the *Appalachian Trail in Pisgah and Cherokee National Forests* and in *Nantahala National Forest*. Each map shows the route of the trail, nearby roads and highways, major forest features, towns, streams, rivers, lakes, trail shelters, recreation areas, water sources, and the like. Maps are available free from: Forest Supervisor, Plateau Building, 50 S. French Broad Ave., Asheville 28801.

North Carolina fishing and hunting regulations, seasons, and information about special permits and free publications may be obtained by writing to: Wildlife Resources Commission, Albemarle Bldg,, 325 N. Salisbury St., Raleigh 27611 (919)733–3391. The following fishing publications are available free from the commission: *Belew Lake, Fish Facts, Fishing at Lake Toisnot, Lake Waccamaw, Largemouth Bass in North Carolina, Rainbow Trout in North Carolina, The Bluegill in North Carolina,* and *The Chowan River*. Free publications about game birds and wildlife published by the commission include *Adventures with the Wood Duck, The Squirrel* (fox and gray), and *The European Boar in North Carolina*. Other free publications and regulations booklets published by the commission include *Boating in North Carolina Waters, Ecology Reprints, Designated Public Mountain Trout· Waters, North Carolina Fishing Rules, North Carolina Game Lands, Hunting & Trapping Regulations,* and *Motorboat Owner's Guide*.

The useful, free publication *Fishing in North Carolina*, a full-color 32–page booklet, contains descriptions and illustrations of popular lures and fish species, a map of the piers on the North Carolina coast, and detailed descriptions of offshore, surf and pier, inshore, inle', and sound, brackish water, midstate, and mountain waters fishing. The free 24–page booklet *Fishing North Carolina Waters*

provides a handy guide to fishing for striped bass, spring shad, fall speckled trout, winter chain pickerel, summer white perch, largemouth bass, trout, and panfish in eastern, western, and Piedmont regions of the state. The 38–page guide *Hunting in North Carolina* contains game species distribution maps and useful information about the black bear, wild boar, whitetail deer, raccoon, opossum, squirrel, rabbit, quail, wild turkey, fox, wildcat, upland game birds, and waterfowl hunting in the state. The free 70–page booklet *Hunting & Fishing Maps for North Carolina Game Lands* contains detailed maps of all state game lands, including the Nantahala, Pisgah, Green River, New Hope, Uwharrie, Holly Shelter, Croatan, Big Pocosin, Goose Creek, and Toxaway state game lands. All four publications are available free from the Wildlife Resources Commission. Four useful, informative publications, *Fishing Currituck Sound, Offshore Fishing in North Carolina, Outer Banks Surf Fishing,* and *Bass Fishing in North Carolina*, are available free from: Travel Development Section, P.O. Box 27687, Raleigh 27611.

Highways & Maps

The Blue Ridge Parkway is shown on the *North Carolina Highway Map*, an invaluable aid to anyone traveling around the state. State and U.S. highways, cities, towns, roads, state and national forests, railroads, ferries, airports, rest areas, park campsites, lakes, rivers, and streams are all shown on the map, which also provides insets showing routes in and through major cities. The map is available free from: Dept. of Natural & Economic Resources, Travel Development Section, Raleigh, NC 27611. See "Pisgah National Forest & The Blue Ridge Parkway" for additional information.

VACATION/ LODGING GUIDE

Cape Hatteras National Seashore & The Outer Banks

The long, narrow, sandy strip of land stretching 175 miles off the coast of North Carolina, known as the Outer Banks, encompasses the world famous island reserve of Cape Hatteras National Seashore—the nation's first national seashore, created more than 40 years ago, preserving 45 square miles on the 70–mile stretch of land between Whalebone Junction and Ocracoke Inlet. Towering waves, undisturbed sand dunes, quaint fishing villages, vast expanses of sand and windblown beach and flora are scenic sights of one of the nation's stormiest coasts. Off shore, the sands of the Outer Bank Islands form a shallow ledge which reaches twelve miles out to sea. On windy days magnificent waves rise like fighting stags and froth over the shoals. These shoals are littered with broken, rusted skeletons of long forgotten ships wrecked by savage storms or destroyed by enemy torpedoes during two world wars. A wild, unspoiled coast and everchanging scenery have added to the mystery and intrigue surrounding this area. During the 1500's Virginia Dare, the first English child born in America, was part of a lost colony on these shores. Her ghost is said to still roam the beaches. Blackbeard, the infamous pirate, is said to have holed up on the beaches of Ocracoke. His fate was met when five pistol shots were heard off Ocracoke Island in 1718—but the remains of his booty are still a mystery. The Air Age saw its birth on the Outer Banks, with the famous experiments conducted by the Wright Brothers on Kitty Hawk and Kill Devil Hills. Today, the Cape's natural treasures reward several million outdoor enthusiasts. Experienced anglers testify that there is no finer place along the East Coast for sport fishing than in the currents around the Outer Banks. Dolphin, sailfish, amberjack, barracuda, bluefin and yellowfin tuna, wahoo, cobia, and white marlin are fished for by fleets of chartered boats based at Oregon Inlet and Hatteras. Hatteras is referred to as "Game-fish Junction", to describe the meeting place of the northern and southern species. It is here that the cold green waters of the northern Labrador current flow against the warm, tropical Gulf Stream waters. The northern flowing Gulf Stream is pushed away from the coast, and over 40 varieties of northern and southern fish can be caught here. The Gulf Stream waters off Cape Hatteras produce some of the country's top-ranked fishing for trophy blue marlin. Catches up to 1,140 pounds have been reeled in off Hatteras, with the average running close to 300 pounds. Marlin begin to appear in the offshore waters late in May and continue to provide prize catches through late October. Hatteras boats fish the twelve miles of turbulent Diamond Shoals and the Gulf Stream waters, which start at Diamond Light Tower stationed on the eastern tip of the shoals. One of the largest fleets of sportfishing boats on the mid-Atlantic coast can be found at Oregon Inlet. From here charter boats fish the Platt and Wimble shoals and the Gulf Stream waters beyond. Porgies, groupers, grunts, triggerfish, red snappers, sea bass plus an occasional amberjack or dolphin are found with "Headboats" that fish out of the harbors' drift and bottom-fish the coral reefs.

There is top-notch fishing along Cape Hatteras for channel bass in the 20 to 50 pound class, bluefish, striped bass during the crisp fall months, spotted sea trout during the rising tide of cool fall mornings plus pompano, flounder and kingfish. The all-tackle world's record bluefish weighing 31 pounds 12 ounces was caught near Hatteras Inlet in 1972. The dunes, marshlands and woodlands of holly, oak, and pine on the Outer Banks provide a refuge for migratory waterfowl and shorebirds. Pea Island National Wildlife Refuge, on the northern tip of Hatteras Island, has paths and trails through 5,580 acres which serve as gathering points for Canada and snow geese, swans

and wild ducks. Some 300 species of birds have been seen on Cape Hatteras and throughout the area visitors can spot herons, egrets, seabirds and soaring gulls. Foxes, raccoons, muskrats, shrews and squirrels also inhabit the Outer Banks, and on Hatteras there are small deer. Camping is one of the best ways to appreciate the outdoor wonders offered on Cape Hatteras National Seashore. There are at least 20 private and five National Park Service Campgrounds. Surf fishermen and family vacationers will find dune buggy rentals, bait and tackle shops, accommodations and supplies at the towns of Rodanthe, Waves, Savo, Avon, Buxton, Hatteras, Ocracoke, and at Oregon Inlet. A free ferry connects Hatteras Island with Ocracoke Island.

Information Sources, Maps & Access

Information about local fishing conditions can easily be obtained from the local marinas and bait and tackle shops. For info write: Avon River and Recreation Enterprises, P.O. Box 35, Avon 27915; Cape Hatteras Fishing Pier, Hatteras 27943; Chicamaconico Enterprises, Rodanthe 27968; and Oregon Inlet Fishing Center, P.O. Box 342, Manteo 27954. Fishing and hunting regulations can be obtained from the North Carolina Wildlife Resources Commission, 325 N. Salisbury St., Raleigh, N.C. 27611, or call toll-free (1–800)662–7137. For detailed information and a free *Cape Hatteras Map/Brochure*, ferry schedules, and free *Birds of the Outer Banks*, *Fort Raleigh*, and *Ocracoke Island* guides, write: Superintendent, Cape Hatteras National Seashore, P.O. Box 457, Manteo 27954 (919)473–2117. The National Seashore recreation area is traversed by State Route 12 and is reached by U.S. Highways 64, 264 and 158. Beginning at Whalebone Junction, the park includes part of Bodie Island (pronounced "body"), Pea Island National Wildlife Refuge, Hatteras Island, and Ocracoke Island. The islands are connected by bridge or ferry, and you can drive the length of the park on Highway 12— a relatively narrow paved road with soft shoulders. The road passes through eight small villages that reflect the culture of the Outer Banks. They are not a part of the park. Stop at Whalebone Junction Information Center for assistance in planning your visit and for current information about accommodations in the area. Free informational brochures and activity schedules are available here and at all visitor centers. SandCastle, a children's activity center on Bodie Island, offers interpretive programs daily in the summer. These programs are geared to children but are open to people of all ages. The wind generator there demonstrates an alternate method of producing energy. At Coquina Beach, the remains of the shipwrecked *Laura A. Barnes* are accessible to the visitor. This four-masted schooner was stranded on a sand bar off Bodie Island in 1921. Nearby, lifesaving operations are reenacted weekly in summer with reproductions of equipment used by the U.S. Life Saving Service. You are invited to visit Pea Island National Wildlife Refuge to see many species of protected birds and animals. The refuge is operated by the U.S. Fish and Wildlife Service. The three lighthouses within the park are located on Bodie Island, Hatteras Island, and Ocracoke Island. The lighthouse tower at Cape Hatteras is open to the public during daylight hours. A ferryboat runs between Hatteras Island and Ocracoke Island during daylight hours. It is free of charge. Ocracoke Island and the tiny village around Silver Lake, because they are somewhat isolated, have retained much of their early charm and character. Blackbeard sold his pirate's booty here in the early 1700s. You might see another reminder of the past on your visit—the remnant of a once-large herd of banker ponies. Toll ferryboats operate between Ocracoke and Cedar Island (2¼ hours) and between Ocracoke and Swanquarter (2 hours) connecting the park with the mainland. Visitors should check ferry schedules well in advance. Reserva-

tions are required. Call Ocracoke (919)928–3841; Cedar Island (919)225–3551.

Outside the park not too far northwest of Whalebone Junction is *Fort Raleigh National Historic Site.* The park commemorates the "Lost Colony," one of several unsuccessful attempts by Sir Walter Raleigh to settle Roanoke Island in the 1580s. You can also visit *Wright Brothers National Memorial,* 14.5 kilometers (9 miles) north of Whalebone Junction. It was on the sand flats at the foot of Kill Devil Hill that Wilbur and Orville Wright flew the first heavier-than-air powered airplane in 1903.

Gateways & Accommodations

Buxton
(Pop. 700; zip code 27920; area code 919) is a picturesque village located on Hatteras Island. It is surrounded by, but not part of, Cape Hatteras National Seashore and acts as a gateway to this section brimming with natural beauty and recreational facilities. Folklore has it that the village of Buxton was the site of the first citrus tree, which grew from an accidentally discarded grapefruit seed. Today many yards contain grapefruit or orange trees, and there is an abundance of Spanish moss gracefully hanging from age-old living oaks. Buxton has a Museum of the Sea, with mementos of the lighthouse keepers' activities and daily lectures and nature walks given by park rangers. The Cape Hatteras Lighthouse rises 198 feet above the seashore, making it the tallest in the United States, and the only one visitors can climb. The outside of the lighthouse has a famous black and white barbershop spiral design. Inside there are 268 steps leading to outstanding views of the treacherous Diamond Shoals. Accommodations: *Falcon Motel* (rates: $24.96 double), with 35 good rooms and family units, swimming pool one mile east of town on the Hatteras Hwy./North Carolina 12 (995–5968); *Outer Banks Motel* (rates: $26 double), with 22 good rooms and family guest cottages, swimming beach, boat rentals, 1 mile east of town on the Hatteras Hwy./North Carolina 12 (995–5601.

Hatteras
(Pop. 1,300; zip code 27943; area code 919) is the largest village on the Outer Banks, with a population relying on fishing or boating for their livelihood. Anglers interested in Gulf Stream fishing have materially aided the town's development, as has the recent influx of

tourists. The character of the town is hearty and colorful. Live, scrubby, stunted seashore oaks and waterbushes contrast with brightly colored houses. The ancestors of these rugged natives are thought to be shipwrecked English sailors—and unmistakable traces of Devon accents fill conversations. Hatteras offers excellent sport fishing and is the site of the International Blue Marlin Tournament in mid-June. There are several fresh water ponds, water sports, and free ferries to Ocracoke Island. Accommodations: *Sea Gull Motel* (rates: $25–30 double), with 30 good rooms, swimming pool and beach, across from restaurant, one mile east of town on the Hatteras Hwy./North Carolina 12 (986–2550).

Kill Devil Hills
(Pop. 360; zip code 27948; area code 919) acts as a gateway to the Outer Banks and the Cape Hatteras National Seashore, in addition to being a self-contained resort area. Numerous hotels, motels, restaurants, shops, stores and recreational facilities can be found in the town's area, which stretches from the ocean to the sound's shores. Kill Devil Hills is adjacent to Kitty Hawk, the site of many of the Wright Brothers' famous flight experiments. The Wright Brothers National Memorial was constructed in 1932 by the Government to honor their achievement. The historic takeoff and landing spots are marked, and replicas of the first airplane as well as exhibits on the story of its invention can be seen. Admission to the exhibits is free. Accommodations: *Holiday Inn at Nags Head* (rates: $49–51 double), with 104 excellent rooms, restaurant, swimming pool and beach, between Milepost 9 and 10 on U.S. 158 Business Route (441–6333); *Quality Inn Sea Ranch* (rates: $40–60 double), with 49 excellent rooms, restaurant, coffeeshop, indoor heated pool, swimming beach, golf and tennis, at Milepost 7 on U.S. 158 Business Route (441–7126).

Nags Head
(Pop. 400; zip code 27959; area code 919), located just south of Kill Devil Hills on the northern limits of Outer Banks, is a year round fishing and beachcombing village. There are sand dunes reaching heights of 135 feet along this sandy, narrow strip of land. Fishing piers, boat rentals, good summer swimming and quiet beach walking can all be enjoyed at Nags Head. The area is chock full of folklore—the White Doe, the reincarnation of Virginia Dare, is said to still roam these hills. Colorful regional tales are told of a headless horseman who gallops over the dunes, and of an eternal bloodstain

on the beach left by a woman slain by her husband, who found her embracing another man and fired his gun before he learned the man was her long-lost brother. Aaron Burr's beautiful daughter left the shores of Nags Head on a small boat and is thought to have been forced to walk the ship's plank by pirates. A portrait of her, found later on the abandoned ship, led to the discovery of her death. Visitors can view artwork by old and modern masters, such as Chagall, Dali, Millet, and Renoir at the Seaside Art Gallery. Performances of the "Lost Colony" can be seen in the Waterside Theatre, which has lovely gardens designed to resemble a Pleasure Garden of the Elizabethan era. For reservations write: The Lost Colony Box 40, Manteo, N.C. 27954. Accommodations: *Ramada Inn* (rates: $53–56 double), with 108 excellent rooms and cottages, restaurant, swimming pool, just south of the U.S. 158 Bypass (441–6315); *Sea Foam Motel* (rates: $32–39 double), with 50 excellent rooms and family units, swimming pool and beach at Milepost 16.5 on U.S. 158 Business Route (441–7320); *The Sea Motel—A Quality Inn* (rates: $36–44 double), with 112 excellent rooms, restaurant, swimming pool and beach at Milepost 16.5 on U.S. 158 Business Route (441–7191).

Ocracoke

(Pop. 550; zip code 27960; area code 919) is considered the most picturesque town on the Outer Banks and is partly built around Silver Lake at the southern end of the banks. Visitors will find excellent bathing, crabbing, oystering, clamming, fishing, watersports, and hunting for wildfowl. A ferry operates from Cedar Island on the mainland to Ocracoke. Ferries are often crowded, and reservations can be made within 30 days by phone or in person at the ferry terminal. (Ocracoke Island terminal 928–3841; Cedar Island terminal 225–3551.) There is a visitors' center located in Ocracoke with history exhibits of the area. The National Park Service presents talks on Ocracoke Island and its history during the summer months. Blackbeard the pirate is believed to have used Ocracoke as his hiding place. The Old Pirate House is the reputed site of his headquarters, and Teach's Hole, an inlet near the village, is said to have been where Blackbeard maintained his ship and the location of his death in 1718. The Ocracoke Lighthouse, built in 1823, still beams its white light for 14 miles. Accommodations: *Harborside Motel* (rates: $28 double), with 18 good rooms and boat dock overlooking the harbor on North Carolina 12 (928–3111).

Rodanthe

(Pop. 460; zip code 27968; area code 919), located on the Outer Banks, the state's most eastern town, a quaint fishing village locally called Chicamaconico for the Coast Guard Station, which operated in the town for 80 years. The town's coastal waters saw more military activity during World Wars I and II than any other area in the United States. It is estimated that at least 29 ships were sunk in these waters. Today, Rodanthe serves as a gateway to the Cape Hatteras National Seashore area, which provides a full range of fishing and water activities. Accommodations: *Hatteras Island Motel* (rates: $19–25 double), with 64 good rooms, restaurant, on North Carolina 12 (987–2345).

Lodges & Resorts

★★★*Blackbeard's Lodge on Ocracoke Island* is 35 miles out in the Atlantic, one in a chain off the coast of North Carolina and part of the historic Outer Banks. It was here that the first explorers—Verrazano, Raleigh, Drake—set foot on this virgin land. The oldest lighthouse on the eastern coast is still in operation here, and the way of life has changed little since 1719. The first white colony was established here and the first white child, Virginia Dare, was born nearby—on Roanoke Island. Ocracoke Island was the homeport of Blackbeard, and this is where he was beheaded. More than 600 recorded shipwrecks have occurred off these banks and many more of which there are no official records. The bleached bones of some of these wrecks can still be seen on the island. The island is part of the Cape Hatteras National Seashore Park, and the National Park Service keeps the island in its natural state. There are no night clubs, movies, golf courses, or amusement parks. But there is one of the most beautiful, sparkling clean and completely unspoiled beaches on the East Coast—with many miles of beach, free to all (there are no private beaches here). The Park Service provides a protected area for swimming. The ocean beach is 15 miles long and never crowded even in summer. Surfing, beachcombing, and shelling are excellent. Pamlico Sound surrounds the island on three sides and provides good fishing grounds, boating, and swimming for children. The Park Service provides lectures and nature walks; boat trips to other islands can be arranged. The island is a favorite place for hunting and fishing enthusiasts and it has been said that more fish are caught off the coast of North Carolina per man than any place in the world. It has also been termed "one of the ten most fascinating places to visit." (This is the home of the famous wild ponies—

a small herd of which still roam a few miles of fenced-in range.) The lodge provides a colorful link with this island's most fascinating history. Its decor is based on pirates, shipwrecks, and buried treasure. The atmosphere is friendly and informal. Rooms are large, comfortable, air-conditioned and range from $19.50–36 double occupancy, depending on the season. All rooms have private baths. Contact Doward H. Brugh, owner-manager, Blackbeard's Lodge, Ocracoke, NC 27960 (919)928–3421.

★★★★*The Island Inn* is located on Ocracoke Island off the coast of North Carolina, 18 miles from the Gulf Stream. It has been called the "Bermuda of the U.S.A.," North Carolina's "Cape Cod" and the "Pearl of the Outer Banks." Much of the island is uninhabited, and filled with scenic wilderness of sand, surf and solitude. Sports minded people are attracted to the island year round to take advantage of the natural setting and opportunities provided by the harbor for fine boating, sailing, and water skiing. The sound and ocean are model beaches for swimming, sunbathing and beachcombing. Or just stroll on the shores to enjoy the silence and beauty of the picturesque seascapes. The coast is a perfect setting for fishing and hunting. The inn does not have planned activities, but maintains the easy-going, relaxed pace of its natural setting. The area has become a haven for artists, photographers and writers. Ocracoke Village, the location of Island Inn, is a collection of cottages, windblown oakes, sandy lanes and rustic docks. The inn has harbor and sunset views, a front porch for easy-paced rocking, and a dining room specializing in fresh seafood from the Ocracoke waters. The inn's rooms have private baths, air-conditioning, TVs, and carpeting. The owners are always ready to exchange conversation and a bit of local history. The cost of meals is not included in rates, but can be added to your bill. Rates: May through October: $22–32; November through April: $18–28. For further information contact: The Island Inn, Ocracoke, NC 27960 (919)928–4351.

Great Smoky Mountains National Park

See "Tennessee" chapter for details.

Nantahala National Forest & Blue Ridge Highlands

This sprawling 420,000–acre forest reserve, once the heart of the Cherokee Indian Nation and named after the Cherokee word for "Land-of-the-Noon-Day Sun," takes in some of the finest fishing, camping, hunting, and wilderness backpacking areas in the East, including the towering 5,000–foot peaks of the Nantahala Range in the northwestern part of the state. Old logging roads and hundreds of miles of rugged wilderness trails, including the Appalachian Trail, provide access to the Joyce Kilmer Forest, Nantahala, Tallulah, and

Little Tennessee rivers; the Snowbird, Valley, Tusquitte, Cheoah, and Cowee Mountains, and to Fontana, Santeetlah, Hiwassee, Chatuge, and Cheoah lakes. The remote Snowbird Creek Wilderness offers some of the finest fishing in the eastern United States for large, wild brook trout. The forest and state wildlife management areas provide top-ranked hunting in season for whitetail deer, wild turkey, grouse, quail, and wild boar. Several large lakes and powerful white-water mountain streams in the Nantahala Forest highlands offer nationally renowned fishing for large rainbow, brown, and brook trout, largemouth and smallmouth bass, and kokanee salmon.

Beautiful Nantahala Lake, formed by the damming of the swift, deep-flowing Nantahala River (a renowned rainbow trout stream that provides natural spawning beds for the large lake-run fish), provides excellent fishing for hook-jawed kokanee and rainbow trout. Large Lake Hiwassee, located to the west of Nantahala Lake and formed by the damming of the Hiwassee River, holds largemouth and smallmouth bass and walleye, as does Lake Santeetlah, formed by the impoundment of the Little Tennessee River. Huge Fontana Lake is bordered on the north by the Great Smoky Mountain National Park, on the west by Cheoah Lake, on the east by the Tuckasegee River Valley, and on the south by the Cheoah Mountains and Nantahala National Forest and is fed by the Nantahala, Little Tennessee, and Tuckasegee rivers and by the cold, clear mountain waters of Hazel, Eagle, Forney, Sawyer, Noland, Panther, and Alaska creeks. Situated at 1,710 feet elevation, the lake has a surface area of 10,670 acres, a 248–mile-long irregularly shaped shoreline, and a maximum depth of 440 feet. Fontana offers renowned fishing for walleye, largemouth and smallmouth bass, crappie, and white bass. The cold, deep blue-green waters of beautiful Cheoah Lake, located just below the great Fontana Dam, hold some huge tackle-busting rainbows. Many small lakes and remote ponds located at elevations ranging from 2,000 to 6,000 feet dot the highlands of the forest and provide good fishing for those willing to hike in for pan-sized trout and bass. These small gemlike lakes and beaver ponds are easily identified on U.S. Geological Survey Maps of the region. The mountain streams of the Cherokee Indian Reservation, north of the forest, are heavily stocked with rainbow and brook trout, and many of the trout are quite large. The Indians and federal authorities manage the Cherokee waters under a special permit system. To get a copy of the regulations and information on the permits, write: Cherokee Fish & Game Management Enterprise, Box 302, Cherokee 28719.

Nine developed campgrounds with more than 400 family units are scattered throughout the forest. Some of the more popular include the 66 sites on Hiwassee Lake, the beautiful new camping area at Cable Cove on Fontana Lake, and the Tsali Campground with 42 sites, also near Fontana Lake. A shore distance southwest of the Great Smoky Mountains National Park lie several remote high country wild areas in the Nantahala National Forest that offer some of the finest backpacking and wilderness fly fishing and camping opportunities in eastern America. The Joyce Kilmer Wilderness Area, a 32,500–acre tract of rugged terrain in the Nantahala National Forest, straddles the Tennessee-North Carolina line. In the heart of the wilderness is the Joyce Kilmer Memorial Forest, dedicated to the author of "Trees." The forest covers 3,840 acres, the entire watershed of Little Santeetlah Creek, and is surrounded by mile-high ridges curving around the stands of virgin timber like a giant horseshoe. In 1935, when the forest tract was chosen, it was recognized as the finest remainder of our eastern primeval forest then in Forest Service ownership. Today, as then, it is a prime example of the wilderness found by white men when they first ventured into the southern Appalachians. Huge poplars and hemlocks in the lower cove create green, canopied chambers with mossy

floors. In the higher elevations, towering oaks and maples predominate. Adjoining the Kilmer Forest is another roadless valley, the watershed of Slickrock Creek. Tributary streams flowing down the steep surrounding ridges have sculpted the valley's sides while the creek itself runs clear and pure, cascading over two beautiful waterfalls. Slickrock is especially famous as one of the finest brown trout streams in the East. First stocked in the 1930s, the creek's fish now reproduce naturally, and grow to trophy weights in the remote, deep-flowing pools.

To the east of Slickrock is the valley of Yellowhammer Creek and on the west, the undeveloped half of the drainage of Citico Creek. All four creeks have carved extraordinary valleys where their tributaries have incised deep V-shaped troughs transforming the mountainsides into a series of serrated furrows. The topography of the wilderness, which includes a total of 10,000 acres of virgin timber, is rugged and steep, ranging in elevation from 1,086 feet at Calderwood Lake to 5,341 feet at Stratton Bald. The high dividing ridges, nearly level for long distances, usually exceed altitudes of 5,000 feet. The entire area is generously crisscrossed with foot trails offering excellent opportunities for hiking, camping, hunting, and fishing. The size of the area offers the backpacker routes on which he can travel for days without doubling back or retracing steps. A large number of trail entry points also make for a variety of day hikes.

Slightly east of the Joyce Kilmer Forest is the Cheoah Bald Wilderness, halfway between Bryson City and Andrews. The central feature of the area, the hub of the whole 19,000–acre tract, is Cheoah Bald itself with an elevation of 5,062 feet. Some 12 miles of the Appalachian Trail, regarded by many as the most spectacular segment of the trail in the Southeast, pass over the top of the Bald, offering a splendid panorama of the Smokies and surrounding terrain. The south slope of Cheoah Bald forms one side of the Nantahala Gorge, a canyon so deep and narrow that sunlight rarely hits the valley floor. The area's steep terrain is covered by substantial stands of virgin timber. The same precipitous slopes create numerous waterfalls and cascades, the best known of which are found along Ledbetter Creek. A few old logging trails, well mossed over, make excellent hiking trails through the remote reaches of the wilderness. Wildlife, including the elusive black bear, is abundant.

The 15,000–acre wilderness area surrounding Snowbird Creek is practically guaranteed to keep wilderness fly fishermen in a state of permanent bliss. This stream and its major tributary, Sassafras Creek, are entirely contained within the Nantahala National Forest and have been rated among the eight best trout fishing streams in western North Carolina. All sections of Snowbird Creek offer excellent fishing, but the stretch above Big Falls offers a population restricted solely to "wild" brook trout, making the creek the largest in the state with a population limited to brook trout. The wilderness is also renowned for its many waterfalls and stands of hardwood and pine, generously nourished by the annual 80–inch rainfall. Trails follow old logging roads up Snowbird Creek and wind through the many spectacular balds of surrounding ridges, including the Snowbird and Cheoah mountains.

Information Sources, Maps & Access

For detailed information and a full-color *Nantahala National Forest Map* (50¢), contact: Supervisor's Office, U.S. Forest Service, P.O. Box 2750, Asheville, NC 28802 (704)258–2850. Nantahala National Forest is accessible via U.S. Highway 19 from Asheville, U.S. Highway 23 from Waynesville; and U.S. 129 from Knoxville, Tennessee. Other nearby towns include Franklin, Andrews, Sylva, and Bryson City.

Gateways & Accommodations

Bryson City

(Pop. 1300; zip code 28713; area code 704) is situated at the entrance to the Great Smoky Mountains National Park at the point where the Little Tennessee and Tuckasegee Rivers flow together, and provides much in the way of fishing, hiking, boating, swimming and camping for the tourist and outdoorsman. Of special interest is Fontana Dam, which is the tallest dam in the TVA system at 480 feet; Nantahala National Forest, with its scenic drives through the Southern Appalachians and sparkling, cascading waterfalls—some dropping 411 feet; and the Joyce Kilmer Wilderness Area with 15,000 acres—providing many activities for all kinds of nature lovers, including camping, swimming, boating, fishing (bass and trout), hunting (deer, wild boar, turkey and ruffed grouse). Accommodations: *Bryson City Motor Court* (rates: $20–22 double), with 18 good rooms and swimming pool at Main and Spring Sts. (488–2127); *Hemlock Inn* (rates: $44–52 Modified American Plan double), with 27 excellent rooms and guest cottages, dining room, in beautiful alpine location three miles east of town off U.S. 19 (488–9820).

Cherokee

(Pop. 8,000; zip code 28719; area code 704) is the site of the Cherokee Indian Reservation, the largest (63,000 acres) east of Wisconsin. There are 8,000 descendants of the Cherokee tribe living here at the edge of the Great Smoky Mountains National Park area. Though progressive in their ideas with schools, hospitals, offices and dorms for living, they still maintain many of their traditions. Nearby is the Museum of the Cherokee Indian, Oconaluftee Indian Village and Museum, Frontierland, Cycolorama of the Cherokee Indian, Santa's Land Park and Zoo. A seasonal event is a drama called "Unto These Hills" recreating the history of the Cherokee Nation. Accommodations: *Carriage Inn Resort Motel* (rates: $24 double), with 25 excellent rooms and swimming pool, across from restaurant, located four miles west of town on U.S. 19 (488–2398); *Craig's Motel* (rates: $22–28 double), with 30 excellent rooms, heated swimming pool and trout stream, located one mile east of town on U.S. 19 (497–3821); *Holiday Inn of Cherokee* (rates: $38 double), with 101 excellent rooms, restaurant, heated pool, one mile west of town on U.S. 19 (497–9181); *Teddy Bear Motel* (rates: $24 double), with 40 excellent rooms, restaurant, heated pool, four miles west of town on U.S. 19 (488–6112).

Franklin

(Pop. 2400; zip code 28734; area code 704) is noted for the beauty of its setting and mountain climate—it overlooks the beautiful valley of the Little Tennessee River and is surrounded by several mountain ranges. It was originally the site of a Cherokee settlement and was in fact occupied by the Cherokees until 1819. The main attraction is the Cowee Ruby Mines—a series of 15 mines in which visitors can dig for precious and semi-precious stones. Nearby is the Nantahala National Forest including the Wayah State Game Refuge, Nantahala Lake and the summit of Wayah Bald—one of the highest mountains in the eastern U.S. The area is rich for fishing, camping, hiking and picnicking. The Appalachian Trail crosses here as it follows the crest of the Nantahala Range. Accommodations: *City Motel* (rates: $22–30 double), with 41 excellent rooms, swimming pool across from restaurant, one mile east of town at the junction of U.S. 23 and 441 bypass (524–6491); *Colonial Inn* (rates: $32 double), with 30 excellent rooms and swimming pool across from restaurant, four miles south of town on U.S. 23/441 (524–6600); *Quality Inn Town* (rates: $24–28 double), with 50 excellent rooms and swimming pool at 277 E. Main St. (524–4451).

Highlands

(Pop. 600; zip code 28741; area code 704) is a summer resort town completely surrounded by the Nantahala National Forest in the "Land of the Waterfalls." Highlands lies on a high plateau in the Appalachians. The variety of plant and animal life in the region makes it an attraction to all naturalists. The road leading northwest from the city and to Cullasaja Gorge passes famous waterfalls, one of which you can stand under and view the surrounding area and river. The area provides picnicking, formal gardens and museums. Of special note is the Biological Museum with a cross section of a 425 year old hemlock from which historical events to the time of Columbus have been traced. Accommodations: (see below for listings).

Robbinsville

(Pop. 800; zip code 28771; area code 704) is a small mountain village and shopping place for the Snowbird Indians who live in the Snowbird Mountains. They are often seen walking through the town. The history of the town goes back to the Battle of Horseshoe Bend and the Creek War in 1814 between the Cherokees and Andrew Jackson. One of the highlights of the town is a ride on the Bear Creek Scenic Railroad—a round-trip steam train ride to the rim of Nantahala Gorge. The Joyce Kilmer Wilderness Area is nearby, and there is much in this area to attract fishermen and huntsmen. Accommodations: *San Ran Motel* (rates: $16 double), with 10 excellent rooms on U.S. 129 bypass (479–3256).

Lodges & Resorts

★★★★*Bear Paw at Lake Hiwassee* is a superb family mountain resort nestled in the Blue Ridge Mountains of the Nantahala National Forest. Beautiful Lake Hiwassee, with 189 miles of scenic shoreline, offers outstanding fishing for trout, pike, crappie, large and smallmouth bass in its crystal clear waters. A 75–slip marina offers boat and motor rentals, launching ramp, tackle shop and all the necessities for exploring the hidden coves around the lake. Accommodations are in rustic wood and stone-crafted one, two, or three bedroom cottages, some with fireplaces, scattered around the hilly woodlands of the resort. Each cottage has its own porch with views of the lake or mountains and a nearby outdoor grill for family cookouts. Cottages are fully equipped and are designed to let you set your own vacation pace. Services and facilities include an Olympic size swimming pool, tennis courts, recreation center, and 2½ miles of marked nature trails bordered by rhododendron, mountain laurel,

dogwood, and other flora. Daily housekeeping cottage rates range from $19–31 per day. For additional information, contact: Bear Paw, Rte. 4, Murphy, NC 28906 (704)644–5451.

★★★*Blue Boar Lodge at the Joyce Kilmer Forest* is nestled on the shores of beautiful Lake Santeetlah in the Nantahala National Forest, bordered by the rare stands of virgin pine in Joyce Kilmer National Forest. The lodge offers airy spacious rooms, delicious southern-style home cooking, and a crackling fire to take the edge off cool nights, even in summer. Fishermen can troll the clear lake waters for small- or large-mouth bass, walleye, pan fish, muskie, or channel catfish. Rowboats, canoes, and motor boats are all rented at the lake dock. Hiking paths lead from the lodge through the unique Joyce Kilmer Forest, and across mountain vistas for panoramic views. Lodge rates, including meals, are $18 per person double occupancy. For more information write: Blue Boar Lodge, Joyce Kilmer Forest Road, Robbinsville, NC 28771 (704)479–8126.

★★★*Boundary Tree Lodge* is located a half-mile from the Great Smoky Mountains National Park amid lovely wooded scenery. Fine fishing is just across the street from the resort in the Oconaluftee River. The resort is owned and operated by the Eastern Band of Cherokee Indians and has a reservation desk for sightseeing plus performances of "Unto These Hills," an outdoor drama depicting the Cherokee history. More Indian lore can be seen in the Oconaluftee Indian Village, a recreated Cherokee village of 200 years ago. The lodge has a heated swimming pool, a children's pool and playground, tennis courts, and hiking trail. In addition to the Great Smoky Mountains National Park, area attractions include Frontierland, Santaland, and Cyclorama. Accommodations include rooms in a modern motel, lodge and cottages. Rooms are carpeted, air-conditioned and have color TVs. Cottages have kitchenettes with all utensils, fireplaces and linen. Daily maid service is provided. Meals are not included in the rates, can be enjoyed in the lodge's two restaurants. Rates: November-May, rooms $18–21; cottage $28; June-September-October, rooms $26–28, cottages $38; July-August, rooms $28–31, cottages $41. For further information contact: Boundary Tree Lodge, P.O. Box 464, Cherokee, NC 28719 (704)497–2155.

★★★*Folkestone Lodge* is a small, charming, old-fashioned mountain lodge located adjacent to the Great Smoky Mountains National Park. The lodge is near Bryson City, a small Appalachian town, only ten miles away from the Cherokee Indian Reservation with tourist sights, museums and historic reenactment dramas. The lodge is furnished with antiques, serves home cooking, and fresh bread daily, and has no television. A mountain lore library is provided for lodge guests. Nature walks, pack trips, and guided wilderness trips are conducted by the lodge which also has bicycle rentals. Nearby in Great Smoky Mountains National Park there is hiking, camping, trout fishing, mountain lore programs, campfire talks, and tubing down Deep Creek. Over 600 miles of maintained hiking trails lead past waterfalls and trout streams to an elevation of 6,600 feet. There is a weekly auction nearby, and the Kranichs add other information about local happenings and history. Rates including breakfast are $22 per day per room (double occupancy). Children up to age 16 are $7. For reservations or information write: Folkestone Lodge, Route 1, Box 310, West Deep Creek Road, Bryson City, NC 28713 (704)488–2730.

★★★*Fontana Village*; is nestled deep in the heart of the Great Smoky Mountains, surrounded by high peaks and crystal clear lakes. It's North Carolina's largest and most complete resort, featuring a wide range of activities and opportunities for relaxing. Fishing for bass and trout can be enjoyed on beautiful 30–mile long Fontana Lake, with never a closed season. Boats, motors, bait, licenses or temporary

permits are available. There is a launching ramp for those with their own boats, and open or covered docking is available. The lake also provides fine waterskiing, canoeing and paddleboating. Guests can also try their fishing abilities out in the trout pond. There are five Laykold lighted tennis courts, a 9–hole par 3 golf course, a marina, two pools (adult and children's), horseback riding, boating excursions, archery and craftmaking. Hiking trails are laced throughout the resort's area. Game facilities are provided, including horseshoes, miniature golf, shuffleboard, softball, basketball, ping-pong, plus a game room. All recreational activities operate on a full scale April through October—including movies, lectures and talent shows. Certain indoor recreation is partially curtailed during May and September to accommodate Square Dance Festivals. Accommodations at the resort can be selected from a new 80–room Inn, the 56–room lodge or more than 300 cottages in a variety of types from one to three bedrooms. Every cottage has a living room, bath and kitchen equipped for light housekeeping. Towels are delivered daily and linens every fourth day. Rooms in the inn have extra length beds, color TV and suites with wood-burning fireplaces. The lodge has maid service, wall-to-wall carpeting, and room air-conditioning. A gourmet menu is featured in the resort's Pioneer Restaurant, and an on-the-premise cafeteria provides quick meals. Meals are not included in rates. Rates: The inn, summer rates $35.75–51.75; cottages, summer rates $29.75–66.75; The lodge, summer $24.75–26.75; all rates are daily double occupancy. For further information contact: Fontana Village, Fontana Dam, NC 28733 (704)498–2238.

Lee's Inn, a spacious colonial inn in Highlands, is located in the highest spot on the eastern seaboard, surrounded by the great slopes of the Great Smoky Mountains. The inn has a large outdoor pool, two new tennis courts nearby, and is close to three lush, rolling golf courses. Fishing, mountain hiking, gem mining, and canoeing can all be enjoyed in the area. Lee's Inn is adjacent to Nantahala National Forest and Great Smoky Mountains National Park, and a short walk from the unique shops and summer theater in Highlands. Nearby are the Dry Falls, so called because they can be walked under without getting wet, and Bridal Veil Falls, which can be driven under. These, and the lovely Cullasaja, Satulah, Glen and Highland Falls make Highlands known as the "Land of Waterfalls." Lee's Inn offers a supervised program for youths ages 6–16, including cookouts, hayrides, gem mining, hiking, mountain crafts, and nature study. All rates include three generous meals daily in the beautiful Rhododendron Room, which features fresh fruits and vegetables and such specialties as southern country ham, under a canopy of live rhododendron in bloom. Inn rooms, depending on what part of the season the room is reserved, are $44–50 for a double room. Motel rooms are $52–54 for a double room. Family inn suites, with two connecting bedrooms and private bath, accommodate 4–6 persons, and are $80–88 for four. Luxury suites, with two bedrooms, private bath, dressing room, sitting room with fireplace and private porch accommodate 4–20 persons, and are $114–128 for four persons. For more information write: Lee's Inn and Motel, Highlands, NC 28741 (704)526–2171.

****Nantahala Outdoor Center** is located where the Appalachian trail crosses the Nantahala River. It is a focal point for some of the most exciting outdoor activities around. For starters they have four whitewater rafting expeditions. Beginners take the 8–mile Nantahala trip, culminating with a run through breathtaking Nantahala Falls. The Ocoee trip, one of the most continuous whitewater trips you can take, was chosen as the site of the 1978 National Championship Wildwater Races. The excitement of "Deliverance" is captured in trips on the Chattooga, the river the movie was filmed on. There are two trips on the Chattooga, varying in difficulty, but both offering

beautiful, remote forest scenery. NOC has an outstanding whitewater instruction program. A library of films and books on paddling is available, and videotape equipment is often used to analyze a student's techniques. In addition to this complete whitewater agenda, NOC offers courses in rock climbing, orienteering and backpacking in an area perfect to practice any of these skills. The mountains can also be enjoyed via horseback with one of NOC's guided trips. In January and February there's cross-country skiing in the backcountry of the Smoky Mountains. Rentals and guidance for beginners are available. And if you wish something more exotic or relaxing, you can send for information on expeditions and trips NOC is planning. Camping facilities are near all whitewater trails. Lodging is available at the NOC motel. Rooms with two double beds, three double beds, kitchenettes and a hotel room with three bunk beds are available. Additional lodging is available at other nearby hotels. NOC has complete outfitting facilities for tents, stove kits, sleeping bags and just about everything else that is needed. Rates: Guided raft trips, $12–25 per person, depending on river. Raft rentals, $20–35. No rafts may be rented for the Chattooga River. Private instruction in whitewater, rockclimbing, backpacking, $30 per person. Guide service for backpacking, canoeing and kayaking $15. Meals are priced $2–4.50. Motel rooms are $14–20 per night. Group rates available. For further information contact: Nantahala Outdoor Center, Star Rt. Box 68, Bryson City, NC 28713 (704)488–2175.

***Nantahala Village**, including a mountain lodge, log cabins, stone and frame cottages, mobile homes, and private mountainside homes, is situated on rolling 215 wooded acres overlooking Fontana Lake and surrounded by the Great Smoky Mountains. The Cherokee Indians named the deep river gorge the Nantahala, the "land of the noonday sun," because only the direct noonday sun penetrates deep into the spectacular mountain cleft formed by the Nantahala River. The sun shines brightly, however, on the tennis courts, swimming pool, miniature golf course, shuffle board courts, and badminton nets on the sprawling lawns of Nantahala Village nearby. There are many scenic horseback riding trails throughout the Smokies, and the Appalachian trail crosses the Nantahala River gorge. Fontana Lake is a man-made lake, 25 miles long, popular for swimming and fishing for largemouth bass, smallmouth white bass, bream, and pike. Outboard motor boats and paddle boats are rented at the lake dock. Whitewater trips can be arranged on the Nantahala River, chosen by the American Canoeing Association as the site of the southeastern

slalom and whitewater championship races. Cherokee heritage is still alive on the nearby reservation, and the story of the Cherokee nation is told in the play "Unto These Hills." Anyone can pay an entrance fee and hunt for rubies and sapphires in the local mines. Four annual rock swaps are held annually in the gorge. The restaurant at the Nantahala Village boasts the finest mountain cooking in the Smokies, which is served family-style in the dining room, with its high beamed ceilings and open hearth. During the summer months there is a supervised activity program for children. A community rec room with ping-pong, pool and large TV room are open to guests. Lodge rooms accommodate 2–4 persons and rates range between $23 and $29 during the summer season, June 15–Labor Day, and between

$16–22 in the spring (April 1–June 14) and fall (Labor Day-November 25). There are eight motel apartments, with two bedrooms, each with twin beds, a private bath, and back porch overlooking the Smoky Mountains. Four of the eight motel apartments also have kitchens. Rates for motel apartments without kitchens range between $26–30 during the summer, and $19–23 in the spring and fall. Motel apartments with kitchens are $32–36 in the summer season, and $25–29 in the spring and fall. Rustic one-room log cabins, nestled in the wooded slope, accommodate 1–4 people and are $24–28 in the summer months, depending on the number of people, and $16–20 in the spring and fall. Stone and frame cottages, which dot the wooded landscape and look out to the blue peaks of the Smokies, have between two and five bedrooms, accommodating 2–8 persons. Many have fireplaces, and the new cottages have air-conditioning and TV. Rates range between $30–48 in the summer, depending on the size of the cabin and the number of people in the party, and $23–37 in the spring and fall. The private topsider mountain view house, with two bedrooms, two private baths, living room with a fireplace and panoramic view of the Smokies is $51–55 in the summer, and $45–48 in the spring and fall, and will accommodate six people. Rates for mobile homes accommodating 4–6 persons range between $40–44. For more information write: Nantahala Village, P.O. Drawer J, Bryson City, NC 28713 (704)488–2826.

★★★*Osceola Lake Inn* hugs the shores of beautiful Lake Osceola, surrounded by the Great Smoky Mountains and the peaks of the Blue Ridge. Osceola Lake is ideal for fishing, and the inn provides guests with boats to explore the wooded coves and lakeshore. There is also a large outdoor pool, a 9–hole putting green, an all-weather tennis court and badminton nets and horseshoe pits on the spacious grounds. Nearby is one of North Carolina's most scenic 18–hole championship golf courses. The Blue Ridge Parkway rises over the crest of the Blue Ridge, providing panoramic views of the surrounding countryside. Bridle paths and hiking trails lead over meadows, past many scenic waterfalls and fast-moving mountain springs. In nearby Hendersonville, Broadway plays are produced weekly by the Flat Rock Playhouse, and there is square dancing in the main street every Monday night. The Osceola Lake Inn is well known for Jewish/American cooking, with fresh fruits and vegetables supplied by the local farms. Spacious air-conditioned rooms are available in the main inn, and there are individual guest lodges with private bath surrounding the main building. Rates vary according to the time of the season. Generally, inn rooms are $14–17 per person daily including breakfast and dinner, and lodges are $15–29 per person daily. Special spring and fall rates are also offered. For more information write: The Osceola Lake Inn, P.O. Box 2258, Hendersonville, NC 28739 (704)692–2544; Winter address: 250 Palm Beach Avenue, Palm Island, Miami Beach, FL 33139 (305)534–8356.

★★★*Skyline Lodge & Village* is a year-round resort constructed of redwood and granite, nestled atop a 4,300–foot mountain overlooking the waterfalls of Big Creek and the scenic surrounding countryside. In the winter months guests can enjoy sleigh riding, skating on Skyline Lake, or skiing on nearby slopes. Warm weather sports include swimming in the resort's heated pool, all-weather tennis courts, and hiking on scenic nature trails. There is golf and horseback riding nearby. Skyline Lake provides fine rainbow and brook trout fishing as well as boating. Nearby attractions include Bridal Veil Falls, Lake Sequoyah, Mirror Lake, Dry Falls; Whiteside Mountain, Bear Pen Mountain, Kelsey Trail, Nantahalal National Forest and gem mines which yield over 200 kinds of minerals and gems. There is also a Biological Museum with a collection of cut stones and a garden with over 400 marked species. Meals are served in the resort's Hearthside Dining Room, which has a panoramic view of the adjacent mountains and streams. Three beautiful open hearths in the dining areas, made of area granite, burn during the fall and winter months. Accommodations include single or double rooms; extra large rooms with panoramic view and refrigerator and some with balconies and bridal suites. Meals are not included in rates. Rates: Rooms $24–45. All rooms are equipped with color TVs. For further information contact: Skyline Lodge & Village, Box 630, Highlands, NC 28741 (704)526–2121.

★★*Snowbird Mountain Lodge* is nestled in the heart of the Nantahala National Forest, high up in the Santeetlah Gap at an elevation of 2,880 feet. Two miles from the lodge is the magnificent Joyce Kilmer Memorial Forest with 3,800 acres of virgin timber, one of the few remaining primeval forests in the Eastern U.S. You can fish, hike, or swim in the mountain streams. Nearby are the Great Smoky Mountains and the entire area is reminiscent of the days when the first settlers came to this region. In fact, the feeling is much like a great primeval forest, almost unchanged since the Indians made it their home. There are well kept hiking paths for those less inclined to venture through the thickets. Activities at the lodge itself include shuffleboard, table tennis, archery, croquet, horseshoes, badminton, miniature bowling, skittles. There are movies (wildlife and travelogues) and color slides of the area to watch. There's a reading room, with a large selection library, gameroom,

and TV room as well. The fishing includes both stream and lake fishing, and boats, motors and bait are available nearby. The lodge is rustic and has accommodations for 36 guests; rates range from $23–28 per person per day. A full American Plan is offered and will be welcomed as the invigorating mountain air will stimulate your appetite. The season is mid-May to November and temperatures range from 60–70°. In any season the views and scenery are breathtaking. For further information contact: Snowbird Mountain Lodge, Joyce Kilmer Forest Road, Robbinsville, NC 28771. Your hosts are Mary and Ed Williams and you can call them at (704)479-3433.

Travel Services

Nantahala Outdoor Center, see above for description.

Smoky Mountain River Expeditions is a member of the Eastern River Outfitters Association and runs white water rafting day trips on the French Broad River in North Carolina, as well as the Ocoee River in Tennessee. Smoky Mountain River Expeditions provides all equipment, including rafts, paddles and life jackets, and operates trips safe enough for anyone 12 years of age or older. Their season is April through November and they book trips for individuals and groups. Rafters must wear sneakers and comfortable clothes. In summer, swimsuits with sun protection are recommended. For cooler weather trips, wet suits, wool clothing, rain suits or nylon wind breakers can make the trip more comfortable. For the *French Broad River* trip, rafters meet at the headquarters in Hot Springs (off Routes 25 & 70) at 9:15 AM and are shuttled to Barnard at 9:30. The run covers 7½ miles of rushing water, winding past beautiful rugged boulders and wooded mountains. The river trip is guided by professionals and takes 5 to 6 hours. Lunch is provided on the trip, but no alcoholic beverages are allowed. Participants are taken back to the Hot Springs headquarters where there are changing rooms, rest rooms and a small shop. Babysitting service is available by prior notice at $10 per day per child. The trip is $22 per person and $20 each in groups of 20 or more. The *Ocoee River* trip goes down a scenic stretch of whitewater between the TVA Dams #1 and #2 on the Ocoee River in Tennessee. This is a five-mile rapids run with very little quiet water. Dress suggestions and equipment provided are the same as on the French Broad River trips, but no lunch is provided. This trip takes two to three hours. Two trips are run three days a week only on Friday, Saturday and Sunday. Each day the first trip starts at 10:30 AM and the second at Tennessee Highway 68 near Ducktown, TN for a safety orientation. Then they are shuttled to the put-in to start the river trip. After the trip, rafters are shuttled back to the Ole Copper Inn. Baby sitting service is not available on this trip and the rate is $15 per person. For information and reservations write: Smoky Mountain River Expeditions, Inc., P.O. Box 398, Hot Springs, NC 28743 (704)622-7260.

Pisgah National Forest & The Blue Ridge Parkway

This renowned hiking, fishing, canoe-camping, and hunting area in northwestern North Carolina covers 478,000 acres of wild rivers, deep gorges, cascading waterfalls, thickets of rhododendron and azalea, and colorful forests of yellow poplar, red oak, sugar maple, spruce, and black cherry. The forest clover provides superb hunting for whitetail deer, black bear, ruffed grouse, wild turkey, and boar.

The biblical name Pisgah was given to a prominent peak near Asheville by a pioneer mountain preacher. Nearby is Rat Mountain, resembling a rodent with tail extended and head lowered between its front paws. When snow covers the northern slope of Pisgah, the twin peaks of Rat and Mount Pisgah are said to resemble a bride and groom standing out in heroic stature against the landscape. In the Toecane district of the forest is Roan Mountain (6286 feet), famed for its spectacular display of native purple rhododendron in bloom the last two weeks of June. Awesome views of the surrounding countryside are available from the trails winding toward the lofty summit. The top of the mountain is relatively broad, level, and almost treeless. Each June the flowering of the rhododendron is celebrated by a festival atop the mountain.

In the forest's Grandfather district, the Linville Gorge area, a 7,600–acre tract, is maintained as a primitive, natural environment, an unspoiled setting for native fauna and flora, including many rare plant species. Cliffs of the Linville Mountains rim the gaping crevice on the west, with the rugged broken range of Jonas Ridge forming the eastern wall of the canyon. The steep sides of the gorge enclose the wild Linville River, which makes a dizzying descent of 2,000 feet in only 12 miles. Hunting and fishing are permitted here under state regulations. Primitive camping is also available. Access is via foot trails leading from State Highway 105. Free permits, available at the district ranger's office, are needed to enter the area. Since the Linville Gorge Wilderness is a challenge to even the most experienced hiker, anyone using the trails is advised to inform the National Forest District Ranger's Office at Marion of all hiking plans within the gorge. Like the Linville Gorge, the Shining Rock Wilderness Area has been set aside as a carefully protected reserve beyond the reach of man's influence. The outstanding feature of this 13,600–acre tract is Shining Rock Mountain, an outcropping of white quartz with elevations ranging from 3,500 to over 6,000 feet. The area is accessible by trails from U.S. 276 North off the Blue Ridge Parkway at Wagon Road Gap. Again, primitive camping is available, and a permit is required to enter the area.

Over 600 miles of trails, including 80 miles of the Appalachian Trail provide access to the remote wilderness highlands, Black Mountain peaks, the scenic waterfalls and virgin hemlock stands of the Craggy Mountain area, to Lakes James and Cane, and the many rivers and streams, including the Cane, Watauga, Big Pigeon, and Broad rivers. Special challenges for the hiker are the Black Mountains and Mount Mitchell, highest peak in the eastern United States. Campsites are available at Bald Mountain, Black Mountain, Carolina Hemlocks, Coontree, Mortener, North Wells River, Powhatan, Rocky Bluff, and White Pines.

Stretching for 460 miles through the southern Appalachians, the Blue Ridge Parkway follows the mountain crests to link Shenandoah National Park in North Carolina and Tennessee. Designed especially for motor recreation, the parkway provides quiet, leisurely travel, free from commercial development and the congestion of high-speed highways. From Shenandoah National Park for 355 miles, the parkway follows the Blue Ridge Mountains, eastern rampart of the Appalachians, entering North Carolina near Cumberland Knob. Then, skirting the southern end of the Black Mountains, it weaves through the Craggies, the Pisgahs, and the Balsams to the Great Smokies.

In North Carolina, the land crossed by the parkway becomes higher and more sparsely settled. Rolling bluegrass pastures terminate in precipitous bluffs. Lush gardens of rhododendron bloom throughout Doughton Park, about 20 miles south of the Virginia-North Carolina line, in early June. Some of the more spectacular sights easily accessible from the parkway include Linville Falls, a rugged gorge and waterfalls reached by a short trail; Craggy Gardens with its lovely purple rhododendron blooming in mid-June; and the Devil's Courthouse, a rock affording 360–degree views across the mountains of

the Carolinas, Georgia, and Tennessee. Many campgrounds, picnic areas, restaurants and self-guiding trails are located along the parkway.

Information Sources, Maps & Access

For detailed information and a full-color *Pisgah National Forest Map* (50¢) and a free *Shining Rock Wilderness Map* and *Linville Gorge Wilderness Map*, contact: Superintendent's Office, U.S. Forest Service, Plateau Bldg., 50 S. French Broad Avenue, Asheville, NC 28801 (704)258–2850. The Pisgah National Forest is reached via U.S. 40 from Asheville. The Blue Ridge Parkway traverses

Shining Rock Wilderness

Linville Gorge Wilderness

U.S. DEPARTMENT OF AGRICULTURE FOREST SERVICE-SOUTHERN REGION

U.S. DEPARTMENT OF AGRICULTURE FOREST SERVICE-SOUTHERN REGION

portions of the forest north and west of Asheville. The *Blue Ridge Parkway Map* for North Carolina and Virginia describes the area traversed and shows the route in its entirety from Shenandoah National Park to the Cherokee Reservation in North Carolina. Points of interest, mileage, campsites, trails, picnic areas, points of access, nearby towns, and major highways are all indicated on the map, which is available free from: Superintendent, Blue Ridge Parkway, P.O. Box 7606, Asheville 28807 (704)258–2850. Another brochure available free from the Parkway Superintendent, *Blue Ridge Parkway Visitor Activities*, lists various attractions and visitor centers in Virginia and North Carolina—Peaks of Otter, Rocky Knob Campground, Doughton Park, Linville Falls, Crabtree Meadows, and others—and gives hours and special features. Self-guiding trails along the parkway are also listed.

Gateways & Accommodations

Asheville

(Pop. 65,000; zip code 28803; area code 704) is an outstanding recreation, vacation, and resort area, one of the most famous in the East. Centered in the Blue Ridge Mountains, it is directly off the Blue Ridge Parkway—one of the most scenic mountain drives in America. The area contains many attractions for the visitor including the Great Smoky Mountains National Park, Pisgah National Forest, Nantahala National Forest, Croatan National Forest, and the Cherokee Indian Reservation. There are many museums, formal gardens, summer theatres, local handicrafts exhibits and fairs, folk festivals, parks, zoos, historic sites and memorials. Nearby are the Wolf Laurel Ski Resort and opportunities for outdoor activities such as golf, fishing, riding, and hiking. Accommodations: *Best Western Inn on the Plaza* (rates: $40–55 double), with 299 superb rooms and suites, restaurants, coffeeshop, swimming pool at 1 Thomas Wolfe Plaza (252–8211); *Forest Manor Motor Lodge* (rates: $48 dou-

ble), with 21 excellent rooms and family units, restaurant, in beautiful location, 4½ miles south of town on U.S.25 at 866 Hendersonville Rd. (274–3531); *Great Smokies Hilton* (rates: $38–50 double), with 280 excellent rooms, restaurant, coffeeshop, swimming pools and sauna at 1 Hilton Dr. (254–3211); *Grove Park Inn* (rates: $47–51 double), a superb resort hotel with 260 rooms and family units, dining rooms, swimming pools, golf and tennis on landscaped grounds, located on Macon St., two miles north of town (252–2711); *Holiday Inn East* (rates: $42 double), with 211 rooms, restaurant, heated pool, five miles east of town on U.S. 70 (298–5611); *Holiday Inn West* (rates: $42 double), with 182 good rooms, restaurant, coffeeshop, swimming pool at 275 Smoky Park Hwy., 3½ miles west of town on U.S. 19/23 (667–4501); *Howard Johnson's Motor Lodge* (rates: $50 double), with 68 excellent rooms and family units, restaurant, heated swimming pool 1½ miles south of town on U.S. 25 (274–2300).

Banner Elk

(Pop. 800; zip code 28604; area code 704), situated in the Elk River Valley and surrounded by mountain peaks 5,000–6,000 feet high, is a small resort area for both summer and winter pleasures. Skiing at Sugar Mountain and Beech Mountain is excellent, and there is also Grandfather Mountain for picnicking, hiking, etc. In the summer months the Land of Oz is open—a walk-thru park with costumed characters from the famous books. Accommodations: *Holiday Inn at Beech Mountains* (rates: $35 double), with 100 excellent rooms, restaurant, swimming pool one mile south of town on North Carolina 184 (898–4571).

Blowing Rock

(Pop. 800; zip code 28605; area code 704) is located directly on the Blue Ridge Parkway and dates back to the 1880's as a stagecoach town and only available access across this rugged mountain terrain. It is one of the oldest resorts in the southern Appalachian area, and the summer temperatures are ideally cool for all outdoor activities. The 8,000 acres around the Blue Ridge Parkway offer opportunities for fishing, hiking, picnicking, riding, climbing; parks in the area offer golf, swimming, tennis, lawn games, and camping. In the winter there are five ski areas from which to choose. Another interest of the area is Tweetsie Railroad, a restored narrow gauge railroad and re-created western town. Blowing Rock is the entrance to Moses Cone Memorial Park which offers 3600 acres of wooded area for walking, riding etc. The area includes Glenburney Falls and Glen Mary Falls and their gorges. The most famous area attraction and namesake is Blowing Rock—an immense cliff—overhanging Johns River Gorge and valley approximately 3,000 feet below. The rock was so named because of wind funnels through the rocky walls of the gorge with such force that an upsurge of air currents is formed and light objects which are cast over the rock will be returned. This phenomenon prompted a cartoon showing it to be the only place in the world where "snow falls upside down." There are, of course magnificent mountain views to be had throughout this entire area. Accommodations: *Azalea Garden Motel* (rates: $29 double), with 17 excellent rooms in a beautiful location on U.S. 221/321 Business Route (295–3272); *Hillwinds Inn* (rates: $28 double), with 18 excellent rooms and restaurant at Sunset Dr. and Ransom St. (295–7660); *Parkway Motel* (rates: $25–29 double), with 18 good rooms and heated pool, two miles north of town on U.S. 221/321 at Blue Ridge Parkway exit (295–7981).

Boone

(Pop. 8754; zip code 28607; area code 704) was named for Daniel Boone, and is located on the famous Daniel Boone Trail at the fork of Wilderness Road. Although Boone is in a plateau-valley, it is the

highest elevation of the Appalachian Mountains, and hence named "the roof of eastern America." The area is surrounded by even higher mountains, on three sides, reaching up to 5,000 ft. Four river systems, flowing north, east, south and west, have their head-waters within this area. The area's streams are filled with trout and bass, the forests with wild game, and the hillsides and valleys offer recreation for sports enthusiasts in all seasons. The seasonal event is "Horn in the West," a re-creation of Daniel Boone's pioneer move west. Accommodations: *Holiday Inn* (rates: $39 double), with 100 excellent rooms, restaurant, swimming pool, two miles south of town on U.S. 221/321 (264-2451); *Ramada Inn* (rates: $36 double), with 117 excellent rooms, restaurant, heated pool, one mile west of town on North Carolina 105 (264-1000).

Brevard

(Pop. 7000; zip code 28712; area code 704) is a mountain resort center located near the entrance to Pisgah National Forest. The area is sometimes referred to as the "Land of the Waterfalls." There are opportunities for fishing, hiking, riding, hunting, camping, picnick-ing, and swimming in the National Forest as well as just for viewing the scenic wonders. The area is also noted for its musical events and in the summer there is a festival of music and arts, with nightly concerts. Accommodations: *Imperial Motor Lodge* (rates: $30 dou-ble), with 74 excellent rooms and heated pool, north of town on U.S. 64/276 (883-3185); *Pisgah Inn* (rates: $31.72 double), with 50 excellent rooms, restaurant, in nice alpine setting located off the Blue Ridge Parkway between mileposts 408 and 409 (235-8228).

Linville

(Pop. 600; zip code 28646; area code 704) is a summer resort area located in a natural park of 16,000 acres. Linville River offers good trout fishing, and Linville Falls is a scenic wonder which cascades over 50 feet of rock and then drops 60 feet into the Gorge, now designated a national wilderness area. The area below the falls is a recreational area and offers picnicking, hiking, and fishing. The resort area offers a golf club. Visible from vantage points in the area are the famous and mysterious Brown Mountain Lights. Linville

Caverns and Grandfather Mountain have attractions for visitors as does Lake Kawana with swimming, boating, etc. Accommodations: *Parkview Motor Lodge* (rates: $14.56-20 double) with 18 good rooms next to restaurant, 12 miles south of town off Blue Ridge Parkway milepost 317 (765-4787).

Little Switzerland

(Pop. 250; zip code 28749; area code 704) is a summer colony resort located on a 1,200 acre tract running along both sides of the Blue Ridge Parkway. Noted for its simplicity and restfulness, it has long attracted writers and artists, as well as many other visitors. Mount Mitchell State Park in the Pisgah National Forest is nearby and offers camping, picnicking, mountain views, a recreation lodge, and restaurants. Lake James, in the area, is well stocked with fish and there are many trout streams as well. The Crabtree Emerald Mine allows you to dig for your own emeralds, and the Museum of North Carolina Minerals offers exhibits of interest. Accommodations: (see "Big Lynn Lodge" and "The Chalet" below).

Maggie Valley—Gateway to the Great Smokies

(Pop. 900; zip code 28751; area code 704) is a rapidly developing tourist area and year-round resort center. It is near the Great Smoky Mountains National Park and four miles from the entrance to the Blue Ridge Parkway. The main attraction is the Ghost Town in the Sky—a mountain top entertainment center with re-built western, mining and mountaineer towns, along with stage shows and gunfights. The area also has much in the way of picnic areas, foliage for nature lovers and, in the winter, skiing at Cataloochee. Accommodations: *Country Manner Motel* (rates: $24 double), with 18 excellent rooms, trout fishing in nice location on U.S. 19 (926-1712); *Covered Wagon Motel* (rates: $25-28 double), with 20 excellent rooms and heated swimming pool on U.S. 19 at 3125 Dellwood Rd. (926-1845); *Holiday Inn at Maggie Valley* (rates: $42 double), with 102 excellent rooms, restaurant, heated pool on U.S. 19 at the junction of 276 (926-0201); *Rocky Waters Motel* (rates: $18-27 double), with 30 good rooms, heated swimming pool, trout stream in nice location one mile west of town on U.S. 19 (926-1585).

Waynesville

(Pop. 7000; zip code 28786; area code 704) is a popular vacation, tourist, and health resort. The Balsam Mountains, with their 5,000–6,000 foot peaks surround the town, with trails for hiking and riding, streams for fishing, and beautiful mountain scenery. The town is near the Cherokee Indian Reservation, the Great Smoky Mountains National Park, and Maggie Valley, with its splendid views. Waynesville was named for "Mad Anthony" Wayne of the Revolutionary War and is said to be the site where the last shot of the Civil War was fired. Accommodations: (see "Maggie Valley" Holiday Inn listing above).

Lodges & Resorts

★★★★*Beech Mountain Resort* is a year-round family resort in the Blue Mountains, on a scenic mountain-top location. Guests can visit the Pinnacle, often surrounded by clouds. During the summer and most of the autumn the Land of Oz outdoor park comes alive with a multi-million dollar re-creation of the Wizard of Oz tales. Other travel attractions include the Tweetsie Railroad; the nationally known Highland Games and Gatering of Scottish Clans; the Horn-In-the-West outdoor drama and Mountaineer Playhouse. Outdoor opportunities also abound. Ski enthusiasts can enjoy fine downhill slopes with instruction and rentals available. The resort is the site of the Snow Carnival of the South, and there are professional ski races at Beech and nearby. There is an 18–hole championship golf course located on the mountain, with lovely scenery from every hole. Natural wonders such as Grandfather Mountain; Linville Gorge and Falls; Blowing Rock; Linville Caverns plus springs brimming with rhododendron blossoms and falls with fiery foliage attract nature enthusiasts. The resort also offers tennis, swimming, canoeing, hiking and other recreational activities with rentals and instruction available for all sports during season. The resort has privately owned homes available for rent near the slopes at Beech Tree Village, chalets, one bedroom apartments to plush seven-room units and special units with golf course or ski slope views are other available accommodations. The resort has a Swiss/Bavarian flair with restaurants, snack shops and accommodation facilities pleasantly nestled on the mountain. Meals are not included in rates. Rates: summer, one-bedroom for 2–4 persons: $35–50 per night; two-bedroom condos from $50–60 per night for four persons; chalets from $65 per person per night; three-bedroom and four-bedroom accommodations for 6–8 persons range from $75–85 per night. For further information contact: Beech Mountain Resort Accommodations, P.O. Box 261, Banner Elk, NC 28604 (704)387–4246.

★★*Big Lynn Lodge & Little Switzerland* is situated in Lynn Gap in the Blue Ridge Mountains, 1,500 feet above a broad valley with range after range of mountain peaks sloping in all directions. This North Carolina village was named Little Switzerland because the superb views in all directions are reminiscent of the Alps. The lodge opens in April, when the dogwood is beginning to bloom, and closes the last weekend in October when the brilliant colors begin to fade with approaching winter. The lodge is surrounded by spectacular hiking trails, and there are shuffleboard courts and horseshoe pits on the lawn. Close by is the championship Spruce Pine golf course, and the Museum of North Carolina Minerals. Weekly square dances are held in Geneva Hall in Little Switzerland. The main lodge has a gift shop, two lounges, two TV rooms, and a restaurant serving home cooked meals family style. Cottages have two beds and private bath. Rates are from $31–38 daily, and $192–241 weekly. For more information write: Big Lynn Lodge, P.O. Box 459, Little Switzerland, NC 28749 (704)765–4257.

Blue Ridge Parkway Lodges are located along an impressive stretch of highway administered by the National Park Service from Shenandoah National Park in Virginia to the Great Smoky Mountains National Park in North Carolina and Tennessee. The mountain scenery is unmatched anywhere and the log cabins, rail fences, and rustic Mabry Mill accentuate the native pioneer culture. There are two accommodations operated by National Park Concessions, Inc.

★★★*Bluffs Lodge* is located at mile post 241 at Doughton Park. It is a 24–room rustic lodge perched at 3,750 feet above sea level overlooking the mountains and valleys. The lodge is conveniently located about midway on the Blue Ridge Parkway. There are complete visitors services at Doughton Park, including a coffee shop, craft and photo shops and a service station. There are also scenic trails for hiking and historic buildings to visit. All the rooms at the lodge have tile baths and steam heat. The season is May 1st through October 31st, and room rates are $23 for two persons with two beds. Each additional person in a room is $3. No pets are allowed. For reservations write: National Park Concessions, Bluffs Lodge, Laurel Springs, NC 28644 or phone Sparta (919)372–4499.

★★★*Rocky Knob Cabins* are at mile post 174 in a secluded glade near the Blue Ridge Parkway in southern Virginia. Cabins have housekeeping facilities with electric kitchens, running water, dishes and utensils. Cabins are open May 30 through Labor Day and are $15 for one or two persons, plus $3 for each additional person. For reservations and information write: National Park Concessions, Inc., Rocky Knob Cabins, Meadows of Dan, VA 24120 or phone Floyd, VA (703)593–3503.

★★★*Cataloochee Ranch at Maggie Valley*, at 5,000 feet, the highest guest ranch in the east, is situated on 1,500 acres in the Great Smokies. Its rich mountaintop pastures and woodlands directly adjoin the wilderness areas of the Great Smoky Mountains National Park. Though there is no planned daily entertainment, numerous diversions are available. They include riding, pack trips, tennis, trout fishing in the two spring-fed ponds, and swimming. There are facilities for table tennis, horseshoes, croquet, plus a well-stocked library. Accommodations are available for up to 40 guests. Ten bedrooms in the main house all have either connecting or private bathrooms. Five family-sized cabins have two bedrooms each, baths, and open fireplaces. The ranch is on the American Plan. Three hearty meals are served daily, ranch style, on long tables in the two dining rooms. Lunches are packed for all-day rides and hikers. North Carolina is "dry," so guests should provide their own alcoholic beverages. The season, lasting from May 11 to October 21, offers daily and weekly rates; rooms in the main house vary from $325–422 weekly for two people. Cabins are available for groups up to six from $77 daily for two people to $960 weekly for six. The variance in rates is determined by location and size of rooms and cabins. Cataloochee Ranch also features a winter ski season from mid-December to mid-March. For further information or reservations contact: Cataloochee Ranch, Rt. 1, Box 500, Maggie Valley, NC 28751 (704)926–1401, or in winter, (704)926–0285.

★★★★*The Chalet on the Blue Ridge Parkway* sits high atop the crest of the Parkway at milepost 334. It is the center of the resort community of Little Switzerland and carries through the Swiss look in the traditional design of its buildings and the costumes in its restaurant. The Chalet is open from May 1 through November 11 (weather permitting). There is a heated pool, playground for the children, shuffleboard, horseshoes and other lawn games. There is also a shopping plaza with gifts, jewelry, clothing, craft items and even an ice cream shop. The Chalet has tournament quality tennis courts, and guests can play golf at two of the finest mountain courses. Golf

and tennis package rates are available on request. The main dining room serves three excellent meals a day and there is a private lounge for guests. The main lodge has a spacious lobby and a fireplace for cool mountain evenings. The lodge runs an Octoberfest every year, cookouts and special events. In the immediate area are mines to explore, museums, old mills, nature trails, train trips and flea markets. The scenery is spectacular, and the Chalet makes the most of the view. Accommodations are in 58 rooms and chalets ranging from $22 to $44 per room double occupancy from May through September 23. After September 23, rates are $24 to $46. All units have private baths, most have mountain or parkway views and many have balconies. There is no charge for children under 10 with parents. For information and reservations contact: The Chalet Lodge and Restaurant, Little Switzerland, NC 28749 (704)765–4089 or 2153.

★★★*Eseeola Lodge* is located at the foot of Grandfather Mountain in the Blue Ridge Mountains of western North Carolina at an altitude of 3,800 feet, just 70 miles from Asheville and 100 miles from Charlotte. The season is from the first of June through the middle of September when warm days and cool nights offer ideal vacation weather. The lodge has an 18–hole championship golf course with bent greens and electric golf carts available. Golf instructions are available from head professional Burl Dale. There are riding stables with an excellent string of horses and beautiful riding trails. Riding instructions are available from Peggy Touchstone, head riding mistress. For tennis players, there are fast all-weather courts. Use of the heated swimming pool, the putting green, the television room, the card room and hiking trails is free to guests. In July and August, the lodge's director organizes recreational programs especially for children. The lodge also has a gift shop, a beauty parlor, a cocktail lounge, a dining room for superb dinners, and the Par-Tee Room in the Clubhouse for lunches. Accommodations include rooms in the lodge, each with its own porch, and cottages with bedrooms and living rooms. American Plan rates including three meals are $76–84 for twin beds and bath, $70–78 for double bed and bath, and a suite (two persons) is $86–94 per day. For information and reservations: The Eseeola Lodge, Linville, NC 28646 (704)733–4311.

★★★*Green Park Inn at Blowing Rock* overlooks the Blue Ridge Mountains from an elevation of 4,300 feet, built atop the eastern continental divide. This elegant inn, almost a century old, has been completely refurnished to blend 20th-century luxury with Victorian charm. A large outdoor heated pool overlooks the rolling fairways and manicured greens of the Blowing Rock Country Club where all visitors of the Green Park Inn are welcome guests. The elegant dining room serves gourmet dishes, fresh baked pastries and home-made desserts. Each evening guests enjoy live entertainment in the Divide Lounge. Each of the 74 deluxe rooms is bright and spacious, and decorated with a special charm. There are also plush suites, each with a large private bedroom and adjoining living room, and private balconies with a view of the lush rolling golf course and the mountains beyond. Rates, including two meals daily are $64–95 per person double occupancy, and $105 daily per person in suites. Special golf packages are also available. For more information write: Green Park Inn, P.O. Box 7, Blowing Rock, NC 28605 (704)295–3141.

★★★★*High Hampton Inn* is a rustic mountain retreat, with pine-paneled rooms and handmade native furniture to give a warm, homey atmosphere. There are 2,000 acres of beautiful grounds with enough diversions to satisfy everyone's tastes. The setting is 3,600 feet above sea level; the architecture blends with the mountain scenery. The elegantly groomed landscape gives way to trails along expansive rocky ridges. Whiteside Mountain, one of the highest sheer precipices in eastern America, towers 1,800 feet above the countryside and the inn. The inn is noted for its programs and

activities which bring people together, and especially for its children's programs which are among the nation's best. Some of these activities include horseback riding, picnic hikes, tennis clinics, golf lessons, hayrides, cookouts, arts and crafts, special beach and swimming areas, and a Noah's Ark building. There are special activities for teens and the inn runs a school of equitation for girls 10–16. While the children are enjoying these activities the adults can take advantage of their leisure time with swimming, sailing, canoeing, paddle boating, fishing, special golf and tennis packages and clinics, nature walks, riding, badminton, shuffleboard, croquet, mountain climbing, trap and skeet shooting. There are eight tennis courts, a pro shop, and a famous well-designed 18–hole golf course, scenic and challenging. Bird watching is a frequent pastime as there are over 150 species, indigenous and migratory, in this area. The food is excellent, home-cooked, home-baked, and home-grown. Rooms are simple but extremely comfortable. There are fireplaces in the cottages and in some of the bedrooms at the inn. The inn is open April 15–November 1 and then for Thanksgiving and Christmas. Rates are based on full American Plan (three meals) and are usually taken on a weekly basis; daily rates can be arranged. Rates range from $28–36.50 per person per day depending on season. The inn has been family owned and operated for the past 50 years. Your host is William McKee and he will be happy to send further information. Contact him at High Hampton Inn & Country Club, Cashiers, NC 28717 (704)743–2411.

★★★*Hound Ears Lodge & Club at Blowing Rock* is a ski, golf, and tennis resort tucked away in a green valley in the Blue Ridge Mountains. Minutes away from the Beech Mountain Ski Area, the highest resort in Eastern U.S., and situated in the heart of North Carolina ski country, Hound Ears Club has its own double chairlift and rope tow. Private and group lessons are taught by Austrian ski professionals, and equipment can be rented throughout the December-March season. In the spring, the rolling, lush, 18–hole golf course opens, dotted with stately pine and surrounded by the hazy mountains of the Blue Ridge. There is also a heated swimming pool, a lounge, tennis courts, and two fine restaurants on the grounds. The lodge, a spacious mountain chalet, looks over the open valley to the Blue Ridge Mountains beyond. Airy lodge rooms are available with two double beds, private bath, and open balcony for $44 per person double occupancy from November 1 until June 14, and $48 per person from June 15 until October 31. Clubhouse suites offer a large bedroom with two double beds, bath, private balcony and a separate sitting room for $48 per person, winter season, and $67 per person from June 15 to the end of October. Executive suites feature two rooms with two double beds, private bath and dressing rooms in each, and a sitting room with adjoining private balcony for $184 for four persons winter season, and $264 for four persons during the spring and summer. All rates include breakfast and dinner. Golf and tennis packages are available, including lodging and meals, 18 holes of golf per day including the use of an electric cart, or two court hours of tennis per day for $99 per person double occupancy. For more information write: Hound Ears Lodge and Club, Blowing Rock, NC 28605 (704)963–4321.

★★★★*Lake Toxaway* has a lodge and cottages set in an area called the Switzerland of America. The lodge and country club is on Lake Toxaway, the largest private lake in the state. The architecture of the lodge brings to mind a turn-of-the-century inn nestled in a setting of tall trees. The club and facilities are open from May through October. There is an 18–hole par 72 golf course with water hazards on the front nine and a shorter back nine. Both nines bring golfers to the pro shop where refreshments are served. The club also has six regulation tennis courts—three all weather and three Har-

Tru. There is a private pool, a marina on the lake, rental boats for fishing or water skiing, and miles of hiking trails. Anglers will find rainbow trout and smallmouth bass. Breakfast and dinner are served in the club dining room, and there is a grill at the golf pro-shop for late breakfasts, lunches and snacks. Daytime dress is casual; and coat and tie are required for evening. Nearby, there are horseback riding, communities with mountain crafts for sale, Pisgah National Forest, the Blue Ridge Parkway Drive and Whiteside Mountain. The club organizes special events including cookouts, dances, bingo and other evening entertainments. Accommodations are in rooms or suites in the lodge and housekeeping cottages and apartments. Rates without meals for two people are $30 per day for lodge rooms and $35 per day for lodge suites, both with private baths. Housekeeping cottages and apartments are $40 per day and $240 per week. There are rates for additional persons and children under 16. In the month of May, all rates are discounted 25% and golf and tennis are free. For information or reservations for the May through October season write: Lake Toxaway Country Club, Lake Toxaway, NC 28747 or call (704)966–4488. For advance reservations, off season, or to inquire about winter accommodations call (704)966–4260.

★★★*The Pines Country Inn in Pisgah Forest* offers over a century of fine tradition, service and rustic country accommodations in the inn and in four guest cabins and cottages scattered throughout 12 acres of pine woods on Hart Mountain overlooking the beautiful Little River Valley. Activities include hiking, fishing, bird watching, swimming and golf. The inn offers guest accommodations on the second floor: two double rooms with private baths and three double rooms share two baths. The Hart Suite is a family room combination which includes adjoining double bedrooms with bath and commands the entire second story porch with its glorious view of the valley and surrounding mountains. The Dining Room, where in-house guests enjoy family style breakfast and dinner, provides real country cooking. The Summer Cottage, small and snug, houses two bedrooms, each with its private entrance and bath. Guests share the open front porch. Gramma's Log Cabin is spacious and homey, with three double rooms and one triple bedroom (for 3 or 4), all with private baths. Grandpa's Log Cabin is especially good for groups or large families. A large living room, complete with fireplace, is shared by all the cabin guests. Two double bedrooms share one bath downstairs; upstairs there are five bedrooms and two baths. The upstairs porch overlooks the mountainside. The Gate Cottage, roomy and private, has two bedrooms, each with bath. The sitting room and porch look out over the rolling green lawn. Daily rates range from $24–35 with meals with special weekly rates and children's rates. For additional information, contact: The Pines Country Inn, P.O. Box 7, Pisgah Forest, NC 28768 (704)877–3131.

★★★*Pisgah View Ranch* is located in a high valley, adjacent to the Pisgah National Forest, surrounded by the Blue Ridge Mountains, with mile-high Mount Pisgah towering majestically over the ranch. The 1,700–acre ranch is completely secluded and has every facility for a complete vacation, including: swimming pool and wading ponds, lake stocked with rainbow trout, tennis, shuffleboard and table tennis, horseback riding and hiking, square dancing, picnic lunches, baby-sitting service, country style cooking with fresh fruits and vegetables, and evening entertainment. There are 52 airy cottage rooms with private baths. You can take scenic sightseeing trips to places nearby such as the Great Smoky Mountains National Park, the Cherokee Indian Reservation, Blue Ridge Parkway, Chimney Rock, Mount Mitchell (highest peak in Eastern United States), and the Land of Waterfalls. Riding parties can be arranged for both morning and afternoon with experienced guides. Rates at the ranch are based on the American Plan which includes all meals and

recreational facilities with the exception of a fee for horseback riding ($5 per hour). Rooms range from $28 per person per day to $175 per week for double occupancy. Pets are not desired and a charge of $5.00 per pet per day will be charged. Contact the owners: Ruby and Chester Cogburn, Pisgah View Ranch, Rt. 1, Candler, NC 28715 (704)667–9100.

★★★*Roaring River Chalets at Blowing Rock* are nestled in lush woods overlooking a free-running trout stream in the Blue Ridge Mountains. Hiking trails through the woods offer panoramic mountain views, and the trout stream promises excellent fishing. Close to horseback riding stables, scenic golf courses, and Beech Mt., Hounds Ears Ski Area, and Appalachian Ski Mountain, Roaring River Chalets are open all year round. Each chalet is two stories, with a private balcony, one or two bedrooms, living rooms, T.V., and fully equipped modern kitchens. One bedroom chalet apartments are $35 for two persons, and $40 for four persons. Two bedroom chalets are $35–$45 weekdays and $40–$60 weekends. For more information write: Roaring River Chalets, Rt. 1, Box 88C, Blowing Rock, NC 28605 (704) 295–3695.

★★★*Sapphire Valley Resort*, located in the Blue Ridge Mountains, sprawls across the valley and encompasses mountain woods, lakes, and streams. The resort is especially proud of its 18–hole championship golf course, close to 3,300 feet high. Golf clinics are directed by the Hall of Famer Louise Suggs and the Hebert brothers, Lionel and Jay. There is a complex of 12 all-weather tennis courts, including all-weather cork turf, hard composition and clay for day or flood lit for night. A clinic is run May and June and instruction is available. Water activities include lake fishing, boating, canoeing, lake or pool swimming. There are miles of horseback riding trails winding upland and hiking ranging from woodland strolls to mountain climbs. A mine, once worked by Tiffany is open for gem hunting. Fine southern skiing, badminton, horseshoes, birdwatching and shuffleboard are other popular resort activities. The resort has accommodations in the Fairfield Inn. Overlooking Lake Fairfield and facing Bald Rock Mountain, the inn, which was built in 1896, is a gracious country retreat. Entertainment at both the inn and club includes dancing, live entertainment and mountain music bands. A social director organizes various games and activities. Accommodations are also available in rustic one and two bedroom cottages and luxury one, two or three bedroom villas. The resort has an optional Modified American Plan, which is available at $16 additional per day, per person and $9 extra per day, for children. Rates: inn rooms: lake front, double room daily $42, weekly $250; tennis court side, double room daily $38, weekly $225. Rustic cottages, one-bedroom daily $55, weekly $350. Luxury villas, daily $50–125, weekly $300–800. For further information contact: Sapphire Valley Resort, Star Route 70, Box 80, Sapphire, NC 28774 (704)743–3441.

★★★*Twinbrook Resort at Maggie Valley* borders the Great Smoky Mountains National Park and the Cherokee Indian Reservation. Anglers will enjoy the excellent fishing in the clear running trout streams. Hiking and bridle trails lead off across the open valley to the mountains, which rise in all directions to 6,000 feet. In addition, Twinbrook has a children's playground, a heated outdoor pool, horseshoe pits, softball fields, shuffleboard courts, and family picnic areas. Within minutes are the excellent ski areas, golf courses, quaint shops and the old ghost town of Maggie Valley. Each private 1-, 2-, and 3-bedroom cottage has its own private setting among the valley hemlocks, wild rhododendron, and mountain laurel. All are completely furnished with modern fully equipped kitchens and open porches. Many have fireplaces. All are provided with electric heat for cool autumn nights and the ski season. Rates are $32–$35 daily for a one-bedroom; $48–$60 daily for a two-bedroom cottage; and $75 daily for a three-bedroom cottage. For additional information contact: Carl and Viola Henry, Rt. 1, Box 683, Maggie Valley, NC 28751 (704)926–1388.

★★★★*Wolf Laurel Resort* is a year round recreational facility operated in conjunction with the Bald Mountain Development. In warm weather guests enjoy a heated swimming pool, Grasstex tennis courts, hiking trails, a children's playground and a well-stocked trout pond. The 18–hole golf course has some outstanding features. No. 12 hole is the highest hole east of the Rockies, at an elevation of 4,785 feet. Golfers play in the shadow of Big Bald Mountain, a 5516-foot peak; there is a golf shop and the resort offers special golf packages. There is a riding stable on the resort property with horses for hire and beautiful trails to follow. In the winter, Wolf Laurel becomes a ski resort with three lifts, snow-making equipment and the Graduated Length Method of instruction. There is a rental shop with 600 pairs of skis and boots. The Lodge at the base of the runs has a grill for snacks, a shop with equipment and ski clothes, and a fireplace for relaxation and conversation. There are ski packages which include lodging, plus rates for skiing only. Whatever the season, guests can enjoy a meal in the Mountain Top Restaurant which serves three meals a day. Wolf Laurel is only 27 miles north of Asheville and easily reached via the New Appalachian Highway U.S. 23. Accommodations include the 78 rooms of the Wolf Laurel Inn. For two persons, rates range from $22 to $30 on weekdays and $24 to $32 on weekends and holidays. Guests can also stay in one of the authentic log cabins in Settler's Village, in cottages, and A-frame contemporary homes with one to five bedrooms. These accommodations are completely furnished and have cooking facilities. Rates are $40 per day or $225 per week, for two in a one-bedroom unit. From March 15 through May 15, when the mountain flowers are in bloom, and from October 15 to December 15 in the autumn weather, rates are 25% off. For information and reservations contact: Wolf Laurel Resort, Route 3, Mars Hill, NC 28754 (704)689–4111.

★★★*Woodfields Inn at Flat Rock* is the oldest operating inn in North Carolina. Built in 1850, and refurnished with antiques, the inn continues its tradition of gracious southern hospitality. The wide verandas command a panoramic view of the shady lawns, brilliant gardens, and the distant Great Smoky Mountains. Three generous meals with fresh garden vegetables are served daily in the elegant dining room. The inn has shuffleboard courts, badminton, ping pong, and card rooms. Close by is the Carl Sandburg Homesite National Monument, and the quaint shops and summer stock theater in Flat Rock. Woodfields Inn is within an hour's drive of the Great Smokies National Park and the Cherokee Indian Reservation, and is surrounded by hiking trails, lakes, and mountain streams ideal for hiking, swimming and fishing. For details write: Woodfields Inn, Flat Rock, NC 28731 (704)693–6016.

OHIO

Introduction

The Buckeye State's terrain unfolds from the highlands of West Virginia and Pennsylvania into soft undulating hills and fertile valleys and flattens out into broad woodlands which reach to Indiana on the west. The mighty Ohio River flows in a sweeping arc forming the state's southern and eastern boundaries, and the southern shoreline of Lake Erie forms a wave-swept boundary along nearly three-quarters of the northernmost reaches of the state. Ohio's 41,222 square miles contain over 500,000 acres of mixed hardwood and conifer forests, meadows, bogs, and beaver flows on state forest and public game lands which provide excellent opportunities for camping, backpacking, cross-country skiing and hunting in season for whitetail deer, waterfowl, small game, and upland game birds. Its 200 square miles of lakes and streams hold trophy-sized largemouth and smallmouth bass, walleye, muskellunge, northern pike, striped bass, hordes of panfish, a limited number of trout, and Great Lakes Chinook and coho salmon.

Accommodations & Travel Information

Descriptions of Ohio's state operated lodges and resorts are found in the "Vacation/Lodging Guide" which follows. For additional vacation lodging and services info, write: Office of Travel & Tourism, 30 E. Broad St., Columbus 43215; Lake Erie Tourist Information Center, 1018 Ramada St. Sandusky 44870, covers North-Central Ohio and Lake Erie Islands; Buckeye Tourist Council, Box 307, Cambridge 43725, covers East-Central Ohio; Tecumseh Tourist Council, RR 2, West Liberty 43357, covers West-Central Ohio; and Toledo Convention & Visitors Bureau, 218 Huron St., Toledo 43604.

Ohio's scenic mixed hardwood and conifer forests, valleys, lakeshores, and meadowlands in the state forest reserve and park lands feature literally hundreds of family campgrounds and primitive backcountry campsites. Descriptions of campgrounds, lodges and cabin accommodations, and reservation information for all of Ohio's state forests and parks are contained in the following publications, available free upon request from: Division of Parks & Recreation, Dept. of Natural Resources, Fountain Sq., Columbus 43224: *Ohio State Forests, Ohio State Parks Lodge & Cabin Accommodations, Ohio State Parks Camping Information, Ohio State Parks Area Facilities*. You can get free *Ohio State Park Maps* for all state park areas from the address above.

A 16–page *Hocking Hills State Park Hiking Trails Guide*, describing the scenic backpacking trails that wind through these rugged, forested hills steeped in Indian and colonial lore, may be obtained free from the Division of Parks & Recreation (address above). Numerous trails reach back through this 10,000–acre backcountry of hills, deep, damp gorges, dry, sandy ridgetops, forests of eastern hemlock, black birch, Canada yew, mountain laurel; and a profusion of ferns and wildflowers to Old Man's Cave, Ash Cave, Cedar Falls, beautiful Conkle's Hollow, the massive cliff of Black Hand sandstone known as "Rock House," and the steep Cantwell Cliffs on Buck Run.

Highways & Maps

The *Ohio Transportation Map*, available free from Dept. of Transportation, 25 S. Front St., Columbus 43215, shows all highways and roads, lakes, rivers, and streams, towns and settlements, county lines, railroads, ferries, tolls, dams, points of interest, state forests, airports, rest areas, parks, fairgrounds, highway patrol posts, and first-aid stations. It includes close-up maps of Cleveland, Cincinnati, Columbus, Youngstown, Dayton, Toledo, and Canton, and an index of state park camping facilities.

Ohio Forests, Lakes & Recreation Areas

The scenic 106,000–acre Wayne National Forest is composed of three forest divisions in southeastern Ohio. The major features of this outstanding backpacking and hunting country of rolling hills, spectacular outcroppings of sandstone and shale, and numerous streams include the Hanging Rock Region, Lake Vesuvius Recreation Area, Dean State Forest, Trimble and Wolf Creek state wildlife areas, Strouds Run State Park, Waterloo State Forest, Burr Oak Reservoir, and Symmes, Hocking, Raccoon, and Little Muskingum rivers. The beautiful Little Muskingum River, with its several covered bridges and scenic woodlands, holds a good population of smallmouth bass. Burr Oak Reservoir holds big largemouth bass and walleyes. This is the state's top hunting area for whitetail deer, red fox, raccoon, wild turkey, and upland game birds.

The Hocking Caves region presents many interesting geological formations. Trails and camping facilities are numerous. Ash Cave was once the site of countless Indian fires, and Old Man's Cave was the longtime residence of an anonymous hermit more than 100 years ago. Ohio's premier fishing area is the vast southern waters of Lake Erie surrounding the famous archipelago north of Sandusky and Port Clinton formed by Kelleys Island, South Bass Island and Put-in-Bay, Middle Bass Island, and North Bass Island and Isle St. George. The reefs, shoals, sandbars, and rock and gravel bottoms surrounding this renowned summer vacation region provide often spectacular fishing for fat yellow perch and scrappy smallmouth bass, and an occasional walleye, muskellunge, northern pike, coho salmon, or sturgeon. The Bass Islands area is one of the hottest smallmouth bass fishing spots in the Midwest. Acrobatic bronzebacks, one of the truly great sport fishes, caught here average from ¾ to 1½ pounds and range up to 7 pounds. Chinook salmon and the beautiful silver-blue coho can be caught in Lake Erie throughout the year and many are taken by shoreline fishermen using large plugs, flashy spinners and spoons, and by offshore trolling. During the fall when the water temperature is 45°–50°, Chinook and coho migrate up such Lake Erie tributaries as the Chagrin River, Conneaut Creek, and Huron River. Northern pike, which once were abundant and grew to monster lengths in Lake Erie before 1900, are today confined to Sandusky Bay, Maumee Bay, and the marshlands and tributary streams adjoining these areas. As the ice breaks up during late February or early March, the great northerns move from Lake Erie into the adjoining bays and marshes to spawn.

Elsewhere in Lake Erie, smallmouth bass are found along the gravel bottoms, shoals, and reefs along Kelleys Island, Huron-Vermilion Reef, and the Port Clinton Reef. Big largemouth bass are found in all boat harbors and weed-filled inlets and bays, along with buckets of scrappy crappies. Legions of white bass are found off the Bass Islands, Kelleys Island, Mouse Island, and the Port Clinton Reef areas. Inland from the once pristine waters of Lake Erie, smallmouth bass are found in clear, cold impoundments and lakes, and streams with good gravel or rock bottoms and a visible current in every county of the Buckeye State, as are largemouth bass, walleye, and crappie.

The cannibalistic muskie, whose name is derived from an Ojibwa Indian word meaning "long snout," is most often caught on live suckers and floating, diving plugs, spoons, jointed lures, and feathered spinners. Muskies were rarely found in Ohio's lakes and reservoirs before the Division of Wildlife started stocking them in 1953. Today, muskies of 5 to 25 pounds and up to 50 pounds are found in Piedmont, Leesville, Rocky Fork, Clear Fork, Dillon, Cowan, Hargus,

Delaware, Knox, and Deer Creek reservoirs, Grand and Little Muskingum rivers, and Paint, Olive, Meigs, Wolf, Rocky Fork, Scioto Brush, Wills, and Ohio Brush creeks.

Trout are limited to several localities in Ohio. Rainbow trout are found in Clear Creek on the Erie and Sandusky county border and in the Mad River. The Mad River rainbows and browns are thought to be fish that have escaped from the privately operated Zanesfield Rod & Gun Club lands during periods of high water. Carry-over rainbows are also found in the Chagrin River. Conneaut Creek, and Beaver Creek in Seneca County and in Punderson, Oberlin, and Forked Run lakes. The state record 13–pound 8–ounce brown and 15–pound 6–ounce rainbow were caught in the privately operated Castalia Trout Club stretch on Cold Creek. Brook trout are found in Cold Creek and in the Mad River and its Macocheek Creek and Cedar Run tributaries. Ohio offers a small but varied selection of scenic canoe streams. These include the Cuyahoga River, the Great Miami River, the Little Miami River, the Maumee River, the Sandusky River, and the Mohican, Walhonding, and Muskingum rivers.

The Little Miami River and Little Beaver Creek are part of the national wild and scenic river system. Little Beaver Creek, noted for its boulder outcroppings and beautiful wooded slopes, is a tributary

of the Ohio River in the extreme southeast corner of the state. The scenic Little Miami River is located just northeast of Cincinnati and offers an unusual unspoiled canoeing experience for Ohio. For detailed information about the state's scenic river system, write: Department of Natural Resources, Div. of Natural Areas & Preserves, Fountain Sq., Columbus 43224.

The Cuyahoga originates in sugarbush country, traveling through glacial plains, and drops over a series of falls and rapids in the Akron-Cuyahoga Falls area, following a wide gorge to Lake Erie. The river flows through scenic pasture and forest land, and the bass fishing is excellent. The current varies from mild to dangerous. The Great Miami offers almost 140 miles of navigable water, ending in the rugged hill country of the southwestern corner of the state. The entire route is mild and easy to canoe, and fishing is good for smallmouth bass. The Little Miami cuts through a deep gorge filled with scenic beauty. Challenging canoeing is the main attraction on the Maumee, with several portages, rapids, and dams. The Sandusky offers picturesque farmland and excellent fishing for smallmouth bass, rock bass, channel catfish, bullhead, crappie, and white bass. The name Sandusky is derived from an Indian word meaning "water within water pools." The continuous stretch formed by confluences of the Mohican, Walhonding, and Muskingum rivers is often considered the most scenic in Ohio. Many colorful river towns are passed, and good fishing conditions are prevalent up and down the route. The mixed hardwood forests along the shores are inhabited by gray squirrels, raccoons, red fox, mink, ducks, deer, blue herons, and osprey.

Information Sources, Maps & Access

For detailed fishing, hunting, camping, and canoeing information, and the following free publications, contact the Ohio Dept. of Natural Resources, Information Office, Fountain Sq., Columbus, OH 43224 (614)466–3066: *Ohio Fishing & Hunting Areas*, which contains listings and a "Map of Public Fishing & Hunting Locations"; a 58–page *Guide to Boating in Ohio*; *Lake Erie Fishing Services*; *Ohio Fishing Regulations Booklet*; *Fish Identification Chart*; the 18–page booklet *When & Where to Fish*; *Ohio Hunting Regulations*; an *Ohio Licensed Shooting Preserves* booklet; and the following Ohio information leaflets. *Bait Fish, Rainbow Trout, Brown Trout, Brook Trout, The Pickerels in Ohio, Muskellunge in Ohio, Muskellunge Fishing in Ohio, Northern Pike in Ohio, Northern Smallmouth Blackbass, Coho Salmon in Ohio, Fish Dehydration Guide, Fish Smoking, Endangered Wild Animals in Ohio, Red Fox in Ohio, Ringnecked Pheasant, Wild Turkey, Whitetail Deer, Woodcocks,* and *Hawks in Ohio.* For more information and the free booklet *Ohio Canoe Adventures*, with descriptions and maps of numerous river trips, write to: Publications Center, Dept. of Natural Resources, Fountain Sq., Columbus 43224. *Lake Contour Maps* showing boat-launching points and harbors, gas stations, wooded areas, highways, towns, bridges, county lines, railroads, and lake features including bottom type, dead timber areas, streams, and depth contours, are available for all major lakes including Seneca, Pymatuning, Killdeer, Logan, Indian, Deer Creek, Burr Oak, Clendening, Buckeye lakes, Lake Erie Islands, and Berlin, Milton, Mosquito, Portage, Mogadore, Atwood, Leesville, Tappan, Piedmont, Pleasant Hill, Delaware, Hoover, Rocky Fork, Grant, Cowan, Acton, Clark, Indian, Kiser, and Dillon. Maps are free up to five copies; over five they are 10¢ each. Each map includes a "peak action calendar." A complete set of bound maps is available for $7.65 from: DNR, Fountain Sq., Columbus 43224.

Ohio's state forests offer excellent backpacking and primitive camping opportunities and good hunting in season for whitetail deer, ruffed

grouse, raccoon, wild turkey, and red fox. Free *State Forest Maps* showing roads, streams, campsites, points of interest, trails, and towns are available from: Division of Forestry and Reclamation, Dept. of Natural Resources, 815 Ohio Depts. Bldg., Columbus 43215. These include Shade River State Forest, Shawnee State Forest, Brush Creek State Forest, Blue Rock State Forest, Scioto Trail State Forest, Dean State Forest, Fernwood State Forest, Hocking State Forest, Maumee State Forest, Mohican and Memorial state forests, Pike State Forest, Tar Hollow State Forest, and Zaleski State Forest.

Complete information and a 50¢ full-color *Wayne National Forest* Map showing all roads and trails, railroads, ranger stations, recreation sites, points of interest, boat-launching sites, and lakes, ponds, and streams are available from: Forest Supervisor, 1615 J St., Bedford, IN 47421. The Wayne National Forest is reached via U.S. Highways 33 and 52, Interstate 70, and Ohio State Highways 7 and 93. Supplies, guides, and outfitters are available at Athens, Ironton, Marietta, Grandview, Wade, Newport, Fly, Ellisonville, Lisman, Hanging Rock, Nelsonville, Corning, New Straitsville, Greendale, and Shawnee.

Lodges & Resorts

Ohio State Park Lodges are operated by Ohio Inns Inc. for the Ohio Department of Natural Resources. There are five parks with these lodges, located throughout the state. All five parks also have housekeeping cabins. Deluxe cabins are heated for year-round use and sleep six in two bedrooms. Standard cabins are for summer use only and sleep four to six persons. Lodge rates vary from lodge to lodge but all require a one night deposit. Cabin rental rates are the same at all parks. Deluxe cabins rent for $40 per day or $176 per week from April 1 through October 31. Off season rate is $34.50 per day or $139 per week. The standard cabins are $29 per day and $139 per week in season; and $27 per day or $96 per week off season (weather permitting). Room rates and cabin rates are subject to change each April 1st. No pets are allowed and credit cards are not honored. From Memorial Day to Labor Day, all weekly cottage rentals must begin and end on Saturday. For reservations and information, the individual parks should be contacted. For information on all parks, lodges and cabins, write Ohio Inns Incorporated, Sales & Services, P.O. Box 550, Cambridge, OH 43725.

★★★*Burr Oak State Park Lodge* is in Ohio's most primitive wildlife area in the rugged hills near Athens. The state park has 3,300 acres and includes a 665–acre crystal-clear lake. There is a marina on the lake with a launching ramp, boat rental and fishing facilities. Boaters are limited to 10–hp motors. The park has an outdoor pool, as well as an indoor heated pool. There are tennis courts, horseback riding, hiking and cycling trails, shuffleboard, horseshoes and a snack bar. Children will enjoy the playground. In winter the park has ice skating, ice fishing, tobogganing and sledding. Nearby attractions are Ohio University at Athens, the Mormon Valley Farm, Millfield Mining Days and McConnelsville Opera House. Burr Oak Lodge is built on a hill and offers a panoramic view. It has 60 rooms which rent for $25 per night for one to four persons. For further information contact: Burr Oak State Park Lodge, RFD #2, Box 128, Glouster, OH 45732 (614)767–2112.

★★★*Cowan Lake State Park* history dates back to the time of the earliest pioneers and settlers. The park surrounds the 700–acre lake. Cabins are nestled in the woods and all are heated, with two bedrooms, bath, living room, kitchen, dining area and screened porch. The campsites are class "A" suitable for tents or trailers. Boating and fishing supplies are also available. Fishing is excel-

lent as is hunting for pheasant, squirrel, rabbit and waterfowl. There's a public beach with bathhouse for swimming and several miles of interesting hiking trails. In the summer months a nature program is conducted. Cabin rates range from $37.50 a night to $165 a week depending on season. Further information is available from Roger O'Dell, Park Manager, Cowan Lake State Park, 729 Beechwood Road, Wilmington, OH 45177 (513)289–2105.

★★*Dillon State Park* is situated on 7,548 acres with a water area of, 1,660 acres surrounded by woodlands, fields and ravines. There's an excellent 1,360-foot sand swimming beach. Fishing and boating are also excellent and all supplies are available. Hunting in season and in restricted areas, with shotgun or longbow only, is good for small game. The park has several short trails for hiking and many scenic picnic areas. Winter sports include sledding, skating, hiking, ice fishing, skiing and ice boating. There's a long sledding run and beginners' ski slope. Campsite areas are grade "A", and there are 29 deluxe housekeeping cabins. There is a sportsman's area with trap and skeet fields, a rifle range and pistol range, an indoor small bore range as well as an archery field. Instructions and classes are provided. Cabin rates range from $32.50 a night to $165 weekly depending on season. For further information contact: Dillon State Park, Route 1, Nashport, OH 43830 Dillon State Park, Route 1, Nashport, OH 43830 (614)453–4377 park office or (614)453–0442 camp office.

★★*Hocking Hills State Park & Forest*. Plant species found in the north mix with those of the south for an interesting display and unusual variety. The mixture of this vegetation and the geological formations are enhanced by the numerous caves which were used by Indian tribes over 2,000 years ago. Today the 1,900 acres of park land includes six separate sites of these ancient landmarks—Old Man's Cave, Ash Cave, Cedar Falls, Conkle's Hollow, Rock House, and Cantwell Cliffs. Several miles of hiking trails pass through the park and forest. Hunting and fishing are permitted, but there is no boating on the 17–mile lake. The park contains a campsite with swimming pool and playground, amphitheater and dining lodge. Deluxe housekeeping cabins are available ranging from $32.50 a night to $165 weekly depending on season. In the summer a nature program is conducted and there are bridle paths for horses. Contact: Hocking Hills State Park, 20160 State Route 664, Logan, OH 43138 (614)385–6841 park office or (614)385–6165 camp office.

★★★*Hueston Woods State Park Lodge* is of rustic construction, decorated with Indian murals and artifacts to commemorate the Miami Indians who once inhabited this area. The lobby of the lodge features a 100–foot high sandstone fireplace. The park is located in the far western part of the state, near Cincinnati. It has 3,600 acres and a 625–acre lake. The park has a naturalist center and historic homes to view. There is an 18–hole golf course on the park grounds, tennis courts, bicycle rental, horseback riding and lawn and indoor games. Sailing is enjoyed on the lake and motors are limited to 10 hp. There is a launching ramp for private craft but no marina facilities. There are heated indoor and outdoor pools,

plus a beach for swimming. Hiking trails are popular, as is fishing. In the winter, there is ice fishing, skating, sledding and tobogganing. The park has a gift shop and a snack shop, plus a 150–seat Dining Room in the lodge. Local spots to visit include the Cincinnati Zoo, the U.S. Air Force Museum, Fort St. Clair Museum, Fort Hamilton Memorial and Kings Island. The park has 25 deluxe cabins for rent all year long, and 35 standard cabins without heat, available during the warm months. The Hueston Woods Lodge has 94 guest rooms which rent for $32 per night for up to four persons in a room. For reservations and further information write: Hueston Woods State Park Lodge, RFD #1, College Corner, OH 45003 (513)523–6381.

Lake Erie Islands State Park consists of a group of three islands offshore in Lake Erie—Catawba Island, Kelleys Island and South Bass Island—which offer recreational activities but no accommodations. *Catawba Island* was once an Indian hunting ground. The nine-acre park is located on the shore of Lake Erie. There's a free public boat launching ramp and a huge fishing pier (the only free one open to the public in this area). A scenic picnicking area provides an excellent view of the harbor. Winter activities include ice fishing and ice boating. Cedar Point, a private amusement park, is nearby. *Kelleys Island* is noted for its extraordinary glacial grooves, up to six feet deep, cut by an advancing glacier. The limestone was gouged by the ice sheet approximately 25,000 years ago. The island

has family campsites open year round. During the summer months nature programs are conducted with talks, movies, hikes and nature aid groups. There's a public sand beach for swimming, a boat launch (marine supplies available), and fishing is excellent. In the winter you can enjoy ice fishing and ice boating. The Glacial Grooves State Memorial, 400 feet of scoured limestone ground out by the glacier, is a natural landmark and point of interest. There is also Inscription Rock preserved by the historical society— a giant boulder where prehistoric Indians incised pictographic writings at least 500 years ago. Bicycles can be rented on the island. The island is accessible by ferry from the mainland. *South Bass Island*'s history goes back to the War of 1812. The 32-acre park houses the ruins of the Victory Hotel, one of the largest hotels in the world. Built in 1891, it was the first hotel to have a swimming pool where men and women were allowed to swim together. Ferry service is available from the mainland. There are campsites, nature programs, boating, fishing, picnicking and winter activities of ice fishing and ice boating. As a point of interest, visit Perry's Cave and Monument (Commodore Perry, 1812). For further information: Lake Erie Is-

lands State Park, 4049 E. Moores Dock Road, Port Clinton, OH 43452. Or contact the islands individually: Catawba Island State Park, 4049 E. Moores Dock Rd., Port Clinton, OH 43452 (419)797–4530. Kelleys Island State Park, Kelley Island, OH 43438 (419)746–4643. South Bass Island State Park, South Bass Island, OH (419)285–2112.

★★*Lake Hope State Park* lies entirely within the 25,490-acre Zaleski State Forest in the valley of Raccoon Creek. It is a rugged, heavily-forested region traversed by steep gorges and narrow ridges. The first inhabitants of the area were prehistoric mound builders— some of these sites still remain. Along with the beautiful scenery, they provide interest to nature lovers and historians alike. The 3,103 acre park and the 120-acre lake are under the supervision of the Division of Parks and Recreation. There are facilities for boating (can be rented), fishing (equipment and licenses available), picnicking, camping, hiking, swimming (400-foot beach), hunting in season, and horseback riding paths with horses available nearby. During the summer months there are nature programs conducted with talks, movies and campfire programs. In the winter, sports include ice skating, ice fishing, sledding, hiking, and camping. Accommodations can be had at the lodge or in a variety of cabins, from deluxe to sleeping, some of which have fireplaces. No pets are allowed in the cabins or at the lodge. Rates vary from $17–37.50 a night or $85–135 weekly. Rooms at the lodge range from $10–17.50 a night. Contact: Lake Hope State Park, Zaleski, OH 45698 (614)596–5253.

★★★*Mohican State Park* was once the hunting grounds of the Delaware Indians. It was also the area where Johnny Appleseed was frequently seen caring for his apple tree nurseries. The Mohican River, which flows through the park, is one of the most popular canoeing rivers in Ohio and there are several canoe liveries in the area which offer a variety of trips. There are three golf courses, a privately owned horse stable nearby, and several miles of bridle paths through the forest. There are formal landscaped gardens, natural woodlands and nature trails, and the famous French provincial style mansion containing 200 sculptured ceramic mushrooms. A country store and grist mill are points of interest as well as Malabar Farm, the home of author Louis Bromfield, through which tours are guided. Clearfork Gorge and the virgin white pine forest have been declared a National Natural Landmark. Hiking trails meander throughout the primitive and scenic areas of the park and forest—especially enjoyable is the self-guided Mohican Nature Trail. Fishing is excellent in the Mohican River or in two nearby lakes; hunting is also permitted in season for small game. There are several picnic areas and the two lakes provide boating and swimming facilities. There is also a swimming pool in the camp areas—there are both class "A" and "B" campsites available. Winter sports include skiing, sledding, hiking, skating and nature programs in summer months. Twenty-five deluxe housekeeping cabins overlook Mohican River and range from $32.50 a night to $165 weekly depending on season. For further information contact Dale Bricker, Park Manager, Mohican State Park Box 22, Loudonville, OH 44842 (419)994–4290.

★★*Pike Lake State Park* was created by the Civilian Conservation Corps. The 600–acre park is surrounded by beautiful Pike State Forest, 10,586 acres located in the wooded rolling hills of southern Ohio. The lake itself is 13 acres and offers boating, fishing and swimming. Picnicking, hiking and camping facilities are excellent. There are well-marked bridle trails, and during the summer months programs in nature study are conducted, including lectures, movies, hikes and a junior program for children from 7–10 years old. The park has one of the finest wildlife displays in Ohio. Other points of interest nearby are a dental museum and an Indian exhibit

pavilion. Cabins are available overlooking the lake, and rates range from $27–37.50 a night and $130–165 weekly. Group cabins are also available. Contact: Pike Lake State Park, Rte 2, Bainbridge, OH 45612 (614)493–2212.

★★★*Punderson State Park Manor House* was once a grand, private residence in the Tudor-style situated to overlook glacial Lake Punderson. The State Park is located in the snow belt, and features winter sports. It does not neglect summer activities, however. There is an 18–hole golf course with a club house, pro shop and golf carts. The marina at the north end of the lake has a boat launching ramp and boats for rent. Only electric motors up to 4 hp are allowed on the lake. There is a swimming beach on the west side of the lake, and for anglers, the lake is restocked each year with rainbow trout. Three tennis courts, several miles of hiking trails, lawn and indoor games and nature programs are also to be found at Punderson State Park. The park has only 890 acres, and the lake is small but enjoyable. There is a camping area with 201 sites, each with electrical hookup. A heated outdoor pool at the manor is for guests of the lodge and cabins only. In winter, visitors will find sledding, tobogganing, ice skating and ice fishing. There is a beginners skiing hill with an electrically-run rope tow, and a ski chalet with a snack bar. There are 26 deluxe cottages for rent year-round. The Manor House has 35 elegant rooms, renting for $25 a night. For more information and reservations, contact: Punderson State Park Manor House, State Route #87, Newbury, OH 44065 (216)564–2201.

★★★*Salt Fork State Park Lodge* is ideally located about two hours drive from Cleveland, Columbus, Pittsburgh and Charleston. The park is especially known for the 3,300–acre lake on which there are no horsepower restrictions for motor boats. The lake has 79 miles of sheltered shoreline for boaters, fishermen and waterskiers. The marina has a launching ramp and boat rentals. Hiking or bicycling the trails on the 20,000–acre park, relaxing in a sauna bath, swimming in the heated indoor pool or outdoor pools, playing tennis or hunting can all be enjoyed at Salt Fork. Winter brings ice skating, sledding and ice fishing. Golfers will enjoy the championship 18–hole course, and everyone can appreciate the snack bar and gift shop. There are many places to visit nearby, including the Cambridge Glass Museum, the Zane Grey Museum, the Buckeye Trail and the Cambridge Barn Theatre. The park has 54 deluxe cabins available all year. The lodge is of modern design and has 148 guest rooms. They rent for $32 a night. For more information write: Salt Fork State Park Lodge, P.O. Box 550, Cambridge, OH 43725 (614)439–2751.

★★★*Shawnee State Park Lodge* is located in the state's largest State Forest with 58,000 acres. It is on the Ohio River in Appalachia and just 12 miles from the southern Ohio city of Portsmouth. The park has a small 70–acre lake, as well as the river. The marina on the Ohio River has boat rentals, launching ramps, and fishing. There are two public beaches for swimming, as well as a heated indoor and outdoor pools. Only electric motors are allowed on boats on the lake. The park has an 18–hole golf course, tennis courts, hiking trails, court games such as badminton and shuffleboard, an indoor game room, and a playground for the children. There are picnic grounds and a snack bar. In winter there is ice fishing, sledding and skating. Nearby, visitors can see the canal locks, Log House Village and the Shawnee Vineyards. There are many local special events such as the Jackson Apple Festival and the River Days Celebration. Shawnee has 25 deluxe cottages. The lodge has 50 guest rooms renting for $25 per night. For reservations and information write: Shawnee State Park Lodge, P.O. Box 98, Friendship, OH 45630 (614)858–6621.

★★★*Tar Hollow State Park*, located on 16,126 acres of state park and forest land, was once the hunting grounds of the Shawnee and Mingo Indians. Today anglers can take advantage of the fine bluegill and pan fish catches on 15–acre Pine Lake. Boating and swimming are also permitted on the lake. There are more than 20 miles of bridle trails in the forest area surrounding the state park. A horsemen's camp near the park provides facilities for 20 units. Hikers can travel along any of the park's trails. There is also a section of the Buckeye Trail which passes through Tar Hollow State Forest and Park and part of the 16-mile loop Chief Logan Trail. Camping facilities within the park area exist for tents and trailers and are rented on a first come, first served basis. The adjacent forest area has primitive campsites and walk-in campsites. Group campers can take advantage of the park's large meeting hall with kitchen, as well as four cabins. Picnicking facilities with tables and grills are located at scenic areas throughout the park and state forest. Rates: Campsites within the park (class "B") $2.25 from November 1–March 31 and $2.50 April 1–October 31. There is no charge for the primitive campsites. Group camp facilities between Memorial Day and Labor Day $130 per day for 175 persons or less; $66 per day for 60 persons or less. For further information contact: The Ohio Department of Natural Resources, Division of Parks and Recreation, Tar Hollow State Park, 16396 Tar Hollow Road, Laurelville, OH 43135 (614)887–4818.

Introduction

Pennsylvania, with its vast tracts of "big-woods" state forest reserves and game lands, wild high country areas, thousands of lakes and ponds, trophy muskellunge and smallmouth bass rivers, scenic canoe routes, and nationally famous limestone trout streams—including the Yellow Breeches, Letort, Brodhead, Big Spring, Loyalstock, and Penns Creek—offers some of the East's finest canoe-camping, fishing, hunting, and backpacking opportunities. In the northwest region of the Keystone State are mixed hardwood forests, rolling hills, marshlands, and hundreds of miles of remote wild trout streams in the beautiful Allegheny National Forest. The scenic Upper Delaware River, which forms the natural boundary between Pennsylvania and New Jersey, is one of the East's top walleye and rainbow trout streams and canoe routes, noted for its deep-flowing pools, islands, rapids, and swirling eddies.

PENNSYLVANIA

Accommodations & Travel Information

The Keystone State's major outdoor vacation lodges, inns, and resorts are described in the "Vacation/Lodging Guide" which follows. For information on travel in the state contact: Bureau of Travel Development, South Office Bldg., Harrisburg, PA 17120 (717)787–5453.

Highways & Maps

To determine the best route to your destination in Pennsylvania, consult the *Official Map of Pennsylvania*. Free copies may be obtained from: Bureau of Travel Development, Dept. of Commerce, South Office Bldg., Harrisburg 17120. The map shows all roads and highways, indicating accumulated mileage between selected points, highway markers, and approximate populations of towns and cities. It also shows airports, state forest lands, state game lands or game farms, state park lands, state or national forest natural areas, fish hatcheries, roadside rest areas, railroads, hiking trails, and other points of interest. There is a chart of public recreation areas showing their locations on the map and which facilities are available at which area.

Pennsylvania Lakes, Forests & Streams

Pennsylvania's sprawling 1.9 million acres of state forest lands encompass some of the most scenic and wild limestone trout streams, virgin hemlock, cove hardwood, spruce fir forests, mountain swamps and bogs, beaver flows, remote lakes and ponds, and primitive trails in the eastern United States. These vast top-ranked fish and game lands offer unsurpassed fishing, backpacking primitive camping, cross-country skiing, and hunting in season for whiteland deer, black bear, red fox, raccoon, snowshoe hare, wild turkey, crow, squirrel, and upland game birds. The north central forests of Elk, Clearfield, and Cameron counties are inhabited by a few protected elk—native to the state more than a century ago.

Information Sources, Maps & Access

For detailed fishing and hunting information and regulations, contact the following state agencies: Fish Commission, P.O. Box 1673, Harrisburg, PA 17120 (717)787–2579 or Game Commission, P.O. Box 1567, Harrisburg, PA 17120 (717)787–6286. The Fish Commission produces an extremely useful, free booklet, *List of Pennsylvania Fishing Waters*, which specifies the state's principal lakes and streams by region and alphabetically within each region by county and indicates the fish species present in every listing. In addition, the commission publishes the following angler's aids, available free upon request: *Fishing in Pennsylvania, Favorite Trout Waters, Favorite Lakes of Eastern Pennsylvania, Favorite Lakes of Western Pennsylvania, Fly Fishing-Only Waters, 100 Best Fishing Spots, Salmon Fishing Guide, Ice Fishing,* and *Pennsylvania Boating Guide.* Waterproof *Lake Contour Maps* showing underwater natural and man-made structures and hydrographics are available for $2.95 each (include 50¢ postage) for the following Pennsylvania lakes and reservoirs: Allegheny, Crooked Creek, East Branch (Clarion), Loyalhanna, Mahoning Creek, Shenango, Tionesta Creek, and Youghiogheny. Order direct from: Lakes Illustrated, Box 4854 GS, Springfield, MO 65804. The Fish Commission publishes a free *Fishing and Boating Map* in cooperation with the Department of Transportation; it has the state road map on one side and a color-coded map on the reverse which indicates the principal streams, lakes, and boating access areas. The accompanying chart contains the following information for each of the 626 fishing spots on the map: location on both maps, type of ownership, type of fish present, and facilities. Fly fishing and fish-for-fun projects are listed along with mileage involved. This useful map can be used in conjunction with the *List of Pennsylvania Fishing Waters* mentioned earlier to gain an overview of the fishing possibilities. The State Game commission will furnish a list of free department literature about various animals and game, conservation projects, wildlife areas, refuges, the hunting regions of the state, plants, and related topics, it also publishes the following free hunter's aids: *Hunting in Pennsylvania* series (Northwest, Northeast, Southwest, Southeast), *Duck Identification Chart, Vanishing Spitfire* (bobcat), *Keystone Bruin* (black bear), *Whitetail Deer, Woodchuck, Ruffed Grouse, Wild Turkey in Pennsylvania, American Woodcock, Beaver in Pennsylvania, After the Buck Season, List of Protected Species, Ten Commandments of Shooting Safety, Deer & Bear Harvest Map,* and the *Wildlife* Notes series (red fox, owl, varying hare, and so forth). The Game Commission also publishes free maps of the State Forests. For Allegheny National Forest information and a full-color *Allegheny National Forest Map* (50¢) contact: Supervisor, Allegheny National Forest, Warren, PA 16365 (814)723–5150. For detailed information on the famous trout streams of south-central Pennsylvania, contact: Yellow Breeches Fly Shop, Box 200, Rte. 174, Boiling Springs, PA 17007 (717)258–6752. Anyone planning to hike the Appalachian Trail in

VACATION/ LODGING GUIDE

Pennsylvania should obtain a copy of the comprehensive *Guide to the Appalachian Trail in Pennsylvania* ($9.25, 150 pp.), published by the Keystone Trails Association. It can be ordered from: Appalachian Trail Conference, P.O. Box 236, Harpers Ferry, WV 25425. The book contains information essential to the trail hiker, including the nature of the trail in Pennsylvania, trail markings, maintenance, fires, shelters and cabins, uniform distress signal, snakes, historical information, and organizations involved in trail maintenance such as the Keystone Trails Association. For comprehensive, detailed information on backpacking and hiking in Pennsylvania, a number of free publications are available. The definitive guide to Pennsylvania trails is the Keystone Trail Association's excellent *Pennsylvania Hiking Trails in State Parks, Game Lands, and Elsewhere*. This 91–page book ($2.50) is available from: Appalachian Trail Conference, P.O. Box 236, Harpers Ferry, WV 25425. It contains useful general information on maps, state game lands, and forests and parks. It also contains a list of motels, restaurants, inns, private campgrounds, etc., located near hiking areas, moderately priced, and where hikers are welcome. Thirty-four major and minor hiking trails are described, with a sketch map of each trail on a facing page. Descriptions of each trail include map information, camping data, and addresses where you can write for further information. The Department of Environmental Resources has two free brochures: *Hiking Trails of Pennsylvania* and *Natural Areas in Pennsylvania*. These publications list and describe popular hiking trails and natural areas. For additional information on trails, you can write to: Keystone Trails Assn., RD2, Coopersburg 18036; or to: Bureau of Forestry, Dept. of Environmental Resources, P.O. Box 1467, Harrisburg 17120.

Pennsylvania has a great variety of scenic and wild-water rivers that provide excellent canoe-camping, white-water, and fishing opportunities along the way for rainbow, brook, and brown trout, largemouth and smallmouth bass, pickerel walleye, and a few voracious muskellunge. The canoe routes found within the state's three major river basins—the Delaware, Susquehanna, and Ohio—are shown and described in detail in the *Pennsylvania Canoe Country Map-Guide*, available free upon request from: Bureau of Travel Development, Dept. of Commerce, South Office Bldg., Harrisburg 17120. This useful guide contains a map showing the major canoe trails during normal water conditions, with color codes to indicate expected degree of difficulty. The guide also contains detailed descriptions of each canoe route and charts showing public lakes available for canoeing as well as facilities available (launch ramps, boat moorings, campgrounds). A 3 × 5-foot *Stream Map of Pennsylvania* is available from Pennsylvania State University for $1 plus 6¢ resident tax. Write: Stream Map of Pennsylvania, Box 6000, University Park 16802. White-water canoeists and kayakers are urged to wear a life vest, a good crash helmet—and, when the water temperature is below 50°, a wet suit to survive the paralyzing effects of ice-water immersion. Canoeists are urged to contact the State Fish Commission in Harrisburg before their trip, to determine water conditions. The Keystone State is served by Interstate 79, 76, and 80, the Pennsylvania Turnpike, and U.S. Highways 19, 422, 30, 22, 220, 119, 219, 522, and 40.

Recreation Areas

Allegheny National Forest

This renowned camping, fishing, and hunting region embraces 495,000 acres of mixed hardwood forests, rolling hills, marshlands, and hundreds of miles of remote, wild trout streams along the Allegheny Plateau in northwest Pennsylvania. The major features include the Hearts Content and Tionesta virgin timber stands, Alle-

gheny Reservoir, Minister Valley Backcountry, State Game Lands #28–29, Beaver Meadows Lake, Tracy Ridge and Hickory Creek wild areas, and the North Country, Tanbark, Twin Lakes, and Tracy Run trails. The forest is a top hunting area for whitetail deer, red fox, wild turkey, ruffed grouse, raccoon, and snowshoe hare.

Bald Eagle State Forest

The 180,000–acre Bald Eagle State Forest in Snyder, Union, Centre, and Mifflin counties encompasses the nationally famous trophy limestone trout fishing waters of Bald Eagle, Penns, Laurel Run, Little Fishing, Buffalo, and Jacks creeks. The forest contains several hundred miles of scenic hiking trails and old logging roads that provide access to the interior backpacking, fishing, hunting, and primitive camping areas in the virgin white pine and hemlock forests of the 77–acre Joyce Kilmer Natural Area; the 5,119–acre Hook Natural Area of mixed oak forest along the North Branch of Buffalo Creek; the old-growth hemlocks and sandstone outcrops of 600–acre Mount Logan Natural Area; the mountain bogs and cranberry, mountain holly and high bush blueberry thickets of the 140–acre Rosecrans Bog; the virgin pine-hemlock and pitch pine wilds of the 500–acre Snyder-Middlesworth Natural Area; the beautiful, remote 1,000–acre Tall Timbers Natural Area on Swift Run, with its second-growth oak, white pine, hemlock, and hard pine-oak forests, and the 3,581–acre White Mountain Wild Area along the deep trout pools and riffles of famous Penns Creek. For detailed information, write: Supervisor, Bald Eagle State Forest, Mifflinburg 17844.

Buchanan State Forest

The 70,000–acre Buchanan State Forest encompasses prime deer and upland game bird country in Fulton, Bedford, and Franklin counties in southcentral Pennsylvania, and includes the virgin hemlock and mixed oak forests of the 1,403–acre Sweet Root Natural Area; the virgin pine forests and abandoned farm settlements of the 568–acre Pine Ridge Natural Area; and the primitive camping areas of the 11,376–acre Martin Hill Wild Area.

Delaware State Forest & The Poconos

The 71,387–acre Delaware State Forest, in Pike and Monroe counties, embraces the broad plateaus of the Pocono Mountains and nationally famous trophy brown trout waters of the Brodhead River and its Paradise Creek headwaters, Wallenpaupack Lake (home of the state record 24–pound brown trout), Spruce Run, Laurel Run, Rattlesnake Creek, and hundreds of remote lakes and ponds; the 67–acre Pine Lake Natural Area, a high mountain bog; the 2,845–acre

wilderness of the glacial Bruce Lake Natural Area; the mountain swamps, rock ledges, and oak forests of the 471–acre Buckhorn Natural Area; the glacial swamps and spruce forests of the 1,931–acre Stillwater Natural Area; and the mountain swamps, sheep laurel, and mixed oak forests of the 936–acre Pennel Run Natural Area.

Elk State Forest & Quehanna Wild Area

The beautiful valleys, meadows, bogs, beaver flows, and evergreen forests of the 172,308–acre Elk State Forest in Elk, Cameron, and Potter Counties in north central Pennsylvania form part of the 800,000–acre area known as the "Black Forest," which includes the 32–acre Lower Jerry Run Natural Area; the northern hardwood forests of the 1,245–acre Wykoff Run Natural Area; the old-field white pines and abandoned farmlands of the 200–acre Pine Tree Trail Natural Area; the wildlands of the 15,682–acre Bucktail Natural Area; and the famous 46,163–acre Quehanna Wild Area and the Quehanna Trail.

Moshannon State Forest & Bald Eagle Creek

The scenic Moshannon State Forest (derived from the Indian name Moss-hanne, meaning "Moose Stream") lies in the heart of the Allegheny Mountains in the "Black Forest" area and includes the Black Moshannon area, named for the color of its stream waters from decaying swamp vegetation—once one of the great logging centers of the state, noted for its giant virgin white pines; Bald Eagle Creek, home of the state record 5 lb. 11½ oz. brook trout; the high mountain bogs, laurel thickets, and forests of the 917–acre Marion Brooks Natural Area; beautiful Black Moshannon Lake, noted for its muskellunge, chain pickerel, and yellow perch; and a portion of the Quehanna Wild Area.

Rothrock State Forest & Bear Meadows

The 85,138–acre Rothrock State Forest in the north-central portion of the state encompasses the famed trout waters of Spruce Creek, Standing Stone, Detweiler Run, Laurel and Shavers creeks; Indian Steps, an old Indian war-path; Bear Meadows, where black spruce, balsam fir, pitcher plant, and sundew grow in rare abundance, 185–acre Detweiler Run Natural Area and the laurel beds of the 142–acre Big Flat Laurel Natural Area; and the 1,757–acre Trough Creek Wild Area and the 1,757–acre Thickhead Mountain Wild Area in the Bear Meadows area.

Sproul State Forest & Pine Creek

The vast Sproul State Forest encompasses 256,000 acres of some of the most rugged and isolated wild country remaining in the state. The forest is located in western Clinton and Centre counties, and includes the 2,180–acre Burn's Run Wild Area; the 4,800–acre Fish Dam Wild Area; the 86–acre Tamarack Swamp Natural Area; the scenic northern hardwood and red pine forests of the 15,682–acre Bucktail Natural Area; the mountain swamps and old growth hemlocks of the 186–acre East Branch Swamp Natural Area; and the beaver dams, mountain bogs, and cranberry thickets of the 144–acre Cranberry Swamp Natural Area. The Bucktail Drive, which parallels the West Branch of the Susquehanna River, is considered the most scenic drive in the state. The sprawling 275,961–acre Susquehannock State Forest is located in the heart of north central Pennsylvania's famed big-game lands in Potter, Clinton, and McKean counties, and includes the 1,500–acre Beech Bottom Hemlocks Natural Area and the headwaters of the Allegheny River and Pine Creek. The Tiadaghton State Forest—the name the Iroquois Indians gave to Pine Creek—encompasses 70,000 acres of prime trout waters and game lands in Sullivan and Lycoming counties, and includes the 3,727–acre Algerine Wild Area and the spruce-fir forests, sphagnum moss, and sundew of the Algerine Swamp; 7,032–acre Wolf Run

Wild Area along Pine Creek; McIntyre Wild Area east of Ralston; the 4,000–acre high plateau country of the Miller Run Natural Area west of Pine Creek; and the old growth hemlocks at the Bark Cabin Run headwaters. The rugged highlands of the 160,000–acre Tioga State Forest, named after a tribe of Seneca Indians, is located in Tioga and Bradford counties, and includes the renowned trout waters of Big Asaph Run, Elk Run, and Pine Creek—noted for its awesome 1,000–foot deep gorge, often referred to as Pennsylvania's "Grand Canyon"—and the 3,931–acre Asaph Wild Area; the old beaver meadows and conifer forests of the 308–acre Black Ash Swamp Natural Area; 5,720–acre Pine Creek Gorge Natural Area; and the high mountains bog and forests of the 1,302–acre Reynolds Spring Natural Area.

Wild & Scenic Trout Waters

Pennsylvania has been famous for trout fishing since classic fly fishing began after the Civil War. The Pocono Mountains area, with its thick hemlock and hardwood forests and beautiful rhododendron- and laurel-shaded streams and rivers, has added a great deal to the literature of fly fishing. Streams such as the twisting Lehigh River System, spilling into the Delaware at Easton; Brodhead Creek and its exquisite feeder, Paradise Creek, flowing into the Delaware at Stroudsburg; the Bushkill to the north; and the Lackawaxen—schooling grounds for author and ardent angler Zane Grey—entering the Delaware upstream at Shohola, have offered fine trout fishing for generations, as well as bass, walleye, and other species in the lower reaches. Lake Wallenpaupack, which drains into the Lackawaxen, contains some of the largest rainbow and brown trout (state record, 24 pounds) in the East, as well as muskies, bass, walleyes, and assorted panfish. Harveys and Crystal lakes, on the western edge of the Poconos, contain lake trout, kokanee, bass, and panfish. To the north of Wallenpaupack in Wayne County is the beautiful, cold Upper Woods Lake, which provides angling for rainbows and kokanee in some of the most scenic country in Pennsylvania. In the center of the state are a series of stream systems, tributaries of the West Branch of the Susquehanna, which offer fine trout fishing for browns and rainbows, as well as brookies in the forest headwaters. The Loyalstock enters the big river to the east of Williamsport at Montoursville. This stream and some of its tributaries, such as the Little Loyalstock and Elk Creek, contain good trout populations, including some large fish. Among the other fine trout streams flowing into the West Branch are the Big Pine Creek System, 15 miles west of Williamsport; Young Woman's Creek at Gleasonton near Hyner Run State Park, with 6 miles of fly-fishing-only water on the right branch; Kettle Creek to the west at Westport; the vast Sinnamahoning Creek watershed which drains an immense, fan-shaped area—the First Fork produces lots of trophy browns; and the famous Bald Eagle Creek and its many noted feeder streams which spill into the Susquehanna just east of Lock Haven. The Bald Eagle yields eye-popping brown trout, as does its limestone tributary, Big Fishing Creek, whose rich, alkaline waters provide some superior fly fishing. Another great trout stream is Penns Creek, a limestone stream complex rising in a ridge system a short distance to the south of Big Fishing Creek and running east into the main Susquehanna above Selinsgrove. Trophy browns await the skilled angler who hits the stream or its Elk and Pine Creek feeders at the right time. South central Pennsylvania contains some world-famous limestone trout streams in the lush region surrounding the beautiful town of Carlisle. This is classic, pastoral fly fishing, reminiscent of the legendary British chalk streams, the Test and the Itchen. Brown and rainbow trout grow long, deep, and heavy in these insect-rich waters, but their elusiveness increases with their weight. A whole school of American limestone fishing technique has arisen with special tackle

and patterns suited to the demanding water conditions and insect hatches, and perfected by expert anglers such as Charles Fox and Vince Marinaro. The best known of these streams are the Letort, Yellow Breeches, and Big Spring creeks. It is advisable to be equipped with local patterns designed for these waters, because the fish are superselective. The Letort Cricket, the Jassid series, and the Leaf Hopper are a few examples of terrestrial flies which were developed for summer fishing on these exacting waters.

Wyoming State Forest & Loyalstock Creek

The Wyoming State Forest takes in 40,000 acres of wildly primitive conifer and northern hardwood forests, high plateaus and ridges, and deep stream canyons, and includes the nationally renowned trout waters of picturesque Loyalstock Creek and its tributaries; Eagles Mere, Mokoma, Splashdam, and Painter Den lakes; the Loyalstock Trail; the famed trout waters of the 774–acre Kettle Creek Gorge Natural Area; the High Knob Natural Area, and the beaver ponds and bogs of Spook Swamp.

Lodges & Resorts

★★★★*Allenberry Resort Inn* is a 57–acre family resort in rural Pennsylvania, near Yellow Breeches Creek. Fine outdoor activities, plus professional theatre in the Allenberry Playhouse, are part of the resort's offerings. Daytime activities include swimming in an Olympic-size heated pool, volleyball, and badminton. The Yellow Breeches Creek which borders Allenberry provides excellent fly fishing all year. Considered one of the best trout streams in the East, it is stocked regularly by the Pennsylvania Fish Commission. There are two Har-tru and two Laykold lighted tennis courts on the grounds with professional instruction available. Nearby Roundtop provides fine skiing, and three professional 18–hole golf courses are a short drive from Allenberry. The Allenberry Playhouse has performances from April through November with a capacity of 400 theatregoers. The Meadow Lodge, rustic cabins, and the Stone Lodge are the three types of overnight accommodations. Meadow Lodge, overlooking South Mountain has 32 motel-type rooms with TV, private baths and double beds. Conferences can be accommodated in its Club

Room. Cabins with an in-the-woods feeling vary in size from one with four private guest rooms, plus a small conference room, to those with two bedrooms. The Stone Lodge, built in 1814 with a charming stone facade, has been completely renovated in colonial decor, contains 15 guest rooms for individuals, couples or small groups. The Carriage Room, one of Allenberry's restaurants, is located here, serving an international menu. More casual meals are served daily buffet style. Meals are not included in rates. Rates: April to November: Meadow & Stone Lodges, singles, $23–25; doubles, $28–30. Cottages, $40–72. Weekly, off-season and ski rates are also available. An American Plan conference rate is also available. For further information contact: Allenberry Resort Inn and Playhouse, Boiling Springs, PA 17007 (717)258–3211.

★★★*The Antlers Inn* is located in Pennsylvania's Canyon Country and operates the White Pine Camping Park and Canyon Cruises. The Antlers Inn is a small rustic inn noted for its good food for the past 30 years. It is centrally located to a quarter of a million acres of public mountain forests and surrounded by many beautiful hiking trails. Owners Edward and Katherine McCarthy run Canyon Cruises down the river of Pennsylvania's Grand Canyon. There are one-day trips and two day weekends. In early spring and summer the waters of Pine Creek offer over 60 miles of swift, clean, white water and majestic scenery. The first day's trip is through the upper canyon from Ansonia to Blackwell with a mid-way, mid-day cookout. The second day's trip begins at Watrous and winds through small towns to Ansonia. Length of the trip depends on group size, water level and experience. The McCarthys equip cruise guests with rubber rafts, lifejackets and paddles. A hot midday lunch is served on the creek and the evening meal is at the Antlers Inn. The weekend package includes two nights' lodging and six meals at the Antlers. Other accommodations are at White Pine Camping Park, operated by the Antlers Inn, an isolated camping area with rustic cabins, hookups for trailers and primitive tent campsites. The camping park has its own play area and is surrounded by public forest land. Campers can use any of five access areas to Pine Creek for canoeing and fishing. For further information contact The Antlers Inn, RD 4, Wellsboro PA 16901 (814)435–6300.

★★★★*Buck Hill Inn*, high in the Pocono Mountains, is the largest all-year-round resort in the Northeast, with more activities and facilities on its 6,000 acres than any resort in the world. It is only a two-hour drive from New York City or Philadelphia, and 240 miles from Washington, DC. There is an indoor ice skating rink open from November through April, a glass-domed heated indoor pool open all year, an outdoor heated Olympic-size pool, Paddle Tennis on two new lighted courts, tennis on eleven Teniko and 3 hard-surface courts, sailing, water skiing, snowmobiling, riding stables with 20 miles of scenic trails, lawn bowling, picnicking and hiking. Golfers have great facilities at Buck Hill Inn. Three separate nine-hole courses adjoin and can be played in any combination, starting and ending at the clubhouse. There are also two top putting greens. In winter, two ski lifts operate for downhill skiing, and there is outdoor ice-skating. The inn welcomes children and families. In July and August, they run a children's day camp and a teenage program. There is also a special offer for families staying more than three nights. On request, children will be given a separate room (adjoining if possible) at no additional charge over the normal one-half rate for children. Guests can meet for cocktails in the new Forest Cocktail lounge and after dinner, dance to orchestra music. There is gracious dining, with jackets required at dinner, in the two dining rooms, or informal meals in the Bluestone Room. The 350 rooms include ultra-modern decor with huge picture windows and rooms in traditional ivy-covered buildings. All rooms are air-conditioned

and have color TV. Daily rates per person double occupancy are $52 with breakfast and dinner and $55 with three meals. For information and reservations contact: Buck Hill Inn, Buck Hill Falls, PA 18323 (800)233–8113 or (717)595–7441.

★★★*Crescent Lodge* is a year-round country lodge located in the heart of the Poconos. It is located near the major Poconos ski areas and offers skiing, tobogganing, sledding, snowmobiling and ice skating, all nearby. The main lodge has a cocktail lounge with dancing and live entertainment. Guests can disco in the Avalanche Room or have a drink with cheese and crackers in the Starting Post Lounge. There is a game room and an elegant dining room. The fireside lounge offers warmth for apres-ski parties. There is a wide variety of accommodations: the lodge has double rooms and country suites, and the motel unit has deluxe rooms with fireplaces and suites with glass-enclosed bath, living room and dinette. Cottages are luxurious and several have fireplaces. For those who want efficiency accommodations, there are cottages with kitchens, utensils, living room and two bedrooms. All rooms have color TV, wall-to-wall carpeting, telephone, private bath and self-controlled heat and air-conditioning. Rates without meals based on double occupancy range from $28 per day mid-week for a lodge room to $60 per day weekends for efficiency cottages. For more information contact: Crescent Lodge, Paradise Valley, Cresco, PA 18326 (717)595–7486.

★★★*The Inn at Starlight Lake* opened in 1909 and maintains the same turn-of-the-century, friendly atmosphere today. Innkeepers Jack and Judy McMahon and Dennis Ebert make guests feel welcome at this country-inn resort located in the Moosic range of the Appalachian Mountains, a three-hour drive from New York City. The inn is surrounded by natural woodlands, is tucked away among the hills at the edge of a spring-fed lake. At the lake, guests enjoy canoeing, sailboats, rowing, fishing and swimming. Parents can enjoy the dockside sundeck and watch their children playing safely in the shallow water. Guests have free use of bicycles, canoes and rowboats. For livelier water sports, arrangements can be made for canoe trips on the nearby Delaware River. The scenery makes a hike an adventure. Hikers can explore the forests and meadows, shady dells, mossy boulders and green hills. Also, there is tennis, croquet and shuffleboard. Fall offers a color display of spectacular variety and the inn welcomes hunters during the November-December season. Then come the winter sportsmen. There are twelve miles of marked, wooded trails with gentle slopes for a bracing day of cross-country skiing. Instruction and rental equipment are available at the pro shop. Downhill skiers can visit Nob-Hill only 15 minutes away or travel 30 minutes to Pennsylvania's largest skiing area, Elk Mountain. The Mainhouse at the inn has 20 rooms and 10 cottage rooms, available from Memorial Day to Columbus Day. Meals are served in the informal, lakeside dining room and dinner often features specialties such as Jaegerschnitzel and Sauerbraten, served with home-baked bread and followed by freshly ground coffee. There are drinks and snacks in the Stovepipe Bar and, in season, live music for dancing. Weekend and holiday rates are $63.25 to $69 per day for two persons with full breakfast and dinner. Weekday rates are 10% less; children's and weekly rates are available. For information and reservations: The Inn at Starlight Lake, Starlight, PA 18461 (717)-798–2519.

★★★★*Seven Springs Resort* is a year-round resort located in western Pennsylvania's Laurel Mountains. Winter sports enthusiasts will enjoy the resort's fine skiing facilities—six double chairlifts, two poma lifts, three rope tows and a triple chairlift. There is night skiing, snow making, ski rentals and a lodge at the base of the slopes. Warm weather sports activities include an 18–hole, 6,700 yard golf course, with private lessons available. There are hard-surface tennis courts and a daily tennis clinic. The resort has both indoor and outdoor swimming pools. In addition the resort has an alpine slide; racquetball and handball facilities; bowling lanes; an 18–hole miniature golf course; a health spa with sauna and jacuzzi; shuffleboard; a recreation room; children's activities and adult evening entertainment. There's hiking on the Laurel Ridge Hiking Trail and ski lift rides to Little Lake Tahoe. Accommodations include rooms or suites in the main lodge; housekeeping chalets, cabins, apartment and townhouses. Meals are not included in rates, but are available three times a day at the resort's dining room. Rates: Main Lodge, rooms $23–26 per person, suites for 4–6 people, $140–170 per person, per day. Chalets with kitchen facilities, $300–400 weekly, $225–275 for a partial stay of two nights. Cabins with kitchens, $350–450 weekly, $250–325 for a partial stay of two nights. Apartments and townhouses at the golf course ¾ mile from the Main Lodge, $275–475 weekly, $175–325 for partial stay of two nights. All apartment units have air-conditioning, complete kitchens with dishwashers, and most have TV, washer and dryers and access to private swimming pool. For further information contact: Seven Springs Resort, Champion, PA 15622 (814)352–7777.

Travel Services

Allegheny Outfitters are located in Scandia Mountains at the Red Oak Campground and offer complete outfitting services for canoeing, backpacking, camping, fishing, and hunting trips in the Allegheny National Forest region. For detailed information, contact: Allegheny Outfitters, RD 1, Box 1730, Russell, PA 16345 (814) 757–8801.

Apple Valley Cross-Country Ski Area has trails through some of the most scenic parts of Pennsylvania. It is located 50 miles from Philadelphia and twelve miles from Allentown. The center has a new ski lodge and offers cross-country ski rentals and instruction. There are one-mile long downhill trails, and 30 more acres of cross-country trails have just been added. All trails are marked and lead through apple and peach orchards, around ponds, over bridges, past campsites, and through open fields. The main trail leads to the

top of a mountain called High Point, which offers a view across the valley to a distance of 10 or 15 miles. Trail fees are $2.75 a day and rentals of cross-country equipment are $5 a day. Lessons are available at $6 per hour per person or $5 each in groups of four or more. For more information write: Apple Valley Cross-Country Ski Area, RD 1, Zionsville, PA 18092 (call the residence phone (215)679–9360 or the ski shop (215)966–5525).

Fenwick Spruce Creek & Seven Springs Fly Fishing Schools. The world-famous Fenwick Corporation operates 2-day fly fishing schools during August on Spruce Creek—one of the fabled Appalachian limestone streams. The school is held on private waters, which include 6 meandering miles of Spruce Creek and a small lake used as a casting pond. Spruce Creek is the stream President Eisenhower used to fish. The Fenwick instruction includes use and types of fly line, rod and reel construction, how to choose tackle, and terminology, entomology, choice of flies and how to match the hatch, fly fishing

knots, casting technique, reading the stream, and playing the fish. Accommodations are available at Spruce Creek Lodge—15 miles west of State College in the center of Pennsylvania. Fenwick also runs 2-day schools at the huge Seven Springs Mountain Lodge in Champion, during April, May, and June. Both schools are open to beginning through advanced fly fishermen. For free literature, rates, and registration information, write: Director, Fenwick Fly Fishing School, Eastern Division, 2202 Glen Court, Rt. 7, Frederick, MD 21707 (301)663–3966.

Fish & Game Frontiers, one of the nation's most renowned firms specializing in outdoor recreation travel, offers guided trips and travel service for freshwater and saltwater fishing, Atlantic salmon fishing, big-game hunting, wingshooting, Africa photo tours, and

special tours, as well as foreign independent travel. Free brochures are available upon request for the following package trips (include air transportation, lodging, meals, and professional guide services): Columbia Special Summer Quail/Dove Hunt; Bird-shooting at Snook Inn on Mexico's Yucatán Peninsula; Trophy Tarpon and Snook Fishing at Casa Mar Lodge, Costa Rica; Bonefishing Adventure at Boca Paila on the Mexican Caribbean; Quebec's Mistassini Reserve Trophy Fishing; Atlantic Salmon Fishing on Iceland's famed Laxa; New Mexico Antelope Hunt; Alaskan Wood River—Tik Chik Lake Chain Wilderness Fishing; Labrador Trophy Squaretail and Salmon Fishing; Rainbow King Lodge—Iliamna Lake, Alaska; African Hunt Safaris; Pheasant Shooting in Denmark; Club Pacifico-Panama Sportfishing Camp; and New Zealand Trophy Trout Fishing. For the trip brochures listed above, rates, and custom travel planning service, write: Fish & Game Frontiers, P.O. Box 161, Pearce Mill Rd., Wexford, PA 15090 (412)931–6640.

Kittatinny Canoes at Dingmans Ferry. Whether you enjoy the challenge of white water, or the wider, placid stretches of the Delaware, Kittatinny Canoes, Inc., will plan individual and group, overnight, day or weekly trips between any of their seven base camps along 135 miles of the Delaware River. Canoes may be rented for $12 daily on weekdays, and $15 weekend days. Five to seven day rentals are $50. Car top carriers are available for $2 daily, or Kittatinny will transport, deliver and pick up 1–12 canoes along any part of the 135 mile stretch of the river. Transportation rates will vary according to distance. For more information write: Kittatinny Canoes, Silver Lake Road, Dingmans Ferry, PA 18328 (717)828–2700.

Kittatinny–Delaware Water Gap Recreation Area Information Center, located off Interstate 80 outside East Stroudsburg, is staffed by National Park Service Rangers who will gladly help you plan your Delaware River canoe trip, supply maps, and recommend local points of interest. From June-October the rangers guide special three-day canoe trips for novices (you must supply your own canoe— rentals are available). For information call the Delaware National Water Gap Recreation Area headquarters in Bushkill at (717)588–6637. The Delaware Water Gap National Recreation Area provides a well-managed, protected backcountry recreation area offering camping, hiking, and canoeing in an area of natural beauty and historical significance. The free-flowing Delaware River's white waters flow through the mountains and valleys of the Appalachian Plateau. The rapids become tamer south of Port Jervis, New York, interspersed with quiet pools up to 20 feet deep. The river passes Bushkill Creek and enters Wallpack Bend, shored on the east by the forests of the Kittatinny Ridge. The famous Flatbrook Creek enters the river in this area. Below it is another stretch of riffles, and beyond them, a group of islands dot the river in an area of boulders deposited by glaciers. This upper, scenic section of the Delaware offers top-ranked fishing for big smallmouth bass, walleyes, rainbow trout, and muskellunge up to the state record 19 pounds. There are no developed canoe-camping areas along the river at present, but islands and shore areas offer a variety of natural campsites. Campers should be careful to choose sites protected from sudden changes in water level, which occur in this area even during relatively good weather. Group camping areas may be reserved by special permit from the park headquarters. Worthington State Park, near the lower section of the national recreation area, provides some campsites. Check weather conditions before you start a canoe trip: foul weather and cold water can turn a pleasant trip into a dangerous and harrowing experience. Early spring and late fall trips require special preparation and knowledge of elementary rescue techniques. The lands surrounding the river are cut by ravines; in some areas they are composed of rocky

slopes, elsewhere of marshlands and swamps, and forests of oak, beech, and hickory trees and rhododendron and hemlock groves. Among the most beautiful areas here are the Pennsylvania Gorges north of Wallpack Bend carved out of the western side of the Delaware Valley. Old logging roads wind along the creek gorges. Trails also lead to Mounts Minsi and Tammany in the immediate vicinity of the divide. The Appalachian Trail runs through the recreation area.

Laurel Highlands River Tours offer wild-water guided raft trips on the Youghiogheny and Cheat Rivers. The Youghiogheny river, the calmer of the trips, slices through the mountains of southwestern Pennsylvania. The river is classic whitewater, with calm pools of clear blue water interrupting the river's brawling rapids. River runners rallys at Ohiopyle State Park and paddle eight miles to Bruner State Run for a total trip time of about seven hours. The Cheat River of West Virginia is truly a wild river, recommended for those with previous paddle experience. The trip covers 11 miles and over 30 rapids in a remote portion of the river. Total trip time is over eight hours from time of rally until you return to your car. Laurel Highlands provides rafts, paddles, life jackets, a smorgasbord-style shore lunch and return transportation to your car. A professional guide, trained in all aspects of river rescue, will accompany each trip. Each raft holds a crew of four. A lodge package consisting of the wild-water raft ride, two nights' lodging, lunch and dinner banquet the day of your return can be arranged with nearby Pine Slope Lodge. Rates: Youghiogheny River trip from May through October weekends and holidays, $25 per person. Weekday discount rate, $20 per person. Cheat River trip from April through mid May, weekends and holidays, $30 per person, weekday discount rates, $25 per person. Group discounts available. For further information contact: Laurel Highlands River Tours, P.O. Box 107, Ohiopyle, PA 15470 (412)329–4501.

Mountain Streams & Trails Outfitters will get you ready to hike the Laurel Highlands in southern Pennsylvania, on the West Virginia and Maryland border. Complete hiking equipment, packs, tents, sleeping bags and food are all available. The Bear Run Trail, the Laurel Ridge Trail system, the Ohiopyle Trail system, and the Laurel Mountain Trail surround Mountain Streams & Trails Outfitters' two shops, Last Resort, 2.5 miles south of Mill Run on 381, and Rivendell, on 381 in Ohiopyle. In the winter, these quiet trails provide excellent cross-country skiing, and skis may be rented from Mountain Streams & Trails Outfitters for $1.50 an hour. Lessons are available twice daily for $6 per person. When the first warm days of spring stir you out of your winter blues and tell you to get moving, Mountain Streams & Trails Outfitters is already running white-water rafting trips down the Canyon of the Cheat River. Trips run each weekend in April and May through Memorial Day weekend, from 7:30 till noon, and are $23 per person on Fridays and Mondays, and $30 per person Saturday and Sunday. Summer is the time for the Youghiogheny River, the water runs fast and high, and guides steer you through the great boulders. Trips run May through October, leaving at 8, 10, and 12, and are $20 per person during the week and $25 per person weekend days. The Gauley River trips start the second weekend in September and continue till October, through the fall foliage. The Gauley run is an overnight trip; full camping facilities, a steak dinner with all the trimmings, and an open bar make the sunset on the river unforgettable. The Gauley River overnight trips are $125 per person. Day trips are run on the upper and lower stretches of the Gauley, and are $45–50 per person during the week, and $40–45 per person on weekend days. Organized groups are welcome, but reserve early. For information write: Mountain Streams and Trails Outfitters, Box 106, Ohiopyle, PA 15470 (412)329–8810.

Pack Shack Adventures at Delaware Water Gap, operated by Joe Greene, offers a complete supply of camping and canoe-tripping gear, canoeing instruction, and guided Delaware River canoe trips in July and August. For detailed information, contact: Pack Shack Adventures, Delaware Water Gap, PA 18327 (717)424–8533.

Wilderness Voyageurs runs whitewater rafting trips on the Youghiogheny River, called the most popular river in the East. The river is in Southwestern Pennsylvania in Ohiopyle State Park. Wilderness Voyageurs runs trips daily every weekend from April through October and weekdays from May to September. Trips begin at 7:30 am, 9:30 am and 11:30 am. It takes five to six wild, exciting hours to travel the 7½ miles of whitewater. At the end of the trip, buses transport rafters back to their cars. The cost includes rafts, paddles, life jackets, lunch, a professional guide and transportation back to your car. On Saturdays, Sundays and holidays the trip is $28 per person and $23 on weekdays. Four people ride in a raft and everyone paddles. Minimum age is 12 years old. Rafters should bring a dry change of clothes; the park has changing facilities. Everyone must wear tennis shoes. Reservations must be made, especially for large groups. For information and reservations: Wilderness Voyageurs, Inc., P.O. Box 97, Ohiopyle, PA 15470 (412)329–4752 or (412)329–5517.

RHODE ISLAND

Introduction

Rhode Island is the smallest, most densely populated state in America, yet it furnishes excellent saltwater angling, sailing, freshwater fishing for trout, bass, kokanee salmon, northern pike, pickerel, and panfish, hiking and cross-country skiing, and hunting for deer, upland game, and waterfowl. The state contains 1,214 square miles and offers the sportsman more than 400 miles of shoreline, island-filled bays, long tidal estuaries, game management areas, streams, and lakes. The Department of Natural Resources deserves a great deal of credit for managing and preserving inland wildlife resources under the most challenging conditions.

Accommodations & Travel Information

Although Rhode Island offers comparitively few full-service lodges and resorts, the state's motel and hotel accommodations are varied and plentiful. For information on where to stay, consult the useful *Guide to Rhode Island*, available free from: Dept. of Economic Development, 1 Weybosset Hill, Providence 02903 (401)277–2614. This booklet contains a listing of accommodations arranged by region, including campgrounds and trailer parks. The traveler is advised to inspect the quarters upon arrival and to obtain information from individual hostelries by phoning or writing in advance.

A free *Camping in Rhode Island* describing all state-managed and commercial campgrounds may be obtained from: Dept. of Economic Development, 1 Weybosset Hill, Providence 02903. The state's major campsites and hiking trails, including the Inter-Park and Appalachian trails, are shown on the *Rhode Island Recreation Map* (See "Highways & Maps"). Winter camping areas are described in the free publication *Winter in Rhode Island*, available free from: Dept. of Economic Development (address above). If you are planning to hike the Rhode Island backcountry be sure to consult the *AMC Massachusetts & Rhode Island Trail Guide* ($7.75), published by: Appalachian Mountain Club, 5 Joy St., Boston, MA 02108. It contains a detailed section on the state's Inter-Park trails, including the Arcadia, John B. Hudson, Breakheart, Narragansett, Mount Tom, Escoheag, Ben Utter, Tippecansett, and Walkabout trails, as well as Audubon sanctuaries and state parks.

Highways & Maps

Anyone planning on participating in any kind of recreational activity in Rhode Island should send for the free *Rhode Island Recreation Map* from: Dept. of Natural Resources, Veterans Memorial Bldg., Providence 02903. Besides providing an excellent road map showing all major highways and other roads, it features a recreation guide legend, which indicates the following on the map: hunting checking stations, limits of stocked areas on trout streams, public boat-launching sites, guest moorings, public and private camping sites, charter boats, hiking trails, horseback trails, archery ranges, public rifle ranges, canoeing areas, areas where shellfishing is prohibited, and fish ladders. The map also features a recreation index showing saltwater beaches, freshwater beaches, yacht clubs, boatyards, yacht harbors and basins, trout ponds and streams (stocked), parks, view sites, and ski areas. All these are location-keyed to the map. The reverse side contains a wealth of recreational information. There is also safety information for boaters (whistle signals, rules for passing/overtaking, meeting head on, and crossing, storm warnings, and a channel buoy guide). Motorboat laws, waterskiing laws, and forestry and fire laws are provided, and there is, of course, an index showing cities, towns, and places of interest and their locations on the map.

Rhode Island Woodlands, Lakes & Coastal Recreation Areas

Rhode Island's rocky, wave-pounded coast and inland forests, trails, lakes and streams offer excellent opportunities for fishing, backpacking, canoeing, and cross-country skiing. The productive waters of Narragansett Bay bite deep into the eastern interior of Rhode Island and contain three major islands, the largest of which gives the state its name. The bay, the adjacent coastal areas stretching west and east from its mouth, and the outstanding waters of Block Island—noted for its superb surf-fishing, coastal hiking trails, rocky bluffs, lighthouse, and pioneer graves—lying 15 miles due south of the mainland across the prolific sweep of Block Island Sound, constitute one of the East Coast's prime saltwater fishing areas. Giant tuna to weights of 1,000 pounds, school bluefins, white marlin, broadbill swordfish, and mako sharks are pursued in the bait-filled tides of Rhode Island and Block Island sounds and the trophy big-game Atlantic Ocean reaches that stretch from Block Island to New York's Montauk Point and the Gulf Stream eddy. Cod, pollack, and an occasional halibut are taken from the offshore reefs, ledges, and wrecks including Shark, Coxes', and Brown ledges. Heavy striped bass, bluefish, bonitos, weakfish (squeteague), fluke, winter flounders, sea bass, porgies (scup), mackerel, blackfish (tautog), tomcods, and other species provide great variety in the bays and estuaries, as well as along the shoreline and in sound waters.

Striped bass are probably the most popular game fish, followed by the savage bluefish, and are found along the beaches and rocky shores of the outer coastline, as well as in the interior waters of Narragansett Bay and the Sakonnet River. The long striper season extends from spring until late fall, and many of the trophy fish to 60 pounds are caught during the fall feeding spree when the linesides fatten up for a long, cold winter. Plugs, bucktails, eel rigs, surgical tubes, spinner and worm combinations, spoons, jigs, feather lures, and natural baits including live eels, menhaden, mackerel, squid, clams, herring, and sea worms are the most popular. Fly casting is gaining in popularity, and sheltered bays, estuaries, tidal rivers, and salt marshes provide ample opportunities to fish with streamers and popping bugs. Bass are well dispersed along the state's saltwater exposure, but inlets, known as breachways, are among the most productive areas and include the favorite channels at Weekapaug, Quonochontaug, Charlestown, Card Ponds, and Jerusalem-Galilee, which are all located west of the mouth of Narragansett Bay, and the various pond outlets at Little Compton to the east of the bay.

Bluefish, which attain weights of more than 20 pounds, are often found in the company of stripers, but are more inclined to pursue schools of menhaden and mackerel several miles offshore. Blues are taken from July until October or November on the same general lures as bass and are swift, powerful battlers. Weakfish have made an impressive comeback, following a severe low in their natural cycle, and once again are landed in weights up to 12 pounds. These spotted, iridescent scrappers, resembling trout in form, prefer bays, inlets, tidal marshes, and beach areas, striking at shrimptail jigs, spoons, spinners, bucktails, and spinner-and-worm combinations. Favorite natural baits include shrimp, sea worms, squid, and minnows, but weaks will also hit flies. Squeteague, as they are locally called, are present from May until low water temperatures in the fall drive them south.

The bottom varieties provide fishing all year long with scup, tautog, sea bass, and fluke avilable during the warmer months, and cod, pollack, tomcods, and winter flounder dominating the winter scene, as well as being taken in deeper cold water during the summer.

**VACATION/
LODGING GUIDE**

Charter and party boat operations can be found at Jerusalem and Galilee, Wickford, Warwick, Pawtuxet, Sakonnet Harbor, world-famous Newport on the island called Rhode Island at the mouth of Narragansett Bay, and Block Island, which can be reached by ferry from Point Judith, Providence, or Newport.

Stream trout fishing is somewhat limited because of the topography and demographics of the state. Most of the fast-water angling is put and take, because many of the watersheds are reduced to warm trickles during the summer heat. The best stream system in the state is the Wood River in southwest Rhode Island. The Wood flows out of Arcadia Management Area south for about 10 miles to Alton, where it meets the Pawcatuck. The entire length to Alton is stocked with brook, brown, and rainbow trout, and the Wood is by far the

most consistent producer of holdover browns to 5 pounds. Tributaries such as Flat and Falls rivers and Breakheart, Roaring, and Parris brooks are also productive. Another Pawcatuck feeder, the Beaver River, furnishes trout fishing from the Pawcatuck at Shannock, upstream for about 4 miles. A few holdover browns are taken, especially near the confluence.

To the north of Arcadia Management Area are two other popular trout streams, both capable of producing an occasional large trout. The Moosup is near the center of the Connecticut border, and with its Bucks Horn Brook feeder provides more than 10 miles of fishing. The Ponaganset River, with its Dolly Cole and Windsor brooks tributaries, is similar in size to the Moosup Watershed and runs from Ponaganset impoundment into Barden Reservoir. The trout

area is contained within Foster township, and the large browns sometimes enter the river from Barden.

Some of Rhode Island's lakes and ponds supply good trout fishing opportunities. Watchaug Pond, in the Burlingame Management Area in southwest Rhode Island, produces occasional browns to 6 pounds, stocked trout, and excellent fishing for both kinds of bass, pickerel, and panfish. Beach Pond, a few miles northwest on the Connecticut border at Beach Pond State Park, holds kokanee salmon, rainbows, browns, largemouths, smallmouths, pickerel, and panfish. The warm-water fish are abundant, but their growth rates are below standard. Beach Pond is shared with Connecticut under reciprocal arrangements. Wallum Lake straddles the Massachusetts border in the northwestern corner of Rhode Island and, like Beach Pond, is a reclaimed trout lake that became reinfested with warmwater species. Brook and rainbow trout, smallmouth bass, and panfish are the major species. Stafford Pond in the southeastern section near Tiverton is the most prolific smallmouth bass lake in Rhode Island, but also produces large quantities of rainbows through generous stocking, as well as pickerel and panfish. Other ponds on the fishing law list supply some good trout fishing; the town of each spot is provided, along with the spot's rating.

Warmwater possibilities are much greater, and there are many ponds, lakes, and brookish waters which have excellent largemouth populations. Both public and private areas produce well; in some cases, permission may be obtained to fish private property.

Worden Pond, skirting the Great Swamp Management Area near Tuckertown in the southeast section, is a marsh-bordered, primitive-looking expanse which lives up to its appearance, providing excellent fishing for largemouth bass, as well as good fishing for smallmouths, pickerel, and panfish. Northern pike are also present in this prolific lake and it is hoped that they will thrive and become a natural population. Nearby Tuckers Pond also boasts a reputation for fine bass fishing. Some other productive public bass, pickerel, and panfish waters include Bowdish, Pascoag, and Waterman reservoirs in West Glocester, Pascoag, and Greenville, respectively, Indian Lake at Mooresfield, Warwick Pond at Warwick, and Brickyard Pond at Barrington.

Rhode Island may seem like a rather unlikely place to hunt, but deer, ruffed grouse, woodcock, pheasant, bobwhite quail, cottontail and snowshoe rabbits, gray squirrels, waterfowl, and other wildlife are found in the fields, woodlands, marshes, ponds, shorelines, and offshore areas. Thirteen game management areas, ranging in size from Arcadia, 7,523 acres, in the southwest of the state, to Newton Swamp, 111 acres, also in the southwest, near Westerly, have a combined total of over 21,000 acres.

Rhode Island has an excellent network of forest campsites and hiking trails. State camping facilities are available at Arcadia State Park, with 25 tent and trailer sites adjacent to a section of the Appalachian Trail; Arcadia Management Area, with 48 sleeping cabins; Burlingame State Park, 755 tent and trailer campsites in a wooded area bordering the shore of Watchaug Pond; Fishermen's Memorial State Park, 140 tent and trailer sites in a shore-meadow area overlooking Block Island and Rhode Island sounds; Frosty Hollow Area in Exeter, two Adirondack shelters on Shelter Trail off Frosty Hollow Road; George Washington Management Area, 60 tent and trailer sites in a wooded area overlooking Bowdish Reservoir; Horseman's Camping Area in West Greenwich, 30 tent and trailer sites; and the Ninigret Conservation Area in Charlestown, 50 sites for self-contained units. There are canoe campsites at the Burlingame Management Area on the shores of the Pawcatuck River, and at the Carolina Management

Area on the Pawcatuck River. The privately owned Indian Acres Canoe Camp is on the Pawcatuck River, a day's paddle down the Wood River; write: LeRoy J. Edwards, 8 Friendship St., Westerly 02891. Reservations for state campgrounds are accepted at the Division of Park & Recreation, 83 Park St., Providence 02903.

Information Sources, Maps & Access

For detailed saltwater and freshwater fishing information contact: Dept. of Natural Resources, Veterans Memorial Bldg., Providence, RI 02903 (401)277–6800. A free *Camping in Rhode Island* describing all state-managed and commercial campgrounds may be obtained from: Dept. of Economic Development, 1 Weybosset Hill, Providence 02903. The state's major campsites and hiking trails, including the Inter-Park and Appalachian trails, are shown on the *Rhode Island Recreation Map*. Winter camping areas are described in the free publication *Winter in Rhode Island*, available free from: Dept. of Economic Development (address above). Rhode Island trails in the forest management areas and parks offer opportunities for cross-country skiing and snowshoeing. For information on ski areas, there are two informative brochures available. *Winter in Rhode Island* is available free from: Dept. of Economic Development, 1 Weybosset Hill, Providence 02903, and *Where to Ski* is obtainable at no charge from: Auto & Travel Club, National Headquarters, 888 Worcester St., Wellesley, MA 02181. Major Rhode Island ski areas offering instruction are *Diamond Hill*, Highway 114, Cumberland 02864 (401)333–5400; *Pinetop*, off I–95; Escoheag 02821 (401)397–5656; *Ski Valley*, Highway 121, Cumberland 02864 (401)333–6406; *Yawgoo Valley*, off Highway 2, Slocum 02877 (401)295–5366. Call or write for further information on rates and type of trails. Ferry service to Block Island is provided by Interstate & Nelseco Navigation, Box 482, New London, CT 06320 (203)442–7891 with daily departures from New London, Providence and Newport. Ferry service from Montauk, NY is provided by Cruises East, Inc., (516)668–2077. Air shuttle service to Block Island is provided by New England Airlines, (401)596–2460).

Lodges & Resorts

See "Accommodations & Travel Information" in the Rhode Island Introduction above.

Boating in RHODE ISLAND

Introduction

The Palmetto State embraces the nationally renowned barrier islands along its beautiful Atlantic Coast and the trophy bass waters of the Santee-Cooper Reservoir and the scenic hiking, fishing, camping, and hunting areas of the Sumpter National Forest and Blue Ridge Mountains in the northwest. The wild and scenic areas include the beautiful Blue Ridge highlands of the Ellicott's Rock Wilderness, the shoulder-high switch cane of the Long Cane Creek Scenic Area, Chattooga River Gorge, Clark Hill Reservoir, Indian Camp Wild Area, and the remote tumbling trout waters of the Chauga, Little, Whitewater, and Toxaway rivers.

Accommodations & Travel Information

Descriptions of South Carolina vacation resorts may be found in the "Vacation/Lodging Guide" which follows. For complete information on and listings of resorts, and hotels and a free, full-color 48–page *South Carolina State Parks Guide*, write to: local Chambers of Commerce or the Dept. of State Parks, Recreation and Tourism, Edgar A. Brown Bldg., 1205 Pendleton St., Columbia 29201 (803)758–2536. The Palmetto State has over 16,000 campsites from the banks of the wild Chattooga in the beautiful Blue Ridge Mountains south through the state to the sand dunes of the Atlantic coastline. Camping areas with complete facilities and services are available in Sumpter and Marion national forests and in all of the state parks. There is a wide variety, from primitive camping areas to full-service family campgrounds.

Highways & Maps

A *South Carolina State Highway Map* is available free from: Map Sales Section, Highway Commission, Drawer 191, Columbia 29202. It shows all roads and highways, towns, lakes, rivers and streams, parks, points of interest, railroads, airfields, national and state forests, fish hatcheries, campgrounds, and rest areas.

SOUTH CAROLINA

South Carolina Forests, Lakes & Coastal Recreation Areas

The state of South Carolina, specifically the famous Santee-Cooper watershed, offers some of the best largemouth and landlocked striped bass fishing in the nation. Roughly a triangle in shape, the state covers 31,055 square miles (775 of which consist of lakes and streams), bordered on the east and north by North Carolina and the beautiful Blue Ridge Mountains (which occupy an area about 500 square miles in the northwest portion of the state), on the west by the wild Chattooga and the Tugaloo, and the historic Savannah River and its Hartwell and Clark Hill reservoirs, and on the south by the warming currents of the Atlantic Ocean. From the scenic highlands of the soft Blue Ridge Mountains the terrain drops gradually to the rolling hills, mixed hardwood and pine forests, and red clay country of the Piedmont plateau and the Sand Hills, to the vast swamplands and tidewaters of the coastal plains, a distance of about 235 miles. The climate ranges from temperate in the Blue Ridge highlands to semitropical in the southeast, with long, hot summers, tempered by sea breezes near the coast.

The scenic 346,000–acre Sumpter National Forest, once the home and hunting grounds of the Cherokee Indians, encompasses the pine, oak, yellow poplar, and hardwood forests of the northwestern section. The forest has three major divisions: the Andrew Pickens district, known as the Gateway to the Mountains, in the Blue Ridge Mountains; and the Enoree and the Long Cane districts, in the rolling Piedmont. Many old logging roads and trails, including the

VACATION/ LODGING GUIDE

Foothills Trail, provide access to such remote interior wild areas as the beautiful highlands of the Ellicott's Rock Wilderness, the shoulder-high switch cane of the Long Cane Creek Scenic Area, Broad River Scenic Area, Chattooga River Gorge, Clark Hill Reservoir, Indian Camp Wild Area, and the trout waters of the Chauga, Little, Whitewater, and Toxaway rivers. This is the state's top hunting area for whitetail deer, quail, and wild turkey. Trout fishing in South Carolina is limited to the cold clear streams of the Blue Ridge Mountains in the Sumpter National Forest. Wilderness fly fishermen will find good fishing along the upper reaches of the wild Chattooga River and its East Fork and Whetstone Creek tributaries for native and stocked rainbows and browns. The Chauga River and its Cedar Bore, Hell Hole, and West Village Creek headwaters are top-ranked brown trout waters surrounded by the scenic Blue Ridge high country and mixed hardwood forests with thick undergrowths of mountain laurel and rhododendrons. The remote wild stretches of the Whitewater River above Lake Jocassee hold large resident populations of rainbow and brown trout. The cold, gin-clear headwaters of Big Eastatoe Creek, a feeder stream of the Keowee-Toxaway Reservoir, hold rainbows and browns. Other top-ranked rainbow and brown trout streams in the forest include North and Middle Saluda rivers, South Pacolet River, and the remote wild

country stretches of Matthews, Cane, and Laurel Fork creeks, which hold native populations of small, orange-bellied brookies.

The major impoundments in Sumpter National Forest, including Yonah, Tugaloo, Keowee, and Jocassee reservoirs, provide good year-round fishing for bream, largemouth bass, crappie, and yellow perch. The Tugaloo River branch of Hartwell Reservoir is noted for its late winter spawning run of walleyes upstream to Yonah Lake Dam. The sprawling, island-studded waters of 61,350–acre Hartwell Reservoir on the Savannah River, and its many branches and feeder streams, provide top-ranked fishing along the shoals, rocky shorelines, and dead-timbered areas for largemouths, and schools of white bass, crappie, bream, and catfish. Huge 78,500–acre Clark Hill Reservoir, a famous impoundment on the Savannah River to the south of Lake Hartwell, bordered on the east by the Long Cane Division of Sumpter National Forest and on the west by Georgia's Piedmont plateau, has huge schools of threadfin shad and provides excellent fall fishing for surface-churning schools of largemouth bass up to trophy weights in the 10–pound-plus class. During the spring spawning run, big bass are caught along the lake's Long Cane, Little River, and Buffalo Creek feeders, and at Hollings Landing and Hester's Bottoms at the mouth of Newford Creek. Clark Hill also offers good year-round fishing for crappies around shallow stump-filled areas, brush piles, and submerged islands, using popping bugs and live worms. Large rainbows are occasionally caught in the cold, dangerous tailrace waters below Clark Hill Dam. The Savannah, which forms the boundary between Georgia and South Carolina, flows south from the dam in a meandering course with numerous oxbows to its mouth at the Atlantic Ocean, and provides often excellent fishing for largemouth bass and spring-run striped bass. The world-famous Santee-Cooper lakes with their 450 miles of shoreline formed by 110,000–acre Lake Marion and 60,400–acre Lake Moultrie, joined by a 7½–mile diversion canal, offer some of the South's finest fishing for trophy largemouth bass and landlocked striped bass up to monster weights during the spring spawning period at the famed Low Falls, Jacks, and Wybow creeks, Santee, Congaree, and Wateree rivers, and the Diversion Canal area. In addition to spectacular bass fishing the Santee-Cooper lakes provide excellent fishing with live minnows around submerged debris during the spring and fall for crappie up to world's record weights, and good but unpredictable fishing for large chain pickerel and catfish. Other top-ranked bass waters in the Santee-Cooper watershed include the 11,400–acre Lake Greenwood and 50,800–acre Lake Murray on the Congaree River and 13,710–acre Lake Wateree on the Wateree River. Marina fish camps, boat landings, and campgrounds are available at all major lakes in the Santee-Cooper country. During the hot summer months, largemouth bass, stripers, and crappies are most successfully caught by trolling over cold deep water holes.

South Carolina's beautiful Atlantic coastline, with its beautiful islands—including Hilton Head, Hunting, Edisto, Seabrook, Bull, Kiawah, and Isle of Palms with their lush maritime forests and diversity of wildlife—provides excellent saltwater fishing during the spring and fall for inshore species including sea bass, porgy, flounder, snapper, and grunt; and offshore trolling in the Gulf Stream waters for sailfish, kings, bonito, marlin, wahoo, barracuda, amberjack, dolphin, kings, mackerel, cobia, and jacks.

Information Sources, Maps & Access

Detailed descriptions of the major lakes and streams, including the Savannah River Watershed, Coosawhatchie, Combahee, and Ashepo watersheds, Santee-Cooper Watershed, Peedee Watershed, and Edisto and Ashley watersheds, are contained in the *Guide to Fishing in South Carolina*, available free upon request from: Wildlife & Ma-

rine Resources Dept., P.O. Box 167, Columbia 29202 (803)758–6314. This invaluable guide also contains a detailed *Watershed Map of the State*, a *Map of Trout Waters in South Carolina*, and a listing of managed public fishing lakes. A free *Guide to South Carolina Hunting & Fishing Regulations* may be obtained from the same address. The 22–page *South Carolina Game Management Areas Guide*, available free from the Dept. of Wildlife & Marine Resources, contains detailed maps and descriptions of the renowned game lands in the scenic Mountain, Western Piedmont, and Central Piedmont hunt units in the Sumpter National Forest. A *South Carolina Boat Landings Map & Guide and Boating Regulations Guide* may be obtained free from: Division of Boating, P.O. Box 167, Columbia 29202.

For the nitty-gritty on Santee-Cooper accommodations, fishing guides, boat rentals, and gear, write: Santee-Cooper Country, P.O. Box 12, Santee 29142, phone (803)854–2131. A *Santee-Cooper Lake Contour Map* ($3) may be obtained from Lakes Illustrated, Box 4854 GS, Springfield, MO 65804. A free *Canoeing the Chattooga Map-Guide* is available from: Sumpter National Forest, 1801 Assembly St., Columbia 29201. A free *Map of South Carolina's Offshore Bottom Fishing & Trolling Areas*, which shows depths, general compass headings frequently used, artificial reefs, buoys, and wrecks, may be obtained from: Wildlife & Marine Resources Dept. (address above). Full-color recreation maps of the *Sumpter National Forest* and the *Andrew Pickens* ranger district, *Enoree and Tyger* districts, and the *Long Cane* division are available for 50¢ each from: Supervisor, Francis Marion & Sumpter National Forests, 1801 Assembly St., Columbia 29201. They show roads and trails, ranger stations, mountains, lakes, streams, recreation sites, and points of interest. Rangers are at Walhalla, Greenwood, Edgefield, and Newberry. Sumpter National Forest is reached via Interstates 20 and 26, U.S. Highways 25 and 176, and South Carolina State Highways 28, 9, and 72. Guides, supplies, and outfitters can be found at Union, Whitmire, Newberry, Greenwood, Walhalla, Augusta, Edgefield, McCormick, and Calhoun Falls.

Lodges & Coastal Resorts

★★★★*Fripp Island*, one of South Carolina's outer islands, can be reached by driving through the scenic Huntington Island State Park and over the Fripp Island Bridge, which spans the blue waters of the Atlantic Ocean. Three thousand acres of lush, rolling lawns and fairways, laced with quiet tidal marshes and cool lagoons make Fripp Island one of the more private, beautiful ocean resorts on the eastern seaboard. The 18–hole golf course, lined with stately palmettos and shady live oaks, presents a challenge to even experienced golfers. Four holes are bordered by the silver-blue waters of the Atlantic, and the 18th hole divides the ocean and sand dunes. There is a new pro shop on the grounds, and Byron Comstock, the resident pro, is on hand all season. The Fripp Island Racquet Club sports eight soft and six hard courts, two of which are open nightly. Butch Trellue, Fripp Island's resident tennis pro will strengthen your serve and sharpen your stroke, using video playback equipment to review your form. Three swimming pools, one Olympic-sized with a double board, offer respite from the Carolina sun. Boats may be chartered for deep-sea fishing at the Marina, or you may prefer the quiet island lakes for freshwater fishing. Three miles of windy beach are open for shell hunting, crabbing, kite flying, or an exuberant plunge in the foamy water. This year, Fripp Island has opened a new jogging and exercise trail. The Plantation Room serves fresh seafood and continental cuisine. The Sandbar Lounge offers nightly entertainment. Golf tournaments, tennis championships, watercolor workshops, and sailing regattas highlight the season. Modern deluxe rooms are

available only a stroll from the beach for $40 daily. One-three bedroom plush villas are available, oceanside, on a tidal creek near the tennis club, overlooking the lagoons by the fairway, or on very secluded sites in the tidal marshes. Rates range between $40 and $120 daily, and $300–600 weekly. Sumptuous private homes, luxuriously furnished with completely equipped kitchens and washers and dryers, are $65–100 daily and $455–840 weekly, depending on the size of the home, and its location. For more information write: Fripp Island Service Corporation, Fripp Island, SC 29920 (803)838–2411.

★★★★*Kiawah Island*, a 10,000–acre year-round resort mecca located 21 miles from historic Charleston, is noted for its serene, primitive beauty and 10–mile wild beach, is one of the last of the great barrier islands between Nags Head and Key West. The island is renowned for its variety of wildlife—including giant loggerhead turtles, alligators, egret, and osprey—golf, tennis, hiking, swimming beaches, and fishing. Everything the vacationer needs is within a three-minute walk of the village center. Kiawah Golf Links, designed by Gary Player, is an 18–hole, par–71 championship layout. The 6,250 yard course winds through forests of live oaks and palmetto and wanders around black-water lagoons. Facilities include a driving range, putting green, locker room and a pro shop offering club storage and the latest in equipment and fashions. Guests may rent clubs if they prefer not traveling with their own; however, advance notice is required and the supply may be limited. The pro shop is open from 8:00 am to dark. Eleven clay and two lighted hard courts are available for guest tennis. A fully-equipped pro shop handles a variety of top-line merchandise. The pro shop is open from 8:00 am to 8:00 pm. Private lessons, group lessons and year-round Stroke-A-Day Clinics are offered by resident professional, Roy Barth, who is uniquely qualified to teach guest and club members. A graduate of the UCLA Tennis Team, he coached the 1975 Wightman Cup Team. Explore Kiawah Island's 10,000 acres on jeep or water safaris. On all tours, a guide will relate the island's history and lore while introducing you to the island's natural beauty. The two-hour Wilderness Jeep Safari travels first through the dense palmetto forests of Kiawah's interior; then, along ten miles of breathtaking beach, with stops for shelling (or beachcombing). The two-hour Canvasback Lake Tour begins with a jeep ride to Canvasback Lake. There, guests travel by boat along six miles of shoreline, as guides identify the abundant wildlife, including alligators and a variety of water fowl. Four-hour island fishing trips in early morning or late afternoon for channel bass, drum, bluefish, or trout can be arranged through the Tours and Transportation Office located in the Straw Market. Guests can choose creek fishing, surf casting or crabbing—or a combination. Price includes tackle, bait, guide and transportation. Fishing

licenses are not necessary. Your beachcombing days on Kiawah Island can range from satisfaction to sheer delight as you collect scallops of varying shades, from bright yellows to deep purple; olive shells, prized for their intricate beauty; tiny auger shells; large brown cockles; delicate angel wings; channeled and knobbed whelks (conchs); tun shells in all sizes from miniature to the giant tun; bulleyes; starfish; elegant disks; sea urchins; and sand dollars. Walk the ten-mile beach on your own or make arrangements with the Tours and Transportation Office for a Shelling Expedition. You'll be taken by jeep to the far end of the beach and can collect shells as you walk back to the village. Other activities include a professionally supervised children's program, hiking, sailing, and annual special events such as seminars on antiques and interior design; the Great Kiawah Island Horse Race, a day of quarter horse races on the beach; and the Kiawah Cup, a USTA sanctioned tennis tournament for amateurs over 35. At Kiawah Island Inn all guest rooms are beautifully furnished, spacious, and equipped with private balconies and double beds. A number of luxurious suites are also available through the villa rental program. All lodges are a short walk from the beach, golf, tennis, spa, shopping, and dining. Dune lodges offer ocean, pool and dune views. Lagoon lodges offer pond, forest and landscape views. Daily inn room rates range from $30–42.50 double occupan-

cy. Shipwatch Villa suites range from $95–180 per day. Villas at Kiawah are beautifully furnished, privately-owned condominiums, townhouses and cottages, overlooking a choice of natural views. Living areas are spacious, air-conditioned and feature complete kitchens. Linens and cooking utensils are included, and washers and dryers are also included or available nearby. Villa rates range from $79–225 per day, and include maid and linen service. Superb dining is available at the Jasmine Porch, Charleston Gallery, and the Straw Market Restaurant and Cafe. East of the Mississippi River, call toll-free (1–800)845–2471. In South Carolina, call (803)559–5571. Write for reservations: Kiawah Island Resort, P.O. Box 12910, Charleston, SC 29412.

★★★★*Sea Pines Plantation at Hilton Head Island* has been called the most complete resort in the United States. It is actually a series of four resort-area villages placed on a 4,500–acre setting. Hilton Head Island is a peninsula paralleling the coastline off South Carolina, 45 miles from historic, picturesque Savannah. There are five miles of Atlantic beachfront on the eastern side and Caliboque Sound on the western side—which houses a 90–slip yacht basin, one of the finest in the world. This sub-tropical paradise offers 54 holes of golf (four courses, and more nearby), 60 tennis courts, and has become known as the world's leading sports resort, hosting 13 nationally televised tennis tournaments (including the World Invitational) and the PGA Heritage Golf Tournament. The golf course is rated one of the top ten in North America. Needless to say there are many tennis and golf packages available, in fact there are more programs than at any other resort in America. Besides golf, tennis and beach activities, there are 13 miles of bicycle trails (another unique feature); there are two sailing schools, more than a dozen swimming pools (including two heated ones), exercise rooms, a marina for smaller boats (if you don't happen to have a yacht); a charter fishing fleet for big game gulf stream adventures; a 572–acre forest and wildlife preserve for jogging and birdwatching, and nature walks; sailboating, surf-sailing, inshore fishing as well as deep sea; riding stables which also offer instruction from beginners to advanced and hold special events as well. There is a magnificent children's program including tennis instruction, crabbing and fishing contests, kite jamborees, specially designed and acclaimed playgrounds, including the famous tree-house area. Many of the activities at Sea Pines for children and adults have received national acclaim, and the accommodations here have as well. The unique architecture has been featured in magazines and the resort itself has won an award from the American Institute of Architects for its planning and design. You have your choice of four areas in which to stay. If you wish a hotel atmosphere there is the 204-room Hilton Head Inn directly on the beach. Or you can choose a villa near the hotel. If you wish something different there are three separate village areas on the island each with one-four bedroom villas. The village areas are exactly that—villages—each with its own resort facilities, swimming pools, tennis courts, shops, restaurants and art galleries. All in all there are approximately 60 restaurants on the island and plenty of night life from which to choose. If all of this is not enough—you can even rent a private home and have your own vacation all by yourself. The food everywhere is superb—seafood, of course, being fresh and most frequently served, but there is also French cuisine. The best part of all of this is the temperature range from 60–90° year round. Rates are approximately $32–150 a day—depending on many variables, season, location, number of bedrooms and whether you wish maid service, a jacuzzi and sunken bathroom. For brochures and reservations contact Sea Pines Plantation, Hilton Head Island, SC 29928 (800)845–6131 toll free.

South Carolina State Park Lodges & Guest Cabins extend from sandy beaches to the Blue Ridge Mountain peaks. They are all open year-round during the daylight hours. There are 126 state park cabins, located in 13 parks and available for year round rental. Many are oceanfront or lakefront or have scenic mountain views. Cabins are air-conditioned and completely furnished for housekeeping with electric ranges, refrigerators, dishes, utensils, linens and bedding. Some of the cabins have fireplaces or redwood decks and bedroom lofts. Prices for cabins range from $60 to $240 per week and cabins sleep four to twelve persons. Reservations from September through May are made on a first come, first served basis by contacting the superintendent of that park. However, during June, July and August, reservations for cabins (except Santee, Hickory Knob and Keowee-Toxaway) are granted by a lottery drawing held in mid-February. Applications for the drawing can be obtained from State Park Cabins, P.O. Box 11647, Columbia, SC 29211. State parks with cabins are classified as Coastal, Midlands, and Piedmont (mountain) parks.

Coastal parks offer sandy beach, pounding surf, isolated sea islands and marshlands. Many of the coastal parks are near large resort cities and historic sites. Three of the coastal parks with cabins, Hunting Island, Edisto Beach and Myrtle Beach, are ocean-front parks. *Hunting Island* is the state's only sea island state park. It is subtropical barrier island with wide sandy beaches and cool lagoons. A 136–foot lighthouse built in 1875 stands as a sentinel over the park's 1,000–foot boardwalk. All except two of the 13 cabins are on the ocean and rent from $25 to $35 per day, accommodating up to ten people. Call (803)838–2011. *Edisto Beach* is made of two miles of tree-lined beaches, 50 miles south of Charleston. Shell collecting is excellent here. The one- and two-bedroom cabins rent for $20 a night and the number to call is (803)869–2156. *Myrtle Beach State Park* is the state's busiest park. It is well-known for its 720–foot salt water fishing pier and its outdoor swimming pool. The five two-bedroom cabins rent for $30 a night and $180 a week. The number is (803)238–5325. *Givhans Ferry State Park* is popular with Charleston area visitors. There is scenic camping, as well as cabins along the moss-draped oaks lining the Edisto River. The cabins with fireplaces are $17 per night and $100 per week. The phone number is (803)873–0692.

The Midlands region has some of the finest historical, cultural, scenic and recreational attractions in the state. It is basically a flat, heavily forested sand hill and lake terrain. *Hickory Knob State Park* along with Baker Creek and Hamilton Branch make up the Clark Hill Recreation Complex on the shores of 72,000–acre Clark Hill Lake. Hickory Knob has 40 lodge rooms and 18 cabins, a restaurant, marina, tennis courts, a pool, riding trails, stables and horses for hire, plus rental boats. Lodge rooms rent for $20 per night and cabins are $35 per night or $120 per week. Nine of the cabins have fireplaces. The number for reservations is (803)443–2151. Tall pines and water highlight *Cheraw State Park*. Activities at this park and the other four in the area center around black water rivers, spring fed lakes and swampy tracts. Redbreast fishing, picnicking and nature trails are popular. The one-bedroom cabins rent for $10 a night and $60 a week. Call (803)537–2215. *Barnwell State Park* has cabins and recreational facilities specially designed for handicapped people. Rates are $22 per night and $132 a week. These cabins are on Lake Marion. The number for reservations is (803)284–2212. *Santee State Park* is also on Lake Marion and has a resort atmosphere with boat ramps and docks, a tackle shop, a campground and a restaurant. Some of the lakefront cottages are on piers and these two-bedroom cabins can sleep six. They rent for $30 a night and $180 a week. Call (803)854–2167. *Poinsett State Park* has a peaceful, woodsy atmosphere. The cabins with fireplaces rent for $11 for one-bedroom units and $17 for two-bedroom cabins. The number is (803)494–8177.

Piedmont region has four parks with cabins: Keowee-Toxaway, Oconee, Pleasant Ridge, and Table Rock—all in the upper Piedmont mountain region. Most of this area's sights can be seen by traveling the Cherokee Foothills Highway #11. Visitors should not miss the wild Chattooga River, Whitewater Falls, Stumphouse Mountain Tunnel and the Keowee-Toxaway Visitors Center. *Keowee-Toxaway* has only one cabin, with three bedrooms that can accommodate ten persons. There are two fireplaces and three bathrooms. Rate per night is $40 and per week, $240. The phone number to call for reservations is (803)868–2605. Keowee-Toxaway is a rugged park with back-packing trails and primitive camping, plus an unusual museum and trail which tell the history of the Cherokee Indians. *Oconee State Park* has 19 very popular cabins, accommodating from four to eight persons. Some of the cabins are lakefront and all have fireplaces. Rates range from $22 to $32 per day and $132 to $192 per week. There are also several cabins with lofts. The park has a restaurant that is also very popular. For reservations and information call (803)638–5353. *Pleasant Ridge* has three secluded modern redwood cabins and camping in a remote mountain setting. They have two bedrooms and range from $22 per night with a fireplace and $11 per night without. The reservations number is (803) 836–6589. *Table Rock* has very popular one- two- and three-bedroom cabins, all with fireplaces, accommodating up to 12 people. Rates range from $20 to $30 per night and $120 to $180 per week. The phone number for reservations is (803)878–9813.

Travel Services

Wildwater Ltd. The Chattooga River, one of the last free-running, wild rivers in the United States, works its way over 40 miles of the most remote, hauntingly beautiful country in the East, from the crest of the Appalachian Mountains in North Carolina, along the Georgia-South Carolina border, to Lake Tugaloo, in Georgia. When Congress elected to preserve the Chattooga as a National Wild and Scenic River, Wildwater Ltd. was selected to carry the U.S. Congressmen, their staffs and families down the Chattooga River. 12 foot voyager rafts, especially built for whitewater use, Coast Guard approved life jackets, and wide blade paddles are provided. Guides instruct each rafter on how to safely run the rapids in the Chattooga, which falls more rapidly than the Colorado River. Trips are seven hours, including lunch, and run every day except Mondays from Memorial Day to Labor Day, and weekends in the spring and fall. Rates are $15 per person on weekdays, and $20 per person on weekend days. Wildwater Ltd. also runs whitewater trips through Nolichuckey Canyon. The Nolichuckey is formed by the confluence of the Toe River and the Cane River in Spruce Pine, North Carolina. Its volume of water is many times that of the Chattooga, and its rapids are faster. Rafters must be experienced and in good physical shape to handle the two miles of continuous Class III rapids which begin the journey, and manipulate their rafts through house-sized boulders and steep rapids. After lunch at the silent site of the old Ghost town of Lost Cove, rafts approach the most challenging rapids of the river, at Souse Hole. After Souse Hole, the river quiets, and rafters are free to take in the deep beauty of the river gorge. Waterfalls shimmer down 2,000–foot cliffs, and tiny green plants cling to the sheer rock walls. The minimum age for the Nolichuckey Canyon Trip is 13. Price is $25 per person. For more information write: Wildwater Ltd. Winter address: 400 West Road, Portsmouth, VA 23707 (804)397–6658; summer address (May-September): Longcreek, SC 29658 (803)647–5336.

TENNESSEE

Introduction

Tennessee contains 42,244 square miles of varied terrain with the scenic Great Valley separating the Cumberland Plateau from the Great Smokies on the eastern border; the rolling hills and bluegrass country of the central basin, sloping to the Mississippi River bottomlands along the western boundary. The Volunteer State contains several famous fishing, hunting, and wild country camping areas, including Reelfoot Lake; the western highlands and remote mountain coves of the Great Smoky Mountains National Park; Cherokee National Forest, which embraces a narrow strip of rugged highlands along the Unaka and Great Smoky mountains; and the trophy bass, walleye, and trout waters of the Tellico River, Doe Creek and Watauga Lake, Dale Hollow Lake, Caney Fork of the Cumberland, Obed River, South Fork of the Cumberland, and South Holston, Wilbur, Norris, Great Falls, and Center Hill lakes.

Accommodations & Travel Information

For detailed information on all aspects of vacation travel in Tennessee, contact: Tennessee Tourist Development, 505 Fessler Lane, Nashville, TN 37210 (615)741–7994. Descriptions of many of the state's lodges and resorts are found in the "Vacation/Lodging Guide" which follows. Over 250 campsites are scattered throughout Tennessee, some near urban centers offering all the comforts of home, others hidden deep in the wilderness far from the sights and sounds of civilization. Tennessee's wild climate makes year-round camping possible in many of the campgrounds that remain open and operative year round. *Camping in Tennessee* lists 252 campsites that have been approved by the Tennessee Department of Public Health, alphabetically by the nearest town or city. Each listing includes the name of the campsite, address and directions where available, seasons, type of camp, and facilities including showers, toilets, boat rentals, hunting and fishing opportunities, swimming, and laundries. Two types of camps are listed in the guidebook: travel camps house provisions for travel trailers, truck coaches or campers, tent campers, tents and vehicles. Whole primitive camps are sites established primarily for tent camping, which permit tents, travel trailers, truck coaches, and tent campers. Camping in Great Smoky Mountains Park in areas other than specified campgrounds requires a special permit, which may be obtained at the Sugarlands Visitor Center. *Camping in Tennessee* is available free from: Tennessee Tourist Development, 505 Fessler La., Nashville 37210.

Anyone seriously planning a trip along the Appalachian Trail should consult the *Guide to the Appalachian Trail in Tennessee and North Carolina*. Published by the Appalachian Trail Conference, the book includes three detailed maps and extensive trail data: mileage, difficulty, directions, points of interest, historical information on the area traversed, national park and forest regulations, etc. The trail is covered from both north to south and south to north, so there is no backtracking of information to find your way. A general history of the Appalachian Trail is also included. Priced at $6.70, the guide may be ordered from: Appalachian Trail Conference, P.O. Box 236, Harpers Ferry, WV 25425. Checks should be in U.S. dollars only, payable to Appalachian Trail Conference. Allow three weeks for delivery or include $1 for special mailing and note the addition with your order. Good opportunities for cross-country skiing are available in Great Smoky Mountains National Park and Cherokee National Forest. Access to Great Smoky is via U.S. 441 to Newfound Gap (elevation 5,048 feet) between Cherokee, North Carolina, and Gatlinburg, Tennessee. A round trip of 14 miles is possible on the Clingmans Dome Road (highest elevation 6,643 feet) during winter months when the road is closed. Tours may also be made either north or south on the Appalachian Trail. Overnight tours require a

camping permit which will not be issued unless clothing, camping gear, equipment, and food are considered safe and adequate upon inspection by a ranger. Trailside shelters are available, but overnight use is by reservation only and plans must be cleared from park headquarters before a permit can be obtained. Day touring parties are urged to inform park headquarters near Gatlinburg or the Oconaluftee Ranger Station near Cherokee of the trip schedule and route.

The Cherokee National Forest encompasses the southern Appalachian Mountains both to the north and south of the Great Smoky Mountains National Park. Although snow conditions are not as reliable as in the park because of lower elevations, there are nonetheless a number of reliable areas exceeding 5,000–foot elevations. These include Camp Creek Bald, site of the former Viking Mountain Ski Area, and Roan Mountain, shared with the Pisgah National Forest in North Carolina. Wind conditions may cause spotty snow in some areas. Several trail shelters are located along the Appala-

chian Trail, which crosses both forests. For more information contact the U.S. Forest Service district rangers at Greeneville (Camp Creek Bald) or Erwin (Big Bald, Roan Mountain, Yellow Mountains). For additional information see the "Vacation/Lodging Guide."

Highways & Maps

The state's scenic and recreation highways and roads that wind through the beautiful forest highlands of the Great Smokies along the eastern border, along the large man-made impounds of the Great Valley of the Tennessee River, and through the Cumberland Mountains, plateau, and the central basin and the famed bluegrass country are shown on the *Official Tennessee Highway Map,* available free from: Division for Tourist Development, 1028 Andrew Jackson Bldg., Nashville 37219. In addition, this useful map shows state parks and recreation areas, campgrounds, lakes and streams, towns, and the Cherokee National Forest lands.

**VACATION/
LODGING GUIDE**

Blue Ridge Parkway

See "Pisgah National Forest & The Blue Ridge Parkway" in the North Carolina chapter.

Cherokee National Forest & Highlands

This 614,000–acre highland reserve, renowned for its outstanding fishing, hunting, hiking, and canoe-camping areas, takes in a long, narrow strip of mountainous terrain along the Great Smoky and Unaka mountains of the Tennessee-North Carolina border. The forest is divided into two major segments—the Unaka and Cherokee divisions—which are connected by the Great Smoky Mountains National Park, shared by Tennessee with North Carolina. Numerous forest roads and hiking trails, including the entire Tennessee section of the Appalachian Trail, provide access to the remote wilderness backpacking and hunting areas within the forest. The scenic mountain streams, with their deep staircased pools and rapids, in the Cherokee National Forest and Great Smoky Mountains National Park provide excellent fishing for wild trout in the remote headwaters of the Unaka and Great Smoky mountains. These wild, turbulent streams are surrounded by lush grass meadows and dense hardwood forests of yellow buckeye, white ash, black cherry, mountain silverbill and beech, colorful hemlock forests of red and sugar maples, yellow and sweet birches, holly, black and pin cherries with undergrowths of rosebay and catawba rhododendrons, and fragrant spruce and fir forests at the higher elevations hold wild brook, rainbow, and brown trout. Many of the most productive trout streams, managed by the state, are in rugged, wild country and are often accessible only by hiking up packhorse trails that follow old Indian paths and logging railroad beds. The most productive streams are located on the several units of the vast Cherokee Wildlife Management Area and include Paint Creek, Laurel Fork Creek, Tellico River, Citico Creek, and Green Cove Pond. Trout fishing in these streams and in the state-designated wild trout streams—North Fork of Citico Creek, North River, Bald River, Sycamore Creek, and their tributaries—is by special permit only, available from: Wildlife Resources Agency, P.O. Box 40747, Nashville 37204.

A number of wilderness areas, small and large pockets of unspoiled natural beauty, lie within Cherokee National Forest. In the southwest section of the forest, bounded by Starr and Chestnut mountains on the west and east and Gee Knob to the south, is the Gee Creek

Wilderness Area, encompassing the entire Gee Creek Watershed. The creek itself contains large numbers of brown trout and flows through a magnificent gorge with 5–25–foot waterfalls. Prime timber and rhododendron thickets cover its steep sides. The heart of the gorge is true wilderness—not even a trail interrupts its primitive setting.

Northeast of the Gee Creek Wilderness in Monroe County are 13,900 acres of mountain terrain comprising the Bald River Wilderness. For virtually its entire length, the Bald River in the southern half of the roughly oval-shaped area is filled with rippling, shooting cascades and many falls beneath which lie deep crystal pools and swift-flowing clear mountain water. As it enters the Tellico, the river makes a dramatic plunge over the 100–foot Bald River Falls. Dense mountain laurel and rhododendron outline all streams in the watershed in a profusion of broad-leafed evergreen and brightly colored blossoms. Populations of rainbow and brown trout reproduce naturally in the Bald and its tributary streams—Henderson Branch, Brookshire Creek, Kirkland Creek, Big Cove Branch, and Waucheesi Creek. The upper reaches also support native populations of brook trout. It is estimated that this watershed alone contains half of the brook trout in the southern section of the forest. Since it is considered part of the Tellico Wildlife Management Area, the Tennessee Game and Fish Commission has imposed certain restrictions on fishing in the wilderness: Henderson Branch is closed to fishermen in order to encourage nature production, and the Bald has been defined as a wild trout stream to be fished with wet or dry flies only with reduced bag and increased size limits.

In the extreme southwestern reaches of the forest is the Frog Mountain Wilderness, a 15,000–acre area adjoining the Cohouta Wilderness in Georgia's Chattahoochee National Forest. Swift streams in the north side of Frog Mountain flow into the broad Ocoee River. A part of the Ocoee Wildlife Management Area, the area supports good populations of game and nature trout. Also included are some lands which now border on the portion of the Conasauga River designated a wild and scenic river by the State of Tennessee. Nearby are campgrounds at Sylco, Tumbling Creek, and Thunder Rock. There are a variety of other scenic attractions in Cherokee National Forest, including a number of lakes—Watauga, Holston, Chilhowee, and Parksville—with nearby campsites. Parksville, a 1,900–acre Tennessee Valley Authority lake, provides beautiful waters for fishing and boating. Seven-acre Chilhowee Lake, nestled on the top of Chilhowee Mountain, provides numerous camping facilities and astounding views of the surrounding countryside. Hiking trails traverse the area and lead to the nearby waterfalls.

Information Sources, Maps & Access

The *Cherokee National Forest Map* shows all major natural features, roads, trails, recreation and campsites, trail shelters, landing fields, district ranger stations, and points of access and is available for 50¢ from: Forest Supervisor, Cherokee National Forest, P.O. Box 400, Cleveland 37311 (for detailed information, call (615)476–5528). Backpackers, hikers, hunters, horseback riders—in short, anyone using roads or trails within the forest—will find the *Road and Trail Maps* for individual ranger districts especially useful. Maps are available for the Tellico, Hiwassee, Ocoee, Nolichuckey, and Unaka ranger districts. Each map shows highways; horse trails; foot trails; paved, gated, all-weather, and gravel roads; National Forest System roads; and routes on which automobiles and motorcycles are permitted. National forest lands are carefully distinguished from private property, and natural features—mountains, lakes, streams, rivers, and the like—are indicated too. Maps are available free from: Forest Supervisor (address above). Be sure to specify which ranger district

you are requesting. For those who prefer to enjoy the park in the relative safety and comfort of an automobile, the Forest Service also publishes a map for a self-guiding 15–mile auto tour through part of the Nolichuckey ranger district of the Cherokee National Forest. The 2–hour trip over well-graded gravel roads winds along the banks of the French Broad River to the crest of Meadow Creek Mountain. The *Brush Creek Auto Map* shows the complete route, describes points of interest along the way, and is available free from: District Ranger, U.S. Forest Service, Greeneville, TN 37743. The *Chilhowee, Quinn Springs, and Parksville Lake Recreation Areas Map* is available free from: Forest Supervisor, Cherokee National Forest, P.O. Box 400, Cleveland 37311, and shows the major features of the area as well as points of access and major roads. A list of campsites and recreation areas is also included.

Another free brochure from the forest supervisor, *Outdoors in the Unaka Mountains*, shows streams, hiking trails, roads, highways, and recreation areas in the Unicoi-Erwin area in the central region of the northern (Unaka) division of the forest. The Rock Creek Recreation Area in this section lies along a cascading mountain stream and provides several trails leading to waterfalls, mountain peaks, and coves in the neighboring mountains. The Raven's Lore Walk, a self-guiding trail, winds through majestic Unaka Mountain and offers an introduction to the history and natural wonders of the area.

Another publication issued free by the Forest Service, *Endangered, Rare and Uncommon Wildflowers*, is a 20–page booklet with beautiful color photographs, describing 62 varieties of rare wildflowers. The booklet tells how to recognize each flower, where to find it, and

includes an index and the scientific name for each species. If you are planning an extended stay in the forest, be sure to write the forest supervisor for *Regulations Governing the Occupancy and Use of National Forest Recreation Sites and Areas*. State Highway 32 and U.S. Highway 25 both provide access to the southern end of the forest's Unaka division from the nearby town of Newport. State Highways 70 and 107 lead from Greeneville to the Unaka division, as does U.S. Highway 23 from Johnson City. The forest's southern or Cherokee division is reached via U.S. Highway 64 from Cleveland and State Highway 30 from Athens and Etowah.

Gateways & Accommodations

Athens

(Pop. 13,000; zip code 37303; area code 615) is the home of Tennessee Wesleyan College and a major western gateway to the Cherokee National Forest. Accommodations: *Sheraton Inn* (rates: $22.88 double), with 103 excellent rooms, restaurant, and swimming pool on Mt. Verde Rd. off I–75 exit 52 (745–1212).

Cleveland—Headquarters of the Cherokee National Forest

(Pop. 26,000; zip code 37311; area code 615) is the headquarters and major western gateway to the superb fishing, hiking, and hunting areas of the vast Cherokee National Forest. One of the major area attractions is the canoeing and fishing waters of the Hiwassee River. Accommodations: *Holiday Inn* (rates: $28 double), with 190 excellent rooms and family units, restaurant, coffeeshop, heated pool on Keith St. (472–1504); *Holiday Inn on I–75* (rates: $28–31 double), with 147 excellent rooms, restaurant, coffeeshop, heated pool, three miles west of town at the junction of I–75 and Tennessee 40 (479–4531); *Quality Inn Chalet* (rates: $25–28 double), with 124 excellent rooms, restaurant, heated pool and sauna two miles northwest of town at the junction of I–75 and Tennessee 60 (476–8511).

Elizabethton

(Pop. 12,000; zip code 37643; area code 615) is a major gateway to the eastern region of the Cherokee National Forest and to the beautiful Alpine Gardens at Roan Mountain State Park, renowned Watauga Lake, and the Sycamore Shoals State Historic Park, west of town on U.S. 321. This historic reconstruction, with its fort and palisade walls, commemorates the first fort west of the Blue Ridge Mountains and was the site of a battle over Indian territorial claims. Another area attraction is the old American covered bridge built in 1882 that spans the Doe River. Accommodations: *Camara Inn* (rates: $28 double), with 60 good rooms, restaurant, swimming pool and sauna at 505 W. Elk Ave. on U.S. 321 (543–3511).

Etowah

(Pop. 3,700; zip code 37331; area code 615) is the site of a Cherokee National Forest District Ranger's Office and a popular gateway to the western highlands and wilderness areas of the forest. Accommodations: *Holiday Terrace Motel* (rates: $14.91 double), with 22 good rooms and swimming pool next to restaurant on North Tennessee Ave., one mile north of town on U.S. 411 (263–7618).

Greeneville

(Pop. 15,000; zip code 37743; area code 615), founded in 1783, was the home of Andrew Jackson and the area birthplace of Davy Crockett. The town is the site of District Ranger's Office of the Cherokee National Forest and serves as a major gateway to the eastern fish and game lands of the forest. Area attractions include the Andrew Jackson National Historic Site and Davy Crockett Park, due east of town on U.S. 11E. Accommodations: *Holiday Inn* (rates:

$22.50–28.50), with 66 good rooms, restaurant, coffeeshop, swimming pool three miles east of town on the U.S. 11E bypass (639–4185).

Johnson City

(Pop. 40,000; zip code 37601; area code 615) is a major tobacco trading center and eastern gateway to the Cherokee National Forest and Watauga Lake area. One of the major area attractions is the guided tours of the Rocky Mount Historic House and Museum built in 1770, which served as the first capitol of the Southwest Territory under William Blount. The site contains a large log house, blacksmith shop, slave barn and cabin, and early American artifacts and costumes. Rocky Mount is located seven miles northeast of town on U.S. 11E. Accommodations: *Camara Inn* (rates: $30 double), with 148 excellent rooms, restaurant, swimming pool, two miles north of town on U.S. 11E at 2312 Brownsmill Rd. (929–1161); *Holiday Inn* (rates: $33 double), with 158 excellent rooms, restaurant, swimming pool, 2¼ miles north of town on U.S. 11E at 2406 N. Roan St. (928–6121).

Newport

(Pop. 7,300; zip code 37821; area code 615) is a major gateway to Douglas Lake, Great Smoky Mountains and the eastern highlands of the Cherokee National Forest, located off Interstate 40. Accommodations: *Holiday Inn* (rates: $30–32 double), with 158 excellent rooms, restaurant, heated pool, 1½ miles south of town on Tennessee 32 (623–8622).

Sweetwater

(Pop. 4,300; zip code 37874; area code 615) is a popular western gateway to the Cherokee National Forest. A major area attraction is the underground tours (337–6616) of the 4½-acre Lost Sea subterranean lake in glass-bottom boats. Accommodations: *Best Western Mar-Vel West* (rates: $25–27 double), with 137 excellent rooms and family units, restaurant, heated indoor pool and sauna three miles west of town on Tennessee 68 (337–3541); *Ramada Inn* (rates: $25.50 double), with 143 excellent rooms and family units, restaurant, coffeeshop, heated pool, three miles west of town on Tennessee 68 (337–3511).

Lodges & Resorts

See "Great Smoky Mountains National Park."

Great Smoky Mountains National Park

The most massive and lofty mountain range in the eastern United States, the Great Smoky Mountains fall within the larger system of the southern Appalachians, a roughly oval-shaped chain of ranges running northeast to southwest. The Great Smokies themselves march for about 70 miles on an almost east-to-west line between North Carolina and Tennessee, bordered on the east by the Big Pigeon River and on the west by the Little Tennessee. In the eastern part of the Smokies, 16 peaks exceed 6,000–foot elevations. To the west, crests are generally lower, forming the bald (or forest) country, where grassy meadows blanket the mountaintops, affording spectacular views in all directions. With outlines softened by dense forest growth, the mountains seem to billow and stretch in sweeping troughs as far as the eye can see. The name Great Smokies is derived from the smokelike haze that envelops the mountains.

Situated between three national forests—the two segments of the Cherokee in Tennessee, and Pisgah and Nantahala forests in North Carolina—the Great Smoky Mountains National Park contains vast areas of virtually unspoiled forests, similar to those found by the early pioneers who settled in isolated mountain valleys. The first

settlers arrived in the area late in the 18th century and established simple farms in the coves and valleys. As the years passed, the outside world changed under the impetus of progress while the mountain culture remained untouched by events beyond the Smokies—an early 19th-century farming community totally oblivious to the trappings of the modern world. Many of the old log cabins and barns still stand as monuments to the pioneer existence that has all but vanished from the mountains.

Fertile soils and heavy rains over a long period have caused a world-renowned variety of flora to develop within the park. Some 1,400 kinds of flowering plants bloom in the hills and valleys. Within the coves, broadleaf trees predominate; along the 6,000-foot-high crests, conifer forests similar to those of Canada find a climate suitable for dense growth.

The main roads offer only a cursory introduction to the beauties of the Smokies. At Cades Cove an 11–mile loop road leads past open fields, pioneer homesteads, and little frame churches where the mountain people lived and worshiped almost unnoticed for a century. Another scenic high mountain road winds its way through Newfound Gap to Clingmans Dome; there, a ½–mile walk to an observation tower provides an excellent panorama of the countryside. Summer brings extremely heavy traffic to this route. For those who prefer to avoid the beaten track, there are 600 miles of horse and foot trails winding along streams and through forests into the high country. The spectacular views and waterfalls on many streams are popular objectives. The Park Headquarters publishes a free list of trails, including Abrams Bald, Laurel Falls, Mingus Creek, Newton Bald, and Spruce Mountain trails. Elevations, hiking difficulty, mileage, and starting points are indicated. It can be obtained free of charge at any ranger station, visitor center, or park headquarters. Because of overcrowding, it has become necessary to ration overnight use of the 68 miles of Appalachian Trail within the park. Four other popular areas, Mount Le Conte, Laurel Gap, Kephart Prong, and Moore Spring, are rationed also. Arrangements for a permit must be made after you arrive in the park. There are many uncrowded trails in the park offering trailside campsites, a list of which (Backcountry Map & Camping Guide) is available from the Park Superintendent at the Gatlinburg address below. Permits for winter camping between November and March will be issued only after winter gear and clothing are approved by a ranger as adequate for survival in deep snow and 20° weather.

In addition to the backcountry camping sites, the park offers seven developed campgrounds (at Smokemont, Balsam Mountain, Cosby, Elkmont, Deep Creek, Cades Cove, and Look Rock) and three primitive camping areas (at Cataloochee, Davenport Gap, and along Abrams Creek). Fees are charged at the developed campgrounds, which feature water, fireplaces, tables, comfort stations, and tent and limited trailer space. Visitors should bring their own tents and other camping equipment, since no shelters are provided. There are no showers or hookups for trailers. From June 1 through Labor Day, the camping limit is seven days. Primitive campgrounds have no developed water supply. All water must be boiled or chemically treated before drinking. Camping at primitive areas is also limited to seven days. Camping permits are not necessary for campgrounds reached by car, but registration is required upon arrival. Write to park headquarters for more details on individual campsites.

Several of the park's remote backcountry areas offer unsurpassed wilderness fishing and primitive camping opportunities. The remote Big Creek area in North Carolina, in the heart of old logging country, provides excellent fishing for wild brook and rainbow trout, and camping at the Big Creek Primitive Campground and the Walnut Bottoms backcountry camp. The area is laced by primitive footpaths, including the Big Creek Trail, which provides access through the scenic hardwood and moss-covered balsam and red spruce forests. The pastoral backcountry surrounding Cataloochee Creek (Cherokee for "wave upon wave of mountains") and Cataloochee Primitive Campground in North Carolina is a renowned backpacking area laced by numerous trails. Numerous hiking trails wind through second-growth forests of river birch, basswood, yellow poplar, majestic eastern hemlocks, oaks, maples, magnolia, and tulip poplar in the backcountry surrounding the trout waters of Deep and Indian creeks and the Patch Pole backcountry camp and Deep Creek campground in North Carolina. Miles of scenic trails wind through hardwood forests, large grassy balds, spruce and fir stands, and tangles of flame azalea and purple rhododendron surrounding the renowned wild trout waters of Noland, Forney, Hazel, Eagle and Twentymile creeks, which feed into the northern shoreline of huge Lake Fontana; backcountry campsites are located along the creeks. Hazel Creek, with its Cold Spring branch, Sugar Fork, and Bone

Valley Creek tributaries, is nationally famous for its trophy rainbow and brook trout fishing. Remnants of old logging railroads that traversed the majestic virgin forests during the early part of this century and spectacular displays of rare yellow-berried dogwoods, yellow iris, kerria bush, monkshood, bluebead lily, wild ginger, pawpaw bushes, and flame azalea border the old Cherokee trails and trout pools that make this area a backpacker's and wilderness fly fisherman's paradise.

Hundreds of miles of primitive trails wind through the scenic meadows, flats, valleys, and high country red spruce and Fraser fir forests and balds throughout the Great Smoky Park to Mount Le Conte, Greenbrier Cove, Little Pigeon River, Little River, Slickrock Creek, Joyce Kilmer Forest, Oconaluftee (Cherokee for "near the river") Valley, and the beautiful, verdant green of Cades Cove. Campers and fishermen should keep in mind that black bear and wild boar are common in many of the remote interior areas.

Two park streams are set aside as "fishing for fun" streams, where trout or bass under 16 inches must be returned immediately. The regular season is from April 15 through September 15. A Tennessee or North Carolina fishing license is required, but not trout stamps. Local regulations are posted on streams and can be obtained at any park ranger station or visitor center. *Camping-Fishing Great Smoky Mountains National Park*, a brochure available free from the Gatlinburg office, lists the various fishing streams, regulations, open waters, campgrounds, and horseback concessionaires.

Most of the neighboring towns have gas, food, lodging, and camping supplies. Many private campgrounds operate outside the park. For information, write the chambers of commerce of nearby towns in North Carolina and Tennessee.

Information Sources, Maps & Access

For detailed information on all aspects of vacation and backcountry travel and a free *Great Smoky Mountains National Park Map*, contact: Superintendent's Office, Great Smoky National Park, Gatlinburg, TN 37738 (615)436-5615. The *Great Smoky Mountains National Park Map* describes points of interest, camping facilities, accommodations, and general park features. The map shows access points, major highways surrounding the park, park roads, campsites, ranger stations, trail shelters, horse and foot trails, creeks, and other features. A U.S. Geological Survey Map, *Great Smoky Mountains National Topographic Map* (2 sheets), is available showing the eastern and western halves of the park. Each is 28 × 32 inches with a scale of 1:62,500 or about 1 inch to 1 mile, and each sheet is priced at $2. A complete *U.S. Geological Survey National Park Map*, scale: 1:125,000, is also available showing the park and adjacent areas. It covers approximately 2,730 square miles and is issued in both contour and shaded-relief editions. This map shows roads, trails, including the Appalachian Trail, shelters, ranger stations, fire towers, and campgrounds. A text printed on the reverse side of the map discusses the geology and history of the region, and offers other information of interest to visitors. Either the contour or relief edition

is priced at $2. Both maps may be ordered from: Distribution Branch, U.S. Geological Survey, 1200 S. Eads St., Arlington, VA 22202. A *1934 Edition of Great Smoky Mountains National Park U.S. Geological Survey Map* may be obtained from: TVA Map Office, 400 Commerce Ave., SW, Knoxville 37902. This full-color topographic map shows old roads, trails, and railroads not shown on the new park map. Set of two sheets, each 28 × 34 inches, scale 1:62,500 (1 inch to 1 mile). Price $4 per set. Write to the superintendent in Gatlinburg for a copy of *Favorite Hiking Trails* in the Great Smokies National Park. For other trails and more detailed information, try the *Hiker's Guide to the Smokies*, a Sierra Club Totebook including a map of the park and environs and 370 pages of detailed information. The guide, coauthored by Dick Murlless and Constance Stallings, offers a brief history of the park, notes on the weather, a geologic history of the Smokies, descriptions of flora and fauna, tips on off-trail hiking, and a list of park regulations. Various trails are described in the Tennessee and North Carolina divisions of the park. The 14 sections on both states are each prefaced by a general history of the area, describing its early settlement and natural attractions. The trails following the introduction are outlined in abundant detail including point-by-point trail data, mileage, difficulty, elevations, U.S. Geological Survey maps covered, trail connections, and more. An invaluable source for the serious hiker in the Smokies, the guide is priced at $7.95 and can be ordered from: Sierra Club, Box 7959, Rincon Annex, San Francisco, CA 94104.

Saddle horses for the Great Smoky pack trails are provided by *Cades Cove Riding Stables*, Cades Cove Star Route, Townsend 37882; *McCarters Riding Stables*, Gatlinburg 37738, at Tuomide Branch; *Smokemont Riding Stables*, Route No. 1, Cherokee, NC 28719, at Smokemont Creek; and *Smoky Mountain Riding Stables*, P.O. Box 445, Gatlinburg 37738, at Dudley Creek. Great Smokies National Park is reached from Nashville via Interstate Highways 24, 40, and 75; from North Carolina via Interstate Highways 26, 40, 59, and 75; from Knoxville via U.S. Highway 129; and from the east via Insterstate 381. Lodging, supplies, and canoe rentals are available at Gatlinburg, Townsend, Maryville, Sevierville, Cherokee, North Carolina, and several other towns and villages surrounding the park in Tennessee and North Carolina.

Scenic auto routes in the park include the spectacular Newfound Gap Road (U.S. 441) from Asheville-Knoxville which winds through the park and the Cherokee Indian Reservation in North Carolina; the Parson Branch, Rich Mountain and Laurel River Roads in the pastoral Cades Cove area, with its old barns, mills, and log cabins; Roaring Fork Loop; and the Heintooga Ridge Road, off the Blue Ridge Parkway and Newfound Gap Road north of the Cherokee Indian Reservation.

Park visitor centers include the Sugarlands Visitor Center, two miles south of Gatlinburg at the junction of U.S. 441 and Little River Road, and the Oconaluftee Visitor Center in North Carolina at the park entrance on U.S. 441. The fascinating Oconaluftee Pioneer Farmstead is situated adjacent to the visitor center. Guide nature hikes and lectures are conducted daily from the Sugarlands Visitor Center from mid-June through Labor Day.

Gateways & Accommodations

Gatlinburg—Headquarters of
Great Smoky Mountains National Park

(Pop. 2,400; zip code 37738; area code 615) is the major gateway and headquarters for the Great Smoky Mountains National Park. The village stretches along the Little Pigeon River to the base of

A Sierra Club Totebook®

Hiker's
Guide
to the
Smokies

by Dick Murlless
and Constance Stallings

Mount Le Conte and the top of Pigeon River Cove. The town is one of the south's major resort and handicrafts centers for woodworking, pottery, and weaving. Area attractions include the scenic Newfound Gap and Roaring Fork Loop roads; Sugarlands National Park Visitor Center at the junction of Newfound Gap Rd. and Little River Rd.; American Historical Wax Museum on U.S. 441; National Bible Museum in River Oaks Center; Windmill Towne on Tennessee 73; Ober Gatlinburg Ski Resort and Aerial Tramway (436–5423); Sweet Fanny Adams Theatre at 964 River Rd. Accommodations: *Best Western Fabulous Chalet* (rates: $23–46 double), with 26 superb rooms, many with fireplaces and balconies with views of the Smokies, heated pool on Sunset Dr. four blocks off U.S. 441 (436–5151); *Brookside Motel* (rates: $28–32 double), with 120 excellent rooms and guest cottages, some with fireplaces, at Tennessee 73, three blocks off U.S. 441, at Roaring Fork Rd. (436–5611); *Downtowner Motor Inn* (rates: $36 double), with 68 excellent rooms, some with fireplaces, restaurant, cocktail lounge, heated pool and sauna, on Tennessee 73 at 128 Roaring Fork Rd. (436–5043); *Gatlinburg Inn* (rates: $30–65 double), with 67 excellent early American-style rooms, suites, tennis, in nice setting at 755 Parkway on U.S. 441 (436–5133); *Glenstone Lodge* (rates: $37.50–41.50 double), with 222 superb rooms and family units, some with fireplaces, dining room, coffeeshop, indoor heated pools, on Airport Rd. off U.S. 441 (436–9361); *Holiday Inn* (rates: $34–38 double), with 406 excellent rooms, restaurant, indoor/outdoor pools, sauna, taproom, on Airport Rd. off U.S. 441 (436–9201); *Howard Johnson's Motor Lodge* (rates: $38 double), with 252 excellent rooms and family units, restaurant, swimming pool on U.S. 441 in town north (436–5621); *Mountain View Hotel & Motor Lodge* (rates: $24–36 double), with 117 excellent rooms, restaurant, heated pools at 500 Parkway on U.S. 441 at junction of Tenn. 73 (436–4132); *Olde English Inn* (rates: $30–37 double), with 46 excellent rooms and suites, heated pool, off Ski Mountain Rd. at 309 Oakley Dr. (436–7813); *River Edge Motor Lodge* (rates: $40–45 double), with 43 excellent rooms, some with fireplaces, heated pool at 948 River Rd. (436–9292); *Rocky Waters Motor Inn* (rates: $34–36 double), with 105 excellent rooms overlooking the Little Pigeon River, some with fireplaces, two heated pools, in town on Park-way/U.S. 441 (436–7861); *Royal Townhouse Motor Inn* (rates: $34–42 double), with 81 excellent rooms, wood burning fireplaces, heated pool, next to Aerial Tramway at 937 Parkway/U.S. 441 (436–5818); *Sheraton Gatlinburg* (rates: $44–48 double), with 315 excellent rooms, restaurant, coffeeshop, cocktail lounge, heated pool at Cherokee Orchard and Airport roads off U.S. 441 (436–9211).

Pigeon Forge

(Pop. 1,400; zip code 37863; area code 615) is an old iron and crafts center located north of Gatlinburg on the scenic Newfound Gap Road (U.S. 441). Area attractions include the Pigeon Forge Pottery Center (453–3883) on Middle Creek Rd.; guided tours of the old gristmill in operation since 1830; Smokey Mountain Car Museum on U.S. 441; Silver Dollar City (453–4616), a replica of an 1800's highland village with pioneer crafts and musicians, steam train, craft shops, log flume rides, one mile north of town off U.S. 441. Accommodations: *Best Western Plaza Motel* (rates: $30 double), with 94 excellent rooms and heated pool across from restaurant on U.S. 441 (453–5538); *Best Western Toni Motel* (rates: $30 double), with 106 excellent rooms and heated pool on U.S. 441 (453–9058); *River Lodge Motel* (rates: $26–48 double), with 51 excellent rooms, restaurant, swimming pool, on N. Parkway/U.S. 441 (453–0801).

Townsend—Gateway to the Cades Cove Area

(Pop. 300; zip code 37882; area code 615) on Tenn. 73 and the Little River, is the major gateway to Great Smoky Mountains National Park and the beautiful Cades Cove Area—a spacious valley noted for its quiet, pastoral scenery and pioneer buildings, old gristmill, and visitors center. The scenic Rich Mountain and Little River Roads provide access to remote areas of the park. Other area features include the Tuckaleechee Caverns, three miles south on Little River Rd. (73) and the Smoky Mountains Passion Play. Accommodations: *Talley-Ho Motel* (rates: $18–24 double), with 34 excellent rooms, Carriage House Restaurant, heated pool, one mile west of town on Tenn. 73 (448–2465); *Valley View Lodge* (rates: $20–22 double), with 26 excellent rooms and swimming pool in center of town on Tenn. 73 (448–2237).

Lodges & Resorts

★★★*The Cobbly Nob Resort* rests in the calm of a valley, at the Great Smoky Mountains National Park. The resort is open all year and the climate is temperate year-round. There's lots to keep you busy including an 18–hole championship golf course designed by Gary Player, four tennis courts, a larger-than-Olympic free-form swimming pool, horseback riding or hiking up the trails in the nearby mountains, fishing in the ponds or streams, and skiing year-round. There are movies and planned activities for children. You'll enjoy some of the best cooking in the area here. Rooms are large and there are suites available. All rooms have queen sized beds, cable TV, and many with fireplaces and balconies. There are weekly discounts and package plans available. Rates range from $27–38 and are based on double occupancy. The setting for the resort is exquisite and the rooms are beautifully decorated and comfortable. Write or call The Cobbly Nob Resort, RFD 3, Gatlinburg, TN 37738 (615)436–9333.

★★★*Le Conte Lodge* is a remote alpine retreat reached by any of five trails up to the lodge in the Great Smoky Mountains; the Alum Cave Bluffs trail (5½ mi.), the Rainbow Falls Trail (6.7 mi.), the Bullhead Trail (7.2 mi.), the Trillium Gap Trail (8 mi.) and the Boulevard Trail (8 mi.). Hike there, or take a horse in the Appalachian tradition. The lodge opens March 24, when wild azalea and rhododendron cover the hillsides, and closes November 5, when the last of the brilliant red and yellow leaves have fallen, and approaching winter greys the mountainsides. This cluster of rustic cabins, built of hand-hewn logs of native timber, overlooks the Great Smoky Mountains National Park from an elevation of 6,400 feet. The smaller cabins sleep up to four people, in private bedrooms with double sized beds arranged bunk style. Two larger cabins, with five bedrooms sleep 10–12. All bedrooms are private. Southern-style country cooking is enjoyed in the family-style dining room, which serves two hearty meals daily. Breathtaking sunsets are seen at Cliff Point, and sunrise over the Smokies is enjoyed in the cool of the morning from Myrtle Point. Rates, including two meals daily, are $17.49 per adult and $12.83 for children, 10 and under. For more information write: Le Conte Lodge, Inc., P.O. Box 350, Gatlinburg, TN 37738 (615)436–4473.

Land Between The Lakes

See "Kentucky" chapter for details.

Other Tennessee Lakes, Recreation Areas & Wild Rivers

Tennessee's spectacular mountains and verdant green valleys, plateau country, turbulent mountain streams, scenic lakes, and timbered bottomlands, extending from the over-6,500–feet elevation of the Great Smoky Mountains in the east to the flatlands bordering the Mississippi River on the west, and encompassing 41,951 square

miles, provide some of the best and most varied fishing and hunting in the eastern United States.

The famous great lake impoundments built by the Tennessee Valley Authority and the U.S. Corps of Engineers range in size from 900–acre Davy Crockett Lake in the Cherokee National Forest in the eastern section of the state to the huge 158,300–acre Kentucky Lake, with its 2,380 miles of shoreline, in the west. The TVA lakes are located on the Tennessee River system stretching from the northeast corner of the state southward into Alabama and then north through western Tennessee. Corps of Engineers impoundments include Dale Hollow on the Obed River, Woods Reservoir on the Elk River, Center Hill on Caney Fork and Barkley, Cheatham, and Old Hickory on the Cumberland. All of the state's major impoundments, including Barkley, Kentucky, Cheatham, Old Hickory, J. Percy Priest, Woods, Tims Ford, Center Hill, Cordell Hull, Nickajack, Great Falls, Dale Hollow, Chickamauga, Watts Bar, Melton Hill, Norris, Fort Loudoun, Chilhowee, Cherokee, Douglas, Fort Patrick Henry, South Holston, Boone, Wilbur, and Watauga reservoirs are renowned to fishermen far and wide for often spectacular fishing for largemouth and smallmouth bass, spotted or Kentucky bass, white and black crappie, walleye, sauger, white bass, rock bass, bluegill, muskellunge, rockfish, rainbow, brown and brook trout, and several species of catfish.

All of the major impoundments have good to excellent fishing for largemouth or smallmouth or both. Dale Hollow Reservoir on the Obed River provides nationally ranked fishing for largemouth bass, walleye, and muskellunge and produced the world's record 11–pound 15–ounce smallmouth bass. The cold tailwaters below Dale Hollow Dam are noted for their outstanding rainbow trout, and produced the state record 26–pound 2–ounce brown trout. Good tailwater fishing for lunker rainbows and brown trout is found below the dams of Lakes Watauga, Norris, Chilhowee, Dale Hollow, South Holston, and Center Hill. The tailwaters flowing through the dams from the bottom of the reservoirs are extremely cold and rich in insect life and schools of minnows and threadfin shad. The best time to fish the tailwaters is when the generators are shut off, and the pots and rapids are easily reached. High water scatters the fish and makes access more difficult. Several of the great lakes are world famous for walleye fishing, including Woods, Dale Hollow, Norris, Watauga, and Old Hickory—which holds the world's record of 25 pounds for this species. A few of the lakes and float streams of the Cumberland Plateau have native populations of muskellunge. Dale Hollow Lake and Woods Reservoir in Franklin County and Norris Reservoir, which backs up the Clinch and Powell rivers, are among the state's best muskie waters. Watauga Lake which impounds the waters of the Watauga River in the beautiful mountain country of Cherokee National Forest offers some of the state's finest trout fishing when rainbows up to 10 pounds move into Doe Creek tributary during their winter spawning run.

Several of the state's large rivers and streams offer good float fishing with a johnboat or canoe. Canoe rentals and float-trip guides are located along most of the major rivers. The major float-fishing waters include the Buffalo River for smallmouth bass, bream, and pickerel; Duck River for smallmouth bass and rock bass in the upper section; Obed River for smallmouth and rock bass; Hiwassee River for brown and rainbow trout; Little Tennessee River for brown and rainbow trout; French Broad River for largemouth bass, catfish, and sauger; the lower portions of the Nolichuckey River for smallmouth bass and channel catfish; and the South Fork Holston River for excellent brown and rainbow trout fishing below South Holston Dam.

Tennessee boasts a number of fine rivers and streams inviting to white-water enthusiasts and fishermen alike. On the Tennessee-Kentucky border, the South Fork of the Cumberland River has hollowed out a wild, magnificent canyon perfect for float trips, which can be divided into two runs; one from New River to Leatherwood Bridge, and the other from the bridge to State Highway 92. The entire trip takes three days or longer, depending on whether one stops to fish or explore the area. Put-in for the upper run is off Highway 27 at the town of New River. The first nine miles travel the placid waters of the New River through a steep-faced canyon. Near the confluence with the South Fork of the Cumberland are some easy rapids followed by a scenic run through a handsome gorge with 400–foot-high sandstone cliffs. Dogwood, hardwoods, and lofty pine trees grow near the river's edge. Next comes Jake's Hole and a series of breathtaking drops as the river rushes through boulder masses, creating a confusion of turbulent, class IV white water, navigable only by experts.

Angel Falls, a boulder garden just below Leatherwood Bridge in Scott State Forest, is no place for the novice either. Experts have run the left side under certain water conditions, but saner and less experienced people portage. Excellent smallmouth bass fishing is available at the gorge as well as several nearby spots for camping. There are Indian cliff dwellings located beneath the canyon rim, but they are accessible only to those with rock-climbing skills and equipment. Just across the Kentucky line is perilous Devil's Jump Falls, which can be run at certain water levels but must be portaged if the river is up.

Like the South Fork of the Cumberland, the Obed National Wild and Scenic River in the Catoosa Wildlife Management Area north of Rockwood, has carved a precipitous and rocky gorge with a floor of unpredictable white water. The 12½–mile trip through the gorge can be made in one day, but the clear pools filled with huge muskie, lovely sand beaches, and natural swimming holes will prove too tempting to pass up. Two or three days with frequent stops will make for a most enjoyable journey.

Tennessee's rugged and scenic Cherokee National Forest highlands and widely scattered wildlife management area lands and public hunting areas provide excellent fall hunting opportunities for whitetail deer, upland game birds, waterfowl, and limited numbers of black bear and wild European boar—both by special permit only. The Pond Mountain, Tellico and Ocoee bear reserves in Cherokee National Forest are closed to bear hunting. The vast hardwood and conifer forests of the Cherokee Wildlife Management Area units in the Cherokee National Forest are among the state's finest public hunting grounds; the Tellico WMA unit (80,000 acres of spectacular mixed hardwood and pine forests), Ocoee WMA unit (40,000 acres of mountainous conifer and hardwood forests), Laurel Fork WMA unit (10,000 acres of mixed hardwoods), Kettlefoot WMA unit (39,000 acres of mixed hardwoods and rugged highlands), and the huge Unicoi WMA provide good hunting for deer, wild boar, grouse, woodcock, raccoon, opossum, bobcat, fox, black bear, rabbit, gray and fox squirrel, and wild turkey.

The state's great reservoirs and lakes are prime resting and nesting areas for large flocks of ducks and Canadian geese. Reelfoot Lake, created by an earthquake, is a bass fisherman's and waterfowl hunter's paradise located up in the extreme northwest corner of the state near the Mississippi River. The Mississippi itself has long been famous as a migration route for large flocks of ducks and honkers.

As a note of caution, both fishermen and hunters should have an eye out for rattlesnakes, copperheads, and a few cottonmouth mocasins found scattered throughout the fish and game regions of the state.

Information Sources, Maps & Access

Tennessee fishing and hunting regulations and information about special permits and seasons are available along with the publications listed below, from: Wildlife Resources Agency, P.O. Box 40747, Nashville 37204. The free *Tennessee Fishing Guide* contains a fishing map of the state, laws and regulations, license information, and a listing of wildlife officers and agency-managed lakes. The free, full-color *Fishing Tennessee* booklet contains illustrations and descriptions of the state's principal game fish, a *Tennessee Fishing Map* showing reservoirs, streams, and major roads, and a *Map of Floatable Streams in Tennessee*. Fishing pamphlets are available from the agency for *Watts Bar, Norris Lake, Fort Loudoun, South Holston, Cherokee, Douglas, Boone,* and *Watauga* reservoirs. The free *Guide to Hunting in Tennessee* contains regulations, laws, license information, and a comprehensive listing and descriptions of the state's Wildlife Management Areas, including the vast Cherokee Wildlife Management Area and its Tellico Pond Mountain and Ocoee bear reserves and Tellico, Ocoee, Andrew Johnson, Kettlefoot, Laurel Fork, and Unicoi game units. The *Tennessee Turkey Hunting Guide* contains a listing of laws, regulations, and county checking stations. The agency also publishes a free *Wildlife Management Areas Map* showing state and Cherokee National Forest game units. A *Reelfoot Wildlife Refuge Map* and a *Directory of Reelfoot Lake Camps* (includes guides, lodging, and boat rentals) may be obtained free from the Refuge Manager, Box 295, Samburg 38254.

The Tennessee Valley Authority has developed some 36 lakes in the seven Tennessee Valley states, offering more than 600,000 acres of water surface and 11,000 miles of shoreline. Detailed recreation maps for nine lakes in Tennessee are available from: TVA Map Office, 400 Commerce Ave., SW, Knoxville 37902, or Chattanooga 37401. Single copies of the maps are free on request. Each lake recreation map describes points of interest in the area, opportunities for fishing, hunting, and outdoor activities, boating requirements and water safety, and the topographic features of the lake. The map shows the lake and surrounding terrain, public and TVA dam reservation lands, commercial boat docks, boat-launching sites, public parks, wildlife management areas, roads, highways, and nearby towns. Maps are available for the following lake areas: *Nickajack Lake* is near Raccoon and Sand mountains on the Tennessee River. The *Upper Holston Lakes* include Fort Patrick Henry Dam, Boone Lake, South Holston Lake, Watauga Dam and Lake, and Roan Creek—all in and around the Cherokee National Forest and the nearby towns of Johnson City, Elizabethton, Bristol, and Kingsport. *Chickamauga Lake* lies between the Watts Bar and Chickamauga dams just outside Chattanooga. Bordering the lake are Harrison Bay and Booker T. Washington state parks, both of which are indicated on the map. The *Cherokee-Douglas Lakes* include Davy Crockett Lake and a segment of the French Broad River. Neighboring towns include Morristown and Rogersville. *Watts Bar Lake* adjoins Chickamauga Lake near Kingston, Harriman, and Rockwood. The map of *Melton Hill Lake* shows the Clinch River Floatway, situated near the towns of Oak Ridge and Clinton. *Fort Loudoun Lake* is just outside of Knoxville on the Tennessee River; *Norris Lake* adjoins the Central Peninsula and Cove Creek Peninsula wildlife management areas near the town of La Follette. The *Hiwassee Lakes* include Apalachia Lake in the Nantahala National Forest of Tennessee and Blue Ridge and Nottely lakes in Georgia's Chattahoochee National Forest.

Navigation charts and maps have also been published by TVA for its major lakes. They show water depths, the location of public recreation

areas, boat docks, resorts, and roads. Charts for the mainstream lakes of the Tennessee River show navigation channels, buoys, lights, and other navigation aids. Maps for tributary lakes show the location of numbered boards the TVA has installed at strategic locations on shore to aid fishermen and recreation boaters in locating their positions. A free index of TVA navigation charts, maps, and other charts may be purchased from: TVA Maps (Knoxville and Chattanooga addresses above).

A brochure published by the TVA, *Recreation on TVA Lakes*, offers a general description of recreational opportunities on the lakes, including fishing, boating, and camping, and a list of addresses for further information. A map of TVA lakes with a detailed listing of recreation areas on each lake giving addresses and facilities is also provided. The brochure, a useful supplement to the recreation maps, is available free from the addresses above.

Tennessee River Tributary Watershed Maps, lithoprinted in color, showing drainage, tropography, woodlands, highways and roads, cities and towns, with a contour interval of 100 feet, are available from: TVA Map Office (addresses above) for *Bear Creek* (45¢), *Upper French Broad River* (45¢), *Sequatchie River* (45¢), *Duck River* (75¢), *Elk River* (75¢), *Little Tennessee River* (75¢), *Emory River* (75¢), and *Hiwassee River* (75¢). Trips along the Obed and Emory are described in *Obed-Emory Canoe Trails*, a brochure and map available free from: Recreation Resources Branch, TVA, Knoxville 37902. Canoe routes described include runs along Daddy's Creek, Clear Creek, and White Creek as well as the Obed and Emory rivers. All information, including location of rapids and pools, river difficulty, portages, trip length, and the like, is provided. The three-color map is fairly explicit, showing roads, highways, the major runs described, towns, paved and gravel roads, and access points. For detailed information on the beautiful Obed National Wild and Scenic River and its Clear Creek Tributary, write: Obed Wild & Scenic River, P.O. Box 477, Oneida 37841.

Tennessee Valley Canoe Trails is another useful aid for river runs in the Tennessee Valley. Varied types of river canoeing from serene trips on certain portions of the French Broad and Nolichuckey rivers to exciting white water on other sections of the same streams are described and identified on a map of the valley. Other bodies of water covered include White's, Clear, and Daddy's creeks; the Obed, Oconaluftee, Hiwassee, Tuckasegee, and Tellico rivers; the Watauga and Raven Fork. Mileage, river difficulty, and stream gauge readings are provided. Point-by-point descriptions of each route are not included. Copies of this brochure and pamphlets on the Obed and Elk rivers and streams in the Little Tennessee Valley Watershed are available free from: Recreation Resources Branch, TVA, Knoxville 37902.

Little Tennessee Valley Canoe Trails is a guide to the middle portion of the Little Tennessee River and four of its tributary streams—the Nantahala, Raven Fork, Oconaluftee, and Tuckasegee rivers—all of which are used extensively by canoers. These streams, which have their beginning on the western side of the Appalachian Mountains in North Carolina, flow generally east to west and provide a variety of river runs, from the easygoing to the treacherous. The guide includes a very basic map showing access points, major routes, bridges, towns, and roads. Detailed descriptions of each stream provide mileage, access points, stream difficulty and stream gauge, and a list of canoe safety tips. The brochure may be obtained free from: TVA Canoe Trails, 301 Cumberland Ave., SW, Knoxville 37902.

Still another guide to Tennessee's waters, the *Elk River Guide*,

describes the river (called Chuwalee by the Indians), which rises on the edge of the Cumberland Plateau in middle Tennessee and flows southwest to the Tennessee River near Wheeler Dam. The Elk is an easy stream to float and is ideal for beginners or family expeditions. The brochure includes a simple map of the river's course between Tims Ford Dam to the Old Stone Bridge near Fayetteville, a distance of a little over 40 miles. Tips on floating the Elk and a brief description of the river are also included in the folder, which is available free from: Elk River Development Assn., Municipal Bldg., P.O. Box 507, Fayetteville 37334.

Buffalo River Canoe Rental will rent 17-foot Grumman 3-man aluminum canoes, paddles, and life jackets for expeditions on the Buffalo River in middle Tennessee. The river is a basically pastoral stretch of water, with some turbulent water in the upper sections. Year-round floating is available, with tributary streams providing interesting diversions. Located on Highway 13, 10 miles south of Linden and 16 miles north of Waynesboro, the company also offers a primitive-type campground at Slink Shoals provided for customers at no cost. A brochure describing the rental service and access sites along the Buffalo and Duck rivers is available free from: *Buffalo River Canoe Rental Co.*, Flatwoods 38458, phone (615)589–2755. The auto access routes serving the state are Interstate Highways 71, 75, 24, 40, 65, 155, and 64.

Lodges & Resorts

★★*Cedar Hill Resort at Dale Hollow Lake* in the Cumberland Mountains of Tennessee is the largest resort near Dale Hollow Dam, the site of one of the largest fish (trout) hatcheries in the U.S. Dale Hollow Lake has superb fishing and was voted the best freshwater lake on this continent—it is truly a sportsman's paradise—and the fishing is excellent year round with no closed season. In addition to the wonderful scenery and fishing, the 850 miles of shore-line provides excellent sightseeing boat trips, and the resort has houseboat rentals available for just that purpose. Fishing boats and outboards are also available for rental as well as the equipment needed and guides. Water skiing is also popular and there is a swimming pool on the premises. The area is also good for hunting waterfowl, deer, squirrel, rabbits, and quail. Hiking, cookouts and camping can be arranged on an island nearby. There is a playground for children and a good restaurant for short-order or complete meals. Docking facilities are extensive on the lake and there are plenty of motor trips you can take in the surrounding areas. There are 20 modern and spacious cottages equipped for light housekeeping. They are all located along the shore and offer excellent views of the lake, near the docks and pool. There is also a motel available for rooming. Rates at the motel range from $18.50–24 (depending on season)—double occupancy. Cottages range from $20 (depending on season and occupancy). Rooms and cottages are also available on a weekly basis. Contact: Dick Roberts, Cedar Hill Resort, Celina, TN 38551 (615)243–3201.

★★★*Newport Resort on Watts Bar Lake* is located near the Great Smoky Mountains. The resort is the bass-tournament center on the lake, which provides over 700 miles of shoreline for both the novice and expert. Guests can bring their own boats or rent them from the marina. Pleasure and houseboats are also available. Nearby Renegade Hunting range has managed hunts, with big game hunting on more than 6,000 acres. Golf is also available nearby. At the resort you can enjoy swimming, a sandy beach, hiking, skiing, and sightseeing. Area attractions include the Lost Sea and Chattanooga. The resort's Rotunda Restaurant is open seven days a week, specializing in fresh seafood. There's a deck surrounding the restaurant for tranquil lounging. Accommodations include modern hotel rooms, motel

apartments, and housekeeping cottages. All are air-conditioned with refrigerators. A grocery store is maintained on the resort's premises. Rates: motel rooms and apartments; $18–80 daily, $110–480 weekly; cottages rentals $25–35 daily, $150–210 weekly. For further information contact: Newport Resort, Route 1, Spring City, TN 37381 (615)365–9521.

State Outdoor Recreation Area System & Lodgings

The state of Tennessee has 17 scenic parks located throughout the state. Some are day use parks only, but others have overnight accommodations including campsites, inns, modern lodges and rustic cabins. Inn room rates are available for single or double occupancy, with a charge of $4 per person for additional individuals. A one night's deposit is required for all rooms and checkout time is 1 P.M. Cabin rates cover occupancy by one to four persons. Each additional person is $4/day or $20/week. Cabins are completely furnished with cooking facilities, utensils and linens, except for overnight cabins which do not have kitchens. From May 1 through September 30, cabins can be rented by the week only; and the rental runs from Monday at 5 P.M. to Monday at 10 A.M. Off-season, there is a two-night minimum in the cabins. Rates quoted are daily rates, but persons renting cabins for a seven-day week pay for only five days. Tent and trailer campsites are on a first-come, first-served basis with no reservations accepted. Only one vehicle is allowed per campsite and maximum stay is two weeks. The rate for one to four persons is $4 per day, 50¢ for each additional person and no charge for children under seven years of age. Campgrounds have showers, tables and grills; and most have ice and camp stores. There is fishing at nearly every State Park. A charge of $1 is levied for small, park-owned lakes, but fishing is free on all TVA lakes and Army Corps of Engineers lakes. Swimming pools open around June 1st, depending on lifeguards, as do beaches. No personally-owned boats are allowed on the small park lakes, but rental boats and canoes are available. For information on all State Parks, write or call: Tennessee Dept. of Conservation, Division of State Parks, 2611 West End Ave., Nashville, TN 37203 (615)741–3251.

Cove Lake State Park Lodgings are located in east Tennessee's Campbell County on the shores of Cove Lake. The lake is situated in a picturesque valley surrounded by the Cumberland Mountains. Canadian geese, attracted by the quiet inlets, marshes and fields of the area, make this their winter home. Visitors come to view these geese, whose natural food is supplemented by the park. Ancient Americans, known as Mound Builders, once prospered in this valley. The University of Tennessee uncovered their mounds and habitation sites in the late 1930's. Some of the earthen remnants are still visible and excavation pictures and artifacts are on display at the park. The surrounding hills, rich in coal, have unfolded many fossils of long-extinct plants and animals. Park naturalists conduct fossil hunting tours of the mountains throughout the summer months. In addition to these fossil tours, planned activities and programs include guided walks, bicycle tours, float trips, arts and crafts, demonstrations, archery lessons, campfires, movies and slide shows. The park has 127 campsites with water and electrical hookups plus picnicking facilities for both campers and day park users. Year-round fishing is permitted on 210–acre Cove Lake. Bass and bluegill are the prime sport fish, and there are good catches of crappie. Rowboat rentals are available. Swimming is provided by the park's Olympic-sized pool, with space for sunbathing. There is a bathhouse and a children's pool equipped with spray showers. In addition to the water sports provided by the lake and pool the park has facilities for badminton, shuffleboard, horseshoes, field games, volleyball,

playgrounds, ping-pong, bicycle rentals, miniature golf and many other activities. Accommodations at the park are in a stone motel, which overlooks the rolling, grassy fields surrounding Cove Lake. Rooms are air-conditioned and have TV's. Meals, which are not included in rates, are available at the park's year-round restaurant, featuring southern cooking at reasonable prices. The restaurant is a prime spot to view the winter geese. Rates: double occupancy $16. Children under 12 free, when accompanied by parents. Weekly rates available. For further information contact: Tennessee Department of Conservation, Division of State Parks, Cove Lake State Day Use Park, Caryville, TN 37714 (615)562–8355.

Cumberland Mountain State Rustic Park is located four miles south of Crossville, between Nashville and Knoxville, on the Cumberland Plateau. This 1,720–acre park has been open since 1940. Most of its buildings are constructed of a unique local sandstone called "Crab Orchard Stone." The park includes the 50–acre Cumberland Mountain Lake which offers swimming from a sandy beach with bathhouses and lifeguards, fishing (with a Tennessee license and park permit) and boating with park rental boats and canoes. The park has two marked hiking trails; one a short one-hour walk, and the second which goes around the lake. There are three

tennis courts, badminton, a softball field, basketball, volleyball, horseshoes, shuffleboard, ping-pong tables and other facilities. A naturalist offers seasonal programs, and in the fall there is a non-flowering plant pilgrimage during which guides point out ferns, mosses, mushrooms, lichens and fungi. The new park restaurant overlooks the lake and is open from 11 a.m. to 9 p.m. serving lunch and dinner. The dining room seats 350 and there are banquet rooms available. Cumberland Mountain is a sanctuary and all plants, animals, rocks, minerals and artifacts are protected. The park has a group lodge, the Old Stone Lodge, which will accommodate 16 people and has a kitchen and a fireplace. It is $3 each per day with a minimum of $30. For campers there are 146 campsites complete with water and electric hookups. There is also a camp store and a dump station. The park has 37 cabins. The deluxe is $30 per day; ultra-modern is $25 per day; modern is $20 per day and the rustic is $12 per day, but is not winterized. For information and reservations write: Superintendent's Office, Cumberland Mountain State Rustic Park, Crossville, TN 38555 (615)484–6138.

Edgar Evins State Rustic Park is located in De Kalb County, in the hills of middle Tennessee. This new park, opened in 1975, is on Center Hill Lake which was formed by the Army Corps of Engineers dam across the Caney Fork River. Swimming in the lake is permitted, but there are no lifeguards. Center Hill Lake is a popular fishing spot, and record catches of smallmouth bass, largemouth bass and walleye pike have been taken. The park boat dock has fishing supplies and boats for rent. Privately-owned boats may be launched from either of the two park launching ramps. The park is made up of 6,000 acres of land that was once an Indian hunting ground for deer, bear, and buffalo. It has steep walled bluffs, narrow ridges, and rolling hills. For recreation, there is a swimming pool for registered cabin guests only. All visitors can enjoy the four playground areas which include facilities for horseshoes, badminton and frisbee tossing. For hiking, there is a marked 1½ mile trail around the lake. The park is a protected wildlife sanctuary. For accommodations, Edgar Evins has a modern, 34–unit village cabin complex. Each one has a one bedroom and is equipped for housekeeping. Cabins are open year-round and rent for $30 a day. There are also 60 unusual trailer and tent campsites. These are platform type sites and are built around the slopes of the lake. The campground is open all year round and sites are $4.24 per night. The grounds also house a campstore, three bathhouses and a dump station. The campstore is open only during the summer season. For information and reservations contact: Superintendent's Office, Edgar Evins State Rustic Park, Route #1, Silver Point, TN 38582 (615)858–2446 office or (615)858–2114 reservations.

***Fall Creek Falls State Resort Park**, in the central part of the state, is the second largest state park with 16,000 acres. It includes Fall Creek Lake and has a boat dock and a fisherman's village. This park is a favorite with golfers, because it has its own 18–hole golf course and pro shop. The scenery is outstanding with deep gorges, virgin timberland, and the spectacular Fall Creek Falls, which plunge 256 feet to a shaded pool. For seeing the sites, visitors can choose backpacking trails, bike trails, or scenic drives. There are two marked backpacking trails which start at the park's nature center. One is an easy 13 miles which traverses the plateau uplands. Campsites are located along this trail. A more difficult 12 mile trail descends and climbs the scenic Cane Creek Gorge. The bike trail goes from the Inn to the dam, and bicycles are available for rent. The park has two swimming pools, one at the inn and the other at the Village Green cabin area. There is also swimming in Fall Creek Lake. Other facilities include a restaurant, picnic areas, snack bars, gift and craft

shops, playgrounds, ball fields, a recreation lodge for checking out playing equipment, a general store and a nature center. For groups, there is a lodge accommodating 96 at $3 each per day ($120 minimum) and two group camping areas. The Inn, perched on the edge of the lake, has rooms for $26 a night double occupancy and suites for $50 a night. Deluxe cabins and chalets, with housekeeping facilities, can be found at Fisherman's Village and Village Green. They rent for $40 a night. For further information and reservations: Fall Creek Falls State Resort Park, Pikeville, TN 37367 (615)881–3241.

***Henry Horton State Resort Park** has a championship golf course, skeet and trap shooting, outstanding accommodations and excellent facilities. It was the first resort park in the Tennessee Outdoor Recreation Area System and is located 40 miles south of Nashville on Highway 31A. The park has 1,135 acres on the shores of the historic Duck River. The Buford Eillington Golf Course, located within the park, has 18 holes and is a par 72 championship course. There is a pro shop with dressing rooms, rentals, carts and golfing accessories for sale. A park golf pro is on duty and the course is open all year. To brush up on technique, golfers can use the practice green near the pro shop. For individuals and gun clubs, Henry Horton has a professional multi-field skeet and trap equipment, vending machines, and rest rooms. A skeet range manager can provide assistance, as well as individual and group instruction. The Olympic-sized swimming pool is open from early summer through Labor Day and has lifeguards, bathhouses and a concession stand. There is also a wading pool for children. Swimming is free for guests of the inn and the cabins. Along the shores of the Duck River are picnic tables, grills, playgrounds and ball fields. For games such as tennis, croquet, horseshoes, badminton, archery, shuffleboard and others, there are courts provided. Special activities are planned by the park's recreation directors throughout the year. They include arts and crafts, hayrides, square dances, movies, slide shows and much more. Weekly activities are posted at the Inn, the recreation center and the park office. Horton Park has a restaurant featuring Southern cuisine and is open all year. Visitors can stay at the Horton Inn. Each room has two double beds, air-conditioning, TV, telephone and carpeting; and there are four suites with kitchenettes. Rooms are $26 per day double occupancy and suites are $45. There are also five modern cabins at $35 per day equipped for housekeeping and sleeping up to six people each. They also have TV, phones and air-conditioning. For those who prefer outdoor accommodations, there are 85 campsites, picturesquely located along the Duck River. Thirty-one are primitive, for tents only, and 54 have electrical hook-ups and grills. The two bathhouses have hot showers. For information and reservations contact: Superintendent's Office, Henry Horton State Resort Park, P.O. Box 128, Chapel Hill, TN 37034 (615) 364–2222.

***Montgomery Bell State Resort Park** is a historic location as well as a recreational area with two lakes, a golf course, hiking trails, outstanding accommodations, and more. Located in the rolling hills of middle Tennessee, this area saw the establishment of Cumberland Iron Works and the beginning of the iron industry here. It is named for Montgomery Bell who purchased the Cumberland furnace and built an iron empire. The remains of the old Laurel furnace and ore pits are within the State Park. Another historic site is the replica of the house in which the Cumberland Presbyterian Church was organized in 1810. The park's 3,782 acres surround two lakes—Acorn and Woodhaven. Both have good fishing, especially for bream and bass. Acorn Lake has a sandy swimming beach with lifeguards and a modern bathhouse enclosing a concession stand and a recreation pavilion. This lake also has a boat dock and rental boats available. No private boats are allowed on either lake. The newest addition to

Montgomery Bell Park is an 18–hole golf course, the Frank G. Clement Course. It has bent grass greens for year-round play, a pro shop, rental gear, carts and concessions. For the hiker, the park has 19 miles of developed foot trails. There is also an 11.7 mile over-night hiking trail with three primitive camping shelters. The recreational facilities include a lighted tennis court, playground, ball field, archery range, horseshoe pits, basketball courts, shuffleboard, and tether-ball. All playing equipment can be checked out free at the inn or the camper check-in station. Planned activities include hayrides, campfire programs, crafts, movies and games. The Montgomery Bell Inn and Restaurant is open all year and is located in a peaceful glade of trees overlooking the 35–acre Acorn Lake. The Inn has 40 rooms renting for $19 to $23 per day double occupancy and $40 per day for suites. Guests at the Inn enjoy a private pool. The restaurant is open to the public and seats 350. Just across a cove from the Inn, and reached via a quaint rustic wooden bridge, are ten two-bedroom cottages. They are completely equipped for housekeeping and rent for $30 a day. Campers will find 110 campsites in a wooded valley complete with bubbling stream. Over half of the sites have water and electricity. For more information and reservations write: Superintendent's Office or Inn, Montgomery Bell State Resort Park, Burns 37029 or call (615)797-3101 for the Inn and (615)797-9051 for the office.

★★★*Paris Landing State Resort Park* is one of the State Parks of Tennessee which offers a variety of facilities and activities appealing to both young and old, outdoorsman or vacationer. This 841–acre park is located on Kentucky Lake, the second largest man-made lake in the world. The area is characterized by gently rolling to relatively steep terrain. The forests consist mostly of oaks, hickories and pines. Nearby attractions include a 170,000 acre 40–mile long peninsula of the TVA's Land Between the Lakes recreation area. There is also a National Military Park and Museum with Civil War replicas. Paris Landing provides a fully equipped campsite, picnic areas, marina for crafts of all sizes, a public, private and children's pools as well as swimming at the beach of the lake. There is plenty of boating and fishing and water skiing available with equipment at the marina of nearby. There is also a beautiful 18–hole golf course and other activities including shuffleboard, archery, volleyball, tennis, softball, croquet, badminton, and ping-pong. Recreation directors are also available and provide planned programs including arts and crafts, movies and slide shows, organized games, instruction in archery. Outdoor entertainment is presented during the summer months in the evenings. Paris Landing is a sanctuary, and all plants and animals and rocks and minerals are protected by state law. The Inn provides a commanding view of the lake and has 103 rooms available ranging from $20–26. The spacious restaurant is noted for its fine Southern cuisine. There are close to 20 state recreational facilities with ac-commodations at inns or cabins, rates varying accordingly. For further information contact Paris Landing State Resort Park, Rte 1, Buchanan, TN 38222 (901)642–4140, (901)642–4311 or Tennessee Dept. of Conservation, Division of State Parks, 2611 West End Avenue, Nashville, TN 37203 (615)741–3251.

★★★*Pickett Rustic State Park* is a wilderness park in the far north central part of the state. It is especially attractive to hikers. The park has 33 miles of foot trails. There are 14 interconnected trails, so that a hiker could start at one end and cover all the trails in series. These trails are connected via the Great Meadow Trail to the trails of the Daniel Boone National Forest, which descend to the gorge of the Big South Fork of the Cumberland River. There is swimming, fishing and boating on Arch Lake. Canoes and rowboats may be rented, but no privately-owned boats can be used on the lake. The park also has a pool with lifeguards, and swimming is free to cabin

guest and $1 for others. Games, horseshoes and archery equipment can be checked out at the office. The park has a variety of cabins. Rustic cabins have kitchens, fireplaces, screened in porches and one or two bedrooms. They rent for $20 a night. The deluxe cabins are similarly equipped but are larger and some have three bedrooms. They are $30 a night. Pickett also has five chalets all adjoining with interconnecting doors. They have two floors with a spiral staircase connecting the bedroom and bath upstairs to the kitchenette and living room downstairs. Each has a fireplace and a patio and rents for $25 a night. Campsites with electrical hookups are available and the campgrounds has a new bathhouse. For more information call or write: Pickett State Rustic Park, Jamestown, TN 38556 (615) 879–5821.

★★★*Pickwick Landing State Resort Park* developed around the old TVA village where a thousand people lived while constructing the Pickwick Dam in the 1930's. It was purchased from the TVA in 1969 and two other tracts of land were added to make up the present day park. The ultra-modern park includes a marina, a golf course, an inn, cabins, recreation areas, as well as the Bruton Branch Primitive Area. This 347–acre area has a swimming beach, boat launching ramp, primitive campsites and motorcycle trails. The park is 11 miles south of Savannah, TN on Pickwick Lake. It has a par 72 18–hole golf course, complete with pro shop, snack bar, rentals, both gasoline and pull carts, a golf pro, and golf accessories for sale. The Pickwick Inn and Restaurant overlooks the lake and has 75 rooms and three suites. Guests at the Inn can enjoy the fine southern cuisine in the dining room, the gift shop, adult and kiddie swimming pools, lighted tennis courts, and playground. Pickwick Park has a fully-equipped marina that can accommodate boats of all sizes. The rental dock has 102 wet storage slips and 32 transient or overnight storage slips. There are also 96 dry storage racks for boats. Piers have water and electrical hook-ups; and the marina has rental boats, fuel, fishing supplies and marine accessories. Boating, sailing, water skiing and fishing can be enjoyed on Pickwick Lake. There are three free public launching ramps and private boats are permitted on the lake. The swimming beaches at Circle Beach and Sandy Beach in the day-use area and at Bruton Branch Primitive Area make up about two miles of sandy, public beachfront. Anglers will find largemouth, smallmouth and striped bass, crappie, bluegill, sauger and catfish in the lake. The park has courts and free use of equipment for volleyball, archery, badminton and many other games. Besides the Inn, there are also accommodations in 10 two-bedroom cabins overlooking the lake. They are equipped for housekeeping and have TV, fireplaces and a patio. They rent for $40 a day. A wooded campground has 48 sites with hookups, table and grill. The bath-house has hot showers and restroom facilities. For more information or reservations contact: Pickwick Landing State Resort Park, P.O. Box 10, Pickwick Dam, TN 38365 (901)689–3129 office or (901)689–3135 inn.

★★★*Pin Oak Lodge in Natchez Trace State Forest & Park* offers spacious lodge rooms and private modern cabins. Fisherman will enjoy the fast running streams in the north end of Natchez Park, and the three clear lakes in its heart. Hiking trails and bike paths explore the paths originally blazed by Indians, and used by boatman journeying home from the Mississippi along Natchez Trace which provided the safest route from highway men and thieves. In the north end of the park stands its most unique feature, the "Big Pecan", a stately tree 118 feet tall and 18 feet in circumference. Tradition has it that this impressive tree grew from a pecan carried by one of Andrew Jackson's men as they returned homeward along this route from the Battle of New Orleans. In addition to the lodge there are several campgrounds with trailer hookups, picnic areas, a

grocery store, bike rentals, and a marina with fishing boats, rowboats and paddleboats for rent. The lodge has a private swimming pool for guest use only, and a pleasant dining room serving delicious southern home-style cooking. Inn rooms are $20 daily for a single room, and $26 for a double. Modern cabins with fully equipped kitchens may be rented on a weekly basis only from May 1-September 30, and for two night minimum stays during the off season. Rates are $22 daily. For more information write: Pin Oak Lodge, Natchez Trace Resort Park, Wildersville, TN 38388 (615)968–8176.

★★★★*Reelfoot Lake State Resort Park* is located in Lake and Obion counties in northwest Tennessee, on 22 miles of the Reelfoot Lake shoreline. The park has a total of 18,725 acres; 18,000 comprised of water. The area is considered one of the nation's greatest hunting and fishing preserves. Almost every kind of shore bird, as well as the golden and bald eagle can be found here. Botany enthusiasts from nationwide come here to explore the area's flowering and non-flowering plants, trees, and shrubs. The legendary bald cypress dominates the margins of the lake. The lake, considered one of the nation's most prolific natural fish hatcheries, provides fine catches of crappie, bream, and largemouth bass. Boat rentals are available, and there is a marina with 75 slips for private boats. Scenic boat cruises are given daily April through October, with guides to explain the natural and cultural history of the lake. Swimming is provided with the park's adult pool, a children's pool and several nearby beaches. Reelfoot has a total of 120 camping sites, with water, electric and grills. Picnicking facilities are provided for both campers and park day users. The park also has recreational activities including tennis, horseshoes, shuffleboard, pool, ping-pong, badminton, archery, basketball, archery, and table games. There is a 600–seat auditorium available for banquets and conventions and a free museum housing Indian artifacts and specimens of area wildlife. Accommodations at the park include an ultra-modern inn and restaurant complex situated over the lake, nestled among the towering cypress trees, and a five unit motel. The Inn has rooms and suites and the motel offers units with kitchenettes. Meals, not included in rates, are available at the park's 100–seat capacity, year-round restaurant. Rates: Inn rates, double occupancy $23. Cabin rates, $40. Children under 12 free when accompanied by parents. Weekly rates are available. For further information contact: Superintendent's Office, Reelfoot Lake State Resort Park, Route 1, Tiptonville, TN 38079 (901)253–7756.

★★★*Standing Stone State Park & Forest* offers rustic accommodations on 11,000 acres of highland forest near Dale Hollow Lake and embraces beautiful Standing Stone Lake. The park takes its name from the "standing stone" that was supposedly used as a boundary line between two Indian tribes. The stone was sandstone and about eight feet tall. It sat upright on a sandstone ledge. After it fell, the Indians placed it on an improvised monument to preserve it. The stone is still preserved at Monterey. Standing Stone State Rustic Park and Forest is situated on the Cumberland Plateau of north central Tennessee. This great plateau or "tableland" extends unbroken from New York to Alabama and was a very real barrier to western migration in the 18th century. At that time, no roads crossed it and only a few foot paths like the great Warriors' Path through the Cumberland Gap gave access to the interior lowlands beyond. This quaint and rustic park is noted for its outstanding scenery, spring wildflowers, fossils and other natural features. The park has 15 rustic cabins and three three-bedroom timberlodges. Each is fully equipped for housekeeping, including appliances, cooking and serving utensils and linens. Reservations should be made through the park office. Rates range from $18–30 daily. The park offers excellent fishing, camping, swimming, and hiking on ten miles of backcountry trails. The park is located in middle Tennessee in Overton County, 20 miles north of Cookeville, on State Route 52 between Livingston and Celina. For reservations and additional information, contact: Superintendent's Office, Standing Stone State Rustic Park, Livingston, TN 38570 (615)823–6347.

★★★*Tims Ford State Rustic Park* was opened in 1978 after the TVA Dam on the Elk River created the Tims Ford Lake in 1970. The 10,700–acre reservoir of Tims Ford has some of the best bass fishing in the Southeast. The park marina accommodates fishermen with a bait shop and a fish-cleaning area. The marina also has rental boats with nine-horsepower motors, a boat launching ramp and dock and boating supplies. A special feature of the park is the huge double L-shaped swimming pool which is one of the largest in the State Park system. It has a 12–foot diving pool, a children's wading pool and a bathhouse with concession stand. Lifeguards are on duty in the summer. There are five miles of paved trails for the bicyclist, which travel from the visitors' center around the picnic area and over a bicycle bridge to the campgrounds. Rental bikes are available. There are picnicking facilities all along the lake, playgrounds, playing fields and game courts. At the recreation center, balls, rackets and other equipment can be checked out free of charge. Plans for expansion of the park include 720 more acres of recreational facilities. Accommodations at Tims Ford include 20 two-bedroom cabins scattered on the wooded slopes. Each cabin has a fireplace, outdoor balconies off the bedrooms and livingroom and completely equipped kitchens. They rent for $40 a day. The park has 50 campsites with water and electrical hookups, and a central bathhouse has hot showers. For further information and reservations: Superintendent's Office, Tims Ford State Rustic Park, Route 4, Winchester, TN 37398 (615)967–4457.

★★★*Watts Bar Resort in the Great Smoky Mountains* is nestled on the shore of Watts Bar Lake. Fishermen can troll the lake waters in pontoon boats, motor boats and aluminum boats available at Watts Bar Resort's private marina. Private boat dockage is also available on the lake, which is ideal for waterskiing and swimming. Watts Bar Resort also has tennis courts, a large outdoor pool, and over 200 miles of hiking trails throughout the Great Smokies and over Cumberland Ridge. Southern home-style cooking is enjoyed in the pleasant dining room overlooking the lake. Watts Bar Resort offers deluxe hotel rooms, suites, and one, two, and three bedroom cottages all completely furnished with fully equipped, modern kitchens. Many hug the lakeshore or are spread out over the spacious lawns and sunlit gardens. The resort is open from April 6 through late October. Rates are $18–20 daily for a deluxe room, $115–130 weekly. One bedroom suites with a small sitting room are $22 daily, $145 weekly. Two bedroom suites are $33 daily, and $215 weekly. Studio cottages, with one bedroom and kitchenette are $25 daily, $165 weekly. One bedroom cottages, with living room/dining areas and kitchenettes are $32 daily, $210 weekly. Two bedroom cottages are $32–45 daily, $224–325 weekly. Three bedroom cottages are $53 daily and $345 weekly. For more information write: Watts Bar Resort, Box 600, Watts Bar Dam, TN 37395 (615)365–9595.

VERMONT

Introduction

Vermont, the beautiful Green Mountain State, with its quaint New England villages and covered bridges, contains several outstanding outdoor recreation meccas, including huge, 110–mile-long Lake Champlain, with its islands, bays, coves, and fjordlike shores; the scenic forests, rolling hills, and trout streams of the Green Mountain National Forest, traversed by the famous 166–mile Long Trail, which climbs along the peaks and valleys of the range in a north-south course from the Vermont-Massachusetts border to the Canadian boundary; the renowned alpine and cross-country skiing areas at Killington, Mt. Snow, Stratton, Pico Peak, Bromley Mountain, Okemo, Stowe, Smugglers Notch, Jay Peak, and Sugarbush; the nationally renowned fly fishing waters of the Batten Kill and the headwaters of Otter Creek; and the famous game lands and trophy fishing lakes of the Northeast Kingdom, dominated by the sprawling, island-dotted waters of Lake Memphremagog.

Accommodations & Travel Information

Vermont's major vacation lodges, sporting camps, inns, ski resorts and cross-country centers are described in detail in the "Vacation/Lodging Guide" which follows. For information on all aspects of travel in the Green Mountain State and a free copy of the *Vermont Visitor's Handbook*, contact: Vermont Development Agency, Montpelier, VT 05602 (802)828–3231. Within Vermont's rugged borders is some of New England's most enjoyable fishing and hunting in surroundings famous for mountainous beauty. The lofty ridges of the Green Mountains form the spine of the state, running from the Massachusetts border north to Quebec, and contain scores of wilderness brook trout waters. Vermont also boasts one of the densest deer herds per square mile in America. Most of Vermont's western border lies on the great bass, pike, and walleye waters of sprawling Lake Champlain, while the east is bounded by the productive Connecticut River. The wild Northeast Kingdom occupies the corner at the top of the state where Vermont, New Hampshire, and Quebec meet; it encompasses a large, unspoiled land of trout streams, beaver dams, salmon lakes, glacial bogs, and profuse wildlife. Rumors persist that remnants of the once plentiful mountain lion and wolf populations still exist in the vastnesses of this largely roadless area. Whether or not the region harbors these feared predators, it does shelter deer, bear, moose, and native trout, and marten, fisher, and Canada lynx prowl the thick forest of maple, birch, beech, spruce, fir, and tamarack (eastern larch) in search of prey.

The state has substantial amounts of public fishing and hunting land, considering its size. Occupying much of southern and central Vermont is the 240,000–acre Green Mountain National Forest. In addition, there are thousands of supplemental acres in state forests and parks, public hunting areas, wildlife management areas, and private tracts where the public is allowed, or where permission can be secured with a polite request. Prospecting with maps, especially the U.S. Geological Survey Topographic Maps, will allow the venturesome angler to hit the jackpot, because Vermont has many wilderness trout ponds, spring-fed, remote beaver ponds, and high country streams where excellent trout fishing can still be found if some boot leather is used. For details about conservation efforts, useful fishing information, and area reports, write to: Fish & Game Dept., 5 Court St., Montpelier 05602 (802)828–3371, for the free booklet *Vermont's Fisheries Annual*. The following fishing and hunting publications may be obtained free upon request from the department: *Digest of Fish & Games Laws and Regulations*; *Vermont Guide to Fishing*, which contains a Fishing Map of Vermont and describes principal game-fish species, streams, lakes, ponds, and

major information sources of interest to the outdoors enthusiast; *Vermont Guide to Hunting*, which includes deer and bear maps, descriptions of principal game species, and tips about planning a hunt, camping, and information sources; and *Vermont Hunting Season Camping List*, which describes and lists sites open for camping through the end of the deer season.

The informative, large-format 202–page guide *Trout and Salmon Fishing in New England Lakes and Ponds* ($8 postpaid) contains detailed descriptions and lake survey maps of Crystal, Willoughby, Great Averill, Little Averill, Seymour, and Echo lakes. It may be ordered from: Partridge Press, Box 422, Campton, NH 03223. Vermont has several excellent canoe routes that provide white-water paddling, fishing, and backcountry camping opportunities. It should be noted, however, that low water flow during the summer months limits canoeing possibilities. Rivers and streams that were at full flow a few weeks earlier are often nothing more than a trickle during July and August, requiring the canoeist to walk his canoe through shallow stretches. The old Indian water trail formed by the Connecticut River, which forms the boundary between Vermont and New Hampshire, is the state's premier canoe route. Known to the Indians as *Quinatucquet* ("long estuary"), the Connecticut flows for 234 miles from its headwaters in New Hampshire's First Connecticut Lake near the Quebec border southward through scenic north woods country and many rapids and over several dams to the Massachusetts border. It offers varied "big-lake" canoeing and river paddling with a few unrunnable sections; 15 dams along the route require carries of varying lengths. The New England Power Company maintains canoe campsites along the Connecticut at Wilder, Bellows Falls, and Vernon ponds. For detailed information, contact: New England Power Co., 20 Turnpike Rd., Westborough, MA 01581.

Extended backcountry canoe trips may also be taken on Otter Creek, the longest river within the state, which rises in the town of Dorset and flows 90 miles northward into Lake Champlain; on the Winooski River from Middlesex through the great valley of the Winooski, where it cuts through the main range of the Green Mountains, to Lake Champlain; the beautiful Lamoille River from Johnson to

Lake Champlain; the Missisquoi (Indian for "much waterfowl and grass") from Richford to Lake Champlain; the White River from Bethel to its junction with the Connecticut; and the West River from Townshend to the Connecticut. Many other streams mentioned in the *AMC River Guide: Volume II* (address below) and shown on the free *Vermont Guide to Fishing* map provide 1– or 2–day trips. "Big-water" canoeing may be found on Lake Champlain, Lake Memphremagog, Lake Willoughby—which lies on a V-shaped trough formed by the downfaulting of a block of the earth's crust between Mounts Pisgah and Hor in the Northeast Kingdom—and on Lake Bomoseen, the largest natural body of water entirely within the state, with an area of eight square miles.

The *Ledyard Canoe Club of Dartmouth*, Robison Hall, Hinman Box 6171, Hanover, NH 03755, offers canoe and kayak rentals for the Connecticut River (603)646–2753. Canoe trip information and rentals are provided by *Stowe Canoe Co.*, Rte. 100, Stowe 05672. Canoe rentals in the state are provided by *Burlington Rent-All*, 340 Dorset St., South Burlington 05401; *Canoe Imports*, 74 S. Willard St., Burlington 05401 (available for rent by the day, week, or month); *Chipman Point Marina & Campgrounds*, Chipman Point, Orwell 05760 (Lake Champlain, available by the day, week, month, or season): *Eddy's Marine and Sports Center*, Rte. 7S, Brandon 05733 (day or week); *Sailing Winds*, Box 93, Wells 05774 (rent by day, week, or month); *Sports Shops*, 139 Lake St., St. Albans 05478 (day or week); *Tudhope Marine Co.*, Rte. 2, North Hero 05474 (day, week, month, or season); and *Waterhouses*, RFD, Salisbury 05769 (day, week, month, or season).

The handy brochure *Vermont Boating Guide* is a necessity for anyone planning to do any boating in Vermont. It provides essential information on canoe trips and fishing access areas. There is plenty of info on historic Lake Champlain, including a listing of marinas on the lake and the services offered by each, and sources of rentals of boating equipment, lodging and camping areas with boating facilities available only to guests, as well as other facilities with available boat rentals on Lake Champlain and elsewhere. This brochure can be obtained free from: Agency of Development & Community Affairs, Montpelier 05602. A very helpful booklet available at no charge from the Division of Recreation & Department of Water Resources, Agency of Environmental Conservation, Montpelier 05602, is *Canoeing on the Connecticut River*. This booklet contains info on everything you will need to know before starting your trip on this river—water conditions, camping, fishing, dams, and falls. The various stretches of the river are described, section by section, and for the convenience of the reader a map is provided on the page facing each section's description. The most comprehensive guide is the *AMC River Guide: Volume II, Central & Southern New England*. This all-inclusive guide to the canoeable waterways of New England is published by Appalachian Mountain Club, 5 Joy St., Boston, MA 02108 ($6.00). Excellent, well-maintained camping facilities are available throughout Vermont in state forest and park recreation areas and in the Green Mountain National Forest. The Department of Forests & Parks operates 36 campgrounds with 2,100 campsites. The campgrounds open officially the Friday preceding Memorial Day and close October 12. There are youth group camping areas at Kettle Pond in the Groton State Forest and at the Underhill Recreation Area in the Mount Mansfield State Forest on the western slope of Mount Mansfield. Special areas in the Groton and Coolidge state forests have been designated as primitive campsites accessible only by foot trails. Some of the campgrounds have Green Mountain lean-tos, which are roofed shelters closed on three sides and fully open on the fourth. They have a 10x13–foot wooden floor about 15 inches above the ground and will accommodate up to five persons.

Detailed information about family camping, registration, time limits, campsite occupancy, pets, reservations, fees, regulations, youth group camping, primitive camping, and day use is contained in the *Vermont Guide to State Parks & Forest Recreation Areas*, available free from: Dept. of Forests & Parks, Montpelier 05602. The guide also contains a useful directory of state parks and forest recreation areas. *Day Hiking in Vermont*, a free guide published by the Green Mountain Club, Box 94, Rutland 05701, provides useful information on the Long Trail. Several useful publications are available from the Green Mountain Club (address above). A *Trail Map of the Mount Mansfield Region* is available for 50¢. The following GMC booklets describing trails and mountains outside the Long Trail system are available for 25¢ each, or five for $1: *Guide to the Lake Willoughby Area, Guide to Mount Cushman & Scraz Mountain; Guide to the Worcester Mountains; Guide to the Essex County Fire Tower Trails*. The Vermont section of the Appalachian trail winds for 134 miles through scenic mixed hardwood and evergreen forests, rolling hills, valleys, meadows, and mountains, from Hanover, New Hampshire, through the scenic highlands and backcountry of the Green Mountain National Forest to the Massachusetts border. The last 95–mile stretch from Sherburne Pass follows south along the famous Long Trail segment, which is maintained by the Green Mountain Club.

The bible for hikers wishing to explore this scenic route is the Appalachian Trail Conference's *Guide to the Appalachian Trail in New Hampshire and Vermont* (publication #22). The format of the book is such that it may be conveniently taken apart so that you need only take with you the section pertaining to the part of the trail you are traveling. The book is packed with essential general information such as trail markings, trail allocations and maintenance, trail precautions, and a section on the equipment you will need. There is a section on the history of the trail, a list of individual trail sections, and a helpful treatise on accommodations along the trail. The chapter on "The Long Trail in Vermont" is broken down into five detailed sections as are the other portions of the trail. You can send $6.60 for this book to: Appalachian Trail Conference, P.O. Box 236, Harpers Ferry, WV 25425. The *Dartmouth Outing Club Trail Guide* ($2.25, 110 pp., maps) provides a guide to trails in eastern Vermont, the Dartmouth regions, and between Hanover, New Hampshire, and Mount Moosilauke. Write: Dartmouth Outing Club, Dartmouth College, Hanover, NH 03755.

The free pamphlet *Day Hiking in Vermont* also contains descriptions of some favorite summer and early fall hikes along the Vermont portions of the trail complete with times allotted for actual hiking. This publication is available free from: Green Mountain Club, Box 94, Rutland 05701. Vermont is blessed with hundreds of miles of trails, abandoned railroad beds, and old logging roads that wind through the Green Mountain National Forest and the state forest backcountry areas, as well as at special ski areas, winter lodges, and ski touring centers. The 288–page *EMS Ski Touring Guide to New England* describes Vermont's major ski touring areas. The EMS guide contains regional maps, trail mileages, and driving directions. It may be obtained for $5.95 (plus 50¢ postage and handling) from: Eastern Mountain Sports, 1041 Commonwealth Ave., Boston, MA 02215.

A detailed *Vermont Ski Guide* may be obtained free from: the Agency of Development & Community Affairs, Montpelier 05602. The Vermont State Chamber of Commerce in Montpelier maintains 24–hour-a-day ski reports; phone (802)223–2957. A *New England Ski Touring Map* is available free by writing: New England Ski Touring Operators' Assn., Box 88, Rochester 05767. Most of Vermont's major touring trails are included in this useful new

publication. For complete information, the *Ski Touring Guide* ($3.50) may be obtained from: Ski Touring Council, West Hill Rd., Troy 05868.

Highways & Maps

Vermont's 2,294 miles of state highways wind through some of the most scenic highlands, valleys, evergreen forest and lake country, woodlands and farmlands in New England. The complete guide to the state's highway and road system is the *Vermont Official Transportation Map*, available free from: Dept. of Highways, Agency of Development & Community Affairs, Montpelier 05602. This attractive full-color map shows all highways and roads, interstate highways, historic sites, towns, museums, state parks and forests, wildlife management areas, campgrounds, state recreation areas, and natural features, including lakes, streams, and mountains.

Green Mountain National Forest & the Long Trail

The northern and southern units of this magnificent forest embrace 240,000 acres of some of the finest backcountry camping, alpine and cross-country skiing, backpacking, and hunting areas in New England. Dominated by the scenic rolling hills of the Green Mountain Range—dotted by rustic farms and charming New England villages with their red barns, historic country inns, white clapboard church steeples and covered bridges—the terrain varies from the rugged heights of Mount Ellen to the quiet secluded hollows of the Lye Brook Backwoods area. The Long Trail winds along the crest of the Green Mountains for 88 miles along a north-south axis and provides access to seldom-explored wilderness camping areas and remote brook trout ponds and beaver flows surrounded by beautiful meadows and mixed hardwood and evergreen forests inhabited by whitetail deer, black bear, and upland game birds. The major lakes in the forest region—Somerset Reservoir, Stratton Pond, Chittenden Reservoir, Silver Lake, and Lake Dunmore—hold smallmouth and largemouth bass, northern pike, walleye, rainbow trout, and panfish. Lake Dunmore with its deep, clear waters is one of Vermont's top-ranked lakes for trophy smallmouth bass, northern pike, and a few landlocked salmon. The remote pools and runs of the White and Mad rivers and the headwaters of the Deerfield River provide fishing for rainbow brook and brown trout in a majestic north country setting. U.S. Forest Service campgrounds are at Texas Falls, Chittenden Brook, Moosalamoo, White Rocks, Hapgood Pond, and Red Mill Brook.

The Lye Brook Backwoods area embraces 16,500 acres in the southern Green Mountain National Forest in Bennington County. The area acquired its name from Lye Brook, which flows northwesterly through the western half of the area. Remnants of old railroad grades and logging roads are found throughout the wilderness. Bourn Pond and numerous small beaver ponds and streams hold native populations of brook and brown trout. The Wallingford Pond Wilderness to the north, near the White Rocks area, embraces 20,000 acres of upland ridges, ponds, and beaver meadows. This outstanding primitive camping area is dominated by the beautiful blue waters of Wallingford Pond, the last large unspoiled natural pond in the state. The Bristol Cliffs Wilderness takes in 4,900 acres at the northern end of the Green Mountain National Forest. The cliffs on the western side of South Mountain provide a spectacular view of the Lake Champlain Valley and Adirondack Mountains in New York. Major features include the New Haven River and two remote natural ponds, North and Gilmore, that support beaver colonies. The backwoods is an outstanding hiking and hunting area for deer, black bear, and ruffed grouse.

The Long Trail is a scenic "wilderness" footpath that winds through beautiful high country forests of evergreens and mixed hardwoods along the crest of the Green Mountains for 262 miles from the Massachusetts boundary north to the Quebec border. The trail passes close to 400 high country lakes and countless beaver ponds, many of which offer superb fishing for native brook trout, bass, and some arm-length chain pickerel. Nearly 100 approach and side trails supplement the Long Trail, creating a trail system of over 435 miles. This system traverses public lands, both state and federal, and also makes extensive use of private lands, thanks to cooperating landowners. Hikers can show their appreciation to all landowners by treating their property as carefully as they would their own.

VACATION/ LODGING GUIDE

Information Sources, Maps & Access

For detailed travel information, contact the Supervisor, Green Mountain National Forest, 151 West St., Rutland, VT 05701 (802)775–2579. The full-color *Green Mountain National Forest Map*, available for 50¢ from the Forest Supervisor shows highways, secondary roads, old logging roads, and major features of the outlying areas, including Okemo, Townshend, Grafton, Proctor, Piper, Rupert, Calvin Coolidge, George Aiken, West Rutland, and Rothbury state forests as well as Lake Bomoseen, Lake Champlain, Lake St. Catharine, Connecticut River, and Wimona, Sunset, and Hortonia lakes. The Appalachian Trail is clearly marked, as are landing fields for planes, fire lookout towers, district ranger stations, spot elevation in feet, forest service recreation sites with and without camping facilities, other recreation sites without camping facilities, winter sports areas, boat access areas, points of interest, trail huts or cabins, trail shelters, forest supervisors' headquarters, and covered bridges. The reverse side of the map contains detailed information on how to get to the Green Mountains. Some notes on the history of the area are provided—this area played a prominent role in the era of the pioneer timber harvests. In 1739 Vermont's first sawmill was making lumber of the virgin white pine, oak, and hemlock forests. By 1835 (12 years after the opening of the Champlain-Hudson River Canal) the towering forests on the slopes of the Green Mountains had been razed.

For specific fishing, hunting, camping, and cross-country skiing information and a free *Bristol Cliffs Wilderness Map & Guide*, write to: Forest Supervisor (address above). Indispensable for Long Trail hikers is the 152–page *Guidebook of the Long Trail* ($3), available from: Green Mountain Club, P.O. Box 94, Rutland 05701. The GMC also publishes the following free leaflets: *Suggestions for Use of the Long Trail by Backpacking Groups* and *Suggestions for Use of the Long Trail in Winter.* The Appalachian Trail Conference's *Guide to the Appalachian Trail in New Hampshire and Vermont* (publication #22) also has an entire section devoted to the Long Trail. This guide may be ordered for $6.00 from: ATC, P.O. Box 236, Harpers Ferry, WV 25425. The forest is reached via several of

New England's most scenic auto routes, including the Calvin Coolidge Memorial Highway (U.S. 4), New England Heritage Trail (U.S. Highway 7), Vermont Routes 9, 100, 11, 125, and 73, and Interstate Routes 89 and 91. Overnight accommodations, supplies, meals and equipment rentals are available at Rutland, Manchester Center, Middlebury, Rochester, and scores of scenic New England hamlets and rural villages.

Gateways & Accommodations

Arlington

(Pop. 1,900; zip code 05250; area code 802.) Located in the southwestern part of Vermont, Arlington has maintained its homespun New England charm, despite great popularity among summer tourists. Settled in 1763, the town's past is laced with the historic enterprises of notables such as Ethan Allen, The Green Mountain Boys and Thomas Chittenden. St. James Church and Cemetery, a testimony to the town's Episcopalian history contains many old headstones with unusual inscriptions. Ethan Allen's first wife, Mary Brownson is buried here. The Martha Canfield Library, one of the state's oldest libraries, with some 4,000 volumes is open to the public. Candle Mill Village built in 1764 by Remember Baker of the Green Mountain Boys, includes a gristmill and candlemaking demonstrations and museum. Area attractions include the township of Shaftsbury, site of the first Baptist Church in Vermont, and the scenic mountain township of Glastenbury with a population of seven. Arlington is the site of much fishing activity on the Batten Kill. Accommodations: *Candlelight Motel* (rates: $19–27 double), with 17 excellent rooms, breakfast room, heated pool, fishing in the Batten Kill, one mile north of town on U.S. 7 (375–6647).

Barre

(Pop. 10,800; zip code 05641; area code 802.) Located in the northeast section of Vermont, Barre is the site of the world's largest granite quarries and granite fishing plant. Barre is a bustling, industrial center situated in contrasting country surroundings. The lively traffic-filled Main Street is dotted with century-old Georgian Colonial style houses recalling this historic town's past with a granite industry dating back to 1812. Visitors can see Rock of Ages Quarry and Craftsman Center, including open quarries and highly skilled artisans creating monuments. The Robert Burns Monument, considered one of the finest granite sculptures in the world, is located on the town's high school lawn. Goddard College provides concerts and theatre. The area also features 24,000–acre Groton State Forest with swimming, fishing, boating, museums and four campgrounds. Accommodations: *The Hollow Motel* (rates: $24–30 double), with 26 superb rooms, swimming pool and sauna at 278 S. Main St. (479–9313); *Sir Anthony Motel* (rates: $20–26 double), with 45 excellent rooms, dining room, cocktail lounge, swimming pool at 173 S. Main St. (476–6678).

Bennington

(Pop. 14,600; zip code 05201; area code 802), located in southwest Vermont, is a gateway to the rural and historic riches of the state. Historically the town was the headquarters of Ethan Allen's Green Mountain Boys during the strife between New York and Vermont. The site of Catamount Tavern, gathering place of the group, can be visited. Old Bennington, two miles west of Bennington, is the site of the original town and hosts a plethora of historic landmarks including colonial houses, church and common. Historic sightseeing includes the Old First Church built in 1762 and Vermont's oldest church; Old Burying Ground, with the graves of those who fell in the Battle of Bennington; the Bennington Museum with Vermont artifacts and Grandma Moses paintings; Bennington Battle Monu-

ment, built in 1891, then the tallest battle monument in the world at 306 feet. Shaftsbury State Park on 26–acre Lake Shaftsbury has swimming, boating and fishing. Annual events in the area include Bennington Battle Day, Antique and Classic Car Show and Antique Show. Accommodations: *Darling Kelly's Motel* (rates: $24–28 double), with 23 excellent guest rooms in charming motel with beautiful view of the Green Mountains in scenic location, heated pool, on U.S. 7, 1¼ miles south of town (442–2322); *New Englander—a Best Western Motel* (rates: $27–36 double), with 51 superb guest rooms, Heritage House Restaurant, cocktail lounge, coffeeshop, heated pool, two miles north of town on U.S. 7 Business Route at 220 Northside Dr. (442–6311); *Paradise Motor Inn & Restaurant* (rates: $28–42 double), with 76 superb guest rooms and family units, heated pool on Vermont 9 at 141 W. Main St. (442–8351).

Killington

(Pop. 50; zip code 05751; area code 802.) Located in the eastern central part of the state, Killington is the gateway to many of Vermont's key winter and summer recreational facilities. Mount Killington ski area is one of the east's most popular slopes with a full range of alpine skiing, cross-country trails, and snowmobiling. A 3½ mile long gondola tramway reaches to the top of 4,241-foot Killington Peak for a breathtaking five-state view. A ¼ mile walk leads to the top of the mountain's summit, where the state was christened "Verd-Mont" in 1763. The area is known for year-round activities including the splendid autumn foliage, fishing, boating, golf, summer theatre, horseback riding, hiking, tennis, and gift and craft shops. Accommodations: (see "Lodges & Resorts" below).

Londonderry

(Pop. 1,000; zip code 05148; area code 802) is situated on the banks of the West River surrounded by forested ridges on the south. Londonderry is the gateway to the popular Vermont ski areas of Magic Mountain and Stratton Mountain. Sightseeing in the area encompasses the quaint Universalist Chapel in Londonderry and the restored village of Weston. In Weston visit the Farrar-Mansur House built in 1797; the Weston Playhouse with murals illustrating the history of the American theatre; the Wilder Memorial Library, built in 1820 as part of the Wilder homestead and the Ross House built by a shoemaker named Emerson Ross in 1830. Each autumn Londonderry hosts the Stratton Arts Festival, with paintings, photography, sculpture, crafts and crafts demonstrations and performing arts. Accommodations (see also "Lodges & Resorts" below): *The Post-Horn Motel* (rates: $26 double), with 15 excellent guest rooms, restaurant, cocktail lounge at Magic Mountain on Vermont Highway 11 (824–3131).

Manchester

(Pop. 1,500; zip code 05254; area code 802). Located in the southwestern portion of the state, Manchester has maintained its position as one of Vermont's favorite summer resort areas for hundreds of years. The town is the headquarter's of the nationally renowned Orvis Company—manufacturer's of outdoor sporting gear and publisher's of the *Orvis Catalog*. Orvis operates the Museum of American Fly Fishing here, just south of town on U.S. 7. The famed Batten Kill flows through here and is popular with fishermen throughout spring and summer. Nearby Dorset is the home base of *Fly Fisherman* magazine. Visitors such as Mrs. Abraham Lincoln, Mrs. U.S. Grant, President Taft and Theodore Roosevelt have graced Manchester. The combination of wide, shady streets, beautiful mountain surroundings and the nearby burgeoning ski areas of Big Bromley, Stratton Mountain, Magic Mountain and others have all played a part in the continued popularity of the town. Mount Equinox, soon to be the site of a Perrier bottling plant, the highest

peak in the Taconic Range; it rises to 3,835 feet providing a spectacular view, along with picnic and parking areas. Emerald Lake State Park and Mt. Aeolus provide outdoor activities akin to the area. Studio Tavern, site of much of Ethan and Ira Allen's activities; Soldiers Monument; and Burr and Burton Seminary's Gymnasium, site of the annual Southern Vermont Artists' Exhibition are all part of Manchester's attractions. Accommodations (see "Barrows House" below): *Erdman's Eyrie Motel* (rates: $30 double), with 15 excellent rooms and guest cottage, breakfast, trout pond in beautiful location in East Dorset on U.S. 7 (362–1208); *Four Winds Country Motel* (rates: $22–34 double), with 18 superb guest rooms, breakfast service, tennis courts, golf in scenic location in Manchester Center 05255 on U.S. 7 (362–1105); *Palmer House Motel* (rates: $39.90 double), with 28 superb rooms, heated pool, tennis on U.S. 7 in Manchester Center 05255 (362–3600); *Weathervane Motel* (rates: $32 double), with 20 luxury rooms in beautiful, scenic location on U.S. 7 (362–2444).

Middlebury

(Pop. 6,500; zip code 05753; area code 802). Located in central Vermont, Middlebury has preserved much of the charm and gracious style of the early Vermont settlers. Both a summer and winter resort, many of its activities center around Middlebury College, which dates back to 1800. Old Stone Row on the campus includes Painter's Hall, the oldest college building in the state (1815) and Starr Library with a fine collection of works by American writers including Robert Frost. The college also has an 18–hole golf course, and a snow bowl which hosts a winter carnival. Other area attractions include the Vermont State Craft Center at Frog Hollow; The Sheldon Art Museum with bits of Vermontiana; The Congregational Church facing Middlebury's Common; the Addison County Fair Exhibition Hall and tours of Vermont homes. Accommodations (see "Middlebury Inn" below): *Blue Spruce Motel* (rates: $18.90–23.10 double), with 18 good rooms and family units, three miles south of town on U.S. 7 (388–7512).

Newfane

(Pop. 900; zip code 05345; area code 802.) Located in southwest Vermont near Brattleboro, this town dates back to 1553. The town's elm-shaded green is flanked by a traditional assortment of Vermont-style buildings. The charm of Vermont's small townships can truly be appreciated in well-preserved, charming Newfane. Sightseeing includes the Windham County Courthouse on the green, considered one of the most beautiful in Vermont and a classic example of the Greek Revival trend; the second oldest hotel in the state, the Newfane Inn; the Congregational Church featuring crisp architectural lines typical of New England buildings. The area serves as a gateway to the mountainous wildlife areas of the state. Townshend State Forest and Jamaica State Park both provide camping and recreational activities which take advantage of the area's varied outdoor offerings. Accommodations: *Four Columns Inn* (rates: $30–45 double), with 14 charming guest rooms, formal dining room, cocktail lounge, at 230 West St. (365–7713); *Old Newfane Inn* (rates: $40 double), with nine charming colonial guest rooms, formal dining room, cocktail lounge on Vermont Highway 30 (365–4427).

Peru—Gateway to Mt. Bromley & Hapgood Pond Recreation Area

(Pop. 240; zip code 05152; area code 802) is a small village serving as a gateway to the fine ski areas of Bromley Mountain and the Green Mountain range. Peru contains homes, town stores and buildings painted white in the neat, severe lines typical of rural New England architecture. Nearby Hapgood Pond Recreation Area, has

been developed by the National Forest Service. Picnicking, boating, fishing, and camping can all be enjoyed here. Accommodations (see "Johnny Seesaw's" below): *Bromley Sun Lodge* (rates: $26–30 double), with 51 excellent guest rooms, restaurant, cocktail lounge, two miles west of town on Vermont Highway 11 (824–6400).

Plymouth—Gateway to Calvin Coolidge State Forest

(Pop. 280; zip code 05056; area code 802) is tucked away in southern central Vermont, best known to sports people as a center for skiing at Round Top Mountain. Scenic and recreational riches of the Plymouth area can be found at Echo Lake, Lake Amherst, Mount Tom, and Black River. History buffs know Plymouth to be the birthplace of Calvin Coolidge. Visitors can see the village store where Coolidge was born, which now operates as a museum, his hillside cemetery, and the President Coolidge Homestead site of his swearing-in as president in 1923. The Calvin Coolidge State Forest lies just beyond Plymouth where foot trails lead to scenic high points. Accommodations: *Farmbrook Motel* (rates: $22–23 double); with 10 good rooms and family units, trout fishing, three miles north of town on Vermont Highway 100A (672–3621).

Rutland

(Pop. 18,900; zip code 05701; area code 802). Located in central southern Vermont in the valley of Otter Creek, Rutland is a hub for much of the state's commerce, industry, and a gateway to the Green Mountain National Forest. It is known as Marble City; the world's deepest marble quarry can be found in West Rutland. Rutland has long been a commercial center, dating back to the 1700's when it was popular for its rich beaver trade. During the Revolutionary War it was a site of a northern outpost and later became the headquarters for state troops. Vermont's oldest newspaper, the *Rutland Herald* was founded here in 1794, and has maintained daily publication since 1861. In spite of Rutland's commercial and industrial past and present, the natural beauty of the area has been largely undisturbed. The Green Mountain peaks of Killington, Shrewsbury and Pico rise to the east and the Taconic Range graces the western view. In town sights include the Main Street park—once the site of the courthouse, jail, pillory and whipping post, it is now a quiet park; the Chaffee Art Center, across from the Main Street Park, featuring art collections and special events. Area attractions include a Marble Exhibit, the scenic Otter Valley Railroad in Proctor 05765 (459–2026) and Hubbardton Battlefield and Museum (273–2282). Annual events include the Mid-Vermont Artists' Outdoor Show and the Vermont State Fair. Accommodations: *Holiday Inn* (rates: $32–38 double), with 100 excellent rooms, restaurant, cocktail lounge, heated pool, on U.S. 7, two miles south of town (775–1911); *Howard Johnson's Motor Lodge* (rates: $34–40 double), with 100 excellent rooms, restaurant, heated pool and sauna on U.S. 7, two miles south of town (775–4303).

Stowe—Gateway to Mt. Mansfield

(Pop. 2,390; zip code 05672; area code 802), in north central Vermont, is one of the state's most popular headquarters for winter and summer sport enthusiasts. Nearby Mt. Mansfield and Spruce Peak ski areas boast long seasons and steep terrain. During the winter months Stowe bustles with the full range of activity from skiers and winter vacationers. Warmer weather attracts hikers, golfers, tennis players, and sightseers. The area offers a plentiful assortment of backroad tours, annual events and interesting activities. Contact Stowe Area Assn. Inc. (253–7321), for details. The Stowe Historical Society Museum in the village houses Vermont artifacts and area history items. The Green Mt. Inn, a tavern built in 1833 to accommodate stagecoach travelers, now serves modern-day tourists.

Mt. Mansfield reaches 4,393 feet, making it the highest peak in Vermont. Several of the mountain's peaks resemble human profiles. Much of the five-mile-long mountain area is encompassed by Mt. Mansfield State Forest. The summit, with its spectacular view can be reached via the Long Trail, as well as several additional routes. Mt. Mansfield State Park provides camping, fishing, boating, and picnicking facilities. Mt. Mansfield has some of Vermont's finest downhill and cross-country ski terrain. Hunting and game refuge areas can also be found at Mt. Mansfield. Accommodations: *Golden Eagle Motel* (rates: $20–44), with 60 superb alpine guest rooms and family units with fireplaces in some, heated pool and sauna, and full range of outdoor recreation activities including trout fishing, cross-country skiing and tennis in beautiful setting just north of town on Vermont 108 (253–4811); *Green Mountain Inn* (rates: $30–70 double), with 61 charming inn and motel rooms, dining room at 212 Main St. (253–7301); *Spruce Pond Inn* (rates: $28–36 double), with 14 superb guest rooms and New England dining room, trout pond, 1¼ miles south of town on Vermont Highway 100 (253–4828); *Toll House Motor Inn* (rates: $65–96 Modified American Plan double), with 58 superb guest rooms and family units, dining room, cocktail lounge, tennis, trout fishing, near ski areas, six miles northwest of town on Vermont 108 (253–7311).

Waitsfield—Gateway to the Mad River

(Pop. 840; zip code 05673; area code 802). Located in central Vermont the village is situated along river flats surrounded by hills. Waitsfield acts as a gateway to the ski areas of Glen Ellen and Mad River Glen. The town dates back to 1789, when it was settled by General Benjamin Wait. Visitors can view the Federal Church, a white clean-lined structure, and the yellow brick Joslin Memorial Library. The Bundy Art Gallery houses exhibitions of contemporary art with a sculpture garden. Crafts are exhibited annually at the Mad River Valley Craft Show. Accommodations: *Madbush Chalet* (rates: $29–62 double, seasonal), with 23 superb guest rooms in beautiful alpine valley setting with natural swimming pool, sauna, tennis court, three miles south of town on Vermont Hwy. 100 (496–3966).

Warren—Gateway to Sugarloaf

(Pop. 600; zip code 05674; area code 802). Located in central Vermont between Warren Pinnacle and Sugarloaf Mountain, Warren acts as a gateway to some of the state's finest ski areas. Outdoor enthusiasts can also enjoy Granville Gulf State Park, located be-

tween Warren and Granville. The park is densely wooded and offers a scenic six-mile ride to Moss Glen Falls, considered Vermont's most beautiful waterfall. Area attractions include The Natural Bridge of Stone, a photogenic sight with a 12–foot arch and the United Church, situated on a knoll with a stonewall base in the center of the town. Accommodations: (see "Sugarbush Inn" below).

West Dover—Gateway to Mt. Snow

(Pop. 100; zip code 05356; area code 802). Located in south-central Vermont, this town is headquarters for skiers destined for the slopes of Mt. Snow. The mountain ski resort has a gondola tramway to the summit and some of Vermont's best skiing. Autumn foliage attracts sightseers and hikers as do warm weather sports such as golf at Mt. Snow Country Club (464–3333) and riding, tennis, swimming at Mt. Snow. In the late summer and early autumn the Festival of Craft at Mt. Snow hosts local artisans' exhibits of crafts from glass to graphics. Accommodations: *Mountaineer Lodge at Mt. Snow* (rates: $24 double), with 22 excellent guest rooms, dining room, tennis court at foot of Mt. Snow off Vermont Highway 100 (464–5406); *Tamarack at Mt. Snow* (rates: $24–27 double), with 17 excellent guest rooms, dining room, swimming pool at Mt. Snow (464–8850); *Yankee Doodle Lodge* (rates: $25 double), with 22 superb ski season guest rooms, dining room, fireplaces and lounge, ½ miles north of West Dover on Vermont Highway 100 (464–5591).

White River Junction

(Pop. 2,380; zip code 05001; area code 802), located in the east-central part of Vermont, is aptly named as the meeting place of the White and Connecticut Rivers. The town has an industrial ambience created by the network of railroads and serves primarily as a gateway for those headed for the activities at Dartmouth College in Hanover, NH, and Woodstock. Visitors can see nearby Quechee Gorge on the Ottauquechee River. Accommodations: *Holiday Inn* (rates: $40 double), with 140 excellent rooms, restaurant, cocktail lounge, swimming pool, kennel at junction of Interstate Highways 91 & 89 (295–7537); *Howard Johnson's Motor Lodge* (rates: $28–33 double), with 112 excellent rooms, restaurant, cocktail lounge, heated pool and sauna at junction of Interstates 89 & 91 (295–3015).

Woodstock

(Pop. 2,600; zip code 05091; area code 802) is located in east-central Vermont, on the banks of the Ottauquechee River, overlooked by Mt. Tom. Woodstock has tenaciously maintained its old-Vermont style and is considered one of the most charming, picturesque towns in New England, with a particularly noteworthy green. Historically Woodstock was a center of the state's publishing activities. Visitors can view the Norman Williams Public Library with one of the largest book and 18th– and 19th–century newspaper collections in the state. The Library also houses the Williams Collection of Japanese Art. The green's sights include the Windsor County Courthouse, a Georgian Colonial style building built in 1855; and the Old White Meeting House, which contains a bell cast by Paul Revere and Sons. There are many beautiful old homes lining Woodstock's streets such as the Johnson House, the Bailey House and the Dana House. These homes, along with others, contain interesting area artifacts and architecture. The town is proud of the relatively new covered bridge built in 1968—the first one built in Vermont since 1895. Recreationally Woodstock is popular as both a summer and winter resort. Riders, golfers, sightseers, and fishermen all find facilities in Woodstock. Mt. Tom, Sonneberg and other nearby areas provide fine downhill and cross-country skiing and tobogganing in beautiful unspoiled settings. Accommodations (see "Woodstock Inn" below): *Valley View Motel* (rates: $18–26 double), with 20

excellent rooms, restaurant, cocktail lounge six miles north of town on Vermont Highway 12 (457–2123).

Lodges, Resorts & Country Inns

★★★★*Barrows House at Dorset-in-the-Mountains* will take you back to the charm of colonial New England. This famous 200–year old inn, in the heart of the picture-book rural village of Dorset, flanked by the Green Mountains, is situated on spacious, park-like grounds with colorful gardens near white clapboard houses and the village green. Four season activities include superb trout fishing in the trophy stretches of the nationally renowned Batten Kill and Metawee rivers and for brook trout in the headwater beaver ponds of Otter Creek near Dorset Mountain; upland game bird and deer hunting in the Green Mountain National Forest; cross-country skiing and hiking on backcountry trails; alpine skiing at Stratton, Bromley, and Magic Mountains. The inn is noted as a winter cross-country skiing center with a doorfront trail to begin your exploring of the countryside. The inn provides a hearty breakfast, picnic lunch with a sauna and hot toddy on your return. The inn facilities include a swimming pool, two tennis courts, bicycle rentals from "The Stable", a gazebo, field house, croquet green, badminton court, main inn and delightful, beautifully appointed colonial guest cottages. During winter, "the Stable" houses a cross-country ski shop. Modified American Plan rates are $36–46 per room. Area attractions include the Dorset Playhouse, scenic drives, barn sales, and auctions. For additional information, contact: Charles & Marilyn Schubert, Barrows House, Dorset, VT 05251 (802)867–4455.

★★*Blue Gentian Lodge* at the base of Magic Mountain is a small, cozy chalet offering 14 comfortable rooms to ski home to at the end of the day. Stratton and Bromley Ski Areas are minutes away. Nearby Viking Touring Center provides cross-country ski lessons and equipment to explore the many trails and frozen ponds of the surrounding mountains. The pine-panelled dining room features home cooking and hot, freshly baked breads on every table. The rustic living room, with a blazing fire and an authentic, stuffed mountain lion, poised and ready to spring, is a perfect place to b.y.o. and relax. There is a game room with bumper pool and TV. In the summer trails open for hiking, and the adjoining ponds and heated pool offer swimming. Tennis, golf, fishing, and horseback riding are all close by. In autumn, the ponds reflect the brilliant foliage. Winter rates are $31 per person double occupancy in a large room and $25 per person for a small room. Rates include breakfast and dinner. Ski week rates are $120 per person from Sunday night dinner to Friday breakfast in a large room and $100 per person in the smaller rooms. Summer rates are $24 for a large single room, $24 small double, $38 larger rooms, and $32 smaller. For more information write: Blue Gentian Lodge, Londonderry, VT 05148 (802)824–5908.

★★★★*Blueberry Hill Inn & Ski Touring Center* is a small Green Mountain country inn with a heritage dating back to 1813 and renowned for elegant, gourmet cooking. This charming four-season inn, located west of Middleburg Gap of the Long Trail, is also one of Vermont's foremost ski-touring centers in the Green Mountain National Forest. Cross-country skiers have access to over 30 miles of groomed trails—from the scenic Silver Lake Trail to the 7-mile trek to the Sucker Brook Shelter on the Long Trail. They offer a complete ski shop with rentals and an expert staff to advise you on trails, waxing, lessons, and gear. Other activities include picnic tours, summer hikes, moonlight tours, inn-to-inn tours, and the American Hennessy Marathon. The inn is small; limited to eight rooms, all with private baths, with a charm you would expect to find only in an early 1800's country inn. Many antiques and homemade

quilts embellish the rooms. The meals are family style, all prepared by Martha's Clark's imaginative gourmet cooking, and pleasantly presented and served in her own style, which is at once informal yet elegant. Blueberry Hill does not have a liquor license, so be sure to bring a bottle of your own choice. Modified American Plan rates are $40 per person per day. For additional information contact Martha and Tony Clark, Blueberry Hill, Goshen, VT 05733 (802)247–6735.

★★★★*Churchill House Inn & Ski Touring Center*, located west of Brandon Gap on the Long Trail, is a three-story farmhouse built in 1871, furnished with high oak bedsteads, blanket chests, and parlor and franklin stoves to retain its 19th–century charm. The Churchill House Inn has organized ski tours in winter, biking tours, hiking and canoeing tours, fly fishing, and a unique renaissance tour, all involving nightly stays in a succession of small country inns throughout the Green Mountains. These tours offer a variety of fine cuisines, a survey of 19th–century Vermont country architecture, exploration of streams, rivers, mountain paths, and backcountry roads. The renaissance tour, organized by the Churchill House Inn, relives the days when inns served as a haven of rest and refreshment after a long day's journey, by offering travel in the mode of our forefathers, and the hospitality of their day. Travel by steam locomotive one day; cross-country by foot the next; cycle; canoe down Vermont's longest river, Otter Creek; horseback ride across country, through woods, and canter across open meadows. Six inns highlight the renaissance tour, offering unique accommodations each night, gourmet specialties, and a fine variety of tap rooms to discuss the days adventure. Similar tours, each traveling from inn to inn, have been organized around hiking, biking, canoeing, fly fishing, and cross-country skiing. In addition, the Churchill House Inn has its own cross-country ski center, offering 22 miles of its own ski-touring trails, and a ski shop specializing in rentals ($7), group lessons ($4), private lessons ($8), and guided tours. In the spring, the nearby Neshobe River is privately stocked with trout, and the surrounding mountain streams, beaver ponds, and rivers offer superlative trout fishing. The Churchill House Inn has its own tackle shop, and rents canoes. Five days of guided fishing instruction and short excursions are available. Churchill House can also organize week-long fishing trips, with nightly stays at three other charming country inns. Rooms, with meals as tempting as pot roast simmered in cranberry and horseradish sauce, run $32–38 per person for a double room, and $40 per person for a single room. For more information write: The

Churchill House Inn, RFD 3, Route 73 East, Brandon, VT 05733 (802)247–3300.

★★★*Combes Family Inn* is situated on acres of rolling meadows in the heart of Vermont's mountain and lake region. The year-round inn is a quaint, newly restored century-old farmhouse. There's swimming and fishing at nearby Echo Lake, bicycling, hiking, picnicking (the inn will be happy to prepare a box lunch), plus golf and tennis nearby. Ski touring enthusiasts will enjoy acres of open meadows and back roads. Tobogganing can be enjoyed on several of the inn's packed runs, using one of their toboggans. Skiing is minutes away at Okemo and Round Top Ski areas. Killington, Pico, Bromley, Magic, and Stratton Mountains are a half-hour away. The area also offers small New England towns for sightseeing, the Coolidge Birthplace and Museum, Steamtown U.S.A. in Bellows Falls, the Alpine slide at Bromley, and cheese and maple factories. And of course, the fall foliage is not to be missed. The inn features comfortable accommodations at the Farmhouse or in adjoining motel units. The "Barnboard" room is the inn's site for cocktails, cards and conversation. Meals are offered on the Modified American Plan and hearty Vermont-style fare is served. The inn is especially proud of the farm-fresh quality of their food and invites you to pick vegetables from their summer garden for your dinner. A ski package at Okemo

Mountain is available, including lodging, breakfast and dinner at the inn and lift tickets at Okemo. Rates: MAP at the inn with shared bath: $18–20. European plan (no meals) at the inn: $10–12. Motel units MAP with private bath and two double beds: $26. Motel unit European plan $18. Ski packages run from $205 for a week for adults to $87 for a three-day mid-week adult package. Children's rates are available. For further information contact: Combes Family Inn, Lake Rescue, R.F.D. 1, Ludlow, VT 05149 (802)228–8799.

★★*Cranberry Inn*, close to Magic Mountain, Stratton, Bromley, Okemo, Ascutney, Round Top, Killington, and Pico Peak ski areas, is a traditional, gabled country inn, built in 1810 and surrounded by forests and meadows perfect for cross-country skiing. A warm hearth to relax by, comfortable lodgings, and country-style meals are offered skiers at this quaint Vermont country inn. In autumn, hike the hills brilliant with red maple and yellow oak. Spring is the time of maple-sugar festivals and country auctions and violets blooming in the woods. In summertime take old-fashioned locomotive rides in nearby Steamboat U.S.A., fish the streams, and enjoy summer theatre in Weston. Cranberry Inn offers rooms with private bath per-person double occupancy at $27. Rooms with shared bath are $25 per person double occupancy. Five-day ski rates, from Sunday dinner to Friday breakfast are offered at a 15% discount. For details write: Cranberry Inn, Chester, VT 05143 (802)875–2525.

★★★*Dostal's Resort on Magic Mountain* is a charming Tyrolean chalet within walking distance of Magic Mountains slopes. After a day of challenging skiing on Magic Mountain's two dozen runs, or exploring the countryside at the nearby Viking Ski Touring Center, relax in a whirlpool bath, or take a dip in the heated indoor pool. Sink down in a comfortable sofa by a roaring fire in the cozy living room embellished with hanging plants. Dostal's sports a billiard room, and an intimate cocktail lounge built of wood and brick with a high beamed ceiling. After a delicious dinner, dance to live music, join in the singing, or catch an old movie on color cable TV in your room. Rates for a single room including meals are $37. Double occupancy per person is $29.50 weekdays and $35 weekends and holidays. Bunk accommodations on weekdays run $23 per person and $25 weekdays and holidays. Dostal's Resort also offers five-day special rate packages from Sunday night to Friday morning, for $165 single accommodation, $129 per person double occupancy, and $100 for bunk accommodations. Additional rooms are available in the Chamois Lodge, an annex of Dostal's. Rates are $34 single occupancy, $26 per person double occupancy weekdays and $32 weekends and holidays. Five day special rates in Chamois Lodge are $135 five day single occupancy, and $115 per person double occupancy. For information write: Dostal's, Magic Mountain, Londonderry, VT 05148 (802)824–6700.

★★★*Edgemont Condominiums at Killington* offer spacious, modern living just ½ mile from the Snowshed lifts at the base of Killington Ski Complex. Ski home after an exhilarating day on Killington's 50 runs, over a half-mile ski trail that leads through the woods right to your door. Cook up a big dinner in the modern kitchen, or relax by a roaring fire in comfortably furnished living rooms with wall-to-wall carpeting. The Edgemont offers one bedroom units, with a separate bedroom with a double bed, a living room with a sofa bed, dining area, fireplace and fully equipped kitchen, for a maximum of four people. Rates vary according to what part of the ski season apartments are rented. Generally, for a ski week, one bedroom units range from $185–290. Weekend rates $90–135. Two bedroom units for a maximum of six people range between $300–475 a ski week and $130–220 weekends. Three bedroom units, with bunkbeds in two of the bedrooms, a double bed in the master bedroom and a

living room sofa bed accommodating eight people range $340–530 a ski week and $150–245 for a ski weekend. For more information write: Edgemont at Killington, 551 Killington Rd., Killington, VT 05751 (802)422–3333.

★★★*Edson Hill Manor & Ski Touring Center at Stowe.* Situated halfway between Stowe and Mt. Mansfield, Edson Hill Manor is a large country house secluded on 400 acres of private woodlands and fields. Skiers will enjoy the comfort of the pine-panelled living room, with a roaring fireplace, and delicious home-cooked country meals in the candlelit dining room. A new cross-country ski center at Edson Hill Manor rents cross-country skis plus the wax of the day for $7.50 full day and $4.75 half day. Special family rates are available on ski rentals. One hour group lessons are offered for $6 and hour long private lessons are available for $10. Fireside lunches are served in the manor lounge. Ski the deep, quiet powder in the surrounding woods through snow-laden pine and birch, or ramble over the fields in snowshoes. The toboggan slope by the manor is floodlit at night. Pine-panelled rooms, many with fireplaces, are $44–48 for a double room. Studio suites accommodating two-six people with fireplaces range from $34–52 depending on the number of people and the location of the rooms. Wing apartments, with one double and two single rooms, plus a private bath, are $38–42. Single rooms are available ranging from $38–46, bunk rooms are $38. Suites accommodating two-four persons with kitchenettes are $40–44. All rates include hearty country-style dinners and breakfasts. Edson Hill Manor also offers a lodging and ski touring package, including five nights' lodging with breakfasts and dinners, ski rentals and lessons for $252–261 in fireplace rooms. In the summer, fish the nearby brooks for trout, or choose a horse from the stables and take advantage of the guided trail rides and riding instruction. Manor guests have privileges at the new Stowe Country Club, with its 18-hole golf course. For more information write: Laurence P. Heath, Edson Hill Manor, Route #1, Stowe, Vermont 05672 (802)253–7371.

★★★*The Fox Run* is a four-season resort with a lovely view of Mt. Okemo. Skiing on Mt. Okemo is just a mile away and Round Top, Killington, Pico Peak, Stratton, Bromley, Magic Mountain and other ski resorts are no more than 45 minutes away. The area also offers excellent cross-country skiing, with instructors and rentals at the resort. The resort also boasts a deep, dark, spring-fed pond well-stocked with rainbows and browns. The nearby Black River offers stream fishing. There is a 9–hole (34 par) golf course, designed by golf-course architect Frank Duane, with instruction available, a 25-meter heated swimming pool with instruction, championship tennis courts with professional instruction, and an ice skating rink. The area also provides fine hiking and horseback riding. In addition to the activities the resort is located in a beautiful area for fall foliage sightseeing, especially the four mile drive up Mt. Okemo. Shops, summer theatre, and antique barns are all nearby. The resort offers 14 large double bedrooms, each with TV. There are also 12 loft suites with two double beds, two twin beds, and TV. There is a cocktail lounge, the Fletcher Room with colonial decor and Franklin stove, a playroom for children, and the Red Fox dining room. Babysitting is available and there is entertainment every Friday and Saturday night. Rates include meals on the Modified American Plan and the resort offers a dinner menu consisting of 10 entrees featuring steak, shrimp and fresh fish. Rates: $39–41 per person per day. Ski weeks, $119–250; ski weekend, $51–110. Juniors 12 and under are half price as extra persons in a room and are served children's portions from the regular menu. For further information contact: The Fox Run Resort, P.O. Box D, Ludlow, Vermont 05149 (802)228–8101.

★★★*Golden Stage Inn*, once a stagecoach stop and a refuge on the underground railroad, has a colorful history of warmth and hospitality, which its present owners have exceeded. Centered near six major ski areas, Okemo Mt., Bromley, Ascutney, Round Top Mt. Killington and Pico Peak, the Golden Stage Inn is nestled on four acres of woods and surrounded by Green Mountain forests. The wrap-around porches, glittering with icicles in the winter, overlook Okemo Mt. and the Black River Valley. Nearby Plymouth Village Ski-Touring Center provides rentals and expert instruction with miles of ski trails over sunlit meadows and quiet wooded paths. In the summer and fall, the Golden Stage Inn is a popular retreat for fisherman, hikers and backpackers. It is also near the Summer Theatre in Weston, and the Fletcher Farm Craft School. In the evening, firelight glows off the copper-topped bar in the rustic barnwood-panelled lounge. Relax with a book from the library by a crackling fire, or linger over dinner, featuring traditional New England and continental dishes, hearty and delicate soups, unusual crepes and quiches. Eight attractive bedrooms with private and semi-private bath are available. Rates are $31 per person including meals in the winter, $14 for children, and $25 per person in the summer for a single, $35/room double occupancy. Children $10. For more information write: Tom and Wende Schaaff, The Golden Stage Inn, P.O. Box 218, Proctorsville, VT 05153 (802)226–7744.

★★*Green Trails Country Inn & Ski Touring Center by the Floating Bridge* in historic Brookfield, south of Montpelier, is in central Vermont near Allis State Park with its more than 400 acres. Natural ski-touring trails around Brookfield go in loops over frozen lakes and ponds, through woods of evergreens and maples, and over rolling meadows. The trails are suitable for all levels of skiers. Showshoeing, tobogganing and sledding are other winter-time outdoor activities. Downhill skiing and ice skating can be found within ten miles at Randolph and Northfield and three of Vermont's great ski areas, Stowe, Sugarbush and Killington, are within an hour's drive. There is swimming, trout fishing and boating in Sunset Lake and golf, tennis, and soaring are found nearby. Auctions, antique shops, arts and crafts shows, summer theater groups and country fairs are all within the nearby area. The inn itself is unique, having been built in 1840. It has six guest rooms, two efficiency apartments and a fireside lounge-game room. With accommodations for a maximum of 25 people, relationships are friendly and informal. The Fork Shop Restaurant was once an old mill and it overlooks the waterfall and Sunset Lake. The best of country dining, with homemade breads

and pies as well as continental specialties is offered. Room rates include a continental breakfast and range from $24 to $30 per night per unit. The family unit costs $60 for five to six people and $72 for seven to eight people. The apartment with its own kitchenette ranges from $42 per night for one to two people to $96 a night for seven to eight people. For further information, contact Green Trails Country Inn, Brookfield, VT 05036 (802)276–2012.

★★★*The Grey Bonnet* is a quiet, modern country inn for skiers. Located at 1,800 feet in the Green Mountains, it's five minutes from Mt. Killington, offering some of the East's finest skiing and miles of lifts. The Grey Bonnet has snowshoeing and carefully maintained cross country ski trails for guests on their premises. Winter activities include an illuminated skating plaza. Adjoining Gifford Woods provides nature trails with a scenic mountain lake. Sailing and canoeing can be enjoyed on the lake. The Appalachian and Long trails are nearby for short or extended hikes. Several excellent golf courses and good salmon or trout fishing are also nearby. The Killington area has excellent summer theatre, tennis, and riding trails. Take the longest aerial gondola ride in the world to enjoy the

spectacular view and sunsets from Killington Peak. The inn has an outdoor swimming pool, lawn games, heated indoor whirlpool, Finnish saunas, game rooms, and a card and party room. Rooms facing the south have views of Gifford Woods and those to the north a panoramic view of the mountains. All have two double beds, carpeting, individual thermostats and bath with tub and shower. Meals are provided on the Modified American Plan. Dinner, served fireside in a candlelit room, offers continental cuisine, salad bar and dessert carts. The inn will make arrangements for lifts, lessons, equipment or car rentals for you. There is transportation to and from the lifts available for $2. Rates: peak season, daily, $32–38; weekly, $214–256. Off season, daily, $26–32; weekly, $162–204. Holiday weeks are an additional $4 daily per person. Children six years of age and under half price. A European Meal Plan is available during the off season. For further information contact: The Grey Bonnet, Killington VT, 05751 (802)775–2537.

★★★★*Hermitage Country Inn & Ski Touring Center* is a charming 19th–century farmhouse inn in the Green Mountains three miles from

Mt. Snow. The inn is situated on 24 acres of scenic lawns, fields, old stone walls and orchards with a trout stream and pond, nature and cross-country ski trails, and beaver ponds. The farmhouse offers a beautiful view of the Deerfield River Valley and distant woodlands and hills. Activities include riding on bridle trails, hiking, fishing, boating at Lake Whitingham, ice skating at the Mt. Snow Base Lodge, alpine skiing at Haystack Mountain and Mt. Snow, sleighrides, snowshoeing, cross-country skiing on marked trails and overnight guided tours to the North Face of Mt. Snow and Stratton Pond. The ski touring center offers equipment rentals and certified instruction. Each of the guest rooms is individually decorated and furnished with antiques. Each room has its own ceramic tiled, thermostatically controlled bath-shower combination. Dining at the Hermitage is continental-casual (no ties required) but civilized. There are four intimate dining rooms—"the Gold Room", "the Pont Mirabeau Room" with its colorful mural of the River Seine in Paris, "the Blue Room" with its wall gallery of fine paintings, and "the Porch", glass-enclosed with wrought-iron furnishings and a lovely view of Haystack's ski trails. The menu is a la carte and offers a selection of fine dishes, prepared to order. Many of the vegetables, herbs and fruits are grown on the premises and home-made rose-hip jelly or freshly boiled maple syrup are only a sampling of the seasonal specialties that make the Hermitage such a unique experience. In addition, the inn has an extensive wine cellar. Modified American Plan rates for a double room with bath are $80 per day. For additional information, contact: The Hermitage, Box 457, Cold Brook Rd., Wilmington, VT 05363 (802)464–3759.

★★*The Highland House* is a small New England inn, right outside of Londonderry, Vermont. With only seven bedrooms, it offers a relaxed, informal atmosphere. Close to Vermont's Green Mountains, it's the perfect place to relax after a day of skiing in the winter. In spring and summer, there is tennis, golf, swimming and trail hiking on the Appalachian and Long trails close by. Picnicking in the National Forest is just minutes away and there's also hunting and trout fishing in the vicinity. Touring backcountry roads in fall offers visitors scenes of Vermont's beautiful landscape. There are also unique antique shops and summer theaters in nearby Weston. The dining room offers home-cooked breakfast and dinners, served family style, with a bring-your-own-bottle bar. Rates are $10 to $15 per person per day. Baths are shared. For groups, there is a housekeeping cottage with two bedrooms and bath, a living room with a Franklin stove, and a complete kitchen. For further information contact Alan and Margaret Unangst, The Highland House, Londonderry, VT 05148 (802)824–3019.

★★★*The Highlander Lodge at Lake Caspian*, a stately colonial Inn, with small private cottages situated on 160–wooded-acres is a delightful summer resort and a quiet retreat for cross-country skiers in winter. The ski touring center rents cross-country skis, boots, poles and the wax of the day for $7, $20 for a family group of four. Skis may be rented by the week for $40. One hour lessons are offered for $6 group and $14 private. Guided tours are available. Trails wander along the shores of the frozen lake, deep into pine forests heavy with snow. The lodge rooms are spacious and comfortably furnished with armchairs, antique dressers, deep pile carpeting and elegant, colonial wallpaper. Private cottages have a living room, bath, porch and one, two or three bedrooms. Generous meals are served in the early-American dining room; candlelight glows in the antique mirrors and pewter. Afterwards relax by the fire in the living room or gather round the grand piano. In the summer, relax on the wide shady porches overlooking the lake. If you were lucky enough to catch a landlocked salmon, perch, lake trout or rainbow, cook it on the beachhouse grills. There are tennis courts, sailboats, canoes, and

paddle-boats to enjoy. A separate recreation house and playground are available for kids. Rates for a single lodge room are daily per person including meals $38 and $27–35 per person double occupancy. Cottage rates vary according to the number of people and the location of the cottage. Generally cottage rates range between $74–134 daily. The Highlander Lodge offers a five day mid-week ski touring package for $145 per person including lodging, two meals daily, ski rentals and instruction. For more information write: Carol and Dave Smith, The Highlander Lodge, Box 125, Greensboro, VT 05841 (802)533–2647.

★★★*Hotel Chateau Jaymont* offers fine lodging and French cuisine, five miles from the Canadian border in the Northern Vermont wilderness. Cross-country and downhill skiing are available at the Jay Peak Ski Area three miles away. There is excellent fishing, several golf courses, long trails for hiking, antique shops and covered bridges nearby for summer treats. Chateau Jaymont has its own tennis court and a large, heated swimming pool. Rooms are spacious and complete with private bath and television. Accommodations are available for a family of six in one room. The cuisine is truly for gourmets with a large selection of imported fine wines. There are two bars for after-skiing enjoyments. Drinks can be served in front of the fireplace or while watching professional entertainment. Rates range from $25–35 per person, per day, Modified American Plan. Packages are available. For further information, contact Hotel Chateau Jaymont, Route 242, Jay Peak, VT 05859 (802)988–4459.

★★★*The Inn at Long Trail.* Built at the junction of Vermont's Long Trail and the Appalachian Trail, and only a mile from Killington, the largest downhill ski complex in the east, the Inn at Long Trail offers comfortable lodging in fireplace suites and dormitories to skiers, snowshoers, mountain climbers, and fishermen who seek the beauty of the Green Mountains. The gift shop represents Vermont artists and craftsmen, selling bright quilts, pottery, weavings, photographs, and drawings. Skiing and hiking equipment are also available. Cross-country ski trails and snowshoe trails begin across the road, where hardwood trees cast long shadows in the winter sunlight, criss-crossed with tracks of deer. The inn has accommodations for 94 mountain enthusiasts, 65 in fireplace suites and rooms with private or semi-private baths, and 29 dormitory spaces. Weekend rates for fireplace suites including meals are $148 for a party of two; single rooms with private bath and including meals are $94, and private rooms with shared bath and meals are $88 for two. Dormitory rates are $34 per person for a two day weekend with meals. Five day weekly rates are: $350 for a fireplace suite for two, $215 for a single private room with bath, $175 for a private room with shared bath, and $95 for a dormitory room. For more information write: The Inn at Long Trail, Sherburne Pass, Rte #1, Killington, VT 05751 (802)775–7181.

★★★*The Inn at Mt. Ascutney* is an intimate country inn located directly across the valley from the Mt. Ascutney Ski Area offering superb views and year-round recreation activities in the surrounding countryside, including alpine and cross-country skiing, fishing, hunting, horseback riding, golf and tennis. The inn is a converted farmhouse, decorated with English and American antiques. The dining room and cocktail lounge have been converted from the old carriage house, leaving low beams and featuring an open hearth and kitchen. The inn offers superb country cooking with a continental touch, prepared by a Cordon Bleu chef. Double occupancy rates are $33–38 and include breakfast and afternoon tea. For information, contact: Eric and Margaret Rothchild, Brook Rd., Brownsville, VT 05037 (802)484–7725.

★★★*Johnny Seesaw's,* a large rustic family inn built 2,000 ft. high on the side of Bromley Mt., is ideal for both cross-country and downhill skiers. The inn is located below Bromley's upper east slopes, and surrounded by the deep-powder trails of the Green Mountain National Forest. Wild Wings and Viking ski centers are nearby to provide rentals and lessons for the cross-country skiing enthusiast. The inn has large, private bedrooms and bunkrooms for children and young adults. Those who prefer more privacy will enjoy cottages with two separate bedrooms and private baths, and a living room with a fireplace and TV, and windows looking out at the surrounding mountains. Parents and grandparents often enjoy staying in the private cottages, while children stay in the bunkhouses. A separate playroom for children with their own TV is located in the main lodge. There is also a library for all, and a large, wood panelled living room, with a circular fireplace, and a raised alcove for listening to music and sing alongs. By tradition, young people usually eat early, while adults enjoy a cocktail by the fire in the oak panelled lounge. Windows look over to Bromley Mountain. Generous, family-style meals are served daily, and hot, home-baked breads and nourishing soups are a specialty. Special ski week plans from Sunday dinner to Friday breakfast, including lifts at Bromley run $148–178 for a private room in the main inn, and $198 per person in a private cottage. Mid-week ski package rates for dormitory rooms are $128. Ski package weeks including lessons and equipment, as well as lodging and lifts are also available. Rooms with meals are daily, per person, $36 for a private cottage, $25–33 for a room in the main inn, and $20 for a bunk room. For more information write: Johnny Seesaw's, Peru, VT 05152 (802)824–5533.

★★★*Kandahar Lodge* is located 2,150 feet up in the beautiful Green Mountain National Forest. This resort is one of the oldest of Vermont's mountain ski lodges, established in 1938. Its new owners, Joan and Doug Melville, are enthusiastic trout fishermen and their eldest son is the manager, as well as a hiking and cross-country skiing expert. In the summer season the main attractions are hiking and fishing. The famous Long Trail passes right by the lodge, and Kandahar is hosting the Green Mountain Fly Fishing School. The Melvilles' youngest son can teach guests to canoe and they soon plan to offer white-water trips. They are also planning three-day golf packages. The resort has an outdoor pool, a sauna, a trout pond and a recreation room, complete with pocket billiards and card tables. A huge stone fireplace in the cozy lounge provides a place for conversation at the end of the day. Winter attractions include both cross-country and downhill skiing. The resort is located between Bromley, Magic Mountain and Stratton ski areas. There is also ice skating and snowshoeing on the mountain trails. The dining room features home-baked breads and pastries, plus a traditional Sunday smorgasbord. Rooms have wall to wall carpeting, ceramic baths, TV, individual heat controls and many have rustic beamed ceilings and panelled walls. For further information contact: Kandahar Lodge & Resort Motel, Junction Rte 11 and 30, Bromley Mountain, Manchester VT 05254 (802)824–5531.

★★★*Kedron Valley Inn & Stables* is a superb country inn dating back to 1828, in the beautiful horse country of the Green Mountains in South Woodstock. The inn offers year-round recreation, including trail rides, swimming in a private pond, cross-country skiing and alpine skiing at the nearby Woodstock Touring Center, Mt. Tom, Suicide Six, Killington Peak and Mt. Ascutney. The inn rents ski-touring equipment, and has three expert nordic skiers on the staff for instruction. Near the Green Mountain Horse Association facilities, the Kedron Valley Inn & Stables, with mounts for beginners and experts are the center of great activity in summer. Aside from renting and boarding horses, they arrange for private lessons, provide wagon rides, sleigh rides, picnic trail rides, horse trekking, and a

guided trail ride. Food from the kitchen is simple and delicious. Each room has its own bath. There are fireplaces in the living rooms which come alive on cool nights. They also have an excellent lounge called the Tavern. Recently constructed motel units just behind the inn are designed with rustic charm in harmony with the rural setting. Rates range from $18–34 per day. Add $11 per person for the Modified American Plan. For information, contact: Kedron Valley Inn, South Woodstock, VT 05071 (802)457–1473.

★★*Killington Country Resort* is located in the heart of the Vermont ski country. The East's best skiing at Killington and Pico is only 15 minutes away, and it's less than an hour to Sugarbush, Glen Ellen, Okemo, Roundtop, Mad River, Mt. Tom, and Suicide Six. Killington Country, a year-round resort, is within an easy drive of a variety of historic sights, including Proctor Marble Exhibit, Shelburne Museum, Bennington Battlefield and Museum, and much more. There are many fine summer theatres, antique shops and country stores for the famous Vermont cheese and maple syrup. The resort occupies ten landscaped acres and includes a large lake with sand beach for swimming and sun-bathing. Fishing, hunting, wooded paths, and plenty of space to relax are also attributes of the resort. Nearby there's horseback riding, hiking on the famous Appalachian and Long trails, tennis, golf and many other sports. A spacious dining room with fireplace offers excellent meals, served in fine style, and the rustic cocktail lounge has a touch of old New England. Accommodations range from a comfortable dorm room in the Deer Brook Lodge to a private room with bath in the motel. Both lodge and motel rates, based on double occupancy, are $25 per night, Modified American Plan. Rates vary with the season. For additional information contact Bill and Pat Kenerson, Killington Country Resort, Rte. 100, Pittsfield, VT 05762 (802)746–8981 or 755–1779.

★★★*Killington Village*. Within walking distance of the Killington Ski Vacation Center, and the Snowshed and Rams Head lifts, Killington Village is a series of eight modern two-story oak buildings, with picture windows and private balconies providing panoramic views. Each building houses 12 soundproof rooms, with private side en-

trances. Killington Village offers a unique combination of standard bedrooms and fireplace rooms with kitchenettes and dining areas. Rent a standard room by itself, and you have a lodge-type room, with the optional modified meal plan, offering candlelight dining in the Angus Tavern Restaurant overlooking the Snowshed slopes. With kitchenettes and dining areas, the fireplace rooms by themselves or combined with an adjoining standard bedroom create an apartment. A cocktail lounge, large game room with TV, and a laundromat are available for guests. Killington Village also offers a variety of two, five, and seven day ski vacation plans in varying combinations of lodging, lifts, meals, lessons and equipment rental to suit every need. A standard room, for example, for two people Saturday and Sunday including meals and unlimited use of Killington lifts is $83. A fireplace room for two with meals and lifts runs $96 for a weekend. For more information write: Killington Village, 212 Killington Rd., Killington VT 05751 (802)422–3613 or 422–3101.

★★★*Liftline Lodge* is an Austrian-style inn set at the base of Stratton Mountain in southern Vermont. The lifts are only one hundred yards away. Stratton has over sixty miles of fine trails for downhill skiers and there is also a Nordic Center for cross-country ski enthusiasts. For summer enjoyment, Stratton offers an eighteen-hole championship golf course, a professional tennis center with both indoor and outdoor courts, canoeing down the West River, fishing, hiking and riding. There are summer stock theaters for entertainment as well as flea markets and many antique shops. Auctions, art shows and craft and music festivals are featured in the fall along with Vermont's world-famous foliage. Liftline Lodge has its own clay tennis court with night lights and its own heated pool. For indoor pleasures, there's a sauna, fireplace, piano bar, game room and a boutique stocked with Austrian antique chests and armoires, colorful enamels and ceramics. The dining room offers the best of Austrian and American dishes with music provided by an Austrian Folk Music Group. There are more than sixty comfortable rooms, each with two double beds and a private bath. There are also four luxurious apartments that sleep six comfortably. Each apartment has two bedrooms, a kitchenette and a living room with a wood-burning fireplace. Room rates are from $38–40 per person double occupancy, Modified American Plan. $27 per person double occupancy, European Plan. Apartments range from $65 to $159 per night, depending on the number of people. For more information and reservations, contact Herbert and Gretel Schachinger, Liftline Lodge, Stratton Mountain, VT 05155 (802)297–2600.

★★★*Long Run Lodge* is a charming, gabled village inn located west of Lincoln Gap on the Long Trail in Lincoln Center on the New Haven River. This popular stop-over on the inn-to-inn tour along the Long Trail began its existence in the 1800's as a lumberjack's hotel. Lodge activities include hiking, swimming, and ski touring in winter. The delicious, countrystyle meals include homemade breads and desserts. Rates are $35 per day and include inn room, dinner, breakfast, box lunch, and snacks. For additional information, contact: Gen and Jim Burke, RD #1, Box 114, Bristol, VT 05443 (802)453–3233.

★★★*Middlebury Inn* is a warm, homey inn, located in the heart of the quaint town of Middlebury. The glory of Middlebury is its combination of historical spots and proximity to fine outdoor activities. The inn receives the cultural, recreational and educational benefits of nearby Middlebury College (a five-minute walk from the inn) and from being the center for many of the community's functions—the result is a real taste of New England life. The inn, situated in the center of the town's National Historic Register District, provides guidance for walking tours of the village. Bits of

American history can be found at the Sheldon Museum, a treasure house of period Vermontiana, plus the many local historic sites or milestones of the American Revolution. Homer Noble Farm, now a National Historic Landmark and Robert Frost's Interpretive Trail, with many of his poems mounted on plaques in scenic settings, are just five miles away. Or take a ferry ride across Lake Champlain to visit Fort Ticonderoga and its collection of American Revolution artifacts. In addition, you can picnic, with a lunch packed by the inn, in the beautiful deep green forests, or lakeside state and national forest settings. There is golf and tennis at Middlebury College or walks along the country roads past hill-farm pastures. During winter, the Middlebury area offers fine skiing nearby. The Middlebury College Snow Bowl has four lifts and a 20-mile downhill slope, with professional instruction. Other downhill skiing is at nearby Sugarbush Valley, Glen Ellen, and Mad River Valley. The Middlebury College Campus boasts the longest, lighted cross-country ski course in the country—3.5 miles long. Fine ski touring with trails past primitive national forest stands and early Vermont settlers' homes is part of the college's offerings. There is also camping, canoeing and horseback riding in the Middlebury area. The Middlebury Inn structure was constructed in 1827, and has since seen many changes of management and improvements. Recently, the present owner received a grant to maintain and restore the building. The homey inn building currently features distinctive rooms for guests, a ballroom, a lounge with entertainment, afternoon teas in the lobby and special Sunday night buffets. The inn's chef is considered one of the inn's special features and he keeps customers coming back with his satisfying New England fare. The inn operates on the European Plan, and meals are available at either the inn or local restaurants. Rates: single room from $16. Double rooms $28–48. Suites $40. Package rates available. For further information contact: Middlebury Inn, 29 Court House Square, Middlebury, VT 05753 (802)388–4961.

★★★★*Millbrook Country Inn in the Mad River Valley* is a charming country inn east of Appalachian Gap on the Long Trail. The inn, renowned for its hospitality and breathtaking views, offers access to superb trout fishing, hiking, and tennis in the spring, summer, and fall and cross-country skiing in winter. The classic cape-style farm house, which dates back to 1865, is the longest established inn in the Valley. Six bedrooms to accommodate guests, a living room with fireplace and "the warming room" with Glenwood stove are all decorated with period furnishings which complement the friendly unhurried atmosphere. Farmstyle meals include home-baked breads and desserts and in season, vegetables fresh from the backyard country garden. A hearty breakfast and single entree dinner are offered to guests. Modified American Plan rates are $30 per person, double occupancy. Millbrook is part of the famed inn-to-inn hiking tours along the Long Trail. For information, contact: Millbrook Country Inn, RFD Box 44, Waitsfield, VT 05673 (802)496–2405.

★★★★*Mount Mansfield Resort* at Mt. Mansfield, Vermont's highest mountain, offers three types of accommodations from which to choose—the Lodge, the Toll House, and the Town Houses. The Lodge, located at the base of Mt. Mansfield, offers guests comfortable accommodations, award-winning French cuisine, a selective wine cellar, and impeccable service in the Continental manner. The Lodge combines rustic charm with outstanding luxury—with a library, living rooms for get-togethers, a game room and a cocktail lounge. The Toll House offers the ultimate in modern accommodations with an easy ski lodge feeling, in a setting of breathtaking beauty. Located right at the Sky slopes, it has 40 luxuriously comfortable rooms and suites. Each has a balcony with a spectacular view of the mountains and valley. Cuisine with a European flair and hearty New England dishes are served in a rustic dining room.

There's a game room and sun deck. The Town Houses offer the charm of a vacation home, combining a two-level design, with a choice of one-three bedrooms. You can ski from the slopes to the door. In spring and summer and fall you can enjoy golf, tennis, hiking, and horseback riding. All this is located at Stowe, and Stowe's world-famous ski school offers the finest instructors. A day-care center is available for children. There are three sport and rental shops and the area offers access to 150–mile trail system of Stowe. At other times of the year Stowe offers a private 18–hole championship golf course, tennis, swimming, fishing, trail riding, hiking, scenic drives, magnificent views, shopping for antiques, country auctions, and summer theatre. There are of course package plans available. Rates: at the Lodge (Modified American Plan) range from $78–128 per day, double occupancy; at the Toll House (Modified American Plan) from $90–120 per day, double occupancy; at the Town Houses (European Plan) from $65–175 with a two day minimum stay. For information and reservations call (802)253–7311 or write Mount Mansfield Resort, Stowe, VT 05672.

★★★★*Mountain Meadows Lodge & Ski Touring Center at Killington*, just east of the entrance to Killington Ski area off Sherburne Pass on the Long Trail, is a secluded hundred-year-old farmhouse and bright red barn, snuggled against the backs of the high surrounding mountains, in a quiet little valley on the shores of 110–acre Kent Pond. The lodge offers cross-country skiing, hiking trails, canoeing, and great homestyle cooking. 15 miles of carefully groomed cross-country ski trails lead from the front door, across the lake and into the

mountains. Mountain Meadows Lodge is also a part of the 50–mile ski trail linking small country inns and mountain lodges in Vermont. The ski shop, located in the converted barn, offers package ski rentals for $6 per adult and $4 for children. Half day ski rentals are also offered. Lessons are available, group lessons are $5, private lessons $10 and video private lessons $18. In addition, Mountain Meadows offers a special ski-week plan, including lessons, guided wilderness tours, moonlight ski tours, and interchangeable skiing at Mountain Top Ski Touring Center, and Blueberry Hill Ski Touring Center, for $37.50 for adults, and $19 per child. Weekly ski rentals are $24. Hearty family-style meals are served in the converted barn, at round wooden tables covered with bright cloth. The adjoining living room offers a comfortable chair before a crackling fire, and full picture windows look out at the broad grey sloping mountains and the quiet open meadows beyond. Daily bulletins listing skiing conditions at Killington and Pico Peak are posted here, and special events, such as moonlight tours, are written on the community chalk board. Altogether, Mountain Meadows has accommodations for 90 skiers; dormitory rooms run $17, including meals; family style rooms sleeping five-six with private bath are $20 per person, children under 12, $10. Double rooms with private bath are $25 per person, and with semi-private bath $20 per person. In the summer the lake offers fishing, canoeing, and swimming, or swim in the pool if you like. The Appalachian Trail is right at the front door of the lodge. Killington and Pico Peak areas offer tennis or golf, or take the 3½ mile Gondola to Killington Peak for a spectacular view of four states. Horseback riding can be arranged at nearby stables. In this season, Mountain Meadows Lodge has accommodations for 45. For more information write: Bill and Joanne Stevens, Mountain Meadows Lodge, 20 Thundering Brook Road, Killington, VT 05751 (802)775–1010.

★★★★*Notch Brook Resort*, a series of contemporary wood and glass structures secluded in a grove of birch overlooking Mt. Mansfield, offers luxurious double rooms, and one, two, and three bedroom modern townhouses to skiers who come to Stowe. Minutes away from Mt. Mansfield and Spruce Peak ski areas, Notch Brook runs a free shuttle bus service for guests. After a day of skiing, relax in the sauna, or take a dip in the heated outdoor pool. All rooms are modern and furnished in earth-tone colors, with large brick fireplaces and picture windows that capture the sunset's deepening shadow on the mountains. Apartments and townhouses come with fully equipped, modern kitchens. Double rooms are $32–34 daily, double occupancy, and $210 weekly. One-bedroom suites are $55 daily and $315 weekly. One-bedroom townhouse, $78 daily and $450 weekly. Two-bedroom townhouses are $110 daily and $650 weekly. Three-bedroom townhouses are $145 daily and $850 weekly. Mid-week packages are also available. Rates include daily maid service, use of saunas, game room, and free shuttle bus service. For more information write: Notch Brook Resort, Notch Brook Road, Stowe, VT 05672 (802)253–4882.

★★★*The Okemo Inn.* Nestled against the slope of Okemo Mountain, and just ten minutes from Round Top Mt. Ski area and ½ mile from Killington and Magic Mt., the inn is a handsome 1810 Vermont homestead which has been restored as a warm, congenial, country inn. Twelve bedrooms accommodate 36 guests. There is a sauna to

relax in after an exhilarating day on the slopes. The dining room serves homemade soups and such hearty entrees as charcoal broiled pork chops and trout in wine sauce. The 1810 Room is a relaxed fireside lounge, and next door is a cozy TV room. Bedrooms are decorated with antiques, and offer spectacular views of the surrounding mountains. Winter rates are $20 daily for a single room without meals, and $35 for a double room. A two-room family suite with bath is $50. Rates including breakfast and dinner are $25 daily per person in a room, and $20 additional for each person sharing the same room. Five-day ski specials, including lodging and meals from Sunday night until Friday morning are $100 per adult and $75 for children under 12. In the summer, rates are $12 single and $20 double, without meals. Fall rates are $15 for one guest, and $25 for two, without meals. For more information write: Ron and Toni Parry, The Okemo Inn, Route 103, Ludlow, VT 05149 (802)228-2031.

★★★*The Old Red Mill.* Once an old saw mill producing desks for schools near Wilmington, Vermont, The Old Red Mill is now a fine country tavern near Mt. Snow, Haystack, Prospect, and Hogback ski areas, still retaining its unique character. The belts, pulleys, and circular saws of the old mill now decorate the walls and hold plants. The mill stream still runs by. Hearty meals and grog are served in the dining room. Steaks and seafood specialties are offered with full salad bar and fresh baked bread on every table. In winter, enjoy the serenity of the cross-country trails; in summer the Marlboro Music Festival and summer theater enliven the area. Single rooms are $15 mid-week, $30 weekends and $35 during holiday weeks. Double rooms are $20 mid-week, $30 weekends and $35 holidays. Triple rooms are $25 mid-week, $35 weekends and $40 holidays. Modified meal plans are offered by the inn $60 per adult per week, and $48 per child. Mid-week ski plans are also available. Single rooms on ski plan are $50 for three nights and $55 five nights. Double rooms on ski plan are $50 for three nights and $60 five nights. Triple rooms are $60 three nights, $70 five nights. For more information write: The Old Red Mill, Route 100, Wilmington, VT 05363 (802)464-3700.

★★★★*The Old Tavern* is a lovely year-round resort in the southern Vermont hills. The tavern boasts authentic Vermont charm, scenery and outdoor recreation akin to the area. There is a natural swimming pond, tennis courts, a croquet court and indoor game room. During the warm weather the resort packs lunches for guests to take on well-marked walking trails winding through the woods. Bicycles can be rented, and horseback riding and three golf courses are nearby. The tavern offers skiers six miles of private cross-country trails. Guests with skates can take advantage of the rink and sleds, toboggans, and snowshoes provided by the tavern. Guaranteed reservations will be made for downhill skiers at nearby Timber Ridge to avoid waiting for lift lines. The area has several antique shops in the village and is close to art galleries, artisan and craft centers, all providing a New England flavor. The tavern is a restored 1801 stagecoach inn, distinctively furnished with antiques. There are no phones in the bedrooms and a TV only in the lounge, to assure guests a quiet stay. There are lots of cozy corners, a fireplace, and a well stocked library. The tavern serves three meals a day—with a real New England touch. Regional dishes include Blueberry Soup and Cheese 'n Bacon Pie. Gentlemen are requested to wear jackets at dinner. (Meals are not included in rates.) Rates: Rooms with private bath $30-45. The resort is open all year except Christmas Eve, Christmas Day, and the month of April. For further information contact: The Old Tavern, Grafton, VT 05146 (802) 843-2375.

★★★*Pico Peak Lodge at Killington* offers year-round recreation. Nestled at the foot of Pico Peak and just five miles from Killington, the Lodge has great skiing from November 'til May. Spring skiers can watch Vermont's famous maple sugaring process in one of the area's many maple sugar houses. Cross-country trails meander throughout the vicinity. In the summer, there's hiking on the Appalachian or Long trails, tennis and golf at nearby locations, and Pico Peak's own swimming pool. The gondolas and chairlifts operate in the fall to provide views of the brilliant Vermont autumn foliage. Rooms range from single doubles with one double bed, TV and bath to twin doubles with two double beds, TV, full bath, access to balcony or terrace, to suites with two bedrooms, living room and kitchenettes. From the traditional carved-to-order Sunday breakfast ham to the delicious country cooking served at all meals, Pico Peak's menus will delight the palate. Steaming drinks accompany piano playing in the Snug. Special ski plans and weekender rates are available. Daily and holiday rates per person, including dinner and breakfast go from $45 to $50 for single occupancy, $30 to $36 for double. For more information and reservations, contact Pico Peak Lodge, Box 10, Killington, VT 05751 (802)773-6331.

★★★★*Snow Lake Lodge* is set on 120 acres at the foot of beautiful Mt. Snow, one of southern Vermont's most exciting and popular ski resorts. The lodge is a quality resort hotel, with hot and cold Japanese dream pools, a cocktail lounge, a game room, movies, parties, dancing and entertainment. Fine food is graciously served—the cuisine is American-Continental and there is a fine selection of wine from the cellar. The accommodations are quite comfortable and the rooms offer wonderful views of the surrounding mountains and countryside. For the summer season the lodge is open from Memorial Day through late October. The Mt. Snow Country Club and Public Golf Course features one of New England's finest 18-hole championship courses. The lodge also has four clay tennis courts and an outdoor swimming pool. The Mt. Snow Summer Playhouse is close by. There are excellent facilities for groups, seminars and meetings and of course, numerous ski packages—including lodging, meals, lessons, lift tickets and equipment—for weeks, weekends or mid-week rates. No pets, please. For full details contact Snow Lake Lodge, Mt. Snow, VT 05356 or call toll free (800)451-4211, or (802)464-3333.

★★★*Stoweflake Nordic Resort* is situated in a broad rolling valley in the heart of Vermont ski country, minutes away from Mt. Mansfield and Spruce Peak. Three nearby ski-touring centers, The Trapp Family Lodge, Topnotch, and Edson Hill Manor, combine to create 150 miles of trails throughout the surrounding mountains. The main lodge has the atmosphere of a New England ski inn, with cozy rooms, firelit lounges, pine panelled tap rooms, and a dining room featuring a large salad bar, fine wines, and hearty dinners. Two modern motels, the Stoweflake and the Nordic Motor Inn, offer large deluxe rooms, fully carpeted and modernly furnished with TV and private bath. Relax in the Stoweflake's sauna and exercise room after a challenging day of skiing. All deluxe rooms in the Nordic Inn have private outside entrances, and a central hall leading to the early American dining room and the lounge area, with brick fireplaces, high-beamed ceilings and windows looking out across snow-covered meadows to the surrounding mountains. In addition, there are plush apartments accommodating four-six people in one, two and three bedrooms. All apartments have fully equipped modern kitchens, and a spacious living room/dining area. The two-story Ski House, the original ski home, accommodates ten people, with a living room, dining room, fireplace, modern kitchen and three private bedrooms with bath on the upper level, and two bunk rooms, a family room and fireplace, and second bath below. Rates

for the ski season range between $75 and $100 a night depending on the number of persons in the group. Deluxe apartments range between $60–90. Rooms in the main lodge are $27–36 single occupancy with breakfast and dinner and $21–28 double occupancy, per person. The Nordic Motor Inn offers single rooms for $28–38 double occupancy; per person $18–23. These rates do not include meals, but modified American Plan rates are available. Stoweflake rooms are $38–48 including meals for single occupancy and $28–33 per person double occupancy, including meals. In addition the Stoweflake Nordic Resort offers a variety of downhill and cross-country ski specials. In the summer, the sprawling lawns encircle two swimming pools, and provide a chip-and-putt course and a practice green on the grounds. Tennis, hiking, biking, fishing, and summer theater are all closeby. For more information write: The Baran Family, Stoweflake Nordic Resort, Box B, Stowe, VT 05672 (802)253–7355.

★★★★*Stowehof Inn*, with its fairytale bell tower and sod roof, offers old world charm in the midst of the recreational skiing excitement of Stowe. A covered walkway, supported by old maple trees, leads the way to the inn, which has 47 individually furnished rooms and fireplace suites. After an exciting day skiing nearby Mt. Mansfield or Spruce Peak, or exploring the 60 miles of ski-touring trails throughout the surrounding countryside, relax by the fire in the multilevel living room with nooks, private alcoves, and gaming boards for cards, chess, and backgammon. A quaint, winding staircase leads upward to a more private living room-library, decorated like the inside of a covered bridge. There is a sauna to relax in, and the Tap Room, a tyrolean bar, serves hot hors d'oeuvres, cheese and meat fondue in the afternoon. The intimate dining room, with stone fireplace and high-beamed ceiling, is known for its fresh baked breads, caesar salads prepared right at your table, and such exquisite specialties as Salzburger Nockerl, sauteed veal piccata, and dover sole amandine. The Stowehof offers special down-hill and cross-

country ski week plans for five days and five nights. Downhill plans, including lodging, with breakfast at the Stowehof, and Mt. Mansfield and Spruce Peak lifts are $310 per person, double occupancy. Cross-country plans are $195 per person including use of 60 miles of trail, one lesson daily, and rentals. Room rates on the Modified American Plan include lodging, breakfast, hors d'oeuvres, candle-light dinner, and late evening demitasse and pastry. Rates on the European Plan (without meals) are also available. Each room has its own private balcony offering superlative views of the surrounding mountains. Standard rooms are daily, per person double occupancy, $42 weekdays and $50 on weekends, and $190 on the five day mid-week special plan. Deluxe rooms are $46 weekdays, $55 weekends, and $210 five day mid-week special. Fireplace suites, with kitchenette and bar available upon request, are $60 weekdays, $270 five-day mid-week, and $70 weekend days. In the summer, the many ski trails become hiking paths to exceptional mountain vistas. There is a trout pond on the grounds, and a patio pool. The Stowehof has four brand new high quality tennis courts, and there is a pro on hand for instruction. Free tennis clinics are available to all guests. Stowehof has a putting range, and guests are welcome to golf the 18–hole championship golf course at the nearby Stowe Country Club. For details write: Stowehof Inn, Edson Hill Road, Stowe, VT 05672 (802)253–8500.

★★★*Stratton Mountain Inn* is located in the Green Mountains with skiing down both sides of the mountain and ski facilities are extensive, including lessons, rentals, patrol, and day care. There are 10 lifts, 59 miles of ski trails and slopes, ski touring, ice skating and indoor tennis for the winter. The summer brings warm days and crisp evenings for peaceful walks or leisurely drives on country roads, summer theaters, antique shops, and arts festivals. On the premises there is golf, tennis, chair-lift rides, swimming, and fishing (down the road). The inn offers congenial service with quiet efficiency, a charming lounge, superb food and wines, and fresh mountain air all year long. Special events include music festivals through summer and fall. There are numerous packages available and winter rates start at $38 per person for double occupancy (Modified American Plan). For further information and reservations phone (802)297–2400 or toll-free (800)451–4261 or write Stratton Vacations, Stratton Mt., VT 05155.

★★★★*The Sugarbush Inn*, long renowned as a winter resort at the base of the Sugarbush Ski Area, has become a complete year-round resort nestled in the heart of the Green Mountains. Sugarbush offers an unsurpassed variety of sports and recreational facilities for every taste and skill. In winter, there is superb skiing—either cross-country (there are 35 miles of groomed trails) or down-hill on the 4,000 foot summit, with a complete rental shop, instruction, base lodge and complete skiing packages available. To this, Sugarbush has added, for the summer months, facilities for golf and tennis. The John Gardiner Tennis Clinic is the finest tennis facility in all of New England. There are 16 tennis courts and packages are available—or if you don't wish to participate in a clinic, you can use the courts free of charge as a guest of the inn. One of the best championship golf courses around has now been completed in a dramatic setting on the grounds of the inn. If you or any members of your party are not tennis or golf fans, there's plenty more to keep you busy— horseback riding, fishing, swimming (outdoor heated pool), sauna, soaring at a nearby airport, hiking, antiquing, historic sights, art galleries, and visits to picturesque towns. For the children there is a playground and programs each day including swimming, riding, hiking arts and crafts, indoor games, and movies. Dining is excellent, with New England dishes and seafood a specialty. For your accommodations you may choose a comfortable guest room at the

inn or a charming chalet or a condominium-style terrace suite. Rates are based on European Plan per day per person and range from $24–48. For further information and reservations contact: Sugarbush Inn, Warren, VT 05674 (802)583–2301.

★★★★*Summit Lodge at Killington* is situated high on a knoll under the peak of Killington Mountain, with a beautiful view of the Green Mountains. Winter months at the Summit provide all the skiing pleasures of Killington Mountain, plus nearby slopes. Killington, often thought of as the ski headquarters of the east, boasts the highest lift in Vermont, and miles of uninterrupted trails. Extensive snowmaking makes Killington the first to open and the last to close. The lodge also offers six tennis courts, with lessons and a ball throwing machine available; an indoor and outdoor pool; a giant Jacuzzi whirlpool; saunas; plus a fully equipped game room. From the lodge you can enjoy summer theater, horseback riding in the mountains, trout fishing and boat rentals on a seven-acre stocked pond, nature trail, galleries, antique shops, and more. There is also a gondola going to the top of Killington for a five-state view. The lodge has a warm rustic atmosphere. There's an intimate Rathskeller with a fireplace and entertainment, and a library and art gallery. The Country Dining Room, noted for its excellent cuisine and friendly service, offers a varied menu. The lodge also provides guests with free shuttle service to and from the ski area and a pick-up service from the local bus station and airport for a nominal fee. Accommodations vary from a small room with bath with shower to a suite with a bedroom, sitting room, full bath, and mountain view. Rooms with balconies and terraces are also available. The lodge operates on a Modified American Plan. Daily rates are $36–54. A seven-day ski week offering special bargain rates and coordinated with Killington's lesson program, is $230–345. Holiday rates slightly higher. Children's rates available. For further information contact: The Summit Lodge at Killington, VT 05751 (802)422–3535.

★★★★*Topnotch at Stowe* is located only minutes from the base of Mt. Mansfield. "Unique" is most appropriate when applied to Topnotch—it is one of a handful of U.S. resorts that retain the charm, graciousness and careful attention to detail of a fine European inn, yet are as relaxed and informal as a country lodge. Travelers are comfortable enough to feel like personal guests— a luxurious home they can make their own hideaway. There is no front desk—the reception area is in a library surrounded by nearly 1,000 books. You are greeted by a concierge. There is no lobby, lounge or sitting room—instead there is an oversized living room with fireplace, antique armoire, occasional chairs and tables, large floor pillows and more than six 12–foot tall picture windows. There are dozens of games and even a telescope. Each guest room is furnished distinctively—each with its own library, valuable antiques and art prints, retractable clothes lines in the showers, perfumed soap in antique dishes, color TV and phone. Townhouses are also available with living rooms, fireplaces, kitchens, dining room and porch. Tea and pastry is served at 4 o'clock but dinner will be the highlight of your day—gourmet dining is by candlelight with a wine to go with every dinner choice. There are ten tennis courts, swimming pool, health spa with sauna, massage, exercise room, whirlpool hydrotherapy, croquet, badminton, outdoor backgammon, ping pong, a fully equipped game room, stables and miles of trails for riding or lessons. There's a golf course just two miles away. Fishing and hunting are excellent. Boating and canoeing can be arranged. Stowe is one of the winter sports capitals of the east, offering alpine skiing, sledding, ice-skating (on their lighted pond), snowshoeing, ski joring, tobogganing, cross-country skiing and ski touring. Year-round, there's sightseeing, antiquing, auctions, concerts, art festivals, handicrafts, barn sales, horse and dog shows,

bicycle races, and hot air balloon festivals. The area also has restored villages and covered bridges. In summer there's a unique movie theater where you can sit cabaret style and enjoy a drink and a film at the same time. There's dancing and entertainment at the Inn in the evenings. Rooms at the Inn based on daily rate per room start at $55 for double occupancy (European Plan). Rates in the townhouses start at $75 per day per unit. Rates are based on room size, location and time of year. Modified American Plan is also available. For further information and reservations contact Mr. Lewis M. Kiesler, President, Topnotch at Stowe, Mt. Mansfield Rd., Stowe, VT 05672 (802)253–8585.

★★★★*Trapp Family Lodge & Ski Touring Center* is nestled in a beautiful alpine valley in the heart of the Green Mountains. When Johannes von Trapp and his famous singing family settled here, they chose this spectacular valley because it reminded them of their native Austria. Edelweiss does not grow here, but Indian pipe and meadow daisies do, and hikers will enjoy the hiking paths, pano-

ramic vistas, and sweeping valleys surrounding the lodge. Two nearby stables provide a fine selection of well-trained horses for riding, and fishermen will enjoy the fast running streams and alpine lakes within easy reach. All guests share golf privileges at the nearby Stowe Country Club, which has one of the most scenic 18–hole championship courses in the nation. In winter, the lodge is a famous cross-country skiing center with a complete ski shop, warming room with fireplace, 60 miles of marked and groomed trails, and a rustic forest cabin that serves lunch. The lodge, a charming Tyrolean Chalet, its windowboxes overflowing with bright flowers, offers a choice of single or double rooms with a shared or private bath. Many rooms have fireplaces or open onto a private balcony with a breathtaking panorama of the mountains. Rates include leisurely dinners featuring international specialties, and hearty mountain breakfasts. Music, dancing and singing are enjoyed in the lovely Tirolerstueberl Bar. Rates are daily $25 for a single room with shared bath and $35 daily with a private bath. Twin double rooms

are $24 per person with shared bath, and $29 per person for a double room with private bath. Deluxe rooms are $36–44 per person double occupancy. For more information write: The Trapp Family Lodge, Stowe, VT 05672 (802)253–8511.

★★★★*Tulip Tree Inn in the Green Mountain National Forest* is a delightful four-season, antique-filled, rambling country inn west of the Long Trail in the Green Mountain National Forest, one mile from the Chittenden Reservoir—a noted landlocked salmon and trout fishery. Both the Appalachian Trail and Long Trail wind their way through the high-country of the national forest to the east and north. The inn has its own swimming pool and trout stream. In winter, the inn has a cross-country ski trail, waxing room, and access to 55 miles of superb cross-country trails maintained by the Mountain Top Ski Touring Center (which see). The Tulip Tree offers ten tastefully appointed guest rooms and is noted for its hearty breakfasts, and gourmet, candlelit dinners and deserts served in the picturesque dining room. Modified American Plan rates, double occupancy, are $26 to $30 per person. For additional information, and details on inn-to-inn hikes, contact: Barbara and Gerald Liebert, Tulip Tree Inn, Chittenden, VT 05737 (802)483–6213.

★★★*Village at Smugglers Notch* is situated in beautiful Stowe Valley in the northern Green Mountains. Activities at this superb four-seasons resort include cross-country skiing on 40 miles of marked trails; alpine skiing at Mt. Mansfield; backpacking and hiking on the scenic Long Trail; trout fishing in Sterling Pond; tennis on 8 Har-tru and 2 all-weather courts; swimming in the 70–foot heated pool; trail riding and instruction at Topnotch stables; summer music festivals and gourmet dining at the Crown & Anchor Old English Public House. Accommodations are in deluxe studios and 3, 4, and 5 bedroom townhouses. For summer and winter rates and special ski packages, contact: The Village at Smugglers Notch, Jeffersonville, VT 05464; call toll-free (800)451–3222.

★★★*Whiffletree Condominiums at Killington*. With its high windows capturing panoramic views of Killington, Whiffletree Condominiums offers luxuriously furnished one, two, three and four bedroom units within walking distance of the Killington lifts. All condominiums are plushly furnished, with high ceilings, wall-to-wall carpet-

ing, fireplaces, spacious dining areas and fully equipped kitchens. Four-bedroom, two bath duplexes comfortably accommodate groups of eight to ten persons. One bedroom units containing a private bedroom with twin beds and a living room sofa bed accommodate a maximum of four persons. Rates vary depending on what part of the season (early, peak, or late) you wish to reserve. Generally, one bedroom, one bath units accommodating a maximum of six vary between $260–450, two bedroom, two bath units, $300–435. Three bedroom, two bath duplexes accommodating eight people maximum, $365–560 and four bedroom two bath duplexes accommodating ten people maximum, $450–615. For more information write: Whiffletree Condominiums, 550 Killington Rd., Killington, VT 05751 (802)422–3101.

★★★★*Woodstock Inn & Ski Touring Center*. Churchbells cast by Paul Revere once rang from four steeples, and now much of the village of Woodstock, Vermont, on the banks of the scenic Ottauquechee River in the foothills of the Green Mountains has been designated a historical district to preserve the handsome, colonial houses dating from the 1700's and the three covered bridges spanning the river in its course through the town. The handsome Woodstock Inn on the Village Green welcomes guests in a hospitable tradition dating back to 1793. History serves only as a setting for exhilarating winter sports and a wide variety of summer recreation offered at this superb inn, which has its own downhill ski center with a 2000' chair lift and 40 miles of backcountry trails maintained by the Woodstock Ski Touring Center. The face of "Suicide Six" skiing area is considered one of the finest slalom hills in the east. Two double chair lifts service 17 runs, challenging every level of skiing ability from beginner to expert. Lift tickets are $7.50 weekdays and $10.50 weekends and holidays. Expert skiing instruction is offered on all levels three times daily. Group lessons are $7, four lessons $24, and eight lessons $40. Private lessons can be arranged by appointment and are $12. Ski rentals are available for $10 a complete outfit in New Base lodge on the face of Suicide Six. Forty miles of marked trails surround the Woodstock Ski Touring Center traversing gentle golf courses, passing deep into the surrounding woods, encircling Amity Pond, and climbing Mt. Tom. Guided tours are available, led by ski instructors who are trained naturalists. The ski center has a wide variety of wax and waxless skis, and snowshoes for rent. Fireside lunches are served in the bar-restaurant of the touring center. The inn also has paddle tennis courts. Old fashioned horse-drawn sleigh rides in the brilliant winter sunlight are a delight. In the spring, enjoy fresh maple syrup on your pancakes, made right on the grounds of the inn. Bicycles are available to explore the historic village and the surrounding countryside. In the summer, the Woodstock Inn opens its ten tennis courts. There is an 18–hole golf course on the surrounding estate and a large pool. The forestry department at the resort, headed by a graduate of the Yale School of Forestry, offers guided nature walks. Anglers can fish in the Ottauquechee River beside a covered bridge. Each guest room in the Woodstock Inn has a homemade quilt on the bed, and is decorated with antiques and colorful local handicrafts. Modern comforts are well blended with quaint New England traditions. The inn is known for its traditional New England dishes and continental cuisine. Rates are generally $34–54 and $36–56 per person for a double room. For more information contact: The Woodstock Inn, Woodstock, VT 05091 toll-free (800)225–1726.

Travel Services

The Bamboo Rod–Green Mountain Fly-Fishing School offers three-day weekend instruction sessions between May and September. The school is held on weekends from Friday through Sunday, but some

Monday through Wednesday sessions may be scheduled as well. The instructor is Bill Cairns, well-known for his practical skills as well as his theoretical teaching of fly-fishing. The instruction includes fly casting, flies and their selection, films and slides, streamside procedure, fish and their environment, knots, visits to local streams, basic stream entomology, and the selection and care of fly-fishing equipment. Students spend three days and two nights at one of Vermont's loveliest inns. The package fee includes two nights lodging (double occupancy), all meals, gratuities, instruction, a three-day Vermont fishing license and use of equipment. The cost of the weekend is $250 per person and reservations can be made by writing The Bamboo Rod–Green Mountain Fly-Fishing School, Route 100, Weston, VT 05161 (802)824–3452.

Cross-Country Outfitters at Stowe offers access to the Stowe area, cross-country trails, expert instruction, equipment rentals, and guided tours. For additional information, contact: Cross-Country Outfitters, Box 1308, Stowe, VT 05672 (802)253–4582.

Green Mountain Touring Center is a superb family cross-country skiing resort located on the 1,200–acre Green Mountain Stock Farm with 15 miles of backcountry trails. Accommodations are at the Inn which accommodates up to 30 guests and serves delicious home-cooked meals. Instruction at the ski touring center is provided by U.S. Ski Team member Bob Gray. A typical weekend package costs $65 and includes meals, instruction, trail use, and gear. For information contact: Green Mountain Touring Center, Green Mountain Stock Farm, Randolph, VT 05060 (802)728–5861.

Killington Adventure offers backpacking camping trips through the Green Mountains the White Mountains of New Hampshire and the Adirondacks of New York. In the Green Mountains one and two week hikes in the southern areas of the mountains afford the hiker moderate mountains, lush growth, streams, ponds and spectacular vistas along the way. A three-week hike covers over 100 miles with some rugged climbing. Arctic flora and fauna can be spotted along this hike. There are two White Mountain area hikes. Some venture into the steeply cut Presidential Range, with 6288 ft. Mt. Washington as the major peak. Most hikes are done in the Pemigewasset Wilderness—climbing deep into the mountains along the Pemigewasset River and to peaks of 5,000 feet. New York's Adirondacks are steep, wild, rugged mountains with abundant streams, lakes and wildlife. Mount Marcy, the highest peak at 5,344 ft. is traversed by three week hikes, while the one and two week hikes travel into the Dix range, just east of the Marcy area. Swimming in mountain waters, nature studies, rock climbing, and the sheer exhilaration of mountain air and scenery are just some of the opportunities hikers will have along the way—many of which can only be experienced in undeveloped mountain areas. Killington Adventure provides prospective hikers with pre-hike training lessons. The soon-to-be hiker learns to prepare meals out-of-doors, how to stay dry and warm in all kinds of weather, how to backpack, fundamentals of rock climbing, river crossing, the basics of navigation, "clean" camping and interesting outdoor information. Hikes are conducted in groups of eight with two guides per group. Each guide is highly skilled in some area of wilderness craft and Killington Adventure considers them one of their most important assets. Hiking groups are available for teenagers, adults, and there is a special program for mentally handicapped people. Equipment is provided on some trips, and others require hikers to provide their own. Killington Adventure will sell the necessary equipment. Each hike has a banquet at the end of the trip that is part of the Killington rate. Rates: Teen, two weeks, $250 for the first session and $225 for each additional session attended the same summer, three week teen, $335 per session.

Adults, one week $200 per session. For further information contact: Dave Langlois, Director Killington Adventure Programs, Killington VT 05751 (802)422–3139.

Mountain Top Ski Touring Center, situated close to Killington, offers a 55–mile backcountry trail system in the Green Mountain National Forest, over beautiful lakes, mountain crests, and open meadows through scenic evergreen and northern hardwood forests. Miles of trail are ideal for the novice tourer. The center, which includes accommodations in the Mountain Top Inn, is set on 500 acres of highcountry and offers instruction, ski shop and rentals, warming hut, guided moonlight tours and horse-drawn sleigh rides. The trail-use fee is $2 per person. For Inn rates and additional information, contact: Mountain Top Ski Touring Center, Chittenden, VT 05737 (802)483–2311.

The Orvis Fly Fishing School offers three days of intensive training in fly fishing. Even a neophyte can gain an understanding of it, as fly casting, fly selection and the skills and lore of fly fishing are all very teachable and when taught the correct way, open a new field of enjoyment for you. You will have a personal instructor who will provide you with a balanced outfit, stay right at your elbow and patiently check all your moves to bring you to the point of long smooth easy casts. There are illustrated lectures on fly selection, stream entomology, knot tying and a fascinating movie on the life cycle of the trout, habits and habitat. You will visit the Batten Kill with a guide for demonstrations of actual fishing under various stream conditions and be given a three day license to fish there in the evenings. You can also visit the Orvis rod factory and try out the famous fly rods. Bring chest waders and hip boots and your own rod or borrow one of theirs with a choice of bamboo, graphite or glass. Your tuition of $225 per person includes all lessons and practice sessions, a room at the lodge, meals and swimming pool. You can sign up for three day weekend or three days during the week. The school runs April-August. Contact Miss Pam Newhouse, The Orvis Fly Fishing School, 10 River Road, Manchester, VT 05254 (802)362–1300.

Quiet Sports—Canoe Service offers canoe rental, trip planning, and car shuttle service for canoeing and fishing trips on the beautiful Otter Creek, Neshobe, Lemon Fair, and Leicester rivers. Area attractions include Lake Dunmore—noted for its lake and rainbow trout—Dead Creek Wildlife Sanctuary, and the exciting brown trout and northern pike fishing on Otter Creek, which flows past farmlands, woodlands and hills, quaint villages, and wildlife areas. Canoe rental rates are $15 for the first day—$10 per day for the duration of your trip or $60 per week. For detailed information, contact: Pen Reed, Quiet Sports, Rte 7, Brandon, VT 05733 (802)247–6320.

Vermont Ski Touring Trail is a 40-mile guided tour between historic country inns in the Green Mountains with access off the Long Trail. For information on inn-to-inn tours and skiing the high route along the crest of the Green Mountains, contact: Ski Tours of Vermont, RFD #1, Chester, VT 05143 (802)875–2631. See also "Blueberry Hill Inn," "Churchill House Inn," "Mountain Meadows Lodge," and "Mountain Top Ski Touring Center" above.

Viking Ski Touring Center offers a superb trail system in the southern Green Mountains in Londonderry with groomed, marked trails, warming hut, the Nordic Trader—a first-rate ski shop—instruction, rentals, and an old-time maple sugar house. Trail fees are $2 per person. For additional information, contact: Viking Ski Touring Center, Little Pond Rd., Londonderry, VT 05148 (802)824–3933.

Wild Wings Ski Touring Center offers groomed and wilderness trails, instruction, equipment rentals, and warming hut in the southern Green Mountains with access to national forest backcountry. For additional information, contact: Wild Wings Ski Touring Center, Peru, VT 05152 (802)824–6793.

Lake Champlain Country

One of the first European discoveries in Vermont by Samuel de Champlain in 1609, the lake reaches southward from Canada for 116 miles and varies in width from one quarter of a mile to 13 miles. The lake is jointly shared by Vermont, New York and the Province of Quebec. Approximately two-thirds of its area is in Vermont, a small portion in Quebec, and the remainder in New York, linking New York City to Montreal and the Great Lakes. Bridges and ferries connect its eastern and western shores. Streams emptying into the lake and hills, mountains and wooded areas comprising the lake's shores make it a popular site of all sorts of outdoor recreation from swimming, fishing, boating to hiking and sightseeing. The Lake Champlain Islands, a group of islands and peninsulas in the lake, are rich in historic lore and offer opportunities for hikers and nature lovers. The State Forest at Burton Island is accessible by boat and provides camping, picnicking, hiking trails, boating, fishing and swimming on 253 lovely acres. This beautiful inland sea ranks with any eastern lake in the beauty of its irregular, cove-filled shoreline, with mountains framing the background of both shores, the rocky, spruce-clad islands dotting the wide northern end, and the variety and productivity of its vast expanse of water. The shallow, weedy waters of the narrow southern end offer light tackle action for largemouth bass, northern pike, pickerel, walleye, and panfish from Whitehall, New York, north past the historic narrows of Fort Ticonderoga and Crown Point, Chimney Point, Basin Harbor, and the mouth of the Otter River and into the broad, deep upper segment of Lake Champlain. As one heads up the lake, smallmouth bass and walleye become more numerous, and lakers, cisco, and whitefish appear in the deep, cold waters off Burlington and up along the shores of Vermont's scenic Grand Isle. The mooneye, *Hiodon tergisus*, is a small herringlike fish which reaches about two pounds in weight and provides great sport on light tackle such as flies and small lures. These lightweight scrappers are abundant off Chimney Point. Occasional muskellunge, landlocked salmon, and big rainbow trout are taken from the lake by fortunate anglers. Lake Champlain holds more state fish records than any other body of water in Vermont. Ice fishing is tremendously popular, and hardy winter anglers erect shanty cities on Champlain ice and take long strings of perch, walleye, smelt, burbot, whitefish, crappie, northern pike, and pickerel, as well as lake, brown, and rainbow trout.

Information Sources, Maps & Access

For detailed information on Lake Champlain contact the Vermont Development Agency, Montpelier 05602 (802)828–3231 or Fish & Game Dept., 5 Court St., Montpelier 05602 (802)828–3371. *Lake Survey Charts of Lake Champlain* may be obtained from: National Ocean Survey, Distribution Branch (C44), Riverdale, MD 20840. The Lake Champlain Region is reached via auto access routes US 7 and Interstate 89.

Gateways & Accommodations

Burlington

(Pop. 36,200; zip code 05401; area code 802). Situated on the shores of Lake Champlain in the northwest area of Vermont, Burlington is known as the "Queen of Vermont". The oldest city in Vermont, and the site of the oldest daily newspaper, it is a combination of a modern commercial city with a historic and educational past. Ethan Allen's body is buried in Greenmount Cemetery and at Ethan Allen Park, part of his farm, can be visited. Battery Park with a scenic view of the lake was a campground during the War of 1812, where three British vessels were repulsed. The University of Vermont houses the Robert Hull Fleming Museum, which contains the finest collection of Vermont Indian relics in existence in addition to a valuable collection of art and archaeology. Scenic ferry rides across Lake Champlain to Port Kent can be enjoyed May through late October. Seasonal events in the area include Champlain Shakespeare Festival at the University of Vermont; the Vermont Mozart Festival and St. Michael's Playhouse performances. The Champlain Valley Exposition is an annual country fair scheduled the week before Labor Day. Accommodations: *Holiday Inn* (rates: $42 double), with 174 excellent rooms, restaurant, cocktail lounge, heated pool on U.S. 2 at Interstate 89 junction (863–6361); *Howard Johnson's Motor Lodge* (rates: $28–37 double), with 89 excellent rooms, restaurant, cocktail lounge, heated pools on US 2 at I–89 Exit 14E, 1½ miles east of town (863–5541).

North Hero—Gateway to Lake Champlain Islands

(Pop. 400; zip code 05474; area code 802) is a popular Lake Champlain vacation area and a gateway to North Hero State Park on the lakeshore. Accommodations: *Holiday Harbor Motel* (rates: $18–24 double), with 11 good guest rooms and family units on Lake Champlain with swimming beach, boat and motor rentals on U.S. 2, 4½ miles north of town (372–4077); *Shore Acres Resort Motel* (rates: $25.50–29.50 double), with 20 excellent rooms, dining room, swimming beach, fishing, on Lake Champlain, just south of town on U.S. 2 (372–8722).

South Hero

(Pop. 870; zip code 05486; area code 802) is located off the shores of northern Vermont bordered by Lake Champlain. South Hero is the headquarters for those visiting the tranquil, lovely areas of Sand Bar State Forest Park and Grand Isle State Park. South Hero's terrain is hilly and uneven with roads leading away from the village to acres of apple orchards, farmland, stretches of island scenery, on Lake Champlain, and mountain peaks. The stone used in the walls of the Old Stone Inn, which was built in 1829 and situated at the crossroads of the village, has produced fossils that indicate that the islands were once underwater. History buffs can visit the restored Hyde Log Cabin, built by Jedediah Hyde Jr. containing items of the Revolutionary War period. The Phelps-Reade House, built in 1819 by an Englishman

believed to be named Hakings, who built many of the homes in South Hero, has been restored and contains many of the original features. Trips across Lake Champlain can be arranged with Lake Champlain Transportation Co. Ferry (802)372–5550.

Lodges & Resorts

★★★★*The Basin Harbor Club* is a magnificent 700-acre summer resort, encircling a jewel-like harbor on Lake Champlain in the Adirondacks. Basin Harbor, owned by the Beach family since 1909, has grown, under their care, from a farmed estate to one of New England's foremost summer resorts. There are lodge rooms available in the main Inn, the historic homestead, and in 65 private cabins that dot the lakefront and border the rolling, 18–hole golf course. There is a pro-shop and electric carts available for guest use, and two 9–hole putting greens. Tennis is also popular at Basin Harbor, which sports two Har-Tru and three all-weather courts. A resident tennis pro is on hand throughout July and August. Lifeguards are on duty at the pool, and swimming instruction is available. There are docks and

floats off the sandy beaches of the lake. Fishermen will find walleyed pike, small mouth bass, pickerel, great northern pike, and yellow perch in Lake Champlain. You can rent an outboard at the harbor ($6.50) or take a canoe ($2.50) if you plan to fish the coves. Lake Cruises on the 28–foot Basin Harbor cruiser "The Happy" leave twice daily from the dock ($2.50 per trip). Badminton, shuffleboard and croquet are all available. Contact: Basin Harbor Club, Vergennes, VT 05491 (802)475–2311.

★★★*Sunset Lodge*, nestled in the Champlain Valley on 32 acres of woods on the shores of Lake Dunmore, offers a quiet summer retreat. Take an outboard and fish the lake for bass, pike, lake trout, landlocked salmon, and perch, or rent a canoe and hunt for waterfalls on the other side. Rent a sailboat and bend to the wind, or hike the Long Trail, and visit Robert Frost's Memorial Cabin nearby. There is a main lodge, with TV and a piano, and bar-b-que pits for cookouts on the lake. Visit the nearby craft center in Middlebury, or explore the covered bridges, apple orchards, and country auctions.

In May and June, September and October one bedroom cottages are $105 per week. Two bedroom cottages are $105–120 per week and three bedroom cottages are $140 per week. During these months cottages may be rented on a daily basis. At the height of the season, during July and August rates are $120 per week for a one bedroom cottage, $120–145 per week two bedroom, and $165 per week three bedroom. For more information write Mr. and Mrs. F. Alfred Patterson, Jr., Sunset Lodge, Salisbury, VT 05769 (before May 15 (802)897–5592, after May 15th (802)352–4290).

★★★*The Tyler Place* is a unique family resort, spread out over 165 private acres, hugging the shores of the Shipyard, Kingfisher, and Edwards Bay on Lake Champlain. An enthusiastic college staff organizes a complete recreational program for children including swimming and diving instruction, archery, softball, arts and crafts, water polo, and water skiing. Toddlers to teens enjoy the outdoors with friends their own age, and parents are free to play tennis on any one of the seven courts, aquaplane, fish the bay for bass and pike, swim in the pool, or canoe across the bay to the wooded Canadian border. Many guests enjoy golfing at the modified 18–hole course at the Champlain Country Club, or drive to Burlington, where there is a championship course. The canoe trip down the river through the 4,600–acre wildlife refuge is a unique wilderness experience. In the evenings children dine separately in special dining rooms for their age groups, evening activities include peanut hunts and marshmallow roasts for the little ones, and teenagers enjoy dances and pool parties. Adults dine privately by candlelight, and enjoy wine and cheese parties, music, and dancing. Rooms and suites in the inn, with six bedroom cottages all with living rooms, fireplaces and kitchenettes range between $43 and 56 per person daily. For more information write: The Tyler Family, The Tyler Place, Highgate Springs, VT 05460 (802)868–3301.

Northeast Kingdom Lakes Country

The wild bogs, sprawling island-dotted lakes, ancient mountains, turbulent rivers, and fragrant north country spruce and fir forests of the Northeast Kingdom form one of New England's great fishing, hunting, and canoe-camping regions. This renowned fish and game country encompasses the northeast corner of Vermont, stretching south from the Quebec border; it contains the renowned trout, landlocked salmon, and smallmouth, bass waters of Lake Memphremagog, Barton River, Brownington Pond, Clyde River, Echo, and Island, Norton, Unknown, Holland, and Lewis ponds. Willoughby Lake is famous for its large lake trout up to 30 pounds, and the Averill, Salem, and Seymour lakes offer the best landlocked

salmon waters in the state. The remote headwaters, ponds, and beaver flows provide exciting early season and early fall fishing for big, orange-bellied squaretails for the wilderness angler who is willing to travel the old logging roads and cross country using topo map and compass. Hunting for whitetail deer and black bear is good throughout the region, particularly in the wild Yellow Bogs area.

Beautiful island-dotted Lake Memphremagog, which sprawls for 32 miles across the Vermont-Quebec boundary, offers some of the East's top "big-lake" canoeing and early season fishing for rainbow and brown trout up to ten pounds, landlocked salmon, trophy smallmouth bass, walleye, pickerel, and a few gray lake trout up to 30 pounds in the deepwater areas. The 6,317–acre Vermont portion can be considered the second-largest body of water in the state. The greater portion of the lake, however, sprawls north into Quebec. The shallow waters of the Vermont section, with its numerous points, coves, and bays, contain the bulk of the lake's spawning beds, which provide often spectacular early season sport. The best fishing during July and August is at Gibraltar Rock, Long Island, Molson Island, Fitch Bay, Owl Head Mountain, Sable Point, Derby Bay, South Bay, Black Island, Horseneck Island, and Holbrook Bay areas.

There are several north-flowing Vermont tributaries of Lake Memphremagog: the Barton River rises in Shadow Lake and flows north for 20 miles into South Bay. It provides excellent early season fishing for big lake-run rainbows, as does its feeder, the Willoughby River. The Barton holds native rainbows and buckskin-flanked browns, as well as brook trout in the remote headwaters area. The lower stretches of the river meander through a broad floodplain surrounded by low, wooded hills. The Black River, which rises from a chain of lakes in its Orleans County headwaters, flows north into South Bay and holds some big browns and rainbows. The Clyde River flows northwest from its Island Pond headwaters for 24 miles through Pensioner, Salem, and Clyde ponds into Lake Memphremagog. The Clyde holds some big squaretails in its headwaters; brown trout in the lower stretches; and rainbow trout in the fast-water areas throughout its length. Island Pond, which covers 598 acres, holds rainbow and brook trout, smallmouth bass, and walleye. Pensioner Pond holds some trophy-sized smallmouths and pickerel. Neighboring Echo Lake and 1,732–acre Seymour Lake hold lake trout, landlocked salmon, rainbow trout, and smallmouth bass. Seymour Lake also holds big brown and brook trout and is renowned for its early season gray trout fishing. Clyde Pond, a dammed portion of the river, provides some excellent walleye and smallmouth bass fishing. To the east of Island Pond the Nulhegan River, a tributary of the Upper Connecticut River, flows through a remote, seldom-traveled high country wilderness of vast swamps, wooded hills, and mountains. The wild Nulhegan holds squaretails in its headwaters and some big browns in the boulder-studded pools and eddies along its lower reaches. The famed Averill Lakes to the north hold big lake trout, landlocked salmon, brook, and rainbow trout. The remote Hurricane Brook Wildlife Management area, just south of the Quebec boundary at the head of the Pherrins River and northeast of Seymour Lake, offers some of the state's top-ranked hunting and unspoiled wilderness trophy brook trout fishing. This wild, roadless "big north" country is laced with a network of old logging trails which wind through dense northern hardwood and spruce and fir forests and provide access to Round and Beaver ponds—two of Vermont's best wild squaretail fisheries. Turtle Pond offers good chain pickerel fishing. Holland Pond, which covers 210 acres, holds some big brook, brown, and rainbow trout. Bow hunters will find good deer hunting along the game and hiking trails. Black bear are most often found along the extensive hardwood ridges. Upland bird hunters will

find ruffed grouse and woodcock. Topo maps are a must in this big country.

Beautiful Lake Willoughby—surrounded by a magnificent north country wilderness dominated by Wheeler Mountain (2,371 feet), Mount Pisgah (2,751 feet), and Bald Mountain (3,315 feet)—is a deep, narrow body of water which covers 1,692 acres and offers top-ranked fishing for landlocked salmon, lake trout, and rainbow trout up to trophy weights. Narrow Crystal Lake to the west covers 712 acres and holds big smallmouth bass, landlocked salmon, lake trout, and rainbow trout. Several scenic trails provide access to the remote headwater ponds and wilderness camping areas surrounding Lake Willoughby. The Wheeler Mountain trail climbs up over open rock and provides panoramic views of the northern Green Mountains and Lake Willoughby. The Mount Pisgah and North trails wind through scenic north woods and provide stunning views of Lake Memphremagog, northern Green Mountains, Lake Willoughby, and the Burke Mountain-Victory Bog wilderness.

The northern hardwood and conifer forests, sedge meadows, swamps, bogs, rocky mountaintops, old fields, brooks, streams, and ponds of the Victory State Forest and Victory Bog Wildlife Management Area are south of Lake Willoughby, ranging from the relatively developed Burke Mountain Area to the remote scenic wilderness of the Umpire Brook-Victory Bog area and the headwaters of the Moose River. Old logging roads, abandoned railroad beds, and primitive trails wind through the low-lying spruce and fir forests to remote fishing, hunting, and wilderness camping areas. The meadows, swamp areas and mountain summits are a naturalist's paradise, inhabited by marsh hawks, osprey, great blue heron, green heron, yellow-bellied sapsuckers, downy woodpeckers, northern water thrush, green heron, and rough-legged hawks, and carpeted by a lush understory of mountain holly, meadow sweet, hobblebush, partridge berry, dogberry, pink lady's slipper, shiny club moss, wild lily of the valley, goldthread, Indian cucumber root, wild sarsaparilla, Labrador tea, swamp candles, cayuga pondweed, painted trillium, starflower, wood sorrel, mountain ash, and dogberry. The evergreen forests are inhabited by deer, moose, black bear, coyote, lynx, marten, fisher, and weasel. Ruffed grouse and woodcock are often found along the hardwood ridges, while otter, beaver, mink, and muskrat inhabit the low-lying swamps and bogs. The Moose River provides scenic wilderness canoeing and fishing for brookies along its upper stretches and for brown trout in the lower reaches.

Information Sources, Maps & Access

The Northeast Kingdom is shown on the following U.S. Geological Survey large-scale, full-color maps, available for $1.25 each from the Distribution Branch, U.S. Geological Survey, 1200 S. Eads St., Arlington, VA 22202: Memphremagog, Island Pond, Averill, Lyndonville, Burke, Guildhall. Public use maps of the *Victory State Forest-Wildlife Management Area* and *Hurricane Brook Wildlife Management Area* may be obtained free upon request from: Fish & Game Dept., Montpelier 05602. These useful maps show roads, trails, cross-country trails, and natural features. The Northeast Kingdom is reached via Vermont Highways 100, 14, 54, and 114 and Interstate 91. Overnight accommodations, resorts, lodges, supplies, and boat and equipment rentals are available at Orleans, Barton, Newport, Island Pond, and many rural hamlets and villages.

Gateways & Accommodations

Newport—Gateway to Lake Memphremagog

(Pop. 4,700; zip code 05855; area code 802) is located in the north central part of Vermont, a few miles from the Canadian border at the southern end of Lake Memphremagog. Newport is referred to as "Border City" and serves as a gateway between Canada and New England. Lake Memphremagog provides scenic camping, boating and swimming. The area was a fishing grounds for the Indians before white settlement and continues to attract anglers. Owl Head Mountain, reaching 3,360 feet, towers over the western end of the lake's shore and provides opportunity for hiking and scenic viewing of the area. Historic sightseeing includes the Orleans County Court House on Main Street; and the Old Stone House, with the Orleans County Historical Society collection. Accommodations: *Best Western Newport City Motel* (rates: $26–28 double), with 65 excellent rooms next to restaurant at 966 E. Main St. (334–6558); *Border Motel* (rates: $28 double), with 65 excellent rooms and family units, dining room, cocktail lounge, heated pool in Derby (05829) on U.S. 5 (766–2213).

Lodges & Resorts

★★★*Burke Mountain Recreation* is located at the base of Burke Mountain surrounded by Darling State Park and 10,000 acres in the Northeast Kingdom. It's hidden away from it all, and provides the perfect year-round escape. During summer and fall, there's camping, hiking, picnicking, jogging, swimming, fishing, golf, and tennis. But the biggest attraction is in winter, with alpine and mountain skiing, touring trails, a ski school, racing academy, ski patrol and of course a ski shop, lodge, and a nursery for care of infants. Cross-country skiing attractions include 32 miles of scenic trails, a warming hut on the McGill Trail, and stop-overs at the Old Cutter Inn. Lodging is provided in deluxe condominiums from studios to four bedroom units, including fireplace/woodstove, linens, kitchens and heat for up to ten people. For further information and rates call or write Burke Mt. Recreation, Inc., East Burke, VT 05832 (802)626–3305.

★★★*Lakeside* offers three cottages on the shores of Lake Willoughby in a lovely forest and mountain area, with a private sand beach for swimming and docking. Fishing is for lake trout, landlocked salmon, and perch. Horsebackriding stables are one mile away and golf facilities seven miles away. Most guests come to enjoy the peaceful nature of the area. The cottages are simple housekeeping units supplied with state tested mountain spring water. The cabins accommodate from two to four with views of the lake and mountains. They are completely set up for housekeeping except for linen. Meals are served at restaurants within walking distance. Rates: $85–100 weekly. For further information contact: (summer) Gerrit Zwart, Barton, VT 05822 (802)525–6639; (winter) Gerrit Zwart, Suffern NY 10901 (914)357–2246.

VIRGINIA

Introduction

Virginia, known as the Old Dominion, encompasses the famed saltwater fishing and waterfowl hunting grounds of the Tidewater region; the rugged slopes, valleys, lakes and streams, and peaks of the beautiful Blue Ridge and Allegheny mountains in the Jefferson and George Washington national forests; the magnificent high camping and hiking areas of the Mount Rogers National Recreation Area; Shenandoah National Park, which extends for 80 miles along the Blue Ridge Mountains, traversed by the scenic Skyline Drive; remote forest reserve and fish and game lands, inhabited by whitetail deer, ruffed grouse, black bear, fox squirrel, red fox, raccoon, and wild turkey; and the nationally renowned smallmouth bass waters of the North and South forks of the Shenandoah River.

Accommodations & Travel Information

Detailed descriptions of Virginia vacation lodges and resorts are found in the "Vacation/Lodging Guide" which follows. For detailed travel information, contact: Virginia Travel Service, 911 E. Broad St., Richmond, VA 23219 (703)786–4484. Virginia's vast national and state forest and park lands offer hundreds of well-maintained campgrounds and recreation cabin facilities. State park recreational campground areas include Bear Creek Lake, adjoining Cumberland State Forest near the Willis River and the town of Dillwyn; Chippokes Plantation State Park, on the James River across from Jamestown; Clayton Lake State Park, near Pulaski and Radford in western Virginia (cabins); Douthat State Park, near the Allegheny Mountains and the city of Clifton Forge (cabins); Fairy Stone State Park, next to the Philpott Reservoir (cabins); Goodwin Lake State Park, off Route 460 in southern Virginia; holiday Lake, on the Appomattox River in south central Virginia; Hungry Mother, just north of Marion and the Mount Rogers National Recreation Area (cabins); Natural Tunnel, in southwest Virginia off Route 23 (cabins, camping); Occoneechee, near Clarksville on Buggs Island Lake; Pocahontas State Forest and Park, about 10 miles southwest of Richmond; Prince Edward, off Route 360 in south central Virginia (cabins); Seashore State Park, near Norfolk and Virginia Beach (cabins); Staunton River State Park, on Buggs Island Lake (cabins); and Westmoreland, on the Potomac (cabins). For information and reservations in state forests and parks containing cabins or campsites write: Divisions of Parks, 1201 State Office Bldg., Richmond 23219.

National park campground facilities along the Blue Ridge Parkway include Otter Creek Campground, about 15 miles northwest of Lynchburg; Peaks of Otter, about 10 miles north of Bedford; Roanoke Mountain, just outside Roanoke; and Rocky Knob, 20 miles west of Philpott Reservoir (cabins). In the Shenandoah National Park, major recreation areas are Big Meadows (cabins); Lewis Mountain (cabins); Loft Mountain, Matthews Arm Campground, and Skyland (cabins). Major national facilities in George Washington National Forest are Sherando Lake and Todd Lake. In Jefferson National Forest, the major recreation areas include Cave Mountain Lake, Cave Springs, and Mount Rogers National Recreation Area.

Highways & Maps

Beginning at the southern end of the Skyline Drive in Rockfish Gap, the Blue Ridge Parkway extends for 469 miles through George Washington and Jefferson national forests to Cherokee, North Carolina, just south of the Great Smoky Mountains National Park. Constructed for recreational purposes only, the route is limited to passenger vehicles and consists of a two-lane roadway running through a strip of parkway varying in width from 500 to 1,200 feet on either side. The landscape bordering the drive has been left as unspoiled as

possible, affording a panorama of striking scenery ranging from superb mountain vistas to quiet rural farmlands.

Originally much of the Blue Ridge Parkway's route through Virginia was part of the Appalachian Trail. The trail has been relocated to lands on either side of the parkway, usually in the national forest preserves. Because it crosses the parkway in many places along its route through the national forests, easy access to the trail is provided by the parkway, making short trips of 1–3 days possible. There are many picnic areas with water supply, toilet facilities, and concession stands in summer along the parkway. Overnight and restaurant accommodations are available at Doughton Park, North Carolina, and Rocky Knob. A free *Blue Ridge Parkway Map-Brochure* describing points of interest and listing mile posts along the parkway may be obtained from: Superintendent, Blue Ridge Parkway, P.O. Box 1710, Roanoke 24008 (703)982–6213. Descriptions of concessions and lodgings with a reservation request form are contained in a leaflet issued free by: National Park Concessions, Blue Ridge Parkway Operations, Laurel Springs, NC 28644.

An *Official Virginia Highway Map* may be obtained free by writing to: Dept. of Highways & Transportation, 1221 E. Broad St., Richmond 23219. This useful full-color map shows state parks and forests, national forests, highways and roads, ferries, travel information stations and rest areas, national and state fish hatcheries, national wildlife refuges, and other points of interest.

VACATION/ LODGING GUIDE

Blue Ridge Parkway

See above and the North Carolina chapter under "Pisgah National Forest & The Blue Ridge Parkway" for details and accommodations.

Shenandoah National Park & The Skyline Drive

Extending for 80 miles along the Blue Ridge Mountains between Front Royal on the north and Waynesboro on the south, the Shenandoah National Park covers about 193,500 acres, over 300 square miles, of northwestern Virginia. Sixty peaks, ranging in elevation from 3,000 to 4,000 feet, rise within the park, providing the backbone for the famous Skyline Drive. Following the older Appalachian Trail most of the way along the crest of the ridge, the drive offers a continuous, almost numbing series of spectacular views over wooded ravines and occasional rocky crags to the undulating Piedmont Plateau on the east end across the rolling farmlands of the Shenandoah Valley to the Alleghenies on the west.

The area presently covered by the park was once farmed and extensively lumbered. Its most prosperous period occurred between the mid–18th and late–19th century when farming and, later, mining were the chief activities of the region. Late in the 19th century the demand for mountain handicrafts waned and a blight destroyed most of the chestnut trees. With the decline of interest in mining and agriculture, families began to move away from the area and the population dwindled. Soon the forest began to take over, and today nearly all the land within the park is heavily wooded with oak, pine, and other species. There are over 900 different kinds of flowering plants in the area. Just as the forest returned after human activity declined, so the wildlife began to make a comeback. Among the larger mammals, white-tailed deer are most common; other animals, including bobcat, gray fox, black bear, and woodchuck, may also be glimpsed in dense forest areas.

In addition, many small feeder streams such as Big Ugly Run, Big Creek, Brokenback Run, Rose River, and Overall Run provide some of the few remaining strongholds of native eastern brook trout in the southeastern United States. Because of the park's long, ridge-like topography, streams tend to be short with steep gradients. Trout found within the streams are small, rarely exceeding 12 inches and usually measuring from 5 to 8 inches. There are several other species of fish within the park streams, but trout are the only fish

that may be legally caught. Because of the size of the streams and density of the forest cover, fishermen will find most of the waters very brushy with little casting room. The best way to fish the streams is from the lower boundaries of the park. Fishing is not permitted near any of the park campgrounds or Skyline Drive. Most of the park is open to "backcountry camping," defined by park officials as any use of portable shelters or sleeping equipment in areas of the park that are more than 250 yards from a paved road, and more than ½ mile from any park facilities other than trails, unpaved roads, and trail shelters. Permits are required and are available from park headquarters, visitor centers, and all entrance stations. There are also 6 fully equipped, locked cabins in backcountry areas, able to accommodate a total of up to 12 people. Reservations are necessary and can be made with Potomac Appalachian Trail Club, 1718 N. St., NW, Washington, DC 20036.

There are 4 family campgrounds within the park. Big Meadows in the central section near Fishers Gap is the largest of these and is open year round; 253 campsites are available as well as showers, a laundry, and nearby food services. Horseback riding, an amphitheater, and fishing streams are additional attractions. Also in the central park section is Lewis Mountain Campground, open mid-May to October and offering 32 sites. Matthews Area in the northern section near Hogback Overlook off Knob Mountain Road offers 186 campsites and is open mid-April to October. Loft Mountain near Big Run Overlook on the Skyline Drive in the southern section offers 31 campsites, showers, a laundry, and a nearby store, and is open mid-April to October. Available only to organized youth groups, Dundo Campgrounds is open April to October and must be reserved in advance from park headquarters. Tables and fireplaces are provided at all campsites, with piped water, comfort stations, and sewage disposal stations nearby. There are no trailer hookups. Camping limit is 14 days.

Information Sources, Maps & Access

For detailed information and a free *Shenandoah National Park Map/Brochure*, contact: National Park Service, Shenandoah National Park, Luray, VA 22835 (703)999–2266. For useful, full-color *U.S. Geological Survey Maps of Shenandoah National Park* (Northern, Central and Southern sections, $2 each), write: Distribution Branch, U.S. Geological Survey, 1200 S. Eads St., Arlington, VA 22202. Trail guides published by the Appalachian Trail Conference are invaluable in following the footpath. For Virginia, three guides to the Appalachian Trail are needed to complete the entire route. *The Susquehanna River to the Shenandoah National Park and Side Trails* ($4.79; no maps) covers the trail from Clarks Ferry Bridge in Pennsylvania through Maryland, West Virginia, and northern Virginia as far as Shenandoah Park. The *Guide to the Appalachian Trail & Side Trails in Shenandoah National Park* ($4.79; no maps) covers the major and minor trails through the whole of the park, between Chester and Rockfish gaps. *Central and Southwestern Virginia* ($6.10 including maps) follows the trail from Rockfish Gap through Jefferson and George Washington national forests to the Tennessee border. Each guide contains profuse trail data (from north to south and from south to north), including mileage, difficulty, points of interest, campgrounds, recreation areas, and points of access and exit. The natural and human history of the area and the story of the Appalachian Trail are provided in some detail. Guides may be ordered from: Appalachian Trail Conference, P.O. Box 236, Harpers Ferry, WV 25425. Please allow 3 weeks delivery, or to expedite shipment include $1 for special mailing and note the addition with your order.

Maps for the trail may also be ordered separately: PATC Map #7

covers the North Virginia trail section from Harpers Ferry to Snickers Gap ($1); PATC Map #8 follows the trail between Snickers and Chester gaps ($1); PATC Maps #9, 10, and 11 show the trail in the Shenandoah National Park ($3.25). Each map shows the Appalachian and side trails, shelters, lookout towers, names of mountain ridges, rivers and creeks, roads, towns, and highways. Maps may be ordered from: ATC (above address). Major routes leading to Shenandoah National Park include Interstate 81 and 66, and Interstate 64 from Richmond. The park is traversed north and south by the scenic Blue Ridge Parkway. Lodging, supplies, and canoe rentals are available at towns and villages surrounding the park, including Front Royal, Luray, Elkton, Waynesboro, and Charlottesville.

Lodges

Shenandoah National Park covers 300 square miles of beautiful Blue Ridge Mountain country. The 105–mile Skyline Drive traverses the park and along this road, visitors will find accommodations in two lodges and a cottage complex. A visit should begin at Dickey Ridge or Big Meadows Visitors Centers where guests of the park will find orientation programs and exhibits. Then there are over 400 miles of scenic trails to explore, including well-marked trails and a 94–mile link of the Appalachian Trail. There are also 25 miles of horseback riding trails and stables with guided trips. Fishing is popular, especially for brook trout in the mountain streams. Wildlife are abundant and include deer, black bear, woodchuck, bobcat, gray fox and nearly 200 species of birds. Visitors can even find seventeen kinds of orchids and a virgin hemlock forest. Reservations in all accommodations, information on the Skyline Drive and other park facilities can be obtained by writing or calling ARA-Virginia Skyline Co., Inc., P.O. Box 727, Luray, VA 22835 (703)743–5108.

★★*Big Meadows Lodge* is in the middle of Skyline Drive and has

accommodations for 250, a dining room, conference room, cocktail lounge and mountain craft shop. Bicycles can be rented at Big Meadows for sightseeing the area, and there are horseback and nature trails as well. All the facilities are open from April 28 through October 30. In winter, from November through April 27, motel rooms only are available and the Big Meadows Wayside with a coffee shop, gift and craft shop, service station and a camp store is open. Accommodations in the main lodge in a room for two persons complete with private bath and terrace overlooking the valley are $29.75 per night. Rooms without the terrace are $21 or $22 per night. Motel rooms with a valley view are $29.75 and cottage rooms with a fireplace are $24. There are one- and two-bedroom suites with living room and fireplace starting at $42 for two persons. For reservations and information write or phone: ARA-Virginia Skyline Co. (703) 999–2221; the winter number is (703)743–5108.

★★*Lewis Mountain* has more rustic cottage accommodations. The modern, furnished cottages, complete with private baths, have attached outdoor cooking and living areas with a concrete floor, roof, fireplace and picnic table. Guests can cook on the outdoor grill and there is an electrical outlet and a water tap outdoors. Families enjoy eating outdoors, and they can rent cooking utensils at the nearby camp store. Lewis Mountain accommodations are open from late April through October and reservations are accepted starting January 1st. A one-room cottage with attached outdoor eating area accommodating up to four persons is $19 a day. A two-bedroom cottage with connecting bath, accommodating six, with a private outdoor area is $32 a day. For reservations and information write or phone: ARA-Virginia Skyline Co. (703)743–5108.

★★*Skyland Lodge* overlooks the Shenandoah Valley from the highest point on Skyline Drive. It is open from late March through early November. Skyland has horseback riding, guided hikes in the summer, and evening programs given by a naturalist. There are accommodations for 400 people, as well as a dining room, a banquet room, a conference hall and a cocktail lounge. Skyland Lodge has motel-lodge rooms, cottage rooms, and suites. Motel rooms have two double beds, a private bath and a view of the valley. One or two persons in a room are $29.75 per night on the European Plan. Cottage rooms have one or two double beds and private baths, but no view. They range from $18 to $20 for one or two persons. There are also suites with one or two bedrooms, connecting to a living room with a fireplace. These range from $43 for a one-bedroom suite for two, to $71 for a two-bedroom suite for 4, 5 or 6 persons. There are no housekeeping accommodations and no meal plans. Information and reservations by writing ARA-Virginia Skyline Co. at the address above or telephoning the lodge at (703)999–2211.

Other Virginia National Forests & Recreation Areas

The George Washington National Forest in northwest Virginia includes over 1 million acres of rugged mountains and hiking, fishing, hunting, and wilderness camping country in a dozen counties. About 100,000 acres of the forest spill over into West Virginia. Hundreds of miles of forest roads, canoe trails, and hiking trails, including the Appalachian Trail, provide access to the Ramseys Draft, Crawford Mountain, Little River, Rich Hole, and Laurel Fork wilderness areas, the Highlands, Little North Mountain, Goshen and Wunder wildlife management areas, the Maury, James, Bullpasture, Dry, Cowpasture, Jackson, and North Fork Shenandoah rivers, and Elkhorn, Hearthstone, and Sherando lakes. The forest and the 70,000 acres of state wildlife management areas have some

of the finest hunting in the East for whitetail deer, black bear, wild turkey, grouse, quail, and raccoon. The highland headwaters offer good fishing for pan-size rainbow and brook trout.

Of particular interest to hunting and fishing enthusiasts is the Ramseys Draft area in the Deerfield and Dry River ranger districts. The draft is a clear trout stream arising about 25 miles northwest of Staunton; it drains the narrow valley between the parallel ridges of the Shenandoah Mountains on the west and Bald Ridge on the east. The area was the first portion of the George Washington National Forest to be purchased when the forest was being established, and it has never been logged. As a consequence, Ramseys Draft is unique in Virginia because of its large area of virgin timber: extremely tall hemlocks, giant white pines, and tulip trees grow in the valley and along the draft and its tributary creeks. This substantial roadless area provides a habitat for many wildlife species including a sizable population of black bear. Still essentially an isolated wilderness with little evidence of human activity, the terrain is characterized by steep slopes almost everywhere except near the eastern periphery.

The 6,000 acres of the Rich Hole Wilderness Area in the James River district are covered by a virgin stand of Appalachian hardwood forest. Along the streams—short offshoots of the Cowpasture River's South Fork—grow large hemlocks of apparent great age. The solitude and unspoiled beauty of the area are such that entering the wilderness from nearby U.S. 60 is like leaving the sights and sounds of our high-speed technology for a walk through the remote past. Northern red oak, basswood, and tulip poplar share the wilderness with a variety of game animals: black bear, white-tailed deer, raccoon, gray squirrel, ruffed grouse, and wild turkey. Two small headwater creeks provide a habitat for the native brook trout which spawn in them, and a pair of trails—Rich Hole and North Branch—meet near Brushy Mountain, in the heart of the wilderness.

Sprawled across 575,000 acres of the Blue Ridge and Allegheny mountains of Virginia, Jefferson National Forest offers many opportunities for just about every form of outdoor recreation. The forest's liberal seasons and bag limits permit excellent hunting opportunities for deer, black bear, wild turkey, ruffed grouse, and fox squirrels. Fishermen will find native brook trout in the high headwater streams of the James River and stream-raised brown and rainbow at lower elevations. The larger streams—Hunting Camp Creek, Laurel Creek, Dry Branch, Johns Creek, and others—are heavily stocked throughout the season. Nearby reservoirs such as the Gatewood and Big Cherry offer fine fishing for small- and largemouth bass, pickerel, panfish, walleye, and muskellunge. The Appalachian Trail winds for 95 miles through the Jefferson National Forest. Through Iron, Walker, Brushy, and Creek mountains the trail is well marked with white paint blazes, standard Appalachian Trail markers, and with Forest Service and state highway signs at intersections, shelters, and points of interest. Immediately adjacent to the Blue Ridge Parkway, the James River Face forms the easternmost portion of the forest and is just 35 miles northeast of busy Roanoke. The wilderness has rugged terrain, with a network of steep ridges and hollows and a precipitous drop to the James River. Views of the James River Gap are particularly spectacular. The area is traversed by a section of the Appalachian Trail, and a number of old logging roads provide additional trails through the area. A trail shelter not far from the James River and campsites near Cave Mountain Lake offer opportunities for a breather or for overnight camping.

The Mount Rogers National Recreation Area and the White Rocks area, the southernmost extension of the forest, duplicate the look and atmosphere of a Swiss alpine setting with stands of deep green spruce and high mountain vegetation. The highest mountain in

Virginia at 5,729 feet, Mount Rogers is joined by a saddle to nearby Pine Mountain (5,526 feet). The area formed by these two mountains, managed as part of the Jefferson National Forest, is unusual for a number of reasons. Fraser fir and red spruce caps, even at the highest elevations, are unique in Virginia. Below these fir caps are northern hardwood forests (beech, oak, and hickory), which are generally indigenous only to the northern United States and Canada. In addition, the high plateau and open meadows characteristic of most of the region give the area a strikingly anomalous alpine flavor, as though a high Swiss mountain plateau had been miraculously transplanted to the rugged lands of southwest Virginia. These features give the Mount Rogers area a feeling of height and vastness, and a mood found nowhere else in the state.

The area abounds in opportunities for outdoor adventures: fishing in Straight Branch, Jones Creek, and the Holston River; horseback riding in the mountain; and hiking on many trails including the Iron Mountain and a section of the Appalachian. Winter sports are popular, as well as swimming, hunting, and canoe trips. There are campgrounds, including some with showers and flush toilets, at Bear Tree, Comers Rock, Grindstone, Hurricane, Shepherds Corner, and Raccoon Branch. Nearby are the New River, Buck Lake, Rural Retreat Fishing Lake, and the Grayson Highlands State Park. The beautiful Blue Ridge Mountains and valley country of central Virginia offer hundreds of miles of wild trout streams, remote blue lakes, and scenic, nationally renowned smallmouth bass waters in the Jefferson and George Washington national forests and Shenandoah National Park. The headwaters of the James River, formed by the Jackson and Cowpasture rivers in the George Washington National Forest, hold good-sized smallmouth bass and trout in the upper sections. The stretch of the Jackson flowing through the Gathright Wildlife Man-

agement Area offers top-ranked fishing for rainbow and brown trout. Beautiful Back Creek, which rises in the Gathright WMA, produced the state record brook trout. The remote mountain streams and ponds of the James River and Warm Springs ranger districts of the George Washington National Forest, particularly the renowned Bullpasture River and Big Lick, Dry Run, and Wolf Run creeks, provide good to excellent fishing for rainbow, brook, and brown trout. The famous smallmouth bass and canoeing waters of the winding North and South forks of the Shenandoah surround the Lee range district of the George Washington National Forest before their union at Front Royal to form the main branch of the Shenandoah.

The headwaters and forest tributaries of the North Fork of the Shenandoah, including the Big and Little Stony creeks, offer trout fishing. Shenandoah National Park offers fishing for wild trout in the Blue Ridge headwaters of the Rapidan, Rivanna, and Moormans rivers. The Rappahannock offers some top-ranked smallmouth bass fishing and canoeing from its headwaters, including the Rapidan and Hazel Creek, downstream to the dam at Fredericksburg. The upper stretches of the Potomac, which forms Virginia's northern border for 156 miles, hold a large population of smallmouth bass.

State-managed "fish-for-fun" areas, where anglers are limited to artificial lures and single barbless hooks and all trout caught must be returned to the stream, are established on the Rapidan River in Madison County, Big Cedar Creek in Russell County, Dan River in Patrick County, Little River in Floyd County, Snake Creek in Carroll County, Little Stony Creek in Carroll County, and on Passage Creek. Large rainbows up to 24 inches and brook trout about a foot long are commonly caught on the fish-for-fun section of the Rapidan. Pay-as-you-go trout fishing is offered on the upper

reaches of Big Tumbling Creek including Laurel Bed Lake and Creek, in the Clinch Mountain Wildlife Management Area and in Douthat State Park Lake, including a portion of Wilson Creek upstream to the park boundary, these are stocked regularly throughout the season. Fishermen are required to buy a $1 daily permit in addition to having an applicable fishing license.

Information Sources, Maps & Access

For detailed recreation information and a full-color *George Washington National Forest Map* (50¢) contact: Supervisor, George Washington National Forest, Federal Bldg., Harrisonburg, VA 22801 (703)433–2491. *Sportsman's Guides to the George Washington National Forest* specifically tailored for hunters and fishermen, showing stocked streams, forest and wildlife management areas, campsites, highways, roads, fish hatcheries, and parking and recreation areas, are available for the Deerfield, Lee, Pedlar, Dry River, James River, and Warm Springs ranger districts. These free maps as well as information on hunting and fishing regulations are available from: Commission of Game & Inland Fisheries, P.O. Box 11104, Richmond, VA 23230.

For a full-color *Jefferson National Forest Map* (50¢), recreation information, and the free *Map of the Appalachian Trail in the Jefferson National Forest, Mt. Rogers National Recreation Area Map*, and *Sportsman's Guides to the Jefferson National Forest*, contact: Supervisor, Jefferson National Forest, 3517 Brandon Ave., SW, Roanoke, VA 24018.

Virginia fishing and hunting regulations, and the following free publications may be obtained by writing to: Commission of Game & Inland Fisheries, P.O. Box 11104, Richmond 23230 (703)257–1000. The free *Boating Access Map to Virginia Waters* shows all boat-launching ramps in the state managed by the commission. The useful free guide *Freshwater Fishing in Virginia* describes license requirements, reservoirs, streams, and public fishing waters; it contains a map of Virginia waters and a Virginia fishing calendar. The free 24–page *Virginia Hunters' Guide* describes license requirements, hunting seasons, distribution of game, hunting methods, and hunting on private lands; it contains a useful map of public hunting lands, and lists and describes bow-hunting areas, shooting preserves, sportsman's organizations, and annual harvest records by county. In addition, the commission publishes two free guides to the state's game lands: *Wildlife Management Areas* and *The Sportsman's Guide to the Goshen-Little North Mountain Wildlife Area in the Remote Western Blue Ridge Mountains*. The *Sportsman's Guide to Virginia's Piedmont State Forests* may be obtained free from: Division of Forestry, Box 3758, Charlottesville 22903. The major routes leading to the George Washington forest are Interstate 64 from the east and west, and Interstate 81 from the north and south. The forest is traversed east and west by U.S. 33 and 250, and by U.S. 220 from the north and south. Lodging, supplies, gear, and canoe rentals are available at many towns and villages in the forest vicinity, including Clifton Forge, Millboro Spring, Staunton, Waynesboro, Head Waters, Sun Rise, Mountain Grove, Brandywine, Sugar Grove, and Natural Bridge. The major routes to Jefferson National Forest are Interstate Highways 81, 77, 581, and 64. Lodging, supplies, fishing, hunting and camp gear, and canoe rentals are available at Wytheville, Bluefield, Rural Retreat, Marion, Tazewell, Narrows, Pearisburg, Blacksburg, Dublin, Pulaski, Buena Vista, New Castle, Salem, Roanoke, and Chilhowie.

Lodges & Resorts

★★★*Boar's Head Inn* looks like a country estate during the days of the American Revolution or back in merrie old England. It is located in the green hills of Virginia near Charlottesville in the heart of Thomas Jefferson country. Massive pine timbers from an 1834 grist mill were used to build the inn's west wing where the two dining rooms are located. Architectural features of the building include the old-fashioned bed alcoves and covered arcades. Antiques and sporting prints add to the mood of Colonial times. There are two lakes on the estate for the enjoyment of guests and the lakes are populated by a flock of several hundred Canadian geese, swans, mallards and other ducks. Visitors can tour the hunt country and the Blue Ridge Mountains, visit the homes of Jefferson, Madison and Monroe, or see the many museums and historical sights in the area. Guests can order breakfast in bed, lunch by the lake or dinner in the charming colonial dining rooms. In the evening, there is dancing in the Downstairs Lounge to a "Big Band" beat. For those who want active recreation, the inn has a Sports Club. Guests at the inn can pay a membership fee of $5 per day per person plus $1 for each additional member of a family. With the Sports Club membership, guests enjoy free use of the three platform tennis courts, lighted for night play; a social round pool; a 75–foot, six-lane pool for lap swimming; a wading pool for youngsters; and separate gym facilities

for men and women. There is a moderate charge for use of the tennis courts, the squash courts and for massages. The Sports Club has four squash courts, including one of the few doubles courts in the state. The ten clay courts have been the site of National Clay Court Championship play and there are also four all-weather Grasstex tennis courts. The Boar's Head Inn room rates are $32 single occupancy, $38 double occupancy and $56 for suites. Children under 12 are free and pets are $2 per day. For more information, contact: The Boar's Head Inn, Ednam Forest, Charlottesville, VA 22903 (804)296–2181.

★★★★*Bryce Resort & Ski Center in the Shenandoah Valley* is a year round resort on 45–acre Lake Laura, surrounded by the mountainous George Washington National Forest. Winter sports include day and night skiing on three runs ranging from beginner to expert. Beginners are given special instructional attention and experts will enjoy the excitement of special racing events. There is a ski boutique with a complete line of ski rentals and a repair shop. Warm weather also brings a full range of activities. Golfers can tee off on an 18–hole course, 1,300 feet above sea level. Golf pro, practice holes, carts and pro shop are all on hand. Tennis buffs can take advantage of five outdoor courts, with three lighted, and two indoor courts. Lake Laura has a fine sandy beach, and swimming. Sailboats, canoes and paddle boats are available. There is scenic horseback

riding and pony rides with instruction available for children. Hikers can enjoy the mountains of George Washington National Forest. A special attraction of the resort is grass skiing. A 25–inch rolling track ski attaches to any ski boot and participants can ski without snow. Rentals and professional instruction are available. The resort has a flight school and a 2,500 foot, lighted landing strip. In addition, guests can enjoy bicycling, an outdoor pool, a sauna and evening entertainment at the resort's lounge. Accommodations include condominiums overlooking the ski slopes; townhouses located directly on the golf course; and chalets in woodsy settings. All accommodations are furnished and have kitchens and fireplaces. The resort has a 300-seat capacity restaurant, plus a snack bar and cafeteria. Rates: condominiums and townhouses, single, weekday are $30, weekends and holidays, $40. Vacation special for six nights and seven days is $300 with four person minimum. Chalets are $70–80, with four person minimum. Vacation special for six nights and seven days is $295–335. Meals are not included in rates, but special packages exist including meals. For further information contact: Bryce Resort, P.O. Box 3, Basye, VA 22810 (703)856–2121.

★★★*Cascades Inn at Hot Springs*, a gracious southern colonial inn, is situated at the head of Cascades gorge in the Allegheny Mountains. The broad veranda of the stately inn overlooks the open lawns, and the large outdoor swimming pool. The Cascades Golf Course, a lush, 18–hole mountain course, bordered by springs and tiny waterfalls, is the new home of Sam Snead. Lower Cascade Course, and Homestead Course only three miles away, triple your golfing challenge. The three mile Cascade Stream is annually stocked with trout, and the staircase falls in the gorge is a favorite picnic spot. Three private cottages are available, secluded on the wooded grounds surrounding the inn. All the inn's guests are free to use the facilities of the nearby Homestead Resort which include dancing, riding, golf, tennis, shooting skeet or trap, a spa, and indoor and outdoor pools. Daily rates at the Cascades Inn include breakfast and dinner and are $45–47 daily per person double occupancy and $47–49 per person single occupancy. Cottages accommodate 2–12 people and are $45–51 daily. For more information write: The Cascades Inn, Drawer U, Hot Springs, VA 24445 (703)839–5355.

★★★★*Mountain Lake Hotel* is in the Allegheny Mountains on the clear blue waters of Mountain Lake, 4,000 ft. above sea level. It is 275 miles from Washington, DC and 229 miles from Richmond. The hotel offers a complete package with lodging in the hotel or rustic cottages, all meals and most recreational facilities included. Fishing in the 250–acre lake stocked with rainbow trout, bass and perch is free with the hotel providing fishing equipment. There is also no charge for use of rowboats, for use of the tennis courts and equipment, for swimming in the lake, or for playing badminton, croquet, ping-pong, horseshoes or pool. The hotel has a rough nine-hole course that can be played at no charge, and there are scenic walks and hiking trails through 2,200 acres of mountains. The hotel has a string of trail horses for hire at $5 per hour. Guests also have golf and pool privileges at New Castle Rock Club where green fees are $4 weekdays and $5 weekends. Evening entertainment includes an orchestra on Saturday nights, bingo twice a week and movies nightly. Meals are served in the hotel dining room and casual dress is permitted. The season is from June 1st through October 1st. Rooms with private bath, American Plan, are $48 to $52 for two persons. There are also rates for children and for connecting rooms with two to four persons. A living room suite for two persons on the American Plan is $66 per day. Multi-unit cottages with one bedroom are $44 to 46 for two persons with all meals included. Individual cottages with two and three bedrooms and two baths range from $50 for two persons to $118 for six persons. For more information and reservations write or call Mountain Lake Hotel, Mountain Lake, VA 24136 (703)626–7121.

Travel Services

Downriver Canoe Company. Located just 10 miles south of Front Royal, Virginia on Rt. 340 in the village of Bentonville, offers the finest in canoes and service on one of America's most scenic rivers, the South Fork of the Shenandoah. The river flows northward through a narrow section of the Shenandoah Valley, between Shenandoah National Park and the George Washington National Forest. Camping and picnicking spots are numerous because of its close proximity to the Appalachian Trail. Many Indian artifacts remain from a by-gone age. Several limestone caves just off the river await the more adventurous. For rates and detailed information, contact: Downriver Canoe Company, Rte. 1, Box 256A, Bentonville, VA 22610 (703)635–5526.

Shenandoah River Outfitters, Inc., located in the George Washington National Forest, two hours from Washington D.C., can provide you with the opportunity to discover the beauty and serenity of the Shenandoah River—by canoe. They are the oldest and largest outfitters in the mid-Atlantic, with eight years of experience. The South Fork of the Shenandoah, flowing between the Blue Ridge and Massanutten mountains, is a show case of nature's wonders with green landscape, an abundance of wildlife, and intricate rock formations. The rapids are navigable for the novice but intricate enough for the advanced canoeist with class III rapids at Compton. The river provides many fine fishing areas for smallmouth bass and perch. Shenandoah River Outfitters will provide all the necessities for your canoe excursion in the backcountry—for one day or two weeks, for two miles to 100 miles. They will provide day canoe rentals for 1 to 300 persons or complete outfitting with all camping gear, food and guides for 2 to 150 persons. Canoe rental is $22 per day, half price on the third day. Excursions with guide for two days is $60, for three days, $80 with all the essentials for the trip being furnished. You need only bring your Virginia fishing license if you wish to fish. Partial outfitting is also available. Special Canoe Steak days are available on request. For further information or reservations contact: Shenandoah River Outfitters, RFD 3, Luray, VA 22835 (703)743–4150.

Introduction

West Virginia is a land of surprises. The Mountain State embraces some of the eastern United States' most spectacular wild country, much of which is reminiscent of the north country of eastern Canada. The Monongahela National Forest in the Allegheny Mountain Range encompasses the arcticlike wild sphagnum and cranberry bogs, mats of heath shrubs, huckleberry plains, beaver ponds, and swift-flowing runs of the Cranberry backcountry—once known as the "Wilds of Pocahontas"—and the often fog-shrouded Dolly Sods backcountry. The forest also takes in the wild trout waters of Seneca Creek, Shavers Fork, and the Cranberry River, which holds transplanted golden-rainbow hybrids; the trophy muskellunge waters of the Elk River; and the wild and scenic South Branch of the Potomac, the best smallmouth bass stream in the East, with a wild 7–mile gorge.

Accommodations & Travel Information

Descriptions of the state's premier lodges and resorts are found in the "Vacation/Lodging Guide" which follows. For detailed information on all aspects of vacation travel in the state, contact: Travel Development Div., Dept. of Commerce, State Capitol, Charleston, WV 25305 (304)348–3456. *West Virginia Hotels & Motels*, an alphabetical listing by town, gives rates, number of units, facilities available, addresses, and phone numbers and can be obtained free from: Dept. of Commerce (address above). Descriptions of the state parks and forests, including detailed information on accommodations and public hunting and fishing areas, are contained in the booklet *West Virginia State Parks and Forests*, also available at no cost from the department. *Camping West Virginia*, a brochure available free from: Travel Development Division, Dept. of Commerce, State Capitol, Charleston 25305, lists all campgrounds alphabetically by city, giving addresses, phone numbers, number and type of campsites, and a brief description of facilities. A list and map of public hunting and fishing area campgrounds is also found in *West Virginia State Parks & Forests*.

Highways & Maps

The state's highway and road system is shown on a full-color *West Virginia Highway & Tourist Map* available free from: Travel Development Division, Dept. of Commerce, State Capitol, Charleston 25305. The map shows all major and secondary roads, airports, points of interest, and state and national forests. It also contains a state park and forest facilities chart and camping information. One of the major features of the state's scenic highway system is the New River Bridge, which carries the Appalachian Corridor "L" highway across a scenic gorge deep in the hills of Fayette County. The bridge is the world's longest steel arch, with a main span of 1,700 feet across the canyon.

WEST VIRGINIA

**VACATION/
LODGING GUIDE**

West Virginia Forests, Lakes & Wild Rivers

West Virginia's rugged Appalachian Highlands, national and state forest lands, remote wild areas, and wild, turbulent rivers and mountain streams offer some of the finest hunting, fishing, backpacking, camping, and cross-country skiing opportunities in the eastern United States. The Wildlife Resources Division of the Department of Natural Resources maintains 35 areas for hunting, fishing, camping, or access to the prime fishing and hunting lands, including the Monongahela and portions of the Jefferson and George Washington national forests, and nine state forests. West Virginia offers over a million acres of public lands to the outdoorsman. Basically the state is divided into two physiographic regions by the Allegheny Front. The Allegheny Plateau covers the western two-thirds of the state, where hundreds of streams cut the region into a maze of wooded valleys and rolling hills. The scenic highlands in the northeast portion of the plateau, where more than 40 peaks exceed 4,000-foot elevations in the Monongahela National Forest, give rise to fast-flowing trout streams that form the headwaters of the state's major rivers, including the famous smallmouth bass waters of the South Branch of the Potomac, and the wild Cheat, Elk, Gauley, Tygart, and Greenbrier rivers. The Monongahela, Kanawha, and the wild New River tributaries of the Ohio River drain an area of approximately 21,000 square miles. The state's principal game fish are the scrappy, acrobatic smallmouth bass, found in most warmwater streams of the state; the elusive muskellunge, found in the big-river tributaries of the Ohio; and brook, brown, and rainbow trout, found in the lakes and streams of the eastern highlands.

The most productive trout fishing is found in the remote backcountry glades of the picturesque Cranberry River in the Monongahela National Forest, and in the Williams, South Branch of the Potomac near Petersburg, North Fork of the Cheat River, Shavers Fork of the Cheat, and the Elk River above Webster Springs. Some of the state's finest trout fishing is found among the tundralike bogs, beaver meadows, and wilderness highlands of the Monongahela National Forest. Access is by hiking trails and packhorse. The state has established quality trout fishing "catch and release" regulations on the Back Fork of the Elk River in Webster County, beginning 2 miles upstream from Webster Springs, extending upstream 4 miles; and on the Shavers Fork, a 5½-mile section in the Monongahela National Forest in Randolph County, north of U.S. 250, extending downstream to the mouth of McGee Run. The Back Fork can be reached from state secondary routes 29 and 24/3; Shavers Fork can be reached from National Forest Route 92, which intersects U.S. 250, 4 miles west of Cheat Bridge.

"Fly fishing only" sections for wild trout enthusiasts have been established on Edwards Run in a marked area within the boundaries of the Edwards Run Public Hunting & Fishing Area in Hampshire County; on Otter Creek and tributaries in the Monongahela National Forest in Randolph and Tucker counties, with year round fishing permitted; and on scenic Rich Creek in a marked area offering year-round fishing in Monroe County. All fish caught in these waters must be released.

The Monongahela National Forest which includes such wilderness areas as Dolly Sods, Otter Creek, and Cranberry Backcountry, stretches over 830,000 acres of the Allegheny Mountain range. The highest peak in this mountainous wilderness and also the highest point in West Virginia is Spruce Knob (4,862 feet), in the Spruce Knob-Seneca Rocks National Recreation Area. To the northeast of Spruce Knob, still within the recreation area, are the Seneca Rocks—sheer-

faced, towering rocks which erupt dramatically nearly 1,000 feet out of the edgeline forest of rolling pasture land. Within the forest boundaries are the headwaters of three major river systems; the Monongahela, Potomac, and Greenbrier.

Auto touring is a popular way of getting around, but there are also many trails for hikers along clear mountain streams, through forested valleys, and across highland bogs. In many reaches of the park, the harsh climate and rocky soil will support little vegetation except mosses, ferns, and sparse shrubbery. Interesting features of the park include Smoke Hole, where cool air from the many caves meets the moist warm air from the gorge, forming a smoky mist, and the Falls of Hills Creek—three stunning waterfalls along a short stretch of the creek. Remnants of a vast virgin spruce forest still stand near Gaudineer Scenic Area. Even though Monongahela's trees were extensively felled during the early part of this century, the second-growth timber that now blankets the area provides a wide diversity of species. The forest is essentially an eastern hardwoods area, but many highland regions are reminiscent of the dense forests of eastern Canada. Forest and valley alike abound with many forms of plant and animal life, including the timid black bear and wild turkey. Trout, muskie,

catfish, and smallmouth bass are found in the park's numerous streams, including the Cranberry, Upper Potomac, and Elk rivers. Members of the plant kingdom are also a source of fascination: the forest floor supports mosses and ferns in lush profusion, and the waxy-leaved laurel and rhododendron have found a comfortable habitat in the cathedral-like spaces between tall trees.

The state's scenic Appalachian highlands, mixed conifer and hardwood forests, valleys, and gently rolling hills offer excellent hunting for ruffed grouse, quail, pheasant, woodcock, wild turkey, gray squirrel, cottontails, raccoon, bobcat, deer, and black bear. The whitetail deer population, near extinction at the turn of the century from logging and mining activities, today is over 100,000 and growing. The best hunting areas are found in the uplands of the Monongahela National Forest region. The dwindling population of black bear, which once roamed in good numbers throughout the state, are now protected in the Otter Creek and Cranberry Glades backcountry areas of the Monongahela National Forest. Wild turkey, brought close to extinction because of slaughter for food during the early pioneer days, have been brought back to former population levels and today offer excellent fall hunting on the state and national

forest public hunting lands. The handsome ruffed grouse is the state's most important upland game bird, found along the primitive roads, streams, and burns in the mountainous state and national forest hunting areas. The bobwhite quail is concentrated along the scenic wooded river valleys and farmlands in the eastern counties. A substantial number of woodcock are shot each year, especially in the Canaan Valley. The state also offers limited shooting for pheasant, wood ducks, and a very few mallards, blacks, teal, and Canada geese.

Information Sources, Maps & Access

West Virginia fishing and hunting regulations, bag and possession limits, opening and closing dates; a trout stocking schedule listing each stream, county location, and frequency stocked; float-fishing waters; a listing of public fishing lakes and ponds, indicating trout waters, stocking schedules, tailwaters, boating, and camping; and bear and turkey hunting maps may all be obtained free by writing: Dept. of Natural Resources, State Capitol, Charleston, WV 25305 (304)348–3381. Detailed information and a free *Spruce Knob-Seneca Rocks Area Map* and a *Monongahela National Forest Map* (50¢)—showing the Dolly Sods, Cranberry, and Otter Creek Backcountry Areas and pioneer villages—may be obtained from: Supervisor's Office, U.S. Forest Service, Box 1231, Elkins, WV 26241 (304)636–1800. The useful *West Virginia Stream Map*, showing the Mountain State's major trout and fishing streams and illustrations of the major game fish, may be obtained free by writing: Division of Wildlife Resources, Dept. of Natural Resources, State Capitol, Charleston 25305. This large, handy map shows the locations of all lakes and streams stocked with trout. The major auto access routes serving the state include Interstate Highways 77, 79, 81, 85, 64, and 95.

Lodges & Resorts

★★★*Mirror Lake in the Monongahela National Forest* is a year-round vacation facility consisting of luxury chalets surrounding a five-acre trout lake. Located 6½ miles south of Davis on Route 32, Mirror Lake is next to Canaan Valley State Park with its nature trails, fine skiing facilities, heated swimming pool, ice rink, tennis courts and championship golf course. Some of the chalets are on Mirror Lake and others are located in the Timberline area with a 45–acre bass and sailing lake, trails for hiking or cross-country skiing, and a conservation area. Mirror Lake provides summer recreation with fishing and swimming from the sandy beach, as well as canoeing in one of the canoes provided free with each chalet. Summer days are comfortable since the 3,200–foot elevation keeps the temperatures below 90 degrees. In wintertime, the area turns into a white wonderland. Chalets are luxurious with wood-burning fireplaces, sun decks, carpeting and tasteful furniture. They are completely equipped for housekeeping with all electric kitchens, linens, dishes, pots and pans, electric heat, firewood, television and telephones. Some have dishwashers, sleeping lofts and garages. All have beautiful views. Chalets sleep from 6 to 14 people, depending on the unit. Winter rates range from $276 to $380 for one week. There are also rates for three night weekends, two nights in midweek and extra days. For further information contact: Charlie and Betsy Reed, Mirror Lake, Route 32, Davis, WV 26260 (304)866–4216.

★★★★*Snowshoe Resort in the Monongahela National Forest*, located in the West Virginia mountains in Pocahontas County offers some of the best alpine and cross-country skiing in the east. Located in the Monongahela National Forest near the site of the pioneering village of Old Spruce, Snowshoe features 10 miles of well-maintained ski touring trails with a system of warming huts. Among the more popular tours are Bear Pen Ramble, 3½ miles from the resort center

on a gradual descent down the northwest bowl returning via Cup Run lift, and Shavers Run, 4 miles from the resort center, southeast around part of Snowshoe basin rim with a gradual descent into the valley terminating at Shavers Pond. For novice skiers there is the Leather Bark Loop, a gentle 1.5–mile loop trail along the top of

Snowshoe basin. Showshoe also offers 4½ miles of slopes, a luxurious lodge and resort center, and special vacation packages. The average 200 inches of snowfall, excellent weather providing long seasons and a 1,500 foot vertical drop on internationally known Cup Run, has made this one of mid-America's favorite ski resorts. Four triple chairlifts, including one of the longest in the world, help keep lines short. The resort features trails, for novice to experts, Super-experts can try the Mephisto trail, a 1,000–foot-long trail with a 450 foot vertical. The ski school boasts instructors like Director Marty Douglass, formerly of Killington Ski School. Instruction is available on all levels, using the American Teaching Method. Snowshoe has your rental equipment waiting when you arrive, which is kept with you throughout your stay. The same procedure is used for lift tickets. Ten miles of marked, maintained cross-country skiing can also be found at Snowshoe. Over the past three years Snowshoe has been under the watchful planning of Dr. Tom Brigham, who has brought the resort to its present high standards. His plan to transform Snowshoe into a year-round resort has brought about summer tennis clinics. Under the direction of Ian Crookenden, a New Zealand Davis Cupper, guests receive five hours a day of training on the seven all-weather championship courts. Snowshoe has recently added two new lodging complexes to the main lodge and has eight chalets, plus a series of condominiums available for overnight use. The structures are simple, modern and functional. Rates: The resort has ski plans available on three levels and covering a wide range of costs. A five day plan including meals on the Modified American Plan and lodging from $90–133. Overnight in condominiums or chalets, $75–200 per person. Summer rates range from $20–315 depending on services, accommodations and length of stay. For further information contact: Snowshoe, Slatyfork, WV 26291 (304)799–6762.

★★★*State Park & Forest Lodgings.* West Virginia has an outstanding system of State Parks and Forests throughout the beautiful Mountain State. Most are easily accessible via the Interstate and the Appalachian Corridor highway system. Visitors find roaring waterfalls, scenic hiking trails, placid blue lakes, rugged peaks for skiing and climbing, boating, fishing, golf, tennis, horseback riding. The parks also have excellent facilities for lodging with a wide variety of accommodations ranging from primitive campsites to deluxe cabins.

Lodge facilities are open year-round, except for the Mountain Creek at Pipestem and Tygart, which are closed in the winter. Lodge rooms are modern, many with air-conditioning, TV and other extras. Most lodges have restaurants; some open all year long. Summer recreation facilities such as swimming pools and tennis courts at the lodges are open from Memorial Day through Labor Day.

Cabins are furnished and completely equipped for housekeeping. Pots and pans, dishes, linens, bedding and flatware are provided in all cabins. Cots and cribs are available. Cabins may be reserved for full weeks only from the second Monday in June to Labor Day. They may be rented by the day or weekend during the rest of the year. Deluxe cabins have open fireplaces, modern kitchens, wood-paneled walls, heat and baths with showers. They are available March through December with the exception of a few open year around. Standard cabins are usually constructed of logs and also have fireplaces, modern kitchens and baths with showers. They may be reserved from the end of April to the end of October. Economy cabins have one room which serves as kitchen, living room and bedroom. These cabins, with built-in double bunks and small baths with shower, are open from Memorial Day through Labor Day. Rustic cabins are equipped in the style of the frontier days. There are gas lamps, woodburning stoves, fireplaces and gas refrigerators. Sanitary facilities are outside and water must be drawn from a well. Rustic cabins are available from April through December.

Camping is another alternative in the state parks and forests. Camp-sites are available on a first-come-first-served basis with no reservations accepted. Only one tent or trailer is permitted per campsite and the stay is limited to two consecutive weeks. Campgrounds are usually operated from mid-April to November weather permitting, except for Canaan Valley and Pipestem which are open year-round (although there are no water hook-ups in the winter). The four types of campsites are: deluxe with flush toilets; grill or stove; tent pad; pull-off for trailers; hot showers; picnic tables; dumping station and hookups for electricity, sewer and water on some sites. Standard are the same as deluxe sites with no hookups available, except a few electric hookups. Rustic campsites have pit toilets and well water; and primitive sites are in undeveloped areas.

Reservations for lodge rooms and cabins can be made by mail or by calling a toll-free number. For West Virginia residents the number is (1–800)642–9058. For surrounding states the number is (1–800)624–8632. Lines are open Monday through Friday 8:30–4:30. For reservations made by phone, the deposit must be received within ten days. When writing for reservations, contact the individual state park or forest. West Virginia residents can make reservations twelve months in advance and out-of-state residents ten months in advance. For full information write: West Virginia Dept. of Natural Resources, Division of Parks and Recreation, 1800 Washington Street East, Charleston, WV 25305.

State Parks

Babcock State Park is located less than 100 miles southeast of Charleston. Its most distinctive natural feature is a fast flowing mountain trout stream that forms fantastic waterfalls and winds through massive boulders. On the banks of this stream is the Glade Creek Grist Mill. The mill was constructed from parts of old mills. It is in operation today to grind cornmeal and buckwheat flour for park visitors. The 3,637–acre park includes a 19–acre lake for fishing and boating. Visitors can rent rowboats, sailboats and paddleboats to enjoy the water. There are also recreational facilities which include a swimming pool, shuffleboard, croquet, badminton, volleyball, archery, ping-pong, horseshoes and tennis. There are marked trails for hiking and the park has a naturalist. Fishermen can enjoy both lake and stream fishing. A restaurant and commissary is open from the last Saturday in April through Labor Day, and there is a souvenir shop. Accommodations include 40 standard campsites with a daily fee of $3.50, 18 standard cabins and 8 economy cabins. For two persons, the standard cabin is $25 first night, $11 each additional night and $80 weekly. Economy cabin for four persons is $27.50 first night, $12.50 each additional night and $90 weekly. For reservations or more information write Babcock State Park, Clifftop, WV 25822 (304)438–6205.

Blackwater Falls State Park gets its name from the famous falls of the Blackwater River which plunges five stories. This dramatic sight can be viewed from observation points, and stairways and boardwalks lead to the base of the falls for a close-up view. The park is popular year round. In summer, visitors swim in the 14–acre Pendleton Lake which has a sandy beach, bathhouse and lifeguards. Rowboats and paddleboats are for rent and there is a golf course just 10 miles away. Hiking, horseback riding, photography and fishing can be enjoyed in the park and in the surrounding Monongahela National Forest where there are long trails for backpacking. In the fall, all 1,688 acres offer a multi-color show. Winter activities include skiing at Canaan Valley, sledding and skiing in the beginners' ski area. In the Blackwater Lodge on the South Rim of the Canyon, there are 55 air-conditioned rooms, a restaurant with banquet room, a gift shop, a lounge and a recreation room. The natural stone and wood lodge has a sweeping view of the park. Lodge rooms are $18 for a single,

$20–22 for a double and $36 for a two room suite. There are also 25 deluxe cabins, open all year, with rates for two persons of $35 the first night, $13 each additional night and $100 per week. The campground has 65 standard campsites with no hookups that cost $3.50 per night for up to six persons. For information and reservations contact: Blackwater Falls State Park, Davis, WV 26260 (304)259–5216.

Bluestone State Park is in the southern part of the state, in the heart of a major recreational area. Besides the 2,145 acres of the State Park, visitors can enjoy Bluestone Lake, the 1800–acre federal reservoir, and the 20,000-acre Bluestone Public Hunting area. Golfers can visit the nearby courses at Pipestem and Willowwood Country Clubs. Water-skiing equipment is for rent, as well as rowboats, canoes and motorboats. For vacationers with their own boats, there are boat launching facilities. Other activities are swimming, shuffleboard, croquet, badminton, volleyball and horseshoes. Children will enjoy the playground. There are hiking trails and a naturalist at the park. Bluestone has 25 deluxe cabins which rent for $35 first night, $13 each additional night and $100 weekly. Weekly rates for four persons are $170 and for six are $220. Eighty-one campsites accommodate tents or trailers for $3–3.50 per night, with standard facilities and no hookups. There are also 400 primitive sites in the nearby Bluestone Public Hunting area which cost $2.50 per night. For information and reservations write: Bluestone State Park, Box 3, Athens Star Route, Hinton, WV 25951 (304)466–1922.

Cacapon State Park is in the far eastern tip of the state. It is dominated by the looming Cacapon Mountain surrounded by a vast plain. The park covers 6,115 acres of rolling foothills crisscrossed by hiking trails. The facilities all have a rustic look, with natural stone, ironwork and logs complementing the natural scene. There is a new golf course designed by Robert Trent Jones. Other outdoor activities include swimming, fishing, horseback riding, tennis, badminton, shuffleboard, and other games. There is a large restaurant with a banquet room, a snack shop, and a souvenir and gift shop. There is a playground for children and a naturalist who can inform visitors about the environment. There are all types of accommodations. Fifty rooms are available in the main lodge which overlooks the golf course. A double room is $20–22 in the summer and $18–20 in the winter. For visitors preferring a quaint and rustic atmosphere in an economical lodge, there is the 11–room Old Inn Lodge. A double room with shared bath is $16; with private bath, it is $19. The Inn is closed in the winter. There are 29 cabins, including 11 deluxe with a weekly rate for four persons of $170; 12 standard cabins at $135 per week for four; and six economy cabins for $90 per week for a group of four. There are no campsites. For further information, write: Cacapon State Park, Berkeley Springs, WV 25411 (304)258–1022.

Canaan Valley, in the mid-Appalachian highlands, is the park system's major winter-sports area. It lies in a verdant mountain valley, 3,000 feet above sea level. Surrounding the valley are rugged mountain peaks rising to over 4,200 feet above sea level, which gives the area a climate similar to many areas in Canada. There are complete facilities for the skier, including chair lifts and snow-making equipment for those days when Mother Nature doesn't provide enough snow. Canaan Valley is a short drive from both Washington, DC and Pittsburgh and attracts skiers from up and down the Eastern seaboard. Winter vacationers can also enjoy the ice skating rink or curl up in front of a cozy fireplace. Although best known for its winter sports, Canaan Valley is a year-round recreation center. There is a championship 18–hole course to please the golfers. Hiking trails on rugged and scenic terrain attract backpackers and day hikers. There are tennis courts, a playground for the children and fishing for all. A naturalist is on hand to describe the flora

and fauna. Boating and horseback riding can be enjoyed at nearby Blackwater Falls. The park has a souvenir shop, a restaurant open year around and a snack bar. A new 250–room lodge and convention center provides modern, comfortable accommodations and there are 15 deluxe cabins and 34 tent or trailer campsites for those who prefer more rustic lodging. Lodge rooms rent for $18/single and $24/double year round. Deluxe cabin rates start with a two-bedroom cabin for $50 the first night, $24 each additional night and $170 per week. There are also three-bedroom and four-bedroom cabin rates. The cabins are open year round. Campsites have hookups for electricity, water and sewer, as well as shower facilities, and are $5 per night. While the campsites are available year round, there are no hookups for water in the winter. For further information contact: Canaan Valley State Park, Route 1, Box 39, Davis, WV 26260 (304)866–4121.

Hawks Nest State Park is the smallest of the state parks—only 276 acres—yet it has the most to offer in scenic views, activities and facilities. It is located in an area many call the "Grand Canyon of the East" because of the spectacular New River Gorge. The lodge is built on the edge of the gorge to offer visitors an impressive view. Guests can enjoy an exciting aerial tramway ride from the lodge down to the lake below. At the lake there is a marina and boat dock, for the use of boaters and fishermen. Another great view can be enjoyed from the park's museum which sits high, overlooking the entire park and canyon. The rustic museum displays early pioneer and Indian artifacts. Hawks Nest is near Charleston and is an excellent stop-over with much to offer. There is swimming, fishing and boating. There are tennis courts and a playground, a souvenir shop and a restaurant. Marked hiking trails offer spectacular scenic views. The park is open year round with accommodations in the 31 lodge rooms. Summer rates are $18 for a single, $20–22 for a double and $22–32 for suites. Winter rates are $16 for a single, $18–20 for a double and $18–28 for suites. There are no campsites or cabins. For reservations and information contact: Hawks Nest State Park, Ansted, WV 25812 (304)658–5212.

Holly River State Park is in the center of the state and encompasses 7,947 acres of densely forested land. It is a peaceful and rustic recreation area. Fishermen come to the park for the fine trout stream that meanders through the woods, and to fish Laurel Fork, a tributary of the Holly River. Hiking trails through the dense woodlands lead to secluded waterfalls and feature a brisk climb to the top of Potato Knob. Climbers of the Knob are rewarded with a scenic view. If all that climbing and fishing works up an appetite, visitors can eat at the park restaurant which is open from the last Saturday in April through Labor Day. Groceries are also available and there is a souvenir shop. There are tennis courts and other game courts, a swimming area, a playground, and a naturalist. The nine standard cabins have fireplaces and rent for $25 first night, $11 each additional night, and $80 weekly for two persons. There are 88 campsites with electric hookup with a $4 fee per night. For information and reservations contact: Holly River State Park, Hacker Valley, WV 26222.

Lost River State Park is historically important for having been the summer retreat of the famous Lee family of Virginia in the early 1800's. To commemorate the era when the Lee family owned this land, a cabin, built during these years, has been restored and set up as a museum. Lost River is also known for the abundance of wildlife in the park. Most every visitor sees deer, raccoon, opossum, groundhogs, red and gray squirrels, and screech owls. Serious wildlife observers with a bit of stealth and patience can see wild turkey, grouse, and even wild goats. The park is in the highlands of eastern West

Virginia on the Virginia border. Lost River has marked hiking trails, one of which leads to the scenic overlooks at "Cranny Crow" offering commanding views of the park and the surrounding area. There is swimming, fishing, horseback riding, game courts, tennis courts and a playground. Indoor facilities include a restaurant, souvenir shop and recreation building. Groceries are also available. This 3,712 acre park is one of the most popular family vacation parks in the state. Accommodations are 9-deluxe and 15-standard cabins. Deluxe cabins accommodate four to eight persons and rates for four are $50 first night, $24 each additional night and $170 weekly. Standard cabins for two to six persons, with rates for three, four or six persons in one cabin. For more information write: Lost River State Park, Mathias, WV 26812 (304)897–5372.

North Bend State Park is located in the northwestern part of the state and is West Virginia's major year-round park in the Ohio Valley. The park is located in the broad valley of the North Fork of the Hughes River, an area rich in the heritage of the oil and gas industry. Its 1,405 acres include the famous horseshoe bend of the

Hughes River, and the modern guest lodge overlooks the bend. A campground is spread along the riverside. The park has a beautiful, large outdoor swimming pool with diving board and lounging area. Hiking trails are marked and there is a naturalist on duty. Summer visitors can enjoy tennis courts and other game courts, fishing and picnicking. In the winter, they can warm up at a fireplace. There is a golf course nearby and also numerous hand-blown glass facilities— a specialty of this area. The restaurant has huge glass windows, so that diners can enjoy the view while they eat. Youngsters can enjoy the playground while Mom shops in the souvenir shop. Lodge rooms and cabins are open all year. Summer rates in the lodge are $18 single, $22 double, $25 for three and $28 for four. Winter rates are $16 single, $20 double, $22 for three and $24 for four. Two-bedroom deluxe cabins rent for $50 the first night and $24 each additional night; and three-bedroom deluxe cabins are $65 the first night and $31 each additional night with weekly rates available. There are 55 standard campsites without hookups for $3.50 per night. Write or call North Bend State Park, Cairo, WV 26337 (304)643–2931.

Pipestem Resort State Park has been given resort status because of the wide range of recreational facilities and the exceptional accommodations at the park. It is located near the popular Bluestone Dam recreation area in the southern part of the state. Pipestem has much to offer the golfer. The park's 18–hole championship course has wooded fairways, large greens and overlooks the beautiful Bluestone Gorge. It has the finest of clubhouse facilities as well. Then there is a 9–hole "executive" three-par course with its own clubhouse. Visitors can swim in an outdoor olympic-size pool or in the indoor pool. Tennis is played on lighted courts. The miles of scenic trails with spectacular lookout points can be traveled on foot, by bicycle (available for rent), or on horseback year round. There are also archery and playground facilities. The Visitors' Center has native art and craft demonstrations and the native handicrafted items are on sale. Visitors can watch the mountain artisans at work. Lodging choices offer something for everyone. The Pipestem Lodge has 113 rooms and sits high above the horseshoe bend of the Bluestone River. Those who really want to get away from it all will prefer the 30 room Mountain Creek Lodge. It is set in the bottom of a thousand-foot-deep canyon and is accessible only by the scenic aerial tramway system. Families may prefer one of the 25 deluxe cabins or camping at one of the 50 campsites equipped with electric, water and sewerage hookups and washing facilities with hot showers and a laundromat. During summer evenings, programs are offered in the outdoor amphitheater, which is nestled in the forested hills near the gorge. Pipestem is easy to reach since it lies between two major interstate corridors, just 46 miles from I–64 and 20 miles from I–77. It is only minutes from two major airports with car rental services; and AM-TRAK from Washington, Cincinnati and other cities connects to Hinton just four miles from Pipestem. Pipestem Lodge is open year round; a double room is $26 in the summer and $20 in the winter. Mountain Creek Lodge is closed from November 1st to March 31st and a double rents for $24 in the summer and $20 in the winter. The 25 deluxe cottages are open year round and range from two-bedroom to four-bedroom units. Summer rates for a two-bedroom are $60 first night, $31 each additional night and $215 weekly. Winter rates for the same unit are $50 first night, $24 each additional night and $170 weekly. For reservations or more information contact: Pipestem Resort State Park, Pipestem, WV 25979 (304)466–1800.

Twin Falls State Park is a 3,776–acre park in the southern highlands area of the state, just a short drive south from Charleston. It is open year round and has full recreational facilities. Golfers enjoy the nine-hole golf course. For history buffs, there is an old pioneer home and farm that has been restored for the inspection of visitors. There is swimming, game courts, tennis and a playground. Indoor facilities include a restaurant, a souvenir shop and a recreation building fully equipped for indoor sports. There are twenty rooms in the lodge which rent for $18–22 for a double in the summer and $16–20 for a double in the winter. There are 13 deluxe cabins which accommodate four to eight persons and rent for $50 first night, $24 each additional night and $170 weekly for a group of four. A 47–site campground and an adjacent 90–site picnic area are under construction and soon to be completed. For information write Twin Falls State Park, P.O. Box 236, Mullens, WV 25882.

Tygart Lake State Park is located in the north-central part of the state, south of Pittsburgh. It features water sports of all types because of the 13–mile long lake, Tygart Lake, that winds through its wooded valleys. The lake was created in the 1930's by the Army Corps of Engineers for flood control. Today it is used by boaters, fishermen, waterskiers, scuba divers and swimmers. The park also offers the services of the Tygart Lake Marina with complete fuel and

repair services, boat loading and launching facilities, and rentals of ski and fishing boats. A beautiful, new 20–room lodge overlooks the lake. In the lodge is a restaurant with high double-window walls for viewing the placid lake. There is a golf course nearby, and the park has game courts and a playground. Tygart Lake Lodge is closed from November 1st to Easter weekend. Rooms rent for $18 single and $22 double. There are also 10 deluxe cabins accommodating up to six persons. Rates for two persons: $35 first night, $13 each additional night, and $100 weekly. There are forty standard campsites which are $3.50 per day. For further information write: Tygart Lake State Park, Route 1, Grafton, WV 26354 (304)265–2320.

Watoga State Park was the first West Virginia state park established and is the largest one in the park system. Covering 10,057 acres of woodland, it is located along the eastern border of the state in the Appalachian highlands. The park's name comes from the Cherokee Indian word "watauga" which means "the river of islands." This refers to the Greenbrier River, which makes up several miles of the park boundary. Visitors will find many recreational opportunities awaiting them at Watoga. There is boating on the park's 11–acre lake, and boat rentals are available. The park has an excellent system of trails and horseback paths, and horses for hire. There is also swimming, fishing, tennis, game courts, picnicking and a playground to be enjoyed. Golf courses are nearby, as are many natural and historic points of interest. Droop Mountain Battlefield State Park is minutes away and is the site of the largest Civil War battle of West Virginia's history. Also nearby are Pearl S. Buck's birthplace, Greenbank National Radio Astronomy Observatory and the Cass Scenic Railroad. Watoga adjoins both the Monongahela National Forest and the Calvin Price State Forest, giving tens of thousands of additional acres of largely undeveloped land to explore. Indoors there is a restaurant, souvenir shop, groceries for sale and a fireplace. Accommodations are cabins and campsites. The eight deluxe cabins rent for $50 first night, $24 each additional night and $170 weekly for four persons. The 25 standard cabin rates begin at $25 first night, $11 each additional night and $80 weekly for two persons. There are 38 campsites with standard facilities which are $3.50 per night. For information and reservations contact: Watoga State Park, Star Route 1, Box 252, Marlinton, WV 24954 (304)799–4087.

State Forests

Cabwaylingo State Forest is named for the four counties in the area—Cabell, Wayne, Lincoln and Mingo—in the southwestern corner of the state. It has 8,123 acres of forest land with swimming, fishing, hunting, hiking trails, picnicking and a playground. Restaurants and grocery stores are nearby. The State Forest has 13 standard log cabins with fireplaces. For two persons, the rates are $20 first night, $10 each additional night, and $70 weekly with rates for four or six persons available. There are 34 rustic campsites which are $3 per night. For more information contact: Cabwaylingo State Forest, Route 1, Dunlow, WV 25511 (304)385–4255.

Camp Creek State Forest is near the southern tip of the state. The 5,897–acre forest is well developed for day use recreation including hiking, fishing, hunting and use of the game courts. For those planning a longer stay, there are 12 rustic campsites at $3 per night. For further information: Camp Creek State Forest, Star Route, Box 310, Camp Creek, WV 25820 (304)425–9481.

Coopers Rock State Forest is up on the northern border of the state near the busy town of Morgantown. It is the state's largest area for

day-use recreation, covering 12,698 acres. Because of its nearness to the city, it is well used, even in the winter. The forest has many unusual rock formations and scenic overlooks. Fishing, hunting, hiking and picnicking are popular. In winter, snow and ice sports are enjoyed. For overnighters, there are 24 standard campsites with hot showers, flush toilets and laundry facilities. The fee is $3.50 per night. For more information write Coopers Rock State Forest, Route 1, Box 270, Bruceton Mills, WV 26525 (304)296–6065.

Greenbrier State Forest is located near the resort town of White Sulphur Springs on the southern border just off the Interstate. There is fishing year-round and hunting in season on the 5,130 wooded acres. There is swimming, boat rental, hiking trails and a playground. A golf course and restaurants are nearby. This forest has some of the most comfortable and the most popular guest cabins in the state. The 12 standard cabins rent for $25 first night, $11 each additional night and $80 weekly for two persons, with rates available for more persons in a cabin. The 16 standard campsites are $3.50 per night. For more information contact Greenbrier State Forest, Caldwell, WV 24925 (304)536–1944.

Kanawha State Forest is just 11 miles south of Charleston near the heavily populated Kanawha Valley. Its picnic areas are probably the most heavily used in the state. There is plenty of hiking on the 9,052 acres as well as swimming and hunting. There is a souvenir shop and a playground. For overnight guests there is a fully-equipped camping area with 43 campsites, many with electric and water hookups. Campsites are $3.50–4 per night. For information and reservations write Kanawha State Forest, Route 2, Box 285, Charleston, WV 25314 (304)346–5654.

Kumbrabow State Forest is for the person who steers clear of developed areas and wants rugged outdoors. It has dense forest growth, making a true wilderness, a few rustic cabins and campsites. There are 9,431 acres, with hiking trails, fishing, hunting and picnicking to be enjoyed. The five rustic cabins are $20 first night, $10 each additional night and $70 weekly for four persons. The seven rustic campsites rent for $3 per night. For additional information: Kumbrabow State Forest, P.O. Box 65, Huttonsville, WV 26273 (304)335–2219.

Panther State Forest is made up of 7,810 acres of rugged hills near the southern border of the state. Visitors can enjoy hunting, day-hiking, fishing, swimming and getting back to nature. There is a playground for the children and picnic sites. For overnight visitors there are six rustic campsites with electric hookups which are $3.50 per night. For further information contact: Panther State Forest, Panther, WV 24872 (304)938–2252.

Seneca State Forest is near major attractions such as the Watoga State Park and Cass Scenic Railroad. Its 11,684 acres are in the Appalachian highlands and the forest is bordered by the famed Greenbrier River. Visitors can enjoy hunting, hiking and just wandering around the lush forest, or try swimming, fishing or boating. For a touch of the frontier life, there are seven rustic cabins which rent for $20 first night, $10 each additional night and $70 weekly for two persons, with rates for more people per cabin. The ten rustic campsites are $3 per night. For more information contact: Seneca State Forest, Dunmore, WV 24934 (304)799–6213.

Travel Services

Appalachian Wildwaters runs whitewater rafting trips in which customers are participants, not passengers. They run one day, overnight, special events and two-day school trips on the Cheat River and the New River. AW provides rafts, lifejackets, paddles, lunch, guides and transportation to and from the river. On overnight trips they supply tents with floors and mosquito netting and all meals on the river. A one-day trip on the Cheat River Canyon is exciting and challenging immediately downstream from the "put-in". Decision Rapids gives rafters a big taste of the river and foretells the thrills of Beach Run Rapids, Old Nasty and Even Nastier on down the river. Lunch is eaten on shore and then it's back to more rapids. This 12–mile trip winds through high canyon walls and in June, the banks of the river are lush with rhododendron. At the end of the trip is Swimmers Rapids, where rafters can dive in to feel the pull of the river first hand. AW uses four to ten person rafts, depending on the water level. After Memorial Day, they use "duckies"—soft, one or two person craft. One-day Cheat River trips are $32.50 per person and are held from April 1 through November 15. New River flows in the same river bed that held the ancient River Teays. It wanders through rocky canyon walls that earn the area the name of "Grand Canyon of the East." Here are some of the biggest rapids in Eastern U.S. At the end of the trip, the rafts pass beneath the New River Gorge Bridge, the highest, longest single-arch steel bridge in the world. The AW 10 person rafts were designed just for these New River trips. The one-day New River adventure is $37.50 per person. Appalachian Wildwaters has three day retreats on the New River, with camping out near the river; overnight trips for families or adults only, rafting the Gauley River when the Summerville Dam is released, and two-day kayak schools on the New River. There are weekday, family and group discounts on all rates. For reservations and information write: Appalachian Wildwaters, P.O. Box 126, Albright, WV 26519 and call toll free (800)624–8060 between 9:30 and 4:30 or in West Virginia (304) 329–1665.

Cheat River Outfitters, Inc. will provide all of the gear you might need to enjoy a raft trip down the Cheat River through the wilderness. A typical trip includes the loan of all the basic equipment (raft, paddles, life jackets, wetpacks, and lunch) and a guided trip down the river. They provide changing rooms, toilet facilities, and a bus to return you to the take-off point. An equipment store and restaurant are available in Albright at the take-off point. Camping facilities abound in the nearby areas; motels and hotels are available as well. The Outfitters offer special packages for whitewater trips. In April, May and June, the weekday trip rate is $25 per person; runs are usually on Mondays and Fridays although any group of 12 people can set up a run on the day of their choice. The weekend day trip rate during April, May, and June is $30 per person with four trips leaving each morning. Trips for the fall months of September and October are newly available and rumored to be the most delightful time to see the incredible beauty of the area. Reservations are taken beginning January 1 for the summer season. For further information contact: Cheat River Outfitters, Inc., P.O. Box 196, Albright, WV 26519 (304)329–9816.

New River Adventures offers whitewater rafting adventures on two fast running class V and class VI rivers, the New River and the Gauley, which carve their way through the Allegheny Plateau. 17–foot vulcanized rubber rafts hold ten people, and are guided by white-water experts skilled in water safety techniques and first aid. Coast-guard-approved life jackets, and helmets especially designed for white-water expeditions equip every adventure. The boisterous New River plunges 17 miles through magnificent scenery from Thurmond to Hawks Nest State Park. Tossing rapids and enormous waves make up most of this challenging river trip, but there are quieter pools, and long placid stretches through Hawks Nest State Park where participants are free to take in the river's beauty. New River trips run every day from mid-April until October, and are $35 on weekdays, including lunch, and $40 per person on weekend

days. The Gauley River trips run through the brilliant Indian Summer days from late September through October. The Gauley plunges through a wild, deep canyon from Summerville Dam to the town of Swiss. There are over 100 turbulent rapids, many class VI. Previous experience on the New River is required before taking on the awesome rapids of the Gauley, with names like "Lost Paddle", "Heaven Help You", and "Pure Screaming Hell". Day trips are run on the upper and lower stretches of the Gauley, and are $50 per person. The steep whitewater rapids of the upper section are for experienced rafters only, and the minimum age is 16. Two day runs on the Gauley, which cover both the upper and lower stretches of the river, and include four meals and overnight camping on the river bank, are $125 per person. For more information write: New River Adventures, Inc., Star Route Box 25, Thurmond, WV 25936 (304)469–9627.

Trans-Montane Outfitters Ltd. The green Allegheny Mountains offer hundreds of miles trails for wilderness hiking and backpacking. There are unexplored caves, carved by springs as they cut inward, and clear lakes, surrounded by forest, as they flow outward. Trans-Montane Outfitters Ltd. located in the heart of these mountains, fills a very real need between camping near your car in a state park and the more rugged expeditions offered by wilderness schools. Trans-Montane will outfit and equip any outdoor adventure you design. You decide the length of the trip, the designation, and whatever skills you would like to learn. Trans-Montane will provide guides, food and equipment. Guided day trips, including lunch, are $16 per person. Two day trips are $40 per person, including meals, instruction and equipment. Longer trips are $20 for each additional day. Special family rates are available at a 10% discount for mate and all children. Groups of ten or more are offered a 10% discount. In addition, Trans-Montane offers caving adventures to age 10 and up, canoeing and rafting day trips or overnights in the lovely Shavers Fork Wilderness Area, and a 12–mile trip by canoe or raft through the Dry Fork Canyon. Backpacking trips lead into the Dolly Sods Wilderness Area, where wildflowers and wild berries abound; in the 18,000 acre Otter Creek Wilderness, filled with swimming holes and

lush vegetation; and the Canaan Mt. Area, through woods, across streams, up onto large rock outcroppings which afford spectacular views of the Allegheny Plateau. In addition, Trans-Montane Outfitters offer photography workshops, mountain crafts, and wildflower hikes. For more information write: Trans-Montane Outfitters Ltd., winter address: 400 West Road, Portsmouth, VA 23707 (804)397–6658; summer address: P.O. Box 325, Davis, WV 26260 (304)259–5117.

Wildwater Expeditions Unlimited, Inc. is an outfitter for rafting adventures on 30 miles of the Western Hemisphere's oldest river, the New. When white water is not cascading over the raft and paddle-power is not required, this adventure offers some of West Virginia's most historic and breathtaking scenery. Wildwater provides trips on both the lower and upper portions of the river. The lower raft trip offers whitewater rapids in classes one through five. These are turbulent, challenging waters, not recommended for non-swimmers. The upper raft trip is ideal for those who prefer leisure and tranquility combined with whitewater excitement. This section offers whitewater rapids in classes one and two, a milder section than the lower raft trip. Wildwater has riverside camping with platformed tents located midway between the upper and lower portions of the river. Primitive camping facilities include a comfort station with cold running water, restroom and picnic shelter. Professional guides and rafts with bow and stern features designed specifically for New River's white waters are part of each trip. Custom fishing and other water-related adventures are available. Wildwater Unlimited is a founding member of the Eastern Professional River Outfitters Association, dedicated to the advancement of professionalism and safety in whitewater rafting. Safety rules are strictly adhered to. Rates: One day trips (upper or lower part of river) including morning coffee, lunch, rafting equipment, transportation back to car and beverage at end of trip, are $42 to 45. An extra day can be added to one day lower section trips for a cost of $90 total, per person. Two day trips with three nights of camping, all meals, raft equipment, transportation to and from nearby stations: $130. For further information write: Wildwater Expeditions Unlimited, Inc., P.O. Box 55, Thurmond, WV 25936 (304)469–2551.

Introduction

Like neighboring Minnesota, northern Wisconsin boasts several of the nation's most renowned fishing, hunting, canoeing, cross-country skiing, wilderness-camping, and family-vacation areas and one of the greatest concentrations of lakes in the world. Over 8,500 have been charted throughout the state, the largest of which is Lake Winnebago, with an area of 215 square miles, but a comparatively shallow average depth of 15 feet. Situated within the Badger State's 56,154 square miles are the scenic evergreen forests and trophy fishing waters of the Northern Highlands; the nationally renowned muskellunge waters of the Chippewa Flowage-Hayward Lakes Region; the historic fur-trade canoe routes of the Bois Brule and Flambeau rivers; the famous trophy trout and smallmouth-bass waters off the evergreen-clad shores of Lake Superior's Apostle Islands; the St. Croix and Namekagon rivers; the scenic Wisconsin River Dells (gorges); and the famed brown-trout waters of the Wolf National Wild River. The virgin forests and waterways of the Badger State were first explored by the French voyageurs in their search to find the legendary "Northwest Passage." Jean Nicolet was the first European to penetrate the Wisconsin Territory in 1634, having been sent by Samuel de Champlain to investigate rumors of a distant race called the "People of the Sea," who, it was believed, might be Asiatics, but were actually the populous tribe of Winnebago Indians.

Accommodations & Travel Information

Wisconsin's major vacation lodges and resorts, north country sporting camps, inns, and cross-country ski centers are described in detail in the "Vacation/Lodging Guide" which follows. For information on all aspects of travel in the state, contact: Wisconsin Vacation & Travel Service, Dept. of Tourism, Madison, WI 53701 (608) 266–2161.

For fishing and hunting regulations, seasons, and information, contact: Dept. of Natural Resources, Box 450, Madison, WI 53701 (608)266–2621. The following useful DNR publications are available free upon request (single copies only): *Fishing, Spearing & Netting Regulations, Wisconsin Game Fish, Wisconsin Trout Streams, Wisconsin Walleye, Wisconsin Lakes, Largemouth Bass, Brook Trout, Brown Trout, The Lake Sturgeon, Muskellunge,* the 68–page guide *Forest Trees of Wisconsin, Wild Flowers of Wisconisn, Wetlands, Upland Trees, Forests,* and *Endangered Animals in Wisconsin.* Also available from the Dept. of Natural Resources are these useful publications: *Fishing Wisconsin's Great Lakes for Trout & Salmon* (25¢), *Wisconsin Muskellunge Waters* (free in single copies), and *Wisconsin Birds of Prey* (50¢).

WISCONSIN

FISHING WISCONSIN'S GREAT LAKES FOR TROUT and SALMON

Lake contour maps for over 30,000 Wisconsin lakes showing lakebottom composition, depth, access, campgrounds, resorts, shore features, vegetation, and fish species present are listed in the 40–page *Wisconsin Mapped Lakes Catalog* ($1), available from Clarkson Map Company, 724 Desnoyer St., Kaukauna 54130. These maps may be ordered direct for 75¢ each (plus 40¢ postage and handling) and are available for every major lake in the state, including such nationally renowned fishing waters as *North Twin Lake, Eagle Lake, Chippewa Flowage, Lac Court Oreilles, Totogatic Flowage, Lac Vieux Desert, Big Sand Lake,* and the *Turtle-Flambeau Flowage.* The Clarkson Map Company also publishes special purpose maps ($1 each) of the famous outdoor recreation areas: *Boulder Junction (Vilas County) Land of the Muskie, Minocqua, Shawano Lake, Wolf River* (includes lakes Poygan, Winneconne, and Butte Des Morts), *Lake Winnebago, Menominee County, Three Lakes* (includes the beautiful 27 lakes chain in Oneida County), *Waukesha Area* (includes Pewaukee, Nagawicka, Oconomowoc, Okauchee lakes), and the *Waupaca Chain.*

Trout stream maps ($2 each) showing fishing, wading, boat conditions, width and depth of channel, trout population, public access, and campgrounds are available for the *Bois Brule* and *Mecan* rivers from Hendrickson's, P.O. Box 207, New Glarus 53574.

A handy guide for campers is the *1976 Visitor's Guide to Wisconsin's State Parks, Forests, and Other Recreation Lands,* a brochure listing campsites throughout the state parks and forests, available free from the Department of Natural Resources at the above address.

Canoe Trails of North-Central Wisconsin ($4.00) describes a variety of trips along ten different streams: the Chippewa, Flambeau, Couderay, Jump, Turtle, Yellow, Manitowish, and Thornapple rivers, and Deertail and Main creeks. Written descriptions include information on rapids, campgrounds, scenery, fishing, and historical points of interest. Maps accompanying each description show rapids, best channels, campsites, boat landings and access, points of interest, hazard ratings, nearby creeks, and other reference points for the canoeist. Similar in format, *Canoe Trails of Northeastern Wisconsin* ($4.75) offers the same kind of information and maps for the Brule, Deerskin, Embarrass, Manitowish, Menominee, Oconto, Pelican, Peshtigo, Pike, Pine, Popple, Red, Spirit, Tomahawk, Wisconsin, and Wolf rivers. *Canoe Trails of Southern Wisconsin* ($4.95) offers maps and descriptions for canoe trips on the Baraboo, Crawfish, Crystal, Fox, Kickapoo, La Crosse, Lemonweir, Manitowoc, Mecan, Milwaukee, Pecatonica, Pine, Rock, Sugar, Waupaca, Wisconsin, and Yellow rivers. The guides are available at the prices quoted above from Wisconsin Trails, P.O. Box 5650, Madison 53705.

Highways & Maps

Travelers to Wisconsin's state and national forests, scenic lakes, wild rivers, and other wilderness areas will appreciate the comprehensive *Wisconsin State Highway Map,* available free from the Dept. of Transportation, Division of Highways, 4802 Sheboygan Ave., Room 2B, P.O. Box 40, Madison 53701. The map indicates every type of road within the state, from unsurfaced county trunks to interstate highways, as well as cities, towns, rivers, lakes, state and national forestlands, airports, information centers, historical sites, wayside facilities, Indian reservations, public hunting and fishing grounds, and other information of interest to visitors and residents alike.

The full-color 111–page *Atlas of Wisconsin* offers a thorough geographic inventory of the state for both sportsmen and visitors. The atlas features all major roads and highways and many minor roads; contours, elevations, forested lands, streams, and lakes; parks and preserves; and township lines. Locations of any of the 14,000 names in the gazetteer (including streams, rivers, lakes, etc.) can be easily found by using the various keys. The clothbound atlas can be ordered for $5.95 from the Wisconsin Sportsman, P.O. Box 1307, Oshkosh 54901. Please include 50¢ for postage and handling. For the serious connoisseurs of ghost towns, the Wisconsin Sportsman publishes a *Map of Ghost Towns, Old Mining and Logging Towns of Northern Wisconsin and Michigan* ($3).

Apostle Islands of Lake Superior

The Bayfield Peninsula, a large promontory off the coast of northern Wisconsin, juts into the waters of Lake Superior like a giant thumb pointing toward Canada. Off the shores of this hilly protrusion lie 22 islands, called the Twelve Apostles by Frenchmen arriving from Sault, who counted only a dozen on first sighting the group. Originally there were probably eight or nine additional islands, now reduced to rocky shoals scattered throughout the archipelago. All of the islands bear evidence of the effects of repeated glaciation and wave erosion, each is composed of red sandstone bedrock blanketed by a layer of glacial till—rocks, clay, and boulders. Along the shores of many of the Apostles, wave action has produced intricate, sometimes grotesque carvings in the 10- to 60-foot cliffs fringing the coastlines. The interior landscapes are characterized by unspoiled white sand beaches, thick evergreen forests, and marshes—habitats of deer, mink, beaver, muskrat, and many species of migratory waterfowl.

The earliest inhabitants of the region were called the Mound Builders, a group of prehistoric Indians who lived near the shores of Lake Superior some 12,000 years ago. More recently, shortly before the discovery of America, Ojibway or Chippewa tribes built a settlement on Madeline Island, the largest of the Apostles, and dubbed the area *Monigwunakauning,* meaning "home of the golden-breasted woodpecker," because of the thousands of birds that stopped on the island during their annual migrations. According to the Chippewa legend, the islands were made by Manitou, or Spirit, who pursued a stag as far as the shores of Lake Superior, unsuccessfully firing arrows at the animal. When the deer jumped in the water, Manitou became so angry that he picked up handfuls of rocks and threw them at the escaping animals. These rocks became the Apostle Islands.

The first white man to visit the Apostles was probably Etienne Brule, who arrived in 1622 in search of the Northwest Passage. Later, other French explorers—Nicolet, Groseilliers, and Radisson—also stumbled on the islands. The two latter built a cabin on Chequamegon Bay, near the present city of Ashland, in 1659. Missionaries and fur traders followed shortly thereafter, building chapels and trading posts with equal zeal. A fort established on Madeline Island in 1693 by Pierre le Sueur became a key wilderness outpost for the fur trade of the Lake Superior region, visited by voyageurs on their long journeys to and from the far North. The Apostles provide a spectacular unspoiled setting for wilderness camping, canoeing, fishing, and hunting. Fishing on the Sioux and Onion bays for lake, brown, and rainbow trout and coho salmon is a popular activity, as is seining for smelts along shallow beach areas during late April. Chequamegon Bay enjoys a reputation for trophy northern pike, smallmouth bass, walleye, yellow perch, and chinook and coho salmon. Bayfield County Forest, Chequamegon National Forest, and Apostle Islands National Lakeshore lands are all open in season for public hunting for black bear, ruffed grouse, snowshoe hare, woodcock, and whitetail deer.

Information Sources, Maps & Access

For detailed information, a free *Apostle Islands Map/Brochure,* a free *Visitor's Guide to Stockton Island,* and a 15-page booklet, *Historic Chequamegon* ($1), contact: National Park Service, Apostle Islands National Lakeshore, 1972 Centennial Dr., Bayfield, WI 54814 (715)779-5732.

Many of the legends connected with the islands and a full history of Madeline are recounted in *Madeline Island & the Chequamegon Region,* a 59-page paperbound narrative. The story of the fur trade in the Apostles is told in full detail as is the subsequent history of the lumbering industry and the archipelago's development as a summer

VACATION/ LODGING GUIDE

resort. The book is priced at $1.00 and is available from the National Park Service, Apostle Islands National Lakeshore. The easiest way to see all 22 of the Apostles is to sign up on one of the excursion-boat cruises that leave the Bayfield City Dock daily from June 10 through the month of September. A 50–mile cruise on the *Chippewa*, offered daily, tours the islands and makes a stop at Devils Island to inspect the sandstone caves and Coast Guard Lighthouse. Two shorter trips of 25 miles each are also made daily aboard the *Islander*. For information, contact Apostle Island Cruise Service, Box 691, Bayfield, WI 54814 (715)779–3925. The town of Bayfield can be reached via State Highway 13 from Park Falls, Mellen, and Ashland. From Duluth, Minnesota, or Superior, take U.S. 535 southeast, then travel northeast on 13.

Gateways & Accommodations

Bayfield

(Pop. 900; zip code 54814; area code 715.) Named for Admiral Henry Bayfield, surveyor of the Great Lakes, the town is a key jumping-off point for the Apostle Islands National Lakeshore and historic Madeline Island. Regular ferry service and sightseeing cruises are available daily from Bayfield, June-October (for information phone 779–3925). Other area attractions include the Red Cliff Indian Reservation, three miles north on Wisconsin Hwy. 13, and Port Mountain Ski Area, with downhill skiing and cross-country trails, three miles south on Hwy. 13. The Bayfield area is popular in season with hunters, deep-sea fishermen, and boating enthusiasts. Charter fishing boats leave the pier daily. Accommodations: *Bay Villa* (rates: $26–35 double), 18 rooms, 6 apartments with 1–2 bedrooms and kitchens, TV, restaurant nearby, on Lake Superior, just north of town via Wisconsin Hwy. 13 (779–3252); *Bayfield Inn* (rates: $31.20 double), 18 rooms overlooking the harbor and Apostle Islands, color TV, restaurant, on Wisconsin Hwy. 13 at head of city harbor (779–3363).

Travel Services

Apostle Islands Outfitters put together camping and hiking trips to Stockton Island and other islands in the Lake Superior chain known as the Apostle Islands. These islands are a National Lakeshore administered by the National Park Service and campsites have been designated on many of the islands. Apostle Islands Outfitters offers a complete outfitting package deal which includes all basic camping equipment, food, packs, floored tents, sleeping bags, cooking and eating outfit, ax, saw, shovel, first aid kit, water carrier, fire grill and map of the island. This averages about $11 per person, per day. Or campers can opt for partial outfitting which allows them to rent equipment item by item and supplement the gear they already have. Not only do Apostle Islands Outfitters provide equipment, they will also assist with the planning—suggesting campsites, pointing out the best hiking areas, noting historical sites or unusual rock formations on the island, and covering all other details to make the outing worry-free. They can plan day hiker-picnic trips or camping trips lasting several days. Excursion boats take campers and day passengers to Stockton Island, the largest of the islands, for $8 per adult camper and $3 per child. Water taxis to the other islands take from one to six passenger with gear and cost from $28 up. The boats also run on sightseeing cruises to see lighthouses, sandstone cliffs, sea caves, quarries and flaming Lake Superior sunsets. For more information on camping on an island, write or phone: Apostle Island Outfitters, #1 Washington Ave., Box 691 P, Bayfield, WI 54814 (715)779–5744.

Spirit Waters–Apostle Islands Voyageur Canoe Tour is operated by ARTA North Country—affiliated with the American River Touring Association. Explore the largest body of fresh water in the world—island-hop a magnificent group of islands off Lake Superior's south shore—in 34–foot Voyageur canoes. Spirit Waters' interpreter-guides will share their knowledge of natural and folk-history of the fur trade era, so you can better understand how the early voyageurs traveled. Starting in Bayfield, Wisconsin, and taking-out in the fishing village of Cornucopia, the voyage will involve island and shore camping in the Apostle Island National Lakeshore area. For additional information, rates, and schedules for this 7–day voyage, contact: Spirit Waters–ARTA North Country, Excelsior, MN 55331 (612)474–5190.

Chequamegon National Forest & The St. Croix

Situated south of the Apostle Islands and Lake Superior's Chequamegon Bay in northwestern Wisconsin, this reserve encompasses 838,000 acres of gently rolling terrain, conifer and hardwood forests, and over 400 evergreen-rimmed lakes, including some of the nation's great muskie waters in the famed Hayward Lakes-Chippewa Flowage area and the adjacent Lac du Flambeau Indian Reservation waters. Its name derives from *sho-wah-ma-gon*, a Chippewa Indian term for the "place of shallow waters," referring to the Chequamegon Bay. The forest's major waterways—the Flambeau, Chippewa, Yellow, and Namekegon—and their tributaries form a network of more than 632 miles of streams, once the travel routes of Indians, missionaries, voyageurs, and loggers. Today these same streams provide superlative canoe routes and excellent fishing for muskie, northerns, walleye, bass, and trout.

Among the more unusual scenic attractions in the forest are the Morgan Falls, fifteen miles west of Mellen, Wisconsin, where a small stream falls over 70 feet down a rock cliff to a small pool, then tumbles downward once again to a second pool fringed by tall conifers. From there the stream flows through a small valley, paralleled for a short distance by high rock bluffs. The highest point within the forest is known as St. Peter's Dome, near Morgan Falls, a lofty, pink granite outcropping affording fine views of Lake Superior 25 miles to the north.

Many superb large and small remote lakes, framed by secluded shores and conifer forests, fall within and adjacent to forestlands.

They range in size from one acre to 17,000–acre Chippewa Lake just outside the southwest corner of the Chequamegon. A number of the large lakes within the forest, and many smaller bodies of water, hold trophy-size northern pike, muskellunge, walleye, small- and large-mouth bass, several species of panfish and trout. Several streams and spring ponds hold rainbow, brook, and brown trout. Several of the deep, cold-water lakes have been treated by the Fisheries Division of the Wisconsin Department of Natural Resources to remove undesirable species; these have been restocked with rainbows, which have reproduced in sufficient quantities to provide good catches.

The forest's populations of black bear, whitetail deer, raccoon, snowshoe rabbit, squirrel, and ruffed grouse offer superb hunting in season, while the many predators, such as coyote, fox, and bobcat may also be taken. During September bear-hunting season, several large, trophy-size black bear have been bagged by successful hunters. In recent years the DNR has permitted the use of bear hounds to hunt bear. In October and November, the ruffed grouse, or "partridge," is the most popular game bird hunted in this area. The forest's most popular big-game animal, whitetail deer, is scattered uniformly throughout the forest. During the late-November season their natural wariness offers a challenge to even the most experienced hunter. Waterfowl hunting in the Chequamegon is limited and considered average at best, although a number of shallow impoundments have been developed in an effort to improve local waterfowl habitat conditions.

A network of old logging roads, seeded to clover and mowed to retard brush growth, and forest service roads provide access to the Riley Lakes Wildlife Area, Blockhouse Lake, the Moquah Barrens Wildlife Area, and to Moose, Teal, Lost Land, Owen, Pigeon, Namekagon, and scores of remote seldom-fished wild-country lakes. Several logging roads are gated during the hunting season and provide the sportsman with many hours of good hunting without being disturbed by motorized hunters. Adjacent to the forest are the superb fishing waters of the Red Cliff Lac Court Oreilles, Lac du Flambeau, and Bad River Indian reservations.

Of the innumerable rivers and streams that flow through the Chequamegon, the Flambeau, Chippewa, and Namekagon rivers are considered top-ranked canoeing waters. Designated a Wild and Scenic River by Congress in 1968, the Namekagon, flowing from Namekagon Lake, is generally runnable for its entire length all summer long and, within forest lands, flows through a relatively unspoiled stretch of terrain and numerous low marshy areas. The river's name derives from an Ojibway expression meaning "where the sturgeons are plentiful"—a deceptive appellation, since one of the outstanding features of the Namekagon stretch is the number of fine trout streams adjoining the river, including Cap Creek and Big Brook. The Jump and Yellow rivers, northwest of Medford, are also good canoeing streams with several white water stretches. The upper reaches of all of these rivers are often shallow in the late summer and early fall, so be prepared to portage around shallow stretches. Specific information on a canoeing stream or lake within the Chequamegon National Forest can be obtained by contacting the District Ranger's Office, cited at the end of this section, nearest your point of interest.

Three major trail systems, complemented by seven short paths, offer fine routes on foot or on horseback. The Flambeau Trail System, a network of almost 100 miles in length, passes through varying types of forest cover and crosses several streams and creeks, including the South Fork of the Flambeau River. Because there are 12 different trails with lengths from one to 24 miles, the system appeals to both the casual hiker and serious backpacker. The seventeen-mile Mount

Valhalla Loop Trail passes through forests of jack pine, aspen, and white birch and winds around the Valhalla Overlook, a high hill offering beautiful views of Lake Superior. The 16–unit Birch Grove Campground and Long Lake Picnic Grounds are situated within easy reach of this route. Other attractions along the Mount Valhalla Trail include a ridge-top section and the Sunbowl, a large valley with exceptional one-mile views from its surrounding rim. Information on the Flambeau and Mount Valhalla trails and other hiking routes within the forest is available from the Forest Supervisor, Chequamegon National Forest, Federal Bldg., Park Falls 54552.

Information Sources, Maps & Access

For detailed information and a full-color *Chequamegon National Forest Map* (50¢), and free maps of the *Flynn Lake, Rainbow Lake,* and *Round Lake Wilderness Areas,* contact: Supervisor, Chequamegon National Forest, Park Falls, WI 54552 (715)762–2461. Detailed information, including trail descriptions, points of interest, and mile-by-mile trail data, and a *Map of the North Country Trail* are available from the District Forest Rangers at Glidden 54527, telephone (1–715)264–2511; at Hayward 54843, telephone (1–715)634–4821; and at Washburn 54891, telephone (1–715)373–2667. North Country Trail is shown on the following U.S. Geological Survey maps: Delta, Drummond, Diamond Lake, Marengo, Grand View. These maps are available for $1.25 each from: Branch Distribution, U.S. Geological Survey, 1200 S. Eads St., Arlington, VA 22202. A free *Flambeau River State Forest Map* may be obtained from: DNR, Box 7921, Madison, WI 53707. Detailed fishing and hunting information for the region may be obtained by contacting, Dept. of Natural Resources Office, Northwest Region, Box 309, Spooner, WI 54801 (715)635–2101. Both the Namekagon and St. Croix rivers are shown on the *St. Croix & Namekagon Wild & Scenic River Map/Brochure* available free, along with detailed travel information, from: Superintendent, National Park Service, P.O. Box 579, St. Croix Falls, WI 54024 (715)483–3287. A *Bois Brule River Canoe Trip Map* and *Brule River State Forest Map/Brochure* may be obtained free from: DNR, Box 7921, Madison, WI 53707. For detailed info on Northern Wisconsin trophy trout stream conditions and hatches, write or call: *Chuck Billie's Northern Wildlife,* P.O. Box 116, Lake Nebagamon 54849 (715)374–2408. Be sure to request a copy of their catalog/newsletter, *The Northern Angler.* This nationally famous firm also offers guided trips on the Bois Brule, White, Namekagon, Iron, and

Black rivers for rainbows, browns, and brookies, and on Lake Superior for trophy trout and salmon.

Chequamegon National Forest is easily reached via State Highway 64 from Medford; via County Route H from Phillips; via state highways 182 and 13 from Park Falls; and via County Road GG from Mellen. From the Bayfield Peninsula and Chequamegon Bay region, the forest is accessible via State Highway 112 from Ashland; from Bayfield and Red Cliff take State Highway 13 south to Washburn, then proceed west on County Road C.

Recreation Areas

The Bois Brule

Long famous for its superb brook-trout fishing, the historic Bois Brule River, once an important exploration and fur-trade route to the headwaters of the St. Croix and thence to the Mississippi, is also one of the North Country's great canoe routes. This scenic northwoods gem provides outstanding fishing for Lake Superior-run rainbows, salmon, and lunker brown trout. Fed by numerous springs and bordered by a dense northern coniferous forest, the river flows in the former channel of a larger waterway which drained the waters of the melting ice of glacial Lake Duluth thousands of years ago. The upper and lower stretches of the Bois Brule River differ greatly in character. The lower Brule, from the start of the Copper Range to its mouth on Lake Superior, is a swift-moving run marked by almost continuous rapids as it flows through a deep and narrow valley. Flanked by forests of aspen, birch, and balsam fir, this section of the river drops 328 feet in 19 miles. The 30–mile section of the upper Brule is by contrast placid and slow-moving, coursing through a broad, flat, bog-filled valley, its banks lined with towering cedar, tamarack, and spruce.

A 33,000–acre forest provides the setting for this majestic river and is prime hunting ground for whitetail deer, black bear, ruffed grouse, and waterfowl in the Merriam Swamp area. The forest also offers excellent opportunities for backpacking and hiking. Winding through the southeastern part of the forest, the Brule-St. Croix Portage Trail crosses a historic carrying place used by Indians, explorers, and fur traders traveling along the Mississippi-Lake Superior waterway. Other trails follow the course of clear fishing streams or explore the shores of Lake Nebagamon and Lake Minnesuing. The 26–mile Brule-St. Croix Lake Trail is groomed for snowmobiling in winter and also offers excellent hiking during the summer months. The trail is marked with standard snowmobile marking signs and parking areas are provided at both ends.

Flambeau River State Forest

Covering over 86,000 acres just south of Chequamegon National Forest, the Flambeau River State Forest was originally created to preserve the great natural wilderness area along the North Fork of the Flambeau. The name "Flambeau" was given to the river by early French voyageurs, who discovered Indians spearing fish by torchlight in the big lake to the east. Ever since that time, the Lac du Flambeau—"Lake of the Torch"—and its river have been famous for both trophy muskellunge fishing and canoeing; today the river and its surrounding wooded terrain are renowned as one of the few unspoiled and noncommercialized areas left in Wisconsin. By far the greatest attraction of the area is the Flambeau River, praised by beginners and experts alike as one of the finest and most scenic canoe runs in the state. A 12–mile run from Nine Mile Creek on Highway 70 to Oxbow passes through acres of virgin hardwood and hemlock and has only one stretch of fast water worth mentioning, the Barnaby Rapids below Nine Mile Creek. Several trout streams, including Butternut and Log creeks, enter this section of the river,

which also passes through Dead Man's Slough, named for an unfortunate logger who met his end during one of the treacherous highwater periods. Still other portions of the river pass through miles of heavy timber, including the "Big Block," a solitary stand of old-growth hemlock running for about three miles, or over perilous white water such as Cedar Falls, Beaver Dam, and Flambeau Falls.

Flynn Lake Wilderness

Three proposed wilderness areas within the Chequamegon have been carefully maintained as unspoiled forest tracts. Approximately one mile north and west of Drummond, the Flynn Lake Wilderness Study Area offers 15 undeveloped lakes and 31 ponds, all of them essentially landlocked, since there are no existing streams with the 6,321-acre area. The Flynn Lake Wilderness offers fine examples of northern hardwood, balsam fir, natural and planted pine, and aspen/paper birch stands on rolling glaciated-lake-country terrain. The only signs of development within this primitive expanse are a one-mile section of the North Country Trail in the northeast corner of the area, numerous old railroad grades and logging roadbeds, and two private cabins located on private lands. Wildlife common to the northern Wisconsin forests include deer, black bear, ruffed grouse, red fox, coyote, skunk, otter, beaver, muskrat, and weasel. Most of the species of fish common to the area are found in the numerous lakes—such as Cisco, Arrowhead, and Star—and provide excellent fishing. At present, the Flynn Lake Wilderness is intended for day use only, but Perch Lakes Campground, some two miles north of the northeast corner of the area, offers 16 sites and is within easy reach of the wilderness. Horses, outboard motors or mechanical devices, motorized vehicles, and nonmotorized wheeled vehicles are forbidden. No special permits are needed to visit the area.

North Country Trail

This 60-mile wilderness trail crosses the northern half of the Chequamegon National Forest from Ruth Lake, three miles south of Iron River on County Trunk A. to Forest Road 390, about 2½ miles west of Mellen. The trail's eastern half winds through the Penokee Hills, a region of granite outcroppings, boulder-strewn ridges, and scenic overlooks. The western half follows a gently rolling combination of upland and swamps. About seven miles from the Ruth Lake entry point, the North Country Trail enters the Rainbow Lake Wilderness, a lake-strewn, forested area encompassing 6,583 acres, carefully maintained in its primitive, unspoiled state, free from motorized vehicles or developed recreational facilities. Hikers should note that a free permit is required to enter the wilderness. Since the trail crosses some 20 roads, the route can be explored in short, easy segments, ideal for weekend or day trips.

Three Adirondack shelters are located along the trail, and are designated specifically for trail use. Fire rings and refuse containers are the only amenities available at the shelters located at Seitz Lake, Marengo River, and Porcupine Lake. There are also four campgrounds adjacent to or within one mile of the trail, offering sites for a small, daily-use fee.

The many wilderness attractions of the route—dense forests, craggy ridges, and a variety of wildlife—are enhanced by the 23 lakes near the trail, all of them fine sources for walleye, northerns, small- and largemouth bass, panfish, and trout. In addition to the larger rivers, such as Brunsweiller and Marengo, there are a number of seldom fished trout streams off the main trail.

Early May, when the spring flowers begin to bloom, is a favorite time for hiking the trail, as is October, when the spectacular fall foliage provides miles of brilliant forest scenery. In winter, the trail may be used for cross-country skiing, although the route does contain many steep hills and sharp turns that may prove difficult for less experienced skiers. The Forest Service sternly warns that all ski travel on the trail should be done with caution and adequate preparation, both for survival and physical ability.

Rainbow Lake Wilderness

Northwest of Flynn Lake is the Rainbow Lake Wilderness, a similarly primitive forest tract covering 6,583 acres and containing 15 lakes and nine ponds. Much the same fauna and flora are found in the area, and, as in the Flynn Lake region, fishing is tops for bass, perch, trout, crappie, bluegill, and northern pike. The only developed recreation facility within the area is the section of cross-country trail; old logging roads provide access to other parts of the area. Permits, available from the District Ranger Offices, are required for entrance to the Rainbow Lake Wilderness.

Round Lake Wilderness

Located 18 miles due east of Park Falls, the Round Lake Wilderness Area encompasses the 2,900-acre Doering Tract, mature stands of aspen, paper birch, and yellow birch, and 25,000 feet of frontage on both sides of the South Fork of the Flambeau River. Aside from Round Lake, other bodies of water within the area include Tucker, Jupa, and Ole's lakes. The South Fork of the Flambeau River rises in the Round-Pike lake chain and flows for some 2½ miles through the wilderness study area. In spring and early summer, the river is navigable by canoe from the Round Lake outlet. Later in the summer, numerous shallows and rapids offer difficulties for less experienced canoeists and may require portaging. The first rapids, Fishtrap, is located on the western boundary of the Round Lake Wilderness. In addition to offering a real challenge in season to white-water enthusiasts, the Flambeau provides fine fishing for walleye, muskellunge, northern pike, bass, and panfish. The only developed recreation facility in the study area is a portage trail between Tucker and Round lakes; primitive type roads and old logging trails provide access to other parts of the area and make excellent hiking trails through this dense northern hardwood forest. There are three nearby national-forest campgrounds and one canoe camp providing overnight facilities to visitors to the wilderness. Round Lake is open for day use only, but no permits are required for entry.

St. Croix & Namekagon National Scenic Rivers

The historic St. Croix, an ancient Indian and fur trade canoe route, flows from its source, the St. Croix Flowage, through scenic north country forests past numerous evergreen-clad islands, swamps, and towering sandstone bluffs, winding southward for 174 miles before emptying into the "Father of Waters," the Mississippi. Near Big Island, the river is joined by its beautiful tributary, the Namekagon (the Chippewa word for sturgeon) which rises high in the Chequamegon National Forest at Lake Namekagon. Its waters swell the St. Croix to more than twice its original size; then for 80 miles the river traces the boundary between Minnesota and Wisconsin. Flowing silently between the sandy banks of an ever-widening glacial valley, the St. Croix is fed by numerous other tributaries, and changes in character from a narrow trout stream to a broad, lakelike flowage of almost imperceptible movement. In the first 12½ miles of its journey, it forms 35 rapids of low to medium risk. The rest of its length is marked by waters with some moderately challenging rapids, currents varying from slow to fast, and one high-risk rapid at Big Fish Trap in the St. Croix River Forest. Historic points of interest along the route include the remains of a primitive Indian village near the confluence with the Lower Tamarack River and Sioux Portage Creek, the main artery of travel for trappers and Indians on their way to Yellow Lake.

Gateways & Accommodations

Hayward—Gateway to
the Northern Lake Country

(Pop. 1,600; zip code 54843; area code 715). Gateway to the Chequamegon National Forest and Wisconsin's northern lake country, Hayward is also surrounded by some of the best deer hunting country in the state. Area attractions include Historyland, 1 mile southeast of Wisconsin Hwy. 27 via County Road B, comprising a replica of an old-time logging camp, a Chippewa Indian Village, and a paddlewheel steamboat offering hourly excursions on the Namekagon River (open mid-May to mid-October, daily, 10 a.m.–8 p.m.; guided tours available); the National Fresh Water Fishing Hall of Fame, on Wisconsin Ave., housing exhibits of all aspects of the sport (open April 1–Nov. 30, daily 10 a.m.–5 p.m.); and the Wilderness Walk, 3 miles south of Hayward on Wisconsin Hwy. 27, an old western town featuring animals in native habitats. Accommodations: *Northern Pines Motel* (rates: $18–26 double), 15 attractive rooms, 2 with kitchens, queen-size beds, TV, golf privileges, 1¼ miles south of town via Wisconsin Hwy. 27 (634–4959); *Wild River Inn* (rates: $18–24 double), 17 rooms, two with kitchens, nearby cafe, bar, located on Namekagon River, canoes available, snowmobile trails, 1 mile south via Wisconsin Hwy. 27 (634–2631).

Ladysmith

(Pop. 3,700; zip code 54848; area code 715.) Located along the Flambeau River, Ladysmith was once a popular rendezvous for trappers, voyageurs, and traders. In 1900, the town was named in honor of the wife of E.D. Smith, who chose the village as the site of a branch factory for the Menasha Wooden Ware Company. The area abounds in recreational opportunities for canoeists and fishermen. Accommodations: *Best Western El Rancho Motel* (rates: $24–27 double), 27 comfortable rooms, queen-size beds, color TV, restaurant and cocktail lounge, 1 mile north of town via Wisconsin Hwy. 27, on Flambeau Ave. (532–6666); *Lakelodge Motel* (rates: $16–18 double), 15 rooms, one efficiency unit, TV, playground, restaurant adjacent, 12 miles south of Ladysmith via Wisconsin Hwy. 27 (532–6446).

Park Falls

(Pop. 3,000; zip code 54552; area code 715). An old lumbering town on the Flambeau River, Park Falls is the headquarters and gateway to the Chequamegon National Forest. Accommodations: *Edge O'Town Motel* (rates: $19–25 double), 12 air-conditioned rooms, color TV, restaurant adjacent, ½ mile north of town via Wisconsin State Hwy. 13 (762–4410); *Park Falls Motel* (rates: $18–22 double), 11 air-conditioned rooms, color TV, snowmobile trails, cross-country skiing, 1 mile north of Wisconsin State Hwy. 13 (762–3191); *Valley Motel* (rates: $19–23 double), 24 air-conditioned rooms, color TV, restaurant adjacent, snowmobile trails, on 4th Ave. S., ½ mile south of town via Wisconsin State Hwy. 13 (762–3245).

St. Croix Falls

(Pop. 1,600; zip code 54024; area code 715). The town is headquarters for the oldest of Wisconsin's state parks, Interstate Park, created cooperatively with Minnesota in 1900. Within the park is the Gorge of the St. Croix River, a deep canyon lined with red cliffs and pine-covered terraces. Remarkable geological formations here include the Old Man of the Dalles, whose craggy profile sits atop the Wisconsin bank of the river, and the Devil's Chair, a tall and slender red spire, also on the Wisconsin side. Boat trips through the gorge leave Taylors Falls, Minnesota, daily, from mid-May through mid-October. St. Croix Falls is also the jumping-off point for numerous good fishing lakes and rivers and for the Trollhaugen Ski Area, 3 miles south of town via Wisconsin State Hwy. 35, a popular winter playground with ski schools, a children's area, and both downhill and cross-country trails. Accommodations: *Best Western Dalles House Motel* (rates: $20–40 double), 52 excellent rooms and suites, color TV, heated indoor pool, dining room and bar, ¾ mile south of town on Wisconsin State Hwy. 35 (483–3206); *Louie's Inn* (rates: $20–24 double), 15 rooms, saunas, restaurant and cocktail lounge, 4 miles south of town on Wisconsin State Hwy. 35 (755–2781).

Spooner

(Pop. 2,600; zip code 54801; area code 715). Named for the railroad magnate and U.S. Senator John Coit Spooner, the town is a gateway to the McKenzie Lake region. Points of interest include the State Fish Hatchery, ¾ mile south of town on U.S. Hwy. 63, the world's largest warmwater hatchery of muskellunge, and the Museum of Woodcarving, 1½ miles south on U.S. Hwy. 63, with over 600 figures of animals and Biblical characters. Accommodations: *Bil-Mar Motel* (rates: $20–26 double), 12 attractive rooms, color TV, trout stream, ski and snowmobile trails, 5 miles north of town in Trego via U.S. Hwy. 53 (635–3204); *Country House Motel* (rates: $25–29 double), 20 rooms, color TV, playground, restaurant, adjacent to fish hatchery, ¾ mile south of town on U.S. 53 (635–8721).

Lodges & Resorts

★★★*Broken Arrow Lodge*, located on beautiful Lac Court Oreilles, is open May through October and provides a fine fishing for bass, crappies, walleye, northern and muskies, from the five outstanding fishing lakes in the immediate area. A 14-ft. Aluma Craft boat is furnished with each cabin and outboard motors may be rented. There is an excellent concrete launching ramp and mooring sites for guests' large private boats. The resort has an excellent sandy beach with a gradual slope, ideal for children to wade, plus an off-shore raft for experienced swimmers. Autumn provides hunting and beautiful foliage. Hayward, ten miles away, offers a variety of shops, indoor- and outdoor theatres and excellent dining. There is the world famous annual Lumberjack Championship, plus deer and animal farms, logging camp and museum, fish hatchery, Indian museum and ceremonials, tennis courts, the National Musky Festival and 9–hole and 18–hole golf courses. All cabins are identical and are spaced for privacy in a wooded setting close to the shoreline with large picture windows offering an excellent view of the lake. All are fully carpeted, have two bedrooms, complete modern kitchens, furnishing, bed linens and a fold-out bed in the living room. Rates: weekly $150–210 depending on the number of people. Daily rates from May to June 2 and after Aug. 31 are $16–32; weekly $100–200. For further information contact: Broken Arrow Lodge, (summers) Route 2, Hayward, WI 54843 (715)634–2025; (winters) 8485 W. Calumet Road, Milwaukee, WI 53224.

★★★*Dun Rovin Lodge at Lake Chippewa*, 17 miles east of Hayward, is a year round family resort with excellent accommodations and recreational facilities surrounded on both sides by 12 miles of undeveloped evergreen shoreline. There are 12 modern housekeeping cottages (three brand-new) and a seven-unit modern housekeeping motel with fireplaces in some of the units. There is a clean, sandy beach, a brand new dock and new tri-hull boats are available for guests to enjoy on the lake. Anglers can find wood and aluminum boats, guides, bait, tackle, to help them hook tiger muskies, giant crappies, walleyes, bass and panfish. There is a fish cleaning house on the premises and freezing service is available. A keepsake trophy is awarded each year to the guest fisherman who hooks the largest musky. For guests who prefer land to water, there are miles of wilderness trails and saddle horses nearby. Winter guests enjoy snowmobiling, cross-country skiing, ice fishing and the warmth of a roaring fire. Dun Rovin Lodge has special facilities and discount rates for fishing and snowmobiling parties. The cabins range in size from one to three bedrooms with a special duplex cabin with three bedrooms on each side—ideal for large groups. All cabins have gas heat, hot and cold running water, fully equipped kitchens, blankets and linens, except towels. Summer rates are $130 to $195 per week and winter rates are $180 to $300 per week. Meal plans vary and reservations can be made for less than a week from September through May. For more information call or write: Joan & Dennis Johnstone, Dun Rovin Lodge, Route 4, Hayward WI 54843 (715)462–3834.

★★★*Eagle's Beak Lakeland Resort* is situated on a strip of land tucked between the Big and Little Couderay Lakes. Lakeland's grounds are pine covered with beautiful views of both lakes. The lakes connect to the entire chain of spring-fed lakes in the area. The water is crystal clear with a safe beach for children. Big and Little Couderay Lakes are both famous for fighting muskies, northerns, walleyes, bass, panfish, and jumbo crappies. Guides are available for guests. There is a diving board and float available to guests for swimming. There is plenty of picnic and playground area with outside grills for barbecuing. One Aluma Craft boat, fish cleaning house and freezer facilities are included in each cottage rental. Extra boats may be rented. Seven modern housekeeping cottages are available on the resort's spacious grounds. They all have screened-in porches and are completely furnished and set up for housekeeping. Rates: Deluxe cabins: $90–165 per week, cabins daily $16–35 and $10 per week for each extra person per cabin. For further information contact: Eagle's Beak Lakeland Resort, Route 2, Stone Lake, WI 54876 (715)865–3711.

★★*Lake Owen Lodge* is located on beautiful Lake Owen, famous for its trophy fishing and water sports. There is a beautiful beach, boats and motors, a screened fish-cleaning house and freezer lockers for guests use. Just minutes from the lodge you can enjoy horseback riding, trout fishing, canoeing, golf, tennis, biking, hiking and excellent hunting. Autumn brings a true color spectacular in this area of the northwoods. Winter offers great skiing on Mount Telemark,

with downhill, as well as cross-country trails. In addition, you can enjoy snowshoeing, snowmobiling, and ice fishing. Comfortable, cozy cottages are available, either housekeeping or American Plan with rates beginning at $44 per day or $76 Modified American Plan. Double occupancy in lodge rooms varies from $22–26, and from $38–42 MAP. Children are welcome, those under age 10 at half price. Pets are not allowed. For more information contact Lake Owen Lodge, Cable, Wisconsin 54821 (715)798–3785.

★★★★*Lakewoods Resort & Ski Touring Center at Lake Namekagon*, high in the northwoods, on a densely wooded land bridge surrounded by the clear blue waters of Lake Namekagon, is a cross-country skiing and ice-fishing center in the winter, and a lake resort in the summer. Deep powder cross-country trails start right at the door of Lakewoods Ski Touring Center, and lead into the evergreen woods, and traverse open meadows. Skis are available from the center for $8

daily. 500 miles of groomed snowmobile trails extend over the adjacent Chequamegon National Forest. Lakewoods rents snowmobiles at their winter center for $12 hourly. Nearby Mt. Telemark will challenge the downhill skier, and Lakewoods is an hour's drive from Indianhead, Big Powder Horn, and White Cap Mountains. The resort has an indoor heated pool, whirlpool baths, and Finnish saunas to relax in after and invigorating day outdoors. The Lake Namekagon dining room serves steaks, fresh seafood, and traditional specialties, overlooking the lake. In the summer, the clear lake waters are ideal for swimming off the sandy beaches, and there is boating, water skiing, and fishing. Lakewoods has an outdoor pool, as well as its indoor pool, whirlpool baths and saunas. Tennis courts, a children's playground, shuffleboard courts, and a private putting green are spread out over the lawns bordered by dense woods. Airy modern motel rooms are available for $18–22 single occupancy; $26–30 double occupancy. There are also deluxe rooms which are $36 double occupancy, and $42 for four persons. Luxurious 1, 2, and 3 bedroom condominiums, fully carpeted with fully equipped kitchens and living rooms with fireplaces, and private balconies, looking over the forest canopy to the blue lake waters range from $55 daily for two in a one-bedroom condominium to $88 daily for six persons in a three-bedroom condominium. For more information write: The Lakewoods, Cable, WI 54821, (715)794–2161.

★★★*Mogasheen Resort at Lake Namekagon*, located in the heart of the Chequamegon National Forest, is a superb northwoods family resort with year-round activities. There is fishing on the lake for walleye, northern pike, large crappies, bass, bluegills and occasionally a musky. Noted trout streams, Lake Superior and deep-water fishing are all close at hand. The resort has a center for fish cleaning and free freezer service. The shore of the lake is dotted with evergreens and northern hardwoods and has a sandy, gradually sloping beach, which is safe for swimming. There is also free-water skiing, with special attention for beginners. Other water activities include free use of the resort's water paddle boat and canoes. There is a weekly organized six-mile canoe trip down the Namekagon River. Swimming can be enjoyed year-round in the indoor heated swimming pool. Sports enthusiasts can take advantage of the resort's new tennis court and hiking on Chequamegon National Forest trails. Excellent golf courses, deer and game farms, and horseback riding facilities are all nearby. During the winter, hunters, ice fishermen, snowmobilers, and cross-country and downhill skiers will appreciate the quiet beauty of the northwoods. Mt. Telemark is 15 miles away in the Chequamegon National Forest and groomed cross-country trails lead out from the resort. The resort has a recreational building with a fireplace. The cottages have screened porches, and are completely furnished for housekeeping. A 14–foot

aluminum boat is furnished with each cottage. All the cottages face the lake and provide a nice view. Restaurants are nearby, and there are portable grills, picnic tables, and dairy products available at the resort. Rates: For deluxe cottage $175–235 weekly per person. Accommodations for up to 50 guests available. For further information contact: Bill and Ruth Sykes, Mogasheen Resort on Lake Namekagon, Route 2, Cable WI 54821 (715)794–2113.

★★★*Northland Lodge* is situated in the Chequamegon National Forest on the shores of spring-fed Lost Land Lake, four miles long and two miles wide with many bays and weed beds, connected with Teal Lake by a scenic, navigable channel, providing 2,500 acres of prime fishing water at the headwaters of the Chippewa Flowage. The lake holds muskellunge, walleye, pike, large and smallmouth bass, crappies, and pan fish. Fiberglass boats are included with each cabin and outboard boats can be rented. There is a fish-cleaning house and free fish-freezer service. While fishing is considered best during the spring, early summer, and fall, the lodge attracts fishermen all season. The lake's beaches are shallow and sandy with gradual slopes, and are safe for children. The forest provides opportunities for hiking through majestic stands of pine and hardwood or drives along the backroads. There is hunting for deer and upland game birds, with particularly fine partridge shooting. Golfers can drive to the nearby Hayward area to enjoy the 18–hole or 9–hole golf courses. Restaurants, movies, horseback riding, and churches are also nearby. The Northland Lodge has a large recreation room with full bar, and light snacks and other items for sale. The accommodations are rustic log cabins situated among pines and silver birch on spacious, well-lighted, level grounds. Most are right on the water's edge, and spaced far apart for privacy. The two-and-three bedroom cabins have living rooms, screened porches, kitchens and baths. They are completely set-up for light housekeeping with linens included. Guests provide their own towels. Rates: Weekly for two bedrooms $150–170, weekly for three bedrooms $190–200. For further information contact: Northland Lodge, On Lost Land Lake, Route 7, Hayward, WI 54843 (summer (715)462–3379; winter (612)546–0641).

★★★★*Ross' Teal Lake Lodge* is located on 150 acres in the center of Chequamegon National Forest. Teal Lake and Lost Land Lake, which are connected by a navigable channel, offer 2,500 acres of Wisconsin's finest musky fishing, plus walleye, bass, and panfish. Fishing these two lakes is especially enjoyable because speed boats are limited to 10 m.p.h. and water skiing is prohibited. Ross' has a staff of experienced guides, canoes, boats and motors to rent, and live bait on hand at all times. There is a well-stocked tackle shop and fishing equipment can be rented. Children will enjoy fishing for pan fish from the 10 piers along one-half mile of lakeshore. There is a large heated swimming pool, a sand beach and a pool-dock for protected lake swimming, a trap shooting site, and a rifle range. There is a two-mile forest hiking trail that is entirely within the resort's grounds. Meals are served in the dining room of the main lodge. The lodge also houses a lounge with a huge stone fireplace. Next door is the Harbor Club recreation center with games and facilities for indoor activities. Nearby is a horse ranch with over 60 mounts, offering riding instruction and beautiful trails. Guests at Ross' have playing privileges at the nearby Hayward Country Club golf course. The resort can direct guests to canoe trips, tours of the world's largest ore docks and grain elevators, harbor boat tours, and picnics among the waterfalls and deep gorges of Copper Falls State Park. Accommodations at Ross are in 21 luxurious guest homes scattered along the lakeshore, well spaced for privacy. The cottages are of a rustic log-cabin design outside, with luxury tile baths, large rooms, roomy closets, and a view of the lake. They range in size

from the "Yellow Birch," a one-bedroom cabin with full bath and glassed-in porch sitting room, to the "Willow," a three-bedroom summer home featuring pine-panelling, a huge stone fireplace, and a large kitchen. Lodging can be reserved with or without meals, including family combinations with adults on American plans and children on modified or European plans. Rates depend on the guest home and the number of occupants. On the American Plan with all meals included, daily rates vary from $32 to $45 per person. There are special rates for children and pets are welcomed at $1 per day. For diagrams of the guest houses and full information write or call: Ross' Teal Lake Lodge, Route 7, Box 225, Hayward, WI 54843 (715)462–3631.

★★★★*The Telemark Lodge & Ski Center* is renowned for its alpine and cross-country skiing facilities, excellent accommodations, and summer recreation. Telemark is a 2000–acre complex located three hours' driving time from Minneapolis and a short flight from Chicago and Milwaukee. In the winter, downhill skiers can enjoy the ten Alpine ski runs and three double chairlifts. There are NASTAR races every weekend and a complete ski shop with rental facilities. The cross-country skiing is even more popular at Telemark. The U.S. Olympic team trains there and the first World Cup cross-country ski race ever held in the U.S. was at Telemark. There are 93 kilometers of machine-tracked trails, moonlight tours, and tours of the Birkebeiner trail. There are several ski packages offered which include lessons for beginners, meals and lodging, and lift tickets. Telemark also has a schedule of special events, races, and nature photography workshops. There is a children's ski program and guests can even enjoy an old fashioned sleigh ride. In the warmer weather, guests can spend time on the four cushioned tennis courts, the Telemark Golf Course, or at the outdoor pool and sundeck. There are canoe trips on the Namekagon Wild & Scenic River with rental canoes and pick-up service available. Horseback riding through the Great Divide Country and hiking or bicycling the trails of Telemark and the Chequamegon National Forest are other seasonal activities. In any weather, guests can swim in the huge indoor pool, relax in the heated hydrotherapy pool or sauna. For the evening hours, there is live entertainment in the Nite Club where entertainers such as Count Basie, Woody Herman and Chubby Checker have performed. Accommodations are in the 300 luxury lodge rooms and the Valhalla townhouses secluded in the woods. The lodge features a 55–foot fireplace built with 155 tons of native stone in the lobby. All rooms have queen-sized beds, a kitchenette, a game table, color TV, and a private balcony. The townhouses have two to four bedrooms and can accommodate up to ten people. Each townhouse has a free-standing fireplace, dishwasher, modern kitchen, sun deck, and electric heat. The townhouses rent for $90 per night for a two-bedroom to $120 per night for a four-bedroom. Midweek lodge rates are $36.50 single occupancy and $44.50 double occupancy per night with no charge for children under 10 in the same room. For more information call or write: Telemark Lodge, Cable, WI 54821 (715)798–3811.

★★★*Virgin Timber Resort* is in the Chequamegon National Forest on Moose Lake, fed by the Chippewa, Big Moose, and Little Moose Rivers. The resort is 425 miles from Chicago and 150 miles from Minneapolis, in the Hayward area. Guests stay in seven rustic log cabins equipped with full housekeeping facilities and a wood burning fireplace. The resort has a lodge with beer bar, pool table, and TV. There is a playground, sand box, and kiddie pool for the children. Adults can enjoy the swimming area, try a ride on the water bike, or sail the pontoon boat. For the angler, fishing licenses, live bait, boats and motors are for rent and guides are available. Hosts Norm and Ruth Scamfer guide guests to the many things to do in the area including visiting Moose Lake's wildlife sanctuary,

the fish hatchery, the deer farm, or the go-cart track. There are also boat cruises, canoe trips, horseback riding stables, a logging camp, an Indian village, and the National Freshwater Fishing Hall of Fame nearby. Accommodations at Virgin Timber Resort range from one- to four-bedroom cabins. All have hot and cold water, showers, flush toilets, gas range for cooking, electric refrigerator and all dishes and utensils. A one-bedroom cabin for two people rents for $131 per week. The largest cabin is a four-bedroom cabin with two baths and two fireplaces accommodating eight people for $225 per week. Pets are welcome at $25 per week. For information and reservations write: Norm & Ruth Scamfer, Rte 4, Box 144, Hayward WI 54843 (715)462–3269.

★★★★*Whitecap Mountains* offers four-season recreation and terrific skiing for families and for individuals who want to get back to nature. Located four hours from Minneapolis and seven hours from Chicago, Whitecap offers downhill skiers eight ski lifts with thirty major runs. There is a bunny bowl, leisurely novice runs, and challenging runs for the expert and daring. The new Quad chair lift carries 2,400 skiers per hour over a 200–acre south bowl. For cross-country skiers, there are 50 kilometers of professionally maintained trails, including a new 25 kilometer trail for the skier who wants a long, scenic trail; a short ski along Lake Weber that leads to the Wine Hut; and—for the romantic—a moonlight ski with night lights for evenings when the moon is under cover. The superb trail system was designed by Sven Wiik and provides access to the Great North Trail. Whitecap hosts three Rossignol sponsored citizens races as well as their own Maple Fest Race in March. There is a ski shop, rentals, a ski repair facility with quick service, a ski school for all levels of expertise, and a game room for relaxation. At the Chalet, there is delicious food, a fireplace, and cozy lounges. For a quick lunch or a snack, there is the Wine Hut, an authentic log cabin hidden in the Valley of Grindelwald. Whitecap is active in the summers, as well. Special sessions from June through August include whitewater trips on the rapids of Northern Wisconsin's rivers, rock climbing and mountaineering with qualified guides, tennis workshops, and sailing in Lake Superior. Rooms are available at the

"Stables," a lodge at the base of the mountain. There are also units (some with kitchenettes) in the Coach Haus and Carriage Haus. Rates for two are $30 in the Stables and $40 in the Coach Haus or Carriage Haus. Units with kitchenettes are $60 to $90 and accommodate two to four persons. There are also special ski packages, weekday rates, long weekends, family reunion specials, and rates which include lodging, meals, lessons, lift tickets and other extras. For full information contact: Whitecap Mountains, Montreal, WI 54550 (715)561–2227.

★★★*Williams' Grindstone Lake Resort* caters to a family clientele on a private estate of 500 acres of pine and white birch forest with two miles of private shoreline along spring-fed Grindstone Lake. The resort welcomes children and provides them with an 18–foot diameter merry-go-round, a gasoline driven train, Shetland ponies, and a well-equipped playground. Outdoor facilities for all ages include archery, badminton, horseshoes, basketball, tether ball, shuffleboard, kayaks, watercycles, canoes, a sailboat, and boats with outboard motors. The sandy beach is equipped with chaise longues for relaxing, a diving platform, a 24–foot water slide, and a water wheel. During July and August, there is evening entertainment including dances featuring a local orchestra, hayrides with weiner roasts, and Chippewa Indian Dances. All facilities and entertainments are for resort guests only and are free, except for boats and motors. Golf and horseback riding are nearby, and fishing for tiger musky and smallmouth bass in Grindstone Lake has resulted in record catches. The resort is operated in summer months only, on the American Plan. The dining room serves hearty portions of fine food. Cottages are panelled in mahogany, knotty pine, and white birch and each has a picture window with a view of the lake or woods. There are also suites and bedrooms with baths in the lodge. With three meals, all facilities and entertainment, cottages are $195 per person per week; suites are $190 and bedrooms are $165. Children's rates are available. For information or reservations write: William's Grindstone Lake Resort, RR 2, Hayward, WI 54843 (715)634–4025. Winter address and phone: 6609 Maple Ave., Morton Grove, Ill. 60053 (312) 966–2225.

Travel Services

Brule River Canoe Rental offers complete outfitting for canoe trips on the wild and scenic Bois Brule. They offer Grumman, Blue Hole, Old Town and Klepper canoes as well as transportation to and from the river. For literature and rates, contact: Brule River Canoe Rental, Inc., Brule, WI 54820 (715)372–4983.

Flambeau Lodge Canoe Service is located eight miles north of Tony on County Road 1 on the Flambeau River. The lodge offers a full-service campground, dining room serving hot meals, and canoe rentals and shuttle service for canoe trips on the historic Flambeau. For information, contact: Felske Enterprises, Inc., Rte. 1, Ladysmith, WI 54848 (715)532–5392.

Northern Wildlife Angling Guide Service is available for the legendary Bois Brule, White, Namekagon, Iron, and Black rivers for brook, and rainbow trout up to trophy weights as well as charter fishing trips on Lake Superior for lake trout, salmon, browns and rainbows. Chuck Billies Northern Wildlife—one of Wisconsin's premier angling shops, located on State Highway B en route to the finest fly-fishing section of the Bois Brule—offers expert, professional guides, shuttle transportation, and canoe rentals. For rates and detailed fishing info, contact: Chuck Billies Northern Wildlife, P.O. Box 116, Lake Nebagamon, WI 54849 (715)374–2408.

Spirit Waters–North Country Flambeau & St. Croix/Namekagon River Tours are sponsored by ARTA North Country, affiliated with the American River Touring Association. The four-day spectacular Flambeau River trip covers 45 river miles from Oxbow to Flambeau Lodge, with some of the best white-water in the midwest. The five-day St. Croix and Namekagon wild and scenic river trip covers 60 miles from Trego to the Snake River Ferry. For detailed trip info, rates, and schedules, contact: Spirit Waters–ARTA North Country, Excelsior, MN 55331 (612)474–5190.

Nicolet National Forest & The Northern Highlands

Bounded on the north by the twisting Brule River, Nicolet National Forest stretches over parts of six northeastern counties, embracing nearly 650,000 acres of mixed hardwoods and evergreens just south of the Northern Michigan-Wisconsin border, and hundreds of sparkling blue lakes, including the famed trophy muskie waters of Big Sand, Lac Vieux Desert, and North Twin lakes, and the headwaters of five of the top-ranked trout streams in the Upper Great Lakes Region—the Pine, Popple, Peshtigo, Oconto, and Wolf. Many of the forest's remote "lost" lakes provide excellent fishing for trout, bass, northern pike, and walleye for the adventuresome wilderness angler. The Pike River, which rises just east of the forest boundary and flows for 90 miles into Lake Michigan's Green Bay, floated the world's record amount of lumber during the logging era, and today its deep marshy waters offer quality fly fishing for large browns and brookies. The famed Deerskin River, home of the old ten pound world-record tiger trout, flows through the northeast corner of the forest.

The forest is named for Jean Nicolet, an early French explorer and emissary of Governor Champlain of New France, who landed near Green Bay in 1634. Certain that he had at last discovered the route to China and, would be greeted by mandarins as soon as he stepped off his ship, Nicolet arrived dressed in elaborate robes, firing pistols with both hands. Instead, groups of naked Indians emerged from the forest, bowing and singing praises before this splendid deity. Though he never did reach the Orient, Nicolet was the first white man to touch soil now governed by Wisconsin, and as such he claimed the land surrounding Green Bay—Indians and all—for New France.

The wild Wolf River, the Pine, the Popple and Wisconsin, the Peshtigo, and the Oconto were well-traveled highways of the fur trade during the eighteenth and early nineteenth centuries. Beaver were so abundant in the forest that Nicolet reported being served 120 of the animals as the main course at a feast given by Indians in his honor. For almost two centuries, pelts, and especially beaver skins, were the standard currency. Today beaver are still present in the national forest sharing the terrain with popular game species, including whitetail deer and ruffed grouse. Many of the more remote beaver ponds shown on the topo maps provide excellent fishing in a wilderness setting for fat orange-bellied brook trout.

Information Sources, Maps & Access

For detailed information and a full-color *Nicolet National Forest Map*, contact: Supervisor, Nicolet National Forest, Rhinelander, WI 54501. For detailed fishing and hunting info, contact the Dept. of Natural Resources Office, North-Central Region, Rhinelander, WI 54501 (715)362–7616. For a free *Northern Highlands State Forest Map*, *Northern Highlands Canoe Trails Map/Brochure*, and a free *American Legion State Forest Map*, contact: DNR, Box 450, Madison, WI 53701. For information on the Wolf Wild & Scenic River, contact: Menominee Restoration Committee, P.O. Box 397, Keshena, WI 54135. Northern Highlands State Forest is accessible from Rhinelander via State Highway 47; via State Highway 70 from Eagle River; via State Highway 182 from Park Falls; and via U.S. Highway 51 from Ironwood, Michigan. Other outfitting centers surrounding or within the forest include Arbor Vitae, Boulder Junction, Star Lake, Manitowish, and Presque Isle. Nicolet National Forest can be reached via State Highway 70 from Eagle River; via U.S. Highway 32 from Crandon; via State Highway 73 or 189 from both Stambaugh and Caspian in Michigan, and via State Highway 17 north from Rhinelander to Eagle River, then east on 70.

Recreation Areas

Northern Highlands State Forest

The Northern Highlands State Forest, established in the early part of this century to protect the headwaters of the two great rivers that lie within its boundaries—the Flambeau and the Wisconsin—covers

140,000 acres of glaciated terrain in north-central Wisconsin. The forest also encompasses many miles of water frontage and provides access to most of the 150 lakes within its borders. The relentless, sweeping action of glaciers, which several times covered the area, created the present rolling topography and numerous crystal-clear lakes, and formed the sandy, gravelly soils that supported the towering pine forests of ages past. Today the predominant tree species in the forest are aspen and white birch, with a secondary cover of pine, oak, maple, tamarack, and black spruce.

Only three other regions in the world can match northern Wisconsin in density of lake surface per square mile—Minnesota, Ontario, and Finland. The high concentration of lakes within the forest is indicated by the fact that although the largest of these bodies of water, Trout Lake, covers only 6½ square miles, the lakes and ponds of Vilas County alone occupy 140 square miles, or over 15 percent of the area. Together with the Flambeau and Wisconsin rivers, these waterways offer unparalleled opportunities for fishing and canoeing, and the Northern Highlands forest area has been especially tailored to meet the growing demands of canoeists, with portages, access points, and canoe-campgrounds located throughout the region.

Three self-guiding trails ranging from ½ to 2½ miles in length explore wooded lakeshores, swamplands, and upland timber groves. Interpretive stations are scattered along the routes. For snowmobilers, the forest offers over 40 miles of interesting trail riding in the Boulder Junction, Sayner, and St. Germain-Arbor Vitae area. A shorter scenic Camp Lake Trail is located west of Highway 15.

The forest's many lakes, including Trout, White Sand, Partridge, and Clear, offer excellent fishing for muskie, walleye, rainbow and brown trout, largemouth and smallmouth bass, and northern pike. Developed boat landings on the major lakes provide easy access. Active timber-management programs within the forest allow access, cover, and food for deer and grouse, and prime habitats for bear, squirrels, and other game animals. In addition, the Powell Marsh Waterfowl Area has increased the number of ducks and geese available to the hunter.

Wolf National Wild & Scenic River

This nationally famous big-water fly fishing stream and national scenic waterway, considered the Badger State's most dangerous canoe trail, forms its headwaters near the small village of Hiles in northeastern Wisconsin and flows south some 400 miles into Lake Poygan. The remote wild stretches of the upper Wolf flow through the Menominee Indian Reservation and Big Smoky Falls area, Wolf Rapids, Otter Slide, Big Eddy Falls, Tea Kettle Rapids, Keshena Falls area, and the beautiful Dalles of the Wolf. Fly fishing in this stunning northwoods wilderness is good for brown trout up to five pounds. Although only one 24–mile stretch of the Wolf has been classified as a wild and scenic river, the shortest such segment included among the first nine rivers protected by the 1968 legislation passed by Congress, many other runs along the river offer equally splendid scenery and adventurous white water. The scenic-river portion of the Wolf runs for 23½ miles between the Menominee-Langlade county line and Keshena Falls. Because of the heavy

concentration of visitor accommodations and other commercial enterprises, the last half-mile before the town of Keshena has been designated "recreational." Most runs along the river include rapids of considerable difficulty, and this particular stretch, encompassing such evocative white-water milestones as Shotgun Eddy, Gilmore's Mistake, White Rapids, and Big Eddy Falls, is no exception. The run is thus not recommended for beginners, and even experts are strongly advised to scout the water situation in advance at Boy Scout, Gilmore's, and Shotgun rapids.

Another run along the Wolf north of the scenic portion of the river follows a 15–mile stretch between the confluence with the Lily River and Langlade in the county of Langlade, Wisconsin. This section of the Wolf—indeed, all of the river above Keshena—is nationally renowned for its brown trout fishing. Rapids vary from easy white water at Big Slough Gundy and Hollister to the more challenging waters of Cedar Rapids, laced with granite boulders and large waves. This stretch can easily be cut into two runs of seven and eight miles each at the takeout/put-in site of Hollister.

The countryside surrounding the Wolf River is hilly, and, for the most part, sparsely populated—a wild region blanketed with white pine and hardwood forests of ash, yellow birch, aspen, and maple, offering spectacular fall scenery. Big-game animals indigenous to the terrain around the river's northern stretches include deer and black bear; of the smaller mammals, porcupine, otter, muskrat, beaver, and snowshoe hare are most common. Fishermen should note that the areas around the Trip Rapids, Ducknest Falls, and Sullivan Falls have been set aside for fly fishing only. Brown trout, along with some walleyes and white bass, are the most popular species taken. The slower-moving, marshy stretches near Lake Poygan are famous for tremendous runs of spring walleye and northerns to thirty pounds.

Gateways & Accommodations

Boulder Junction

(Pop. 800; zip code 54512; area code 715). Known as the "Muskie Capital of the World," this small village in the northern part of Wisconsin is surrounded by the unspoiled lakes and woodlands of the Northern Highland-American Legion State Forest. The hundreds of lakes in the Boulder Junction region are renowned among fishermen nation-wide for excellent catches of muskellunge. Each year in mid-August a Muskie Jamboree is held to celebrate this native fish. In winter, the surrounding countryside is a vast playground for downhill and cross-country skiing, snowmobiling, and ice skating. The Aqualand Fish and Wildlife Exhibit, eight miles southeast of town on County Road K, has six marine bowls of Wisconsin aquatic life, plus a wildlife area with native species. Accommodations: *Northern Highland Motor Lodge* (rates: $24 double), 12 air-conditioned rooms, TV, sauna (385-2150).

Eagle River

(Pop. 1400; zip code 54521; area code 715). Named for the bald eagles that were once common in the surrounding woods, Eagle River is the gateway to the Eagle chain of 28 navigable lakes and to the sprawling Nicolet National Forest. A District Ranger's office is located in town. Eagle River is also popular with winter sports enthusiasts; within the national forest are facilities for skiing, tobogganing, skating, and snowmobiling. Accommodations: *Hiawatha Motor Inn* (rates: $27 double), 28 comfortable rooms, TV, indoor pool, playground, fishing dock, boats and motors, supper club and restaurant, 2½ miles north on U.S. Hwy. 45 and Wisconsin Hwy. 17 (479-6431); *Persian Paradise* (rates: $21-29 double), 24 excellent

rooms, overlooking lake, private beach, swimming, fishing, boats and motors, restaurant, 2¼ miles south on U.S. Hwy. 45 (479-9779); *Traveler's Inn Motel* (rates: $17.50-24 double), 24 good rooms, ten with kitchens, TV, recreation room, in town at 318 Wall St. (479-4403).

Lac du Flambeau

(Pop. 1,900; zip code 54538; area code 715). French traders called the villate "Lake of the Torch" after the Chippewa practice of night fishing from torch-lit canoes. Located in the center of an Indian reservation, Lac du Flambeau is the tribal headquarters for 900 Chippewa living in the area and a popular gateway to the Chequamegon National Forest. There are many resorts and more than 100 beautiful lakes within a five-mile radius of the village. Accommodations: *Schaefers' Tower* (rates: $21.50 double), 14 rooms, six with kitchens, TV, playground, groceries, on Lake Haskill, four miles south of town at junction of County Road D and Wisconsin Hwy. 70 (588-3341).

Land O'Lakes

(Pop. 700; zip code 54540; area code 715). This picturesque village on the Michigan border near the Ottawa National Forest is surrounded by some 135 lakes, including the Cisco Lakes that loop in a 140–mile chain along the state line. Just east of town is Lac Vieux Desert, source of the Wisconsin River. Accommodations: *Bel-Air Motel* (rates: $18 double), 11 attractive rooms, TV, 3600–foot airstrip, snowmobile trails, indoor pool and golf course adjacent, two blocks east of U.S. Hwy. 45 (547-3343); *Pineaire Motel* (rates: $17-19 double), ten excellent rooms on pine-shaded grounds, fronting Moon Lake, private beach, swimming, dock, fishing, boats and motors available, coffeeshop, airport transportation, attractive early American decor, one mile north of town via U.S. 45, just across Michigan state line (906)544-3800.

Manitowish Waters

(Pop. 500; zip code 54545; area code 715). Located in the Northern Highland State Forest, the village is surrounded by a maze of forested rivers and lakes, 14 of which are navigable by canoe, without portaging. Fishing, tennis, horseback riding, waterskiing, boating, and cross-country skiing are all available in season. Best bets in restaurants are the dining room at *Deer Park Lodge* (see below) and the *Little Bohemia Lodge*, two miles south of town via U.S. Hwy. 51, which specializes in roast duck and homemade pastries served in an attractive 1920's atmosphere, (543-8433).

Minocqua

(Pop. 3,000; zip code 54548; area code 715). The hub of the northern lakes region, Minocqua is located on an isthmus jutting into Lake Kewaguesaga. The town has been popular with summer vacationers since the 1920's, when resorts and lakeside retreats first dotted the surrounding forests and lakeshores. In recent years, Minocqua has become a focal point for winter sports. Area attractions include Jim Peck's Wildwood, two miles west of town on Wisconsin State Hwy. 70, with more than 100 species of native mammals and birds, plus a picnic area and swamp walk (open May-mid-October; phone 356-5588 for information); and the Warbonnet Zoo, nine miles south on U.S. 51 (open May-Oct., 8am-7pm). Accommodations: *Cross Trails Motel* (rates: $22-24 double), 17 excellent rooms, TV, lawn games, snowmobile trails, near small wildlife refuge, restaurant adjacent, one mile north of town via U.S. Hwy. 51 at junction with Wisconsin State Hwy. 70 (356-5202); *Lakeview Motor Lodge* (rates: $25-35 double), 25 excellent rooms and chalet units, on Lake Minocqua, dock, fishing, swimming, restaurant nearby, in town on U.S. Hwy. 51 (356-5208); *Pines Motel* (rates: $22-26 double), 30 attractive rooms, color TV, some queen-size beds, 1¼ miles north of town at junction of U.S. 51 and Wisconsin Hwy. 70 (356–5228).

Rhinelander—Headquarters of the Nicolet National Forest

(Pop. 8,200; zip code 54501; area code 715). Located at the junction of the Wisconsin and Pelican rivers, Rhinelander is headquarters for the Nicolet National Forest and a key gateway for the 230 lakes and 13 trout streams that lie within a 12–mile radius. The Rhinelander Logging Museum, in Pioneer Park on U.S. Highway 8, houses one of the most complete displays of old-time lumbering equipment in the Midwest. On the museum grounds are a reproduction of a pioneer logging camp and the last narrow-gauge locomotive to work Wisconsin's north woods. A pair of Paul Bunyan's shoes and a replica of the "Hodag," Rhinelander's answer to the Loch Ness monster, are also on display here. (The museum is open daily 10am–7pm, late May-late Sept.) Other points of interest include the self-guiding auto tour of Consolidated Papers' forestland, which begins 12 miles east of town near the junction of U.S. Hwys. 8 and 45, and Nicolet College, two miles south on County Rd. G and Oneida Ave., noted for its handsome architecture and wooded setting. The Supervisor's office for the Nicolet National Forest is located in town in the Federal Building. Accommodations: *Claridge Motor Inn* (rates: $29.50–37.50 double), 80 excellent rooms, color TV, heated indoor pool, airport bus, trout pond, dining room and cocktail lounge, in town at 70 N. Stevens St. (362–7100); *Holiday Inn* (rates: $32 double), 103 excellent rooms and suites, heated indoor pool, saunas wading pool, airport bus, dining room and cocktail lounge, two miles west of town at Junction of U.S. Hwy. 8 and Wisconsin State Hwy. 47 (369–3600).

Shawano—Gateway to the Wolf Wild & Scenic River

(Pop. 7,000; zip code 54166; area code 715). Once the site of an Indian Village, Shawano takes its name from the Menominee word for "south." In its heyday the town resounded with the buzzing of sawmills and the thudding rush of logs down the nearby Wolf River. Today the chief industries are dairying and paper production. Area attractions include Lake Shawano, two miles east on Wisconsin State Hwy. 22, and the Navarino Hills Ski Area, 15 miles south on Wisconsin State Hwy. 187. Accommodations: *River View Motel* (rates: $12–18 double), seven air-conditioned rooms, TV, nearby restaurant, ½ mile south of town on Wisconsin State Hwy. 22 (524–4493); *Shawano Motel* (rates: $16–20 double), 21 air-conditioned rooms, color TV, snowmobile trails, nearby restaurant, at 1244 E. Green Bay St. (526–6173).

Three Lakes

(Pop. 1,400; zip code 54562; area code 715). The town is a popular gateway to the Nicolet National Forest and the series of 27 beautiful lakes on the forest's west boundary. Accommodations: *Oneida Village Motor Inn* (rates: $20–25 double), 47 rooms, six with kitchens, restaurant and cocktail lounge, disco entertainment in summer, fishing guides available, in town at 501 Superior St. (546–3373).

Tomahawk

(Pop. 3,900; zip code 54487; area code 715). Tomahawk is a year-round resort center and the state headquarters for forest fire protection. The town takes its name from one of the nearby lakes, which vaguely resembles an ax-blade. Lakes and streams in the area provide excellent fishing; deer and small game hunting is also good in season. In the summer there are water-skiing shows three nights a week in Memorial Park. Winter sports are equally popular; two

miles north of town is the Camp 10 ski area, with T-bars, rope tows, rentals, a ski school, and children's area. The Tomahawk Regional Chamber of Commerce, downtown on U.S. 51, offers travel and recreation information (phone 453–2353). Accommodations: *Four Seasons Motel* (rates: $24.50 double), 20 attractive rooms, three kitchen units, color TV, heated pool, snowmobile trails, airport transportation ¾ mile north of town via U.S. Hwy. 51 (453–5345); *Nokomes Motel* (rates: $18–20 double), 10 rooms and one three-bedroom kitchen cottage, color TV, nearby restaurant, package store, five miles north of town on U.S. 51 (453–4151).

Woodruff

(Pop. 1,300; zip code 54568; area code 715). The town is a jumping-off point and outfitting center for visitors to the Northern Highland-American Legion State Forest, an 81,000–acre preserve with excellent beaches, fishing lakes, and campgrounds. Points of interest include the Woodruff State Fish Hatchery, 2¾ miles east of town on County Road J, and Henkelmann's Museum, three miles northeast of town on Wisconsin State Hwy. 70, housing displays of mounted game animals and antiques (open late May to mid October, daily 9am–9pm). Accommodations: *Arbor Vitae Motel* (rates: $19–24 double), 20 rooms on lake with private sand beach, fishing, boats, cross-country skiing, 1½ miles north of town via U.S. Hwy. 51, at junction with Wisconsin State Hwy. 70 (356–3393); *Jolin's Deer Path Resort* (rates: $16–19 double), 12 motel rooms, 11 cottages with kitchens and one-three bedrooms, pleasant grounds on Upper Gresham Lake, sand beach, fishing, boats, guides available, 13 miles northwest of town via U.S. 51 (385–2123).

Lodges & Resorts

★★★★*Chain O'Lakes Resort* is located in on the shore of Twin Lake of the Flambeau Chain of Lakes. Twin Lake, along with numerous additional lakes in the chain, has long been the favorite fishing grounds for the Chippewa Indians, and members of the tribe still fish in these waters. Pike, muskies, bass and panfish can be caught, with guides available for scenic boat trips into the lakes and to fishing hot spots. Row boats, motor boats, and water skiing facilities are available for guests. In the autumn guests can stroll in wooded areas with colorful foliage and hunt in the backcountry. Winter sports include ice fishing, tobogganing, and skiing. Snowmobile rentals are available from the resort, for trails running on the resort's property through wooded areas. Accommodations at the resort are deluxe, fully-equipped housekeeping cottages open all year. Rates: $175 week for two-bedroom cottage; $190 week for three bedrooms; $225 for four bedrooms. For further information contact: Siech's Chain O'Lakes Resort, R.R. 1, Minocqua, WI 54548 (715)356–5144.

★★★*Chanticleer Inn* offers active, family fun in all seasons. Located in Eagle River, the inn's specialty is winter sports. For the downhill skier there is a ski hill at the resort, and famous ski areas such as Sheltered Valley and Powderhorn are nearby. The cross-country skier will enjoy miles of marked and developed trails. There are more than 500 miles of marked and groomed country snowmobile trails. There is an annual snowmobile derby on Dollar Lake which the Chanticleer Inn originated. Ski equipment and snowmobiles can be rented or you can bring your own. A special Snow-Fun package includes three days of fun, two nights lodging, three meals and extras for only $38.50. In the summer, there is just as much activity. The Chanticleer is in the middle of the 28–lake Eagle Chain and is located on a 100–acre spring-fed lake. Fishing for muskie, walleye, bass and panfish is popular. There are docking facilities for all sizes of boats, plus canoes, sailboats, pontoon boats and power boats for rent. Waterskiing and swimming at the two private beaches are popular.

Outdoor facilities include two tennis courts and an archery range. There are three types of accommodations: condominiums, motel rooms, and cottages. The townhouse condominiums have one to three floors for one to ten people. There is color TV, fireplace, kitchen and dining facilities on the main floor and air-conditioning in the studios and upstairs units. All accommodations are available on Modified American, American and lodging only plans, and there are special economy condominium rates. Cottages have fireplaces, hot water, and a view of the lake. Motel rooms have TV, air-conditioning, refrigerator, phone and bed vibrator. With breakfast, dinner, maid service and use of the facilities cottages and motel rooms rent for $24.50–$25.50 per day or $163.50–$169.50 weekly, per person, double occupancy. Condominiums can be rented by the floor and range from $29.50–$34.50 per person. Children two to seven get a 50% discount and for eight-eleven year olds deduct 15%. For more information, write or call the Alwards at: Chanticleer Inn, Route 3, Eagle River, WI 54521 (715)479–4486.

★★★*Deer Park Lodge*, situated on the shores of beautiful Lake Manitowish, offers you relaxation in an atmosphere of unhurried, carefree, out-of-doors enjoyment. Tall northern pines, sparkling lakes, and bracing Wisconsin air beckon the hiker, fisherman, the camera bug, or the person who just wants to unwind. The lake invites you to try your hand at great fishing, water skiing, or other water sports. The heated swimming pool, the 18– and 9–hole golf courses (free in July and August), and other sporting facilities invite the active family. A special feature of Deer Park is their qualified instructors who cater to, feed, and entertain your children for eight hours every day. All services for children are at no additional charge. Babysitters are available during the evening at nominal rates. By day, Deer Park offers a wide selection of activities for adults. They include swimming in the beautiful glassed-in pool, riding, hiking, tennis on any of the four courts, waterskiing, fishing, archery, and skeet shooting. At night you will dine on truly delicious food (special diets are available), have leisurely cocktails in the lounge, attend the special shows, and dance. Facilities include a hotel/lodge and guest hourses on the lake. Rates during June are $38 per adult per day, including all accommodations. During the season, July 1 through August 26, daily rates at the hotel are $42; weekly at $185 per person. Guest house accommodations are at $56 daily and weekly at $250. Children's rates vary depending on the number of accompanying adults and the number of rooms. For information write: Deer Waters, Park Lodge, Manitowish WI 54545; Labor Day through Feb. 1: (305)733–1749. Toll-free numbers are as follows: Feb. 1–May 2 (800)327–1012, May 6–Sept. 1 (800)826–7215.

★★★★*Dillman's Sand Lake Lodge*, in Lac du Flambeau, offers clear lakes, evergreen forests, some of the best and all-inclusive recreational facilities, and the friendliness of a resort that has been family owned for the past 44 years. The resort is on 250 acres, 15 acres of which are a peninsula that juts out into White Sand Lake. Because of the peninsula, the resort has two separate swimming beaches—one the length of a city block with gradually sloping white sand for sunbathing and children's swimming. The other beach has a sudden drop-off, used for a diving pier and water skiing. Free swimming and water skiing lessons are offered on weekdays. The spring-fed lake holds big muskies, bass and walleye. Indian guides will take guests to the best fishing spots and cook the day's catch. Dillman's covered marina has canoes, sailboats, rowboats, motorboats, and speedboats for rent. Scuba diving is also popular in the lake, and rental gear is available at a nearby sporting goods shop. Guests have free use of the three beautiful tennis courts in a wooded setting. The resort even provides rackets and balls. There is a golf practice fairway, archery equipment, and hiking trails. Bicycles can be rented for $1 an hour, there are

two golf courses nearby, and horseback riding is available at nearby stables. The Lac du Flambeau area is the home of the Chippewa Indians, and every Tuesday and Thursday night there is a Pow-Pow with authentic dances. Social directors arrange games and activities for children and there are various tournaments for adults throughout the week. Meals are served in a lakeview dining room. Lodging is in cottages, chalets, and motel rooms which can accommodate 120 persons. Most units have a view of the lake and seven have fireplaces. Rooms rent for $14.50–$15.60 per day. Cottages range from $28.40 for two adults to $39.00 for two adults and a child on up to $93.60 for six adults, with various rates in between. A food plan including dinner and breakfast adds $9.50 per day or $66.50 per week for adults. For more information contact: Dillman's Sand Lake Lodge, Lac du Flambeau, WI 54538 (715)588–3143.

★★★*Dorich's Pine Isle* is located on the shores of Upper Boom Lake on 25 acres of evergreen-covered land. By walking across a small bridge guests can visit the resort's island with its own picnic house among tall pines and birch. Fishing at the resort is excellent for walleyes, northern pike, and muskies on Upper Boom Lake with access to the Wisconsin River. After you have cleaned your catch in the fish cleaning house the resort will gladly freeze them for you at no charge. One boat is furnished with each cottage at no charge. During the winter months fishermen ice-fish on the lake. The lake has a small beach with a roped-off area for children and a raft for more experienced swimmers. Winter sports include duck and small-game hunting and the fall offers excellent deer hunting, with both bow and arrow and rifle. Forty-five miles of snowmobiling trails are part of the resort's system with maintained trails starting at the resort, leading to miles of connecting trails. Skiers can travel to nearby Camp Ten for fine downhill slopes. The resort's grounds provide a playground for children, shuffleboard, badminton, volleyball, and horseshoes. There is a recreation building overlooking the beach area with a large sun deck. Barbecue grills are at all the cottages and there are picnic tables on the grounds. Cottages are all modern with paneled interiors. They are completely equipped for light housekeeping with everything provided except linens. Rates: $130–175 weekly. For further information contact: Dorich's Pine Isle, Route 1, Box 1970, Rhinelander, WI 54501 (715)369–2255.

★★★★*Eagle Waters Resort* offers private rooms in country cottages and plush suites deep in the northwoods on the shores of the beautiful Eagle Lake. The resort has two competitive tennis courts, an adjoining nine-hole golf course, and a heated pool with a poolside bar. There is superb fishing for walleyes, muskies, bass, northern pike and pan fish. Horseback riding and hiking trails meander through the backwoods. In addition, Eagle Waters Resort offers a supervised children's program. All rooms in the country cottages are pine panelled, have private entrances, individual bath and heat. Rooms are $40 for one-four days, and $36.50 for longer stays. Deluxe rooms are $53 for one-four days and $47.50 for stays lasting five days or more. The new Eagle Roost apartments, with luxurious living rooms, two private bedrooms, complete kitchen with bar, and private patio deck on the lake front are $60 nightly for one-four days, and $55 nightly for longer stays. Country breakfasts, served in the dining hall overlooking the lake, feature home-baked breads and hot pastries each morning. Dinners include fresh trout, walleye or whitefish; prime rib, or freshly spiced home-baked ham. All desserts are homemade, including fresh strawberry tarts and apple strudel fresh from the oven. Midnight snacks are a special feature of the Eagle Waters resort, fine Wisconsin cheese, breads, and coldcuts are spread out, all-you-can-eat every night. The main lounge offers a comfortable armchair to sink down in in front of a roaring fire on cool north country evenings, a cocktail lounge serving hot hors d'oeuvres, an open game room with pool and ping-pong tables, and dancing to live music after dinner. For more information write: The Eagle Waters Resort, winter address: 6536 North Maplewood Ave., Chicago, Ill. 60645 (312)274–2671; summer address: Eagle River, WI 54521 (715)479–4411.

★★★*Edgewater Beach Resort at Lac Vieux Desert* is located in the northwoods at the headwaters of the Wisconsin River on one of the largest spring-fed lakes in Wisconsin, at an elevation of 1,930 feet. The resort is informal, homey and rustic with housekeeping cottages equipped with complete cooking facilities. The resort has the only natural harbor in the area, ideal for docking boats and launching private craft. Whatever the conditions on the lake, boats are safe on the calm harbor waters. There is a boatman on duty to assist guests with resort boats or their own, and to supply bait, tackle and advice. The resort boats are 14-foot fiberglass craft and one boat is included free with the weekly rental of a cottage. Rentals of 5 hp and 10-hp motors are available. Guests are also welcome to bring their own boats. For those who like to fish from shore, there is a 50–foot pier. Along the 49–mile shoreline of Lac Vieux Desert, fishermen will find trophy muskie, walleye and northern pike, as well as crappie, perch and other pan fish. There are also numerous streams nearby where brook, brown, and rainbow trout can be caught. The resort has a playground for children, croquet, badminton, volleyball, basketball, and a horseshoe pit. In the evening the adults can gather around the rustic cedar bar and enjoy the recreation room. All cabins have automatic gas heat and modern kitchens and bathrooms. Several have a view of the lake, screened porches, and living rooms. Rates vary according to the capacity of the cottage, with cottages for two renting for $85 per week and the deluxe log cabin for six renting for $235 per week. Daily rates, baby cribs, rates for pets and rates for extra occupants in a cottage are available. Free transportation to and from the Land O'Lakes Airport can be arranged. For further information, contact: Mr. & Mrs. H. Kuehling, Edgewater Beach Resort, Land O'Lakes, WI 54540 (715)547–3696.

★★★*Forest Lodge* is a summer vacation resort located on High Lake, the uppermost lake of the Manitowish Chain of lakes. It offers American Plan rates that include not only three meals a day and maid service but also a free boat with each cabin, use of sports equipment, and free water skiing. Fishing guides are available and motors can be rented. The lodge has a private sand beach and a playground for children. There are horseshoe, badminton and shuffleboard courts, and golf and horseback riding are nearby. Each cabin has a fireplace, refrigerator, private bath, and porch. All are located along the lakeshore. Meals are served family-style in the rustic dining room. After dinner, guests can relax in the new recreation room with movies, ping pong, games or TV. American Plan daily rates range from $35 to $38 per person. There are special rates for children, as well as group rates. One special cabin, called "The Cabin on the Hill," is located 150 yards from the main lodge, away from the lake. It has one large room, separate bath, and a fully-equipped L-shaped kitchen. On the American Plan, this cabin is $32 per person per day for two. It can also be reserved for two weeks on a Housekeeping plan for $300. For more information, contact: Jim or Pat Wagen, Forest Lodge, Star Route, Land O'Lakes, WI 54540 (715)385–2128.

★★★*Froelich's Sayner Lodge* overlooks the blue waters of Plum Lake and is surrounded by giant 200–year-old pines, in the center of the Northern Highlands State Forest. The lodge has been welcoming guests for 88 years and William Froelich, Jr. has owned and operated it for 24 years. It has a reputation for friendly, informal hospitality. The resort recently underwent a complete remodeling. The newly decorated dining room has knotty birch walls, beamed ceilings, and fireplaces at each end. A long wall of picture windows looks out on the stately pines and lake. There is a large heated outdoor swimming pool and two lighted tennis courts. The sandy beach slopes off gently and has a roped-off area for children, a raft and long piers with sundeck chairs for relaxing. Bicycles are provided free and there are several bicycles-built-for-two. There is a pitch-and-putt course on the grounds. A fine nine-hole golf course adjoins the resort and can be played for a modest fee. A boathouse on the waterfront houses canoes, boats, and motors for rent. There is a library in the recreation building, and TV can be enjoyed there, in the lounge or in the cocktail lounge. The resort can guide you to side trips to the Porcupine Mountains, the cranberry marshes, the Indian reservation, Aqualand, Pleasure Island, Sayner's Historical Museum, the world's largest muskie hatchery, iron ore mines, mink ranches, and other local attractions. They will pack a lunch for all-day excursions. Plum Lake is over seven miles long and holds walleye, muskie, bass and northern pike. There are over 1,300 lakes in the county. Fish service includes cleaning, wrapping and freezing, and a nearby ex-guide will smoke fish to be taken home. Accommodations include cottages for two or three people, four plush cabanas facing the pitch-and-putt golf course, five deluxe main lodge rooms, and standard rooms with private baths. All rates are American Plan and range from $37 to $43 per person for cottages, $39 to $45 for cabanas or deluxe rooms and $35 to $40 for main lodge rooms, depending on the season. The resort is open from early May through October, and has special children's and weekly rates. For information and reservations: Froelich's Sayner Lodge, Box R79, Sayner, WI 54560 (715)542–3261.

★★*McPartlin's Cottages at Land O'Lakes* are nestled on the wide, wooded shores of sparkling Lac Vieux Desert, known for its fishing for walleye, northern pike, muskie, and numerous species of panfish. McPartlin's own fleet of Thompson wood boats supplies each cottage with its own craft, and motors can be rented. Complete facilities are available for cleaning the days catch, and freezer storage space is provided. There is a sand beach and a separate play area for children. Cottages have one-four wood-panelled rooms, with lake views, complete kitchens, private bath, and bed linens provided. Cabins accommodate one-four persons, and are $105–175 weekly throughout

June, July, and August, and may be reserved on a daily basis during the other months. For more information write: McPartlin's Cottages, Lac Vieux Desert, Star Route, Land O'Lakes, WI 54540 (715)547-3401.

★★★*Miller's Resort of the Woods* is situated on the shore of Boulder Lake, part of the 26–lake Manitowish Chain of Lakes. Boulder Lake has six miles of shoreline, and an area of 525 acres. Tall pines and white birches border the lakeshore. Weed beds and rock bars provide fishermen with excellent spots for musky fishing as well as for, walleyes, northerns, crappies, bass, and panfish. Streams and 194 lakes in a nine mile radius offer superb fishing. A guide will outfit and teach the novice, or take the expert over just the right fishing grounds. The resort has a fish cleaning shanty and free freezer service. Boating facilities include aluminum, fiberglass, paddle boats, sailing, pontoon boat, wooden guide-model boats and motors, and dock facilities. The lake also provides fine swimming with a gradually sloping beach, sunbath piers and raft. Guests can waterski and water cycle. Nature enthusiasts will enjoy guided or unguided nature walks and hikes on forest trails. There is a full range of recreational activities for both children and adults at the resort and weekly competition for trophies. The American Plan, European Plan, and housekeeping plan are available at the resort. Rates: American Plan, including maid service and all meals, $115–130; European Plan $15 per day; housekeeping plan $175–300 weekly. Special package plans for weekends are available. For further information contact: Miller's Resort of the Woods, P.O. Box 50, Boulder Junction, WI 54512 (715)385-2137.

★★★★*The Musky Inn Resort* is an informal, rustic resort nestled among towering pines on the shores of Big St. Germain Lake. Level landscaped grounds, plus a shorefront location gives guests a full view of the spectacular sunsets. The tiger muskie, king of fresh water, is found here, along with walleyes, northerns, bass, and panfish. Boats, motors, and fishing guides are available. Over 500,000 acres of cross-country ski trails wind through picturesque northern fields. The best downhill skiing in the Midwest is 45 minutes away. Swimming, sailing, and canoeing are all part of the warm-weather activities. Golf, tennis and horseback riding are nearby. Supervised trips for children are provided by the resort. The main lodge is beautifully constructed from virgin pines. It contains the main dining room, a fireside bar, and an indoor game room—all overlooking the lake. The upstairs rooms of the main lodge is often used by groups. Each guest unit continues the rustic flavor of Musky Inn, while providing all the comforts of home, plus a view of the lake. Rates: summer with American Plan $27–35 per day per adult; spring and fall, weekdays $19–24; weekends $24–28. Packages available with or without meals. Winter, three night weekend is $75–100 per couple; weekly $125–145 per couple. For further information contact: The Musky Inn, St. Germain, WI, 54558 (715)542-3768.

★★★*Pride-O-Th' North* is a year-round resort located on the north shore of Little St. Germain Lake, in a pleasant setting on 90 acres of woodland. Little St. Germain Lake is long and narrow and sheltered from the wind, with many coves for fishing. The lake has varied cover and depths and is noted for muskie, walleye, bass, large crappie, and bluegill. Fresh fish-freezing facilities, licenses, motors and life preservers are available. The swimming area has a gradual slope with no sudden drops. There are sailboats, canoes, floater loafers, surfboards, bronco boards and water skiing equipment available. In addition there is basketball, badminton, volleyball, croquet, horseshoes, and archery, with a playground for children. In the winter you can enjoy tobogganing, sledding, snowmobiling, cross-country skiing. Their private hiking trails connect to some of the longest public trails in the state. All trails are well marked and groomed. All cottages are located on the lake shore and have their own private piers. They are spacious, attractive, and equipped for easy, modern housekeeping. Your rental will include a boat, utilities, cooking utensils, blankets, and linens. Rates depend on season and number of people per cabin. For further information contact Pride-O-Th' North, Box 68F, St. Germain, WI 54558 (715)542-3793.

★★★★*Red Arrow Lodge* is in the northwoods on the shores of Lake Alice, with its 12 islands and 30 miles of shoreline. The resort is near the center of 25 lakes and four rivers. Fishing in the area is excellent for muskies and northern pike. Many of the guest participate in a weekly fishing contest with trophies awarded for the biggest fish caught in each of the classifications, plus bigger trophies in each class for the largest of the entire season. The resort will clean and freeze your catch, provide free use of a boat, motor with pontoon boat rentals. Hiking trails that wind and twist through valleys and over ridges unfold an area rich in wildlife and scenic beauty. There are also eight-foot-wide hiking paths through the woods for easy hiking. Bicycling is also popular. The lake and lodge provides swimming, a beach, a pier extending into the lake, row boating, diving platforms, and out-of-the-way nooks for private swimming. Speedboating, waterskiing, and aquaplane lessons are provided by the lodge. Golfers have playing privileges at nearby Maple Birch Golf Course, a nine-hole course with excellent greens. Children can take advantage of the Kiddie Korral, with everything from swings to a real log cabin. Every evening the lodge provides entertainment including get-togethers, parties, live music and square dancing. The resort provides three meals a day and specializes in northwoods delicacies. Accommodations include cabins, cottages, and lodge rooms. Some offer a lake view, and others are tucked away for seclusion. Rates: a cabin including two bedrooms (each with one double bed), living room, shower bathroom, screen porch and lake view is $120 weekly for four people. A one bedroom cabin with shower bathroom is $120 weekly for two guests. Hotel rooms in the main lodge are $110–115. Rooms in the Log Guest House are $110–115. For further information contact: Red Arrow Lodge, P.O. Box 156, Tomahawk, WI 54487.

★★*Steed's Wolf River Lodge* is a small, rustic lodge that specializes in rafting on the Wolf River, with a whitewater canoe school and cross-country skiing. It's a place for a secluded vacation—the whole county has less than 20,000 residents, and the lodge has only eight rooms. The rafting season starts at the end of April. Rafts can be rented at the lodge and accommodate two adults each. The canoe school offers a five-day program of instruction, tailored to the experience of the students. Guests arrive Sunday night and stay until Friday afternoon, with lodging from Sunday through Thursday, all meals, taxes, tips, equipment and instruction are included in the $300 package. In the winter the attraction is cross-country skiing. The lodge rents and sells skis, and gives cross-country skiing instruction. The lodge is an old log building and guests share common bathrooms. Drinks are served in the living room in front of the fireplace. The cook brings in eggs from neighboring farms and trout from the local streams, and makes homemade bread and jams. There is also a campground on the premises. The rate is $1.50 per person, per night and includes outdoor privies, picnic tables and wood. Trout fishing and lake fishing are good in season, and there are golf courses and tennis courts nearby. Summer, spring and fall, the weekend rate for two nights lodging and five meals is $65 per guest double occupancy. Winter weekend rates are $75 per guest and include ski services. Call or write for more information and available dates: Steed's Wolf River Lodge, White Lake, WI 54491 (715)882-2182.

★★★*Timberlands Resort* is secluded among 10 acres of tall trees, only five miles away from Eagle River with recreation, shops, restaurants and services for the tourist. The resort consists of six new rental vacation homes, fully equipped for housekeeping. Each home has 100 feet of frontage on Eagle Lake, one of the 28 lakes of the largest inland chain of lakes in the world. A free 14–foot aluminum boat comes with every weekly rental. Motors and canoes can be rented. Hosts Ed and Dee Leibly keep Timberlands Resort open year-round so that guests can enjoy early spring fishing, the fall "Colorama," and winter sports: snowmobiling, ice-fishing, skiing, sledding and skating. Snowmobiles and sled are rented in the snow season. Each

of the vacation homes has a fireplace, automatic heat, a picture window and panelling throughout. Two-bedroom homes rent for $195 per week in summer and $234 in winter for four persons or less. The deluxe two-bedroom is $205 and $246 per week. A three-bedroom home for six persons or less is $295 in summer and $354 in winter. There is also a one-bedroom home for two at $140 per week, not open in the winter. There are rates for extra persons, discount weekly rates in spring and fall, and weekend accommodations in spring, fall and winter. For more information and reservations, contact: Ed & Dee Leibly, Timberlands Resort, Route 3, Box 607, Eagle River, WI 54521 (715)479–4700.

★★★★*Twin Waters Resort* is tucked away in a quiet forest of tall pines and hardwoods on the shore of Big St. Germain Lake. The resort aims to provide quiet, restful and enjoyable vacations, in an area well-known for its year round scenic splendor and recreational opportunities. In warm weather vacationers can enjoy a wide range of birding. You can watch the spring bird migration, observe shore and woodland birds, hear the cry of the loon, see bald eagles and osprey and keep a watchful eye for the elusive pileated woodpecker. Wildflowers scent the forests and paint it with color. There are often sights of stirrings among the wildlife from the spotted white-tailed fawn to the beaver busy repairing dams. And warm weather brings the opening of the fishing season for walleye, northern pike, muskellunge, bass, trout and panfish. The resort is a photographer's paradise and guided bird and nature walks are available. Water activities include swimming, waterskiing, a sandy beach to relax on; canoes, boats and motors are available. In winter months the resort boasts excellent cross-country skiing right from your door on maintained and marked trails. State and other local trails are also nearby. Beginners can receive help getting started and maps are provided. Snowmobiling can be enjoyed on marked trails with 100- and 500-mile patch rides. Golf, tennis and horseback riding facilities are nearby, along with supper clubs and shopping center. The cottages are well-equipped for housekeeping with linen service available. All the cottages have carpeting in the living rooms and most have solid pine panelling. Guests can choose from a range of accommodations including one room efficiency cottage to a three bedroom cottage. Rates: Summer (June 30–August 25) are $115–235; early summer (June 9–30) $105–210; spring and fall savings (May 1–June 9, August 25–mid-November) $92–188; winter (mid-November to May 1) $210–250. Daily rates are available for some cottages. For further information contact: Twin Waters Resort, St. Germain, WI 54558 (715)542–3486.

★★★*Voss' Birchwood Lodge* overlooks Spider Lake in the Manitowish Waters Chain of Lakes, famous for muskellunge, walleye, and bass fishing. The resort has been operated by the Voss family for 68 years. Accommodations in the rustic main lodge include suites and rooms with private baths and comfortable furnishings. There are also individual guest cottages overlooking the lake that have picture windows, screened or glassed-in porches, and private baths. Many of the rooms and cottages have fireplaces and all have automatic heat for those cool northwoods nights. A recreation building on the grounds has a coffee shop, soda fountain, yarn shop, recreation area with ping pong tables, and four new specialty shops. Outdoor sports that can be enjoyed on the spacious resort grounds include swimming from the private beach, tennis, shuffleboard, horseshoes, hiking, and horseback riding. Golfers will enjoy the nine-hole and 18–hole golf courses nearby. For fishermen, boats, motors and guides are available. Side trips can be planned to view Copper Falls, Porcupine Mountains, the Indian Reservation, or Black River Harbor. The Birchwood Lodge is run mostly on the Modified American Plan, which includes breakfast and a dinner with homemade bread and pastries, served in the lodge dining room overlooking the lake. Cocktail hour is enjoyed in the fireside lounge. Cottages range from one to four bedrooms with rates from $175 to $210 weekly per person; M.A.P. Suites in the lodge are $175 and up, M.A.P. per week per person (double occupancy). A few housekeeping cottages are available to accommodate two to seven people at $150 to $250 weekly. For reservations, write or call: Voss' Birchwood Lodge, Manitowish Waters, WI 54545 (715)543–8441. Winter address Dec. thru April 15: 533 Northwest 1st Ave., Delray Beach, FL 33444 (305)278–4936.

★★★★*Wildcat Lodge* is a four-season resort with excellent facilities and year-round activities, located just outside Boulder Junction on Wildcat and Kitten Lakes—a seven hour drive from Chicago and five hours from Milwaukee. Its 120 acres are surrounded by the Northern Highland State Forest in an area with the world's largest concentration of lakes—194 lakes in a nine mile radius. Summer at Wildcat Lodge revolves around water sports. The 52 acres of Big and Little Kitten Lake provide quiet waters for swimming from the sandy beach; using the sailboat, pontoon boat, one of the 14–foot, fiberglass or aluminum boats or a canoe. A short channel takes guests into the 320–acre Wildcat Lake with five islands and bays for fishing. The resort also runs a fishing clinic for guests led by a registered guide meetings in the lounge on Monday nights. Extra minnow buckets, nets and seat cushions are available free, and they also have some rental rods and reels. Plus, there are maps of the lake and advice on "hot spots." The resort provides equipment for many warm-weather activities at several recreation areas on the grounds. There is archery, swings, volleyball, shuffleboard, badminton, cycling, tennis; and a skeet and trap range are nearby. Another summer activity is the Wildcat canoe trips. The resort started running these seven years ago and now makes one or two trips each week. A staff member leads the trips, which can be planned for fishing down the Manitowish River for a few hours or a full day, complete with picnic lunch. There are trails for hiking and in the Northern Highland State Forest; there are three self-guided nature trails with guides available during the summer. Wildcat Lodge also provides guests with info on nearby places of interest such as wildlife museums, water ski shows, Indian dances and amusement areas. In the wintertime, the snow sports take over. Wildcat has developed a half dozen trails from 1 kilometer to 10 kilometers, all starting at the lodge, and designed for cross-country skiing. The average snowfall is over 100 inches with snow cover up to 120 days. The lodge can make arrangement for equipment rentals. For the snowmobiler, Vilas County has over 500 miles of groomed connecting trails. One of the main trails between Boulder Junction and Presque Isle goes right across the entrance to Wildcat Lodge. Snowmobiles can be rented in the area by the day or week. Wildcat Lodge is only 40 miles from downhill skiing with the greatest vertical drop in the midwest. Copper Peak Ski Flying Hill, the largest ski jump in the Western Hemisphere, is nearby. And, there is ice fishing, snowshoeing, ice skating and tobogganing. Accommodations are in ten cabins on the Modified American Plan which are not open in the winter; and four ultramodern four-bedroom vacation homes, open year-round. The ten cabins have separate living rooms overlooking the lake. Rates include breakfast and dinner, and each cabin has a refrigerator but no cooking facilities. Daily rate is $27.25 per person or $25.25 on a weekly basis. There are special rates for children under 14, 10 and 3, as well as for families with more than two children. The vacation homes are built into the side of a hill overlooking the lake. Each has four bedrooms, two baths, a living room with a fireplace and a complete kitchen. Weekly rates for 2 to 4 people are $275, for 5 to 6 people are $325 and for 7 to 8 people are $375. There are also daily rates and minimum rentals during certain seasons. For reservations and information: Wildcat Lodge, Box 138, Boulder Junction, WI 54512 (715)385–2421.

★★*Zastrow's Lynx Lake Lodge* is a year-round resort with comfortable, spacious cottages nestled in the northwoods. Their own sand beach has a shallow floor, and is safe for children. Enjoyment of a water bike, canoe, raft and sailboat is free to all guests. Their fishing boats are ready at the dock to take guests on all-day fishing trips with picnic lunches provided by the lodge. They also have boats on Annabelle, Crab, Little Bass, Little Horsehead, Mabel, Mud, and Red Bass lakes. On the grounds, children can enjoy the playgrounds and guests of all ages can play shuffleboard, horseshoes,

croquet, badminton, and many other lawn games. There are marked nature trails for hiking. In the winter, snowmobilers are welcome and there are trails for cross-country skiing. Meals in the lodge dining room are generous and include a huge salad bar and entrees such as T-bone steak, a smorgasbord with five different meats, fresh walleye from the nearby lakes, and roast duck. Cabins have one to three bedrooms, with free TV and a refrigerator in each unit. American Plan rates per person are $28.50 per day or $175 per week. Children's rates and housekeeping plans are available. For further information, contact: Zastrow's Lynx Lake Lodge, Box 277B, Boulder Junction, WI 54512 phone (715)686–2249.

Travel Services

Thunder Lake Ski Touring Center is principally a ski school with equipment sales and rentals plus cross-country skiing excursions. They do, however, arrange cross-country ski packages which include meals, lodging, tours and instruction. At the ski touring center, there is a special practice oval, and beginners can see their mistakes on video tape. The center has four top instructors who will tailor lessons and excursions to the abilities of the individual or group. They teach downhill techniques and turns, cross-country skiing, and use of map and compass for ski touring. As the ultimate experience for the seasoned ski tourer, they plan and lead winter camping trips. Group lessons are $5 an hour, full day excursions are $12 per person and there are special family rates and rates for schools, clubs and organizations. For more information, write Thunder Lake Ski Touring Center, Box 164, Eagle River, WI 54521 (715)479–7008.

Trees For Tomorrow Environmental Center offers a variety of canoe workshops, ski touring, hunting mushrooms and edible wild plants, classes and forestry-for-the-layman programs in the spectacular northwoods along a chain of 28 lakes. The center, situated in the heart of northern Wisconsin's lake region, offers four modern dormitory units with private rooms sleeping 2–4 persons, a pleasant dining hall serving all-you-can-eat meals cafeteria style, and a 40–acre environmental complex. Beginning and advanced canoe workshops include lessons in water safety, river reading and tactics, and runs down the Eagle River, beginning with the wider, gentle river stretches on Saturday and concluding with an exhilarating plunge down the Eagle Sunday morning. Canoe workshops are held June 15–17, and

are $67.50 per adult, and $37.50 per child under 14, including five generous meals, two nights lodging, professional instruction, canoe shuttles and bus transportation from the center. Canoes will be provided for those who come without their own for a slight additional fee. Mini-vacation plans from June 29–July 2 include trips to the breath-taking Bonds Falls in the upper Michigan Peninsula, canoe trips, day hikes, and afternoon swims in the Ottawa National Forest-Sylvania Recreation Area, float trips on the Eagle Chain of Lakes, and all-you-can-eat barbeques in the evening. Rates are $42.50 adults, $32.50 children. An additional day trip featuring a tour of Star Lake Plantation, one of Wisconsins oldest pine plantations, is offered separately with one night's lodging and meals for $14 adults, $12.50 children. Forestry-for-the-layman courses combine classroom sessions on everything from forest management to marketing forest products with float boat rides, barbeques, swims, hikes and a ski show program. The program will be held August 31–September 3 and is $60 per adult, $45 for children. Mushroom hunting and edible plants courses train the eye to distinguish the dangerous mushroom from the gourmet's treat, with lectures, slide presentations, and field trips. Mushroom hunts are held September 7–9 when the northwoods are cool and moist after the showery weather of July and August. Rates are $41 per adult, and $31 for children including lodging, meals, lectures by experienced mycophagists, and transportation to field areas. For details, write: Trees For Tomorrow, P.O. Box 609, Eagle River, Wisconsin 54521 (715)479–6456.

Other Wisconsin Lodges & Resorts

★★★★*The Farm* emphasizes country living in the summer and ski touring in the winter. It is an 800–acre timber and dairy farm with 500 acres of woodland and 300 acres of cropland, a herd of 50 milk cows, horses and other livestock. Guests are invited to participate in the farm activities. It is an especially educational experience for children. They will be fascinated by milking time. They can ride haywagons and see alfalfa harvested. They can even see honey being made in a working beehive. There is recreation to be enjoyed as well; horseback riding along wooded trails; hiking in northwoods country; fishing in the Somo River, which winds through The Farm, or fishing for more avid anglers in the nearby lakes. And in the evening, hayrides and popcorn roasts. Guests stay in rooms in the home of Art and Toinee Palmguist or in one of two cottages. Family style meals are served and the cuisine is Finnish-American. Behind the house is an authentic, wood-burning Finnish sauna. In the winter, Art Palmquist, an expert skier, leads guests on cross-country ski trails. Trails lead through the 800-picturesque acres of The Farm and wind in and out of snow-covered evergreens. There is instruction available for novices and trails to delight the experts. Snowmobilers are welcome and The Farm also offers sleighrides in the winter. Rates summer and winter are $145 per week for adults and $85 per week for children under 12 accompanied by an adult. Children without parents are $125 per week. There are also special weekend ski packages and ski rental is $6 per day. For more information write or call: The Farm, Brantwood, WI 54513 (715)564–2558.

★★★*Glidden Lodge* perches on the shore of Lake Michigan and is the only resort in Door County with a natural sand beach on the lake. The lodge is 12 miles north of Sturgeon Bay and only a one-hour drive from Green Bay. The architecture is charming with wave-washed beach stone walks, a rustic stone lodge and dining room, and white stone planters overflowing with flowers on the patio. There are well-maintained tennis, shuffleboard, volleyball, badminton and basketball courts, plus an archery range and a nine-hole putting green. Swing sets and bicycles are provided for the children, and children even have a separate recreation room with indoor

games, special parties and movies. Swimming from the white sand beach in the crystal-clear waters is fun for all ages. For fishermen eager to drop a line in Lake Michigan, a charter fishing boat leaves the Glidden dock twice daily. Golf and horseback riding are nearby, as are acres of tall pines. Meals are served in the dining room and feature fresh-baked bread and pastries. The dinner hour is informal and homey. The lodge is open from May 25 to Oct. 15 with in-season rates in effect from June 22 through Sept. 4. Accommodations include rooms in the main lodge, lake front motel units, and efficiency cottages with fireplaces and modern kitchens that sleep five to nine people. In-season rates for lodging with no meals included are $26 for motel units and $16 for lodge rooms per person per day. Efficiency cottages range from $320 to $500 per week for two to four bedroom units. Off season and children's rates are available. Write or phone the Schmocks, Glidden Lodge, Sturgeon Bay, WI 54235 (414)743–4944.

★★★*Gordon Lodge* is a secluded luxury resort on the shores of Lake Michigan at North Bay. By car, it is only four hours from Milwaukee and six hours from Chicago. Its grounds are extremely well-kept and its facilities are modern. The motif is nautical with a huge anchor adorning the bicycle path, a ship's wheel in the "Top Deck" cocktail lounge, and nautical lamps lighting the dining room. There are plenty of outdoor activities on the 130 acres. Swimmers can enjoy a dip in the new, heated pool, or try the crystal blue waters of Lake Michigan from the sandy beach along the lodge's mile of shoreline. Golfers can practice on the 18–hole putting green and then use their skills on the two golf courses just ten minutes from the lodge. Guests can sail their boat rather than drive their car to Gordon Lodge, then use the free dockage for registered guests. Shuffleboard, two lighted badminton courts and bicycles are available free. Guests stay in waterfront villas with private bath and a fireplace. Huge picture windows, covering almost a full wall, offer a view of the lake. The main lodge also has rooms with patios that overlook the dock and the water. In addition, there are cottages nestled among the pines. The main lodge includes an elegant dining room where gourmet food is served, a lounge with an open pit fireplace, and the "Top Deck" cocktail lounge with music and dancing. There is entertainment every night. The main lodge and all accommodations are air conditioned and heated, and there are telephones and TV in every room. Rates are based on double occupancy and include breakfast and dinner. The waterfront villas range from $48 to $60 per person per day; the main lodge rooms with private bath and two beds are $45 per person; and cottages range from $38 to $45. For reservations and information contact: Gordon Lodge, North Bay, Baileys Harbor, WI 54202 (414)839–2331.

★★★*Leathem Smith Lodge* is located on the famous Door County Peninsula at the edge of Sturgeon Bay, just hours from Chicago, Milwaukee, and Minneapolis. Because of its location, boaters can come to the lodge via private sail or power boat from the waters of Lake Michigan or Green Bay. There is a 300–foot pier and marina facilities to accommodate boaters who plan to fish for the big lake trout and salmon or simply cruise the picturesque offshore islands, with charter boats available. The modern resort has a king-size swimming pool that is heated, and surrounded by a patio for hours of sunning and relaxation. Tennis buffs will enjoy the four tennis courts. For those whose game is golf, there is the a putting green, as well as a driving range. Shuffleboard courts are lighted for night play, and there are facilities for volleyball, badminton and softball. Bicycles are free and babysitters are available. The dining room offers good food and fine wines, as well as a picture-window view of the lake. After dinner, there is entertainment in the lounge with a cocktail to relax. All guest rooms have air-conditioning, TV, telephone

and a private bathroom. Rooms on the lower level have patios and each room on the upper level has a private balcony. There are also two- and three-bedroom cottages with all the facilities and comforts of the guest rooms, plus a large living room and a sundeck. The lodge is open year-around and rates vary with the season. They range from $20 to $40 single occupancy and $27 to $49 double occupancy for rooms; $30 to $75 for suites; and cottages for three persons are $42.50 to $67.50 with an additional charge for persons over three. For information: Leathem Smith Lodge, Sturgeon Bay, WI 54235 (414)743–5555.

★★★★*The Olympia* is a luxury resort hotel with first-class accommodations, a health spa and active sports facilities for year-round enjoyment. It is located just two hours from Chicago and 30 minutes from Milwaukee near the Kettle Moraine Natural Forest. The resort has 400 acres of forestland, hills, rivers and lakes, including a privately stocked lake for fishing. The challenging 18–hole golf course measures more than 6,600 yards and there is a clubhouse with a pro shop, carts and lockers. The Olympia has indoor and outdoor tennis courts plus handball, volleyball, badminton, shuffleboard and croquet. Warm-weather guests can water ski, sail, bicycle, horseback ride or hike along nature trails. In the winter, guests downhill ski on the resort's own hill reached by a double chairlift. There are cross-country ski trails, as well as ice skating, ice boating and ice fishing on nearby lakes. To warm up, guests can sit by the roaring fire with a hot buttered rum in the Apres Ski Chalet. There

is an enclosed shopping mall with an art gallery and shops for gifts, clothing, antiques, jewelry and local crafts. The evenings are active, too, at the Olympia. Dinner is served in an elegant, candlelit main dining room which offers a panoramic view of the sunset and the surrounding terrain through glass window walls. The menu has European and American gourmet dishes and wines from the world's finest vineyards. For guests who don't want to dress for a formal dinner, the Beach House at Silver Lake serves seafood, steaks and chops. The resort is also known for its Sunday brunches which feature French omelettes made to order. There are several cocktail lounges and a night club where top performers and musical groups provide entertainment and music for dancing. There are even twin cinemas showing movies nightly. The hotel has a grandiose lobby with high-beamed ceilings and a fireplace sweeping up to massive skylights. The 500 rooms all have double or king-sized beds and plush carpeting. Suites have open fireplaces and private bars. There are also deluxe villas sleeping four to eight persons. European Plan rates (no meals included) in the hotel are $35 to $42 single occupancy and $40 to $50 double occupancy for deluxe bedrooms. Suites are $95 to $98. Villas start at $75 per night for four and range to $125 for eight persons, with weekly rates as well. The Olympia offers special Learn-to-Ski weekend and mid-week ski packages; plus holiday houseparties for Thanksgiving, Christmas and New Year's Eve. For information or reservations, write Olympia Resort & Spa, Oconomowoc, WI 53066 (toll-free (800)558–9573; in Wisconsin (414)567–0311).

★★★★*Woodside Ranch & Cross-Country Ski Center* is a dude ranch offering all the fun of riding and western life in the spring and fall, plus a cross-country skiing resort in the winter. It is located just 20 miles northwest of Wisconsin Dells on over 800 acres. Riding is the favorite sport at the ranch, which has a stable of excellent horses. Riding is free, except in snow season. For children, there is a pony ring, with small, gentle ponies. Older youngsters can ride larger ponies in the corral. For adults, the day begins with a breakfast ride. Later, guests can take a dip in the heated, sheltered, private pool or enjoy shuffleboard, tennis, archery, ping pong, croquet, badminton, horseshoes or boating. Equipment is furnished and lessons are available. Informal clothes are all that are needed, even at dinner. Meals are served ranch style and feature fruits and vegetables from the ranch's own garden; fresh milk, cream, and eggs and spring chicken twice a week. In the Trading Post's new "Round Up Room" there are snacks, cocktails, pizza, beer, electronic games and pool tables. Fish the Enchanted Pond or visit the deer and buffalo sanctuary. There is even a sauna, and wilderness canoe trips can be arranged. Later, there are twilight hay rides and surrey rides, square dancing, and amateur and stunt nights. Wranglers bunk in air-conditioned rooms in the ranch house and each have a private bath. Log cabins with built-in fireplaces sleep two to eight people. There are also cottages with screened-in porches. As soon as there is snow on the ground, the winter sports take over. There are cross-country ski trails for novices and experts. Miles of snowmobile trails are marked and snowmobiles can be rented. Cross-country and downhill skiing equipment can also be rented. The rope tow is free and there is night skiing on lighted slopes. Or guests can ice skate on the Enchanted Pond, go tobogganing, or take a sleigh ride. The Trading Post serves hot buttered rum, hot cider and hot chocolate in the wintry months. And every Saturday night there is a "Hoedown" in the dance hall. Rates range from $35 to $38 per person per day, but there are many special packages including weekends, three-day and six-day rates, children's discount, lower rates in the ranch house and weekly rates. For all the information write or call: Woodside Ranch, Mauston, WI 53948 (608)847–4275.

INDEX

ABOUT THE AUTHOR

VAL LANDI was born and raised in Ringwood, New Jersey. He is the author of the highly acclaimed Bantam *Great Outdoors Guide* and a contributor to several of the nation's leading magazines. Mr. Landi now divides his time between New York City and research trips throughout the United States and Canada for his forthcoming traveler's field guide and ecology series.

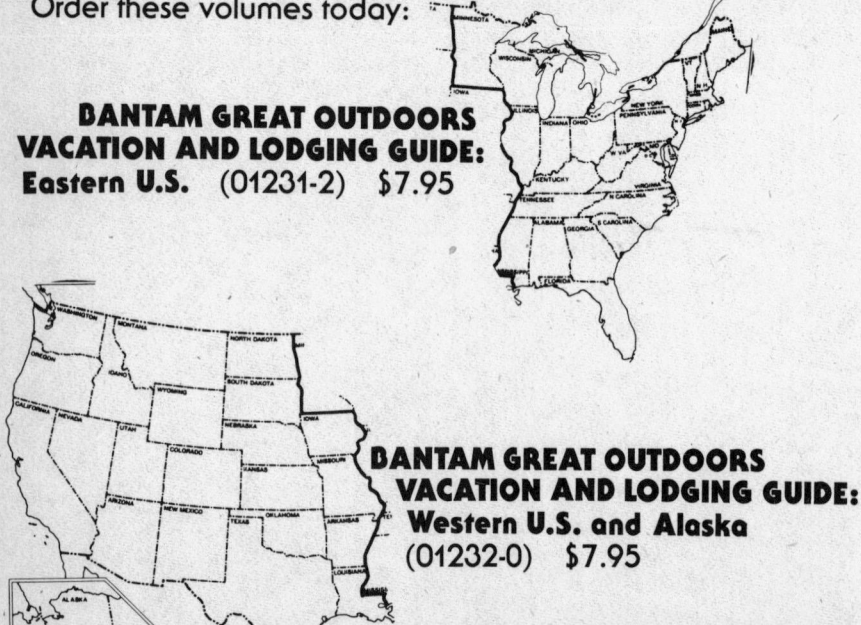